Indianapolis & vicinity
street guide

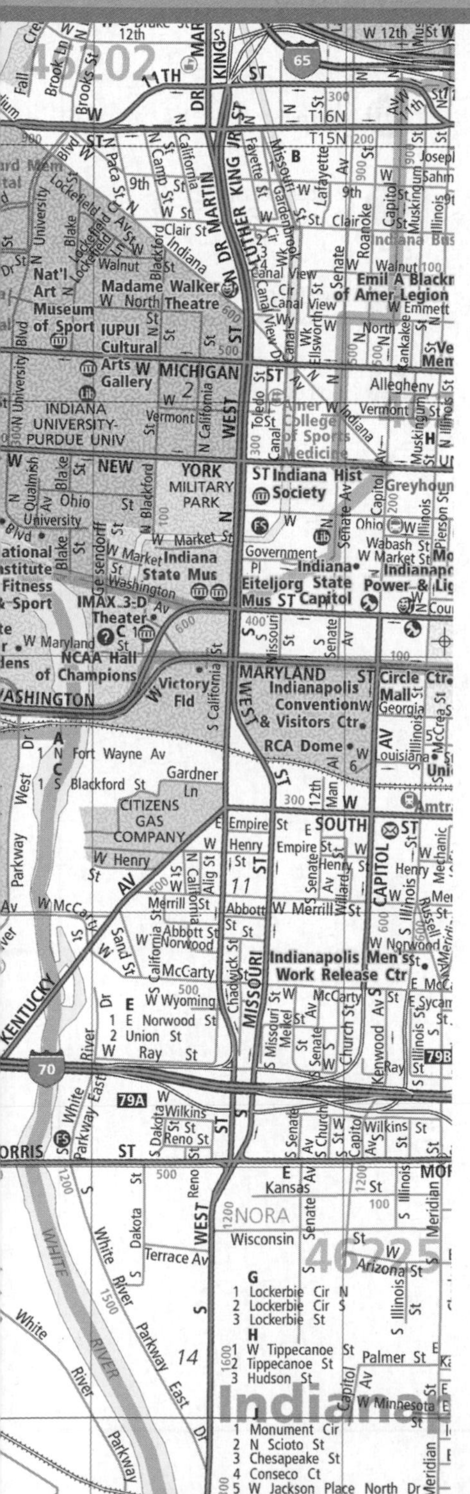

comment card on last page

Contents

Introduction

Maps

Lists and Indexes

PageFinder™ Map U.S. Patent No. 5,419,586
          Canadian Patent No. 2,116,425
          Patente Mexicana No. 188186
©2006 Rand McNally & Company. Portions ©2005 NAVTEQ.
NAVTEQ ON BOARD is a trademark of NAVTEQ.
All rights reserved. Rand McNally is a registered trademark of Rand McNally & Company. Made in U.S.A. All rights reserved.

RAND McNALLY

Rand McNally Consumer Affairs
P.O. Box 7600
Chicago, IL 60680-9915
randmcnally.com

For comments or suggestions, please call
(800) 777-MAPS (-6277)
or email us at:
consumeraffairs@randmcnally.com

NAVTEQ
ON BOARD™

Legend

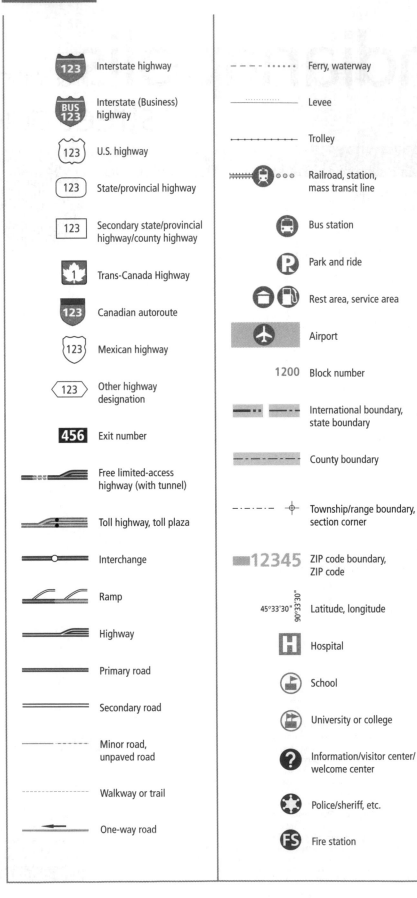

123	Interstate highway
BUS 123	Interstate (Business) highway
123	U.S. highway
123	State/provincial highway
123	Secondary state/provincial highway/county highway
1	Trans-Canada Highway
123	Canadian autoroute
123	Mexican highway
123	Other highway designation
456	Exit number
	Free limited-access highway (with tunnel)
	Toll highway, toll plaza
	Interchange
	Ramp
	Highway
	Primary road
	Secondary road
	Minor road, unpaved road
	Walkway or trail
	One-way road

	Ferry, waterway
	Levee
	Trolley
	Railroad, station, mass transit line
	Bus station
P	Park and ride
	Rest area, service area
	Airport
1200	Block number
	International boundary, state boundary
	County boundary
	Township/range boundary, section corner
12345	ZIP code boundary, ZIP code
45°33'30" 90°33'30"	Latitude, longitude
H	Hospital
	School
	University or college
?	Information/visitor center/ welcome center
	Police/sheriff, etc.
FS	Fire station

	City/town/village hall and other government buildings
	Courthouse
	Post office
Lib	Library
	Museum
	Border crossing/ Port of entry
	Theater/ performing arts center
	Golf course
●	Other point of interest

we've got you COVERED

Rand McNally's broad selection of products is perfect for your every need. Whether you're looking for the convenience of write-on wipe-off laminated maps, extra maps for every car, or a Road Atlas to plan your next vacation or to use as a reference, Rand McNally has you covered.

Street Guides

Fort Wayne

Indianapolis & Vicinity w/CD

Lake & Porter Counties

South Bend

Folded Maps

EasyFinder® Laminated Maps

Carmel/ Fishers/ Noblesville

Evansville

Fort Wayne

Indianapolis

Indianapolis & Vicinity Regional

South Bend/ Osceola/ Mishawaka

Paper Maps

Elkhart/ Goshen

Fort Wayne

Indianapolis

Northwest Indiana

South Bend

Wall Maps

Indianapolis & Vicinity Regional

Road Atlases

Road Atlas

Road Atlas & Travel Guide

Large Scale Road Atlas

Midsize Road Atlas

Deluxe Midsize Road Atlas

Pocket Road Atlas

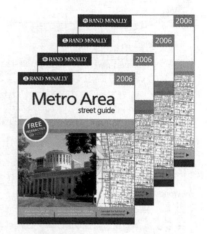

Wherever Rand McNally products are sold or at

www.randmcnally.com

Downtown Indianapolis

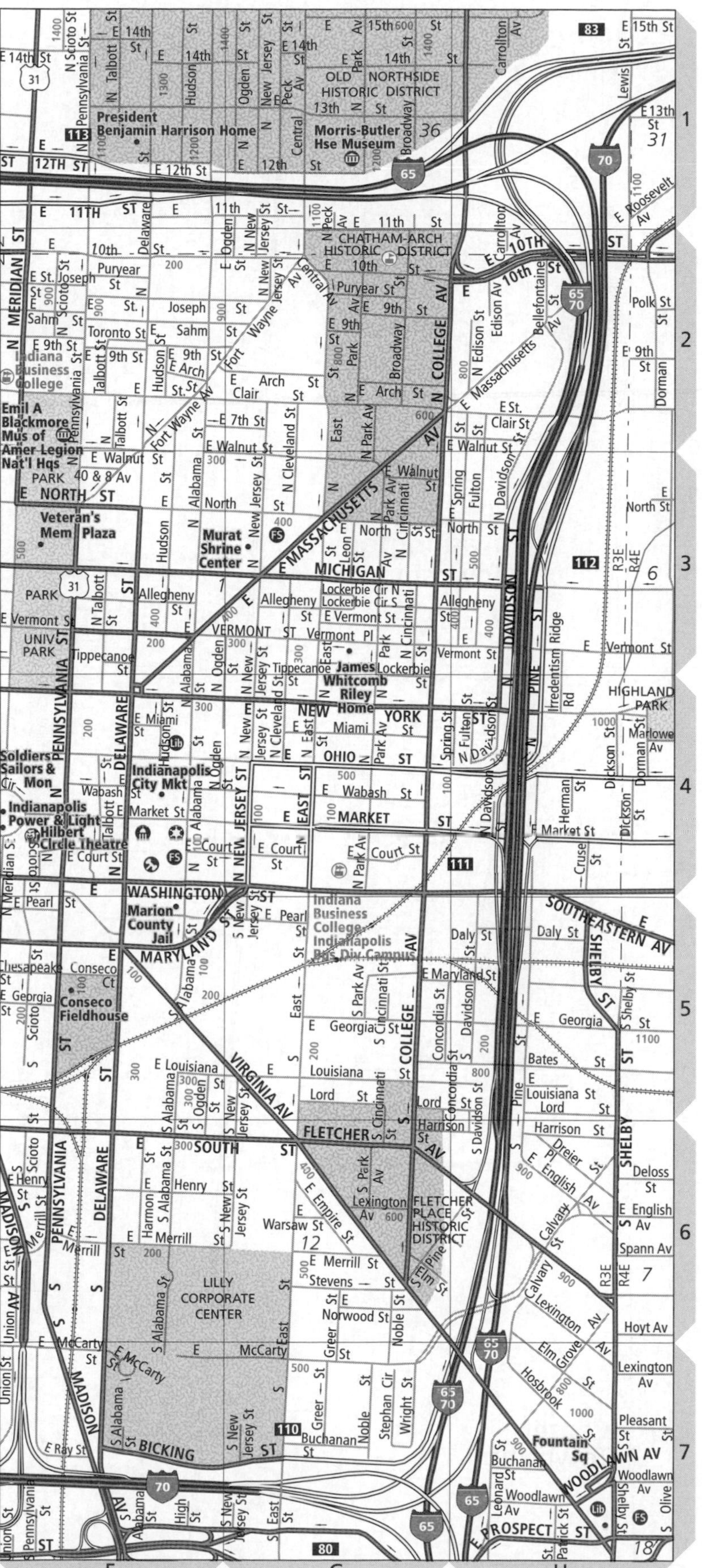

Points of Interest

1 in. = 1400 ft.

0   0.25   0.5

miles

MAP
1567

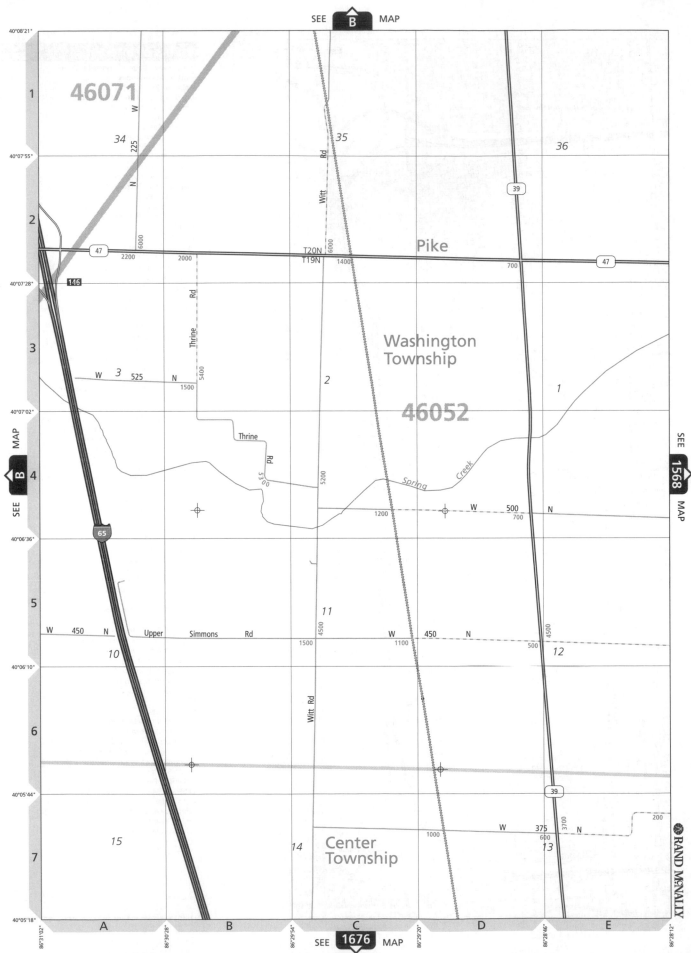

1:24,000
1 in. = 2000 ft.
0   0.25   0.5
miles

46071

W 225 N 6000

34

47 2200 2000

146

Thrine Rd

W 3 525 N 1500

5400

Thrine

Rd 5300

5200

65

Witt Rd

35

36

39

Pike

T20N 6000 1400
T19N

47 700 47

Washington
Township

2

1

46052

Spring Creek

W 500 N
1200 700

11

Upper Simmons Rd

W 450 N
10

4500 1500

W 1100 450 N
500

4500

12

Witt Rd

39

W 375 N
1000 600 3700

200

15

14

Center
Township

13

RAND McNALLY

SEE 1568 MAP

SEE B MAP

A B C D E

SEE 1676 MAP

MAP
1568

1:24,000
1 in. = 2000 ft.
0   0.25   0.5
miles

SEE **1567** MAP

SEE **1569** MAP

Victor
6700 Rd
Browns Wonder
Creek
Caldwell
6600 Rd

36   31   32   33

Spring Creek
47   T20N   47
700   T19N   2000

R1W R1E
1
Washington
Township
6

Elm Swamp Rd

Clinton Township
5   4

46052

W 500   E   500   N
5000

Elm Swamp Rd

12
W 450
N
Upper Simmons Rd
7
4500

E   450   N
1200   8   9 2200

Jo Honan Rd
R1W R1E

Spring Creek

N 175 E   175

E

N

W 375
N
Small Rd
13   18
FAIR WAY
GOLF COURSE

E   375   N
1200   17   16   225
3700
1700   3400

Center Township

John St

RAND McNALLY

A   B   C   D   E

MAP
1569

1:24,000
1 in. = 2000 ft.

0   0.25   0.5

miles

SEE **B** MAP

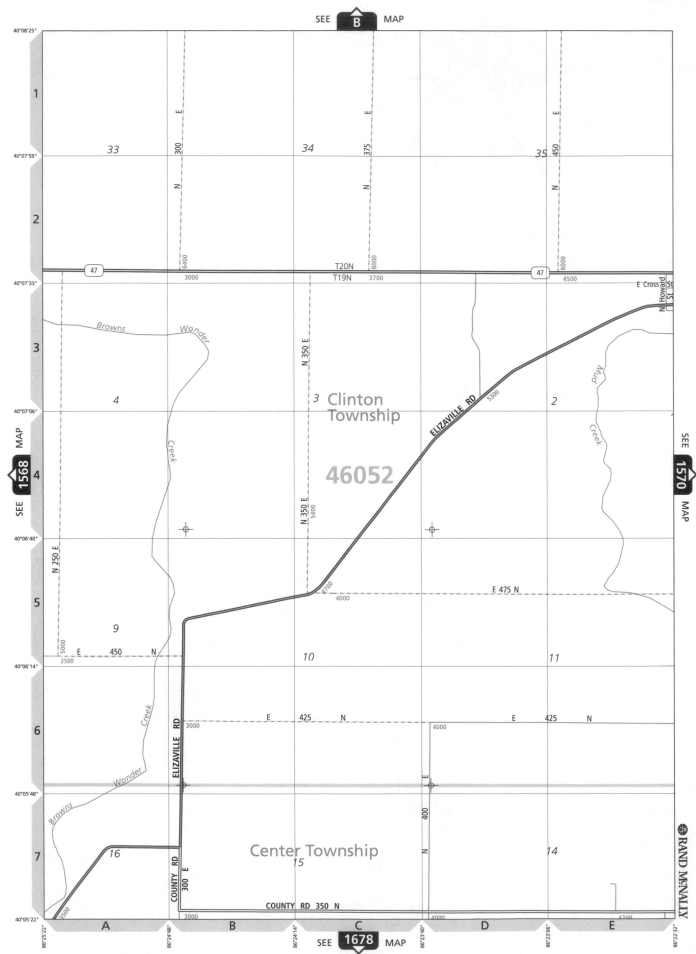

40°08'25"

1

40°07'59"

33

300 E

34

375 E

35

450 E

2

N

N

N

6400

6000

6000

47

T20N

47

40°07'33"

3000

T19N

3700

4500

E Cross Howard St

N Howard St

Browns

Wonder

3

N 350 E

Clinton
Township

Elizaville Rd

5300

2

4

4

46052

Creek

Creek

40°07'06"

40°06'40"

N 250 E

N 350 E

5400

E 475 N

4700

4000

5

9

5000

E   450   N

2500

10

11

40°06'14"

Creek

Elizaville Rd

3000

E   425   N

4000

E   425   N

6

Wonder

Browns

Elizaville Rd

400 E

40°05'48"

Center Township

7

16

County Rd 300 E

15

400 N

14

3500

3000

County Rd 350 N

4000

4700

40°05'22"

A   B   C   D   E

86°25'22"   86°24'48"   86°24'14"   86°23'40"   86°23'06"   86°22'32"

SEE **1678** MAP

SEE **1568** MAP

SEE **1570** MAP

MAP
1570

1:24,000
1 in. = 2000 ft.

0   0.25   0.5

miles

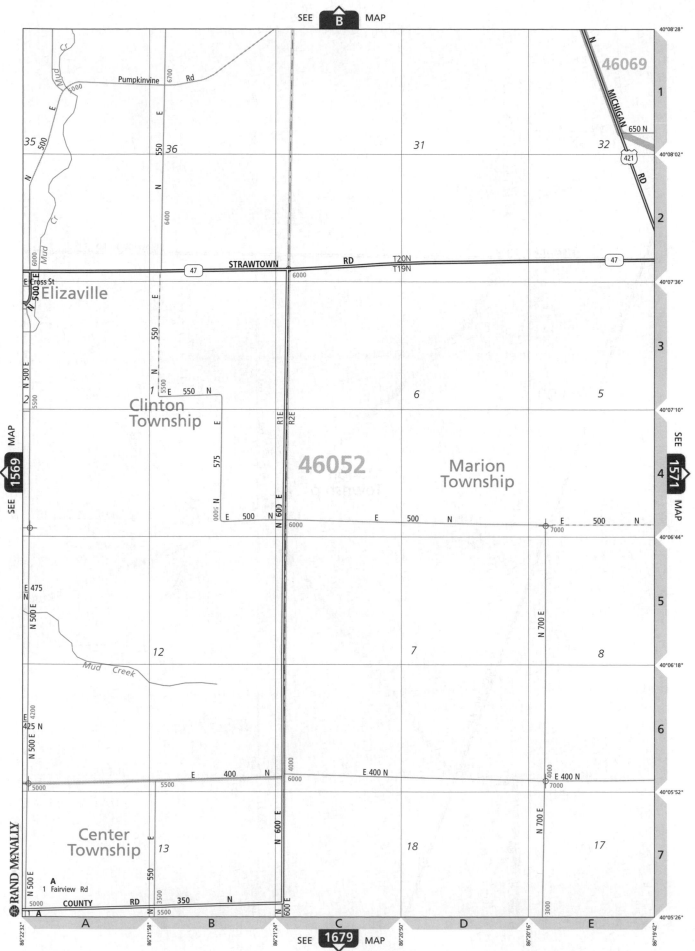

SEE **B** MAP

46069

Pumpkinvine Rd

MICHIGAN RD

650 N

421

35   36

31   32

47   STRAWTOWN   RD   T20N
T19N   47

E Cross St

Elizaville

Clinton Township

6000

46052

Marion Township

6   5

E 550 N

E 500 N   E 500 N   E 500 N

7000

SEE **1569** MAP

SEE **1571** MAP

E 475

12

Mud Creek

7   8

425 N

E 400 N   E 400 N   E 400 N

5000   5500   6000   7000

Center Township

13   18   17

A
1 Fairview Rd

COUNTY   RD   350   N

5000   5500

SEE **1679** MAP

A   B   C   D   E

RAND MCNALLY

MAP
1571

1:24,000
1 in. = 2000 ft.

0   0.25   0.5

miles

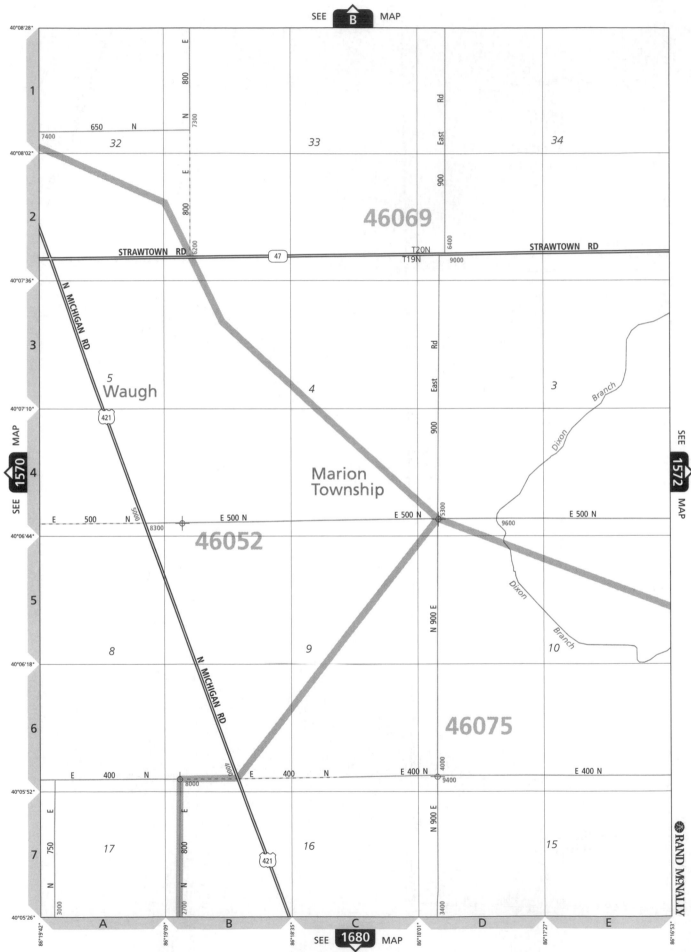

SEE 🅱 MAP

40°08'28"

1

650   N

7400

32

33

34

E

800

N

7300

Rd

East

900

6400

40°08'02"

2

46069

STRAWTOWN RD

6200

47

T20N

T19N

STRAWTOWN RD

9000

E

800

N MICHIGAN RD

40°07'36"

3

5

Waugh

4

3

Rd

East

900

Branch

Dixon

40°07'10"

421

MAP

SEE 1570

4

Marion
Township

SEE 1572 MAP

E   500   N

5000

8300

E 500 N

E 500 N

5300

E 500 N

9600

46052

40°06'44"

5

8

9

N 900 E

Dixon

Branch

10

40°06'18"

6

N MICHIGAN RD

46075

E   400   N

4000

8000

E   400   N

E 400 N

4000

9400

E 400 N

40°05'52"

7

17

16

421

15

E

750

N

3000

E

800

N

2700

N 900 E

3400

40°05'26"

A   B   C   D   E

86°19'42"   86°19'09"   86°18'35"   86°18'01"   86°17'27"

SEE 1680 MAP

*E5.91.98

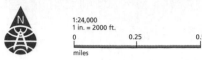

1:24,000
1 in. = 2000 ft.
0   0.25   0.5
miles

N

40°08'32"

1000
34   35   36   31

241ST ST
W

40°08'06"

COUNTY RD
Branch
6000
BOONE CO
HAMILTON CO
West Rd
6000
23600

40°07'40"

STRAWTOWN RD
10000
Dixon
47
T20N
T19N
R2E R3E

Big Springs Rd
5900

Big
Springs
Rd

11000
650 N

6200

Big Springs Rd

46069

Marion Township

3   2   1   6

Rd
West
Creek
Eagle

40°07'14"

SEE 1571 MAP

SEE 1573 MAP

Big Springs Rd
5530
5000

E 500 N
10600

11800

Eagle Creek

Creek

E 500 N

1200 E

W   226TH   ST
22600
3600

40°06'48"

Adams
Township

11   12   7

5

Big Springs Rd
4800

Dixon
Branch

40°06'21"

E
1150
N
3600

6

R2E R3E

E 400 N
10000

11100

E 400 N
11600

W   216TH   ST
3600

40°05'55"

15   14   13   18

Washington
Township

Eagle Creek
3000

Big Springs Rd

E   350   N
11000

1200 E

Kreager   Ditch

7

40°05'29"

86°16'53"   A   86°16'19"   B   86°15'45"   C   86°15'11"   D   86°14'37"   E   86°14'03"

MAP
1573

1:24,000
1 in. = 2000 ft.

0   0.25   0.5
miles

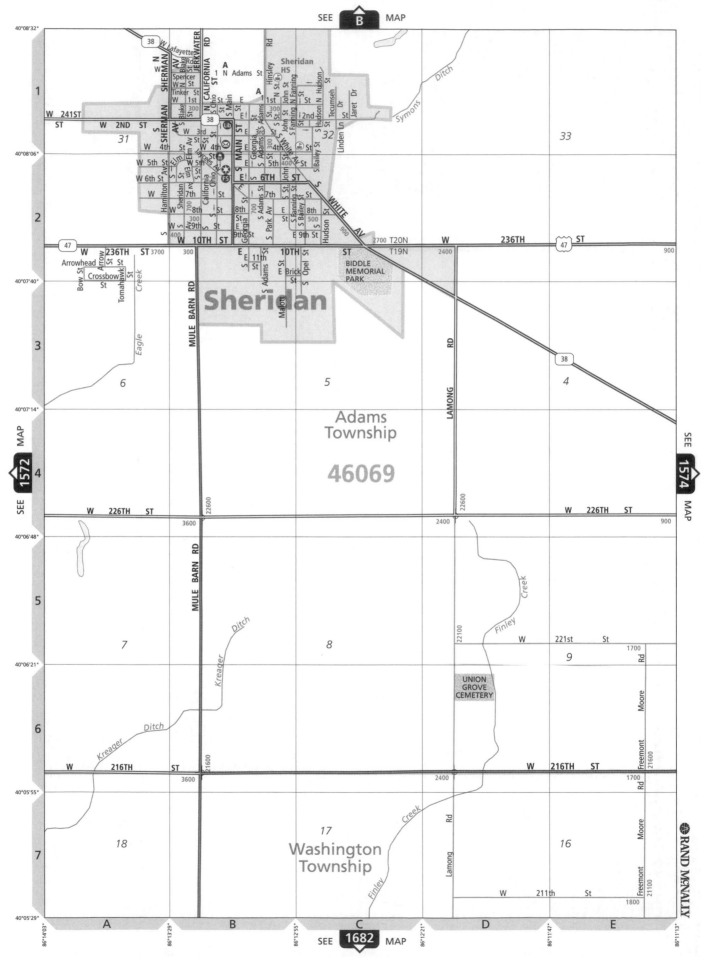

SEE ▲ MAP
B

40°08'32"

W Lafayette
38
JERKWATER RD
W Lafayette

N SHERMAN AV
Blake
Spencer
Tinker St
W 1st
300
CALIFORNIA ST
N OHIO
N Ohio St
S Main
A
N Adams St
Hinsley
N St
John St
N Fanning
N Hudson
Sheridan HS
Tecumseh
Symons Ditch

1

W 241ST ST
W 2ND ST
38
SHERMAN AV
W 3rd
Blake
300
S Ohio
3rd S Adams
1st
E
300
John St
John St
S White Av
Hudson
2nd
Linden Ln
Jaret Dr

31
W 4th
Frances Av
W 4th St
S Elm
S Elm Av
S Main ST
Georgia
3rd S
Georgia
4th
5th
S White Av
S Bailey St
32
33

40°08'06"

W 5th St
Hamilton
S Elm Av
W Sheridan
S California
S Ohio St
E 6TH ST
E Georgia St
400
S Adams
S John St
5th
E
S Fanning St
S Bailey
S Hudson
900

W 6th St
7th
S Park Av
7th
E
8th

W 8th
700
S California St
8th
E
8th
500

W 9th ST
Georgia
S Adams St
S Fanning St
E 9th St
S Hudson

2
S 400
W 10TH ST
E
10th St
W 236TH ST
47
2700 T20N
W 236TH ST
47
2400
900

47
W 236TH ST 3700
300
E 11th St
S Adams St
10th St
T19N

Arrowhead St
Arrow St
Bow St
Crossbow St
Tomahawk St
Creek
MULE BARN RD
S Opel St
E Brick St
S Mallott
BIDDLE MEMORIAL PARK
1000

40°07'40"
Sheridan

6
Eagle Creek
3
5
LAMONG RD
38
4

40°07'14"

Adams Township

46069

SEE
◄ **1572** MAP
4

SEE
1574 ► MAP

40°06'48"
W 226TH ST
22600
3600
22600
2400
W 226TH ST
900

40°06'21"
MULE BARN RD
7
Kreager Ditch
8
22100
Finley Creek
W 221st St
1700
9
Rd
Moore

5

UNION GROVE CEMETERY

6
Kreager Ditch
21600
Freemont Rd
21600

40°05'55"
W 216TH ST
3600
2400
W 216TH ST
1700
Rd
Moore

18
17
Finley Creek
Lamong Rd
16
Moore Rd
Freemont 21100

7
Washington Township
W 211th St
21100
1800

40°05'29"

| A | B | C | D | E |

86°14'03"   86°13'29"   86°12'55"   86°12'21"   86°11'47"

SEE **1682** MAP

•ε·LL·86

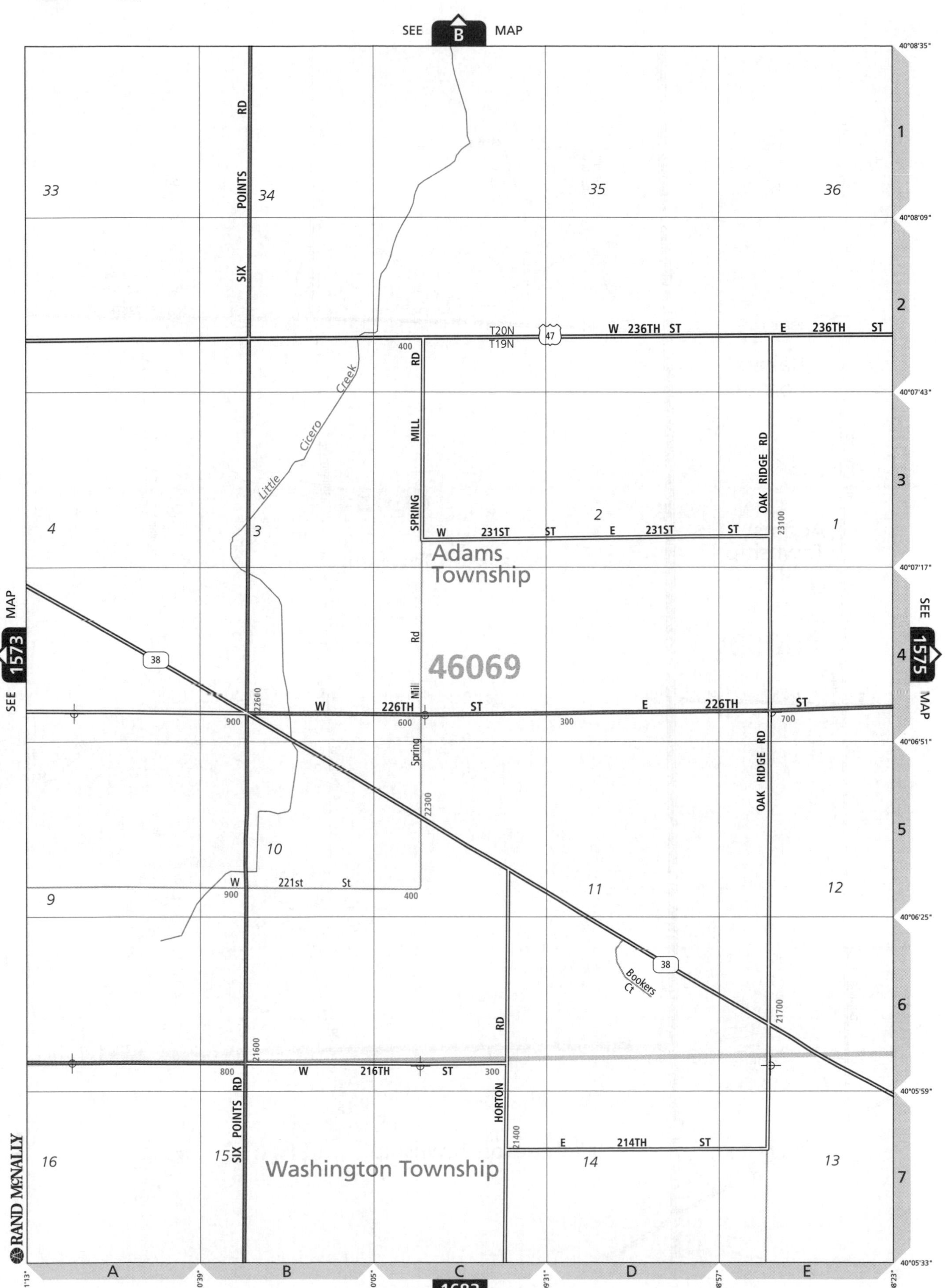

MAP
1574

1:24,000
1 in. = 2000 ft.

0   0.25   0.5
miles

SEE **B** MAP

40°08'35"

33   34   35   36   1

SIX POINTS RD

40°08'09"

40°07'43"

Little Cicero Creek

MILL   RD

SPRING   RD

W 236TH ST   E 236TH ST

47

T20N
T19N

OAK RIDGE RD

400

4   3   2   1   3

Adams
Township

W 231ST ST   E 231ST ST

23100

40°07'17"

46069

Rd

Mill

SEE **1573** MAP

38

40°07'17"

4

SEE **1575** MAP

22660

W 226TH ST   E 226TH ST

900   600   300   700

OAK RIDGE RD

40°06'51"

Spring

22300

5

10

W 221st St

900   400

9   11   12

40°06'25"

38

Bookers Ct

21700

6

RD

21600

800

W 216TH ST   300

HORTON

40°05'59"

21400

16   15   14   13   7

SIX POINTS RD

E 214TH ST

Washington Township

40°05'33"

MAP
1575

1:24,000
1 in. = 2000 ft.

0   0.25   0.5
miles

SEE [B] MAP

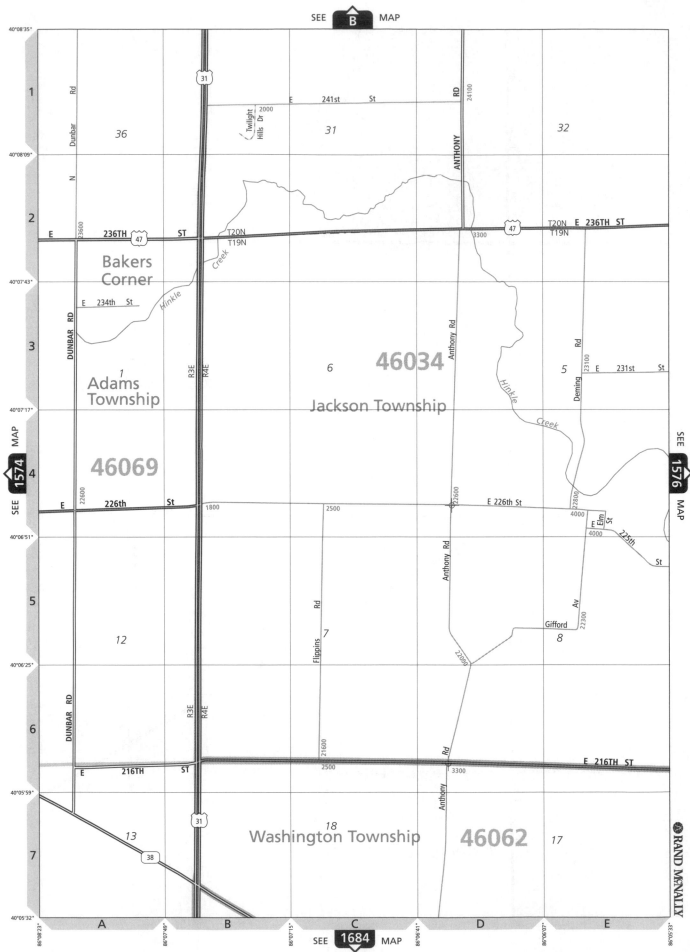

40°08'35"

1

Dunbar Rd

36

31

E 241st St

2000
Twilight Hills Dr

31

ANTHONY RD

24100

32

40°08'09"

N

2

E 23600 236TH [47] ST

T20N
T19N

Hinkle Creek

T20N
T19N
[47] 3300

E 236TH ST

40°07'43"

Bakers Corner

E 234th St

DUNBAR RD

Hinkle

3

1

Adams Township

6

46034

Anthony Rd

Hinkle Creek

5

Deming Rd

23100

E 231st St

R3E R4E

40°07'17"

Jackson Township

SEE 1574 MAP

46069

SEE 1576 MAP

4

E 22600 226th St

1800

2500

22600

E 226th St

22800

4000

E Elm St
4000

225th

St

40°06'51"

5

12

Flippins Rd

7

Anthony Rd

Gifford Av

22300

8

40°06'25"

22000

DUNBAR RD

6

R3E R4E

21600

2500

Anthony Rd

3300

E 216TH ST

E 216TH ST

40°05'59"

7

13

[31]

[38]

18

Washington Township

46062

17

40°05'32"

A   B   C   D   E

86°08'23" 86°07'49" 86°07'15" 86°06'41" 86°06'07" 86°05'33"

SEE 1684 MAP

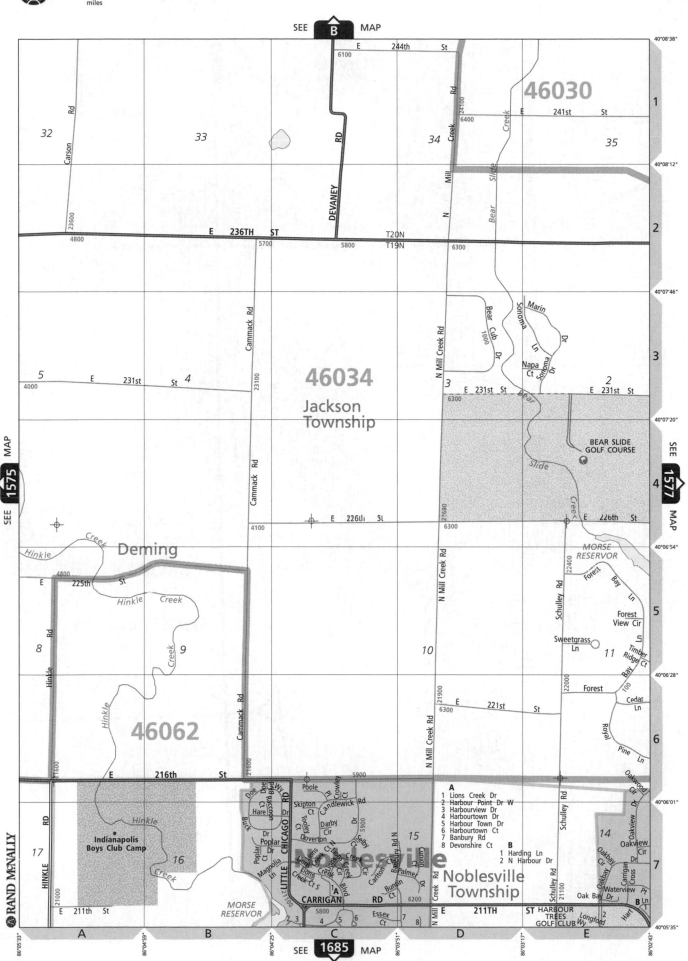

SEE B MAP

46030

46034
Jackson
Township

Deming

46062

Noblesville

Noblesville
Township

E 244th St
E 241st St
E 236TH ST
T20N
T19N
DEVANEY RD
N Mill Creek Rd
Carson Rd
Cammack Rd
Bear Slide Creek
Bear Cub Dr
Sonoma Ln
Marin Dr
Napa Ct
Sonoma Dr
E 231st St
BEAR SLIDE GOLF COURSE
E 226th St
MORSE RESERVOIR
Hinkle Creek
E 225th St
Hinkle Rd
Schulley Rd
Forest Bay Ln
Forest View Cir
Sweetgrass Ln
Timber Ridge Ct
Forest
Cedar Ln
Royal Pine Ln
E 221st St
E 216th St
Indianapolis Boys Club Camp
HINKLE RD
E 211th St
LITTLE CHICAGO RD
CARRIGAN RD
E 211TH ST
HARBOUR TREES GOLF CLUB
Oakwood Cir
Oakview Dr
Oakview Cir
Oakbay Cir
Oak Bay Dr
Carrigan Cross
Waterview Pt
Hart
Longford Wy
Essex Ct
Banbury Rd N
Palmer Dr
Bunbury Ct
Carlton Ct
Poole Pl
Crowley Ct
Candlewick Rd
Skipton Ct
Tooley Ct
Darby Cir
Doverton
Selby Cir
Lions Creek Ct N
Lions Creek Ct S
Lions Creek Cir
Lions Creek Blvd
Doe Ct
Doe Wy
Raccoon Blvd
Hare Dr
Buck
Poplar Ct
Poplar Dr
Magnolia Ln

A
1 Lions Creek Dr
2 Harbour Point Dr W
3 Harbourview Dr
4 Harbourtown Dr
5 Harbour Town Dr
6 Harbourtown Ct
7 Banbury Rd
8 Devonshire Ct

B
1 Harding Ln
2 N Harbour Dr

SEE 1575 MAP
SEE 1577 MAP
SEE 1685 MAP

MAP
1577

1:24,000
1 in. = 2000 ft.

0   0.25   0.5

miles

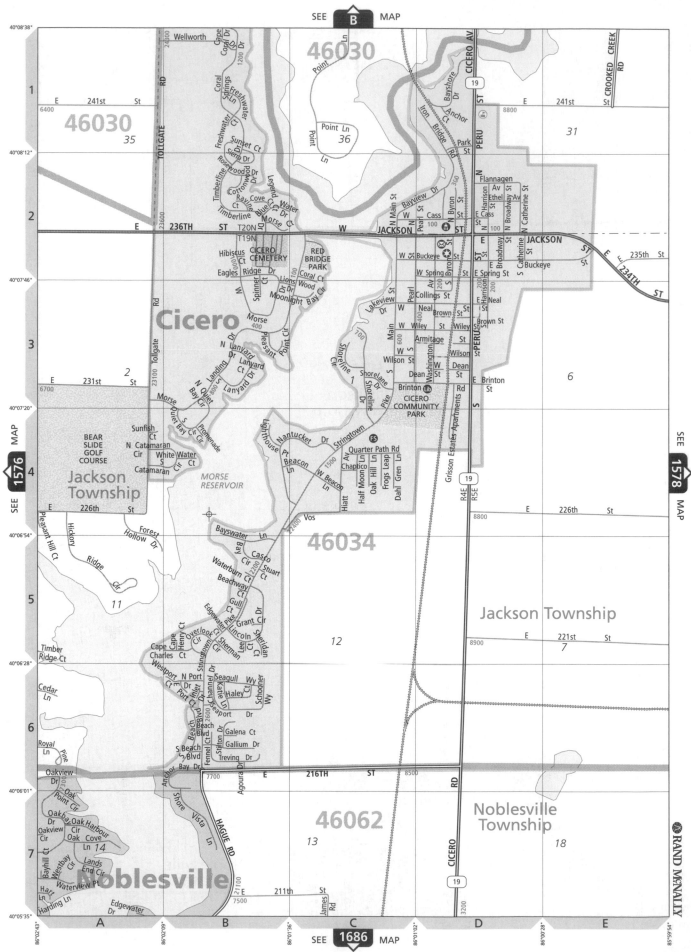

SEE **B** MAP

46030

46030
35

Cicero

Jackson
Township

BEAR
SLIDE
GOLF
COURSE

2

11

MORSE
RESERVOIR

SEE **1576** MAP

36

RED
BRIDGE
PARK

CICERO
CEMETERY

1

CICERO
COMMUNITY
PARK

46034
12

31

JACKSON

6

Jackson Township
7

SEE **1578** MAP

Grisson Estates Apartments

13
46062

Noblesville
Township
18

Noblesville
14

RAND MCNALLY

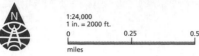

1:24,000
1 in. = 2000 ft.

0   0.25   0.5
miles

MAP
1578

SEE B MAP

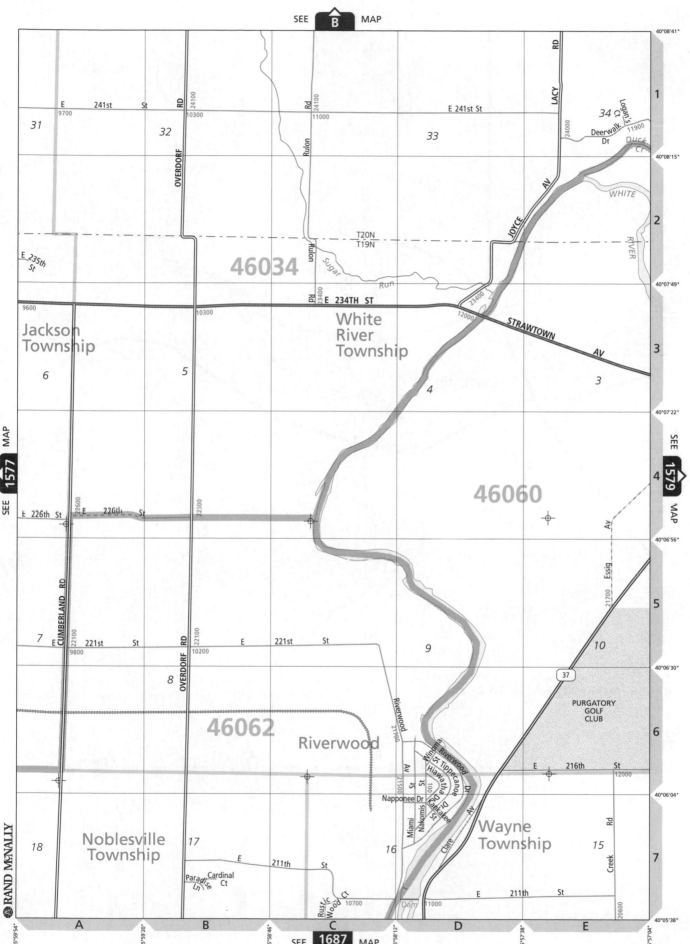

40°08'41"

E   241st   St   RD   24100   Rd   24100   E 241st St   LACY   RD   1

31   *32*   10300   11000   *33*   34   Logan's Ct   40°08'15"

OVERDORF   JOYCE   AV   Deerwalk Dr   Duck Cr   11900

T20N   Rulon   Rd   Sugar   Run   WHITE   RIVER   2

T19N   40°07'49"

E 235th St   Rd   23400   E 234TH ST   23400   STRAWTOWN   40°07'49"

9600   10300   12000

Jackson   White   River   AV   3
Township   Township

6   *5*   *4*   *3*   40°07'22"

46034

SEE 1557 MAP   SEE 1579 MAP   40°07'22"

46060   Essig   Av   40°06'56"

E 226th St   22600   E 226th St   22500   4

CUMBERLAND   RD   40°06'56"

E   221st   St   OVERDORF   RD   22100   E   221st   St   *9*   21700   Essig   *10*   5

7   22100   10200   37   40°06'30"

9800   *8*   PURGATORY   GOLF   CLUB

46062   Riverwood   21700   E   216th   St   6

Riverwood   12000   40°06'04"

Winamac   Tippecanoe   Dr   Riverwood   Dr   40°06'04"

Av   Hiawatha   Dr   100

Napponee Dr   Kankakee   St   Clare   Av

Miami   Nakomis   St   Wayne   Creek   Rd   7

18   Noblesville   *17*   *16*   Township   *15*

Township   E   211st   St

Paradise   Cardinal   Ct   Rustic   Wood Ct   10700   Dam   11000   E   211th   St   20600   40°05'38"

Ln

A   85°59'54"   B   85°59'20"   C   85°58'46"   85°58'12"   D   85°57'38"   E   85°57'04"

MAP
1579

1:24,000
1 in. = 2000 ft.

0   0.25   0.5
miles

SEE **B** MAP

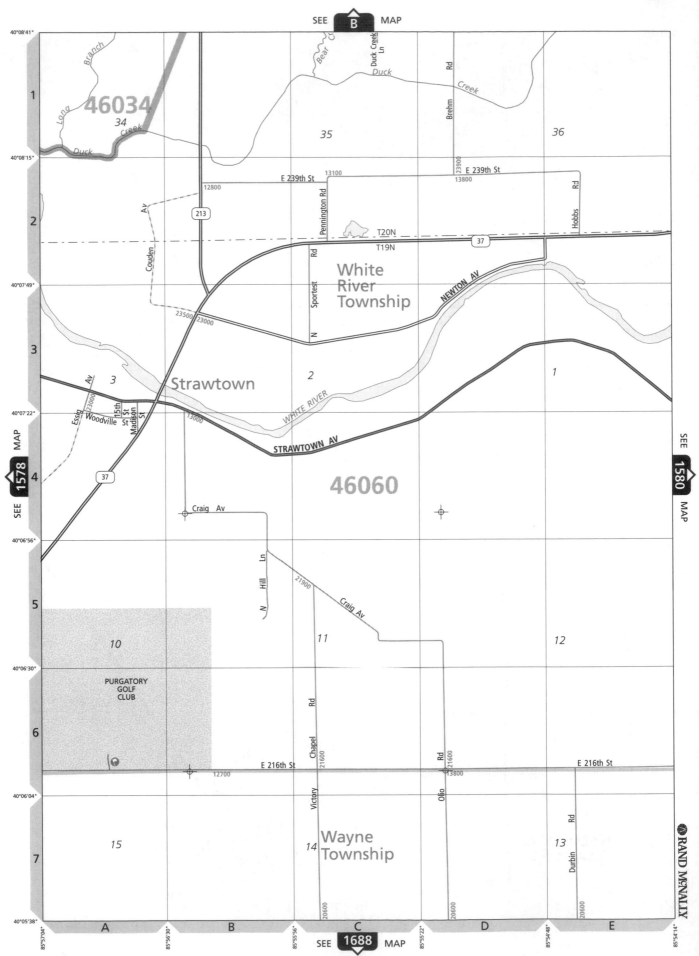

40°08'41"

1

46034
34

Long Branch

Bear C

Duck Creek Ln

Duck

Brehm Rd

Creek

35

36

40°08'15"

13100

E 239th St

12800

E 239th St

13800

23900

Av

213

Pennington Rd

Hobbs Rd

2

Couden

T20N

37

T19N

40°07'49"

Sportest Rd

N

White River Township

Newton Av

23500 23000

3

Av

3

2

1

Strawtown

Essig

15th St

Woodville

Madison St

23000

13000

White River

40°07'22"

Strawtown Av

46060

37

4

40°06'56"

Craig Av

5

N Hill Ln

21900

Craig Av

10

11

12

Purgatory Golf Club

Chapel Rd

21600

Olio Rd

21600

6

E 216th St

12700

13800

E 216th St

Durbin Rd

40°06'04"

15

Victory

14

Wayne Township

13

7

20600

20600

20600

40°05'38"

A   B   C   D   E

85°57'04"   85°56'30"   85°56'56"   85°55'22"   85°54'48"   85°55'58"

SEE 1578 MAP

SEE 1580 MAP

SEE 1688 MAP

RAND McNALLY

SEE B MAP

Perkinsville
Mulberry St
W Center
9800
St
Walnut St
St
WATER ST
N Washington St
Madison St
13
ANDERSON-HAMILTON RD
Florida Rd
Cornell Rd
Pipe Cr
WHITE RIVER
36
31
37
32
33
E ATLANTIC RD
N
T20N
T19N
15800
STRAWTOWN AV
Cornell Rd
HAMILTON CO
MADISON CO
Dyers Creek
R5E R6E
1
6
5
46011
4
Jackson Township
1700
14800
White River Township
46060
W 125 N
E 226th St
W 100 N
1000
12400
5800
Prairie Baptist Rd
CYNTHEANNE RD
RD
12
7
8
9
ATLANTIC
R5E R6E
13
N
21600
E 216th St
21600
5800
E 216th St
100
E
W 10 N
46051
Stony Creek Township
RD
Prairie Baptist Rd
21000
14800
13
18
Wayne Township
17
E 211th St
16
ATLANTIC
20600

40°08'43"
40°08'17"
40°07'51"
40°07'25"
40°06'59"
40°06'33"
40°06'07"
40°05'40"
1
2
3
4
5
6
7
A
B
C
D
E
85°54'14"
85°53'40"
85°53'06"
85°52'32"
85°51'58"
85°51'24"

SEE 1579 MAP
SEE B MAP
SEE 1689 MAP

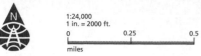

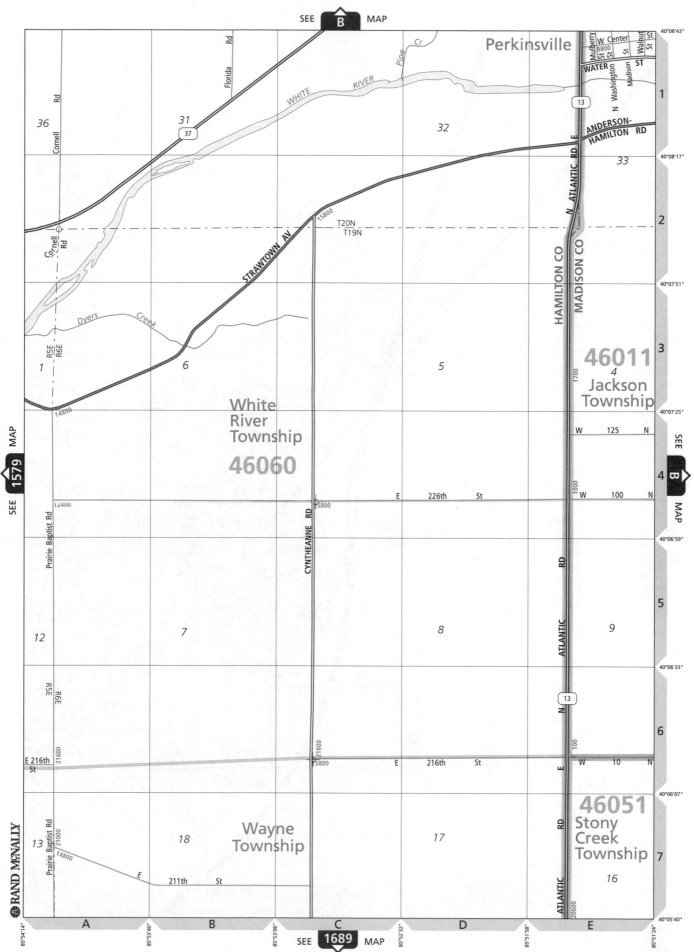

MAP
1676

1:24,000
1 in. = 2000 ft.

0   0.25   0.5
miles

SEE 1567 MAP

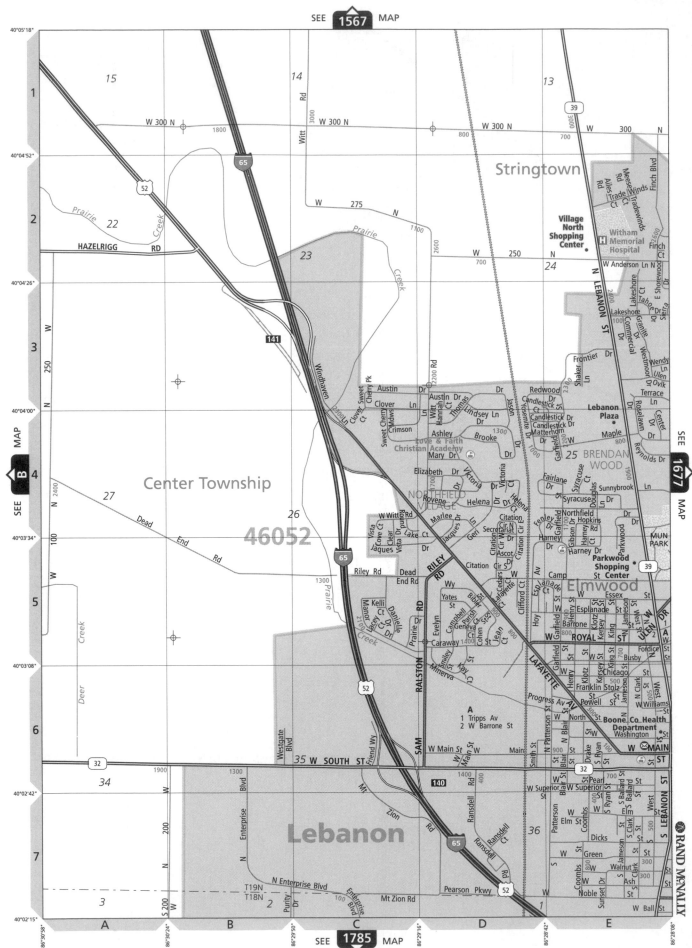

Stringtown

Village North Shopping Center

Witham Memorial Hospital

Center Township

46052

NORTHFIELD VILLAGE

Love & Faith Christian Academy

Lebanon Plaza

BRENDAN WOOD

Elmwood

Parkwood Shopping Center

MUN PARK

A
1 Tripps Av
2 W Barrone St

Boone Co. Health Department

Lebanon

SEE 1677 MAP

SEE B MAP

RAND McNALLY

T19N
T18N

A   B   C   D   E

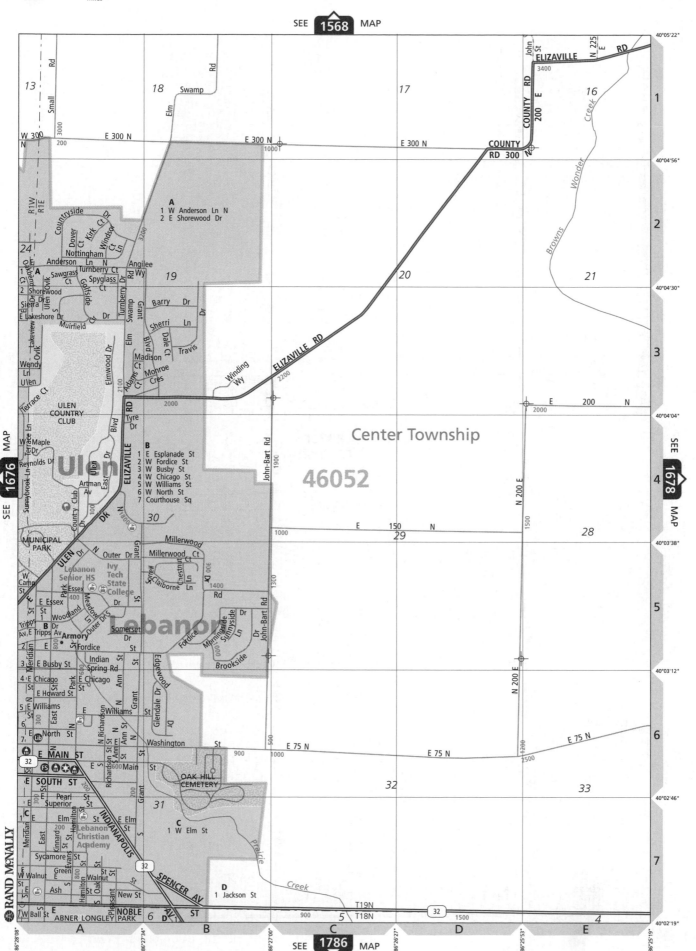

1:24,000
1 in. = 2000 ft.

0   0.25   0.5
miles

N

40°05'22"

13   18   Swamp Rd   17   Elizaville   16   40°04'56"
John St   N 225 E   RD

W 300 N   E 300 N   E 300 N   E 300 N   COUNTY RD 300 N   COUNTY   200 E

A
1 W Anderson Ln N
2 E Shorewood Dr

24   Countryside   19   20   21   40°04'30"

Anderson Ln N   Angilee Wy

Turnberry Ct   Spyglass Ct   Barry Dr

Sherri Ln   Travis   Dale Ct   Madison

ELIZAVILLE RD

Monroe Cres   Winding Wy   2200   40°04'04"

ULEN COUNTRY CLUB   2000   E 200 N   2000

Center Township

Ulen   B
1 E Esplanade St
2 W Fordice St
3 W Busby St
4 W Chicago St
5 W Williams St
6 W North St
7 Courthouse Sq

46052

John-Bart Rd   1900

N 200 E   1500   40°04'04"

SEE 1676 MAP   30   E 150 N   29   28   40°03'38"
1000

MUNICIPAL PARK   Millerwood Dr   Millerwood Ct   1300   N 200 E   1500

Lebanon Senior HS   Ivy Tech State College   Claiborne Ln   Chestnut Ln   1400   Rd

Lebanon   SEE 1678 MAP

Essex   Woodland   Somerset Dr   Fordice   Morningside   Sunnyside Ln   John-Bart Rd   40°03'12"

Armory   Brookside   500   E 75 N   N 200 E   40°03'12"

Indian Spring Rd   E Chicago St   Ann   Grant   Edgewood Dr   Glendale Dr   E 75 N   E 75 N   200   40°03'12"

E Howard St   Williams   2500   6

E North   Washington St   500   E 75 N   1000   E 75 N   2500   40°02'46"

E MAIN ST   32   Main St   OAK HILL CEMETERY   32   33   40°02'46"

SOUTH ST   Grant St   31   32   33

Pearl   Superior   E Elm St

C
1 W Elm St

Lebanon Christian Academy   INDIANAPOLIS

32   Walnut   SPENCER AV   Prairie Creek

D
1 Jackson St   T19N   32   1500   40°02'19"
T18N

RAND McNALLY   ABNER LONGLEY   NOBLE PARK   6   5   900   4

A   B   C   D   E

86°28'08"   86°27'34"   86°27'00"   86°26'27"   86°25'53"   86°25'19"

MAP 1678

SEE 1569 MAP

1:24,000
1 in. = 2000 ft.

0   0.25   0.5
miles

SEE 1677 MAP

SEE 1679 MAP

SEE 1787 MAP

RAND McNALLY

MAP
1679

1:24,000
1 in. = 2000 ft.

0   0.25   0.5
miles

SEE 1570 MAP

SEE 1678 MAP

SEE 1680 MAP

SEE 1788 MAP

13   18   17

Fairview Rd

550 N   600 N

E 300 N

Marion
Township

E 275 N

Slabtown Rd

Mounts   Run

N 675 E

19   20

E 250 N
2500 N
5000   24   5500

N 600 E

N 675 E

E 200   7100 N

Center
Township

46052

2200

1400

R2E

25   30   29

E 150 N

N 600 E

1300   1500

46075

N 650 E

5000   E 100 N   6500   E 100 N

800

Union
Township

36   31   32

N 600 E

R1E R2E 700

Mounts   Run

600

N 100

RAND MCNALLY

Gadsden

W BASE LINE RD   T19N   32

A   B   C   D   E

40°05'26"
40°05'00"
40°04'34"
40°04'08"
40°03'41"
40°03'15"
40°02'49"
40°02'23"

86°22'29"   86°21'55"   86°21'21"   86°20'47"   86°20'13"   86°19'39"

MAP 1680

SEE 1571 MAP

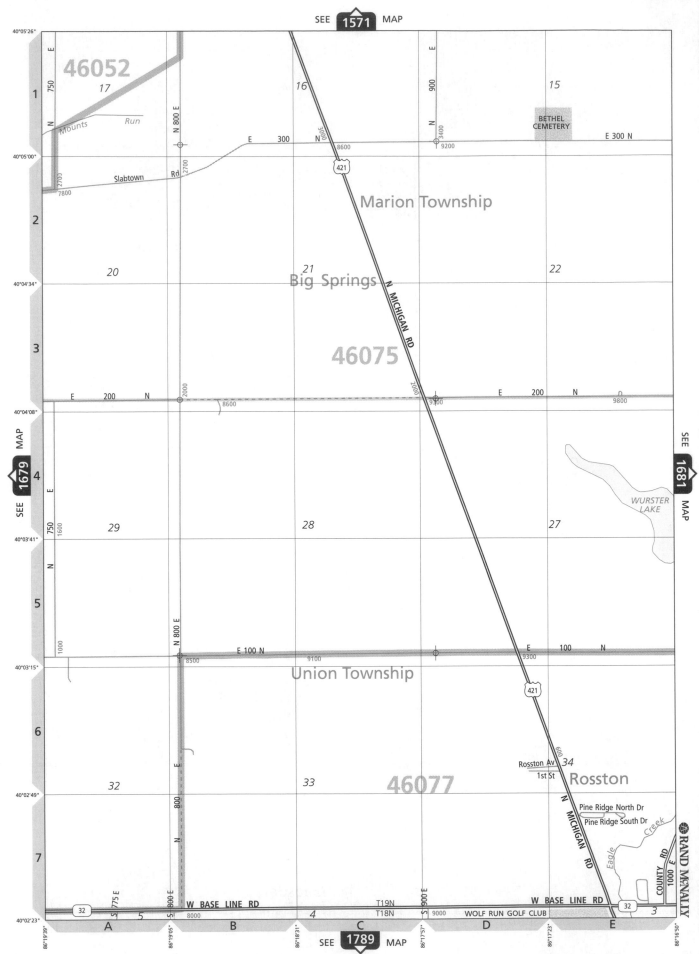

46052

17

Mounts   Run

16

15

BETHEL
CEMETERY

E 300 N

N 800 E

E 300 N
8600
9200

421

Slabtown   Rd

Marion Township

7800

2

20

21

Big Springs

22

46075

N MICHIGAN RD

3

E 200 N
2000

E 200 N
9800
8600
2000
9300

SEE 1679 MAP

SEE 1681 MAP

4

WURSTER
LAKE

29

28

27

750
1600

5

1000

N 800 E

E 100 N
8500
9100
E 100 N
9300

Union Township

6

421

Rosston Av   34
1st St

Rosston

32

33

46077

N MICHIGAN RD

Pine Ridge North Dr
Pine Ridge South Dr

Eagle   Creek

7

800 N

COUNTY RD E 1000

RAND McNALLY

S 775 E
S 800 E

W BASE LINE RD
8000

T19N
T18N
S 900 E
9000

W BASE LINE RD

WOLF RUN GOLF CLUB

32

32

A   5   B   4   C   D   E   3

MAP
1681

1:24,000
1 in. = 2000 ft.

0   0.25   0.5
miles

SEE **1572** MAP

40°05'29"

15

14

13

18

1

COUNTY RD 1000 E

E 300 N   E 300 N   W 206TH ST

10800   11900   4100

Stuckey
Farm
Market

40°05'03"

Marion
Township

1200 E

Ditch

Kreager

2

22

23

24

19

40°04'37"

R2E | R3E

BOONE CO | HAMILTON CO

Big Springs Rd

Creek

Eagle

2400

46069

3

19600

2000

PARR-
JONES
CEMETERY

E 200 N   E 200 N   W 196th St

10900   11700   4400

40°04'11"

SEE **1680** MAP

N 1100 E

Washington
Township

SEE **1682** MAP

27

WURSTER
LK

26

25

30

4

COUNTY RD 1000 E

40°03'45"

Union
Township

1200 E

5

1000

E 100 N   10900   E 100 N   W 186TH ST

10600 11300   4100

40°03'19"

Eagle

Creek

Creek

Finley

6

35

36

31

N 1100 E

400

46077

R2E | R3E

40°02'53"

34

17600

7

32

T19N
T18N   W BASE LINE RD   T19N
T18N   W 176TH ST

Taylor Rd

3   2   11000   Indianapolis Terry Arpt 1   46074 6   4100

40°02'27"

86°16'50"   86°15'42"   86°15'08"   86°14'34"   86°14'00"

A   B   C   D   E

SEE **1790** MAP

MAP
1682

1:24,000
1 in. = 2000 ft.

0   0.25   0.5
miles

SEE **1573** MAP

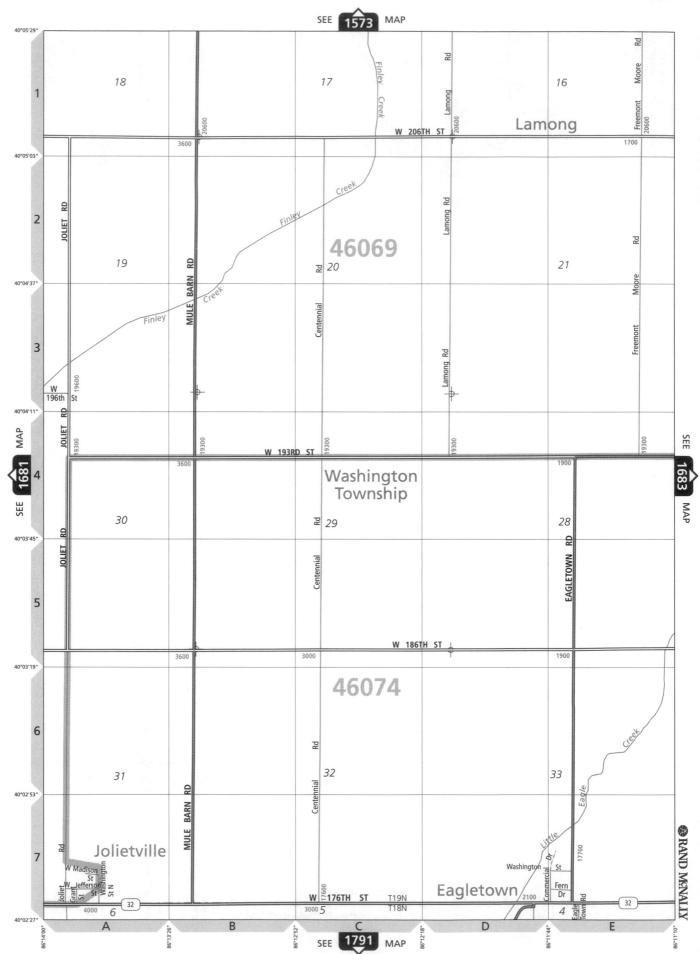

18

17

16

Finley Creek

Rd

Moore Rd

Lamong Rd

1

W 206TH ST

Lamong

20600

3600

20600

1700

JOLIET RD

2

MULE BARN RD

19

Finley Creek

Creek

46069

Rd

Centennial

20

Lamong Rd

21

Rd

Moore Rd

19600

3

Finley Creek

Lamong Rd

Freemont

W 196th St

SEE **1681** MAP

JOLIET RD

19300

4

W 193RD ST

3600

19300

19300

19300

Washington
Township

1900

19300

SEE **1683** MAP

JOLIET RD

30

Rd

Centennial

29

28

EAGLETOWN RD

5

W 186TH ST

3600

3000

1900

46074

6

Centennial Rd

Creek

Eagle

31

MULE BARN RD

32

33

Little

7

Rd

Jolietville

Washington

Commercial Dr

17700

W Madison St

Fern Dr

W Jefferson St

Washington St N

Joliet St

Grant St

Eagletown

Eagle Town Rd

32

W 176TH ST

T19N

2100

32

4000

6

W 17600

3000

5

T18N

4

RAND McNALLY

86°14'00"   A   86°13'26"   B   86°12'52"   C   86°12'18"   D   86°11'44"   E

40°05'29"
40°05'03"
40°04'37"
40°04'11"
40°03'45"
40°03'19"
40°02'53"
40°02'27"

·01·11·98

MAP
1683

1:24,000
1 in. = 2000 ft.

0   0.25   0.5
miles

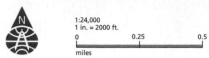

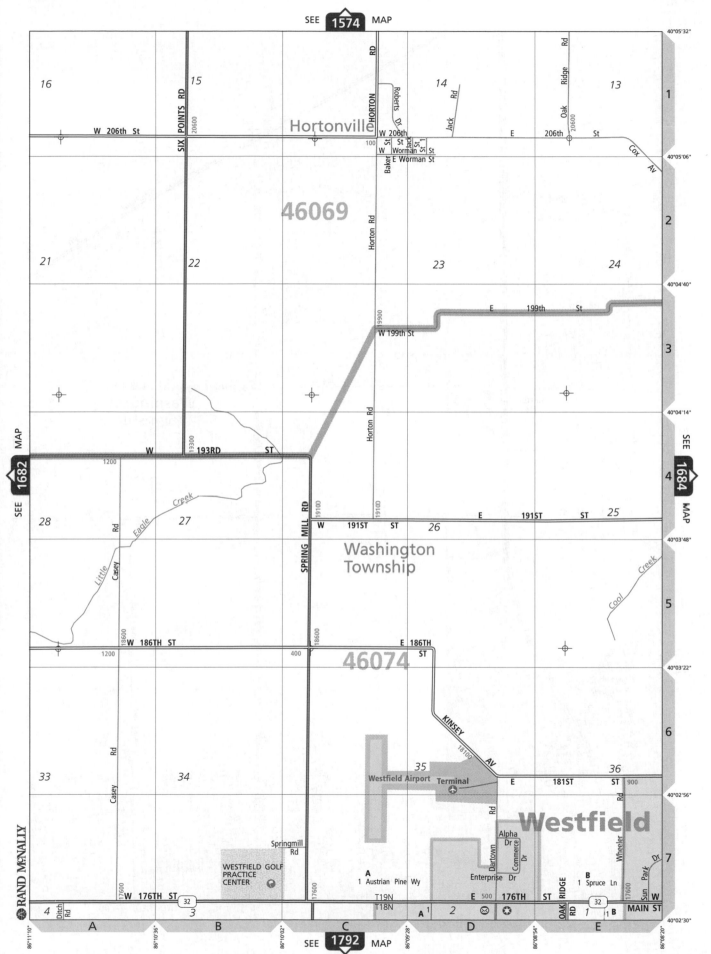

SEE **1574** MAP

40°05'32"

16   15

Oak   Ridge   Rd

Hortonville   14   13

W 206th St

SIX POINTS RD

20600

HORTON RD

Roberts Dr

Jack Rd

Oak   20600

E   206th   St

W 206th St

Cox Av

40°05'06"

100   St   St Jack St 1 St

W Worman   St St St
Baker   E Worman St

46069

Horton Rd

1

2

21   22   23   24

40°04'40"

E   199th   St

19900

W 199th St

3

Creek

Horton Rd

SEE **1682** MAP

1200   W   **193RD**   ST

19300

19100

19100

40°04'14"

SEE **1684** MAP

4

28   27

Little   Eagle   Rd

Casey   Rd

E   **191ST**   ST   25

W   **191ST**   ST   26

40°03'48"

Washington
Township

SPRING MILL RD

Cool Creek

5

18600   W   **186TH**   ST

1200

18600

E **186TH**
ST

40°03'22"

46074

400

6

33   34

Casey   Rd

KINSEY

18100

AV

35   E   **181ST**   ST   900

40°02'56"

Westfield Airport   Terminal

E

Westfield

Rd

36

Alpha
Dr

Springmill
Rd

Commerce
Dr

Wheeler Rd

17600

Sun Park Dr

7

WESTFIELD GOLF
PRACTICE
CENTER

A
1 Austrian Pine Wy

Dartown Rd

Enterprise   Dr

B
1 Spruce Ln

17600   W   **176TH**   ST

32

17600

T19N
T18N

E   500   **176TH**   ST

OAK RIDGE RD

32

W

MAIN ST

4   Ditch Rd   3   A ¹   2   D   1   ¹ B

A   B   C   D   E

40°02'30"

86°11'10"   86°10'36"   86°10'02"   86°09'28"   86°08'54"   86°08'20"

SEE **1792** MAP

MAP
1684

1:24,000
1 in. = 2000 ft.

0   0.25   0.5

miles

SEE 1575 MAP

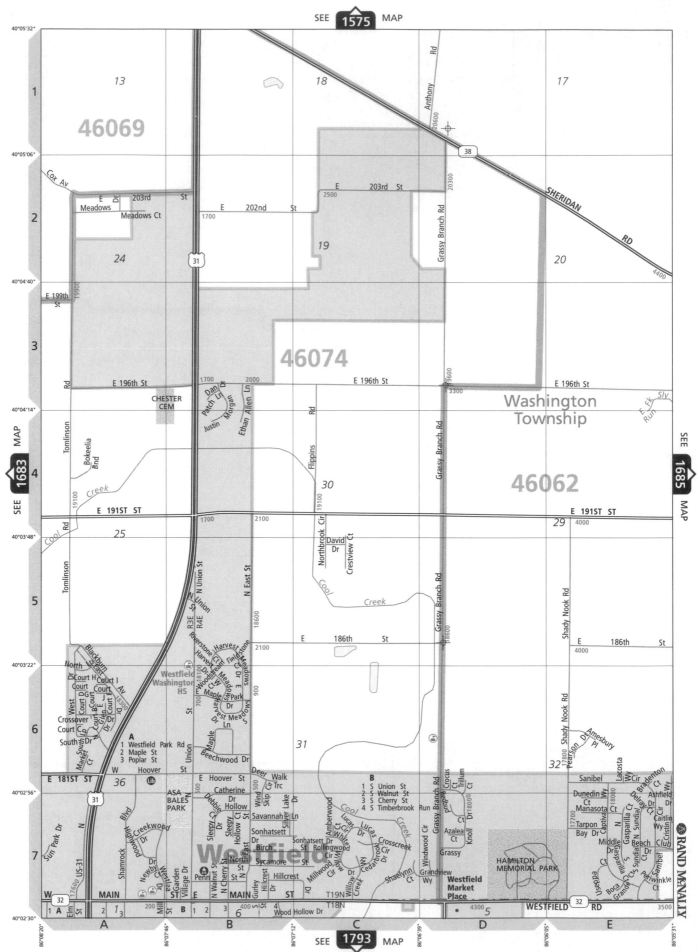

40°05'32"

13

18

17

46069

40°05'06"

Rd

Anthony

20600

38

SHERIDAN RD

Cox Av

E   203rd   St

20300

E Dr   203rd   St

Meadows

2500

Meadows Ct

E   202nd   St

1700

Grassy Branch Rd

40°04'40"

24

31

19

20

4400

E 199th St

19900

40°04'14"

Rd

E 196th St

1700

2000

46074

E 196th St

9600

3300

E 196th St

CHESTER CEM

Dan Patch Ln

Justin Morgan

Ethan Allen Ln

Washington Township

E Fk Sly Run

SEE 1683 MAP

Tomlinson

Bokeelia Bnd

Rd

Flippins

Grassy Branch Rd

46062

SEE 1685 MAP

19100

Creek

30

19100

E 191ST ST

E 191ST ST

Cool Rd

40°03'48"

25

1700

2100

Northbrook Cir

David Dr

Crestview Ct

29

4000

Tomlinson

N Union St

N East St

Cool

Creek

Grassy Branch Rd

Shady Nook Rd

R3E R4E

18600

18500

18600

E   186th   St

E   186th   St

2100

4000

40°03'22"

Blackburn

North

Riverstone Ct

Hansel

Harvest Fieldstone

Meadows

900

Westfield Washington HS

18300

18100

700

Woodstream

Maple

Harvest Meadows Ln

Maple Park Dr

31

Shady Nook Rd

17800

Pearson Dr

Amesbury Pl

Lacosta

Court H

Court I

Court D

Court C

Glen E

Court F

West Court

Crossover Court

South Dr

South Ct

N

Market Ct

A

1 Westfield Park Rd

2 Maple St

3 Poplar St

Union St

Maple

Beechwood Dr

32

17700

Sanibel

Dunedin Ct

Manasota Ct

Tarpon Bay Dr

Delray Wy

18000

Gasparilla Ct

Cir

Ashfield Dr

Caitlin Dr

Cristin

Sanibel

E 181ST ST

36

W Hoover

40°02'56"

31

Lib

E Hoover St

500

Deer Walk Trc

Wind Skip

500

Silver Lake Dr

B

1 S Union St

2 S Walnut St

3 S Cherry St

4 S Timberbrook St

Grassy Branch Rd

Crocus Ct

Trillum Ct

Middle

Boca Grande Dr

Beach

Club

ASA BALES PARK

Catherine Dr

Debbie Ct

Sleepy Hollow Ct

Sleepy Hollow Dr

Savannah

Sonhatsett Dr

Amberwood

Lucas Ct

Lucas Dr

White

Crosscreek Cir

Cedarbrook Cir

Cool Creek

Windwood Cir

Azalea Knoll

Grassy Dr

Sundial

Manasota

Usepa

Sundial

Periwinkle

Westfield

Sun Park Dr

Shamrock Blvd

1600 US-31

Newby Ct

Creekwood Dr

Penn

N Walnut St

N Cherry St

North St

Birch St

Sycamore St

Gurley Ct

Hillcrest St

Hillcrest

Millwood Dr

Willow Dr

Rollingwood

Shaelynn Ct

Grandview Wy

Run

Westfield Market Place

HAMILTON MEMORIAL PARK

40°02'30"

W

32

1 A

Elm St

Main

2

1 3

200

Mill St

B

1 2

6

3

400

4

Wood Hollow Dr

T19N

T18N

WESTFIELD RD

4300

5

3500

32

A   B   C   D   E

86°08'20"   86°07'46"   86°07'12"   86°06'39"   86°06'05"

SEE 1793 MAP

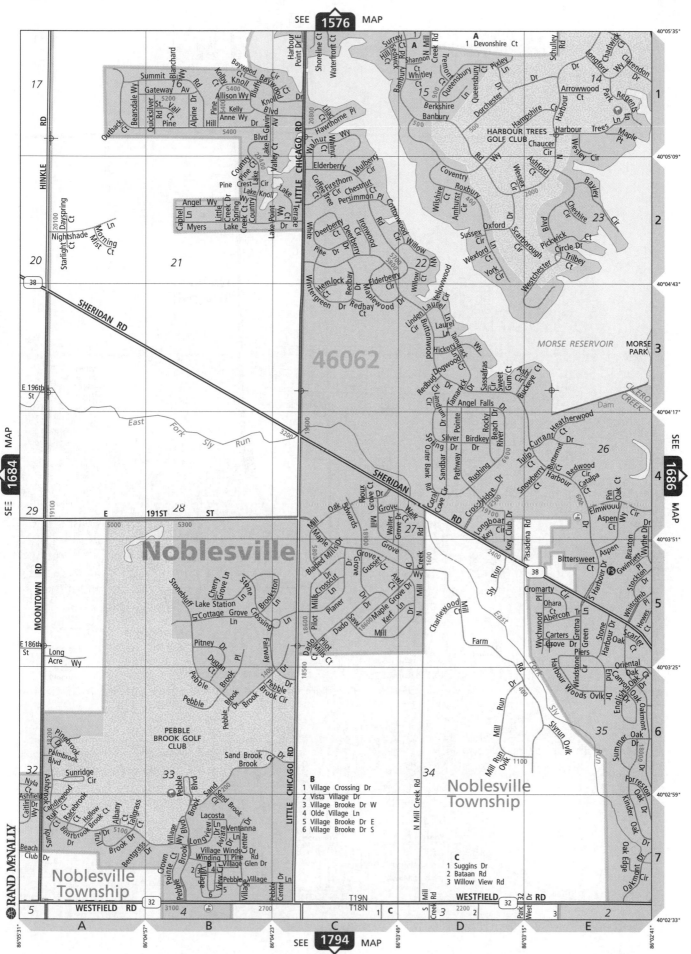

MAP
1685

1:24,000
1 in. = 2000 ft.

0   0.25   0.5
miles

SEE 1576 MAP

SEE 1684 MAP

SEE 1686 MAP

Noblesville

46062

MORSE RESERVOIR

MORSE PARK

CICERO CREEK

Dam

HARBOUR TREES GOLF CLUB

SHERIDAN RD

PEBBLE BROOK GOLF CLUB

Noblesville Township

Noblesville Township

B
1 Village Crossing Dr
2 Vista Village Dr
3 Village Brooke Dr W
4 Olde Village Ln
5 Village Brooke Dr E
6 Village Brooke Dr S

C
1 Suggins Dr
2 Bataan Rd
3 Willow View Rd

SEE 1794 MAP

WESTFIELD RD

T19N
T18N

WESTFIELD RD

MAP
1686

1:24,000
1 in. = 2000 ft.
0   0.25   0.5
miles

SEE 1577 MAP

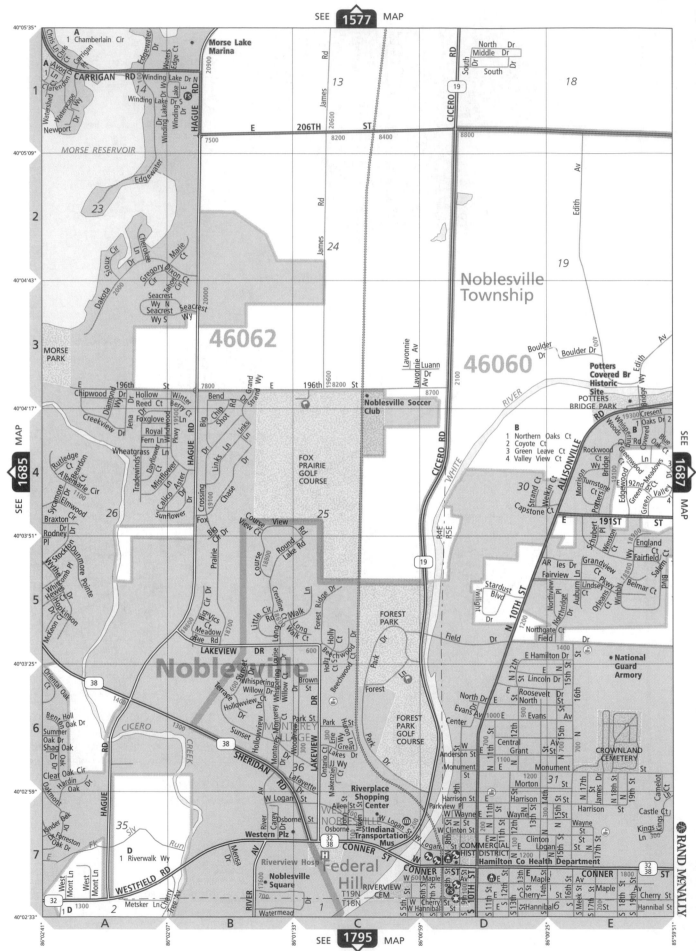

SEE 1685 MAP

SEE 1687 MAP

46062

Noblesville
Township

46060

MORSE RESERVOIR

MORSE PARK

Noblesville Soccer Club

FOX PRAIRIE GOLF COURSE

Noblesville

FOREST PARK

FOREST PARK GOLF COURSE

Potters Covered Br Historic Site
POTTERS BRIDGE PARK

B
1 Northern Oaks Ct
2 Coyote Ct
3 Green Leave Ct
4 Valley View Ct

National Guard Armory

CROWNLAND CEMETERY

Riverplace Shopping Center

WEST NOBLESVILLE

Indiana Transportation Mus

COMMERCIAL HIST DISTRICT
Hamilton Co Health Department

D
1 Riverwalk Wy

Riverview Hosp

Federal Hill

Western Plz

Noblesville Square

RIVERVIEW CEM

RAND McNALLY

MAP
1687

1:24,000
1 in. = 2000 ft.

0   0.25   0.5
miles

SEE 1578 MAP

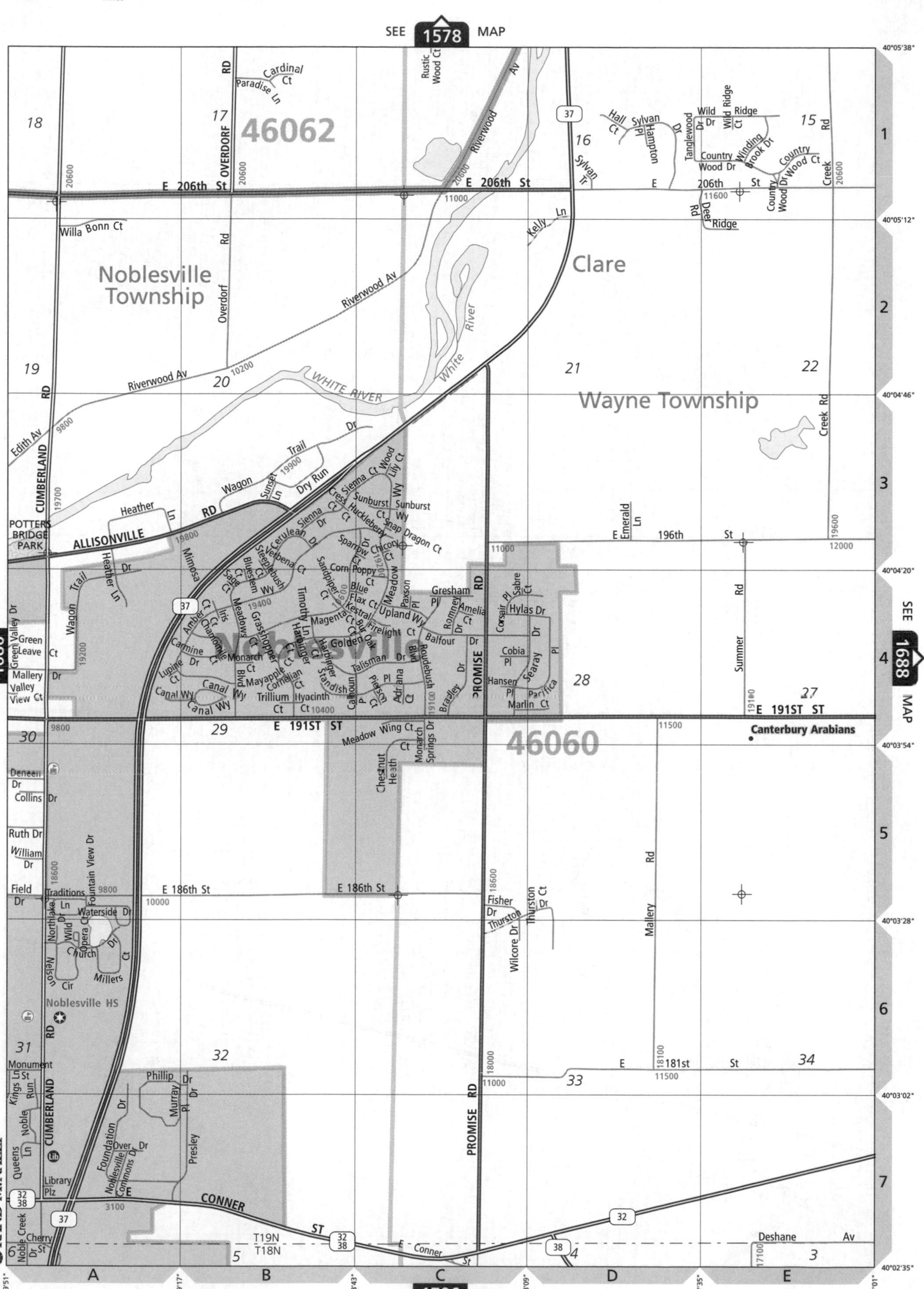

SEE 1686 MAP

SEE 1688 MAP

46062

18
17
19
20
21
22
16
15

Noblesville
Township

Clare

Wayne Township

Noblesville

46060

Canterbury Arabians

30
29
31
32
33
34
27
28

RAND McNALLY

SEE 1796 MAP

A   B   C   D   E

40°05'38"
40°05'12"
40°04'46"
40°04'20"
40°03'54"
40°03'28"
40°03'02"
40°02'35"

85°59'51"   85°59'17"   85°58'43"   85°58'09"   85°57'35"   85°57'01"

1   2   3   4   5   6   7

MAP
1688

1:24,000
1 in. = 2000 ft.
0   0.25   0.5
miles

SEE 1579 MAP

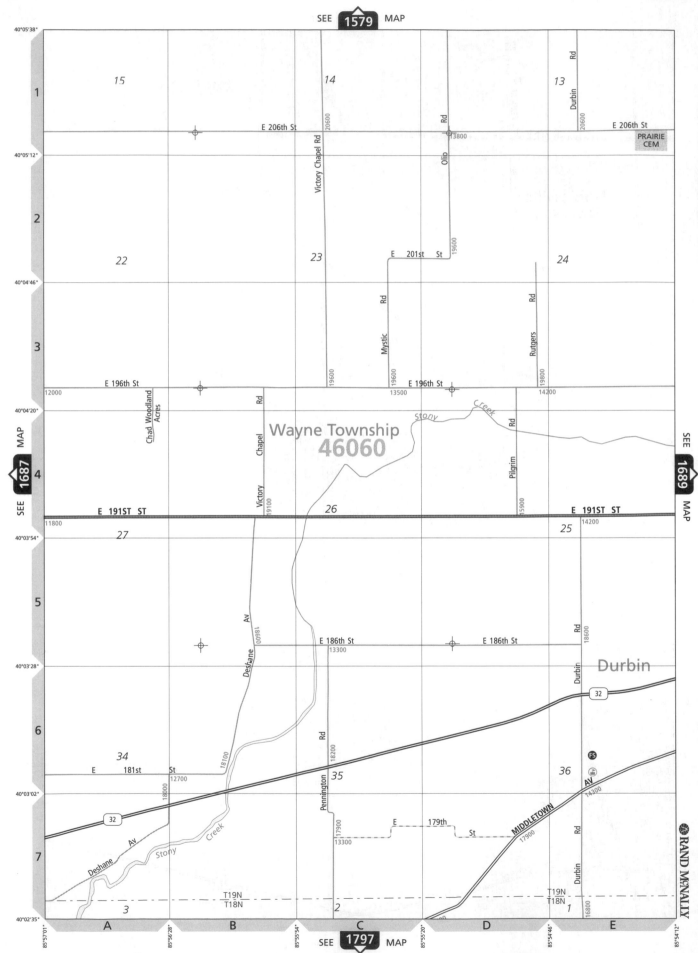

SEE 1687 MAP

SEE 1689 MAP

SEE 1797 MAP

RAND McNALLY

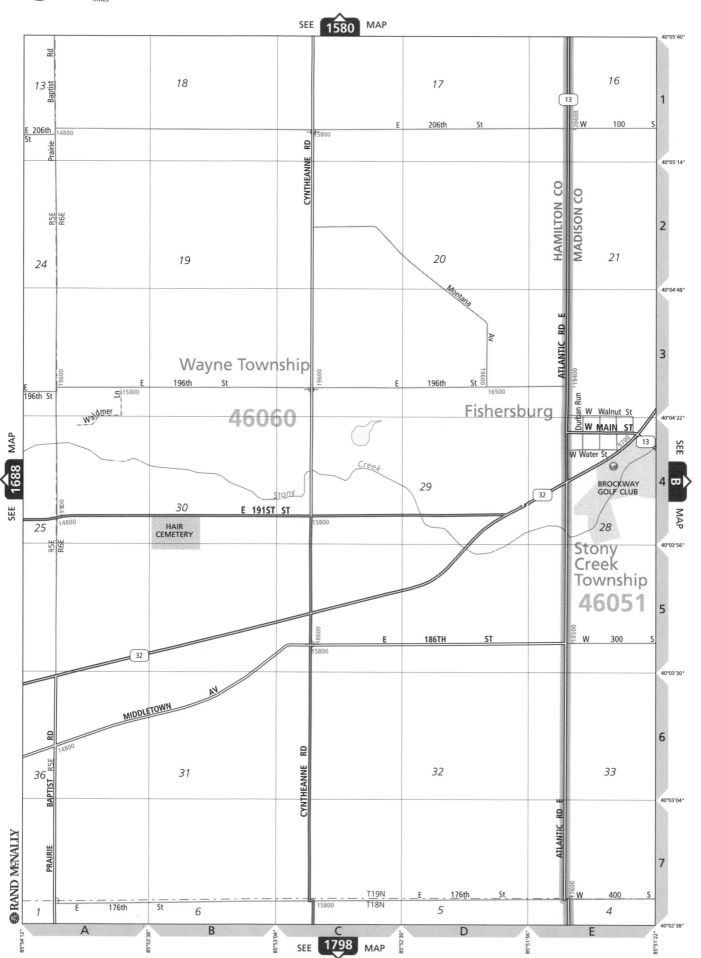

MAP
1689

1:24,000
1 in. = 2000 ft.

0   0.25   0.5

miles

SEE **1580** MAP

40°05'40"

13   Baptist Rd   18   17   16

13   W   W 100 S   1

E 206th St   14800   E   206th   St   15800   120600   40°05'14"

Prairie

R5E R6E

24   19   20   21   2

Montana   Av   40°04'48"

HAMILTON CO   MADISON CO

Wayne Township

46060   3

19600   ATLANTIC RD E   40°04'22"

E 196th St   E   196th   St   19600   E   196th   St   16500   19400   W MAIN ST

Fishersburg   Durbian Run   W Walnut St   13

Waldmer Ln   15000   46060   Creek   W Water St   40°04'22"

SEE **1688** MAP   Stony   29   BROCKWAY GOLF CLUB   SEE **B** MAP

30   E 191ST ST   32

9800   14800   HAIR CEMETERY   15800   32   28   40°03'56"

25   R5E R6E   Stony Creek Township   **46051**   5

40°03'30"

32   E   186TH   ST   18500   W 300 S

18600   15800

MIDDLETOWN   AV   6

14800   40°03'04"

36   BAPTIST RD   31   CYNTHEANNE RD   32   33   ATLANTIC RD E

7

PRAIRIE   T19N   E   176th   St   17600   W 400 S

1   E   176th   St   6   15800   T18N   5   4

40°02'38"

A   B   C   D   E

85°54'12"   85°53'38"   85°53'04"   85°52'30"   85°51'56"   85°51'22"

SEE **1798** MAP

RAND McNALLY

MAP
1785

1:24,000
1 in. = 2000 ft.
0   0.25   0.5
miles

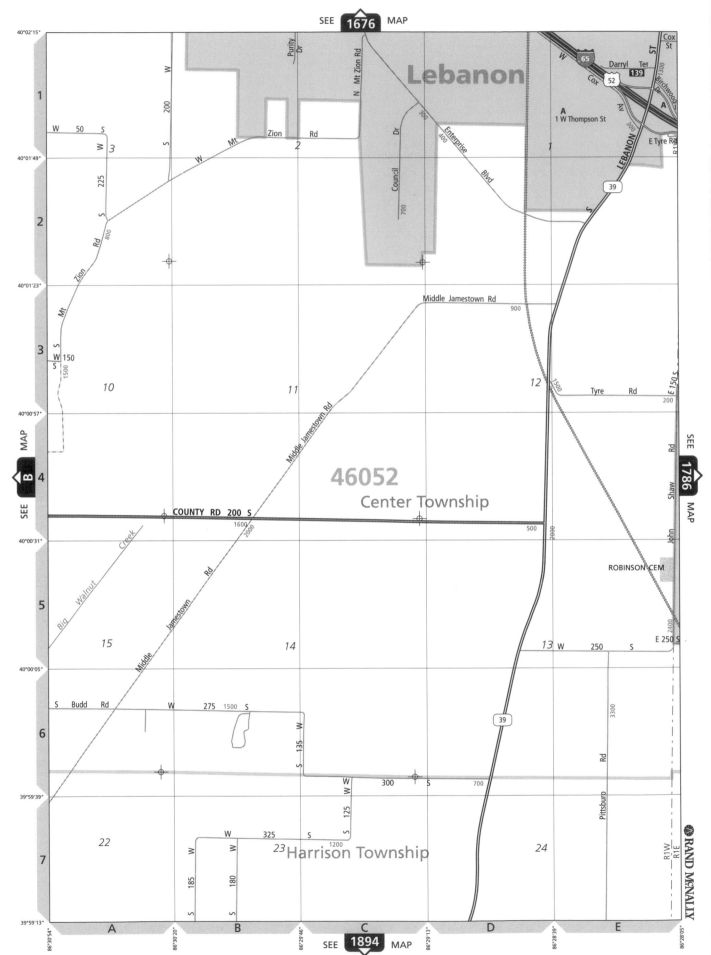

SEE 1676 MAP

Lebanon

I-65
139
Cox St
Darryl Ter
52
Birchwood
A
1 W Thompson St
E Tyre Rd
Lebanon
39

Purity Dr
Mt Zion Rd
N
Zion   Rd
2
W   Mt
W   50   S
W   3
S
S
200
S
225
S
800
Mt   Zion   Rd
W   150
S
1500
S
Council Dr
300
400
700
Enterprise   Blvd
S

10
11
12

Middle Jamestown Rd
900
1500
Tyre   Rd
E 150 S
200

SEE B MAP

B

SEE 1786 MAP

46052
Center Township

Middle Jamestown Rd

COUNTY RD 200 S
1600
2000
500
2000
John Shaw Rd

ROBINSON CEM

Big   Walnut   Creek
Middle   Jamestown   Rd

15
14
13   W   250   S
E 250 S

S Budd Rd   W   275   1500 S

W
S
135
W

39

3300
Pittsburg   Rd

W   300   S   700

W
S
125

22
W   325   S
1200
23 Harrison Township
24

S
185
W
S
180
W

7

RAND McNALLY
R1W R1E

40°02'15"
40°01'49"
40°01'23"
40°00'57"
40°00'31"
40°00'05"
39°59'39"
39°59'13"

86°30'54"
86°30'20"
86°29'46"
86°29'13"
86°28'39"
86°28'05"

A   B   C   D   E

1
2
3
4
5
6
7

1:24,000
1 in. = 2000 ft.

0   0.25   0.5
miles

MAP
1786

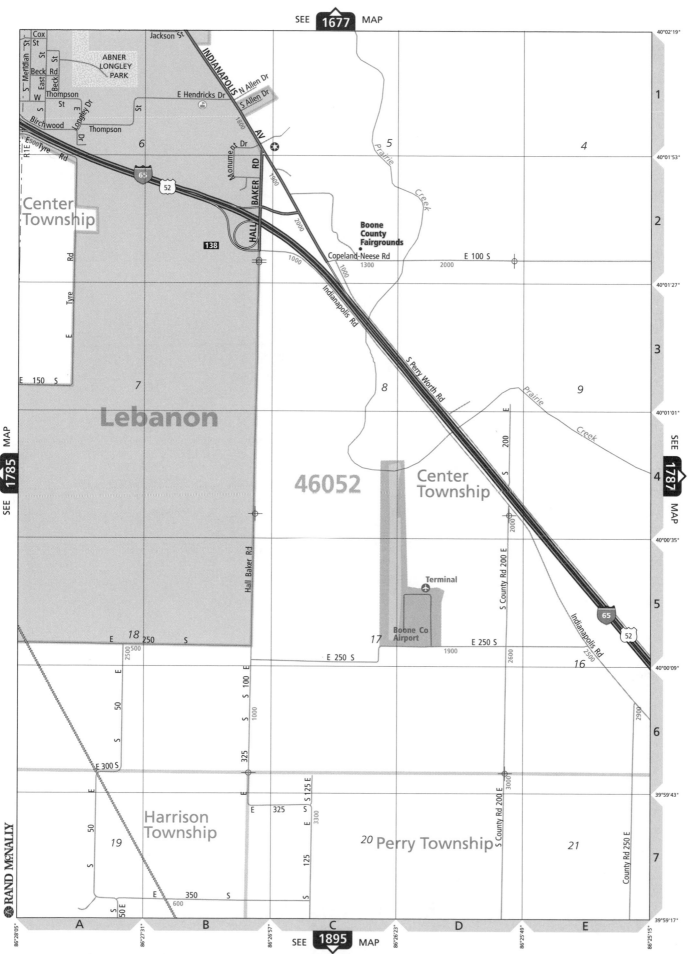

SEE ◆ 1677 MAP

Jackson St

ABNER
LONGLEY
PARK

Cox
St

S Meridian St
Beck St
East St
W

Beck Rd

Thompson
St

Longley Dr
E

Birchwood Dr

Thompson

E 500 Tyre Rd
R1E

Center
Township

N Allen Dr
E Hendricks Dr
S Allen Dr

INDIANAPOLIS AV

Monument Dr

BAKER RD

HALL

65
52

138

6

Tyre Rd
E

Tyre
E

E 150 S

7

Lebanon

5

4

1

40°02'19"

40°01'53"

Boone
County
Fairgrounds

Copeland-Neese Rd
1300

E 100 S
2000

1800

1900

2000

1000

1000

2

40°01'27"

Indianapolis Rd

8

S Perry Worth Rd

Prairie

Creek

9

3

40°01'01"

SEE ◆ 1785 MAP

SEE ▶ 1787 MAP

46052

Center
Township

E
S

200

4

40°00'35"

2000

S County Rd 200 E

Indianapolis Rd

65
52

5

Terminal

Boone Co
Airport

Hall Baker Rd

18

E 250 S

2500 500

E

17

E 250 S
1900

E 250 S

2600

2500

16

5

40°00'09"

S 100 E
1000

325

E

S

50

E

S

E 300 S

325

E
S 125 E
3300

125

S

Harrison
Township

19

50

S
E

E 350 S

600

50 E
S

S County Rd 200 E

3000

20 Perry Township

County Rd 250 E

21

2900

6

40°59'43"

7

40°59'17"

A   B   C   D   E

SEE ◆ 1895 MAP

86°28'05"   86°27'31"   86°26'57"   86°26'23"   86°25'49"   86°25'15"

RAND McNALLY

MAP
1787

1:24,000
1 in. = 2000 ft.

0   0.25   0.5
miles

SEE 1678 MAP

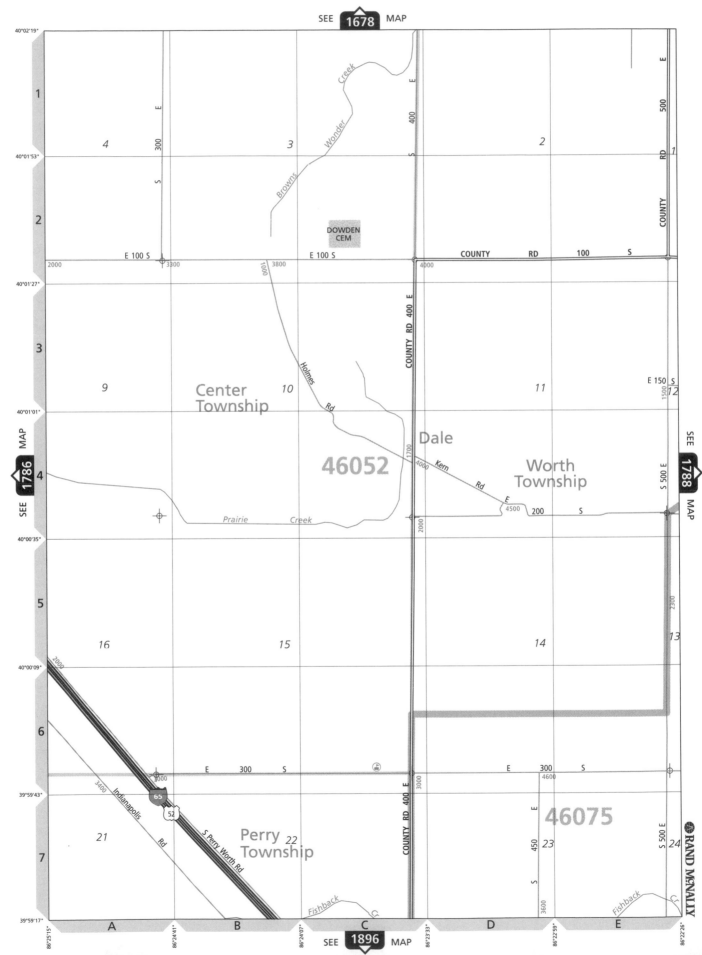

40°02'19"

1

4

E 300

S

3

Browns   Wonder   Creek

2

500 E

COUNTY   RD   1

40°01'53"

2

DOWDEN
CEM

COUNTY

40°01'27"

E 100 S   3800   E 100 S   COUNTY   RD   100   S

2000   3300   1000   4000

3

9

Center
Township   10

Holmes   Rd

11

E 150 S

1500   12

40°01'01"

MAP
1786
SEE

Dale

46052

1700   4000   Kern   Rd   E   4500   200   S

Worth
Township

S 500 E

SEE 1788 MAP

40°00'35"

Prairie   Creek

2000

5

16

15

14

2300

13

40°00'09"

2000

6

Indianapolis   Rd

3400

65

52

E   300   S   3000   E   300   S

3000   4600

39°59'43"

S Perry Worth Rd

Perry
Township   22

COUNTY   RD   400   E

46075

E

21

450   23

S 500 E

24

7

3600

Fishback   Fishback

39°59'17"

86°25'15"   86°24'41"   86°24'07"   86°23'33"   86°22'59"   86°22'26"

A   B   C   D   E

SEE 1896 MAP

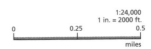

RAND M9NALLY

1:24,000
1 in. = 2000 ft.

0   0.25   0.5
miles

MAP
1788

SEE 1679 MAP

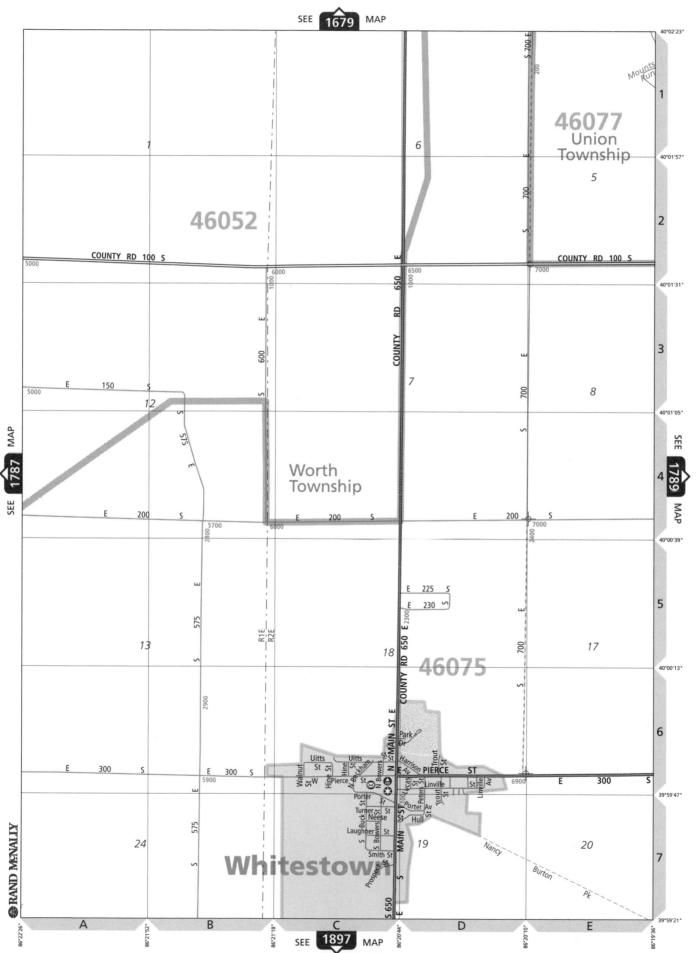

40°02'23"

46077
Union
Township

1

5

S 700 E
200

S 700

S

40°01'57"

2

COUNTY RD 100 S

46052

5000

COUNTY RD 100 S

5000

6000
1000

E

6500
1000

7000

40°01'31"

6

600 E

S

COUNTY RD 650

E

3

E   150   S

5000

7

8

700 E

S

12

575 E

S

40°01'05"

SEE 1787 MAP

SEE 1789 MAP

Worth
Township

E   200   S

5700
2400

6000

E   200   S

7000
2400

E   200   S

40°00'39"

575 E

S

E   225   S
E   230   S

COUNTY RD 650 E   2300 E

13

18

46075

17

700 E

S

40°00'13"

2900

R1E
R2E

E   300   S

5900

E   300   S

Walnut St W

Uitts St

Uitts St

Hine St

Hine St

N Beckham St

Pierce St

N Bowers St

N MAIN ST E

Park Dr

Harrison

Trout St

PIERCE   ST

Linville St

6900

E   300   S

39°59'47"

575 E

S

Porter St

S Buck St

Turner St

Neese St

Laughner St

S Bowers St

Smith St

Prospect St

N 100 E

S MAIN ST E

Lucas St

Peters Av

Porter Av

Hull

Trout St

Linville Av

Nancy

Burton Pk

24

19

20

7

Whitestown

S 650 E

86°22'26"   A   86°21'52"   B   86°21'18"   C   86°20'44"   D   86°20'10"   E   86°19'36"

39°59'21"

SEE 1897 MAP

MAP
1789

1:24,000
1 in. = 2000 ft.

0   0.25   0.5
miles

SEE 1680 MAP

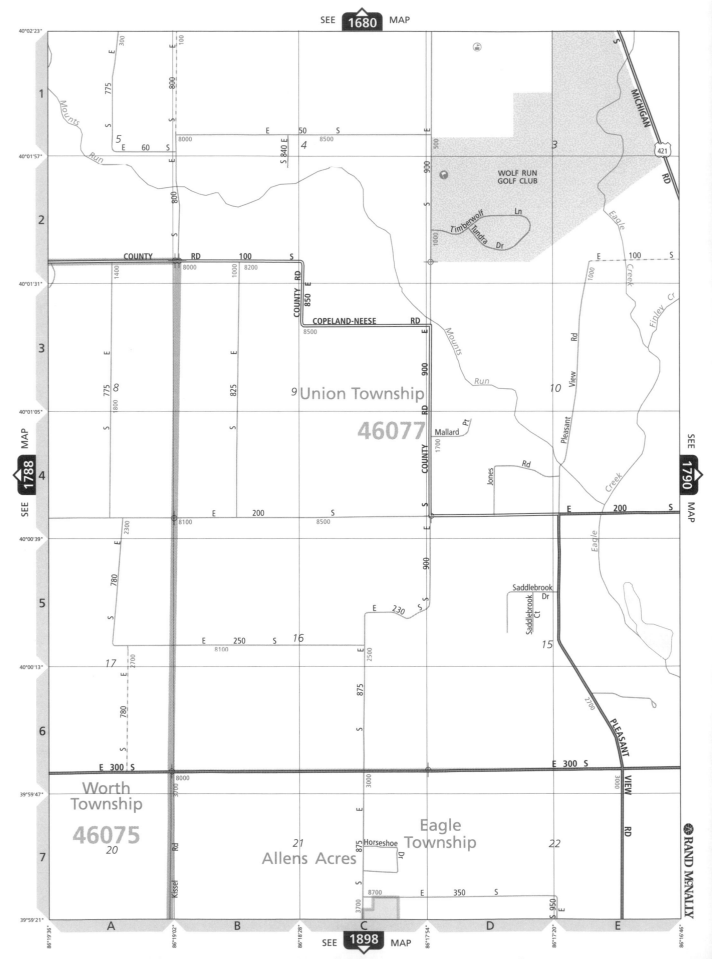

WOLF RUN
GOLF CLUB

MICHIGAN

RD

421

Timberwolf   Ln
Tundra
Dr

Eagle

COUNTY   RD   100   S

COUNTY RD

850 E

COPELAND-NEESE   RD

Mounts Run

Finley Cr

View   Rd

Pleasant

Creek

Eagle

Union Township

46077

9

10

Mallard   Pt

Jones   Rd

COUNTY RD

900 E

900

Saddlebrook
Dr
Saddlebrook
Ct

15

16

17

**Worth
Township**

46075
20

Eagle
Township

Allens Acres

21

Horseshoe
Dr

22

PLEASANT

VIEW

RD

Kissel Rd

RAND MCNALLY

SEE 1788 MAP

SEE 1790 MAP

SEE 1898 MAP

A   B   C   D   E

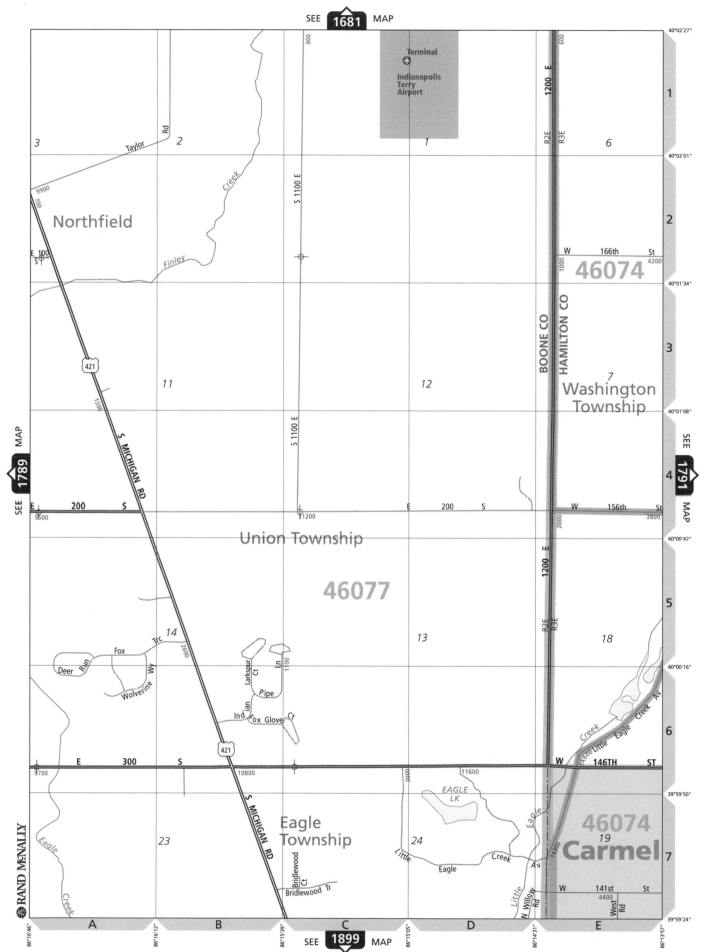

MAP
1790

1:24,000
1 in. = 2000 ft.

0   0.25   0.5
miles

SEE **1681** MAP

800

600

1200 E

R2E R3E

Terminal
Indianapolis
Terry
Airport

1

3   Taylor   Rd   2

1

6

40°02'27"

40°02'01"

9900

700

Northfield

Creek

S 1100 E

2

40°02'01"

E 100
S

Finley

W   166th   St
1000   4200

46074

40°01'34"

BOONE CO

HAMILTON CO

421

1500

11

S 1100 E

12

7
Washington
Township

3

40°01'08"

SEE **1789** MAP

SEE **1791** MAP

4

E   200   S
9600

S. MICHIGAN RD

S 1100 E
1200

E   200   S

W   156th   St
2000   3800

40°00'42"

Union Township

46077

1200 E

R2E R3E

5

40°00'16"

14
Trc

Fox

2600

Deer   Run   Wy

Wolverine

Larkspur   Ct
Ct   Ln
1100

Pipe

13

18

Creek   Little   Eagle   Creek   Av

6

Ind   Fox Glove   Ct
ian

421

E   300   S
9700

10800

11600

W   146TH   ST

Eagle

3000

14300

EAGLE
LK

Little   Eagle

Eagle   Av

39°59'50"

46074
19
Carmel

7

Eagle
Township

23

24

Little

Bridlewood   Ct

Bridlewood   Tr

Little   N Willow   Rd

W   141st   St
4400
West   Rd

Creek

Eagle   Creek

A   B   C   D   E

86°16'46"   86°16'12"   86°15'39"   86°15'05"   86°14'31"   86°13'57"

39°59'24"

SEE **1899** MAP

RAND M°NALLY

MAP
1791

1:24,000
1 in. = 2000 ft.
0   0.25   0.5
miles

SEE **1682** MAP

40°02'27"

1

Joliet Rd

6   5   4

Little Eagle Creek Av

Washington St S

Town Rd

TOWNE RD

40°02'01"

2

16600

W 166th St   W 166th St   W   166th   St

3100   2400   16600

40°01'34"

Joliet Rd

3

Little Eagle Creek

7

Eagle Creek Av

8 Washington Township

9

16100

W   161ST   ST

2100

40°01'08"

Joliet Rd

Little

Little   Little

W   159th   St

2400

46074

BENT TREE GOLF CLUB

SEE **1790** MAP
SEE **1792** MAP

SUGAR GRV CEM
4

15600   15600

W 156th St   EAGLE CREEK CEMETERY

W   156th   St

1400

46077

40°00'42"

Little Eagle Creek

Shelborne Rd

TOWNE RD

F5

5

15100

17

W   151st   St   W   151st   St

2400   1800

Country Place Rd

Little

18

16

40°00'16"

6

14600   14600

W 146TH ST   W 146TH ST

39°59'50"

1700

Woods Dr

Chariots   Whisper Dr

Autumn

Autumn Woods Dr

Esprit

Carmel
7

Shelborne Rd

19   20

21
Megan Dr

Nicholas Dr

Chase

Charity Cir

Equina Ct
Stallion Ct
Breeders Ct
Beaumont
Secretariat Blvd
Chase Ct
Mustang Dr

Charity Chase Dr

14100

A
1 Primo Wy

W 141st St   W 141st St

141st   St

Sweet Saddle Ct

39°59'24"

3600

Giovanni Dr

Da Vinci Dr

Amblewind Pl

46032

B
1 Magic Stallion Dr

Honey Tree Dr

B
1

A
1

Inglenook Ln
2300
14100

A   B   C   D   E

86°13'57"   86°13'23"   86°12'49"   86°12'15"   86°11'41"

SEE **1900** MAP

RAND McNALLY

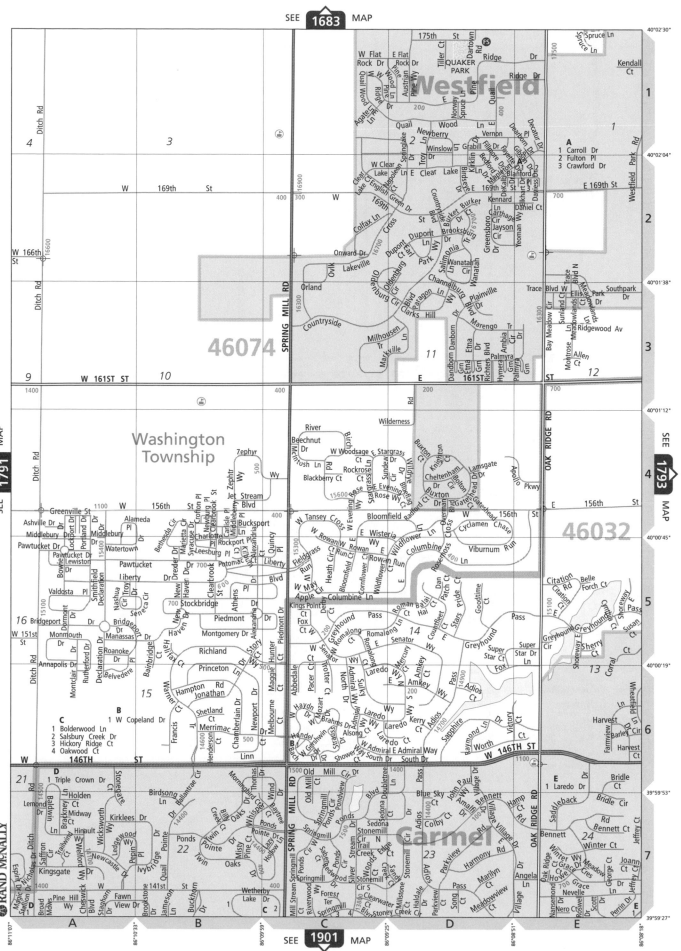

MAP
1792

1:24,000
1 in. = 2000 ft.
0   0.25   0.5
miles

Westfield

Washington Township

Carmel

46074

46032

A
1 Carroll Dr
2 Fulton Pl
3 Crawford Dr

C
1 Bolderwood Ln
2 Salsbury Creek Dr
3 Hickory Ridge Ct
4 Oakwood Ct

B
1 W Copeland Dr

D
1 Triple Crown Dr

E
1 Laredo Dr

RAND McNALLY

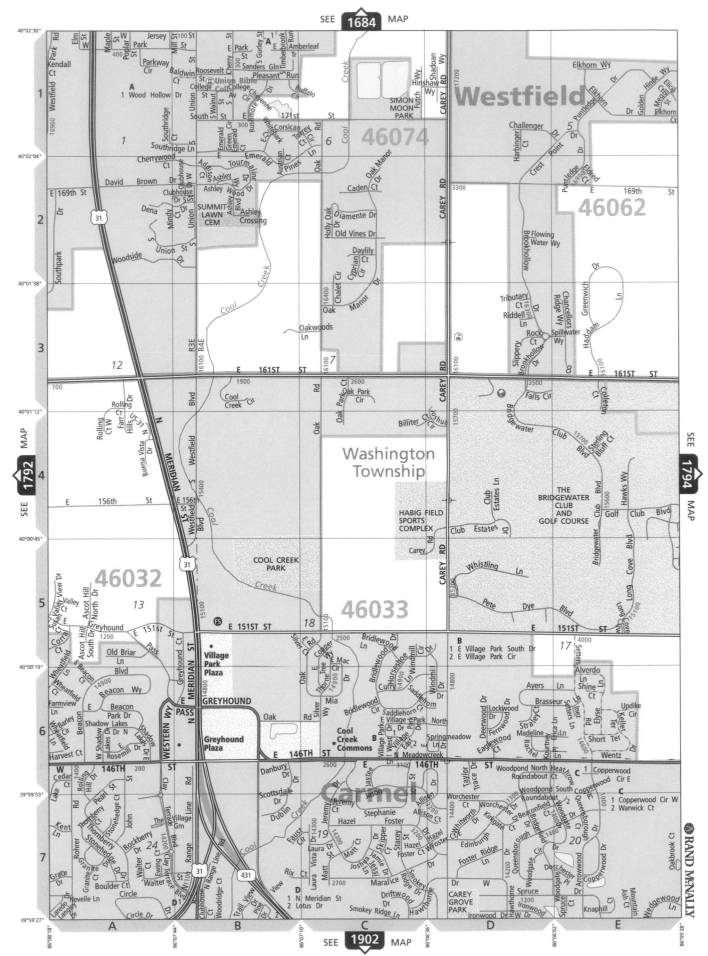

MAP
1793

1:24,000
1 in. = 2000 ft.

0   0.25   0.5
miles

SEE **1684** MAP

Westfield

46074

46062

Washington
Township

46032

46033

THE
BRIDGEWATER
CLUB
AND
GOLF COURSE

COOL CREEK
PARK

HABIG FIELD
SPORTS
COMPLEX

Carmel

CAREY
GROVE
PARK

SEE **1792** MAP

SEE **1794** MAP

SEE **1902** MAP

RAND MCNALLY

MAP
1794

1:24,000
1 in. = 2000 ft.

0   0.25   0.5
miles

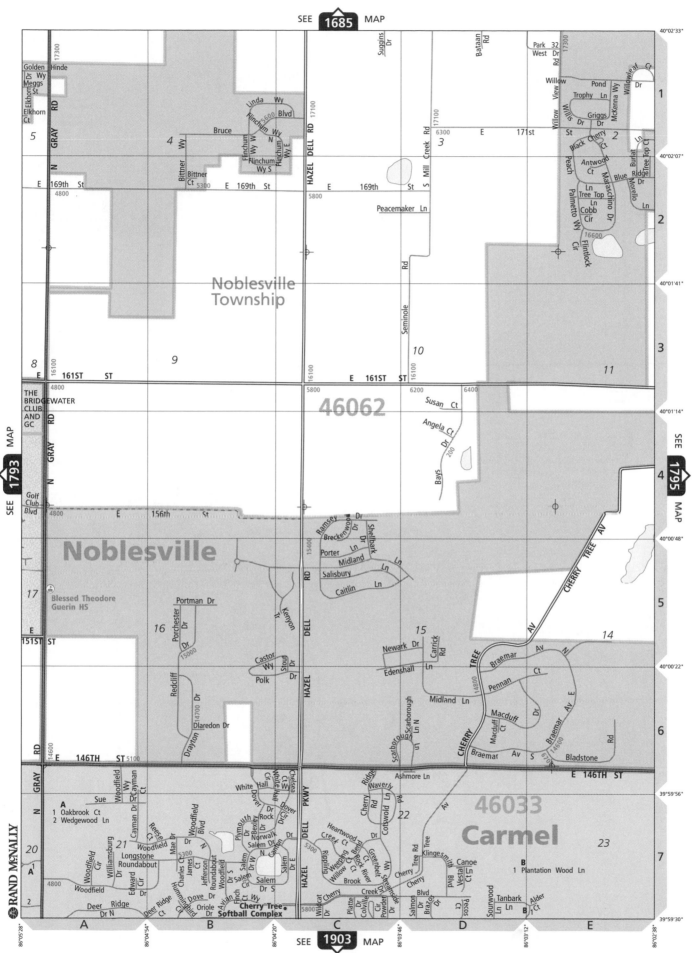

SEE 1685 MAP

SEE 1793 MAP

SEE 1795 MAP

SEE 1903 MAP

40°02'33"
40°02'07"
40°01'41"
40°01'14"
40°00'48"
40°00'22"
39°59'56"
39°59'30"

86°05'28"
86°04'54"
86°04'20"
86°03'46"
86°03'12"
86°02'38"

Noblesville
Township

46062

Noblesville

THE
BRIDGEWATER
CLUB
AND
GC

Blessed Theodore
Guerin HS

46033
Carmel

A
1 Oakbrook Ct
2 Wedgewood Ln

B
1 Plantation Wood Ln

Cherry Tree
Softball Complex

RAND McNALLY

MAP
1795

1:24,000
1 in. = 2000 ft.
0   0.25   0.5
miles

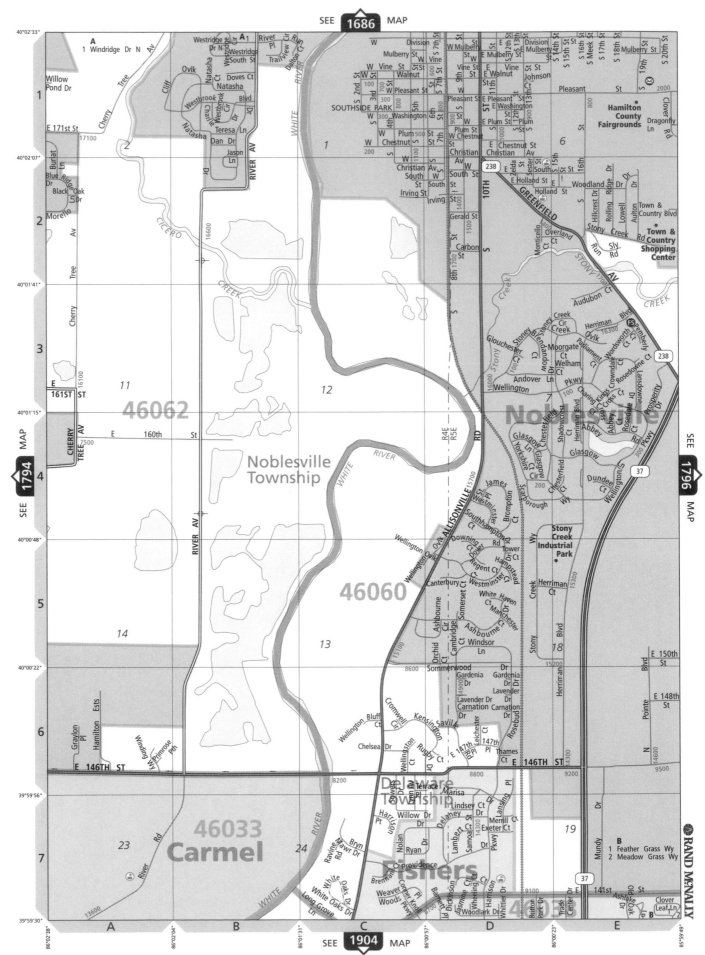

SEE 1686 MAP

SEE 1794 MAP

SEE 1796 MAP

SEE 1904 MAP

RAND McNALLY

40°02'33"
40°02'07"
40°01'41"
40°01'15"
40°00'48"
40°00'22"
39°59'56"
39°59'30"

86°02'38" 86°02'04" 86°01'31" 86°00'57" 86°00'23" 85°59'49"

46062
46060
46033
Carmel
Noblesville
Township

Hamilton
County
Fairgrounds

Town &
Country
Shopping
Center

Stony Creek
Industrial
Park

Delaware
Township

Fishers

A   B   C   D   E

MAP
1796

1:24,000
1 in. = 2000 ft.

0   0.25   0.5

miles

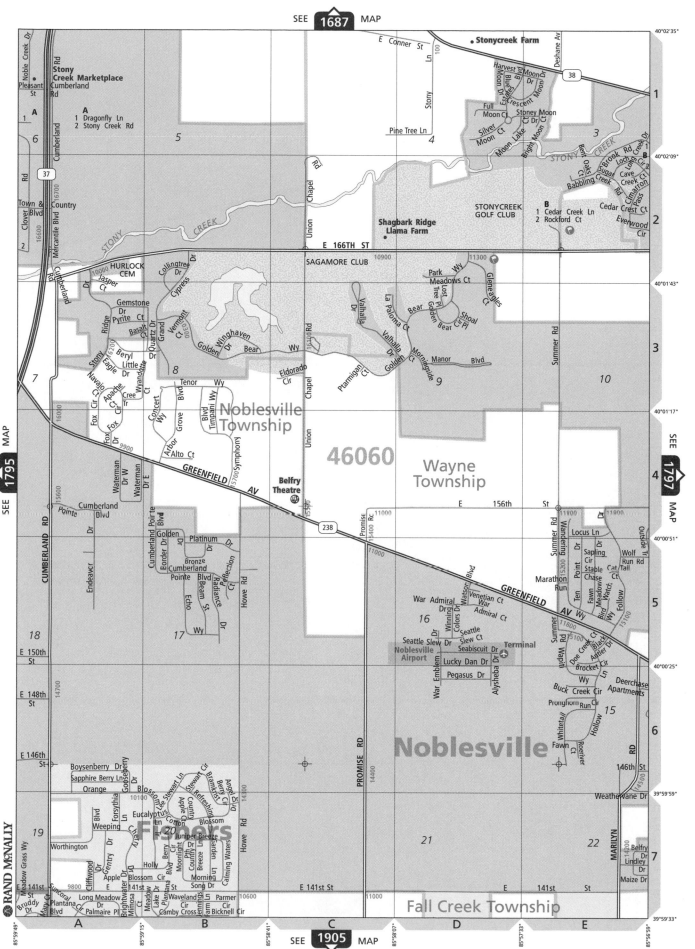

SEE 1687 MAP
SEE 1795 MAP
SEE 1797 MAP
SEE 1905 MAP

RAND McNALLY

MAP
1797

1:24,000
1 in. = 2000 ft.
0   0.25   0.5
miles

SEE 1688 MAP

40°02'35"
40°02'09"
40°01'43"
40°01'17"
40°00'51"
40°00'25"
39°59'59"
39°59'33"

STONY CREEK

Pennington Rd
17400
17400
17300 AV
MIDDLETOWN
17200

STONY CREEK CEM

38

Foote Trail
Cir
Long Creek
Folly Brook
Leewood
Ct
Cedar
Pass
Creek
Cimarron
Rd
Loch
Ln
Blackbird
Ln
Ct
Everwood
Cir

3

2

Mystic   Rd   16900

Durbin   Rd   16800

Clarksville

Hill   St
St
Lehr   St
Mason St

BODEN RD

Greenview Rd
Greenview
Cir

E 166TH ST
12100

13400

E   166th   St
13800

38

Wayne Township

BODEN RD

OLIO RD

10

11

12

Sand   Creek

40°00'25"

SEE 1796 MAP

46060

E   156th   St
15600
12800

E   156th   St
13800

E   156th   St

SEE 1798 MAP

Runaway
Ln
Outside   Tr
Outside
Trail Ct
Dry Creek Rd
Dusty   Rd
Inside   Tr
Wolf   Run
Wolf
Run Ct

Cricket   Rd
Stream Ln   Song
Cold   Blue
Fox   Lake Ct
Dr   Rally
Ct
238

Sand   Creek

14

13

Deer Trail
Dr
Deerview
Lovely   Dr
Dove Ln
Dry Creek Rd
15

BODEN RD
14600

Verizon
Wireless
Music
Center
E 146th St

ERVIN
CEMETERY

Gallant Fox Dr
Whitway
Dr
Gallant
Fox
A
Whitway
Dr
GREENFIELD   AV

A
1 Deerchase Apartments

E   146TH   ST
12900
13800
14600

146th St

SCHOOL   RD

Weathervane
Dr   Dr
Black   Farm
Banister Dr
Belfry
Dr   Cuppola Dr
Lindley   Dr
Maize
Dr
Woods

22

BROOKS
13600

Sand   Creek

Campus Pkwy

Corporate   Pkwy

238

FRONTAGE
RD

23

Bergen   Blvd

Tegler

Dr

13800

24

Noblesville

E   141st   St

A   B   C   D   E

85°56'59"   85°56'25"   85°55'51"   85°55'17"   85°54'43"   85°54'09"

SEE 1906 MAP

MAP
1798

1:24,000
1 in. = 2000 ft.

0   0.25   0.5
miles

SEE **1689** MAP

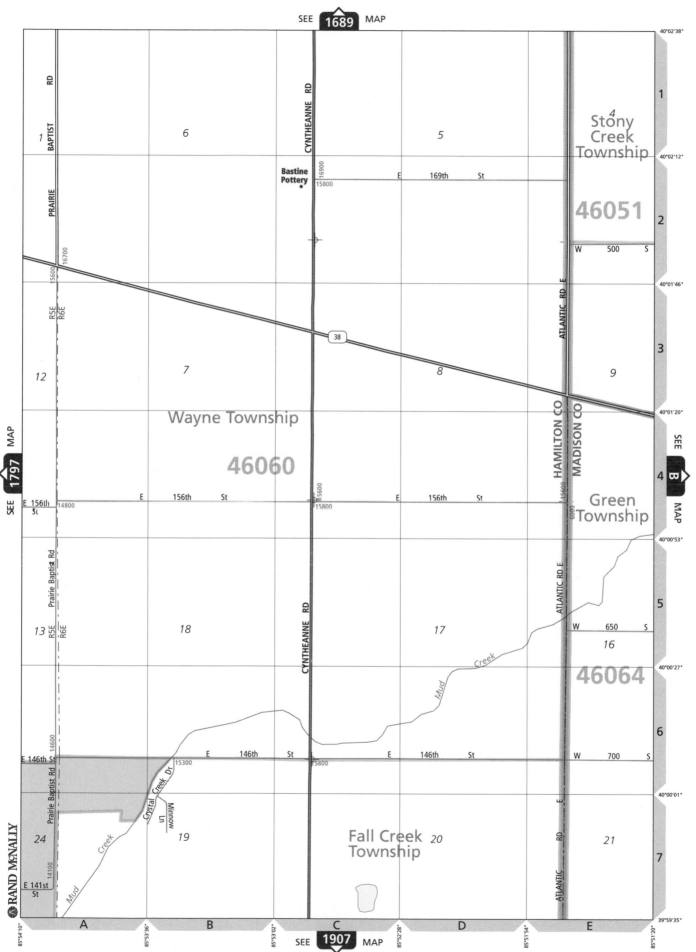

N

RD

BAPTIST

1

PRAIRIE

CYNTHEANNE RD

6

5

Stony
Creek
Township

Bastine
Pottery

16900
15800

E   169th   St

46051

16700

W   500   S

15600

40°02'38"

1

40°02'12"

2

40°01'46"

R5E R6E

38

12

7

8

9

3

40°01'20"

Wayne Township

46060

HAMILTON CO

MADISON CO

ATLANTIC RD E

SEE **1797** MAP

SEE **B** MAP

4

E 156th
St

14800

E   156th   St

15600
15800

E   156th   St

15600

6000

Green
Township

40°00'53"

Prairie Baptist Rd

R5E R6E

13

18

CYNTHEANNE RD

17

ATLANTIC RD E

W   650   S

16

46064

5

40°00'27"

14600

6

40°00'01"

E 146th St

E   146th   St

15300

E   146th   St

15800

E   146th   St

W   700   S

Prairie Baptist Rd

24

Crystal Creek Dr

Minnow
Ln

19

Mud   Creek

Fall Creek
Township

20

Mud   Creek

ATLANTIC   RD   E

21

7

14100

E 141st
St

39°59'35"

RAND McNALLY

A   B   C   D   E

85°54'10"   85°53'36"   85°53'02"   85°52'28"   85°51'54"   85°51'20"

SEE **1907** MAP

MAP
1894

1:24,000
1 in. = 2000 ft.

0   0.25   0.5

miles

N

SEE **1785** MAP

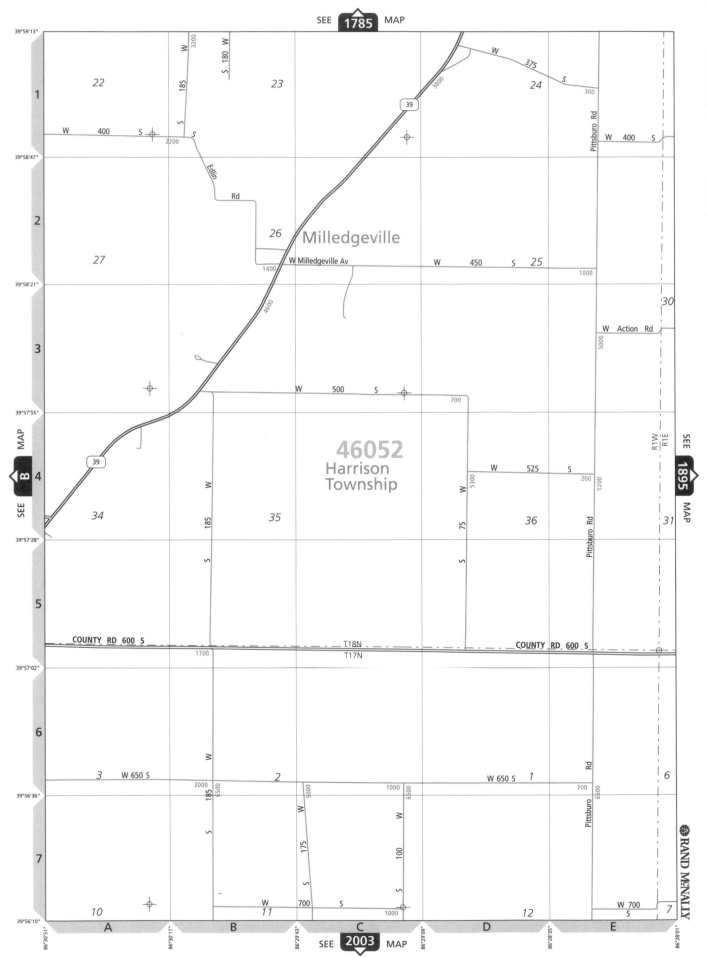

39°59'13"

1

22

W   3200

S 180 W

23

W   375   S

24

W

185

S

2200

39°58'47"

W   400   S

300

Pittsburo Rd

W   400   S

39

3800

2

Edlin

Rd

26   Milledgeville

27

W Milledgeville Av

25

W   450   S

1400

1000

39°58'21"

30

4600

W   Action   Rd

3

5000

39°57'55"

W   500   S

700

R1W
R1E

SEE **1895** MAP

MAP

B

SEE

39

46052

Harrison
Township

W   525   S

200

5300

5200

4

34

W   185   S

35

W   75   S

36

Pittsburo Rd

31

39°57'28"

5

39°57'02"

COUNTY RD 600 S

1700

T18N

T17N

COUNTY   RD   600   S

39°56'36"

6

3   W 650 S

W   185   S

2

W   6500   S

W   5000   S

1000

W   650   S

1

6500

Rd

6

Pittsburo

6500

2000

39°56'10"

7

10

W   175   S

11

W   700   S

1000

W   100   S

12

Pittsburo

W   700   S

7

A   B   C   D   E

86°30'51"   86°30'17"   86°29'43"   86°29'09"   86°28'35"   86°28'08"

SEE **2003** MAP

MAP
1895

1:24,000
1 in. = 2000 ft.

0   0.25   0.5
miles

SEE 1786 MAP

19

20

21

1

E 400 S

S 50 E

125

3500

E

S

E 400 S

500

4500

4000

39°59'17"

39°58'51"

S 50 E

30

29

28

2

S 100 E

E   450   S

4500

1200

E

250

Rd

County

S County Rd 200 E

4500

39°58'25"

E Action
Rd

E

40

3

E 500 S   Action Rd

E 500 S

S 100 E

800

5000

5000

E 500 S

1500

2000

39°57'59"

SEE 1894 MAP

Shepherd

SEE 1896 MAP

Harrison
Township

46052

4

S 50 E

S 100 E

31

E 550 S

32

E 550 S

33

COUNTY   RD   550   S

500

1000

1700

5500

39°57'32"

Perry Township

Herr

5

COUNTY RD 600 S

T18N
T17N

6000

39°57'06"

6

S

6

50

E

5

County   Rd   650   S

2300

4

S County Rd 200 E

39°56'40"

7

E 700 S

S 50
E

7

600

E 700 S

8

9

39°56'14"

A   B   C   D   E

SEE 2004 MAP

86°28'01"   86°27'27"   86°26'53"   86°26'19"   86°25'45"   86°25'12"

MAP
1896

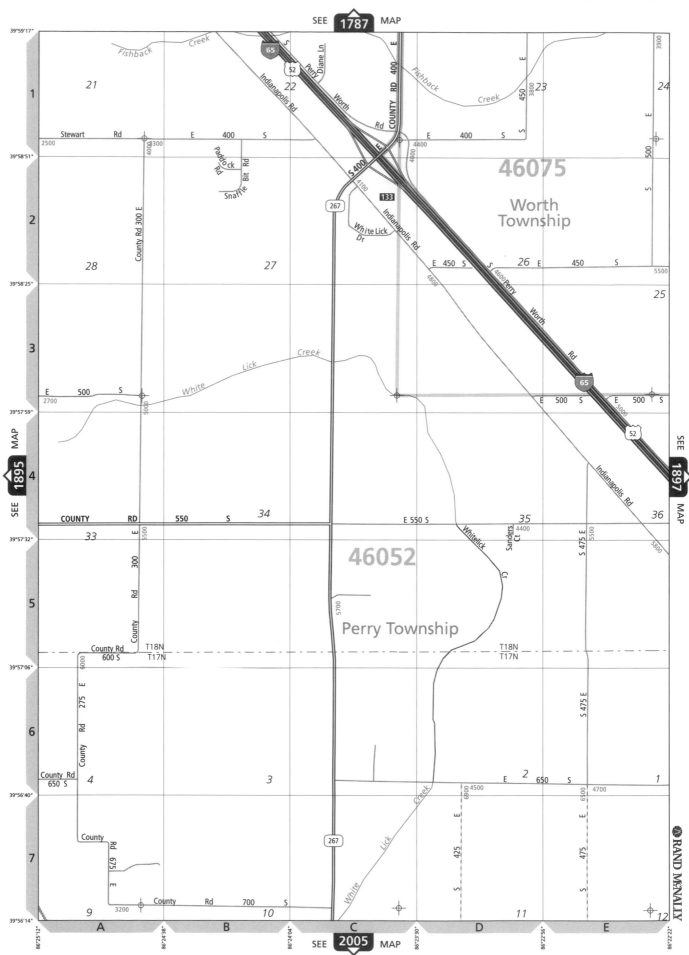

SEE **1787** MAP

39°59'17"

Fishback Creek

I-65
52
Perry
Diane Ln
Worth
Indianapolis Rd
COUNTY RD 400
Fishback Creek

21   22   23   24

Stewart Rd   E   400   S
2500   4300   400
39°58'51"   4400   400   500   **46075**

Paddock Rd
Snaffle Bit Rd   267   133

Worth Township

White Lick Dr   Indianapolis Rd

28   27   E   450   S   26   E   450   S
5500

25

39°58'25"

White Lick Creek

E   500   S
2700   5000   White

3   Lick   Creek   E   500   S   E   500   S
I-65
52

SEE **1895** MAP ◄   Indianapolis Rd

SEE **1897** MAP ►

COUNTY RD   550   S   34   E 550 S   35   36
33   Whitelick   Sanders Ct   4400
39°57'32"   **46052**   S 475 E   5500
5600

County Rd 300 E   Perry Township   S 475 E

5   5700

County Rd   T18N
600 S   T17N   T18N
T17N
39°57'06"

County Rd 275 E   S 475 E

6

County Rd
650 S   4   3   E   2   650   S   1
4500   4700
6900
6500
39°56'40"

County
Rd 675 E   267   White Lick Creek   S 425   S 475

7   3200   County Rd   700   S
9   10   11   12
39°56'14"

A   B   C   D   E

86°25'12"   86°24'38"   86°24'04"   86°23'30"   86°22'56"   86°22'22"

SEE **2005** MAP

RAND McNALLY

MAP
1897

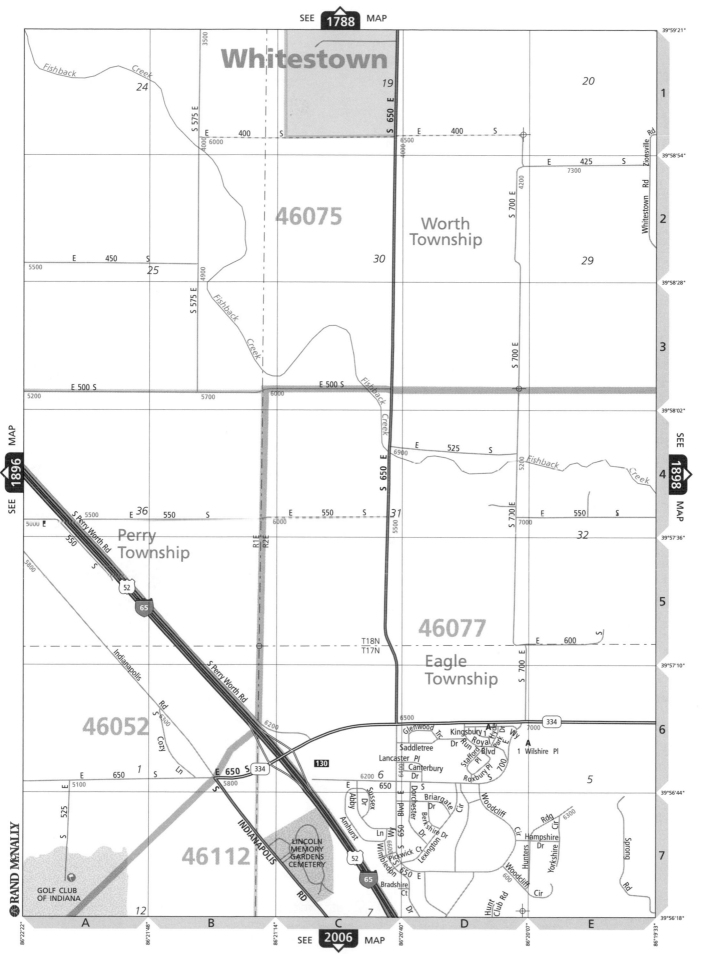

1:24,000
1 in. = 2000 ft.

0   0.25   0.5
miles

Whitestown

24
Fishback Creek
46075
19
20
1

S 575 E
400
E
400
S
Zionsville Rd

Worth Township
E 425 S
S 700 E
Whitestown Rd

2
30
29
39°58'28"

E 450 S
25
Fishback Creek
46077

E 500 S
E 500 S
Fishback Creek
3

SEE 1896 MAP
SEE 1898 MAP

E 525 S
S 650 S

Perry Township
E 36 550 S
E 550 S
31
E 550 S
S 700 E
32
4

I-65
US 52
Indianapolis Rd
S Perry Worth Rd

46077
Eagle Township
E 600 S
S 700 E
5

T18N / T17N

46052
334
130
6
Glenwood Trc
Kingsbury Dr
Royal Run
Saddletree
Lancaster Pl
Canterbury Dr
1 Wilshire Pl
E 650 S 334
E 650 S

46112
INDIANAPOLIS RD
LINCOLN MEMORY GARDENS CEMETERY
Indianapolis
US 52
I-65
7

GOLF CLUB OF INDIANA

RAND McNALLY

A   B   C   D   E

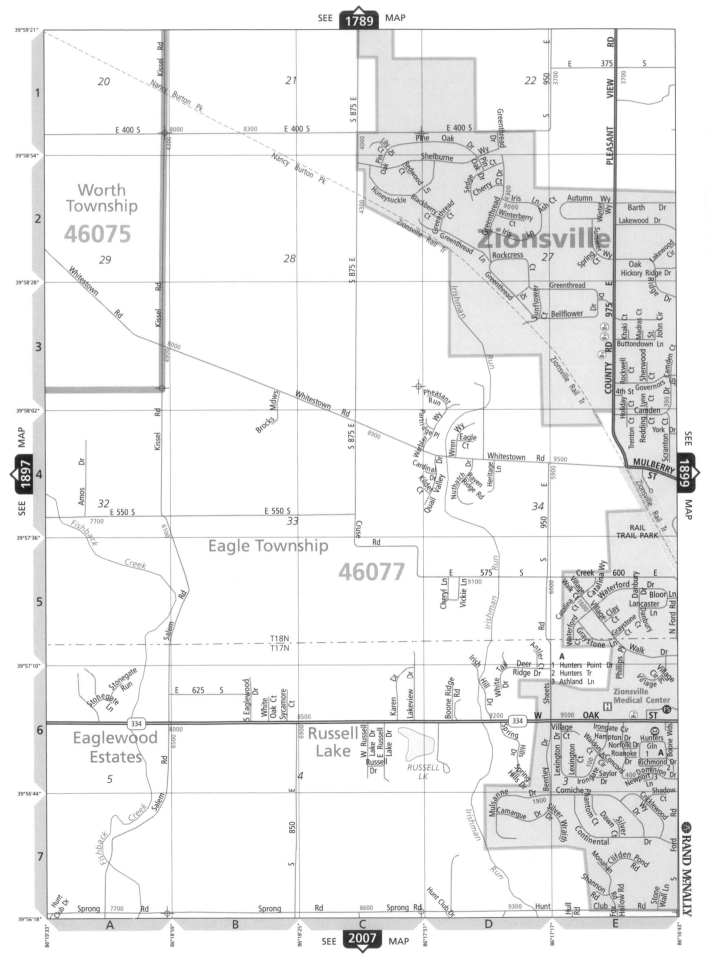

1:24,000
1 in. = 2000 ft.
0 0.25 0.5
miles

SEE 1789 MAP

SEE 1897 MAP

SEE 1899 MAP

Worth Township
46075

Eagle Township
46077

Zionsville

Eaglewood Estates

Russell Lake

RAIL TRAIL PARK

Zionsville Medical Center

A
1 Hunters Point Dr
2 Hunters Tr
3 Ashland Ln

Whitestown Rd
E 400 S
E 550 S
E 575 S
E 600 S
E 625 S
S 875 E
S 850 E
S 950 E
Kissel Rd
Salem Rd
Cruse Rd
Sprong Rd
Hunt Club Rd
Nancy Burton Pk
Zionsville Rail Tr
Fishback Creek
Irishman Run
COUNTY RD 975
PLEASANT VIEW RD
MULBERRY ST
W OAK ST
334
T18N
T17N

SEE 2007 MAP

MAP
1899

1:24,000
1 in. = 2000 ft.
0   0.25   0.5
miles

SEE 1790 MAP

SEE 1898 MAP

SEE 1900 MAP

SEE 2008 MAP

Eagle Township

46077

46074

Carmel

Eagle Village

Clay Township

Zionsville

46033

BOONE CO
HAMILTON CO

RAND McNALLY

1:24,000
1 in. = 2000 ft.
0 0.25 0.5
miles

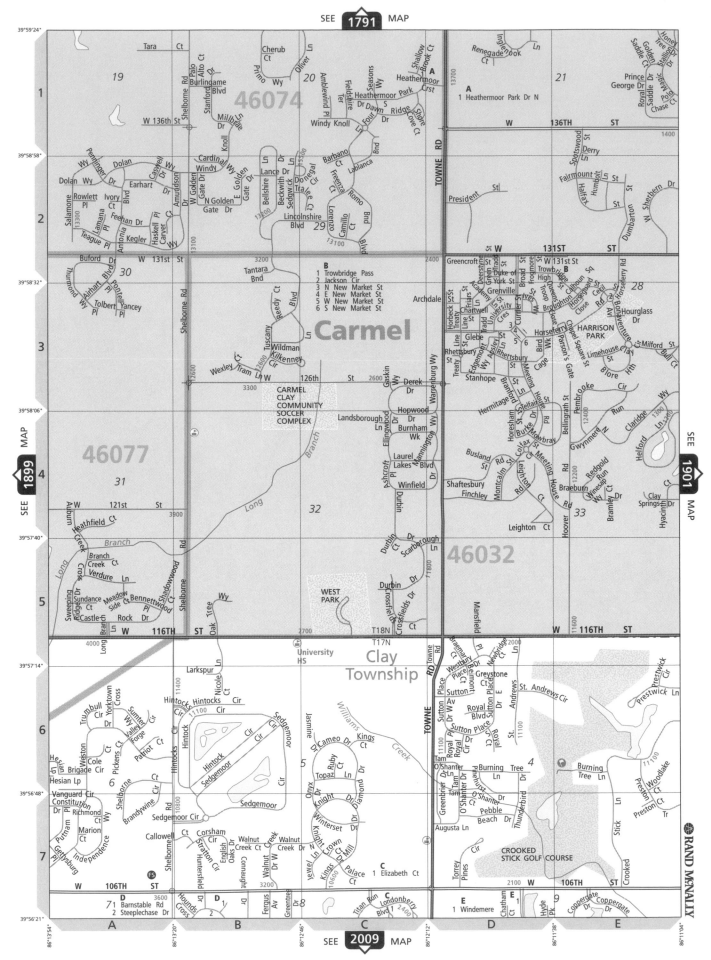

SEE 1791 MAP

SEE 1899 MAP

SEE 1901 MAP

SEE 2009 MAP

Carmel

Clay Township

46074

46077

46032

A
1 Heathermoor Park Dr N

B
1 Trowbridge Pass
2 Jackson Cir
3 N New Market St
4 E New Market St
5 W New Market St
6 S New Market St

C
1 Elizabeth Ct

D
1 Barnstable Rd
2 Steeplechase Dr

E
1 Windemere

CARMEL CLAY COMMUNITY SOCCER COMPLEX

WEST PARK

HARRISON PARK

CROOKED STICK GOLF COURSE

University HS

W 136TH ST

W 131ST ST

W 126th St

W 121st St

W 116TH ST

W 106TH ST

TOWNE RD

Shelborne Rd

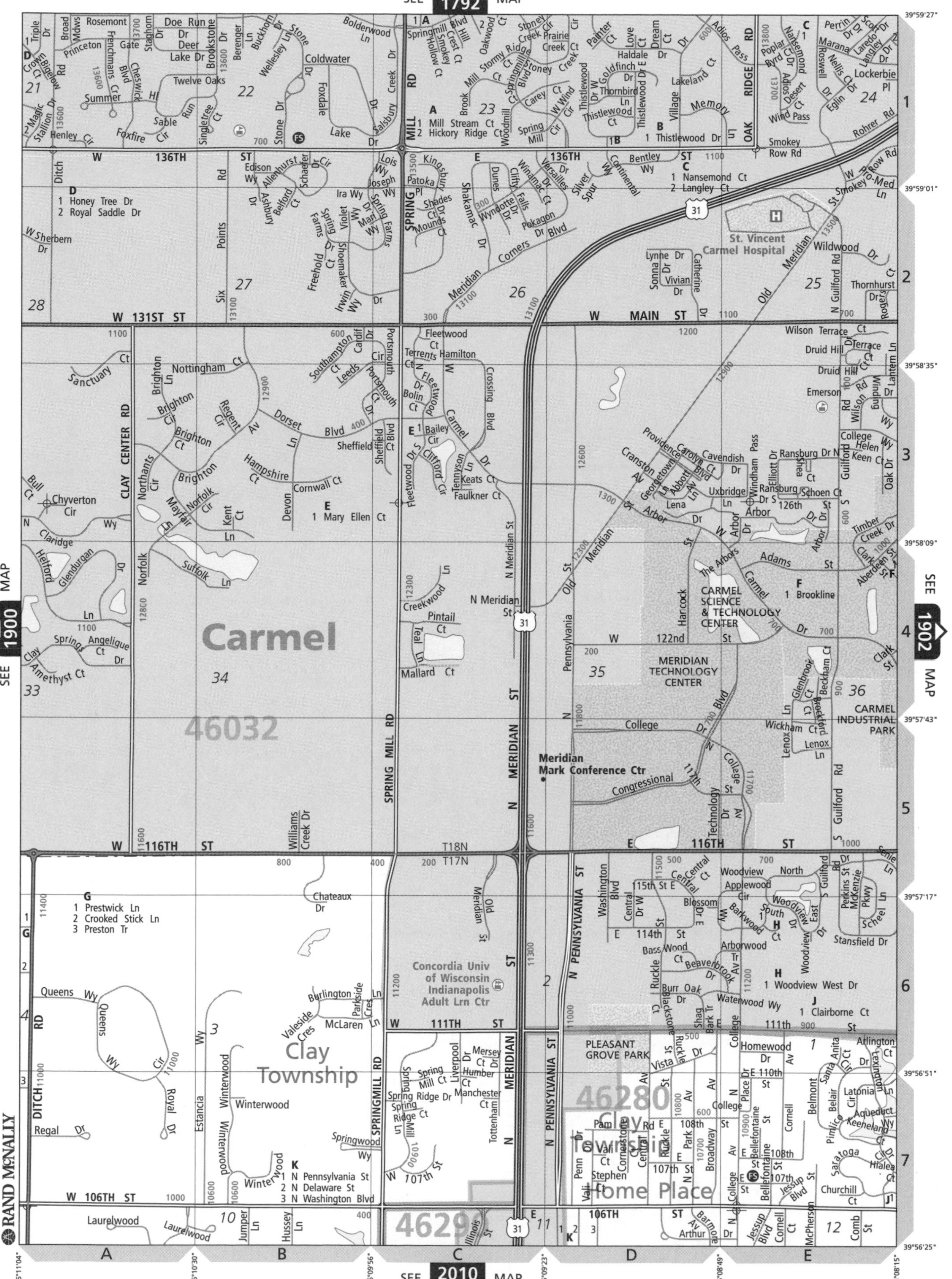

MAP
1901

1:24,000
1 in. = 2000 ft.

0   0.25   0.5
miles

SEE 1792 MAP

39°59'27"
39°59'01"
39°58'35"
39°58'09"
39°57'43"
39°57'17"
39°56'51"
39°56'25"

SEE 1900 MAP

SEE 1902 MAP

Carmel

46032

Clay Township

46280
Clay Township

Home Place

46290

Concordia Univ
of Wisconsin
Indianapolis
Adult Lrn Ctr

St. Vincent
Carmel Hospital

CARMEL SCIENCE
& TECHNOLOGY
CENTER

MERIDIAN
TECHNOLOGY
CENTER

CARMEL
INDUSTRIAL
PARK

Meridian
Mark Conference Ctr

PLEASANT
GROVE PARK

W 136TH ST
W 131ST ST
W MAIN ST
W 116TH ST
W 111TH ST
W 107th ST
W 106TH ST
E 116TH ST
E 110th
106TH ST

RAND McNALLY

SEE 2010 MAP

86°11'04"
86°10'30"
86°09'56"
86°09'23"
86°08'49"
86°08'15"

MAP
1902

1:24,000
1 in. = 2000 ft.

0   0.25   0.5
miles

SEE 1793 MAP

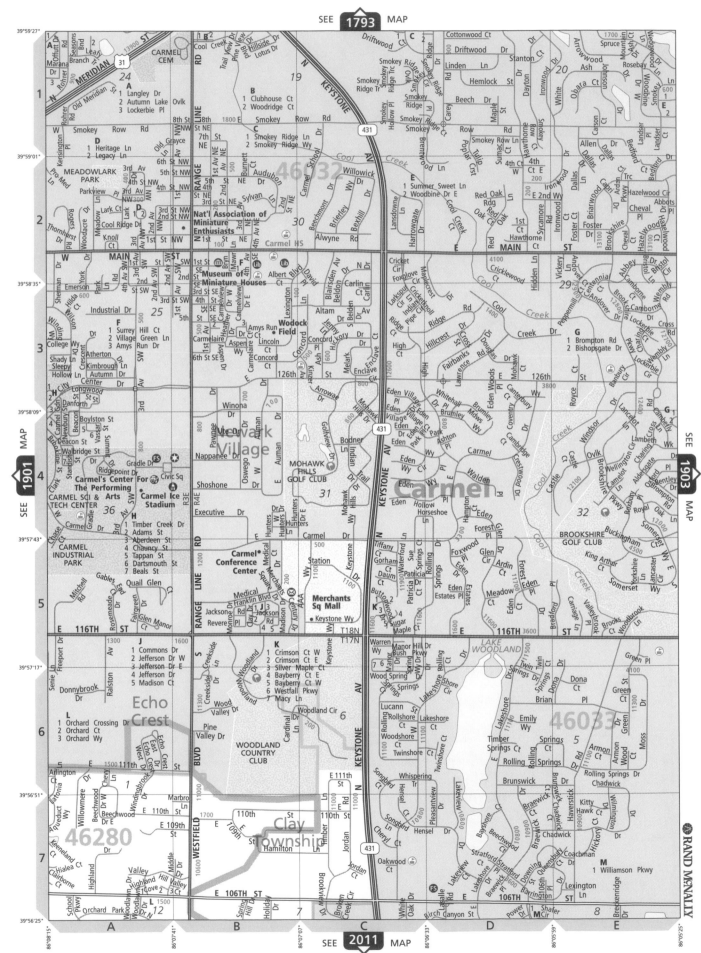

SEE 1901 MAP

SEE 1903 MAP

SEE 2011 MAP

RAND McNALLY

*525.50.98

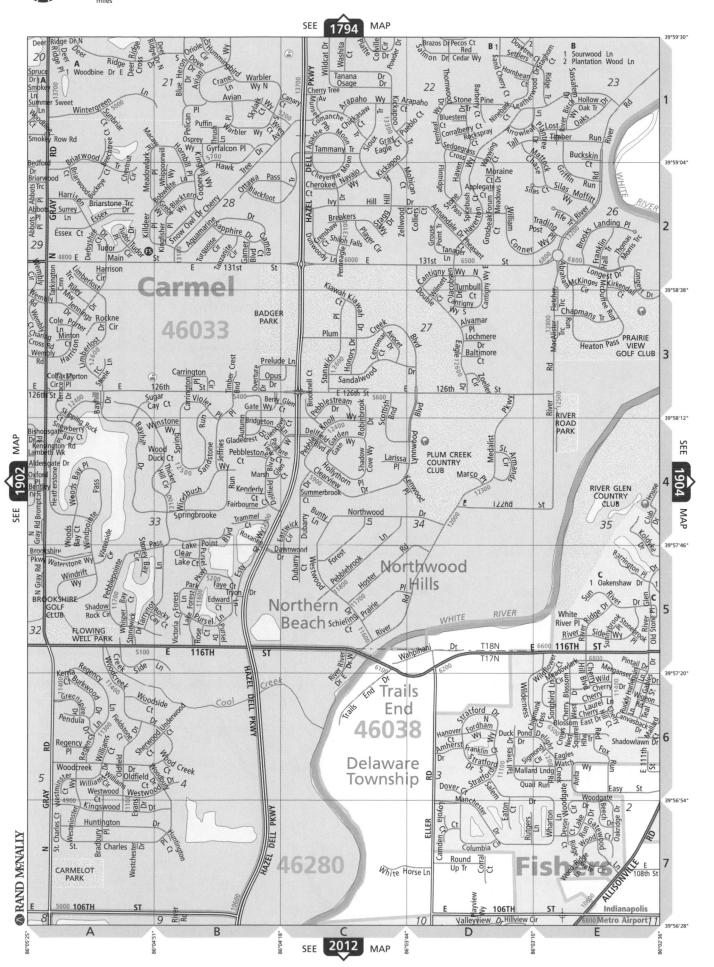

MAP
1903

N

1:24,000
1 in. = 2000 ft.

0   0.25   0.5
miles

SEE 1794 MAP

SEE 1902 MAP

SEE 1904 MAP

SEE 2012 MAP

Carmel

46033

Northwood Hills

Northern Beach

Trails End

46038

Delaware Township

46280

Fishers

Indianapolis

Metro Airport

RAND MCNALLY

BADGER PARK

PRAIRIE VIEW GOLF CLUB

PLUM CREEK COUNTRY CLUB

RIVER ROAD PARK

RIVER GLEN COUNTRY CLUB

BROOKSHIRE GOLF CLUB

FLOWING WELL PARK

CARMELOT PARK

WHITE RIVER

MAP
1904

1:24,000
1 in. = 2000 ft.
0   0.25   0.5
miles

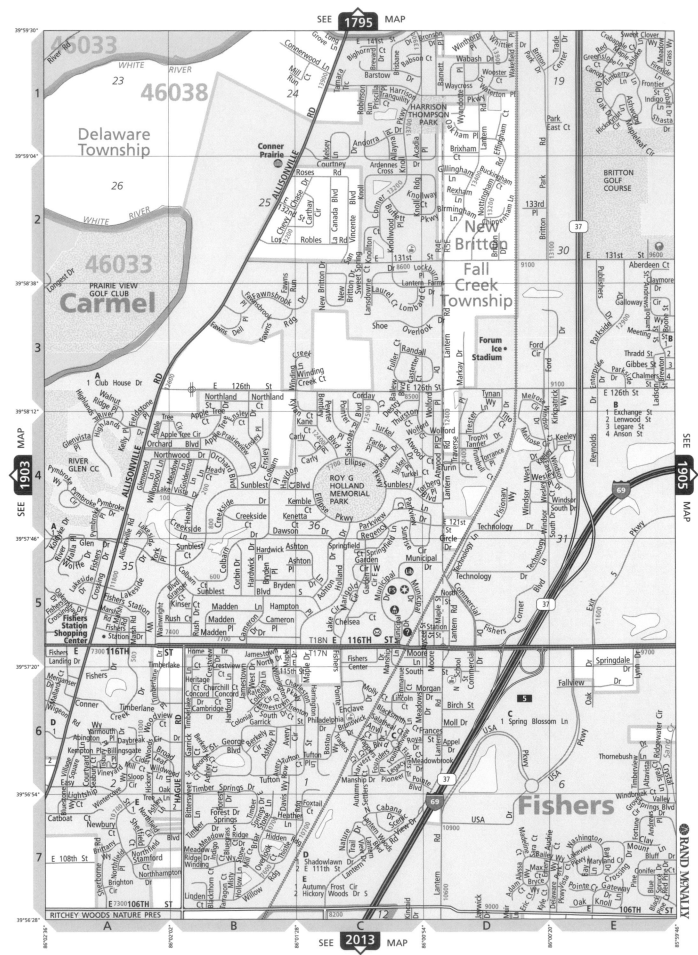

SEE 1795 MAP

SEE 1903 MAP

SEE 1905 MAP

SEE 2013 MAP

RAND McNALLY

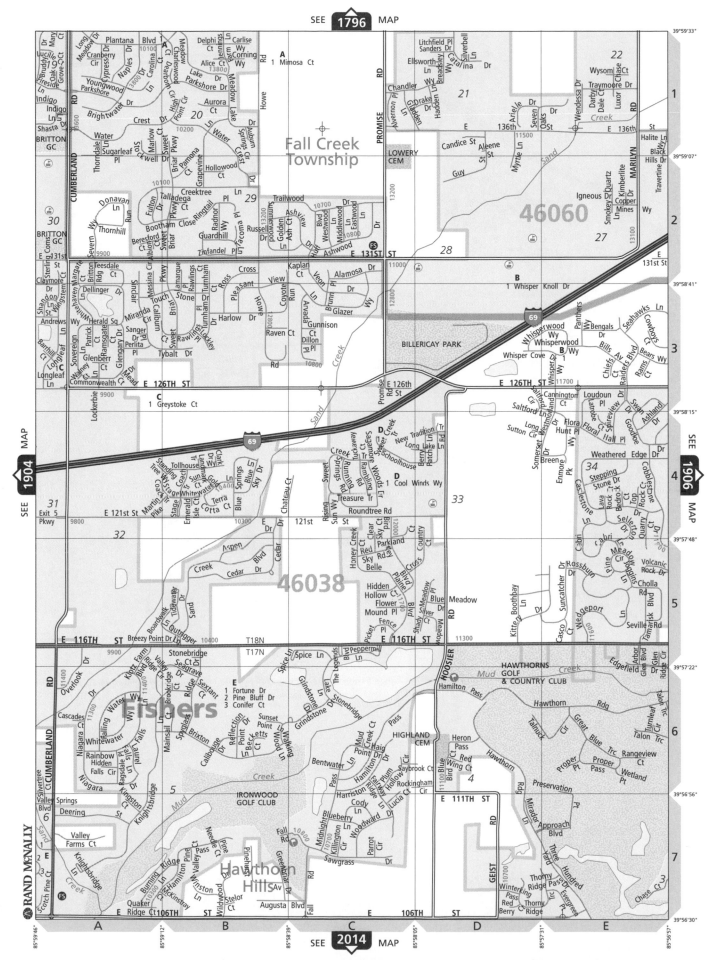

MAP
1905

1:24,000
1 in. = 2000 ft.
0   0.25   0.5
miles

N

39°59'33"
39°59'07"
39°58'41"
39°58'15"
39°57'48"
39°57'22"
39°56'56"
39°56'30"

Fall Creek
Township

LOWERY
CEM

46060

BRITTON
GC

BRITTON
GC

BILLERICAY PARK

46038

Fishers

HAWTHORNS
GOLF
& COUNTRY CLUB

HIGHLAND
CEM

IRONWOOD
GOLF CLUB

Hawthorn
Hills

SEE 1904 MAP

SEE 1906 MAP

RAND M^cNALLY

1:24,000
1 in. = 2000 ft.

0 0.25 0.5
miles

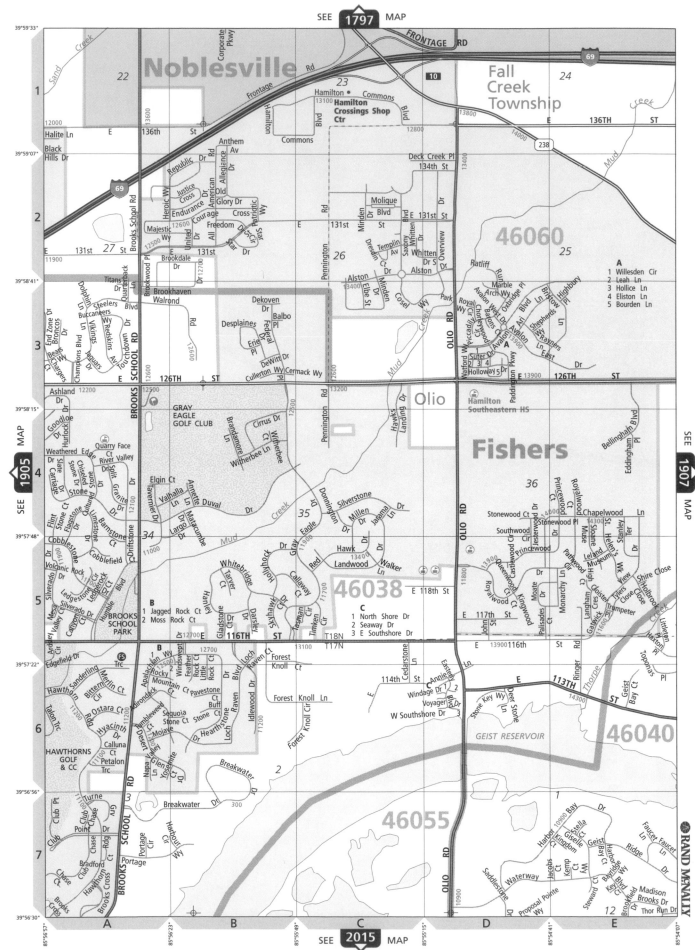

SEE 1797 MAP

Noblesville

Fall Creek Township

Fishers

Olio

46060

46038

46040

46055

GRAY EAGLE GOLF CLUB

Hamilton Crossings Shop Ctr

Hamilton Southeastern HS

BROOKS SCHOOL PARK

HAWTHORNS GOLF & CC

GEIST RESERVOIR

A
1 Willesden Cir
2 Leah Ln
3 Hollice Ln
4 Eliston Ln
5 Bourden Ln

B
1 Jagged Rock Ct
2 Moss Rock Ct

C
1 North Shore Dr
2 Seaway Dr
3 E Southshore Dr

SEE 1905 MAP

SEE 1907 MAP

SEE 2015 MAP

MAP
1907

1:24,000
1 in. = 2000 ft.

0   0.25   0.5
miles

SEE 1798 MAP

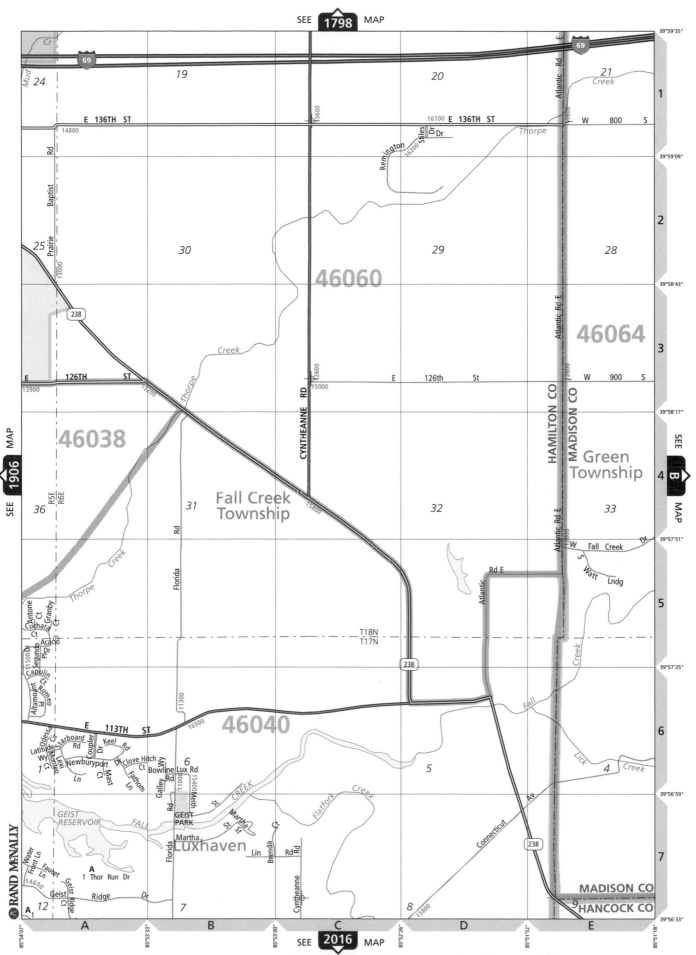

Cr

I-69

Mud

24

19

20

21
Creek

1

E 136TH ST

14800

16100 E 136TH ST

Stiles Dr

Dr

Thorpe

W 800 S

39°59'35"

39°59'09"

Rd

Baptist

Remington

16200

Atlantic Rd E

13600

2

Prairie

25

30

29

28

13000

238

46060

46064

39°58'43"

Creek

Thorpe

3

E 126TH ST

12600

E 126th St

W 900 S

13900

15200

15000

2600

39°58'17"

SEE 1906 MAP

46038

R5E
R6E

Cyntheanne Rd

Hamilton Co

Madison Co

Green
Township

B

39°58'17"

SEE B MAP

4

36

31

Fall Creek
Township

32

33

13800

Atlantic Rd E

13000

W Fall Creek Dr

39°57'51"

Rd

Thorpe

Creek

Florida

Atlantic Rd E

S Watt Lndg

5

Antone Ct

Granby Ct

Cuchara Ct

T18N
T17N

238

Creek

39°57'25"

Acacio Ct

Segundo Pl

1500 Dr

Capulin Ct

Romeo

Fall

39°57'25"

Altamount Rd

E 113TH ST

16500

46040

11300

6

Odessa Cir

Latitude Wy

Starboard Rd

Coupler Dr

Keel Rd

Monroe Ct

Lexi Ln

Newburyport Ct

Clove Hitch Ct

Mast Ln

Fathom Ln

Bowline Rd

6

Lux Rd

5

4

Lick Creek

39°56'59"

Galley Wy

1100

15400 Meith St

CREEK

Flatfork Creek

Connecticut Av

238

Florida Rd

Martha St

Martha St

Brenda Ct

Lin Rd

Cyntheanne Rd

15800

GEIST
RESERVOIR

FALL

Geist Park

Martha St

Luxhaven

7

Water Front Ln

Fauquet Ln

A
1 Thor Run Dr

Geist Ridge Ct

14600

Geist Ridge Dr

A1

12

7

8

9

MADISON CO

HANCOCK CO

39°56'59"

39°56'33"

A

85°54'07"

B

85°53'33"

C

85°53'00"

D

85°52'26"

E

85°51'52"

81°51'15"

MAP
2003

1:24,000
1 in. = 2000 ft.

0   0.25   0.5
miles

SEE 1894 MAP

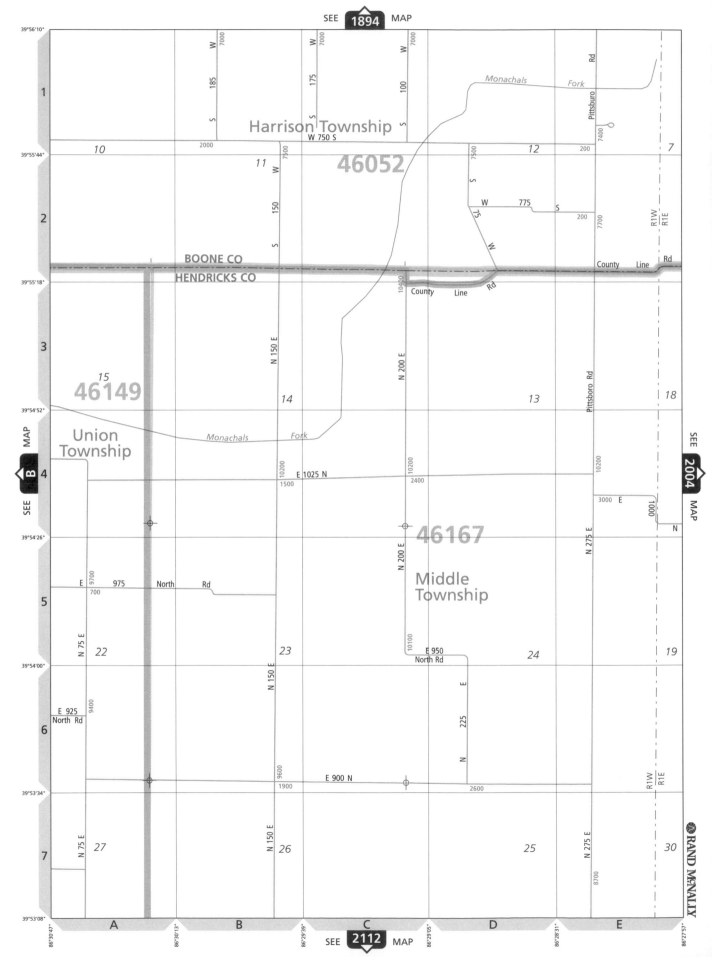

39°56'10"

1

W 7000
185 S
W 7000
175 S
W 7000
100 S

Pittsburo Rd

Monachals   Fork

Harrison Township

W 750 S

39°55'44"

10   2000   11   W 7500   46052   12   7400   200   7
W 7500

2   W 150 S   S   W   775   S   7700   R1W R1E
75 W   200

BOONE CO   County   Line   Rd
HENDRICKS CO   County   Line   Rd

39°55'18"   10400

3   N 150 E   N 200 E   Pittsboro Rd   18

15

46149   14   13

39°54'52"

Monachals   Fork

SEE MAP B

Union Township   10200   10200   10200

4   E 1025 N   2400   3000 E   1000

1500

SEE 2004 MAP

39°54'26"   N 275 E

46167

N 200 E

E 9700   975   North   Rd   **Middle Township**
5   700

N 75 E   10100   N 275 E
22   23   E 950   24   19
North Rd

N 150 E   E 225

39°54'00"

E 925   9400   N
6   North Rd

9600   E 900 N   2600   R1W R1E
1900

39°53'34"

N 75 E   N 150 E   N 275 E
7   27   26   25   30

8700

39°53'08"

A   86°30'13"   B   86°29'39"   C   86°29'05"   D   86°28'31"   E   86°27'57"

86°30'47"

RAND McNALLY

MAP
2004

1:24,000
1 in. = 2000 ft.

0   0.25   0.5
miles

SEE 1895 MAP

39°56'14"

1

7

Harrison
Township

46052   8

Perry
Township

COUNTY   RD   750   S
2000   9

S COUNTY RD 200 E

39°55'48"

2

BOONE CO   County Line Rd
500
HENDRICKS CO

39°55'22"

3

SEE 2003 MAP

18

West   Fork   White   Lick   Creek

17

N 550 E

16

39°54'56"

SEE 2005 MAP

4

471

N 10000 E   1000

N

5300   6300
3000

46167

39°54'30"

Middle
Township

N 500 E

20

Brown
Township

46112   21

5

39°54'04"

E   951   North   Rd
3800
19

White   Lick   Creek

9900

N 425 E

9900 Tara   Wy

Beckoning

Country
View Dr

Country
View Ct

6

Dr

E   900   N
9000   5600   6100

N 500 E

West   Fork

5100   6900

39°53'38"

30

29

28

7

9300

N 400 E

E   850   N
4200

39°53'12"

A   B   C   D   E

86°27'57"   86°27'24"   86°26'50"   86°26'16"   86°25'42"   86°25'08"

SEE 2113 MAP

RAND MCNALLY

MAP
2005

1:24,000
1 in. = 2000 ft.
0   0.25   0.5
miles

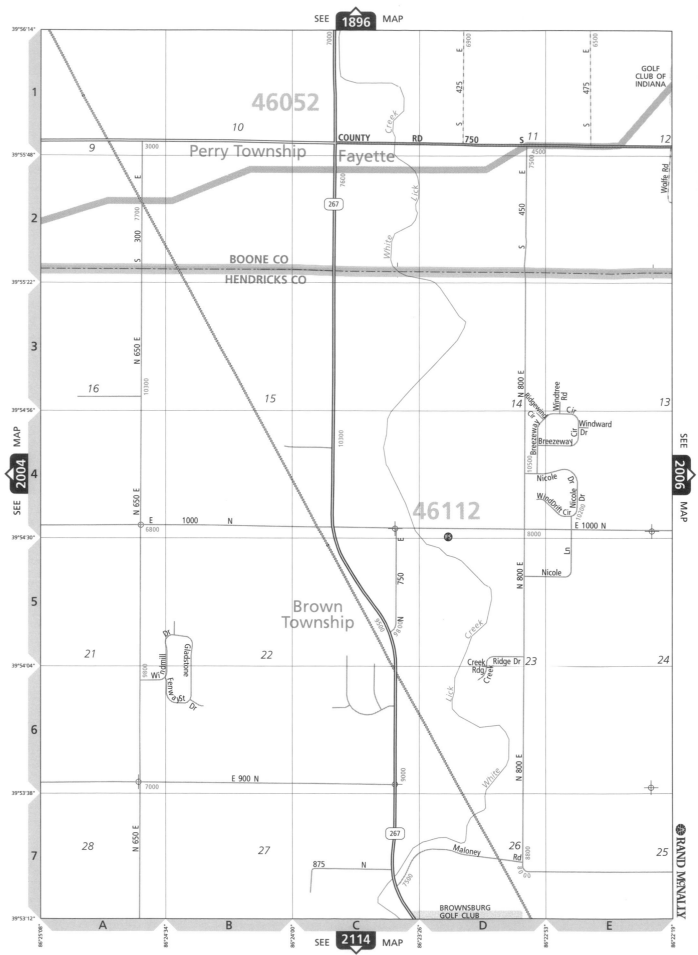

SEE **1896** MAP

46052

GOLF
CLUB OF
INDIANA

10

COUNTY   RD   750   S   11   12

9   3000   Perry Township   Fayette   450   4500

267   Wolfe Rd

2   300   7700   7600   S   475

BOONE CO
HENDRICKS CO

3   N 650 E   10300

16   15   N 800 E   Windtree
Rd   14   Windward
Dr   13

Ridgewind
Cir   Windtree
Cir

1050   Breezeway

Breezeway

SEE
2004
MAP   46112   Nicole   Nicole
Dr   WindDrift Cir   Nicole Dr   10200 Dr   SEE
2006
MAP

4   N 650 E   E   1000   N
6800   FS   8000   E 1000 N   Ln

Nicole

5   750   9800N   Brown
Township   N 800 E

Lick   Creek

21   Gladstone   22   Creek
Rdg   Ridge Dr   23   24

Wi   0980   Creek   Lick   Creek

6   Fenway St
Dr   N 800 E

White

E 900 N
7000   9000

267

7   28   N 650 E   27   26   Maloney
Rd   8800   25

875   N   7500   800

BROWNSBURG
GOLF CLUB

A   B   C   D   E

RAND MCNALLY

SEE **2114** MAP

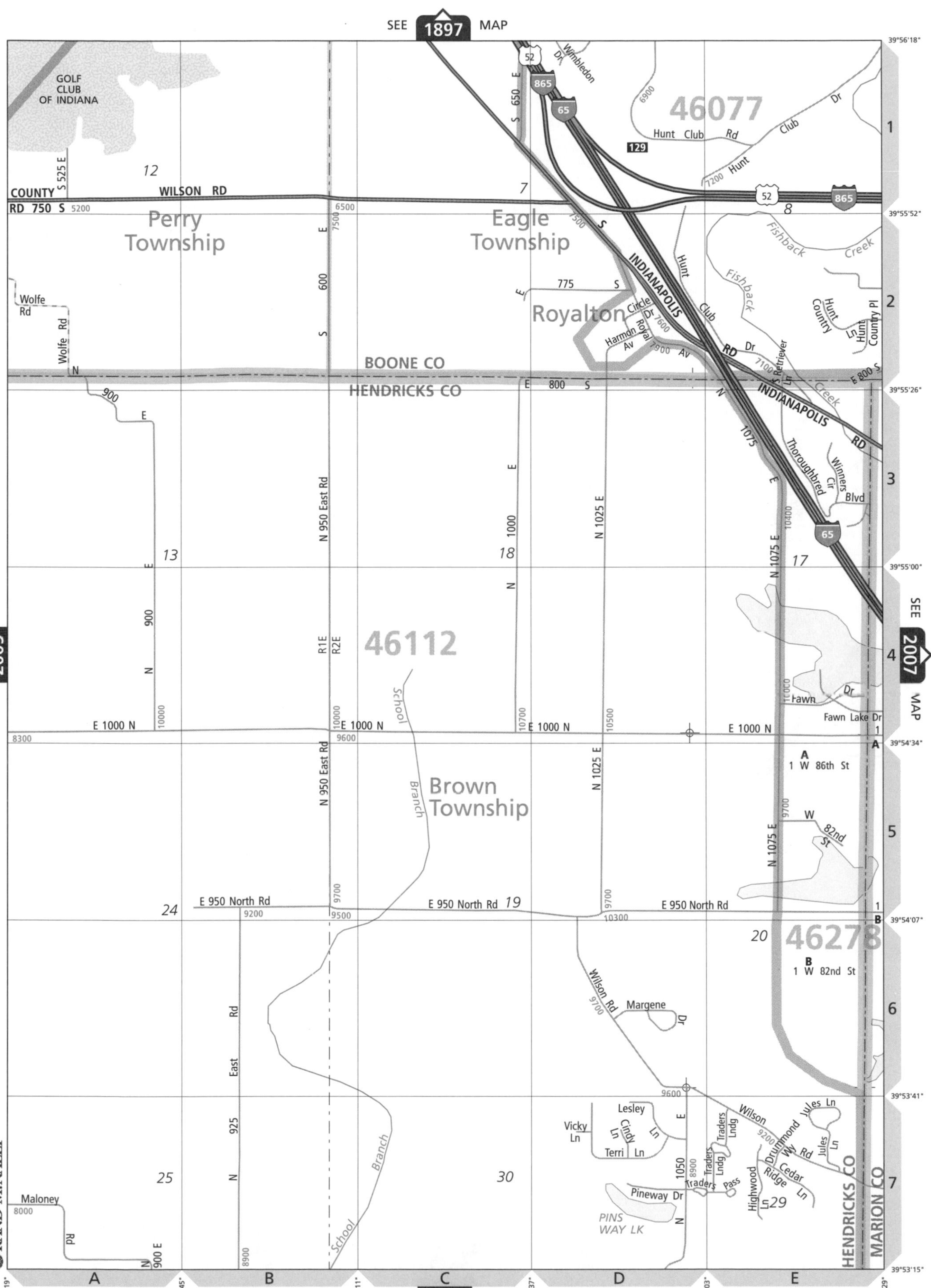

MAP
2006

1:24,000
1 in. = 2000 ft.

0   0.25   0.5
miles

SEE 1897 MAP

GOLF
CLUB
OF INDIANA

Wymbledon Dr

52

865

65

46077

129

6900

Hunt Club Rd

Club Dr

Hunt

7200

S 525 E

12

52

865

8

COUNTY
RD 750 S 5200

WILSON   RD

6500

7

Fishback Creek

39°55'52"

Perry
Township

7500 E

Eagle
Township

7500 S

INDIANAPOLIS

Wolfe
Rd

600 S

775 S

E

Royalton

Circle Dr

Harmon
Av

7600

Royal

2900 Av

Hunt

Club

Fishback

Hunt
Country
Ln

Hunt
Country Pl

39°55'26"

Wolfe Rd

N

900

E

BOONE CO

HENDRICKS CO

800 S

E

RD

Retriever Ln

Creek

7100

Dr

INDIANAPOLIS   RD

E 800 S

13

N 950 East Rd

N

900

E

10000

E

1000

N

N 1025 E

1075

Thoroughbred

E

Winners
Cir

Blvd

10400 E

65

17

39°55'00"

SEE 2005 MAP

R1E
R2E

46112

School

18

10700

10500 E

N 1075 E

11000 E

Fawn

Dr

Fawn Lake Dr

SEE 2007 MAP

39°54'34"

8300

10000

E 1000 N

9600

N 950 East Rd

E 1000 N

Branch

Brown
Township

10700

E 1000 N

N 1025 E

10500

E 1000 N

1

A
1 W 86th St

A

9700

W

N 1075 E

82nd
St

W

5

39°54'07"

24

E 950 North Rd

9200

9700

9500

E 950 North Rd

19

9700

E 950 North Rd

10300

1

B
1 W 82nd St

B

20

46278

6

39°53'41"

East   Rd

Wilson Rd

9700

Margene

Dr

9600

Wilson

9200

Jules Ln

Drummond

Jules Ln

Wy Rd

925

N

School   Branch

25

8900

30

Vicky
Ln

Lesley
Ln

Cindy
Ln

Terri   Ln

1050

E

Traders
Lndg

8900

Traders
Lndg

Traders
Lndg

Cedar
Ln

Ridge

Highwood

29

Traders
Pass

Maloney

8000

Rd

900 E

N

8900

Pineway Dr

PINS
WAY LK

1050

N

HENDRICKS CO

MARION CO

39°53'15"

A   B   C   D   E

SEE 2115 MAP

RAND McNALLY

86°22'19"   86°21'45"   86°21'11"   86°20'37"   86°20'03"   86°19'29"

39°56'18"

MAP
2007

1:24,000
1 in. = 2000 ft.

0   0.25   0.5
miles

N

SEE 1898 MAP

39°56'18"

Fishback Ct

46077
Eagle Township

Cooper Ln S

7000

850 E

Club Dr

Smith Ln
Ford Ln
Sunset Ct
Beaumont Valley Ct
Valley Dr

1

Hull Rd
Fox Rd

Hunt Club Ln

Hunt Ln

Hunt Club Ln

Sullivan Pl
Woodbridge

Irishman's Hull Rd
Irishman Run
Overlook Pt

Irishmans
Fox Hollow Rd
Hollow Ct

8900

39°55'52"

8
Salem Rd

9
52   865

10

Irishmans Run Pl
Irishmans Ln

Fox Hollow Rd

Ford Ln

850 S

7010

2

Hunt
Country Ln

Soaring Hawk Rd

W 96TH ST

6700

S FORD RD

Eagle Run

E 800 S

W 96TH ST

8200

Pineview Dr

7600

BOONE CO
MARION CO

39°55'26"

KISSEL RD

N Doe

Thorn Dr

Stones Ferry Wy
Bend Rd
8200

7200

9300

MOORE RD

3

Fishback

LAFAYETTE

Spring Dr

17

Stones Ferry Rd
Stones Ferry Pl

Stones

8400

Lambeth Ct Ln

9100 Cooper Rd

W 93rd St

Fanchon Dr   W 92nd St

W 92nd St

16

Mill Rd

Tenton Ct

Cockerham Cir

Tilly Dr

15

39°55'00"

Fishback

Shetland Ct

Shetland

N Nature Dr

N Nature RD

Tilly

8900

W

8800

8200

W 88TH ST

7200

N

Waterside Dr

Waterside Ct

4

SEE 2006 MAP

Fawn Lake Dr
Fawn Cir

Shetland Ln

Rohan Ct

W 86th St

Shetland Ln

Cooper Rd

W 87th St

Glen Willow Ln

Meadowmor Ln

Santana Ln
Santana Cir

Brookmont Ct

Gordonshire Dr
Gordonshire Ct

Gordonshire Dr

Waterside Residence Dr

Greenridge Dr

SEE 2008 MAP

39°54'34"

W Lake 86th St

W 86TH ST

8400

8200

7700

W 86TH ST

N Silver Ridge Ct

7200

N Silverleaf Ct

W 86th St

Falcon Rdg

5

20

Olin St

W 85th St

84th St

W

Walden Trace Dr

Walden Trace

Walden Glen Ct

Traders

Hollow Ln

7800

Traders Hollow Ct

PLEASANT HILL CEMETERY

BIG EAGLE CREEK

22

Thoroughbred Ct
Thoroughbred Dr

8300

Sunray Ct
Fox Lk N
Fox Lk S Dr

Wellsbrook Rd

8000

39°54'07"

W 82nd St

8500

W 82nd St

8100

46278

MOORE RD

N

Indianapolis

Fox Lake Ct
Fox Gunnery Rd
Gunnery Cir
Fox Run Rd
Fox Run Cir

Conarroe Rd

6

W 81st St

Upland Dr
Fawnwood Dr

Mesic Ct

Stream Cir

Pond Ln

Mill

7900 N

W 79TH ST

7300

6900

39°53'41"

Fishback

Fishback Rd

Preservation Wy

Woodreed Dr

7000

Shady Hills Dr W

Shady Hills Dr E
Shady Hills Dr

Shady Hills Dr

Lafayette RD

La Tour Cir

7700

Cabernet Wy
Blvd

7

29

Wilson Rd

7600

Preservation Wy
Crown

Point

CROWN POINT CEM

8200

28

TRADERS POINT

W Traders Ct

FS

Traders

Noel Forest Ct

Noel Rd

7400 N

Maison Ct
Chablis Ct

Almaden Ct
Almaden Dr
Chablis Palais Cir

27

Randle Dr

Andre Dr

W Andre Ct
Kimkris Ct

Dubonnett Ct

Sauterne Dr

Normandy Wy

Perrier Dr

Salterne Dr

D

39°53'15"

A   B   C   D   E

86°19'29"   86°18'55"   86°18'22"   86°17'48"   86°17'14"   86°16'40"

SEE 2116 MAP

RAND McNALLY

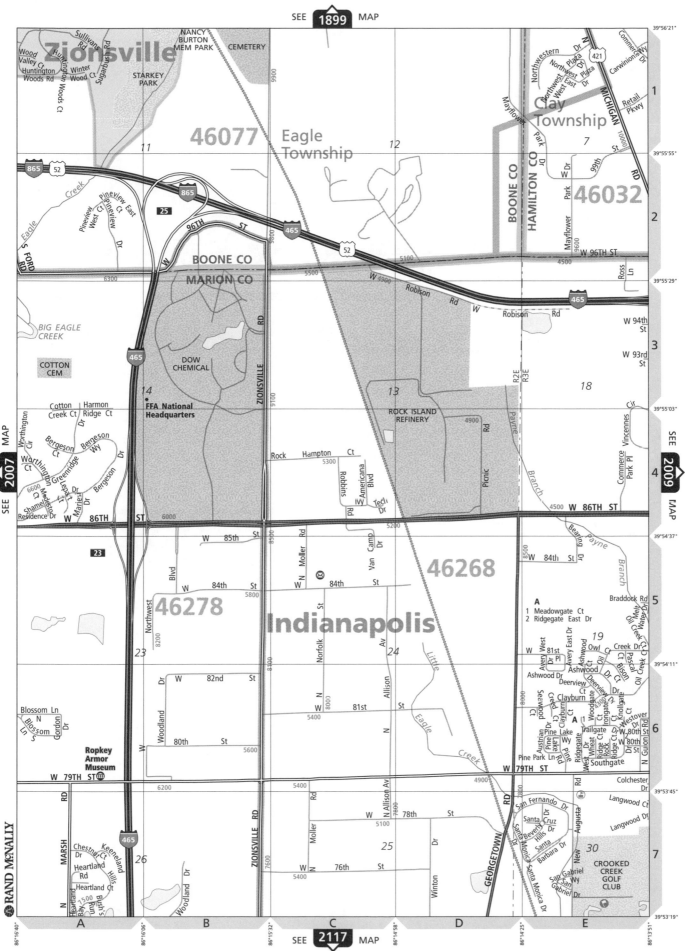

MAP
2008

1:24,000
1 in. = 2000 ft.
0   0.25   0.5
miles

SEE 1899 MAP

Zionsville

Wood Valley Ct
Huntington Woods Rd
Sullivans Dr
Pushville Rd
Winter Wood Ct

NANCY BURTON MEM PARK
CEMETERY

STARKEY PARK

46077

Eagle Township

Clay Township

Northwestern Dr
Northwest Plaza Dr
Northwest Plaza Dr
Northwest West East Dr
Commerce Dr
Carwinion Wy
Retail Pkwy

421

MICHIGAN RD

Mayflower Park Dr

BOONE CO
HAMILTON CO

7

46032

12

865 52

25

865

Pineview West Ct
Pineview Ct
Pineview East
Pineview Dr

96TH ST

465

52

Mayflower Dr
W Dr
99th St

W 96TH ST

9600

N FORD RD

S FORD RD

BOONE CO
MARION CO

Creek
Eagle

6300

5500

W 4900

5100

4500

Robison Rd

W Robison Rd

465

Ross Ln

W 94th St

BIG EAGLE CREEK

465

ZIONSVILLE RD

DOW CHEMICAL

9100

13

R2E R3E

18

W 93rd St

COTTON CEM

14 •FFA National Headquarters

ROCK ISLAND REFINERY

4900

Payne

Branch

Vincennes Cir

SEE 2009 MAP

Worthington Cir
Cotton Creek Ct
Harmon Ridge Ct
Bergeson Ct
Berneson Wy
Greenridge Lepat Dr
Worthington Ct
Madelor Ct
6600
Shamel Dr
Maries Dr
Bergeson Dr
Bergeson Dr
Residence Dr

SEE 2007 MAP

W 86TH ST

6000

Rock Hampton Ct
5300
Robbins Rd
Ivy
Americana Blvd
Tech Dr

Picnic Rd

4900

Branch

4500 **W 86TH ST**

Commerce Park Pl

W 85th St
8500
N Moller Rd
Van Camp Dr
5200

Bearing Dr

Payne Branch

8500 W 84th St

46268

23

Northwest Blvd
8200

W 84th St
5800

N
W 84th St

Braddock Rd

A
1 Meadowgate Ct
2 Ridgegate East Dr

Melvil
Oil Creek
Water Dr

46278

Indianapolis

Norfolk St

Allison Av

24

19

Avery West Dr
Avery East Dr
81st Pl
Owl Creek Ct
Pascal Ct
Oil Creek Ct
Bison

W 81st

Ashwood
Ashwood Ct
Ashwood Dr
Deerview Dr
Deerview Dr
Sewood Ct
Clayburn Ct
Woodgate
Irongate
Knollgate
Westover Ct

Dr W 82nd St
Woodland Dr
8100
Little Eagle Creek

N 8008
W 81st St
5400

Blossom Ln
N Blossom Ln
S Blossom Dr
Gordon Dr

W 80th St
5600

A
Trailgate
Austrian Pine Wy
Pine Lake Wy
Pine Lake Ridge Ln
Pine Lake Ridge Ct
Ridgegate West
N Wheat Dr
Pine Rock Dr
Ridge Rd
N 80th St
N Guion Rd
W 80th St

Ropkey Armor Museum

W 79TH ST

6200

5400

Pine Park Ln

Southgate

Eagle Creek

W 79TH ST

4900

Colchester Dr

Langwood Ct

MARSH RD

N Allison Av

7800
W 78th St
5100

ZIONSVILLE RD

Moller Rd

Dr

GEORGETOWN RD

San Fernando Dr
Santa Cruz Dr
Santa Beverly Hills Dr
Santa Monica Dr
Santa Barbara Dr

Augusta Rd
Langwood Dr

30

Chestnut Ct
Keeneland Hills Dr
Heartland Rd
Heartland Ct
N Heartland Bay
1500
Bush's Run

465

26

7600
Woodland Dr

25

Winton Dr

W 76th St
5400

San Gabriel Wy
New
San Gabriel Dr

CROOKED CREEK GOLF CLUB

A   B   C   D   E

SEE 2117 MAP

1 2 3 4 5 6 7

39°56'21"
39°55'55"
39°55'29"
39°55'03"
39°54'37"
39°54'11"
39°53'45"
39°53'19"

86°16'40" 86°16'06" 86°15'32" 86°14'58" 86°14'25" 86°13'51"

1:24,000
1 in. = 2000 ft.
0 0.25 0.5
miles

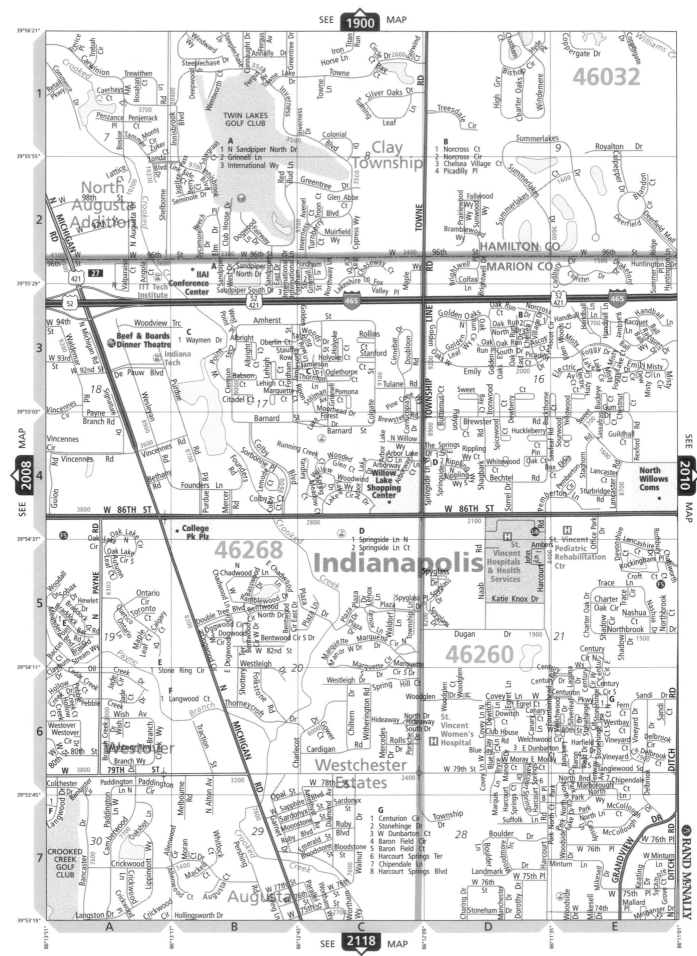

SEE 1900 MAP

SEE 2008 MAP

SEE 2010 MAP

A
1 N Sandpiper North Dr
2 Grinnell Ln
3 International Wy

B
1 Norcross Ct
2 Norcross Cir
3 Chelsea Village Ct
4 Picadilly Pl

C
1 Waymen Dr

D
1 Springside Ln N
2 Springside Ln Ct

E
1 Stone Ring Cir

F
1 Langwood Ct

G
1 Centurion Cir
2 Stonehinge Dr
3 W Dunbarton Ct
4 Baron Field Cir
5 Baron Field Ct
6 Harcourt Springs Ter
7 Chipendale Ln
8 Harcourt Springs Blvd

46032

46268

46260

Indianapolis

Clay Township

North Augusta Addition

Westover

Westchester Estates

Augusta

TWIN LAKES GOLF CLUB

CROOKED CREEK GOLF CLUB

HAMILTON CO

MARION CO

IIAI Conference Center

ITT Tech Institute

Beef & Boards Dinner Theatre

Indiana Tech

College Pk Plz

Willow Lake Shopping Center

North Willows Coms

St. Vincent Hospitals & Health Services

St. Vincent Pediatric Rehabilitation Ctr

St. Vincent Women's Hospital

W 96th St

W 86TH ST

MICHIGAN RD

TOWNE RD

TOWNSHIP LINE RD

GRANDVIEW DR

A B C D E

1 2 3 4 5 6 7

SEE 2118 MAP

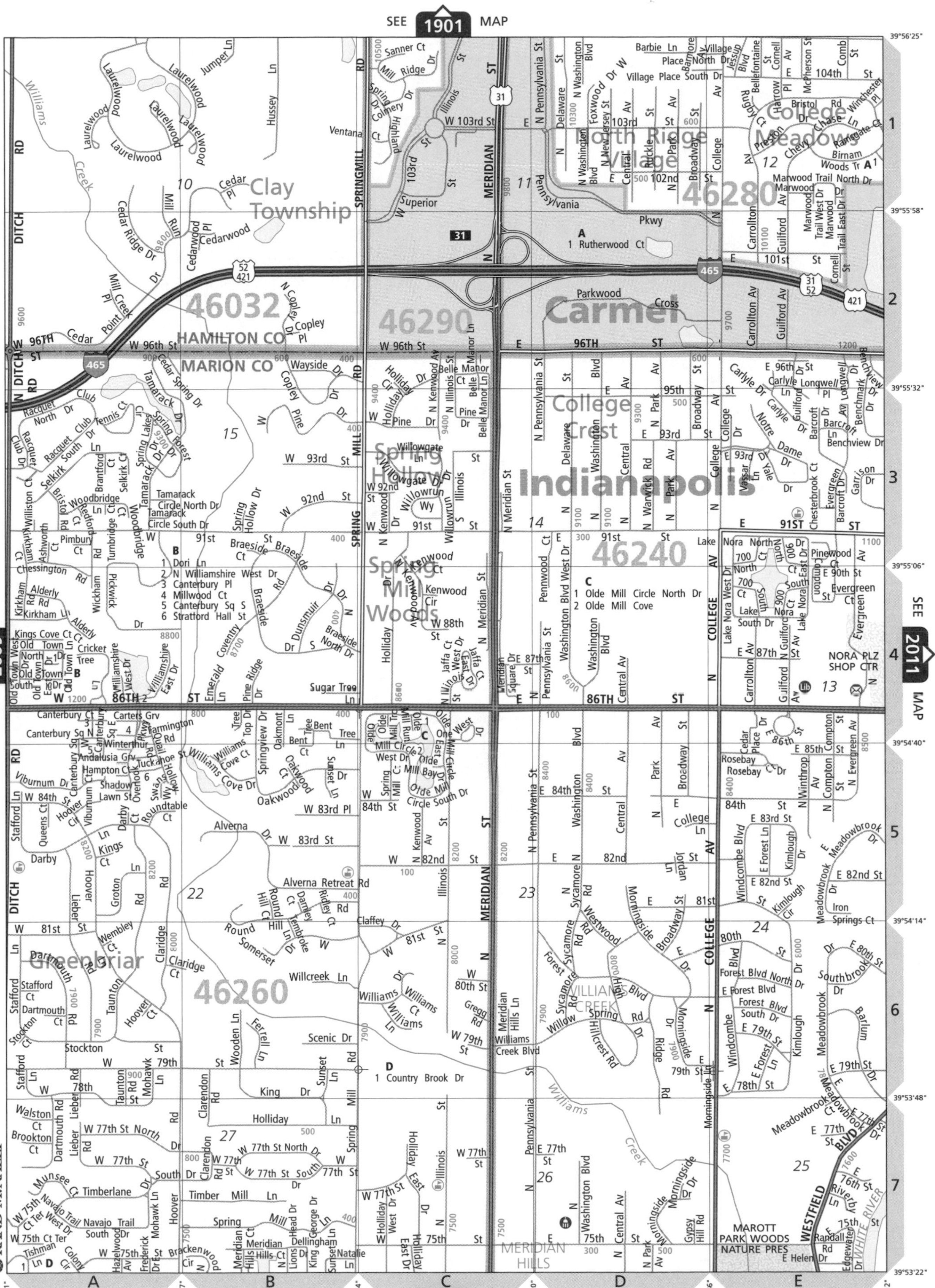

MAP
2010

1:24,000
1 in. = 2000 ft.

0   0.25   0.5
miles

SEE 2009 MAP

SEE 2011 MAP

RAND McNALLY

1:24,000
1 in. = 2000 ft.
0 0.25 0.5
miles

SEE 1902 MAP

SEE 2010 MAP

SEE 2012 MAP

Orchard Park

Home Place

Hunting Hills and Dales

Carmel

46033

46280

Clay Township

Chesterton

HAMILTON CO

MARION CO

SUNRISE GOLF

Driftwood Hills

SHERWOOD FOREST

OUR LADY OF PEACE CEMETERY

UNION CHAPEL CEM

Indiana Wesleyan University

Keystone at the Crossing Fashion Mall

Nora Plz Shopping Center

North Central HS

Indianapolis

Fashion Mall Commons

Clearwater Crossing

46240

46250

WHITE RIVER

Pleasant Acres

N KEYSTONE AV

WESTFIELD BLVD

E 96TH ST

86TH ST

E 82ND ST

DEAN RD

SEE 2120 MAP

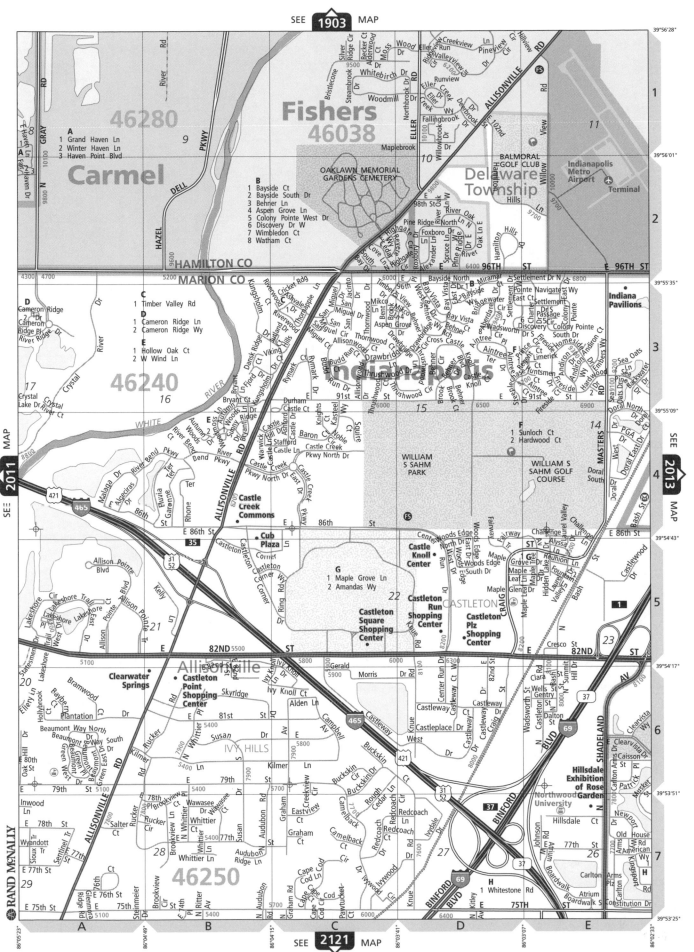

MAP
2012

N

1:24,000
1 in. = 2000 ft.
0   0.25   0.5
miles

Fishers
46038

Carmel
46280

A
1 Grand Haven Ln
2 Winter Haven Ln
3 Haven Point Blvd

B
1 Bayside Ct
2 Bayside South Dr
3 Behner Ln
4 Aspen Grove Ln
5 Colony Pointe West Dr
6 Discovery Dr W
7 Wimbledon Ct
8 Watham Ct

C
1 Timber Valley Rd

D
1 Cameron Ridge Ln
2 Cameron Ridge Wy

E
1 Hollow Oak Ct
2 W Wind Ln

Indianapolis

46240

Delaware
Township

Indianapolis
Metro
Airport

BALMORAL
GOLF CLUB

OAKLAWN MEMORIAL
GARDENS CEMETERY

Indiana
Pavilions

F
1 Sunloch Ct
2 Hardwood Ct

WILLIAM
S SAHM
PARK

WILLIAM S
SAHM GOLF
COURSE

Castle
Creek
Commons

Cub
Plaza

G
1 Maple Grove Ln
2 Amandas Wy

Castle
Knoll
Center

Castleton
Square
Shopping
Center

Castleton
Run
Shopping
Center

Castleton
Plz
Shopping
Center

Allisonville

Clearwater
Springs

Castleton
Point
Shopping
Center

IVY HILLS

46250

Hillsdale
Exhibition
of Rose
Garden

Northwood
University

H
1 Whitestone Rd

SEE 2011 MAP

SEE 2013 MAP

RAND MCNALLY

MAP
2013

1:24,000
1 in. = 2000 ft.

0   0.25   0.5
miles

SEE 1904 MAP

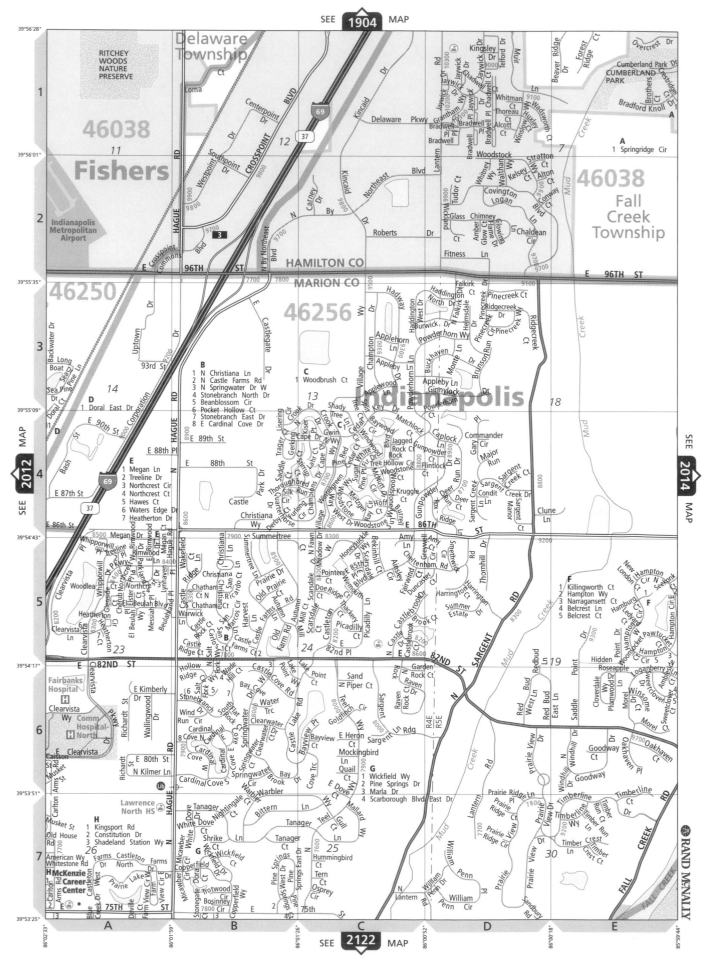

SEE 2012 MAP

SEE 2014 MAP

SEE 2122 MAP

RAND MCNALLY

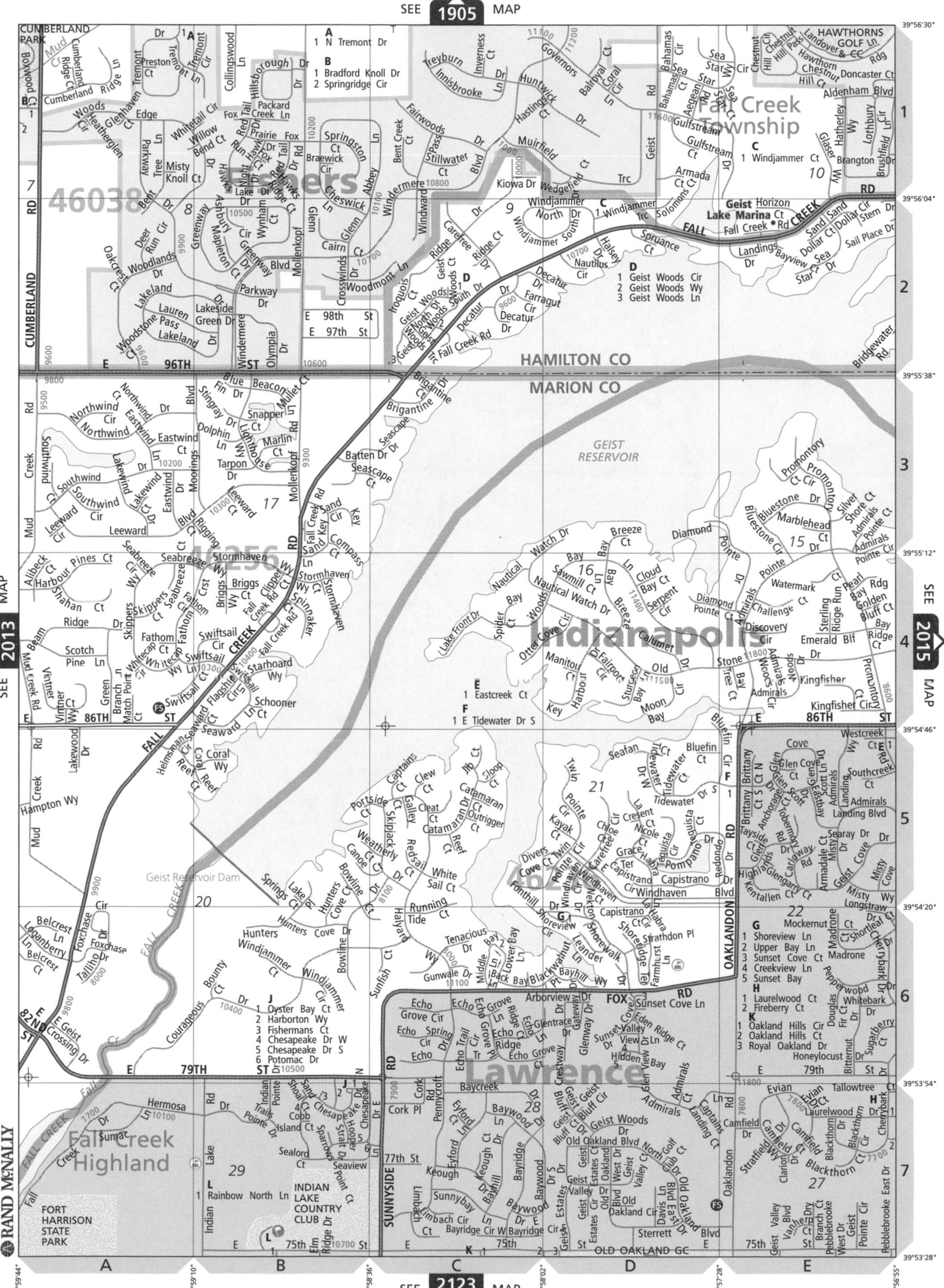

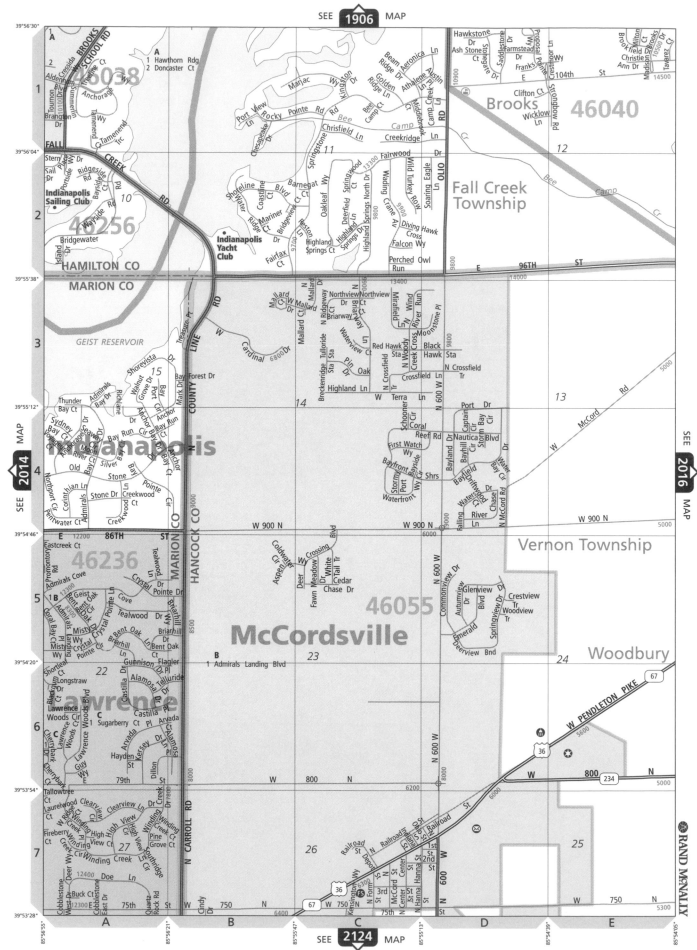

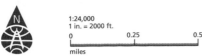

1:24,000
1 in. = 2000 ft.

0   0.25   0.5
miles

MAP
2016

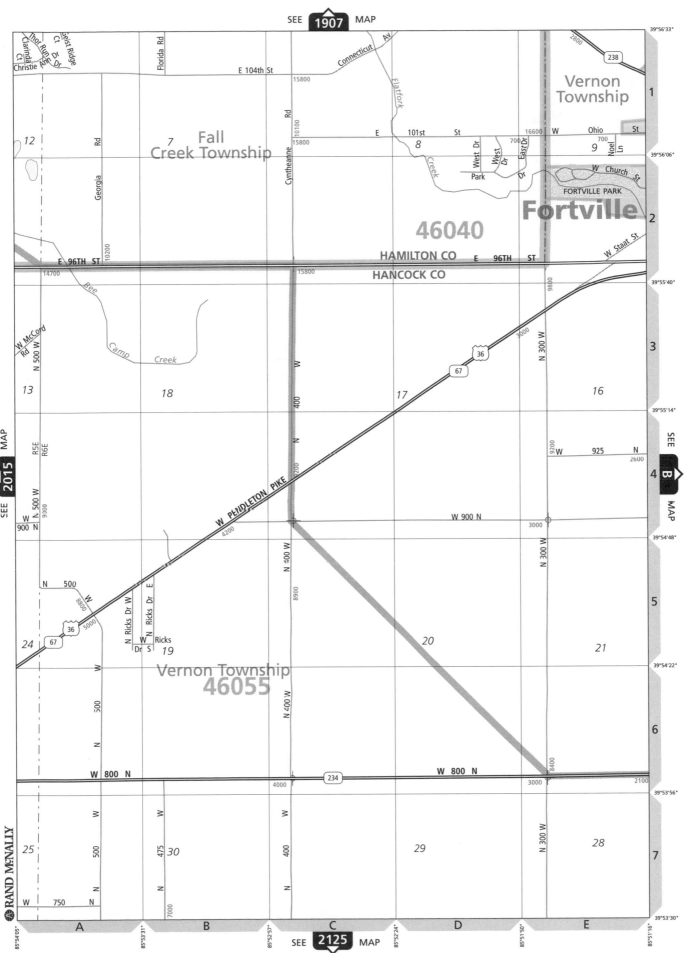

SEE 1907 MAP

SEE 2015 MAP

SEE B MAP

SEE 2125 MAP

RAND McNALLY

39°56'33"
39°56'06"
39°55'40"
39°55'14"
39°54'48"
39°54'22"
39°53'56"
39°53'30"

85°54'05"
85°53'31"
85°52'57"
85°52'24"
85°51'50"
85°51'16"

Vernon Township

Fall Creek Township

Fortville

FORTVILLE PARK

46040

HAMILTON CO
HANCOCK CO

Vernon Township
46055

W PENDLETON PIKE

W 96TH ST   E 96TH ST

W 800 N

W 900 N

E 104th St

Connecticut Av

E 101st St

W Ohio St

W Church St

W Staat St

MAP
2112

1:24,000
1 in. = 2000 ft.

0   0.25   0.5

miles

SEE 2003 MAP

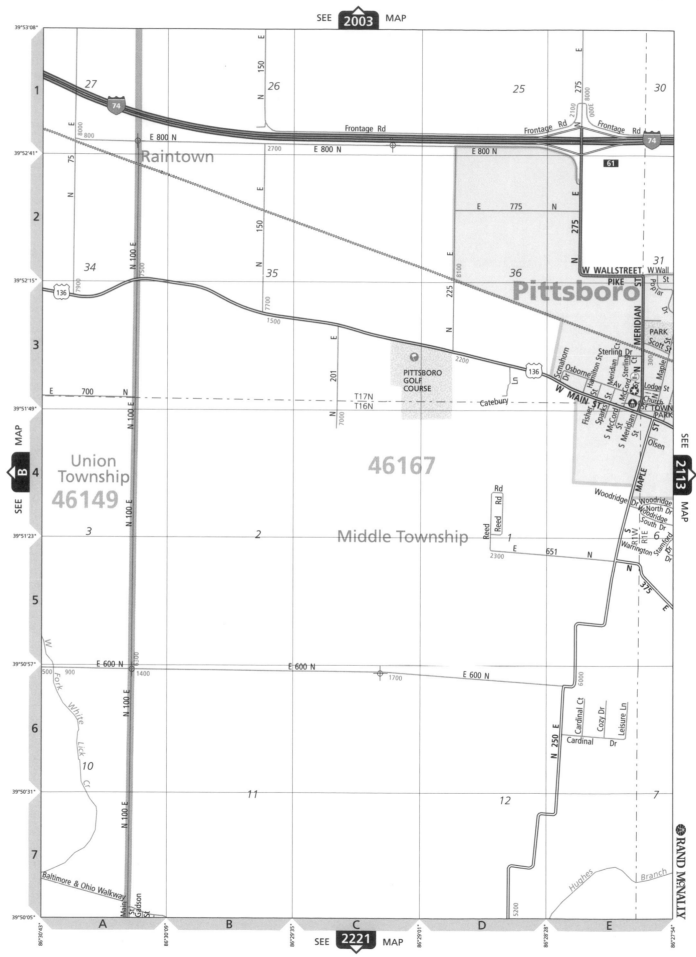

Raintown

27

26

25

30

Frontage Rd

Frontage Rd   Frontage   Rd

E 800 N

E 800 N

E 800 N

Pittsboro

34   35   36   31

W WALLSTREET   W Wall St

PIKE

W MAIN ST

PARK

Scott St

Sterling Dr

Scnahom Dr

Osborne

Hamilton St

Meridian

Sterling

Sterling Ct

Maple

Lodge St

Church St

PITTSBORO
GOLF
COURSE

Catebury   Ln

T17N
T16N

E   700   N

Fisher St

Sparks St

S McCord St

S Meridian St

Olsen

TOWN
PARK

SEE 2113 MAP

Union
Township
46149

46167

MAPLE

Woodridge Dr

Woodridge Dr

North Dr

Woodridge
South Dr

S R I W

RIE

Warrington

Stamford Dr

3   2   Middle Township   1

Reed   Reed   Rd

Rd

E   651   N

375

E 600 N   E 600 N   E 600 N

N 100 E

W

Fork

White

Lick

Cr

500   900

1400

1700

6000

Cardinal Ct

Cozy Dr

Leisure Ln

Cardinal
Dr

N 250 E

10

11   12   7

Baltimore & Ohio Walkway

Main St

Gadson St

Hughes   Branch

A   B   C   D   E

SEE 2221 MAP

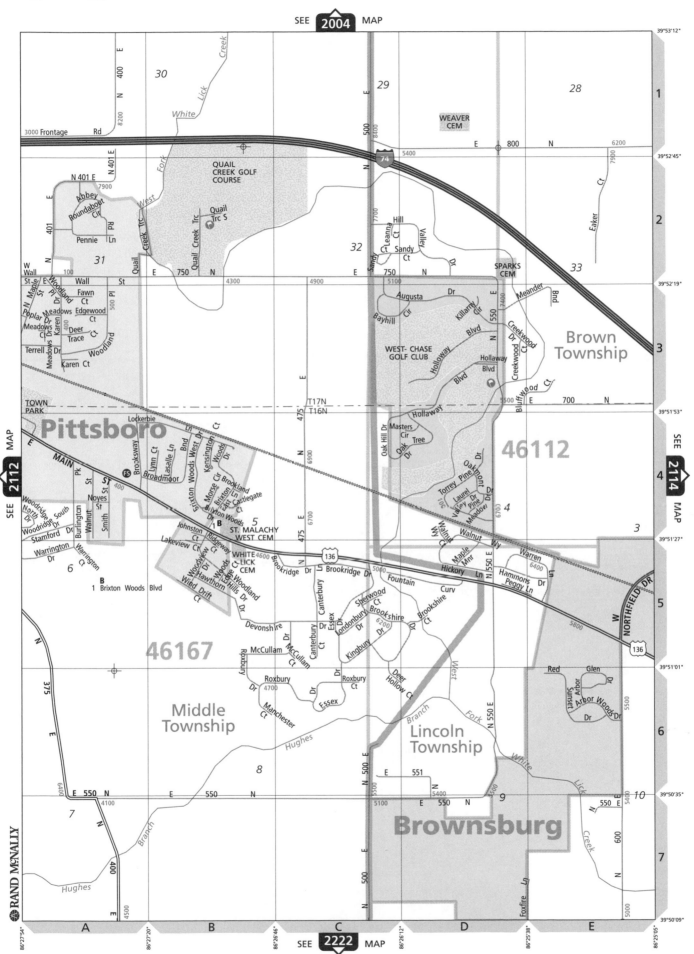

MAP
2113

1:24,000
1 in. = 2000 ft.
0   0.25   0.5
miles

SEE 2004 MAP

39°53'12"

30
29
28

1

WEAVER
CEM

3000 Frontage Rd

39°52'45"

800 N
6200
7900

QUAIL
CREEK GOLF
COURSE

Quail
Trc S

I-74
5400

Eaker Ct

2

N 401 E
7900

Abbey
Roundabout
Cir

Pennie Ln
Rd

401

31

Hill
Leanna Ct
Sandy Ct

Valley Dr

SPARKS
CEM

33

39°52'19"

W Wall St
100
Wall St
Woodland Pl
Fawn Ct
Meadows Dr
Edgewood Ct
Poplar Dr
Karen
Meadows Ct
Deer Trace Ct
Terrell Dr
Woodland
Karen Ct

Quail Creek Trc
E   750   N

4300
4900
5100

750

Augusta Dr
Bayhill Cir

Killarney Cir

Meander Bnd

Creekwood

WEST-
CHASE
GOLF CLUB

Holloway Blvd

Hollaway Blvd

Creekwood Dr

Brown
Township

3

TOWN
PARK

T17N
T16N

Holloway Blvd

Bluffwood Ct

5500
700
N

39°51'53"

SEE 2112 MAP

Pittsboro

Lockerbie

Brooksway
Broadmoor

Lynn Ct
Lasalle Ln

Brixton Woods West Dr
Kensington Bnd
Woods Dr

Masters
Cir
Oak Hill Dr
Oak Tree Dr

46112

MAIN ST
400

Pk St
Noyes St
Smith St

Morse Cir
Brixton Woods East

Brookland
Castlegate

Oakmont Dr
Torrey Pine Dr
Laurel Valley Dr
Pine Meadow
Pine

4

Woodridge North Dr
Woodridge South Dr
Stamford Dr
Burlington Dr
Walnut

Johnston Ridgeway
Ct

Dr
5

ST. MALACHY
WEST CEM

Walnut Wy

3

39°51'27"

Warrington Dr
Warrington Ct

Lakeview Ct
Woodview Dr
Hawthorn Dr
Eagle Hills Dr
Woodland

WHITE
LICK
CEM
4600

Brookridge Dr

Brookridge Dr
Fountain Dr

Maple Mnr
Hickory Ln
Warren Ln
6400
Hammons Dr
Peggy Ln

N 550 E

5

6

B 1 Brixton Woods Blvd

Wind Drift Dr

Devonshire Dr
McCullam

Canterbury Ct
Essex Ct
Londonbury Dr
Sherwood Ct
6200
Kingbury Dr

Brookshire Dr
Brookshire Dr

Curv

46167

Roxbury Dr

McCullam

Canterbury Dr

Deer Hollow Ct

W
e
s
t

Red Glen Dr
Arbor Sunset Dr
Arbor Woods Dr

NORTHFIELD DR
5800

US 136

39°51'01"

375

Middle
Township

Roxbury Dr
4700
Essex Dr

Roxbury Ct

Manchester Ct

8

Lincoln
Township

F
o
r
k

N 550 E

W
h
i
t
e

L
i
c
k

6

E 550 N
6400
4100

E   550   N

500

5100

551
5400
550
N

9

550
5400

10

39°50'35"

7

400

H
u
g
h
e
s

B
r
a
n
c
h

Brownsburg

Foxfire Ln

600

5000

7

39°50'09"

A
B
C
D
E

SEE 2222 MAP

MAP 2114

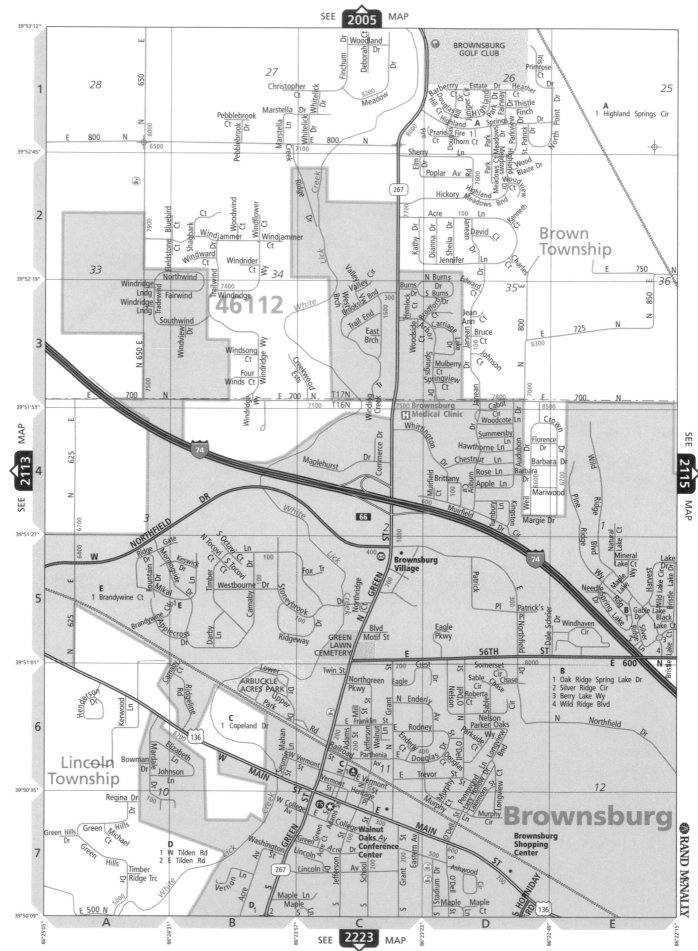

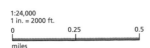

MAP
2115

1:24,000
1 in. = 2000 ft.

0   0.25   0.5
miles

SEE 2006 MAP

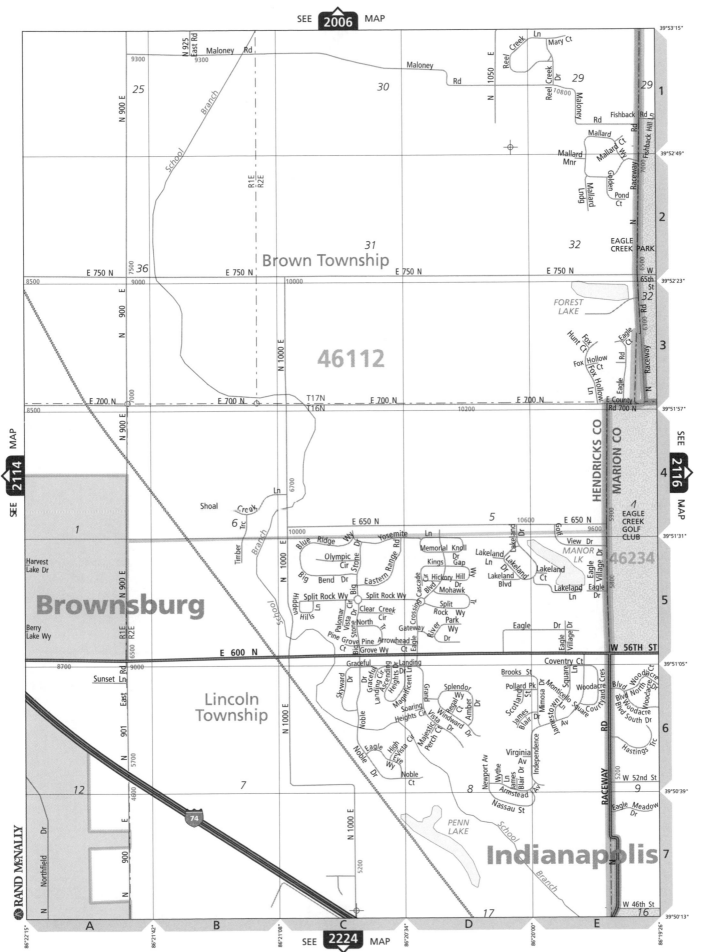

SEE 2114 MAP

SEE 2116 MAP

SEE 2224 MAP

RAND McNALLY

MAP
2116

1:24,000
1 in. = 2000 ft.
0   0.25   0.5
miles

SEE 2007 MAP

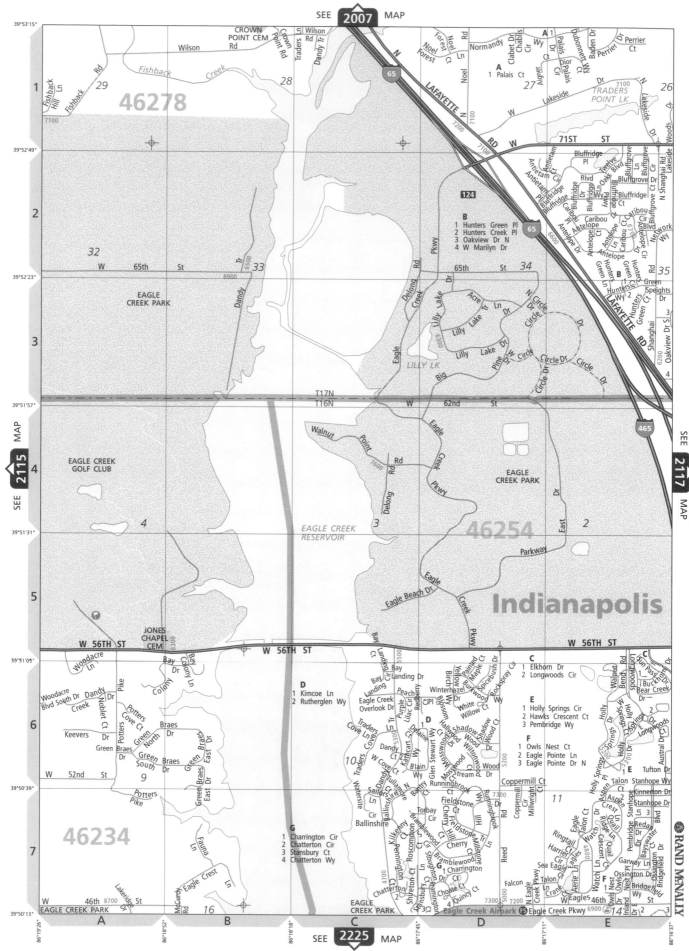

39°53'15"

CROWN POINT CEM Rd

Wilson

Wilson Rd

Traders Rd

Dandy Tr

A

Forest

Noel Rd

Normandy

Chablis

Clabet Dr

A

Palais Wy

Dior Dr

Palais Ct

Dubornet Dr

Baden Dr

Perrier Dr

Perrier Ct

Fishback Creek

Noel Forest Ct

Noel Cir

A
1 Palais Ct

27

Lakeside Dr

Dr

TRADERS POINT LK

26

7100

Lakeside

Woods

1

Fishback Hill Ln

Fishback Rd

Fishback Rd

29

46278

28

LAFAYETTE RD

7200

7100

71ST ST

7100

Lakeside Dr

39°52'49"

7100

Bluffridge Pl

Antietam Cir

Antietam Pl

Bluffridge

Bluffridge Ln

Oaks Blvd

Twelve

Bluffgrove Ln

Bluffgrove Dr

Bluffridge Blvd

Bluffridge Dr

Bluffridge Ct

Lakeside

2

32

124

65

6600

Caribou Cir

Caribou Ct

Antelope

Antelope Dr

Caribou Cir

Caribou Cir

Antelope Cir

Antelope Ct

Caribou Dr

Antelope Dr

NetWork Wy

B
1 Hunters Green Pl
2 Hunters Creek Pl
3 Oakview Dr N
4 W Marilyn Dr

Pkwy

35

W   65th   St

Tr

6500

33

Dandy

8900

65th   St

34

Green Speights Dr

Hunters Green Ln

Hunters Green Ct

Green Ln

Hunters Green Rd

B

39°52'23"

EAGLE CREEK PARK

Delong Creek Rd

Acre Ln

Lilly Lake Ln

N Circle Dr

Circle Dr

Shanghai

Lafayette Rd

6200

Oakview Dr S

3

Lilly Lake Dr

Lilly Lake

Lilly Lake

Pine W Dr

Circle Dr

Circle Dr

Circle Dr

Circle Dr

6300

LILLY LK

Eagle

Big

Circle Dr

39°51'57"

T17N
T16N

W   62nd   St

465

SEE 2117 MAP

Walnut

Point

7600

Eagle Creek Rd

Eagle Creek Pkwy

EAGLE CREEK PARK

4

EAGLE CREEK GOLF CLUB

4

Delong Rd

3

46254

2

East Dr

SEE 2115 MAP

39°51'31"

EAGLE CREEK RESERVOIR

Parkway

Indianapolis

5

Eagle Beach Dr

Eagle Creek Pkwy

Bay

39°51'05"

JONES CHAPEL CEM

W 56TH ST

W 56TH ST

W 56TH ST

8300

Landing Ct

5500

C
1 Elkhorn Dr
2 Longwoods Cir

Sun Pass Ct

Walpole Bend Rd

Buckhorn Dr

Bear Creek Dr

C

6

Woodacre Ln

Woodacre Blvd South

Dandy Dr

Noblet Ct

Pike

Creek

Dandy Dr

Bay Dr

Bay Colony Ln

Bay Colony Ln

D
1 Kimcoe Ln
2 Rutherglen Wy

Bay Landing Cir

Bay Landing Dr

Bay Landing Dr

Eagle Creek Overlook Dr

Purple Lilac Cir

Peachy CPl

Birchy Wy

Painted Yellow Wy

Burkwood Dr

Winterhazel Dr

Rockspray Cir

White Willow

Shadow Wood

E
1 Holly Springs Cir
2 Hawks Crescent Ct
3 Pembridge Wy

Holly Springs

Holly Springs Dr

Holly

Longwoods Dr

E

Keevers Dr

Potters Cove Ct

Braes North Dr

Green Braes Dr

Green Braes East Dr

Traders Cove Ln

Dandy Ct

W Cove Ct

Delaine Dr

Blain

Kathcart

Glen Stewart Wy

Blossom Wy

Hallway

Mosswood

Shadow Wood

Willomwood

Wood

Wood

F
1 Owls Nest Ct
2 Eagle Pointe Ln
3 Eagle Pointe Dr

5200

Austral Dr

Tufton Dr

E

6

Potters Pike

Green Braes Dr

Green Braes South Dr

Green Braes East Dr

10

Sailors Cir

Tullamore

Bantry Wy

Running-brook Ct

Runningbrook

Mosswood Stream Ct

Wood

Coppermill Ct

5300

7300

11

Eagle Talon Ct

Aspen Crest Dr

Stanhope Wy

Kinnerton Dr

Stanhope Dr

Aspen Pl

Reda Dr

W   52nd   St

9

Potters Pike

Watersite Cir

Fieldstone

Ballinshire N

Torbay

Kilkenny

Fieldstone Dr

Millstone

Cherry Hill

Runningbrook

Coppermill Ct

Millwright Ct

Holly Springs Ct

Eagle Talon Ct

Aspen Ct

Quail Ridge Ln

Pembridge

Stanhope

Bayswater Dr

39°50'39"

46234

Fauna Ln

G
1 Charrington Cir
2 Chatterton Cir
3 Stansbury Ct
4 Chatterton Wy

Ballinshire

Pennington

Roscommon

Stoughton Dr

Bramblewood Dr

Cherry

Cherry

Reed Rd

G
1 Charrington

Harriett

Ringtail

Eagle Talon Ct

Eagle Watch

Quail Crescent

Crescent Ct

Garway Dr

Ossington Dr

Bridgefield

7

Eagle Crest Ln

McCurdy Rd

Lakeridge St

16

Chatterton Cir

Shireton Ct

Ransbury Ct

Flamington

Choate Ct

4 Quincy Ct

7300

5000

7200

N Eagle Creek Pkwy

6900

Falcon

Sea Eagle

N Eagle

Crane

Inland

Eagles Wy

Aerie

W 46th St

Owls Nest Ct

Owls Nest

Bridge

Owls

Ossington Dr

Inland Dr

F

14

39°50'13"

EAGLE CREEK PARK

W   46th   St

8700

EAGLE CREEK PARK

Eagle Creek Airpark

Eagle Creek Pkwy

A   B   C   D   E

86°19'26"   86°18'52"   86°18'18"   86°17'45"   86°17'11"   86°16'37"

SEE 2225 MAP

RAND M?NALLY

MAP
2117

SEE 2008 MAP

Indianapolis

SEE 2116 MAP

SEE 2118 MAP

SEE 2226 MAP

RAND McNALLY

MAP
2118

SEE 2009 MAP

1:24,000
1 in. = 2000 ft.
0   0.25   0.5
miles

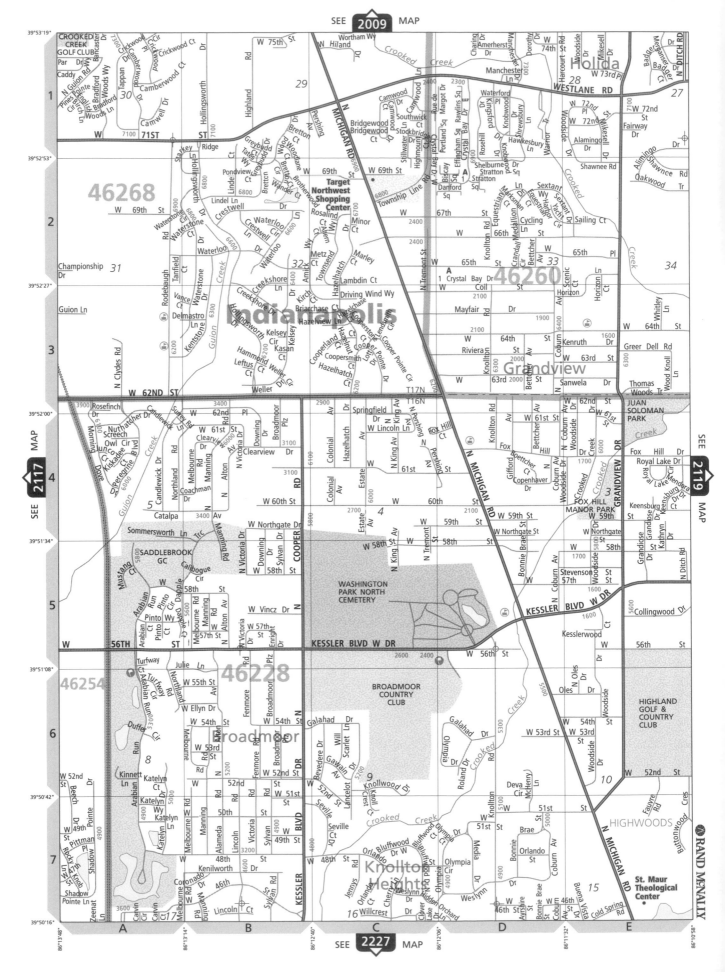

SEE 2117 MAP

SEE 2119 MAP

SEE 2227 MAP

46268

46260

46228

46254

Indianapolis

Grandview

Highwoods

Knollton Heights

Broadmoor

RAND McNALLY

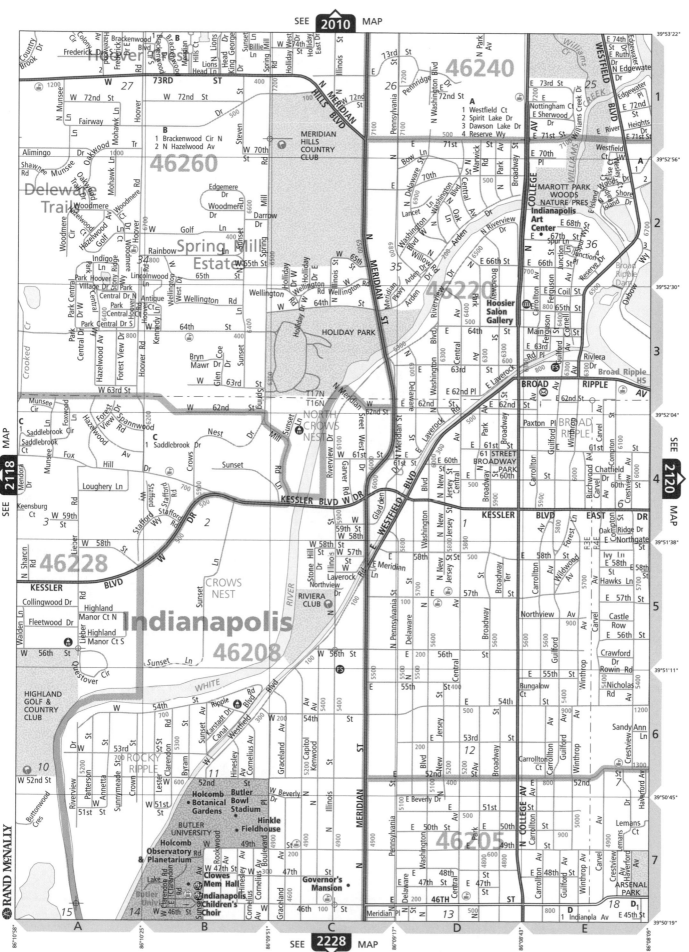

MAP
2119

1:24,000
1 in. = 2000 ft.
0   0.25   0.5
miles

RAND MCNALLY

SEE 2010 MAP
SEE 2118 MAP
SEE 2120 MAP
SEE 2228 MAP

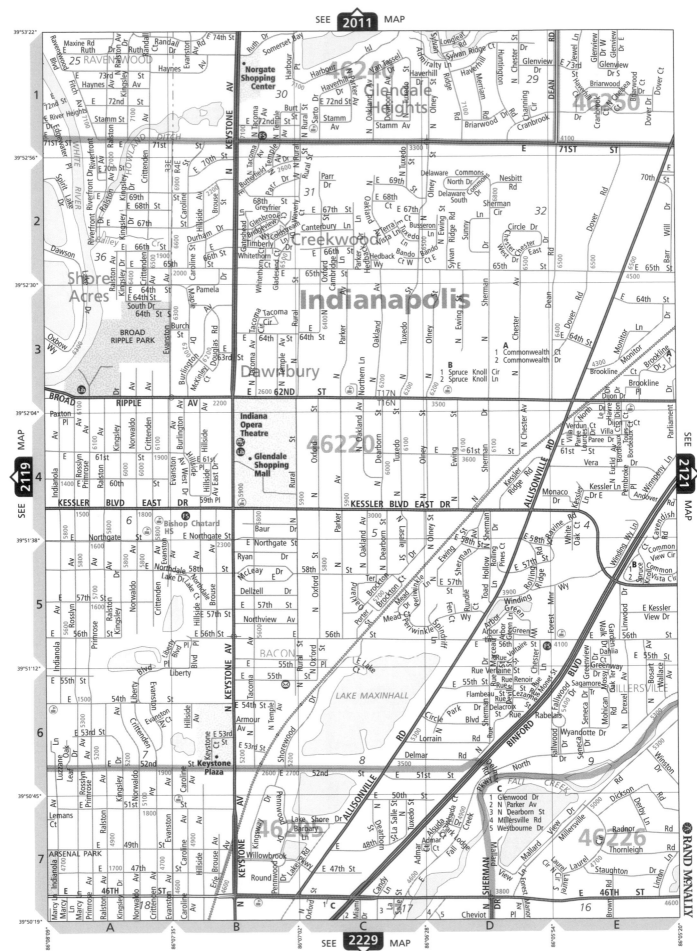

MAP
2120

1:24,000
1 in. = 2000 ft.
0   0.25   0.5
miles

SEE 2011 MAP

SEE 2119 MAP

SEE 2121 MAP

SEE 2229 MAP

RAND McNALLY

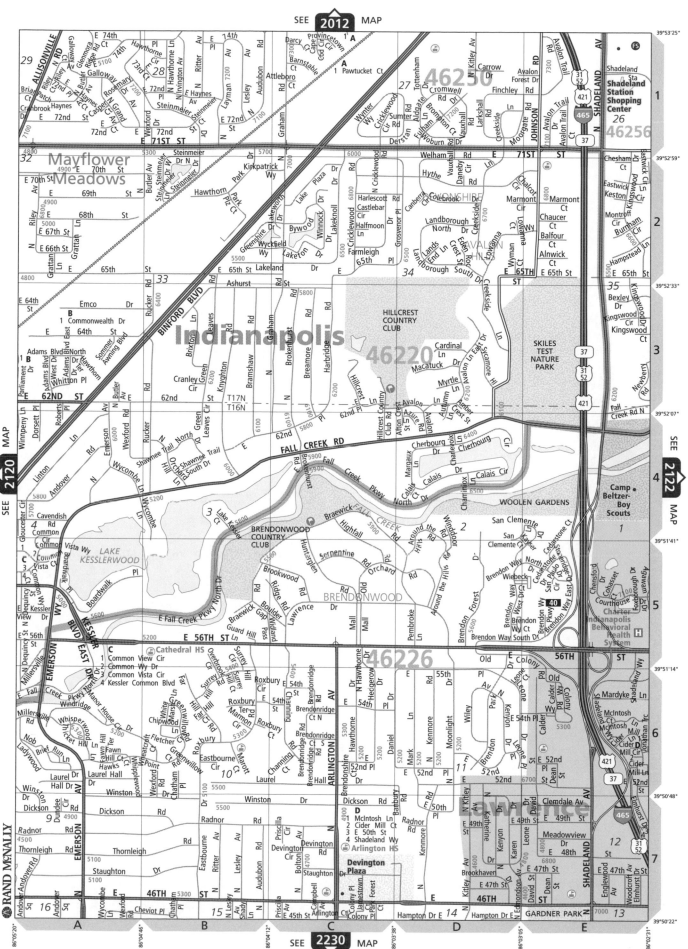

MAP
2121

MAP
2122

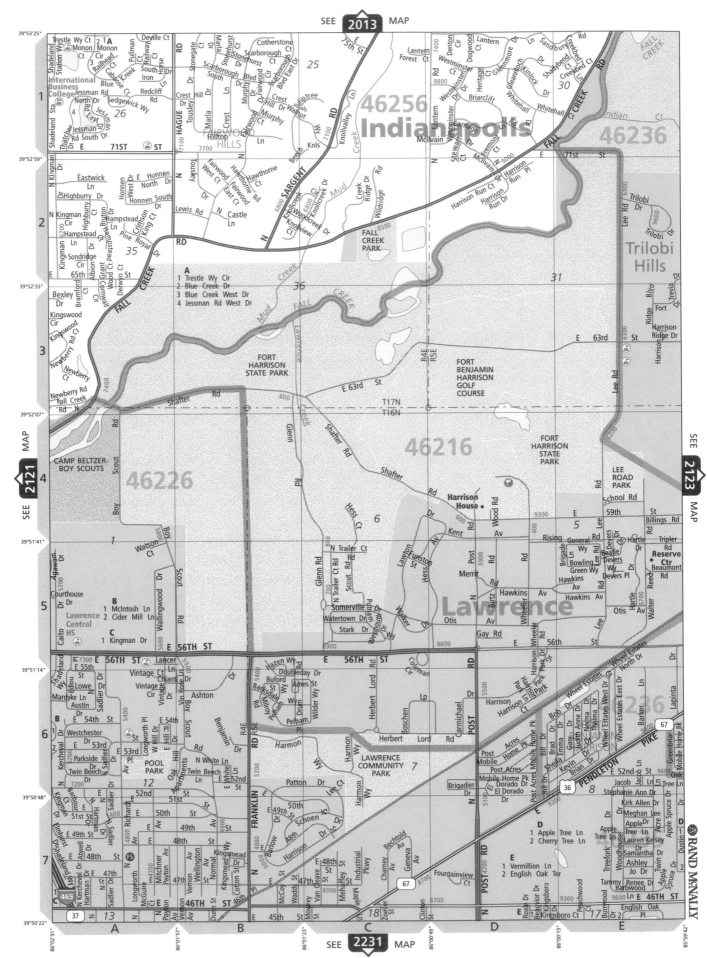

SEE 2013 MAP

SEE 2121 MAP

SEE 2123 MAP

SEE 2231 MAP

46256
Indianapolis

46236

Trilobi
Hills

46226

46216

Lawrence

FORT
HARRISON
STATE PARK

FORT
BENJAMIN
HARRISON
GOLF
COURSE

FORT
HARRISON
STATE
PARK

CAMP BELTZER-
BOY SCOUTS

FALL
CREEK
PARK

RAND McNALLY

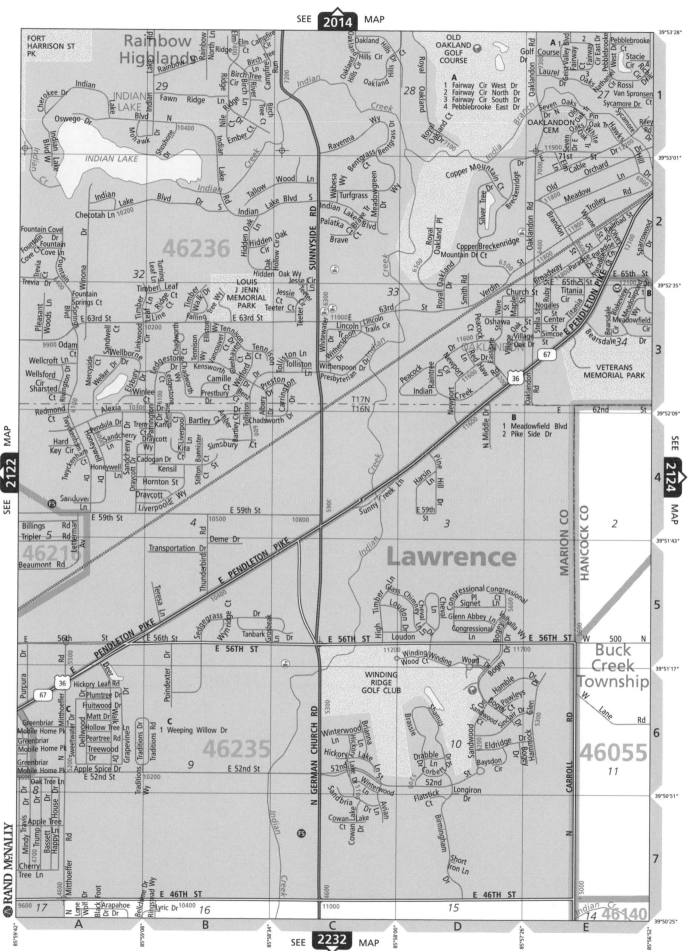

MAP
2123

1:24,000
1 in. = 2000 ft.

0   0.25   0.5
miles

SEE 2014 MAP

SEE 2122 MAP

SEE 2124 MAP

SEE 2232 MAP

RAND MCNALLY

MAP 2124

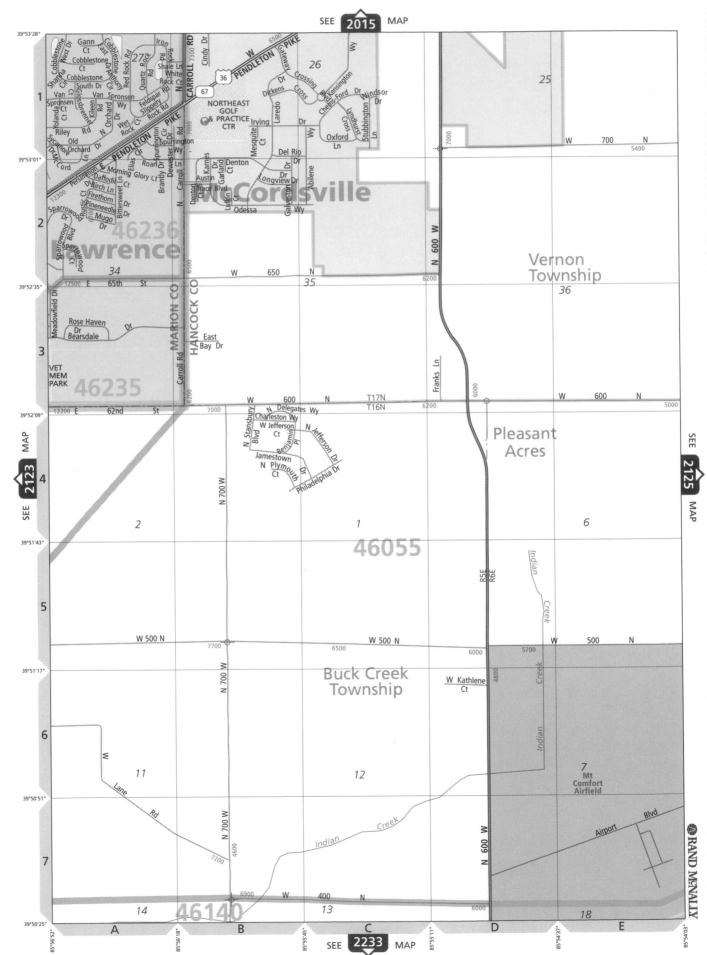

1:24,000
1 in. = 2000 ft.
0   0.25   0.5
miles

SEE 2015 MAP

SEE 2123 MAP

SEE 2125 MAP

SEE 2233 MAP

McCordsville

46236
Lawrence

46235

46055

46140

Vernon Township

Pleasant Acres

Buck Creek Township

Mt Comfort Airfield

NORTHEAST GOLF & PRACTICE CTR

VET MEM PARK

MARION CO
HANCOCK CO

RAND McNALLY

MAP
2125

1:24,000
1 in. = 2000 ft.

0   0.25   0.5
miles

SEE **2016** MAP

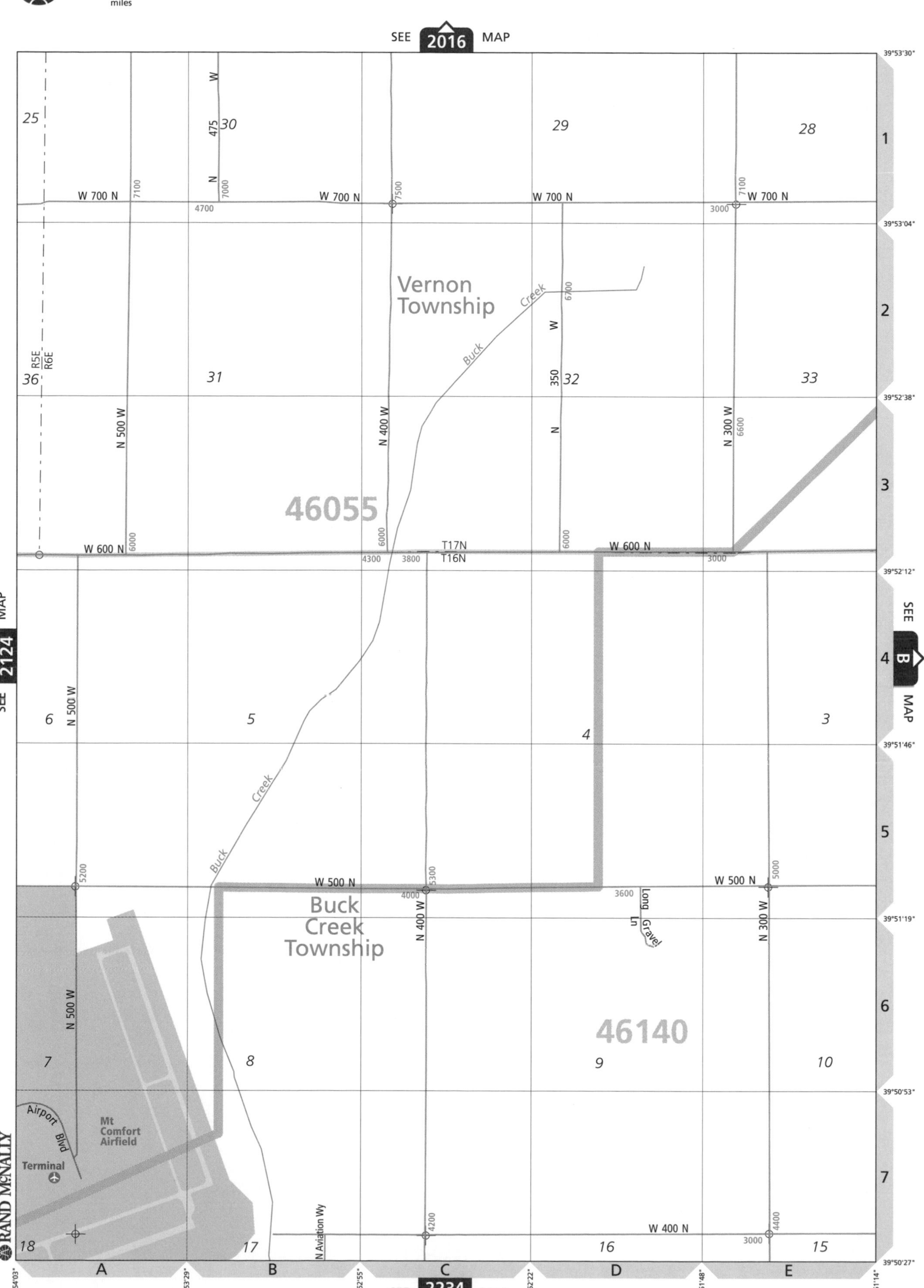

25

W
475 30

29

28

1

W 700 N   7100   N 7000   4700   W 700 N   7500   W 700 N   3000   7100   W 700 N

39°53'30"

39°53'04"

Vernon
Township

Buck Creek

6700

W

46055

31

R5E R6E

36

N 500 W   6000

350 32   N

33

2

39°52'38"

3

N 400 W   6000

N 300 W   6600

W 600 N   6000   4300   3800   T17N T16N   6000   W 600 N   3000

39°52'12"

SEE **2124** MAP

SEE **B** MAP

6   N 500 W

5

Buck Creek

4

3

4

39°51'46"

5

5200

W 500 N   4000   5300   N 400 W   3600   Long Gravel Ln   W 500 N   5000   N 300 W

39°51'19"

Buck
Creek
Township

46140

6

N 500 W

7

8

9

10

39°50'53"

Airport Blvd

Mt
Comfort
Airfield

Terminal

7

N Aviation Wy   4200   W 400 N   3000   4400

18

17

16

15

39°50'27"

85°54'03"   85°53'29"   85°52'55"   85°52'22"   85°51'48"   85°51'14"

A   B   C   D   E

SEE **2234** MAP

MAP
2221

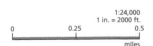

1:24,000
1 in. = 2000 ft.
0   0.25   0.5
miles

N

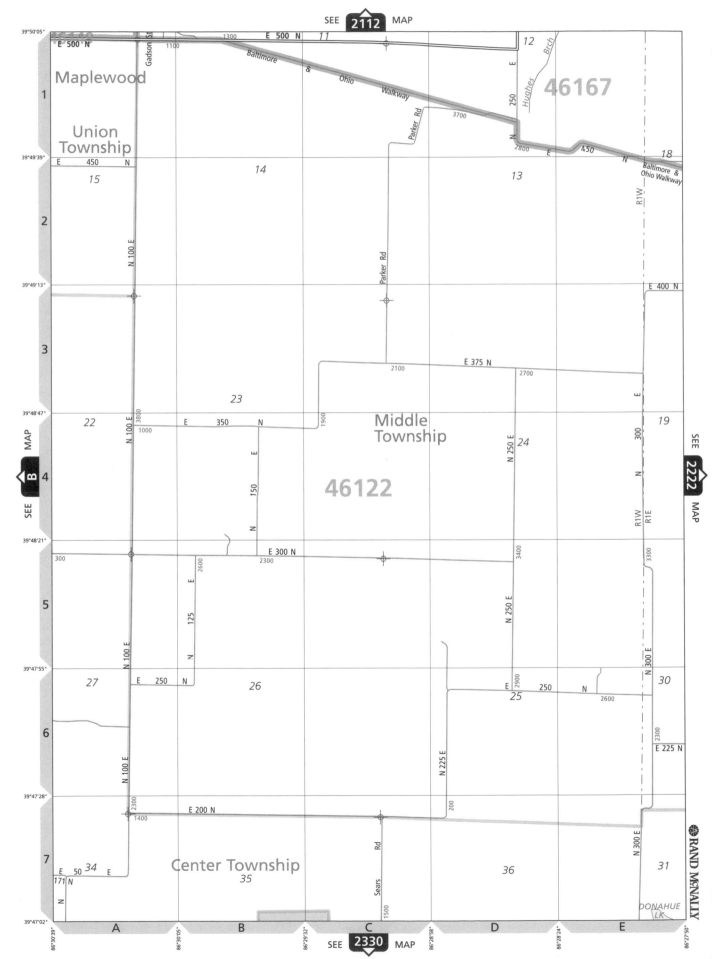

SEE 2112 MAP

39°50'05"
E 500 N
Maplewood
Gadson St
1100   1300   E 500 N   11   12
Baltimore   &   Ohio   Walkway
Hughes Brch
46167
250
E
3700

Union
Township
Parker Rd
2800   E   450   N   18
Baltimore &
Ohio Walkway

1

39°49'39"
E   450   N
15   14   13   R1W

2

39°49'13"
E 400 N

Parker Rd
E

3

E 375 N
2100   2700

23   E
39°48'47"
22   N 100 E 3800   E   350   N   1900   Middle
Township   300   19
1000   46122   N 250 E   24
E   150   R1W R1E

B   MAP   4
SEE

SEE 2222 MAP

N

39°48'21"
300   2600   E 300 N   3300
E   2300   3400

5
125   N 250 E   300 E

N   E

39°47'55"
27   E   250   N   26   2900   250   N   30
E   25   2600
N 225 E   2300
E 225 N

6

N 100 E   200

39°47'28"
2300   E 200 N   200
1400   N 300 E

7
E   50   34   E   Center Township   Sears Rd   36   31
171   N   35
N   1500   DONAHUE
LK

39°47'02"
86°30'39"   A   86°30'05"   B   86°29'32"   C   86°28'58"   D   86°28'24"   E   86°27'58"

RAND M\cNALLY

SEE 2330 MAP

1:24,000
1 in. = 2000 ft.
0   0.25   0.5
miles

MAP
2222

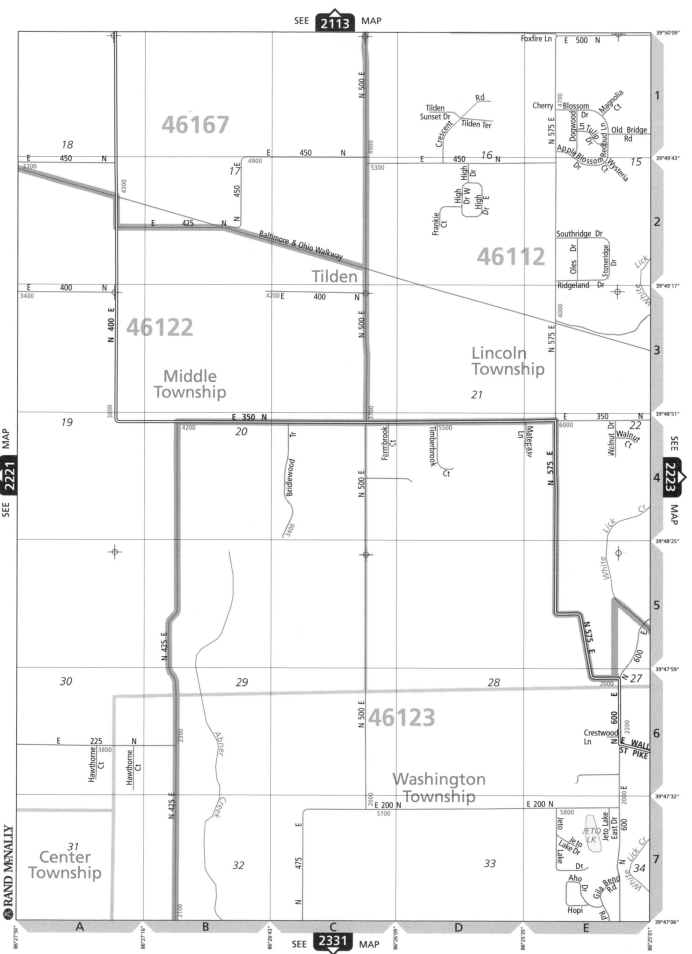

SEE 2113 MAP

39°50'09"

Foxfire Ln   E 500 N

1

46167

Tilden   Rd

Tilden Sunset Dr   Tilden Ter

Crescent

Cherry   Blossom   Magnolia Ct

Dogwood Ln   Tulip Dr   Redbud Ct   Old Bridge Rd

Apple Blossom Dr   Wysteria

4700

N 575 E

18

E 450 N
3300

E 450 N   4900   17
450 E

450 N

E 425 N   N

5300   16 N   E 450 N   15

39°49'43"

2

Baltimore & Ohio Walkway

High Dr

High Dr W   High Dr E

Frankie Ct

Southridge Dr

Oles Dr   Stoneridge Dr

Ridgeland Dr

46112

Lick

Tilden

N 500 E

E 400 N
3400

4200 E   400 N

4000

N 575 E

White

39°49'17"

46122

N 400 E

Middle
Township

Lincoln
Township

3

21

19   E 350 N   4200   20   3700

Farmbrook Ct

Timberbrook
5500
Ct

Matepaw Ln

E 350 N   6000   22

N 575 E

Walnut Dr   Walnut Ct

39°48'51"

4

SEE 2221 MAP

SEE 2223 MAP

Bridlewood Tr

3400

N 500 E

Lick Cr

White Lick

39°48'25"

5

N 575 E

600 E

30   29   28   N 27   2000

39°47'59"

N 425 E   2300

Abner

46123

N 500 E

600 E   2200

6

E 225 N   N
3800

Hawthorne Ct   Hawthorne Ct

Washington
Township

Creek

Crestwood Ln   E WALL ST PIKE

2000 E

39°47'32"

N 425 E   2100

31   32   475 N   33   34

Center
Township

E 200 N   5700   2000   E 200 N

5800   Jeto Lake East Dr

Jeto Lake Dr   JETO LK

Jeto Lake Dr

Aho Dr   Gila Bend Rd

Hopi Rd

600 E   White Lick Cr

39°47'06"

A   B   C   D   E

86°27'50"   86°27'16"   86°26'43"   86°26'09"   86°25'36"   86°25'01"

SEE 2331 MAP

RAND McNALLY

MAP
2223

1:24,000
1 in. = 2000 ft.
0   0.25   0.5
miles

SEE 2114 MAP

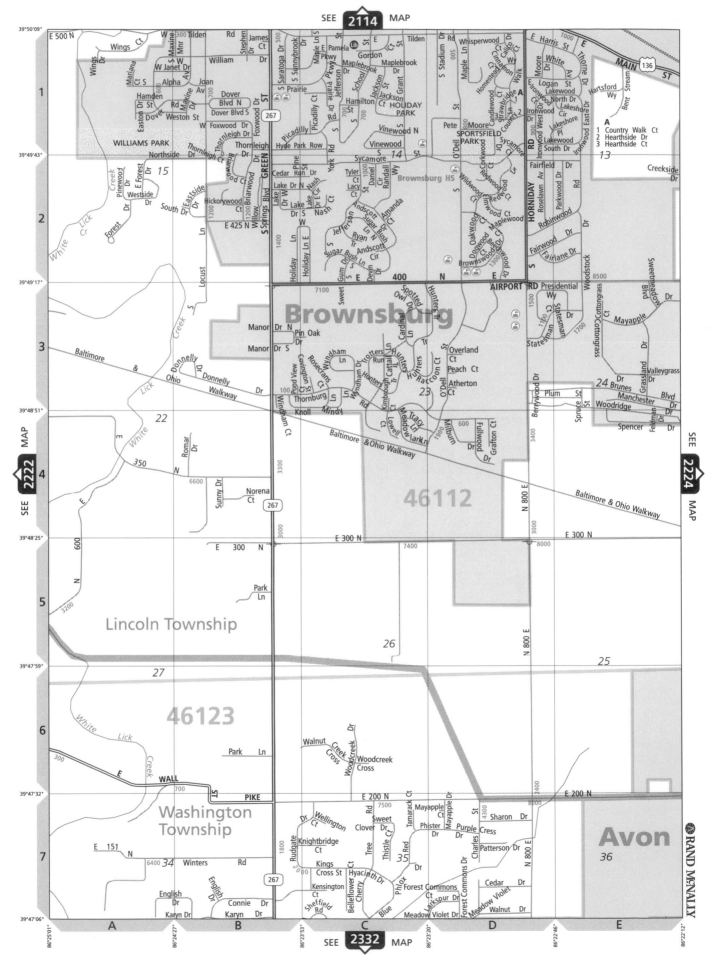

SEE 2222 MAP

SEE 2224 MAP

SEE 2332 MAP

WILLIAMS PARK

Brownsburg

46112

Lincoln Township

46123

Washington Township

Avon

RAND MCNALLY

A   B   C   D   E

A
1 Country Walk Ct
2 Hearthside Dr
3 Hearthside Ct

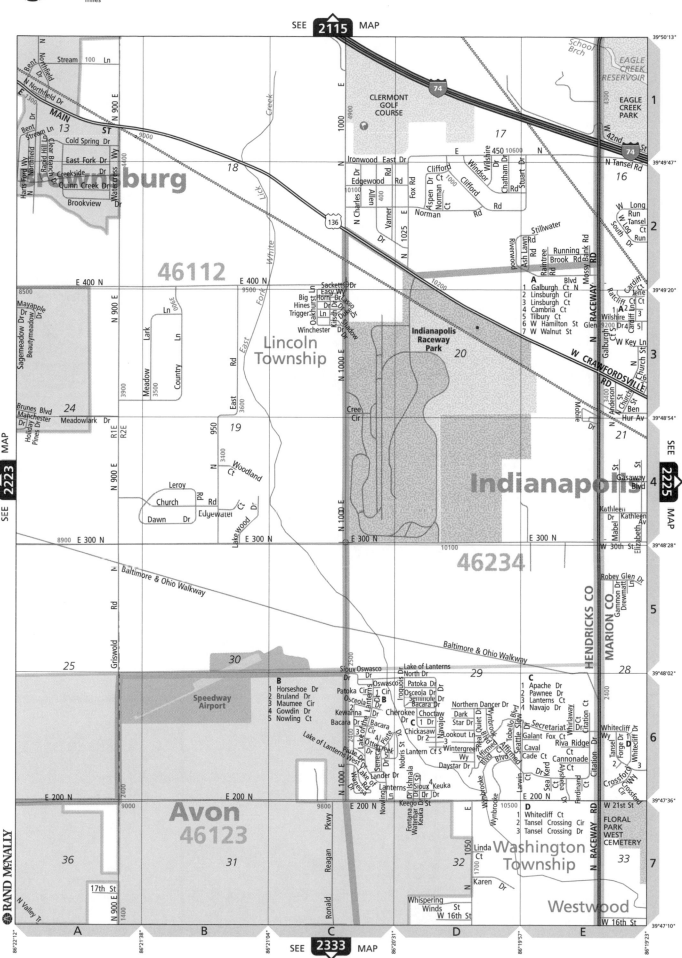

MAP
2224

1:24,000
1 in. = 2000 ft.

0   0.25   0.5

miles

SEE 2115 MAP

SEE 2223 MAP

SEE 2225 MAP

EAGLE CREEK RESERVOIR

EAGLE CREEK PARK

School Brch

CLERMONT GOLF COURSE

Brownsburg

Lincoln Township

46112

Indianapolis

Indianapolis Raceway Park

46234

Avon
46123

Washington Township

Westwood

Speedway Airport

MARION CO

HENDRICKS CO

RAND McNALLY

39°50'13"
39°49'47"
39°49'20"
39°48'54"
39°48'28"
39°48'02"
39°47'36"
39°47'10"

86°22'12"
86°21'38"
86°21'04"
86°20'31"
86°19'57"
86°19'23"

MAIN ST

Baltimore & Ohio Walkway

A
1 Galburgh Ct
2 Linsburgh Cir
3 Linsburgh Ct
4 Cambria Ct
5 Tilbury Ct
6 W Hamilton St
7 W Walnut St

B
1 Horseshoe Dr
2 Bruland Dr
3 Maumee Cir
4 Gowdin Dr
5 Nowling Ct

C
1 Apache Dr
2 Pawnee Dr
3 Lanterns Ct
4 Navajo Dr

D
1 Whitecliff Ct
2 Tansel Crossing Cir
3 Tansel Crossing Dr

1:24,000
1 in. = 2000 ft.
0 0.25 0.5
miles

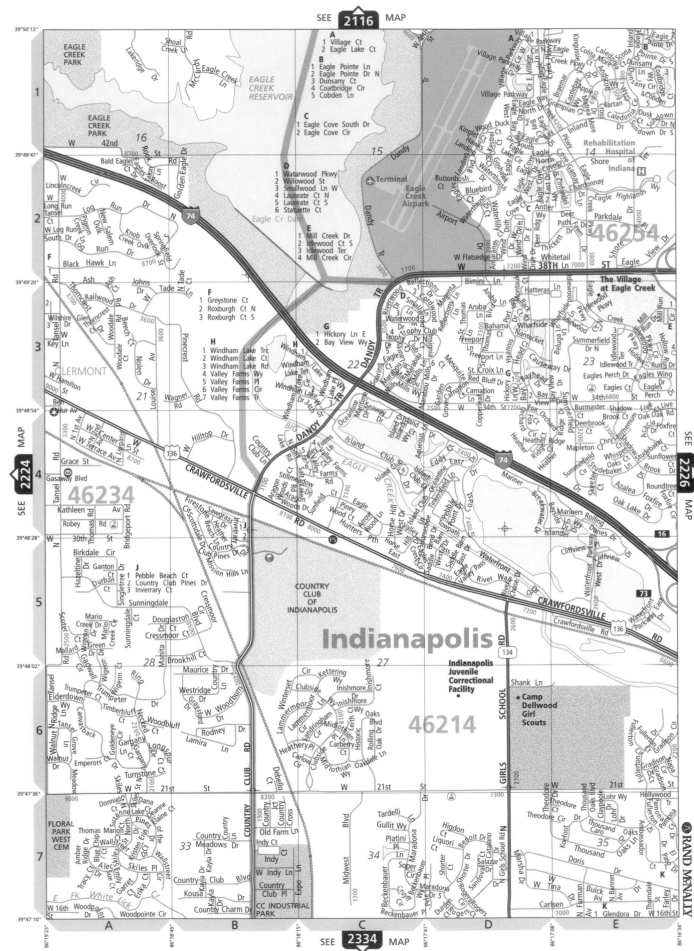

SEE 2116 MAP

A
1 Village Ct
2 Eagle Lake Ct

B
1 Eagle Pointe Ln
2 Eagle Pointe Dr N
3 Dunsany Ct
4 Coatbridge Cir
5 Cobden Ln

C
1 Eagle Cove South Dr
2 Eagle Cove Cir

D
1 Waterwood Pkwy
2 Willowood St
3 Smallwood Ln W
4 Laureate Ct N
5 Laureate Ct S
6 Statuette Ct

E
1 Mill Creek Dr
2 Idlewood Ct S
3 Idlewood Ter
4 Mill Creek Cir

F
1 Greystone Ct
2 Roxburgh Ct N
3 Roxburgh Ct S

G
1 Hickory Ln E
2 Bay View Wy

H
1 Windham Lake Trc
2 Windham Lake Ct
3 Windham Lake Rd
4 Valley Farms Wy
5 Valley Farms Pl
6 Valley Farms Cir
7 Valley Farms Tr

J
1 Pebble Beach Ct
2 Country Club Pines Dr
3 Inverrary Ct

EAGLE CREEK PARK
EAGLE CREEK RESERVOIR
Eagle Creek Airpark
Terminal
Rehabilitation Hospital of Indiana
The Village at Eagle Creek
CLERMONT
46254
46234
46214
Indianapolis
COUNTRY CLUB OF INDIANAPOLIS
Indianapolis Juvenile Correctional Facility
Camp Dellwood Girl Scouts
FLORAL PARK WEST CEM
CC INDUSTRIAL PARK
CRAWFORDSVILLE RD
W 38TH ST
DANDY TR
COUNTRY CLUB RD
GIRLS SCHOOL RD

SEE 2224 MAP
SEE 2226 MAP
SEE 2334 MAP

MAP
2226

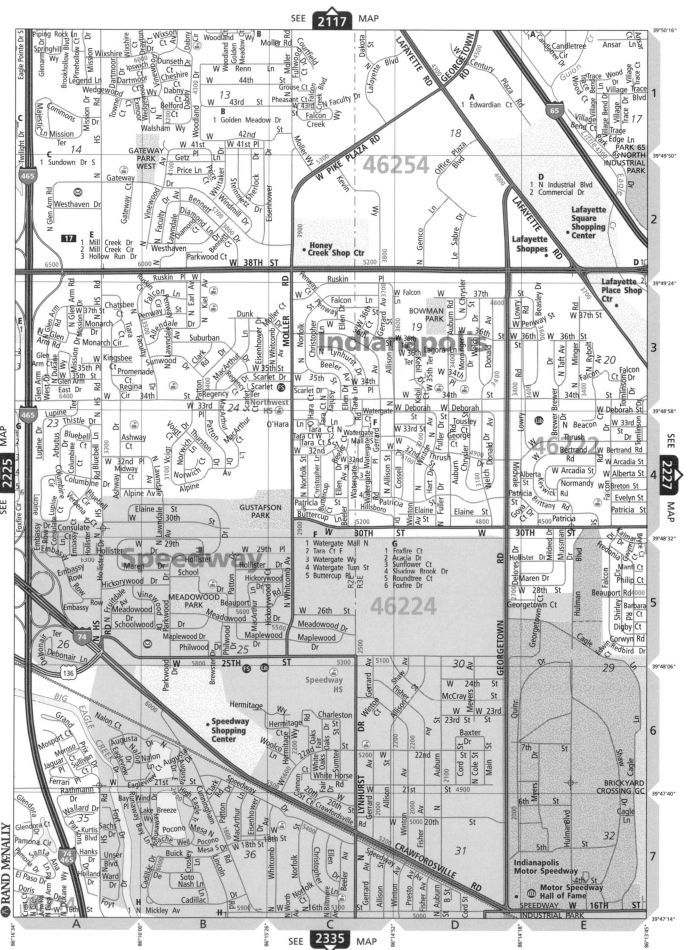

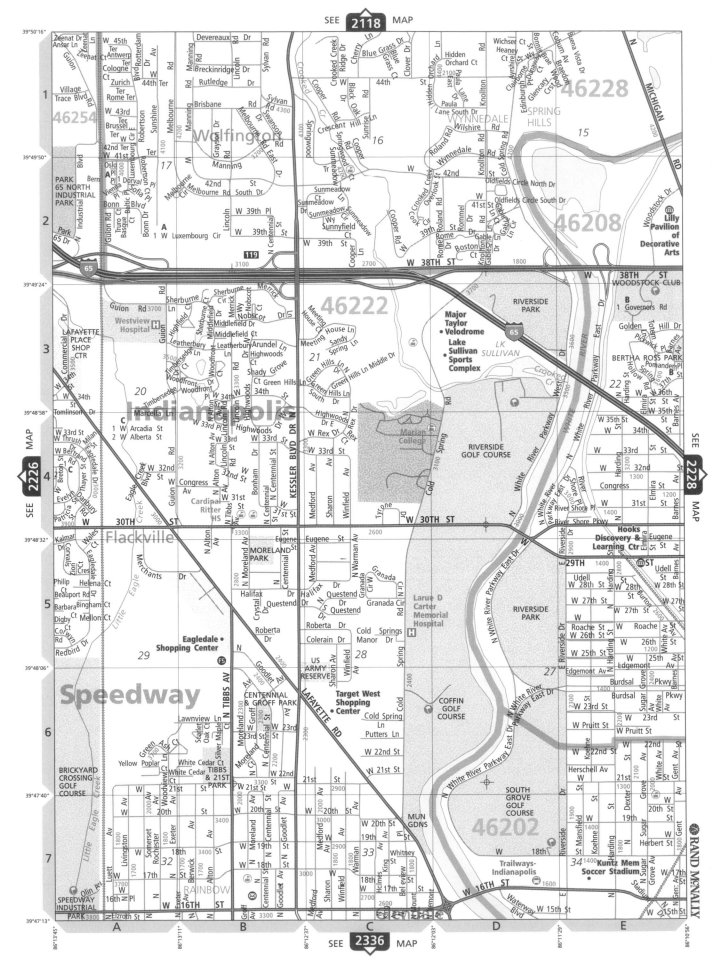

MAP
2227

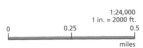
1:24,000
1 in. = 2000 ft.
0   0.25   0.5
miles

SEE 2118 MAP

SEE 2336 MAP

MAP
2228

1:24,000
1 in. = 2000 ft.

0   0.25   0.5
miles

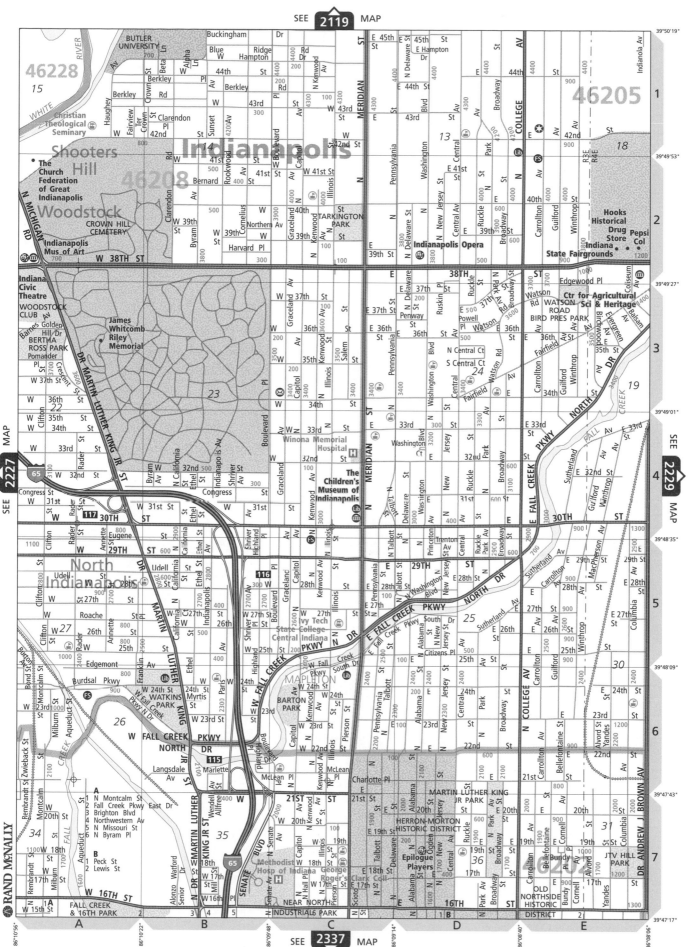

RAND McNALLY

MAP
2229

1:24,000
1 in. = 2000 ft.

0   0.25   0.5
miles

SEE 2120 MAP

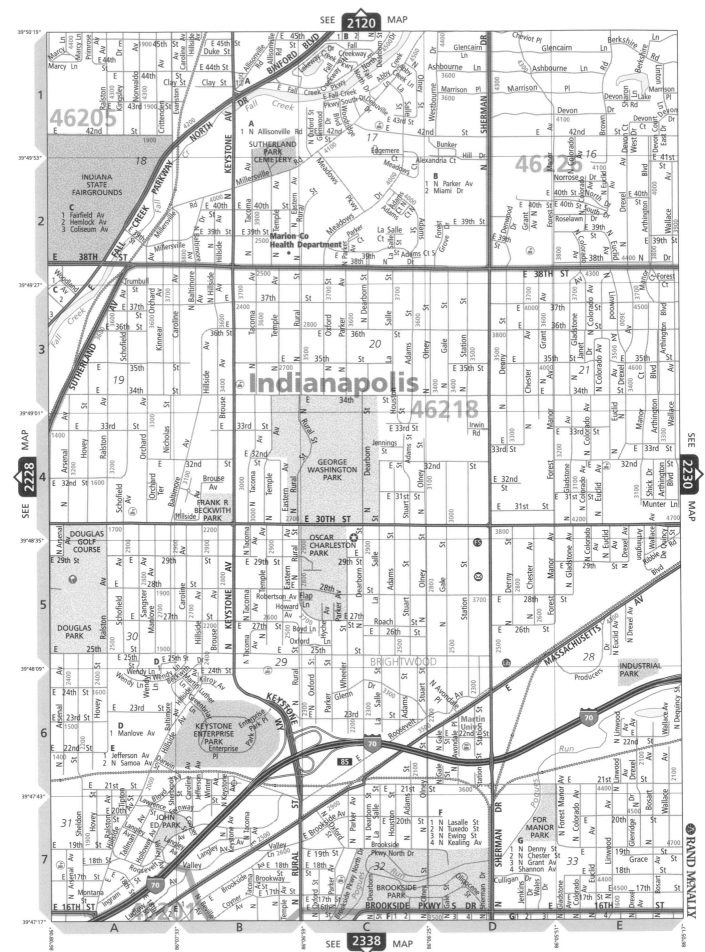

SEE MAP 2228

SEE MAP 2230

SEE 2338 MAP

RAND MCNALLY

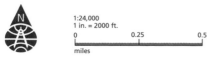

MAP
2230

1:24,000
1 in. = 2000 ft.

0   0.25   0.5
miles

SEE **2121** MAP

SEE **2229** MAP

SEE **2231** MAP

SEE **2339** MAP

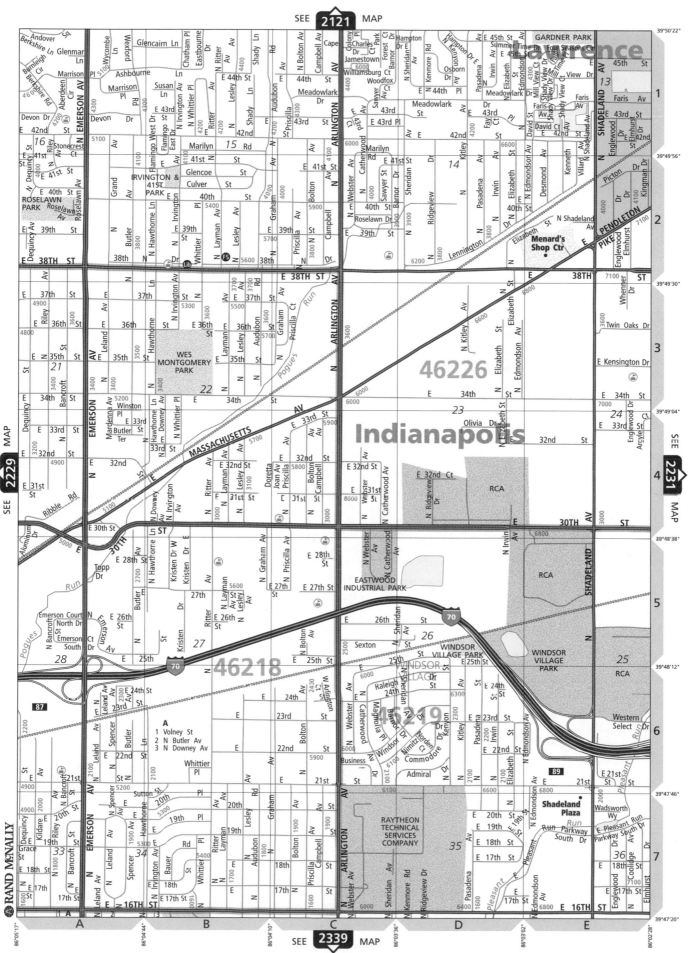

Lawrence

46226

Indianapolis

46218

46219

GARDNER PARK

ROSELAWN PARK

IRVINGTON & 41ST PARK

WES MONTGOMERY PARK

Menard's Shop Ctr

RCA

RCA

RCA

EASTWOOD INDUSTRIAL PARK

WINDSOR VILLAGE PARK

WINDSOR VILLAGE PARK

Western Select

Shadeland Plaza

RAYTHEON TECHNICAL SERVICES COMPANY

A
1 Volney St
2 N Butler Av
3 N Downey Av

RAND McNALLY

MAP
2231

1:24,000
1 in. = 2000 ft.
0   0.25   0.5
miles

SEE 2122 MAP

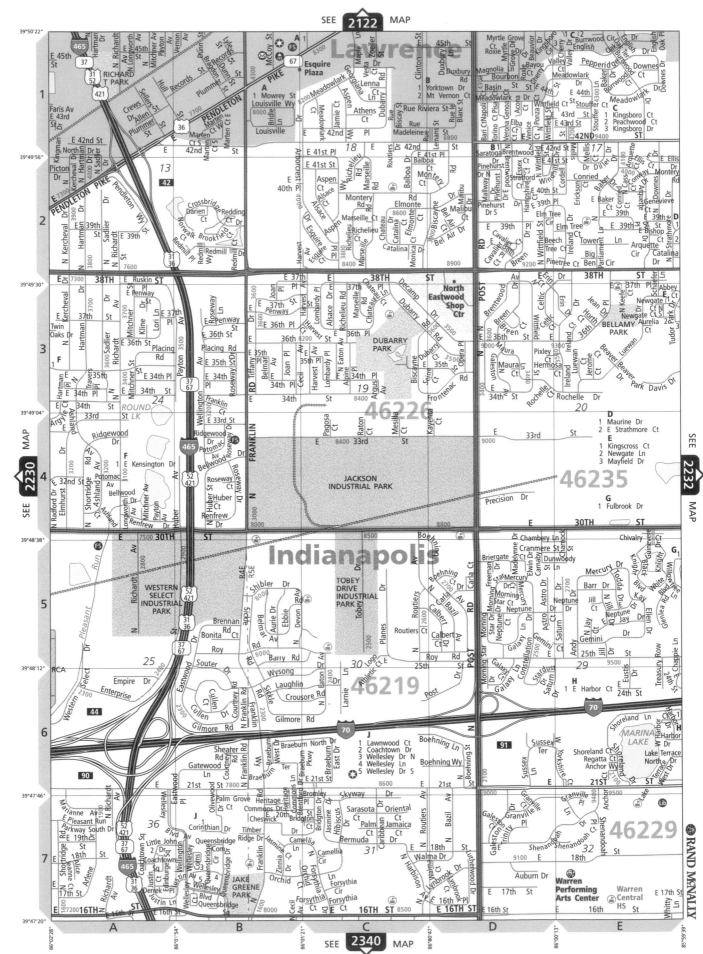

Lawrence

Indianapolis

46226

46235

46219

46229

JACKSON
INDUSTRIAL
PARK

DUBARRY
PARK

TOBEY
DRIVE
INDUSTRIAL
PARK

WESTERN
SELECT
INDUSTRIAL
PARK

MARINA
LAKE

JAKE
GREENE
PARK

BELLAMY
PARK

North
Eastwood
Shop
Ctr

Esquire
Plaza

RICHARD
T PARK

Warren
Performing
Arts Center

Warren
Central
HS

SEE 2230 MAP
SEE 2232 MAP
SEE 2340 MAP

RAND M?NALLY

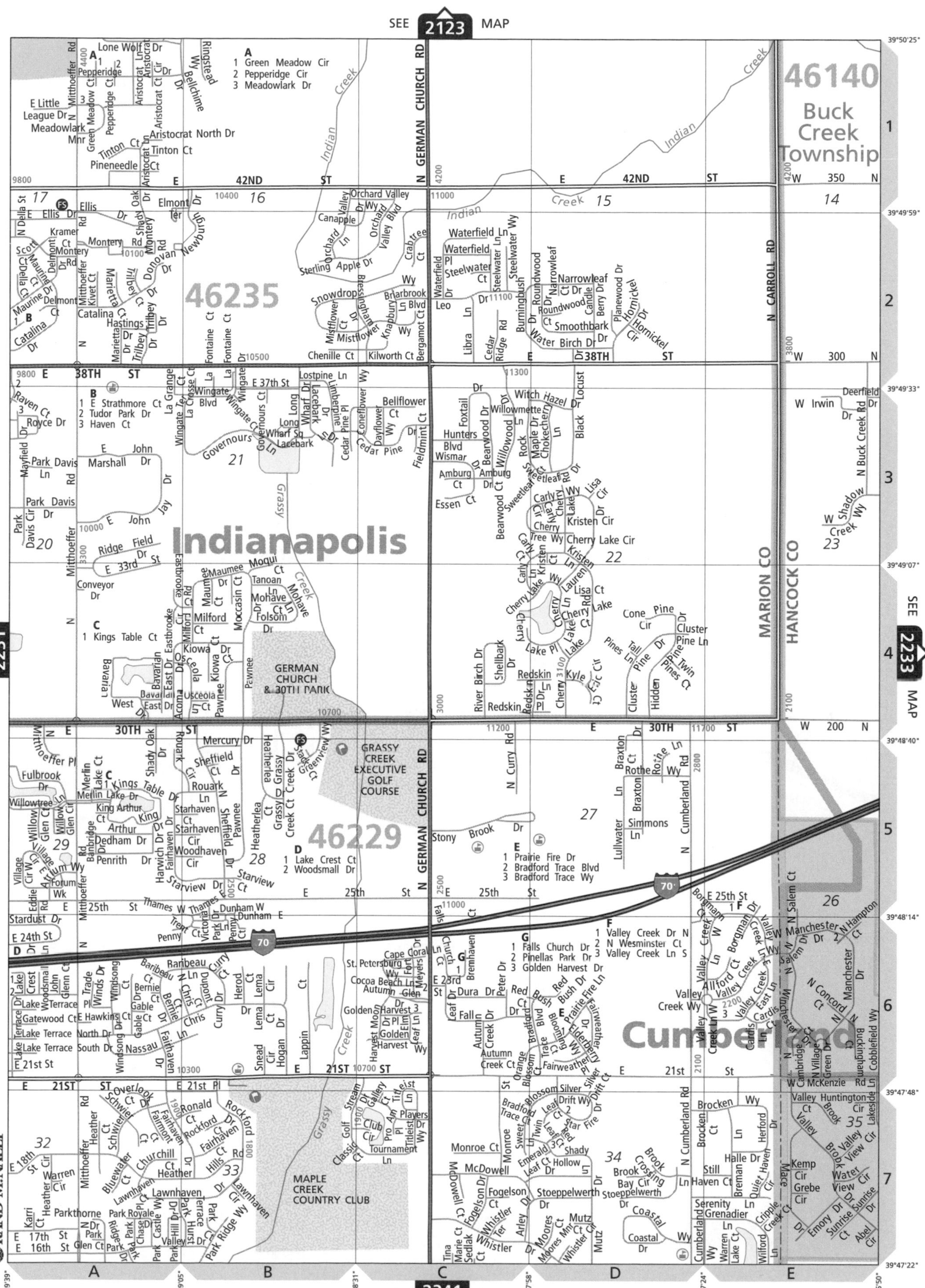

MAP
2232

SEE 2123 MAP

SEE 2231 MAP

SEE 2233 MAP

SEE 2341 MAP

1:24,000
1 in. = 2000 ft.
0   0.25   0.5
miles

46140
Buck Creek Township

46235

Indianapolis

46229

Cumberland

MARION CO
HANCOCK CO

GRASSY CREEK EXECUTIVE GOLF COURSE

GERMAN CHURCH 30TH PARK

MAPLE CREEK COUNTRY CLUB

RAND McNALLY

MAP
2233

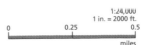

1:24,000
1 in. = 2000 ft.

0   0.25   0.5
miles

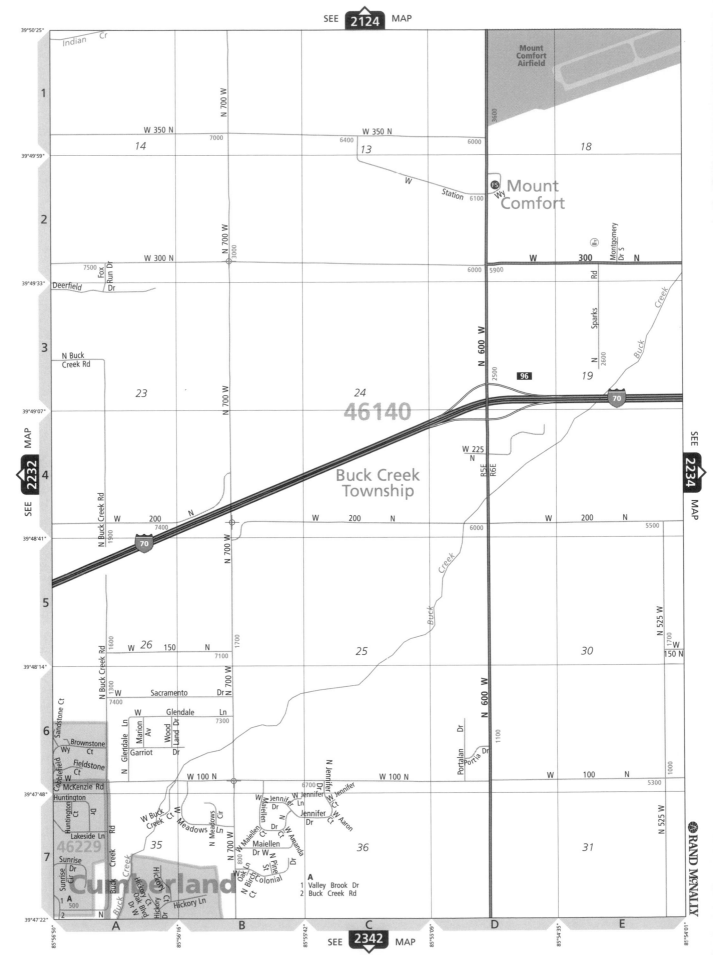

39°50'25"
Indian Cr

1

W 350 N   7000   W 350 N   6400   13   6000   18

Mount
Comfort
Airfield

3600

14

39°49'59"

2

N 700 W

W 300 N   3000   W 300 N   6000 5900

7500   Fox Run Dr

39°49'33"
Deerfield Dr

FS Mount
Comfort

Montgomery Dr S

W   300   N

Sparks Rd

Buck Creek

3

N Buck
Creek Rd

23   N 700 W   24

46140

N 600 W

2500   96   2600   19   70

39°49'07"

N Buck Creek Rd

W 225 N

4

Buck Creek
Township

R5E R6E

W   200   N   6000   W   200   N   5500

1900

70

39°48'41"

N 700 W

SEE 2232 MAP

SEE 2234 MAP

Buck Creek

5

N 525 W

W 26   150   N   1700

1600

1700   W 150 N

25   30

39°48'14"

N Buck Creek Rd   1300   W   Sacramento   Dr   N 700 W

7400

26   N

7100

Portalan Dr
Portia Dr   1100

6

Sandstone Ct

W   Glendale   Ln   7300

N Glendale Ln
Marion Av   Wood Land Dr
Garriot   Dr

W   100   N   5300

1000

Brownstone Wy
Fieldstone Ct
Cobblefield
McKenzie Rd   W   100   N

6700   W Jennifer Dr   N Jennifer
W Jennifer Ln   W Jennifer Ct
W Maiellen Dr   W Aaron
Jennifer Dr   W Aaron

W   100   N

N 525 W

39°47'48"
Huntington Ct
Huntington Dr
Lakeside Ln

46229

W Buck Creek Rd
Meadows Ct
Meadows Cir
N Meadows Ln

N 700 W   800   W Maiellen Dr W
W Maiellen Dr
Maiellen Dr W
W Amanda Dr

N 525 W

7

Sunrise Dr
Sunrise Cir

35   Oak Ln
W Birch Ct
Colonial Pine St

36   31

A
1 Valley Brook Dr
2 Buck Creek Rd

Hickory Ct
Hickory Oak Blvd
Oak Dr W
Hickory Ln

Cumberland   Buck Creek

1 A   500
2   N

39°47'22"

A   B   C   D   E
85°56'50"   85°56'16"   85°55'42"   85°55'09"   85°54'35"   85°54'58"

RAND McNALLY

MAP
2234

1:24,000
1 in. = 2000 ft.

0   0.25   0.5

miles

SEE 2125 MAP

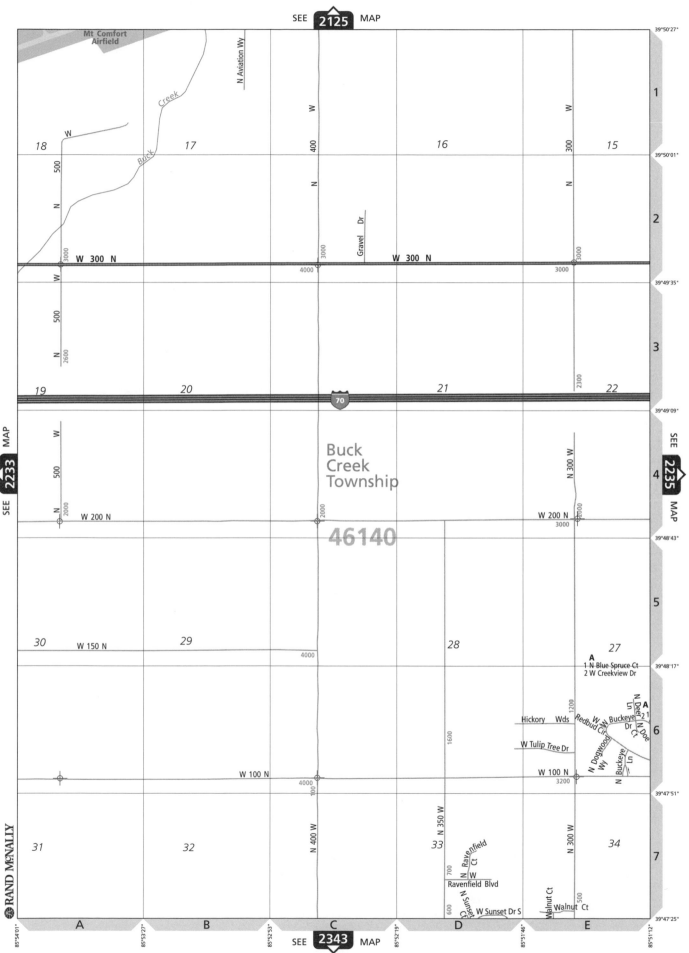

Mt Comfort
Airfield

N Aviation Wy

Buck Creek

W

18   17   16   15

39°50'27"

1

39°50'01"

W 300 N

Gravel Dr

W 300 N

39°49'35"

2

3

19   20   21   22

70

39°49'09"

SEE 2233 MAP

SEE 2235 MAP

Buck
Creek
Township

46140

N 300 W

4

W 200 N   W 200 N

39°48'43"

5

30   29   28   27

W 150 N

A
1 N Blue Spruce Ct
2 W Creekview Dr

39°48'17"

Hickory Wds

Redbud Cir
W Buckeye
N Deer Ln
N Doe Ct
21
A

W Tulip Tree Dr

N Dogwood Wy
N Buckeye Ln

6

W 100 N   W 100 N

39°47'51"

N 400 W

N 350 W

N 300 W

31   32   33   34

Ravenfield Ct
N W

Ravenfield Blvd

N Sunset Cir
W Sunset Dr S

Walnut Ct
Walnut Ct

7

39°47'25"

A   B   C   D   E

85°54'01"   85°53'27"   85°52'53"   85°52'19"   85°51'46"   85°51'12"

SEE 2343 MAP

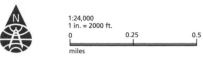

MAP
2235

1:24,000
1 in. = 2000 ft.

0   0.25   0.5
miles

N

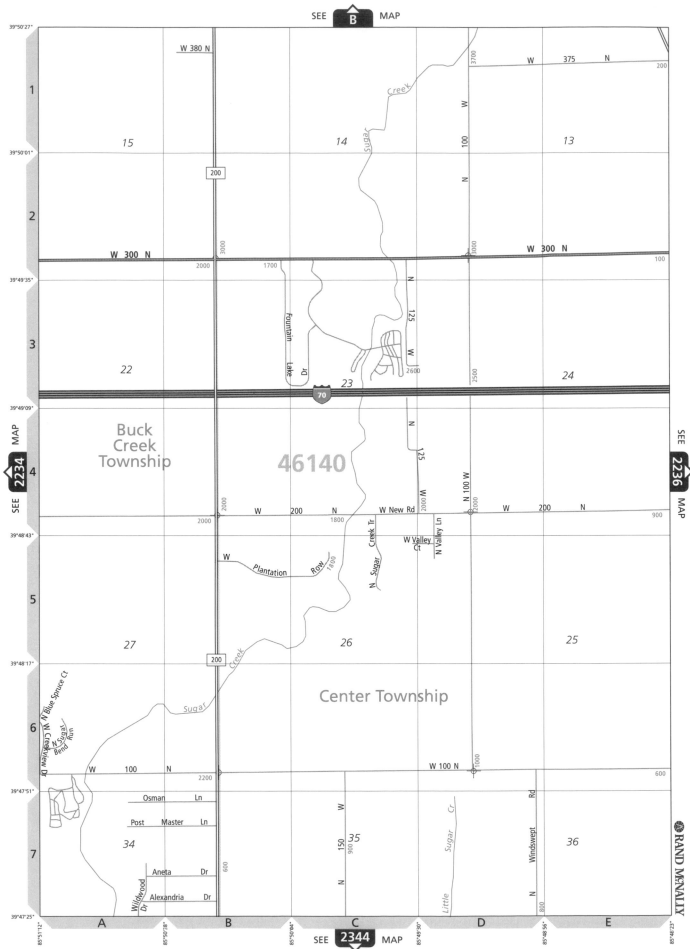

39°50'27"

W 380 N

W 375 N
200

1

3700

W

15

14

100

13

Sugar   Creek

N

39°50'01"

200

2

3000

3000

W 300 N

W 300 N

39°49'35"

2000

1700

100

N

Fountain   Lake

125

3

22

W

2600

2500

24

Dr

23

◉70◉

39°49'09"

Buck
Creek
Township

46140

N

4

125

2000

N 100 W

W 0002

W 200 N

W New Rd

W 200 N

2000

2000

900

39°48'43"

1800

W Valley
Ct

N Valley Ln

W

Plantation   Row

1800

N Sugar Creek Tr

5

N

27

26

25

39°48'17"

200

Sugar   Creek

Center Township

N Blue Spruce Ct

W Creekview Dr

N Sugar
Bend Run

Sugar

6

W 100 N

W 100 N

1000

W   100   N

2200

600

39°47'51"

Osman   Ln

Post   Master   Ln

W

Rd

34

150

35

Windswept

36

7

600

Aneta   Dr

900

N

Little   Sugar   Cr

N

Wildwood
Dr

Alexandria   Dr

800

39°47'25"

A   B   C   D   E

85°51'12"   85°50'38"   85°50'04"   85°49'30"   85°48'56"   85°48'23"

RAND McNALLY

MAP
2236

1:24,000
1 in. = 2000 ft.

0   0.25   0.5
miles

SEE ◆B◆ MAP

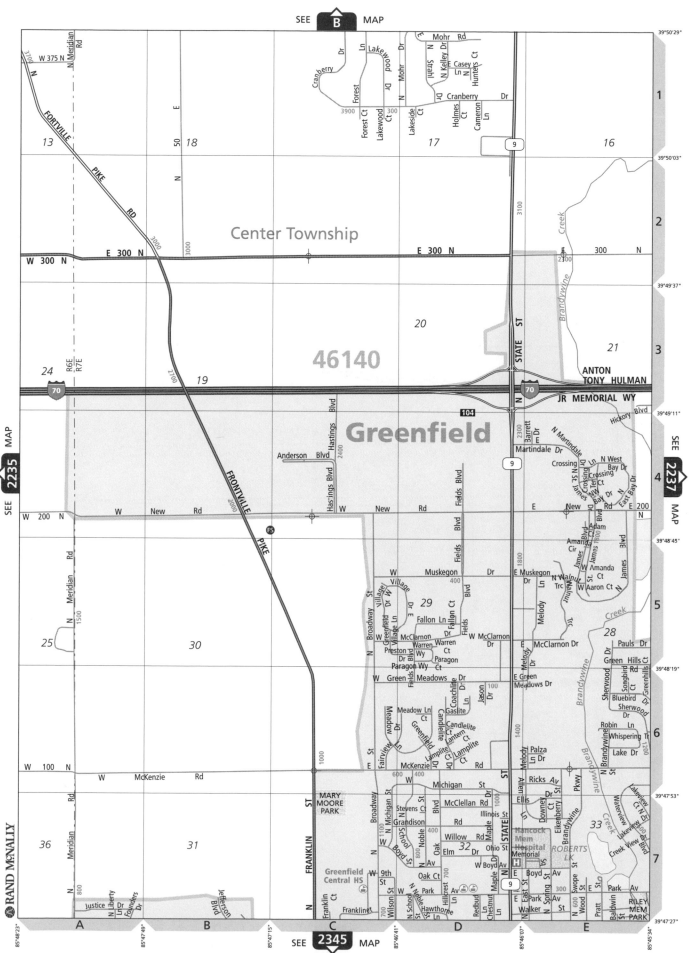

39°50'29"

Mohr   Rd

Cranberry Dr

Lakewood Ln

Mohr

N Kelley Dr

E Casey Ln

Hunters Ct

Shahti

Forest

Cranberry   Dr

Holmes

Cameron Ln

1

Forest Ct

Lakewood Dr 300

Lakeside Ct

3900

300

17

9

16

39°50'03"

13

18

2

Center Township

50

N

3000

3000

3100

Brandywine

Creek

E 300 N

E 300 N

300   N

W 300 N

E 2100

39°49'37"

20

3

46140

21

24

R6E
R7E

2700

**ANTON
TONY HULMAN**

I-70

19

N

I-70

STATE ST

JR MEMORIAL WY

Hickory Blvd

39°49'11"

SEE
2235
MAP

104

Barrett

N Martindale

Greenfield

Hastings Blvd

2400

2300

Martindale Dr

N West
Bay Dr

SEE
2237
MAP

Anderson   Blvd

Fields Blvd

9

Crossing

N St. James
Crossing
Crossing
Wy
Bay Dr

4

2000

W   New   Rd

W   New   Rd

E

New   Dr

Bay Rd

East Bay Dr

200

N

W 200 N

Fields   Blvd

E

Adam
Blvd 1800

39°48'45"

Amanda
Cir

James St
James Blvd

James Blvd

25

Meridian   Rd

1500

N

Fields

Muskegon   Dr

400

1800

E Muskegon
Dr

W Amanda
Ct

N Walnut Ct
Walnut Trc

N Aaron Ct

5

30

Village St

Broadway   St

Village
Village Ln
Dr
E

29

Fields Blvd

Fallon Ct

Fields

Melody

Creek

28

Greenfield Blvd

Fallon Ln
Dr

W McClarnon

Dr

E
Melody

McClarnon Dr

Pauls Dr

McClarnon

Warren
Warren
Ct

Green Hills Rd

Preston
Dr

Paragon Wy

Paragon
Ct

W

E

Songbird
Dr

Greenhills

Sherwood
Dr

Bluebird

39°48'19"

W   Green   Meadows   Dr

E Green
Meadows Dr

Sherwood
Dr

Coachlite

Jason
Dr

100

Brandywine

Robin
Ln

Meadow Ln
Ct

Gaslite

N Brandywine St

Whispering Tr

1200

6

Meadow
Dr

Candlelite

Candlelite
Lantern
Ct

1400

Lake Dr

Fairview

Greenfield

Lamplite
Ct

Lamplite
Ct

Melody
Ln

Palza
Dr

Lakeview Ct N

1000

McKenzie   Dr

600   400

St

Ricks   Av

Waterview

Lakeview Ct N

39°47'53"

W   100   N

W   McKenzie   Rd

Michigan   St

Ellis

Downey

Eikenberry St

Brandywine Pkwy

Creek View Blvd

**MARY
MOORE
PARK**

Broadway St

N Michigan St

Stevens
Ct

McClellan Rd

Illinois St

1000

Hancock
Mem
Hospital
Memorial

33

Grandison
Rd

400

ROBERTS
LK

36

Meridian   Rd

800

31

Franklin   St

1100

School St

N Noble

Willow   St

Oak

Elm

32

Maple

Ohio St

H

Boyd   Av

Swope St

Park Av

7

Jefferson   Blvd

Greenfield
Central HS

9th
St

W School St
N Noble St

Oak Ct

W Boyd Av

Maple

N

9

Park Av

300 N

Baldwin St

**RILEY
MEM
PARK**

Justice
Liberty
Founders
Ln
Dr

Franklin
Ct

Franklin
et

Wilson St

Hawthorne

Hillcrest
Av

Redbud
Ln

Chestnut
St

East St

N Spring St

Walker   St

600 Wood St

Pratt   St

9

SEE **2345** MAP

39°47'27"

A   B   C   D   E

85°48'23"   85°47'49"   85°47'15"   85°46'41"   85°46'07"   85°45'34"

MAP
2237

1:24,000
1 in. = 2000 ft.

0   0.25   0.5
miles

N

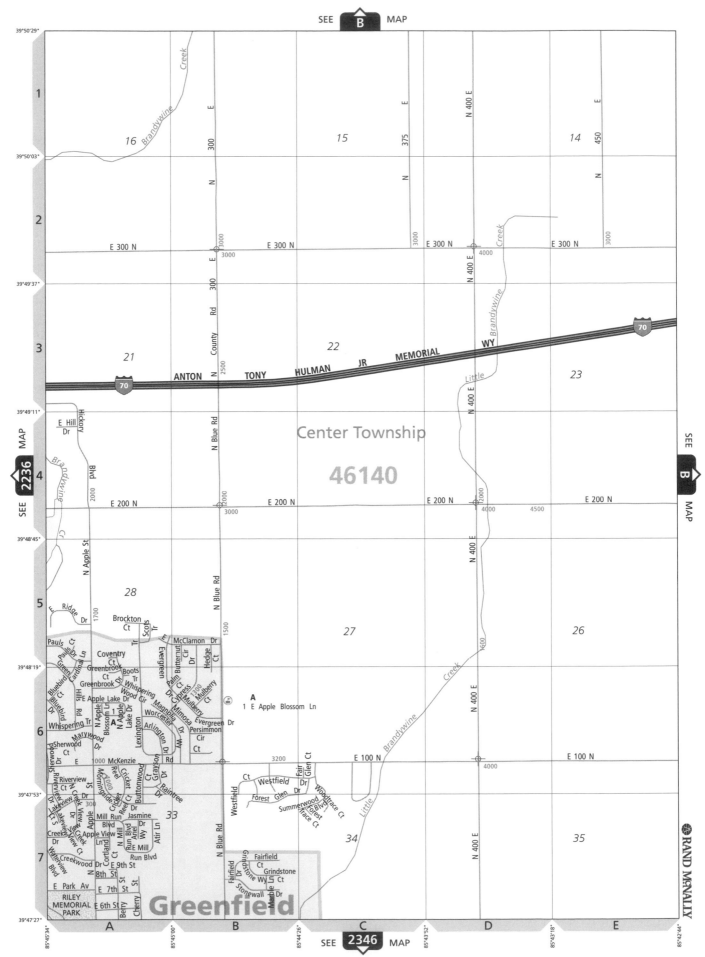

Center Township

46140

Greenfield

RILEY MEMORIAL PARK

SEE ◄ **2236** MAP

SEE **B** ► MAP

RAND MCNALLY

A   B   C   D   E

1   2   3   4   5   6   7

A
1 E Apple Blossom Ln

MAP
2329

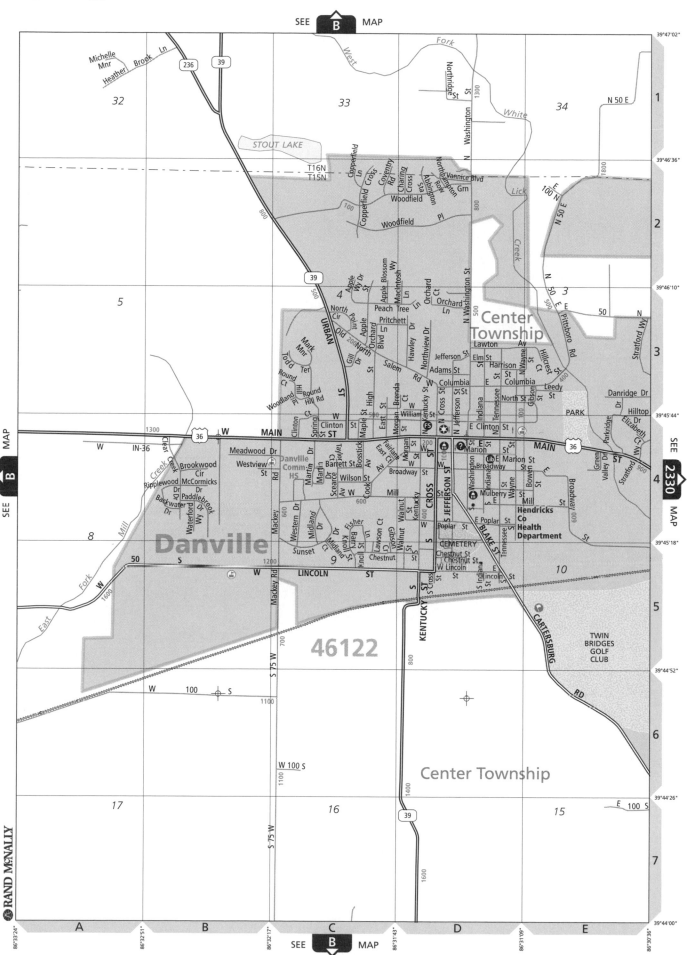

1:24,000
1 in. = 2000 ft.
0   0.25   0.5
miles

SEE B MAP

N

39°47'02"

West   Fork

32   33   34   N 50 E

White

Northridge St   1300

STOUT LAKE

T16N
T15N   39°46'36"

Washington

Copperfield Ln
Coventry Rd
Charing Cross
Copperfield Cross
Northampton Row
Abbington
Vannice Blvd
Woodfield Sta   Grn   Lick

39   100   2

500   Woodfield Pl   800   Creek

N 50 E

Apple Blossom Wy   100 N
39   Apple Wy Dr   Machntosh   N 50 E
Apple Dr St   Orchard Ct   50 E
4   North   Peach Tree Ln   Orchard Ln   39°46'10"
Cir   Apple   Pritchett   Center   50   N
5   North Point   Orchard   Hawley   Northview Dr   500 E   Township   3
URBAN   Old North   Blvd   Dr   N Washington St   Pittsboro Rd   400 E   Stratford Wy
200   Salem Rd   Lawton   Av
Mark   Gill St   Jefferson St   Hillcrest   3
Mnr   Todd   Adams St   Elm St   Harrison   Danridge Dr
Round   Hill   Round   Columbia   E   St Columbia   Wayne St   Leedy   Hilltop
Ct   Woodland Pl   Hill Rd   High St   N Kentucky St   N Cross St   St   Indiana   North St   Gibson St   Parkridge   Dr   Elizabeth
Clinton   W   Maple St   East St   Brenda   William Ct   N Jefferson St   Tennessee St   100   PARK   Dr   Stratford Wy   39°45'44"
1300   W   Spring St   Clinton St   Morgan   E Clinton St   Green   SEE
W   IN-36   MAIN   W   St   W   St   MAIN   36   Valley Dr   2330
Brookwood   Meadwood Dr   Martin Dr   Bosstick   Fairlane Ct   200   Marion   E Marion St   Stratford   MAP
Cir   Westview   Danville   Barrett St   Scearce   Cooley Av   Morgan St   W   St   Lib E   Broadway   Bowen   4
Ripplewood   McCormicks   St   Rd   Comm   Martin   Wilson St   Av   Broadway   Washington St   Wayne   Mill   Broadway 009
Dr   Dr   Paddlebrook   HS   Dr   Cook St   Mill   S Kentucky St   Mulberry St   St   Hendricks
Backwater   Dr   Wy   600   S Cross St   S Jefferson St   E Poplar St   Co
Dr   Waterford   Western Dr   Midland Dr   Fisher Dr   Lawson Ct   Walnut St   Poplar St   Tennessee St   Health   39°45'18"
8   Mill   Sunset   Midland Ct   Barry St   Gibson St   Walnut St   CEMETERY   E Poplar   Department
50   9   Knoll St   Chestnut St   Chestnut St   Chestnut St
Fork   W   1200   LINCOLN   ST   W Lincoln St   S Indiana St   10
Mackey Rd   S Kentucky St   S Blake St   S Lincoln St
700   CARTERSBURG   39°44'52"
46122   TWIN
800   BRIDGES
W   100   S   1100   GOLF
1100   CLUB   5
S 75 W
RD

W 100 S   Center Township   39°44'26"

17   16   39   15   E 100 S

1400

1600   39°44'00"

A   B   C   D   E

RAND M°NALLY

MAP
2330

1:24,000
1 in. = 2000 ft.
0   0.25   0.5
miles

SEE 2221 MAP

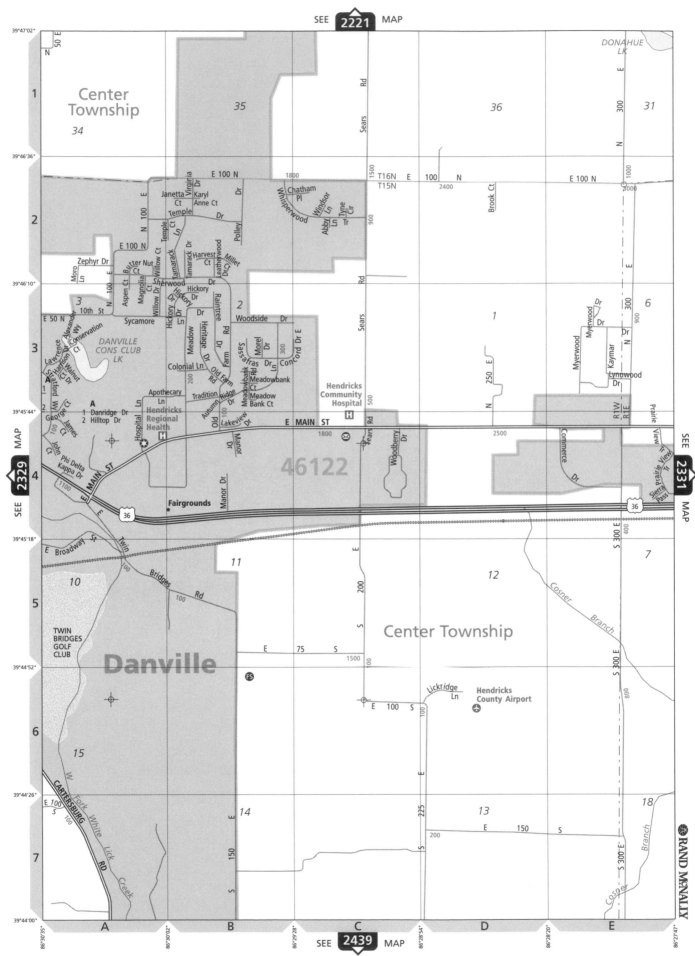

DONAHUE LK

Center Township
34

1

35

Sears Rd

36

300 N

31

39°47'02"

39°46'36"

E 100 N

1800

1500   T16N   E   100   N

E 100 N

Brook Ct

1000
3000

Janetta Ct
Virginia Dr
Karyl Anne Ct
Temple Dr
Polley Dr
Chatham Pl
Whisperwood
Windsor Ln
Abby Ln
Tyne Cir

900

2

100 N

Temple Ct
Temple Ln

E 100 N

Zephyr Dr
Moro Ln
Butter Nut Ct
Willow Ct
Tamarack Dr
Harvest Ct
Leatherwood Dr
Millet Dr

Sears Rd

250 E

1

300 E

6

Myerwood Dr
Myerwood Dr

Aspen Ct
Magnolia Ct
Sherwood
Hickory Dr
Hickory Dr
Hickory Dr
Raintree Rd
Heritage Dr
Old Farm Rd

900

Willow Dr
10th St

3

Sycamore

2

Woodside Dr

Myerwood Dr
Kaymar Dr
Lynnwood Dr

E 50 N
Lawrence Wy
Alexander Wy
Hanson Dr
Walnut Ct Dr
Stratford Wy

DANVILLE CONS CLUB LK

Meadow Dr
Colonial Ln

Morel Dr
Sassafras Rd
Concord Dr E

300

3

A
1

250 E

N

Meadowbank
Meadowbank Ct
Meadow Bank Ct

Hendricks Community Hospital H

R1W R1E

Prairie View Tr

SEE 2331 MAP

2

A
1 Danridge Dr
2 Hilltop Dr

Apothecary Ln
Tradition Ln
Autumn Ridge
Lakeview Dr

500

39°45'44"

George Ct
James Ct
John Ct

Hendricks Regional Health H

Hospital Ln

Manor Dr

E MAIN ST

1800

2500

Prairie View Tr
Sierra Pass

Commerce Dr

SEE 2329 MAP

Phi Delta Kappa Dr

E MAIN ST

46122

Woodberry Dr

Sears Rd

4

1100

Manor Dr

Fairgrounds

36

S 300 E
400

36

39°45'18"

E Broadway St
Twin

11

850

200 S

7

5

10

Bridges Rd
100

100

12

Cosner Branch

TWIN BRIDGES GOLF CLUB

Center Township

S 300 E
800

39°44'52"

F5

E   75   S
1500

100

6

15

Lickridge Ln

Hendricks County Airport ✈

E   100   S
100

Danville

W Fork White

39°44'26"

CARTERSBURG

E 100 S
100

14

150 S

225 S
200

13

E   150   S

18

S 300 E

7

Lick Creek

Cosner Branch

RAND McNALLY

39°44'00"

A   86°30'35"   B   86°30'02"   C   86°29'28"   D   86°28'54"   E   86°28'20"   86°27'47"

SEE 2439 MAP

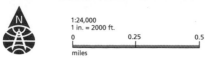

1:24,000
1 in. = 2000 ft.
0   0.25   0.5
miles

MAP
2331

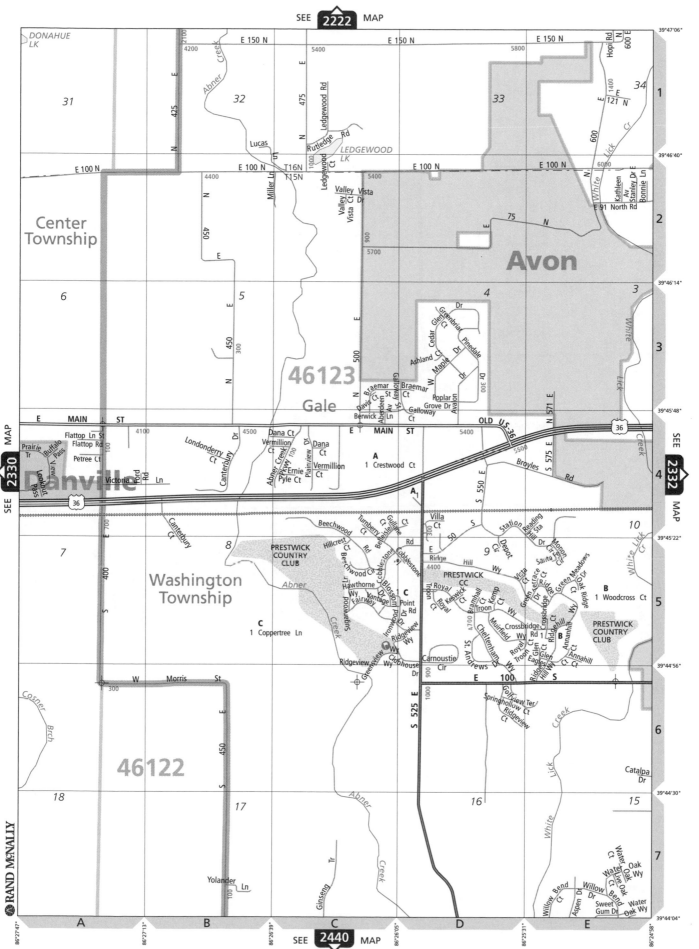

SEE 2222 MAP

DONAHUE LK

39°47'06"

E 150 N   E 150 N   E 150 N
4200   5400   5800

31   32   33   34

Ledgewood Rd

Lucas
Rutledge
LEDGEWOOD LK
Ledgewood Rd

E 100 N   E 100 N   E 100 N   E 100 N
T16N
T15N
4400   5400   6080

Center Township

Miller Ln
Victoria

Valley Vista Dr
Valley Vista Ct

E 91 North Rd
Kathleen Av
Stanley Dr
Bonnie Ln

39°46'40"

39°46'14"

Avon

6   5   4   3

Greenbriar Dr
Glen Ct
Cedar
Ashland Ct
Maple
Pinedale
Dr 300

39°45'48"

46123
Gale

Braemar Ct
Davis Ct
Aberdeen
Keystone Av
Braemar
Galloway
Poplar Grove Dr
Avalon
Galloway
Berwick Ln

OLD US 36
36
S 571 E

E MAIN ST   E MAIN ST
4100   4500   5400   5500

Flattop Ln St
Flattop Rd
Prairie Tr
Buffalo Pass
Petree Ct
Lookout Pass

Danville
36

Londonderry Ct
Canterbury
Ford Rd
Ln

Dana Ct
Vermillion Ct
Abner Creek Pkwy 700
Ernie Pyle Ct
Dana Dr
Plainview Dr
Vermillion Ct

A 1 Crestwood Ct

Broyles Rd
S 550 E
S 575 E

A 1

Villa Ct
Station
Reading
Hill Dr
Sta
Depot
Cir
Monon

39°45'22"

7

Canterbury Ct

8

Beechwood Ct
Turnberry Ct
Belleisle Ct
Gullane Ct

PRESTWICK COUNTRY CLUB

Hillcrest
Beechwood Rd
Hawthorne Wy
Fairway
Snugborough
Cobblestone
Cobblestone
Blossom
Vantage
Dr
C

Ridge
Wy 4400
E 50
Hill Wy

9
PRESTWICK CC

Royal
Troon
Royal
Keswick Ct
Bramhall
Kemp Ct
Troon
Green Meadows
Ridge
Vista
Saints Ct
Green estate
Crossbridge
Oak Ridge Dr

10

B 1 Woodcross Ct

Washington Township

Abner Creek

C 1 Coppertree Ln

Ironwood
Point Rd
Ridgeview Wy
Ridgeview Wy
Greenview Wy
Clubhouse
Dr
Carnoustie Cir

Mulfield
Royal
Troon
Wy
Crossbridge Rd
Glen
Ridge
Eagles
Glen
Hill Wy
Annahill
Annahill Ct

PRESTWICK COUNTRY CLUB

St Andrews
Cheltenham

39°44'56"

E 100 S
S 525 E
1000
S 900

W Morris St
300

Golfview Ter
Springhollow Ct
Ridgeview
Ct

39°45'22"

46122

18   17   16   15

450 S

Cosner Brch

Abner Creek

White Lick Creek

Catalpa Dr

39°44'30"

Yolander Ln
100

Ginseng Tr

Willow Bend Ct
Aspen Dr
Willow Bend Dr
Water Oak Ct
Water Oak Ct
Live Oak Wy
Sweet Gum Dr
Water Oak Wy

39°44'04"

A   B   C   D   E

SEE 2440 MAP

SEE 2330 MAP
SEE 2332 MAP

MAP
2332

1:24,000
1 in. = 2000 ft.

0   0.25   0.5
miles

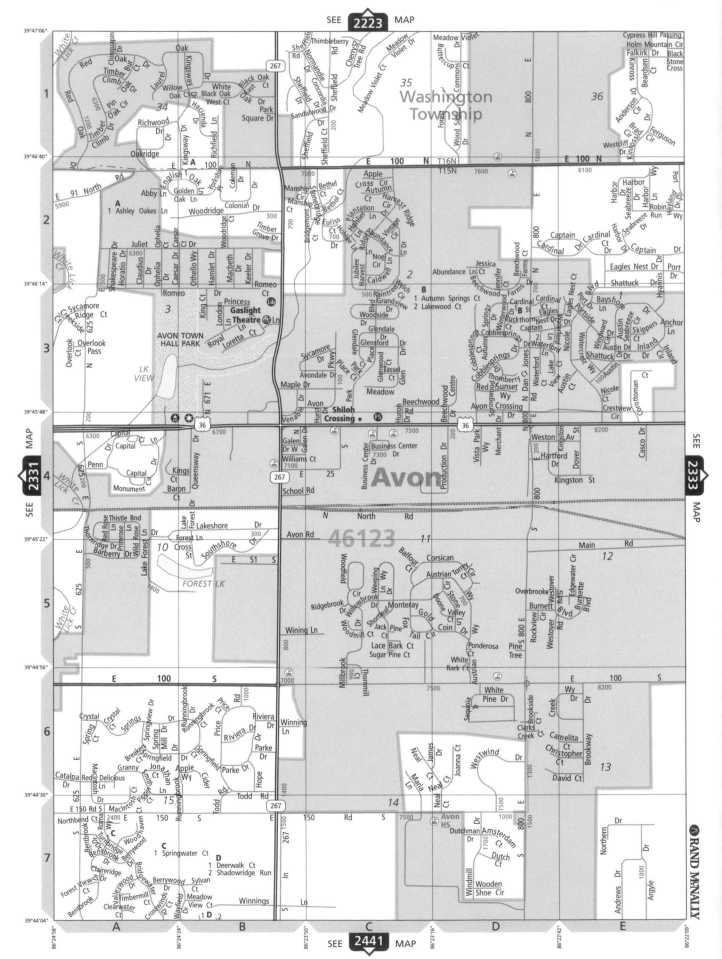

SEE 2223 MAP

SEE 2331 MAP

SEE 2333 MAP

SEE 2441 MAP

RAND McNALLY

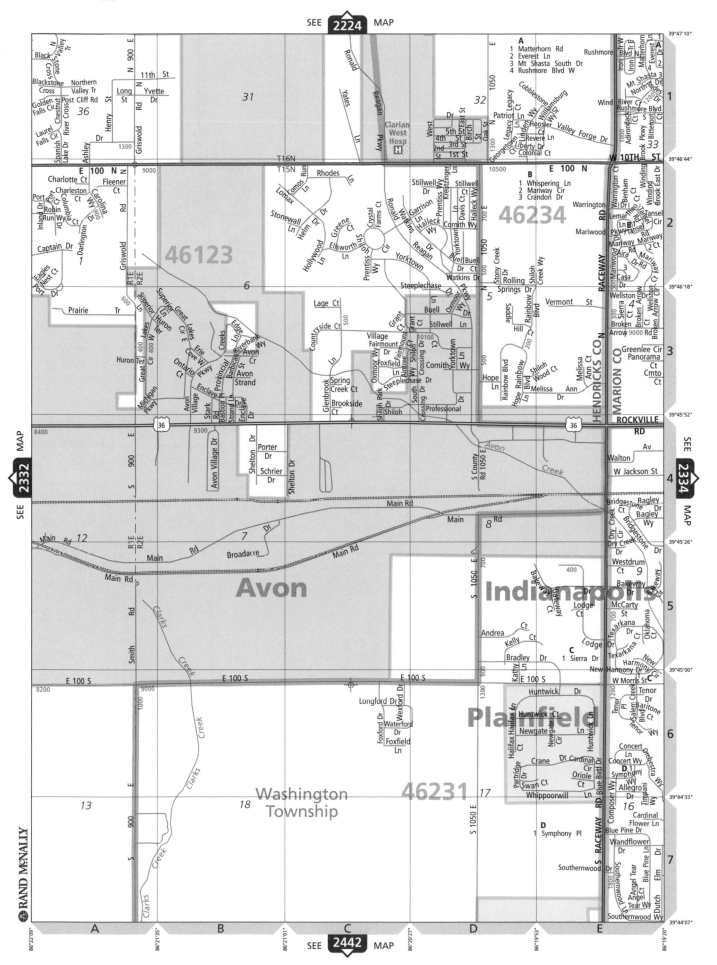

MAP
2333

1:24,000
1 in. = 2000 ft.
0   0.25   0.5
miles

SEE 2224 MAP

SEE 2332 MAP

SEE 2334 MAP

SEE 2442 MAP

A
1 Matterhorn Rd
2 Everest Ln
3 Mt Shasta South Dr
4 Rushmore Blvd W

B
1 Whispering Ln
2 Mariway Cir
3 Crandon Ln

C
1 Sierra Dr

D
1 Symphony Pl

46234
46123
46231

Avon
Indianapolis
Plainfield
Washington Township

W 10TH ST

Clarian West Hosp

HENDRICKS CO
MARION CO

ROCKVILLE RD

RAND McNALLY

MAP
2334

1:24,000
1 in. = 2000 ft.

0   0.25   0.5
miles

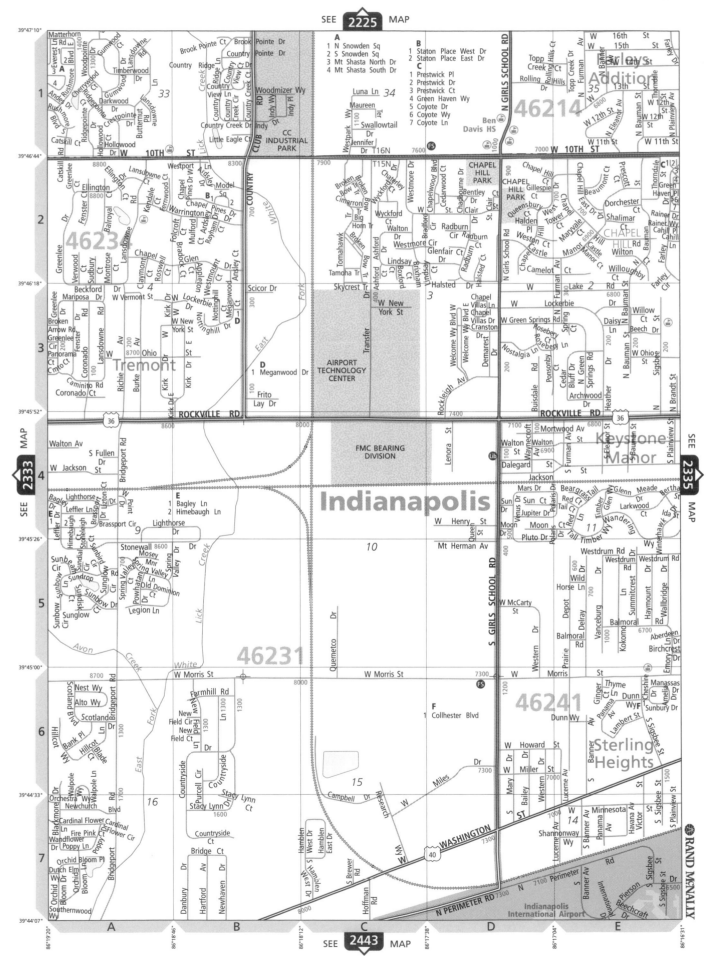

SEE 2225 MAP

A
1 N Snowden Sq
2 S Snowden Sq
3 Mt Shasta North Dr
4 Mt Shasta South Dr

B
1 Staton Place West Dr
2 Staton Place East Dr

C
1 Prestwick Pl
2 Prestwick Dr
3 Prestwick Ct
4 Green Haven Wy
5 Coyote Dr
6 Coyote Wy
7 Coyote Ln

D
1 Meganwood Dr

E
1 Bagley Ln
2 Himebaugh Ln

F
1 Collhester Blvd

46214

46234

46231

46241

Indianapolis

Tremont

CC INDUSTRIAL PARK

CHAPEL HILL PARK

CHAPEL HILL PARK

CHAPEL HILL

AIRPORT TECHNOLOGY CENTER

FMC BEARING DIVISION

Barlows Addition

Keystone Manor

Sterling Heights

Indianapolis International Airport

SEE 2333 MAP

SEE 2335 MAP

SEE 2443 MAP

W 10TH ST

ROCKVILLE RD

ROCKVILLE RD

W NEW YORK ST

WASHINGTON

N PERIMETER RD

W MORRIS ST

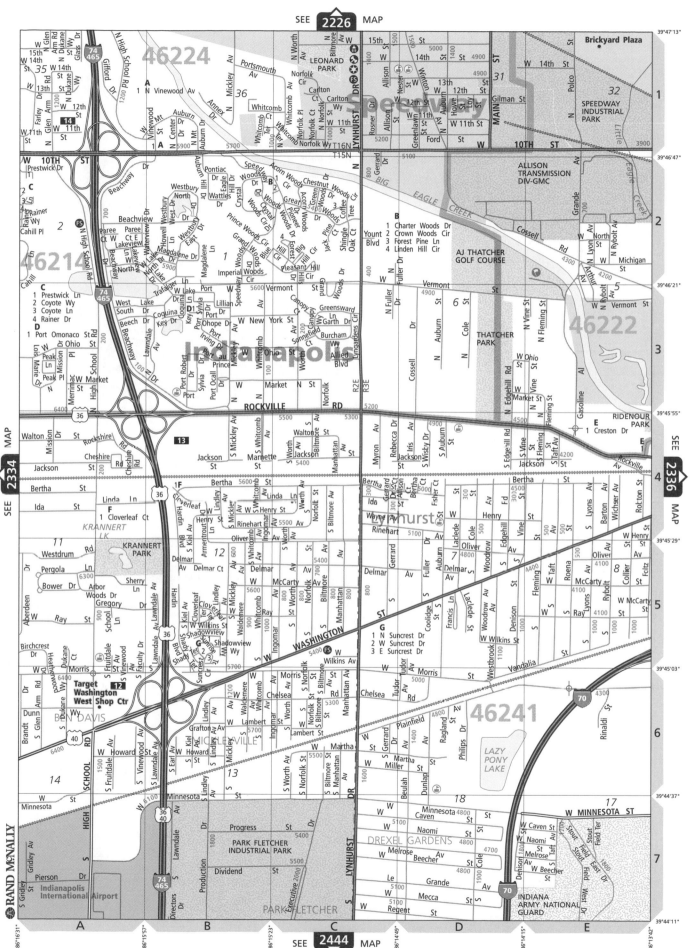

MAP
2335

SEE 2226 MAP

1:24,000
1 in. = 2000 ft.
0   0.25   0.5
miles

N

SEE 2334 MAP

SEE 2336 MAP

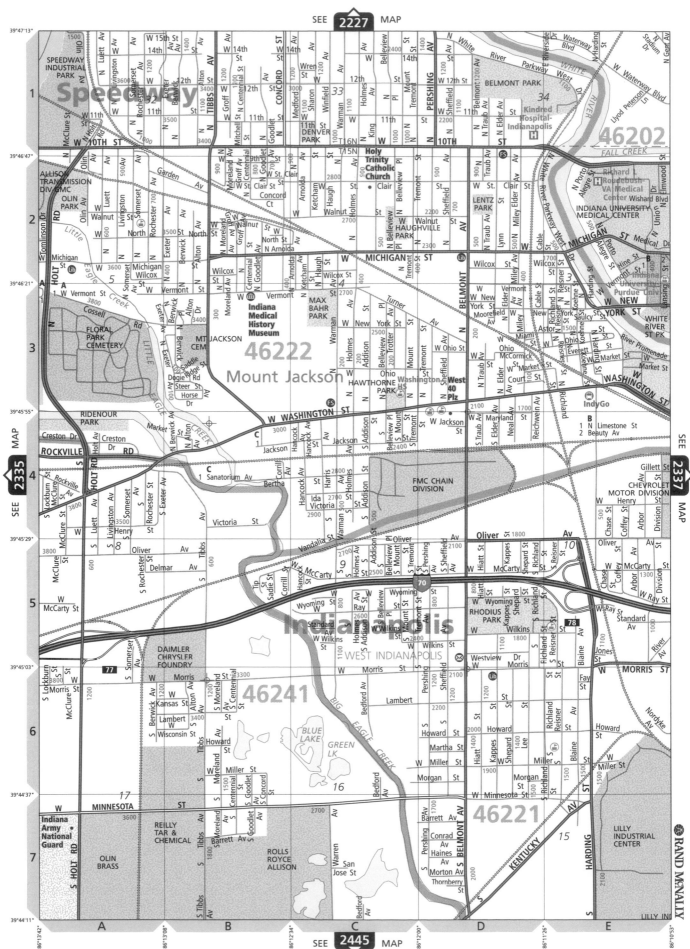

MAP
2336

1:24,000
1 in. = 2000 ft.

0   0.25   0.5

miles

SEE 2335 MAP

SEE 2337 MAP

46202

46222

Mount Jackson

46241

46221

Speedway

Indianapolis

SPEEDWAY INDUSTRIAL PARK

BELMONT PARK

Kindred Hospital-Indianapolis

Richard Roudebush VA Medical Center

INDIANA UNIVERSITY MEDICAL CENTER

Holy Trinity Catholic Church

ALLISON TRANSMISSION DIV-GMC

OLIN PARK

Indiana University Purdue Univ

FLORAL PARK CEMETERY

MT JACKSON CEM

Indiana Medical History Museum

MAX BAHR PARK

WHITE RIVER ST PK

River Promenade

RIDENOUR PARK

HAWTHORNE PARK

West 40 Plz

IndyGo

CHEVROLET MOTOR DIVISION

FMC CHAIN DIVISION

RHODIUS PARK

WEST INDIANAPOLIS

DAIMLER CHRYSLER FOUNDRY

BLUE LAKE

GREEN LK

Indiana Army National Guard

OLIN BRASS

REILLY TAR & CHEMICAL

ROLLS ROYCE ALLISON

LILLY INDUSTRIAL CENTER

LILLY IND

RAND McNALLY

MAP
2337

1:24,000
1 in. = 2000 ft.

0   0.25   0.5
miles

N

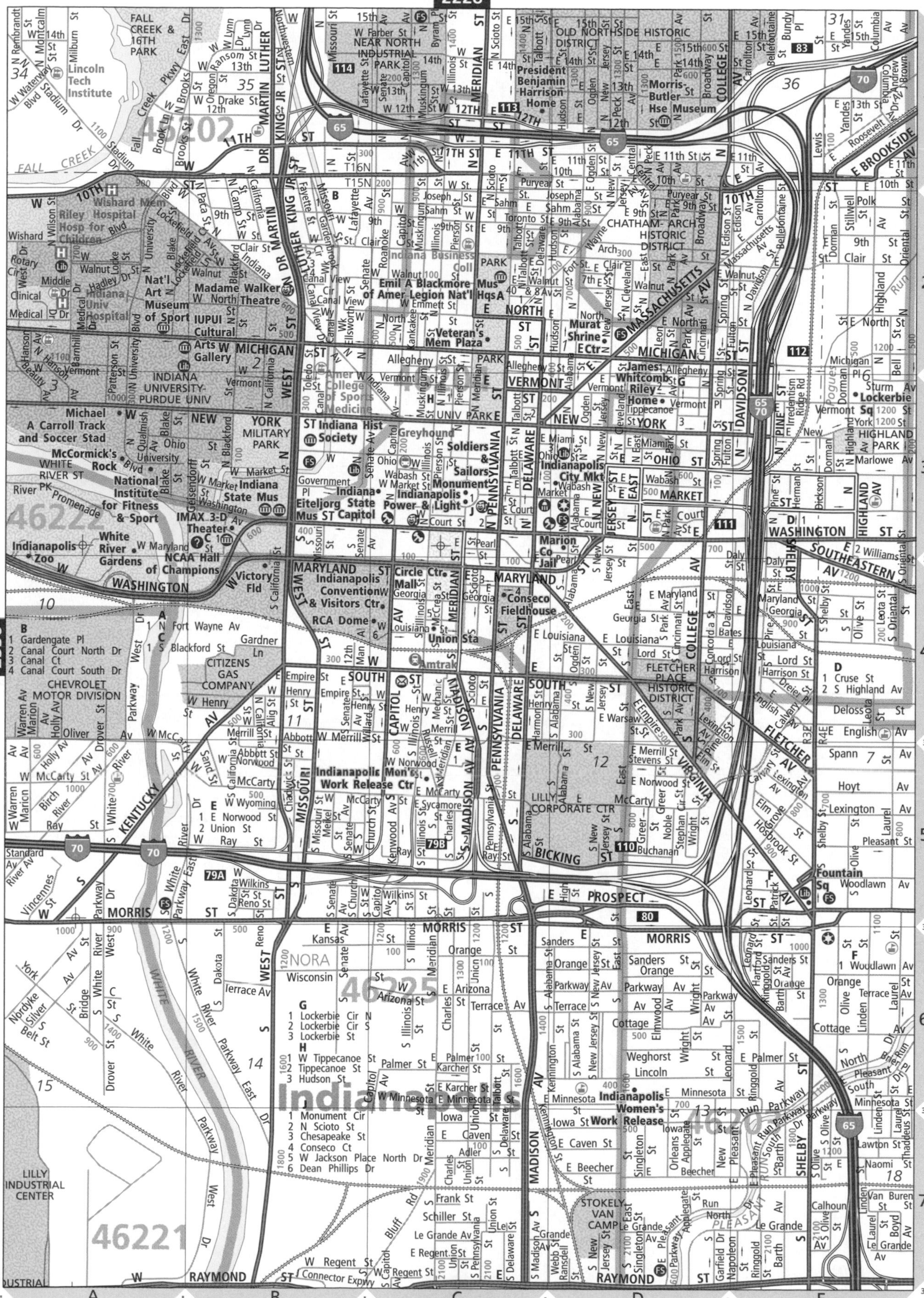

SEE 2336 MAP

SEE 2338 MAP

RAND McNALLY

FALL CREEK & 16TH PARK

Lincoln Tech Institute

OLD NORTHSIDE HISTORIC DISTRICT

NEAR NORTH INDUSTRIAL PARK

President Benjamin Harrison Home

Morris-Butler Hse Museum

Wishard Mem Riley Hospital Hosp for Children

CHATHAM-ARCH HISTORIC DISTRICT

Nat'l Art Museum of Sport

Madame Walker Theatre

Indiana Business Coll

Emil A Blackmore Mus of Amer Legion Nat'l Hqs A

IUPUI Cultural

Murat Shrine E Ctr

Arts Gallery

Veteran's Mem Plaza

HIGHLAND PARK

INDIANA UNIVERSITY-PURDUE UNIV

Amer College of Sports Medicine

James Whitcomb Riley Home

NY MILITARY PARK

Indiana Hist Society

Soldiers & Sailors Monument

Michael A Carroll Track and Soccer Stad

Greyhound

Indianapolis City Mkt

McCormick's Rock

National Institute for Fitness & Sport

Government

Indiana State Mus

Indianapolis Power & Light

Indiana State Capitol

Eiteljorg State Mus

Marion Co Jail

WHITE RIVER ST PK

IMAX 3-D Theater

NCAA Hall of Champions

Indianapolis Zoo

White River Gardens

Victory Fld

Circle Ctr Mall

Indianapolis Convention & Visitors Ctr

Conseco Fieldhouse

RCA Dome

Union Sta

FLETCHER PLACE HISTORIC DISTRICT

CITIZENS GAS COMPANY

CHEVROLET MOTOR DIVISION

Amtrak

Indianapolis Mon Work Release Ctr

LILLY CORPORATE CTR

BICKING

Fountain Sq

NORA

Indianapolis Women's Work Release

LILLY INDUSTRIAL CENTER

STOKELY VAN CAMP

B
1 Gardengate Pl
2 Canal Court North Dr
3 Canal Ct
4 Canal Court South Dr

D
1 Cruse St
2 S Highland Av

G
1 Lockerbie Cir
2 Lockerbie Cir
3 Lockerbie Cir

H
1 W Tippecanoe
2 Tippecanoe St
3 Hudson St

H
1 Monument Cir
2 N Scioto St
3 Chesapeake St
4 Conseco Ct
5 W Jackson Place North Dr
6 Dean Phillips Dr

46202
46222
46221
46225
46220

Indianapolis

MAP
2338

1:24,000
1 in. = 2000 ft.

0   0.25   0.5
miles

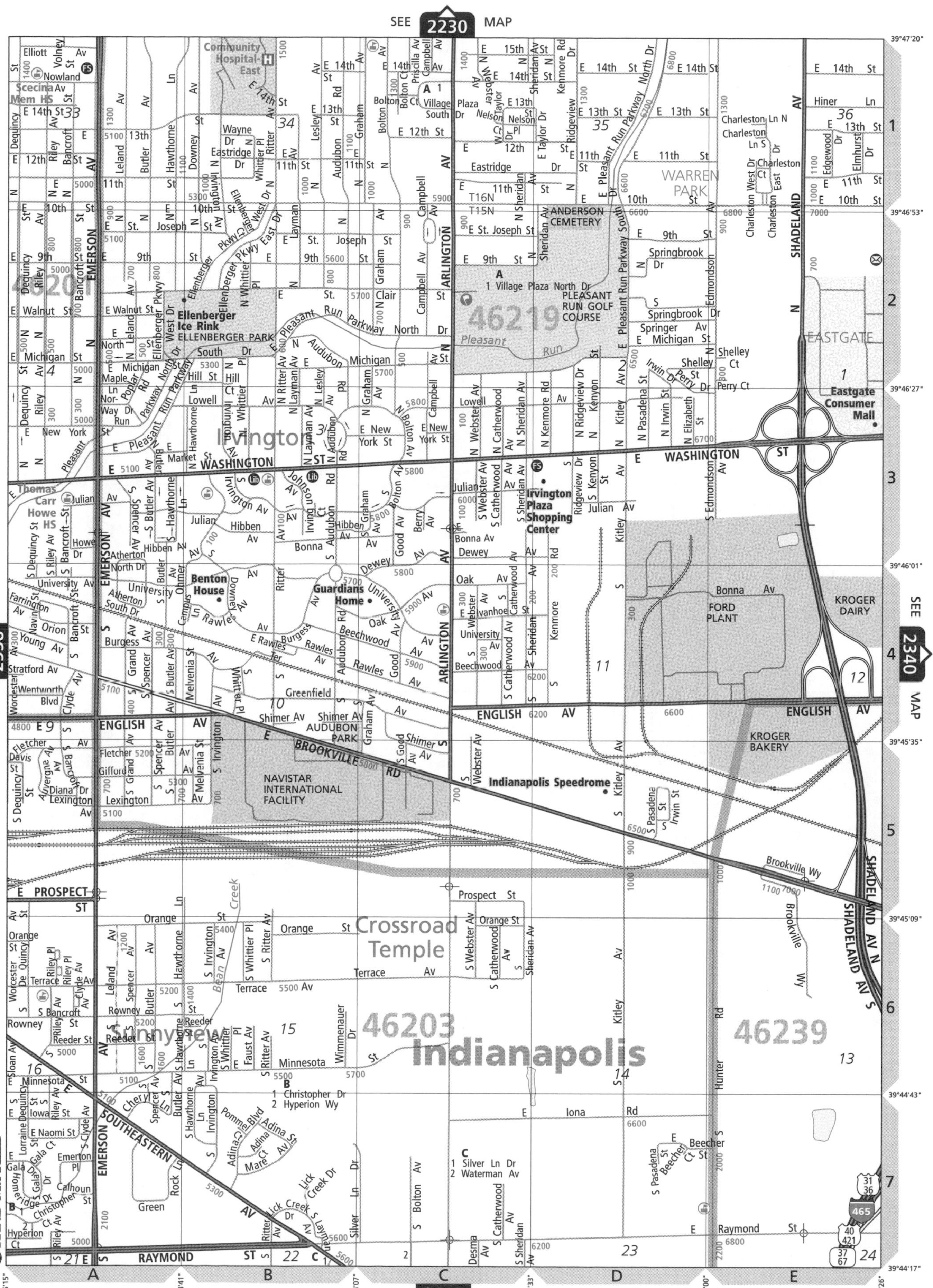

MAP
2339

1:24,000
1 in. = 2000 ft.
0   0.25   0.5
miles

SEE 2230 MAP

SEE 2338 MAP

SEE 2340 MAP

SEE 2448 MAP

RAND McNALLY

MAP
2340

1:24,000
1 in. = 2000 ft.

0   0.25   0.5
miles

SEE 2231 MAP

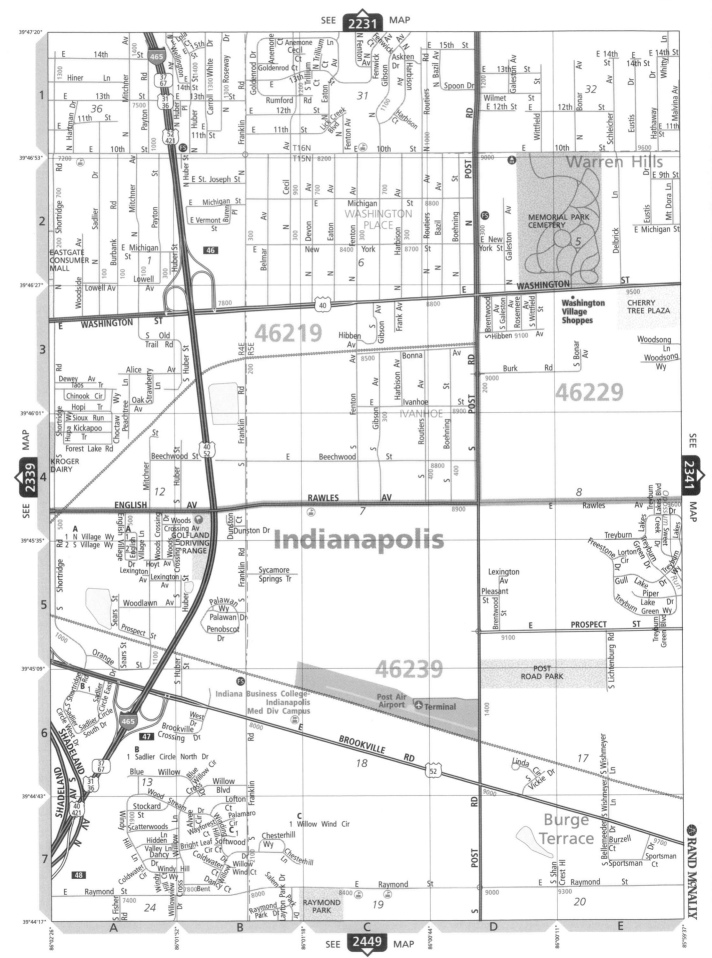

39°47'20"

E 14th Av

1400

Hiner   Ln

1300

E 13th St

7500   31   36   37   67

11th St

E 10th St

1000

52   421

39°46'53"

7200

Shortridge Rd

Sadlier Rd

Mitcher

Payton

Burbank

E Michigan St

EASTGATE
CONSUMER
MALL

Woodside

Lowell Ave

Lowell Av

39°46'27"

E WASHINGTON ST

S Old
Trail Rd

Dewey Av

Taos   Tr

Alice   Av

Chinook Cir

Hopi St

Strawberry

Oak   Av

Peachtree

39°46'01"

Shortridge

Hupa   Kickapoo
Tr

Sioux Run

Choctaw

Forest Lake Rd

KROGER
DAIRY

Beechwood St

Mitcher

Huber St

39°46'01"

SEE 2339 MAP

2339

ENGLISH   AV

39°45'35"

A
1 N Village Wy
2 S Village Wy

English

Abella Ln

Village Ln

Shortridge Rd

Sears St

Woodlawn Av

Prospect St

Hoyt Av

Lexington
Av

Huber St

Woods Crossing

Woods
Crossing Av

GOLFLAND
DRIVING
RANGE

Dunston
Ct

Dunston Dr

Franklin Rd

Sycamore
Springs Tr

Palawan
Wy

Palawan Dr

Penobscot
Dr

Indianapolis

39°45'09"

Orange

Sears St

1000

1100

B
1 Sadlier Circle East

Sadlier
Circle

Sadlier
Circle
South Dr

S Shortridge Rd

S-Sadlier Circle West Dr

465

47

Brookville
Crossing

West
Dr

Indiana Business College-
Indianapolis
Med Div Campus

8000

39°44'43"

37   67

31   36

40   421

48

SHADELAND   AV   S

B
1 Sadlier Circle North Dr

Blue   Willow

Blue
Willow Cir

Willow
Cir

13

Wood Stream

Willow
Blvd

Lofton
Ct

Stockard
St

Alvee Dr

Windy

Scatterwoods
Ln

Wayforest
Dr

Palamaro
Cir

C
1

Hidden
Valley Ln

Bright Leaf
Cir Ct

Softwood
Ct

C
1 Willow Wind Cir

Chesterhill
Wy

Dancy
Dr

Coldwater
Cir

Windy Hill

Franklin Rd

Chesterhill

Salem Dr

Willow Wind Ct

Dancy Ct

7

39°44'17"

A

E Raymond St

24

7400

Willowhead Dr

Windy Hill Cir

S Fisher Rd

Coldwater Cir

Raymond
Park Dr

Layton Park Dr

7800 Bent

8000

RAYMOND
PARK

86°02'26"   86°01'52"   86°01'18"   86°00'44"

Center section (46219 area)

46219

R4E R5E

200

Hibben
Av

Gibson Av

Frank Av

Belmar

New

Devon

Eaton

Fenton

York

300

Cecil

Bazil

Harbison

40

Hibben
Av

Harbison Av

Bonna

Fenton

Gibson

Ivanhoe

Routiers

Boehning

IVANHOE

300

8500

8800

8900

40   52

Beechwood

8800

400   400

RAWLES   AV

8

7   8900

E   Rawles   Av

Lexington
Av

Pleasant
St

Brentwood
Av

E   PROSPECT   ST

9100

46239

POST
ROAD PARK

Post Air
Airport

Terminal

FS

1400

E   BROOKVILLE   RD

8000

52

18

9000

Linda Cir

Vickie Dr

17

POST   RD   S

Burge
Terrace

S Shan
Crest Hl

Bellemeeder Dr

S Wishmeyer

Burzell
Ct

Sportsman

Sportsman Ct

9700

9300

E Raymond St

19

20

8400

86°00'11"   85°55'58"

Right section (46229 area)

E 14th St

14th
St

E 14th
St

Whitly Av

32

Malvina Av

Hathaway

Eustis

Schleicher

Bonar

12th St

Wittfield

10th

E 9th St

Eustis

Mt Dora Av

Delbrick

E Michigan St

Galeston Av

13th St

Wilmet

E 12th St

Spoon Dr

Harbison

Ct

N Bazil

Routiers Rd

1200

1100

9000

9600

WARREN HILLS

MEMORIAL PARK
CEMETERY

5

9500

WASHINGTON   ST

Brentwood
Av

S Galeston

Rosemere

S Wittfield

Washington
Village
Shoppes

CHERRY
TREE PLAZA

Hibben   9100   Av

Burk   Rd

9000

S Bonar Av

Woodsong
Ln

Woodsong
Wy

46229

POST   RD

N New
York

FS

E New
York

Galeston

200

Treyburn
Lakes Blvd

9600

Treyburn
Lakes Blvd

Treyburn
Creek
Sweet Dr

Freestone Lorton
Dr Cir

Treyburn
Green Dr

Gull   Lake

Treyburn
Lake Dr

Piper
Lake Dr

Treyburn
Green Blvd

Brentwood
Av

S Lichtenburg Rd

Treyburn
Green Blvd

39°46'53"   T16N   T15N   8200

8400   8700

9000   FS   N

N 1000

8800

N POST   RD

7800

7500

T16N

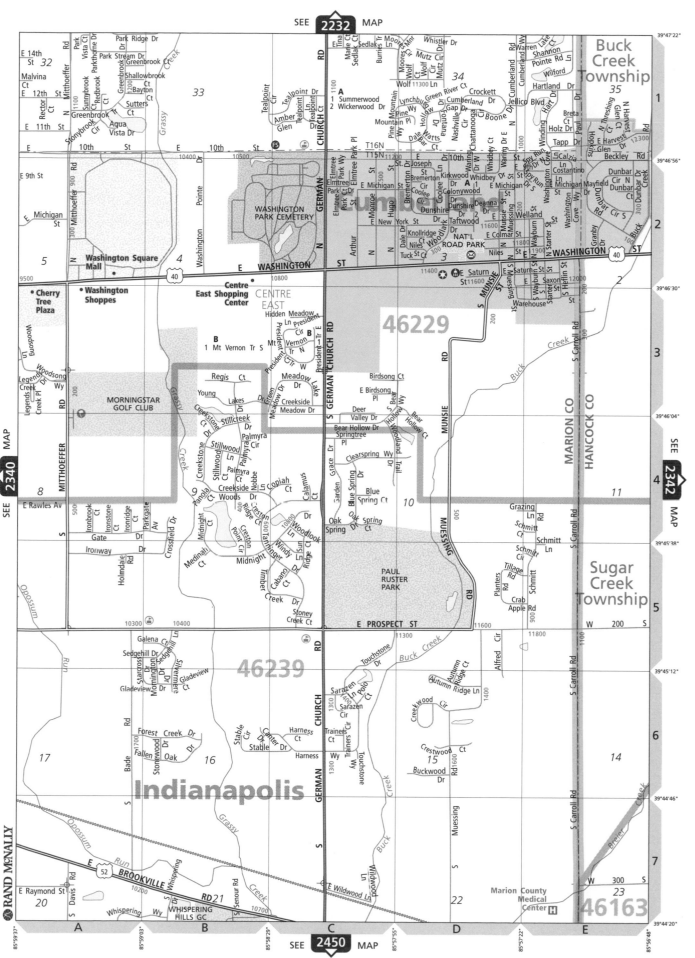

MAP
2341

1:24,000
1 in. = 2000 ft.
0   0.25   0.5
miles

SEE 2232 MAP

Buck Creek Township

46229

MARION CO
HANCOCK CO

SEE 2340 MAP

SEE 2342 MAP

Washington Square Mall

Cherry Tree Plaza

Washington Shoppes

Centre East Shopping Center

CENTRE EAST

MORNINGSTAR GOLF CLUB

PAUL RUSTER PARK

Sugar Creek Township

46239

Indianapolis

Marion County Medical Center

46163

Whispering Hills GC

SEE 2450 MAP

RAND McNALLY

Cumberland

MAP
2342

1:24,000
1 in. = 2000 ft.
0   0.25   0.5
miles

SEE 2233 MAP

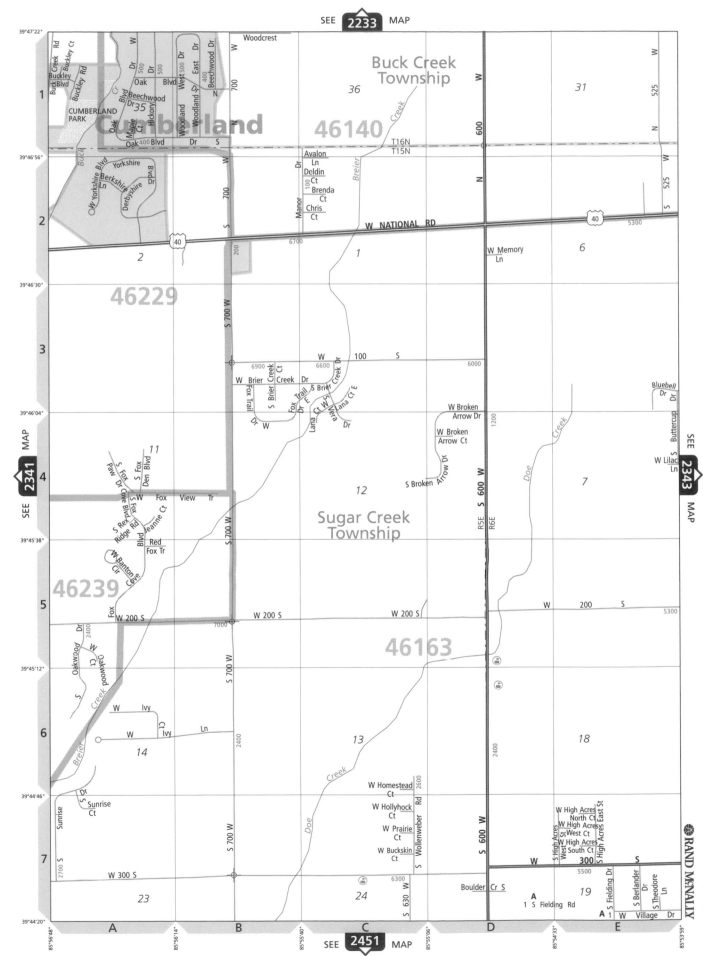

Woodcrest

Buck Creek
Township

Buckley Creek Rd
Buckley Ct
Buckley Rd
Buck Blvd
Buckley Blvd
Oak Blvd
Maple Dr
Beechwood Dr
Hickory Dr
West 500 Dr
Woodland Dr
East 500 Dr
Beechwood Dr
500 Dr
700 N
Woodcrest

CUMBERLAND
PARK
35

Cumberland

36

46140

31

T16N
T15N

Oak Blvd

Yorkshire Blvd
W Yorkshire Blvd
Berkshire Ln
Derbyshire Dr

Avalon Ln
Deldin Ct
Brenda Ct
Chris Ct
Manor Dr

W NATIONAL RD

40

525 N

525 S

40

5300

2

46229

200 S

6700

2

1

W Memory Ln

6

S 700 W

3

W 100 S

6900
6600
6000

W Brier Creek Dr
S Brier Creek Ct
Fox Trail Dr W
S Brier Creek Dr
Lana Ct W
Vera
Lana Ct E
Dr

Bluebell Dr

W Broken Arrow Dr
W Broken Arrow Ct
S Broken Arrow Dr

1200

Buttercup

W Lilac Ln

SEE 2343 MAP

SEE 2341 MAP

11

S Fox Paw Dr
S Fox Cove Blvd
S Fox Den Blvd
W Fox View Tr
S Fox Ct
Jeanne Ct
S Rex Ridge Rd
Blvd
Red Fox Tr
W Benton Creve Cir

4

12

7

Doe Creek

R5E   R6E
S 600 W

**Sugar Creek
Township**

S 700 W

S 700 W

46239

Fox
W 200 S
7000
2400
Oakwood Dr
W Oakwood Ct
S

W 200 S

W 200 S

46163

W 200 S

5300

5

W Ivy Ct
W Ivy Ln

14

Creek Brier

2400

13

18

2400

S 700 W

Sunrise Dr
S Sunrise Ct

Doe Creek

W Homestead Ct
2600
W Hollyhock Ct
W Prairie Ct
W Buckskin Ct
Wollenweber Rd

W High Acres North Ct
W High Acres West Ct
W High Acres South Ct
S High Acres West St
S High Acres East St

S 600 W

6

7

2700 S

W 300 S

6300 W

S 630 W

Boulder Cr S

W 300 S

5500

S Fielding Dr
S Berlander Dr
S Theodore Ln

23

24

19

A
1 S Fielding Rd
W Village Dr
A 1

A   B   C   D   E

SEE 2451 MAP

RAND MCNALLY

MAP
2343

1:24,000
1 in. = 2000 ft.
0   0.25   0.5
miles

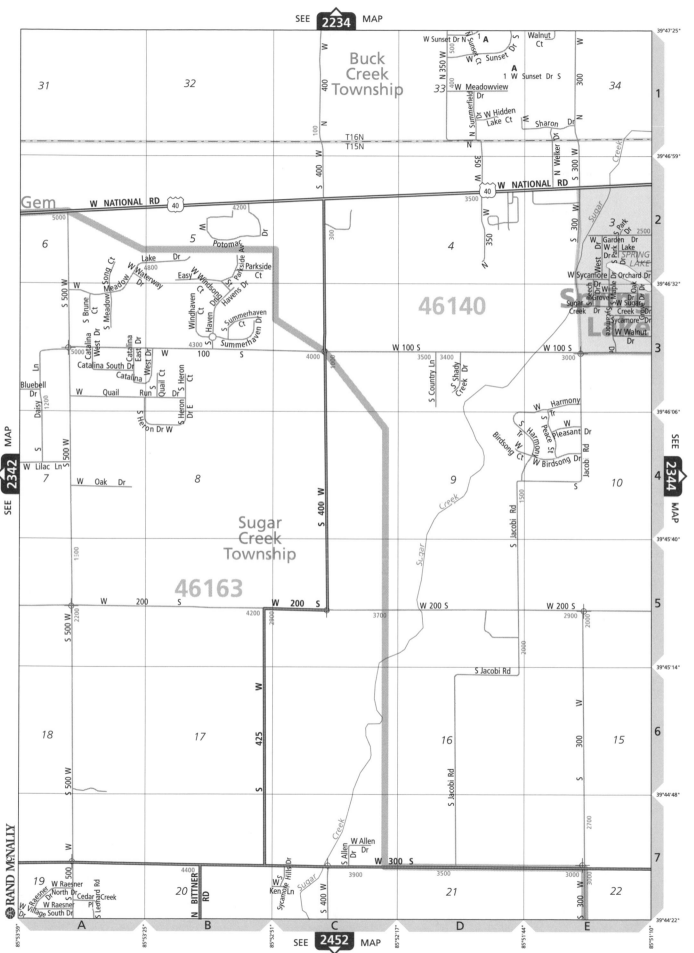

SEE 2234 MAP

Buck
Creek
Township

W Sunset Dr N
W Sunset Ct
W Sunset Dr
Walnut
Ct
Sunset Dr S

31   32   33   W Meadowview
Dr   34   1

T16N
T15N

W National Rd 40
W Welker Dr

39°47'25"

39°46'59"

Gem   W NATIONAL RD 40   W NATIONAL RD   40   39°46'32"

6   5   4   3   2
Potomac Dr
Lake Dr   Park Dr   Spring Lake
W Waterway   Parkside
Easy Windsong   Parkside Ct   W Garden Dr
W Meadow Song Ct   Havens Dr   W Park Lake Dr
S Brune Ct   Windhaven Ct   Summerhaven   W Sycamore Dr   Orchard Dr
Catalina West Dr   Haven Dr   Summerhaven Ct   Sugar Creek   Beech Dr   Maple Dr   Oak Dr
Catalina East Dr   Summerhaven   Grove Dr   W Sugar Creek Dr
Catalina South Dr   100   S   4000   W 100 S   Sycamore Dr   W 100 S   39°46'32"
Catalina West Dr   W Walnut Dr

7   8   9   10   4
Bluebell Dr
Daisy   Quail Ct   S Shady Creek Dr   Harmony Tr
Quail Run   Quail Dr   S Country Ln   W Pleasant Dr   Jacobi Rd
S Heron Dr E   W Harmony Tr   Birdsong Ct
S Heron Dr W   S Peace St   W Birdsong Dr

W Lilac Ln   Sugar Creek   S Jacobi Rd   39°46'06"
W Oak Dr

Sugar
Creek
Township

46140

46163

W 200 S   W 200 S   W 200 S   W 200 S   39°45'40"

18   17   16   15   6
S Jacobi Rd   39°45'14"

W 300 S   39°44'48"

19   W Raesner Dr   North Dr   Cedar Rd   20   21   22   7
W Raesner   Leonard Creek   N Bittner Rd   S Allen Dr   W Allen Dr
W Village South Dr   Sycamore Hills Dr   W Kenard Ln   W 300 S

A   B   C   D   E
SEE 2452 MAP

SEE 2342 MAP
SEE 2344 MAP

RAND McNALLY

39°44'22"
85°53'59"   85°53'25"   85°52'51"   85°52'17"   85°51'44"   85°51'10"

MAP
2344

1:24,000
1 in. = 2000 ft.
0   0.25   0.5
miles

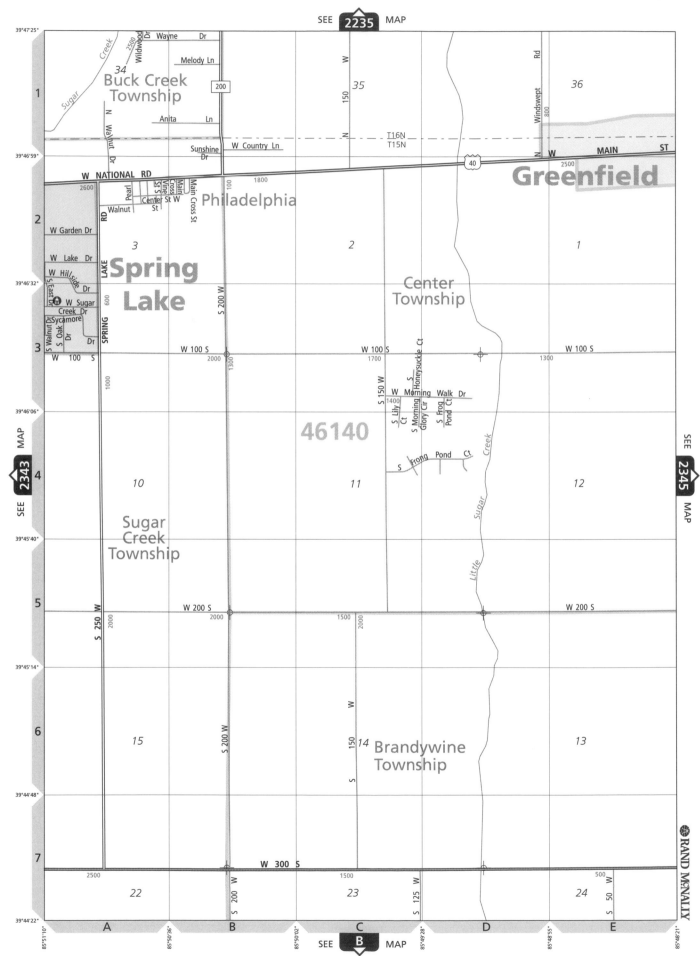

SEE 2235 MAP

Sugar Creek

2500
Wildwood Dr   Wayne   Dr

Melody Ln

34
Buck Creek
Township

200
N Walnut

Anita   Ln

Sunshine Dr   W Country Ln

T16N
T15N

W   150   N

W   800   Windswept Rd

36

35

W   MAIN   ST
N   W   2500
US 40
Greenfield

W   NATIONAL   RD
2600
Pearl   Main Vine St   Main Cross St
Center St W   St S
Walnut   Center St
RD   St
LAKE   Philadelphia

1800
100

W Garden Dr

2   3   2   1

W Lake Dr

Spring
Lake
W Hillside Dr

S Easton   W Sugar Creek Dr
Sycamore Dr
S Walnut Dr   S Oak Dr

Center
Township

SPRING   600   LAKE RD

W 100 S

W 100 S
2000
1300

W 100 S
1700

W 100 S
1300

S 200 W

1000

S 150 W   1400
W Morning   Honeysuckle Ct
S Lily Ct   S Morning Glory Cir   Walk Dr
S Frog Pond Ct

46140

S Frong Pond Ct

SEE 2343 MAP

10   11   12

Sugar
Creek
Township

Little   Sugar   Creek

SEE 2345 MAP

S 250 W   2000
W 200 S   2000
W 200 S   1500   2000
W 200 S

W   150   S

15   14   13
Brandywine
Township

S 200 W

W 300 S
2500   1500   500

S 200 W   S 125 W   S 50 W

22   23   24

A   B   C   D   E

SEE B MAP

85°51'10"   85°50'36"   85°50'02"   85°49'28"   85°48'55"   85°48'21"

39°47'25"
39°46'59"
39°46'32"
39°46'06"
39°45'40"
39°45'14"
39°44'48"
39°44'22"

1   2   3   4   5   6   7

RAND McNALLY

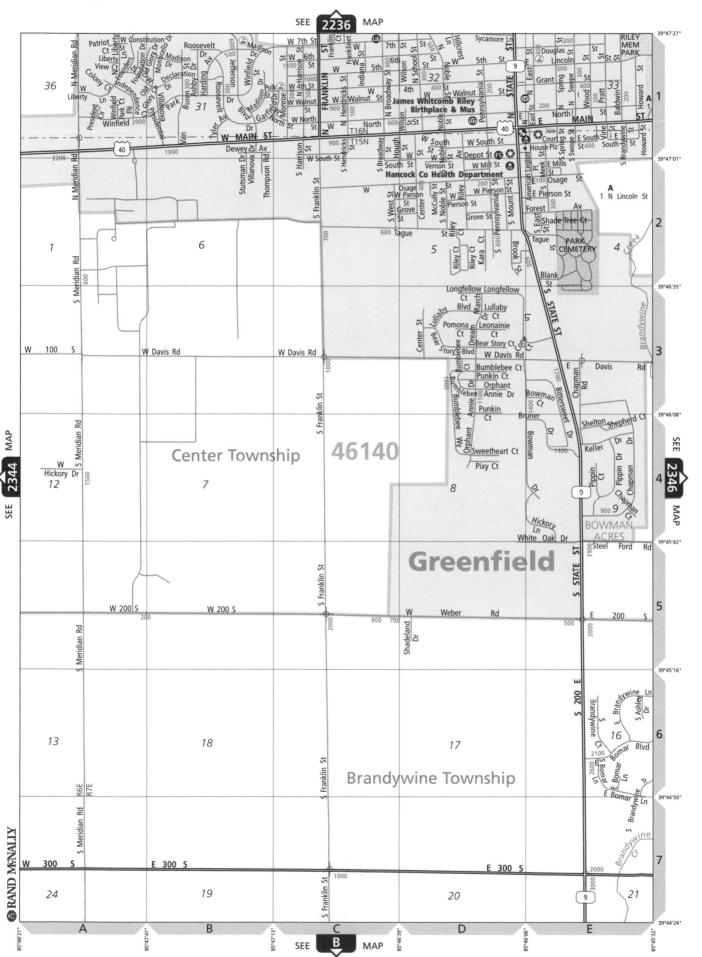

MAP **2345**

1:24,000
1 in. = 2000 ft.

0   0.25   0.5
miles

39°47'27"
39°47'01"
39°46'35"
39°46'08"
39°45'42"
39°45'16"
39°44'50"
39°44'24"

Center Township

46140

Greenfield

Brandywine Township

RAND MCNALLY

RILEY MEM PARK
PARK CEMETERY
BOWMAN ACRES

James Whitcomb Riley Birthplace & Mus
Hancock Co Health Department

A   B   C   D   E

85°48'21"   85°47'47"   85°47'13"   85°46'39"   85°46'06"   85°45'32"

MAP
2346

1:24,000
1 in. = 2000 ft.
0   0.25   0.5
miles

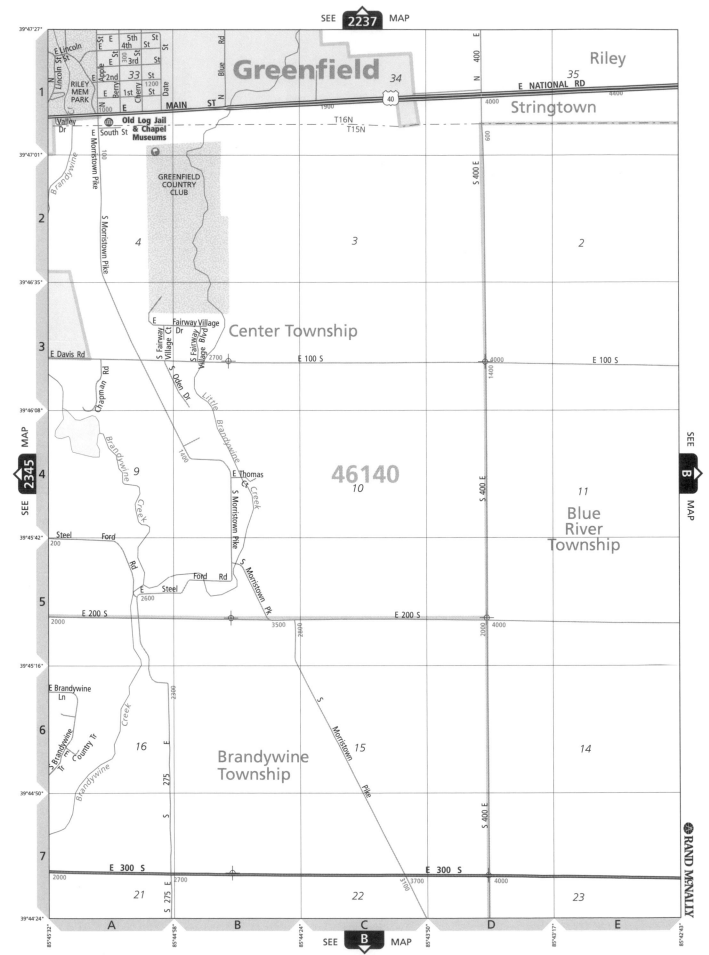

SEE **2237** MAP

Greenfield

34

Riley

E NATIONAL RD
35
4400

40

Stringtown

T16N
T15N

1

39°47'27"

RILEY
MEM
PARK

E Lincoln
St

E
5th St
4th St
3rd St
2nd St
1st St

E MAIN ST

Blue Rd

400 N

600

1900
4000

E Lincoln
St

Lincoln St

Apple
Berry
Cherry
Date

33

1200

E

1000

N

Valley
Dr
E South St

Old Log Jail
& Chapel
Museums

S Morristown Pike

39°47'01"

GREENFIELD
COUNTRY
CLUB

2

4

3

2

S 400 E

39°46'35"

E Fairway Village
Dr

Center Township

E Davis Rd

Fairway Village Blvd
S Fairway Village Ct

3

S Oden Dr

E 100 S

2700

4000
1400

E 100 S

39°46'08"

SEE **2345** MAP

Chapman Rd

Little Brandywine Creek

1400

46140

9

10

11

S 400 E

SEE **B** MAP

39°45'42"

Steel
Ford

E Thomas Ct

Brandywine Creek

200

S Morristown Pike

**Blue
River
Township**

5

Ford Rd

E Steel

E 200 S

2600

2000

3500

2800

E 200 S

2000
4000

39°45'16"

E Brandywine
Ln

S 300 E

S Morristown Pike

39°44'50"

6

S Brandywine
Tr

Country Tr

Brandywine Creek

16

S 275 E

**Brandywine
Township**

15

14

S 400 E

7

E 300 S

E 300 S

2000

2700

S 275 E

3500

3700

4000

39°44'24"

21

22

23

A
85°45'32"

B
85°44'58"

C
85°44'24"

D
85°43'50"

E
85°43'17"
85°42'58"

SEE **B** MAP

RAND MCNALLY

MAP
2439

1:24,000
1 in. = 2000 ft.

0   0.25   0.5
miles

SEE **2330** MAP

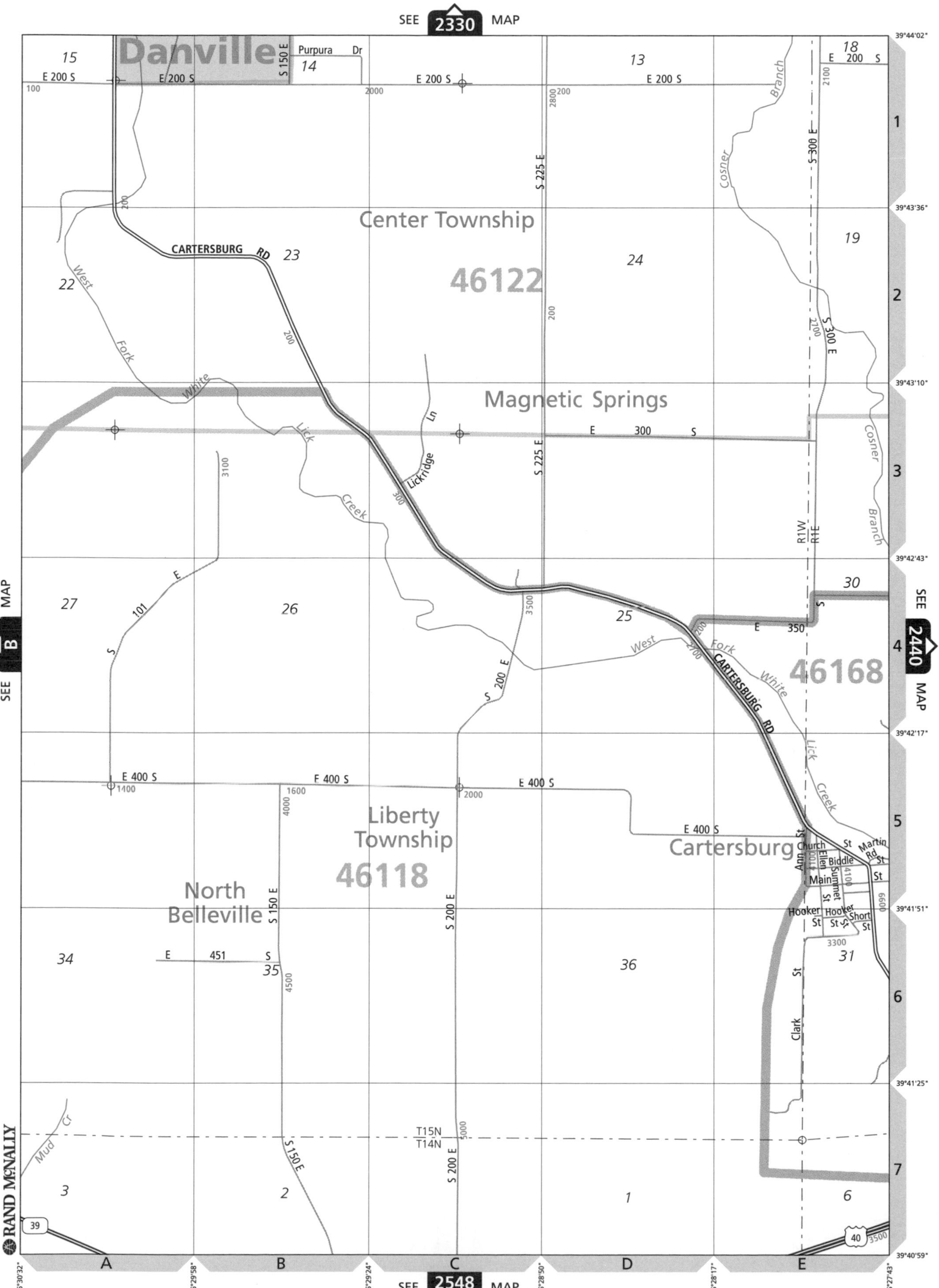

Danville

15   Purpura   Dr   13   18
E 200 S   14   E 200 S
E 200 S   E 200 S   E 200 S   E 200 S
100   2000   200

Center Township

46122

22   CARTERSBURG RD   23   24   19

West Fork White

Lick Creek   Lickridge Ln

Magnetic Springs

E 300 S

27   26   25   30

46168

West Fork White

CARTERSBURG RD

Lick Creek

E 400 S   E 400 S   E 400 S
1400   1600   2000

Liberty
Township
46118

E 400 S

Cartersburg

North
Belleville

34   E 451 S   35   36   31

3   2   1   6

SEE **2548** MAP

SEE **2440** MAP

39°44'02"
39°43'36"
39°43'10"
39°42'43"
39°42'17"
39°41'51"
39°41'25"
39°40'59"

1
2
3
4
5
6
7

A   B   C   D   E

39
40

SEE 2331 MAP

SEE 2439 MAP

SEE 2441 MAP

Center Township
Washington Township
Guilford Township
Liberty Township
Plainfield
46122
46123
46168
46118
OAK TREE GOLF COURSE
Plainfield Correctional Facility
Arthur Campbell HS
1 Andrews Blvd East Dr

SEE 2549 MAP

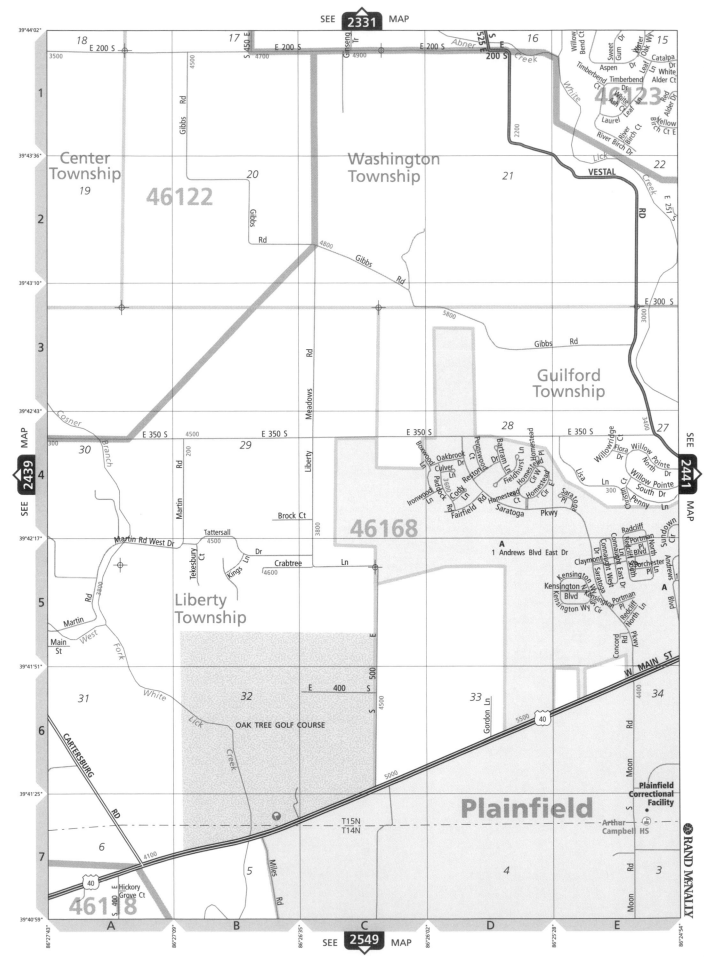

MAP
2441

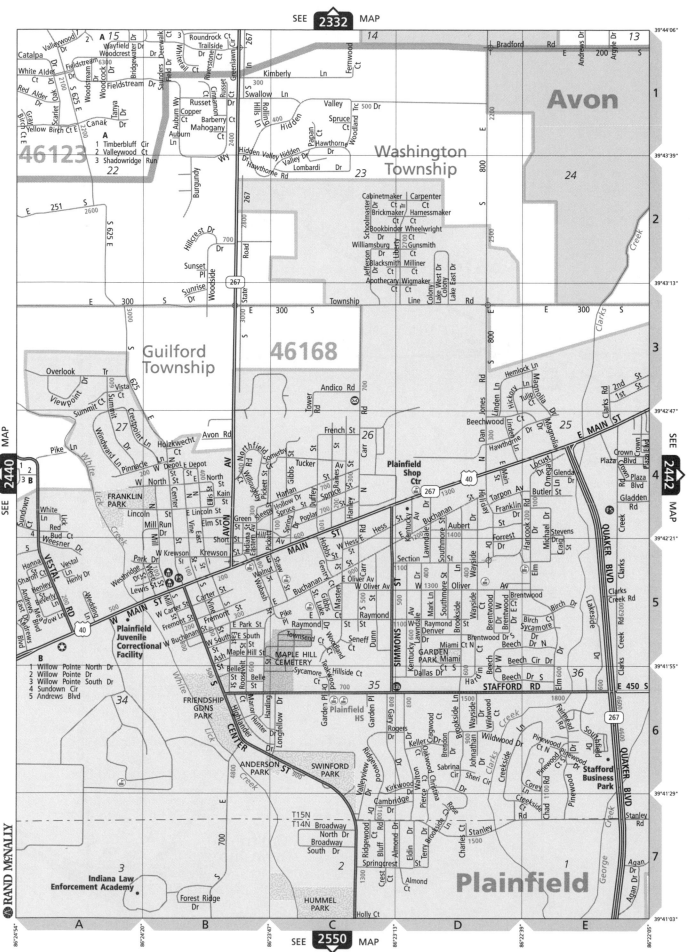

1:24,000
1 in. = 2000 ft.
0   0.25   0.5
miles

SEE 2332 MAP

SEE 2550 MAP

SEE 2440 MAP

SEE 2442 MAP

Avon

Washington Township

Guilford Township

46123

46168

Plainfield

RAND M?NALLY

MAP
2442

1:24,000
1 in. = 2000 ft.

0   0.25   0.5
miles

N

SEE 2333 MAP

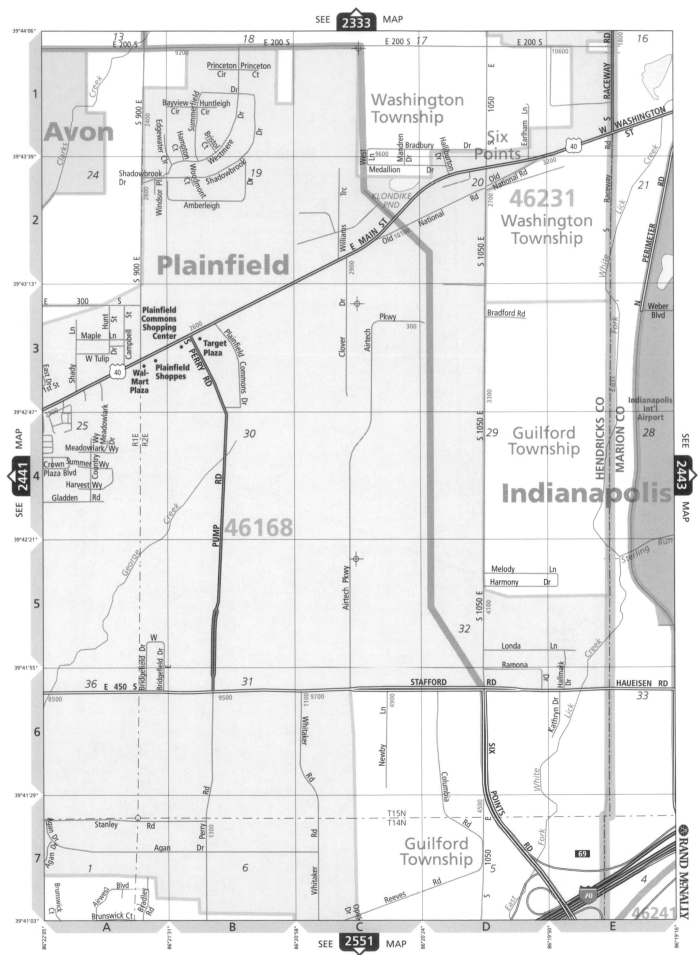

Avon

Plainfield

Washington
Township

Six
Points

46231
Washington
Township

Guilford
Township

Indianapolis

46168

Guilford
Township

SEE 2441 MAP

SEE 2443 MAP

SEE 2551 MAP

RAND McNALLY

46241

Indianapolis
Int'l
Airport

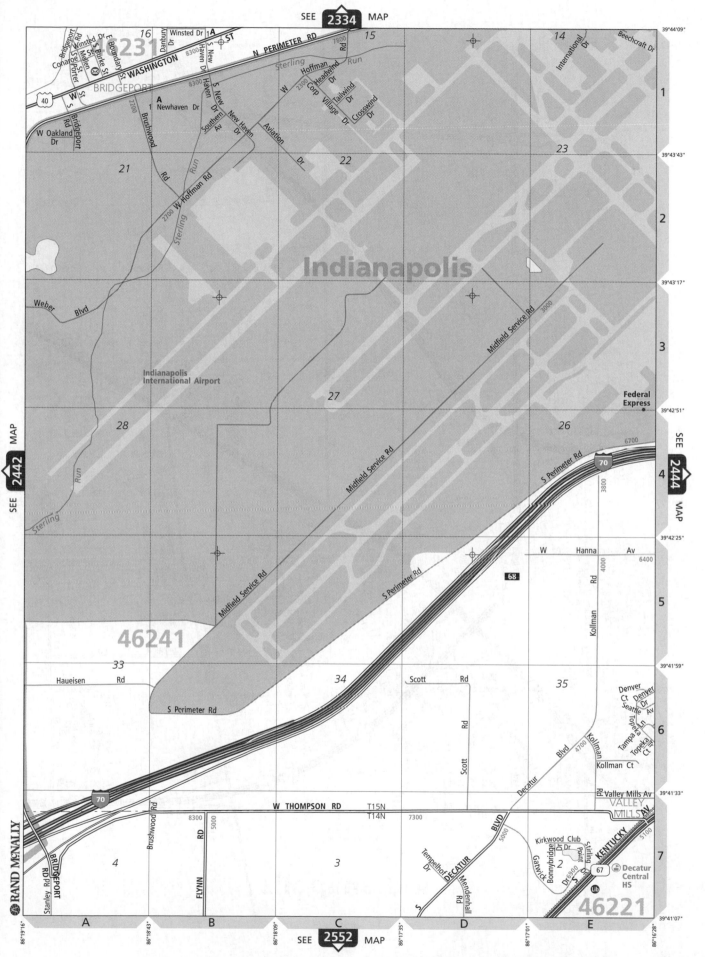

MAP 2443

1:24,000
1 in. = 2000 ft.

0   0.25   0.5

miles

SEE 2334 MAP

SEE 2442 MAP

SEE 2444 MAP

SEE 2552 MAP

Indianapolis

Indianapolis
International Airport

46231

46241

46221

RAND McNALLY

Federal
Express

Decatur
Central
HS

Streets/labels:
Winsted Dr
Danbury
Bridgeport Rd
Winsted Dr
E Boundary
S Melien St
S Porter St
S Burke St
Conarove Rd
N PERIMETER RD
Sterling Run
WASHINGTON
BRIDGEPORT
40
Newhaven Dr
Haven Dr
S New Haven Dr
Southern Av
New Haven Dr
Aviation Dr
Hoffman Dr
Headwind Dr
Tailwind Dr
Corp Village Dr
Crosswind Dr
W Oakland Dr
Bridgeport Rd
Brushwood Rd
W Hoffman Rd
Sterling Run
Weber Blvd
Midfield Service Rd
Midfield Service Rd
S Perimeter Rd
S Perimeter Rd
Sterling Run
70
68
W Hanna Av
Kollman Rd
Haueisen Rd
Scott Rd
Scott Rd
Denver Ct
Denver Dr
Seattle Av
Topeka Ln
Tampa Av
Topeka Ct
Kollman Ct
Kollman Blvd
Decatur
Rd Valley Mills Av
VALLEY MILLS AV
W THOMPSON RD
T15N
T14N
Brushwood Rd
FLYNN RD
Tempelhof Dr
DECATUR BLVD
Mendenhall Rd
Kirkwood Club Dr
Bonnybridge Dr
Gatwick Dr
Stirling Point
KENTUCKY
67
Stanley Rd
Bridgeport Rd

Grid numbers: 16, 15, 14, 21, 22, 23, 27, 28, 26, 33, 34, 35, 4, 3, 2

MAP 2444

1:24,000
1 in. = 2000 ft.
0   0.25   0.5
miles
N

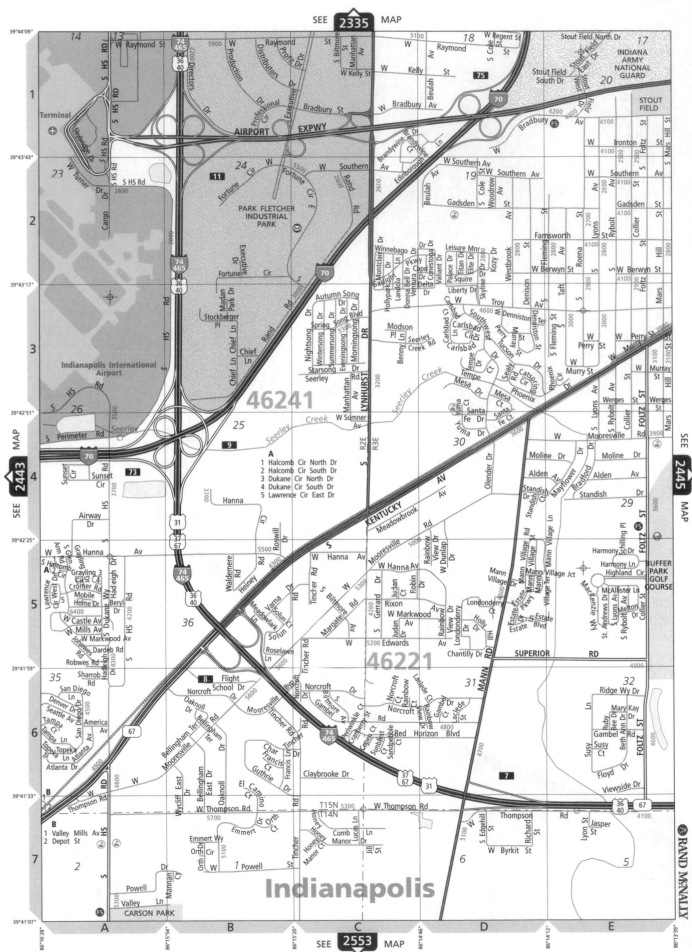

SEE 2335 MAP

Indianapolis

RAND McNALLY

MAP **2445**

SEE **2336** MAP

1:24,000
1 in. = 2000 ft.
0   0.25   0.5
miles

INDIANA ARMY NATIONAL GUARD
STOUT FIELD
OLIN BRASS
REILLY TAR & CHEMICAL
HOLT RD
AIRPORT
W Kelly St EXPWY
W RAYMOND ST
Old
Greencycle Dr
Raymond St
Belmont
W RAYMOND ST 1500
CTR

17
16
2900
Warren Av
Bedford St
Maywood Rd

Bradbury Av
W Ironton St
2400
2500

46241
20
Farnsworth St
2800

W Southern Av
Gadsden St
Lockburn
McClure
2800

MAYWOOD
W Southern Av
Gooden Av
S Moreland Av
Centennial St
Maywood St
Concord St
Arnold Rd
2800

Rolls Royce Allison

21
2600
2400

22

Belmont
Hudnut
Blvd
2300

Administration
Flotation
Activator Av
N Hudnut Blvd
Eagle Creek Av
Belmont
Levee Rd
Hudnut Pl
Hudnut Blvd
Hudnut Blvd
S Hudnut Blvd

RIVER

46225
W TROY AV
2700
1000

1

2

W Berwyn St
S
MARS HILL
S Tibbs Av
W Troy Av
W Troy Av
KENTUCKY AV
MAYWOOD GARDENS
3500
2800

46221

BIG EAGLE CREEK
WHITE

INDIANAPOLIS DISPOSAL PLANT

HARDING ST
W Murray St
Chase St
Coffey St
Arbor St
3300
3300
3000

39°43'20"

3

W Troy Av
W Murray St
Mooresville Dr
5th Av E
4th
Perry Av
Davis
W Carr Av
6th Av E
Bowen Pl
Perry Av
Winings Av
Murray St
Davis Dr
Christie Ct
3100
3700
3300
3700

S Tibbs Av
3300

W Sumner Av
Division St
1400
3500

39°42'54"

SEE 2444 MAP

BUFFER PARK GOLF COURSE

29
28

Indianapolis

27

INDIANAPOLIS POWER & LIGHT

Hanna Av
3900
W

SEE 2446 MAP

4

WHITE RIVER

32
33

46217
34

Terminal Rd

5

67
74 465
36 40
T15N
THOMPSON
T14N
RD

67
67
74 465
4
37
Knights Wy
Harding Ct
S Harding St
FS
Thompson Rd

6

SANDHURST DR
5100
3400
3400
5300
5000
Tibbs
Byrkit St
Newhart
SUNSHINE GARDENS
Concord St
3100
W 2800
Warman Av
5100

5
4
3

Belmont Av
W EPLER AV
37
BELL CEM
S HARDING ST
Harding Ln
Cliff Ridge Dr
Cliff Ridge Ln
Cliff Ridge Ct
Bluff View Blvd
Bluff View Dr

7

RAND McNALLY

A   B   C   D   E

SEE **2554** MAP

86°13'39"   86°13'05"   86°12'31"   86°11'57"   86°11'24"   86°10'50"

39°44'12"
39°43'46"
39°41'36"
39°42'02"
39°42'28"
39°41'10"

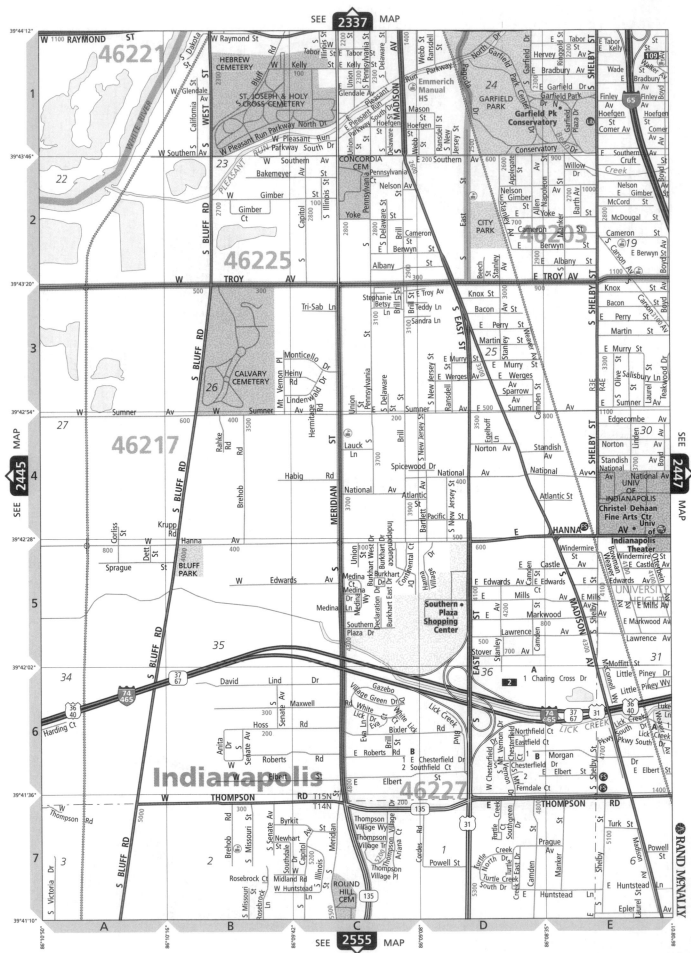

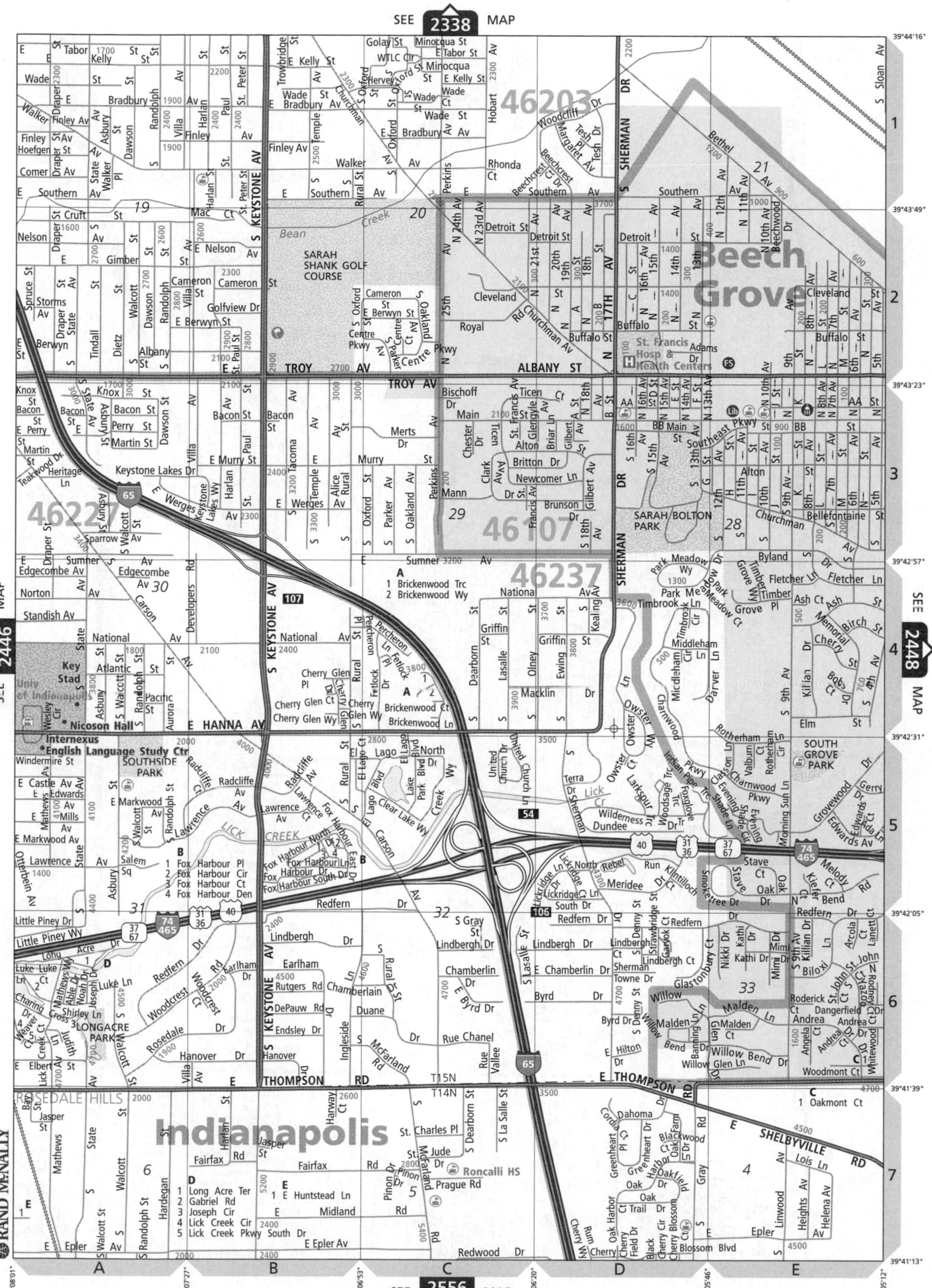

MAP
2447

1:24,000
1 in. = 2000 ft.

0   0.25   0.5
miles

SEE 2338 MAP

SEE 2446 MAP

SEE 2448 MAP

SEE 2556 MAP

46203

Beech Grove

46227

46107

46237

Indianapolis

ROSEDALE HILLS

RAND McNALLY

A   B   C   D   E

1:24,000
1 in. = 2000 ft.
0 0.25 0.5
miles

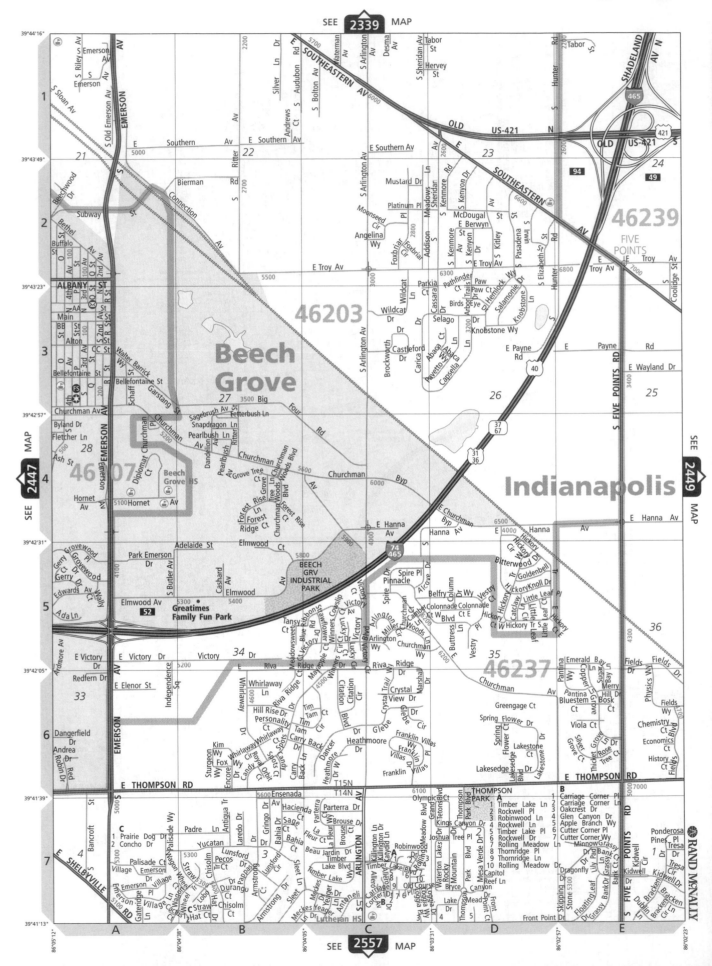

SEE 2339 MAP

Beech Grove

Indianapolis

46239
46203
46107
46237

FIVE POINTS

BEECH GRV INDUSTRIAL PARK

Greatimes Family Fun Park

THOMPSON PARK

A
1 Timber Lake Ln
2 Rockwell Pl
3 Robinwood Ln
4 Rockwell Ln
5 Timber Lake Pl
6 Rockwell Dr
7 Rolling Meadow Ln
8 Thornridge Pl
9 Thornridge Ln
10 Rolling Meadow Dr

B
1 Carriage Corner Pl
2 Carriage Corner Ln
3 Oakcrest Dr
4 Glen Canyon Dr
5 Apple Branch Wy
6 Cutter Corner Pl
7 Cutter Corner Wy

C
1 Prairie Dog Dr
2 Concho Dr

SEE 2447 MAP

SEE 2449 MAP

SEE 2557 MAP

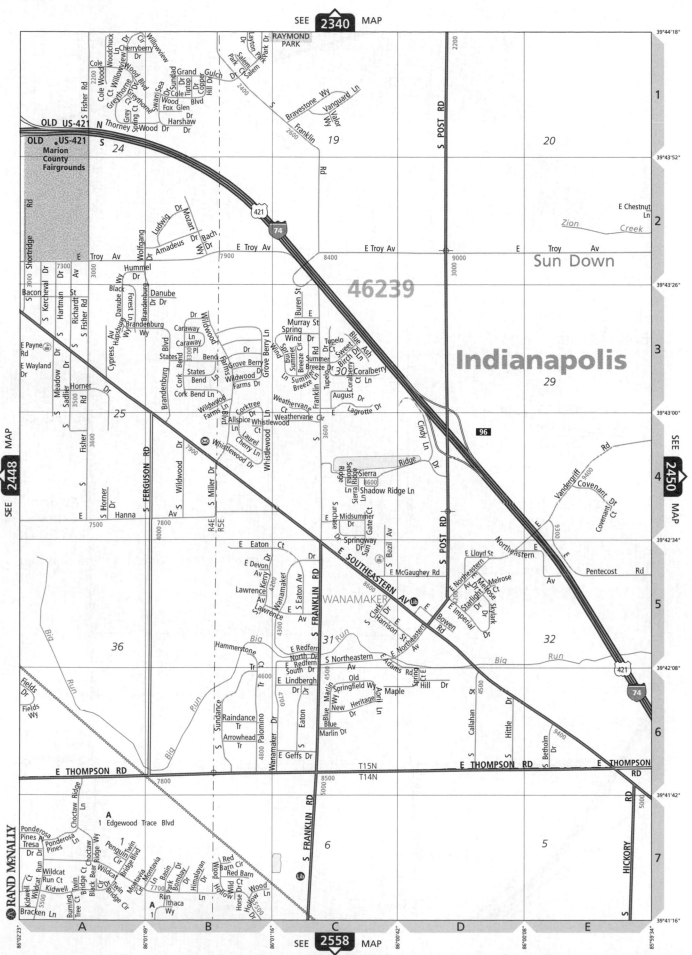

MAP
2449

1:24,000
1 in. = 2000 ft.
0   0.25   0.5
miles

SEE 2340 MAP

SEE 2448 MAP

SEE 2450 MAP

SEE 2558 MAP

RAYMOND PARK

OLD US-421 N
OLD US-421 S
Marion County Fairgrounds

Indianapolis

Sun Down

46239

29

WANAMAKER

RAND McNALLY

A 1 Edgewood Trace Blvd

MAP
2450

1:24,000
1 in. = 2000 ft.

0   0.25   0.5
miles

SEE 2341 MAP

SEE 2449 MAP

SEE 2451 MAP

SEE 2559 MAP

39°44'18"
39°43'52"
39°43'26"
39°43'00"
39°42'34"
39°42'08"
39°41'42"
39°41'16"

1
2
3
4
5
6
7

A   B   C   D   E

BROOKVILLE RD

Julietta

52

Whispering Hills Golf Course

Belle Arbor

Indianapolis

46239

Sugar Creek Township

46163

46126

Moral Township

MARION CO
HANCOCK CO

MARION CO
SHELBY CO

RAND McNALLY

MAP
2451

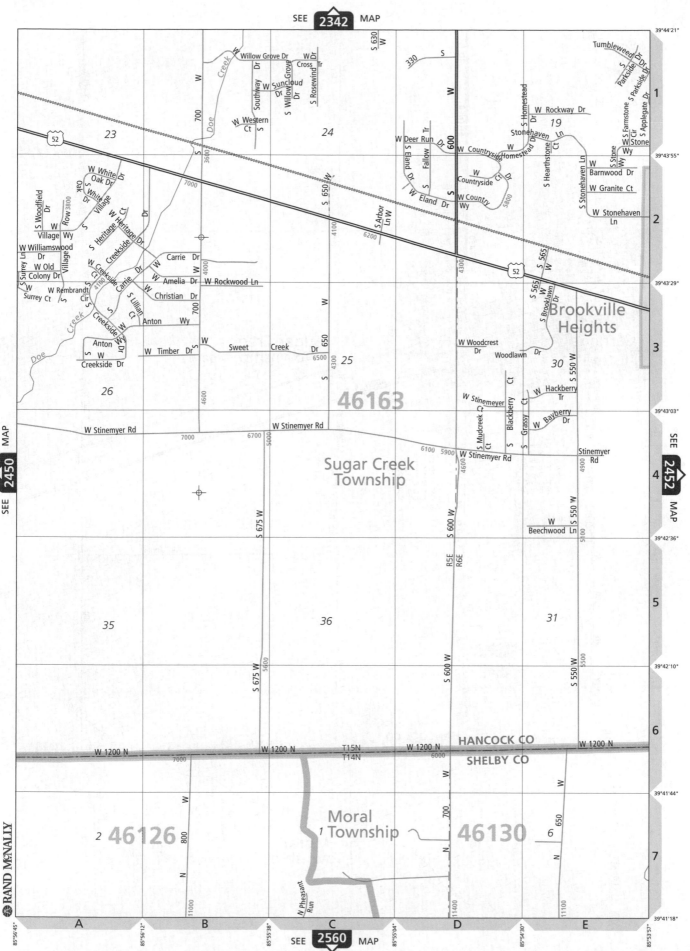

MAP
2452

1:31,000
1 in. = 2000 ft.

0   0.25   0.5
miles

SEE 2343 MAP

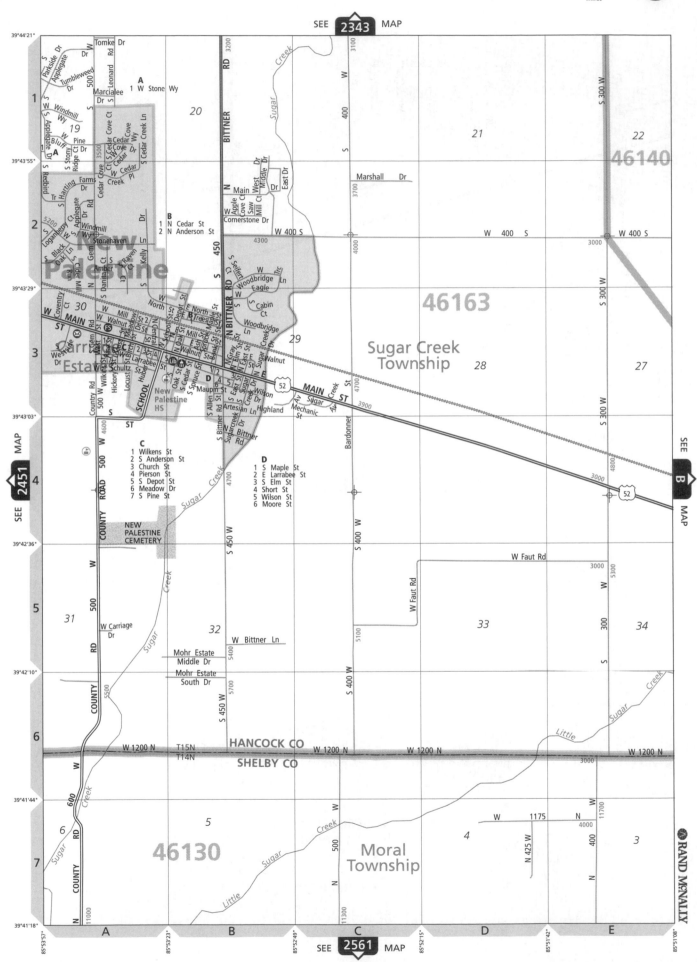

39°44'21"

Tomke Dr
Parkside Dr
Applegate Dr
S
Tumbleweed Dr
Leonard Rd
500
S
Marcialee Dr
A
1 W Stone Wy
20
BITTNER RD
3200
3100
W
400
S
21
S 300 W
22
46140

19
Windmill Wy
S
Applegate Dr
A
Stony Ridge Ct
Pine Dr
S Cedar Cove Ct
S Cedar Cove Ct
Cedar Cove Wy
S Cedar Cove Wy
W Cedar
Cedar Creek Ln
S Cedar Creek Pl

39°43'55"
Redbird Tr
Harting Farms Dr
Applegate Dr
Cedar Cove Dr
Cedar Creek Pl
B
1 N Cedar St
2 N Anderson St
N Main
Apple Cove Dr
West Dr
Saw Mill Dr
Middle Dr
East Dr
Marshall   Dr
3700

Loganberry Ct
5200
Windmill Wy
Stonehaven
Black Oak Ln
Gem Ct
Amber Danita
Kelly Ln
Raven
Cornerstone Dr
W 400 S
4300
W 400 S
4000
W 400 S
3000
W 400 S

39°43'29"
Coventry Ct
30
W MAIN ST
Mill Rd
N Depot
E North St
Treesdale St
Seifert Ct
Woodbridge Ln
Eagle Ln
Cabin Ct
Woodbridge Ln
46163
S 300 W

New Palestine

W Walnut
Mill St
Meadow Dr
School St
N Oak St
N Mill St
Blank St
N Gray St
N Elm St
N East St
Sugar Creek
Walnut
29
Sugar Creek Township
28
S 300 W
4700
27

3
Carriage Estates
Gem St
Wenke Dr
Schultz Dr
Hickory St
Wilkins St
500 W
Larrabee
Hubel
S Cedar St
S Spruce St
S Maupin St
S Allen St
Sugarcreek Rd
S East St
S Sugar Creek Ct
S Wilson Dr
Highland
Artesian Ln
Mechanic St
52
MAIN ST
Creek St
3900
Bardonner
4700
4800
52

39°43'03"
SCHOOL ST
New Palestine HS
D
Oak St
Bittner Rd
Bittner Rd
S Bittner Rd
S Sugar Creek
W

SEE 2451 MAP

W
4600
500 W
W
SCHOOL ST

C
1 Wilkens St
2 S Anderson St
3 Church St
4 Pierson St
5 S Depot St
6 Meadow Dr
7 S Pine St

D
1 S Maple St
2 E Larrabee St
3 S Elm St
4 Short St
5 Wilson St
6 Moore St

S 400 W

3000

SEE B MAP

COUNTY ROAD 500 W
S 450 W
4700

NEW PALESTINE CEMETERY
S 400 W

39°42'36"

W Faut Rd
3000

39°42'10"
31
500 W
W Carriage Dr
5500
32
W Bittner Ln
5400
Mohr Estate Middle Dr
Mohr Estate South Dr
S 450 W
5700
S 400 W
5100
W Faut Rd
33
300 S
5300
34

5
COUNTY RD 600 W

39°41'44"

HANCOCK CO
T15N
W 1200 N
T14N
SHELBY CO
W 1200 N
W 1200 N
W 1200 N
3000

Little Sugar Creek

5
46130
Sugar Creek
500 N
Moral Township
4
W   1175   N
N 425 W
400 N
11700
4000
3

39°41'18"
COUNTY RD 600 W
N 11000

85°53'57"   A   85°53'23"   B   85°52'49"   C   85°52'15"   D   85°51'42"   E   80°15'58"

RAND McNALLY

MAP 2548

SEE 2439 MAP

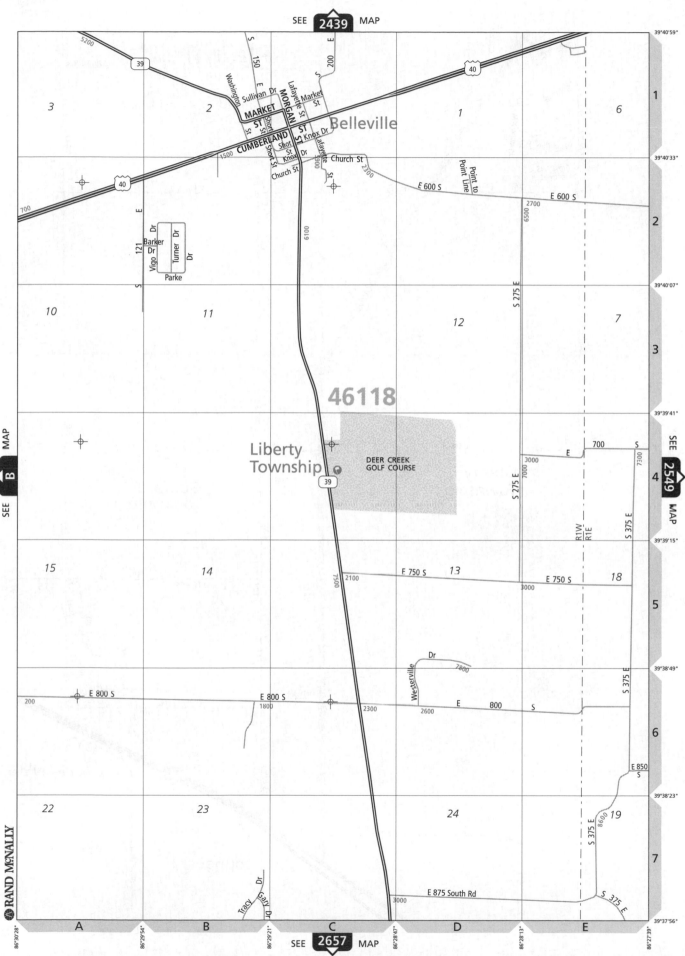

1:24,000
1 in. = 2000 ft.

0   0.25   0.5
miles

SEE 2549 MAP

SEE B MAP

Belleville

Liberty
Township

46118

DEER CREEK
GOLF COURSE

RAND MCNALLY

SEE 2657 MAP

MAP
2549

1:24,000
1 in. = 2000 ft.

0   0.25   0.5
miles

SEE 2440 MAP

Plainfield

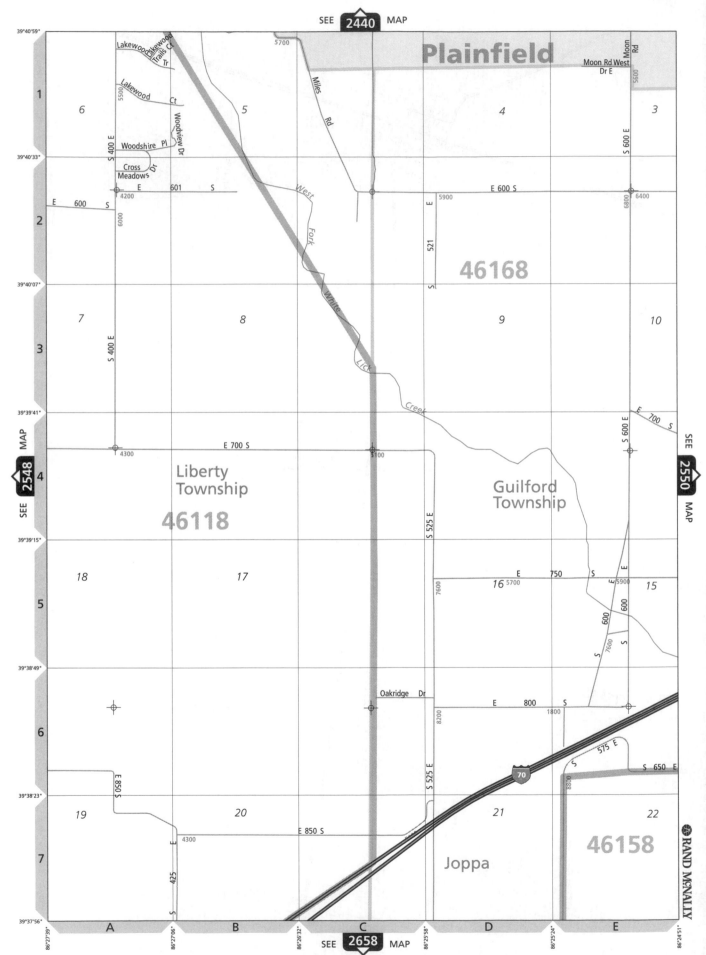

5700

Moon Rd

Moon Rd West
Dr E

5600

S 600 E

39°40'59"

1   6   5   4   3

Lakewood Lakewood
Trails Ct
Tr

Lakewood

5500

Lakewood Ct

Woodview Dr

Woodshire Pl

Cross
Meadows Dr

S 400 E

Miles Rd

West Fork

39°40'33"

E   601   S

4200

E 600 S

5900

6800   6400

E   600   S

6000

521 S 521 E

2

46168

39°40'07"

7   8   White   9   10

S 400 E

3

Lick

Creek

39°39'41"

E 700 S

4300

E 700 S

S 600 E

S 600 E

SEE 2548 MAP

4

**Liberty
Township**

46118

3100

**Guilford
Township**

SEE 2550 MAP

39°39'15"

5   18   17

S 525 E

7600

E   750   S

16 5700

E 5900

600

600

S

7600

S

15

39°38'49"

Oakridge   Dr

E   800   S

8200

1800

S 525 E

6

575 E

70

S

S 650 E

8800

39°38'23"

E 850 S

19   20

4300

E   425   S

E 850 S

21

Joppa

46158

7

S

39°37'56"

A   B   C   D   E

86°27'39"   86°27'06"   86°26'32"   86°25'58"   86°25'24"   86°24.98"

RAND McNALLY

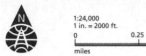

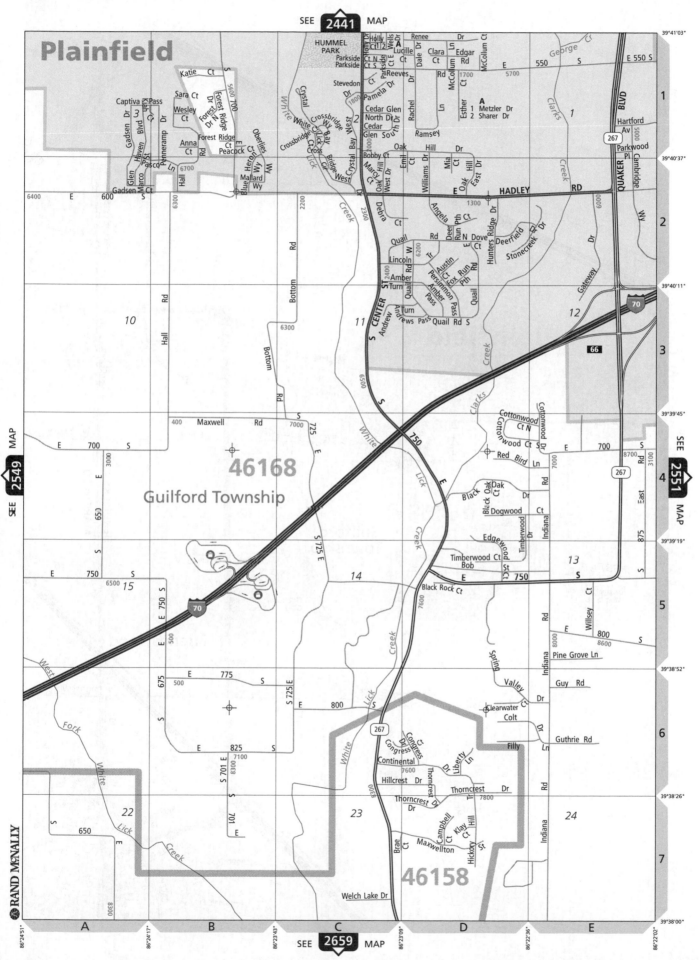

SEE 2441 MAP

Plainfield

46168

Guilford Township

46158

SEE 2549 MAP

SEE 2551 MAP

SEE 2659 MAP

RAND McNALLY

MAP
2551

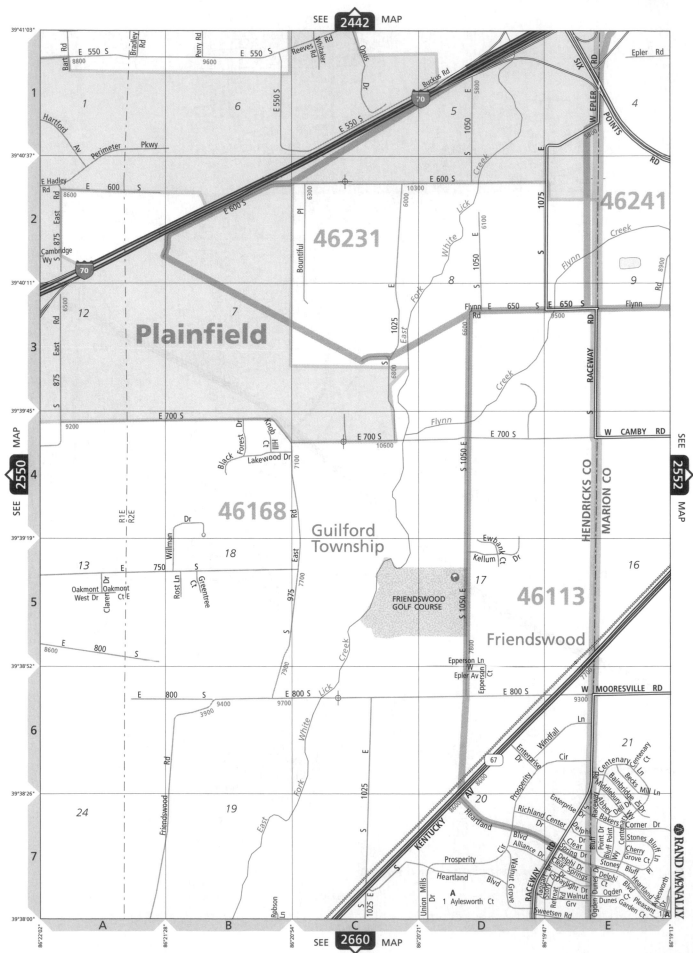

SEE 2442 MAP

39°41'03"

E 550 S
Bart Rd
8800
Bradley Rd
Perry Rd
E 550 S
Reeves Rd
Whitaker Rd
Opus Dr
9600

1

6

E 550 S

Buckus Rd

70

5

5800
1050 S

E
Six

Epler Rd

Epler Rd
W Epler Rd

4

Hartford Av
Perimeter Pkwy

39°40'37"

E Hadley Rd
8600
E 600 S

E 600 S

White Lick Creek

1075 S

46241

E 875 S
East Rd

Cambridge Wy S

70

E 600 S

Bountiful Pl
6300
46231

10300

6000 E

6100 E
1050 E

Flynn Rd

8900

9

39°40'11"

70

12
6500
East Rd

7

Plainfield

East Fork White Lick Creek

1025 S

6800 S

8
1050 E

Flynn Rd
6600 E
E 650 S
E 650 S
9500
Flynn

RACEWAY RD

39°39'45"

E 700 S

9200

Black Forest Dr
Knob Hill Ct
Lakewood Dr
7100

East Rd

Creek
Flynn

E 700 S
10600
E 700 S

W CAMBY RD

SEE
2550
MAP

R1E R2E

46168

Dr
Willman

East Rd

HENDRICKS CO
MARION CO

SEE
2552
MAP

39°39'19"

13
E 750 S

18

Rost Ln
Greentree Ct

975 S
7700

Guilford Township

Ewbank Dr
Kellum Ct

16

Oakmont West Dr
Clarendon Dr
Oakmont Ct E

17

FRIENDSWOOD GOLF COURSE

S 1050 E

46113

E 800 S
8600

7900

Lick Creek

7800

Friendswood

39°38'52"

E 800 S
3900
9400
E 800 S
9700

White Fork

1025 E

Epperson Ln
W
Epler Av
Epperson Ct

E 800 S
9300

W MOORESVILLE RD

6

24

Friendswood Rd

19

East Fork

1025 S

67

KENTUCKY AV
8600

Windfall Ln

Enterprise Dr

Cir

20

Prosperity Dr

Heartland

Centenary Ln
Centenary Ct

Becks Mill Ln
Middlebury Dr
Abbey Dell Dr
Bakers Corner Dr

21

39°38'26"

Enterprise Dr

Richland Center Dr

Delphi Dr
Clear Spring Dr

RACEWAY RD

Middlebury
Bluff Point Wy
Bluff Point
Stones Bluff Ln

Stones Bluff Blvd

Cherry Grove Ct

7

Robson Ln

Prosperity Blvd

Heartland Blvd

Walnut Grove Ct

Union Mills Rd

A
1 Aylesworth Ct

Blvd Alliance Dr
Clear Springs

Delphi Ct
Taggart Dr
Story Dr
Retreat Dr
Daylight Dr
Delphi Blvd

Grv
Ogden Dunes Ct
Ogden Dunes Garden Ct
Sweetsen Rd

Delphi Blvd
Heartland Blvd
Ogden Ct Pleasant
Walnut
Aylesworth Dr

1 A

RAND MCNALLY

39°38'00"

A   B   C   D   E

SEE 2660 MAP

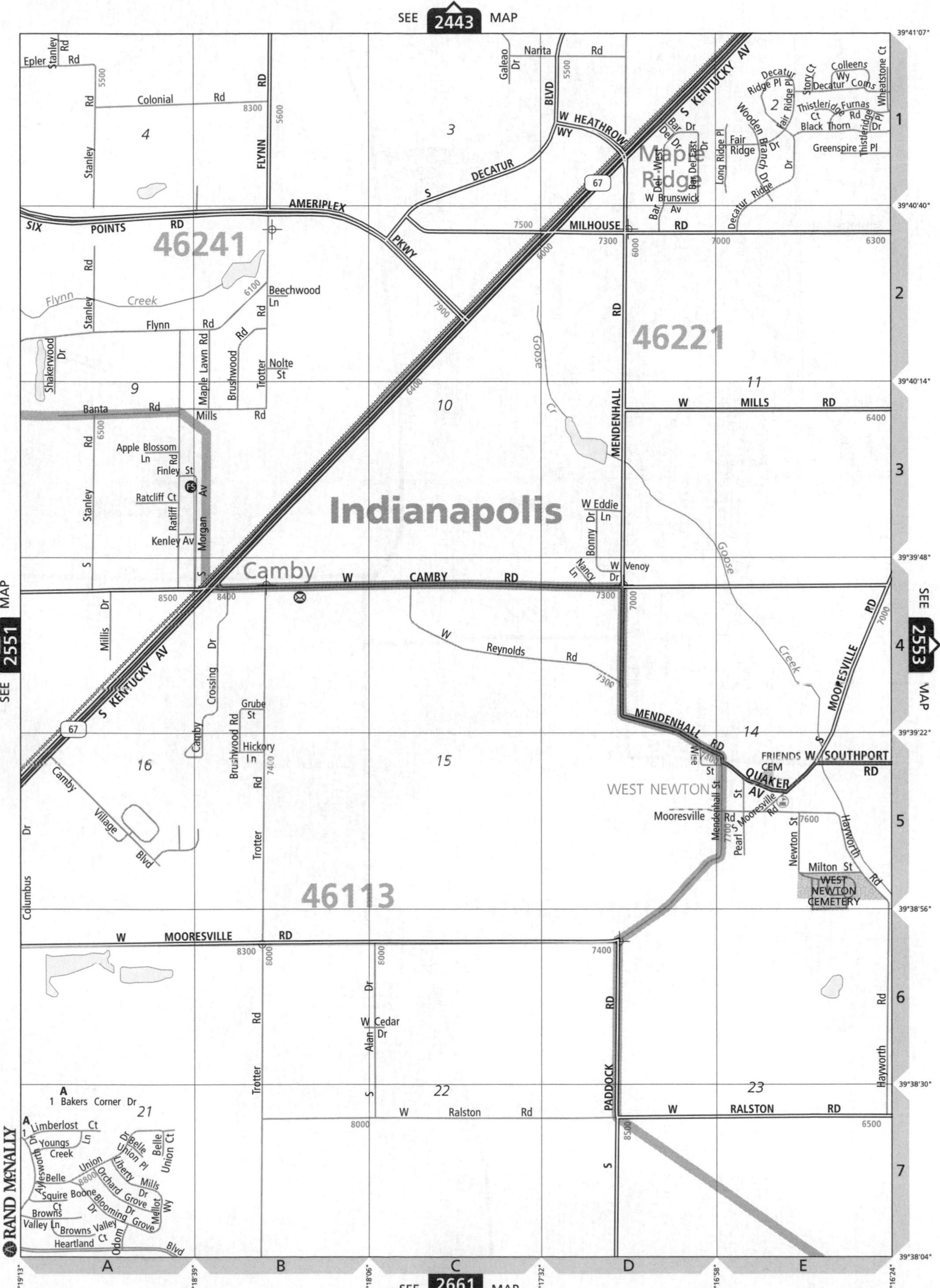

MAP
2552

N

1:24,000
1 in. = 2000 ft.

0   0.25   0.5
miles

SEE 2443 MAP

39°41'07"

Epler Stanley Rd
Stanley Rd
5500
Colonial Rd
8300
Stanley Rd
FLYNN RD
5600

Narita Dr
Galeao Dr
Rd
BLVD
5500
W HEATHROW
WY
DECATUR
S
67
Milhouse
7500
W Brunswick Av
Del Dr West
Bar Dr
Del Dr East
Bar Dr
Long Ridge Pl
Wooden Branch Dr
Fair Ridge
MENDENHALL RD

Decatur Ridge Pl
Fair Ridge Pl
Decatur Ridge
Colleens Wy
Decatur Coms
Thistleridge Ct
Black Thorn
Furnas Rd
Greenspire Pl
Thistleridge Pl
Wheatstone Ct
Ston Ct
2
1

4

3

AMERIPLEX
SIX POINTS RD
PKWY
46241

39°40'40"

7300
6000
6300
7000
6300

Flynn Creek
Stanley Rd
6500
Flynn Rd
Maple Lawn Rd
Brushwood Rd
Trotter Rd
Beechwood Ln
Nolte St
6100

Shakerwood Dr
9
Banta Rd
Mills Rd

10

46221
W MILLS RD
11
6400

2

39°40'14"

Apple Blossom Ln
Finley St
Morgan Av
Ratcliff Ct
Ratliff
Kenley Av
S
Goose Cr
Mendenhall RD
W Eddie Ln
Bonny Dr
W Venoy Dr
Nancy Ln

Indianapolis

3

39°39'48"

Camby
W CAMBY RD
8500
8400
7300
7000
Goose Creek

SEE 2551 MAP

W Reynolds Rd
7300

Millis Dr
S KENTUCKY AV
67
Camby Crossing Dr

Grube St
Brushwood Rd
7400
Hickory Ln
Camby
16
Camby Dr
Village Blvd

15
MENDENHALL RD
14
MOORESVILLE RD

FRIENDS CEM
W SOUTHPORT RD
QUAKER AV
WEST NEWTON
Mooresville Rd
Pearl St
Aisle St
Newton St
Hayworth Rd
Milton St
WEST NEWTON CEMETERY
7600
S Mooresville Rd
Mendenhall Rd

SEE 2553 MAP

4

39°39'22"

5

39°38'56"

Columbus Dr
46113
W MOORESVILLE RD
8300
8000
8000
Trotter Rd
Alan Dr
W Cedar Dr
PADDOCK RD
7400

6

39°38'30"

A
1 Bakers Corner Dr
21
Trotter Rd
S
22
W Ralston Rd
8000
23
W RALSTON RD
8500
S
6500
Hayworth Rd

7

A
1 Limberlost Ct
Ln
Youngs Creek
Aylesworth Dr
Belle
Squire Boone Ct
Browns Valley Ln
Heartland
Belle Pl
Union Pl
Orchard Grove Dr
Blooming Grove Dr
Odom Dr
Liberty Dr
Union Mills Dr
Mellot Wy
Browns Valley
Blvd
Belle
Union Ct
8800

RAND McNALLY

A   B   C   D   E

SEE 2661 MAP

86°19'13"   86°18'39"   86°18'06"   86°17'32"   86°16'58"   86°16'24"

39°38'04"

MAP
2553

N

SEE 2444 MAP

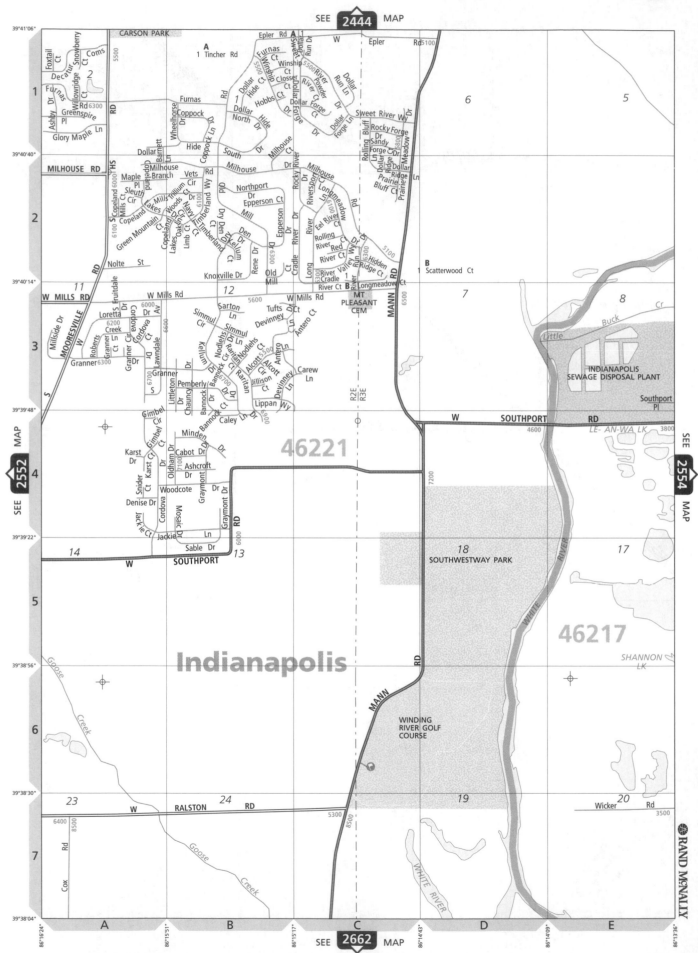

CARSON PARK

39°41'06"

A
1 Tincher Rd

Epler Rd

Epler   Rd 5100

Foxtail Ct   Snowberry Ct   Coms

Decatur   Willowridge Ct

2

Furnas
Ashby Dr   Rd 6300
Greenspire
Pl
Glory Maple Ln

1

Furnas

Coppock

Wheelhouse Dr

Dollar
Barnett Ln

Hide

South

Milhouse Dr

Furnas Dr

Winship Ct

Dollar Hide Ct   Closser Ct

Hobbs Ct

Dollar Forge Ct

Dollar North Dr

Milhouse Dr

River Run Dr

Winship

Powder River   River Forge Dr

Dollar Run Dr

Dollar Forge Dr

Sweet River Wy

Rocky Forge Dr
Sandy Forge Dr
Dollar Ridge Ln

Rolling Bluff Dr

Prairie Bluff Ct

Prairie Meadow Dr

6

5

39°40'40"

MILHOUSE RD

Maple Pl   Milhouse Branch

Dollar

Sleuth Cir

Copeland   6000

Vets Cir

Trillium Ct   Old

Northport Dr   Epperson Ct

Epperson Mill Dr

Milhouse Dr

Rocky River Dr

Riversport

Longmeadow Ct

Mills Ct   Copeland

Copeland Lakes

Green Mountain

Lakes Oak Ct   Woods

Limb Ct   Timberland Ct

Dry Den Ct   Kellum

Den Dr

Rene Dr

Eel River Ct

River Dr

Rolling River Wy

Red River Ct

River Valley Wy

Hidden Ridge Ct

Scatterwood Ct
B

2

RD

Nolte St

Knoxville Dr

Old Mill Dr

Long Cradle Ct

River Cradle Ct

Longmeadow Ct
B

7

8

39°40'14"

11

W MILLS RD

12

Fruitdale

W Mills Rd

5600

W Mills Rd

MT PLEASANT CEM

Sarton Ln

Tufts Dr   Ct

Devinney

Antero Ct

Millside Dr

MOORESVILLE

Loretta Dr
Cordova   6000 Av
Cordova Dr
Cordova Ct

Roberts

Granner Ct

Granner Dr   6600

Granner 6300

Lawndale

Simmul Cir

Simmul Cir

Kellum Dr

Nodlehs Dr

Raritan Ct

Alcott Dr   5500

Alcott Ct

Devinney Ln

Antero Ln

Carew Ln

3

Littleton Dr   6700

Granner S

Pemberly Dr

Chauncy Ct

Bannock Dr   5700

Raritan Dr

Jillison Ct

Lippan Wy

6900

39°39'48"

Gimbel Cir

Gimbel Ct

Caley Ln

Minden Dr

Cabot Dr

SOUTHPORT   RD

4600

LE-AN-WA LK   3800

SEE 2554 MAP

Karst Dr   Karst Ct

Oldham Dr

Ashcroft Dr

Bannock Dr

46221

7200

INDIANAPOLIS SEWAGE DISPOSAL PLANT

Southport Pl

4

SEE 2552 MAP

Snider Ct

Denise Dr

Woodcote Dr

Cordova

Mosaic Dr

Graymont Dr

Graymont RD   6000

39°39'22"

Jackie Ct

Jackie Dr

Sable Dr

14

13

W   SOUTHPORT

18   SOUTHWESTWAY PARK

17

5

Indianapolis

MANN RD

46217

SHANNON LK

39°38'56"

6

Goose Creek

WINDING RIVER GOLF COURSE

WHITE RIVER

39°38'30"

23

24

RALSTON   RD

W

5300

19

20
Wicker   Rd
3500

7

6400
8500

Cox Rd

Goose Creek

WHITE RIVER

39°38'04"

A   B   C   D   E

86°16'24"   86°15'51"   86°15'17"   86°14'43"   86°14'09"

SEE 2662 MAP

RAND MCNALLY

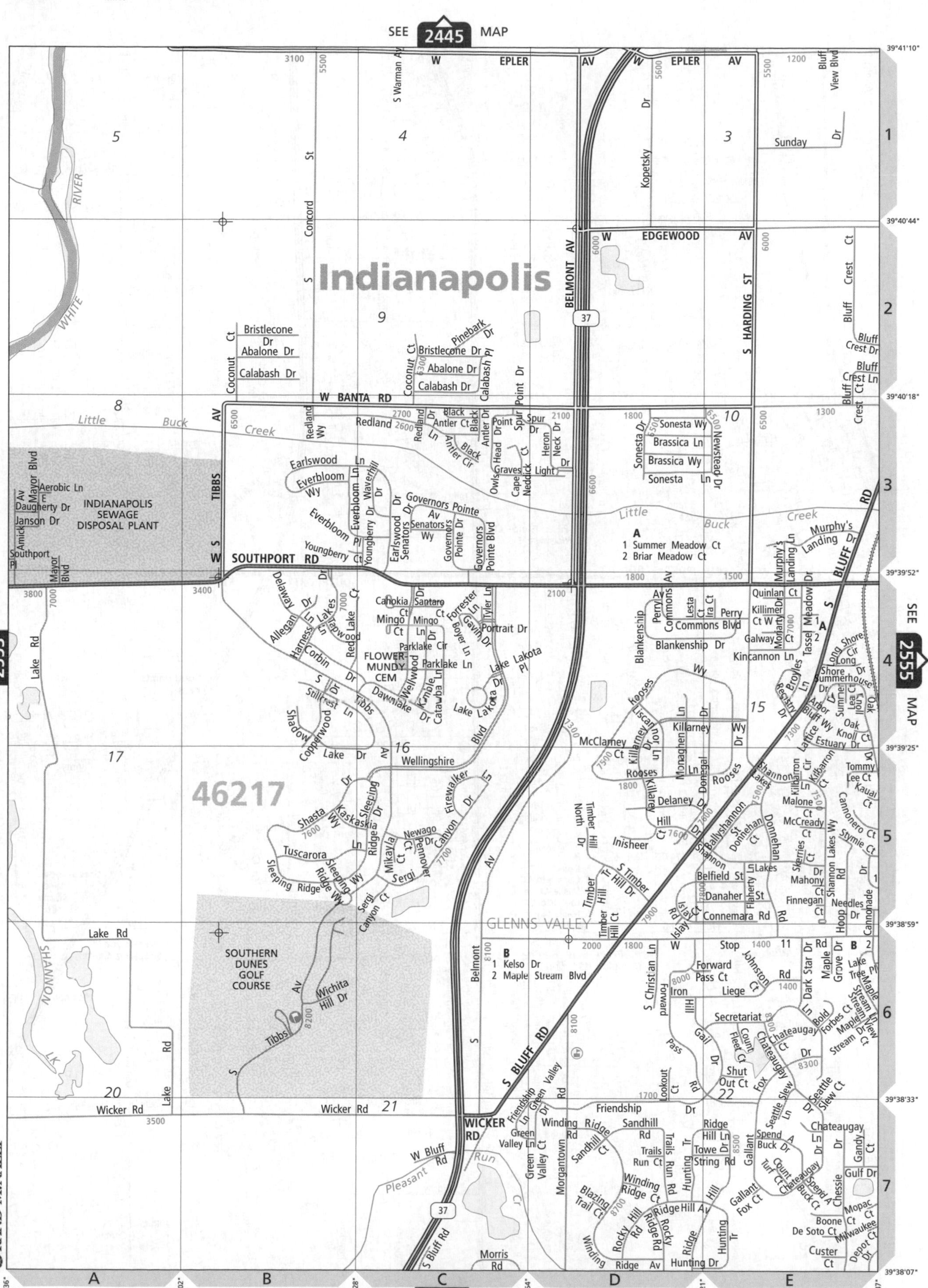

MAP
2554

1:24,000
1 in. = 2000 ft.

0   0.25   0.5
miles

SEE 2445 MAP

39°41'10"
39°40'44"
39°40'18"
39°39'52"
39°39'25"
39°38'59"
39°38'33"
39°38'07"

W   EPLER   AV   W   EPLER   AV

3100 5500   5600   5500   1200

Bluff View Blvd

S Warman Av

Kopetsky Dr

Sunday   Dr

5   4   3   1

S Concord St

Indianapolis

9

W   EDGEWOOD   AV

6000   6000

Belmont Av   S Harding St

Bluff Crest Ct

Bluff Crest Dr

Bluff Crest Ln

2

37

Bristlecone
Dr
Abalone Dr

Coconut Ct   Calabash Dr

Pinebark   Dr

Bristlecone Dr   Pl

Coconut Ct   Abalone Dr

Calabash Dr

Point Dr

Calabash Dr

W   BANTA   RD

Bluff Crest Dr

Little   Buck   Creek

8   6500

Redland Wy

Redland   2700   Black Antler Ct Dr   2100

Redland   2600   Antler Ln   Black Antler Cir   Black Antler Dr

Point   Spur Dr

Heron Neck Dr

Sonesta Wy   Ct   Newstead St

1800   6500   1300

Sonesta Dr

Brassica Ln

Brassica Wy

Sonesta   Ln   Dr

10

Earlswood Ln   Waverhill

Everbloom Wy

Everbloom Ln   Pl

Owl's Head   Cape Neddick Light   Graves Ct

6600   6500

TIBBS   AV   S

S   W   TIBBS   AV

Everbloom Pl

Youngberry Dr   Everbloom Dr

Governors Pointe

Earlswood   Av   Senators   Wy

Senators   Governors Pointe Blvd

Governors   Pointe Blvd

Little   Buck   Creek

A
1 Summer Meadow Ct
2 Briar Meadow Ct

Murphy's Landing Dr

SOUTHPORT   RD

1800   1500

Murphy's Landing

Quinlan Ct

Bluff   RD   S

3800   7000   3400   2100

Lake Rd

Delaway   Dr

Allegan   Harness Lakes   Tapwood

Cahokia   Santaro

Mingo   Mingo Ct   Ct

Forrester   Dr

Boyer Ln   Gavin Dr   Tyler Ln

Portrait Dr

Blankenship

Perry   Lesta   Ira Ct

Commons   Commons Blvd   Perry Ct W   Killimer Ct

Blankenship Dr   Galway   Moriarty   S Tassel Meadow Ct

Kincannon Ln   A

Long Shore Cir   Long

Summerhouse Dr   Shore

SEE 2553 MAP

Lorbin   Red Lake   Dr   Wellwood

FLOWER-MUNDY CEM   Parklake Cir   Parklake Ln

Dumble   Catawba   Dawnlake

Lake Lakota Pl

Lake Lakota Dr

Lake Lakota Blvd

7060   7300   7300

Lattice   Arbor Wy   Bluff Knoll Ct   Lea Ct

Registry   Oak   Lou

Summer   Lee Oak

Estuary Dr

Stillcrest   Ln   Tibbs   Av   Copperwood

Shadow Lake Dr

16

Wellingshire Dr

Rooses   Wy

Liscannor Ln   Killarney   Monaghen Ln

McClarney   Killarney Wy

Rooses

15

Tommy Lee Ct   Kauai Ct

Killarron Ct   Kilbarron Ct

Malone   7300

Cannonero Ct   Stymie Ct

17   46217

Shasta   Wy   7600

Kaskaskia   Sleeping   Ridge   Dr

Newago   Pennover   Dr   Mikayla   Firewalker Dr   Canyon   Av

Sergi   Ct

Killarney

Delaney Dr   Rooses

Hill   1800   Killarney

Inisheer   Shannon Lakes   Ballyshannon

Donnehan   Dr

McCready   Dr

Mahony Dr   Skerries Ct

Shannon Lakes Rd   Finnegan Ct

Tuscarora   Ln

Sleeping Ridge   Wy

Sleeping Ridge Wy   Sergi Canyon Ct

Timber Hill North Dr   S Timber Hill Dr   Timber Hill Dr

Shannon   Ballyshannon

Belfield St   Filherty   Lakes Dr

Danaher St   Hoop Dr   Needles Dr   Connemara Rd   Cannonade

GLENNS VALLEY

2000   1800   7900   8300

B
1 Kelso Dr
2 Maple Stream Blvd

Belmont   S

8100

Stop   1400   11

Forward Pass Ct

Liege

Forward Iron

Dark Star Dr   Maple Grove Dr   Lake   Maple   Tree Pl

8000   1400

Secretariat   Bold

Count Fleet Ct   Chateaugay Dr   8300

B   2

Maple Stream Dr   Stream Ct   View

Lake Rd

SOUTHERN DUNES GOLF COURSE

Tibbs Av   S   8200   Wichita Hill Dr

Tibbs   S

Gail   Pass   Gail Dr   Shut Out Ct   Fox   Chateaugay Dr

Seattle Slew Ln   Seattle Slew Ct   Chateaugay Dr

Lookout Ct   Spend A Buck Dr   Gallant   Gandy

1700   22

20   Wicker Rd   Lake Rd   Wicker Rd   21

3500   Friendship Ln   Friendship Dr   Ridge Hill Ln   Chateaugay Ct

WICKER   RD

Green Valley Ln   Winding Ridge Rd   Sandhill Rd   Towe Ct   String Rd   Spend A Buck Ct   Gallant Dr

W Bluff Rd   Green Valley Ct   Sandhill Ct   Trails Run Ct   Hunting   Chessie

Pleasant   Run   Morgantown Rd   Winding Ridge Ct   Trails Run Rd   Ridge Hill   Gallant Fox Ct   Chateaugay Ct   Mopac

37   Blazing Trail Ct   8700   Ridge Hill Av   Hunting   Boone Ct   Milwaukee

Morris Rd   Rocky Hill Rd   Rocky Ridge Rd   Winding Ridge Av   Ridge   Hunting Dr   De Soto Ct   Depot Dr   Custer Ct

SEE 2555 MAP

A   B   C   D   E

SEE 2663 MAP

86°13'36"   86°13'02"   86°12'28"   86°11'54"   86°11'21"   86°10'47"

RAND McNALLY

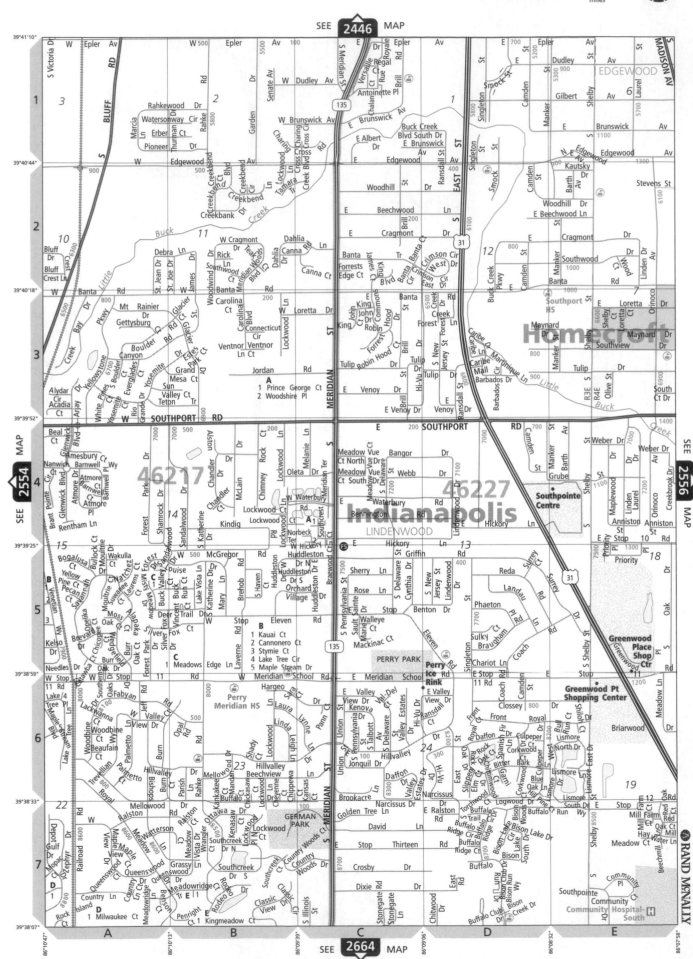

MAP 2555

1:24,000
1 in. = 2000 ft.

0   0.25   0.5
miles

SEE 2446 MAP

SEE 2554 MAP

SEE 2556 MAP

SEE 2664 MAP

RAND McNALLY

MAP
2556

1:24,000
1 in. = 2000 ft.

0   0.25   0.5
miles

39°41'13"

39°40'47"

1

46227

39°40'21"

PERRY MANOR

2

Horcroft

Indianapolis

39°39'55"

SEE 2555 MAP

SEE 2557 MAP

TWIN BROOKS

3

Southport

65

E SOUTHPORT RD

4

46237

39°39'28"

5

B1

B

39°39'02"

1 Santolina Dr
2 Wallien Ct
3 Whichman Wy
4 Preidt Pl
5 Brookfield Dr
6 Pearson Pl

6

21

SMOCK MUNICIPAL
GOLF COURSE

39°38'36"

D
1 Country Walk Dr
2 Summer Walk Dr S
3 Sunburst Cir
4 S Country Walk Dr

C
1 Paso del Norte Dr
2 Del Prado Dr
3 Punto Alto Ct
4 Punto Alto Cir

E COUNTRY LINE RD

7

39°38'10"

COMMUNITY
HOSPITAL - SOUTH

RAND MCNALLY

31

A   B   C   D   E

86°07'58"   86°07'24"   86°06'51"   86°06'17"   86°05'43"   86°05'09"

MAP 2557

1:24,000
1 in. = 2000 ft.
0   0.25   0.5
miles

SEE 2448 MAP

Indianapolis

46239

46237

SEE 2556 MAP

SEE 2558 MAP

46259

A
1 Wagon Wheel Tr
B
1 Quail Feather Ct
2 Overcrest Dr

C
1 Iron Oaks Ct
D
1 Apple Branch Wy

E
1 Southern Trails Dr
F
1 Seabrook Dr
2 Streamwood Ln
3 Shores Edge Pl
4 Shores Edge Wy

G
1 Lovage Ct

H
1 Ehlerbrook Rd
J
1 Buck Pond Pl

K
1 N Combs Rd

St. Francis Hospital

RAND McNALLY

SEE 2666 MAP

MAP
2558

1:24,000
1 in. = 2000 ft.
0   0.25   0.5
miles

SEE 2449 MAP

46239

46259
Indianapolis

SEE 2557 MAP

SEE 2559 MAP

FRANKLIN TOWNSHIP COMMUNITY PARK

Franklin Central HS

DAKOTA LANDING GOLF CLUB

A 1 Silver Lake Dr
B 1 N Matthews Rd

MARION CO
JOHNSON CO

RAND MCNALLY

SEE 2667 MAP

MAP
2559

1:24,000
1 in. = 2000 ft.

0   0.25   0.5
miles

SEE 2450 MAP

46239

Charlesmac Village

SOUTHEASTWAY PARK

46126

Indianapolis

46259

SEE 2558 MAP

SEE 2560 MAP

MARION CO

SHELBY CO

Moral Township

MARION CO

JOHNSON CO

SEE 2668 MAP

A B C D E

RAND McNALLY

MAP
2560

1:24,000
1 in. = 2000 ft.

0   0.25   0.5
miles

SEE 2451 MAP

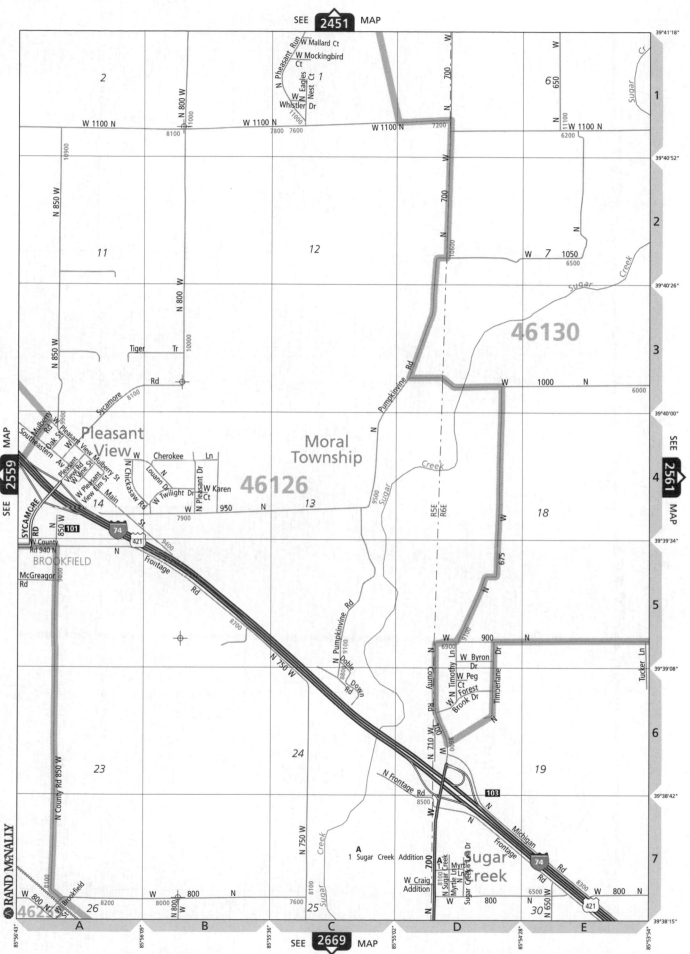

SEE
2559
MAP

SEE
2551
MAP

N Pheasant Run
W Mallard Ct
W Mockingbird Ct
N Eagles Nest Ct
W Whistler Dr

W 1100 N
W 1100 N
W 1100 N

N 800 W
N 850 W
N 850 W

Tiger Tr
Sycamore Rd

Pleasant View

Mulberry Rd
Oak St
N Pleasant View Av
Pleasant View Rd
W Vine St
W Pleasant View Elm St
N Chickasaw Rd
Cherokee Ln
Louann Dr
N Twilight Dr
W Pleasant Dr
W Karen Ct
N Mulberry St
Main St

Southeastern

SYCAMORE RD
N 850 W
101
74
421

W County Rd 940 N

BROOKFIELD

McGreagor Rd

N County Rd 850 W

Frontage Rd

N 750 W

Pumpkinvine Rd
N Doble Down Rd

Moral Township
46126

46130

Sugar Creek

Pumpkinvine Rd

R5E R6E

W 1000 N

W 900 N
W Byron Dr
W Peg Ct
W Timothy Ln
Forest Bronk Dr
Timberlane Dr
Tucker Ln

N County Rd 700 W

N Frontage Rd
103
74
Michigan Frontage Rd

Sugar Creek

A
1 Sugar Creek Addition
A
Myrtle Ln
Sugar Creek Lea Dr
W Craig Addition
N Sugar Creek
Myrtle Ln

W 800 N
W Brookfield
4625
W 800 N
W 800 N
421

A   B   C   D   E

MAP
2561

1:24,000
1 in. = 2000 ft.

0   0.25   0.5
miles

SEE 2452 MAP

39°41'18"

6   5   W   1120   N   4   3

1   4800 W
500 W   490 W W1110 480 W   1110   460   W 1100 N   400 W
                                    N   W   N   N   1100
W 1100 N   5300   4000

39°40'52"

Little Sugar Creek

N COUNTY RD 600 W

Sugar Creek

2   7   W 1050 N 8   9   W 1050 N   10
                    5100

39°40'26"

46130

3   W 1000 N   W 1000 N
          5300   4200

39°40'00"

Moral Township

SEE 2560 MAP

4   16

          18   17   W   950   N   15
                                        4200

39°39'34"

N 500 W

5   5300
                              5100

N COUNTY RD 600 W

W 900 N   9200   W 900 N
5800   5100   4100

SEE B MAP

39°39'08"

N 400 W

6   19   20   21   22

46126

39°38'42"

Dry Fork

7   W 800 N
                              5000

          8000   9000   W 800 N
          7500
30   29   28   27

39°38'16"

85°53'54" A   85°53'21" B   85°52'47" C   85°52'13" D   85°51'39" E   .90.l5.s58

SEE 2670 MAP

RAND McNALLY

MAP
2657

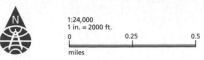

1:24,000
1 in. = 2000 ft.

0   0.25   0.5
miles

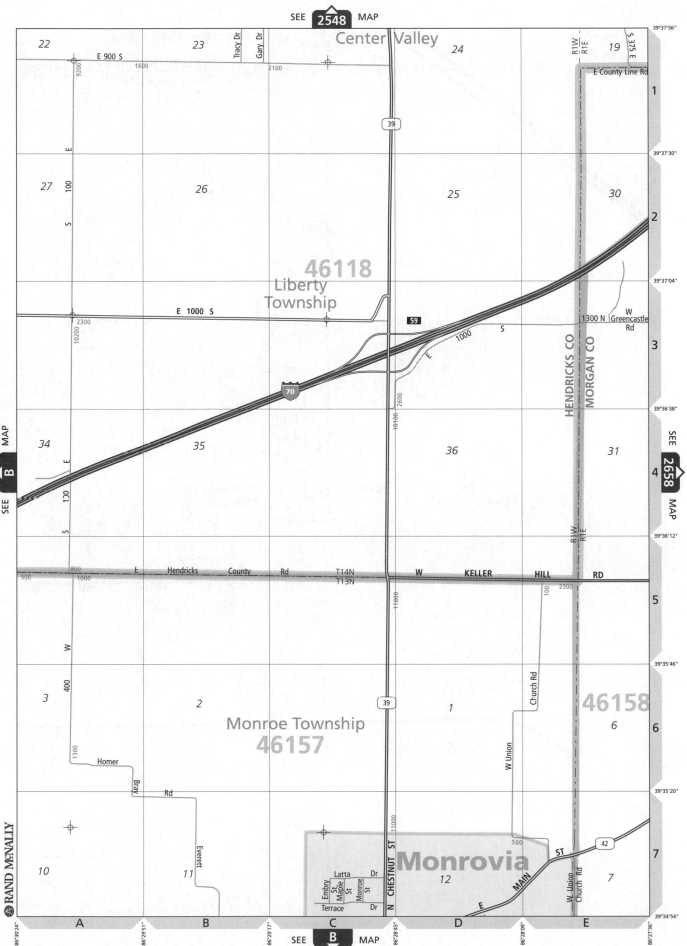

Center Valley

22   23   Tracy Dr Gary Dr   24   R1W R1E   19   S 375 E

E 900 S

9200   1600   2100   E County Line Rd   1

27   100   26   25   30

E   2

S   46118

S   Liberty
                 Township

E 1000 S

2300   59   1300 N W
10200   1000 S Greencastle
                                                                                        Rd   3

                                                    E

                                                                  70   2600

34   E   35   36   31

130   S   SEE 2658 MAP

                                                                          R1W R1E

                                                                                  39°36'12"   4

SEE B MAP

800   E   Hendricks   County   Rd   T14N   W   KELLER   HILL   RD
500   1000   T13N   2300   5
                                                                  100

                                              11800

                                                                        Church Rd

3   W   2   1   46158

400   6

1300   Homer   6
        Bray
        Rd   W Union
                Everett   ST 42
10   11   7

                        Latta Dr   Monrovia   12   MAIN   7
                   Embry St Maple St Monroe St   E
                   Terrace Dr   N CHESTNUT ST   500   W Union Church Rd

A   B   C   D   E

RAND MCNALLY

MAP
2658

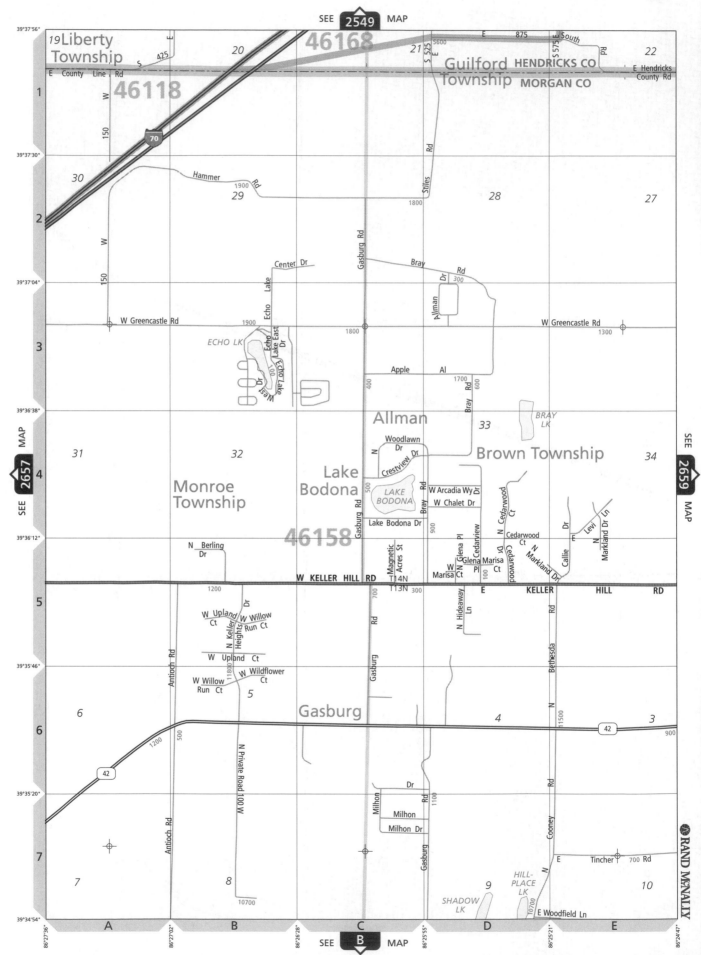

SEE 2549 MAP

1:24,000
1 in. = 2000 ft.

0   0.25   0.5
miles

39°37'56"

19 Liberty
Township

20

46168

21

Guilford
Township HENDRICKS CO

22

E 425

S

E County Line Rd

E Hendricks
County Rd

S 525

S 575

E South
Rd

5600

E 875

46118

HENDRICKS CO
MORGAN CO

1

W 150

70

39°37'30"

30

Hammer

1900

Rd

28

27

29

Stiles

Rd

1800

W 150

2

Gasburg Rd

Bray

Rd

Dr 300

Center Dr

39°37'04"

Echo Lake

W Greencastle Rd

1900

1800

Allman

W Greencastle Rd

1300

3

ECHO LK

Echo
Lake East
Dr

Echo Lake

400

Apple

Al

1700

Bray Rd

600

West Dr

39°36'38"

BRAY
LK

Allman

33

SEE 2657 MAP

31

32

Woodlawn
Dr

N

Crestview Dr

Brown Township

34

SEE 2659 MAP

Lake
Bodona

Monroe
Township

LAKE
BODONA

500

Bray Rd

W Arcadia Wy Dr

W Chalet Dr

Cedarwood

Ct

N

Cedarwood

Lewi

Dr

N

Markland Dr

Ln

4

39°36'12"

Gasburg Rd

46158

Lake Bodona Dr

900

Cedarview

Cedarwood

Ct

Cedarwood

Ct

Cedarwood

100

Callie

Dr

E

N

Markland Dr

N Berling
Dr

Magnetic
Acres St

T14N

N Glena Pl

Glena Marisa
Pl Ct

39°36'12"

W Keller Hill Rd

T13N

700

E

KELLER

W Marisa

HILL

RD

1200

300

N Hideaway
Ln

Bethesda Rd

5

W Upland
Ct

N Keller
Heights

Willow
Run Ct

Dr

39°35'46"

Antioch Rd

11800

W Upland Ct

W Wildflower
Ct

6

W Willow
Run Ct

5

Gasburg Rd

Gasburg

4

42

900

3

39°35'20"

6

1200

500

N Private Road 100 W

42

11500

Cooney Rd

Milhon

Dr

Milhon

1100

Milhon Dr

7

39°35'20"

Antioch Rd

Gasburg Rd

HILL-
PLACE
LK

E

Tincher

700 Rd

7

8

10700

9

SHADOW
LK

10700

E Woodfield Ln

10

39°34'54"

A

B

C

D

E

86°27'36"

86°27'02"

86°26'28"

86°25'55"

86°25'21"

SEE B MAP

SEE 2550 MAP

Guilford Township
HENDRICKS CO
MORGAN CO
46168
E HENDRICKS COUNTY RD
W Fk White Lick Cr
S 650 E
Indiana Rd
22
23
24
25
26
27
6900
6300
7700
8300
8600

Sharon Ct
Star Ln
Northpointe Dr
Westwood Dr
Delwood Dr
Devonwood Dr
Northfield Dr
McKinley Dr
Fairwood Dr
Canaan Ct
Fairlane
Trinity
Wagon Tr
Pioneer Ct
Pioneer Pl
Wagon Trail Cir
Wagon Trail Ct
Victor
Victor Dr
Oak Grove Ct
Cottonwood Dr
Sherwood Dr
Sugarwood Dr
Willow Dr
Raesta
Estate Dr
Williams Dr
Westbrook Dr
Dunn Dr
Edgewood Dr
Eastview Dr
Wy
Holiday Ln
Divinity Ct
Locust Ln
Solomon St
Sweetwood Dr
Pine Ct
Hadley Woodland St
North Center Dr
Nelson Dr
Sunset Mnr
Greenwood Dr
Carolyn Ln
Crestwood Dr
Highland Dr
Maryvale Ct
Sunbury Dr
White Lick Rd
300
267
A
1 Parkview Dr
Denny Dr
Northridge Dr
Mooresville HS
INDIANA
N
Morningstar Dr
Church St
Clair St
Arlington Dr
Brentwood Dr
Rose Ln
Terrace Tr
Campus Ct
Styleline Dr
Carlisle St
Carlisle St
Maple St
Bishop St
Taylor St
Wheeler Av
Churchill Dr
Stormy Ln
Circle Dr
Hadley St
Bridge St
W Greencastle Rd
900
W Greencastle Rd
Academy Building Museum
Taegart Dr
Morgan Dr
Carter Dr
Jefferson St
Northeast St
Bolton Av
Memorial Dr
Memorial
N MONROE ST
Washington St
Concord St
Lincoln Ln
E Washington St
Franklin St
Main St
Commerce Dr
West St
Harrison Av
600
E MAIN ST
W MAIN ST
W Harrison
Harrison St
Clay St
Madison St
Broad St
Al
200
Mooresville
S MONROE ST
Broad St
Concord Dr
E HIGH ST
CEM
42
HIGH ST
Lockerbie St
W
Jefferson St
South St
South St
Park Dr
Keller Dr
Bingham Rd
400
35
34
46158
36
OLD TOWN PARK
Brown Township
White Lick Creek
E Moore St
67
The Village Shopping Center
2100
ROSS-WISE LK
Southbridge St
S Indiana St
Southbridge Shopping Center
Park
E KELLER HILL RD
900
T14N
T13N
100
E Jessup Ct
Jessup
Jessup Wy
Jessup Ct
Trace Run
Evergreen Ln
Lambert Ct
1800
Oldfield Ln
Oldfield Dr
Oldfield Ln
S Oldfield Ln
BETHEL RD
Charmil Dr
1
2
3
42
800
White Lick Cr
Bunker Hill Rd
Brown Township
E Tincher Rd
700
MANN LK
10
11
12
CROSBY RD
2200
400
11000
Sundown Manor
67
B
1 Eastwood Dr
2 S Old IN-67
Worth Ct
Woodside Dr
Center Ct
South
Rainbow Ln
Rosewood Dr
Bethel Church Rd
400
800
E Fk White Lick

39°38'00"
39°37'34"
39°37'08"
39°36'42"
39°36'16"
39°35'50"
39°35'24"
39°34'58"
1
2
3
4
5
6
7
A
B
C
D
E
86°24'47"
86°24'13"
86°23'40"
86°23'06"
86°22'32"
86°21'58"

SEE 2658 MAP
SEE 2660 MAP
SEE B MAP

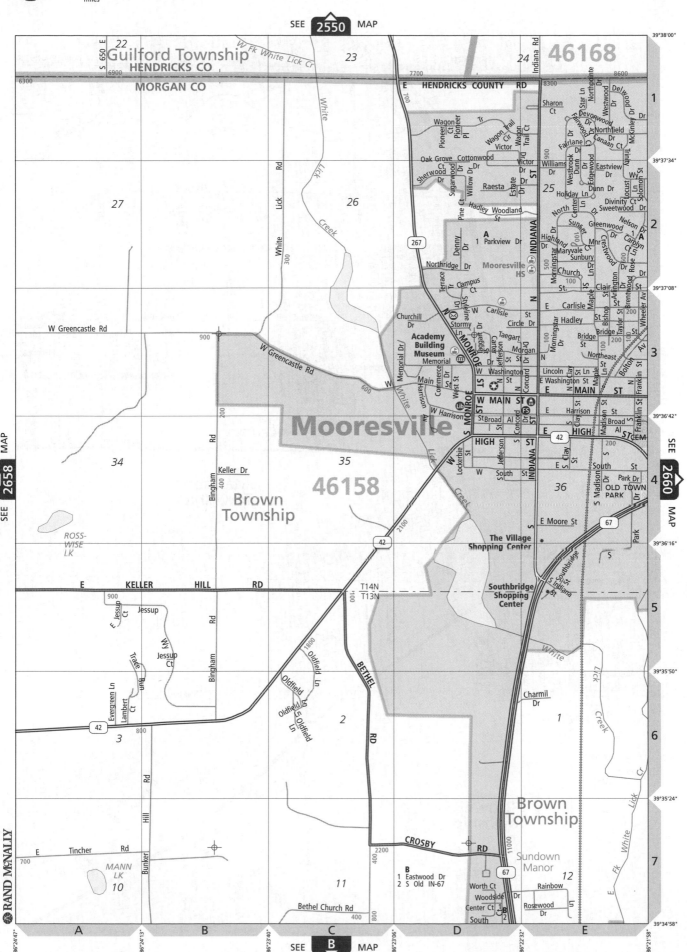

MAP
2660

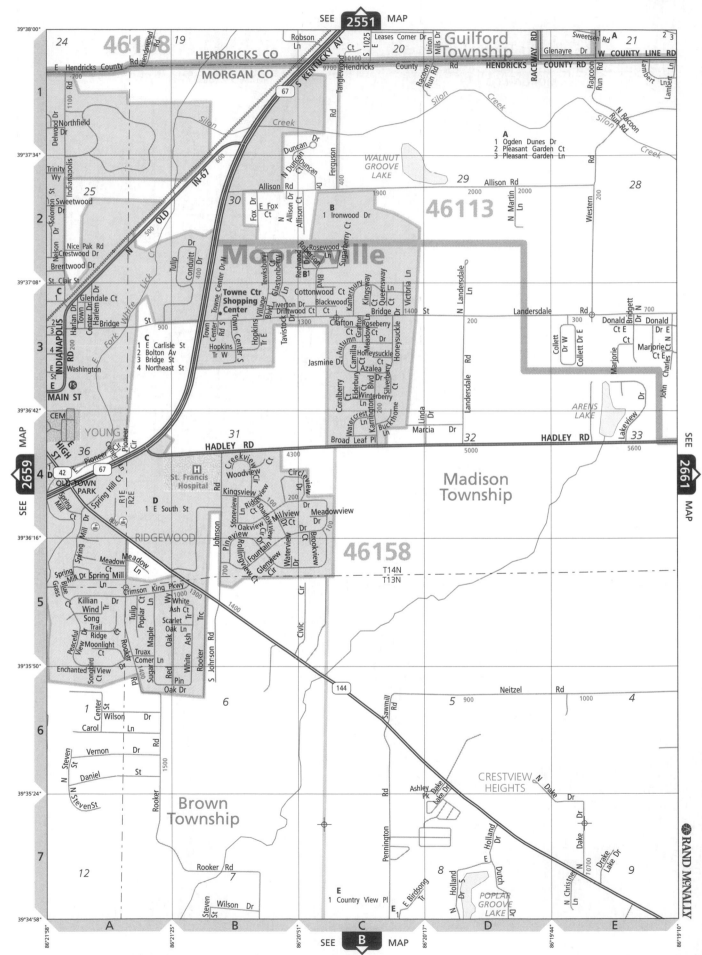

SEE 2551 MAP

24   46158   19   Robson Ln   Leases Corner Dr   Union   20   Guilford Township   Glenayre Dr   W COUNTY LINE RD   21   2 3

HENDRICKS CO / MORGAN CO

E Hendricks County Rd

HENDRICKS COUNTY RD

RACEWAY RD

A
1 Ogden Dunes Dr
2 Pleasant Garden Ct
3 Pleasant Garden Ln

Silon Creek

WALNUT GROVE LAKE

46113

Allison Rd

29   Allison Rd   28

1   Northfield Dr   Delwood Dr

25   Indianapolis St   Sweetwood Dr

Nice Pak Rd
Crestwood Dr
Brentwood Dr

2   Duncan Dr   Allison Rd   E Fox Ct   Fox Dr   30   B
1 Ironwood Dr
Sugarberry Ct

Rosewood

Moorsville

St. Clair St   C 1   Glendale Ct   Conduitt Dr   Tulip Dr   Towne Ctr Shopping Center   Cottonwood Ct   Kingsway   Queensway   Victoria Ln   N Landersdale Rd   Landersdale Rd   Donald Ct E   Bridgett Dr   Donald Dr E

3   Indianapolis Rd   Harlan Dr   Town Center Dr   Bridge St   Hopkins Village Blvd   Tiverton Dr   Driftwood Ct   Bridge St   Collett Dr W   Collett Dr E   Marjorie Ct   Marjorie Dr   Marjorie Ct E   John Charles Dr

C
1 E Carlisle St
2 Bolton Av
3 Bridge St
4 Northeast St

Washington   Jasmine Dr   Camilla Dr   Azalea   Honeysuckle   Landersdale Rd

MAIN ST   E   Coralberry   Elderbury Blvd   Winterberry   Silverberry   Karrington Ln   Linda Dr   ARENS LAKE   Lakeview Dr

CEM   YOUNG   36   31   Broad Leaf Pl   32   HADLEY RD   33

SEE 2659 MAP   HIGH ST   Pioneer Cir   HADLEY RD   Creekview Ct   4300

42   67   Woodview Cir   Circleview Dr   5000   Madison Township   5600

4   D 1   OLD TOWN PARK   St. Francis Hospital   Kingsview Ct   Ridgeview Ct   Millview Ct   Meadowview Dr   SEE 2661 MAP

Spring Hill Ct   Stoneview Ct   Shadowview   Brookview Dr

RIDGEWOOD   Pineview Ct   Oakview Ct   Glenview Cir   Waterview Dr

46158

D
1 E South St   Rollingview Ct   Fountain Dr   T14N / T13N

Spring Mill   Meadow Ct   Meadow Ln   Blue Grass   Spring Mill Dr

5   Killian Wind Tr   White Tulip Wy   Ash Ct   Scarlet Oak Ln   Civic Cir   5   900   1000   4

Song Trail   Poplar Ct   Maple Dr   White Ash Trc   Neitzel Rd

Ridge   Moonlight Ct   Truax Comer Ln   Sugar Ln   Red Pin Oak Dr

Peaceful View   Songbird Ct   Enchanted View Ct   Rooker Dr   S Johnson Rd

6   1 Center St   Wilson Dr   6   144   Sawmill Rd

Carol Ln

Vernon Dr   Rooker Rd

N Steven St   Daniel St   1500   CRESTVIEW HEIGHTS   N Dake Dr

39°35'24"   Ashley Pk   Lake Dr   Holland Dr   Dake Dr

Brown Township   Pennington Rd   Dutch Dr   Drake Lake Dr

7   12   Rooker Rd   7   8   E Birdsong Tr   Holland Dr   POPLAR GROVE LAKE   N Christner Ln   10700   9

Steven St   Wilson Dr   E
1 Country View Pl   E 1

SEE B MAP

A   B   C   D   E

RAND McNALLY

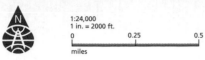

1:24,000
1 in. = 2000 ft.
0   0.25   0.5
miles

MAP
2661

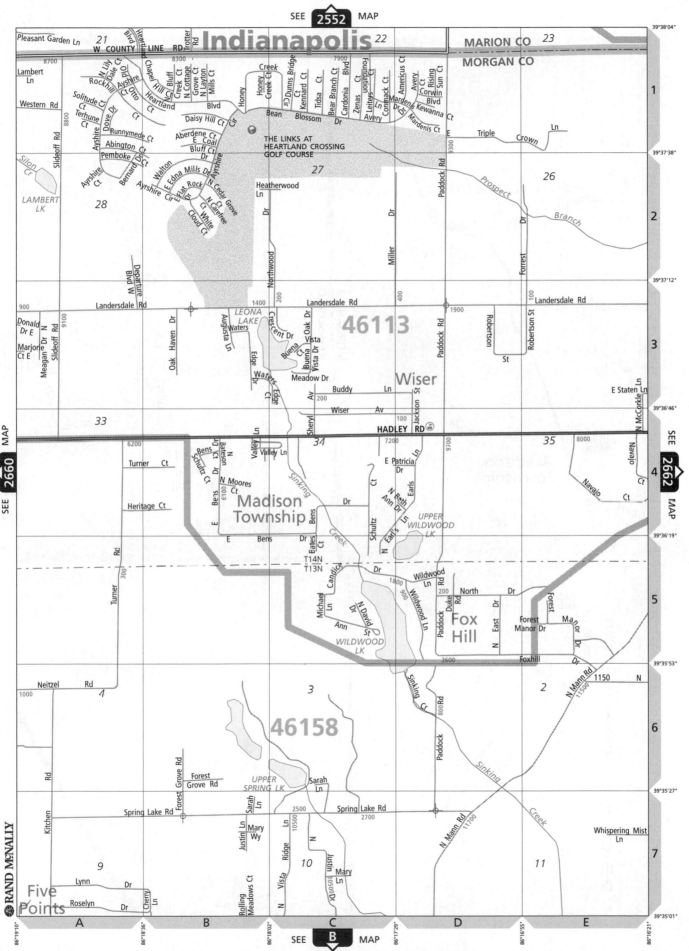

SEE **2552** MAP

Indianapolis

Pleasant Garden Ln   21   22   MARION CO   23
W COUNTY LINE RD Trotter Rd   MORGAN CO

Lambert Ln   N Lily Dale Ct   Creek   7900
8700   Rockhill Ct Otto Ct Bluff Ct N Cottage   Honey   Creek Ct   Foundation Ct Americus Ct   1
Western Rd   Solitude Ct Dove Dr   N Layton Ct Honey Creek Cir Dunns Bridge Ct Bear Branch Ct Zenas Leiters Connack Avery Ct Corwin Blvd Rising Sun Ct
8800   Terhune Ct   Grove Ct Blvd   Kennard Ct Tidsa Cardonia Ct Avery Dr Mardene Ct Kewanna Ct
                  Ayshire Ct Runnymede Ct   Daisy Hill Ct   Bean Blossom Dr   Mardenis Ct
                  Abington Ct Aberdene Ct E Coal Ct   9300 E Triple Crown Ln
Silon Cr   Pemboke Ct Bernard Bluff Ct   THE LINKS AT   Paddock Rd
                  Ayrshire Ct Walton E Edna Mills Dr Ayrshire   HEARTLAND CROSSING   Prospect
LAMBERT LK   28   Ayrshire Cir Flat Rock Dr N Cedar Grove GOLF COURSE 27   Dr Forrest Branch 26
Slideoff Rd   G White N Carefree   Heatherwood Ln   2
                  Cloud Ct Carefree   Dr   Miller
                  Departure Blvd W   Northwood 200   Dr   Forrest
900   Landersdale Rd   1400   Landersdale Rd 400   1900 100 Landersdale Rd
Donald Dr E   9100 Slideoff Rd   Oak Haven Dr Augusta Ln LEONA Waters Buena Oak Dr 46113   Robertson Landersdale Rd 3
Marjorie Ct E   Meagan Dr E   Crescent Dr LAKE Vista Buena Vista Dr   Paddock Rd St Robertson St 100
                                                Edge Meadow Dr   Wiser E Staten Ln
                  33   Waters Edge Ct   Buddy Ln   Jackson St   N McCorkle Ln
                                                Av 200 Wiser Av   100   SEE
                                                Sheryl   HADLEY RD   2662
                  6200   Bateson Dr Valley Ln 34   7200   9700   35 8000   MAP
Turner Ct   Bens Dr Schultz Ct N Moores Ct   E Patricia Dr   Navajo 4
                  Schultz Ct 6100   Earls Reth Ann Dr Ct   Navajo Ct
Heritage Ct   Bens E Dr   Bens   Schultz Dr N Earls Ln UPPER WILDWOOD LK   Ct
Turner Rd 300   Bens E   Bens Dr Eates Ct Creek   N Dr   Wildwood Ln North Dr Forest 5
                  Madison Township   T14N T13N   1800 Wildwood Rd 200 Duke Rd Forest Manor Dr Manor Dr
                  Michael Ln N David St   Candice Dr 900 Wildwood Ln Fox Hill N East Dr Foxhill Dr
                  WILDWOOD LK   Ann   2600 Foxhill Dr
Neitzel Rd   1000   4   3   Sinking Cr 800 Rd   N Mann Rd 1150 N
                                                                                             11500
46158   Forest Grove Rd   Paddock   Sinking 6
                  Forest Grove Rd UPPER SPRING LK Sarah Ln   Rd   Creek
Rd Kitchen   Spring Lake Rd Forest Grove Rd Sarah Ln 2500 Spring Lake Rd 2700   N Mann Rd 11700 Whispering Mist 7
                  Justin Ln Mary Wy 10500 N Vista Ridge 10 Justin Ln Mary Ln 9   N Mann Rd   Ln
9   Lynn Dr Cherry Ln Rolling Meadows Ct N 10500 Dr 11   2
Five Points   Roselyn Dr

RAND McNALLY

SEE **B** MAP

A   B   C   D   E

MAP
2662

1:24,000
1 in. = 2000 ft.

0   0.25   0.5
miles

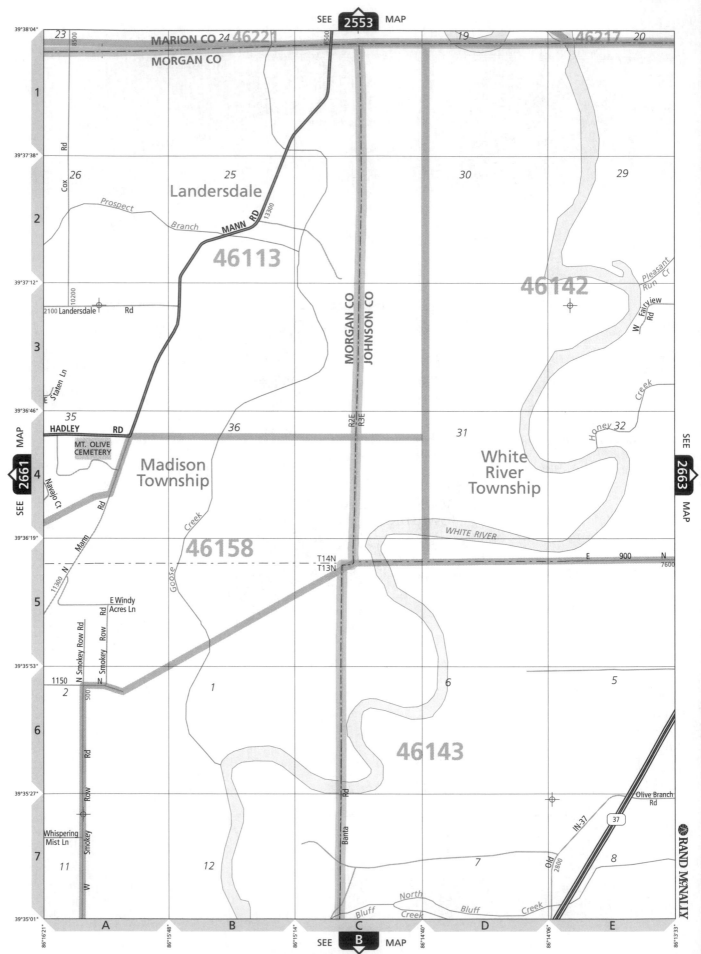

SEE **2553** MAP

39°38'04"
23   8500   MARION CO 24 **46221**   19   **46217** 20
MORGAN CO

1

39°37'38"
26   Cox Rd   25   Landersdale   30   29

Prospect
2   Branch   MANN RD   13300
46113

39°37'12"
110200
10200
2100 Landersdale   Rd   **46142**   Pleasant Run Cr
3   Staten Ln   MORGAN CO   JOHNSON CO   W Fairview Rd   Creek

39°36'46"
35   HADLEY   RD   36   R2E R3E   31   Honey 32
MT. OLIVE
CEMETERY
4   Madison
Township   White
River
Township
Navajo Ct

SEE 2661 MAP
SEE 2663 MAP

39°36'19"
46158   Goose Creek   Mann Rd   11300 N   WHITE RIVER
T14N
T13N   E   900   N   7600

5   E Windy
Acres Ln
N Smokey Row Rd   N Smokey Row Rd

39°35'53"
1150   1   6   5
2   500

6   Rd   **46143**

39°35'27"
Row Rd   Banta Rd   Olive Branch Rd
Old 2800   IN-37   37

7   Whispering
Mist Ln   W Smokey
11   12   7   8

39°35'01"
North Bluff Creek   Bluff   Creek
86°16'21"   A   86°15'48"   B   86°15'14"   C   86°14'40"   D   86°14'06"   E   86°13'33"

SEE **B** MAP

RAND McNALLY

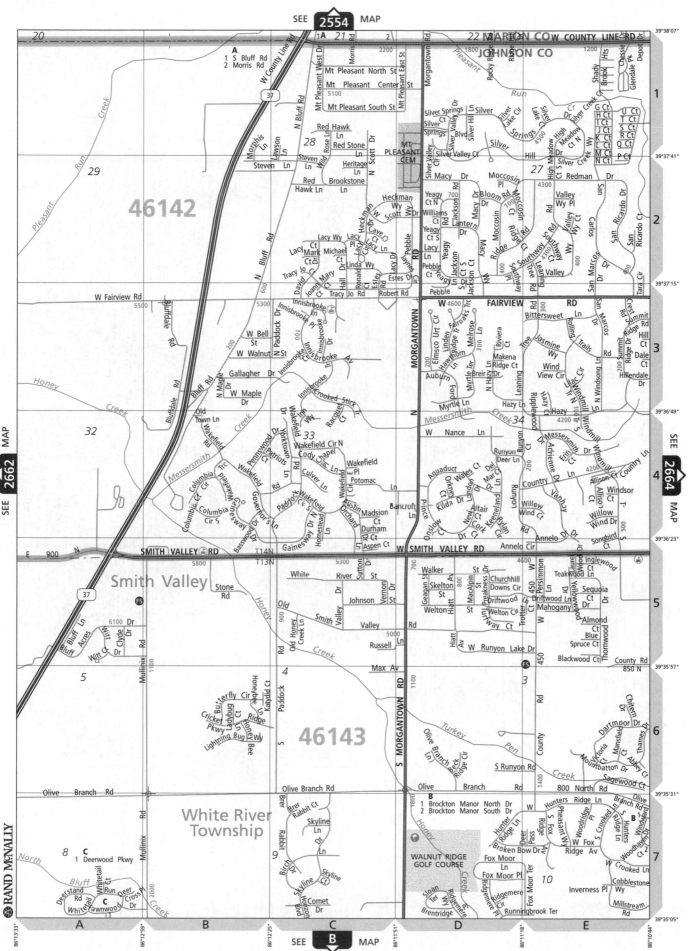

MAP 2663

1:24,000
1 in. = 2000 ft.
0 0.25 0.5
miles

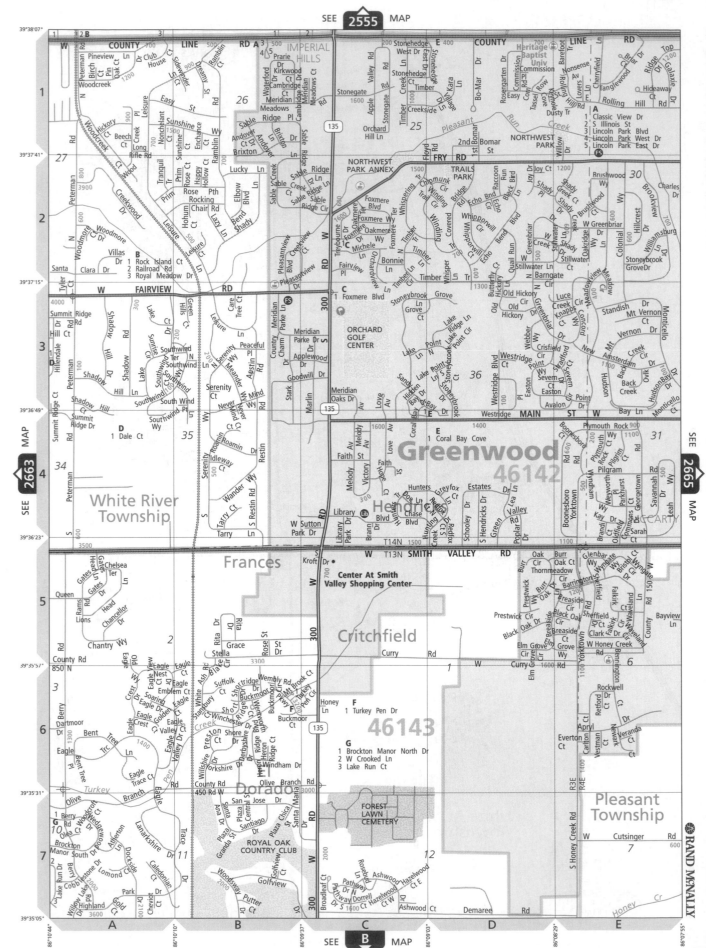

SEE 2555 MAP

SEE 2663 MAP

SEE 2665 MAP

SEE B MAP

Greenwood
46142
46143
White River Township
Pleasant Township
Frances
Critchfield
Dorado
Hendricks
McCarty
IMPERIAL HILLS
NORTHWEST PARK
NORTHWEST PARK ANNEX
TRAILS PARK
ORCHARD GOLF CENTER
Center At Smith Valley Shopping Center
FOREST LAWN CEMETERY
ROYAL OAK COUNTRY CLUB
Heritage Baptist Univ

W COUNTY LINE RD
FRY RD
W FAIRVIEW RD
W MAIN ST
W SMITH VALLEY RD
COUNTY RD 850 N
County Rd 450 Rd W
W Curry Rd
W Cutsinger Rd
300 W
135
T14N
T13N
R3E
R4E

A
1 Classic View Dr
2 S Illinois St
3 Lincoln Park Blvd
4 Lincoln Park West Dr
5 Lincoln Park East Dr

B
1 Rock Island Ct
2 Railroad Rd
3 Royal Meadow Dr

C
1 Foxmere Blvd

D
1 Dale Ct

E
1 Coral Bay Cove

F
1 Turkey Pen Dr

G
1 Brockton Manor North Dr
2 W Crooked Ln
3 Lake Run Ct

39°38'07"
39°37'41"
39°37'15"
39°36'49"
39°36'23"
39°35'57"
39°35'31"
39°35'05"

86°10'44" 86°10'10" 86°09'37" 86°09'03" 86°08'29" 86°07'55"

A B C D E
1 2 3 4 5 6 7

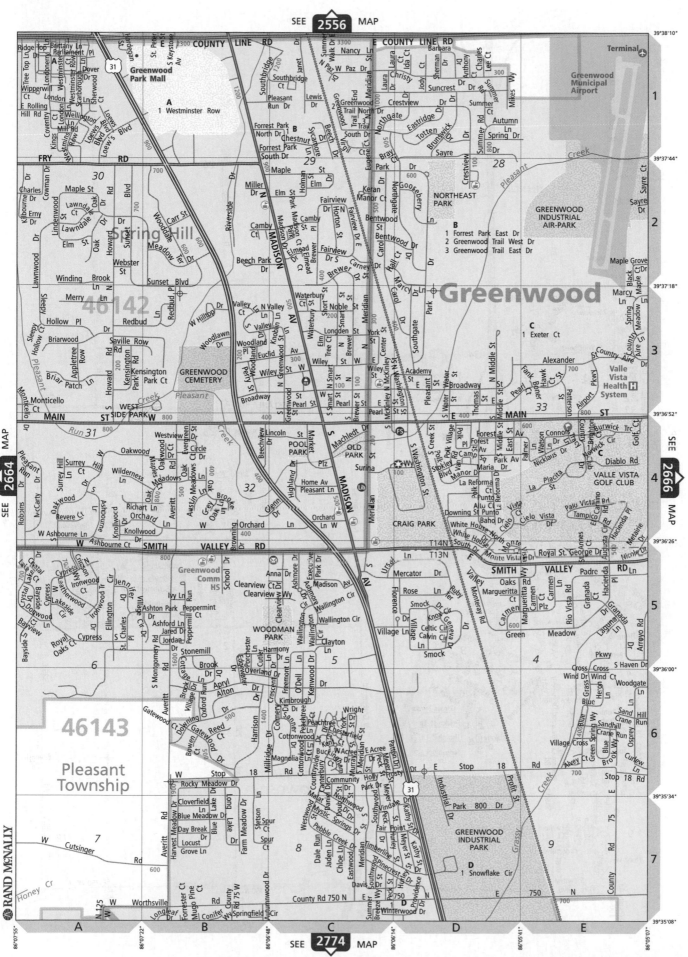

MAP
2665

1:24,000
1 in. = 2000 ft.

0   0.25   0.5

miles

SEE **2556** MAP

SEE **2664** MAP

SEE **2666** MAP

SEE **2774** MAP

RAND M?NALLY

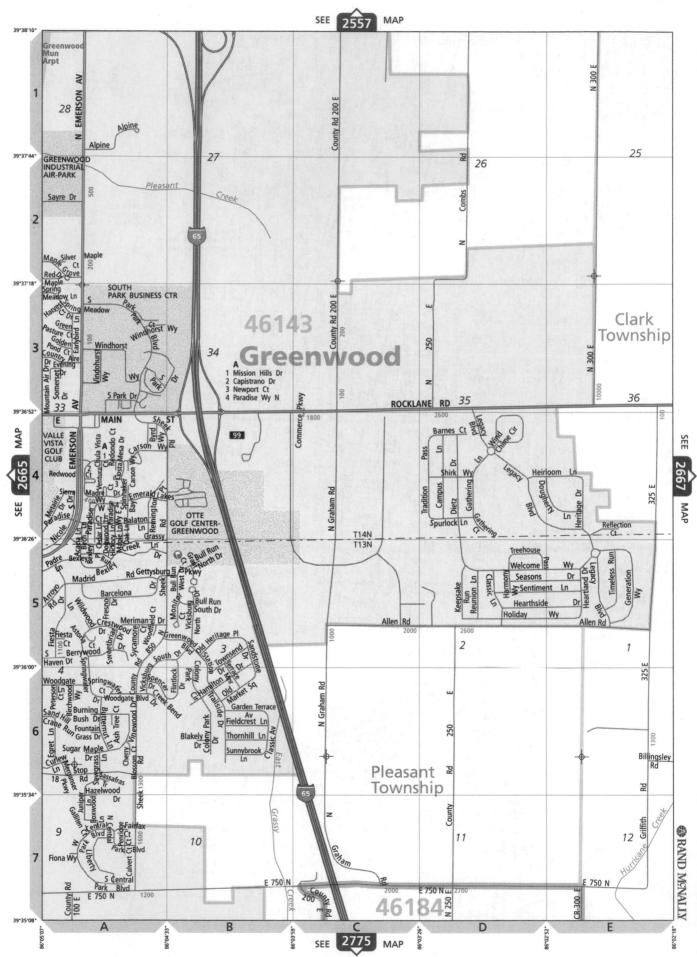

MAP
2666

1:24,000
1 in. = 2000 ft.
0   0.25   0.5
miles

SEE 2557 MAP

Greenwood
Mun
Arpt

28

GREENWOOD
INDUSTRIAL
AIR-PARK

Sayre Dr

Pleasant   Creek

27

26

25

N 300 E

County Rd 200 E

Combs   Rd

N

Silver
Ct
Maple
Grove
Red Ct
Maple
Spring
Meadow Ln
Harvest Spring Dr
Green Ct
Golden
Pasture Ct
Aire
Pond Ct
Country
Evening Dr
Somerset Dr
Mountain Air Dr

Maple
Maple

200

500

S Meadow

SOUTH
PARK BUSINESS CTR

Windhorst
Windhorst Wy
Windhorst Blvd
S Park Dr
Windhorst Wy
Wy
Wy
S
Park
Dr

100

34

46143

Greenwood

A
1 Mission Hills Dr
2 Capistrano Dr
3 Newport Ct
4 Paradise Wy N

County Rd 200 E

200

250

100

E

Clark
Township

N 300 E

N

10000

ROCKLANE RD   35

36

SEE 2665 MAP

E
MAIN   ST

VALLE
VISTA
GOLF
CLUB

Redwood

Sierra
Madre
W

EMERSON

S   AV

Metairie
Paradise
Nicole
Dr

400

Ventura
Chula Vista
Costa Mesa Dr
Ct
Bay
Paradise
W
Oak Ln
Balaton
Kensington Ln

Sheek
Byrd
Redondo Ct
Carson
Wy
Rd

Carson

Wy

Redondo Ct
A

Splinaker

Emerald Lakes

OTTE
GOLF CENTER-
GREENWOOD

Grassy

99

Commerce Pkwy

1800

N Graham Rd

2600

Barnes Ct

Pass
Ln
Shirk
Dr
Wy

Campus
Tradition
Dietz
Spurlock Ln

Legacy
Blvd
Wind
Chime Ctr
Ln
Legacy

Gathering

Ct
Gathering

Heirloom   Ln

Dougherty
Blvd

Heritage Dr
Ln

Reflection
Ct

325 E

SEE 2667 MAP

100

T14N
T13N

Acacia Ln
Birch
Cedar Ln
Dogwood Ln
Hickory
Bexley
Bexley
Padre
Ln

Arroyo
Rd
Ln

Crestwood
Dr

Fresno

Astoria
Ct

Wildwood

Creek
Lrl
Rd
Gettysburg

Madrid

Barcelona

Grassy
Dr
Bull Run
Bull Run
North Dr
Monroe
Sheek Rd
West Dr
Bull Run
Pkwy
Vicksburg
North
Bull Run
South Dr
Ct

Treehouse

Welcome   Pass   Wy
Seasons   Dr
Wy
Ln
Sentiment
Ln
Harmony
Classic Ln
Hearthside
Holiday   Wy

Keepsake
Run
Reunion Ln

Heartland Dr

Lowell Dr

Timeless Run

Generation
Wy

Allen Rd

1000

2000

2600

Allen Rd

325 E

Meriman Dr
Sweetbriar Ct

Sycamore
Ct
Woodfield Ct
County
Rd
Vicksburg
South Dr

850
Greenwood Blvd
Old
Colony
Park
Dr

Station
Dr

Old Heritage Pl

3

Townsend
Dr
Neville

Sandstone

Fiesta
Fiesta Ct
Berrywood
Haven Dr

1100
S

Flintlock

4

Creek Bend

Colony Park
Ct

Hamilton
Av
Trailside Dr
Old
Market Sq

Garden Terrace
Av
Fieldcrest Ln

Thornhill Ln

Blakely
Dr

Sunnybrook
Ln

2

1

Woodgate

Peterson Ln
Sand Hill
Crane Ln
Egret Ln

Springwater Ct
Birchwood
Burning
Bush Dr
Fountain
Grass Dr

Vinewood Dr
Butternut Ct
Ash Tree
Ct

Woodgate Blvd

Classic Av

East

N Graham Rd

Rd

250

E

Pleasant
Township

Billingsley
Rd

1300

Sugar Maple
Dr
Curlew
Merganser
Stop
18
Tr
Rd
Hazelwood
Dr

Sassafras

Blossom Ct

Cherry

Sheek 1300

Juniper
Galliton W
Fiona Wy

9

Liberty
Park
Boxwood
Central Ct
Penridge Ct
Blvd

1600

Fairfax
Ct

S Central
Park Blvd

Calvert Ct
Blvd

10

County Rd
100 E

1200

E 750 N

Grassy

I-65

Graham
N
Rd

Creek
200 E

County Rd

E 750 N

11

250

E

County
Rd

E 750 N
N 250 E

2000

2700

46184

CR-300 E

12

Griffith   Creek

Hurricane   Creek

1300

325 E

Rd

E 750 N

CR-300 E

SEE 2775 MAP

A   B   C   D   E

RAND McNALLY

MAP
2667

1:24,000
1 in. = 2000 ft.

0   0.25   0.5
miles

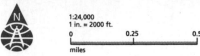
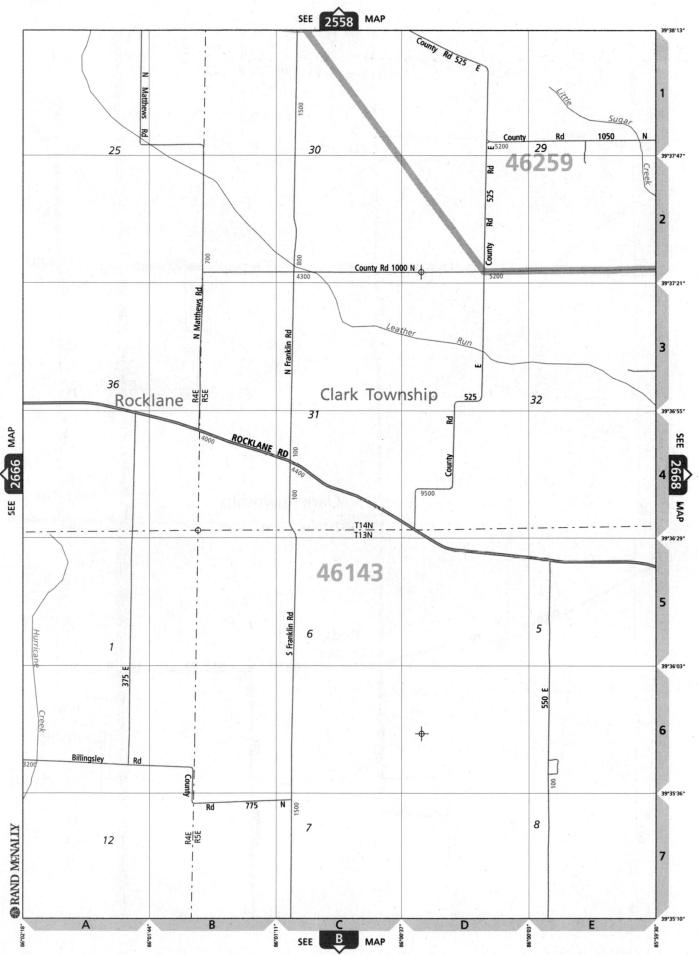

SEE **2558** MAP

39°38'13"

County Rd 525 E

1

Little

Sugar

N Matthews Rd

County   Rd   1050   N

25   30   5200

46259   29

County Rd 525 E

Creek

39°37'47"

2

700   800

County Rd 1000 N

4300   5200

39°37'21"

N Matthews Rd

N Franklin Rd

Leather   Run

3

E

36

Rocklane   R4E | R5E   **Clark Township**   525   32

31   County Rd   39°36'55"

4000   ROCKLANE RD   100

4400

100   9500

SEE **2666** MAP

SEE **2668** MAP

4

39°36'29"

T14N
T13N

46143

Hurricane

1   S Franklin Rd   6   5   5

550 E

375 E

39°36'03"

6

Creek

100

3200   Billingsley   Rd

County

Rd   775   N

1500

R4E | R5E

12   7   8

39°35'36"

7

39°35'10"

A   B   C   D   E

86°02'18"   86°01'44"   86°01'11"   86°00'37"   86°00'03"   85°59'30"

SEE **B** MAP

RAND McNALLY

MAP
2668

1:24,000
1 in. = 2000 ft.
0   0.25   0.5
miles

SEE 2559 MAP

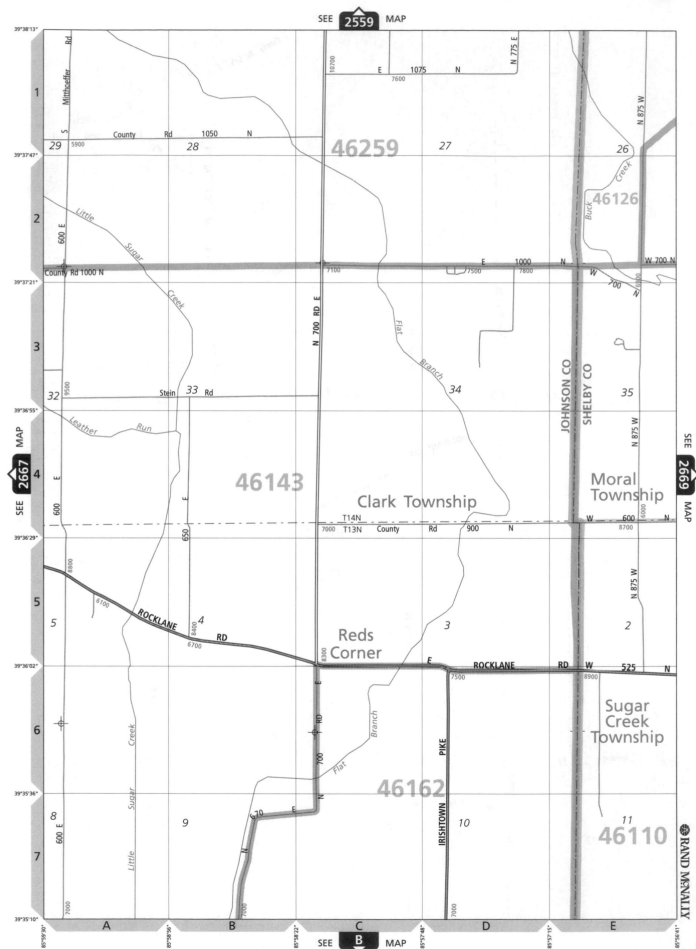

39°38'13"

Mittheeffer Rd

10700

N 775 E

E   1075   N
7600

N 875 W

1

S

County   Rd   1050   N

29   5900

28

46259

27

26

39°37'47"

Little

Buck Creek

46126

600 E

Sugar

2

Creek

County Rd 1000 N

E   1000   N
7100   7500   7800

W   700 N

W 700

6900

39°37'21"

N 700 RD E

Flat

JOHNSON CO

SHELBY CO

3

32   9500

Stein   33   Rd

Branch

34

35

N 875 W

39°36'55"

Leather   Run

E

E

46143

Clark Township

Moral
Township

4

600

E

W   600   N
8700   6000

39°36'29"

650

7000 T13N   County   Rd   900   N

T14N

8800

N 875 W

5

6100

5

ROCKLANE

8400   4

RD

6700

3

2

8300

Reds
Corner

E

ROCKLANE   RD   W   525   N
7500   8900

39°36'02"

RD

E

6

600 E

Little

Sugar

Creek

700

N

Flat   Branch

PIKE

IRISHTOWN

Sugar
Creek
Township

39°35'36"

8   600 E

670   E

9

46162

10

11

46110

N

7

7000

7000

39°35'10"

A   B   C   D   E
85°59'30"   85°58'56"   85°58'22"   85°57'48"   85°57'15"   85°56'58"

SEE B MAP

SEE 2667 MAP

SEE 2669 MAP

RAND M°NALLY

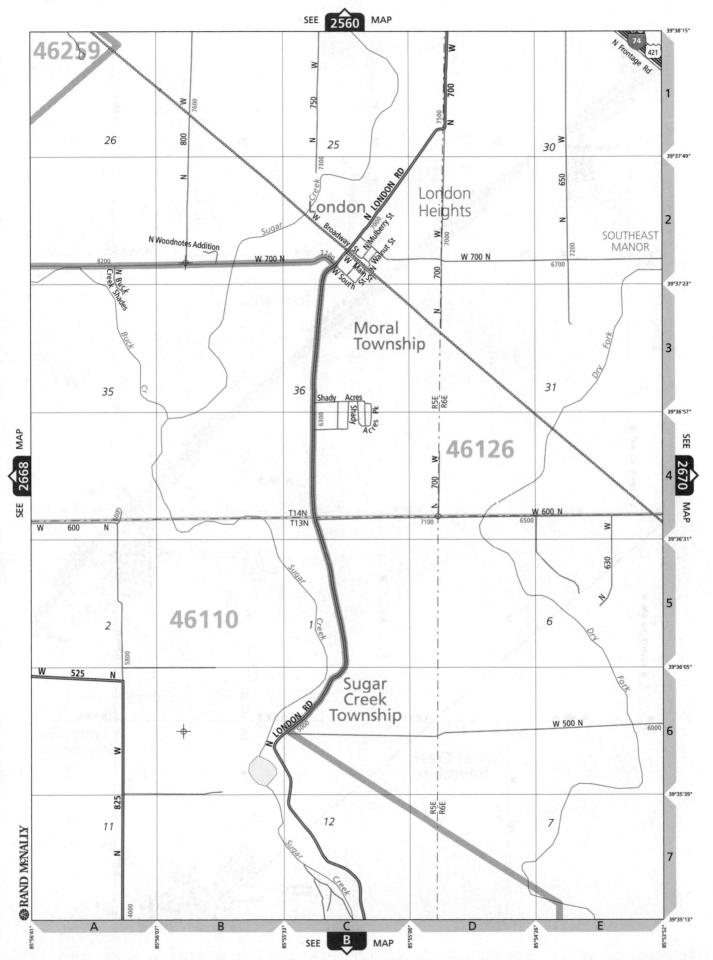

MAP
2669

1:24,000
1 in. = 2000 ft.
0   0.25   0.5
miles

SEE 2560 MAP

46259

N Frontage Rd
74 421

1

26

7600

800
N
W
750
N
Creek
7300

25

30

650
N
W
7200

39°38'15"

39°37'49"

London

N LONDON RD

London
Heights

2

SOUTHEAST
MANOR

N Woodnotes Addition

W Broadway St
N Mulberry St
N Walnut St

8200
W 700 N
7700
W Main St
W South St

W 700 N

7000
W

700

6700

39°37'23"

N Buck
Creek Shades

Buck
Cr

Moral
Township

N
700

Dry Fork

3

35

36

31

R5E
R6E

39°36'57"

SEE 2668 MAP

Shady Acres
6300
Shady
Acres Pk

46126

W
700

4

SEE 2670 MAP

W 600 N
T14N
T13N
7100

6500
W 600 N

W
630
N

39°36'31"

W 600 N

Sugar
Creek

39°36'05"

46110

5800

2

1

6

Dry Fork

5

W 525 N
W
825
N

N LONDON RD
5000

Sugar
Creek
Township

W 500 N
6000

6

39°35'39"

11

12

7

R5E
R6E

Sugar
Creek

4000

7

39°35'13"

85°56'41"
A
85°56'07"
B
85°55'33"
C
85°55'00"
D
85°54'26"
E
85°53'52"

MAP
2670

1:24,000
1 in. = 2000 ft.
0   0.25   0.5
miles

SEE 2561 MAP

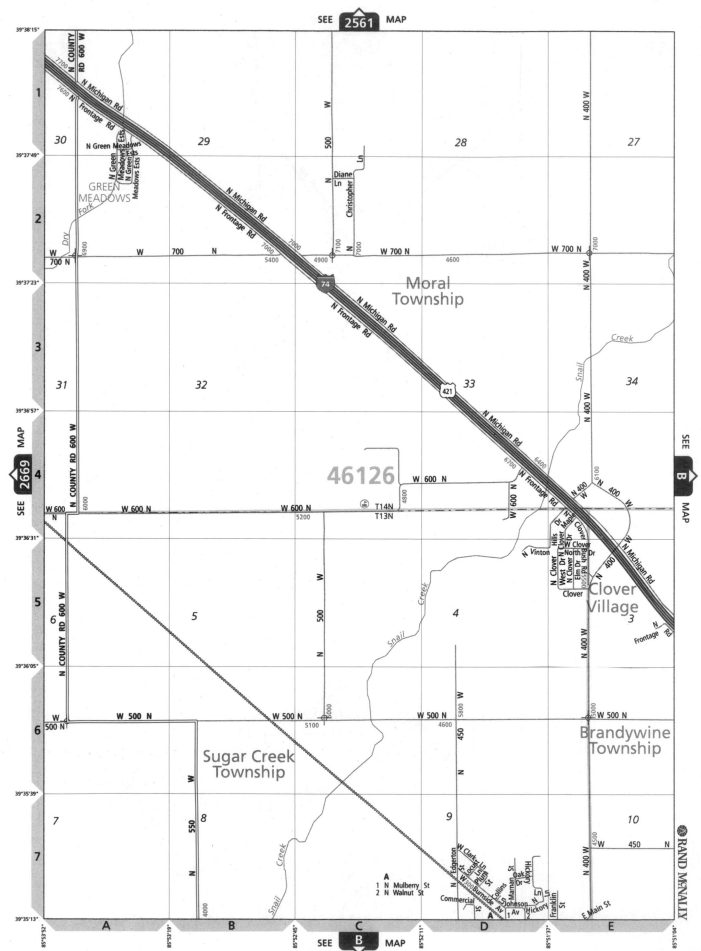

39°38'15"

N COUNTY RD 600 W
7700 N
7600 N
N Michigan Rd
N Frontage Rd

30   29   28   27

39°37'49"
N Green Meadows Ests
N Green Meadows Ests
N Green Meadows Ests
N Green Meadows Ests
GREEN MEADOWS
Dry Fork

Diane Ln
Christopher Ln

2

W 500 W

39°37'23"
700 N
6900
W 700 N
5400   4900
7100
W 700 N
7000
4600
W 700 N
7000
N 400 W

74
Moral Township

N Michigan Rd
N Frontage Rd

Creek

3

Snail

31   32   33   34
7000
421

39°36'57"
N COUNTY RD 600 W
6000
6700
6400
N Michigan Rd
N 400 W

SEE 2669 MAP

46126

W 600 N
4800
N Frontage Rd
W 600 N
N 400 W
6100
400 W

SEE B MAP

39°36'31"
W 600 N
6000
W 600 N
5200
T14N
T13N
N 400 W

Hills
N Clover
West Dr
N Clover
Clover
W Clover
N Clover
North
N Clover
Maple
Clover Dr
Bush Rd
Elm Dr
5500
N Vinton
Clover

Clover Village

5

N COUNTY RD 600 W
6 5

W 500 W
5000
Snail Creek

4   3

N 400 W
N Frontage Rd

39°36'05"

W 500 N
N 400 W
4500

Brandywine Township

6
500 N
W 500 N
5100
6000
W 500 N
4600
450
5800
W 500 N
W 500 N
5000
W 500 N
N 400 W

Sugar Creek Township

39°35'39"

W 500 W

7   8   9   10

550 N
450 N
N 400 W
4500 W   450 N

RAND McNALLY

7

4000
Snail Creek

A
1 N Mulberry St
2 N Walnut St

W Clarke Ln
Edgerton
Locust Ln
Plum St
Collins Ln
N Maple St
Oak Dr
Hickory Dr
Burnside Av
Commercial St
Johnson Av
Hickory St
1 Av
Franklin St
E Main St
N 300

39°35'13"

85°53'52"   85°53'19"   85°52'45"   85°52'11"   85°51'37"

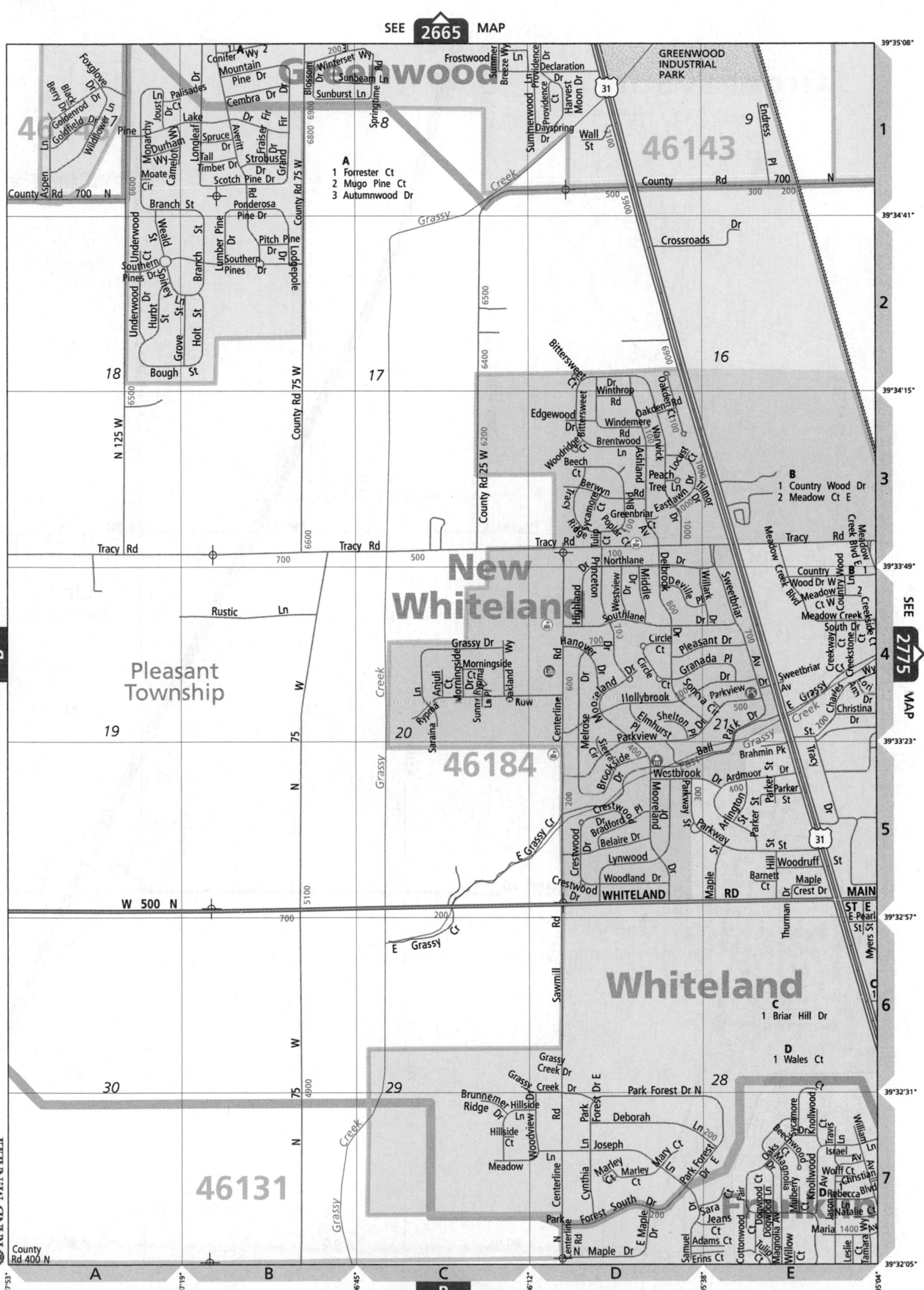

MAP
2774

1:24,000
1 in. = 2000 ft.
0   0.25   0.5
miles

SEE 2665 MAP

GREENWOOD
INDUSTRIAL
PARK

Greenwood

46143

A
1 Forrester Ct
2 Mugo Pine Ct
3 Autumnwood Dr

County Rd 700 N

B
1 Country Wood Dr
2 Meadow Ct E

SEE 2775 MAP

New
Whiteland

46184

Pleasant
Township

WHITELAND   RD

Whiteland

C
1 Briar Hill Dr

D
1 Wales Ct

46131

Franklin

SEE B MAP

SEE B MAP

RAND McNALLY

MAP
2775

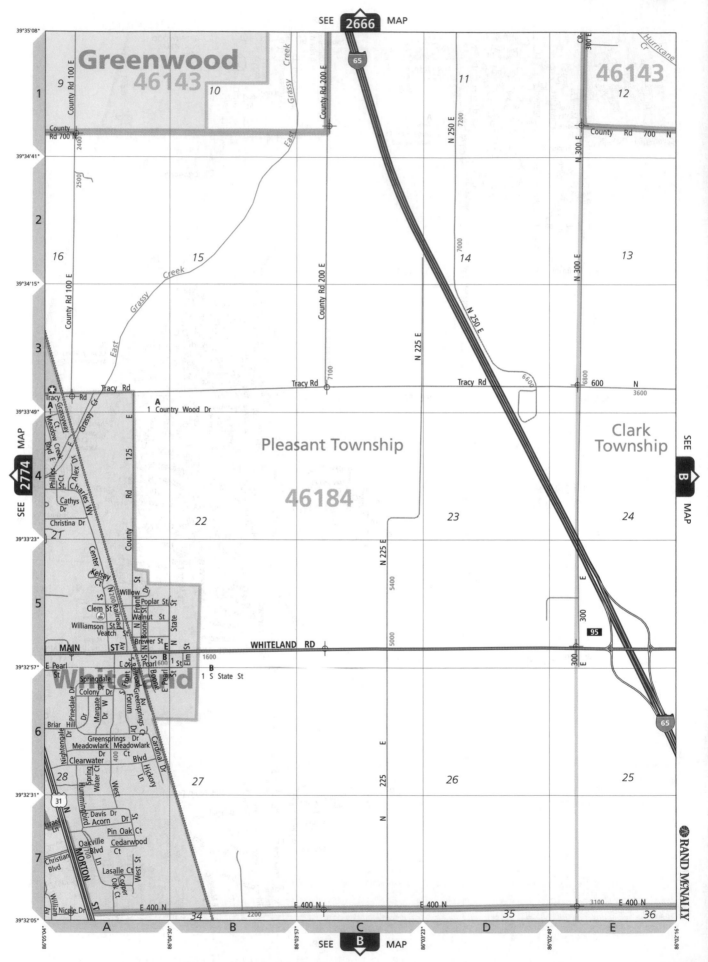

1:24,000
1 in. = 2000 ft.

0   0.25   0.5
miles

N

Greenwood
46143

46143
12

Pleasant Township
46184

Clark
Township

Whiteland

WHITELAND RD

RAND McNALLY

Cities and Communities

Community Name	Abbr.	County	ZIP Code	Map Page	Community Name	Abbr.	County	ZIP Code	Map Page	Community Name	Abbr.	County	ZIP Code	Map Page
Acton		Marion	46259	2559	Gadsden		Boone	46052	1679	Northwood Hills		Hamilton	46033	1903
Adams Township	AdmT	Hamilton	46069	1574	Gale		Hendricks	46123	2331	Olio		Hamilton	46038	1906
Allens Acres		Boone	46077	1789	Gasburg		Morgan	46158	2658	Orchard Park		Hamilton	46280	2011
Allisonville		Marion	46250	2012	Gem		Hancock	46140	2343	Perkinsville		Hamilton	46060	1580
Allman		Morgan	46158	2658	Glendale		Marion	46222	2227	Perry Township	PryT	Boone	46052	1896
Augusta		Marion	46268	2009	Glendale Heights		Marion	46240	2120	Philadelphia		Hancock	46140	2344
* Avon	AVON	Hendricks	46123	2332	Grandview		Marion	46260	2118	Pike		Boone	46052	1567
Bakers Corner		Hamilton	46069	1575	Green Township	GrnT	Madison	46064	1907	* Pittsboro	PTBR	Hendricks	46167	2112
* Beech Grove	BHGV	Marion	46107	2447	Greenbriar		Marion	46260	2010	* Plainfield	PNFD	Hendricks	46168	2441
Belle Arbor		Marion	46239	2450	* Greenfield	GNFD	Hancock	46140	2345	Pleasant Acres		Hancock	46055	2124
Belleville		Hendricks	46118	2548	* Greenwood	GNWD	Johnson	46142	2665	Pleasant Acres		Marion	46240	2011
Big Springs		Boone	46075	1680	Guilford Township	GfdT	Hendricks	46168	2550	Pleasant Township	PltT	Johnson	46184	2775
Blue River Township	BRvT	Hancock	46140	2346	--Hamilton County	HlnC				Pleasant View		Shelby	46126	2560
--Boone County	BneC				--Hancock County	HnkC				Rainbow Highlands		Marion	46236	2123
Brandywine Township	BwnT	Hancock	46140	2345	Harrison Township	HsnT	Boone	46052	1894	Raintown		Hendricks	46167	2112
Broadmoor		Marion	46228	2118	Hawthorn Hills		Hamilton	46038	1905	Reds Corner		Johnson	46143	2668
Brooks		Hamilton	46040	2015	Hendricks		Johnson	46142	2664	Riley		Hancock	46140	2346
Brookville Heights		Hancock	46163	2451	--Hendricks County	HdkC				Riverwood		Hamilton	46062	1578
Brown Township	BrnT	Hendricks	46112	2005	Herr		Boone	46052	1895	Rocklane		Johnson	46143	2667
Brown Township	BrnT	Morgan	46158	2658	Holaday Hills & Dales		Hamilton	46032	2011	Rosston		Boone	46077	1680
* Brownsburg	BNBG	Hendricks	46112	2114	Holida		Marion	46260	2118	Royalton		Boone	46077	2006
Buck Creek Township	BCkT	Hancock	46140	2234	* Homecroft	HMCT	Marion	46227	2556	Russell Lake		Boone	46077	1898
Burge Terrace		Marion	46239	2340	Home Place		Hamilton	46280	1901	--Shelby County	SbyC			
Camby		Marion	46221	2552	Hoover Crest		Marion	46260	2119	Shepherd		Boone	46052	1895
* Carmel	CRML	Hamilton	46032	1902	Hortonville		Hamilton	46069	1683	* Sheridan	SRDN	Hamilton	46069	1573
Carriage Estates		Hancock	46163	2452	* Indianapolis	INPS	Marion	46204	2337	Shooters Hill		Marion	46208	2228
Cartersburg		Hendricks	46168	2439	Irvington		Marion	46219	2339	Shore Acres		Marion	46220	2120
Center Township	CtrT	Hancock	46140	2237	Jackson Township	JknT	Hamilton	46034	1576	Six Points		Hendricks	46231	2442
Center Township	CtrT	Hendricks	46122	2439	Jackson Township	JknT	Madison	46011	1580	Smith Valley		Johnson	46143	2663
Center Valley		Hendricks	46118	2657	--Johnson County	JhnC				Snacks		Marion	46254	2117
Charlesmac Village		Marion	46239	2559	Jolietville		Hamilton	46069	1682	* Southport	SPRT	Marion	46227	2556
Chesterton		Hamilton	46280	2011	Joppa		Hendricks	46168	2549	* Speedway	SDWY	Marion	46224	2335
* Cicero	CCRO	Hamilton	46034	1577	Julietta		Marion	46239	2450	Spring Hill		Johnson	46142	2665
Clare		Hamilton	46060	1687	Keystone Manor		Marion	46241	2334	Spring Hollow		Marion	46260	2010
Clark Township	ClkT	Johnson	46143	2667	Knollton Heights		Marion	46228	2118	* Spring Lake	SGLK	Hancock	46140	2344
Clarksville		Hamilton	46060	1797	Lake Bodona		Morgan	46158	2658	Spring Mill Estates		Marion	46260	2119
Clay Township	ClyT	Hamilton	46032	1900	Lamong		Hamilton	46069	1682	Spring Mill Woods		Marion	46260	2010
Clinton Township	CtnT	Boone	46052	1569	Landersdale		Morgan	46113	2662	Sterling Heights		Marion	46241	2334
Clover Village		Shelby	46126	2670	* Lawrence	LWNC	Marion	46226	2231	Stony Creek Township	SCkT	Madison	46051	1689
College Crest		Marion	46240	2010	* Lebanon	LEBN	Boone	46052	1677	Strawtown		Hamilton	46060	1579
College Meadows		Hamilton	46280	2010	Legendary Hills		Marion	46278	2117	Stringtown		Boone	46052	1676
Creekwood		Marion	46220	2120	Liberty Township	LtyT	Hendricks	46118	2548	Stringtown		Hancock	46140	2346
Critchfield		Johnson	46143	2664	Lincoln Township	LcnT	Hendricks	46112	2224	Sugar Creek		Shelby	46126	2560
Crossroad Temple		Marion	46203	2339	London		Shelby	46126	2669	Sugar Creek Township	SCkT	Hancock	46163	2343
* Cumberland	CBLD	Hancock	46229	2341	Luxhaven		Hamilton	46040	1907	Sugar Creek Township	SgCT	Shelby	46110	2668
* Cumberland	CBLD	Marion	46229	2341	Lynhurst		Marion	46241	2335	Sun Down		Marion	46239	2449
Dale		Boone	46052	1787	--Madison County	MdnC				Sunnyview		Marion	46203	2339
* Danville	DNVL	Hendricks	46122	2329	Madison Township	MdnT	Morgan	46113	2661	Tilden		Hendricks	46112	2222
Dawnbury		Marion	46220	2120	Magnetic Springs		Hendricks	46122	2439	Trails End		Hamilton	46038	1903
Delaware Township	DelT	Hamilton	46038	1903	Maple Ridge		Marion	46221	2552	Tremont		Marion	46234	2334
Deleware Trails		Marion	46260	2119	Maplewood		Hendricks	46167	2221	Trilobi Hills		Marion	46236	2122
Deming		Hamilton	46034	1576	--Marion County	MrnC				* Ulen	ULEN	Boone	46052	1677
Driftwood Hills		Marion	46240	2011	Marion Township	MrnT	Boone	46052	1571	Union Township	UnnT	Boone	46077	1789
Durbin		Hamilton	46060	1688	Mayflower Meadows		Marion	46220	2121	Union Township	UnnT	Hendricks	46149	2112
Eagle Township	EglT	Boone	46077	1898	* McCordsville	MCVL	Hancock	46055	2015	Vernon Township	VrnT	Hancock	46055	2015
Eagle Village		Boone	46077	1899	Middle Township	MdlT	Hendricks	46167	2112	Warren Hills		Marion	46229	2340
Eagletown		Hamilton	46074	1682	Milledgeville		Boone	46052	1894	Washington Township	WshT	Boone	46052	1567
Eaglewood Estates		Boone	46077	1898	Monroe Township	MnrT	Morgan	46158	2658	Washington Township	WshT	Hamilton	46069	1682
Echo Crest		Hamilton	46280	1902	* Monrovia	MNVA	Morgan	46157	2657	Washington Township	WshT	Hendricks	46123	2331
El Dorado		Johnson	46143	2664	* Mooresville	MRVL	Morgan	46158	2659	Waugh		Boone	46052	1571
Elizaville		Boone	46052	1570	Moral Township	MrlT	Shelby	46130	2561	Wayne Township	WynT	Hamilton	46060	1688
Elmwood		Boone	46052	1676	--Morgan County	MgnC				Westchester Estates		Marion	46268	2009
Fall Creek Highland		Marion	46236	2014	Mt Comfort		Hancock	46140	2233	* Westfield	WTFD	Hamilton	46074	1684
Fall Creek Township	FCkT	Hamilton	46040	1907	Mount Jackson		Marion	46222	2336	Westover		Marion	46268	2009
Farleys Addition		Marion	46214	2334	Needham Township	NdmT	Johnson	46131	2775	Westwood		Marion	46234	2224
Fayette		Boone	46052	2005	Newark Village		Hamilton	46032	1902	White River Township	WRvT	Hamilton	46034	1579
Federal Hill		Hamilton	46060	1686	New Britton		Hamilton	46038	1904	White River Township	WRvT	Johnson	46142	2663
* Fishers	FSHR	Hamilton	46038	1904	* New Palestine	NPLN	Hancock	46163	2452	* Whiteland	WTLD	Johnson	46184	2774
Fishersburg		Madison	46051	1689	* New Whiteland	NWTD	Johnson	46184	2774	* Whitestown	WTWN	Boone	46075	1788
Five Points		Morgan	46158	2661	* Noblesville	NBVL	Hamilton	46060	1686	Wiser		Morgan	46113	2661
Flackville		Marion	46222	2227	Noblesville Township	NbvT	Hamilton	46062	1795	Wolfington		Marion	46228	2227
* Fortville	FTVL	Hancock	46040	2016	N Augusta Addition		Hamilton	46032	2009	Woodbury		Hancock	46055	2015
Fox Hill		Morgan	46113	2661	North Belleville		Hendricks	46118	2439	Woodstock		Marion	46228	2228
Frances		Johnson	46143	2664	Northern Beach		Hamilton	46033	1903	Worth Township	WrhT	Boone	46052	1788
* Franklin	FKLN	Johnson	46131	2774	Northfield		Boone	46077	1790	* Zionsville	ZNVL	Boone	46077	1899
Franklin Township	FknT	Johnson	46131	2775	North Indianapolis		Marion	46208	2228					
Friendswood		Hendricks	46113	2551	North Ridge Village		Hamilton	46280	2010					

*Indicates incorporated city

List of Abbreviations

Admin	Administration	Cto	Cut Off	Lp	Loop	Ste.	Sainte
Agri	Agricultural	Dept	Department	Mnr	Manor	Sci	Science
Ag	Agriculture	Dev	Development	Mkt	Market	Sci	Sciences
AFB	Air Force Base	Diag	Diagonal	Mdw	Meadow	Sci	Scientific
Arpt	Airport	Div	Division	Mdws	Meadows	Shop Ctr	Shopping Center
Al	Alley	Dr	Drive	Med	Medical	Shr	Shore
Amer	American	Drwy	Driveway	Mem	Memorial	Shrs	Shores
Anx	Annex	E	East	Metro	Metropolitan	Skwy	Skyway
Arc	Arcade	El	Elevation	Mw	Mews	S	South
Arch	Archaeological	Env	Environmental	Mil	Military	Spr	Spring
Aud	Auditorium	Est	Estate	Ml	Mill	Sprs	Springs
Avd	Avenida	Ests	Estates	Mls	Mills	Sq	Square
Av	Avenue	Exh	Exhibition	Mon	Monument	Stad	Stadium
Bfld	Battlefield	Expm	Experimental	Mtwy	Motorway	St For	State Forest
Bch	Beach	Expo	Exposition	Mnd	Mound	St Hist Site	State Historic Site
Bnd	Bend	Expwy	Expressway	Mnds	Mounds	St Nat Area	State Natural Area
Bio	Biological	Ext	Extension	Mt	Mount	St Pk	State Park
Blf	Bluff	Frgds	Fairgrounds	Mtn	Mountain	St Rec Area	State Recreation Area
Blvd	Boulevard	ft	Feet	Mtns	Mountains	Sta	Station
Brch	Branch	Fy	Ferry	Mun	Municipal	St	Street
Br	Bridge	Fld	Field	Mus	Museum	Smt	Summit
Brk	Brook	Flds	Fields	Nat'l	National	Sys	Systems
Bldg	Building	Flt	Flat	Nat'l For	National Forest	Tech	Technical
Bur	Bureau	Flts	Flats	Nat'l Hist Pk	National Historic Park	Tech	Technological
Byp	Bypass	For	Forest	Nat'l Hist Site	National Historic Site	Tech	Technology
Bywy	Byway	Fk	Fork	Nat'l Mon	National Monument	Ter	Terrace
Cl	Calle	Ft	Fort	Nat'l Park	National Park	Terr	Territory
Cljn	Callejon	Found	Foundation	Nat'l Rec Area	National Recreation Area	Theol	Theological
Cmto	Caminito	Frwy	Freeway	Nat'l Wld Ref	National Wildlife Refuge	Thwy	Throughway
Cm	Camino	Gdn	Garden	Nat	Natural	Toll Fy	Toll Ferry
Cap	Capitol	Gdns	Gardens	NAS	Naval Air Station	TIC	Tourist Information Center
Cath	Cathedral	Gen Hosp	General Hospital	Nk	Nook	Trc	Trace
Cswy	Causeway	Gln	Glen	N	North	Trfwy	Trafficway
Cem	Cemetery	GC	Golf Course	Orch	Orchard	Tr	Trail
Ctr	Center	Grn	Green	Ohwy	Outer Highway	Tun	Tunnel
Ctr	Centre	Grds	Grounds	Ovl	Oval	Tpk	Turnpike
Cir	Circle	Grv	Grove	Ovlk	Overlook	Unps	Underpass
Crlo	Circulo	Hbr	Harbor/Harbour	Ovps	Overpass	Univ	University
CH	City Hall	Hvn	Haven	Pk	Park	Vly	Valley
Clf	Cliff	HQs	Headquarters	Pkwy	Parkway	Vet	Veterans
Clfs	Cliffs	Ht	Height	Pas	Paseo	Vw	View
Clb	Club	Hts	Heights	Psg	Passage	Vil	Village
Cltr	Cluster	HS	High School	Pass	Passenger	Wk	Walk
Col	Coliseum	Hwy	Highway	Pth	Path	Wall	Wall
Coll	College	Hl	Hill	Pn	Pine	Wy	Way
Com	Common	Hls	Hills	Pns	Pines	W	West
Coms	Commons	Hist	Historical	Pl	Place	WMA	Wildlife Management Area
Comm	Community	Hllw	Hollow	Pln	Plain		
Co.	Company	Hosp	Hospital	Plns	Plains		
Cons	Conservation	Hse	House	Plgnd	Playground		
Conv & Vis Bur	Convention and Visitors Bureau	Ind Res	Indian Reservation	Plz	Plaza		
Cor	Corner	Info	Information	Pt	Point		
Cors	Corners	Inst	Institute	Pnd	Pond		
Corp	Corporation	Int'l	International	PO	Post Office		
Corr	Corridor	I	Island	Pres	Preserve		
Cte	Corte	Is	Islands	Prov	Provincial		
CC	Country Club	Isl	Isle	Rwy	Railway		
Co	County	Jct	Junction	Rec	Recreation		
Ct	Court	Knl	Knoll	Reg	Regional		
Ct Hse	Court House	Knls	Knolls	Res	Reservoir		
Cts	Courts	Lk	Lake	Rst	Rest		
Cr	Creek	Lndg	Landing	Rdg	Ridge		
Cres	Crescent	Ln	Lane	Rd	Road		
Cross	Crossing	Lib	Library	Rds	Roads		
Curv	Curve	Ldg	Lodge	St.	Saint		

STREET Block City ZIP Map# Grid

US-31 N Meridian St
10600 ClyT 46032 1901 C7
10600 CRML 46032 1901 C7
13900 CRML 46032 1902 A1
14800 WTFD 46032 1793 B6
14800 WTFD 46033 1793 B6
15100 WshT 46032 1793 B5
15100 WshT 46033 1793 B5
US-31 N Morton St
3800 FKLN 46131 2775 A7
3800 FKLN 46184 2775 A7
3800 FknT 46184 2775 A7
3800 WTLD 46131 2775 A7
3800 WTLD 46184 2775 A7
US-31 US Highway 31 N
300 GNWD 46142 2665 B3
1200 GNWD 46227 2665 A1
US-31 US Highway 31 S
200 GNWD 46142 2665 B4
600 GNWD 46143 2665 C5
1400 GNWD 46143 2774 E5
US-36
- BHGV - 2447 D5
- BHGV - 2448 D4
- CtrT 46122 2330 E4
- CtrT 46122 2331 A4
- CtrT 46123 2331 A4
- DNVL 46122 2331 A4
- INPS - 2231 A2
- INPS - 2335 B7
- INPS - 2339 E7
- INPS - 2340 A6
- INPS - 2444 B1
- INPS - 2445 C7
- INPS - 2446 A6
- INPS - 2447 D5
- INPS - 2448 D4
- INPS 46224 2335 A4
10 DNVL 46122 2329 E4
900 DNVL 46122 2330 A4
1200 CtrT 46122 2329 B4
3000 VrnT 46040 2016 D3
3000 VrnT 46055 2016 D3
5000 VrnT 46055 2015 D6
5200 WshT 46123 2331 A4
5600 MCVL 46055 2015 D6
5800 AVON 46123 2331 E4
5800 WshT 46123 2332 D4
6200 INPS 46214 2335 A4
6400 AVON 46123 2332 B4
6400 INPS 46214 2334 E4
6400 INPS 46241 2334 E4
6500 LWNC 46236 2124 B1
6500 MCVL 46055 2124 B1
6500 MCVL 46236 2124 B1
7300 INPS 46231 2334 E4
7500 LWNC 46226 2231 B1
8300 INPS 46234 2334 A4
8400 AVON 46123 2333 B4
8400 LWNC 46226 2122 E6
8800 INPS 46231 2333 E4
8800 INPS 46234 2333 E4
9000 LWNC 46235 2122 E6
9000 LWNC 46236 2122 E6
9400 WshT 46123 2333 B4
10000 LWNC 46235 2123 A6
10000 LWNC 46236 2123 A6
10500 AVON 46234 2333 E4
US-36 E Main St
10 DNVL 46122 2329 D4
900 DNVL 46122 2330 A4
US-36 W Main St
10 DNVL 46122 2329 E4
1200 CtrT 46122 2329 B4
US-36 E Pendleton Pike
7500 INPS 46226 2231 B1
7500 LWNC 46226 2231 B1
8400 LWNC 46226 2122 E6
9000 LWNC 46235 2122 E6
9000 LWNC 46236 2122 E6
10000 LWNC 46235 2123 A6
10000 LWNC 46236 2123 A6
12300 LWNC 46236 2124 A2
12600 MCVL 46055 2124 B1
12600 MCVL 46236 2124 B1
US-36 W Pendleton Pike
3000 VrnT 46040 2016 E3
3000 VrnT 46055 2016 C4
5000 VrnT 46055 2015 D6
5600 MCVL 46055 2015 D6
6500 LWNC 46236 2124 B1
6500 MCVL 46055 2124 B1
6500 MCVL 46236 2124 B1
US-36 Rockville Rd
- INPS 46224 2335 A4
6200 INPS 46214 2335 A4
6200 INPS 46241 2335 A4
6400 INPS 46214 2334 E4
6400 INPS 46241 2334 E4
7300 INPS 46231 2334 E4
8300 INPS 46234 2334 A4
8800 INPS 46231 2333 E4
8800 INPS 46234 2333 E4
US-37
- INPS - 2444 B5
US-40
- BHGV - 2447 B6
- BHGV - 2448 D3
- INPS - 2339 E7
- INPS - 2340 A7
- INPS - 2444 B5
- INPS - 2445 C7
- INPS - 2446 A6
- INPS - 2447 D5
- INPS - 2448 D3
10 CtrT 46140 2344 D2
10 GNFD 46140 2344 D2
10 GNFD 46140 2345 D1
100 PNFD 46168 2441 D4
1500 CtrT 46140 2346 C1
1500 GNFD 46140 2346 C1
1600 PNFD 46168 2440 A7
2100 SCkT 46140 2344 E1
2200 LtyT 46118 2548 D1
2300 PNFD 46168 2442 A3
US-40
2600 SGLK 46140 2344 D2
2700 SCkT 46140 2343 D2
2700 SGLK 46140 2343 D2
3100 PNFD 46231 2442 E1
3200 WshT 46231 2442 E1
3300 LtyT 46118 2439 E7
3600 LtyT 46118 2440 A7
4100 LtyT 46168 2440 A7
4200 SCkT 46163 2343 B2
4800 GfdT 46168 2440 D6
5000 SCkT 46140 2342 E2
5000 SCkT 46163 2342 E2
6000 INPS 46241 2335 A6
6600 INPS 46241 2334 D7
6700 CBLD 46163 2342 B2
7000 CBLD 46229 2342 B2
7000 SCkT 46229 2342 B2
7300 INPS 46231 2334 D7
7300 SCkT 46229 2341 E2
7500 INPS 46219 2340 B4
8000 INPS 46231 2443 A1
9000 INPS 46229 2340 C3
9200 INPS 46231 2442 E1
9500 INPS 46229 2341 B2
11000 CBLD 46229 2341 B2
US-40 Cumberland St
- LtyT 46118 2548 C1
US-40 E Main St
10 GNFD 46140 2345 D1
100 PNFD 46168 2441 A5
900 GNFD 46140 2346 C1
1000 CtrT 46140 2346 C1
2300 PNFD 46168 2442 A3
3100 PNFD 46231 2442 E1
3200 WshT 46231 2442 E1
US-40 W Main St
10 GNFD 46140 2345 D1
100 PNFD 46168 2441 D4
1600 PNFD 46168 2440 A7
2200 GNFD 46140 2344 D2
2500 CtrT 46140 2344 D2
US-40 E National Rd
1500 CtrT 46140 2346 B1
1500 GNFD 46140 2346 B1
US-40 W National Rd
10 CtrT 46140 2344 D2
10 GNFD 46140 2344 D2
2100 SCkT 46140 2344 B2
2600 SGLK 46140 2344 A2
2700 SCkT 46140 2343 D2
2700 SGLK 46140 2343 D2
4200 SCkT 46163 2343 B2
5000 SCkT 46140 2342 E2
5000 SCkT 46163 2342 E2
6700 CBLD 46163 2342 B2
7000 CBLD 46229 2342 B2
7000 SCkT 46229 2342 B2
7300 SCkT 46229 2341 E2
7600 CBLD 46229 2341 E2
US-40 E Washington
7700 CBLD 46229 2341 E2
7700 SCkT 46229 2341 E2
US-40 E Washington St
7800 CBLD 46229 2341 E2
7800 INPS 46219 2340 C3
7800 SCkT 46229 2341 E2
9000 INPS 46229 2340 C3
9500 INPS 46229 2341 A2
US-40 W Washington St
6000 INPS 46241 2335 A6
6600 INPS 46241 2334 D7
7300 INPS 46231 2334 D7
8000 INPS 46231 2443 A1
9200 INPS 46231 2442 E1
9200 PNFD 46231 2442 E1
9200 WshT 46231 2442 E1
US-47
10 AdmT 46069 1574 D2
10 AdmT 46069 1575 A2
900 AdmT 46069 1573 E2
2400 SRDN 46069 1573 E2
US-47 E 236th St
10 AdmT 46069 1574 D2
10 AdmT 46069 1575 A2
US-47 W 236th St
10 AdmT 46069 1574 D2
900 AdmT 46069 1573 E2
2400 SRDN 46069 1573 E2
US-52
- ClyT - 2010 B2
- CRML - 2010 E2
- CRML - 2011 B3
- CtrT - 1786 E5
- CtrT - 1787 A7
- CtrT 46052 1676 A2
- EglT - 1897 C7
- EglT - 2006 D1
- EglT - 2007 C2
- EglT - 2008 C2
- INPS - 2008 A2
- INPS - 2009 E3
- INPS - 2010 B2
- INPS - 2011 B3
- INPS - 2012 B5
- INPS - 2121 E3
- INPS - 2231 B5
- INPS - 2340 A1
- LEBN - 1676 D7
- LEBN - 1785 E1
- LEBN - 1786 B2
- LWNC - 2121 E7
- LWNC - 2122 A7
- LWNC - 2231 A1
- PryT - 1787 A7
- PryT - 1896 E4
- PryT - 1897 A5
- WrhT - 1896 C1
- ZNVL - 2008 A2
10 NPLN 46163 2452 B3
2000 SCkT 46163 2452 E4
5300 SCkT 46163 2451 D2
7300 INPS 46163 2450 E1
7300 SCkT 46163 2450 E1
9600 INPS 46239 2341 A7
US-52
10700 INPS 46239 2450 E1
US-52 E Brookville Rd
7700 INPS 46239 2340 D6
9600 INPS 46239 2341 A7
10700 INPS 46239 2450 E1
US-52 E Main St
10 NPLN 46163 2452 B3
4000 SCkT 46163 2452 C3
US-52 W Main St
10 NPLN 46163 2452 B3
US-67
- INPS - 2444 C6
US-136
10 BNBG 46112 2114 B6
10 PTBR 46167 2112 D3
10 PTBR 46167 2113 C5
200 LcnT 46112 2114 B6
300 UnnT 46149 2112 A3
500 MdlT 46167 2112 D3
800 MdlT 46149 2112 A3
1000 BNBG 46112 2223 E1
1300 BNBG 46112 2224 C2
1400 LcnT 46112 2224 C2
4200 MdlT 46167 2113 C5
4800 LcnT 46167 2113 C5
5500 LcnT 46167 2113 E5
5700 BNBG 46112 2113 E5
6200 SDWY 46224 2226 A6
6300 INPS 46224 2226 A6
6600 INPS 46214 2225 E5
6600 INPS 46214 2226 A6
8300 INPS 46234 2225 B4
9100 INPS 46234 2224 C2
9200 LcnT 46234 2224 C2
US-136 Crawfordsville Rd
6200 SDWY 46224 2226 A6
6300 INPS 46224 2226 A6
6600 INPS 46214 2225 E5
6600 INPS 46214 2226 A6
US-136 W Crawfordsville Rd
8300 INPS 46234 2225 B4
9100 INPS 46234 2224 E3
9200 LcnT 46234 2224 E3
US-136 E Main St
10 BNBG 46112 2114 C7
10 PTBR 46167 2112 E4
10 PTBR 46167 2113 A4
1000 BNBG 46112 2223 E1
1300 BNBG 46112 2224 A1
1400 LcnT 46112 2224 A1
US-136 W Main St
10 BNBG 46112 2114 C6
10 PTBR 46167 2112 E4
200 LcnT 46112 2114 B6
500 MdlT 46167 2112 E3
US-421
- BwnT - 2670 D3
- ClyT - 2010 B2
- CRML - 2010 E2
- CRML - 2011 B3
- INPS - 2009 E3
- INPS - 2010 B2
- INPS - 2011 B3
- INPS - 2012 A4
- INPS - 2121 E1
- INPS - 2231 B5
- INPS - 2339 E7
- INPS - 2340 A1
- INPS - 2448 E1
- INPS - 2449 B2
- INPS - 2450 A7
- INPS - 2559 B1
- LWNC - 2121 E6
- LWNC - 2122 A7
- LWNC - 2231 A1
- MrlT - 2559 D3
- MrlT - 2560 A5
- MrlT - 2669 E1
- MrlT - 2670 D3
- SgCT - 2670 D3
10 UnnT 46077 1680 D6
10 UnnT 46077 1789 E1
700 UnnT 46077 1790 A3
1000 MrnT 46075 1680 C2
1000 UnnT 46075 1680 D6
3000 EglT 46077 1790 B6
3000 MrnT 46075 1571 B7
3400 EglT 46077 1899 C2
4000 MrnT 46052 1571 B7
4500 ZNVL 46077 1899 C2
6000 ClyT 46077 1899 E7
6100 MrnT 46052 1570 E2
6100 MrnT 46069 1570 E2
9500 INPS 46268 2009 A2
9600 ClyT 46032 2009 A2
9600 INPS 46032 2009 A2
9800 ClyT 46032 2008 E1
10000 ClyT 46077 2008 E1
10500 ClyT 46032 1899 E7
US-421 N Michigan Rd
- ZNVL 46077 1899 E6
10 UnnT 46077 1680 D6
1000 MrnT 46075 1680 C2
1000 UnnT 46075 1680 D6
3000 MrnT 46075 1571 B7
4000 MrnT 46052 1571 B7
6100 MrnT 46052 1570 E2
6100 MrnT 46069 1570 E2
9500 INPS 46268 2009 A2
9600 ClyT 46032 2009 A2
9600 INPS 46032 2009 A2
9800 ClyT 46032 2008 E1
10000 ClyT 46077 2008 E1
10500 ClyT 46032 1899 E7
10500 ClyT 46077 1899 E7
US-421 S Michigan Rd
10 UnnT 46077 1789 E1
700 UnnT 46077 1790 A3
3000 EglT 46077 1790 B6
3400 EglT 46077 1899 C2
4500 ZNVL 46077 1899 C2
6000 ClyT 46077 1899 E7

A

A St
- BHGV 46107 2447 D2
AA St
- BHGV 46107 2447 D3
- BHGV 46107 2448 A3
AAA Wy
1100 CRML 46032 1902 C5
W Aaron Ct
6800 BCkT 46140 2233 C7
6800 GNFD 46140 2236 E5
Abaca Ct
3200 INPS 46203 2448 D3
Abaca Wy
6200 INPS 46203 2448 D3
Abalone Dr
- INPS 46217 2554 B2
Abbedale Ct
300 WshT 46032 1792 C6
Abbey Ct
100 NBVL 46060 1795 E4
1500 WRvT 46143 2663 E6
9800 INPS 46235 2231 E3
Abbey Dr
4300 CRML 46033 1902 E2
Abbey Rd
- PTBR 46167 2113 A2
100 NBVL 46060 1795 E4
Abbey Dell Dr
8300 INPS 46113 2551 E7
Abbington Sta
800 DNVL 46122 2329 D2
Abbots Pl
4700 CRML 46033 1902 E2
13100 CRML 46033 1903 A2
Abbott Av
12700 CRML 46032 1901 D3
Abbott St
500 INPS 46225 2337 B5
Abby Ln
1900 DNVL 46122 2330 C2
6500 AVON 46123 2332 A2
6500 EglT 46077 1897 C7
6500 WshT 46123 2332 A2
Abby Creek Ln
4300 INPS 46205 2229 C1
Abel Cir
12100 CBLD 46229 2232 E7
Abercon Tr
6700 NBVL 46062 1685 E5
Abercromby Cir
5600 INPS 46254 2117 B5
Aberdare Dr
- DelT 46250 2012 D3
9300 INPS 46250 2012 D3
Aberdeen Av
- WshT 46123 2331 C4
Aberdeen Cir
4300 INPS 46226 2230 A1
Aberdeen Ct
9600 FSHR 46038 1904 E2
Aberdeen Dr
600 INPS 46241 2335 A5
900 INPS 46241 2334 E5
Aberdeen St
500 CRML 46032 1901 E4
500 CRML 46032 1902 A5
Aberdene Ct
- MdnT 46113 2661 B1
Abilene Wy
- MCVL 46055 2124 C2
Abington Ct
- MdnT 46113 2661 A1
N Abington Dr
4600 INPS 46254 2117 E7
Abington Pl
11200 FSHR 46038 1904 A6
W Abington Wy
4600 INPS 46254 2117 D7
Able Dr
4600 INPS 46227 2447 A6
Abner Creek Pkwy
10 WshT 46123 2331 C4
Abraham Run
12900 CRML 46033 1903 E2
Abundance Ln
- AVON 46123 2332 C2
Acacia Dr
3200 INPS 46214 2225 E4
3200 INPS 46214 2226 D5
Acacia Ln
- GNWD 46143 2666 A5
Acacio Dr
14600 FCkT 46040 1907 A5
Academy Dr
600 ZNVL 46077 1899 B6
Academy Ln
- CRML 46032 1900 D3
Academy St
100 GNWD 46143 2665 D3
Acadia Ct
1000 INPS 46217 2555 A3
Acadia Pl
13600 FSHR 46038 1904 C1
Acoma Dr
3000 INPS 46235 2232 B4
Acona Ct
4200 INPS 46235 2231 D1
Acorn Dr
- WTLD 46184 2775 A7
Acorn Ln
5300 INPS 46254 2117 C5
Acorn Woods Cir
5500 INPS 46224 2335 B2
Acorn Woods Dr
700 INPS 46224 2335 C2
Acre Av
300 BNBG 46112 2114 B7
Acre Ln
- INPS 46278 2116 D3
10 BrnT 46112 2114 D2
E Acree Dr
10 GNWD 46143 2665 C6
W Acree Dr
10 GNWD 46143 2665 C6
Action Rd
400 HsnT 46052 1895 A3
E Action Rd
10 HsnT 46052 1895 A3
W Action Rd
10 HsnT 46052 1894 E3
Activator Av
- INPS 46221 2445 D2
Acton Rd
- INPS 46239 2559 C1
S Acton Rd
- INPS 46239 2559 C1
6000 INPS 46259 2559 C1
8900 ClkT 46259 2559 C7
Ada Ln
200 BHGV 46107 2447 E5
200 BHGV 46107 2448 A5
Adam Ct
500 GNFD 46140 2236 E4
10600 FSHR 46038 1904 D7
Adams Ct
10 WTLD 46131 2774 D7
100 LEBN 46052 1677 A3
Adams Ct N
- INPS 46205 2229 C2
Adams Ct S
3400 INPS 46205 2229 C2
Adams Dr
10 BHGV 46107 2447 D2
E Adams Rd
8800 INPS 46239 2449 C5
Adams St
10 DNVL 46122 2329 D3
600 CRML 46032 1901 E4
1000 CRML 46032 1902 A4
3300 INPS 46218 2229 C3
3800 INPS 46205 2229 C2
N Adams St
10 BNBG 46112 2114 C6
100 AdmT 46069 1573 B1
100 SRDN 46069 1573 B1
1900 INPS 46218 2229 C7
S Adams St
10 BNBG 46112 2114 C7
300 SRDN 46069 1573 B1
Adams Blvd East Dr
6200 INPS 46220 2121 A3
Adams Blvd North Dr
4900 INPS 46220 2121 A3
Adams Blvd West Dr
6200 INPS 46220 2121 A3
Adamson Ct
6500 INPS 46268 2117 D2
Addison Ct
17000 WTFD 46074 1793 B2
N Addison St
10 INPS 46222 2336 C3
S Addison St
200 INPS 46222 2336 C4
800 INPS 46221 2336 C5
Addison Meadows Ln
- INPS 46203 2448 D2
Adelaide St
5300 BHGV 46203 2448 B5
Adina Blvd
1800 INPS 46203 2339 B7
Adina Ct
5400 INPS 46203 2339 B7
Adina St
5500 INPS 46203 2339 B7
Adios Ct
400 WshT 46032 1792 D6
Adios Pass
13700 CRML 46032 1901 E1
13900 CRML 46032 1792 D7
14600 WshT 46032 1792 D6
Adirondack Ct
1100 INPS 46234 2333 E1
12600 FSHR 46038 1906 A6
Adler St
10 INPS 46225 2337 C7
Admar Ct
3400 INPS 46205 2120 D7
Administration Av
- INPS 46221 2445 D2
Admiral Dr
2100 INPS 46219 2230 D6
Admiral Wy
200 WshT 46032 1792 C6
Admirals Ct
7800 LWNC 46236 2014 D7
Admirals Ln
11500 LWNC 46236 2014 D7
Admirals Bay Dr
9100 INPS 46236 2015 A3
Admirals Cove
8400 LWNC 46236 2015 A5
Admirals Landing Blvd
12100 LWNC 46236 2014 E5
12200 LWNC 46236 2015 B6
Admirals Landing Pl
8200 LWNC 46236 2015 A5
Admirals Landing Wy
8400 INPS 46236 2014 E5
8400 LWNC 46236 2014 E5
Admirals Pointe Cir
12000 INPS 46236 2014 E3
Admirals Pointe Ct
9100 INPS 46236 2014 E3
Admirals Pointe Dr
8800 INPS 46236 2014 E4
Admirals Woods Cir
8700 INPS 46236 2014 E4
Admirals Woods Dr
8600 INPS 46236 2014 E4
Admiralty Ln
3400 INPS 46240 2120 C1
E Admiral Way South Dr
10 WshT 46032 1792 D6
W Admiral Way South Dr
10 WshT 46032 1792 C6
Admiral Wy North Dr
14800 WshT 46032 1792 C6
W Adonis Dr
5600 INPS 46278 2117 B2
Adriana Ct
19100 NBVL 46060 1687 C4
Adrienne Dr
200 WRvT 46142 2663 E4
Advisory Wy
3500 INPS 46240 2011 D3
3600 CRML 46240 2011 D3
Advisory Link
3700 INPS 46240 2011 D3
Aegean Rd
9900 FCkT 46038 2014 D1
Aerie Ln
4600 INPS 46254 2116 E7
Aerobic Ln E
- INPS 46217 2554 A3
Aeronica Ln
10500 FCkT 46055 2015 C1
Affirmed Ct
- WshT 46234 2224 D6
Affirmed Dr
- WshT 46234 2224 D6
Afton Crest St
6100 INPS 46220 2121 D4
Agan Dr
- PNFD 46168 2442 A7
1300 PNFD 46168 2441 E7
Agate Ln
17100 WTFD 46074 1792 C1
Agawam Dr
5700 LWNC 46226 2121 E5
5700 LWNC 46226 2122 A5
Agoura Dr
- CCRO 46034 1577 B6
Ahern Ct
6600 INPS 46268 2118 C2
Aho Dr
5700 WshT 46123 2222 E7
Aigner Ct
7100 INPS 46278 2116 D1
Ailes Rd
- LEBN 46052 1676 E2
Ainsley Cir
8400 INPS 46256 2013 C5
Aintree Ct
6600 INPS 46250 2012 E3
Aintree Dr
9100 INPS 46250 2012 D3
Aintree Pl
6500 INPS 46250 2012 D3
Aintree Ter
6500 INPS 46250 2012 D3
Aintree Wy
200 AVON 46123 2333 C3
200 WshT 46123 2333 C3
Aira Dr
400 INPS 46234 2333 E2
Airtel Blvd
12900 CRML 46077 1900 A3
Airport Blvd
- BCkT 46055 2124 E7
- BCkT 46055 2125 A7
Airport Dr
3900 INPS 46254 2225 D2
Airport Expwy
- INPS 46241 2444 B1
- INPS 46241 2445 A1
Airport Pkwy
10 GNWD 46143 2665 E3
E Airport Rd
800 BNBG 46112 2223 D3
Airtech Pkwy
300 PNFD 46168 2442 C5
Airway Dr
6300 INPS 46241 2444 A4
Airwest Blvd
2200 GfdT 46168 2442 A7
N Alabama St
10 INPS 46204 2337 D3
700 INPS 46202 2337 D2
1500 INPS 46202 2228 D7
2500 INPS 46205 2228 D5
S Alabama St
300 INPS 46204 2337 D4
900 INPS 46225 2337 C5
Alameda Pl
15500 WshT 46074 1792 A4
Alameda Rd
4800 INPS 46228 2118 B7
Alamingo Dr
1700 INPS 46260 2118 E1
Alamosa Dr
8100 LWNC 46236 2015 A6
10800 FSHR 46038 1905 C2
Alamosa Ln
7900 LWNC 46236 2015 A6
S Alan Dr
8000 INPS 46113 2552 C6
Alapaka Ct
7700 INPS 46217 2555 A5
Albany Ct
17800 NBVL 46062 1685 A7
Albany St
10 BHGV 46107 2448 A3
100 INPS 46225 2446 C2
500 BHGV 46107 2447 C2
1800 INPS 46107 2447 C2
1900 INPS 46203 2447 A2
E Albany St
900 INPS 46203 2446 E2
Albemarle Cir
1100 NBVL 46062 1686 A4
Albert Ct
10 CRML 46032 1902 B2
E Albert Dr
10 INPS 46227 2555 C1
Alberta St
- INPS 46222 2226 E4
W Alberta St
4000 INPS 46222 2226 E4
4000 INPS 46222 2227 A4
Albion Ct
- FSHR 46060 1905 A2
Albion Dr
6500 INPS 46256 2122 A2
Albright Ct
3100 INPS 46268 2009 B3
Albury Dr
6100 LWNC 46236 2123 B3
Alcona Dr
8200 INPS 46237 2556 D6
Alcott Cir
5500 INPS 46221 2553 B3
Alcott Ct
- FSHR 46038 2013 D1
Alcott Ln
5500 INPS 46221 2553 B3
Alcove Dr
4100 INPS 46237 2448 C5
Alden Av
4300 INPS 46221 2444 D4
Alden Ln
5800 INPS 46250 2012 C6
Aldenham Blvd
12000 FCkT 46038 2014 E1
12000 FSHR 46038 2014 E1
12200 FSHR 46038 2015 A1
Alder Ct
5900 CRML 46033 1794 E7
6500 INPS 46268 2117 D2
Alderly Ct
8800 INPS 46260 2010 A4
Alderly Rd
1100 INPS 46260 2010 A4
Aldersgate Dr
4500 CRML 46033 1902 E4
4500 CRML 46033 1903 A4
Alderwood Ct
10400 FSHR 46038 2012 C1
Aldgate Ln
7100 INPS 46250 2121 D1
Alec Dr
8700 INPS 46234 2225 A7
Aleene St
- FSHR 46060 1905 D1
Alex Dr
10 WTLD 46184 2775 A4
Alexander Ln
9600 FSHR 46038 2012 D2
Alexander St
700 GNWD 46143 2665 E3
7700 INPS 46259 2559 C5
Alexander Wy
- DNVL 46122 2330 A3
Alexandria Ct
3600 INPS 46205 2229 C2
15400 WshT 46074 1792 B5
Alexandria Dr
2300 BCkT 46112 2235 A7
15200 WshT 46074 1792 B5
Alexia Dr
9900 LWNC 46236 2123 A4
Alfred Cir
1100 INPS 46239 2341 D5
Algeciras Dr
8600 INPS 46250 2012 A4
Alibeck Ct
8900 INPS 46256 2014 A4
Alice Av
3000 INPS 46237 2447 B3
7300 INPS 46219 2340 A3
Alice Ct
10300 FSHR 46060 1905 B1
Alice Jeanne Ct
1700 INPS 46219 2231 A7
Alig St
- INPS 46225 2337 B4
Alimingo Dr
1100 INPS 46260 2119 A1
1200 INPS 46260 2118 E2
All American Rd
13100 FSHR 46060 1906 B2
S Allan Ct
5600 INPS 46239 2450 C7
Allayna Pl
13600 FSHR 46038 1904 C1
Allegan Dr
7000 INPS 46217 2554 B4
Allegheny St
- INPS 46202 2337 D2
- INPS 46204 2337 C2
Allegiance Dr
13300 FSHR 46060 1906 B2
Allegro Dr
9100 INPS 46231 2333 E6
Allen Av
2600 INPS 46203 2446 D2
Allen Ct
700 WshT 46074 1792 E3
Allen Dr
400 LcnT 46112 2224 C2
4500 CRML 46033 1902 E1
N Allen Dr
100 CtrT 46052 1786 B1
S Allen Dr
100 LEBN 46052 1786 B1
2900 SCkT 46163 2343 C7
W Allen Dr
3800 SCkT 46163 2343 C7
Allen Ln
100 GNFD 46140 2236 D6
Allen Rd
2000 GNWD 46143 2666 C5
2000 PltT 46143 2666 C5
2600 ClkT 46143 2666 E5
Allen St
- NBVL 46060 1686 C7
7500 LWNC 46226 2231 A1
S Allen St
10 NPLN 46163 2452 B3
Allendale Dr
5800 INPS 46224 2226 B3
Allenhurst Cir
600 CRML 46032 1901 B1
Allenwood Cir
7600 INPS 46268 2009 A7
Allenwood Ct
7500 INPS 46268 2009 A7

STREET
Block City ZIP Map# Grid

Allero Av
5400 INPS 46237 2448 C7
Allero Dr
5300 INPS 46237 2448 C7
Allford Ct
2300 INPS 46229 2232 E6
Allfree St
2100 INPS 46202 2228 B7
Alliance Dr
- GfdT 46168 2551 D7
Allied Blvd
- INPS 46224 2335 C3
N Allison Av
7800 INPS 46268 2008 C7
Allison Ct
- WRvT 46142 2663 E4
10 BrnT 46113 2660 C2
200 INPS 46241 2335 D4
3100 CRML 46033 1793 C7
Allison Dr
14300 CRML 46033 1793 C7
N Allison Dr
13300 BrnT 46113 2660 B2
Allison Rd
- BrnT 46158 2660 B2
10 MRVL 46113 2660 B2
100 BrnT 46113 2660 B2
900 MdnT 46113 2660 B2
Allison St
1000 SDWY 46224 2335 C1
1600 SDWY 46224 2226 C7
N Allison St
3200 INPS 46224 2226 C3
Allison Wy
5400 NBVL 46062 1685 B1
Allison Pointe Blvd
8200 INPS 46250 2012 A5
Allison Pointe Tr
8200 INPS 46250 2012 A5
Allisonville Rd
4300 INPS 46205 2229 B1
4500 INPS 46205 2120 C7
5100 INPS 46220 2120 C7
7100 INPS 46250 2120 D4
7100 INPS 46250 2121 A1
8700 INPS 46250 2012 B4
9400 FSHR 46038 2012 D1
9600 FSHR 46250 2012 D1
9800 DelT 46038 2012 D1
10500 FSHR 46038 1903 E7
10600 DelT 46038 1903 E7
11000 DelT 46038 1904 A4
11000 FSHR 46038 1904 A4
14200 DelT 46060 1795 D4
14200 FSHR 46060 1795 D4
14400 NbvT 46060 1795 D4
15100 NBVL 46060 1795 D4
19100 NBVL 46060 1686 E4
19100 NbvT 46060 1686 E4
19400 NBVL 46060 1687 A3
19400 NbvT 46060 1687 A3
N Allisonville Rd
- INPS 46205 2229 B1
Allisonwood Ct
5900 INPS 46250 2012 C3
Allisonwood Dr
9100 INPS 46250 2012 C3
Allman Dr
10 BrnT 46158 2658 D3
Allmon Dr
- BrnT 46158 2658 D3
Allport Dr
6200 INPS 46254 2117 A7
Allspice Ln
8000 INPS 46239 2449 B4
Almaden Ct
7600 INPS 46278 2007 D7
Almaden Dr
7100 INPS 46278 2007 D7
Almond Ct
1300 PNFD 46168 2441 D7
4200 WRvT 46143 2663 E5
Almond Dr
1200 PNFD 46168 2441 D7
7800 INPS 46237 2557 D5
Alnwick Ct
6800 INPS 46220 2121 E2
Aloda St
3800 INPS 46203 2338 D6
Alonzo Watford Senior Dr
1600 INPS 46202 2228 B7
S Alpha Av
500 BNBG 46112 2223 A1
Alpha Dr
- WTFD 46074 1683 D7
Alpha Ln
4400 INPS 46208 2228 B1
Alpine
- GNWD 46143 2666 A1
Alpine Av
6000 INPS 46224 2226 A4
Alpine Dr
20600 NBVL 46062 1685 B1
Alpine Pl
3400 INPS 46226 2231 C3
Alsace Ct
4000 INPS 46226 2231 C2
Alsace Dr
3600 INPS 46226 2231 C3
Alsace Pl
3800 INPS 46226 2231 C2
Alsong Ct
14700 WshT 46032 1792 C6
Alston Dr
7000 INPS 46217 2555 B4
13300 FSHR 46060 1906 C2
Alsuda Ct
- INPS 46205 2120 D7
Alsuda Dr
4700 INPS 46205 2120 D7
Altair Ct
4800 WRvT 46142 2663 D4
Altam Av
500 CRML 46032 1902 C3
Altamount Dr
11300 FCkT 46040 1907 A6
Altavista Ct
11000 FSHR 46038 1904 E6
Alto Ct
10200 NbvT 46060 1796 B4
Alto Wy
8800 INPS 46231 2334 A6
N Alton Av
1000 INPS 46222 2336 B1
3300 INPS 46222 2227 B3
5900 INPS 46228 2118 B4
7700 INPS 46268 2009 B7
S Alton Av
1200 INPS 46241 2336 B6
Alton Ct
9100 FSHR 46038 2013 D2
Alton Dr
300 INPS 46222 2336 B3
400 GNWD 46143 2665 B6
Alton St
100 BHGV 46107 2448 A3
1700 BHGV 46107 2447 C3
Aluminum Dr
4900 INPS 46218 2230 A5
Alvamar Pl
5300 CRML 46033 1903 D3
Alvee Cir
1900 INPS 46239 2340 B7
Alverdo Ln
4200 WTFD 46033 1793 E6
Alverna Dr
600 INPS 46260 2010 B5
Alverna Retreat Rd
- INPS 46260 2010 B5
Alvernon Pl
- FSHR 46060 1905 C1
Alvey Ct
700 GNWD 46143 2665 E6
Alvord St
1600 INPS 46202 2228 E7
2200 INPS 46205 2228 E6
Alwyne Dr
2000 INPS 46227 2556 A7
Alwyne Rd
600 CRML 46032 1902 C2
Alydar Cir
1000 INPS 46217 2555 A3
Alysheba Dr
- WshT 46234 2224 E6
15000 NBVL 46060 1796 D6
Alyssa Ln
6800 INPS 46250 2012 E5
Alyssa Wy
10700 FSHR 46038 1904 D7
Amadeus Dr
7700 INPS 46239 2449 B2
Amalfi Dr
10 CRML 46032 1792 D7
Amanda Cir
500 GNFD 46140 2236 E5
Amanda Ct
10 BNBG 46112 2223 C2
W Amanda Ct
- BCkT 46140 2233 B7
6900 GNFD 46140 2236 E5
Amandas Wy
6800 INPS 46250 2012 C5
Amaranth Ct
3800 INPS 46254 2225 D2
Amarillo Dr
8100 INPS 46237 2557 C6
Amarillo Wy
6300 INPS 46237 2557 D5
Amaryllis Ct
4900 INPS 46254 2117 D5
Ambassador Ct
1800 INPS 46214 2225 E7
Amber Ct
6100 LWNC 46236 2123 B4
S Amber Ct
4100 NPLN 46163 2452 A2
Amber Dr
- LcnT 46112 2115 D6
Amber Wy
19200 NBVL 46060 1687 B4
Amber Crest St
6500 INPS 46220 2121 D3
Amber Glen Dr
10800 INPS 46229 2341 C1
Amber Glow Ct
9600 FSHR 46038 2013 D2
E Amberleaf Tr
400 WTFD 46074 1793 B1
Amberleigh Dr
- PNFD 46168 2442 B2
Amber Pass
6300 PNFD 46168 2550 D3
Amber Ridge Dr
1800 INPS 46234 2225 A7
Amber Springs Dr
- INPS 46237 2557 E2
Amber Springs Wy
6700 INPS 46237 2557 E2
Amber Turn
7700 PNFD 46168 2550 C2
Amber Valley Dr
6900 INPS 46237 2557 E2
Amber Valley Ln
6000 INPS 46237 2557 E2
Amberwood Ct
17900 WTFD 46074 1684 C7
Ambia Cir
- WTFD 46074 1792 D3
Amble Wy
8100 INPS 46237 2557 D6
Ambleside Ct
8200 INPS 46256 2013 E6
Amblewind Pl
13600 CRML 46074 1900 C1
14000 CRML 46074 1791 C7
Ambry Wy
7800 INPS 46259 2558 B4
Amburg Ct
11000 INPS 46235 2232 C3
Amburg Dr
11100 INPS 46235 2232 C3
Amelia Ct
10900 NBVL 46060 1687 C4
Amelia Dr
1200 INPS 46241 2334 E6
W Amelia Dr
7000 SCkT 46163 2451 B3
Amerherst Dr
2000 INPS 46260 2118 D1
America Av
6300 INPS 46241 2444 A6
American Wy
7000 INPS 46256 2012 E7
7100 INPS 46256 2013 A7
Americana Blvd
8600 INPS 46268 2008 C4
American Legion Pl
10 GNFD 46140 2345 E2
Americus Ct
- MdnT 46113 2661 D1
Ameriplex Pkwy
- INPS 46221 2552 B2
7900 INPS 46241 2552 B2
Ames St
8200 LWNC 46216 2122 B6
Amesbury Ct
900 INPS 46217 2555 A4
Amesbury Pl
- WshT 46062 1684 E6
Amethyst Av
7700 INPS 46268 2009 C6
Amethyst Ct
12300 CRML 46032 1901 A4
Amherst Dr
6200 FSHR 46038 1903 D6
Amherst St
2600 INPS 46268 2009 B3
Amhurst Cir
200 NBVL 46062 1685 D2
Amhurst Wy
- EglT 46077 1897 C7
Amick Av
- INPS 46217 2554 A3
Amick Wy
6400 INPS 46268 2118 B2
Amigo Av
3800 INPS 46237 2556 D3
Amkey Ct
14900 WshT 46032 1792 D6
E Amkey Wy
100 WshT 46032 1792 D6
Amos Dr
500 EglT 46077 1898 A4
Amsterdam Ct
7800 WshT 46123 2332 D7
Amundson Dr
13100 CRML 46074 1900 B2
Amy Ct
8700 INPS 46256 2013 D5
Amy Ln
8600 INPS 46256 2013 C5
Amys Run Ct
100 CRML 46032 1902 B3
Amys Run Dr
100 CRML 46032 1902 A3
Anchor Ct
10 CCRO 46034 1577 D1
2100 INPS 46229 2231 E7
Anchor Ln
- AVON 46123 2332 E3
Anchor Wy
9500 INPS 46229 2231 E6
Anchorage Ct
8400 LWNC 46236 2014 E5
Anchorage Dr
8800 INPS 46236 2015 A4
Anchorage Wy
12400 FCkT 46236 2015 A1
12400 FSHR 46038 2015 A1
Anchor Bay Ct
8800 INPS 46236 2015 B4
Anchor Bay Dr
8900 INPS 46236 2015 A4
21500 CCRO 46034 1577 B6
21500 CCRO 46062 1577 B6
21500 NBVL 46034 1577 B6
21500 NBVL 46062 1577 B6
Anchor Mark Dr
9000 INPS 46236 2015 A4
Andalusia Grv
1000 INPS 46260 2010 A5
Anderson Blvd
900 GNFD 46140 2236 C4
Anderson Cir
- WshT 46123 2332 E1
E Anderson Ln N
10 LEBN 46052 1677 A2
W Anderson Ln N
10 LEBN 46052 1676 E2
10 LEBN 46052 1677 B2
200 CtrT 46052 1676 E2
N Anderson St
10 NPLN 46163 2452 B2
3400 INPS 46234 2224 E3
S Anderson St
10 NPLN 46163 2452 A4
W Anderson St
- NBVL 46060 1686 D6
Anderson-Hamilton Rd
9000 JknT 46011 1580 E1
Andes Dr
9000 INPS 46234 2333 E1
9000 INPS 46234 2334 A1
Andico Rd
600 PNFD 46168 2441 C3
Andiron Ct
9300 INPS 46250 2012 E3
Andiron Dr
9100 INPS 46250 2012 E3
Andiron Wy
9100 INPS 46250 2012 E3
Andorra Dr
8400 FSHR 46038 1904 C1
Andover Ct
3100 GNWD 46142 2664 B1
13000 CRML 46033 1902 E2
Andover Dr
800 GNWD 46142 2664 B1
12800 CRML 46033 1902 E3
Andover Ln
200 NBVL 46060 1795 D3
Andover Rd
4600 INPS 46226 2121 A7
5700 INPS 46220 2120 E4
5700 INPS 46220 2121 A4
Andover Sq
4700 INPS 46226 2121 A7
4700 INPS 46226 2230 A1
Andrade Dr
10600 EglT 46077 1899 D7
10600 ZNVL 46077 1899 D7
W Andre Ct
7100 INPS 46278 2007 D7
W Andre Dr
6900 INPS 46278 2007 E7
Andrea Ct
10 BHGV 46107 2447 E6
10700 WshT 46231 2333 D5
Andrea Dr
500 BHGV 46107 2447 E6
Andrews Blvd
100 PNFD 46168 2441 A5
200 PNFD 46168 2440 E5
Andrews Ct
2500 INPS 46203 2448 B1
Andrews Dr
1200 WshT 46123 2332 E7
1200 WshT 46123 2441 E1
Andrews Pl
10900 FSHR 46038 1904 E7
Andrews Blvd East Dr
200 PNFD 46168 2440 D5
200 PNFD 46168 2441 A5
Andrews Pass
7700 PNFD 46168 2550 C3
Andrew Turn
7600 PNFD 46168 2550 C3
Andrusia Ln
8300 INPS 46237 2556 D6
Andscott Cir
10 BNBG 46112 2223 C2
Andscott Dr
300 BNBG 46112 2223 C2
4400 INPS 46254 2225 E1
Andy Dr
2500 INPS 46229 2231 E5
Anemone Ct
1400 INPS 46219 2340 B1
Anemone Ln
8000 INPS 46219 2340 B1
Aneta Dr
2000 BCkT 46140 2235 A7
Angel Wy
5300 NBVL 46062 1685 B2
Angela Ct
10 BHGV 46107 2447 E6
200 NbvT 46062 1794 D4
1200 PNFD 46168 2550 D2
Angela Ln
10 CRML 46032 1792 E7
Angel Berry Cir
14400 FSHR 46060 1796 B6
Angel Falls Dr
6400 NBVL 46062 1685 D3
Angelina Wy
6000 INPS 46203 2448 C2
Angelique Ct
1100 CRML 46032 1901 A4
Angelique Dr
5000 INPS 46254 2117 C7
Angel Tear Ct
1900 INPS 46231 2333 E7
Angel Tear Wy
9100 INPS 46231 2333 E7
Angilee Wy
900 LEBN 46052 1677 A2
Angola Ct
9500 INPS 46268 2009 A2
Anita Dr
4600 INPS 46217 2446 B6
Anita Ln
2300 BCkT 46140 2344 A1
Anjuli Ct
10 NWTD 46184 2774 C4
Ann St
1000 MdnT 46113 2661 C5
4000 LtyT 46118 2439 E5
4000 LtyT 46168 2439 E5
N Ann St
200 LEBN 46052 1677 A6
S Ann St
- LEBN 46052 1677 A6
Anna Ct
6700 PNFD 46168 2550 B1
Anna Dr
300 GNWD 46143 2665 C5
Annahill Ct
5800 WshT 46123 2331 E5
Annally Dr
3100 ClyT 46032 2009 B1
Annandale Dr
5700 CRML 46033 1903 D2
Annapolis Dr
- WshT 46074 1792 A6
5800 INPS 46254 2117 C4
Annelo Cir
4500 WRvT 46142 2663 D5
Annelo Dr
4400 WRvT 46142 2663 E5
Annetta St
5100 INPS 46208 2119 A7
Annette Ln
12100 FSHR 46038 1906 B4
Annette St
2500 INPS 46208 2228 A5
Annex Dr
1100 INPS 46224 2335 B1
Annie Ln
300 FCkT 46038 1906 D6
Anniston Dr
200 SPRT 46227 2556 B4
Anniston St
1400 INPS 46227 2555 E4
1400 INPS 46227 2556 A4
Ann Marie Wy
5900 INPS 46254 2117 B4
Ansar Ct
4100 INPS 46254 2117 E7
4100 INPS 46254 2226 E1
Ansar Ln
4100 INPS 46254 2226 E1
4100 INPS 46254 2227 A1
Ansley Ct
400 INPS 46234 2334 B2
Anson St
9600 FSHR 46038 1904 E4
Antelope Blvd
6700 INPS 46278 2116 E2
Antelope Cir
6600 INPS 46278 2116 E2
Antelope Ct
6600 INPS 46278 2116 E2
Antelope Dr
6800 INPS 46278 2116 E2
Antelope Ln
6600 INPS 46278 2116 E2
Antero Ct
5400 INPS 46221 2553 C3
Antero Ln
6600 INPS 46221 2553 B3
Anthem Av
12800 FSHR 46060 1906 B1
Anthony Cir
7300 LWNC 46236 2124 A1
Anthony Ct
1100 GNWD 46143 2665 D1
Anthony Rd
20600 JknT 46062 1575 D7
20600 WshT 46062 1575 D7
20600 WshT 46062 1684 D1
20600 WTFD 46062 1684 D1
21600 JknT 46034 1575 D5
Antietam Cir
6900 INPS 46278 2116 D2
Antietam Ct
6900 INPS 46278 2116 E2
Antietam Pl
6800 INPS 46278 2116 D2
Antigua Tr
5000 INPS 46237 2448 B7
Antioch Rd
100 MnrT 46158 2658 B6
Antique Ct
800 INPS 46260 2119 B3
Antler Ct
6200 EglT 46077 1898 D5
Antler Wy
7000 INPS 46254 2225 D2
Antoinette Pl
10 INPS 46227 2555 C1
S Anton Wy
4300 SCkT 46163 2451 A3
W Anton Wy
7000 SCkT 46163 2451 B3
Antone Ct
11600 FCkT 46040 1907 A5
E Antoneli Dr
5800 INPS 46237 2557 C1
Antoneli Ln
5400 INPS 46237 2448 C7
5400 INPS 46237 2557 C1
Antonia Blvd
13100 CRML 46074 1900 A2
Anton Tony Hulman Jr Mem Wy
- CtrT - 2236 E3
- CtrT - 2237 B3
- GNFD - 2236 E3
Anton T Hulman Jr Mem Wy I-70
- CtrT - 2236 E3
- CtrT - 2237 B3
- GNFD - 2236 E3
Antwerp Ter
3700 INPS 46228 2227 A1
Antwood Ct
6900 NBVL 46062 1794 E2
Anvil Ct
8400 FSHR 46038 1904 C6
Apache Ct
300 NbvT 46060 1796 A3
6100 INPS 46254 2117 A7
Apache Dr
2300 WshT 46234 2224 E6
W Apache Dr
6000 INPS 46254 2117 A7
Apache Moon
5200 CRML 46033 1903 C1
Apache Well
5900 SDWY 46224 2226 B7
Apalachian Wy
11100 FSHR 46038 1906 A6
Apilita Ct
3000 CRML 46033 2011 C1
Apollo Pkwy
500 WshT 46074 1792 D4
Apollo Wy
6400 INPS 46278 2117 B2
Apothecary Ct
7500 PNFD 46168 2441 C3
Apothecary Ln
- DNVL 46122 2330 A3
Appaloosa Wy
7300 INPS 46278 2117 A1
Appel Dr
8800 FSHR 46038 1904 D6
Apple Al
1700 BrnT 46158 2658 C3
1700 MnrT 46158 2658 C3
Apple Ln
700 BNBG 46112 2114 D4
Apple St
- DNVL 46122 2329 C3
3500 INPS 46203 2338 D6
N Apple St
10 GNFD 46140 2346 A1
600 GNFD 46140 2237 A7
1500 CtrT 46140 2237 A5
Apple Blossom Cir
10100 FSHR 46060 1796 A7
Apple Blossom Ct
5700 LcnT 46112 2222 E1
Apple Blossom Ln
8600 INPS 46113 2552 A3
E Apple Blossom Ln
1000 GNFD 46140 2237 B6
N Apple Blossom Ln
1300 GNFD 46140 2237 A6
Apple Blossom Wy
- DNVL 46122 2329 C3
Apple Branch Ct
5700 INPS 46237 2557 D1
Apple Branch Ln
6500 INPS 46237 2557 D1
Apple Branch Wy
5500 INPS 46237 2448 E7
5500 INPS 46237 2557 D2
Appleby Ln
8400 INPS 46256 2013 C3
Apple Cider Wy
6400 WshT 46123 2332 B6
Apple Cove Ct
3800 SCkT 46163 2452 B2
Apple Cross Cir
7300 AVON 46123 2332 C2
Apple Cross Dr
4300 INPS 46254 2225 E1
Applecross Dr
100 BNBG 46112 2114 A5
Applegate Ct
5800 CRML 46033 1903 D2
S Applegate Dr
- NPLN 46163 2452 A2
3400 SCkT 46163 2451 E1
3500 SCkT 46163 2452 A1
Applegate St
2000 INPS 46203 2337 D7
2600 INPS 46203 2446 D2
Applehorn Ln
8500 INPS 46256 2013 C3
E Apple Lake Dr
1000 GNFD 46140 2237 A6
N Apple Lake Dr
1300 GNFD 46140 2237 A6
Apple Spice Dr
10000 LWNC 46235 2123 A6
Apple Spruce Dr
- LWNC 46235 2122 E7
Appleton Ct
400 INPS 46234 2334 B2
Appleton Dr
2300 INPS 46227 2556 B6
Appleton Ter
2500 INPS 46227 2556 B6
Apple Tree Cir
10 FSHR 46038 1904 A4
Apple Tree Ct
100 FSHR 46038 1904 B4
Apple Tree Dr
300 FSHR 46038 1904 B4
Apple Tree Ln
9700 LWNC 46235 2122 D7
9800 LWNC 46235 2123 A7
Appletree Row
10 GNWD 46142 2665 A3
Apple Valley Rd
1000 GNWD 46142 2664 C1
Apple View Ln
1000 GNFD 46140 2237 A7
Applewood Cir
11500 CRML 46032 1901 E5
Applewood Dr
- GNWD 46142 2664 B3
Applewood Ln
8500 INPS 46256 2013 C3
Apple Wy Dr
700 DNVL 46122 2329 C3
Approach Blvd
11600 FSHR 46038 1905 E7
April Ln
- INPS 46239 2449 C6
Apryl Dr
- GNWD 46143 2664 E6
- GNWD 46143 2665 B6
Apsley Ln
12600 CRML 46032 1900 D3
Aquaduct Dr
4600 WRvT 46142 2663 D4
Aquamarine Dr
5600 CRML 46033 1903 B2
Aqua Vista Dr
1100 INPS 46229 2341 A1
Aqueduct St
1600 INPS 46202 2228 A7
2300 INPS 46208 2228 A6
Aqueduct Wy
1100 ClyT 46280 1901 E7
1100 ClyT 46280 1902 A7
Aqueous Ln
3200 INPS 46214 2225 C4
Arabian Ct
5600 INPS 46228 2118 A5
Arabian Run
5500 INPS 46228 2118 A6
Aragon Woods Ct
3000 INPS 46214 2225 B4
Aragon Woods Dr
8100 INPS 46214 2225 B4
Arapaho Ct
5200 CRML 46033 1903 C1
Arapaho Wy
5200 CRML 46033 1903 C1
Arapahoe Dr
10000 INPS 46235 2123 A7
Arbor Av
400 INPS 46221 2336 E4
Arbor Dr
200 CRML 46032 1901 D3
S Arbor Ln W
- SCkT 46163 2451 C2
Arbor St
3000 INPS 46217 2445 E3
Arbor Bluff Wy
- INPS 46217 2554 E4
Arbor Creek Dr
5200 INPS 46254 2117 A6
Arborcrest Dr
3800 INPS 46226 2231 B1
Arbor Glen Blvd
- FSHR 46038 1905 E5
Arbor Glen Dr
- BNBG 46112 2113 E6
Arbor Green Ln
- INPS 46220 2120 D5
Arbor Green Wy
3700 INPS 46220 2120 D5
Arbor Grove Blvd
15800 NbvT 46060 1796 B4
Arborhill Dr
11600 EglT 46077 1899 D2
Arbor Lake Ct
8700 INPS 46268 2009 C4
Arbor Lake Dr
8700 INPS 46268 2009 C4
Arbor Lake Ln
2400 INPS 46268 2009 C4
Arbor Springs Dr
- BNBG 46112 2114 C3
Arbor Trails Dr
- INPS 46203 2448 D3
Arborview Dr
11300 LWNC 46236 2014 C6
Arborway Ct
8700 INPS 46268 2009 C4
Arborway Ln
- INPS 46268 2009 C4
Arborwood Tr
11100 CRML 46032 1901 E6
Arbor Woods Dr
- BNBG 46112 2113 E6
- LcnT 46112 2113 E6
700 INPS 46241 2335 A5
Arbutus Dr
3100 INPS 46224 2226 A4
W Arcadia St
3800 INPS 46222 2227 A4
4200 INPS 46222 2226 E4
W Arcadia Wy
100 BrnT 46158 2658 D4
E Arch St
200 INPS 46204 2337 D2
300 INPS 46202 2337 D2
Archdale St
- CRML 46032 1900 C3
Archwood Dr
6900 INPS 46214 2334 E3
Arcola Ct
1300 BHGV 46107 2447 E6
Arden Ct
13200 CRML 46033 1902 E2
Arden Dr
100 INPS 46220 2119 D2
Ardennes Dr
8400 FSHR 46038 1904 C2
8500 DelT 46038 1904 C2
Ardin Ct
- CRML 46033 1902 D5
Ardmoor Dr
200 WTLD 46184 2774 E5
400 NWTD 46184 2774 E5
Ardmore Av
1300 BHGV 46107 2447 E6
1300 BHGV 46107 2448 A6
Ardsley Cir
11500 FSHR 46038 1906 A5
Ardsley Dr
- INPS 46234 2334 B2
Ardwell Ct
7600 INPS 46237 2557 E5
Ardwell Dr
7500 INPS 46237 2557 E5
Argus Av
3400 INPS 46226 2231 C3
Argyle Ct
3200 INPS 46226 2230 E4
3300 INPS 46226 2231 A4
Argyle Dr
1200 WshT 46123 2332 E7
1800 WshT 46123 2441 E1
Ari Ln
12700 FSHR 46060 1906 D3
Ariana Ct
5000 INPS 46227 2446 C7
Ariel Wy
900 GNFD 46140 2237 A7
Arielle Dr
- FSHR 46060 1905 D1
Aristocrat Cir
4400 INPS 46235 2232 A1
Aristocrat Ct
4400 INPS 46235 2232 A1
Aristocrat Ln
4200 INPS 46235 2232 A1
Aristocrat North Dr
10200 INPS 46235 2232 A1
E Arizona St
10 INPS 46225 2337 C6
W Arizona St
10 INPS 46225 2337 C6
Arjay Dr
6800 INPS 46217 2555 A3
Arlene Dr
1700 INPS 46219 2231 A7
AR les Dr
1400 NBVL 46060 1686 D5
Arley Dr
1600 INPS 46229 2232 C7
N Arlington Av
10 INPS 46219 2339 C2
2100 INPS 46218 2230 C7
2100 INPS 46219 2230 C7

Indianapolis Street Index

STREET
Block City ZIP Map# Grid

N Arlington Av
3000 INPS 46226 2230 C3
4500 INPS 46226 2121 C6
S Arlington Av
10 INPS 46219 2339 C4
900 INPS 46203 2339 C4
2200 INPS 46203 2448 C1
3300 BHGV 46203 2448 C3
4200 INPS 46237 2448 C7
5500 INPS 46237 2557 C2
Arlington Cir
4300 INPS 46237 2448 C5
Arlington Ct
1000 ClyT 46280 1901 E6
1000 ClyT 46280 1902 A6
6000 INPS 46226 2121 C7
W Arlington Ct
2400 INPS 46218 2230 C6
Arlington Dr
500 MRVL 46158 2659 E3
1200 GNFD 46140 2237 A6
Arlington St
200 WTLD 46184 2774 E5
Arlington Wy
6000 INPS 46237 2448 C5
Armada Ct
11600 FCkT 46038 2014 D1
11600 FSHR 46038 2014 D1
Armada Dr
3900 INPS 46237 2556 D6
Armadale Ct
8200 LWNC 46236 2014 E5
Armentrout Ln
400 INPS 46241 2335 B5
Armistead Ln
8400 INPS 46227 2556 D7
Armitage St
100 CCRO 46034 1577 D3
Armon Ct
4100 CRML 46033 1902 E6
Armon Dr
11100 CRML 46033 1902 E6
Armour Av
2400 INPS 46220 2120 B6
Armstead Av
- LcnT 46112 2115 D6
Armstrong Ct
5400 INPS 46237 2448 B7
Armstrong Dr
5300 INPS 46237 2448 B7
Arnold Av
- INPS 46241 2445 B2
N Arnolda Av
500 INPS 46222 2336 B2
N Aronson Dr
9400 CRML 46240 2011 C3
9400 INPS 46240 2011 C3
Around the Hills Rd
6300 INPS 46226 2121 D5
Arquette Cir
9800 INPS 46235 2231 E2
Arquette Ct
4100 INPS 46235 2231 E2
Arquette Dr
3800 INPS 46235 2231 E2
Arrow St
- AdmT 46069 1573 A2
Arrowae Dr
10 CRML 46032 1902 C3
Arrowhead Ct
- LcnT 46112 2115 C5
Arrowhead St
- AdmT 46069 1573 A2
Arrowhead Tr
8000 INPS 46239 2449 B6
Arrowleaf Ln
5800 CRML 46033 1903 D1
Arrowwood Ct
- NBVL 46062 1685 E1
Arrowwood Dr
700 CRML 46033 1793 E7
700 CRML 46033 1902 E1
1000 WTFD 46033 1793 E7
Arrow Wood Ln
3000 INPS 46214 2225 C4
Arroyo Rd
900 GNWD 46143 2665 E5
900 GNWD 46143 2666 A5
N Arsenal Av
10 INPS 46201 2338 A3
3000 INPS 46218 2229 A4
S Arsenal Av
100 INPS 46201 2338 A4
Artesian Ln
10 NPLN 46163 2452 B3
Arthington Blvd
3400 INPS 46218 2229 E3
3800 INPS 46226 2229 E2
Arthur Av
400 INPS 46222 2335 E2
400 SDWY 46222 2335 E2
Arthur Dr
500 ClyT 46280 1901 D7
Arthur St
10 CBLD 46229 2341 C2
Artman Av
100 ULEN 46052 1677 A4
Aruba Ln
7400 INPS 46214 2225 D3
Arundel Ln
3100 INPS 46222 2227 B3
Arvada Ct
7900 LWNC 46236 2015 A6
Arvada Pl
7900 LWNC 46236 2015 A6
10800 FSHR 46038 1905 C3
Asbury St
1500 INPS 46203 2338 A7
2400 INPS 46203 2447 A1
3000 INPS 46237 2447 A3
3300 INPS 46227 2447 A3
Ascending Heights Dr
- LcnT 46112 2115 C6
Ascot Cir
9200 INPS 46260 2009 E3
Ascot Ct
1900 INPS 46260 2009 D3
Ascot Dr
1300 LEBN 46052 1676 D5
Ascot Hill North Dr
15100 WshT 46032 1793 A5
Ascot Hill South Dr
15000 WshT 46032 1793 A5
Ash Cir
100 NBVL 46062 1685 D3
Ash Ct
10 BHGV 46107 2447 E4
4300 ZNVL 46077 1898 D2
8800 INPS 46234 2225 A3
Ash Dr
400 CRML 46032 1902 C3
Ash Rd
3700 INPS 46234 2225 A2
Ash St
- NPLN 46163 2452 B3
- PNFD 46168 2441 B5
400 BHGV 46107 2447 E4
400 BHGV 46107 2448 A4
E Ash St
- LEBN 46052 1677 A7
10 ZNVL 46077 1899 B5
W Ash St
10 ZNVL 46077 1899 B5
200 LEBN 46052 1676 E7
Ashbourne Cir
10 NBVL 46060 1795 D5
Ashbourne Ct
800 GNWD 46142 2665 A5
Ashbourne Dr
10 NBVL 46060 1795 D5
10 NbvT 46060 1795 D5
Ashbourne Ln
3600 INPS 46205 2229 D1
3800 INPS 46226 2229 D1
5100 INPS 46226 2230 A1
S Ashbourne Ln
600 GNWD 46142 2665 A4
W Ashbourne Ln
800 GNWD 46142 2665 A4
Ashbrook Dr
4800 NBVL 46062 1685 A6
Ashbury Cir
10000 FSHR 46038 2014 B2
Ashbury Dr
13500 CRML 46032 1901 B2
Ashby Dr
400 GNFD 46140 2345 B1
5700 INPS 46221 2553 A1
Ashcroft Dr
5700 INPS 46221 2553 B4
Ashcroft Pl
12000 CRML 46032 1900 C4
Ashfield Dr
4700 WTFD 46062 1685 A7
Ashford Ct
200 NBVL 46062 1685 E2
400 INPS 46214 2334 C3
Ashford Dr
500 INPS 46214 2334 C2
Ashford Ln
700 GNWD 46143 2665 B5
Ashford Castle Dr
8900 INPS 46250 2012 C4
Ashlake Ln
9400 FSHR 46038 1795 E7
13900 FSHR 46038 1904 E1
Ashland Av
1000 NWTD 46184 2774 D3
3000 INPS 46226 2231 A4
Ashland Ct
200 WshT 46123 2331 D3
3000 INPS 46226 2231 A4
Ashland Dr
- FSHR 46038 1906 A3
12000 FSHR 46038 1905 E4
Ashland Ln
200 ZNVL 46077 1898 E6
Ash Lawn Rd
- LcnT 46112 2224 E2
- LcnT 46234 2224 E2
Ashley Blvd
- WTFD 46074 1793 B2
Ashley Ct
11100 FSHR 46038 1904 B6
Ashley Dr
- WshT 46123 2333 A1
1300 LEBN 46052 1676 D4
S Ashley Dr
2400 BwnT 46140 2345 E6
Ashley Ln
3200 INPS 46224 2226 C3
11200 FSHR 46038 1904 A7
Ashley Pk
- MdnT 46158 2660 C6
Ashley Pl
11100 FSHR 46038 1904 B6
Ashley Wy
- WTFD 46074 1793 B2
Ashley Crossing
- WTFD 46074 1793 B2
Ashley Jo Dr
- LWNC 46235 2122 E7
Ashley Oakes Ln
900 WshT 46123 2332 A2
Ashley Wood Dr
- WTFD 46074 1793 B2
Ashmore Dr
700 GNWD 46143 2665 C5
Ashmore Ln
5900 CRML 46033 1794 C6
Ash Stone Ct
13800 FCkT 46040 2015 D1
Ashton Dr
7800 FSHR 46038 1904 C5
7900 LWNC 46226 2122 B6
Ashton Ln
7800 FSHR 46038 1904 B5
Ashton Pl
900 CRML 46033 1902 D4
7800 FSHR 46038 1904 B5
Ashton Park Dr
800 GNWD 46143 2665 B5
Ash Tree Ct
- GNWD 46143 2666 A6
Ashtree Ct
7700 INPS 46259 2558 B5
Ashtree Dr
7700 INPS 46259 2558 B5
Ashurst St
5300 INPS 46220 2121 B3
Ashvale Dr
5700 INPS 46250 2012 C3
Ashview Dr
5500 INPS 46237 2557 B6
10600 FSHR 46060 1905 C2
Ashville Dr
- WshT 46074 1792 A4
Ashway Ct
6000 INPS 46224 2226 A4
Ashway Dr
3100 INPS 46224 2226 A4
Ashwood Cir
10 BNBG 46112 2114 D7
Ashwood Ct
1500 WRvT 46143 2664 C7
4700 ZNVL 46077 1899 A3
8100 INPS 46268 2008 E5
Ashwood Dr
1500 WRvT 46143 2664 C7
4200 INPS 46268 2008 E6
10700 FSHR 46060 1905 C2
Ashwood Ln
9400 FSHR 46038 1904 E1
Ashworth Ct
9000 INPS 46260 2010 A3
Askren Dr
8700 INPS 46219 2340 C1
Aspen Ct
- WRvT 46142 2663 C5
500 NBVL 46062 1685 E4
600 DNVL 46122 2330 A3
8300 INPS 46226 2231 C2
Aspen Dr
300 CRML 46032 1902 B3
2000 WshT 46123 2331 E7
2000 WshT 46123 2440 E1
4300 LcnT 46112 2224 D2
10400 FSHR 46038 1905 B5
Aspen Ln
- GNWD 46143 2774 A1
Aspen Wy
- MCVL 46055 2015 B5
100 CRML 46032 1902 B3
100 NBVL 46062 1685 E5
4200 INPS 46226 2231 C1
Aspen Crest Ln
4900 INPS 46254 2116 E7
Aspen Grove Dr
6000 INPS 46250 2012 C3
Aspen Grove Ln
9400 INPS 46250 2012 B2
Aspen Talon Ct
4900 INPS 46254 2116 E7
Assembly Ln
5800 INPS 46254 2117 C5
Association Ct
9600 CRML 46280 2011 D2
Astor St
1300 INPS 46222 2336 D3
Astoria Ct
- GNWD 46143 2666 A5
Astro Ct
2600 INPS 46229 2231 D5
Astro Dr
2700 INPS 46229 2231 D5
Athalene Ln
10400 FCkT 46055 2015 C1
Athens Ct
8400 INPS 46226 2231 C1
Athens Pl
400 WshT 46074 1792 B5
Atherton Ct
10 BNBG 46112 2223 D3
Atherton Dr
300 CRML 46032 1902 A3
Atherton Ln
3800 WRvT 46143 2664 A7
Atherton North Dr
5100 INPS 46219 2339 A3
Atherton South Dr
5100 INPS 46219 2339 A4
Atir Ln
900 GNFD 46140 2237 A7
Atlanta Av
4600 INPS 46241 2444 A6
Atlanta Dr
6400 INPS 46241 2444 A6
N Atlantic Rd
100 JknT 46011 1580 E5
100 SCkT 46011 1580 E5
100 WRvT 46011 1580 E5
100 WRvT 46060 1580 E5
100 WynT 46011 1580 E5
100 WynT 46060 1580 E5
N Atlantic Rd SR-13
100 JknT 46011 1580 E5
100 SCkT 46011 1580 E5
100 WRvT 46011 1580 E5
100 WRvT 46060 1580 E5
100 WynT 46011 1580 E5
100 WynT 46060 1580 E5
N Atlantic Rd E
- JknT 46011 1580 E2
- WRvT 46011 1580 E2
1000 WRvT 46060 1580 E2
1500 JknT 46060 1580 E2
N Atlantic Rd E SR-13
- JknT 46011 1580 E2
- WRvT 46011 1580 E2
1000 WRvT 46060 1580 E2
1500 JknT 46060 1580 E2
Atlantic Rd E
3000 SCkT 46060 1689 E7
Atlantic St
300 INPS 46227 2446 C4
Atlantic St
1700 INPS 46227 2447 A4
Atlantic Rd E
100 SCkT 46051 1580 E7
100 WynT 46051 1580 E7
100 WynT 46051 1689 E3
100 WynT 46060 1580 E7
1000 WynT 46060 1689 E3
4000 SCkT 46051 1689 E7
4000 SCkT 46051 1798 E3
4000 SCkT 46060 1798 E3
4000 WynT 46060 1798 E3
5000 GmT 46051 1798 E3
5000 GmT 46060 1798 E3
6000 GmT 46064 1798 E5
8000 FCkT 46060 1907 E3
8000 FCkT 46064 1907 E3
8000 GmT 46064 1907 E3
11300 FCkT 46040 1907 D5
13900 FCkT 46060 1798 E7
13900 FCkT 46064 1798 E7
Atlantic Rd E SR-13
100 SCkT 46051 1580 E7
100 SCkT 46051 1689 E3
100 WynT 46051 1580 E7
100 WynT 46051 1689 E3
100 WynT 46060 1580 E7
100 WynT 46060 1689 E3
Atmore Ct
900 INPS 46217 2555 A4
Atmore Dr
7100 INPS 46217 2555 A4
Atmore Pl
900 INPS 46217 2555 A4
Atrium Wy
9900 INPS 46229 2232 A5
Atrium Boardwalk S
6800 INPS 46250 2012 E7
Atrium Boardwalk W
7500 INPS 46250 2012 E7
Attleboro Ct
5800 INPS 46250 2121 B1
Atwell Dr
4800 LWNC 46226 2122 A7
Atwood Ct
8000 FSHR 46038 1904 C4
Atwood Pl
12400 FSHR 46038 1904 D4
Aubert St
1300 PNFD 46168 2441 D4
Auburn Dr
1100 BNBG 46112 2114 D4
9100 INPS 46229 2231 D7
Auburn Ln
6700 WshT 46168 2441 B1
18800 NBVL 46060 1686 E5
Auburn Rd
3600 INPS 46224 2226 D3
N Auburn St
200 INPS 46224 2335 D3
1000 SDWY 46224 2335 D1
1800 INPS 46224 2226 D6
S Auburn St
- INPS 46241 2335 D4
Auburn Wy
2200 WshT 46168 2441 B1
Auburn Creek Cross
11700 CRML 46077 1900 A4
Auburn Ford
4700 WRvT 46142 2663 D3
Auburn Hill Dr
800 INPS 46224 2335 B2
Auburn Springs Cir
13500 FSHR 46060 1905 B1
Audrey Av
5000 INPS 46254 2117 D7
Audrey Cir
5000 INPS 46254 2117 D7
Audrie Ct
10800 FSHR 46038 1904 E7
Audubon Ct
16500 NBVL 46060 1795 E3
Audubon Dr
100 CRML 46032 1902 B2
1200 BNBG 46112 2114 D4
N Audubon Rd
- INPS 46226 2230 B3
10 INPS 46219 2339 B3
3400 INPS 46218 2230 B3
4300 INPS 46226 2121 B7
7100 INPS 46250 2121 B1
7500 INPS 46250 2012 B7
S Audubon Rd
10 INPS 46219 2339 B3
2300 INPS 46203 2448 B1
Audubon Ridge Ln
5500 INPS 46250 2012 B7
August Dr
3500 INPS 46239 2449 C3
Augusta Blvd
10600 FCkT 46038 1905 B7
10700 FSHR 46038 1905 B7
Augusta Cir
10 GNWD 46143 2665 E5
Augusta Ct
7500 INPS 46268 2009 B7
Augusta Dr
10 BNBG 46112 2113 D3
5800 SDWY 46224 2226 B6
N Augusta Dr
9600 ClyT 46032 2009 A2
9600 INPS 46032 2009 A2
Augusta Dr E
2100 SDWY 46224 2226 B6
Augusta Dr N
5900 SDWY 46224 2226 A6
Augusta Ln
400 MdnT 46113 2661 B3
2200 ClyT 46032 1900 D7
Aulton Dr
16600 NBVL 46060 1795 E2
16600 NbvT 46060 1795 E2
E Auman Dr
700 CRML 46032 1902 B4
W Auman Dr
700 CRML 46032 1902 B4
Aurelia Ct
3600 INPS 46235 2231 E3
Aurie Dr
2500 INPS 46219 2231 B5
Aurora Ct
10300 FSHR 46060 1905 B1
Aurora St
3700 INPS 46227 2447 A4
Austin Ct
7800 PNFD 46168 2550 D2
8100 AVON 46123 2332 E3
Austin Dr
- LEBN 46052 1676 C3
- WRvT 46142 2663 C4
100 AVON 46123 2332 E3
7300 LWNC 46226 2122 A6
Austin Ln
400 GNWD 46142 2665 B4
Austin Pl
10400 FCkT 46055 2015 D1
Austin Rd
- WRvT 46142 2664 B3
Austin Trc
4600 EglT 46077 1899 D3
Austin Trace Blvd
- MCVL 46055 2124 B2
Austral Dr
5200 INPS 46254 2116 E6
Austrian Ct
16900 WTFD 46074 1793 B2
Austrian Wy
500 AVON 46123 2332 C5
Austrian Pine Dr
7900 INPS 46268 2008 E6
Austrian Pine Wy
17300 WTFD 46074 1792 D1
17500 WTFD 46074 1683 C7
Autumn Ct
7300 AVON 46123 2332 C2
Autumn Dr
- CRML 46032 1902 A3
1100 MRVL 46158 2660 C3
Autumn Ln
400 GNWD 46143 2665 D1
6100 INPS 46220 2121 D3
Autumn Wy
- ZNVL 46077 1898 E2
Autumn Breeze Ln
5700 INPS 46237 2557 B4
Autumn Creek Ct
11100 INPS 46229 2232 C6
Autumn Creek Dr
2100 INPS 46229 2232 C6
Autumn Crest Ct
4300 INPS 46268 2117 E1
Autumn Frost Cir
7500 FSHR 46038 1904 C7
Autumn Gate Wy
- CRML 46033 1903 B4
Autumn Glen Dr
10900 INPS 46229 2232 C6
Autumn Harvest Dr
11100 FSHR 46038 1904 C7
Autumn Lake Ovlk
13600 CRML 46032 1902 A1
Autumn Leaf Ct
8400 INPS 46268 2009 A5
Autumn Mill Ct
8300 INPS 46256 2013 B5
Autumn Mill Ln
8200 INPS 46256 2013 B5
Autumn Ridge Ct
1200 INPS 46239 2341 D6
Autumn Ridge Dr
10 DNVL 46122 2330 B4
Autumn Ridge Ln
11400 INPS 46239 2341 D6
Autumn Song Dr
5300 INPS 46241 2444 C3
Autumn Springs Ct
- AVON 46123 2332 C3
Autumn Springs Dr
400 AVON 46123 2332 D3
Autumnwood Dr
2100 GNWD 46143 2665 C7
2100 GNWD 46143 2774 B1
Autumn Woods Dr
8900 INPS 46250 2012 B4
14100 CRML 46074 1791 E7
Autumview Dr
- MCVL 46055 2015 D5
Auvergne Av
700 INPS 46203 2339 A5
Avalon Blvd
- FSHR 46060 1906 D3
Avalon Cir
1200 GNWD 46142 2664 D3
Avalon Dr
10 WshT 46123 2331 D3
Avalon Ln
10 SCkT 46140 2342 C1
6100 INPS 46220 2121 D3
Avalon Rd
6100 INPS 46220 2121 D4
Avalon East Dr
13900 FSHR 46060 1906 D3
Avalon Forest Dr
6600 INPS 46250 2121 D1
Avalon Ln East Dr
6200 INPS 46220 2121 D3
Avalon Trail Ct
7100 INPS 46250 2121 E1
Avalon Trail Dr
7100 INPS 46250 2121 E1
Avalon Trail Rd
7300 INPS 46250 2121 E1
Avalon West Dr
- FSHR 46060 1906 D3
Avenel Ct
9600 ClyT 46032 2009 C2
Averitt Rd
- GNWD 46143 2774 B1
- GNWD 46184 2774 B1
Averitt Rd
200 GNWD 46142 2665 B4
700 GNWD 46143 2665 B6
1600 PltT 46143 2665 B6
Avery Cir
11200 FSHR 46038 1904 B6
Avery Ct
- MdnT 46113 2661 D1
Avery Dr
- MdnT 46113 2661 C1
Avery Row
11100 FSHR 46038 1904 B6
Avery East Dr
8100 INPS 46268 2008 E5
Avery West Dr
8100 INPS 46268 2008 E6
Avian Ln
5000 LWNC 46235 2123 C7
Avian Wy
5100 CRML 46033 1903 B1
14200 CRML 46033 1794 B7
Aviara Dr
17800 NBVL 46062 1685 B7
Aviation Dr
2300 INPS 46241 2443 B1
N Aviation Wy
3800 BCkT 46140 2125 B7
3800 BCkT 46140 2234 B1
Avila Wy
- DelT 46038 1903 E6
- FSHR 46038 1903 E6
Aviva Ln
8400 INPS 46237 2557 D6
Aviva Wy
6700 INPS 46237 2557 D7
Avocet Dr
12600 CRML 46033 1903 C3
Avon Av
100 PNFD 46168 2441 B4
200 INPS 46201 2338 D4
Avon Av SR-267
100 PNFD 46168 2441 B4
Avon Cr
9400 AVON 46123 2333 B3
Avon Ln
100 NBVL 46062 1686 A1
Avon Pkwy
10 AVON 46123 2332 C3
Avon Rd
500 GfdT 46168 2441 B4
2300 AVON 46123 2332 B4
Avon Crossing Dr
- AVON 46123 2332 D3
Avondale Dr
7200 AVON 46123 2332 B3
N Avondale Pl
2100 INPS 46218 2229 D6
Avon Strand
9400 AVON 46123 2333 B3
Avon Village Dr
200 AVON 46123 2333 B4
Avon Village Pkwy
- AVON 46123 2333 B3
Awl Ct
6200 NBVL 46062 1685 C5
Ayers Ln
3700 WTFD 46033 1793 D6
Aylesworth Ct
- INPS 46113 2551 D7
Aylesworth Dr
8600 INPS 46113 2552 A7
8700 INPS 46113 2551 E7
Ayrshire Cir
- MdnT 46113 2661 B2
Ayrshire Ct
- MdnT 46113 2661 A2
Ayrshire St
4400 INPS 46228 2227 D1
4500 INPS 46228 2118 D7
Ayshire Ct
- MdnT 46113 2661 A1
Azalea Ct
3300 WTFD 46062 1684 D7
Azalea Dr
- MRVL 46158 2660 C3
6700 INPS 46214 2225 E4
Azure Ln
6200 INPS 46220 2121 D4

B

B St
- BHGV 46107 2447 D2
- SDWY 46224 2226 D7
Babbling Brook Rd
12000 NBVL 46060 1796 E2
Babette Ct
3300 INPS 46227 2556 C4
Babette Dr
2900 SPRT 46227 2556 C4
3200 INPS 46227 2556 C4
Babson Ct
3200 INPS 46268 2009 B3
8500 FSHR 46038 1904 C1
Bacara Cir
10100 WshT 46234 2224 C6
Bacara Dr
10000 WshT 46234 2224 C6
Baccus Ct
8100 INPS 46268 2009 A5
Bach Dr
7900 INPS 46239 2449 B2
14600 WshT 46032 1792 C6
Back Bay Ct
7300 INPS 46214 2225 D3
Back Bay Ln
11200 INPS 46236 2014 C6
Back Creek Cir
200 GNWD 46142 2664 E3
Back Creek Ovlk
10 GNWD 46142 2664 E3
Backwater Dr
1400 DNVL 46122 2329 B4
9100 INPS 46250 2012 E3
9200 INPS 46250 2013 A3
Bacon St
- INPS 46239 2449 A3
500 INPS 46227 2446 D3
1500 INPS 46227 2447 A3
1600 INPS 46237 2447 A3
S Bade Rd
1100 INPS 46239 2341 A6
Baden Dr
7400 INPS 46278 2116 E1
Badger Ct
7300 INPS 46260 2118 E1
Badger Dr
1400 INPS 46260 2118 E1
Bagley Dr
9000 INPS 46231 2333 E4
9000 INPS 46231 2334 A4
Bagley Ln
400 INPS 46231 2334 B4
Bagley Wy
9100 INPS 46231 2333 E4
Bahama Ct
7300 INPS 46214 2225 D3
Bahamas Cir
10000 FCkT 46038 2014 D1
Bahamas Ct
10000 FCkT 46038 2014 D1
Bahia Ct
5700 INPS 46237 2448 B7
Bahia Dr
5000 INPS 46237 2448 B7
Bailey Cir
300 CRML 46032 1901 C3
Bailey Ct
100 ZNVL 46077 1899 B5
Bailey Dr
1400 INPS 46241 2334 D7
S Bailey St
700 SRDN 46069 1573 C2
Bailey Wy
8900 FSHR 46038 1904 D7
Bainbridge Ct
15000 WshT 46074 1792 B6
Bainbridge Dr
9000 INPS 46113 2551 E6
Bakemeyer St
10 INPS 46225 2446 B2
E Baker Ct
9500 INPS 46235 2231 E2
Baker Dr
4300 INPS 46235 2231 E1
N Baker Dr
3900 INPS 46235 2231 E2
S Baker Rd
8800 ClkT 46259 2559 D7
8800 INPS 46259 2559 D7
Baker St
20500 WshT 46069 1683 C2
Bakers Corner Dr
8900 INPS 46113 2551 E7
8900 INPS 46113 2552 A7
Bakeway Cir
600 INPS 46231 2333 E5
Bakeway Dr
700 INPS 46231 2333 D5
700 WshT 46231 2333 D5
Balai Hai Ct
10 WshT 46032 1792 D5
Balaton Ln
- GNWD 46143 2666 A4
Balbo Pl
13000 FSHR 46038 1906 B3
Balboa Ct
8700 INPS 46226 2231 C2
Balboa Dr
4000 INPS 46226 2231 C2
Bald Eagle Ct
8700 INPS 46234 2225 A2
Baldwin Ct
10 WTFD 46074 1793 B1
Baldwin Ln
14400 CRML 46032 1792 A7
Baldwin St
200 GNFD 46140 2345 E1
400 GNFD 46140 2236 E7
Balfour Ct
500 AVON 46123 2332 C5
6800 INPS 46220 2121 E2
Balfour Dr
10800 NBVL 46060 1687 C4
W Ball St
100 LEBN 46052 1676 E7
100 LEBN 46052 1677 A7
Ballantrae Cir
14500 CRML 46032 1792 B7
14500 WshT 46032 1792 B7
S Ballard St
- LEBN 46052 1676 E7
Ballew Blvd
- FSHR 46038 1904 C3
Ballinshire N
7500 INPS 46254 2116 C7
Ballinshire S
7500 INPS 46254 2116 C7
Ball Park Dr
- NWTD 46184 2774 E5
Ballyshannon St
7600 INPS 46217 2554 E5
Balmoral Ct
10 ZNVL 46077 1899 A6
Balmoral Rd
6900 INPS 46241 2334 E5
Balroyal Ct
600 INPS 46234 2334 A2
10400 FSHR 46038 2014 D1
Balsam Av
3500 INPS 46205 2228 E3
Baltic Pl
4000 INPS 46228 2227 A2
Baltimore Av
2500 INPS 46218 2229 B4
N Baltimore Av
3700 INPS 46218 2229 B3
3800 INPS 46205 2229 B2
Baltimore Ct
5300 CRML 46033 1903 D3

STREET Block City ZIP Map# Grid

Baltimore & Ohio Walkway
- BNBG 46112 2223 C4
- INPS 46234 2224 D5
- LcnT 46112 2222 B2
- LcnT 46112 2223 A3
- LcnT 46112 2224 A5
- LcnT 46167 2222 B2
- LcnT 46234 2224 D5
- MdlT 46122 2221 E2
- MdlT 46122 2222 B2
- MdlT 46167 2221 E2
- MdlT 46167 2222 B2
- UnnT 46149 2112 A7
- UnnT 46167 2112 A7
- WshT 46234 2224 D5
Banbridge Dr
2600 INPS 46229 2232 A5
Banbury Cir
12600 CRML 46033 1902 E3
Banbury Rd
100 NBVL 46062 1576 D7
300 NBVL 46062 1685 D1
5000 INPS 46226 2121 D7
Banbury Rd N
21100 NBVL 46062 1576 C7
Bancaster Cir
7800 INPS 46268 2009 A7
Bancaster Dr
7400 INPS 46268 2009 A7
7400 INPS 46268 2118 A1
S Bancroft Av
700 INPS 46203 2339 A5
Bancroft Ln
- WRvT 46142 2663 C4
N Bancroft St
500 INPS 46201 2339 A2
3100 INPS 46218 2230 A3
S Bancroft St
100 INPS 46201 2339 A3
4700 INPS 46237 2448 A7
Bando Ct E
3500 INPS 46220 2120 D2
Bando Ct W
3400 INPS 46220 2120 C2
Bangor Dr
200 INPS 46227 2555 C4
Banister Dr
14200 FCkT 46060 1797 A7
14200 NBVL 46060 1797 A7
Bank Pl
1300 INPS 46231 2334 A6
Bank St
- NPLN 46163 2452 B3
Bankers Ln
10 INPS 46201 2338 E3
N Banner Av
1300 INPS 46214 2334 E1
1600 INPS 46214 2225 E7
S Banner Av
1200 INPS 46241 2334 E6
Banning Ln
4800 BHGV 46107 2447 D6
Bannister Ct
6000 LWNC 46236 2123 B4
Bannock Cir
6800 INPS 46221 2553 B3
Bannock Ct
6900 INPS 46221 2553 B4
Bannock Dr
6800 INPS 46221 2553 B4
Banta Cir
6400 INPS 46227 2555 C2
Banta Ct
6300 INPS 46227 2555 C2
Banta Rd
- MdnT 46143 2662 C7
- WRvT 46143 2662 C7
8600 INPS 46113 2552 A3
8600 INPS 46241 2552 A3
E Banta Rd
10 INPS 46227 2555 C3
1400 HMCT 46227 2555 E2
1400 HMCT 46227 2556 A2
1400 INPS 46227 2556 A2
W Banta Rd
10 INPS 46217 2555 B3
1100 INPS 46217 2554 B3
Banta Tr
10 INPS 46227 2555 C2
W Banton Cir
7300 SCkT 46239 2342 A5
Bantry Ct
5100 INPS 46254 2116 C7
Banyan Ln
8300 INPS 46237 2557 A6
Barbados Cir
6800 INPS 46227 2555 D3
Barbados Dr
600 INPS 46227 2555 D3
Barbano Ct
2700 CRML 46074 1900 C2
Barbara Ct
10 INPS 46222 2226 E5
10 INPS 46222 2227 A5
Barbara Dr
- BNBG 46112 2114 D4
- BrnT 46112 2114 D4
200 GNWD 46143 2665 D1
Barbary Ln
2700 INPS 46205 2120 B7
Barberrry Ct
- BrnT 46112 2114 D1
Barberry Ct
6900 WshT 46168 2441 B1
13800 CRML 46033 1903 D1
Barberry Dr
6200 AVON 46123 2332 A5
6300 WshT 46123 2332 A5
Barbican St
- AVON 46123 2333 B3
Barbie Ln
500 ClyT 46280 2010 D1
Barbour Ct
5100 LWNC 46226 2122 A6

Barbwood Ln
- LWNC 46235 2122 E7
Barcelona Dr
1000 GNWD 46143 2666 A5
Barclay Ct
4100 INPS 46240 2011 E3
Barcroft Dr
9200 INPS 46240 2010 E3
Barcroft Ln
9400 INPS 46240 2010 E3
Bar Del Dr
- INPS 46221 2552 D1
Bar Del East Dr
5600 INPS 46221 2552 D1
Bar Del West Dr
5600 INPS 46221 2552 D2
Bardonner St
4300 SCkT 46163 2452 C4
Barefoot Tr
1200 GNWD 46142 2664 E1
Barharbor Ct
4300 INPS 46268 2117 E1
Bari Ct
4200 INPS 46235 2231 D1
Baribeau Ct
10200 INPS 46229 2232 A6
Baribeau Ln
10200 INPS 46229 2232 A6
Baritone Ct
9100 INPS 46231 2333 E6
Barker Dr
1200 LtyT 46118 2548 B2
Barker Ln
5400 LWNC 46236 2122 E6
Barksdale Wy
8000 LWNC 46216 2122 B6
Barkwood Ct
700 CRML 46032 1901 E6
Barlby Dr
5400 INPS 46237 2557 B4
Barlby Pl
5400 INPS 46237 2557 B4
Barley Cir
1000 WTFD 46032 1792 E6
1100 WTFD 46032 1793 A6
Barlow Dr
4800 LWNC 46226 2122 B7
Barlum Dr
7800 INPS 46240 2010 E6
7800 INPS 46240 2011 A7
Barmore Av
10400 ClyT 46280 2010 D1
10500 ClyT 46280 1901 D7
Barnard St
2600 INPS 46268 2009 C4
Barnegat Ct
13200 FCkT 46055 2015 B2
Barnes Av
- INPS 46208 2227 E3
- INPS 46208 2228 A3
Barnes Ct
- GNWD 46143 2666 D4
Barnett Ct
500 WTLD 46184 2774 E5
Barnett Ln
5900 INPS 46221 2553 A2
Barnett Pl
13800 DelT 46038 1904 D1
13800 FSHR 46038 1904 D1
14000 FSHR 46038 1795 D7
Barngate Cir
1200 GNWD 46142 2664 D2
Barnhill Dr
400 INPS 46202 2337 A2
Barnor Dr
2200 INPS 46219 2230 C6
4300 INPS 46226 2230 C1
Barnstable Ct
5800 INPS 46250 2121 C1
Barnstable Rd
3700 ClyT 46032 1900 A7
Barnstone Ct
12300 FSHR 46038 1906 A4
Barnwell Ct
- INPS 46217 2555 A4
Barnwell Pl
7100 INPS 46217 2555 A4
Barnwell Wy
900 INPS 46217 2555 A4
W Barnwood Dr
5200 SCkT 46163 2451 E2
Barnwood Rd
4800 INPS 46268 2117 D2
Barnwood Trc
6700 INPS 46268 2117 D2
Baron Ct
5800 INPS 46250 2012 C4
6500 AVON 46123 2332 A4
Baron Field Cir
7900 INPS 46260 2009 C7
Baron Field Ct
7900 INPS 46260 2009 C7
Baron Field Dr
7900 INPS 46260 2009 E6
Barons Ct
12700 FSHR 46060 1906 D3
Barr Dr
9300 INPS 46229 2231 E5
Barrett Av
- INPS 46241 2336 B7
2100 INPS 46221 2336 D7
Barrett Dr
- GNFD 46140 2236 E4
Barrett St
600 DNVL 46122 2329 C4
Barrhill Ct
9600 FSHR 46038 1905 A3
Barrington Av
1500 INPS 46203 2338 B6
Barrington Dr
1100 GNWD 46143 2664 E5
3700 CRML 46033 1902 D7
Barrington Pl
6700 FSHR 46038 1903 E5

Barrone St
300 LEBN 46052 1676 E5
W Barrone St
200 LEBN 46052 1676 D6
Barr Will Dr
6500 INPS 46220 2120 E2
Barry Dr
1000 LEBN 46052 1677 B3
Barry Rd
8000 INPS 46219 2231 B5
Barry Knoll St
700 DNVL 46122 2329 C4
Barstow Dr
8300 FSHR 46038 1904 C1
Bart Rd
- GfdT 46168 2551 A1
- PNFD 46168 2551 A1
Barth Av
1200 INPS 46203 2337 E6
2700 INPS 46203 2446 E2
7000 INPS 46227 2555 E4
Barth Dr
9900 ZNVL 46077 1898 E2
9900 ZNVL 46077 1899 A2
Bartlett Av
3700 INPS 46227 2446 D4
Bartley Ct
6100 LWNC 46236 2123 B4
Bartley Dr
10400 LWNC 46236 2123 B4
Barton Av
300 INPS 46241 2335 E4
Bartram Ln
- PNFD 46168 2440 D4
Basalt Ct
10100 NBVL 46060 1796 A3
W Base Line Rd
4000 CtrT 46052 1678 D7
4000 WrhT 46052 1678 D7
5000 CtrT 46052 1679 C7
5000 WrhT 46052 1679 C7
6000 UnnT 46052 1679 C7
6500 UnnT 46075 1679 C7
6500 WrhT 46075 1679 C7
6900 UnnT 46077 1679 C7
6900 WrhT 46077 1679 C7
7100 UnnT 46075 1680 B7
7100 UnnT 46077 1680 B7
10000 UnnT 46077 1681 B7
W Base Line Rd SR-32
4000 CtrT 46052 1678 D7
4000 WrhT 46052 1678 D7
5000 CtrT 46052 1679 C7
5000 WrhT 46052 1679 C7
6000 UnnT 46052 1679 C7
6500 UnnT 46075 1679 C7
6500 WrhT 46075 1679 C7
6900 UnnT 46077 1679 C7
6900 WrhT 46077 1679 C7
7100 UnnT 46075 1680 B7
7100 UnnT 46077 1680 B7
10000 UnnT 46077 1681 B7
Bash St
8600 INPS 46256 2012 E4
8700 INPS 46256 2013 A4
N Bash St
8000 INPS 46250 2012 E6
Basil Ct
4800 INPS 46237 2556 E4
Basin St
9000 LWNC 46235 2231 D1
Basin Park Dr
5300 INPS 46239 2449 B7
Basque Ct
3900 INPS 46228 2227 A2
Bassett Dr
4700 LWNC 46235 2123 A7
Bass Wood Ct
11100 CRML 46032 1901 D6
Basswood Dr
400 WRvT 46142 2663 B5
7800 INPS 46227 2556 B5
8300 INPS 46268 2009 B5
Bastani Pl
6300 INPS 46237 2557 D2
Bastille Dr
- INPS 46254 2117 A5
Bastille Ln
5700 INPS 46254 2117 B5
Bastille Wy
5900 INPS 46254 2117 A5
Bastion Pl
200 AVON 46123 2333 B4
Bataan Rd
17400 NbvT 46062 1685 D7
17400 NbvT 46062 1794 D1
Bates Ct
- MdnT 46113 2661 C5
Bates St
700 INPS 46202 2337 D4
1400 INPS 46201 2338 A4
N Bateson Ct
10 MdnT 46113 2661 B4
Batten Dr
10700 INPS 46256 2014 B3
Bauer Dr
9600 CRML 46280 2011 D2
Bauer Dr W
3700 CRML 46280 2011 D2
Bauer Rd
1800 INPS 46218 2230 B7
N Bauman St
1000 INPS 46214 2334 E1
S Bauman St
10 INPS 46241 2334 E4
Baur Dr
2400 INPS 46220 2120 B4
Bavarian East Dr
3000 INPS 46235 2232 A4
Bavarian West Dr
3000 INPS 46235 2232 A4
Baxter Dr
4800 SDWY 46224 2226 D6
Bay Ct
2700 ClyT 46032 2009 C1

NW Bay Dr
- GNFD 46140 2236 E4
Bay Ln
10700 FSHR 46038 1904 E7
Bay St
5000 INPS 46227 2447 A7
Bayard Dr
7800 INPS 46259 2558 B4
Bayberry Ct
8000 INPS 46250 2012 A6
Bayberry Ct E
3000 CRML 46033 1902 B6
Bayberry Ct W
3000 CRML 46033 1902 B6
W Bayberry Dr
5600 SCkT 46163 2451 E4
Bayberry Ln
4700 ZNVL 46077 1899 C3
Bay Breeze Ct
9000 INPS 46236 2014 D3
Bay Breeze Ln
8800 INPS 46236 2014 D4
Bay Brook Dr
8000 INPS 46256 2013 B6
Bay Cir Dr
- INPS 46268 2009 C2
Bay Colony Dr
8400 INPS 46234 2116 B6
Bay Colony Ln
5500 INPS 46234 2116 B5
Bay Cove
8000 INPS 46256 2013 B6
Baycreek Dr
11000 LWNC 46236 2014 C7
Bayfield Dr
- MCVL 46055 2015 D4
Bay Forest Dr
12700 INPS 46236 2015 B3
Bayfront Shrs
- MCVL 46055 2015 C4
Bay Harbor Dr
5300 INPS 46254 2117 A6
Bay Harbor Ln
6400 INPS 46254 2117 A6
Bay Head Dr
3400 INPS 46214 2225 D3
Bayhead Dr
7100 INPS 46214 2225 D3
Bayhill Cir
- MCVL 46055 2015 D4
10 BNBG 46112 2113 C3
Bayhill Ct
21100 NBVL 46062 1577 A7
Bayhill Dr
7600 LWNC 46236 2014 C7
12500 CRML 46033 1903 A3
Bayhill Wy
11300 INPS 46236 2014 D6
Bayland Dr
- MCVL 46055 2015 D4
Bay Landing Cir
5500 INPS 46254 2116 C6
Bay Landing Ct
5500 INPS 46254 2116 C5
Bay Landing Dr
7700 INPS 46254 2116 C6
Bay Leaf Cir
4100 INPS 46237 2556 E4
Bayley Cir
100 NBVL 46062 1685 E2
Bay Meadow Cir
- WshT 46074 1792 E3
- WTFD 46074 1792 E3
Bayou Ct
9100 LWNC 46235 2231 D1
Bay Point Dr
3200 INPS 46240 2011 C5
Bay Pointe Cir
8600 INPS 46236 2015 A4
Bay Port Cir
9100 INPS 46236 2015 A3
Bay Rd North Dr
3300 INPS 46240 2011 C6
Bay Rd South Dr
3200 INPS 46240 2011 C6
Bayridge Cir E
11100 LWNC 46236 2014 C7
Bayridge Cir W
11100 LWNC 46236 2014 C7
Bay Ridge Ct
12100 INPS 46236 2014 E4
Bayridge Dr
7500 LWNC 46236 2014 C7
Bayridge Wy
10700 FCkT 46040 1906 E7
Bay Run Cir
12500 INPS 46236 2015 A4
Bay Run Ct
12500 INPS 46236 2015 A4
Bays Dr
100 NbvT 46062 1794 D1
Baysdon Cir
5200 LWNC 46235 2123 D6
Bayshore Ct
10 CRML 46033 1902 D7
Bay Shore Dr
7700 INPS 46240 2011 B6
Bayshore Dr
10 CCRO 46034 1577 D1
Bayshore Ln
8300 AVON 46123 2332 E3
Bayside Cir
- MCVL 46055 2015 C4
Bayside Ct
900 GNWD 46143 2665 A5
6300 INPS 46250 2012 B2
12300 FCkT 46256 2015 A2
Bayside Dr
800 GNWD 46143 2665 A5
3000 INPS 46214 2225 D4
Bayside Wy
6400 INPS 46250 2012 D3
Bayside North Dr
6300 INPS 46250 2012 D2

Bayside South Dr
6300 INPS 46250 2012 B2
Bayswater Blvd
- INPS 46254 2116 E7
Bayswater Ln
1100 CCRO 46034 1577 B4
Bayton Ct
10200 INPS 46229 2341 A1
Bay Tree Ct
8700 INPS 46236 2014 E4
Baytree Ct
400 CRML 46032 1792 C7
Bayview Cir
- PNFD 46168 2442 B1
Bayview Ct
8200 INPS 46256 2013 C6
9600 FCkT 46256 2014 E2
Bay View Dr
- INPS 46214 2225 D3
Bayview Dr
10 CCRO 46034 1577 C2
Bayview Ln
900 GNWD 46143 2664 E5
900 GNWD 46143 2665 A5
Bayview Pt
7900 INPS 46256 2013 C6
Bay View Wy
3400 INPS 46214 2225 C3
Bay Vista Ct
6300 INPS 46250 2012 D3
Bay Vista East Dr
6300 INPS 46250 2012 D3
9500 FSHR 46250 2012 D3
Bay Vista West Dr
9300 INPS 46250 2012 D3
9500 FSHR 46250 2012 D3
Bay Wind Pl
6000 SDWY 46224 2226 A7
Baywood Cir
8900 INPS 46256 2013 C4
Baywood Ct
300 NBVL 46062 1685 B1
Baywood Dr
- NBVL 46062 1685 B1
Baywood Dr E
11100 LWNC 46236 2014 C7
Baywood Dr S
7500 LWNC 46236 2014 C7
Baywood Ln
11100 LWNC 46236 2014 C7
N Bazil Av
1300 INPS 46219 2340 D1
1800 INPS 46219 2231 D7
S Bazil Av
4000 INPS 46239 2449 C5
BB St
- BHGV 46107 2447 D3
- BHGV 46107 2448 A3
Beach Av
2400 INPS 46240 2011 B6
E Beach Av
2000 INPS 46240 2011 B6
Beach Blvd
- CCRO 46034 1577 B6
S Beach Blvd
3100 CCRO 46034 1577 B6
Beach Club Dr
- WshT 46062 1684 E7
4500 WTFD 46062 1684 E7
4600 WshT 46062 1685 A7
4600 WTFD 46062 1685 A7
Beachview Dr
5800 INPS 46224 2335 A2
Beachway Ct
1300 CCRO 46034 1577 B5
Beachway Dr
500 INPS 46224 2335 A2
Beacon Blvd
14600 WTFD 46032 1793 A6
E Beacon Ct
1200 WTFD 46032 1793 A6
N Beacon Ct
3300 INPS 46222 2226 E4
Beacon Ln
900 CCRO 46034 1577 C4
10400 INPS 46256 2014 B3
W Beacon Ln
- CCRO 46034 1577 C4
Beacon St
- CRML 46032 1902 A4
E Beacon Wy
1300 WTFD 46032 1793 A6
Beacon Cove Pl
5800 INPS 46237 2557 B6
Beacon Cove Wy
5800 INPS 46237 2557 B6
Beaconfield Ct
1400 CRML 46033 1793 D7
Beacon Park Dr
14700 WTFD 46032 1793 A6
Beal Ct
1000 INPS 46217 2555 A4
Beals St
400 CRML 46032 1902 A5
Beam St
- NBVL 46060 1796 B5
Beam Ridge Dr
9800 INPS 46256 2014 A4
13700 FCkT 46055 2015 C1
Beanblossom Cir
7800 INPS 46256 2013 B3
Bean Blossom Dr
- MdnT 46113 2661 C1
Bear Branch Ct
- MdnT 46113 2661 C1
Bear Creek Dr
6600 INPS 46254 2116 E6
Bear Cub Dr
1000 JknT 46034 1576 D3
Beardon Ct
1100 NBVL 46062 1686 A4
Beardsen Ct
- WshT 46123 2332 E1
Beargrass Ct
6900 INPS 46241 2334 E4

Bear Hollow Ct
11300 INPS 46229 2341 D4
Bear Hollow Dr
11000 INPS 46229 2341 C4
S Bear Hollow Wy
200 INPS 46229 2341 C3
Bearing Dr
8400 INPS 46268 2008 E4
Bears Wy
12000 FCkT 46038 1905 E3
12100 FCkT 46038 1906 A3
Bearsdale Cir
6300 LWNC 46235 2123 E3
Bearsdale Dr
12000 LWNC 46235 2123 E3
12200 LWNC 46235 2124 A3
12500 VrnT 46235 2124 A3
Bearsdale Wy
20600 NBVL 46062 1685 A1
Bear Story Blvd
300 GNFD 46140 2345 D3
Bear Story Ct
200 GNFD 46140 2345 D3
Bearwood Ct
3500 INPS 46235 2232 C3
Bearwood Dr
3500 INPS 46235 2232 C3
Beasley Dr
3400 INPS 46222 2226 E3
Beatle Dr
5800 LWNC 46216 2122 E5
Beaufain Ct
900 INPS 46217 2555 A6
Beaufort Ln
5800 INPS 46254 2117 C5
Beau Jardin Dr
5800 INPS 46237 2448 C7
Beaumont Blvd
- CRML 46074 1791 D7
Beaumont Ct
800 INPS 46214 2334 E2
7000 EglT 46077 2007 E1
Beaumont Rd
100 LWNC 46216 2122 E5
100 LWNC 46216 2123 A5
Beaumont Green Pl
7900 INPS 46250 2012 A6
Beaumont Green East Dr
7900 INPS 46250 2012 A6
Beaumont Green West Dr
7900 INPS 46250 2012 A6
Beaumont Way North Dr
5000 INPS 46250 2012 A6
Beaumont Way South Dr
5000 INPS 46250 2012 A6
Beauport Rd
4000 INPS 46222 2226 E5
4000 INPS 46222 2227 A5
5400 SDWY 46224 2226 B5
Beauty Av
300 INPS 46202 2337 A2
400 INPS 46202 2336 E4
Beautymeadow Dr
- BNBG 46112 2224 A3
Beauvior Dr
4400 LWNC 46235 2231 D1
4500 LWNC 46235 2122 D7
Beaver Ct
3500 INPS 46235 2231 E3
Beaver Dr
3400 INPS 46235 2231 E3
Beaverbrook Dr
500 CRML 46032 1901 D6
Beaver Ridge Dr
10300 FCkT 46038 2013 E1
Bechtel Rd
1900 INPS 46260 2009 D4
Bechtold Av
4800 LWNC 46226 2122 C7
Beck Rd
- LEBN 46052 1786 A1
Beck St
1300 LEBN 46052 1786 A1
Beckenbauer Ln
1600 INPS 46214 2225 C7
Beckenbauer Pl
7700 INPS 46214 2225 C7
Beckenbauer Wy
1600 INPS 46214 2225 C7
Becker Ct
500 ZNVL 46077 1899 C4
10400 FSHR 46038 2012 C1
Becker Dr
1100 ZNVL 46077 1899 C4
Becketts Ct
10600 FSHR 46038 1905 B6
Beckford Dr
8800 INPS 46234 2334 A3
N Beckham
- WTWN 46075 1788 C6
Beckham Ct
11700 CRML 46032 1901 E4
Beckley Rd
12200 CBLD 46229 2341 E1
Beckoning Dr
9000 BrnT 46112 2004 E6
Beck Ridge Cir
1500 WRvT 46143 2663 D6
Becks Mill Ln
8300 INPS 46113 2551 E6
Beckwith Dr
2300 INPS 46218 2229 A6
13100 CRML 46074 1900 B2
Bedford Av
- INPS 46241 2336 C6
- INPS 46241 2445 C1
1200 INPS 46221 2336 C6
Bedford Ct
4600 CRML 46033 1902 E1
Bedford Dr
400 WTFD 46074 1792 D2
4700 CRML 46033 1902 E2
4700 CRML 46033 1903 A2
Bedrock Ct
12200 FSHR 46038 1905 E4

Bee Camp Ct
10200 FCkT 46055 2015 C1
Beech Ct
10 NWTD 46184 2774 D3
10 WRvT 46142 2664 A1
3600 INPS 46234 2225 A3
Beech Dr
300 GNWD 46142 2665 C1
3300 CRML 46033 1902 D1
4900 INPS 46254 2118 A6
6000 INPS 46224 2335 A3
6600 INPS 46214 2334 E3
11000 FSHR 46038 1903 E7
S Beech Dr
700 SGLK 46140 2343 E3
Beech Dr N
1600 PNFD 46168 2441 D5
Beech Dr S
1600 PNFD 46168 2441 D6
Beech Dr W
600 PNFD 46168 2441 D6
Beech Knls
8100 INPS 46256 2122 B2
Beech Pl
3300 ClyT 46032 2009 B2
Beech St
500 ZNVL 46077 1899 B5
2900 INPS 46203 2446 D2
Beech Cir Dr
1600 PNFD 46168 2441 D5
Beechcraft Dr
6700 INPS 46241 2334 E7
6700 INPS 46241 2443 E1
Beechcrest Ct
2500 INPS 46203 2447 C1
Beechcrest Dr
2400 INPS 46203 2447 D1
2500 BHGV 46203 2447 D1
Beecher Ct
6600 INPS 46203 2339 D7
E Beecher St
200 INPS 46225 2337 D7
500 INPS 46203 2337 D7
2000 INPS 46203 2338 B7
6600 INPS 46203 2339 D7
W Beecher St
4700 INPS 46241 2335 D7
Beech Hollow Ct
4900 INPS 46254 2117 D4
Beech Hollow Dr
5800 INPS 46254 2117 D5
Beechmill Ln
8500 INPS 46227 2555 E7
Beechmont Dr
10 CRML 46032 1902 C2
Beechnut Dr
- WshT 46074 1792 C4
Beech Park Dr
400 GNWD 46142 2665 B2
Beech Tree Ct
9200 INPS 46235 2231 D2
Beechtree Ct
5000 CRML 46033 1903 A2
Beechview Dr
200 GNWD 46142 2665 B4
Beechview Ln
10 INPS 46217 2555 B6
Beechwood Av
5600 INPS 46219 2339 B4
Beechwood Cir
5100 WshT 46123 2331 C5
Beechwood Ct
10 CRML 46033 1902 D7
300 NBVL 46060 1686 C6
1600 PNFD 46168 2441 D4
4100 FKLN 46131 2774 E7
Beechwood Dr
- AVON 46123 2332 D4
- BCkT 46140 2342 B1
- BHGV 46107 2448 A2
- INPS 46107 2448 A2
- INPS 46203 2448 A2
10 WTFD 46074 1684 B6
300 NBVL 46060 1686 C5
400 BHGV 46107 2447 E2
400 CBLD 46140 2342 A1
1400 BNBG 46112 2223 D2
Beechwood Dr E
10900 ClyT 46280 1902 A7
Beechwood Dr W
10900 ClyT 46280 1902 A7
Beechwood Ln
- INPS 46241 2552 B2
200 ZNVL 46077 1899 A5
E Beechwood Ln
10 INPS 46227 2555 C2
W Beechwood Ln
5500 SCkT 46163 2451 E4
Beechwood Rd
400 WshT 46123 2331 C4
Beechwood St
7700 INPS 46219 2340 A4
E Beechwood St
7900 INPS 46219 2340 C4
Beechwood Centre Rd
7400 AVON 46123 2332 C3
Beechwood Farms Ct
- AVON 46123 2332 D2
Beechwood Farms Dr
- AVON 46123 2332 D2
Beeler Av
1600 SDWY 46224 2226 C7
3400 INPS 46224 2226 C3
Beeler Ct
3100 INPS 46224 2226 C4
Behner Cir
9100 INPS 46250 2012 D3
Behner Cross
6200 INPS 46250 2012 D3
Behner Ln
9500 INPS 46250 2012 B2
Behner Wy
6200 INPS 46250 2012 D3
Behner Brook Ct
9100 INPS 46250 2012 D3

STREET
Block City ZIP Map# Grid

Behner Brook Dr
9100 INPS 46250 2012 D3
Behner Rch
6200 INPS 46250 2012 D3
Beisinger Pl
5700 INPS 46237 2557 B2
Bekinhill Ct
8400 INPS 46256 2013 C5
Bel Air Ct
8800 INPS 46226 2231 D2
Bel Air Dr
8700 INPS 46226 2231 D2
Belair Dr
10700 ClyT 46280 1901 E7
Belaire Dr
10 NWTD 46184 2774 D5
Belcrest Ct
8200 INPS 46256 2013 E5
8200 INPS 46256 2014 A6
Belcrest Ln
9700 INPS 46256 2013 E5
9800 INPS 46256 2014 A6
S Belden Dr
300 CRML 46032 1902 C3
Beldon Dr N
100 CRML 46032 1902 C3
Belfield St
1600 INPS 46217 2554 E5
Belford Ct
5900 INPS 46254 2226 B1
13400 CRML 46032 1901 B2
Belfry Dr
12100 FCkT 46060 1796 E7
12100 NBVL 46060 1796 E7
12100 NBVL 46060 1797 A7
Belfry Wy
6200 INPS 46237 2448 D5
Bell St
400 INPS 46202 2337 E2
W Bell St
5600 WRvT 46142 2663 B3
Bellchime Dr
4400 INPS 46235 2232 B1
4500 INPS 46235 2123 A7
Belle St
- PNFD 46168 2441 B6
Belleflower Ct
1500 WshT 46123 2223 C7
Bellefontaine St
100 BHGV 46107 2448 A3
400 BHGV 46107 2447 E3
1500 INPS 46202 2337 E1
2100 INPS 46202 2228 E6
2200 INPS 46205 2228 E6
10400 ClyT 46280 2010 E1
10600 ClyT 46280 1901 E7
Belle Forch Ct
15200 WshT 46032 1792 E5
Belleisle Ct
5100 WshT 46123 2331 C5
Belle Manor Ct
10 INPS 46260 2010 C2
Belle Manor Ln
9300 INPS 46260 2010 C3
9500 CRML 46290 2010 C3
S Bellemeeder Dr
2000 INPS 46239 2340 E7
Belle Plaine Blvd
10800 FSHR 46038 1905 C5
Belle Union Ct
8500 INPS 46113 2552 A7
Belle Union Dr
8500 INPS 46113 2552 A7
Belle Union Pl
8600 INPS 46113 2552 A7
N Belleview Pl
1000 INPS 46222 2336 C1
1600 INPS 46222 2227 C7
S Belleview Pl
10 INPS 46222 2336 C4
800 INPS 46221 2336 C5
Bellflower Ct
10800 INPS 46235 2232 C3
Bellflower Dr
9600 ZNVL 46077 1898 E3
Bellingham Blvd
- FSHR 46038 1906 E4
Bellingham Ter
5800 INPS 46221 2444 B6
Bellingham East Dr
4700 INPS 46221 2444 B7
Bellingrath St
1900 CRML 46032 1900 E4
Bellshire Ln
13200 CRML 46074 1900 B2
Bellwood Dr
- INPS 46226 2231 A4
Belmar Av
10 INPS 46219 2340 B2
2500 INPS 46219 2231 B5
3400 INPS 46226 2231 B3
Belmar Ct
9500 NBVL 46060 1686 E5
Belmont Av
- INPS 46221 2445 D2
5000 INPS 46217 2445 D7
5500 INPS 46217 2554 D2
N Belmont Av
10 INPS 46222 2336 D3
S Belmont Av
10 INPS 46222 2336 D7
300 INPS 46221 2336 D7
2200 INPS 46221 2445 D1
7300 INPS 46217 2554 C6
Belmont Cir
1000 ClyT 46280 1901 E7
Belmont Ct
11500 ClyT 46032 1900 D6
Bel Moore Blvd
8000 INPS 46259 2557 E6
Bel Moore Cir
7000 INPS 46259 2557 E6
S Belt St
1100 INPS 46221 2337 A6

Beluga Ln
3400 INPS 46214 2225 E3
Belvedere Pl
1000 WshT 46074 1792 A6
Benchmark Dr
9300 INPS 46240 2010 E3
Benchview Dr
- CRML 46240 2010 E2
9300 INPS 46240 2010 E2
9300 INPS 46240 2011 A3
N Bend Rd
500 BHGV 46107 2447 E5
Benderfield Dr
400 ZNVL 46077 1899 A5
Bengals Dr
11800 FCkT 46038 1905 E3
Benham Ct
800 INPS 46234 2333 E2
Ben Hur Av
9000 INPS 46234 2224 E3
9000 INPS 46234 2225 A3
9200 LcnT 46234 2224 E3
Benjamin Dr
7800 LWNC 46226 2122 B6
Benjamin Pl
- BCkT 46055 2124 B4
Bennett Ct
700 CRML 46032 1792 E7
3800 INPS 46254 2226 B2
Bennett Dr
- INPS 46224 2226 B2
3800 INPS 46254 2226 B2
Bennett Rd
10 CRML 46032 1792 E7
Bennettwood Pl
11600 CRML 46077 1900 A5
Bennington Ct
- GNWD 46143 2664 E5
Bennington Dr
10 ZNVL 46077 1899 A4
Bennington Rd
10 INPS 46227 2555 C4
Benny Ln
3100 INPS 46241 2444 C3
Benoit Dr
7300 INPS 46214 2225 D7
Bens Dr
200 MdnT 46113 2661 B4
E Bens Dr
6000 MdnT 46113 2661 B4
Benson Ct
8800 INPS 46217 2555 A7
Bent Brook Dr
9300 INPS 46250 2012 C3
9500 FSHR 46250 2012 C3
Bentbrook Dr
- WshT 46123 2332 A7
4800 NBVL 46062 1685 A7
Bent Creek Ct
10200 FSHR 46038 2014 C1
Bentgrass Ct
11100 LWNC 46236 2123 C2
Bentgrass Dr
6900 LWNC 46236 2123 C1
17700 NBVL 46062 1685 A7
Bentley Blvd
12400 FSHR 46038 1904 C3
Bentley Dr
- CRML 46033 1903 A4
300 ZNVL 46077 1898 D6
4600 CRML 46033 1902 E4
7300 INPS 46214 2334 D2
Bentley Wy
1200 CRML 46032 1901 D1
Bentley Bend Ct
8000 INPS 46259 2558 B6
Bentley Commons Dr
7800 INPS 46259 2558 B6
Bentley Farms Dr
8100 INPS 46259 2558 B6
Bentley Farms Pl
8100 INPS 46259 2558 B6
Bent Oak Cir
8300 LWNC 46236 2015 A5
Bent Oak Ct
12700 LWNC 46236 2015 A5
Bent Oak Dr
8300 LWNC 46236 2015 A5
Bent Oak Ln
12600 LWNC 46236 2015 A5
Bent Oaks Ct
- NBVL 46060 1796 E1
Benton Dr
200 INPS 46227 2555 C5
Benton Oak Dr
18000 NBVL 46062 1686 A6
Bentonville Pl
8400 INPS 46227 2556 C7
Bent Stream
- BNBG 46112 2223 E1
- LcnT 46112 2223 E1
Bent Stream Ln
100 LcnT 46112 2224 A1
200 BNBG 46112 2224 A1
Bent Tree Ct
8500 INPS 46260 2010 B5
Bent Tree Ln
400 INPS 46260 2010 B4
3700 WRvT 46143 2664 A6
10000 FSHR 46038 2014 A2
Bent Tree Pl
1400 WRvT 46143 2664 A6
Bentwater Ln
10800 FSHR 46038 1905 C6
Bent Willow Dr
7800 INPS 46239 2340 B7
Bentwood Dr
100 GNWD 46143 2665 C2
Bentwood St
10 GNWD 46143 2665 C2
Bentwood Cir East Dr
8200 INPS 46268 2009 B5
Bentwood Cir North Dr
3000 INPS 46268 2009 B5

Bentwood Cir S Dr
3000 INPS 46268 2009 B5
Bentwood Cir W Dr
8200 INPS 46268 2009 B5
Bentworth Wy
6400 INPS 46237 2557 B2
Benz Ct
6100 LWNC 46236 2123 B3
Berenger Ln
13800 CRML 46032 1901 B1
Beresford Ct
10100 FSHR 46060 1905 A2
Bergamot Ct
3900 INPS 46235 2232 C2
Bergen Blvd
- NBVL 46060 1797 C7
Bergeson Ct
6500 INPS 46278 2008 A4
Bergeson Dr
8700 INPS 46278 2008 A4
Bergeson Wy
6300 INPS 46278 2008 A4
Berkely Cir
11200 FSHR 46038 1904 B6
Berkely Ct
11200 FSHR 46038 1904 B6
Berkley Pl
600 INPS 46208 2228 B1
Berkley Rd
600 INPS 46208 2228 A1
Berkshire Dr
6700 EglT 46077 1897 D7
Berkshire Ln
100 NBVL 46062 1685 D1
4600 INPS 46226 2229 E1
4600 INPS 46226 2230 A1
7400 CBLD 46229 2342 A2
Berkshire Rd
4200 INPS 46226 2230 A1
4400 INPS 46226 2229 E1
S Berlander Dr
3000 SCkT 46163 2342 E7
N Berling Dr
12100 MnrT 46158 2658 B5
Bermuda Dr
8300 INPS 46219 2231 C7
Bern Pl
3700 INPS 46228 2227 A2
Bernard Dr
- MdnT 46113 2661 A2
Bernard St
300 INPS 46208 2228 B2
Bernie Ct
10100 INPS 46229 2232 A6
Bernie Dr
2200 INPS 46229 2232 A6
Berry Av
100 INPS 46219 2339 C3
Berry Ct
9700 ClyT 46032 2009 B2
Berry Rd
900 WRvT 46143 2664 A6
Berry St
10 GNFD 46140 2346 A1
600 GNFD 46140 2237 A7
Berry Glen Ct
5700 CRML 46033 1903 B3
Berry Lake Wy
- BNBG 46112 2114 E6
- BNBG 46112 2115 A5
Berry Patch Ln
- FSHR 46038 1905 D4
Berrywood Dr
- GNWD 46143 2666 A5
1800 LcnT 46112 2223 D4
6600 WshT 46123 2332 A7
Bertha Ct
200 INPS 46241 2335 D4
Bertha St
2600 INPS 46222 2336 B4
5000 INPS 46241 2335 C4
6300 INPS 46241 2334 E4
W Bertrand Rd
3800 INPS 46222 2227 A4
4200 INPS 46222 2226 E4
N Berwick Av
1000 INPS 46222 2336 B1
1600 INPS 46222 2227 B7
S Berwick Av
1200 INPS 46241 2336 A6
2700 INPS 46241 2445 B2
Berwick Ln
5000 WshT 46123 2331 C4
Berwick Pl
300 INPS 46222 2336 B3
Berwyn Rd
1000 NWTD 46184 2774 D3
E Berwyn St
- INPS 46203 2446 E2
100 INPS 46225 2446 C2
2800 INPS 46203 2447 C2
3600 INPS 46203 2448 D2
W Berwyn St
3800 INPS 46241 2445 A2
4100 INPS 46241 2444 E2
Beryl Dr
6200 INPS 46241 2444 A5
10000 NBVL 46060 1796 A3
10000 NbvT 46060 1796 A3
Beta Ln
4400 INPS 46208 2228 B1
Beth Ann Dr
4500 INPS 46221 2444 E6
N Beth Ann Dr
12000 MdnT 46113 2661 D4
Bethany Rd
3600 INPS 46268 2009 A4
Bethel Av
100 BHGV 46107 2448 A2
500 BHGV 46107 2447 E1
1200 BHGV 46203 2447 E1
1200 INPS 46203 2447 E1
2200 INPS 46203 2338 B6
E Bethel Av
- INPS 46203 2338 D7

Bethel Ct
7100 WshT 46123 2332 C2
Bethel Rd
100 BrnT 46158 2659 C5
4900 INPS 46254 2117 C7
Bethel Church Rd
400 BrnT 46158 2659 C7
Bethesda Cir
15500 WshT 46074 1792 B5
Bethesda Ln
5400 INPS 46254 2117 C3
N Bethesda Rd
11500 BrnT 46158 2658 E6
Bethesda Wy
6100 INPS 46254 2117 C4
Bethol Ct
7100 WshT 46123 2332 C2
S Betholm Dr
4800 INPS 46239 2449 E6
Betsy Ln
100 INPS 46227 2446 C3
Bettcher Av
6000 INPS 46228 2118 D4
6500 INPS 46260 2118 D2
Beulah Av
1400 INPS 46241 2335 D6
2200 INPS 46241 2444 D1
Beulahland Pl
8300 INPS 46256 2013 A5
Bevedere Dr
5200 INPS 46228 2118 C6
Beverly Dr
400 ZNVL 46077 1899 B3
E Beverly Dr
100 INPS 46205 2119 D7
W Beverly Dr
200 INPS 46208 2119 C6
Beverly Ln
700 PNFD 46168 2441 A5
Beverly Hills Dr
7700 INPS 46268 2008 E7
N Beville Av
1500 INPS 46201 2229 B7
1500 INPS 46201 2338 A2
1500 INPS 46218 2229 B7
S Beville Av
10 INPS 46201 2338 B3
Bevington Ln
4300 INPS 46240 2011 E3
Bexhill Dr
10 CRML 46032 1902 C2
Bexley Dr
- GNWD 46143 2666 A5
7000 INPS 46256 2121 E3
7100 INPS 46256 2122 A3
14400 CRML 46033 1794 B7
Bexley Pl
700 GNWD 46143 2666 A5
Bexley Run
- GNWD 46143 2666 A5
Bibler St
800 LEBN 46052 1676 D5
Bicking St
200 INPS 46225 2337 C5
Bicknell Cir
10300 FSHR 46060 1796 B7
Biddle St
3300 LtyT 46168 2439 E5
Bierman Rd
5100 INPS 46203 2448 B2
Big Ben Cir
9400 INPS 46235 2231 E2
Big Bend Dr
- LcnT 46112 2115 C5
- NBVL 46062 1686 B4
Big Cir Dr
- NBVL 46062 1686 B4
Bigelow Ct
13900 CRML 46032 1901 A1
Big Four Rd
3500 BHGV 46203 2448 B3
Big Hill Cir
400 INPS 46224 2335 C2
Bighorn Ct
8300 FSHR 46038 1904 C1
Big Horn Dr
9800 LcnT 46112 2224 C3
Big Horn Tr
7800 INPS 46214 2334 C2
Big Oak Dr
5700 INPS 46254 2117 D5
Big Pine Dr
- INPS 46254 2116 D3
- INPS 46278 2116 D3
Big Springs Rd
2000 MrnT 46069 1681 C2
2000 UnnT 46069 1681 C2
6200 MrnT 46069 1572 C2
Big Stone Dr
- LcnT 46112 2115 C5
Bill Dr
- LWNC 46235 2122 D6
5100 LWNC 46236 2122 D6
Billie Ln
400 INPS 46260 2119 B1
Billings Rd
100 LWNC 46216 2122 E4
100 LWNC 46216 2123 A4
Billingsgate Pl
11100 FSHR 46038 1904 A6
Billingsley Rd
3200 ClkT 46143 2666 E6
3200 ClkT 46143 2667 A6
Billiter Ct
15900 WTFD 46033 1793 C4
Bills Av
11800 FCkT 46038 1905 E3
Billy Creek Ct
14400 CRML 46032 1792 B7
Biloxi Ln
1300 BHGV 46107 2447 E6
N Biltmore Av
1500 SDWY 46224 2226 C7
1500 SDWY 46224 2335 C1

S Biltmore Av
300 INPS 46241 2335 C4
4100 INPS 46221 2444 C5
S Biltmore St
1400 INPS 46241 2335 C6
2200 INPS 46241 2444 C1
Bimini Ln
7300 INPS 46214 2225 D3
Binford Blvd
- INPS 46205 2120 D6
- INPS 46205 2229 B1
- INPS 46220 2120 D6
- INPS 46220 2121 B3
- INPS 46250 2012 D7
- INPS 46250 2121 B3
Bing Ct
3900 INPS 46237 2556 D1
Bingham Ct
10 INPS 46222 2227 A5
Bingham Rd
100 BrnT 46158 2659 B4
100 MRVL 46158 2659 B4
Birch Av
500 INPS 46221 2337 A5
Birch Ct
10 WRvT 46142 2664 A1
1600 PNFD 46168 2441 E5
N Birch Ct
800 BCkT 46140 2233 B7
Birch Dr
1800 PNFD 46168 2441 E5
Birch Ln
- GNWD 46143 2666 A5
5200 WRvT 46143 2663 C7
12400 LWNC 46236 2124 A2
Birch St
- AVON 46234 2233 D1
- NPLN 46163 2452 A3
400 WTFD 46074 1684 B7
500 BHGV 46107 2447 E4
8800 FSHR 46038 1904 D6
Birch Canyon St
3100 CRML 46033 2011 C1
3200 CRML 46033 1902 D7
Birchcrest Dr
6400 INPS 46241 2334 E5
6400 INPS 46241 2335 A5
Birch Tree Cir
10700 LWNC 46236 2123 B1
Birch Tree Ct
10700 LWNC 46236 2123 B1
Birch Tree Ln
10700 LWNC 46236 2123 B1
Birchwood Av
3400 INPS 46205 2228 E3
5900 INPS 46220 2119 E4
Birchwood Ct
9900 ClyT 46280 2011 B1
Birchwood Dr
100 LEBN 46052 1785 E1
100 LEBN 46052 1786 A1
Birchwood Wy
- GNWD 46143 2666 A6
Bird Branch Dr
5000 INPS 46268 2117 D3
Bird Cage Wk
- CRML 46032 1900 D3
Bird Key Blvd
11800 FSHR 46038 1905 C4
Birdkey Dr
6400 NBVL 46062 1685 D4
Birds Eye Dr
6300 INPS 46203 2448 D3
Birdseye Dr
- WTFD 46074 1792 D2
Birdsong Ct
11200 INPS 46229 2341 C3
W Birdsong Ct
3200 SCkT 46140 2343 D4
W Birdsong Dr
3000 SCkT 46140 2343 E4
Birdsong Ln
600 CRML 46032 1792 B7
E Birdsong Pl
11200 INPS 46229 2341 C3
E Birdsong Tr
4800 MdnT 46158 2660 C7
Bird Watch Wy
15100 NBVL 46060 1796 E5
Birkdale Cir
8800 INPS 46234 2225 A5
Birmingham Dr
4600 INPS 46235 2123 D7
4600 LWNC 46235 2123 D7
Birmingham Ln
100 FCkT 46038 1904 D2
Birnam Woods Tr
1100 ClyT 46280 2010 E1
1100 ClyT 46280 2011 A1
Biron Wy
5900 INPS 46254 2117 B5
Birtz Rd
400 LWNC 46216 2122 D5
Biscay Sq
2200 INPS 46260 2118 D2
Biscayne Rd
3400 INPS 46226 2231 C3
Bischoff Dr
2300 BHGV 46107 2447 C3
2300 INPS 46107 2447 C3
Bishop Cir
10400 ClyT 46032 2009 D1
E Bishop Ct
9800 INPS 46235 2231 E2
Bishop St
200 MRVL 46158 2659 E3
Bishops Ln
8100 INPS 46217 2555 A6
Bishopsgate Dr
4700 CRML 46033 1902 E3
4700 CRML 46033 1903 A4
Bison Ct
1600 INPS 46268 2008 E6
Bison Club Dr
8800 INPS 46227 2555 D7

Bison Creek Dr
700 INPS 46227 2555 D7
Bison Lake Cir
8600 INPS 46227 2555 D7
Bison Lake Dr
8500 INPS 46227 2555 D7
Bison Lake South Dr
8600 INPS 46227 2555 D7
Bison Run Wy
700 INPS 46227 2555 D7
Bison Woods Ct
8500 INPS 46227 2555 D7
Bitter Bark Ln
500 INPS 46227 2555 D6
Bittern Cir
12300 FSHR 46038 1906 A6
Bittern Ln
8000 INPS 46256 2013 B7
Bitternut Dr
7900 LWNC 46236 2014 E6
Bitteroot Ct
1100 INPS 46234 2333 E1
Bittersweet Ct
- NWTD 46184 2774 D2
- PltT 46184 2774 D2
10 NBVL 46062 1685 E5
Bittersweet Dr
200 NWTD 46184 2774 D3
1400 GNFD 46140 2345 E3
Bittersweet Ln
4100 WRvT 46142 2663 E3
6700 LWNC 46236 2124 A2
10700 FSHR 46038 1904 B7
Bitterwood Dr
6600 INPS 46203 2448 D5
Bittner Ct
5300 NBVL 46062 1794 B2
W Bittner Ln
4200 SCkT 46163 2452 B5
N Bittner Rd
10 NPLN 46163 2452 B3
3200 SCkT 46163 2343 B7
3200 SCkT 46163 2452 B1
S Bittner Rd
10 NPLN 46163 2452 B4
Bittner Wy
16900 NBVL 46062 1794 B2
Bixler Rd
10 INPS 46227 2446 C6
Black Antler Cir
6600 INPS 46217 2554 C3
Black Antler Ct
2400 INPS 46217 2554 C3
Black Antler Dr
- NBVL 46060 1796 E5
6500 INPS 46217 2554 C3
Black Bear Cir
5400 INPS 46239 2449 A7
Blackberry Ct
200 WshT 46074 1792 C4
9200 ZNVL 46077 1898 C2
S Blackberry Ct
4500 SCkT 46163 2451 D4
Black Berry Dr
- GNWD 46143 2774 A1
Blackbird Ct
16600 NBVL 46060 1797 A2
Black Bird Ln
700 GNWD 46142 2664 D2
Blackburn Av
18300 WTFD 46074 1684 A5
18400 WshT 46074 1684 A5
Black Cherry Cir
5500 INPS 46237 2447 D7
5500 INPS 46237 2556 D1
Black Cherry Ct
17000 NBVL 46062 1794 E1
Black Farm Dr
14300 FCkT 46060 1797 A7
14300 NBVL 46060 1797 A7
Black Foot Dr
4500 INPS 46235 2123 A7
Blackfoot Tr
5500 CRML 46033 1903 B2
N Blackford St
100 INPS 46202 2337 B3
S Blackford St
- INPS 46204 2337 A4
Black Forest Dr
7000 GfdT 46168 2551 B4
Black Forest Ln
3000 INPS 46239 2449 A3
Blackgum Ct
8100 LWNC 46236 2015 A6
Black Hawk Ln
8900 INPS 46234 2225 A2
Black Hawk Sta
6000 MCVL 46055 2015 D3
Black Hills Dr
- FSHR 46060 1905 E1
- FSHR 46060 1906 A1
Black Knight Blvd
2700 INPS 46229 2231 E5
Black Lake Ct
- BNBG 46112 2114 E5
Blackley Ct
6000 INPS 46254 2117 A4
Blackley Ln
5900 INPS 46254 2117 B4
Black Locust Dr
- INPS 46235 2232 D3
Black Maple Ct
200 GNWD 46143 2665 E2
Blackmore Dr
1600 INPS 46231 2334 A7
Black Oak Cir
1200 GNWD 46143 2664 E5
Black Oak Ct
8000 GfdT 46168 2550 D4
Black Oak Dr
- NBVL 46062 1795 A2
1200 GNWD 46143 2664 D5
1600 GfdT 46168 2550 D4
4200 INPS 46228 2227 C1

S Black Oak Ln
4000 NPLN 46163 2452 A2
Black Oak East Ct
8000 AVON 46123 2332 B1
Black Oaks Wy
6100 INPS 46237 2557 C1
Black Oak West Ct
2600 AVON 46123 2332 B1
Black Pine Ct
9600 FSHR 46038 1904 E7
Black Rock Ct
1400 GfdT 46168 2550 D5
Blacksmith Ct
7500 PNFD 46168 2441 C2
8400 FSHR 46038 1904 C6
Blackstone Av
5700 INPS 46237 2556 D1
Black Stone Cross
- WshT 46123 2332 E1
- WshT 46123 2333 A1
Blackstone Cross
8600 WshT 46123 2333 A1
Blackstone Ct
11100 CRML 46032 1901 D6
Blackstone Dr
4300 INPS 46237 2556 E1
4700 INPS 46237 2557 A1
Blackstone Pl
10 ZNVL 46077 1899 A4
Blacktern Wy
13200 CRML 46033 1903 B2
Blackthorn Cir
7700 LWNC 46236 2014 E7
Blackthorn Ct
7600 LWNC 46236 2014 E7
10600 FSHR 46038 1904 B7
Black Thorn Dr
6600 INPS 46221 2552 E1
Blackthorn Dr
7700 LWNC 46236 2014 E7
Blackwalnut Pt
11200 INPS 46236 2014 C6
Blackwell Cir
6800 INPS 46237 2557 E2
Blackwood Ct
1200 MRVL 46158 2660 C3
4000 INPS 46237 2447 D7
4200 WRvT 46143 2663 E5
Blade Ct
8800 INPS 46231 2334 A6
Bladed Mills Dr
18900 NBVL 46062 1685 C5
Bladstone Rd
6700 NBVL 46062 1794 E6
Blain Wy
7600 INPS 46254 2116 C6
Blaine Av
1000 INPS 46221 2336 E5
Blair St
- LEBN 46052 1676 E6
N Blair St
200 LEBN 46052 1676 E6
Blairsden Av
10 CRML 46032 1902 C3
Blake Cir
3400 WRvT 46143 2664 B6
Blake St
10 DNVL 46122 2329 D4
10 INPS 46202 2337 A3
300 AdmT 46069 1573 B1
N Blake St
100 SRDN 46069 1573 B1
700 INPS 46202 2337 A2
S Blake St
100 SRDN 46069 1573 B1
Blakely Dr
- GNWD 46143 2666 B6
Blakeview Dr
1400 LWNC 46235 2123 E3
Blanchard Wy
5200 NBVL 46062 1685 B1
Blanford Pl
400 WTFD 46074 1792 D2
Blank St
- GNFD 46140 2345 E2
Blankenship Av
7000 INPS 46217 2554 D4
Blankenship Dr
1500 INPS 46217 2554 D4
Blazing Trail Ct
1900 INPS 46217 2554 D7
Bloodstone St
- INPS 46268 2009 C7
Bloom Dr
4500 WRvT 46142 2663 D2
Bloomfield Ct
11300 INPS 46259 2559 C3
15400 WshT 46074 1792 C5
Bloomfield Dr
6600 INPS 46259 2559 C3
Bloomfield Dr E
6800 INPS 46259 2559 D3
Bloomfield Dr S
11300 INPS 46259 2559 C4
E Bloomfield Ln
10 WshT 46074 1792 C4
Bloomfield Ter
11300 INPS 46259 2559 C3
Blooming Ct
2100 INPS 46229 2232 D6
Blooming Grove Dr
8600 INPS 46113 2552 A7
Bloor Ln
- ZNVL 46077 1898 E5
600 ZNVL 46077 1899 A5
Blore Hth
1800 CRML 46032 1900 E3
Blossom Dr
- WshT 46123 2331 C5
2200 GNWD 46143 2774 B1
Blossom Ln N
6400 INPS 46278 2008 A6
6600 INPS 46278 2007 E6
Blossom Ln S
6500 INPS 46278 2008 A6

STREET Block City ZIP Map# Grid

Blossom Wy
11500 CRML 46032 1901 D6
Bloyd Av
1900 INPS 46218 2229 A7
N Blue Rd
10 GNFD 46140 2237 B7
10 GNFD 46140 2346 B1
600 CtrT 46140 2237 B7
Blue Ash Ln
3200 INPS 46239 2449 C3
Bluebell Cir
3000 INPS 46224 2226 A4
Bluebell Ct
6300 INPS 46224 2226 A4
Bluebell Dr
5200 SCkT 46163 2343 A3
5400 SCkT 46163 2342 E3
Bluebell Ln
3000 INPS 46224 2226 A4
Blueberry Ln
10700 FSHR 46038 1905 C7
Blue Bird Ct
- FSHR 46038 1905 D6
Bluebird Ct
10 GNFD 46140 2237 A6
7400 INPS 46254 2225 D2
7700 BrnT 46112 2114 A2
Blue Bird Dr
- PNFD 46231 2333 E6
Bluebird Dr
1300 GNFD 46140 2236 E6
1300 GNFD 46140 2237 A6
Blue Brook Wy
1400 GNWD 46143 2665 E6
Blue Chip Ct
1800 INPS 46234 2225 A7
Blue Creek Dr
4300 CRML 46033 2011 E1
7400 INPS 46256 2013 A7
7400 INPS 46256 2122 B3
Blue Creek South Dr
7300 INPS 46256 2122 A1
Blue Creek West Dr
7300 INPS 46256 2122 B3
Bluefin Cir
8400 INPS 46236 2014 D4
Bluefin Ct
11600 INPS 46236 2014 D5
Blue Fin Dr
10300 INPS 46256 2014 B3
Blueflag Ct
15600 WshT 46074 1792 D4
Blue Flax Ct
10600 NBVL 46060 1687 C4
Blue Fox Ln
6000 INPS 46237 2557 B2
Blue Grass Ct
600 MRVL 46158 2660 A5
2500 INPS 46228 2227 C1
Bluegrass Ct
10700 FSHR 46038 1904 B7
Blue Grass Dr
2500 INPS 46228 2227 C1
Blue Grass Pkwy
1200 GNWD 46143 2665 E6
Blue Heron Dr
14100 CRML 46033 1903 B1
Blue Heron Ln
1200 GNWD 46143 2665 E6
Blue Heron Wy
5900 PNFD 46168 2550 B2
Blue Hill Cir
5500 INPS 46224 2335 B2
Blue Jay Ct
2100 INPS 46260 2009 D6
Blue Jay Ln
7900 INPS 46260 2009 D6
Blue Lake Ct
- WynT 46060 1797 A5
Blue Lake Dr
- GNWD 46143 2665 B7
- PltT 46143 2665 B7
Blue Marlin Dr
8500 INPS 46239 2449 C6
Blue Marlin Wy
- INPS 46239 2449 C6
Blue Meadow Dr
- GNWD 46143 2665 B7
- PltT 46143 2665 B7
11200 FSHR 46038 1905 D5
Blue Moon Dr
17200 NBVL 46060 1796 D1
Blue Oak Ct
19400 NBVL 46060 1686 E4
Blue Oak Ln
800 INPS 46227 2555 D6
Blue Phlox Dr
1500 WshT 46123 2223 C7
Blue Pine Dr
9100 INPS 46231 2333 E7
Blue Pine Ln
1800 INPS 46231 2333 E7
Blue Ribbon Rd
4300 INPS 46203 2448 C5
Blue Ridge Dr
- NBVL 46062 1794 E2
- NBVL 46062 1795 A2
Blue Ridge Rd
100 INPS 46208 2228 B1
Blue Ridge Wy
- LcnT 46112 2115 C5
Blue Sky Ct
14400 CRML 46032 1792 D7
Blue Sky Dr
10400 FSHR 46038 1905 B5
Blue Spring Ct
11100 INPS 46239 2341 C4
Blue Spring Dr
400 INPS 46239 2341 C4
Blue Springs Ln
10400 FSHR 46038 1905 B4
Blue Spruce Ct
4200 WRvT 46143 2663 E5
N Blue Spruce Ct
1200 BCkT 46140 2234 E6
1200 BCkT 46140 2235 A6
Blue Spruce Dr
10700 FSHR 46038 1904 E7
Bluespruce Dr
5600 INPS 46237 2557 B1
Bluestem Ct
5800 CRML 46033 1903 D1
6800 INPS 46237 2448 E6
10300 NBVL 46060 1687 B3
Bluestone Cir
9100 INPS 46236 2014 E3
Bluestone Dr
11900 INPS 46236 2014 E3
Bluestone Wy
10900 FSHR 46038 1904 A7
Bluewater Ct
1700 INPS 46229 2232 A7
Blue Water Dr
10 CCRO 46034 1577 B2
Blue Willow Cir
1700 INPS 46239 2340 B6
Blue Willow Dr
7700 INPS 46239 2340 A6
Bluff Ln
900 WRvT 46143 2663 A5
Bluff Rd
100 WRvT 46142 2663 B3
1200 PNFD 46168 2441 C7
N Bluff Rd
100 WRvT 46142 2663 B2
S Bluff Rd
1900 INPS 46225 2337 C7
2200 INPS 46225 2446 B1
3000 INPS 46217 2446 B3
5500 INPS 46217 2555 A1
6500 INPS 46217 2554 E3
8800 INPS 46217 2663 B1
8800 WRvT 46217 2663 B1
W Bluff Rd
8600 INPS 46217 2554 C7
Bluff Acres Dr
6000 WRvT 46143 2663 A5
N Bluff Creek Ct
13800 MdnT 46113 2661 B1
Bluff Crest Ct
6000 INPS 46217 2554 E2
Bluff Crest Dr
1100 INPS 46217 2554 E2
1100 INPS 46217 2555 A2
Bluff Crest Ln
1100 INPS 46217 2554 E2
1100 INPS 46217 2555 A2
Bluffdale Rd
100 WRvT 46142 2663 B3
Bluffgrove Cir
6900 INPS 46278 2116 E2
Bluffgrove Ct
6800 INPS 46278 2116 E2
Bluffgrove Dr
6700 INPS 46278 2116 E2
Bluffgrove Ln
6900 INPS 46278 2116 E2
Bluff Point Dr
8400 INPS 46113 2551 E7
Bluff Point Wy
8400 INPS 46113 2551 E7
Bluffridge Blvd
6900 INPS 46278 2116 D2
Bluffridge Ct
6700 INPS 46278 2116 E2
Bluffridge Dr
6800 INPS 46278 2116 E2
Bluffridge Ln
6800 INPS 46278 2116 E2
Bluffridge Pkwy
6700 INPS 46278 2116 E2
Bluffridge Pl
6900 INPS 46278 2116 E2
Bluffridge Wy
6900 INPS 46278 2116 E2
Bluffs Cir
200 NBVL 46062 1685 B1
Bluff View Blvd
5400 INPS 46217 2445 E7
5400 INPS 46217 2554 E1
Bluff View Dr
5200 INPS 46217 2445 E7
Bluffwood Ct
2400 INPS 46228 2118 C7
7100 BrnT 46112 2113 D3
Bluffwood Dr N
4600 INPS 46228 2118 C7
Bluffwood Dr W
2500 INPS 46228 2118 C7
Boardwalk Ln
11700 FSHR 46038 1905 A5
Boardwalk Pl
5000 INPS 46220 2121 A5
Bob Dr
9300 LWNC 46236 2122 D6
Bob St
1500 GfdT 46168 2550 D5
Bobby Ct
2100 PNFD 46168 2550 C2
Bobcat Trail Dr
7100 INPS 46237 2557 D4
Bobs Ct
700 BHGV 46107 2447 E4
Bobwhite Ln
4900 INPS 46254 2117 D4
13200 CRML 46033 1903 B2
Boca Grande Ct
4300 WTFD 46062 1684 E7
Boden Rd
14600 NBVL 46060 1797 B6
14600 WynT 46060 1797 B6
Bodner Ln
700 CRML 46032 1902 C4
Boehning Av
2500 INPS 46219 2231 C4
Boehning Ct
8800 INPS 46219 2231 D5
Boehning Ln
8700 INPS 46219 2231 C6
N Boehning St
10 INPS 46219 2340 D2
2100 INPS 46219 2231 D6
S Boehning St
100 INPS 46219 2340 D4
Boehning Wy
- INPS 46219 2231 C6
Boettcher Ct
5800 INPS 46228 2118 D4
Bogalusa Ct
900 INPS 46217 2555 A5
Bogart Av
- INPS 46203 2338 E6
Bogey Dr
5200 LWNC 46235 2123 D6
Boggs Creek Ct
5400 INPS 46237 2557 B6
Boggs Creek Dr
8400 INPS 46237 2557 B6
Boine Cir
3800 CRML 46033 2011 D2
Bokeelia Bnd
1100 WshT 46074 1684 A4
Bolderwood Ln
400 CRML 46032 1792 A6
400 CRML 46032 1901 B1
Bold Forbes Ct
8100 INPS 46217 2554 E6
Bold Ruler Dr
5700 INPS 46237 2557 B2
Bolin Ct
300 CRML 46032 1901 C3
Bolton Av
- MRVL 46158 2660 A3
200 MRVL 46158 2659 E3
N Bolton Av
300 INPS 46219 2339 C1
2100 INPS 46218 2230 C6
4400 INPS 46226 2230 C1
4600 INPS 46226 2121 C7
S Bolton Av
10 INPS 46219 2339 C3
1900 INPS 46203 2339 C7
2400 INPS 46203 2448 C1
Bolton Cir
- WTFD 46074 1792 D4
Bolton Ct
1300 INPS 46219 2339 C1
E Bomar Blvd
2000 BwnT 46140 2345 E6
Bo-Mar Dr
1100 GNWD 46142 2664 D1
1100 INPS 46142 2664 D1
E Bomar Ln
2000 BwnT 46140 2345 E6
S Bomar Ln
2500 BwnT 46140 2345 E6
Bombay Dr
5300 INPS 46239 2449 B7
Bonanza Ln
6300 INPS 46254 2117 A7
N Bonar Av
1000 INPS 46229 2340 E1
S Bonar Av
100 INPS 46229 2340 E3
Bonaventure Av
12000 CRML 46032 1900 E3
Bond St
2400 INPS 46208 2228 A6
Bonham Dr
3100 INPS 46222 2227 B4
Bonita Ct
7800 INPS 46219 2231 B5
Bonn Blvd
3700 INPS 46228 2227 A2
Bonn Dr
3900 INPS 46228 2227 A2
Bonna Av
- INPS 46219 2339 E4
8500 INPS 46219 2340 C3
E Bonna Av
6000 INPS 46219 2339 C3
Bonneville Dr
6300 INPS 46237 2557 D1
Bonneville Wy
5800 INPS 46237 2557 D1
Bonnie Ln
- WshT 46123 2331 E2
1600 GNWD 46142 2664 C2
Bonnie Brae St
4500 INPS 46228 2227 D1
5700 INPS 46228 2118 D5
Bonny Dr
6800 INPS 46221 2552 D3
Bonnybridge Dr
5100 INPS 46241 2443 E7
Bookbinder Dr
7500 PNFD 46168 2441 C2
Bookers Ct
- AdmT 46069 1574 D6
Boone Ct
1300 INPS 46217 2554 E7
Boone Dr
11500 INPS 46229 2341 D1
Boone St
12800 FSHR 46038 1904 E3
N Boone St
- WTLD 46184 2775 A5
S Boone St
100 WTLD 46184 2775 A6
Boone Vil
10 ZNVL 46077 1899 A6
Boone Ridge Rd
- EglT 46077 1898 D6
Boonesboro Ct
1200 GNWD 46142 2664 E4
Boonesboro Rd
600 GNWD 46142 2664 E4
Boone Wds
10 ZNVL 46077 1898 E6
Bootham Close
10100 FSHR 46060 1905 A2
Boothbay Ln
11500 FCkT 46038 1905 D5
Boots Tr
10 GNFD 46140 2237 A6
Bordeaux Ct
6100 INPS 46220 2120 E4
Border Dr
- NBVL 46060 1796 B5
Borgman Dr
2300 INPS 46229 2232 E6
Borgmann Ct
2400 INPS 46229 2232 D5
Bosahan Ct
10400 ClyT 46032 2009 A1
N Bosart Av
500 INPS 46201 2338 E2
1500 INPS 46201 2229 E7
1600 INPS 46218 2229 E7
5300 INPS 46220 2120 E6
S Bosart Av
200 INPS 46201 2338 E4
500 INPS 46203 2338 E5
Boschen Lp
- LWNC 46216 2122 C6
Bosinney Cir
7800 INPS 46256 2013 B7
Bosk Ct
6900 INPS 46237 2448 E6
Bosloe Dr
10200 ClyT 46032 2009 A1
Bosstick Av
100 DNVL 46122 2329 C4
Boston Ct
2100 INPS 46228 2227 D2
Boston Wy
11100 FSHR 46038 1904 C6
Boston Ridge Ct
6600 INPS 46237 2557 D3
Bottom Rd
2200 GfdT 46168 2550 C3
Bough St
- GNWD 46184 2774 A2
Boulder Cr S
- SCkT 46163 2342 D7
Boulder Ct
200 CRML 46032 1793 A7
S Boulder Ct
6700 INPS 46217 2555 A3
Boulder Dr
100 NbvT 46060 1686 E3
1900 INPS 46260 2009 D7
Boulder Ln
7600 INPS 46260 2009 D7
Boulder Rd
600 INPS 46217 2555 A3
Boulder Gap
- INPS 46226 2121 B5
Boulevard Pl
2100 INPS 46202 2228 B6
3000 INPS 46208 2228 B4
4500 INPS 46208 2119 B7
Boulevard Motif St
10 BNBG 46112 2114 C5
E Boundary St
2300 INPS 46231 2443 A1
Bountiful Pl
6300 GfdT 46231 2551 C2
Bounty Ct
8000 INPS 46236 2014 B6
Bourbon St
9000 LWNC 46235 2231 D1
Bourden Ln
- FSHR 46060 1906 E3
Bow Ln
100 INPS 46220 2119 D2
Bow St
- AdmT 46069 1573 A3
Bowen Ct
1500 GNWD 46143 2665 B6
Bowen Pl
3400 INPS 46221 2445 A3
E Bowen Rd
8800 INPS 46239 2449 D5
Bowen St
200 DNVL 46122 2329 E4
Bower Dr
6300 INPS 46241 2335 A5
N Bowers St
- WTWN 46075 1788 C6
S Bowers St
100 WTWN 46075 1788 C7
Bowie Dr
- WshT 46074 1792 A5
Bowie Ln
5900 INPS 46254 2117 B4
Bowline Ct
8100 INPS 46236 2014 B5
Bowline Dr
8000 INPS 46236 2014 B6
Bowline Rd
- FCkT 46040 1907 B6
Bowling Green Wy
9400 LWNC 46216 2122 E5
Bowman Av
4000 INPS 46227 2446 E5
Bowman Ct
10 GNFD 46140 2345 E3
Bowman Dr
- BNBG 46112 2114 A6
1200 GNFD 46140 2345 E4
Box Elder Ct
1800 INPS 46260 2009 D4
Boxford Ct
400 INPS 46214 2334 C2
Boxwood Ct
10300 FSHR 46038 2014 A1
Boxwood Dr
3200 INPS 46227 2556 C5
3200 SPRT 46227 2556 C5
Boxwood Ln
- GNWD 46143 2666 A7
- PNFD 46168 2440 C4
Boyd Av
- INPS 46227 2446 E3
2000 INPS 46203 2337 E7
2200 INPS 46203 2446 E1
E Boyd Av
10 GNFD 46140 2236 E7
W Boyd Av
400 GNFD 46140 2236 C7
Boyd Ln
2800 INPS 46218 2229 B5
Boyer Ln
2400 INPS 46217 2554 C4
Boylston St
300 CRML 46032 1902 A4
Boy Scout Rd
5200 LWNC 46226 2122 B6
Boysenberry Dr
9900 FSHR 46060 1796 A6
Bracken Cir
5500 INPS 46239 2448 E7
Bracken Ct
3700 CRML 46033 2011 E2
Bracken Dr
5200 INPS 46239 2448 E7
Bracken Ln
7100 INPS 46239 2448 E7
7100 INPS 46239 2449 A7
Brackenwood Blvd
- INPS 46260 2119 A1
Brackenwood Cir N
7400 INPS 46260 2010 A7
7400 INPS 46260 2119 B1
Brackenwood Cir S
7300 INPS 46260 2119 B1
Brackenwood Dr
7300 INPS 46260 2119 B1
Brackney Ln
14400 CRML 46032 1792 A7
Brad Cir
- WshT 46123 2332 E1
Brad Dr
5100 LWNC 46236 2122 D6
E Bradbury Av
1100 INPS 46203 2446 E1
1500 INPS 46203 2447 A1
W Bradbury Av
3800 INPS 46241 2445 A1
4900 INPS 46241 2444 C1
Bradbury Dr
9600 WshT 46231 2442 C1
10300 PNFD 46231 2442 C1
Bradbury Pl
11000 CRML 46033 1903 A7
Bradbury St
5400 INPS 46241 2444 C1
Braddock Dr
3900 INPS 46268 2009 A5
Braddock Rd
- INPS 46268 2008 E5
3900 INPS 46268 2009 A5
Bradenton Ct
4500 WTFD 46062 1684 E6
Bradenton Pl
- INPS 46254 2117 D7
Bradford Cir
600 INPS 46214 2334 D2
Bradford Ct
- BNBG 46112 2114 D3
12400 FSHR 46038 1906 A7
Bradford Dr
3400 INPS 46221 2444 E4
Bradford Pl
10 NWTD 46184 2774 D5
11600 CRML 46033 1902 E5
Bradford Rd
1600 AVON 46123 2441 D1
1600 AVON 46168 2441 D1
11100 GfdT 46231 2442 D3
11100 PNFD 46231 2442 D3
Bradford Knoll Dr
9600 FSHR 46038 2013 E1
9700 FSHR 46038 2014 B1
Bradford Meadow Cir
6200 INPS 46268 2117 C3
Bradford Trace Blvd
- INPS 46229 2232 C5
Bradford Trace Ct
11200 INPS 46229 2232 C7
Bradford Trace Wy
1900 INPS 46229 2232 C5
Bradford Woods Ln
4100 INPS 46268 2118 A1
Bradford Woods Wy
7100 INPS 46268 2118 A1
N Bradley Av
10 INPS 46201 2338 D3
S Bradley Av
10 INPS 46201 2338 D3
1100 INPS 46203 2338 D6
Bradley Dr
- NBVL 46060 1687 C4
- PNFD 46231 2333 D5
5300 WshT 46231 2333 D5
Bradley Rd
5300 GfdT 46168 2442 A7
5400 GfdT 46168 2551 A1
Bradock Ct
400 INPS 46234 2334 B2
Bradshire Ct
6400 EglT 46077 1897 C7
Bradston Wy
5500 INPS 46237 2557 B1
Bradwell Pl
8800 FSHR 46038 2013 D1
Brae Ct
8500 GfdT 46158 2550 C7
Braeburn Dr
1800 CRML 46032 1900 E4
Braeburn Pkwy
2100 INPS 46219 2231 C6
Braeburn Ter
8100 INPS 46219 2231 B6
Braeburn East Dr
2100 INPS 46219 2231 C6
Braeburn North Dr
8100 INPS 46219 2231 B6
Braeburn West Dr
2100 INPS 46219 2231 B6
Braedon Wood
4400 INPS 46228 2227 E1
Braemar Av E
14600 NBVL 46062 1794 E6
Braemar Av N
- NBVL 46062 1794 D5
Braemar Av S
6400 NBVL 46062 1794 D6
Braemar Ct
- WshT 46123 2331 D3
11500 ClyT 46032 1900 D5
Braemar Dr
4200 INPS 46254 2225 E1
Braemar St
5000 WshT 46123 2331 C3
Braeside Ct
700 INPS 46260 2010 B3
Braeside Dr N
400 INPS 46260 2010 B3
Braeside Dr S
400 INPS 46260 2010 B4
Braeside North Dr
400 INPS 46260 2010 B4
Braewick Cir
10600 FSHR 46038 2014 B1
Braewick Ct
100 CRML 46033 1902 D7
Braewick Dr
10700 CRML 46033 1902 D7
Braewick Pl
3600 CRML 46033 1902 D7
Braewick Rd
- INPS 46226 2121 B5
Braewood Ct
7400 INPS 46217 2555 C5
Bragdon St
4300 LWNC 46226 2231 B1
Brahmin Pk
500 WTLD 46184 2774 E5
Brahms Dr
14600 WshT 46032 1792 C6
Braided Stream Wy
3900 INPS 46268 2009 A5
Brambleberry Ct
5800 INPS 46239 2558 C1
Brambleberry Dr
8100 INPS 46239 2558 B1
Bramblewood Cir
7500 INPS 46254 2116 C7
Bramblewood Ln
7300 INPS 46254 2116 D7
Bramblewood Wy
9600 ClyT 46032 2009 D2
Bramford Ct
6400 INPS 46256 2122 A3
Bramhall Ct
700 WshT 46123 2331 D5
Bramkrist Dr
- NBVL 46060 1796 B6
10300 FSHR 46060 1796 B6
Bramley Ct
12000 CRML 46032 1900 E4
Bramshaw Rd
6100 INPS 46220 2121 B3
Bramwood Ct
8000 INPS 46250 2012 A6
Branch St
- GNWD 46184 2774 A1
Branch Wy
3600 INPS 46268 2009 A6
Branch Creek Ct
3800 CRML 46077 1900 A5
Branch Creek Dr
7900 INPS 46268 2009 A6
Branch Creek Wy
7900 INPS 46268 2009 A6
Brandamore Ln
12300 FSHR 46038 1906 B4
Brandenburg Blvd
3300 INPS 46239 2449 B3
Brandenburg Dr
3000 INPS 46239 2449 B3
Brandenburg Wy
7600 INPS 46239 2449 A3
Brandi Ct
- GNWD 46142 2664 E4
Brandon Ct
9800 ClyT 46032 2009 E2
Brandon St
6500 LWNC 46236 2123 E2
Brandt Dr
1200 INPS 46241 2335 A6
Brandt Rd
9100 INPS 46240 2011 E3
9300 CRML 46240 2011 E3
N Brandt St
10 INPS 46214 2334 E3
Brandywine Cir
- BNBG 46112 2114 A5
3600 ClyT 46032 1900 A7
Brandywine Ct
- BNBG 46112 2114 A5
2500 INPS 46241 2444 C1
S Brandywine Ct
- BwnT 46140 2345 E6
Brandywine Dr
5000 INPS 46241 2444 C2
E Brandywine Ln
2200 BwnT 46140 2345 E6
2200 BwnT 46140 2346 A6
Brandywine Pkwy
1000 GNFD 46140 2236 E7
N Brandywine St
- GNFD 46140 2236 E6
S Brandywine St
10 GNFD 46140 2345 E1
S Brandywine Tr
2500 BwnT 46140 2345 E7
2500 BwnT 46140 2346 A6
Branford St
12400 CRML 46032 1900 D3
Brangton Dr
12200 FSHR 46038 2014 E1
12200 FSHR 46038 2015 A1
Brann Dr
- GNWD 46142 2664 C4
Brantford Ct
9200 INPS 46260 2010 A3
Brantly Dr
- LWNC 46236 2124 A2
Brant Pointe Cir
7100 INPS 46217 2555 A4
Brasseur Ln
3700 WTFD 46033 1793 D6
Brassica Ln
1700 INPS 46217 2554 D3
Brassica Wy
1700 INPS 46217 2554 D3
Brassie Dr
5200 LWNC 46235 2123 D6
Brassport Cir
8800 INPS 46231 2334 A4
Brassport Dr
300 INPS 46231 2334 A4
Braugham Rd
500 INPS 46227 2555 D5
Brave Ct
11000 LWNC 46236 2123 C2
Brave Tr
6600 LWNC 46236 2123 C2
Bravestone Wy
8300 INPS 46239 2449 C1
Bravo Pl
8000 INPS 46237 2556 E6
Braxton Ct
2900 INPS 46229 2232 D5
Braxton Dr
2600 INPS 46229 2232 D5
7100 NBVL 46062 1685 E5
7100 NBVL 46062 1686 A4
Bray Ct
10 GNWD 46143 2665 C1
Bray Rd
10 BrnT 46158 2658 C2
10 MnrT 46158 2658 C2
Brazos Dr
- CRML 46033 1794 D7
- CRML 46033 1903 D1
5300 INPS 46237 2557 A1
Breadsley Wy
- FSHR 46060 1905 D1
Breakers Ct
6400 WshT 46123 2332 A6
Breakers Wy
5200 CRML 46033 1903 C2
Breakwater Dr
100 FCkT 46038 1906 A7
3000 INPS 46214 2225 D4
Breamore Rd
6100 INPS 46220 2121 C3
Breaside Cir
1200 GNWD 46143 2664 E5
Breaside Ct
1200 GNWD 46143 2664 E5
Breaside Ln
800 GNWD 46143 2664 D5
Breckenridge Cir
4300 CRML 46033 2011 D1
Breckenridge Ct
4300 CRML 46033 2011 E1
11600 LWNC 46236 2123 D2
Breckenridge Dr
6500 LWNC 46236 2123 D2
10400 CRML 46033 2011 E1
10500 CRML 46033 1902 E7
Breckenridge Sta
9600 MCVL 46055 2015 C3
Breckenwood Dr
15400 NBVL 46062 1794 C5
Breckinridge Dr
3200 INPS 46228 2227 B1
Breeders Ct
14100 CRML 46074 1791 D7
Breeds Hill Ct
6500 INPS 46237 2557 D2
Breeds Hill Dr
6400 INPS 46237 2557 D3
Breen Ct
9100 INPS 46235 2231 D3
Breen Dr
3800 INPS 46235 2231 D2
Breen Wy
- FCkT 46038 1905 E4
Breezeway Cir
10300 BrnT 46112 2005 D4
Breezeway Ct
6300 INPS 46254 2117 A7
Breezy Point Dr
10100 FSHR 46038 1905 A5
Brehm Rd
23900 WRvT 46060 1579 D1
Brehob Rd
3500 INPS 46217 2446 B4
7500 INPS 46217 2555 B5
Breir Dr
4600 WRvT 46142 2663 D3
Breman Ln
1700 INPS 46229 2232 E7
Bremerton Cir
11300 CBLD 46229 2341 D2
Bremerton Dr
600 CBLD 46229 2341 D2
Bremhaven Ct
2300 INPS 46229 2232 C6
Brenda Ct
10 DNVL 46122 2329 D3
10 SCkT 46140 2342 C2
10700 FCkT 46040 1907 B7
Brendandow Ct
400 NBVL 46060 1795 D3
Brendon Dr
900 PNFD 46168 2441 D6
Brendon Wy
10 ZNVL 46077 1899 A6
Brendon Forest Dr
5600 INPS 46226 2121 D5
Brendon Park Dr
5200 INPS 46226 2121 D6

STREET
Block City ZIP Map# Grid

Brendonridge Ct N
5900 INPS 46226 2121 C6
Brendonridge Ct S
5900 INPS 46226 2121 C6
Brendonridge Rd
5200 INPS 46226 2121 C6
Brendonshire Ct
5100 INPS 46226 2121 C6
Brendon Way East Dr
5600 INPS 46226 2121 E5
Brendon Way North Dr
6800 INPS 46226 2121 D5
Brendon Way South Dr
6500 INPS 46226 2121 D5
Brendon Way West Dr
5600 INPS 46226 2121 D5
Brendon Wy Ct
5600 INPS 46226 2121 D5
Brendon Wy Pkwy
5600 INPS 46226 2121 E5
Bren Lee Ct
3400 INPS 46227 2556 C4
Brennan Ct
8300 FSHR 46060 1795 C7
Brennan Rd
7800 INPS 46219 2231 B5
Brent Av
8100 INPS 46240 2011 A6
Brentford Dr
1900 INPS 46219 2231 C7
Brentridge Pl
4800 WRvT 46143 2663 D7
Brentwood Av
11000 ZNVL 46077 1899 C3
N Brentwood Av
3400 INPS 46235 2231 D3
S Brentwood Av
10 INPS 46229 2340 D3
Brentwood Ct
1600 PNFD 46168 2441 D5
4500 ZNVL 46077 1899 C3
9100 INPS 46235 2231 D1
Brentwood Dr
10 MRVL 46158 2659 E3
10 MRVL 46158 2660 A2
N Brentwood Dr
4000 INPS 46235 2231 D2
Brentwood Dr E
500 PNFD 46168 2441 D5
Brentwood Dr S
1600 PNFD 46168 2441 D5
Brentwood Dr W
500 PNFD 46168 2441 D5
Brentwood Ln
100 NWTD 46184 2774 D3
13500 CRML 46033 1902 C1
Brentwood St
800 INPS 46239 2340 D5
Brer Rabbit Ct
5300 WRvT 46143 2663 C7
Brer Rabbit Dr
1700 WRvT 46143 2663 C7
Bressingham Dr
3800 INPS 46235 2232 B2
Breta Ct
11900 INPS 46229 2341 E1
W Breton St
4000 INPS 46222 2226 E4
4000 INPS 46222 2227 A4
Bretton Cir
6800 INPS 46268 2118 B2
Bretton Ct
3100 INPS 46268 2118 B1
Bretton Wood Dr
6800 INPS 46268 2118 B2
Brevard Dr
800 INPS 46217 2555 A5
13800 FSHR 46038 1904 C1
Brewer Dr
300 GNWD 46142 2665 C2
2100 INPS 46227 2556 B5
3300 INPS 46222 2226 E3
Brewer Pl
400 GNWD 46142 2665 C2
S Brewer Rd
1900 INPS 46231 2334 C7
Brewer St
600 WTLD 46184 2775 A5
N Brewer St
10 GNWD 46142 2665 C3
S Brewer St
100 GNWD 46142 2665 C4
Brewster Dr
2500 SDWY 46224 2226 B6
Brewster Rd
1400 INPS 46260 2009 D4
2400 INPS 46268 2009 C4
Brewton St
12600 FSHR 46038 1904 E3
Brian Dr
9300 LWNC 46236 2122 E6
Brian Pl
3500 CRML 46033 1902 D6
Brianna Ln
5200 LWNC 46235 2123 C6
Briar Cir
3400 CRML 46033 2011 D1
Briar Ct
1000 GNWD 46142 2664 E1
Briar Dr
3400 CRML 46033 2011 D1
Briar Ln
10 BHGV 46107 2447 D3
Briar Pl
3400 CRML 46033 2011 D1
Briarbrook Blvd
- INPS 46235 2232 C2
Briarchase Ct
2900 INPS 46268 2118 B3
Briarclift Rd
8800 INPS 46256 2122 D1
9200 LWNC 46256 2122 D1
Briar Creek Ln
3400 CRML 46033 2011 D1
Briar Creek Pl
10300 CRML 46033 2011 D1
Briargate Ct
6200 EglT 46077 1897 D7
Briar Hill Dr
100 WTLD 46184 2775 A6
300 WTLD 46184 2774 E6
Briarhill Dr
12600 LWNC 46236 2015 A5
Briarhill Ln
8100 LWNC 46236 2015 A5
Briarhill Wy
8300 LWNC 46236 2015 B5
Briar Meadow Ct
1300 INPS 46217 2554 D3
Briar Patch Ct
4700 INPS 46250 2121 A1
Briar Patch Ln
800 GNWD 46142 2665 A3
Briarstone Dr
7500 INPS 46227 2556 A5
Briar Stone Ln
10600 FSHR 46038 1904 B7
Briarstone Ln
7600 INPS 46227 2556 A5
Briarstone Trc
5000 CRML 46033 1903 A2
Briarstone Wy
1600 INPS 46227 2556 A5
Briarway Ct
6300 MCVL 46055 2015 C3
N Briarway Ln
9600 MCVL 46055 2015 C3
Briar Way Center Dr
12000 MrlT 46259 2559 E2
Briar Way North Dr
12000 MrlT 46259 2559 E2
Briar Way South Dr
1200 MrlT 46259 2559 E2
Briarwood Ct
100 BNBG 46112 2223 B2
4800 CRML 46033 1903 A2
7200 INPS 46250 2120 E1
Briarwood Dr
800 GNWD 46142 2665 A3
900 BNBG 46112 2223 B2
3700 INPS 46240 2120 D1
4100 INPS 46250 2120 E1
8000 INPS 46227 2555 E6
8000 INPS 46227 2556 A6
Briarwood Tr
4800 CRML 46033 1903 A2
Briarwood Trc
4600 CRML 46033 1902 E2
4700 CRML 46033 1903 A2
E Brick St
400 SRDN 46069 1573 B2
Brickenwood Ct
3100 INPS 46227 2447 C4
Brickenwood Ln
3100 INPS 46227 2447 C4
Brickenwood Trc
3800 INPS 46227 2447 C4
Brickenwood Wy
3100 INPS 46227 2447 C4
Brickmaker Ct
7500 PNFD 46168 2441 C2
Bridge Ct
8300 INPS 46231 2334 B7
Bridge St
100 MRVL 46158 2659 E3
300 MRVL 46158 2660 A3
900 BrnT 46158 2660 A3
1200 INPS 46221 2337 A6
Bridgefield Dr
1200 CRML 46033 1793 D7
4700 INPS 46254 2116 E7
Bridgefield Dr E
4400 PNFD 46168 2442 A6
Bridgefield Dr W
4200 PNFD 46168 2442 A6
Bridgefield Wy
6700 INPS 46254 2116 E7
Bridgemont Ct
7000 WshT 46123 2332 C2
Bridgeport Dr
1000 WshT 46074 1792 A5
Bridgeport Rd
- INPS 46234 2225 A5
10 INPS 46231 2334 A4
1700 INPS 46231 2443 A1
4500 INPS 46231 2442 E6
4500 INPS 46241 2442 E6
5100 INPS 46241 2443 A7
S Bridgeport Rd
2400 INPS 46231 2443 A1
2400 INPS 46241 2443 A1
Bridger Ct
6600 INPS 46268 2117 D2
Bridger Dr N
3400 CRML 46033 2011 D1
Bridger Dr S
3600 CRML 46033 2011 D2
Bridgestone Ct
9200 INPS 46231 2333 E4
Bridgestone Dr
300 INPS 46231 2333 E4
Bridgeton Ln
5700 CRML 46033 1903 B4
Bridgett Dr N
12800 MdnT 46113 2660 E3
Bridgeview Ct
13000 FCkT 46055 2015 B2
Bridgeview Wy
2600 INPS 46220 2120 B2
Bridgewater Cir
9400 INPS 46250 2012 D3
Bridgewater Dr
1500 WshT 46123 2332 A7
1900 WshT 46123 2441 A1
Bridgewater Rd
12100 FCkT 46256 2014 E2
12300 FCkT 46256 2015 A2
Bridgewater Club Blvd
- WTFD 46033 1793 D3
Bridgewood Ct
2500 INPS 46268 2118 C1
Bridgewood Dr
7100 INPS 46268 2118 C1
Bridgton Ct
1900 INPS 46219 2231 B7
Bridgton Dr
1900 INPS 46219 2231 C7
Bridle Cir
800 CRML 46032 1792 E7
Bridle Ct
800 CRML 46032 1792 E6
Bridle Ln
4200 LWNC 46226 2231 B1
Bridlewood Cir
2800 WTFD 46033 1793 C6
Bridlewood Ct
3400 EglT 46077 1790 C7
Bridlewood Dr
14800 WTFD 46033 1793 C6
Bridlewood Ln
2900 WTFD 46033 1793 C5
Bridlewood Tr
3400 MdlT 46123 2222 C4
10100 EglT 46077 1790 C7
Brief Run
5200 INPS 46226 2121 A6
Brier Pl
1600 INPS 46203 2337 E6
S Brier Creek Ct
1000 SCkT 46163 2342 B3
S Brier Creek Dr
6500 SCkT 46163 2342 C3
W Brier Creek Dr
6600 SCkT 46163 2342 B3
Briergate Ct
9000 INPS 46229 2231 D5
Brierley Wy
100 CRML 46032 1902 C2
Brigade Cir
3800 ClyT 46032 1900 A6
Brigade Ln
5800 LWNC 46216 2122 E5
Brigadier Dr
8900 LWNC 46226 2122 D6
Brigantine Ct
9500 INPS 46256 2014 C3
Brigantine Dr
10800 INPS 46256 2014 C3
Briggs Ct
10400 INPS 46256 2014 B4
Briggs Wy
8900 INPS 46256 2014 B4
Bright Leaf Cir
7700 INPS 46239 2340 B7
Bright Moon Ct
- NBVL 46060 1796 E1
Brighton Av
12800 CRML 46032 1901 A3
Brighton Blvd
1400 INPS 46202 2228 A7
Brighton Ct
7300 FSHR 46038 1904 A7
12800 CRML 46032 1901 A3
Brighton Ct
200 GNWD 46143 2665 E4
12900 CRML 46032 1901 A3
Brighton Ln
12800 CRML 46032 1901 A3
Brightwater Dr
9800 FSHR 46060 1905 A1
13900 FSHR 46060 1796 A7
Brightwell Dr
9500 INPS 46260 2009 D3
Brightwell Pl
2200 INPS 46260 2009 D2
Brill Rd
5500 INPS 46227 2555 C1
Brill St
2600 INPS 46225 2446 C2
3000 INPS 46227 2446 C3
6000 INPS 46227 2555 C2
Brinton Rd
10 CCRO 46034 1577 C3
E Brinton St
- CCRO 46034 1577 D3
- JknT 46034 1577 D3
Brinwood Dr
8600 INPS 46240 2011 A4
Brisbane Dr
13800 FSHR 46038 1904 C1
Brisbane Rd
3200 INPS 46228 2227 B1
Bristlecone Dr
- INPS 46217 2554 B2
5900 FSHR 46038 2012 C1
Bristle Lake Ct
- BNBG 46112 2114 E6
Bristle Lake Dr
- BNBG 46112 2114 E5
Bristol Cir
4500 CRML 46033 1902 E2
Bristol Ct
- PNFD 46168 2442 B1
700 GNWD 46143 2664 E5
Bristol Ln
4400 CRML 46033 1902 E2
Bristol Rd
700 ClyT 46280 2010 E1
9100 INPS 46260 2010 A3
Bristow Ln
12700 FSHR 46060 1906 D3
Brittainy Ln
900 GNWD 46142 2665 A1
Brittany Cir
1100 BNBG 46112 2114 D4
Brittany Ct N
8400 LWNC 46236 2014 E5
Brittany Ct S
8300 LWNC 46236 2014 E5
Brittany Dr
4300 EglT 46077 1899 C2
Brittany Ln
- GNWD 46142 2665 A1
Brittany Rd
4400 INPS 46222 2226 E4
Brittany Wy
7300 FSHR 46038 1904 A7
Britton Dr
1900 BHGV 46107 2447 C3
13100 FCkT 46038 1904 D2
Britton Rdg
13000 FSHR 46038 1905 A2
Britton Park Dr
- FSHR 46038 1795 D7
- FSHR 46038 1904 D1
Britton Park Rd
13100 FSHR 46038 1904 D2
Brixham Ct
300 FCkT 46038 1904 D1
400 INPS 46214 2334 C2
Brixton Dr
3000 GNWD 46142 2664 B1
Brixton Ln
900 GNWD 46142 2664 B1
6200 INPS 46220 2121 B3
10200 FSHR 46038 1905 B6
Brixton Woods Blvd
100 MdlT 46167 2113 A5
100 PTBR 46167 2113 A5
Brixton Woods Dr
- PTBR 46167 2113 B4
Brixton Woods East Dr
100 PTBR 46167 2113 B4
Brixton Woods West Dr
100 PTBR 46167 2113 B4
Broad Al
- MRVL 46158 2659 D4
Broad Mdws
13700 CRML 46032 1901 A1
13900 CRML 46032 1792 A7
Broad St
12800 CRML 46032 1900 D3
Broadacre Dr
1100 AVON 46123 2333 B5
Broadleaf Ct
1800 WRvT 46143 2664 C7
Broad Leaf Ln
7400 FSHR 46038 1904 A6
Broad Leaf Pl
100 MRVL 46158 2660 C4
Broadmead Dr
7400 INPS 46259 2558 B4
Broadmead Wy
7800 INPS 46259 2558 B4
Broadmoor Bnd
- PTBR 46167 2113 B4
Broadmoor Plz
6100 INPS 46228 2118 B4
Broad Ripple Av
700 INPS 46220 2119 E3
1300 INPS 46220 2120 A3
Broadview Ct
3300 INPS 46227 2556 C5
Broadview Dr
7800 INPS 46227 2556 C5
Broadway Av
10600 ClyT 46280 1901 D7
Broadway St
10 CCRO 46034 1577 D2
1200 INPS 46202 2337 D1
2100 INPS 46202 2228 D6
3700 INPS 46205 2228 D3
4400 INPS 46205 2119 D6
6200 INPS 46220 2119 D2
9300 INPS 46240 2010 D3
10100 ClyT 46280 2010 D1
11800 LWNC 46236 2123 E2
E Broadway St
10 DNVL 46122 2329 E4
10 GNWD 46143 2665 D3
900 DNVL 46122 2330 A5
N Broadway St
10 CCRO 46034 1577 D2
10 GNFD 46140 2345 C1
700 GNFD 46140 2236 C7
S Broadway St
10 GNFD 46140 2345 C2
W Broadway St
10 DNVL 46122 2329 D4
7400 MrlT 46126 2669 C2
Broadway St W
10 GNWD 46142 2665 B3
Broadway Ter
5700 INPS 46220 2119 D5
Broadway North Dr
900 PNFD 46168 2441 C7
Broadway South Dr
800 PNFD 46168 2441 C7
Brobeck Ct
5700 INPS 46254 2117 B5
Brobeck Ln
5800 INPS 46254 2117 B5
Brock Ct
4500 LtyT 46168 2440 B4
Brock St
4900 INPS 46254 2117 D7
Brocken Ct
1900 INPS 46229 2232 E7
Brocken Wy
11700 INPS 46229 2232 E7
Brocket Cir
11800 NBVL 46060 1796 E6
Brockford Ct
11700 CRML 46032 1901 E4
Brocks Mdws
- EglT 46077 1898 B4
Brockton Ct
- CtrT 46140 2237 A5
5700 INPS 46220 2120 C5
Brockton Dr
5700 INPS 46220 2120 C5
Brockton Manor North Dr
- WRvT 46143 2663 D7
3900 WRvT 46143 2664 C6
Brockton Manor South Dr
- WRvT 46143 2663 D7
3900 WRvT 46143 2664 A7
Brockworth Dr
6000 INPS 46203 2448 C3
Broken Arrow Cir
300 INPS 46234 2333 E3
Broken Arrow Ct
300 INPS 46234 2333 E3
W Broken Arrow Ct
- SCkT 46163 2342 D4
S Broken Arrow Dr
1200 SCkT 46163 2342 C4
W Broken Arrow Dr
6100 SCkT 46163 2342 D3
Broken Arrow Rd
9000 INPS 46234 2333 E3
9000 INPS 46234 2334 A3
Broken Bow Dr
4400 WRvT 46143 2663 D7
Broken Bow Tr
600 INPS 46214 2334 C2
Broken Creek Cir
10500 CRML 46032 1902 C7
Brokenhurst Rd
- INPS 46220 2121 C4
N Brokenhurst Rd
6000 INPS 46220 2121 C3
Bromley Pl
8100 INPS 46219 2231 C7
Brompton Ct
600 NBVL 46060 1795 D4
7100 INPS 46250 2121 D1
Brompton Rd
12200 CRML 46033 1903 A4
12400 CRML 46033 1902 E3
Broncos Dr
12600 FCkT 46038 1906 A3
Bronson Dr
8600 FSHR 46038 1904 D1
8800 DelT 46038 1904 D1
Bronze Dr
- NBVL 46060 1796 B5
Brook Ct
5100 CtrT 46122 2330 D2
8700 INPS 46256 2013 C5
Brook Dr
600 GNWD 46143 2665 B5
Brook Ln
1100 INPS 46202 2337 A1
Brook St
600 GNFD 46140 2345 D2
Brookacre Ln
10 INPS 46217 2555 C6
10 INPS 46227 2555 C6
Brook Bay Cir
11500 INPS 46229 2232 D7
Brook Crossing Ln
11600 INPS 46229 2232 D7
Brookdale Dr
6300 INPS 46227 2556 A2
12500 FCkT 46060 1906 A2
Brooke Dr
1300 LEBN 46052 1676 D4
Brookfield Ct
7800 INPS 46226 2231 B2
Brookfield Dr
4800 INPS 46237 2556 E6
4900 INPS 46237 2557 A6
14400 FCkT 46040 1906 E7
14400 FCkT 46040 2015 E1
W Brookfield St
8500 MrlT 46259 2560 A7
Brookhaven Dr
6600 LWNC 46226 2121 D7
6700 INPS 46226 2121 D7
12500 FCkT 46060 1906 A3
Brookhill Ct
8500 INPS 46234 2225 B5
Brookhollow Blvd
4400 INPS 46254 2226 A1
4500 INPS 46254 2117 A7
Brookhollow Dr
16200 WTFD 46062 1793 D2
Brookland Ln
10 PTBR 46167 2113 B4
S Brooklawn Dr
4400 SCkT 46163 2451 E3
Brookline
12400 CRML 46032 1901 E4
12400 CRML 46032 1902 A4
Brookline Ct
4400 INPS 46220 2120 E3
Brookline Dr
6200 INPS 46220 2120 E3
Brookline Pl
4300 INPS 46220 2120 E3
Brookmeadow Blvd
- INPS 46254 2117 E5
Brookmeadow Dr
4400 INPS 46254 2117 E5
Brook Mill Ct
1400 CRML 46032 1901 C1
Brookmont Ct
8100 INPS 46278 2007 B4
Brooknell Ct
12400 CRML 46033 1903 C3
Brook Pointe Ct
8400 INPS 46234 2334 B1
Brook Pointe Dr
1400 INPS 46234 2334 B1
Brookridge Ct
10400 FSHR 46038 1905 B6
Brookridge Dr
4600 MdlT 46167 2113 B5
4800 LcnT 46167 2113 C5
Brooks Bnd
100 BNBG 46112 2114 C3
Brooks Cross
12400 FSHR 46038 1906 A7
12400 FSHR 46038 2015 A1
Brooks Ct
11600 CRML 46033 1902 E5
Brooks St
- LcnT 46112 2115 D6
1000 INPS 46202 2337 A1
N Brooks St
1200 INPS 46202 2337 A1
Brooks Bend Blvd
6300 INPS 46237 2557 D5
Brooks Bend Dr
2800 CRML 46032 2011 C1
Brooksburg Dr
300 WTFD 46074 1792 D2
Brooks Farm Ln
8300 INPS 46237 2556 D6
Brookshire Ct
6000 LcnT 46167 2113 D5
Brookshire Dr
6000 LcnT 46167 2113 C5
6300 MdlT 46167 2113 C5
Brookshire Pkwy
4500 CRML 46033 1902 E4
4700 CRML 46033 1903 A5
E Brookside Av
1000 INPS 46202 2337 E1
1300 INPS 46201 2337 E1
1600 INPS 46201 2338 A1
2100 INPS 46201 2229 B7
2200 INPS 46218 2229 B7
Brookside Ct
1100 AVON 46123 2332 D6
9900 WshT 46123 2333 C3
Brookside Dr
100 NWTD 46184 2774 D5
1000 LEBN 46052 1677 B5
Brookside Ln
200 PNFD 46168 2441 D5
Brookside Pkwy North Dr
1400 INPS 46201 2338 A1
3000 INPS 46218 2229 C7
Brookside Pkwy S Dr
2000 INPS 46201 2338 B1
3000 INPS 46201 2229 C7
3000 INPS 46218 2229 C7
Brooks Landing Pl
13100 CRML 46033 1903 E2
Brooks School Rd
10100 FCkT 46038 2015 A1
10100 FSHR 46038 2015 A1
10300 FCkT 46038 1906 A7
10300 FSHR 46038 1906 A7
13100 FSHR 46060 1906 A4
13400 FCkT 46060 1906 A2
13600 NBVL 46060 1797 A7
13600 NBVL 46060 1906 A2
Brookston Ln
- NBVL 46062 1685 B5
Brookstone Cr
5000 INPS 46268 2117 C3
Brookstone Dr
13600 CRML 46032 1901 B1
14000 CRML 46032 1792 B7
Brookstone Ln
5000 INPS 46268 2117 C3
5300 WRvT 46142 2663 C2
Brookstone Wy
5000 INPS 46268 2117 D3
Brooksway
- PTBR 46167 2113 A4
Brookton Ct
1300 INPS 46260 2010 A7
Brookview Cir
7500 INPS 46250 2012 B7
Brookview Ct
200 MRVL 46158 2660 C4
5300 INPS 46250 2012 B7
Brookview Dr
- BNBG 46112 2224 A2
600 GNWD 46142 2664 E2
10500 ClyT 46032 1902 C7
10500 CRML 46032 1902 C7
10500 CRML 46032 2011 C1
Brookview Ln
7600 INPS 46250 2012 B7
Brook Village Dr
- GNWD 46143 2665 B6
Brookville Av
600 INPS 46203 2338 D5
Brookville Rd
11800 INPS 46239 2450 E1
E Brookville Rd
3800 INPS 46201 2338 E4
4800 INPS 46201 2339 B5
5100 INPS 46219 2339 B5
6800 INPS 46239 2339 B5
7400 INPS 46239 2340 C6
9600 INPS 46239 2341 A7
10700 INPS 46239 2450 C1
E Brookville Rd US-52
7700 INPS 46239 2340 C6
9600 INPS 46239 2341 A7
10700 INPS 46239 2450 C1
Brookville Wy
1100 INPS 46239 2339 E5
Brookville Crossing Dr
- INPS 46239 2340 A6
Brookville Lake Dr
5700 INPS 46254 2117 B6
Brook Vista
2800 CRML 46032 2011 C1
Brookway Dr
1000 AVON 46123 2332 E6
Brookway St
2500 INPS 46218 2229 B7
Brookwood Cir
1300 DNVL 46122 2329 B4
Brookwood Pl
12900 FCkT 46060 1906 A3
Brookwood Rd
5700 INPS 46226 2121 B5
Brothers Ct
10300 FSHR 46038 2013 E1
Brotherwood Ct
3100 INPS 46268 2118 B2
Broughton St
1800 CRML 46032 1900 D3
Brouse Av
3100 INPS 46218 2229 B4
4600 INPS 46205 2120 B7
5600 INPS 46220 2120 B5
Brouse Ct
5100 INPS 46237 2448 C7
Brouse Dr
5800 INPS 46237 2448 C7
Brouse St
6700 INPS 46220 2120 B2
Brown Rd
4100 INPS 46226 2229 E1
4500 INPS 46226 2120 E7
Brown St
- CCRO 46034 1577 D3
400 NBVL 46060 1686 C6
Browning Dr
400 GNWD 46142 2665 B5
8400 INPS 46227 2556 B6
Brownstone Ct
- CBLD 46140 2233 A6
Browns Valley Ct
8700 INPS 46113 2552 A7
Browns Valley Ln
8800 INPS 46113 2552 A7
Brownswood Dr
10 BNBG 46112 2223 D2
Broyles Ln
7200 INPS 46217 2554 E4
Broyles Rd
2000 WshT 46123 2331 D4
5800 AVON 46123 2331 D4
Bruce Blvd
5300 NBVL 46062 1794 B1
Bruce Ct
7200 BrnT 46112 2114 D3
Bruddy Dr
9600 FSHR 46038 1796 A7
13800 FSHR 46038 1905 A1
Bruin Dr
7100 INPS 46237 2557 D4
Bruland Dr
2300 WshT 46234 2224 C6
Brumley Mdws
3500 CRML 46033 1902 D3
Brumley Wy
3500 CRML 46033 1902 D4
S Brune Ct
600 SCkT 46163 2343 A3
Bruner Dr
1500 GNFD 46140 2345 D4
Brunes Blvd
- BNBG 46112 2223 E3
- BNBG 46112 2224 A3
1000 LcnT 46112 2223 E3
Brunn Pl
12900 FSHR 46038 1905 C3
Brunnemer Ridge Dr
10 WTLD 46184 2774 C7
Brunson Dr
200 BHGV 46107 2447 D3
Brunson Run
9100 INPS 46256 2013 D3
E Brunswick Av
600 INPS 46227 2555 E1
1300 INPS 46227 2556 A1
3800 INPS 46237 2556 D1
W Brunswick Av
10 INPS 46217 2555 B1
7000 INPS 46221 2552 D1
Brunswick Ct
100 CRML 46033 1902 D6
8600 GfdT 46168 2442 A7
8600 GfdT 46168 2551 A1
Brunswick Dr
100 GNWD 46143 2665 D1
3500 CRML 46033 1902 D6
8000 FSHR 46038 1904 C6
Brush Run
6300 INPS 46268 2117 C3
Brushfield Ln
10000 FSHR 46038 2014 E1
Brushwood Ct
600 GNWD 46142 2664 E2
Brushwood Rd
2200 INPS 46241 2443 A1
6200 INPS 46241 2552 B3
7300 INPS 46113 2552 B5
Brushwood Wy
600 GNWD 46142 2664 E2
Brussel Ter
3700 INPS 46228 2227 A1
Bruton Dr
6600 INPS 46256 2122 A2
Bryan Ct
3500 INPS 46227 2556 C6
Bryan Dr
5800 INPS 46227 2556 C1
Bryant Ct
9100 INPS 46250 2012 B3
Bryant Ln
9100 INPS 46250 2012 B3
Bryce Ct
10 INPS 46222 2226 E4
Bryce Wy
8900 FSHR 46038 1904 D7
Bryce Canyon Dr
6200 INPS 46237 2448 D7
Bryce Manor Dr
7900 INPS 46260 2009 D6
Bryden Dr
7700 FSHR 46038 1904 B5
Bryden Pl
11800 FSHR 46038 1904 B5
Bryn Mawr Dr
500 INPS 46260 2119 B3
14300 DelT 46060 1795 C7
Bryn Mawr Ln
10 CRML 46032 1902 B2
Buccaneers Wy
12400 FCkT 46038 1906 A3
Buchanan St
500 INPS 46203 2337 D5
E Buchanan St
100 PNFD 46168 2441 C5
W Buchanan St
200 PNFD 46168 2441 B5
Buck Blvd
6000 INPS 46237 2557 C2
Buck Ct
12300 LWNC 46236 2015 A7

Indianapolis Street Index

STREET
Block City ZIP Map# Grid

Buck Dr
5500 NBVL 46062 1576 B7
S Buck St
100 WTWN 46075 1788 C7
Buck Creek Cir
11800 NBVL 46060 1796 E6
W Buck Creek Ct
7200 BCkT 46140 2233 A7
Buck Creek Pkwy
6300 INPS 46227 2555 D3
Buck Creek Rd
10 CBLD 46229 2341 E2
10 SCkT 46229 2341 E2
10 SgCT 46229 2341 E2
300 BCkT 46229 2341 E2
300 BCkT 46229 2342 A1
300 CBLD 46229 2342 A1
400 BCkT 46229 2233 C7
400 CBLD 46229 2233 C7
N Buck Creek Rd
500 BCkT 46229 2233 A7
500 CBLD 46229 2233 A7
800 CBLD 46140 2233 A6
1900 BCkT 46140 2233 A4
2400 BCkT 46140 2232 E3
Buck Creek Blvd South Dr
300 INPS 46227 2555 C1
N Buck Creek Shades
6800 MrlT 46110 2669 A2
Buckeye Ct
700 NBVL 46062 1685 E3
4900 CRML 46033 1903 A2
9000 INPS 46260 2009 E3
W Buckeye Dr
2700 BCkT 46140 2234 E6
N Buckeye Ln
2800 BCkT 46140 2234 E6
E Buckeye St
10 CCRO 46034 1577 D2
9300 JknT 46034 1577 D2
W Buckeye St
10 CCRO 46034 1577 D2
Buckhaven Dr
8700 INPS 46256 2013 D3
Buckhorn Dr
6600 INPS 46254 2116 E6
14000 CRML 46032 1792 B7
14000 CRML 46032 1901 B1
Buckingham Ct
200 FCkT 46038 1904 D2
1500 GNWD 46143 2665 C6
4500 CRML 46033 1902 E4
N Buckingham Ct
1000 CBLD 46140 2232 E6
Buckingham Dr
100 INPS 46208 2228 B1
Buckley Blvd
12300 CBLD 46229 2342 A1
Buckley Ct
1300 CBLD 46229 2342 A1
Buckley Rd
1200 CBLD 46229 2342 A1
Buckmoor Cir
1200 WRvT 46143 2664 B6
Buckmoor Ct
3100 WRvT 46143 2664 B6
Buckmoor Pkwy
3100 WRvT 46143 2664 B6
Buck Pond Ct
5500 INPS 46237 2557 B6
Buck Pond Pl
5400 INPS 46237 2557 B7
Buckridge East Dr
6800 INPS 46227 2556 A3
Buckridge North Dr
- HMCT 46227 2556 A3
1600 INPS 46227 2556 A3
Buckridge West Dr
6800 INPS 46227 2556 A3
Buck Rill Dr
5700 INPS 46237 2557 C1
Buck Run Ct
7600 INPS 46217 2555 B5
Buckskin Cir
6000 INPS 46250 2012 C6
Buckskin Ct
5900 CRML 46033 1903 E1
6000 INPS 46250 2012 C6
W Buckskin Ct
6300 SCkT 46163 2342 C7
Buckskin Dr
7800 INPS 46250 2012 C6
Bucksport Ln
600 WshT 46074 1792 B4
Buckthorn Ct
7900 AVON 46123 2332 D3
Buckthorne Ct
9000 INPS 46260 2009 D4
Buckthorne Ln
100 MRVL 46158 2660 C4
Buck Trail Rd
6000 INPS 46237 2557 C2
Buckus Rd
- PNFD 46168 2551 D1
Buck Valley Ct
7600 INPS 46217 2555 A5
Buck View Dr
6300 INPS 46259 2559 D2
Buckwood Dr
11300 INPS 46239 2341 D6
S Budd Rd
2200 CtrT 46052 1785 A6
Budd Run Ct
5900 INPS 46250 2012 C3
Budd Run Dr
9100 INPS 46250 2012 C3
Buddy Ln
200 MdnT 46113 2661 C3
Buell Ct
10300 WshT 46123 2333 D2
Buell Dr
- AVON 46123 2333 D3
10200 WshT 46123 2333 D2

Buell Ln
6000 INPS 46254 2117 B4
Buena Vista Ct
100 MdnT 46113 2661 C3
Buena Vista Dr
- WTFD 46032 1793 A4
- WTFD 46033 1793 A4
100 MdnT 46113 2661 C3
4500 INPS 46228 2118 E7
4500 INPS 46228 2227 E1
15600 WshT 46032 1793 A4
Buffalo Cir
17200 WTFD 46074 1793 C1
Buffalo Dr
100 INPS 46217 2555 B6
Buffalo St
300 BHGV 46107 2448 A2
1200 BHGV 46107 2447 D2
Buffalo Pass
1000 DNVL 46122 2331 A4
Buffalo Ridge Cir
500 INPS 46227 2555 D7
Buffalo Ridge Ct
500 INPS 46227 2555 D7
Buffalo Ridge Dr
8500 INPS 46227 2555 D7
Buffalo Run Dr
500 INPS 46227 2555 D7
Buffalo Run Wy
800 INPS 46227 2555 D7
Buffalo Trail Cir
500 INPS 46227 2555 D7
Buffett Pkwy
8600 FSHR 46038 1904 C2
8700 DelT 46038 1904 C2
Buff Stone Ct
12700 FSHR 46038 1906 B6
Buford Dr
4000 CRML 46077 1900 A2
Buford St
8000 LWNC 46216 2122 B6
Buick Dr
5800 SDWY 46224 2226 B7
W Buick Dr
6700 INPS 46214 2225 E7
Buisdale Rd
10 INPS 46214 2334 D3
Bull Ct
- CRML 46032 1900 E3
- CRML 46032 1901 A3
Bullock Ct
7500 INPS 46217 2555 A5
Bull Run Ct
8200 INPS 46227 2555 E6
Bull Run North Dr
1200 GNWD 46143 2666 B5
Bull Run South Dr
1200 GNWD 46143 2666 B5
Bull Run West Dr
900 GNWD 46143 2666 B5
Bumblebee
- GNFD 46140 2345 D3
Bumblebee Ct
- GNFD 46140 2345 D3
Bumblebee Wy
1000 GNFD 46140 2345 D3
Bundy Pl
1500 INPS 46202 2337 E1
1600 INPS 46202 2228 E7
Bungalow Ct
700 INPS 46220 2119 E6
Bunker Hill Dr
3600 INPS 46205 2229 D1
Bunkerhill Dr
10700 ClyT 46032 1899 E7
Bunker Hill Rd
10 BrnT 46158 2659 B7
Bunker Hill Crst
7200 INPS 46259 2558 A4
Buntin Ct
400 NBVL 46062 1576 C7
Bunty Ln
5900 CRML 46033 1903 C4
Burbank Rd
10 INPS 46219 2340 A2
Burch St
2000 INPS 46220 2120 B3
Burcham Wy
5300 INPS 46224 2335 C3
Burdsal Pkwy
800 INPS 46208 2228 A6
1100 INPS 46208 2227 E6
Buren Pl
400 INPS 46219 2340 B2
Buren St
3100 INPS 46239 2449 C3
Burgess Av
5100 INPS 46219 2339 A4
Burgundy Wy
2200 WshT 46168 2441 B2
Burk Rd
9000 INPS 46229 2340 D3
Burke Av
10 INPS 46234 2334 A3
Burke Ct
3900 INPS 46240 2011 D7
Burke Dr
12400 CRML 46032 1900 D4
S Burke St
2100 INPS 46231 2443 A1
Burket Ct
16800 WTFD 46074 1792 D2
Burket Dr
16700 WTFD 46074 1792 D2
Burkhart Dr
- INPS 46227 2446 C5
Burkhart East Dr
4200 INPS 46227 2446 C5
Burkhart West Dr
4200 INPS 46227 2446 C5
Burkwood Dr
11400 CRML 46033 1903 A6
Burkwood Wy
7300 INPS 46254 2116 D6

Burlat Ln
- NBVL 46062 1794 E2
- NBVL 46062 1795 A2
- NbvT 46062 1794 E2
Burlingame Blvd
- CRML 46074 1900 B1
Burlington Av
6200 INPS 46220 2120 B3
Burlington Ln
400 ClyT 46032 1901 B6
400 CRML 46032 1901 B6
Burlington Pk
- MdlT 46167 2113 A4
- PTBR 46167 2113 A4
Burmaster Ct
6900 INPS 46214 2225 E4
Burn Ct
8300 INPS 46217 2555 A6
Burnett Blvd
8100 AVON 46123 2332 D5
Burnett Ct
2400 CRML 46032 1902 B2
Burnette Blvd
- AVON 46123 2332 E5
Burnham Cir
7000 INPS 46256 2121 E2
Burnham Wk
2400 CRML 46032 1900 C4
Burning Bush Dr
- GNWD 46143 2666 A6
Burningbush Dr
3800 INPS 46235 2232 C2
Burning Ridge Ln
10600 FSHR 46038 1905 A7
Burning Tree Ct
5500 INPS 46239 2449 A7
Burning Tree Ln
2000 ClyT 46032 1900 D6
Burnleigh Cir
4800 INPS 46226 2230 A1
Burns Dr
7600 BNBG 46112 2114 C3
N Burns Dr
10 BNBG 46112 2114 D2
S Burns Dr
10 BNBG 46112 2114 D3
W Burnside Av
200 SgCT 46126 2670 D7
Bur Oak Ct
1200 AVON 46123 2332 A1
10600 NBVL 46060 1687 C4
Bur Oak Dr
- INPS 46254 2117 C4
Bur Oak Pl
5700 INPS 46254 2117 D5
Burrell Ln
8600 INPS 46256 2013 C4
Burries Tr
1500 INPS 46229 2341 C1
Burr Oak Cir
1200 GNWD 46143 2664 D5
Burr Oak Ct
1200 GNWD 46143 2664 E5
7800 INPS 46217 2555 A5
Burr Oak Dr
500 CRML 46032 1901 D6
700 GNWD 46143 2664 D5
800 INPS 46217 2555 A5
Burrwood Cir
9400 LWNC 46235 2231 E1
Burrwood Ct
9500 INPS 46235 2231 E1
Burrwood Dr
4200 INPS 46235 2231 E1
4500 LWNC 46235 2122 E7
4500 LWNC 46235 2231 E1
Burt St
2600 INPS 46240 2120 B1
Burton Av
2500 INPS 46208 2227 E5
2500 INPS 46208 2228 A5
Burwick Dr
8800 INPS 46256 2013 C3
Burwick Trc
800 GNWD 46143 2665 E4
Burzell Ct
9500 INPS 46239 2340 E7
E Busby St
200 LEBN 46052 1677 A5
W Busby St
100 LEBN 46052 1677 B4
200 LEBN 46052 1676 E5
Bush Pkwy
3000 CRML 46033 1902 C5
Bush's Run
7400 INPS 46278 2008 A7
Business Dr
6000 INPS 46219 2230 C6
Business Center Dr
7300 AVON 46123 2332 C4
Busland St
- CRML 46032 1900 D4
Busseron Ln
3500 INPS 46220 2120 C2
Busy Bee Ln
3200 INPS 46227 2556 C2
4100 INPS 46237 2556 D2
N Butler Av
800 INPS 46219 2339 A1
1300 INPS 46219 2230 B6
3200 INPS 46218 2230 A2
3800 INPS 46226 2230 A2
6200 INPS 46220 2121 A3
7200 INPS 46250 2121 A1
S Butler Av
10 INPS 46219 2339 A3
1200 INPS 46203 2339 A6
4100 BHGV 46203 2448 A5
Butler St
10 PNFD 46168 2441 E4
Butler Ter
5100 INPS 46218 2230 A4
Buttercup Ct
3000 INPS 46224 2226 C4
7600 WshT 46123 2333 D1

S Buttercup Dr
1300 SCkT 46163 2342 E4
Buttercup Ln
5300 INPS 46224 2226 C4
Buttercup Pl
3000 INPS 46224 2226 C5
Buttercup Wy
5600 INPS 46254 2117 D6
Butterfield Dr
2400 INPS 46220 2120 B2
Butterfly Cir
- WRvT 46143 2663 B6
Butterfly Ct
500 GNWD 46142 2664 D3
Butternut Cir
1400 GNFD 46140 2237 B6
Butter Nut Ct
700 DNVL 46122 2330 A2
Butternut Ct
100 NBVL 46062 1685 E4
8900 INPS 46260 2009 D4
Butternut Ln
- GNWD 46143 2666 A6
1000 INPS 46234 2334 A1
Buttonbush Ct
7400 INPS 46254 2225 D2
Buttondown Ln
9800 ZNVL 46077 1898 E3
Buttonwood Cres
4800 INPS 46228 2118 E7
4900 INPS 46228 2119 A7
Buttonwood Ct
1100 GNFD 46140 2237 A7
Buttonwood Dr
5200 NBVL 46062 1685 D3
5200 NbvT 46062 1685 D3
11600 CRML 46033 1902 C5
Buttress Ln
- INPS 46237 2448 D5
Buxton Ct
- WTFD 46074 1792 D4
4400 INPS 46254 2117 E7
Buxton Dr
- WTFD 46074 1792 D4
Byland Dr
400 BHGV 46107 2447 E3
400 BHGV 46107 2448 A4
1100 INPS 46107 2447 E3
Byram Av
3800 INPS 46208 2228 B2
N Byram Pl
1500 INPS 46202 2228 A7
1500 INPS 46202 2337 C1
Byram St
5200 INPS 46208 2119 B6
Byrd Dr
3800 INPS 46237 2447 D6
E Byrd Dr
3100 INPS 46227 2447 C6
Byrd Wy
10 GNWD 46143 2666 A4
Byrkit St
10 INPS 46217 2446 B7
2800 INPS 46217 2445 B7
W Byrkit St
4500 INPS 46221 2444 D7
W Byron Dr
6700 MrlT 46130 2560 D5
N Byron St
10 CCRO 46034 1577 D2
S Byron St
10 CCRO 46034 1577 D2
Bywood Dr
5800 INPS 46220 2121 C2

C

C St
- BHGV 46107 2447 D2
- INPS 46221 2337 A6
N Cabana Dr
8400 FSHR 46038 1904 C7
Cabano Ct
800 INPS 46239 2341 C5
Cabernet Wy
6800 INPS 46278 2007 E7
S Cabin Ct
4200 NPLN 46163 2452 B3
Cabin Creek Ct
5400 INPS 46237 2557 B6
Cabin Creek Dr
8200 INPS 46237 2557 B6
Cabinetmaker Ct
7500 PNFD 46168 2441 C2
Cable Dr
11800 LWNC 46236 2123 E2
Cable St
500 INPS 46222 2336 D2
Caboose Ct
7300 INPS 46256 2122 A1
Cabot Cir
700 BNBG 46112 2114 D3
Cabot Dr
5800 INPS 46221 2553 B4
Cabri Ln
11900 FSHR 46038 1905 E5
Cactus Ct
5200 INPS 46237 2448 A7
Cadbury Cir
9500 INPS 46260 2009 E2
Caddy Wy
4000 INPS 46268 2117 E1
4000 INPS 46268 2118 A1
Caden Ct
- WTFD 46074 1793 C2
Cadillac Dr
5700 SDWY 46224 2226 B7
Cadogan Dr
10200 LWNC 46236 2123 A4
Cadwell Cir
6800 INPS 46237 2557 E3
Caerhays Ct
3800 ClyT 46032 2009 A1
Caesar Ct
600 AVON 46123 2332 B2

Caesar Dr
600 AVON 46123 2332 B2
Cagle Ln
- INPS 46222 2226 E5
- SDWY 46222 2226 E6
Cahill Ln
400 INPS 46214 2335 A3
600 INPS 46214 2334 E2
Cahill Pl
6500 INPS 46214 2334 E2
6500 INPS 46214 2335 A2
Cahokia Ct
2700 INPS 46217 2554 C4
Caisson St
7000 INPS 46256 2012 E6
7100 INPS 46256 2013 A6
Caitlin Ln
5800 NBVL 46062 1794 C5
Caitlin Wy
17900 WTFD 46062 1684 E7
17900 WTFD 46062 1685 A7
Caito Dr
5600 LWNC 46226 2122 A5
Calabash Dr
- INPS 46217 2554 B2
Calabash Pl
6300 INPS 46217 2554 C2
Calais Cir
6500 INPS 46220 2121 D4
Calais Ct
5900 INPS 46220 2121 D4
Calais Dr
6300 INPS 46220 2121 D4
Calamus Ct
400 INPS 46239 2341 C4
Calaveras Wy
2100 INPS 46240 2011 B5
Calbert Ct
8700 INPS 46219 2231 D5
Calbert Dr
2500 INPS 46219 2231 D5
Calder Wy
- LWNC 46226 2121 E6
Caldwell Ln
- AVON 46123 2332 C2
N Caldwell Rd
6000 CtnT 46052 1568 C1
Caledonia Cir
6800 INPS 46254 2225 E1
Caledonia Wy
4200 INPS 46254 2225 E1
Caledonian Ct
1900 WRvT 46143 2664 A7
Caley Ln
5700 INPS 46221 2553 B4
Calgary Ct
8200 INPS 46268 2009 A5
Calhoun Ct
1900 INPS 46203 2338 E7
Calhoun Pl
19100 NBVL 46060 1687 B4
Calhoun Sq
- CRML 46032 1900 E3
Calhoun St
1300 INPS 46203 2337 E7
4500 INPS 46203 2338 E7
4800 INPS 46203 2339 A7
Calibogue Cir
3500 INPS 46228 2118 B5
Calibouge Dr
10400 FSHR 46038 1905 B6
Caliburn Ct
10200 FSHR 46038 1905 A3
Calico Ct
10 BNBG 46112 2223 D1
Calico Aster Dr
19100 NBVL 46062 1686 A4
California Ct
2600 INPS 46208 2228 B5
N California St
- INPS 46225 2337 B4
100 AdmT 46069 1573 B1
100 SRDN 46069 1573 B1
800 INPS 46202 2337 B1
3100 INPS 46208 2228 B4
S California St
- INPS 46204 2337 B4
- INPS 46225 2337 B4
100 SRDN 46069 1573 B2
2200 INPS 46225 2446 B1
S Callahan St
4500 INPS 46239 2449 D6
Calla Lily Dr
6500 INPS 46237 2557 D5
Callan Dr
5000 INPS 46254 2117 D6
Callaway Ct
13000 FSHR 46038 1906 B5
Callie Dr
12000 BrnT 46158 2658 E5
Callowell Ct
3500 ClyT 46032 1900 A7
Calluna Ct
12300 FSHR 46038 1906 A6
Calming Waters
14100 FSHR 46060 1796 B7
Calumet Ct
10 ZNVL 46077 1899 A7
Calumet Dr
8700 INPS 46236 2014 D4
Calvary St
900 INPS 46203 2337 E4
1000 INPS 46202 2337 E4
Calvert Ct
- GNWD 46143 2666 A7
Calvin Cir
200 GNWD 46143 2665 D5
Calvin St
1700 INPS 46203 2338 B7
Calzia Ln
11800 CBLD 46229 2341 E1
Camargue Dr
1900 ZNVL 46077 1898 D7
Camber Ln
4100 INPS 46237 2448 C5

Camberly Ln
12300 CRML 46033 1902 E4
Camberwood Ct
3600 INPS 46268 2118 A1
Camberwood Dr
7100 INPS 46268 2118 A1
7400 INPS 46268 2009 A7
Camborne Ct
12900 CRML 46033 1902 E2
Camborne Dr
4400 CRML 46033 1902 E3
Cambria Ct
3600 INPS 46234 2224 E3
Cambridge Ct
100 NBVL 46060 1795 D5
3100 GNWD 46142 2664 B1
3700 CRML 46033 1902 D4
N Cambridge Ct
1100 CBLD 46140 2232 E6
Cambridge Dr
1000 GNWD 46142 2664 C1
1000 PNFD 46168 2441 C7
7500 FSHR 46038 1904 B6
Cambridge Ln
6500 INPS 46220 2120 C3
Cambridge Wy
5000 PNFD 46168 2550 E2
6100 PNFD 46168 2551 A2
Camby Cross
10300 FSHR 46060 1796 B7
Camby Ct
400 GNWD 46142 2665 B2
W Camby Rd
- INPS 46241 2552 C4
6500 INPS 46221 2552 C4
7300 INPS 46113 2552 C4
8800 INPS 46113 2551 E4
Camby St
300 GNWD 46142 2665 C2
Camby Crossing Dr
7300 INPS 46113 2552 B5
Camby Village Blvd
- INPS 46113 2552 A5
Camden Ct
100 ZNVL 46077 1898 E3
10800 FSHR 46038 1903 D7
Camden Dr
100 ZNVL 46077 1898 E4
Camden St
3300 INPS 46227 2446 D4
5200 INPS 46227 2555 D1
Camelback Ct
5900 INPS 46250 2012 C7
Camelback Dr
7500 INPS 46250 2012 C7
Camelita Ct
8100 AVON 46123 2332 D6
Camellia Cir
8200 INPS 46219 2231 C7
Camellia Ln
8000 INPS 46219 2231 B7
Camelot Ct
500 NBVL 46060 1686 E7
6900 INPS 46214 2334 D2
Camelot Ln
4400 CRML 46033 1902 E4
Camelot Wy
- GNWD 46184 2774 A1
Cameo Ct
13200 CRML 46033 1903 B2
Cameo Dr
2900 ClyT 46032 1900 C6
Cameron Dr
11600 FSHR 46038 1904 B5
Cameron Ln
10 CtrT 46140 2236 D1
Cameron Pl
7800 FSHR 46038 1904 B5
Cameron St
300 INPS 46225 2446 C2
800 INPS 46203 2446 D2
1900 INPS 46203 2447 A2
Cameron Ridge Dr
4600 INPS 46240 2011 D3
4600 INPS 46240 2012 A3
Cameron Ridge Ln
- INPS 46240 2012 B3
9300 INPS 46240 2011 E3
Cameron Ridge Pl
4600 INPS 46240 2011 D3
4600 INPS 46240 2012 A3
Cameron Ridge Wy
9300 INPS 46240 2012 B3
Camfield Ct
7700 LWNC 46236 2014 E7
Camfield Dr
11800 LWNC 46236 2014 E7
Camfield Wy
7700 LWNC 46236 2014 E7
Camilla Ct
100 MRVL 46158 2660 C3
Camille Ct
10500 LWNC 46236 2123 B3
Camillo Ct
13200 CRML 46074 1900 C2
Caminito Ct
9000 INPS 46234 2333 E3
9000 INPS 46234 2334 A3
Caminito Rd
8800 INPS 46234 2334 A3
Cammack Rd
21600 JknT 46034 1576 B6
21600 JknT 46062 1576 B6
21600 NbvT 46034 1576 B6
21600 NbvT 46062 1576 B6
N Camp St
800 INPS 46202 2337 B2
W Camp St
100 LEBN 46052 1676 E5
100 LEBN 46052 1677 A5
Campbell Av
900 INPS 46219 2339 C1
3000 INPS 46218 2230 C4
4400 INPS 46226 2230 C1
4500 INPS 46226 2121 C7

Campbell Av
7900 INPS 46250 2012 C6
Campbell Ct
8400 GfdT 46158 2550 D7
Campbell Dr
- INPS 46231 2334 C7
Campbell St
- LEBN 46052 1676 D5
3400 PNFD 46168 2442 A3
Camp Creek Ln
10300 FCkT 46055 2015 D1
Campfire Cir
10700 LWNC 46236 2123 B1
Campfire Run
7300 LWNC 46236 2123 B1
Campus Ct
400 MRVL 46158 2659 D2
Campus Ln
- GNWD 46143 2666 D4
300 INPS 46219 2339 B4
Campus Pkwy
- NBVL 46060 1797 B7
Camwell Dr
7100 INPS 46268 2118 A1
Camwood Ct
7100 INPS 46268 2118 C1
Camwood Dr
2400 INPS 46268 2118 C1
Camwood Ln
7200 INPS 46268 2118 C1
Canaan Ct
200 MRVL 46158 2659 E1
Canak Dr
6200 WshT 46123 2441 A1
Canal Blvd
5300 INPS 46208 2119 B6
Canal Ct
700 INPS 46202 2337 A4
Canal Wk
300 INPS 46202 2337 B3
Canal Wy
10100 NBVL 46060 1687 A4
Canal Court North Dr
400 INPS 46202 2337 A4
Canal Court South Dr
400 INPS 46202 2337 A4
Canal View Cir
400 INPS 46202 2337 B2
Canal View Dr
600 INPS 46202 2337 B2
Canal View Wy
400 INPS 46202 2337 B2
Canapple Dr
4100 INPS 46235 2232 B2
Canary Ct
1900 INPS 46260 2009 D6
5200 CRML 46033 1903 C1
Canary Ln
7900 INPS 46260 2009 D6
Canberra Cir
6800 INPS 46220 2121 D2
Candice Dr
1800 MdnT 46113 2661 C5
Candice St
- FSHR 46060 1905 D1
Candle Ct
4600 INPS 46254 2117 B7
Candle Berry Dr
3800 INPS 46235 2232 D2
Candlelite Ct
10 GNFD 46140 2236 D6
Candlelite Dr
1200 GNFD 46140 2236 D6
Candlestick Ct
2100 LEBN 46052 1676 D3
Candlestick Dr
1000 LEBN 46052 1676 D4
Candletree Cir
4500 INPS 46254 2226 E1
Candletree Dr
- INPS 46254 2226 E1
4500 INPS 46254 2117 E7
Candlewick Dr
5900 INPS 46228 2118 A4
Candlewick Ln
- INPS 46228 2118 A3
Candlewick Rd
21300 NBVL 46062 1576 C7
Candlewood Ct
10 BNBG 46112 2223 D1
17900 NBVL 46062 1685 A7
Candlewood Ln
4600 INPS 46250 2011 E7
Candy Ln
- INPS 46205 2120 C7
Candy Cane Dr
3600 INPS 46227 2556 D4
Candy Spots Ct
4800 INPS 46237 2448 B6
Candy Spots Dr
4500 INPS 46237 2448 B6
Cane Ridge Ct
6500 INPS 46268 2117 C2
Canna Ct
6400 INPS 46217 2555 C2
Canna Rd
100 INPS 46217 2555 B2
Cannington Ct
- FCkT 46038 1905 E3
Cannon Ct
5600 SDWY 46224 2226 C6
Cannonade Ct
- WshT 46234 2224 E6
Cannonade Dr
7800 INPS 46217 2554 E6
Cannonero Ct
1200 INPS 46217 2554 E5
1200 INPS 46217 2555 B5
Canoe Ct
10700 INPS 46236 2014 B5
Canoe Ln
- CRML 46033 1794 D7
Canopy Ct
5400 INPS 46224 2335 C3

STREET Block City ZIP Map# Grid

Canopy Ln
9400 FSHR 46038 1904 E1
Canopy Wy
200 INPS 46224 2335 C3
Canter Dr
1500 INPS 46239 2341 B6
Canterbury Ct
10 WshT 46123 2331 B4
500 NBVL 46060 1795 D5
1100 INPS 46260 2010 A4
3700 CRML 46033 1902 D3
6000 MdlT 46167 2113 C5
Canterbury Dr
- EglT 46077 1897 D6
- WshT 46123 2331 B4
1100 GNWD 46143 2665 C6
Canterbury Ln
2700 INPS 46220 2120 C2
6200 MdlT 46167 2113 C5
Canterbury Pl
8500 INPS 46260 2010 A4
Canterbury Sq E
8500 INPS 46260 2010 A5
Canterbury Sq N
1100 INPS 46260 2010 A4
Canterbury Sq S
1100 INPS 46260 2010 A4
Canterbury Sq W
8500 INPS 46260 2010 A5
Cantigny Wy E
12900 CRML 46033 1903 D3
Cantigny Wy N
5600 CRML 46033 1903 D2
Cantigny Wy S
5700 CRML 46033 1903 D3
Canton Dr
5500 CRML 46033 1794 B7
Canvasback Dr
2100 INPS 46234 2225 A6
6900 FSHR 46038 1903 E6
Canyon Ct
11600 FSHR 46038 1906 A5
Canyon Rd
600 INPS 46217 2555 A3
Canyon Oak Dr
18300 NBVL 46062 1685 E6
Cape Dr
8800 INPS 46256 2013 C4
Cape Dr N
8100 INPS 46256 2013 C4
Cape Charles Ct
- CCRO 46034 1577 A5
Cape Charles Dr
6000 INPS 46226 2230 C1
Cape Cod Cir
7300 INPS 46250 2121 C1
7400 INPS 46250 2012 C7
Cape Cod Ct
5900 INPS 46250 2012 C7
Cape Cod Ln
7500 INPS 46250 2012 C7
Cape Coral Dr
1100 CCRO 46034 1577 B1
Cape Coral Ln
10900 INPS 46229 2232 C6
Cape Henry Ct
- CCRO 46034 1577 B5
Capel Dr
7200 INPS 46259 2558 B4
Cape Neddick Ct
6600 INPS 46217 2554 C3
Caphel Ln
20200 NBVL 46062 1685 B2
Capistrano Cir
11500 INPS 46236 2014 D5
Capistrano Ct
11400 INPS 46236 2014 D6
Capistrano Dr
400 GNWD 46143 2666 B3
11600 INPS 46236 2014 D5
Capital Ct
6300 WshT 46123 2332 A4
Capital Dr
10 WshT 46123 2332 A4
Capital Ln
6400 WshT 46123 2332 A4
Capitol Av
- INPS 46225 2337 C6
N Capitol Av
10 INPS 46204 2337 C3
200 INPS 46202 2337 C3
1600 INPS 46202 2228 C7
2200 INPS 46208 2228 C6
4500 INPS 46208 2119 C6
S Capitol Av
10 INPS 46204 2337 C4
100 INPS 46225 2337 C4
2600 INPS 46225 2446 C2
5100 INPS 46217 2446 C7
Capitol Reef Ln
6400 INPS 46237 2448 D7
Caplock Ln
8700 INPS 46256 2013 D4
Capri Dr
5000 INPS 46241 2444 C2
13100 CRML 46033 1902 E2
Capricorn Dr
- INPS 46237 2557 D7
Capsella Ln
3200 INPS 46203 2448 D3
Capstone Ct
9100 NBVL 46060 1686 D4
Captain Cir
- MCVL 46055 2015 D4
Captain Dr
- WshT 46123 2333 A2
8000 WshT 46123 2332 E2
8500 AVON 46123 2332 D3
Captains Ct
8400 INPS 46236 2014 C5
Captains Landing Ct
7800 LWNC 46236 2014 D7
Captiva Wy
17700 WTFD 46062 1684 E7
Captiva Pass
- PNFD 46168 2550 A1
Capulin Ct
- FCkT 46040 1907 A6
Caraway Ln
7800 INPS 46239 2449 B3
Caraway Pl
7800 INPS 46239 2449 B3
Caraway St
1300 LEBN 46052 1676 D5
Carberry Ct
7900 INPS 46214 2225 C6
Carbon St
800 NBVL 46060 1795 D2
Cardamon Ct
4400 INPS 46237 2556 E4
Cardif Dr
13000 CRML 46032 1901 B2
Cardiff Ct
3700 INPS 46234 2224 E2
Cardiff Ln
3600 INPS 46234 2224 E3
Cardigan Rd
2600 INPS 46268 2009 C6
Cardinal Cir
- PNFD 46231 2333 E6
Cardinal Ct
- NbvT 46062 1578 B7
- WshT 46123 2332 E2
5900 MdlT 46167 2112 E6
8200 AVON 46123 2332 D3
10200 NbvT 46062 1687 B1
Cardinal Dr
- WshT 46123 2332 D2
300 WTLD 46184 2775 A6
900 EglT 46077 1898 C4
1700 INPS 46227 2556 A2
2500 MdlT 46167 2112 E6
4000 INPS 46237 2556 D2
W Cardinal Dr
6800 MCVL 46055 2015 B3
Cardinal Ln
10 ClyT 46032 1902 B6
10 CRML 46032 1902 B6
1000 GNFD 46140 2237 A6
1700 BNBG 46112 2223 C3
6300 INPS 46220 2121 D3
Cardinal St
8100 AVON 46123 2332 D3
Cardinal Wy
- CRML 46074 1900 B2
Cardinal Cove E
7900 INPS 46256 2013 B6
Cardinal Cove N
7700 INPS 46256 2013 B6
Cardinal Cove S
7700 INPS 46256 2013 B6
Cardinal Cove W
7900 INPS 46256 2013 B6
E Cardinal Cove Dr
7700 INPS 46256 2013 B4
Cardinal Flower Cir
- INPS 46231 2334 A7
Cardinal Flower Ln
8800 INPS 46231 2334 A7
9000 INPS 46231 2333 E7
Cardis Ct
11800 INPS 46229 2232 E6
Cardis Ln
2200 INPS 46229 2232 E6
Cardonia Blvd
- MdnT 46113 2661 C1
Carefree Cir
8300 INPS 46236 2014 D5
N Carefree Ct
- MdnT 46113 2661 B2
Carefree Dr
9800 FCkT 46256 2014 C2
Caressa Wy
6500 INPS 46259 2558 C2
Care Tree Ct
100 WRvT 46142 2664 B3
Carew Ln
5400 INPS 46221 2553 C3
Carey Ct
1300 CRML 46032 1901 C1
Carey Dr
100 NBVL 46062 1686 B7
Carey Rd
800 CRML 46033 1902 D1
1000 CRML 46033 1793 D5
15400 WshT 46033 1793 C5
15400 WTFD 46033 1793 C5
16100 WshT 46062 1793 D2
16100 WshT 46074 1793 D3
16100 WTFD 46062 1793 D2
16100 WTFD 46074 1793 D3
17200 WshT 46074 1684 D7
17200 WTFD 46062 1684 D7
Cargo Dr
2600 INPS 46241 2444 A2
Caribbean Dr
1800 INPS 46219 2231 C7
Caribe Dr
6600 INPS 46227 2555 D3
Caribe Ln
6600 INPS 46227 2555 D3
Caribe Mall
500 INPS 46227 2555 D3
Caribou Cir
6700 INPS 46278 2116 E2
Caribou Ct
6700 INPS 46278 2116 E2
Caribou Dr
6900 INPS 46278 2116 E2
Caribou Pl
6600 INPS 46278 2116 E2
Carica Dr
3200 INPS 46203 2448 C3
Caring Cove
5300 INPS 46268 2117 C3
Carl St
- INPS 46239 2559 C1
Carla Ct
2700 INPS 46219 2231 D5
Carla Dr
8700 INPS 46219 2231 D5
Carlin Ct
700 CRML 46032 1902 C3
Carlin Dr
10 CRML 46032 1902 C3
Carlise Wy
10300 FSHR 46060 1905 B1
Carlisle Pl
- WshT 46074 1792 B4
E Carlisle St
200 MRVL 46158 2659 E3
300 MRVL 46158 2660 A3
W Carlisle St
100 MRVL 46158 2659 D3
Carlow Cir
8100 INPS 46214 2225 B6
Carloway Rd
8200 LWNC 46236 2014 E5
Carlsbad Cir
4800 INPS 46241 2444 D3
Carlsbad Ct
3000 INPS 46241 2444 D3
Carlsbad Dr
3000 INPS 46241 2444 D3
Carlsbad Ln
3000 INPS 46241 2444 D3
Carlsen Av
6700 INPS 46214 2225 D7
Carlton Ct
- GNWD 46143 2664 E6
5400 SDWY 46224 2335 C1
21200 NBVL 46062 1576 C7
Carlton Wy
5300 SDWY 46224 2335 C1
Carlton Arms Dr
7800 INPS 46256 2012 E6
Carlton Arms Plz
- INPS 46256 2012 E7
Carlton Arms Rd
7500 INPS 46256 2013 A7
Carly Cir
3400 INPS 46235 2232 D3
Carly Ct
3300 INPS 46235 2232 C3
7700 FSHR 46038 1904 B4
Carly Ln
3300 INPS 46235 2232 C4
Carly Pl
7700 FSHR 46038 1904 C4
Carly Wy
11300 INPS 46235 2232 D3
Carlyle Dr
9500 INPS 46240 2010 E2
Carlyle Ln
900 INPS 46240 2010 E2
Carlyle Pl
500 INPS 46201 2338 E2
E Carmel Dr
10 CRML 46032 1902 C4
3100 CRML 46033 1902 D4
W Carmel Dr
10 CRML 46032 1902 A4
600 CRML 46032 1901 E4
Carmel Gdn
12400 CRML 46032 1902 A4
Carmelaire Ct
300 CRML 46032 1902 B3
Carmelaire Dr
100 CRML 46032 1902 B3
Carmel School Dr
- CRML 46032 1902 C2
Carmelview Dr E
200 CRML 46032 1902 B3
Carmelview Dr W
100 CRML 46032 1902 B3
Carmen Ct
900 GNWD 46143 2665 E5
Carmen Ln
800 GNWD 46143 2665 E5
Carmen Plz
500 GNWD 46143 2665 D5
Carmichael Dr
- LWNC 46216 2122 D6
Carmine Dr
10200 NBVL 46060 1687 A4
Carnaby Ct
- BNBG 46112 2114 A6
Carnaby Dr
10 BNBG 46112 2114 B5
Carnaby St
2900 INPS 46229 2231 D5
Carnation Ct
3400 INPS 46214 2225 D3
Carnation Dr
8800 NBVL 46060 1795 D6
Carnation Ln
7400 INPS 46214 2225 D3
Carney Dr
10 GNWD 46142 2665 C2
9800 FSHR 46038 2013 C2
Carnoustie Cir
4800 WshT 46123 2331 D5
Caro Dr
6800 INPS 46214 2225 E7
Carob Ct
5100 INPS 46237 2557 A6
Carol Dr
400 GNWD 46143 2665 C3
Carol Ln
10 BrnT 46158 2660 A6
Carolee Ct
3600 INPS 46227 2556 D4
Carolina Blvd
6500 INPS 46217 2555 B3
Carolina Ct
400 INPS 46217 2555 B3
13800 FSHR 46060 1905 A1
Carolina Wy
800 WshT 46123 2333 A2
Caroline Av
3400 INPS 46218 2229 B3
4400 INPS 46205 2229 B1
5100 INPS 46205 2120 B6
Caroline St
6500 INPS 46220 2120 B2
N Caroline St
7400 INPS 46240 2011 B7
Carolling Wy
7300 INPS 46237 2556 D5
Carolyn Ct
10 MRVL 46158 2659 E2
300 CRML 46032 1901 D3
Carpenter Cir
1800 INPS 46203 2338 C7
Carpenter Ct
3200 INPS 46203 2338 C7
7700 PNFD 46168 2441 D2
W Carr Av
3400 INPS 46221 2445 B3
N Carr Rd
- GfdT 46168 2441 C4
100 PNFD 46168 2441 C4
S Carr Rd
100 PNFD 46168 2441 C5
Carr St
- GNWD 46142 2665 B2
W Carriage Dr
4900 SCkT 46163 2452 A5
Carriage Ln
8900 INPS 46256 2122 D1
11600 CRML 46033 1902 E5
Carriage Corner Dr
- INPS 46237 2448 C7
Carriage Corner Ln
5400 INPS 46237 2448 E7
Carriage Corner Pl
5400 INPS 46237 2448 E7
Carriage Lake Dr
- BNBG 46112 2114 D3
Carriage Stone Dr
12200 FSHR 46038 1906 A4
Carrick Rd
- NBVL 46062 1794 D5
Carrie Cir
6200 INPS 46237 2557 C4
Carrie Ct
6100 INPS 46237 2557 C4
Carrie Dr
7000 INPS 46237 2557 C4
S Carrie Dr
4000 SCkT 46163 2451 A3
W Carrie Dr
7000 SCkT 46163 2451 B2
Carrie Pl
6100 INPS 46237 2557 C4
Carrigan Cross
21100 NBVL 46062 1576 E7
Carrigan Pt
200 NBVL 46062 1686 A1
Carrigan Rd
- NBVL 46062 1686 A1
7000 NBVL 46062 1576 C7
Carrington Cir
5100 CRML 46033 1903 B3
Carrington Dr
6100 LWNC 46236 2123 C3
Carrington Pl
12600 CRML 46033 1903 B3
Carroll Dr
500 WTFD 46074 1792 E1
Carroll Rd
6200 BCkT 46055 2124 B3
6200 BCkT 46235 2124 B3
6200 LWNC 46235 2124 B3
6200 VrnT 46055 2124 B3
6200 VrnT 46235 2124 B3
E Carroll Rd
2600 INPS 46163 2450 E3
2600 INPS 46239 2450 E3
2600 SCkT 46163 2450 E3
N Carroll Rd
2100 BCkT 46140 2232 E2
2100 BCkT 46235 2232 E2
2100 INPS 46140 2232 E2
2100 INPS 46235 2232 E2
3400 BCkT 46140 2123 E6
3400 INPS 46140 2123 E6
3400 INPS 46235 2123 E6
4000 BCkT 46055 2123 E6
5600 BCkT 46235 2123 E6
5600 LWNC 46235 2123 E6
6500 LWNC 46236 2124 B2
6500 MCVL 46055 2124 B2
6500 MCVL 46236 2124 B2
6500 VrnT 46055 2124 B2
6500 VrnT 46236 2124 B2
7500 LWNC 46236 2015 B7
7500 MCVL 46055 2015 B7
7500 MCVL 46236 2015 B7
9000 INPS 46236 2015 B7
S Carroll Rd
10 CBLD 46229 2341 E3
10 SCkT 46229 2341 E3
300 INPS 46229 2341 E4
300 INPS 46239 2341 E4
1100 SCkT 46163 2341 E7
1100 SCkT 46239 2341 E7
2300 INPS 46163 2341 E7
2300 INPS 46163 2450 E1
3500 INPS 46239 2450 E4
3500 SCkT 46163 2450 E4
4500 MrlT 46163 2450 E6
4500 MrlT 46239 2450 E6
4500 SCkT 46239 2450 E6
5000 INPS 46126 2450 E7
5000 INPS 46239 2559 E1
5000 MrlT 46126 2450 E7
5000 MrlT 46126 2559 E1
5000 MrlT 46239 2559 E1
Carrollton Av
1500 INPS 46202 2337 E1
2100 INPS 46202 2228 E6
3200 INPS 46205 2228 E3
4400 INPS 46205 2119 E7
6300 INPS 46220 2119 E3
8600 INPS 46240 2010 E4
9600 CRML 46280 2010 E2
9600 INPS 46280 2010 E2
Carrollton Av
9900 ClyT 46280 2010 E2
Carrollton Ct
700 INPS 46220 2119 E6
Carroll White Dr
1000 INPS 46219 2340 B1
Carrousel Dr
5700 INPS 46254 2117 A5
Carrow Dr
6500 INPS 46250 2121 D1
Carry Back Dr
5700 INPS 46237 2448 B6
Carry Back Ln
4800 INPS 46237 2448 B6
S Carson Av
2800 INPS 46203 2446 E2
2800 INPS 46227 2446 E3
3100 INPS 46227 2447 A4
Carson Ct
600 CRML 46033 1902 E1
Carson Rd
23600 JknT 46034 1576 A1
Carson Wy
- GNWD 46143 2666 A4
Carter St
100 MRVL 46158 2659 D3
100 PNFD 46168 2441 B5
W Carter St
200 PNFD 46168 2441 B5
Carters Grv
1000 INPS 46260 2010 A4
Cartersburg Rd
10 CtrT 46122 2329 E5
10 CtrT 46122 2330 A6
10 DNVL 46122 2329 E5
10 DNVL 46122 2330 A6
100 CtrT 46122 2439 A2
100 DNVL 46122 2439 A2
200 CtrT 46118 2439 A2
200 LtyT 46118 2439 A2
200 LtyT 46122 2439 A2
2700 LtyT 46168 2439 E4
4300 LtyT 46168 2440 A6
Carters Grove Dr
6800 NBVL 46062 1685 E5
Carthage Cir
500 WTFD 46074 1792 D2
Carthay Cir
8300 DelT 46038 1904 C2
Carvel Av
4600 INPS 46205 2119 E7
6100 INPS 46220 2119 E4
Carver Ct
13100 CRML 46074 1900 A2
Carvin Cir
4500 INPS 46228 2118 A7
Carvin Ct
4500 INPS 46228 2118 A7
Carwinion Wy
3700 ClyT 46032 2009 A1
3900 ClyT 46032 2008 E1
Cary Lake Dr
7300 INPS 46259 2558 A4
Casa Dr
9200 INPS 46234 2333 E2
Cascade Cir
- LcnT 46112 2115 D5
Cascades Ct
9800 FSHR 46038 1905 A6
Casco Ct
11600 FCkT 46038 1905 E5
Casco Dr
100 AVON 46123 2332 E4
Casco Bay Cir
1200 CCRO 46034 1577 B5
E Casey Ln
1600 CtrT 46140 2236 D1
Casey Rd
17600 WshT 46074 1683 A7
Cashard Av
4100 BHGV 46203 2448 B5
Casper Ct
5100 INPS 46250 2121 A1
N Cass Ct
4000 INPS 46235 2231 E2
E Cass St
10 CCRO 46034 1577 D2
W Cass St
10 CCRO 46034 1577 D2
Cassara Dr
3000 INPS 46203 2448 D3
Cassidy Ln
7700 INPS 46260 2009 E7
Castetter Ct
12600 FSHR 46038 1904 C3
Castilla Dr
8100 LWNC 46236 2015 A6
Castilla Pl
12500 LWNC 46236 2015 A6
E Castle Av
800 INPS 46227 2446 E5
1400 INPS 46227 2447 A5
W Castle Av
6300 INPS 46241 2444 A5
Castle Ct
100 NBVL 46060 1686 E7
12200 CRML 46033 1902 E4
N Castle Dr
8200 INPS 46256 2013 C5
N Castle Ln
7800 INPS 46256 2122 B2
Castle Ovlk
4300 CRML 46033 1902 E4
Castle Row
1100 INPS 46220 2119 E5
Castlebar Cir
6000 INPS 46220 2121 C2
Castlebay Wy
4300 INPS 46254 2225 E1
Castlebrook Ct
8200 INPS 46256 2013 C5
Castlebrook Dr
8200 INPS 46256 2013 C5
Castle Cove Rd
8000 INPS 46256 2013 B6
Castle Creek Pkwy East Dr
8600 INPS 46250 2012 C4
Castle Creek Pkwy North Dr
5500 INPS 46250 2012 B4
Castle Farms Ct
8000 INPS 46256 2013 B5
Castle Farms Rd
8200 INPS 46256 2013 B5
N Castle Farms Rd
8200 INPS 46256 2013 B3
Castleford Dr
6000 INPS 46203 2448 C3
Castlegate Ct
- MdlT 46167 2113 B4
10 PTBR 46167 2113 B4
E Castlegate Dr
9100 INPS 46256 2013 B3
Castle Hill Dr
5700 INPS 46250 2012 B4
Castle Knoll Blvd
9100 INPS 46250 2012 D3
Castle Knoll Ct
6500 INPS 46250 2012 D3
Castle Lake Rd
7900 INPS 46256 2013 B6
Castle Manor Ct
500 INPS 46214 2334 E2
Castle Manor Dr
6700 INPS 46214 2334 D2
Castle Park Dr
8600 INPS 46256 2013 B4
Castleplace Dr
6300 INPS 46250 2012 D6
Castle Ridge Ct
7700 INPS 46256 2013 B5
Castle Ridge Ln
8200 INPS 46256 2013 B5
Castle Rock Ct
8200 INPS 46256 2013 B5
Castle Rock Dr
3800 CRML 46077 1900 A5
Castlestone Dr
11800 FSHR 46038 1905 E4
Castleton Blvd
8200 INPS 46256 2013 C5
N Castleton Rd
8000 INPS 46250 2012 E6
Castleton Corner Dr
8200 INPS 46250 2012 B5
Castleton Corner Ln
5500 INPS 46250 2012 B5
Castleton Corner Wy
5600 INPS 46250 2012 B5
Castleton Farms North Dr
7300 INPS 46256 2013 A7
Castleton Farms West Dr
7500 INPS 46256 2013 A7
Castleway Ct
6300 INPS 46250 2012 D6
Castleway Ct W
8000 INPS 46250 2012 D6
Castleway Dr
7900 INPS 46250 2012 D6
Castleway West Dr
5900 INPS 46250 2012 C6
Castlewood Cir
11800 FSHR 46038 1906 D5
Castlewood Dr
6900 INPS 46250 2012 E5
Castle Woods Cove
9600 CRML 46280 2011 A2
Castor Wy
5600 NBVL 46062 1794 B5
Caswell Dr
- CRML 46074 1900 A2
Caswell St
7600 INPS 46259 2559 D5
Catalano Dr
1700 INPS 46214 2225 D7
Catalina Ct
10 ZNVL 46077 1898 E5
3800 INPS 46226 2231 C2
Catalina Dr
- FSHR 46060 1905 D1
6000 INPS 46259 2559 C2
8600 INPS 46226 2231 C2
9800 INPS 46235 2231 E2
9800 INPS 46235 2232 A2
Catalina Wy
1600 ZNVL 46077 1898 E5
Catalina East Dr
1000 SCkT 46163 2343 A3
Catalina South Dr
4700 SCkT 46163 2343 A3
Catalina West Dr
1100 SCkT 46163 2343 A3
Catalpa Av
3300 INPS 46228 2118 A4
Catalpa Ct
300 NBVL 46062 1685 E4
Catalpa Dr
- WshT 46123 2440 E1
- WshT 46123 2441 A1
6200 WshT 46123 2332 E7
6200 WshT 46123 2332 A6
N Catamaran Cir
1300 CCRO 46034 1577 A4
1300 JknT 46034 1577 A4
S Catamaran Cir
1300 CCRO 46034 1577 A4
1300 JknT 46034 1577 A4
Catamaran Ct
11100 INPS 46236 2014 C5
Catamaran Dr
8300 INPS 46236 2014 C5
Catawba Ct
7900 INPS 46217 2555 A6
Catawba Ln
- INPS 46217 2554 C4
Catboat Ct
7200 FSHR 46038 1904 A7
Catclaw Ln
4200 INPS 46203 2448 D5
Catebury Ln
6200 MdlT 46167 2112 D3
Catherine Dr
10 CRML 46032 1901 D2
10 WTFD 46074 1684 B7
N Catherine St
10 CCRO 46034 1577 D2
S Catherine St
10 CCRO 46034 1577 D2
N Catherwood Av
10 INPS 46219 2339 C3
2800 INPS 46219 2230 C5
4000 INPS 46226 2230 C2
S Catherwood Av
10 INPS 46219 2339 C3
1200 INPS 46203 2339 C6
Cathys Dr
10 WTLD 46184 2775 A4
Catskill Ct
9000 INPS 46234 2334 A1
Catskill Rd
1000 INPS 46234 2334 A2
Catspring Cir
3200 INPS 46241 2444 D3
Cat Tail Ct
11900 NBVL 46060 1796 E5
Cattail Ln
10 BNBG 46112 2223 C3
Causeway Dr
7200 INPS 46214 2225 D3
Caval Cade Ct
- WshT 46234 2224 E6
Cavalier Ct
9000 INPS 46235 2231 D2
Cave Ct
5100 WRvT 46142 2663 C2
Cave Creek Ct
12000 NBVL 46060 1796 E2
E Caven St
10 INPS 46225 2337 C7
W Caven St
4700 INPS 46241 2335 D7
Cavendish Dr
1000 CRML 46032 1901 D3
Cavendish Rd
4600 INPS 46220 2120 E4
4700 INPS 46220 2121 A4
Cave Springs Ct
5600 INPS 46237 2557 B6
Cawi Ct
4500 INPS 46268 2117 E2
Cayman Ct
5400 CRML 46033 1794 A6
Cayman Dr
5300 CRML 46033 1794 A7
Cayuga Ct
6400 INPS 46268 2117 C2
CC St
- BHGV 46107 2448 A3
Cecil Av
3400 INPS 46226 2231 C3
N Cecil Av
10 INPS 46219 2340 B2
1500 INPS 46219 2231 B7
Cecil Ct
8200 INPS 46219 2340 B1
Cecil St
1800 CRML 46032 1900 E3
Cedar Dr
900 WshT 46123 2223 D7
10300 FSHR 46038 1905 B5
W Cedar Dr
7900 INPS 46113 2552 C6
Cedar Ln
- GNWD 46143 2666 A5
10 JknT 46034 1576 E6
10 JknT 46034 1577 A6
Cedar Pl
700 ClyT 46032 2010 B1
E Cedar St
10 ZNVL 46077 1899 B6
N Cedar St
- NPLN 46163 2452 B2
S Cedar St
- NPLN 46163 2452 B3
W Cedar St
200 ZNVL 46077 1899 B6
Cedar Bluff Dr
10 INPS 46214 2334 E3
Cedarbrook Dr
7600 SPRT 46227 2556 B5
17700 WTFD 46074 1684 C7
Cedar Chase Dr
- MCVL 46055 2015 C5
Cedar Cove Ct
- NPLN 46163 2452 A2
S Cedar Cove Ct
3600 NPLN 46163 2452 A1
Cedar Cove Dr
- NPLN 46163 2452 A1
Cedar Cove Ln
9600 FSHR 46250 2012 C2
W Cedar Cove Wy
4900 NPLN 46163 2452 A2
Cedar Creek Ct
8100 INPS 46268 2009 A6
Cedar Creek Ln
16600 NBVL 46060 1797 A1
16900 NBVL 46060 1796 E1
S Cedar Creek Ln
3500 NPLN 46163 2452 A1
Cedar Creek Pl
- SCkT 46163 2343 A7
W Cedar Creek Pl
4800 NPLN 46163 2452 A2
Cedar Crest Ct
12100 NBVL 46060 1796 E2
Cedar Crest Rd
10 ZNVL 46077 1899 A5
Cedar Glen Dr
200 WshT 46123 2331 D3
Cedar Glen North Dr
1000 PNFD 46168 2550 C1

STREET
Block City ZIP Map# Grid

Cedar Glen South Dr
1000 PNFD 46168 2550 C1
N Cedar Grove Ct
- MdnT 46113 2661 B2
Cedar Key Dr
8300 INPS 46256 2013 C4
Cedar Lake Ct
500 CRML 46032 1793 A6
Cedar Lake Dr
5800 INPS 46254 2117 B6
Cedar Mill Ct
10 ZNVL 46077 1899 A3
Cedar Pine Dr
10800 INPS 46235 2232 C3
Cedar Pine Pl
3600 INPS 46235 2232 B3
Cedar Place Dr
8500 INPS 46240 2010 E5
Cedar Point Dr
9600 ClyT 46032 2010 A2
Cedar Ridge Dr
9900 ClyT 46032 2010 A1
Cedar Ridge Ln
7600 BrnT 46112 2006 E7
Cedar Ridge Rd
3800 INPS 46235 2232 C2
Cedar Run Dr
10 BNBG 46112 2223 B2
Cedars Ct
1100 LEBN 46052 1676 D5
Cedar Spring Dr
9500 INPS 46260 2010 A2
Cedarstone Ct
5800 INPS 46226 2121 E5
Cedarstone Dr
6800 INPS 46226 2121 E5
Cedarstone Ln
- FCkT 46038 1906 C6
Cedarview Dr
100 BrnT 46158 2658 D5
Cedarwood
800 ClyT 46032 2010 B2
Cedarwood Ct
10 WTLD 46184 2775 A7
100 BrnT 46158 2658 D4
800 INPS 46214 2334 D2
N Cedarwood Ct
12200 BrnT 46158 2658 D4
Cedarwood Dr
100 BrnT 46158 2658 D5
Cedarwood Pl
800 ClyT 46032 2010 B2
Celtic Cir
200 GNWD 46143 2665 D5
Celtic Ct
9200 INPS 46235 2231 D3
Celtic Dr
3600 INPS 46235 2231 D3
Cembra Dr
- GNWD 46143 2774 B1
Centenary Ct
9000 INPS 46113 2551 E6
Centenary Dr
2300 ClyT 46032 2011 B1
8300 INPS 46113 2551 E7
Centenary Ln
9100 INPS 46113 2551 E6
Centennial Ct
4200 CRML 46033 1902 E3
Centennial Rd
17600 WshT 46074 1682 C7
19300 WshT 46069 1682 C3
N Centennial St
1100 INPS 46222 2336 B1
3000 INPS 46222 2227 B4
3900 INPS 46228 2227 B2
S Centennial St
1200 INPS 46241 2336 B6
2500 INPS 46241 2445 B2
Center Ct
200 MRVL 46158 2659 D7
Center Dr
800 NBVL 46060 1686 D6
2100 LEBN 46052 1676 E4
N Center Dr
1000 INPS 46224 2335 B1
Center Ln
10 MRVL 46158 2659 E2
Center St
10 BrnT 46158 2660 A6
10 GNFD 46140 2345 D2
10 GNWD 46143 2665 C3
10 WTLD 46184 2775 A5
7600 MCVL 46055 2015 C7
11800 LWNC 46236 2123 E3
N Center St
100 PNFD 46168 2441 B4
600 GfdT 46168 2441 B4
7500 MCVL 46055 2015 C7
S Center St
100 PNFD 46168 2441 B6
1700 PNFD 46168 2550 C3
2300 GfdT 46168 2550 C3
W Center St
8700 INPS 46234 2225 A4
9700 JknT 46011 1580 E1
Center St W
2200 SCkT 46140 2344 A2
Centerline Rd
10 NWTD 46184 2774 D4
10 PltT 46184 2774 D4
4400 WTLD 46184 2774 D7
N Centerline Rd
4000 PltT 46131 2774 D7
4000 WTLD 46131 2774 D7
Centerpoint Dr
7900 FSHR 46256 2013 B1
Center Run Dr
8200 INPS 46250 2012 D4
Central Av
1000 INPS 46202 2337 D1
1100 NBVL 46060 1686 D6
1600 INPS 46202 2228 D7
2100 INPS 46205 2228 D6
4500 INPS 46205 2119 D7

Central Av
5200 INPS 46220 2119 D6
8200 INPS 46240 2010 D5
10100 ClyT 46280 2010 D1
10600 ClyT 46280 1901 D7
N Central Av
6900 INPS 46220 2119 D2
9100 INPS 46240 2010 D3
9500 CRML 46240 2010 D3
Central Ct
2700 CRML 46280 2011 C2
11400 CRML 46032 1901 D5
N Central Ct
500 INPS 46205 2228 D3
S Central Ct
500 INPS 46205 2228 D3
Central Dr
- MrlT 46259 2559 E2
Central Dr E
11300 CRML 46032 1901 D5
Central Dr W
11300 CRML 46032 1901 D6
N Central St
- NPLN 46163 2452 A3
N Central Park Blvd
- GNWD 46143 2666 A7
S Central Park Blvd
- GNWD 46143 2666 A7
W Central Park Blvd
- GNWD 46143 2666 A7
Centre Ct
2900 INPS 46203 2447 C2
Centre Pkwy
2800 INPS 46203 2447 B2
Centurion Cir
1600 INPS 46260 2009 C7
Centurion Pkwy
1700 INPS 46260 2009 E6
Century Cir E
8100 INPS 46260 2009 E6
Century Cir N
1700 INPS 46260 2009 E5
Century Cir S
1700 INPS 46260 2009 E6
Century Cir W
8100 INPS 46260 2009 E6
Century Dr
1300 CRML 46032 1902 B5
1700 INPS 46260 2009 D6
Century Wy
1700 INPS 46260 2009 D6
Century Oaks Ct
500 ZNVL 46077 1899 C4
Century Oaks Dr
500 ZNVL 46077 1899 C3
W Century Plaza Rd
4700 INPS 46254 2226 D1
Cermack Wy
- FSHR 46038 1906 B3
Cerromar Ct
12600 CRML 46033 1903 C3
Cerulean Dr
10300 NBVL 46060 1687 B3
Chablis Cir
7400 INPS 46278 2007 D7
7400 INPS 46278 2116 D1
Chablis Ct
7200 INPS 46278 2007 D7
Chad Rd
1100 PNFD 46168 2441 E7
Chadbourne Dr
800 INPS 46214 2334 D2
Chadsworth Dr
10800 LWNC 46236 2123 B4
Chadwell Ct
9000 FSHR 46038 2013 D1
Chadwick Ct
100 CRML 46033 1902 E7
100 NBVL 46062 1685 E1
Chadwick Dr
3600 CRML 46033 1902 D7
Chadwick St
700 INPS 46225 2337 B5
E Chadwood Ln
8300 INPS 46268 2009 B5
N Chadwood Ln
3100 INPS 46268 2009 B5
W Chadwood Ln
8300 INPS 46268 2009 B5
Chad Woodland Acres
- WynT 46060 1688 A4
Chadworth Ct
5200 LWNC 46236 2123 B3
Chadworth Wy
6100 LWNC 46236 2123 B3
Chalan Ct
5500 INPS 46227 2555 C1
Chalcot Cir
6900 INPS 46220 2121 D2
Chaldean Cir
9700 FSHR 46038 2013 D2
Chalet Cir
16400 WTFD 46074 1793 C3
W Chalet Dr
100 BrnT 46158 2658 D4
Challenge Ct
11800 INPS 46236 2014 E4
Challenge Ln
6900 INPS 46250 2012 E4
Challenger Dr
3600 WTFD 46062 1793 D1
Chalmers St
9500 FSHR 46038 1904 E3
Chamberlain Cir
200 NBVL 46062 1686 A1
Chamberlain Dr
2700 INPS 46227 2447 B6
14700 WshT 46074 1792 B6
Chamberlin Dr
3100 INPS 46227 2447 C6
E Chamberlin Dr
3300 INPS 46237 2447 D6
Chambers Ct
6600 INPS 46237 2557 D1

Chambery Ln
9200 INPS 46229 2231 D5
Chambray Dr
9800 ClyT 46280 2011 B2
Chaminiox Ln
5900 INPS 46220 2121 D4
Chamomile Ct
10200 NBVL 46060 1687 B4
Champions Blvd
12600 FCkT 46038 1906 A3
Champions Dr
8600 INPS 46256 2013 C4
Championship Dr
4000 INPS 46268 2117 E3
4000 INPS 46268 2118 A2
Champton Dr
9100 INPS 46256 2013 C3
Chancellor Dr
3800 WRvT 46143 2664 A5
Chancellors Ridge Wy
16100 WTFD 46062 1793 E3
Chandler Ct
7100 INPS 46217 2555 B4
Chandler Dr
7000 INPS 46217 2555 B4
Chandler Wy
- FSHR 46060 1905 C1
Channel Dr
1000 CCRO 46034 1577 B6
Channelburg Blvd
- WTFD 46074 1792 D2
Channing Cir
3900 INPS 46240 2120 D1
Channing Ct
5200 INPS 46226 2121 C6
Channing Rd
5200 INPS 46226 2121 C6
Chantilly Dr
4700 INPS 46221 2444 D5
Chantry Wy
3800 WRvT 46143 2664 A5
Chapel Pl
200 WRvT 46142 2663 C4
Chapel Glen Dr
8300 INPS 46234 2334 A2
Chapel Hill Ct
- MdnT 46113 2661 B1
7100 INPS 46214 2334 D2
Chapel Hill Rd
600 INPS 46214 2334 E2
Chapel Hill East Dr
700 INPS 46214 2334 E2
Chapel Hill West Dr
400 INPS 46214 2334 D2
Chapel Pines Dr
8300 INPS 46234 2334 B2
Chapel Pines Dr W
700 INPS 46234 2334 B2
Chapel Square St
12800 CRML 46032 1900 E3
Chapel Villas Dr
7300 INPS 46214 2334 D3
Chapel Villas Ln
7300 INPS 46214 2334 D3
Chapelwood Blvd
800 INPS 46214 2334 D2
Chapelwood Ct
6400 INPS 46268 2117 C3
Chapelwood Ln
11900 FSHR 46038 1906 E4
Chapman Ct
10 GNFD 46140 2345 E4
Chapman Dr
900 GNFD 46140 2345 E4
Chapman Rd
- GNFD 46140 2345 E3
1000 CtrT 46140 2346 A3
Chapmans Tr
5900 CRML 46033 1903 E3
Chappie Ln
2400 INPS 46229 2231 E6
Chaptico
- CCRO 46034 1577 C4
Char Dr
5400 INPS 46221 2444 B6
Chardonnay Dr
- INPS 46254 2225 E2
Chargers Ct
12600 FCkT 46038 1906 A3
Charing Cross
800 DNVL 46122 2329 D2
Charing Dr
7500 INPS 46260 2009 D7
7500 INPS 46260 2118 D1
Charing Cross Cir
5900 INPS 46217 2555 C1
Charing Cross Ct
100 NBVL 46060 1795 E3
Charing Cross Dr
1400 INPS 46227 2446 E6
1400 INPS 46227 2447 A6
Charing Cross Rd
10 INPS 46217 2555 B1
12500 CRML 46033 1902 E3
12800 CRML 46033 1903 A3
Chariot Ln
500 INPS 46227 2555 D5
Chariots Whisper Dr
14100 CRML 46074 1791 D7
Charity Chase Cir
14100 CRML 46074 1791 E7
Charity Chase Dr
1500 CRML 46074 1791 E7
Charlecot Dr
7900 INPS 46268 2009 C6
Charlemagne Dr
10700 INPS 46259 2559 B2
Charles Ct
1100 PNFD 46168 2441 D7
5200 CRML 46033 1794 B7
7500 BrnT 46112 2114 D2
Charles Dr
900 GNWD 46142 2665 A2
N Charles Dr
400 LcnT 46112 2224 C2

Charles St
1200 INPS 46225 2337 C6
1700 WshT 46123 2223 D7
S Charles St
800 INPS 46225 2337 C5
Charles Lee Ct
1100 GNWD 46143 2665 D1
1100 PltT 46143 2665 D1
Charleston Ct
6900 INPS 46219 2339 E1
8400 WshT 46123 2333 A2
Charleston Ln N
6900 INPS 46219 2339 E1
Charleston Ln S
6900 INPS 46219 2339 E1
Charleston Pkwy
11300 FSHR 46038 1904 B6
Charleston St
5300 SDWY 46224 2226 C6
Charleston Wy
- BCkT 46055 2124 B4
Charleston East Dr
1000 INPS 46219 2339 E2
Charleston West Dr
1000 INPS 46219 2339 E2
Charleswood Ct
13800 FSHR 46060 1905 B1
Charlevoix Ln
6000 INPS 46220 2121 D4
Charlie Dr
400 NBVL 46062 1795 B1
Charliewood Ct
100 NbvT 46062 1685 D5
Charlotte Ct
8300 WshT 46123 2333 A2
Charlotte Pl
100 INPS 46202 2228 C6
700 WshT 46074 1792 B5
Charmil Dr
100 BrnT 46158 2659 E6
Charney Av
4700 LWNC 46226 2122 C7
Charnock St
2900 INPS 46229 2231 E5
Charnwood Pkwy
500 BHGV 46107 2447 E5
500 INPS 46107 2447 D4
Charrington Ct
7400 INPS 46254 2116 D7
Charter Dr
- DelT 46250 2012 E3
9300 INPS 46250 2012 E3
Charter Oak Cir
1600 INPS 46260 2009 E5
Charter Oak Dr
8300 INPS 46260 2009 E5
Charter Oaks
10300 ClyT 46032 2009 D1
Charter Woods Dr
700 INPS 46224 2335 D2
Chartwell St
- CRML 46032 1900 D3
Chase Blvd
1500 GNWD 46142 2664 C4
Chase Cir
4300 EglT 46077 1899 C2
Chase Ct
1400 CRML 46032 1902 A5
10700 FSHR 46038 1905 E7
10700 FSHR 46038 1906 A7
Chase St
500 INPS 46221 2336 E4
3000 INPS 46217 2445 E3
Chase Oak Ct
4500 EglT 46077 1899 D2
Chaseway Ct
2400 INPS 46268 2009 C2
Chateau Ct
3700 INPS 46226 2231 C3
12100 FCkT 46038 1905 B4
Chateau Dr
3800 INPS 46226 2231 C2
Chateau Ln
3600 INPS 46226 2231 C3
Chateaugay Ct
1400 INPS 46217 2554 E6
Chateaugay Dr
8300 INPS 46217 2554 E6
Chateaugay Ln
1200 INPS 46217 2554 E7
Chateaux Dr
- ClyT 46032 1901 B6
Chaterley Ct
7700 INPS 46214 2334 C2
Chatfield Dr
1000 INPS 46220 2119 E4
Chatham Ct
10500 ClyT 46032 1900 D7
10500 ClyT 46032 2009 D1
S Chatham Ct
7700 INPS 46256 2013 B5
Chatham Ct N
7700 INPS 46256 2013 B5
Chatham Dr
4400 LcnT 46112 2224 D2
Chatham Pl
1700 DNVL 46122 2330 C2
4400 INPS 46226 2230 B1
4500 INPS 46226 2121 B7
Chatsbee Ct
3600 INPS 46224 2226 A3
Chatsworth Ct
8400 INPS 46260 2009 E5
Chattanooga Cir
1100 INPS 46229 2341 D1
Chatterton Cir
4600 INPS 46254 2116 C7
Chatterton Dr
7500 INPS 46254 2116 C7
Chatterton Wy
- INPS 46254 2116 C7
Chaucer Cir
100 NBVL 46062 1685 E1
Chaucer Ct
6800 INPS 46220 2121 E2

Chauncy Dr
6700 INPS 46221 2553 B4
Chauncy St
500 CRML 46032 1902 A5
Checotah Ln
10000 LWNC 46236 2123 A2
Chelsea Ct
11600 FSHR 46038 1904 C5
14500 CRML 46033 1794 C6
N Chelsea Ct
7200 INPS 46250 2120 E1
Chelsea Dr
8500 NbvT 46060 1795 C6
Chelsea Rd
5000 INPS 46241 2335 C6
W Chelsea Rd
5300 INPS 46241 2335 B6
Chelsea Ter
900 WRvT 46143 2664 A5
Chelsea Village Ct
1900 INPS 46260 2009 D2
Chelsea Village Dr
9200 INPS 46260 2009 D3
Cheltenham Dr
- WTFD 46074 1792 D4
Cheltenham Rd
8700 INPS 46256 2013 C5
Cheltenham Wy
700 WshT 46123 2331 D5
Chemistry Ct
7100 INPS 46239 2448 E6
Chems-Ford Dr
- MCVL 46055 2124 C1
Chenille Ct
10700 INPS 46235 2232 B2
Chensford Dr
5700 LWNC 46226 2121 E5
Cherbourg Cir
6400 INPS 46220 2121 D4
Cherbourg Dr
6200 INPS 46220 2121 D4
Cheri Cir
6000 INPS 46237 2557 C5
Cheri Ct
6100 INPS 46237 2557 C5
Cherington Ct
1700 INPS 46227 2556 A6
Cherington Dr
8000 INPS 46227 2556 A6
Cherokee Ct
5200 CRML 46033 1903 C2
Cherokee Dr
7200 LWNC 46236 2123 A1
10200 WshT 46234 2224 C6
Cherokee Ln
100 NBVL 46062 1686 A2
W Cherokee Ln
8200 MrlT 46126 2560 B4
Cherry Ct
4200 ZNVL 46077 1898 D2
Cherry Ln
- MdnT 46158 2661 B7
4400 INPS 46228 2118 C7
4400 INPS 46228 2227 C1
Cherry St
10 GNFD 46140 2346 A1
400 BHGV 46107 2447 E4
600 GNFD 46140 2237 A7
1900 NBVL 46060 1686 E7
1900 NBVL 46060 1687 A7
E Cherry St
1000 NBVL 46060 1686 D7
N Cherry St
10 WTFD 46074 1684 B7
S Cherry St
10 WTFD 46074 1684 C7
10 WTFD 46074 1793 B1
W Cherry St
500 NBVL 46060 1686 D7
Cherrybark Ct
7900 LWNC 46236 2015 A6
Cherrybark Dr
7900 LWNC 46236 2014 E6
7900 LWNC 46236 2015 A6
Cherryberry Dr
7600 INPS 46239 2449 A1
Cherry Birch Dr
5500 INPS 46237 2556 D1
Cherry Blossom Blvd
3800 INPS 46237 2447 D7
Cherry Blossom Ct
- GNWD 46143 2666 A6
5500 INPS 46237 2447 D7
5500 INPS 46237 2556 D1
Cherry Blossom Dr
5700 LcnT 46112 2222 E1
Cherry Blossom East Dr
6700 FSHR 46038 1903 E6
Cherry Blossom West Dr
6700 FSHR 46038 1903 E6
Cherry Creek Blvd
5800 CRML 46033 1794 C7
Cherry Field Dr
- INPS 46237 2447 D7
5500 INPS 46237 2556 D1
Cherryfield Ln
1000 GNWD 46142 2664 E1
Cherry Glen Ct
2600 INPS 46227 2447 B4
Cherry Glen Dr
3800 INPS 46227 2447 B4
Cherry Glen Pl
2600 INPS 46227 2447 B4
Cherry Glen Wy
2600 INPS 46227 2447 B4
Cherry Grove Ct
9100 INPS 46113 2551 E7
Cherry Grove Ln
- NBVL 46062 1685 B5
Cherry Hill Blvd
11400 FSHR 46038 1903 E5
Cherry Hill Ct
4900 INPS 46254 2116 D7
11300 FSHR 46038 1903 E6

Cherry Hill Dr
7300 INPS 46254 2116 D7
Cherry Lake Cir
11400 INPS 46235 2232 D3
Cherry Lake Ct
11100 INPS 46235 2232 D4
Cherry Lake Ln
3100 INPS 46235 2232 D4
Cherry Lake Pl
10900 INPS 46235 2232 C4
Cherry Lake Rd
- INPS 46235 2232 D3
Cherry Lake Wy
11000 INPS 46235 2232 C4
Cherry Laurel Ln
6700 FSHR 46038 1903 E6
Cherry Ridge Rd
14400 CRML 46033 1794 C7
Cherry Tree Av
13100 CRML 46033 1903 B2
14100 CRML 46033 1794 D7
14200 NBVL 46033 1794 D6
14600 NBVL 46062 1794 D6
14800 NBVL 46062 1795 A4
14800 NbvT 46062 1794 E5
14800 NbvT 46062 1795 A4
17100 NbvT 46062 1686 A7
Cherry Tree Ln
9700 LWNC 46235 2122 D7
9800 LWNC 46235 2123 A7
Cherry Tree Rd
1400 WshT 46123 2332 C1
1500 WshT 46123 2223 C7
14200 CRML 46033 1794 D7
Cherry Tree Wy
11300 INPS 46235 2232 D3
Cherry Valley Ct
9300 INPS 46235 2231 D1
Cherry Valley Dr
4400 INPS 46235 2231 E1
Cherrywood Ct
1500 WTFD 46074 1793 A2
8900 INPS 46234 2334 A1
Cherub Ct
3000 CRML 46074 1900 B1
Cherub Pl
8300 INPS 46256 2013 A5
Chervil Ct
4700 INPS 46237 2556 E5
Cheryl Ct
10700 CRML 46033 1902 C7
Cheryl Ln
5200 INPS 46203 2339 A7
6200 EglT 46077 1898 D5
Chesapeake Dr
10000 FCkT 46055 2015 B2
Chesapeake Dr E
7700 LWNC 46236 2014 B7
Chesapeake Dr N
10600 LWNC 46236 2014 B7
Chesapeake Dr S
10600 LWNC 46236 2014 B6
Chesapeake Dr W
7700 LWNC 46236 2014 B6
Chesapeake St
10 INPS 46204 2337 B7
Chesham Ct
7000 INPS 46256 2121 E2
Cheshire Cir
200 NBVL 46062 1685 E2
Cheshire Ct
5900 INPS 46254 2226 B1
Cheshire Dr
1200 INPS 46241 2334 E6
Cheshire Rd
6100 INPS 46241 2335 A4
Chessie Dr
8500 INPS 46217 2554 E7
8900 INPS 46217 2663 E1
8900 WRvT 46217 2663 E1
Chessington Rd
1100 INPS 46260 2010 A4
N Chester Av
2600 INPS 46218 2229 D5
6100 INPS 46220 2120 D4
7800 INPS 46240 2011 D7
S Chester Av
200 INPS 46201 2338 D4
1100 INPS 46203 2338 D6
Chester Dr
10 BHGV 46107 2447 C3
9900 ClyT 46032 2011 C1
Chester Ln
5500 INPS 46220 2120 D6
Chester Rd
9900 CRML 46033 2011 C1
N Chester St
1200 INPS 46201 2338 D1
1500 INPS 46201 2229 D7
7200 INPS 46240 2120 D1
7600 INPS 46240 2011 D7
S Chester St
10 INPS 46201 2338 D3
Chesterbrook Ct
9100 INPS 46240 2010 E3
Chester East Dr
6500 INPS 46220 2120 D2
Chesterfield Ct
100 NBVL 46060 1795 E4
1300 GNWD 46143 2665 C6
4800 INPS 46227 2446 D6
Chesterfield Dr
10 NBVL 46060 1795 D4
E Chesterfield Dr
4700 INPS 46227 2446 D6
S Chesterfield Dr
600 INPS 46227 2446 D6
W Chesterfield Dr
4700 INPS 46227 2446 D6
Chesterhill Ln
8000 INPS 46239 2340 B7
Chesterhill Wy
8000 INPS 46239 2340 B7
Chesterton Cir
7000 INPS 46237 2557 B4

Chesterton Dr
9800 ClyT 46280 2011 B2
Chesterton Ln
7100 INPS 46237 2557 B4
Chesterton Pl
5400 INPS 46237 2557 B4
Chester West Dr
6500 INPS 46220 2120 D2
Chestnut Cir
5100 CRML 46033 1903 A2
Chestnut Ct
10 ZNVL 46077 1899 A6
1600 NBVL 46062 1685 C2
9000 INPS 46260 2009 E4
Chestnut Dr
100 GNWD 46142 2665 C1
Chestnut Ln
600 BNBG 46112 2114 D4
600 GNFD 46140 2236 D7
1200 LEBN 46052 1677 B5
E Chestnut Ln
9700 INPS 46239 2449 E2
9700 INPS 46239 2450 A2
Chestnut St
300 DNVL 46122 2329 C5
E Chestnut St
1000 NBVL 46060 1795 D1
N Chestnut St
300 MNVA 46157 2657 C7
N Chestnut St SR-39
300 MNVA 46157 2657 C7
W Chestnut St
200 NBVL 46060 1795 C1
Chestnut Heath Ct
- NBVL 46060 1687 C5
Chestnut Hill Cir
10500 FSHR 46038 2014 E1
Chestnut Hill Ct
10500 FSHR 46038 2014 E1
Chestnut Hill Pass
- FSHR 46038 2014 E1
Chestnut Hills Blvd
7200 INPS 46278 2117 A1
Chestnut Hills Dr
7500 INPS 46278 2008 A7
Chestnut River Cross
1100 WshT 46123 2333 A1
Chestnut Woods Dr
5400 INPS 46224 2335 C2
Cheswick Blvd
13600 CRML 46032 1901 A1
13800 CRML 46032 1792 A7
Cheswick Dr
8000 INPS 46219 2231 B7
Cheswick Ln
10100 FSHR 46038 2014 B1
Cheval Ct
13100 CRML 46033 1902 E2
Cheval Dr
5600 LWNC 46235 2123 D5
Cheval Ln
5600 LWNC 46235 2123 D5
Cheval Pl
4600 CRML 46033 1902 E2
Cheviot Ct
2100 WRvT 46143 2664 A7
Cheviot Pl
3600 INPS 46205 2120 D7
3600 INPS 46205 2229 D1
3800 INPS 46226 2120 D7
3800 INPS 46226 2229 D1
5200 INPS 46226 2121 A7
Chevy Ln
11000 ClyT 46280 1902 A6
11000 CRML 46280 1902 A6
Chevy Chase Dr
13200 DelT 46038 1904 B2
Chevy Chase Ln
900 ClyT 46280 2010 E1
Cheyenne Cir
2000 WTFD 46074 1793 B1
Cheyenne Ct
8400 INPS 46217 2555 B7
Cheyenne Moon
5200 CRML 46033 1903 C2
Chianti Dr
7700 LWNC 46226 2122 A6
E Chicago St
200 LEBN 46052 1677 A6
W Chicago St
100 LEBN 46052 1677 B4
200 LEBN 46052 1676 E6
Chickasaw Ct
5200 CRML 46033 1903 C1
8400 INPS 46217 2555 B7
Chickasaw Dr
10300 WshT 46234 2224 D6
N Chickasaw Rd
9600 MrlT 46126 2560 A4
Chico Grey Dr
5300 INPS 46237 2557 B2
Chicopee Ct
7800 INPS 46217 2555 A5
Chicory Ct
19200 NBVL 46060 1687 C3
Chief Ln
3200 INPS 46241 2444 B3
Chiefs Ct
12600 FCkT 46038 1905 E3
Chiltern Dr
7900 INPS 46268 2009 C6
Chimney Rock Ct
7000 INPS 46217 2555 B4
Chinook Cir
7200 INPS 46219 2340 A3
Chinquapin Ct
9900 CRML 46033 2011 C1
Chinquapin Dr
- AVON 46123 2332 A1
Chipendale Ct
1500 INPS 46260 2009 E6
Chipendale Ln
1500 INPS 46260 2009 C7
Chipmunk Cir
1400 GNWD 46142 2664 C2

STREET
Block City ZIP Map# Grid
Chipmunk Cross
11200 FSHR 46038 1903 E6
Chipmunks Run
5700 INPS 46254 2117 C4
Chippenham Ln
100 FCkT 46038 1904 D2
Chippewa Ct
8400 INPS 46217 2555 B6
Chipping Ct
6600 INPS 46268 2117 E2
Chip Shot Rd
- NBVL 46062 1686 B4
Chipwood Dr
7300 NBVL 46062 1686 A3
Chipwood Ln
5300 INPS 46226 2121 B6
Chiseled Stone Dr
12200 FSHR 46038 1906 A4
Chisolm Ct
5400 INPS 46237 2448 B7
Chisolm Tr
5200 INPS 46237 2448 B7
5500 INPS 46237 2557 B1
Chitern Dr
1300 WRvT 46143 2663 E6
Chittimwood Dr
8400 INPS 46227 2555 D6
Chitwood Dr
8900 INPS 46227 2555 D7
Chivalry Ct
9600 INPS 46229 2231 E5
Chloe Ct
11500 INPS 46236 2014 D5
Chloe Ln
- GNWD 46143 2665 C7
Choate Ct
7500 INPS 46254 2116 D7
Choctaw Dr
10300 WshT 46234 2224 D6
Choctaw Wy
400 INPS 46219 2340 A4
Choctaw Ridge Ln
5000 INPS 46239 2449 A7
Choctaw Ridge Wy
5200 INPS 46239 2449 A7
Chokecherry Ln
3500 INPS 46235 2232 D3
Cholla Ct
1800 INPS 46240 2011 A4
Cholla Rd
8600 INPS 46240 2011 A4
12000 FSHR 46038 1905 E5
N Cholla Rd
- INPS 46240 2011 A4
Cholla Ter
1700 INPS 46240 2011 A4
Chorleywood Cir
12800 FSHR 46060 1906 D3
Chris Ct
10 SCkT 46140 2342 C2
300 NBVL 46062 1686 A1
N Chris Ct
2200 INPS 46229 2232 B6
Chris Dr
10000 INPS 46229 2232 B6
Chris Ln
400 NBVL 46062 1686 A1
Chris Anne Cir
7700 INPS 46237 2557 C5
Chris Anne Ct
6100 INPS 46237 2557 C5
Chris Anne Dr
7500 INPS 46237 2557 C4
Chrisfield Ln
13300 FCkT 46055 2015 C1
Christian Av
800 NBVL 46060 1795 D1
W Christian Av
300 NBVL 46060 1795 C2
Christian Blvd
- FKLN 46131 2774 E7
- FKLN 46131 2775 A7
W Christian Dr
7200 SCkT 46163 2451 B3
S Christian Ln
8000 INPS 46217 2554 D6
Christiana Ln
8200 INPS 46256 2013 B5
N Christiana Ln
8200 INPS 46256 2013 B5
Christiana Wy
7900 INPS 46256 2013 B4
Christie Ct
3400 INPS 46221 2445 A3
Christie Ann Dr
14400 FCkT 46040 2015 E1
14800 FCkT 46040 2016 A1
Christin Ct
- GfdT 46168 2440 E4
Christina Ct
900 PNFD 46168 2441 D6
3700 CRML 46033 2011 E1
Christina Dr
200 WTLD 46184 2774 E4
200 WTLD 46184 2775 A4
N Christner Ln
10 MdnT 46158 2660 E7
Christopher Ct
700 BrnT 46112 2114 B1
4800 INPS 46203 2339 A7
8000 AVON 46123 2332 D6
Christopher Dr
4800 INPS 46203 2339 B7
Christopher Ln
1600 SDWY 46224 2226 C7
3500 INPS 46224 2226 C3
N Christopher Ln
7000 MrlT 46126 2670 C2
Christy Dr
- PltT 46143 2665 D1
10 GNWD 46143 2665 D1
Chrysanthemum Ct
6800 INPS 46214 2225 E4
Chrysler St
3100 INPS 46224 2226 D4
Chrysler St
6800 INPS 46268 2117 D2
N Chrysler St
3600 INPS 46224 2226 D3
Chula Vista Ct
1000 GNWD 46143 2666 A4
Church Dr
300 NBVL 46060 1687 A6
Church Rd
9000 LcnT 46112 2224 B4
Church St
- NPLN 46163 2452 A4
- PTBR 46167 2112 E3
10 MRVL 46158 2659 E2
10 SPRT 46227 2556 B4
1800 LtyT 46118 2548 C2
3000 LtyT 46168 2439 E5
11700 LWNC 46236 2123 D3
N Church St
3400 INPS 46234 2224 E3
S Church St
1100 INPS 46225 2337 B5
W Church St
300 FTVL 46040 2016 E2
Churchhill Downs Cir
4600 WRvT 46143 2663 D5
Churchill Ct
400 FSHR 46038 1904 B6
1000 ClyT 46280 1901 E7
10100 INPS 46229 2232 A7
Churchill Dr
10 MRVL 46158 2659 D3
Churchman Av
10 BHGV 46107 2448 A3
1700 BHGV 46107 2447 C2
2000 INPS 46203 2338 B7
2200 INPS 46203 2447 B1
2400 INPS 46107 2447 B1
5100 BHGV 46203 2448 A4
E Churchman Av
6000 INPS 46237 2448 D6
Churchman Byp
5800 BHGV 46203 2448 C4
E Churchman Byp
6300 BHGV 46203 2448 D4
6300 INPS 46203 2448 D4
Churchman Ct
4300 INPS 46237 2448 C5
Churchman Pl
300 BHGV 46107 2448 A4
300 BHGV 46203 2448 A4
Churchman Wy
6100 INPS 46237 2448 C5
Churchman Woods Blvd
3800 BHGV 46203 2448 B4
Chyverton Cir
12500 CRML 46032 1901 A3
Cicero Av
24300 JknT 46030 1577 D1
Cicero Av SR-19
24300 JknT 46030 1577 D1
Cicero Rd
100 NBVL 46060 1686 D4
700 NbvT 46060 1686 D4
1300 NbvT 46062 1686 D4
3200 JknT 46062 1577 D7
3200 NbvT 46062 1577 D7
Cicero Rd SR-19
100 NBVL 46060 1686 D4
700 NbvT 46060 1686 D4
1300 NbvT 46062 1686 D4
3200 JknT 46062 1577 D7
3200 NbvT 46062 1577 D7
Cider Mill Cir
7100 LWNC 46226 2121 E6
Cider Mill Ct
7100 LWNC 46226 2121 C7
7500 FSHR 46038 1904 A6
Cider Mill Ln
- LWNC 46226 2122 A5
5200 LWNC 46226 2121 E6
S Cider Mill Run
4000 NPLN 46163 2452 A2
Cielo Vista Ct
- GNWD 46143 2665 D4
Cielo Vista Dr
400 GNWD 46143 2665 E4
Cimarron Tr
7800 INPS 46214 2334 C2
Cimarron Pass
16600 NBVL 46060 1796 E2
16900 NBVL 46060 1797 A2
N Cincinnati St
600 INPS 46202 2337 D2
S Cincinnati St
100 INPS 46202 2337 D4
Cindy Dr
7300 MCVL 46055 2015 B7
7300 MCVL 46055 2124 B1
Cindy Ln
- INPS 46239 2449 D4
8900 BrnT 46112 2006 D7
Cinnamon Ct
10 BNBG 46112 2223 D1
2100 WshT 46168 2441 B1
Cinnamon Dr
7300 INPS 46237 2556 E4
Cinnamon Pl
4700 INPS 46237 2556 E4
Cinnebar Dr
8900 INPS 46268 2009 C3
Circle Blvd
3500 INPS 46220 2120 D6
Circle Ct
600 NWTD 46184 2774 D4
2700 ClyT 46032 2009 C1
Circle Dr
- INPS 46278 2116 D3
- NBVL 46062 1685 E2
10 CRML 46032 1793 A7
10 CRML 46032 1902 A1
10 MRVL 46158 2659 D3
700 GNWD 46142 2665 B4
3800 INPS 46220 2120 D2
7900 EglT 46077 2006 D2
Circle Dr
8800 FCkT 46038 1904 D5
N Circle Dr
- INPS 46278 2116 D3
W Circle Dr
- INPS 46278 2116 D3
Circleview Dr
200 MRVL 46158 2660 B4
Cirrus Dr
12400 FSHR 46038 1906 B4
Citadel Ct
3100 INPS 46268 2009 B3
Citation Blvd
4500 INPS 46237 2448 C6
Citation Cir
4600 INPS 46237 2448 C6
Citation Cir E
1300 LEBN 46052 1676 D5
Citation Cir N
1500 LEBN 46052 1676 D4
Citation Cir S
1300 LEBN 46052 1676 D5
Citation Cir W
1200 LEBN 46052 1676 D5
Citation Ct
- WshT 46234 2224 E6
10 WshT 46032 1792 E5
Citation Dr
- WshT 46234 2224 E6
Citation Rd
700 WshT 46032 1792 E5
Citizens Pl
300 INPS 46205 2228 D5
Citrin Pl
1500 INPS 46227 2556 A5
City Center Dr
- CRML 46032 1902 A3
Civic Cir
11700 BrnT 46158 2660 C5
Civic Sq
10 CRML 46032 1902 A4
Clabet Dr
7400 INPS 46278 2116 D1
Claffey Dr
200 INPS 46260 2010 C6
Claiborne Ln
800 LEBN 46052 1677 B5
Clairborne Ct
1100 ClyT 46280 1901 E7
1100 ClyT 46280 1902 A7
Clairborne Wy
4400 INPS 46228 2227 D1
Claire Dr
4000 INPS 46240 2011 D5
4100 INPS 46250 2011 D5
Claireridge Dr
- WshT 46123 2332 A7
Clara Ct
1300 PNFD 46168 2550 D1
Clara St
6700 INPS 46250 2012 E6
Clare Av
21200 WynT 46060 1578 D7
Claren Dr
7500 GfdT 46168 2551 A5
Clarendon Dr
100 NBVL 46062 1686 A1
600 NBVL 46062 1685 E1
Clarendon Pl
700 INPS 46208 2228 B1
Clarendon Rd
3800 INPS 46208 2228 B2
5100 INPS 46208 2119 B6
7600 INPS 46260 2010 B7
E Clarendon Rd
4600 INPS 46208 2119 B7
W Clarendon Rd
4600 INPS 46208 2119 B7
Claridge Ct
800 INPS 46260 2010 A6
Claridge Rd
8000 INPS 46260 2010 A6
N Claridge Wy
- CRML 46032 1901 A3
1200 CRML 46032 1900 E4
Clarinda Ct
14700 FCkT 46040 2016 A1
Clarion Dr
7700 LWNC 46236 2014 E7
Clark Av
200 BHGV 46107 2447 C3
Clark Dr
1100 GNWD 46143 2664 E5
12300 FSHR 46038 1905 B4
S Clark Dr
4300 INPS 46239 2449 C5
W Clark Ln
300 SgCT 46126 2670 D7
Clark Rd
1900 SDWY 46224 2226 B6
3500 INPS 46224 2226 B3
Clark St
- CRML 46032 1901 E4
- CRML 46032 1902 A4
3100 LtyT 46168 2439 E6
N Clark St
400 LEBN 46052 1676 E6
S Clark St
800 LEBN 46052 1676 E7
Clarks Rd
- PNFD 46168 2441 E4
Clarks Creek Ct
- AVON 46123 2332 D6
Clarks Creek Rd
3600 PNFD 46168 2441 E5
Clarks Hill Wy
- WTFD 46074 1792 D3
Clarkson Dr
4900 INPS 46254 2117 D7
Clarkston Ct
4700 ZNVL 46077 1899 C3
Clarkston Rd
11200 ZNVL 46077 1899 C3
Classic Av
- GNWD 46143 2666 B6
Classic Cir
8800 INPS 46217 2555 B7
Classic Ct
10800 INPS 46229 2232 B7
Classic Ln
- GNWD 46143 2666 D5
Classic View Dr
8800 GNWD 46217 2664 E1
8800 INPS 46217 2555 B7
8800 INPS 46217 2664 E1
Classon Ln
900 BHGV 46107 2447 E5
900 INPS 46107 2447 E5
Claudius Dr
500 AVON 46123 2332 A2
Clay Cir
- CRML 46032 1900 E3
Clay Ct
10 ZNVL 46077 1898 E5
Clay Dr
1300 CRML 46032 1902 B5
Clay St
2000 INPS 46205 2229 A1
N Clay St
10 MRVL 46158 2659 E3
S Clay St
300 MRVL 46158 2659 E4
Claybrooke Dr
5300 INPS 46221 2444 C6
Clayburn Ct
8000 INPS 46268 2008 E6
Clayburn Dr
4100 INPS 46268 2008 E6
8100 INPS 46268 2009 A6
Clay Center Rd
11600 CRML 46032 1901 A3
Claymont Blvd
5900 PNFD 46168 2440 E5
Claymont Ct
400 INPS 46234 2334 A3
Claymore Dr
9600 FSHR 46038 1904 E2
9700 FSHR 46038 1905 A2
Clay Mount Ln
9400 FSHR 46038 1904 E7
Claypoole Dr
2000 INPS 46214 2225 E7
Clay Springs Dr
1100 CRML 46032 1901 A4
1200 CRML 46032 1900 E4
Clay Terrace Blvd
14500 CRML 46032 1793 A6
Clayton Av
2800 INPS 46201 2338 C4
Clayton Ln
- GNWD 46143 2665 C5
Clear Branch Dr
- BNBG 46112 2224 A1
Clearbrook St
15400 WshT 46074 1792 B4
Clear Creek Cir
- LcnT 46112 2115 C5
Clear Creek Dr
- CtrT 46122 2329 B4
300 DNVL 46122 2329 B4
Clear Lake Ct
- WTFD 46074 1792 C2
5100 CRML 46033 1903 B5
E Clear Lake Ln
200 WTFD 46074 1792 D2
W Clear Lake Ln
10 WTFD 46074 1792 C2
Clear Lake Wy
2800 INPS 46227 2447 C5
Clear Oak Cir
7200 NBVL 46062 1686 A6
Clear Sky Ct
12000 FSHR 46038 1905 C4
Clear Spring Dr
10800 GfdT 46113 2551 E7
Clearspring Wy
11000 INPS 46239 2341 C4
Clear Springs Dr
- GfdT 46113 2551 E7
- INPS 46113 2551 E7
Clearview Cir
7800 LWNC 46236 2015 A7
Clearview Ct
400 GNWD 46143 2665 B5
Clearview Dr
400 GNWD 46143 2665 C5
3100 INPS 46228 2118 B4
5900 CRML 46033 1903 C4
Clearview Ln
12400 LWNC 46236 2015 A7
Clearview Wy
300 GNWD 46143 2665 B5
Clear Vista Dr
- LEBN 46052 1676 C5
E Clearvista Dr
7000 INPS 46256 2012 E6
7200 INPS 46256 2013 A6
Clearvista Ln
7200 INPS 46256 2013 A5
Clearvista Pkwy
8000 INPS 46256 2013 A5
Clearvista Pl
8200 INPS 46256 2013 A5
Clearvista Wy
7000 INPS 46256 2012 E6
7000 INPS 46256 2013 A6
Clearwater Blvd
300 WTLD 46184 2775 A6
Clearwater Cir
3500 INPS 46240 2011 D6
Clearwater Ct
1400 CRML 46032 1792 C7
6400 WshT 46123 2332 A7
7900 INPS 46256 2013 B6
8000 GfdT 46168 2550 D6
Clearwater Dr
8000 INPS 46256 2013 B6
Clearwater Pkwy
8000 INPS 46240 2011 D5
Clearwater Cove Dr
7800 INPS 46240 2011 D6
Clearwater Pointe
8100 INPS 46240 2011 D5
Cleat Ct
8400 INPS 46236 2014 C5
Clem St
- WTLD 46184 2775 A5
Clemdale Av
6800 LWNC 46226 2121 E7
Clemson St
8900 INPS 46268 2009 B3
Cleveland St
1200 BHGV 46107 2447 C2
N Cleveland St
200 INPS 46204 2337 D3
600 INPS 46202 2337 D2
Clew Ct
8400 INPS 46236 2014 C5
Clifden Pond Rd
10 ZNVL 46077 1898 E7
Cliff Ovlk
200 NBVL 46062 1795 A1
Clifford Cir
12800 CRML 46032 1901 C3
Clifford Ct
1000 LEBN 46052 1676 D5
10400 LcnT 46112 2224 D2
Clifford Pl
- INPS 46201 2338 B1
Clifford Rd
1000 LcnT 46112 2224 D2
Clifford St
- INPS 46201 2338 B1
Cliff Ridge Ct
1300 INPS 46217 2445 E7
Cliff Ridge Dr
5200 INPS 46217 2445 E7
Cliff Ridge Ln
1300 INPS 46217 2445 E7
Cliffview Dr
6800 INPS 46214 2225 E5
Cliffview Pl
2900 INPS 46214 2225 E5
Cliffwood Dr
14100 FSHR 46060 1796 A7
Clifton Ct
- FCkT 46040 2015 D1
Clifton St
2500 INPS 46208 2228 A5
Clifty Falls Dr
13400 CRML 46032 1901 C1
Clinical Dr
500 INPS 46202 2337 A2
Clinton Ct
10 DNVL 46122 2329 C4
Clinton St
4300 LWNC 46226 2231 C1
4500 LWNC 46226 2122 C7
E Clinton St
10 DNVL 46122 2329 D4
1000 NBVL 46060 1686 D7
W Clinton St
10 DNVL 46122 2329 C4
800 NBVL 46060 1686 D7
Clipper Ct
9000 INPS 46256 2014 B4
Cloister Dr
1600 ClyT 46260 2009 E2
1600 INPS 46260 2009 E2
Closser Ct
5500 INPS 46221 2553 B1
Clossey Dr
600 INPS 46227 2555 D6
Cloud Bay Ct
9000 INPS 46236 2014 D4
Clove Ct
4100 INPS 46237 2556 D4
Clove Hitch Ct
15100 FCkT 46040 1907 A6
Clovelly Ct
4300 INPS 46254 2117 E7
Clover
- BwnT 46126 2670 E5
- SgCT 46126 2670 E5
Clover Ct
- LEBN 46052 1676 C4
Clover Dr
2800 PNFD 46168 2442 C3
4400 INPS 46228 2227 C1
Clover Ln
- LEBN 46052 1676 C3
Clover Rd
16600 NBVL 46060 1796 A2
16700 NBVL 46060 1795 E1
N Clover Bush Rd
5500 BwnT 46126 2670 E4
5500 SgCT 46126 2670 E4
5800 MrlT 46126 2670 E4
Cloverdale Wy
8200 INPS 46256 2013 E6
N Clover Elm Dr
5600 SgCT 46126 2670 E5
Cloverfield Ln
- GNWD 46143 2665 B7
Clover Lake Dr
- INPS 46228 2227 C1
4500 INPS 46228 2118 C7
Cloverleaf Ct
5900 INPS 46241 2335 A4
Cloverleaf Dr
5800 INPS 46241 2335 B4
Clover Leaf Ln
9500 FSHR 46038 1795 E7
Cloverleaf Ter
800 INPS 46241 2335 B5
N Clover Maple Dr
5700 SgCT 46126 2670 E5
W Clover North Dr
4000 SgCT 46126 2670 E5
N Clover West Dr
5600 SgCT 46126 2670 E5
Club Cir
10800 INPS 46229 2232 C7
Club Pt
- FSHR 46038 1906 A7
Club Chase
10700 FSHR 46038 1906 A7
Club Estates Dr
- WshT 46033 1793 D4
3300 WTFD 46033 1793 D4
Club Estates Ln
15500 WTFD 46033 1793 D4
Club House Ct
3800 WRvT 46142 2664 A1
3800 WRvT 46217 2664 A1
Clubhouse Ct
1000 CRML 46032 1793 B7
1000 CRML 46032 1902 B1
Club House Dr
9600 ClyT 46032 2009 B2
9600 INPS 46032 2009 B2
11900 FSHR 46038 1904 A3
12000 FSHR 46038 1903 E4
Clubhouse Dr
- WshT 46123 2331 C5
Clubhouse Dr S
10 WTFD 46074 1793 A2
Clubhouse Dr W
800 WTFD 46074 1793 B2
Club House Rd
8000 INPS 46260 2009 D6
Club Point Dr
10800 FSHR 46038 1906 A7
Clubside Pl
2100 INPS 46214 2225 C6
Clubside Wy
8100 INPS 46214 2225 C6
Clune Ln
9200 INPS 46256 2013 D4
Cluster Pine Dr
3000 INPS 46235 2232 D4
Cluster Pine Ln
11700 INPS 46235 2232 D4
Clyde Av
1200 INPS 46203 2339 A6
S Clyde Av
400 INPS 46201 2339 A4
500 INPS 46203 2339 A4
Clyde Dr
700 WRvT 46143 2663 A5
N Clydes Rd
6200 INPS 46268 2118 A3
Clymer Ln
8000 INPS 46250 2011 E6
CO-200
10 SCkT 46140 2344 B1
200 BCkT 46140 2344 B1
200 CtrT 46140 2344 B1
400 BCkT 46140 2235 B5
400 CtrT 46140 2235 B5
Coach Rd
700 INPS 46227 2555 D5
Coachlite Dr
1400 GNFD 46140 2236 D6
Coachman Dr
3500 INPS 46228 2118 B4
3600 CRML 46033 1902 E7
Coachtown Dr
- INPS 46219 2231 C6
Coachtown Sq
1700 INPS 46219 2231 A7
E Coal Bluff Ct
- MdnT 46113 2661 B1
Coast Dr
2900 INPS 46214 2225 D4
Coastal Dr
11500 INPS 46229 2232 D7
Coastal Wy
11500 INPS 46229 2232 D7
Coastline Ct
12900 FCkT 46055 2015 B2
Coatbridge Cir
6700 INPS 46254 2225 C1
Coatbridge Wy
4300 INPS 46254 2225 E1
Cobalt Dr
13700 FSHR 46038 1904 E1
Cobb Cir
6900 NBVL 46062 1794 E2
Cobb Island Ct
10600 LWNC 46236 2014 B7
Cobblefield Ct
12300 FSHR 46038 1906 A5
Cobblefield Wy
1000 CBLD 46140 2232 E6
1100 CBLD 46140 2233 A6
Cobblesprings Ct
200 AVON 46123 2332 D3
Cobblesprings Dr
7800 AVON 46123 2332 D3
Cobblestone Ct
12200 LWNC 46236 2124 A1
Cobblestone Dr
4000 WRvT 46143 2664 A7
10600 WshT 46234 2333 D1
11700 FSHR 46038 1906 A5
11900 FSHR 46038 1905 E4
Cobblestone Pl
500 WshT 46123 2331 D5
Cobblestone Rd
700 WshT 46123 2331 C5
Cobblestone Wy
4100 WRvT 46143 2663 E7
Cobblestone East Dr
7300 LWNC 46236 2124 A1
7400 LWNC 46236 2015 A7
Cobblestone South Dr
12300 LWNC 46236 2124 A1
Cobblestone West Dr
7300 LWNC 46236 2124 A1
7400 LWNC 46236 2015 A7
Cobden Ct
6600 INPS 46254 2225 E1
Cobden Ln
6700 INPS 46254 2225 C1
Cobham Ln
6500 INPS 46237 2557 A3
Cobham Wy
5100 INPS 46237 2557 A3
Cobia Pl
- NBVL 46060 1687 C4
Coburn Av
4500 INPS 46228 2118 D7
4500 INPS 46228 2227 D1
N Coburn Av
5900 INPS 46228 2118 D4
6200 INPS 46260 2118 D3
Cockerham Cir
8900 INPS 46278 2007 B4
Cocoa Beach Ln
10900 INPS 46229 2232 C6
Coconut Ct
- INPS 46217 2554 B2
Cody Ln
5300 PNFD 46168 2440 D4
5300 WRvT 46142 2663 C4
10800 FSHR 46038 1905 C7
Coffee Tree Cir
700 INPS 46224 2335 C2
Coffee Tree Ct
800 NBVL 46062 1685 C2
Coffey St
500 INPS 46221 2336 E4
3000 INPS 46217 2445 E3
Coffman Rd
7200 INPS 46268 2117 D1
N Coffman Rd
6200 INPS 46268 2117 D3
Cohasset Ct
7000 LWNC 46226 2121 E5
Cohen St
800 LEBN 46052 1676 D5
E Coil St
800 INPS 46220 2119 E3
W Coil St
1900 INPS 46260 2118 D3
2300 INPS 46268 2118 D3
Colbarn Ct
500 FSHR 46038 1904 B5
Colbarn Dr
400 FSHR 46038 1904 B5
Colbarn Pl
12200 FSHR 46038 1904 B4
Colby Blvd
8600 INPS 46268 2009 B4
Colby Ct
3000 INPS 46268 2009 B4
14300 CRML 46032 1792 D7
Colchester Dr
4000 INPS 46268 2009 A6
Cold Harbor Dr
3200 INPS 46227 2556 C6
Cold Spring Dr
- BNBG 46112 2224 A1
Cold Spring Ln
2500 INPS 46222 2227 C6
Cold Spring Rd
2000 INPS 46222 2227 C6
4000 INPS 46228 2227 D2
4500 INPS 46228 2118 E7
Cold Springs Manor Dr
2500 INPS 46222 2227 C5
Coldstream Ln
2700 INPS 46220 2120 B2
Cold Stream Rd
- NBVL 46060 1797 A5
- WynT 46060 1797 A5
Coldwater Cir
- MCVL 46055 2015 B5
2100 INPS 46239 2340 A7
Coldwater Ct
2000 INPS 46239 2340 B7
Coldwater Dr
13700 CRML 46032 1901 B1
Cole Ct
3700 ClyT 46032 1900 A6
N Cole St
100 INPS 46224 2335 D3
2100 SDWY 46224 2226 D6
S Cole St
200 INPS 46241 2335 D4
2100 INPS 46241 2444 D1
Colebrook Dr
6200 INPS 46220 2121 D2
Coleman Cir
- LWNC 46216 2122 C5
Coleman Dr
- WshT 46123 2332 B2
Cole Porter Ln
4700 CRML 46033 1903 A3
Colerain Dr
2800 INPS 46222 2227 C5
Cole Wood Blvd
- INPS 46239 2449 A1
Cole Wood Ct
2400 INPS 46239 2449 A1
Colfax Cir
- CRML 46032 1900 D4
5000 CRML 46033 1903 A3
Colfax Ln
2200 INPS 46260 2009 D2
16700 WshT 46074 1792 C2
16700 WTFD 46074 1792 C2
Colgate St
9000 INPS 46268 2009 C4
Coliseum Av
3600 INPS 46205 2228 E3
3600 INPS 46205 2229 A2
Colita More Ct
7000 INPS 46254 2225 E1
Colleens Wy
6600 INPS 46221 2552 E1
College Av
200 WTFD 46074 1793 B1
E College Av
10 BNBG 46112 2114 C7
N College Av
10 INPS 46202 2337 D1
600 INPS 46204 2337 D1
1600 INPS 46202 2228 E6
2200 INPS 46205 2228 E6
4400 INPS 46205 2119 E7

INDEX 15

N College Av — Indianapolis Street Index — E Country Tr

STREET
Block City ZIP Map# Grid

N College Av
6400 INPS 46220 2119 E2
7100 INPS 46240 2119 E2
7300 INPS 46240 2010 E4
9600 ClyT 46280 2010 E1
9600 CRML 46280 2010 E3
10500 ClyT 46280 1901 E7
11600 CRML 46032 1901 E5
S College Av
10 INPS 46202 2337 D4
400 INPS 46203 2337 D4
W College Av
10 BNBG 46112 2114 B7
College Dr
- CRML 46032 1901 D5
9200 INPS 46240 2010 E3
College Ln
600 INPS 46240 2010 D5
College St
10 WTFD 46074 1793 B1
College Wy
600 CRML 46032 1902 A3
700 CRML 46032 1901 E3
College Place Dr
10900 ClyT 46280 1901 D7
Colleton Ct
16000 WTFD 46033 1793 E3
Collett Dr E
200 MdnT 46113 2660 E3
Collett Dr W
100 MdnT 46113 2660 E3
Collhester Blvd
- INPS 46241 2334 D6
Collier St
400 INPS 46241 2335 E5
2300 INPS 46241 2444 E2
3100 INPS 46221 2444 E4
Colliers Ct
13200 CRML 46033 1903 D2
Collings St
100 CCRO 46034 1577 D3
Collingswood Ln
10400 FCkT 46038 2014 B1
Collingtree Dr
16400 NBVL 46060 1796 B2
Collingwood Dr
800 INPS 46228 2119 A5
1100 INPS 46228 2118 E5
Collins Dr
9600 NbvT 46060 1687 A5
Collins Ln
- SgCT 46126 2670 D7
E Colmar St
11600 CBLD 46229 2341 D2
Colmery Dr
- GNWD 46143 2665 C6
300 ClyT 46290 2010 C1
Cologne Ct
3700 INPS 46228 2227 A1
Colonial Av
6000 INPS 46228 2118 C4
Colonial Cir
7700 FSHR 46038 1904 B6
Colonial Ct
7600 FSHR 46038 1904 B6
10600 WshT 46234 2333 D1
Colonial Dr
900 WshT 46123 2332 B2
9700 ClyT 46032 2009 C1
W Colonial Dr
6700 BCkT 46140 2233 B7
Colonial Ln
1300 DNVL 46122 2330 B3
Colonial Rd
8300 INPS 46241 2552 A1
Colonial Wy
600 GNWD 46142 2664 E2
Colonist Cir
5600 INPS 46254 2117 B5
Colonnade Ct E
6300 INPS 46237 2448 D5
Colonnade Ct W
6200 INPS 46237 2448 D5
Colony Cir
7400 INPS 46260 2010 A7
7400 INPS 46260 2119 A1
Colony Ct
10 GNFD 46140 2345 A1
10 ZNVL 46077 1899 A4
2500 ClyT 46280 2011 C2
Colony Dr
400 WTLD 46184 2775 A6
Colony Pl
4500 INPS 46226 2121 C7
4500 INPS 46226 2230 C1
Colony Wy
1000 ZNVL 46077 1899 A4
Colony Lake East Dr
2800 PNFD 46168 2441 D3
Colony Lake West Dr
2800 PNFD 46168 2441 D3
Colony Mill Ln
6000 INPS 46254 2117 C4
Colony Park Cir
- GNWD 46143 2666 B5
Colony Park Dr
- GNWD 46143 2666 B6
Colony Pointe East Dr
9300 INPS 46250 2012 E3
9500 FSHR 46250 2012 E3
Colony Pointe South Dr
6700 INPS 46250 2012 E3
Colony Pointe West Dr
9300 INPS 46250 2012 B2
Colonywood Dr
11500 CBLD 46229 2341 D2
N Colorado Av
10 INPS 46201 2338 E3
3400 INPS 46218 2229 E3
3800 INPS 46226 2229 E2
S Colorado Av
10 INPS 46201 2338 E3
1400 INPS 46203 2338 E6
Colt Dr
8100 GfdT 46168 2550 D6
Colt Rd
1700 INPS 46227 2556 A6
Columbia Av
1200 INPS 46202 2337 E1
1600 INPS 46202 2228 E7
2200 INPS 46205 2228 E7
Columbia Cir
- WRvT 46142 2663 B4
6300 FSHR 46038 1903 D7
Columbia Cir S
- WRvT 46142 2663 B4
Columbia Ct
- WRvT 46142 2663 B4
800 WshT 46123 2333 A2
Columbia Rd
- GfdT 46168 2442 D6
E Columbia St
100 DNVL 46122 2329 D3
W Columbia St
10 DNVL 46122 2329 D3
Columbine Cir
3100 INPS 46224 2226 A4
Columbine Ct
3100 INPS 46224 2226 A4
Columbine Dr
6300 INPS 46224 2226 A4
E Columbine Ln
10 WshT 46074 1792 D5
W Columbine Ln
10 WshT 46074 1792 C5
Columbus Dr
- INPS 46113 2551 E5
- INPS 46113 2552 A6
Column Dr
4200 INPS 46237 2448 D5
Colville Cir
13900 CRML 46033 1903 C1
14000 CRML 46033 1794 C7
Comanche Ln
4900 INPS 46254 2117 A7
Comanche Tr
5200 CRML 46033 1903 C1
Comb St
10400 ClyT 46280 2010 E1
10500 ClyT 46280 1901 E7
N Combs Rd
10 GNWD 46143 2666 D2
10 INPS 46143 2557 C7
10 PltT 46143 2557 C7
10 PltT 46143 2666 D2
S Combs Rd
6800 INPS 46237 2557 D3
Comer Av
1100 INPS 46203 2446 E1
1500 INPS 46203 2447 A1
Comer Ln
- MRVL 46158 2660 A4
10 BrnT 46158 2660 A4
Comet Dr
5200 WRvT 46143 2663 C7
Commander Cir
8900 INPS 46256 2013 D4
Commerce Av
1800 INPS 46201 2338 A1
Commerce Cir
5100 INPS 46237 2557 A5
Commerce Dr
- ClyT 46032 1899 E7
- ClyT 46032 2008 E1
- ClyT 46032 2009 A1
10 BNBG 46112 2114 C4
10 MRVL 46158 2659 D3
100 CtrT 46122 2330 E4
100 DNVL 46122 2330 E4
17700 WTFD 46074 1683 D7
Commerce Pkwy
- GNWD 46143 2666 C4
Commerce Crossing Blvd
3400 INPS 46240 2011 C4
Commerce Park Pl
8600 INPS 46268 2008 E4
Commerce Square Dr
5100 INPS 46237 2557 A5
Commercial Dr
- INPS 46222 2226 E2
2400 LEBN 46052 1676 E3
3500 INPS 46222 2227 A3
11600 FSHR 46038 1904 D5
17600 WshT 46074 1682 E7
Commercial St
- SgCT 46126 2670 D7
Commission Pl
1300 GNWD 46142 2664 D1
Commission Rd
1100 GNWD 46142 2664 D1
Commodore Dr
6100 INPS 46219 2230 D6
Common Cir
5800 INPS 46220 2121 A4
Commons Dr
1800 CRML 46032 1902 A5
6300 INPS 46254 2226 A1
Common View Cir
4600 INPS 46220 2120 E5
4600 INPS 46220 2121 A5
Commonview Dr
- MCVL 46055 2015 D5
Common Vista Cir
4600 INPS 46220 2120 E5
4600 INPS 46220 2121 A6
Common Vista Ct
4900 INPS 46220 2121 A5
Common Vista Wy
4600 INPS 46220 2121 A5
Commonwealth Ct
6200 INPS 46220 2120 D3
Commonwealth Dr
4600 INPS 46220 2120 D3
4600 INPS 46220 2121 A3
8900 FSHR 46038 1905 A3
Common Wy Ct
5700 INPS 46220 2121 A5
Common Wy Dr
5700 INPS 46220 2121 A6
Community Ct
1200 INPS 46227 2555 E7
Community Dr
10 GNWD 46143 2665 C6
Community Pl
1200 INPS 46227 2555 E7
Comos Run Ln
- WshT 46123 2333 C2
Company Dr
7000 INPS 46237 2557 A4
Compass Ct
10700 INPS 46256 2014 B3
Composer Wy
1500 INPS 46231 2333 E7
N Compton Ct
9500 INPS 46240 2011 A2
Compton St
5800 INPS 46220 2119 E4
8900 INPS 46240 2010 E3
N Compton St
8300 INPS 46240 2010 E5
9100 INPS 46240 2011 A3
Conaroe St
8800 INPS 46231 2443 A1
Conarroe Rd
7900 INPS 46278 2007 E6
Concert Ln
9100 INPS 46231 2333 E6
Concert Wy
9100 INPS 46231 2333 E6
15800 NbvT 46060 1796 B4
Concho Dr
5300 INPS 46237 2448 B7
5300 INPS 46237 2557 B1
Concord Cir
1500 ZNVL 46077 1898 E6
Concord Ct
10 CRML 46032 1902 B3
500 FSHR 46038 1904 B6
3100 INPS 46222 2336 B2
N Concord Ct
1100 CBLD 46140 2232 E6
Concord Dr
7600 FSHR 46038 1904 B6
N Concord Dr
10 MRVL 46158 2659 E3
S Concord Dr
10 MRVL 46158 2659 D4
Concord Dr E
300 DNVL 46122 2330 B3
Concord Ln
200 CRML 46032 1902 C3
Concord Pl
600 CRML 46032 1902 C3
Concord Rd
1000 PNFD 46168 2440 E5
N Concord St
400 INPS 46222 2336 B1
S Concord St
1500 INPS 46241 2336 B6
2500 INPS 46241 2445 B2
5000 INPS 46217 2445 B7
5500 INPS 46217 2554 B2
Concord Wy
2000 GNWD 46142 2664 E3
Concordia Dr
1300 WshT 46123 2332 C1
Concordia St
100 INPS 46202 2337 D4
Condit Ln
8900 INPS 46256 2013 D4
Conduitt Dr
400 MRVL 46158 2660 B2
Cone Ct
10 GNFD 46140 2345 D3
Coneflower Wy
3600 INPS 46235 2232 C3
Cone Pine Cir
11600 INPS 46235 2232 D4
Conestoga Dr
2800 INPS 46241 2444 D2
W Congress Av
3300 INPS 46222 2227 B4
Congress Ct
7600 GfdT 46158 2550 C6
Congress Dr
7800 GfdT 46158 2550 D6
Congress St
1000 INPS 46208 2228 A4
1100 INPS 46208 2227 E4
Congressional Blvd
100 CRML 46032 1901 D5
Congressional Ct
11600 LWNC 46235 2123 D5
Congressional Ln
5600 LWNC 46235 2123 D5
Congressional Pl
5600 LWNC 46235 2123 D5
Conifer Ct
7700 INPS 46250 2011 E7
9600 FSHR 46038 1904 E7
9700 FSHR 46038 1905 B6
Conifer Wy
- GNWD 46143 2665 B7
- GNWD 46143 2774 B1
Conmack Ct
- MdnT 46113 2661 C1
Connaught Dr
10300 ClyT 46032 2009 B1
10400 ClyT 46032 1900 B7
Connaught East Dr
4400 PNFD 46168 2440 E4
Connaught West Dr
4400 PNFD 46168 2440 E5
Connecticut Av
15800 FCkT 46040 1907 D7
15800 FCkT 46040 2016 C1
Connecticut Cir
300 INPS 46217 2555 B3
Connection Av
- BHGV 46107 2448 A2
- BHGV 46203 2448 A2
- INPS 46107 2448 A2
- INPS 46203 2448 A2
Connemara Rd
1500 INPS 46217 2554 E5
Conner St
10 NBVL 46060 1686 C7
Conner St SR-32
10 NBVL 46060 1686 C7
Conner St SR-38
100 NBVL 46060 1686 C7
E Conner St
1000 NBVL 46060 1686 E7
1900 NBVL 46060 1687 B7
3100 NbvT 46060 1687 B7
3100 WynT 46060 1687 C7
5000 WynT 46060 1796 C1
E Conner St SR-32
1000 NBVL 46060 1686 E7
1900 NBVL 46060 1687 B7
3100 NbvT 46060 1687 B7
3100 WynT 46060 1687 B7
E Conner St SR-38
1000 NBVL 46060 1686 E7
1900 NBVL 46060 1687 B7
3100 NbvT 46060 1687 B7
3100 WynT 46060 1687 B7
W Conner St
500 NBVL 46060 1686 C7
W Conner St SR-32
500 NBVL 46060 1686 C7
W Conner St SR-38
500 NBVL 46060 1686 C7
Conner Creek Dr
500 FSHR 46038 1904 A6
Conner Knoll Pkwy
13100 FSHR 46038 1904 C2
14100 FSHR 46060 1795 C7
Connerwood Ln
8800 DelT 46038 1904 B1
Connie Ct
6100 INPS 46237 2557 C5
Connie Dr
6900 WshT 46123 2223 B7
7700 INPS 46237 2557 C5
Connors Dr
600 GNWD 46143 2665 E4
Conover Ct
4800 INPS 46237 2556 E6
Conrad Av
2100 INPS 46221 2336 D7
Conried Ct
3900 INPS 46235 2231 E2
Conried Dr
9400 INPS 46235 2231 E2
Conseco Ct
200 INPS 46204 2337 B7
Conservation Ct
- DNVL 46122 2330 A3
Conservatory Dr
- INPS 46203 2446 D1
Constellation Dr
2400 INPS 46229 2231 D6
Constitution Dr
3800 ClyT 46032 1899 E7
3800 ClyT 46032 1900 A7
7000 INPS 46256 2012 E7
7000 INPS 46256 2013 A7
W Constitution St
1900 GNFD 46140 2345 A1
Consulate Ct
6400 SDWY 46224 2226 A4
Consulate Ln
2900 SDWY 46224 2226 A5
Continental Ct
4000 INPS 46227 2446 C5
Continental Dr
1400 ZNVL 46077 1898 E7
7600 GfdT 46158 2550 C6
Continental Wy
13500 CRML 46032 1901 D1
Conveyor Dr
10000 INPS 46235 2232 A4
Conway Ct
9200 FSHR 46038 2013 D2
Conway Dr
9800 INPS 46235 2231 E2
Cook Av
200 DNVL 46122 2329 C4
Cook Cir
3900 INPS 46228 2227 C2
Cool Creek Blvd
100 CRML 46032 1902 B1
Cool Creek Cir
10 WTFD 46033 1793 B3
Cool Creek Ct
10 CRML 46033 1902 D2
Cool Creek Dr
1300 CRML 46033 1902 D3
Coolee Cir
11300 CBLD 46229 2341 D2
Coolee Ln
600 CBLD 46229 2341 D2
N Coolidge Av
1600 INPS 46219 2230 E7
Coolidge St
800 INPS 46241 2335 D5
S Coolidge St
3000 INPS 46239 2448 E3
Cool Ridge Dr
400 CRML 46032 1902 A2
Cool Winds Wy
- FSHR 46038 1905 C4
Coombs St
700 LEBN 46052 1676 E7
N Cooney Rd
10700 BrnT 46158 2658 E7
Cooper Ln
3800 INPS 46228 2227 C2
8200 EglT 46077 2007 B1
Cooper Rd
4200 INPS 46228 2227 C1
7900 EglT 46077 2007 B3
7900 INPS 46077 2007 B3
8700 INPS 46278 2007 B4
N Cooper Rd
5600 INPS 46228 2118 B5
Cooper St
- INPS 46218 2229 B7
Cooperland Ct
2800 INPS 46268 2118 C3
Cooper Pointe Cir
2600 INPS 46268 2118 C3
Cooper Pointe Dr
6200 INPS 46268 2118 C3
Coopers Hawk Dr
5700 CRML 46033 1903 B2
Coopersmith Ct
2800 INPS 46268 2118 C3
Cooperstone Ct
6300 INPS 46268 2118 C3
Copeland Av
5500 INPS 46227 2556 A1
Copeland Dr
100 BNBG 46112 2114 B6
W Copeland Dr
300 WshT 46032 1792 A6
Copeland Rd
7000 INPS 46259 2557 E7
7000 INPS 46259 2558 A7
Copeland Lakes Dr
- INPS 46221 2553 A2
Copeland Lakes Ln
6100 INPS 46221 2553 B2
Copeland Mills Ct
6000 INPS 46221 2553 A2
Copeland Mills Dr
5800 INPS 46221 2553 A2
Copeland-Neese Rd
1200 CtrT 46052 1786 C2
8500 UnnT 46077 1789 C3
Copen Ct
4700 INPS 46221 2444 C6
Copenhaver Dr
1900 INPS 46228 2118 D4
Copiah Ct
10800 INPS 46239 2341 C4
Copley Dr
9500 ClyT 46260 2010 B2
9500 INPS 46260 2010 B2
N Copley Dr
9600 ClyT 46032 2010 B2
Copley Pl
500 ClyT 46032 2010 B2
Coppel Ln
8400 INPS 46259 2558 C3
Copper Ct
6300 INPS 46237 2557 A2
6700 WshT 46168 2441 B1
Copper Ln
5100 INPS 46237 2557 A2
Copperfield Cross
500 DNVL 46122 2329 C2
Copperfield Dr
7700 INPS 46256 2013 B7
Copperfield Ln
- DNVL 46122 2329 C2
Copperfield Wy
7500 INPS 46256 2013 B7
Coppergate Dr
- ClyT 46032 1900 E7
- ClyT 46032 2009 E1
Copper Grove Dr
4500 INPS 46237 2448 E5
Copper Hill Dr
2400 INPS 46239 2449 B1
Copperleaf Dr
3400 INPS 46214 2225 D4
Coppermill Cir
5000 INPS 46254 2116 D7
Coppermill Ct
7100 INPS 46254 2116 D6
Copper Mines Wy
- FSHR 46060 1905 E2
Copper Mountain Ct
6800 LWNC 46236 2123 D2
Copper Mountain Dr
11600 LWNC 46236 2123 D2
Copper Oak Ct
- WTLD 46184 2775 A7
Copper Oaks Ct
6200 INPS 46237 2557 C1
Coppertree Ln
5100 WshT 46123 2331 B5
E Copper Tree Wy
2500 WTFD 46033 1793 C5
Copperwood Cir E
1500 CRML 46033 1793 E6
Copperwood Cir W
1500 CRML 46033 1793 E7
Copperwood Dr
- INPS 46217 2554 B5
800 CRML 46033 1793 E7
Copperwood Pl
1500 CRML 46033 1793 E7
Coppock Dr
5800 INPS 46221 2553 B1
Coppock Ln
5800 INPS 46221 2553 B2
Coquina Key Dr
5900 INPS 46224 2335 B3
Coquina Key Ln
300 INPS 46224 2335 B3
Coral Cir
10400 FSHR 46038 2014 D1
Coral Ct
600 CCRO 46034 1577 C2
Coral Bay Ct
8200 LWNC 46236 2015 A5
Coral Bay Dr
- GNWD 46142 2664 C4
Coral Bay Cove
- GNWD 46142 2664 D4
Coralberry Ct
100 MRVL 46158 2660 C3
3400 INPS 46239 2449 C3
Coralberry Ln
8400 INPS 46239 2449 C3
Coral Cove Cir
- NBVL 46062 1685 D4
Coral Reef Ct
8400 INPS 46256 2014 B5
Coral Reef Rd
- MCVL 46055 2015 C4
Coral Reef Wy
10200 INPS 46256 2014 B5
Coral Springs Dr
1000 CCRO 46034 1577 B1
Corbett Dr
11400 LWNC 46235 2123 D6
Corbin Dr
2900 INPS 46217 2554 B4
11800 FSHR 46038 1904 B5
Cord St
2100 SDWY 46224 2226 D6
Corday Ct
7800 FSHR 46038 1904 C3
Cordell St
4000 INPS 46235 2231 E2
Cordes Rd
5000 INPS 46227 2446 D7
Cordia Ct
5000 INPS 46237 2447 D7
Cordova Ct
6600 INPS 46221 2553 A3
Cordova Dr
6500 INPS 46221 2553 A3
Cordwood Ln
3600 INPS 46214 2225 D3
Corey Ct
7800 SPRT 46227 2556 C5
Corey Dr
2700 SPRT 46227 2556 B5
E Corey Dr
3200 INPS 46227 2556 C5
Corey Ln
900 PNFD 46168 2441 E6
Corinth Pl
8300 INPS 46227 2556 C6
Corinthian Dr
7700 INPS 46219 2231 B7
Corinthian Ln
8600 INPS 46236 2015 A4
Cork Ct
4700 WRvT 46142 2663 D4
Cork Pl
10900 LWNC 46236 2014 C7
Cork Rd
- LWNC 46236 2014 C7
Cork Bend Dr
3200 INPS 46239 2449 B3
Cork Bend Ln
7900 INPS 46239 2449 B3
Corktree Dr
8000 INPS 46239 2449 B4
Corkwood Ct
10 BNBG 46112 2223 D2
800 INPS 46227 2555 D6
Corkwood Dr
8200 INPS 46227 2555 D6
Corliss St
3800 INPS 46217 2446 A4
Cornelian Ct
10500 NBVL 46060 1687 B4
Cornelius Av
3800 INPS 46208 2228 B2
5200 INPS 46208 2119 B6
Cornell Av
1600 INPS 46202 2228 E7
6300 INPS 46220 2119 E3
10400 ClyT 46280 2010 E1
10800 ClyT 46280 1901 E7
11000 CRML 46032 1901 E7
11000 CRML 46280 1901 E7
Cornell Ct
10500 ClyT 46280 1901 E7
Cornell Rd
24000 WRvT 46060 1580 A2
Cornell St
9800 ClyT 46280 2010 E2
E Cornerbrook Ct
1800 INPS 46240 2011 A4
Cornerstone Ct
10700 ClyT 46280 1901 D7
W Cornerstone Dr
4300 SCkT 46163 2452 B2
Cornflower Ct
15400 WshT 46074 1792 C5
Corniche Dr
1500 ZNVL 46077 1898 E7
Corning Wy
10300 FSHR 46060 1905 B1
Cornith Wy
- AVON 46123 2333 D3
10200 WshT 46123 2333 D2
Corn Poppy Ct
10600 NBVL 46060 1687 B4
Corn Tassel Row
1100 GNWD 46142 2664 D1
Cornucopia Dr
8900 INPS 46268 2009 C4
Cornwall Cir
6400 INPS 46256 2122 A2
Cornwall Ct
500 CRML 46032 1901 B3
Cornwallis Ln
3800 ClyT 46032 1899 E7
Coronado Ct
8800 INPS 46234 2334 A3
Coronado Dr
3400 INPS 46228 2118 A7
Coronado Rd
10 INPS 46234 2334 A3
Corottoman Ct
300 AVON 46123 2332 E3
300 WshT 46123 2332 E3
Corporate Cir
6800 INPS 46278 2117 B2
Corporate Dr
3500 INPS 46278 2117 B2
Corporate Pkwy
- NBVL 46060 1797 B7
- NBVL 46060 1906 B1
Corporate Wy
6000 INPS 46278 2117 B3
Corporation Dr
8700 INPS 46256 2013 A4
9200 FSHR 46256 2013 A4
Corp Village Dr
2200 INPS 46241 2443 C1
Corral Ct
100 DelT 46038 1903 D7
15000 WshT 46032 1793 A5
15000 WTFD 46032 1792 E6
15000 WTFD 46032 1793 A5
Corralberry Ct
5800 CRML 46033 1903 D1
Corrill Av
200 INPS 46222 2336 B4
Corrill St
800 INPS 46221 2336 B5
Corsair Pl
- NBVL 46060 1687 C4
Corsham Cir
3500 ClyT 46032 1900 B7
Corsican Cir
7600 AVON 46123 2332 D5
E Corsican Cir
2100 WTFD 46074 1793 B1
Cortland Ct
900 GNFD 46140 2237 A7
Corvalis Cres
2800 INPS 46222 2227 A5
Corwin Blvd
- MdnT 46113 2661 D1
Corwyn Rd
3900 INPS 46222 2226 E5
3900 INPS 46222 2227 A5
Cosel Wy
12800 FSHR 46060 1906 C3
Cossell Dr
10 INPS 46224 2335 D3
3100 INPS 46224 2226 D4
Cossell Rd
- SDWY 46224 2335 D2
3400 INPS 46222 2336 A3
4000 INPS 46222 2335 D2
4400 SDWY 46222 2335 D2
Costa Mesa Dr
400 GNWD 46143 2666 A4
Costantino Ln
11800 CBLD 46229 2341 E2
Costino Ln
5800 INPS 46254 2117 B7
Cotherstone Ct
7300 INPS 46256 2122 B1
Cotswold Ln
14300 CRML 46033 1794 C7
Cottage Av
500 INPS 46203 2337 D6
4300 INPS 46203 2338 E6
Cottage Ct
4300 INPS 46203 2338 E6
Cottage Ln
600 GNWD 46143 2665 B5
N Cottage Grove Ct
13800 MdnT 46113 2661 B1
Cottage Grove Ln
- NBVL 46062 1685 B5
Cotton St
4600 LWNC 46226 2122 B7
Cotton Bay Dr N
6300 INPS 46254 2117 A6
Cotton Bay Dr W
5200 INPS 46254 2117 A6
Cotton Blossom Dr
10200 FSHR 46060 1796 B7
Cotton Creek Ct
6400 INPS 46278 2008 A3
Cottongrass Ct
- BNBG 46112 2223 E3
Cottongrass Dr
- BNBG 46112 2223 E3
Cottonwood Cir
1400 NBVL 46062 1685 C2
Cottonwood Ct
1100 CRML 46033 1902 D1
1200 MRVL 46158 2660 C3
1400 GNWD 46143 2665 C6
4000 FKLN 46131 2774 E7
10300 ZNVL 46077 1899 A3
Cottonwood Ct N
8100 GfdT 46168 2550 D4
Cottonwood Ct S
1600 GfdT 46168 2550 D4
Cottonwood Dr
100 CCRO 46034 1577 B2
300 MRVL 46158 2659 D1
800 GfdT 46168 2550 E3
7700 INPS 46227 2556 B5
10300 ZNVL 46077 1899 A3
Cottonwood Ln
200 GNWD 46143 2665 C6
Couden Av
23500 WRvT 46060 1579 A2
Cougar Ct
6500 INPS 46237 2557 D4
Council Dr
700 LEBN 46052 1785 C2
Counselors Row
9100 INPS 46240 2011 D3
Count Fleet Ct
8300 INPS 46217 2554 E6
Countfleet Ct
15100 WshT 46032 1792 D5
Country Cross
1900 INPS 46214 2225 B7
Country Jct
2000 INPS 46214 2225 B7
Country Ln
- WRvT 46142 2663 E4
800 INPS 46217 2555 A7
2400 INPS 46234 2225 B6
3500 LcnT 46112 2224 B3
S Country Ln
1100 SCkT 46140 2343 D3
W Country Ln
1700 CtrT 46140 2344 B1
E Country Tr
2300 BwnT 46140 2346 A6

STREET Block City ZIP Map# Grid

Country Wy
- PNFD 46168 2442 A4
W Country Wy
5900 SCkT 46163 2451 D2
Country Aire Dr
900 GNWD 46143 2665 E3
900 GNWD 46143 2666 A3
Country Aire Ln
100 GNWD 46143 2665 E3
Country Apple Ct
14400 FSHR 46060 1796 B7
Country Breeze Ln
14100 FSHR 46060 1796 B7
Countrybrook Ct
4800 INPS 46254 2117 D4
Country Brook Dr
7300 INPS 46260 2010 C6
7300 INPS 46260 2118 E1
7300 INPS 46260 2119 A1
Countrybrook Ln
4800 INPS 46254 2117 D4
Countrybrook Rd
6000 INPS 46254 2117 D4
Countrybrook Ter
4800 INPS 46254 2117 E4
Countrybrook Wy
4800 INPS 46254 2117 D4
Country Charm
- GNWD 46142 2664 B3
Country Charm Dr
8300 INPS 46234 2225 B7
Country Club Blvd
8300 INPS 46234 2225 B7
Country Club Dr
- GNWD 46143 2665 E4
100 LEBN 46052 1677 A4
100 ULEN 46052 1677 A4
Country Club Ln
3200 INPS 46214 2225 B4
Country Club Pl
8100 INPS 46214 2225 B7
Country Club Rd
10 INPS 46214 2334 B2
10 INPS 46234 2334 B2
1600 INPS 46214 2225 B7
1600 INPS 46234 2225 B7
Country Club Pines Dr
8300 INPS 46234 2225 A5
Country Creek Cir
1200 INPS 46234 2334 B1
Country Creek Ct
1200 INPS 46234 2334 B1
Country Creek Dr
8300 INPS 46234 2334 B1
E Country Estates Dr
2600 INPS 46227 2556 B7
Country Lake Blvd
20100 NBVL 46062 1685 B2
Country Ln Ct
8800 INPS 46217 2555 A7
Country Meadows Dr
8300 INPS 46234 2225 B7
Country Pine Ct
20400 NBVL 46062 1685 B2
Country Place Rd
3900 WshT 46074 1791 A5
Country Pointe Dr
1400 INPS 46234 2334 B1
Country Ridge Dr
8300 INPS 46234 2334 B1
Country Ridge Ln
1200 INPS 46234 2334 B1
Country Road 500 W
4500 NPLN 46163 2452 A3
4500 SCkT 46163 2452 A3
Countryside Blvd
- WTFD 46074 1792 C3
Countryside Ct
1700 INPS 46231 2334 B7
10300 WshT 46123 2333 C3
W Countryside Ct
5900 SCkT 46163 2451 D2
Countryside Dr
500 LEBN 46052 1677 A2
1200 INPS 46231 2334 B6
1300 GNWD 46143 2665 C6
W Countryside Dr
5800 SCkT 46163 2451 D1
Countryside Ln
1300 INPS 46231 2334 B6
Country View Ct
1300 INPS 46234 2334 B1
5600 BrnT 46112 2004 D6
Country View Dr
5700 BrnT 46112 2004 E6
Country View Ln
8300 INPS 46234 2334 B1
Country View Pl
- MdnT 46158 2660 C7
Country Walk Cir
3600 INPS 46227 2556 D7
Country Walk Ct
- BNBG 46112 2223 E1
8800 INPS 46227 2556 C7
Country Walk Dr
500 BNBG 46112 2223 D1
8700 INPS 46227 2556 D7
E Country Walk Dr
3500 INPS 46227 2556 C7
S Country Walk Dr
8900 INPS 46227 2556 D7
Country Wood Ct
700 WynT 46060 1687 E1
Country Wood Dr
- WTLD 46184 2775 A3
10 WTLD 46184 2774 E3
300 WynT 46060 1687 E1
Country Wood Dr W
100 WTLD 46184 2774 E4
Country Wood Ln
- WTLD 46184 2774 E4
Country Woods Ct
8700 INPS 46217 2555 B7
Country Woods Dr
10 INPS 46217 2555 C7

Count Turf Ct
8600 INPS 46217 2554 E7
County Line Rd
- HsnT 46052 2003 C3
- MdlT 46052 2003 C3
10 HsnT 46167 2003 E2
10 MdlT 46167 2003 E2
200 HsnT 46052 2004 C2
200 MdlT 46052 2004 C2
200 MdlT 46167 2004 C2
500 BrnT 46052 2004 C2
500 BrnT 46167 2004 C2
500 PryT 46052 2004 C2
E County Line Rd
- LtyT 46118 2657 E1
- MnrT 46118 2657 E1
10 GNWD 46142 2664 D1
10 GNWD 46227 2664 D1
10 INPS 46143 2665 C1
10 INPS 46227 2664 D1
10 INPS 46227 2665 B1
10 PltT 46143 2665 C1
100 GNWD 46143 2665 C1
200 INPS 46237 2665 C1
300 GNWD 46142 2665 B1
300 INPS 46142 2664 D1
400 INPS 46143 2556 E7
400 INPS 46237 2556 E7
400 LtyT 46118 2658 A1
400 MnrT 46118 2658 A1
400 PltT 46143 2556 E7
500 GNWD 46143 2556 E7
2200 GNWD 46143 2557 C7
2200 INPS 46143 2557 C7
2200 INPS 46237 2557 C7
2200 PltT 46143 2557 C7
2900 GNWD 46227 2665 B1
3200 INPS 46142 2665 C1
5500 GNWD 46237 2557 A7
N County Line Rd
9400 INPS 46236 2015 B4
9400 MCVL 46055 2015 B4
9400 MCVL 46236 2015 B4
9600 INPS 46055 2015 B4
S County Line Rd
6000 MrlT 46259 2559 E2
6900 INPS 46259 2559 E4
W County Line Rd
10 GNWD 46142 2664 A1
10 GNWD 46217 2664 A1
10 INPS 46217 2664 A1
500 WRvT 46142 2664 A1
500 WRvT 46217 2664 A1
1000 INPS 46217 2663 E1
1000 WRvT 46142 2663 E1
1000 WRvT 46217 2663 E1
2600 INPS 46142 2663 C1
7800 INPS 46113 2661 A1
7800 MdnT 46113 2661 A1
8900 INPS 46113 2660 E1
8900 MdnT 46113 2660 E1
County Rd 25 W
6000 PltT 46184 2774 C3
6200 NWTD 46184 2774 C3
County Rd 75 E
2200 GNWD 46143 2665 E7
County Rd 75 W
6600 GNWD 46184 2774 B2
6600 PltT 46184 2774 B3
6900 GNWD 46143 2665 B7
6900 GNWD 46143 2774 B2
County Rd 100 E
2200 GNWD 46143 2666 A7
2200 GNWD 46143 2775 A1
2400 PltT 46184 2775 A1
County Rd 100 S
4000 WrhT 46052 1787 D2
5000 WrhT 46052 1788 A2
6500 WrhT 46075 1788 E2
7000 UnnT 46075 1788 E2
7000 UnnT 46077 1788 E2
7000 WrhT 46077 1788 E2
7500 UnnT 46077 1789 A2
7500 WrhT 46075 1789 A2
7500 WrhT 46077 1789 A2
7700 UnnT 46075 1789 A2
County Rd 125 E
- PltT 46184 2775 A5
- WTLD 46184 2775 A5
County Rd 150 W
- GNWD 46143 2664 E5
S County Rd 200 E
2000 CtrT 46052 1786 D5
3000 PryT 46052 1786 D7
3000 PryT 46052 1895 D3
7000 PryT 46052 2004 D2
7500 BrnT 46052 2004 D2
7500 MdlT 46052 2004 D2
County Rd 200 E
10 GNWD 46143 2666 C3
200 GNWD 46143 2557 C7
200 INPS 46143 2557 C7
200 PltT 46143 2666 C3
3000 CtrT 46052 1677 E1
7100 PltT 46143 2775 C1
7100 PltT 46184 2666 C7
7100 PltT 46184 2775 C3
County Rd 200 S
500 CtrT 46052 1785 B4
County Rd 200 W
- BCkT 46140 2344 B1
- CtrT 46140 2344 B1
County Rd 250 E
- PltT 46143 2666 D7
2900 CtrT 46052 1786 E7
2900 PryT 46052 1786 E7
2900 PryT 46052 1895 E3
County Rd 275 E
6000 PryT 46052 1896 A6
N County Rd 300 E
2500 CtrT 46140 2237 B3
County Rd 300 E
3500 CtrT 46052 1569 B7
4000 PryT 46052 1896 A2

County Rd 300 N
1800 CtrT 46052 1677 D1
County Rd 350 N
3000 CtrT 46052 1569 B7
5000 CtrT 46052 1570 A7
County Rd 400 E
1000 CtrT 46052 1787 C3
1000 WrhT 46052 1787 C3
2000 CtrT 46075 1787 C7
2000 WrhT 46075 1787 C7
3000 PryT 46052 1787 C7
3000 PryT 46052 1896 C1
3000 PryT 46075 1787 C7
3000 PryT 46075 1896 C1
3000 WrhT 46075 1896 C1
County Rd 400 E SR-267
- PryT 46052 1896 C1
- PryT 46075 1896 C1
- WrhT 46075 1896 C1
County Rd 400 N
1600 FknT 46131 2774 A7
1600 PltT 46131 2774 A7
County Rd 450 W
900 WRvT 46143 2663 E6
County Rd 450 Rd W
- WRvT 46143 2664 B6
County Rd 500 E
10 WrhT 46052 1787 E2
County Rd 500 W
4600 SCkT 46163 2452 A4
County Rd 525 E
9500 ClkT 46143 2667 D4
9500 ClkT 46259 2558 C7
9500 ClkT 46259 2667 D1
9500 INPS 46259 2558 C7
County Rd 525 Rd E
- ClkT 46143 2667 D2
- ClkT 46259 2667 D2
County Rd 550 S
- PryT 46052 1895 D4
- PryT 46052 1896 A4
N County Rd 600 W
- SgCT 46126 2670 A4
7500 MrlT 46126 2561 A5
7500 MrlT 46126 2670 A1
9000 MrlT 46130 2561 A5
11000 MrlT 46130 2452 A7
11000 SCkT 46130 2452 A7
County Rd 600 S
- HsnT 46052 1895 B5
- PryT 46052 1895 B5
- PryT 46052 1896 A5
10 HsnT 46052 1894 D5
County Rd 650 E
10 WrhT 46052 1788 C3
10 WrhT 46075 1788 C3
2600 WTWN 46075 1788 D6
County Rd 650 S
2000 PryT 46052 1895 D6
2300 PryT 46052 1896 A6
County Rd 675 E
2700 PryT 46052 1896 A7
E County Rd 700 N
10900 BrnT 46112 2115 E3
10900 INPS 46112 2115 E3
10900 INPS 46234 2115 E3
N County Rd 700 W
8500 MrlT 46126 2560 D6
8600 MrlT 46130 2560 D6
County Rd 700 N
- GNWD 46184 2774 A1
- PltT 46184 2774 A1
10 GNWD 46143 2774 D1
10 GNWD 46143 2775 A1
10 PltT 46143 2774 D1
10 PltT 46184 2775 A1
3200 ClkT 46143 2775 E1
3200 ClkT 46184 2775 E1
County Rd 700 S
3200 PryT 46052 1896 A7
County Rd 750 N
- GNWD 46143 2665 C7
County Rd 750 S
2000 PryT 46052 2004 D1
2000 PryT 46052 2005 C1
4200 PryT 46112 2005 C1
5000 PryT 46112 2006 A1
County Rd 775 N
- ClkT 46143 2667 B6
N County Rd 850 W
8100 MrlT 46126 2560 A7
8100 MrlT 46259 2560 A7
County Rd 850 E
1000 UnnT 46077 1789 C3
County Rd 850 N
- GNWD 46143 2666 A6
- WRvT 46143 2663 E5
- WRvT 46143 2664 A5
S County Rd 900 E
1200 UnnT 46077 1789 D4
County Rd 900 N
7000 ClkT 46143 2668 C4
W County Rd 940 N
9300 MrlT 46126 2560 A5
9300 MrlT 46259 2560 A5
County Rd 975 E
4400 ZNVL 46077 1898 E3
5000 EglT 46077 1898 E3
County Rd 1000 E
10 UnnT 46077 1680 E7
10 UnnT 46077 1681 A5
1000 UnnT 46069 1681 A5
1000 UnnT 46075 1681 A5
2000 MrnT 46069 1681 A1
2000 MrnT 46075 1681 A1
3000 MrnT 46075 1572 A5
6000 MrnT 46069 1572 A2
County Rd 1000 N
4000 ClkT 46143 2667 C2
4300 ClkT 46259 2667 C2
5200 ClkT 46143 2668 A2
5200 ClkT 46259 2668 A2
S County Rd 1050 E
100 AVON 46123 2333 D4

County Rd 1050 N
5200 ClkT 46259 2667 D1
5400 ClkT 46259 2668 A1
Coupler Dr
- FCkT 46040 1907 A6
Courage Cross
12500 FSHR 46060 1906 B2
Courageous Dr
10300 INPS 46236 2014 A6
Course View Ct
- NBVL 46060 1686 B4
Course View Rd
18800 NBVL 46060 1686 B5
Court St
1700 INPS 46222 2336 D3
E Court St
100 INPS 46204 2337 C3
600 INPS 46202 2337 D3
W Court St
- INPS 46204 2337 C3
Court B
- WTFD 46074 1684 A6
Court C
- WTFD 46074 1684 A6
Court D
- WTFD 46074 1684 A6
Court E
- WTFD 46074 1684 A6
Court F
- WTFD 46074 1684 A6
Courtfield Dr
4400 INPS 46254 2226 C1
Court G
- WTFD 46074 1684 A6
Court H
- WTFD 46074 1684 A6
Courthouse Dr
- LWNC 46226 2122 A5
7000 LWNC 46226 2121 E5
Court House Plz
10 GNFD 46140 2345 E1
Courthouse Sq
400 LEBN 46052 1677 B4
Court I
- WTFD 46074 1684 A6
Court J
- WTFD 46074 1684 A6
Courtney Dr
8200 FSHR 46038 1904 C2
Courtney Rd
2100 INPS 46219 2231 B6
Courtyard Cres
- LcnT 46112 2115 E6
Courtyard Wy
11000 FSHR 46038 1904 A6
Cove Ct
10 CCRO 46034 1577 B2
W Cove Ct
7700 INPS 46254 2116 C6
Cove Trc
7900 INPS 46256 2013 C6
Covenant Ct
3900 INPS 46239 2449 E4
Covenant Dr
9500 INPS 46239 2449 E4
Coventry Ct
- LcnT 46112 2115 E5
10 GNFD 46140 2237 A5
10 NPLN 46163 2452 A3
1000 GNWD 46142 2665 A1
Coventry Rd
800 DNVL 46122 2329 C2
8700 INPS 46260 2010 B4
Coventry Wy
100 NBVL 46062 1685 D2
3700 CRML 46033 1902 D4
Covered Bridge Rd
400 GNWD 46142 2664 D2
4800 INPS 46268 2117 D2
Covered Bridge Trc
6600 INPS 46268 2117 D2
Covered Bridge Wy
- NbvT 46060 1686 E4
19300 NBVL 46060 1686 E4
Covey Cir
4500 INPS 46237 2556 E2
Covey Ln N
7900 INPS 46260 2009 D6
Covey Ln W
- INPS 46260 2009 D6
Covington Av
1800 INPS 46227 2556 A5
Covington Blvd
8800 FSHR 46038 2013 D2
Covington St
10 BNBG 46112 2223 B3
Cowan Lake Ct
11000 LWNC 46235 2123 C7
Cowan Lake Dr
5000 LWNC 46235 2123 C7
Cowboys Ct
12000 FCkT 46038 1905 E3
Cowman Dr
600 GNWD 46142 2665 A2
Cowslip Ct
4300 INPS 46203 2448 C5
Cox Av
700 WshT 46069 1683 E1
700 WshT 46069 1684 A2
W Cox Av
300 LEBN 46052 1785 E1
Cox Rd
8500 INPS 46113 2662 A2
8500 INPS 46221 2553 A7
8500 INPS 46221 2662 A2
10200 MdnT 46113 2662 A2
Cox St
- LEBN 46052 1786 A1
100 LEBN 46052 1785 E1
Coyner Av
2200 INPS 46201 2338 A2
2200 INPS 46218 2229 B7
Coyote Ct
9600 NBVL 46060 1686 D4

Coyote Dr
800 INPS 46214 2334 C1
Coyote Ln
6500 INPS 46214 2334 C1
6500 INPS 46214 2335 A1
Coyote Run
10600 FSHR 46038 1905 B3
Coyote Wy
800 INPS 46214 2334 C1
800 INPS 46214 2335 A3
Cozy Dr
5900 MdlT 46167 2112 E6
S Cozy Ln
6400 PryT 46052 1897 B6
CR-300 E
- ClkT 46143 2666 E7
- ClkT 46143 2775 E1
- ClkT 46184 2666 E7
- ClkT 46184 2775 E1
- PltT 46184 2666 E7
- PltT 46184 2775 E1
CR-1050 N
- ClkT 46259 2667 D1
Crabapple Ct
9400 FSHR 46038 1904 E1
Crab Apple Rd
1700 INPS 46239 2341 D5
Crabtree Ct
4000 INPS 46235 2232 C2
Crabtree Ln
4600 LtyT 46168 2440 B5
Cradle River Ct
5300 INPS 46221 2553 C2
Cradle River Dr
6100 INPS 46221 2553 C2
Crafton Ct
1300 MRVL 46158 2660 C3
E Cragmont Dr
10 INPS 46227 2555 C2
4100 INPS 46237 2556 E2
W Cragmont Dr
200 INPS 46217 2555 B2
Cragwood Ct
800 PNFD 46168 2441 D6
Craig Av
12500 WRvT 46060 1579 C5
Craig St
10 PNFD 46168 2441 E5
8000 INPS 46250 2012 D5
W Craig Addition
7000 MrlT 46126 2560 D7
Cranberry Cir
9800 FSHR 46060 1905 A1
Cranberry Dr
300 CtrT 46140 2236 D1
Cranberry St
4700 INPS 46221 2444 C6
Cranbrook Ct
7200 INPS 46250 2120 E1
Cranbrook Dr
3800 INPS 46240 2120 D1
4000 INPS 46250 2120 D1
4600 INPS 46250 2121 A1
Crandall Cir
6500 INPS 46260 2118 D2
Crandon Dr
400 INPS 46234 2333 D2
Crane Ct
7000 INPS 46254 2116 E7
Crane Dr
- PNFD 46231 2333 D6
Crane Ln
5100 CRML 46033 1903 B1
Cranley Cir
5400 INPS 46220 2121 B3
Cranmere St
9200 INPS 46229 2231 D5
Cranston Av
200 CRML 46032 1901 D3
Cranston Dr
7300 INPS 46214 2334 D3
Crawford Dr
500 WTFD 46074 1792 E2
1200 INPS 46220 2119 E5
Crawfordsville Rd
- INPS 46214 2226 C7
- SDWY 46222 2226 D7
5300 SDWY 46224 2226 C7
6300 INPS 46224 2226 C7
6600 INPS 46214 2225 E5
Crawfordsville Rd US-136
- INPS 46214 2226 A5
6200 SDWY 46224 2226 A5
6300 INPS 46224 2226 A6
6600 INPS 46214 2225 D5
W Crawfordsville Rd
8300 INPS 46234 2225 B4
9000 INPS 46234 2224 E3
9200 LcnT 46234 2224 E3
W Crawfordsville Rd US-136
8300 INPS 46234 2225 B4
9000 INPS 46234 2224 E3
9200 LcnT 46234 2224 E3
Cree Cir
10300 LcnT 46234 2224 C3
Cree Tr
100 NbvT 46060 1796 A3
7700 INPS 46250 2011 E7
Creed Ct
8000 INPS 46268 2008 E6
Creek Rd
19600 WynT 46060 1687 E3
20600 WynT 46060 1578 E7
21000 WRvT 46060 1578 E7
Creek Rdg
7800 BrnT 46112 2005 D5
S Creek St
200 GNWD 46143 2665 D4
Creek Wy
4000 INPS 46227 2447 C5
Creek 600 E
9500 EglT 46077 1898 E5
9500 ZNVL 46077 1898 E5

Creekbank Dr
400 INPS 46217 2555 B2
Creek Bay Dr
6500 INPS 46217 2555 A3
Creekbed Ct
- INPS 46256 2122 E1
Creekbed Ln
- INPS 46256 2122 E1
Creekbend Blvd
6000 INPS 46217 2555 B2
Creekbend Cir
6000 INPS 46217 2555 B2
Creekbend Ct
6000 INPS 46217 2555 B2
Creek Bend Dr
- GNWD 46143 2666 A6
5300 CRML 46033 1794 C7
Creekbend Ln
300 INPS 46217 2555 B2
Creekbrook Dr
7200 INPS 46227 2555 E4
7200 INPS 46227 2556 A4
Creek Crossing Dr
6200 INPS 46268 2117 D3
Creek Forest Dr
6500 INPS 46227 2555 D3
Creek Forest Ln
400 INPS 46227 2555 D3
Creek Ridge Dr
- BNBG 46112 2114 B1
- BrnT 46112 2114 B1
6700 INPS 46256 2122 C2
7800 BrnT 46112 2005 D6
Creekridge Ln
13500 FCkT 46055 2015 C1
Creeks Edge
9400 AVON 46123 2333 B3
9400 WshT 46123 2333 B3
Creekshore Dr
3200 INPS 46268 2118 B3
Creekshore Ln
6300 INPS 46268 2118 B3
Creekside Ct
200 WTLD 46184 2774 E4
1600 PNFD 46168 2441 D7
6100 WshT 46123 2332 A3
7600 FSHR 46038 1904 B4
W Creekside Ct
7500 SCkT 46163 2451 A2
Creekside Dr
- BNBG 46112 2223 E2
- BNBG 46112 2224 A2
- LcnT 46112 2223 E2
1700 CRML 46032 1902 B6
7600 FSHR 46038 1904 B4
S Creekside Dr
3700 SCkT 46163 2451 A2
W Creekside Dr
7200 SCkT 46163 2451 A3
Creek Side Ln
11500 CRML 46033 1903 A5
Creekside Ln
10 FSHR 46038 1904 B4
1200 PNFD 46168 2441 D6
1400 GNWD 46142 2664 C1
1700 CRML 46032 1902 B5
6300 INPS 46220 2121 D2
7100 INPS 46250 2121 D1
Creekside Meadow Dr
10800 INPS 46229 2341 C3
Creekside Pass
4300 EglT 46077 1899 D2
Creekside Woods Dr
10500 INPS 46239 2341 B4
Creekstone Ct
200 WTLD 46184 2774 E4
300 INPS 46239 2341 B3
Creekstone Dr
300 INPS 46239 2341 B4
Creekstone Wy
11800 EglT 46077 1899 D3
Creektree Ln
- FCkT 46060 1905 B2
10100 FSHR 46060 1905 B2
Creekview Cir
200 MRVL 46158 2660 B4
7800 INPS 46250 2012 C7
Creek View Ct
100 GNFD 46140 2237 A7
Creekview Ct
400 GNWD 46142 2664 B2
Creek View Dr
200 GNFD 46140 2236 E7
200 GNFD 46140 2237 A7
4200 INPS 46237 2556 E3
Creekview Dr
10400 NBVL 46062 1686 A4
N Creek View Dr
1100 GNFD 46140 2237 A7
W Creekview Dr
2700 BCkT 46140 2235 A6
2800 BCkT 46140 2234 E6
Creekview Ln
6300 FSHR 46038 2012 D1
11500 LWNC 46236 2014 E6
Creekway Ct
200 WTLD 46184 2774 E4
Creekwood Cir
11400 INPS 46239 2341 D6
Creekwood Ct
7200 BrnT 46112 2113 D3
12500 INPS 46236 2015 A4
Creekwood Dr
10 WTFD 46074 1684 A7
100 GNFD 46140 2237 A7
1500 BrnT 46112 2113 D3
1600 BNBG 46112 2113 D3
3800 WRvT 46142 2664 A2
Creekwood Ests
7000 BrnT 46112 2114 B3
Creekwood Ln
8600 INPS 46236 2015 A4
12200 CRML 46032 1901 C4
Creek Wy Dr
8200 AVON 46123 2332 D6

Crenshaw Ct
5200 CRML 46033 1903 C2
Crescent Dr
10 MdnT 46113 2661 B3
1000 GNWD 46143 2665 C6
12600 CRML 46032 1902 A3
Crescent Rd
4600 LcnT 46112 2222 D1
Crescent St
3600 INPS 46208 2228 A3
Crescent Hill Ln
2600 INPS 46228 2227 C1
Crescent Moon Dr
17200 NBVL 46060 1796 D1
Cresco St
6700 INPS 46250 2012 E5
Cresent Ct
11500 INPS 46236 2014 D5
Cresent Oaks Dr
9500 NBVL 46060 1686 E4
Cress Ct
10400 NBVL 46060 1687 B3
Cressida Wy
10300 FSHR 46038 2015 A1
Cressmoor Cir
2600 INPS 46234 2225 B5
Cressmoor Ct
8500 INPS 46234 2225 A5
Crest Ct
1300 PNFD 46168 2441 C7
1600 INPS 46214 2226 A7
Crest Ln
7100 INPS 46256 2122 B1
Crest Rd
300 WRvT 46142 2663 E3
Crest Hill Dr
8000 INPS 46256 2122 B1
Crestline Ct
18600 NBVL 46060 1686 B5
Crestmoor Ln
- FCkT 46040 2015 E1
Creston Dr
3600 INPS 46222 2336 A4
3700 INPS 46222 2335 E4
3700 INPS 46241 2335 E4
3700 INPS 46241 2336 A4
Creston Point Cir
600 INPS 46239 2341 B4
Creston Ridge Ct
500 INPS 46239 2341 B4
Crest Point Dr
3700 WTFD 46062 1793 D2
Crestpoint Ln
300 PNFD 46168 2441 A4
Crestpointe Dr
8700 INPS 46234 2334 A1
Crestridge Ct
10300 FSHR 46038 2013 E1
Crestview Av
4600 INPS 46205 2119 E7
5200 INPS 46220 2119 E6
Crestview Cir
8300 AVON 46123 2332 E3
Crestview Ct
200 FSHR 46038 1904 B6
18900 WshT 46074 1684 C5
Crestview Dr
10 BrnT 46158 2658 C4
10 GNWD 46143 2665 C1
10 MnrT 46158 2658 C4
11400 FSHR 46038 1904 B6
N Crestview Dr
9100 INPS 46240 2011 A3
Crestview Tr
- MCVL 46055 2015 D5
Crestway Dr
7900 LWNC 46236 2014 D6
Crestwell Dr
3000 INPS 46268 2118 B2
Crestwell Ln
6600 INPS 46268 2118 B2
Crestwood Ct
500 WshT 46123 2331 C4
1600 INPS 46239 2341 D6
Crestwood Dr
- GNWD 46143 2666 A5
10 MRVL 46158 2659 E2
10 MRVL 46158 2660 A2
10 NWTD 46184 2774 D5
12100 CRML 46033 1902 D4
Crestwood Ln
2900 WshT 46123 2222 E6
Crews Dr
7500 LWNC 46226 2231 A1
Cricket Cir
1000 CRML 46033 1902 C2
Cricket Rdg
5700 INPS 46250 2012 C3
Cricketknoll Ln
10 CRML 46033 1902 C3
Cricket Reel
1100 GNFD 46140 2237 A6
Cricket Reel Ct
1000 GNFD 46140 2237 A7
Cricket Ridge Pkwy
- WRvT 46143 2663 B6
Cricket Song Ln
- NBVL 46060 1797 A5
Cricket Tree Ln
8600 INPS 46260 2010 A4
Cricklewood Cir
7100 INPS 46250 2121 C1
Cricklewood Ct
12900 CRML 46033 1902 D2
Cricklewood Rd
6500 INPS 46220 2121 C2
N Cricklewood Rd
- INPS 46220 2121 C2
Cricklewood Wy
1400 ZNVL 46077 1898 E7
Crickwood Cir
3600 INPS 46268 2009 A7
3600 INPS 46268 2118 A1
Crickwood Ct
3600 INPS 46268 2118 A1

Indianapolis Street Index

STREET
Block City ZIP Map# Grid

Crickwood Dr
3200 INPS 46268 2009 A7
Crickwood Ln
7400 INPS 46268 2009 A7
Crickwood Pl
7300 INPS 46268 2118 A1
7400 INPS 46268 2009 A7
Crimson Ct E
3000 CRML 46033 1902 B5
Crimson Ct W
3000 CRML 46033 1902 B5
Crimson Ln
- LEBN 46052 1676 C4
Crimson Wy
700 GNWD 46143 2665 A5
Crimson Cir East Dr
6300 INPS 46227 2555 C2
Crimson Cir West Dr
6300 INPS 46227 2555 D2
Crimson King Ct
6700 INPS 46256 2122 A2
Crimson King Pkwy
1000 MRVL 46158 2660 A5
Cripple Creek Ct
1600 INPS 46229 2232 E7
Crisfield Cir
1200 GNWD 46142 2664 D3
Cristin Wy
17800 WTFD 46062 1684 E7
Crittenden Av
4200 INPS 46205 2229 A1
4500 INPS 46205 2120 A7
6600 INPS 46220 2120 A2
7100 INPS 46240 2120 A2
Crockett Dr
11500 INPS 46229 2341 D1
Crocus Ct
3400 WTFD 46062 1684 D6
Croft Ct
1400 INPS 46260 2009 E5
Crofton Pl
15500 WshT 46074 1792 B4
Cromarty Cir
18700 NBVL 46062 1685 E5
Cromer Rd
6300 INPS 46241 2444 A5
Cromwell Cir
10 NbvT 46060 1795 C6
Cromwell Rd
6200 INPS 46250 2121 D1
Crook Dr
8900 INPS 46256 2013 C4
Crook Dr N
8100 INPS 46256 2013 B4
S Crooked Ln
1700 WRvT 46143 2663 E7
W Crooked Ln
4100 WRvT 46143 2663 E7
4100 WRvT 46143 2664 C6
Crooked Creek Dr
5900 INPS 46228 2118 E4
Crooked Creek Rd
24100 JknT 46034 1577 E1
Crooked Creek Overlook St
4000 INPS 46228 2227 C2
Crooked Creek Ridge Dr
4400 INPS 46228 2227 C1
Crooked Stick Ln
10700 ClyT 46032 1900 E7
11100 ClyT 46032 1901 A6
Crooked Stick Tr
5300 WRvT 46142 2663 C3
Crosby Dr
10 INPS 46227 2555 C7
Crosby Rd
2200 BrnT 46158 2659 D7
2400 MRVL 46158 2659 D7
Crosley Ln
1700 SDWY 46224 2226 B7
Cross St
700 WshT 46123 2332 B5
1300 CRML 46033 1902 D3
E Cross St
5900 CtnT 46052 1569 E3
5900 CtnT 46052 1570 A3
N Cross St
10 DNVL 46122 2329 D3
S Cross St
10 DNVL 46122 2329 D4
S Cross St SR-39
10 DNVL 46122 2329 D4
W Cross Tr
6500 SCkT 46163 2451 C1
Crossbend Rd
2800 INPS 46227 2556 B6
Crossbow St
- AdmT 46069 1573 A2
Cross Bridge Cir
5900 PNFD 46168 2550 C1
Crossbridge Ct
800 WshT 46123 2331 E5
5700 PNFD 46168 2550 C1
Crossbridge Dr
6500 NBVL 46062 1685 D4
6500 NbvT 46062 1685 D4
7700 INPS 46226 2231 B2
Crossbridge Rd
700 WshT 46123 2331 D5
Crossbridge Wy
700 PNFD 46168 2550 C1
Cross Country Ct
11900 FSHR 46038 1905 C5
Cross Creek Blvd
5900 INPS 46217 2555 C2
Cross Creek Cir
5700 INPS 46254 2117 D5
Crosscreek Cir
2800 WTFD 46074 1684 C7
Cross Creek Ct
4800 INPS 46254 2117 C4
Cross Creek Dr
5700 INPS 46254 2117 D4
Cross Creek Ln
4800 INPS 46254 2117 D5
Crosscut Ln
5800 NBVL 46062 1685 C5
Crosser Cir
8200 INPS 46237 2557 D6
Crosser Dr
8200 INPS 46237 2557 D6
Crossfield Dr
500 INPS 46239 2341 B5
Crossfield Ln
6100 MCVL 46055 2015 C3
N Crossfield Tr
6200 MCVL 46055 2015 C3
Crossfields Ct
2400 CRML 46032 1900 C5
Crossfields Dr
11600 ClyT 46032 1900 C5
11600 CRML 46032 1900 C5
Crossford Cir
2100 INPS 46234 2224 E6
Crossford Wy
2100 INPS 46234 2224 E6
Crossgate Ln
7600 SPRT 46227 2556 B5
Crossing Blvd
- MCVL 46055 2015 C5
Crossing Ct
2000 GNFD 46140 2236 E4
Crossing Dr
8000 INPS 46227 2556 B6
9200 FSHR 46038 1904 E7
Crossing Ln
2100 GNFD 46140 2236 E4
Crossing Ter
2100 GNFD 46140 2236 E4
Cross Key Ct
5000 INPS 46268 2117 D2
Cross Key Dr
6500 INPS 46268 2117 C2
Cross Key Dr W
6700 INPS 46268 2117 D2
Crossman Dr
1700 INPS 46227 2556 A6
Cross Meadows Dr
5800 LtyT 46118 2549 A2
Crossover Dr
- WTFD 46074 1684 A6
Crosspoint Blvd
9700 FSHR 46256 2013 B2
Crosspoint Commons Blvd
7600 FSHR 46038 2013 A2
7600 FSHR 46256 2013 A2
Crossroads Dr
- PltT 46184 2774 D2
10 GNWD 46184 2774 D2
Cross Willow Blvd
7700 INPS 46239 2340 B6
Cross Willow Ln
1900 INPS 46239 2340 B7
Cross Wind Ct
800 GNWD 46143 2665 E6
Cross Wind Dr
- GNWD 46143 2665 E6
Crosswind Dr
7700 INPS 46241 2443 C1
Crosswinds Ct
6500 WshT 46123 2332 A7
Crosswinds Dr
9900 FSHR 46038 2014 B2
Croton Cir
5800 INPS 46254 2117 B5
Crousore Rd
8100 INPS 46219 2231 B6
Crowley Ct
21400 NBVL 46062 1576 C6
Crown Ct
10600 ClyT 46032 1900 C7
Crown Dr
6500 BNBG 46112 2114 D4
6500 BrnT 46112 2114 D4
Crown Pt
1000 ZNVL 46077 1899 A4
Crown St
4200 INPS 46208 2228 B1
5100 INPS 46208 2119 A6
Crowndale Ct
100 NBVL 46060 1795 E3
Crown Plaza Blvd
1900 PNFD 46168 2441 E4
2000 PNFD 46168 2442 A4
Crown Point Rd
8200 INPS 46278 2007 B7
8200 INPS 46278 2116 B1
Crown Pointe Ct
17700 NBVL 46062 1685 B7
Crown Vetch Pl
5600 INPS 46254 2117 C5
Crown Woods Cir
5500 INPS 46224 2335 D2
Crows Nest
11300 FSHR 46038 1903 E6
Crows Nest Dr
- INPS 46260 2119 B4
5900 INPS 46208 2119 B4
5900 INPS 46228 2119 B4
Cruft St
1400 INPS 46203 2446 E2
1500 INPS 46203 2447 A2
Cruse Rd
5500 EglT 46077 1898 C4
Cruse St
10 INPS 46202 2337 E4
Cruyff Cir
7700 INPS 46214 2225 C7
Crystal Ct
1100 WshT 46123 2332 A6
Crystal Dr
2700 INPS 46222 2227 B5
Crystal Bay Dr
2200 INPS 46260 2118 D2
Crystal Bay Dr E
6900 INPS 46260 2118 D1
Crystal Bay Dr W
- INPS 46260 2118 C1
- INPS 46268 2118 C1
Crystal Bay West Dr
5500 PNFD 46168 2550 C1
Crystal Creek Dr
14300 FCkT 46060 1798 B7
Crystal Falls Ln
11000 FSHR 46038 1904 E6
Crystal Farms Ct
- WshT 46123 2333 C2
Crystal Lake Ct
900 GNWD 46143 2665 A5
Crystal Lake Dr
- INPS 46240 2011 E4
700 GNWD 46143 2665 A5
Crystal Pointe Cir
12400 LWNC 46236 2015 A5
Crystal Pointe Dr
12700 LWNC 46236 2015 A5
Crystal Pointe Ln
8300 LWNC 46236 2015 A5
Crystal Ridge Cir
6400 INPS 46259 2557 E2
Crystal Ridge Ct
7000 INPS 46259 2557 E2
Crystal River Ct
- INPS 46240 2012 A3
Crystal River Dr
- CRML 46240 2012 A3
8800 INPS 46240 2011 E4
8800 INPS 46240 2012 A3
Crystal Springs Dr
6200 WshT 46123 2332 A6
Crystal Trail Wy
4500 INPS 46237 2448 C6
Crystal View Dr
6000 INPS 46237 2448 C6
Crystal Water Dr
5900 INPS 46237 2557 C2
Crystal Woods Cir
600 INPS 46224 2335 B2
Crystal Woods Dr
5600 INPS 46224 2335 B2
Cuchara Ct
- FCkT 46040 1907 A5
Cullen Ct
2300 INPS 46219 2231 B6
Cullen Dr
7700 INPS 46219 2231 B6
Cullerton Wy
12900 FSHR 46038 1906 B3
Culligan Dr
3800 INPS 46218 2229 D7
Culpeper Ct
800 INPS 46227 2555 D6
Culpeper Dr
8200 INPS 46227 2555 D6
Culpepper Dr
9900 ClyT 46032 2009 E1
Cultured Stone Dr
12200 FSHR 46038 1906 A4
Culver Ln
5300 PNFD 46168 2440 D4
5300 WRvT 46142 2663 C4
Culver St
5300 INPS 46226 2230 B2
Cumberland Rd
7600 NBVL 46060 1687 A7
9600 FCkT 46038 2014 A2
9600 FSHR 46038 2014 A2
10600 FCkT 46038 1905 A6
10600 FSHR 46038 1905 A2
13100 FCkT 46060 1905 A2
13100 FSHR 46060 1905 A2
13900 FSHR 46038 1796 A5
13900 FSHR 46060 1796 A5
14100 FCkT 46060 1796 A5
15600 NbvT 46060 1796 A5
17100 NBVL 46060 1796 A1
18400 NbvT 46060 1687 A7
20600 JknT 46034 1578 A5
20600 JknT 46062 1578 A5
20600 NbvT 46062 1578 A5
20600 NbvT 46062 1687 A3
20600 WRvT 46034 1578 A5
20600 WRvT 46062 1578 A5
N Cumberland Rd
1000 INPS 46229 2341 D1
1400 INPS 46229 2232 D7
Cumberland St
- LtyT 46118 2548 B1
Cumberland St US-40
- LtyT 46118 2548 B1
Cumberland Wy
1400 INPS 46229 2341 D1
1500 INPS 46229 2232 D7
Cumberland Gap Dr
11400 INPS 46229 2341 D1
Cumberland Park Dr
10500 FSHR 46038 2013 E1
10500 FSHR 46038 2014 A1
Cumberland Pointe Blvd
- NBVL 46060 1796 A4
Cumberland Ridge Ct
10400 FCkT 46038 2014 A1
Cumberland Ridge Ln
9800 FCkT 46038 2014 A1
Cunion Ct
21200 NBVL 46062 1576 D7
Cunningham Rd
1600 SDWY 46224 2226 B6
Cuppola Dr
14200 NBVL 46060 1797 A7
Curlew Ln
- GNWD 46143 2665 E6
- GNWD 46143 2666 A6
Currant Dr
500 NBVL 46062 1685 E4
Currier St
- CRML 46032 1900 D3
Curry Ct
10400 INPS 46229 2232 B6
Curry Dr
2200 INPS 46229 2232 B6
Curry Ln
2900 WTFD 46033 1793 C6
Curry Rd
- GNWD 46143 2664 C5
- WRvT 46143 2664 C5
N Curry Rd
2700 INPS 46229 2232 C5
W Curry Rd
1300 GNWD 46143 2664 D6
1300 WRvT 46143 2664 D6
Custer Ct
1300 INPS 46217 2554 E7
Cutler Ln
- GNWD 46143 2665 B5
W Cutsinger Rd
600 GNWD 46143 2664 E7
600 PltT 46143 2664 E7
600 PltT 46143 2665 A7
Cutter Corner Pl
5400 INPS 46237 2448 E7
Cutter Corner Wy
5400 INPS 46237 2448 E7
Cyclamen Chase
10 WshT 46074 1792 D4
Cycling Ln
2000 INPS 46260 2118 D2
Cyntheanne Rd
9600 FCkT 46040 2016 C2
9600 VrnT 46040 2016 C2
12100 FCkT 46040 1907 C4
12100 FCkT 46060 1907 C4
13600 FCkT 46060 1798 C6
13600 WynT 46060 1798 C6
17600 WynT 46060 1689 C7
20600 WynT 46060 1580 C5
21600 WRvT 46060 1580 C5
Cynthia Ct
10 WshT 46032 1792 E5
Cynthia Dr
7500 INPS 46227 2555 C5
Cynthia Ln
500 WTLD 46184 2774 D7
Cypress N
800 GNWD 46143 2665 A5
Cypress S
700 GNWD 46143 2665 A5
Cypress W
800 GNWD 46143 2665 A5
Cypress Av
- INPS 46239 2449 A3
Cypress Dr
1200 GNFD 46140 2237 B6
13800 FSHR 46060 1905 A1
Cypress Wy
9600 ClyT 46032 2009 C2
Cypress Hill Passing
- WshT 46123 2332 E1
Cyprian Cir
16400 WTFD 46074 1793 C2

D

D St
- BHGV 46107 2447 D3
Dabny Cir
4400 INPS 46254 2226 B1
Dabny Ct
5900 INPS 46254 2226 B1
Dabny Dr
4200 INPS 46254 2226 B1
Dado Ct
- NBVL 46062 1685 C5
Dado Dr
5900 NBVL 46062 1685 C5
Daffodil Ct
12400 LWNC 46236 2124 A2
Daffon Dr
200 INPS 46227 2555 C6
Dahl Gren Ln
- CCRO 46034 1577 C4
Dahlgren Ln
8400 INPS 46227 2556 C6
Dahlia Ct
4200 INPS 46220 2120 E5
Dahlia Dr
6300 INPS 46217 2555 B2
Dahlia Ln
10 INPS 46217 2555 B2
Dahoma Dr
3800 INPS 46237 2447 D7
Daisy Ln
6800 INPS 46214 2334 E3
S Daisy Ln
1000 SCkT 46163 2343 A4
Daisy Hill Ct
- MdnT 46113 2661 B1
N Dake Dr
10700 MdnT 46158 2660 E7
Dake Lake Dr
10 MdnT 46158 2660 D6
Dakota Dr
1900 NBVL 46062 1686 A3
N Dakota St
4500 INPS 46254 2117 C7
4500 INPS 46254 2226 C1
S Dakota St
1000 INPS 46225 2337 B5
2200 INPS 46225 2446 B1
Dale Ct
10 WRvT 46142 2663 E3
10 WRvT 46142 2664 A4
2100 LEBN 46052 1677 B3
Dale Dr
100 CBLD 46229 2341 D2
1600 PNFD 46168 2550 D1
Dale Run
- GNWD 46143 2665 C7
Dalegard St
6900 INPS 46241 2334 D4
Dale Hollow Dr
1600 CBLD 46229 2341 D1
1000 INPS 46229 2341 D1
Dale Schrier Dr
6800 BNBG 46112 2114 E5
Dallas Ct
13500 CRML 46033 1902 E1
Dallas Dr
1100 PNFD 46168 2441 D6
13500 CRML 46033 1902 E2
Dallas Ln
13400 CRML 46033 1902 E2
Dalton Ct
17400 NBVL 46062 1795 B1
Dalton St
6700 INPS 46250 2012 E6
Daly St
900 INPS 46202 2337 E4
Dan Dr
500 NBVL 46062 1795 B1
Dana Ct
- WshT 46123 2331 C4
8700 INPS 46234 2225 A7
Danaher St
1500 INPS 46217 2554 E5
Danborn Dr
- WTFD 46074 1792 D3
Danbury Ct
10 ZNVL 46077 1898 E5
Danbury Dr
600 ZNVL 46077 1898 E5
1800 INPS 46231 2334 B7
2100 INPS 46231 2443 B1
14500 CRML 46033 1793 B6
Danbury Rd
3000 INPS 46222 2227 A4
Dancer Dr
4700 INPS 46237 2448 C6
Dancy Ct
2100 INPS 46239 2340 B7
Dancy Dr
7600 INPS 46239 2340 A7
Dandborn Grn
16100 WTFD 46074 1792 D3
Dandelion Av
3500 BHGV 46203 2448 B4
Dandy Ct
7700 INPS 46254 2116 C6
Dandy Tr
3100 INPS 46234 2225 C4
3500 INPS 46214 2225 C3
3800 INPS 46254 2225 C2
4600 INPS 46254 2116 C6
6200 INPS 46278 2116 B3
Dandy Creek Dr
8800 INPS 46234 2116 A6
Daneby Cir
6900 INPS 46220 2121 D2
Danford Sq
2200 INPS 46260 2118 D2
Danforth St
300 CRML 46032 1902 A3
Dangerfield Dr
300 BHGV 46107 2447 E6
300 BHGV 46107 2448 A6
Daniel Cir
10 BNBG 46112 2223 C2
Daniel Ct
600 WTFD 46074 1792 E2
Daniel Dr
1600 GNWD 46143 2665 C7
5200 INPS 46226 2121 C6
Daniel St
10 BrnT 46158 2660 A6
Danielle Dr
800 LEBN 46052 1676 C5
S Danita Ct
4100 NPLN 46163 2452 A2
N Dan Jones Rd
- AVON 46123 2332 D3
100 PNFD 46168 2441 D4
Danny Dr
400 ZNVL 46077 1899 B3
Dan Patch Ct
6100 INPS 46237 2557 C2
15200 WshT 46032 1792 D5
Dan Patch Dr
5800 INPS 46237 2557 C2
Dan Patch Ln
1800 WTFD 46074 1684 B3
Danridge Dr
10 DNVL 46122 2329 E3
10 DNVL 46122 2330 A4
Dansk Ridge Ct
9100 INPS 46250 2012 B3
Danube Dr
7700 INPS 46239 2449 B3
Danube Wy
3000 INPS 46239 2449 A3
Danver Ln
500 INPS 46107 2447 E4
Daphne Dr
5700 INPS 46278 2117 B2
Dapple Ct
10 ZNVL 46077 1899 A7
5600 INPS 46228 2118 A5
Dapple Trc
5600 INPS 46228 2118 A5
Darby Cir
5800 NBVL 46062 1576 C7
Darby Ct
8300 INPS 46260 2010 A5
Darby Ln
10 BNBG 46112 2114 B5
1000 INPS 46260 2010 A5
Darby Dale Ct
- FSHR 46060 1905 E1
Darby Dan Dr
5500 INPS 46237 2557 B6
Darcy Ct
5800 INPS 46250 2121 C1
Dardeb Rd
6300 INPS 46241 2444 A5
Darien Ct
7800 INPS 46226 2231 B2
Dark Oak Ln
7100 INPS 46237 2556 D4
Dark Star Dr
- WshT 46234 2224 D6
8000 INPS 46217 2554 E6
Darkwood Dr
8700 INPS 46234 2334 A1
Darlington Dr
800 WshT 46123 2333 A2
Darnley Ct
8100 INPS 46260 2010 B5
Darrow Dr
300 INPS 46260 2119 B2
Darryl Ter
- LEBN 46052 1785 E1
Darsley Dr
11700 FCkT 46038 1906 B5
11700 FSHR 46038 1906 B5
Dartmoor Ct
6000 INPS 46254 2226 A1
Dartmoor Dr
- WRvT 46143 2663 E6
4000 WRvT 46143 2664 A6
4300 INPS 46254 2226 A1
Dartmouth Ct
7900 INPS 46260 2010 A6
Dartmouth Rd
7900 INPS 46260 2010 A6
Dartown Rd
17500 WTFD 46074 1683 D7
17500 WTFD 46074 1792 D1
17700 WshT 46074 1683 D7
Dartsmouth St
300 CRML 46032 1902 A5
Darwin St
1900 INPS 46218 2229 A6
Date St
10 GNFD 46140 2346 A1
Daugherty Dr
- INPS 46217 2554 A3
5200 EglT 46077 1899 D4
Daum Ct
3000 CRML 46033 1902 C5
David Ct
6800 INPS 46226 2230 E1
7900 BrnT 46112 2114 D2
8000 AVON 46123 2332 D6
David Dr
400 WRvT 46142 2663 C3
2500 WshT 46074 1684 C5
N David Dr
800 MdnT 46113 2661 C5
David Ln
10 INPS 46227 2555 C7
David Pl
10 CRML 46032 1902 C2
David St
4200 INPS 46226 2230 E1
4600 INPS 46226 2121 E7
4600 LWNC 46226 2121 E7
David Brown Dr
10 WTFD 46074 1793 A2
David Lind Dr
10 INPS 46217 2446 B6
N Davidson St
600 INPS 46202 2337 E2
S Davidson St
10 INPS 46202 2337 D4
Daviess Dr
- WTFD 46074 1792 E2
Da Vinci Dr
2900 CRML 46074 1791 B7
Davis Ct
100 WshT 46123 2331 C3
600 WshT 46123 2333 D2
Davis Dr
- WTLD 46184 2775 A7
10 GNWD 46143 2665 C7
3300 INPS 46221 2445 A4
S Davis Dr
3000 INPS 46221 2445 A3
Davis Ln
7500 LWNC 46236 2014 D7
E Davis Rd
200 GNFD 46140 2345 E3
300 CtrT 46140 2346 A3
300 GNFD 46140 2346 A3
S Davis Rd
2100 INPS 46239 2341 A7
2200 INPS 46239 2450 A1
W Davis Rd
- CtrT 46140 2345 C3
- GNFD 46140 2345 C3
Davis St
4800 INPS 46203 2339 A5
Davis Wy
10800 FSHR 46038 1904 B7
Dawn Dr
4800 INPS 46268 2117 D2
9300 LcnT 46112 2224 B4
Dawnlake Dr
2600 INPS 46217 2554 C4
Dawn Ridge Dr
2400 CRML 46074 1900 C1
Dawnwood Ct
7600 INPS 46227 2556 D5
Dawnwood Dr
- CRML 46033 1903 B5
3500 INPS 46227 2556 C5
Dawson Dr
7800 FSHR 46038 1904 B4
Dawson St
800 INPS 46203 2338 A5
2300 INPS 46203 2447 A1
3000 INPS 46237 2447 A3
Dawsondale Ct
6200 INPS 46227 2556 C2
Dawson Lake Dr
6300 INPS 46220 2119 D1
6300 INPS 46220 2120 A2
Day Dr
9600 ClyT 46280 2011 C2
Daybreak Cir
7500 FSHR 46038 1904 A6
Day Break Dr
- GNWD 46143 2665 B7
Dayflower Ct
7600 NBVL 46062 1686 A4
Dayflower Wy
3600 INPS 46235 2232 C3
Daylight Ct
3500 INPS 46227 2556 C5
Daylight Dr
10800 GfdT 46113 2551 E7
10900 INPS 46113 2551 E7
Daylily Ct
2500 WTFD 46074 1793 C2
Day Lily Dr
7800 INPS 46237 2557 D5
Dayspring Ct
20200 NbvT 46062 1685 A2
Dayspring Dr
- GNWD 46143 2774 D1
Daystar Dr
- WshT 46234 2224 D6
Dayton Av
1500 INPS 46203 2338 E6
S Dayton Av
500 INPS 46203 2338 E5
Dayton Ct
4700 INPS 46203 2338 E7
Dayton Dr
600 CRML 46033 1902 D1
Deacon St
500 CRML 46032 1902 A4
Dead End Rd
- CtrT 46052 1676 C5
- LEBN 46052 1676 C5
Dean Rd
6200 INPS 46220 2120 E3
7100 INPS 46240 2120 E1
7100 INPS 46250 2120 E1
7900 INPS 46240 2011 E6
7900 INPS 46250 2011 E6
Dean St
10 CCRO 46034 1577 D3
4600 INPS 46226 2121 E7
5200 LWNC 46226 2121 E6
W Dean St
- CCRO 46034 1577 C3
Deandra Dr
- EglT 46077 1899 D7
- ZNVL 46077 1899 D7
Dean Grove Wy
7600 INPS 46240 2011 D7
Deanna Dr
11600 CBLD 46229 2341 D2
Deanne Elaine Ct
8600 INPS 46234 2225 A7
Dean Phillips Dr
- INPS 46225 2337 B7
Dearborn Av
7100 INPS 46240 2120 C1
Dearborn Cir
13800 FSHR 46060 1905 B1
Dearborn Dr
- WTFD 46074 1792 D1
N Dearborn St
10 INPS 46201 2338 C3
1400 INPS 46201 2229 C7
3600 INPS 46218 2229 C3
4500 INPS 46205 2229 C1
4800 INPS 46205 2120 C7
5900 INPS 46220 2120 C4
S Dearborn St
10 INPS 46201 2338 C3
3700 INPS 46237 2447 C4
5000 INPS 46227 2447 C7
Deauville Dr
4300 INPS 46205 2229 C1
Debbie Ct
10 WTFD 46074 1684 B7
Debello Ct
2100 INPS 46214 2225 B6
Debonair Ln
6300 SDWY 46224 2226 A5
Debonair Ter
2500 SDWY 46224 2226 A5
Deborah Ct
2700 BrnT 46112 2114 C1
Deborah Ln
200 WTLD 46184 2774 D7
W Deborah St
4000 INPS 46222 2226 E4
5000 INPS 46224 2226 D3
Debra Ct
6000 PNFD 46168 2550 C2
Debra Ln
500 INPS 46217 2555 A2
Decamp Dr
3500 INPS 46226 2231 C3
Decatur Blvd
4700 INPS 46241 2443 D7
S Decatur Blvd
4900 INPS 46241 2443 D7
5200 INPS 46241 2552 C1
Decatur Coms
6300 INPS 46221 2553 A1
6600 INPS 46221 2552 E1
Decatur Dr
600 WTFD 46074 1792 E1
9600 FCkT 46256 2014 C2
Decatur Ridge Dr
5500 INPS 46221 2552 E2
Decatur Ridge Pl
6800 INPS 46221 2552 E1
Deck Creek Pl
- FSHR 46060 1906 C2
Declaration Dr
- GNWD 46143 2774 D1
4300 INPS 46227 2446 C5
15200 WshT 46074 1792 A5
W Declaration Dr
1900 GNFD 46140 2345 B1
Dedham Dr
10000 INPS 46229 2232 A5
Deep Run Ct
6500 INPS 46268 2117 E2
Deepwood Tr
10500 ClyT 46032 2009 B1
Deer
- MCVL 46055 2015 C5
N Deer Ln
1200 BCkT 46140 2234 E6
Deer Rdg
3800 INPS 46254 2225 D2

STREET
Block City ZIP Map# Grid

Deer Run
2600 UnnT 46077 1790 A6
Deer Wy
7600 LWNC 46236 2015 A7
Deerberry Ct
200 NBVL 46062 1685 C2
Deerberry Dr
500 NBVL 46062 1685 C2
Deerbrook Ct
6900 INPS 46214 2225 E4
Deerbrook Dr
100 FSHR 46038 2012 D1
Deerchase Apartments
- NBVL 46060 1796 E6
- NBVL 46060 1797 A6
Deer Creek Av
5300 INPS 46254 2117 D6
Deer Creek Ct
5100 INPS 46254 2117 C5
Deer Creek Dr
5200 INPS 46254 2117 D6
Deer Creek Pl
5000 INPS 46254 2117 D5
Deer Cross Pl
- WRvT 46143 2663 A7
Deerfield Cir
9700 ClyT 46032 2009 E2
Deerfield Dr
1500 PNFD 46168 2550 D2
7200 BCkT 46140 2233 A3
7600 BCkT 46140 2232 E3
Deerfield Ln
9800 FCkT 46055 2015 C2
Deerfield Mall
9600 ClyT 46032 2009 E2
Deer Hollow Ct
5900 LcnT 46167 2113 C6
Deerhurst Wy
- INPS 46237 2557 B2
Deering St
9800 FSHR 46038 1905 A7
Deer Lake Dr
900 CRML 46032 1901 A1
Deer Pass
1800 WRvT 46143 2663 E7
Deer Path Dr
7000 INPS 46254 2225 E2
Deer Ridge Cross
4900 CRML 46033 1903 A1
Deer Ridge Ct
5000 CRML 46033 1794 B7
Deer Ridge Dr
9300 EglT 46077 1898 D6
Deer Ridge Dr N
4800 CRML 46033 1903 A1
4900 CRML 46033 1794 A7
Deer Ridge Dr S
4800 CRML 46033 1903 A1
Deer Ridge Pl
13600 CRML 46033 1903 A1
Deer Ridge Rd
20400 WynT 46060 1687 E1
Deer Run Cir
10000 FSHR 46038 2014 A2
Deer Run Ct
8800 INPS 46256 2013 D4
Deer Run Dr
8700 INPS 46256 2013 D4
W Deer Run Dr
6000 SCkT 46163 2451 D1
Deer Run Pth
6200 PNFD 46168 2550 D2
Deerstand Rd
6200 WRvT 46143 2663 A7
Deer Stone Ln
14000 FCkT 46038 1906 D6
Deerstyne Green St
- CRML 46032 1900 D2
Deer Trace Ct
200 PTBR 46167 2113 A3
Deer Trail Dr
500 INPS 46217 2555 A5
14900 NBVL 46060 1797 A6
Deer Valley Dr
11000 INPS 46229 2341 C3
Deerview Bnd
- MCVL 46055 2015 D5
Deerview Ct
4400 INPS 46268 2008 E6
Deerview Dr
8000 INPS 46268 2008 E6
12300 NBVL 46060 1797 A6
Deerwalk Ct
1800 WshT 46123 2332 B7
1800 WshT 46123 2441 B1
Deer Walk Dr
5200 LWNC 46235 2123 A6
Deerwalk Dr
11800 WRvT 46034 1578 E1
Deer Walk Trc
400 WTFD 46074 1684 B6
Deerwood Ct
5900 INPS 46254 2117 D4
Deerwood Dr
14600 WTFD 46033 1793 D6
Deerwood Pkwy
2200 WRvT 46143 2663 A7
DeKalb Dr
400 WTFD 46074 1792 D2
Dekoven Dr
- FSHR 46038 1906 B3
Delaine Ct
7600 INPS 46254 2116 C6
Delaney Dr
1700 INPS 46217 2554 D5
8800 FSHR 46060 1795 D7
Delaware Pkwy
- FSHR 46038 1904 E7
- FSHR 46038 2013 C1
N Delaware St
10 INPS 46204 2337 C3
800 INPS 46202 2337 C2
1600 INPS 46202 2228 D7
4400 INPS 46205 2228 D1
5100 INPS 46205 2119 D7

STREET
Block City ZIP Map# Grid

N Delaware St
6800 INPS 46220 2119 D2
9100 INPS 46240 2010 D3
9500 CRML 46240 2010 D3
10200 ClyT 46280 2010 D1
10300 ClyT 46280 1901 B7
S Delaware St
10 INPS 46204 2337 C4
2000 INPS 46225 2337 C7
2400 INPS 46225 2446 C1
3400 INPS 46227 2446 C3
7100 INPS 46227 2555 C4
Delaware Commons North Dr
3500 INPS 46220 2120 D2
Delaware Commons South Dr
3500 INPS 46220 2120 D2
Delaway Ln
3100 INPS 46217 2554 B4
Delbrick Ln
10 INPS 46229 2340 E2
Delbrook Cir
1400 INPS 46260 2009 E6
Delbrook Ct
1400 INPS 46260 2009 E6
Delbrook Dr
500 NWTD 46184 2774 D3
7700 INPS 46260 2009 E6
Deldin Ct
10 SCkT 46140 2342 C2
Delegates Row
9100 INPS 46240 2011 D3
9500 CRML 46240 2011 D3
N Delegates Wy
5900 BCkT 46055 2124 B3
Delight Creek Rd
11100 FSHR 46038 1903 E6
Della Ct
3900 INPS 46235 2232 A2
N Della St
4000 INPS 46235 2232 A2
Dellfield Blvd E
- CRML 46033 1903 C4
Dellfield Blvd W
- CRML 46033 1903 B4
Dellinger Dr
12900 FSHR 46038 1905 A3
Dellingham Dr
500 INPS 46260 2010 B7
Dellwood Dr
5200 LWNC 46235 2123 A6
Dellzell Dr
2400 INPS 46220 2120 B5
Delmar Av
3400 INPS 46241 2336 A5
5900 INPS 46241 2335 B5
Del Mar Ct
4600 WRvT 46142 2663 D4
Delmar Ct
5800 INPS 46241 2335 B5
Delmar Rd
3500 INPS 46205 2120 D6
3500 INPS 46220 2120 C6
Delmastro Ln
3500 INPS 46268 2118 A3
Delmont Ct
9900 INPS 46235 2232 A2
Delmont Dr
3800 INPS 46235 2232 A2
Delong Rd
5900 INPS 46254 2116 C4
6200 INPS 46278 2116 C3
Delores Dr
2800 INPS 46222 2226 D5
Deloss St
1100 INPS 46202 2337 E4
1100 INPS 46203 2337 E4
1300 INPS 46201 2337 E4
3700 INPS 46201 2338 D4
Delphi Ct
9200 INPS 46113 2551 E7
10300 FSHR 46060 1905 B1
Delphi Dr
- GfdT 46113 2551 E7
- INPS 46113 2551 E7
Del Prado Ct
8400 INPS 46227 2556 B7
Del Prado Dr
2700 INPS 46227 2556 B6
Delray Ct
4400 WTFD 46062 1684 E7
Delray Dr
600 INPS 46241 2334 E5
Del Rio Dr
- MCVL 46055 2124 B1
Delta Dr
5000 INPS 46241 2444 D3
Delwood Dr
1000 MRVL 46158 2659 E1
1000 MRVL 46158 2660 A1
Demaree Rd
- GNWD 46143 2664 D7
1100 WRvT 46143 2664 D7
Demarest Dr
100 INPS 46214 2334 D3
Deme Dr
10600 LWNC 46236 2123 B5
Deming Rd
22800 JknT 46034 1575 E3
Democracy Dr
5800 INPS 46254 2117 C5
Dena Dr
100 WTFD 46074 1793 A2
Deneen Dr
9600 NbvT 46060 1687 A5
Denise Dr
6000 INPS 46221 2553 A4
Denison St
800 INPS 46241 2335 D5
2600 INPS 46241 2444 D3
Denniston St
3000 INPS 46241 2444 D3
Denniston Ter
4400 INPS 46241 2444 D3

STREET
Block City ZIP Map# Grid

Denny Dr
500 MRVL 46158 2659 D2
N Denny St
1000 INPS 46201 2338 D1
1500 INPS 46201 2229 D7
2600 INPS 46218 2229 D5
S Denny St
10 INPS 46201 2338 D3
1700 INPS 46203 2338 D7
4700 INPS 46237 2447 D6
Denton Cir
7400 INPS 46256 2122 D1
Denton Ct
- MCVL 46055 2124 B2
Denton Dr
- MCVL 46055 2124 B2
Denver Ct
4500 INPS 46241 2443 E6
Denver Dr
1400 PNFD 46168 2441 D5
6400 INPS 46241 2444 A6
6500 INPS 46241 2443 E6
Denwood Dr
3800 INPS 46226 2229 D2
Departure Blvd W
- MdnT 46113 2661 A2
De Pauw Blvd
3500 INPS 46268 2009 A3
DePauw Rd
2400 INPS 46227 2447 B6
Depot Cir
400 WshT 46123 2331 D5
Depot Dr
8500 INPS 46217 2555 A7
8800 INPS 46217 2554 E7
8800 INPS 46217 2663 E1
8800 WRvT 46217 2663 E1
Depot St
- INPS 46221 2444 A7
- MCVL 46055 2015 C7
200 GNFD 46140 2345 D1
4900 INPS 46241 2444 A7
E Depot St
- PNFD 46168 2441 B4
N Depot St
10 NPLN 46163 2452 B3
10 SCkT 46163 2452 B3
S Depot St
10 NPLN 46163 2452 A4
W Depot St
- PNFD 46168 2441 B4
Dequincy Av
- INPS 46226 2230 A2
De Quincy St
2900 INPS 46218 2229 E5
Dequincy St
3100 INPS 46218 2230 A4
N Dequincy St
500 INPS 46201 2339 A2
1600 INPS 46218 2230 A7
2200 INPS 46218 2229 E6
3900 INPS 46226 2230 A3
5400 INPS 46220 2121 A5
S De Quincy St
1100 INPS 46203 2339 A6
S Dequincy St
200 INPS 46201 2339 A4
700 INPS 46203 2339 A5
Derby Ct
8600 INPS 46256 2013 B4
15100 WshT 46032 1792 C5
Derby Ln
4900 INPS 46226 2120 E7
Derbyshire Ct
13100 CRML 46033 1903 A2
Derbyshire Dr
100 CBLD 46229 2342 A2
1400 WRvT 46143 2664 B6
Derbyshire Rd
6000 INPS 46227 2556 B2
6800 SPRT 46227 2556 B3
Derek Dr
2400 CRML 46032 1900 C3
Derrek Pl
7600 INPS 46219 2231 A7
Derry Ln
- CRML 46032 1900 E1
Derstan Rd
7100 INPS 46250 2121 C1
Derwyn Ct
6400 INPS 46256 2122 A3
Desert Glen Dr
11300 FSHR 46038 1906 A6
Desert Wind Ct
800 CRML 46032 1901 E1
Deshane Av
17100 WynT 46060 1687 E7
17100 WynT 46060 1688 A7
17100 WynT 46060 1796 E1
Desma Av
- INPS 46203 2339 C7
- INPS 46203 2448 C1
Desmond Av
4000 INPS 46226 2230 E2
De Soto Ct
1300 INPS 46217 2554 E7
De Soto Ln
1600 SDWY 46224 2226 B7
Desplaines Dr
12700 FSHR 46038 1906 B3
Destry Pl
7900 FSHR 46038 1904 C4
Detroit St
100 INPS 46201 2338 A4
2100 BHGV 46107 2447 C2
Dett St
4000 INPS 46217 2446 A5
Deva Cir
1900 INPS 46228 2118 D6
Devaney Rd
23600 JknT 46034 1576 C2
Developers Rd
3400 INPS 46227 2447 B4
Devereaux Dr
3200 INPS 46228 2227 B1

STREET
Block City ZIP Map# Grid

Devers Dr
5700 LWNC 46216 2122 E5
Devers Pl
9500 LWNC 46216 2122 E5
Devers Wy
9500 LWNC 46216 2122 E5
Deville Ct
7400 INPS 46256 2013 A7
7400 INPS 46256 2122 A1
Deville Pl
300 NWTD 46184 2774 D4
Devin Dr
- BNBG 46112 2223 C2
Devington Cir
5800 INPS 46226 2121 C7
Devington Rd
5900 INPS 46226 2121 C7
Devinney Dr
6500 INPS 46221 2553 B3
Devinney Ln
6700 INPS 46221 2553 B3
E Devon Av
8200 INPS 46239 2449 B5
N Devon Av
10 INPS 46219 2340 C2
2500 INPS 46219 2231 B5
Devon Ct
4500 INPS 46226 2229 E1
11000 FSHR 46038 1903 E7
Devon Dr
4500 INPS 46226 2229 E1
5100 INPS 46226 2230 A1
Devon Ln
12600 CRML 46032 1901 B3
Devon Court East Dr
4200 INPS 46226 2229 E1
Devon Ct West Dr
4200 INPS 46226 2229 E1
Devon Lake Rd
4400 INPS 46226 2229 E1
Devonshire Ct
300 NBVL 46062 1576 D7
300 NBVL 46062 1685 D1
8400 INPS 46260 2009 E5
Devonshire Dr
- LcnT 46167 2113 B5
4900 MdlT 46167 2113 B5
Devonwood Dr
10 MRVL 46158 2659 E1
Dew Cir
9100 INPS 46260 2009 E3
Dewberry Ct
9000 INPS 46260 2009 D4
Dewester Dr
7000 LWNC 46236 2124 B2
Dewey Av
100 GNFD 46140 2345 B1
5800 INPS 46219 2339 C4
7200 INPS 46219 2340 A3
DeWitt Dr
- FSHR 46038 1906 B3
N Dexter St
1800 INPS 46202 2227 E7
Diablo Rd
1100 GNWD 46143 2665 E4
Diamente Dr
- WTFD 46074 1793 C2
Diamond Av
- INPS 46268 2009 C7
Diamond Ct
3900 INPS 46254 2226 B2
Diamond Dr
10700 ClyT 46032 1900 C7
Diamond Ln
3900 INPS 46254 2226 B2
Diamond Wy
19400 NBVL 46062 1686 A4
Diamond Pointe Ct
11600 INPS 46236 2014 D4
Diamond Pointe Dr
9000 INPS 46236 2014 D3
Diana Dr
4900 INPS 46203 2339 A5
5700 INPS 46278 2117 B2
E Diana Dr
5600 INPS 46278 2117 B2
Diane Ln
3700 PryT 46052 1896 C1
4900 MrlT 46126 2670 C2
Dianna Dr
7600 BrnT 46112 2114 D2
Dickens Cross
- MCVL 46055 2124 B1
Dickinson Ct
8800 FSHR 46060 1795 D7
Dickinson Ln
7000 INPS 46259 2558 A4
Dicks St
200 LEBN 46052 1676 E7
Dickson Rd
4400 INPS 46226 2120 E7
6000 INPS 46226 2121 C7
Dickson St
200 INPS 46202 2337 E3
Dietz Dr
- GNWD 46143 2666 D4
Dietz St
2600 INPS 46203 2447 A2
3000 INPS 46237 2447 A2
Digby Ct
10 INPS 46222 2226 E5
10 INPS 46222 2227 A5
Digital Wy
6200 INPS 46278 2117 A2
Dijon Ct
6100 INPS 46220 2120 E4
Dijon Dr
- INPS 46220 2120 E3
Dill Ct
5500 INPS 46237 2557 B4
Diller Dr
4100 INPS 46235 2231 E2
Dillon Pl
700 LWNC 46236 2015 A6
10800 FSHR 46038 1905 C3

STREET
Block City ZIP Map# Grid

Dior Ct
7000 INPS 46278 2116 E1
Diplomat Ct
100 BHGV 46107 2448 A4
Directors Dr
2200 INPS 46241 2444 B1
Discovery Cir
11800 INPS 46236 2014 E4
Discovery Dr S
6500 INPS 46250 2012 E3
Discovery Dr W
9300 INPS 46250 2012 B2
Distributors Dr
2200 INPS 46241 2444 B1
Ditch Rd
- ClyT 46032 1901 A7
- INPS 46260 2010 A2
- WshT 46074 1683 A7
7900 INPS 46260 2009 E6
9600 ClyT 46032 2010 A2
13100 CRML 46032 1901 A1
13800 CRML 46032 1792 A7
14100 CRML 46074 1792 A7
14600 WshT 46074 1792 A6
N Ditch Rd
- INPS 46260 2010 A2
5700 INPS 46228 2118 E5
7300 INPS 46260 2118 E1
7500 INPS 46260 2009 E7
Divers Cove Ct
11400 INPS 46236 2014 C5
Dividend St
5500 INPS 46241 2335 B7
Diving Hawk Cross
- FCkT 46055 2015 C2
Divinity Ct
100 MRVL 46158 2659 E2
Division St
300 INPS 46221 2336 E4
3400 INPS 46217 2445 E4
E Division St
1000 NBVL 46060 1795 D1
W Division St
100 NBVL 46060 1795 C1
Dix Rd
7700 INPS 46259 2559 D6
8500 MrlT 46259 2559 D6
Dixie Dr
10 INPS 46227 2555 C7
Dixon Ct
7600 NBVL 46062 1686 B2
Dlaredon Dr
5400 NBVL 46062 1794 B6
Dobbs Ferry Dr
5600 INPS 46254 2117 B5
Doble Down Rd
- MrlT 46126 2560 C5
Dobson St
7200 INPS 46268 2117 E1
N Dobson St
7100 INPS 46268 2117 E1
Dockside Dr
1700 WRvT 46143 2664 A7
Doe Blvd
- NBVL 46062 1576 B6
Doe Cir
5000 INPS 46254 2117 D6
N Doe Ct
1100 BCkT 46140 2234 E6
Doe Ln
1500 GNWD 46142 2664 C4
7500 LWNC 46236 2015 A7
Doe Wy
5500 NBVL 46062 1576 B6
Doe Creek Ct
15000 NBVL 46060 1796 E5
Doe Ridge Ct
8200 INPS 46256 2013 C5
Doe Run Dr
900 CRML 46032 1901 A1
Doe Spring Dr
9100 INPS 46278 2007 A3
Dogie Rd
3500 INPS 46222 2336 B3
E Dogwood Cir
8200 INPS 46268 2009 B5
N Dogwood Cir
3200 INPS 46268 2009 B5
S Dogwood Cir
3200 INPS 46268 2009 B5
W Dogwood Cir
- INPS 46268 2009 B5
Dogwood Ct
600 NBVL 46062 1685 D3
1200 BNBG 46112 2223 D2
1700 GfdT 46168 2550 D4
4100 FKLN 46131 2774 E7
7400 INPS 46256 2122 D1
Dogwood Dr
7800 INPS 46227 2556 B5
Dogwood Ln
- FKLN 46131 2774 E7
- GNWD 46143 2666 A5
900 GNWD 46143 2665 A5
3200 ClyT 46032 2009 B2
4500 LcnT 46112 2222 E1
N Dogwood Wy
1000 BCkT 46140 2234 E6
Dokey Ln
6300 INPS 46237 2557 D2
Dolan Wy
- CRML 46074 1900 A2
Dollar Forge Ct
5300 INPS 46221 2553 C1
Dollar Forge Dr
5500 INPS 46221 2553 B1
Dollar Forge Ln
5300 INPS 46221 2553 C1
Dollar Hide Ct
5600 INPS 46221 2553 B1
Dollar Hide North Dr
5500 INPS 46221 2553 B1
Dollar Hide South Dr
5500 INPS 46221 2553 A1

STREET
Block City ZIP Map# Grid

Dollar Ridge Ct
5900 INPS 46221 2553 C2
Dollar Ridge Ln
5000 INPS 46221 2553 C2
Dollar Run Dr
- INPS 46221 2553 C1
Dollar Run Ln
5600 INPS 46221 2553 C1
Dolphin Ln
- FCkT 46038 1906 A3
10300 INPS 46256 2014 B3
Dominion Dr
200 ZNVL 46077 1898 E6
Dona Ct
3700 CRML 46033 1902 E6
Dona Dr
11300 CRML 46033 1902 E6
Donald Av
3400 INPS 46224 2226 D3
Donald Ct E
5500 MdnT 46113 2660 E3
Donald Dr E
5700 MdnT 46113 2660 E3
5700 MdnT 46113 2661 A3
Donavan Ln
9900 FCkT 46060 1905 A2
Doncaster Ct
12100 FSHR 46038 2014 E1
12100 FSHR 46038 2015 A1
Donegal Cir
3100 CRML 46074 1900 C2
Donegal Dr
7300 INPS 46217 2554 E5
Donington Cir
6700 INPS 46237 2557 E2
Donna Bell Dr
2700 INPS 46241 2444 C3
Donnehan Ct
7500 INPS 46217 2554 E5
Donnehan Rd
7500 INPS 46217 2554 E5
Donnelly Dr
10 LcnT 46112 2223 B3
Donner Ln
5000 INPS 46268 2117 D2
Donnie Ct
8700 INPS 46234 2225 A7
Donnington Dr
12000 FSHR 46038 1906 C4
Donnybrook Dr
1200 CRML 46032 1902 A6
Donovan Dr
3900 INPS 46235 2232 A2
Doone Valley Ct
7600 AVON 46123 2332 D5
Dora Ct
7500 INPS 46256 2013 B7
Doral Ct
9000 INPS 46250 2012 E4
9000 INPS 46250 2013 A4
Doral East Dr
8800 INPS 46250 2012 E4
8900 INPS 46250 2013 A3
Doral North Dr
7000 INPS 46250 2012 E3
Doral South Dr
7000 INPS 46250 2012 E4
Doral West Dr
8700 INPS 46250 2012 E4
Dorchester Ct
6700 INPS 46214 2334 E2
Dorchester Dr
200 EglT 46077 1897 D6
500 NBVL 46062 1685 D1
Dorchester Pl
1500 CRML 46033 1793 D7
Doretta Joan Av
- INPS 46218 2230 B4
Dori Ln
1200 INPS 46260 2010 A3
Doris Dr
6400 INPS 46214 2226 A7
6600 INPS 46214 2225 E7
Dorkin Ct
4700 INPS 46254 2117 E7
Dorman St
800 INPS 46202 2337 E2
Dormont Dr
- WshT 46074 1792 A5
Dornock Dr
7400 INPS 46237 2557 E5
E Dornock Wy
6900 INPS 46237 2557 E5
Dorothy Dr
7400 INPS 46260 2009 D7
7400 INPS 46260 2118 D1
Dorrell Ct
1600 WRvT 46143 2664 C7
Dorset Blvd
400 CRML 46032 1901 B3
Dorsett Pl
6000 INPS 46220 2121 A4
Dorval Pl
3700 INPS 46228 2227 A2
Doty Ln
3600 CRML 46033 2011 D1
Doub St
1700 GNWD 46143 2665 C7
Doubleday Dr
8000 LWNC 46216 2122 B6
Double Eagle Dr
12600 CRML 46033 1903 D3
Double Tree Blvd
3000 INPS 46268 2009 B5
Doubletree Ln
14000 CRML 46032 1792 C7
Doubloon Rd
9100 INPS 46268 2009 C3
Dougherty Ln
- GNWD 46143 2666 D4
Douglas Ct
400 BNBG 46112 2114 D6
Douglas Dr
1400 CRML 46033 1902 D3

STREET
Block City ZIP Map# Grid

E Douglas Dr
400 BNBG 46112 2114 C6
Douglas Ln
1600 LEBN 46052 1676 E4
Douglas Rd
2100 INPS 46220 2120 B3
Douglas St
10 GNFD 46140 2345 E1
Douglas Fir Ct
8000 LWNC 46236 2014 E6
Douglas Hill Ct
- BrnT 46112 2114 D1
Douglas Hill Dr
- BrnT 46112 2114 D1
Douglaston Ct
8500 INPS 46234 2225 A5
Dove Ct
7900 PNFD 46168 2550 D2
E Dove Ct
8300 INPS 46256 2013 C6
Dove Dr
- MdnT 46113 2661 A1
14100 CRML 46033 1903 B1
14200 CRML 46033 1794 B7
Dover Blvd N
100 BNBG 46112 2223 B1
Dover Blvd S
100 BNBG 46112 2223 B1
Dover Cir
5500 CRML 46033 1794 C7
Dover Ct
2600 LEBN 46052 1677 A2
6200 FSHR 46038 1903 D6
7200 INPS 46250 2120 E1
Dover Dr
800 GNWD 46142 2665 A1
7200 INPS 46250 2120 E1
14500 CRML 46033 1794 B7
Dover Rd
100 NBVL 46060 1795 D5
200 BNBG 46112 2223 A1
6500 INPS 46220 2120 E2
Dover St
- AVON 46123 2332 E4
Doverton Dr
5700 NBVL 46062 1576 C7
Doves Ct
7800 NBVL 46062 1795 B1
Dovetree Ct
5800 CRML 46033 1903 D1
Dowitch Ct
2100 INPS 46260 2009 D6
Dowitch Ln
7900 INPS 46260 2009 D6
Downes Ct
9600 INPS 46235 2231 E1
Downes Dr
4300 INPS 46235 2231 E1
N Downes Dr
3900 INPS 46235 2231 E2
N Downey Av
900 INPS 46219 2339 B1
1300 INPS 46219 2230 B6
3000 INPS 46218 2230 B4
S Downey Av
10 INPS 46219 2339 B4
Downey Ct
10 GNFD 46140 2236 E7
Downing Ct
100 NBVL 46060 1795 D5
Downing Dr
500 GNWD 46143 2665 B6
700 PltT 46143 2665 B6
6000 INPS 46228 2118 B4
Downing St
- GNWD 46143 2665 D4
10700 CRML 46033 1902 D7
Drabble Ln
11400 LWNC 46235 2123 D6
Dragonfly Dr
- INPS 46237 2448 E7
Dragonfly Ln
17000 NBVL 46060 1795 E1
17000 NBVL 46060 1796 A1
Drake Dr
- FSHR 46060 1905 D1
Drake St
100 LEBN 46052 1676 E6
W Drake St
500 INPS 46202 2337 B1
Drakeford Dr
9500 INPS 46260 2009 E2
Drake Lake Dr
10700 MdnT 46158 2660 E7
Dr Andrew J Brown Av
1400 INPS 46201 2337 E1
1400 INPS 46202 2337 E1
1600 INPS 46202 2228 E7
1600 INPS 46218 2228 E7
2100 INPS 46205 2228 E7
Draper St
- INPS 46227 2447 A3
1500 INPS 46203 2338 A6
2400 INPS 46203 2447 A1
Drawbridge Cir
9300 INPS 46250 2012 D3
Drawbridge Ct
9300 INPS 46250 2012 C3
Drawbridge Ln
6000 INPS 46250 2012 C3
Draycott Av
10200 LWNC 46236 2123 A4
Draycott Dr
5900 LWNC 46236 2123 A4
Draycott Wy
10200 LWNC 46236 2123 B4
Drayton Ct
- INPS 46254 2226 B1
Drayton Dr
14600 NBVL 46062 1794 B6
Dream Ct
400 CRML 46032 1901 D1
Dream March Dr
800 GNFD 46140 2345 D3

STREET
Block City ZIP Map# Grid

Dreamy St
900 WRvT 46142 2664 B1
Dreier Pl
900 INPS 46202 2337 E4
900 INPS 46203 2337 E4
Dresden St
6500 HMCT 46227 2556 A3
6500 INPS 46227 2556 A3
Dresdin Ct
12900 FSHR 46060 1906 C2
Drewmatt Ln
- INPS 46234 2224 E5
N Drexel Av
10 INPS 46201 2338 E3
1500 INPS 46201 2229 E7
3200 INPS 46218 2229 E3
3800 INPS 46226 2229 E2
5400 INPS 46220 2120 E6
S Drexel Av
200 INPS 46201 2338 E4
500 INPS 46203 2338 E5
Drexler Dr
- WshT 46074 1792 B5
Driftstone Dr
11900 FSHR 46038 1906 A5
Driftwood Ct
- MCVL 46055 2015 D4
1200 MRVL 46158 2660 B3
3100 CRML 46033 1902 C1
Driftwood Dr
1100 CRML 46033 1902 D1
8600 INPS 46240 2011 B4
13800 CRML 46033 1793 C7
Driftwood Ln
4400 WRvT 46143 2663 D5
Driving Wind Wy
2800 INPS 46268 2118 C3
Dr Martin Luther King Jr St
- INPS 46208 2228 A3
1000 INPS 46202 2337 B1
2100 INPS 46202 2228 A5
N Dr Martin Luther King Jr St
600 INPS 46202 2337 B2
1600 INPS 46202 2228 B7
Drover St
400 INPS 46221 2337 A5
Druid Hill Ct
10 CRML 46032 1901 E3
Druid Hill Dr
10 CRML 46032 1901 E2
Drum Rd
5300 LWNC 46216 2122 B6
Drummond Wy
- BrnT 46112 2006 E7
Dry Run
100 NbvT 46060 1687 B3
Dry Branch Ct
7500 LWNC 46236 2014 E7
Dry Creek Cir
400 INPS 46231 2333 E4
Dry Creek Dr
9200 INPS 46231 2333 E5
Dry Creek Rd
- NBVL 46060 1797 A4
Dry Den Ct
6100 INPS 46221 2553 B2
Dry Den Dr
5600 INPS 46221 2553 B2
Duane Dr
2700 INPS 46227 2447 C6
Dubarry Ct
3500 INPS 46226 2231 C3
11700 CRML 46033 1903 C5
Dubarry Dr
11800 CRML 46033 1903 C4
Dubarry Rd
3500 INPS 46226 2231 C3
Dublin Dr
14400 CRML 46033 1793 B7
Dublin Ln
7000 INPS 46239 2448 E7
7000 INPS 46239 2557 E1
7000 INPS 46239 2558 A1
Dubonnett Ct
7000 INPS 46278 2007 D7
Dubonnett Wy
7400 INPS 46278 2007 E7
7400 INPS 46278 2116 E1
Duck Creek Ln
100 WRvT 46060 1579 C1
Duck Pond Dr
6500 FSHR 46038 1903 D6
E Dudley Av
600 INPS 46227 2555 E1
1500 INPS 46227 2556 A1
4100 INPS 46237 2556 D1
W Dudley Av
10 INPS 46217 2555 C1
Dudley Avenue South Dr
4200 INPS 46237 2556 E1
Dudley Av North Dr
4200 INPS 46237 2556 E1
Duffer Cir
3600 INPS 46228 2118 A6
Duffey St
100 PNFD 46168 2441 C4
Dugan Ct
500 NBVL 46062 1685 B5
Dugan Dr
1900 INPS 46260 2009 D5
Dukane Ct
1000 INPS 46241 2335 A5
N Dukane Wy
1300 INPS 46214 2335 A1
1500 INPS 46214 2226 A7
3500 INPS 46224 2226 A3
S Dukane Wy
1200 INPS 46241 2335 A6
4100 INPS 46241 2444 A5
Dukane Cir North Dr
6300 INPS 46241 2444 B4
Dukane Cir South Dr
6300 INPS 46241 2444 B4

Duke Dr
9800 LcnT 46112 2224 C3
9800 LcnT 46234 2224 C3
Duke Rd
10 MdnT 46113 2661 D5
Duke St
2200 INPS 46205 2229 B1
Duke of York St
- CRML 46032 1900 D2
Dumbarton St
13100 CRML 46032 1900 E2
Dunaway Ct
1700 INPS 46228 2227 D1
Dunbar Cir N
12100 CBLD 46229 2341 E2
Dunbar Cir S
12200 CBLD 46229 2341 E2
Dunbar Ct
12200 CBLD 46229 2341 E2
Dunbar Dr
100 CBLD 46229 2341 E2
Dunbar Rd
21500 WshT 46069 1575 A6
21600 AdmT 46069 1575 A6
N Dunbar Rd
23600 AdmT 46069 1575 A1
E Dunbarton Ct
1900 INPS 46260 2009 D6
W Dunbarton Ct
1900 INPS 46260 2009 C7
N Duncan Ct
10 BrnT 46113 2660 B2
Duncan Dr
300 BrnT 46113 2660 C2
Duncaster Ct
8400 INPS 46256 2013 C5
Dundee Cir
5000 INPS 46226 2121 A7
Dundee Ct
100 NBVL 46060 1795 E4
Dundee Dr
3600 INPS 46237 2447 D5
Dunedin Ct
4100 WTFD 46062 1684 E7
Dunes Dr
13400 CRML 46032 1901 C1
Dunham E
10400 INPS 46229 2232 B6
Dunham W
10300 INPS 46229 2232 B5
Dunk Dr
5200 INPS 46224 2226 B3
Dunlap Av
1300 INPS 46241 2335 D6
W Dunlap Dr
3900 INPS 46221 2444 D5
Dunmore Dr
5900 INPS 46254 2117 C4
Dunmore Pointe
7400 NBVL 46062 1686 A5
Dunn Dr
10 MRVL 46158 2659 E2
Dunn St
400 PNFD 46168 2441 C5
4400 LWNC 46226 2231 B1
4500 LWNC 46226 2122 B7
Dunn Wy
6300 INPS 46241 2335 A6
6900 INPS 46241 2334 E6
Dunns Bridge Ct
- MdnT 46113 2661 C1
Dunsany Cir
4300 INPS 46254 2225 E1
Dunsany Ct
4300 INPS 46254 2225 C1
Dunsany Ln
6600 INPS 46254 2225 E1
Dunseth Ct
5900 INPS 46254 2226 B1
Dunshire Dr
11300 CBLD 46229 2341 D2
Dunsmuir Dr
8800 INPS 46260 2010 B4
Dunster St
3000 INPS 46227 2556 C6
Dunston Ct
500 INPS 46239 2340 B4
Dunston Dr
7900 INPS 46239 2340 B4
Dunwoody Ln
9200 INPS 46229 2231 D5
13100 CRML 46033 1903 C2
Dupont Ct
- WTFD 46074 1792 D2
2200 INPS 46229 2232 B6
Dupont Ln
200 WTFD 46074 1792 D2
Dura Dr
11000 INPS 46229 2232 C6
Durango Ct
5400 INPS 46237 2448 B7
Durban Ct
8800 INPS 46234 2225 A5
Durban Run
- SCkT 46051 1689 E4
Durbin Ct
2500 CRML 46032 1900 C5
Durbin Dr
2400 CRML 46032 1900 C5
Durbin Rd
16600 WynT 46060 1797 E2
20600 WRvT 46060 1579 E7
20600 WynT 46060 1579 E7
20600 WynT 46060 1688 E1
Durden Ct
1600 INPS 46214 2225 D7
Durham Ct
- WRvT 46142 2663 C4
Durham Dr
2200 INPS 46220 2120 B2
Durham Wy
- GNWD 46184 2774 A1
Durham Castle Ct
5700 INPS 46250 2012 C3

Dusk Ct
6700 INPS 46254 2225 E1
Dustin Dr
4700 LWNC 46235 2122 E7
Dusty Tr
- NBVL 46060 1797 A5
1200 GNWD 46142 2664 D1
Dutch Ct
7800 WshT 46123 2332 D7
E Dutch Dr
5000 MdnT 46158 2660 D7
Dutch Elm Dr
1800 INPS 46231 2333 E7
Dutch Elm Wy
- INPS 46231 2334 A7
Dutchman Dr
7700 WshT 46123 2332 D7
Duval Dr
12500 FSHR 46038 1906 B4
Duxbury Ln
4400 LWNC 46226 2231 D1
Duxbury Rd
8800 LWNC 46226 2231 D1

E

E St
- BHGV 46107 2447 D3
Eagle Ct
- BrnT 46112 2115 E3
900 EglT 46077 1898 D4
3600 WRvT 46143 2664 B6
Eagle Dr
- LcnT 46112 2115 D5
Eagle Pkwy
800 BNBG 46112 2114 D5
Eagle Rd
7000 BrnT 46112 2115 E3
7000 INPS 46112 2115 E3
Eagle Trc
1400 WRvT 46143 2664 A6
3700 WRvT 46143 2664 A6
W Eagle Trc
4200 NPLN 46163 2452 B3
Eagle Bay Cir
4200 INPS 46254 2225 D1
Eagle Bay North Dr
7100 INPS 46254 2225 D1
Eagle Bay South Dr
7100 INPS 46254 2225 D1
Eagle Bay West Dr
4200 INPS 46254 2225 D1
Eagle Beach Dr
7500 INPS 46254 2116 C5
Eagle Cove Cir
4000 INPS 46254 2225 C1
Eagle Cove Ct
4000 INPS 46254 2225 D2
Eagle Cove Dr
7100 INPS 46254 2225 D2
Eagle Cove East Dr
4000 INPS 46254 2225 D2
Eagle Cove North Dr
7100 INPS 46254 2225 D2
Eagle Cove South Dr
7100 INPS 46254 2225 C1
Eagle Cove West Dr
4000 INPS 46254 2225 D2
Eagle Creek Blvd
- INPS 46222 2227 A4
Eagle Creek Cir
600 ZNVL 46077 1899 C6
Eagle Creek Ct
600 ZNVL 46077 1899 C6
Eagle Creek Ln
- INPS 46234 2225 B1
Eagle Creek Pkwy
- INPS 46254 2116 D4
- INPS 46278 2116 C3
3400 INPS 46214 2225 E3
4400 INPS 46254 2225 D1
N Eagle Creek Pkwy
- INPS 46254 2116 D7
Eagle Creek Levee Rd
- INPS 46221 2445 D2
Eagle Creek Overlook Dr
7800 INPS 46254 2116 C6
Eagle Crest Ct
3700 WRvT 46143 2664 A6
Eagle Crest Dr
600 BNBG 46112 2114 C6
1200 WRvT 46143 2664 A6
Eagle Crest Ln
8300 INPS 46234 2116 B7
Eagle Crossing Blvd
- BrnT 46112 2115 D5
- LcnT 46112 2115 D5
Eagledale Dr
2500 INPS 46222 2227 A5
Eagle Emblem Ct
3600 WRvT 46143 2664 B6
Eagle Eye Wy
- LcnT 46112 2115 C6
Eagle Highlands Wy
- INPS 46254 2225 E2
Eagle Hill Dr
800 INPS 46224 2335 B2
Eagle Lake Cir
7200 INPS 46254 2225 D1
Eagle Lake Ct
7100 INPS 46254 2225 C1
Eagle Lake Dr
4000 INPS 46254 2225 D2
Eagle Meadow Dr
9100 INPS 46234 2115 E7
Eagle Nest Dr
3600 WRvT 46143 2664 A6
Eagle Pointe Dr
6600 INPS 46254 2225 E1
Eagle Pointe Dr N
6600 INPS 46254 2116 D6
6600 INPS 46254 2225 C1
Eagle Pointe Dr S
6600 INPS 46254 2225 E1
6600 INPS 46254 2226 A1

Eagle Pointe Ln
6800 INPS 46254 2116 D6
6800 INPS 46254 2225 C1
Eagles Ct
6800 INPS 46214 2225 E3
Eagles Crest Cir
2800 INPS 46214 2225 C5
Eagles Landing Blvd
- INPS 46254 2225 D2
Eagles Nest Ct
- WshT 46123 2333 A2
500 AVON 46123 2332 E3
N Eagles Nest Ct
11000 MrlT 46126 2560 C1
Eagles Nest Dr
8200 WshT 46123 2332 E2
8600 AVON 46123 2332 D3
Eagles Perch Dr
6600 INPS 46214 2225 E3
Eagles Ridge Dr
1000 CCRO 46034 1577 B2
Eagles Roost Dr
4000 INPS 46234 2225 A2
Eagles Watch
6600 FSHR 46038 1903 E6
Eagles Watch Dr
4600 INPS 46254 2116 E7
Eagles Watch Ln
4600 INPS 46254 2116 E7
Eagles Wing Dr
6600 INPS 46214 2225 E3
Eagle Talon Ct
4900 INPS 46254 2116 E7
Eagle Town Rd
16600 WshT 46074 1682 E7
16600 WshT 46074 1791 E2
Eagletown Rd
17600 WshT 46074 1682 E5
Eagle Trace Ct
1400 WRvT 46143 2664 A6
Eagle Trace Dr
1400 WRvT 46143 2664 A6
Eagle Trace Wy
7100 INPS 46237 2557 D4
Eagle Valley Ct
3600 WRvT 46143 2664 A6
Eagle Valley Dr
1200 WRvT 46143 2664 A6
Eagle Valley Pass
7400 INPS 46214 2225 C4
Eagle View Ct
1200 WRvT 46143 2664 A6
Eagleview Ct
500 ZNVL 46077 1899 B7
6000 SDWY 46224 2226 A6
Eagle View Dr
3800 INPS 46254 2225 E2
Eagleview Dr
2100 SDWY 46224 2226 A6
Eagle Village Dr
- LcnT 46112 2115 E5
Eagle Vista Pl
7300 INPS 46259 2558 A4
Eaglewood Ct
3600 WTFD 46033 1793 D6
S Eaglewood Dr
800 EglT 46077 1898 B6
Eaker Ct
7900 BrnT 46112 2113 E2
Earhart Dr
3600 CRML 46074 1900 A2
Earhart St
800 INPS 46203 2338 C5
N Earl Av
3600 INPS 46224 2226 B3
S Earl Av
1400 INPS 46241 2335 B6
Earl Ct
7400 SPRT 46227 2556 B4
Earl Dr
3000 SPRT 46227 2556 C4
Earlham Dr
2300 INPS 46227 2447 B6
Earlham Ln
2200 PNFD 46231 2442 D1
2200 WshT 46231 2442 D1
Earl Park Wy
200 WTFD 46074 1792 D2
Earls Ln
4000 MdnT 46113 2661 D4
N Earl's Ln
12000 MdnT 46113 2661 C5
Earlswood Dr
6600 INPS 46217 2554 C3
Earlswood Ln
2800 INPS 46217 2554 B3
Earlybird Ln
100 GNWD 46143 2666 A3
East Brch
10 BNBG 46112 2114 C3
East Dr
- SCkT 46163 2452 B2
- WTFD 46074 1684 A6
200 FCkT 46040 2016 E1
200 PNFD 46168 2442 A3
200 ULEN 46052 1677 A4
N East Dr
500 MdnT 46113 2661 D5
S East Dr
600 SGLK 46140 2344 A3
East Rd
- INPS 46227 2555 D7
East St
- AVON 46234 2333 D1
10 DNVL 46122 2329 C4
200 GNWD 46143 2665 D4
N East St
- NPLN 46163 2452 B3
10 GNFD 46140 2345 E1
10 INPS 46204 2337 D3
10 WTFD 46074 1684 B7
100 LEBN 46052 1677 A6
100 PNFD 46168 2441 B4
300 INPS 46202 2337 D2
600 GNFD 46140 2236 E7

N East St
600 WshT 46074 1684 B7
S East St
- NPLN 46163 2452 B3
10 INPS 46202 2337 D4
10 INPS 46204 2337 D4
10 PNFD 46168 2441 B5
100 LEBN 46052 1677 A7
400 INPS 46203 2337 D5
400 INPS 46225 2337 D5
500 GNFD 46140 2345 E2
1300 LEBN 46052 1786 A1
2500 INPS 46203 2446 D2
2500 INPS 46225 2446 D2
3000 INPS 46227 2446 D3
5500 INPS 46227 2555 D2
S East St US-31
- INPS 46227 2446 D7
5500 INPS 46227 2555 D2
East Bay Dr
- VrnT 46055 2124 B3
Eastbay Dr
8300 LWNC 46236 2014 E5
N East Bay Dr
2000 GNFD 46140 2236 E4
Eastbourne Cir
5400 INPS 46226 2121 B6
Eastbourne Dr
4400 INPS 46226 2121 B7
4400 INPS 46226 2230 B1
Eastbrooke Cir
3200 INPS 46235 2232 A4
Eastbrooke Ct
3200 INPS 46235 2232 A3
Eastcreek Ct
12200 LWNC 46236 2014 C4
12200 LWNC 46236 2015 A5
Easterly Blvd
- FCkT 46038 1906 D6
Eastern Av
10 BNBG 46112 2114 C7
100 PNFD 46168 2441 B5
500 INPS 46201 2338 B2
3000 INPS 46218 2229 B4
N Eastern Av
3900 INPS 46205 2229 B2
Eastern Range Rd
- LcnT 46112 2115 C5
Eastfield Ct
700 INPS 46227 2446 D6
East Fork Dr
- BNBG 46112 2224 A2
Eastgate St
6200 LWNC 46236 2123 D3
Eastlawn Dr
1000 NWTD 46184 2774 D3
Easton Dr
700 BNBG 46112 2223 A1
Easton Point Dr
1200 GNWD 46142 2664 D3
Easton Point Wy
10 GNWD 46142 2664 D3
Eastridge Dr
10 GNWD 46143 2665 D1
5400 INPS 46219 2339 B1
Eastside Dr
4200 LcnT 46112 2223 B2
Eastview Ct
5800 INPS 46250 2012 C7
Eastview Dr
10 MRVL 46158 2659 E2
Eastwick Cir
6900 INPS 46256 2121 E1
11900 CRML 46033 1903 C4
Eastwick Ln
7000 INPS 46256 2121 E2
7200 INPS 46256 2122 A2
Eastwind Ct
3300 INPS 46227 2556 C5
10200 INPS 46256 2014 A3
Eastwind Dr
9200 INPS 46256 2014 A3
Eastwind Ln
9300 INPS 46256 2014 A3
Eastwind St
3500 INPS 46227 2556 C5
3800 INPS 46237 2556 D5
Eastwood Dr
- MRVL 46158 2659 D7
2300 INPS 46219 2231 B6
Eastwood Ln
13200 FSHR 46060 1905 C2
Eastwood Pl
2100 INPS 46219 2231 B7
Eastwood St
1700 GNWD 46143 2665 C7
Easy Ln
- INPS 46239 2558 A1
Easy St
- DelT 46038 1903 E6
- FSHR 46038 1903 E6
- SCkT 46163 2343 B2
1200 GNWD 46142 2664 D1
4000 WRvT 46142 2664 A1
7400 FSHR 46038 1904 A6
Easy Wy
9800 LcnT 46112 2224 C3
N Eaton Av
1100 INPS 46219 2340 C1
2300 INPS 46219 2231 C6
3400 INPS 46226 2231 C3
S Eaton Av
4100 INPS 46239 2449 C5
6000 INPS 46259 2558 C2
Eaton Ct
6000 INPS 46259 2558 C1
10900 FSHR 46038 1903 D7
E Eaton Ct
8000 INPS 46239 2449 B5
S Eaton Dr
4700 INPS 46239 2449 C6
Ebbie Rd
2500 INPS 46219 2231 B5
Echo Bnd
1100 GNWD 46142 2664 D2

Echo Cir
600 GNWD 46142 2664 D2
Echo Ct
6300 INPS 46278 2117 B3
Echo Ln
6500 INPS 46278 2117 B2
N Echo Ln
6800 INPS 46278 2117 B2
Echo Tr
10900 LWNC 46236 2014 C6
Echo Wy
- NBVL 46060 1796 B5
5700 INPS 46278 2117 B3
Echo Bend Blvd
500 GNWD 46142 2664 D2
Echo Crest East Dr
11100 CRML 46280 1902 A6
Echo Crest West Dr
11100 CRML 46280 1902 A6
Echo Grove Cir
10900 LWNC 46236 2014 C6
Echo Grove Ct
11200 LWNC 46236 2014 C6
Echo Grove Ln
11000 LWNC 46236 2014 C6
Echo Grove Pl
7900 LWNC 46236 2014 C6
Echo Lake Center Dr
- MnrT 46158 2658 B3
Echo Lake East Dr
10 MnrT 46158 2658 B3
Echo Lake West Dr
10 MnrT 46158 2658 B3
Echo Ridge Ct
7900 LWNC 46236 2014 C6
Echo Ridge Ln
11200 LWNC 46236 2014 C6
Echo Spring Cir
10900 LWNC 46236 2014 C6
Echo Trail Cir
7900 LWNC 46236 2014 C6
N Ecole St
8100 INPS 46240 2011 A6
Economics Ct
7100 INPS 46239 2448 E6
W Eddie Ln
7300 INPS 46221 2552 D3
Eddie Rd
2400 INPS 46229 2232 A5
Eddingham Pl
- FSHR 46038 1906 E4
Eddington Rd
2600 SPRT 46227 2556 B5
Eddy Ct
3200 INPS 46214 2225 D4
Eden Ct
3500 CRML 46033 1902 D5
N Eden Ct
4600 INPS 46254 2117 E7
Eden Pl
3600 CRML 46033 1902 D5
Eden Wy
3200 CRML 46033 1902 C4
Eden Estates Dr
11600 CRML 46033 1902 D5
Eden Estates Pl
11700 CRML 46033 1902 D5
Eden Glen Dr
11600 CRML 46033 1902 D4
Eden Hollow Pl
3200 CRML 46033 1902 C4
Eden Park Dr
3200 CRML 46033 1902 C4
Eden Park Pl
3300 CRML 46033 1902 C4
Eden Ridge Ct
11500 LWNC 46236 2014 D6
Eden Roc Crest St
6600 INPS 46220 2121 D2
Edenshall Ln
- NBVL 46062 1794 C6
Eden Village Ct
700 CRML 46033 1902 C4
Eden Village Dr
3300 CRML 46033 1902 C3
5600 INPS 46254 2117 D5
Eden Village Pl
3300 CRML 46033 1902 C3
Eden Village Wy
5700 INPS 46254 2117 D5
Eden Woods Ct
9200 INPS 46260 2009 E3
Eden Woods Pl
700 CRML 46033 1902 D3
Eden Wy Cir
3200 CRML 46033 1902 C4
Eden Wy Pl
3200 CRML 46033 1902 C4
Edgar Rd
1300 PNFD 46168 2550 D1
Edgecombe Av
1100 INPS 46227 2446 E4
1400 INPS 46227 2447 A4
Edgefield Dr
11900 FSHR 46038 1905 E5
12100 FSHR 46038 1906 A6
N Edgehill Rd
10 INPS 46222 2335 D3
S Edgehill Rd
10 INPS 46241 2335 D4
S Edgehill St
5000 INPS 46221 2444 D7
Edgemanor Ct
7800 INPS 46239 2558 B1
Edgemanor Dr
7700 INPS 46239 2558 A1
Edgemere Ct
4100 INPS 46205 2229 C1
Edgemere Dr
400 INPS 46260 2119 B2
Edgemont Av
600 INPS 46208 2228 A6
1400 INPS 46208 2227 E6
Edgemont Wy
12700 CRML 46032 1900 D3

N Edgerton St
300 SgCT 46126 2670 D7
Edgewater Cir
- PNFD 46168 2442 A1
2200 AVON 46123 2332 E5
Edgewater Ct
10 LcnT 46112 2224 B4
1300 CCRO 46034 1577 B5
Edgewater Dr
- GNWD 46143 2665 B5
100 NBVL 46062 1686 A2
7300 INPS 46240 2119 E1
7400 INPS 46240 2010 E7
20900 NBVL 46062 1577 A7
N Edgewater Dr
7300 INPS 46240 2119 E1
Edgewater Pl
7100 INPS 46240 2119 E1
7100 INPS 46240 2120 A1
E Edgewood Av
10 INPS 46227 2555 C1
3300 INPS 46227 2556 D1
3800 INPS 46237 2556 D1
4800 INPS 46237 2557 A1
7000 INPS 46239 2557 D1
7000 INPS 46239 2558 A1
7000 INPS 46259 2557 D1
7000 INPS 46259 2558 A1
9800 INPS 46239 2559 B1
9800 INPS 46259 2559 B1
N Edgewood Av
- INPS 46227 2555 E1
W Edgewood Av
10 INPS 46217 2555 B2
1000 INPS 46217 2554 D2
Edgewood Ct
200 PTBR 46167 2113 A3
1700 GfdT 46168 2550 D4
Edgewood Dr
100 NWTD 46184 2774 D3
500 LEBN 46052 1677 B5
800 MRVL 46158 2659 E2
1100 INPS 46219 2339 E1
Edgewood Ln
19100 NBVL 46060 1686 E4
19100 NbvT 46060 1686 E4
Edgewood Pl
900 INPS 46205 2228 E3
Edgewood Rd
10100 LcnT 46112 2224 C2
Edgewood Trace Blvd
5500 INPS 46239 2449 A7
5500 INPS 46239 2558 B1
Edinborough Ln
4900 INPS 46241 2444 C2
Edinburge Sq
1700 INPS 46219 2231 A7
Edinburgh Dr
1300 CRML 46033 1793 D7
Edinburgh Pt
4400 INPS 46228 2227 D1
Edison Av
- INPS 46202 2337 E2
N Edison St
800 INPS 46202 2337 D2
Edison Wy
600 CRML 46032 1901 B1
Edith Av
200 NbvT 46060 1686 E3
200 NbvT 46060 1687 A3
S Edlin Rd
4000 HsnT 46052 1894 B2
Edlou Pl
5400 LWNC 46226 2122 A6
N Edmondson Av
10 INPS 46219 2339 E2
2200 INPS 46219 2230 E6
4200 INPS 46226 2230 D1
4500 INPS 46226 2121 D7
S Edmondson Av
10 INPS 46219 2339 E3
E Edna Mills Dr
- MdnT 46113 2661 B2
Edward Cir
14100 CRML 46033 1794 A7
Edward Ct
5200 CRML 46033 1903 B5
7400 BrnT 46112 2114 D3
Edwardian Cir
4600 INPS 46254 2117 D7
Edwardian Ct
- INPS 46254 2226 D1
4500 INPS 46254 2117 D7
Edwards Av
100 BHGV 46107 2448 A5
300 BHGV 46107 2447 E5
E Edwards Av
500 INPS 46227 2446 D5
1400 INPS 46227 2447 A5
W Edwards Av
10 INPS 46217 2446 B5
4800 INPS 46221 2444 C5
Edwards Ct
10 BHGV 46107 2447 E5
E Edwards Ct
800 INPS 46227 2446 E5
Edwards Grove Dr
18700 NBVL 46062 1685 C4
Edwin Ct
10 INPS 46222 2226 E5
Eel River Ct
5300 INPS 46221 2553 C2
Effingham Ct
13500 FCkT 46038 1904 D1
Effingham Sq
7100 INPS 46260 2118 D2
Egelhoff Ln
3500 INPS 46227 2446 D4
Eglin Dr
13600 CRML 46032 1901 E1
Egret Ct
2000 INPS 46260 2009 D6
Egret Ln
- GNWD 46143 2666 A6
8000 INPS 46260 2009 D6

STREET Block City ZIP Map# Grid

E Ehler Dr
4900 INPS 46237 2557 A6
Ehlerbrook Rd
8100 INPS 46237 2556 E6
8300 INPS 46237 2557 A7
Eiderdown Wy
9000 INPS 46234 2225 A6
S Eight St
- ZNVL 46077 1899 B6
Eikenberry St
100 GNFD 46140 2236 E7
Eisenhower Dr
1800 SDWY 46224 2226 B7
3500 INPS 46224 2226 B3
3800 INPS 46254 2226 C2
Elaine St
4900 INPS 46224 2226 D4
5700 SDWY 46224 2226 A4
S Eland Dr
3500 SCkT 46163 2451 D2
W Eland Dr
6000 SCkT 46163 2451 D2
Elba Ct
4200 INPS 46235 2231 D1
Elbe St
12800 FSHR 46060 1906 C3
E Elbert St
10 INPS 46227 2446 C6
1400 INPS 46227 2447 A6
W Elbert St
10 INPS 46217 2446 B6
El Beulah Blvd
7400 INPS 46256 2013 A5
El Beulah Wy
- INPS 46256 2013 A5
Elbow Bend Blvd
600 WRvT 46142 2664 B2
El Camino Ct
4800 INPS 46221 2444 B6
El Camino Rd
400 GNWD 46143 2665 E4
N Elder Av
10 INPS 46222 2336 D3
S Elder Av
10 INPS 46222 2336 D4
Elderberry Cir
100 NBVL 46062 1685 C3
Elderberry Rd
5200 NBVL 46062 1685 C2
Elderberry Wy
2100 INPS 46229 2232 D6
Elderbury Ct
100 MRVL 46158 2660 C3
Eldin Dr
1200 PNFD 46168 2441 D7
Eldorado Cir
- NbvT 46060 1796 C3
El Dorado Dr
9000 LWNC 46226 2122 D6
Eldor Flower Dr
- ClyT 46032 1899 E6
Eldred Ct
4100 WTFD 46062 1793 E2
Eldridge Dr
11600 LWNC 46235 2123 D6
N Eleanor Av
1000 INPS 46214 2334 E1
S Eleanor St
10 INPS 46241 2334 E4
Electric Av
1700 INPS 46260 2009 E3
Electric Ct
9100 INPS 46260 2009 E3
E Elenor St
5100 BHGV 46203 2448 A6
5100 INPS 46203 2448 A6
Elgin Ct
12500 FSHR 46038 1906 A4
Elias Cir
7000 LWNC 46236 2124 A2
Elicia Ct
4600 WTFD 46062 1793 E1
Elise Ct
6900 INPS 46220 2119 E2
Eliston Ln
- FSHR 46060 1906 E3
Elite Dr
2800 INPS 46241 2444 D2
Elizabeth Ct
- DNVL 46122 2329 E4
10500 ClyT 46032 1900 C7
Elizabeth Dr
1400 LEBN 46052 1676 D4
Elizabeth Ln
- BNBG 46112 2114 A6
Elizabeth St
3000 INPS 46234 2224 E5
N Elizabeth St
10 INPS 46219 2339 D3
2000 INPS 46219 2230 D6
4300 INPS 46226 2230 D1
S Elizabeth St
2800 INPS 46203 2448 D2
Elizaville Rd
1900 LEBN 46052 1677 A4
1900 ULEN 46052 1677 A4
3400 CtrT 46052 1677 E1
3400 CtrT 46052 1678 A1
3500 CtrT 46052 1569 B6
4500 CtnT 46052 1569 B6
Elkhart Dr
500 WTFD 46074 1792 E2
Elkhorn Ct
4600 WTFD 46062 1793 E1
4600 WTFD 46062 1794 A1
Elkhorn Dr
- WTFD 46062 1794 A1
4000 WTFD 46062 1793 E1
5500 INPS 46254 2116 D6
Elkhorn Wy
4000 WTFD 46062 1793 E1
Ella Dobbs Ln
7800 INPS 46227 2556 A5
El Lago Blvd
4000 INPS 46227 2447 C5
El Lago Ct
4100 INPS 46227 2447 C5
El Lago North Dr
2800 INPS 46227 2447 B5
Ellen Dr
1600 SDWY 46224 2226 C7
3400 INPS 46224 2226 C3
Ellen St
4000 LtyT 46168 2439 E5
Ellenberger Ct
5400 INPS 46219 2339 B1
Ellenberger Pkwy East Dr
800 INPS 46219 2339 B2
Ellenberger Pkwy West Dr
500 INPS 46219 2339 A2
Eller Rd
9900 FSHR 46038 2012 D1
10600 DelT 46038 1903 D7
10700 FSHR 46038 1903 D7
Eller Run
- FSHR 46038 2012 D1
Eller Creek Dr
6200 FSHR 46038 2012 D1
Eller Creek Wy
6200 FSHR 46038 2012 D1
Ellery Ln
4600 INPS 46250 2011 E6
4600 INPS 46250 2012 A6
Ellington Cir
700 GNWD 46143 2665 A5
Ellington Ct
800 INPS 46234 2334 A2
Ellington Dr
8700 INPS 46234 2334 A2
Ellingwood Dr
12100 CRML 46032 1900 C4
Elliott Av
4900 INPS 46201 2339 A1
Elliott Dr
800 CRML 46032 1901 E3
Ellipse Pkwy
7700 FSHR 46038 1904 C4
E Ellis Ct
9700 INPS 46235 2231 E2
Ellis Dr
10 GNFD 46140 2236 D7
10000 INPS 46235 2232 A1
E Ellis Dr
9800 INPS 46235 2231 E2
9800 INPS 46235 2232 A2
Ellis St
300 PNFD 46168 2441 B4
Ellis Park Dr
- WTFD 46074 1792 E3
Elliston Wy
- LWNC 46236 2123 B3
Ellsworth Ln
- FSHR 46060 1905 C1
- WshT 46123 2333 C2
Ellsworth St
600 INPS 46202 2337 B2
W Ellyn Dr
3400 INPS 46228 2118 B6
Elm Av
- SRDN 46069 1573 B2
S Elm Av
100 SRDN 46069 1573 B2
Elm Dr
10 PNFD 46168 2441 E5
100 GNFD 46140 2236 D7
200 GNWD 46142 2665 C2
7800 BmT 46112 2114 C2
9600 ClyT 46032 2009 B2
9600 INPS 46032 2009 B2
Elm Ln
- LWNC 46236 2123 E2
- ZNVL 46077 1899 B5
Elm St
- DNVL 46122 2329 D3
10 WTFD 46074 1684 A7
10 WTFD 46074 1793 A1
10 WTLD 46184 2775 B5
200 GNWD 46142 2665 C2
200 PNFD 46168 2441 B4
600 BHGV 46107 2447 E4
700 INPS 46203 2337 D5
22800 JknT 46034 1575 E4
E Elm St
200 LEBN 46052 1677 A7
N Elm St
- NPLN 46163 2452 B3
400 ZNVL 46077 1899 B5
S Elm St
- NPLN 46163 2452 B4
10 ZNVL 46077 1899 B6
100 SRDN 46069 1573 B2
W Elm St
100 LEBN 46052 1677 B7
800 LEBN 46052 1676 E7
Elmberry Ln
9300 FSHR 46038 1904 E1
Elm Branch Ct
8100 INPS 46259 2558 B5
Elmbury Ct
7400 INPS 46237 2557 B4
Elm Ct Dr
100 ZNVL 46077 1899 B5
Elmead Ct
300 GNWD 46142 2665 C2
Elmead Dr
300 GNWD 46142 2665 C2
Elm Grove Cir
- GNWD 46143 2664 D5
Elm Grove Wy
1200 GNWD 46143 2664 D5
Elmhurst Dr
1100 INPS 46219 2339 E1
1600 INPS 46219 2230 E7
3000 INPS 46226 2231 A4
3800 INPS 46226 2230 E2
4200 LWNC 46226 2230 E1
4600 LWNC 46226 2121 E7
4900 LWNC 46226 2122 A7
Elmhurst Pl
500 NWTD 46184 2774 D4
Elmira St
3500 INPS 46208 2227 E3
Elm Leaf Ln
2100 INPS 46229 2232 C6
Elmont Ter
4100 INPS 46235 2232 A1
Elmonte Ct
3900 INPS 46226 2231 C2
Elmonte Dr
8600 INPS 46226 2231 C2
Elm Ridge Ct
10700 LWNC 46236 2123 B1
Elm Ridge Dr
7200 LWNC 46236 2123 B1
7400 LWNC 46236 2014 B7
Elmsco Urt Cir
300 WRvT 46142 2663 D3
Elm Swamp Rd
2100 LEBN 46052 1677 A3
2100 ULEN 46052 1677 A3
3600 CtrT 46052 1568 B5
3600 CtrT 46052 1677 B1
3800 WshT 46052 1568 B5
Elm Tree Cir
9200 INPS 46235 2231 D2
Elm Tree Ct
10 GNWD 46142 2665 C3
9300 INPS 46235 2231 E2
Elmtree Park Ct
900 CBLD 46229 2341 C2
Elmtree Park Dr
11000 CBLD 46229 2341 C2
Elmtree Park Pl
900 CBLD 46229 2341 C2
Elmtree Park Wy
900 CBLD 46229 2341 C2
Elmwood Av
1300 INPS 46203 2337 D6
5100 BHGV 46203 2448 A5
Elmwood Cir
700 NBVL 46062 1685 E4
800 NBVL 46062 1686 A4
Elmwood Ct
10 BNBG 46112 2223 D2
5500 BHGV 46203 2448 B5
Elmwood Dr
2300 ULEN 46052 1677 A3
N Elmwood St
- INPS 46202 2336 E2
El Paso Dr
6500 INPS 46214 2226 A7
6600 INPS 46214 2225 E7
Elrico Dr
8600 INPS 46240 2011 B4
Elsbury Dr
6100 LWNC 46236 2123 A3
Elster Ct
8300 INPS 46256 2013 A5
Elwin Dr
2800 INPS 46229 2231 D5
Elyse Ln
14700 WTFD 46033 1793 E6
Elzroth St
3700 INPS 46222 2227 A7
Embassy Ct
2900 SDWY 46224 2226 A5
Embassy Row
2700 SDWY 46224 2226 A5
Ember Ct
7100 LWNC 46236 2123 B1
Embers Wy
9200 INPS 46250 2012 E3
Embry St
400 MNVA 46157 2657 C7
Emco Dr
4900 INPS 46220 2121 A3
Emerald Blf
12000 INPS 46236 2014 E4
Emerald Blvd
- MCVL 46055 2015 D5
Emerald Ct
17000 WTFD 46074 1793 B1
Emerald Ln
100 WynT 46060 1687 D3
8600 INPS 46260 2010 B4
Emerald St
- INPS 46268 2009 C7
Emerald Bay Ln
6800 INPS 46237 2448 E5
Emerald Green Cir
17000 WTFD 46074 1793 B1
Emerald Hill Ct
- INPS 46237 2557 A3
Emerald Isle Ct
12100 FSHR 46038 1905 B4
Emerald Lakes
1100 GNWD 46143 2666 A4
Emerald Leaf Ct
1800 INPS 46229 2232 C7
E Emerald Pines Ln
1700 WTFD 46074 1793 B2
Emerson Av
- INPS 46107 2448 A4
3700 BHGV 46107 2448 A4
3800 BHGV 46203 2448 A4
N Emerson Av
10 GNWD 46143 2666 A1
1400 INPS 46201 2339 A2
1400 INPS 46219 2339 A2
2500 INPS 46218 2230 A5
3800 INPS 46226 2230 A1
4400 INPS 46226 2121 A7
5800 INPS 46220 2121 A4
S Emerson Av
10 INPS 46201 2339 A4
10 INPS 46219 2339 A4
100 GNWD 46143 2666 A4
2100 INPS 46203 2339 A7
2600 INPS 46203 2448 A1
4200 BHGV 46107 2448 A6
4200 BHGV 46203 2448 A6
4600 BHGV 46237 2448 A6
4600 INPS 46107 2448 A6
S Emerson Av
4600 INPS 46237 2448 A6
5400 INPS 46237 2557 A1
Emerson Rd
400 CRML 46032 1902 A3
700 CRML 46032 1901 E3
Emerson Wy
5200 INPS 46226 2121 A6
5400 INPS 46220 2121 A6
Emerson Court North Dr
5000 INPS 46218 2230 A5
Emerson Ct South Dr
5000 INPS 46218 2230 A5
Emerson Village Dr
5100 INPS 46237 2448 A7
Emerson Village Ln
5100 INPS 46237 2448 A7
Emerson Village Pl
5100 INPS 46237 2448 A7
Emerton Pl
5000 INPS 46203 2339 A7
Emery Wy
10700 FSHR 46038 1904 D7
Emil Ct
5900 PNFD 46168 2550 D2
Emily Dr
1600 INPS 46260 2009 E3
Emily Wy
3500 CRML 46033 1902 D6
Emily Sue Ct
1700 INPS 46234 2225 A7
Emma Dr
5100 LWNC 46236 2122 E6
Emmanuel Ct
11300 FSHR 46038 1904 C6
Emmert Dr
5000 INPS 46221 2444 B7
Emmert Wy
5800 INPS 46221 2444 B7
W Emmett St
100 INPS 46204 2337 C2
Emory Dr
12000 CBLD 46229 2232 E7
Emory Ln
1000 INPS 46241 2334 E6
Emperors Ct
8900 INPS 46234 2225 A6
Empire Dr
7200 INPS 46219 2231 A6
E Empire St
- INPS 46203 2337 D4
200 INPS 46225 2337 B4
Enchance Ct
700 WRvT 46142 2664 B1
Enchanted View Dr
1100 MRVL 46158 2660 A6
Enclave Cir
800 CRML 46032 1902 C3
Enclave Ct
12600 CRML 46032 1902 C3
Enclave Dr
200 AVON 46123 2333 B3
200 WshT 46123 2333 B4
8200 FSHR 46038 1904 C6
Encore Dr
4800 INPS 46237 2448 B6
Endeavor Dr
- NBVL 46060 1796 A5
N Enderly Av
400 BNBG 46112 2114 C6
Enderly Ct
400 BNBG 46112 2114 C6
Endicott Ct
8000 INPS 46259 2557 E5
Endicott Dr
7000 INPS 46259 2557 E6
Endicott Wy
7000 INPS 46259 2557 E6
Endress Pl
2300 GNWD 46143 2774 E1
Endsley Dr
2400 INPS 46227 2447 B6
Endurance Dr
12600 FSHR 46060 1906 B2
End Zone Dr
12600 FCkT 46038 1906 A3
England Ct
9500 NBVL 46060 1686 E5
Englewood Av
4600 LWNC 46226 2121 E7
Englewood Dr
1600 INPS 46219 2230 E7
3800 INPS 46226 2230 E2
4100 LWNC 46226 2230 E1
Englewood Rd
8200 INPS 46240 2011 A5
English Av
6800 INPS 46219 2339 C4
6800 INPS 46239 2339 E4
7200 INPS 46219 2340 A4
7200 INPS 46239 2340 A4
E English Av
900 INPS 46202 2337 E4
900 INPS 46203 2337 E4
1300 INPS 46201 2337 E4
1500 INPS 46201 2338 A4
1500 INPS 46203 2338 A4
4800 INPS 46201 2339 A4
4800 INPS 46203 2339 A4
5100 INPS 46219 2339 A4
English Dr
600 WshT 46123 2223 A7
English Birch Ln
7100 INPS 46268 2118 A1
English Green Dr
10 WTFD 46074 1792 C2
English Oak Dr
7000 NBVL 46062 1685 E6
9300 INPS 46235 2231 E1
9300 LWNC 46235 2231 E1
English Oak Ln
6500 WshT 46123 2332 A2
English Oak Pl
9600 LWNC 46235 2122 E7
9600 LWNC 46235 2231 E1
English Oak Ter
4500 LWNC 46235 2122 D7
4500 LWNC 46235 2231 E1
English Oaks Dr
10700 ClyT 46032 1900 B7
English Village Dr
500 INPS 46239 2340 A4
English Village Ln
600 INPS 46239 2340 A5
Enmore Pk
- FCkT 46038 1905 E4
Ennis Dr
8400 INPS 46237 2557 E7
Ennis Wy
6700 INPS 46237 2557 D6
Enright Dr
5600 INPS 46228 2118 B5
Ensenada Av
5600 INPS 46237 2448 B6
Ensley Ct
5600 INPS 46254 2117 E5
7600 FSHR 46038 1904 B4
Ensley Dr
12300 FSHR 46038 1904 B4
Ensley Pl
12400 FSHR 46038 1904 B4
Enterprise Blvd
- LEBN 46052 1676 C7
300 CtrT 46052 1785 D1
300 LEBN 46052 1785 D1
N Enterprise Blvd
100 LEBN 46052 1676 B7
Enterprise Dr
- FSHR 46038 1904 E3
- GfdT 46113 2551 D6
- INPS 46113 2551 E7
- WTFD 46074 1683 D7
9600 CRML 46280 2011 D2
Enterprise St
2300 INPS 46219 2231 A6
Enterprise Park Pl
- INPS 46218 2229 B6
E Epler Av
10 INPS 46217 2555 C1
100 INPS 46227 2555 C1
1100 INPS 46227 2446 E7
1500 INPS 46227 2447 A7
4100 INPS 46237 2447 E7
W Epler Av
10 INPS 46217 2555 B1
1900 INPS 46217 2445 D7
1900 INPS 46217 2554 C1
9400 GfdT 46113 2551 D6
Epler Rd
5400 INPS 46221 2553 B1
8800 INPS 46241 2552 A1
8900 INPS 46241 2551 E1
W Epler Rd
5100 INPS 46221 2553 C1
5500 INPS 46231 2551 E1
5500 INPS 46241 2551 E1
5500 PNFD 46231 2551 E1
5500 PNFD 46241 2551 E1
Epperson Ct
5500 INPS 46221 2553 B2
7800 GfdT 46113 2551 D6
Epperson Dr
6000 INPS 46221 2553 B2
Epperson Ln
10500 GfdT 46113 2551 D5
Equestrian Ct
6800 INPS 46260 2118 D2
Equestrian Ln
6700 INPS 46260 2118 D2
Equina Ct
14100 CRML 46074 1791 D7
Erber Ct
500 INPS 46217 2555 A1
Eric Cir
3000 INPS 46235 2232 D4
Eric Ct
10600 FSHR 46038 1904 D7
Erica Ln
14700 WTFD 46033 1793 E6
Erickson Ct
3900 INPS 46235 2231 E2
Erie Av
4600 INPS 46205 2120 B7
Erie Pl
12700 FSHR 46038 1906 B3
Erie Wy
300 NBVL 46060 1686 C6
Erie Cove W
300 AVON 46123 2333 B3
Erika Ct
1700 INPS 46234 2225 A7
Erin Ct
200 WRvT 46142 2663 E4
3700 INPS 46235 2231 D2
Erin Dr
3600 INPS 46235 2231 E3
Erins Ct
- WTLD 46131 2774 D7
Ernie Pyle Ct
4700 WshT 46123 2331 C4
Erny Dr
900 GNWD 46142 2665 A2
Espirit Dr
1400 CRML 46074 1791 E7
14000 CRML 46074 1792 A7
Esplanade Ct
1100 LEBN 46052 1676 D5
E Esplanade St
- LEBN 46052 1677 B4
W Esplanade St
200 LEBN 46052 1676 E5
Esquire Ct
3800 INPS 46226 2231 C2
Esquire Pl
3800 INPS 46226 2231 C2
Essen Ct
11000 INPS 46235 2232 C3
Essex Ct
100 NBVL 46062 1576 C7
4000 INPS 46235 2231 D2
Essex Ct
4800 CRML 46033 1903 A2
Essex Dr
- MdlT 46167 2113 C5
200 LEBN 46052 1677 A5
4800 CRML 46033 1903 A2
E Essex St
- LEBN 46052 1677 A5
W Essex St
200 LEBN 46052 1676 E5
Essig Av
21700 WRvT 46060 1578 E5
21700 WRvT 46060 1579 A4
Estancia Wy
10600 ClyT 46032 1901 B7
Estate Av
5800 INPS 46228 2118 C4
Estate Blvd
4400 INPS 46221 2444 D5
Estate Dr
- BmT 46112 2114 D1
10 MRVL 46158 2659 D2
4200 INPS 46221 2444 D5
Estate Ln
4500 INPS 46221 2444 D5
Estate Pkwy
- INPS 46221 2444 D5
Estates Blvd
17200 NBVL 46060 1796 D1
Estates Dr
1300 GNWD 46142 2664 D4
Estelle St
7800 INPS 46227 2556 A5
Estep Dr
9900 ClyT 46280 2011 B1
Estes Dr
5000 WRvT 46142 2663 C2
Estes Rd
400 WRvT 46142 2663 C3
Estes Park Ct
500 INPS 46217 2555 B3
Esther Ct
1700 PNFD 46168 2550 D1
Estuary Dr
1200 INPS 46217 2554 E4
Esty Wy
11700 CRML 46033 1903 B5
Ethan Allen Ln
19400 WTFD 46074 1684 B4
Ethel Av
100 CCRO 46034 1577 D2
10300 ClyT 46280 2011 A1
Ethel St
3000 INPS 46208 2228 B4
Etna Dr
- WTFD 46074 1792 D3
Etna Grn
16100 WTFD 46074 1792 D3
Eucalyptus Ln
- FSHR 46060 1796 A7
Euclid Av
300 GNWD 46142 2665 B3
N Euclid Av
1000 INPS 46201 2338 E1
3000 INPS 46218 2229 E4
3800 INPS 46226 2229 E2
6000 INPS 46220 2120 E4
S Euclid Av
10 INPS 46201 2338 E3
1400 INPS 46203 2338 E6
Eugene Ct
- GNWD 46142 2665 C2
Eugene St
500 INPS 46208 2228 A5
1100 INPS 46208 2227 E5
1300 INPS 46222 2227 C5
Euliss Ct
7100 WshT 46123 2332 C2
Eustis Dr
1000 INPS 46229 2340 E1
2400 INPS 46229 2231 E6
Eva Ct
4700 INPS 46227 2446 C6
Eva Ln
4600 INPS 46227 2446 C6
Evans Av
900 NBVL 46060 1686 D6
E Evans Av
1000 NBVL 46060 1686 D6
Evans Dr
11100 CRML 46033 1903 A7
S Evans St
500 LEBN 46052 1677 A7
Evanston Av
4200 INPS 46205 2229 B1
4500 INPS 46205 2120 A7
6200 INPS 46220 2120 A3
7300 INPS 46240 2120 B1
7400 INPS 46240 2011 B7
N Evanston Av
7400 INPS 46240 2011 A7
Evanston Ct
5300 INPS 46220 2120 A6
Evanston Rd
7900 INPS 46240 2011 A6
Evelyn St
3900 INPS 46222 2227 A4
4000 INPS 46222 2226 E4
Evelyn Wy
1000 LEBN 46052 1676 D5
Evening Dr
900 GNWD 46143 2666 A3
E Evening Rose Wy
10 WshT 46074 1792 C4
W Evening Rose Wy
10 WshT 46074 1792 C4
Evening Shade Cir
1000 BHGV 46107 2447 E5
Evening Shade Ln
900 BHGV 46107 2447 E5
900 INPS 46107 2447 E5
Eveningsong Dr
3000 INPS 46241 2444 C3
Everbloom Ln
6600 INPS 46217 2554 C3
Everbloom Pl
- INPS 46217 2554 B3
Everbloom Wy
2900 INPS 46217 2554 B3
Everest Dr
1400 INPS 46234 2333 E1
Everest Ln
1400 INPS 46234 2333 D1
1400 INPS 46234 2334 A1
Everett
- MnrT 46157 2657 B7
Everett St
1300 INPS 46222 2336 E3
Everglades Ct
6700 INPS 46217 2555 A3
Evergreen Av
3500 INPS 46205 2228 E3
9400 INPS 46240 2010 E3
N Evergreen Av
8400 INPS 46240 2010 E5
Evergreen Ct
1100 INPS 46240 2010 E4
Evergreen Dr
- CtrT 46140 2237 A5
1300 GNFD 46140 2237 A5
Evergreen Ln
10 BmT 46158 2659 A6
Evergreen Pt
10600 FSHR 46038 1905 E7
Evergreen St
200 GNWD 46142 2665 B4
Everton Ct
- GNWD 46143 2664 E6
Everwood Cir
12000 NBVL 46060 1796 E2
12000 NBVL 46060 1797 A2
Evian Ct
7800 LWNC 46236 2014 E7
Evian Dr
7700 LWNC 46236 2014 E7
Evison St
1100 INPS 46203 2338 A6
Ewbank Ct
7300 GfdT 46113 2551 D5
Ewing Ct
100 CRML 46032 1793 A7
N Ewing St
1000 INPS 46201 2338 D1
1400 INPS 46201 2229 D7
6500 INPS 46220 2120 D2
S Ewing St
10 INPS 46201 2338 D3
1000 INPS 46203 2338 D5
3700 INPS 46237 2447 D4
Excalibur Ct
6400 INPS 46268 2117 D3
Exchange St
9600 FSHR 46038 1904 E4
11000 INPS 46259 2559 C5
Executive Dr
10 CRML 46032 1902 B4
1700 INPS 46241 2335 C7
2200 INPS 46241 2444 B1
Executive Park Dr
700 GNWD 46143 2665 C5
N Exeter Av
1000 INPS 46222 2336 B1
1600 INPS 46222 2227 A7
S Exeter Av
400 INPS 46241 2336 B4
Exeter Ct
300 GNWD 46143 2665 E3
9000 FSHR 46060 1795 D7
Exit 5 Pkwy
11600 FSHR 46038 1904 E5
11600 FSHR 46038 1905 A4
Exmoor Ct
4300 INPS 46254 2226 A1
Expo Ln
1600 INPS 46214 2225 C7
Eyford Ct
7800 LWNC 46236 2014 C7
Eyford Ln
7700 LWNC 46236 2014 C7

F

F St
- BHGV 46107 2447 D3
Fable St
6500 INPS 46227 2556 A3
Fabyan Rd
500 INPS 46217 2555 A6
N Faculty Dr
3400 INPS 46224 2226 A3
3800 INPS 46254 2226 B2
S Faculty Dr
1100 INPS 46241 2335 A6
Fahey Dr
2000 ClyT 46280 2011 B1
Fairbanks Dr
1000 CRML 46033 1902 D3
Fairbourne Ct
- CRML 46033 1903 B4
Fairfax Ct
- GNWD 46143 2666 A7
13000 FCkT 46055 2015 B2
Fairfax Rd
2400 INPS 46227 2447 B7
Fairfield Av
500 INPS 46205 2228 D3
1400 INPS 46205 2229 A2
Fairfield Blvd
18700 NBVL 46060 1686 E5
Fairfield Ct
1600 GNFD 46140 2237 B7
Fairfield Dr
10 BNBG 46112 2223 D2
800 GNFD 46140 2237 B7
Fairfield Rd
6200 PNFD 46168 2440 D4
Fair Glen Ct
1700 CtrT 46140 2237 C6
Fairgreen Dr
11600 CRML 46032 1902 A5

STREET Block City ZIP Map# Grid

Fairgrove Ct
8200 INPS 46227 2556 D6
Fairgrove Dr
3600 INPS 46227 2556 C6
Fairhaven Ct
10300 INPS 46229 2232 B7
Fair Haven Dr
- CRML 46033 2012 A2
9900 CRML 46033 2011 E1
Fairhaven Dr
2500 INPS 46229 2232 A5
Fairhope Dr
1600 INPS 46227 2556 A2
4100 INPS 46237 2556 E2
Fairlane Dr
10 BNBG 46112 2223 D2
10 MRVL 46158 2659 E1
1100 LEBN 46052 1676 E4
6000 INPS 46259 2559 B2
Fairlane East Ct
10 DNVL 46122 2329 C4
Fairlane West Dr
6200 INPS 46259 2559 B2
Fairmead Rd
800 PNFD 46168 2441 E6
Fairmont Ct
1900 INPS 46229 2232 A7
Fairmount Ct
200 WshT 46123 2333 C3
Fairmount Dr
10100 AVON 46123 2333 C3
10100 WshT 46123 2333 C3
Fairmount St
- CRML 46032 1900 E2
Fair Oaks Dr
2100 SDWY 46224 2226 C6
4000 FKLN 46131 2774 E7
Fairoaks Trc
- WRvT 46142 2663 D3
Fair Point Dr
10 GNWD 46143 2665 C7
Fairport Cir
11300 INPS 46236 2014 D4
Fair Ridge Dr
6800 INPS 46221 2552 E1
Fair Ridge Pl
5500 INPS 46221 2552 E1
Fairview Dr
1200 GNFD 46140 2236 C6
Fairview Dr E
700 GNWD 46142 2665 C2
Fairview Dr N
100 GNWD 46142 2665 C2
Fairview Dr S
100 GNWD 46142 2665 C2
Fairview Pkwy
9300 NBVL 46060 1686 E5
9300 NbvT 46060 1686 E5
Fairview Pl
400 GNWD 46142 2664 C2
Fairview Rd
1000 CtrT 46052 1679 A2
3400 CtrT 46052 1570 A7
W Fairview Rd
3000 GNWD 46142 2664 A3
3300 WRvT 46142 2664 A3
4000 WRvT 46142 2663 D3
5500 WRvT 46142 2662 E3
Fairview Ter
4200 INPS 46208 2228 A1
Fairway Av
6500 INPS 46250 2012 D5
Fairway Ct
7300 LWNC 46236 2123 E1
Fairway Dr
- BrnT 46112 2114 D1
100 INPS 46260 2119 A1
100 NBVL 46062 1685 B5
1500 INPS 46260 2118 E1
3100 ClyT 46032 2009 B2
4800 WshT 46123 2331 C5
Fairway Tr
8500 INPS 46250 2012 D4
Fairway Cir East Dr
7300 LWNC 46236 2123 E1
Fairway Cir North Dr
11800 LWNC 46236 2123 D1
Fairway Cir South Dr
11900 LWNC 46236 2123 D1
Fairway Cir West Dr
7300 LWNC 46236 2123 D1
Fairway Ridge Ln
10800 FSHR 46038 1905 C6
S Fairway Village Blvd
900 CtrT 46140 2346 B3
S Fairway Village Ct
- CtrT 46140 2346 A3
E Fairway Village Dr
2700 CtrT 46140 2346 B3
Fairweather Dr
2100 INPS 46229 2232 D6
Fairweather Pl
11300 INPS 46229 2232 D6
Fairwind
- BNBG 46112 2114 A3
Fairwind Ct
2600 ClyT 46032 2009 C1
8400 INPS 46256 2013 C5
Fairwood Cir
7300 INPS 46256 2122 B1
Fairwood Ct
100 MRVL 46158 2659 E1
Fairwood Dr
10 BNBG 46112 2223 D2
13100 FCkT 46055 2015 C2
N Fairwood Dr
6600 INPS 46256 2122 B1
Fairwood East Ct
6800 INPS 46256 2122 B2
Fairwoods Dr
10800 FSHR 46038 2014 C1
Fairwood West Ct
6800 INPS 46256 2122 B2
Faith St
1500 GNWD 46142 2664 C4
Falcon Ct
4200 INPS 46222 2226 E3
Falcon Dr
3400 INPS 46222 2226 E3
Falcon Ln
5900 INPS 46224 2226 B3
W Falcon Ln
5100 INPS 46224 2226 D3
Falcon Rdg
1000 CRML 46280 2011 A2
6700 INPS 46278 2007 E5
Falcon Wy
- FCkT 46055 2015 C2
Falcon Creek Blvd
4300 INPS 46254 2226 C1
Falcon Creek Wy
5300 INPS 46254 2226 C1
Falcon Grove Ct
6000 INPS 46254 2117 B6
Falcon Grove Dr
4700 INPS 46254 2117 A7
Falcon Pointe Ln
6300 INPS 46237 2557 D4
Falcon Run Wy
4600 INPS 46254 2117 B7
Falcon Talon Ln
7000 INPS 46254 2116 D7
Falkirk Cir
900 GNWD 46143 2664 E5
Falkirk Ct
1100 GNWD 46143 2664 E5
8800 INPS 46256 2013 D3
Falkirk Dr
- WshT 46123 2332 E1
N Falkirk Dr
9400 INPS 46256 2013 D3
Fall Dr
11000 INPS 46229 2232 C6
Fall Rd
10600 FCkT 46038 1905 C7
10600 FSHR 46038 1905 C7
Fall Creek Dr
7700 LWNC 46236 2014 A7
W Fall Creek Dr
9300 GrnT 46064 1907 E5
9700 FCkT 46040 1907 E5
9700 FCkT 46064 1907 E5
Fall Creek Rd
- FSHR 46038 2014 D2
- FSHR 46038 2015 A1
- FSHR 46256 2014 D2
4900 INPS 46220 2121 C4
6700 INPS 46226 2121 C4
7000 INPS 46226 2122 A3
7000 INPS 46256 2121 C4
7000 INPS 46256 2122 A3
7000 LWNC 46226 2121 C4
7000 LWNC 46226 2122 A3
7000 LWNC 46256 2122 A3
9400 INPS 46256 2013 E7
9400 LWNC 46256 2013 E7
9700 INPS 46256 2014 A5
10500 FCkT 46256 2014 C2
11600 FCkT 46038 2014 D2
11700 FCkT 46038 2015 A1
11700 FCkT 46055 2015 A1
11700 FCkT 46236 2015 A1
11700 FCkT 46256 2015 A1
Fall Creek Rd N
- INPS 46226 2122 A3
- INPS 46256 2121 E3
- INPS 46256 2122 A3
- LWNC 46226 2122 A3
- LWNC 46256 2122 A3
E Fall Creek Parkway North Dr
3900 INPS 46205 2229 A2
Fall Creek Pkwy East Dr
1100 INPS 46202 2337 A1
1300 INPS 46202 2228 A7
W Fall Creek Pkwy N Dr
- INPS 46202 2228 B6
10 INPS 46205 2228 B6
400 INPS 46208 2228 B6
Fall Creek Pkwy North Dr
4400 INPS 46205 2229 C1
E Fall Creek Pkwy North Dr
- INPS 46220 2121 A6
10 INPS 46205 2228 C5
10 INPS 46208 2228 C5
4300 INPS 46205 2229 B1
4500 INPS 46205 2120 D7
5200 INPS 46220 2120 D7
5400 INPS 46226 2121 A6
W Fall Creek Pkwy North Dr
- INPS 46202 2228 B6
- INPS 46208 2228 B6
E Fall Creek Pkwy South Dr
10 INPS 46205 2228 C5
10 INPS 46208 2228 C5
2800 INPS 46205 2229 C1
W Fall Creek Pkwy South Dr
10 INPS 46205 2228 C6
10 INPS 46208 2228 C6
Fall Creekway E
3100 INPS 46205 2229 C1
Fall Creekway N
4300 INPS 46205 2229 C1
Fallen Oak Dr
10200 INPS 46239 2341 A6
Fallingbrook Dr
400 FSHR 46038 2012 D1
Falling Tree Wy
6400 LWNC 46236 2123 B3
Falling Water Wy
11200 FSHR 46038 1905 A6
Falling Waters Dr
- MCVL 46055 2015 D4
Fallon Ct
1600 GNFD 46140 2236 D5
Fallon Ln
200 GNFD 46140 2236 D5
S Fallow Tr
3500 SCkT 46163 2451 D2
Falls Cir
3800 WTFD 46033 1793 D3
Falls Church Ct
2300 INPS 46229 2232 C5
Falls Church Dr
11000 INPS 46229 2232 C6
Fall Time Pl
6800 INPS 46226 2230 E1
Fallview Dr
- FSHR 46038 1904 E6
9700 FCkT 46038 1904 E6
Fallwood Dr
5200 INPS 46220 2120 E6
Fallwood Wy
2100 ClyT 46032 2009 D2
Fanchon Dr
9100 INPS 46278 2007 D3
Fank Boner Ct
600 GNWD 46143 2665 E3
N Fanning St
100 SRDN 46069 1573 B1
S Fanning St
100 SRDN 46069 1573 B1
W Farber St
200 INPS 46202 2337 C1
Far Hill Ct
5300 INPS 46226 2121 B6
Far Hill Rd
5300 INPS 46226 2121 B6
Farina Wy
7800 INPS 46259 2558 B6
Faris Av
6800 INPS 46226 2230 E1
7000 LWNC 46226 2230 E1
7000 LWNC 46226 2231 A1
Farley Cir
6600 INPS 46214 2334 E3
Farley Dr
1000 INPS 46214 2335 A1
1500 INPS 46214 2334 E1
1600 INPS 46214 2225 E7
12400 FSHR 46038 1904 C4
Farley Pl
7800 FSHR 46038 1904 C4
Farmbrook Ct
3300 LcnT 46123 2222 C4
Farmhill Rd
8300 INPS 46231 2334 B6
Farmhurst Ln
8000 INPS 46236 2014 D6
Farmington Rd
- INPS 46260 2010 A4
Farmleigh Dr
6000 INPS 46220 2121 C2
Farm Meadow Dr
- GNWD 46143 2665 B7
Farmstead Dr
- FCkT 46040 2015 D1
S Farmstone Cir
3600 SCkT 46163 2451 E1
Farm View Cir E
7500 INPS 46256 2013 A7
Farm View Cir W
7500 INPS 46256 2013 A7
Farmview Ln
900 WTFD 46032 1792 E6
1100 WTFD 46032 1793 A6
Farnsworth St
3500 INPS 46241 2445 A2
3900 INPS 46241 2444 D2
Farragut Cir
9600 FCkT 46256 2014 C2
Farr Hills Dr
15900 WshT 46032 1793 A4
Farrington Av
4500 INPS 46201 2338 E4
4800 INPS 46201 2339 A4
Fathom Cir
10200 INPS 46256 2014 A4
Fathom Ct
10100 INPS 46256 2014 A4
Fathom Ln
11000 FCkT 46040 1907 A6
Fathom Crst
8800 INPS 46256 2014 A4
Faucet Ln
- FCkT 46040 1906 E7
14400 FCkT 46040 1907 A7
Faulkner Ct
200 CRML 46032 1901 C3
Fauna Ln
4800 INPS 46234 2116 B7
Faust Av
1500 INPS 46203 2339 B6
Faust Cir
2500 CRML 46033 1793 B7
W Faut Rd
3000 SCkT 46163 2452 C5
Fauvre Rd
5000 INPS 46228 2118 E7
Fawn Ct
200 PTBR 46167 2113 A3
Fawn Dr
3800 INPS 46254 2225 E2
9100 BrnT 46278 2006 E4
Fawn Hill Ct
5200 INPS 46226 2121 A6
Fawn Hill Ter
5200 INPS 46226 2121 A6
Fawn Hollow Ln
14600 NBVL 46060 1796 E6
N Fawn Lake Cir
8600 INPS 46278 2007 A4
Fawn Lake Dr
9100 INPS 46278 2006 E4
9100 INPS 46278 2007 A4
Fawn Meadow Dr
- MCVL 46055 2015 C5
15200 NBVL 46060 1796 E5
N Fawn Meadow Dr
8500 INPS 46256 2013 C5
Fawn Ridge Ln
10300 LWNC 46236 2123 B1
Fawns Rdg
12900 FSHR 46038 1904 B3
Fawns Run
13000 FSHR 46038 1904 B3
Fawnsbrook Dr
8100 FSHR 46038 1904 B3
Fawnsbrook Pl
8100 FSHR 46038 1904 B3
Fawns Dell Pl
12900 FSHR 46038 1904 B3
Fawn View Dr
900 CRML 46032 1792 A7
Fawnwood Dr
6000 WRvT 46143 2663 A7
8000 INPS 46278 2007 B6
Fay Ct
10 INPS 46226 2230 D1
Fay St
- INPS 46221 2336 E6
Faye Ct
5200 CRML 46033 1903 B5
Fayette Dr
500 WTFD 46074 1792 D1
N Fayette St
800 INPS 46202 2337 B2
Feather Grass Wy
9500 FSHR 46038 1795 E7
Feather Rock Ct
11400 FSHR 46038 1906 B6
Feather Run Cir
7200 INPS 46237 2557 D4
Feather Run Dr
- INPS 46237 2557 D4
Federal Pl
- FSHR 46038 1906 B3
Federalist Ct
5600 INPS 46254 2117 B5
Feehan Dr
3800 CRML 46074 1900 A2
Feldman Dr
- BNBG 46112 2223 E4
Feldspar Rd
12600 LWNC 46236 2124 A1
Fen Ct
5600 INPS 46220 2120 D5
Fendler Ct
8000 INPS 46259 2557 E6
Fendler Dr
8100 INPS 46259 2557 E6
Fenley Dr
1100 LEBN 46052 1676 D4
Fenmore Rd
5200 INPS 46228 2118 B6
Fennel Ct
900 CCRO 46034 1577 B6
7900 INPS 46237 2557 A5
Fennick Dr
5300 INPS 46237 2557 A2
Fenster Ct
600 INPS 46234 2334 A2
Fenster Dr
100 INPS 46234 2334 A3
N Fenton Av
- INPS 46219 2340 C1
S Fenton Av
10 INPS 46219 2340 C3
5800 INPS 46239 2558 C1
Fenway Av
7800 INPS 46260 2009 E6
Fenway St
6700 BrnT 46112 2005 B6
N Fenwick Av
1300 INPS 46219 2340 C1
Fenwick Ct
1500 INPS 46219 2340 C1
Ferdinand Ct
- WshT 46234 2224 E6
Fergus Av
- ClyT 46032 2009 B1
10400 ClyT 46032 1900 B7
Ferguson Cir
- WshT 46123 2332 E1
Ferguson Rd
400 BrnT 46113 2660 C2
400 MdnT 46113 2660 C2
S Ferguson Rd
3600 INPS 46239 2449 B4
Ferguson St
6300 INPS 46220 2119 E3
Fern Ct
1600 INPS 46260 2009 E6
Fern Dr
1900 WshT 46074 1682 E7
Ferncliff Av
3300 INPS 46227 2556 C1
Ferndale Ct
700 INPS 46227 2446 D6
Fernleaf Wy
13700 CRML 46033 1903 D1
Fernway St
2000 INPS 46218 2229 A7
Fernwood Ct
700 INPS 46234 2334 A2
1100 WshT 46168 2441 C1
Fernwood Dr
14700 WTFD 46033 1793 D6
Ferrari Pl
6400 INPS 46224 2226 A6
Ferrell Ln
7900 INPS 46260 2010 B6
Fetlock Dr
3700 INPS 46227 2447 C4
Fetlock Pl
2900 INPS 46227 2447 C4
Fetterbush Ln
5400 BHGV 46203 2448 B4
Field Dr
1000 NBVL 46060 1686 D5
1000 NbvT 46060 1686 D5
1600 NBVL 46060 1687 A5
1600 NbvT 46060 1687 A5
Fieldcrest Ln
- GNWD 46143 2666 B6
Fieldfare Wy
8300 INPS 46237 2556 D6
Fieldgrass Run
- WshT 46074 1792 C5
Fieldhurst Ln
3500 PNFD 46168 2440 D4
S Fielding Dr
3000 SCkT 46163 2342 E7
S Fielding Rd
3100 SCkT 46163 2342 D7
Field Master Dr
4200 EglT 46077 1899 C2
Fieldmint Ct
3600 INPS 46235 2232 C3
Fields Blvd
1600 GNFD 46140 2236 D5
4700 INPS 46239 2448 E6
Fields Dr
7000 INPS 46239 2448 E5
7100 INPS 46239 2449 A6
Fields Wy
7100 INPS 46239 2448 E6
7200 INPS 46239 2449 A6
Fieldshire Ter
13600 CRML 46074 1900 C1
Fieldstone Ct
2000 WTFD 46074 1684 B5
7400 INPS 46254 2116 D7
7500 BrnT 46112 2114 B2
7600 CBLD 46140 2233 A6
11300 CRML 46033 1903 A6
Fieldstone Pl
12500 FSHR 46038 1904 A4
Fieldstone Tr
4800 INPS 46254 2116 D7
Fieldstream Dr
6200 WshT 46123 2441 A1
6700 WshT 46168 2441 A1
Fiesta Ct
900 GNWD 46143 2666 A5
6300 INPS 46237 2557 C1
Fiesta Dr
800 GNWD 46143 2666 A5
Fiesta St
6300 INPS 46237 2557 D1
Fife Tr
5800 CRML 46033 1903 E2
Fillmore Dr
400 WTFD 46074 1792 D1
Filly Ln
8100 GfdT 46168 2550 D6
Finch Blvd
2500 LEBN 46052 1676 E2
2700 CtrT 46052 1676 E2
Finch Ct
100 LEBN 46052 1676 E2
14300 CRML 46033 1794 B7
Finchley Rd
2300 CRML 46032 1900 D4
6500 INPS 46250 2121 D1
Finchum Dr
2700 BrnT 46112 2114 C1
Finley Av
1100 INPS 46203 2446 E1
1500 INPS 46203 2447 A1
Finley St
8500 INPS 46113 2552 A3
Finnegan Ct
1400 INPS 46217 2554 E5
Fiona Wy
- GNWD 46143 2666 A7
Fir Ct
4000 INPS 46250 2011 E7
Fireberry Ct
12200 LWNC 46236 2014 E6
12200 LWNC 46236 2015 A7
Firelight Ct
10700 NBVL 46060 1687 C4
Fire Pink Ct
8800 INPS 46231 2334 A7
Fireside Cir
9300 INPS 46250 2012 E3
Fireside Ct
9100 INPS 46250 2012 E3
Fireside Dr
9100 INPS 46250 2012 E3
Fireside Ln
- FSHR 46038 1904 E1
9600 FSHR 46038 1905 A1
Firestone Cir
3000 INPS 46234 2225 B4
Firethorn Ct
700 NBVL 46062 1685 C2
Fire Thorn Ct
- BrnT 46112 2114 D1
Firethorn Dr
12400 LWNC 46236 2124 A2
Firewalker Ln
7500 INPS 46217 2554 C5
First Lady Blvd
6000 INPS 46237 2557 C1
First Watch Wy
- MCVL 46055 2015 C4
Fishback Rd
7000 BrnT 46112 2115 E1
7000 INPS 46112 2115 E1
7000 INPS 46278 2115 E1
7100 INPS 46278 2116 A1
7400 INPS 46278 2007 A6
Fishback Hill Ln
7200 INPS 46278 2115 E1
7200 INPS 46278 2116 A1
Fisher Av
1600 SDWY 46224 2226 D7
Fisher Ct
200 INPS 46241 2335 D4
Fisher Dr
100 WynT 46060 1687 C5
Fisher Ln
- DNVL 46122 2329 C4
S Fisher Rd
- INPS 46239 2340 A7
2200 INPS 46239 2449 A1
Fisher St
- PTBR 46167 2112 E4
Fishermans Ct
7800 LWNC 46236 2014 B6
Fishers Dr
11500 FSHR 46038 1904 A6
Fishers Center Dr
8400 FSHR 46038 1904 C5
Fishers Corner Blvd
11600 FSHR 46038 1904 D5
Fishers Crossing Dr
7200 FSHR 46038 1904 A5
Fishers Landing Dr
7200 FSHR 46038 1904 A5
Fishers Pointe Blvd
8400 FSHR 46038 1904 C5
11400 DelT 46038 1904 C5
Fishers Station Dr
- FSHR 46038 1904 A5
Fishers Station Wy
- FSHR 46038 1904 A5
Fishlake Dr
5300 INPS 46254 2117 A6
Fitch Av
7100 INPS 46220 2120 A1
7100 INPS 46240 2120 A1
Fitch Pl
300 ZNVL 46077 1899 B5
Fitness Ln
8800 FSHR 46038 2013 D2
S Five Points Rd
3000 INPS 46203 2448 E4
3000 INPS 46239 2448 E4
4000 INPS 46237 2448 E4
5300 INPS 46237 2557 E2
5300 INPS 46239 2557 E2
6000 INPS 46259 2557 E2
Fjord Dr
5500 INPS 46250 2012 B3
Flagler Pl
12600 LWNC 46236 2015 A6
Flagship Cir
8700 INPS 46256 2014 B4
Flagstaff Ct
6300 INPS 46237 2557 C6
Flagstone Dr
12000 FSHR 46038 1906 A4
Flaherty Ln
7800 INPS 46217 2554 E5
Flame Wy
4800 INPS 46254 2117 B7
Flamingo East Dr
4100 INPS 46226 2230 B1
Flamingo West Dr
4100 INPS 46226 2230 B2
Flannagen Av
10 CCRO 46034 1577 D2
Flap Ln
2800 INPS 46218 2229 C5
Flat Branch Ct
8100 INPS 46259 2558 B5
E Flat Branch Dr
8200 INPS 46259 2558 B5
Flat Rock Ct
8000 INPS 46256 2013 B6
E Flat Rock Dr
- MdnT 46113 2661 B2
10 WTFD 46074 1792 D1
W Flat Rock Dr
10 WTFD 46074 1792 C1
W Flatsedge Dr
7300 INPS 46254 2225 D2
Flatstick Ct
11400 LWNC 46235 2123 D7
Flattop Rd
- CtrT 46122 2331 A4
- WshT 46122 2331 A4
Flattop Ln St
3900 CtrT 46122 2331 A4
3900 WshT 46122 2331 A4
Fleener Ct
8800 WshT 46123 2333 A2
Fleetwood Ct
300 CRML 46032 1901 C2
Fleetwood Dr
800 INPS 46228 2119 A5
N Fleetwood Dr
12900 CRML 46032 1901 C3
Fleetwood Dr S
12800 CRML 46032 1901 C3
N Fleming St
200 INPS 46222 2335 E3
S Fleming St
10 INPS 46241 2335 E4
2600 INPS 46241 2444 E2
Fletcher Av
500 INPS 46202 2337 E4
500 INPS 46203 2337 E4
3600 INPS 46203 2338 D5
4800 INPS 46203 2339 A5
5100 INPS 46219 2339 A5
Fletcher Ct
5300 INPS 46226 2121 B6
Fletcher Ln
400 BHGV 46107 2447 E4
400 BHGV 46107 2448 A4
Fletcher Trc
13000 CRML 46033 1903 E3
Flick Dr
6800 INPS 46237 2557 E6
Flick Wy
8400 INPS 46237 2557 D6
Flicker Ct
8300 INPS 46237 2556 D6
Flight School Dr
5600 INPS 46221 2444 B6
Flinchum Wy E
16900 NBVL 46062 1794 C2
Flinchum Wy N
5600 NBVL 46062 1794 B1
Flinchum Wy S
5500 NBVL 46062 1794 B2
Flinchum Wy W
17000 NBVL 46062 1794 B2
Flintlock Cir
16600 NBVL 46062 1794 E2
Flintlock Ct
8700 INPS 46256 2013 D4
Flintlock Dr
- GNWD 46143 2666 B6
Flintridge Pass
13400 CRML 46033 1903 D2
Flint Stone Ct
12000 FSHR 46038 1906 A4
Flintstone Dr
5100 INPS 46237 2557 A2
Flippins Rd
19100 WshT 46074 1684 C4
21600 JknT 46034 1575 C5
Floating Leaf Dr
5400 INPS 46237 2448 E7
Flora Dr
- GfdT 46168 2440 E4
Flora Hunt Pl
- FCkT 46038 1905 E4
- FSHR 46038 1905 E4
Floral Hall Pl
- FSHR 46038 1905 E4
Florence Dr
100 GNWD 46143 2665 C5
8000 BrnT 46112 2114 D4
Florida Rd
10400 FCkT 46040 1907 B7
10400 FCkT 46040 2016 B1
23600 WRvT 46060 1580 B1
Flotation Av
- INPS 46221 2445 D2
Flower Mound Pl
10800 FSHR 46038 1905 C5
Flowing Water Wy
3800 WTFD 46062 1793 D2
Floyd Dr
4000 INPS 46221 2444 E6
Floyd Rd
800 GNWD 46142 2664 D1
Fluvia Ter
8600 INPS 46250 2012 B4
Flynn Rd
- GfdT 46113 2551 D3
- GfdT 46231 2551 D3
5000 INPS 46241 2443 B7
5000 INPS 46241 2552 B1
8900 INPS 46113 2551 E3
8900 INPS 46241 2551 E3
Fogelson Ct
11100 INPS 46229 2232 C7
Fogelson Dr
1600 INPS 46229 2232 C7
Foggy Ct
9100 INPS 46260 2009 E3
Foggy Dr
1600 INPS 46260 2009 E3
Folcroft Ct
600 INPS 46234 2334 B2
Folkstone Rd
8000 INPS 46268 2009 B6
Follow Dr
15100 NBVL 46060 1796 E5
15500 WynT 46060 1796 E5
Folly Brook Rd
16900 NBVL 46060 1797 A1
Folsom Dr
10500 INPS 46235 2232 B4
Foltz St
400 INPS 46241 2335 E5
2600 INPS 46241 2444 E3
3000 INPS 46221 2444 E4
S Foltz St
2400 INPS 46241 2444 E1
Fontana Dr
1100 INPS 46229 2341 D1
2300 WshT 46234 2224 D7
Fonthill Dr
11200 INPS 46236 2014 C5
Foolish Pleasure Ln
5700 INPS 46237 2557 C2
Foote Trail Cir
17100 NBVL 46060 1797 A1
Ford Cir
9000 FSHR 46038 1904 D3
Ford Dr
12500 FSHR 46038 1904 E3
Ford Rd
- WshT 46123 2331 A4
N Ford Rd
300 ZNVL 46077 1899 A6
600 ZNVL 46077 1898 E5
S Ford Rd
700 ZNVL 46077 1898 E7
7000 EglT 46077 2007 E2
7000 ZNVL 46077 2007 E2
7900 EglT 46077 2008 A2
7900 EglT 46278 2007 E2
7900 EglT 46278 2008 A2
Ford St
4900 SDWY 46224 2335 D1
Fordham Ln
2900 INPS 46268 2009 C2
Fordham St
8900 INPS 46268 2009 B3
Fordham Wy
6300 FSHR 46038 1903 D6
Fordice Rd
800 LEBN 46052 1677 B5
E Fordice St
100 LEBN 46052 1677 A5
W Fordice St
100 LEBN 46052 1676 E5
100 LEBN 46052 1677 B4
Ford Valley Ln
- EglT 46077 2007 E1
Forest Av
- GNWD 46143 2665 D4
10 GNFD 46140 2345 E2
N Forest Av
10 INPS 46201 2338 B3
S Forest Av
10 INPS 46201 2338 B4
Forest Blvd
100 INPS 46240 2010 D6
700 ZNVL 46077 1899 C5

STREET Block City ZIP Map# Grid

E Forest Blvd
700 INPS 46240 2010 E6
Forest Ct
100 CtrT 46140 2236 C1
4700 INPS 46218 2229 E2
Forest Dr
1700 INPS 46227 2556 A2
4000 LcnT 46112 2223 A2
7500 FSHR 46038 1904 B7
7500 INPS 46217 2555 A5
11600 CRML 46033 1902 D5
E Forest Dr
4400 BNBG 46112 2223 A2
4400 LcnT 46112 2223 A2
Forest Dr N
- GfdT 46168 2550 B1
Forest Ln
- NBVL 46060 1686 C6
700 CtrT 46140 2236 C1
5800 INPS 46220 2119 E5
6500 WshT 46123 2332 B5
11800 CRML 46033 1903 C5
E Forest Ln
8200 INPS 46240 2010 E5
Forest Mnr
- INPS 46220 2120 E5
Forest Pl
- CRML 46033 1902 D4
Forest Ter
13800 CRML 46032 1792 C7
Forest Bay Ln
10 JknT 46034 1576 E5
Forest Blvd North Dr
800 INPS 46240 2010 E6
Forest Blvd South Dr
800 INPS 46240 2010 E6
W Forest Brook Dr
6700 MrlT 46130 2560 D6
Forest Commons Ct
- WshT 46123 2223 C7
Forest Commons Dr
1000 WshT 46123 2332 D1
1600 WshT 46123 2223 D7
Forest Creek Dr
10200 INPS 46239 2341 B6
Forest Glen Dr
1000 CtrT 46140 2237 B7
Forest Grove Dr
3800 INPS 46205 2229 D2
Forest Grove Rd
100 MdnT 46158 2661 B6
Forest Hills Dr
400 INPS 46224 2335 C2
Forest Hollow Dr
10 JknT 46034 1577 A4
Forest Knoll Cir
11400 FCkT 46038 1906 B6
Forest Knoll Ct
200 FCkT 46038 1906 B5
Forest Knoll Ln
100 FCkT 46038 1906 B6
Forest Lake Rd
7200 INPS 46219 2340 A4
Forest Manor Av
2600 INPS 46218 2229 D5
3800 INPS 46226 2229 E2
4500 INPS 46226 2120 D7
N Forest Manor Av
1900 INPS 46218 2229 E7
Forest Manor Dr
- MdnT 46158 2661 E5
Forest Park Dr
7000 INPS 46217 2555 A4
Forest Park Ln
11600 CRML 46033 1903 B5
Forest Pine Ln
5300 INPS 46224 2335 D2
Forest Ridge Ct
10 FCkT 46038 2013 E1
1600 GfdT 46168 2550 B1
5500 BHGV 46203 2448 B4
Forest Ridge Dr
- PNFD 46168 2441 B7
600 NBVL 46060 1686 C5
1500 GfdT 46168 2550 B1
Forest Rise Ct
5600 BHGV 46203 2448 B4
Forest Rise Ln
3800 BHGV 46203 2448 B4
Forest Trace Ct
900 CtrT 46140 2237 C7
Forest View Cir
10 JknT 46034 1576 E5
Forest View Ct
- WshT 46123 2332 A7
Forest View Dr
6000 INPS 46228 2119 A4
6300 INPS 46260 2119 A3
N Form St
7500 MCVL 46055 2015 C7
Forrest Dr
100 MdnT 46113 2661 E2
1600 PNFD 46168 2441 D5
Forrest Commons Blvd
6400 INPS 46227 2555 C3
Forrester Ct
- GNWD 46143 2665 B7
- GNWD 46143 2774 B1
Forreston Oak Dr
17800 NBVL 46062 1685 E6
17800 NBVL 46062 1686 A7
Forrest Park East Dr
1100 GNWD 46142 2665 D2
Forrest Park North Dr
400 GNWD 46142 2665 B1
Forrest Park South Dr
400 GNWD 46142 2665 B1
Forrests Edge Ct
10 INPS 46227 2555 C2
Forsythia Cir
8200 INPS 46219 2231 C7
Forsythia Ct
8100 INPS 46219 2231 B7
N Forsythia Dr
1600 INPS 46219 2231 C7
Forsythia Ln
14300 FSHR 46060 1796 A7
Fort Dr
9700 LWNC 46236 2122 E3
Fort Meyers Dr
10900 INPS 46229 2232 C6
Fort Sumter Dr
8300 INPS 46227 2556 C6
Fortune Cir E
2600 INPS 46241 2444 B2
Fortune Cir S
5500 INPS 46241 2444 B2
Fortune Cir W
5600 INPS 46241 2444 B2
Fortune Dr
9400 FSHR 46038 1904 E7
9600 FCkT 46038 1905 B6
9600 FSHR 46038 1905 B6
N Fortville Pike Rd
3000 CtrT 46140 2236 A1
3700 CtrT 46140 2235 E1
Fort Wayne Av
600 INPS 46204 2337 D2
800 INPS 46202 2337 D2
N Fort Wayne Av
- INPS 46204 2337 A4
Forum Dr
100 WTLD 46184 2775 A6
Forum Wk
9900 INPS 46229 2232 A5
Forum Meadows Dr
13400 CRML 46033 1903 D2
Forward Pass Ct
1600 INPS 46217 2554 D6
Forward Pass Rd
8000 INPS 46217 2554 D6
Foster Ct
13100 CRML 46033 1902 E2
Foster Dr
4600 CRML 46033 1902 E2
Foster Ridge Ln
3300 CRML 46033 1793 D7
Foundation Dr
400 GNFD 46140 2345 A1
17800 NBVL 46060 1687 A7
Foundation Ln
10 MdnT 46113 2661 C1
Founders Dr
400 GNFD 46140 2236 A7
400 GNFD 46140 2345 A1
Founders Ln
3200 INPS 46268 2009 B4
Founders Pl
11100 FSHR 46038 1904 C6
Founders Rd
8600 INPS 46268 2009 B4
Fountain Curv
5200 LcnT 46167 2113 C5
Fountain Dr
100 MRVL 46158 2660 B5
400 BNBG 46112 2114 A5
Fountain Ln
6800 INPS 46250 2012 E5
Fountain Cove Ct
6600 LWNC 46236 2123 A2
Fountain Cove Dr
9900 LWNC 46236 2123 A2
Fountain Cove Ln
9900 LWNC 46236 2123 A2
Fountain Grass Dr
- GNWD 46143 2666 A6
Fountainhead Dr
8000 INPS 46260 2009 E6
Fountain Lake Dr
10 CtrT 46140 2235 B3
Fountain Springs Blvd
6300 LWNC 46236 2123 A2
Fountain Springs Ct
10000 LWNC 46236 2123 A3
Fountainview Ct
8800 LWNC 46226 2122 D7
Fountain View Dr
- NBVL 46060 1687 A5
Fountainview Ln
11200 FSHR 46038 1904 C6
Four Seasons Cir
4400 INPS 46226 2230 E1
Four Seasons Wy
13700 CRML 46074 1900 C1
Four Winds Ct
6800 BrnT 46112 2114 B3
Fox Cir
100 NbvT 46060 1796 A4
Fox Ct
300 WshT 46032 1792 C5
E Fox Ct
10 BrnT 46113 2660 B2
Fox Dr
- NbvT 46060 1796 A4
300 BrnT 46113 2660 B2
300 MRVL 46113 2660 B2
Fox Lk N
6800 INPS 46278 2007 E6
Fox Lk S
6800 INPS 46278 2007 E6
Fox Ln
400 WshT 46032 1792 D6
Fox Rd
3700 LcnT 46112 2224 D2
10800 INPS 46236 2014 D6
10800 LWNC 46236 2014 D6
Fox Tr
10 BNBG 46112 2114 C5
Fox Trc
10000 UnnT 46077 1790 A5
Fox Wy
5400 INPS 46237 2448 B6
Foxboro Ln
9700 FSHR 46038 2012 D2
Foxborough Dr
7000 LWNC 46226 2121 E5
Foxbriar Cir
6100 INPS 46203 2448 C2
Foxbriar Pl
2800 INPS 46203 2448 C2
Foxchase Cir
8100 INPS 46256 2014 A6
Fox Chase Dr
8000 NBVL 46062 1686 B4
Foxchase Dr
8000 INPS 46256 2014 A6
Fox Cove Blvd
- SCkT 46239 2342 A5
S Fox Cove Blvd
1500 SCkT 46229 2342 A4
1500 SCkT 46239 2342 A4
Fox Creek Ln
10400 FSHR 46038 2014 B1
Foxdale Lake Dr
13600 CRML 46032 1901 B1
S Fox Den Blvd
- SCkT 46229 2342 A4
Foxfield Ln
10100 WshT 46231 2333 C6
10200 AVON 46123 2333 C3
10200 WshT 46123 2333 C3
Foxfire Cir
900 CRML 46032 1901 A1
3000 INPS 46214 2225 E4
3000 INPS 46214 2226 A4
Foxfire Ct
6600 INPS 46214 2226 D5
Foxfire Dr
3100 INPS 46214 2226 D5
6600 INPS 46214 2225 E4
Foxfire Ln
10 LcnT 46112 2222 E1
5700 BNBG 46112 2113 D7
5700 LcnT 46112 2113 D7
Foxford Dr
1000 WshT 46231 2333 C6
Fox Glen Dr
7800 INPS 46239 2449 B1
Foxglove Cir
1000 CRML 46033 1902 C2
Fox Glove Ct
1100 UnnT 46077 1790 B6
Foxglove Dr
- GNWD 46143 2774 A1
Foxglove Ln
5600 INPS 46254 2117 C6
7500 NBVL 46062 1686 A4
Foxglove Trc
4200 INPS 46237 2447 D5
Fox Harbour Cir
4200 INPS 46227 2447 A5
Fox Harbour Ct
2500 INPS 46227 2447 A5
Fox Harbour Dr
2400 INPS 46227 2447 B5
Fox Harbour Ln
2400 INPS 46227 2447 B5
Fox Harbour Pl
4200 INPS 46227 2447 A5
Fox Harbour Den
2500 INPS 46227 2447 A5
Fox Harbour East Dr
4200 INPS 46227 2447 B5
Fox Harbour North Dr
2500 INPS 46227 2447 B5
Fox Harbour South Dr
2400 INPS 46227 2447 B5
Fox Hill Ct
2300 INPS 46228 2118 C4
Fox Hill Dr
- INPS 46208 2119 A4
700 INPS 46228 2119 A4
1300 INPS 46228 2118 E4
Foxhill Dr
2600 MdnT 46113 2661 E5
2700 MdnT 46158 2661 E5
Fox Hollow Ct
- BrnT 46112 2115 E3
7400 EglT 46077 2007 E1
Fox Hollow Ln
7000 BrnT 46112 2115 E3
Fox Hollow Rd
7000 EglT 46077 1898 E7
7000 EglT 46077 2007 E1
Fox Hunt Ct
7200 BrnT 46112 2115 E3
Fox Lake Ct
6800 INPS 46278 2007 E6
Foxmere Blvd
1600 GNWD 46142 2664 C2
Foxmere Dr
1600 GNWD 46142 2664 C2
Foxmere Ter
600 GNWD 46142 2664 C2
Foxmere Wy
1600 GNWD 46142 2664 C2
Fox Moor Ln
4600 WRvT 46143 2663 D7
Fox Moor Pl
4600 WRvT 46143 2663 D7
Fox Moor Ter
1900 WRvT 46143 2663 E7
Fox Orchard Cir
3300 INPS 46214 2225 D4
Fox Orchard Ct
7100 INPS 46214 2225 D4
S Fox Paw Dr
- SCkT 46229 2342 A4
- SCkT 46239 2342 A4
Fox Pointe Ct
4500 INPS 46268 2117 E2
S Fox Ridge Av
1800 WRvT 46143 2663 E7
W Fox Ridge Av
4200 WRvT 46143 2663 E7
Fox Ridge Ln
8600 INPS 46256 2013 D4
Fox Run Cir
6700 INPS 46278 2007 E6
Fox Run Ct
10400 FSHR 46038 2014 B1
Fox Run Dr
2800 BCkT 46140 2233 A2
Fox Run Pth
7800 PNFD 46168 2550 D2
N Fox Run Rd
7900 INPS 46278 2007 E6
Fox Tail Cir
7500 AVON 46123 2332 C5
Foxtail Ct
5500 INPS 46221 2553 A1
7700 FSHR 46038 1904 C7
Foxtail Dr
3600 INPS 46235 2232 C3
Fox Trail Dr E
1100 SCkT 46163 2342 B3
Fox Trail Dr W
1100 SCkT 46163 2342 B3
Fox Valley Pl
2400 INPS 46268 2009 C3
W Fox View Tr
- SCkT 46229 2342 A4
- SCkT 46239 2342 A4
Foxwood Dr
- BNBG 46112 2223 B1
W Foxwood Dr
100 BNBG 46112 2223 B1
Foxwood Dr W
10300 ClyT 46280 2010 D1
Foxwood Ln
6000 INPS 46228 2119 A4
Foxwood Pl
11900 CRML 46033 1902 D5
Foyt Dr
1600 SDWY 46224 2226 A7
Fraiser Fir Dr
- GNWD 46184 2774 B1
Framington Ct
4600 INPS 46254 2116 D7
Frances St
8700 FSHR 46038 1904 D6
Francis Ct
5500 INPS 46221 2444 B6
14600 WshT 46074 1792 B6
Francis Ln
- INPS 46241 2335 D5
4700 INPS 46221 2444 B6
Frank Av
- INPS 46219 2340 C3
Frank St
10 INPS 46225 2337 C7
Frankdale Ct
8200 INPS 46259 2558 B6
Frankenberger Dr
6500 INPS 46237 2557 D7
Frankie Ct
4300 LcnT 46112 2222 D2
Franklin Blvd
1800 CRML 46032 1902 B5
Franklin Ct
700 GNFD 46140 2236 C7
700 GNFD 46140 2345 C1
6300 FSHR 46038 1903 D6
7900 INPS 46226 2231 B3
9900 ClyT 46280 2011 B1
Franklin Dr
1600 PNFD 46168 2441 D4
Franklin Pl
2300 INPS 46208 2228 B6
N Franklin Rd
10 INPS 46219 2340 B1
100 ClkT 46143 2667 C3
2100 INPS 46219 2231 B6
3000 INPS 46226 2231 B4
4200 LWNC 46226 2231 B4
4500 LWNC 46226 2122 B7
5400 LWNC 46216 2122 B7
S Franklin Rd
10 INPS 46219 2340 B4
100 ClkT 46143 2667 C5
500 INPS 46239 2340 B7
2200 INPS 46239 2449 C1
5600 INPS 46239 2558 C1
6000 INPS 46259 2558 C6
8400 ClkT 46143 2558 C6
8400 INPS 46143 2558 C6
Franklin St
- SgCT 46126 2670 E7
800 LEBN 46052 1676 E6
E Franklin St
10 BNBG 46112 2114 C6
N Franklin St
10 GNFD 46140 2345 C1
10 MRVL 46158 2659 E3
600 CtrT 46140 2345 C1
700 CtrT 46140 2236 C7
700 GNFD 46140 2236 C7
S Franklin St
10 GNFD 46140 2345 C2
10 MRVL 46158 2659 E4
500 CtrT 46140 2345 C2
1000 BrnT 46140 2345 C7
Franklin Trc
700 ZNVL 46077 1899 A4
900 ZNVL 46077 1898 E4
Franklin Wy
2100 INPS 46219 2231 B6
Franklinet
- GNFD 46140 2236 C7
- GNFD 46140 2345 C1
Franklin Hall Tr
13100 CRML 46033 1903 E2
Franklin Parke Blvd
7000 INPS 46259 2558 A4
7400 INPS 46259 2557 E4
Franklin Parke Ct
7300 INPS 46259 2558 A4
Franklin Parke Ln
7200 INPS 46259 2558 A3
Franklin Parke Wds
7400 INPS 46259 2558 A4
Franklin Villas Dr
4800 INPS 46237 2448 C6
Franklin Villas Pl
4800 INPS 46237 2448 C6
Franklin Villas Wy
6000 INPS 46237 2448 C6
Franks Ln
6000 VrnT 46055 2124 D3
Franks Wy
14000 FCkT 46040 2015 D1
Fraser Ct
5700 INPS 46254 2117 A4
Frederick Dr E
7300 INPS 46260 2010 A7
7300 INPS 46260 2119 A1
Frederick Dr S
1000 INPS 46260 2119 A1
Fredonia Rd
2500 INPS 46222 2226 E5
Fredricksburg Dr
3500 INPS 46227 2556 C6
Fred's Ct
6300 INPS 46237 2556 E2
Freedom Ct
5500 INPS 46254 2117 C5
Freedom Dr
12700 FSHR 46060 1906 B2
Freedom Pass
7300 INPS 46259 2558 A4
Freedom Woods Dr
7600 INPS 46259 2558 A4
Freehold Ct
13300 CRML 46032 1901 B2
Freeman Ct
3800 ClyT 46032 1899 E7
Freeman Dr
2800 INPS 46229 2231 D5
Freemont Ln
1100 GNWD 46143 2665 C6
Freemont Moore Rd
19300 WshT 46069 1682 E3
20600 WshT 46069 1573 E7
21100 AdmT 46069 1573 E6
Freenza Ct
13300 CRML 46074 1900 C2
Freeport Dr
11500 CRML 46032 1902 A5
Freeport Ln
7300 INPS 46214 2225 D3
Freestone Dr
700 INPS 46239 2340 E5
Fremont Ct
7000 INPS 46256 2122 D1
Fremont St
100 PNFD 46168 2441 B5
French St
700 PNFD 46168 2441 C4
Frenchmans Cr
13600 CRML 46032 1901 A1
Freshwater Ct
1000 CCRO 46034 1577 B1
Freshwater Ln
1000 CCRO 46034 1577 B1
Fresno Dr
900 GNWD 46143 2666 A5
Freyn Dr
5000 INPS 46254 2117 C7
Friar Ct
9200 INPS 46240 2011 A3
Friars Ln
- CRML 46032 1900 D3
Friend Wy
500 LEBN 46052 1676 C6
Friendship Cir
6400 INPS 46268 2117 C3
Friendship Dr
1500 INPS 46217 2554 D7
Friendship Ln
8500 INPS 46217 2554 C7
Friendswood Rd
3900 BrnT 46158 2660 A1
3900 BrnT 46168 2660 A1
3900 GfdT 46168 2551 B7
3900 GfdT 46168 2660 A1
Frisco Pl
2200 INPS 46240 2011 B6
Frisco Wy
8100 INPS 46240 2011 B6
Frito Lay Dr
8100 INPS 46214 2334 B3
Frogmore St
13000 CRML 46032 1900 D2
S Frog Pond Ct
- CtrT 46140 2344 D3
Frogs Leap
- CCRO 46034 1577 C4
S Frong Pond Ct
1400 CtrT 46140 2344 C4
N Front St
100 WTLD 46184 2775 A5
S Front St
10 WTLD 46184 2775 A6
Frontage Rd
- FSHR 46060 1906 B1
- NBVL 46060 1797 C7
- NBVL 46060 1906 B1
2100 MdlT 46167 2112 C1
3000 MdlT 46167 2113 A1
E Frontage Rd
10800 INPS 46239 2559 B1
N Frontage Rd
5500 BwnT 46126 2670 E5
5900 MrlT 46126 2670 D4
7600 MrlT 46126 2669 E1
8700 MrlT 46126 2560 B5
Frontenac Rd
8700 INPS 46226 2231 D3
Frontier Dr
2300 CtrT 46052 1676 E3
2300 LEBN 46052 1676 E3
Frontier St
9500 FSHR 46038 1904 E1
Front Point Ct
5500 INPS 46237 2448 D7
Front Point Dr
6300 INPS 46237 2557 D1
6600 INPS 46237 2448 D7
Front Royal Ct
8100 INPS 46227 2555 D6
Front Royal Dr
600 INPS 46227 2555 D6
Frontville Pike
1000 CtrT 46140 2236 B4
Frontville Pike
1900 GNFD 46140 2236 B4
Frostwood Ln
- GNWD 46143 2774 C1
Frosty Dr
- GNWD 46143 2665 C6
N Fruitdale Av
2600 SDWY 46224 2226 A5
S Fruitdale Av
1100 INPS 46241 2335 A5
S Fruitdale Dr
6500 INPS 46221 2553 A3
Fruitwood Dr
10100 LWNC 46235 2123 A6
Fry Rd
300 GNWD 46142 2665 A2
900 GNWD 46142 2664 D2
E Frye Rd
7700 INPS 46259 2558 B5
Fulbrook Dr
9800 INPS 46229 2231 E4
9800 INPS 46229 2232 A5
Fulham Dr
7100 INPS 46250 2121 D1
Fullcry Ct
4400 EglT 46077 1899 C2
S Fullen Dr
- INPS 46231 2334 A4
Fullenwider St
1700 INPS 46203 2338 B7
Fuller Ct
12600 FSHR 46038 1904 C3
N Fuller Dr
300 INPS 46224 2335 C3
3000 INPS 46224 2226 D4
S Fuller Dr
500 INPS 46241 2335 D5
Fullerton Cir
2200 INPS 46214 2225 E6
Fullerton Ct
2200 INPS 46214 2225 E6
Fullerton Dr
1800 INPS 46214 2225 E7
Full Moon Ct
11400 NBVL 46060 1796 D1
Fullwood Ct
4300 INPS 46254 2226 C1
Fullwood Dr
- BNBG 46112 2223 D4
Fulton Dr
13400 FSHR 46060 1905 A2
Fulton Pl
16900 WTFD 46074 1792 E2
Fulton St
200 INPS 46202 2337 D3
Funston St
600 LWNC 46216 2122 C5
Furlong Cir
8200 INPS 46256 2013 B4
N Furman Av
1300 INPS 46214 2334 E1
1500 INPS 46214 2225 E7
S Furman Av
10 INPS 46241 2334 E4
Furnas Ct
5500 INPS 46221 2553 B1
Furnas Rd
5500 INPS 46221 2553 B1
6500 INPS 46221 2552 E1
Futch Wy
17100 WshT 46074 1793 C1

G

G Ct
- WRvT 46142 2663 E1
G St
- BHGV 46107 2447 E3
Gable Ct
10100 INPS 46229 2232 A6
Gable Dr
2200 INPS 46229 2232 A6
Gable Lake Dr
- BNBG 46112 2114 E5
Gable Ln Cir
3900 INPS 46228 2227 D2
Gable Ln Ct
2000 INPS 46228 2227 D2
Gable Ln Dr
3800 INPS 46228 2227 D2
Gables Dr
11400 FSHR 46038 1903 E6
Gables End Ct
11700 CRML 46032 1902 A5
Gabriel Rd
1400 INPS 46227 2447 B7
Gadsden St
3800 INPS 46241 2445 A2
4100 INPS 46241 2444 D2
Gadsen Ct
- PNFD 46168 2550 A2
Gadsen Dr
- PNFD 46168 2550 A1
Gadson St
1000 MdlT 46167 2112 A7
1000 MdlT 46167 2221 A1
Gadwall Cir
2500 INPS 46234 2225 A5
Gainesville Ct
3200 INPS 46227 2556 C7
Gainesville Dr
8400 INPS 46227 2556 C7
Gainesway Dr
- WRvT 46142 2663 B4
Gainesway Dr N
400 WRvT 46142 2663 C5
Gainsborough Ct
5200 INPS 46254 2117 E6
Gala Ct
1900 INPS 46203 2339 A7
E Gala Dr
4800 INPS 46203 2339 A7
S Gala Dr
1900 INPS 46203 2339 A7
Galahad Dr
2800 INPS 46228 2118 C6
Galant Fox Ct
- WshT 46234 2224 E6
Galaxie Dr
9100 GNWD 46142 2664 E1
Galaxy Ct
2400 INPS 46229 2231 D5
Galaxy Ln
2500 INPS 46229 2231 D5
Galburgh Ct N
3600 INPS 46234 2224 E3
Galburgh Ct S
3600 INPS 46234 2224 E3
N Gale St
1000 INPS 46201 2338 D1
1400 INPS 46201 2229 D7
3300 INPS 46218 2229 D3
7600 INPS 46240 2011 D7
S Gale St
200 INPS 46201 2338 D4
1000 INPS 46203 2338 D5
5700 INPS 46227 2556 C1
Galeao Dr
5500 INPS 46241 2552 C1
N Galen Dr
300 AVON 46123 2332 C4
Galen Dr W
7100 AVON 46123 2332 B4
Galena Ct
3000 CCRO 46034 1577 B6
10300 INPS 46239 2341 A5
Galeston Av
- INPS 46229 2340 D1
N Galeston Av
10 INPS 46229 2340 D2
3400 INPS 46235 2231 D3
S Galeston Av
10 INPS 46229 2340 D3
Galeston Ct
1900 INPS 46229 2231 D7
Galeston Dr
1800 INPS 46229 2231 D7
Gallagher Dr
5400 WRvT 46142 2663 B3
Gallant Fox Ct
1400 INPS 46217 2554 E7
Gallant Fox Dr
- NBVL 46060 1796 E6
- NBVL 46060 1797 A6
8300 INPS 46217 2554 E7
Gallery Ct
2000 INPS 46229 2232 C7
Galley Ct
8300 INPS 46236 2014 C5
Galley Wy
11000 FCkT 46040 1907 B6
Galliten Ct
- GNWD 46143 2666 A7
Gallium Dr
- CCRO 46034 1577 B6
Galloway Av
7200 INPS 46250 2121 A1
Galloway Cir
12900 FSHR 46038 1904 E3
Galloway Ct
10 WshT 46123 2331 D4
7400 INPS 46250 2121 A1
Galloway St
10 WshT 46123 2331 C3
Galveston Dr
- MCVL 46055 2124 B2
Galway Ct
1400 INPS 46217 2554 E4
Gamay Ln
4000 INPS 46254 2225 E2
Gambel Ct
4500 INPS 46221 2444 D6
Gambel Rd
3900 INPS 46221 2444 E6
Gammon Dr
- INPS 46234 2224 E5
Gandy Ct
8500 INPS 46217 2554 E7
Gann Ct
12300 LWNC 46236 2124 A1
Ganton Ct
8800 INPS 46234 2225 A5
Garamy Ct
5000 INPS 46254 2117 B6
Garamy Dr
5500 INPS 46254 2117 B7
Garden Av
3400 INPS 46222 2336 A2
Garden Cir E
11700 FSHR 46038 1904 C5
Garden Cir W
11700 FSHR 46038 1904 C5
Garden Dr
5500 INPS 46217 2555 B1
W Garden Dr
2500 SCkT 46140 2344 A2
2500 SGLK 46140 2343 E2
2500 SGLK 46140 2344 A2
Garden Pl
- PNFD 46168 2441 C6
Garden Pt
10 ZNVL 46077 1899 A3
Gardenbrook Cir
- INPS 46202 2337 B2
Gardengate Pl
900 INPS 46202 2337 A4
Garden Gate Wy
5800 CRML 46033 1903 C4
Garden Grace Dr
300 INPS 46239 2341 C4
Garden Grove Dr
3400 INPS 46214 2225 D3
Gardenia Dr
8800 NBVL 46060 1795 D6
Garden Ridge Rd
8000 INPS 46237 2557 D6
Garden Rock Ct
8600 INPS 46256 2013 C6

STREET Block City ZIP Map# Grid

Garden Terrace Av
- GNWD 46143 2666 B6
Garden Village Dr
10 WTFD 46074 1684 B7
Garden Walk Dr
5500 INPS 46220 2120 E5
Gardner Ln
500 INPS 46225 2337 B4
Garfield Dr
100 GNFD 46140 2345 B1
E Garfield Dr
900 INPS 46203 2446 E1
S Garfield Dr
2100 INPS 46203 2337 D7
2200 INPS 46203 2446 D1
Garfield St
1200 LEBN 46052 1676 E4
Garfield Park Dr N
- INPS 46203 2446 E1
Garfield Park Center Dr
- INPS 46203 2446 D1
Garfield Plaza Dr
- INPS 46203 2446 E1
Gargany Ct
2100 INPS 46234 2225 A6
Gargany Ln
8700 INPS 46234 2225 A6
Garland Ct
- MCVL 46055 2124 B2
Garnet Blvd
13200 CRML 46033 1903 B2
Garnet Dr
- INPS 46268 2009 B7
Garni Ct
8400 INPS 46227 2555 D6
Garonne Ter
8600 INPS 46250 2012 B4
Garret Ct
1700 INPS 46234 2225 A7
Garrick Ct
11200 FSHR 46038 1904 B6
Garrick St
7500 FSHR 46038 1904 B6
Garriot Dr
- BCkT 46140 2233 A6
Garrison Dr
9100 INPS 46240 2010 E3
9100 INPS 46240 2011 A3
Garrison Ln
700 WshT 46123 2333 D2
Garstang St
10 BHGV 46107 2448 A3
10 BHGV 46203 2448 A3
Garth Dr
5300 INPS 46224 2335 C3
Garver Rd
6000 INPS 46208 2119 C4
Garvok Ct
4500 INPS 46237 2447 D6
Garway Ln
6700 INPS 46254 2116 E7
Gary Dr
800 PNFD 46168 2441 C6
5200 LWNC 46236 2122 E6
8800 LtyT 46118 2548 B7
8800 LtyT 46118 2657 B1
Gary Pl
8800 INPS 46256 2013 D4
Gasaway Blvd
9000 INPS 46234 2224 E4
9000 INPS 46234 2225 A4
Gasburg Rd
10 BmT 46158 2658 C2
700 MnrT 46158 2658 C6
Gaskin Wy
12200 CRML 46032 1900 C3
Gaslight Pkwy
5000 INPS 46241 2444 C3
Gaslite Ln
200 GNFD 46140 2236 D6
Gasoline Al
10 INPS 46222 2335 E4
100 SDWY 46222 2335 E4
N Gasparilla Ct
17800 WTFD 46062 1684 E7
S Gasparilla Ct
17700 WTFD 46062 1684 E7
Gate Cir
10800 FSHR 46038 1903 E7
Gate Dr
10000 INPS 46239 2341 A4
Gateridge Ln
5400 INPS 46237 2448 A7
5400 INPS 46237 2557 A1
Gateshead Ct
- WTFD 46074 1792 D4
Gateshead Dr
- WTFD 46074 1792 D4
Gates Head Ln
- WRvT 46143 2664 A5
Gateshead Ln
6600 INPS 46220 2120 B2
Gateway Av
5100 NBVL 46062 1685 B1
Gateway Ct
- WshT 46231 2333 E5
3900 INPS 46254 2226 A2
Gateway Dr
- INPS 46236 2014 D6
- LcnT 46112 2115 C5
- LWNC 46236 2014 D6
5500 INPS 46254 2226 A2
6000 PNFD 46168 2550 E3
10600 FCkT 46038 1904 E7
10600 FSHR 46038 1904 E7
Gateway Crossing Blvd
- MCVL 46055 2124 B1
Gatewood Ct
- GNWD 46143 2665 B6
9800 INPS 46229 2232 A6
Gatewood Dr
500 GNWD 46143 2665 B6
500 PltT 46143 2665 B6
Gatewood Ln
7700 INPS 46219 2231 B6
Gatewood Ln
10800 FSHR 46038 1903 E7
Gathering Ct
- GNWD 46143 2666 D4
Gathering Ln
- GNWD 46143 2666 D4
Gattling Ct
1600 INPS 46227 2556 A6
Gatwick Dr
6900 INPS 46241 2443 E7
Gatwick View Dr
- FCkT 46038 1906 E5
11600 FSHR 46038 1906 E5
Gavin Av
20600 NBVL 46062 1685 B1
Gavin Dr
7000 INPS 46217 2554 C4
Gawain Av
2800 INPS 46228 2118 C6
Gay Rd
- LWNC 46216 2122 D5
Gazebo Dr
10 INPS 46227 2446 C6
Geagan St
700 WRvT 46143 2663 D5
E Geffs Dr
8300 INPS 46239 2449 C6
Geisendorff St
10 INPS 46204 2337 B3
10 INPS 46202 2337 B3
Geist Rd
9600 FCkT 46038 2014 D1
9600 FCkT 46256 2014 D1
9700 FSHR 46038 2014 D1
10600 FCkT 46038 1905 D7
10600 FSHR 46038 1905 D7
Geist Bay Ct
11300 FCkT 46040 1906 E6
Geist Bluff Cir
11400 LWNC 46236 2014 D7
Geist Bluff Ct
11300 LWNC 46236 2014 D7
Geist Bluff Dr
7700 LWNC 46236 2014 D7
Geist Cove Dr
12000 LWNC 46236 2014 E5
12200 LWNC 46236 2015 A5
E Geist Crossing Dr
9800 INPS 46256 2014 A6
Geist Estates Cir
7600 LWNC 46236 2014 D7
Geist Estates Ct
7700 LWNC 46236 2014 D7
Geist Estates Dr
7500 LWNC 46236 2014 D7
Geist Pointe Cir
7500 LWNC 46236 2014 E7
Geist Ridge Ct
10500 FCkT 46040 1907 A7
10500 FCkT 46040 2016 A1
Geist Ridge Dr
14300 FCkT 46040 1906 E7
14600 FCkT 46040 1907 A7
Geist Valley Blvd
7400 LWNC 46236 2014 E7
7400 LWNC 46236 2123 E1
Geist Valley Ct
7600 LWNC 46236 2014 D7
Geist Valley Dr
11400 LWNC 46236 2014 D7
Geist Woods Cir
11000 FCkT 46256 2014 D2
Geist Woods Ct
9600 FCkT 46256 2014 C2
Geist Woods Dr
11400 LWNC 46236 2014 D7
Geist Woods Ln
10800 FCkT 46256 2014 D2
Geist Woods Trc
9600 FCkT 46256 2014 C2
Geist Woods Wy
9600 FCkT 46256 2014 D2
Geist Woods North Dr
10800 FCkT 46256 2014 C2
Geist Woods South Dr
10800 FCkT 46256 2014 C2
N Gem Rd
3700 NPLN 46163 2452 A2
S Gem Rd
4300 NPLN 46163 2452 A3
N Gemco Ln
3800 INPS 46254 2226 D2
Gemini Ct
9200 INPS 46229 2231 D5
Gemini Dr
9300 INPS 46229 2231 E5
Gemstone Dr
10000 NBVL 46060 1796 A3
General Wy
9400 LWNC 46216 2122 E5
Generation Wy
- GNWD 46143 2666 E5
Geneva Av
4700 LWNC 46226 2122 C7
Geneva Ct
1400 LEBN 46052 1676 D5
Geneva Dr
900 GNWD 46143 2665 D5
Genevieve Ct
9700 INPS 46235 2231 E2
Genoa Ct
4200 INPS 46235 2231 D1
Gent Av
2100 INPS 46202 2227 E6
N Gent Av
1400 INPS 46202 2336 E1
1500 INPS 46202 2227 E7
Gentry Ct
- PNFD 46168 2441 C5
Gentry Dr
9900 FSHR 46060 1796 A7
Gentry St
6600 INPS 46250 2012 E6
George Ct
10 INPS 46224 2226 D4
George Ct
100 DNVL 46122 2330 A4
14300 CRML 46032 1792 E7
Georgetown Ct
4600 INPS 46222 2226 D5
4600 SDWY 46222 2226 D5
10500 WshT 46234 2333 D2
Georgetown Ln
- CRML 46032 1901 D3
Georgetown Rd
10 GNWD 46142 2664 E4
1600 SDWY 46222 2226 D6
1600 SDWY 46224 2226 D6
2900 INPS 46224 2226 D6
3700 INPS 46222 2226 D5
4300 INPS 46254 2226 D1
6000 INPS 46254 2117 D4
6200 INPS 46268 2117 D2
7100 INPS 46268 2008 D7
Georgia Rd
10200 FCkT 46040 2016 A2
10200 VrnT 46040 2016 A2
E Georgia St
10 INPS 46204 2337 C4
500 INPS 46202 2337 D4
S Georgia St
100 SRDN 46069 1573 B2
W Georgia St
10 INPS 46225 2337 C4
Georgiana Ln
8400 INPS 46226 2231 C1
Gerald St
800 NBVL 46060 1795 D2
Gerald Morris Dr
5900 INPS 46250 2012 C6
Geri Dr
1500 LEBN 46052 1676 D5
Gerking Ct
8800 INPS 46256 2013 B4
N German Church Rd
10 CBLD 46229 2341 C2
10 INPS 46229 2341 C2
1500 INPS 46229 2232 C5
3000 INPS 46235 2232 C5
4200 INPS 46235 2123 C6
4600 LWNC 46235 2123 C6
S German Church Rd
10 CBLD 46229 2341 C3
10 INPS 46229 2341 C3
200 INPS 46239 2341 C3
Germander Ln
7600 INPS 46237 2557 A5
Gerrard Av
2300 SDWY 46224 2226 C6
3000 INPS 46224 2226 C4
Gerrard Ct
200 INPS 46241 2335 C4
Gerrard Dr
- SDWY 46224 2335 C2
S Gerrard Dr
300 INPS 46241 2335 C5
4100 INPS 46221 2444 C5
Gerry Ct
10 BHGV 46107 2448 A5
Gerry Dr
200 BHGV 46107 2448 A5
400 BHGV 46107 2447 E5
W Gershwin Dr
300 WshT 46032 1792 C6
Gettysburg Ct
600 INPS 46217 2555 A3
Gettysburg Pkwy
- GNWD 46143 2666 A5
Gettysburg Pl
10700 ClyT 46032 1899 E6
10700 ClyT 46032 1900 A7
Getz Ln
5800 INPS 46254 2226 B2
Gibbes St
9500 FSHR 46038 1904 E3
Gibbs Ct
600 PNFD 46168 2441 C5
Gibbs Rd
1600 WshT 46122 2440 B2
1600 WshT 46168 2440 C2
5000 GfdT 46168 2440 C2
Gibbs St
400 PNFD 46168 2441 C4
N Gibson Av
10 INPS 46219 2340 C1
S Gibson Av
10 INPS 46219 2340 C3
Gibson Cr
- DNVL 46122 2329 C4
Gibson Dr
500 WTFD 46074 1792 E1
1600 LEBN 46052 1676 E5
Gibson St
200 DNVL 46122 2329 E3
Gifford Av
2200 JknT 46034 1575 E5
5000 INPS 46203 2339 A5
5100 INPS 46219 2339 A5
5900 INPS 46228 2118 D4
Gifford Dr
6300 INPS 46224 2335 A1
Gila Bend Rd
1600 WshT 46123 2222 E7
Gilbert Av
200 BHGV 46107 2447 D3
600 INPS 46227 2555 E1
1500 INPS 46227 2556 A1
Gill Dr
10 DNVL 46122 2329 C3
Gillespie Ct
7100 INPS 46214 2334 D2
Gillett St
300 INPS 46221 2336 E4
Gillingham Ln
8700 FCkT 46038 1904 D2
Gilman St
4800 SDWY 46224 2335 D1
Gilmore Rd
7700 INPS 46219 2231 B6
Gimbel Cir
6000 INPS 46221 2553 A4
Gimbel Ct
7000 INPS 46221 2553 A4
Gimber Ct
300 INPS 46225 2446 B2
E Gimber St
700 INPS 46203 2446 D2
1500 INPS 46203 2447 A2
W Gimber St
10 INPS 46225 2446 B2
3500 INPS 46241 2445 B2
Ginger Ct
1200 INPS 46241 2334 E6
Ginnylock Dr
8700 INPS 46256 2013 D3
Ginseng Tr
1900 WshT 46123 2331 C7
1900 WshT 46123 2440 C1
Giovanni Dr
- CRML 46074 1791 B7
N Girls School Rd
400 INPS 46214 2334 D2
1700 INPS 46214 2225 D7
N Girls School Rd SR-134
2600 INPS 46214 2225 D5
S Girls School Rd
10 INPS 46231 2334 D5
10 INPS 46241 2334 D5
Giroud Dr
7400 INPS 46259 2558 A6
Giroud Pl
8300 INPS 46259 2558 A6
Giroud Wy
8300 INPS 46259 2558 A6
Giselle Wy
10700 FCkT 46040 1906 E7
Glacier Ct
6500 INPS 46217 2555 B3
Glacier Dr
6500 INPS 46217 2555 B3
Gladden Dr
6000 INPS 46220 2119 C4
Gladden Ln
- FCkT 46060 1905 C1
- FSHR 46060 1905 C1
Gladden Rd
1900 PNFD 46168 2441 E4
1900 PNFD 46168 2442 A4
Gladecrest Dr
12400 CRML 46033 1903 B4
Gladesend Ct
6500 INPS 46220 2120 B3
Gladeview Ct
10400 INPS 46239 2341 B6
Gladeview Dr
10300 INPS 46239 2341 A6
N Gladstone Av
10 INPS 46201 2338 E3
3400 INPS 46218 2229 E3
S Gladstone Av
10 INPS 46201 2338 E3
1900 INPS 46203 2338 E7
5500 INPS 46237 2556 E1
Gladstone Ct
- FCkT 46038 1906 B5
- FSHR 46038 1906 B5
Gladstone Dr
9500 BmT 46112 2005 B5
Glaser Wy
11000 FCkT 46038 2014 E1
Glasgow Ct
200 NBVL 46060 1795 D4
Glasgow Ln
100 NBVL 46060 1795 D4
Glass Dr
1400 INPS 46214 2335 A1
Glass Chimney Ln
5600 LWNC 46235 2123 C5
8800 FSHR 46038 2013 D2
Glastonberry Ln
400 MRVL 46158 2660 B3
Glastonbury Ct
4500 INPS 46237 2447 D6
Glazer Wy
10800 FSHR 46038 1905 C3
Gleannloch Dr
9100 INPS 46256 2122 D1
Glebe Cir
6100 INPS 46237 2448 C6
Glebe Dr
6000 INPS 46237 2448 C6
Glebe St
2200 CRML 46032 1900 D3
Glen Cir
- CRML 46033 1902 D5
Glen Ct
4400 WshT 46123 2331 E5
N Glen Dr
- WTFD 46074 1684 A6
Glena Pl
100 BrnT 46158 2658 D5
N Glena Pl
100 BrnT 46158 2658 D5
Glen Abbe Ct
3400 ClyT 46032 2009 C2
Glen Arm Ct
6500 INPS 46224 2226 A3
Glenarm Dr
4400 INPS 46254 2226 A1
N Glen Arm Rd
1000 INPS 46214 2335 A1
1500 INPS 46214 2226 A7
3500 INPS 46224 2226 A3
3900 INPS 46254 2226 A2
S Glen Arm Rd
1200 INPS 46241 2335 A6
4000 INPS 46241 2444 A5
Glen Arm East Dr
3400 INPS 46224 2226 A3
Glen Arm West Dr
3400 INPS 46224 2226 A3
Glenayre Dr
10700 GfdT 46113 2660 D1
Glenayre Dr
10700 INPS 46113 2660 D1
Glenbar Wy
700 GNWD 46143 2664 E5
Glenberr Ct
9800 FSHR 46038 1905 A3
Glenbrook Ct
11700 CRML 46032 1901 E4
Glenbrook Dr
2400 INPS 46220 2120 B2
Glenbrook Ln
10 WshT 46123 2333 C3
Glencairn Ln
3600 INPS 46205 2229 D1
3800 INPS 46226 2229 D1
5300 INPS 46226 2230 A1
Glen Canyon Dr
5500 INPS 46237 2448 E7
5500 INPS 46237 2557 D1
Glencary Crst
1600 INPS 46228 2227 D1
Glen Coe Dr
6300 INPS 46260 2119 B3
Glencoe St
5400 INPS 46226 2230 B2
Glen Cove Ct
11900 LWNC 46236 2014 E5
Glencove Ct
12500 CRML 46033 1903 B4
Glen Cove Dr
11800 LWNC 46236 2014 E5
Glencrest Dr
5600 INPS 46237 2557 B6
Glenda Dr
10 PNFD 46168 2441 E4
E Glendale Av
10 INPS 46225 2446 C1
W Glendale Av
500 INPS 46225 2446 B1
Glendale Ct
- MRVL 46158 2660 A3
200 AVON 46123 2332 C3
Glendale Dr
500 LEBN 46052 1677 B6
7200 AVON 46123 2332 C3
N Glendale Ln
1200 BCkT 46140 2233 A6
W Glendale Ln
7300 BCkT 46140 2233 A6
Glendale Pk
10 WRvT 46142 2663 E1
10 WRvT 46217 2663 E1
Glendora Ct
6500 INPS 46214 2226 A7
Glendora Dr
1800 INPS 46214 2225 E7
1800 INPS 46214 2226 A7
Glendurgan Dr
12400 CRML 46032 1901 A4
Glen Eagles Ct
5700 WshT 46123 2331 E5
Gleneagles Ct
16400 NBVL 46060 1796 D2
Glenfair Ct
7400 INPS 46214 2334 D2
Glen Flint Ct
6200 INPS 46254 2117 A6
Glengarry Ct
8200 LWNC 46236 2014 E5
Glengary Dr
12600 FSHR 46038 1905 A3
Glengyle Av
10 BHGV 46107 2447 D3
Glen Haven Blvd
- PNFD 46168 2550 A2
Glenhaven Ct
6200 LWNC 46236 2123 B3
10000 FSHR 46038 2014 A1
Glen Highlands Dr
8300 LWNC 46236 2014 E5
Glen Hill Dr
2400 INPS 46240 2011 B4
Glenlea Rd
- INPS 46229 2231 E5
Glen Manor Ct
1500 CRML 46032 1902 A5
Glenmar Ln
5000 INPS 46226 2230 A1
Glenmora Ridge Rd
7400 INPS 46250 2012 A7
7400 INPS 46250 2121 A1
Glenn Dr
400 GNWD 46142 2665 C4
3000 INPS 46218 2229 C6
Glenn Rd
700 LWNC 46216 2122 B4
Glenn Abbey Ln
10000 FSHR 46038 2014 B2
11500 LWNC 46235 2123 D5
Glenn Cairn Ct
10600 FSHR 46038 2014 B2
Glenn Meade Dr
6600 INPS 46241 2334 E4
Glennmore Dr
7300 INPS 46256 2122 D1
Glen Ridge Cir
11500 FSHR 46038 1905 E5
Glenridge Dr
1900 INPS 46218 2229 E7
Glen Scott Dr
11900 LWNC 46236 2014 E5
Glen Scott Ln
8400 LWNC 46236 2014 E5
Glensford Dr
7300 AVON 46123 2332 C3
Glenshire Cir
7400 INPS 46237 2557 D4
Glenshire Ln
6200 INPS 46237 2557 C4
Glenshire Wy
6500 INPS 46237 2557 D4
Glenside Ct
8300 INPS 46256 2013 A5
Glen Stewart Wy
5200 INPS 46254 2116 D6
Glentrace Dr
11300 LWNC 46236 2014 C6
Glenview Cir
100 MRVL 46158 2660 B5
Glen View Dr
7900 LWNC 46236 2014 D7
Glenview Dr
- MCVL 46055 2015 D5
3800 INPS 46240 2120 D1
Glenview Dr E
7300 INPS 46250 2011 E7
7300 INPS 46250 2120 E1
Glenview Dr S
4200 INPS 46250 2120 E1
Glenview Dr W
7300 INPS 46250 2011 E7
7300 INPS 46250 2120 E1
Glenvista Pl
7400 FSHR 46038 1904 A4
Glenway Dr
7900 LWNC 46236 2014 D6
Glenwick Blvd
7200 INPS 46217 2555 A4
Glen Willow Ln
8200 INPS 46278 2007 B4
Glenwood Ct
200 AVON 46123 2332 C3
Glenwood Dr
- INPS 46205 2120 D7
4200 INPS 46205 2229 C1
Glenwood Ln
100 FSHR 46038 1904 A4
Glenwood Trc
6400 EglT 46077 1897 D6
Glory Maple Ln
6400 INPS 46221 2553 A1
Glossbrenner Ct
7200 LWNC 46236 2124 A1
Gloucester Cir
5800 INPS 46220 2121 A4
Glouchester Ct
300 NBVL 46060 1795 D3
Glowing Flame Dr
9600 FSHR 46038 2013 D2
Golay St
1300 INPS 46203 2338 C6
2200 INPS 46203 2447 C1
Gold Ct
2100 WRvT 46143 2664 A7
Gold Coin Dr
7600 AVON 46123 2332 C5
Golden Dr
- NBVL 46060 1796 B4
Golden Ash Ct
13200 FSHR 46060 1905 B2
Golden Bear Cir
11300 NBVL 46060 1796 D3
Golden Bear Wy
10200 NBVL 46060 1796 B3
10900 WynT 46060 1796 C3
Goldenbell
6500 INPS 46203 2448 D5
Golden Bluff Ct
12100 INPS 46236 2014 E4
Golden Eagle Ct
1300 WRvT 46143 2664 A6
Golden Eagle Dr
4000 INPS 46234 2225 B2
Goldeneye Cir
2200 INPS 46234 2225 A6
Golden Falls Cir
8600 WshT 46123 2333 A1
E Golden Gate Dr
- CRML 46074 1900 B2
N Golden Gate Dr
- CRML 46074 1900 B2
W Golden Gate Dr
- CRML 46074 1900 B2
Golden Harvest Dr
- INPS 46229 2232 C6
Golden Harvest Pl
10800 INPS 46229 2232 B6
Golden Harvest Wy
10800 INPS 46229 2232 C6
Golden Hill Dr
- INPS 46208 2228 A3
1100 INPS 46208 2227 E3
Golden Hinde Wy
4300 WTFD 46062 1793 E1
4700 WTFD 46062 1794 A1
Golden Leaf Wy
9100 INPS 46260 2009 D3
Golden Meadow Ct
4500 INPS 46254 2117 B7
4500 INPS 46254 2226 B1
Golden Meadow Dr
4500 INPS 46254 2117 B7
4500 INPS 46254 2226 B1
Golden Meadow Wy
19100 NBVL 46060 1687 B4
Golden Oak Ln
6500 WshT 46123 2332 B2
Golden Oaks E
9100 INPS 46260 2009 D3
Golden Oaks N
2100 INPS 46260 2009 D3
Golden Oaks W
9100 INPS 46260 2009 D3
Golden Pond Ct
900 GNWD 46143 2666 A3
7800 BrnT 46112 2115 E2
Goldenrain East Ct
4700 INPS 46237 2556 E1
4700 INPS 46237 2557 A1
Goldenrain West Ct
4600 INPS 46237 2556 E1
Golden Ridge Ln
8200 INPS 46237 2557 D6
13600 FCkT 46055 2015 C1
Goldenrod Ct
8000 INPS 46219 2340 B1
Goldenrod Dr
- GNWD 46143 2774 A1
1200 INPS 46219 2340 B1
Goldenrod Ln
100 FSHR 46038 1904 B4
Golden Saddle Ct
13800 CRML 46032 1900 E1
Golden Tree Ln
- INPS 46227 2555 C7
Golden Woods Dr
9200 INPS 46268 2009 C3
Goldfield Dr
- GNWD 46143 2774 A1
Goldfinch Cir
8300 INPS 46256 2013 C6
Goldfinch Dr
1200 CRML 46032 1901 D1
Golf Ct
- GNWD 46143 2665 E4
Golf Ln
900 INPS 46260 2119 A2
W Golf Ln
400 INPS 46260 2119 B2
Golf Club Blvd
- WTFD 46033 1793 E4
- WTFD 46033 1794 A4
Golf Club Ct
7700 LWNC 46236 2014 D7
Golf Course Dr
11800 LWNC 46236 2123 D1
Golfside Dr
10 LEBN 46052 1677 A2
Golf Stream Dr
1900 INPS 46229 2232 B7
Golfview Ct
2000 WRvT 46143 2664 B7
Golf View Dr
10700 BmT 46112 2115 E4
10700 LcnT 46112 2115 E4
Golfview Dr
800 CRML 46032 1902 C4
2300 INPS 46203 2447 B2
3000 WRvT 46143 2664 B7
Golfview Ter
5600 WshT 46123 2331 D6
Good Av
100 INPS 46219 2339 C3
S Good Av
600 INPS 46219 2339 C5
N Goodlet Av
400 INPS 46222 2336 B2
2200 INPS 46222 2227 B6
S Goodlet Av
1500 INPS 46241 2336 B6
2600 INPS 46241 2445 B2
Goodloe Dr
- FSHR 46038 1906 A4
12400 FSHR 46038 1905 E4
Goodtime Ct
15100 WshT 46032 1792 D5
Goodway Ct
9400 INPS 46256 2013 E6
Goodway Dr
7800 INPS 46256 2013 E6
Goodwill Dr
- GNWD 46142 2664 B3
Gooseberry Dr
14500 FSHR 46060 1796 A6
Gooseberry Ln
600 GNWD 46143 2665 D2
Gordon Ct
100 BNBG 46112 2223 C1
Gordon Dr
7900 INPS 46278 2008 A6
Gordon Ln
- PNFD 46168 2440 D6
4500 GfdT 46168 2440 D6
Gordon Wy
7400 INPS 46237 2557 E5
Gordonshire Ct
7600 INPS 46278 2007 C4
Gordonshire Dr
8600 INPS 46278 2007 C4
Gorham Ct
3000 CRML 46033 1902 C5
Goshawk Ct
4100 INPS 46254 2225 D2
Gould Dr
3600 CRML 46033 2011 D1
Government Pl
- INPS 46202 2337 B3
- INPS 46204 2337 B3
Governors Ln
100 ZNVL 46077 1899 A4
Governor's Ln
300 WRvT 46142 2663 B4
Governors Ln
700 ZNVL 46077 1898 E3
11100 FSHR 46038 2014 D1
Governors Rd
3700 INPS 46208 2227 E3
Governors Pointe Av
2400 INPS 46217 2554 C3
Governors Pointe Blvd
6800 INPS 46217 2554 C3
Governors Pointe Dr
6800 INPS 46217 2554 C3
Governours Ct
3600 INPS 46235 2232 B3
Governours Ln
10300 INPS 46235 2232 B3
Gowdin Dr
2200 WshT 46234 2224 C6
Gower Ct
8000 INPS 46268 2009 C6
Goya Ct
10 INPS 46222 2226 D4
Graber Wy
8300 INPS 46259 2558 B6
Grabill Dr
400 WTFD 46074 1792 D1
Grace Ct
700 CRML 46032 1792 E7
Grace Dr
700 CRML 46032 1792 E7
900 CRML 46032 1793 A7
Grace St
- INPS 46234 2225 A4

STREET
Block City ZIP Map# Grid

Grace St
3100 WRvT 46143 2664 B5
4500 INPS 46218 2229 E7
Grace Ter
11400 INPS 46236 2014 D5
Graceful Landing Cir
- LcnT 46112 2115 C6
Graceful Landing Dr
- LcnT 46112 2115 C6
Graceland Av
3000 INPS 46208 2228 C4
5200 INPS 46208 2119 C6
Gradison Cir
2300 INPS 46214 2225 E6
Gradison Ct
2100 INPS 46214 2225 E6
Gradison Dr
2100 INPS 46214 2225 E6
Gradle Dr
200 CRML 46032 1902 A4
Grafton Av
5800 INPS 46241 2335 B6
Grafton Ct
- BNBG 46112 2223 D4
Grafton Meadow Ln
- MRVL 46158 2660 C3
Graham Av
7600 INPS 46250 2012 C7
N Graham Av
1000 INPS 46219 2339 C1
3500 INPS 46218 2230 C3
3800 INPS 46226 2230 C2
S Graham Av
100 INPS 46219 2339 C3
Graham Ct
5800 INPS 46250 2012 C7
N Graham Rd
10 GNWD 46143 2666 C4
1000 PltT 46143 2666 C6
6100 INPS 46220 2121 C3
7100 INPS 46250 2121 C1
7400 INPS 46250 2012 C7
Grampian Wy
6800 INPS 46254 2225 E1
Granada Cir
2500 INPS 46222 2227 C5
Granada Cir N
2700 INPS 46222 2227 C5
Granada Cir W
2700 INPS 46222 2227 C5
Granada Ct
900 GNWD 46143 2665 E5
Granada Dr
700 GNWD 46143 2665 E5
Granada Pl
300 NWTD 46184 2774 D4
Granby Ct
11600 FCkT 46040 1907 A5
Granby Dr
100 CBLD 46229 2341 E2
N Grand Av
3800 INPS 46226 2230 A2
7200 INPS 46250 2121 A1
S Grand Av
300 INPS 46219 2339 A4
Grand Cypress Dr
- NbvT 46060 1796 B3
16400 NBVL 46060 1796 B3
Grande Av
500 INPS 46222 2335 E2
700 SDWY 46222 2335 E2
Grand Fir Dr
- GNWD 46143 2774 B1
- GNWD 46184 2774 B1
Grand Gulch Dr
7800 INPS 46239 2449 B1
Grand Haven Ln
4600 CRML 46033 2011 E1
4600 CRML 46033 2012 A1
Grandiose Dr
5900 INPS 46228 2118 E4
Grandison Rd
100 GNFD 46140 2236 D7
Grand Mesa Ct
600 INPS 46217 2555 B3
Grand Oak Av
3800 INPS 46237 2556 D4
Grand Oak Pl
3800 INPS 46237 2556 D4
Grand Prix Dr
2300 INPS 46224 2226 A6
Grand Ritz Ln
7100 INPS 46237 2556 D4
Grand Strand Wy
- NBVL 46062 1686 B3
- NbvT 46062 1686 B3
Grand Tetons Blvd
5000 INPS 46237 2448 D7
Grandview Ct
9400 NBVL 46060 1686 E5
Grandview Dr
5100 INPS 46228 2118 E4
6200 INPS 46260 2118 E4
7400 AVON 46123 2332 C3
7400 INPS 46260 2009 E7
Grandview Wy
3100 WTFD 46074 1684 D7
Grand Vista Dr
- LcnT 46112 2115 D6
Grand Woods Dr
500 INPS 46224 2335 B2
Granger Ct
300 FSHR 46038 1904 B5
5000 INPS 46268 2117 D2
Granger Ln
6600 INPS 46268 2117 D2
Granite Ct
10 CRML 46032 1793 A7
5200 INPS 46237 2557 A3
W Granite Ct
5300 SCkT 46163 2451 E2
Granite Dr
10 CRML 46032 1793 A7
2300 LEBN 46052 1676 E3
Granner Cir
6700 INPS 46221 2553 A3
Granner Ct
6700 INPS 46221 2553 A3
Granner Dr
5800 INPS 46221 2553 A3
Granny Smith Ln
6600 WshT 46123 2332 A6
N Grant Av
1000 INPS 46201 2338 D1
1400 INPS 46201 2229 D7
3300 INPS 46218 2229 D3
S Grant Av
200 INPS 46201 2338 D4
1100 INPS 46203 2338 D6
Grant Av N
3900 INPS 46226 2229 D2
Grant Blvd
2000 LEBN 46052 1677 A3
Grant Cir
1100 CCRO 46034 1577 B5
Grant Ct
- AVON 46123 2333 C3
- WshT 46123 2333 C3
800 GNWD 46143 2666 B5
Grant St
10 GNFD 46140 2345 E1
17600 WshT 46069 1682 A7
E Grant St
1000 NBVL 46060 1686 D6
N Grant St
10 BNBG 46112 2114 C6
800 LEBN 46052 1677 A5
S Grant St
10 BNBG 46112 2114 C7
100 LEBN 46052 1677 B7
500 BNBG 46112 2223 C1
Grantham Wy
10300 FSHR 46038 2013 D1
Grant Wood Ct
6500 INPS 46256 2122 A2
Granville Ct
9100 INPS 46229 2231 D7
Granville Ln
9100 INPS 46229 2231 D7
Granville Pl
9300 INPS 46229 2231 E7
Grapevine Dr
5200 LWNC 46235 2123 A6
Grapevine Ln
13500 FSHR 46060 1905 B2
Grasshopper Ct
10400 NBVL 46060 1687 B4
Grassland Dr
- BNBG 46112 2223 E3
E Grassy Cr
- NWTD 46184 2774 E4
- PltT 46184 2774 C6
- WTLD 46184 2774 E4
- WTLD 46184 2775 A4
S Grassy Ct
4600 SCkT 46163 2451 E4
Grassy Dr
10 NWTD 46184 2774 C4
Grassy Ln
500 INPS 46217 2555 B4
Grassy Bank Ct
5300 INPS 46237 2448 E7
Grassy Bank Dr
5400 INPS 46237 2448 E7
5400 INPS 46237 2557 E1
Grassy Branch Rd
17600 WTFD 46062 1684 D7
17600 WTFD 46074 1684 D7
18000 WshT 46062 1684 D4
18000 WshT 46074 1684 D4
Grassy Creek Ct
2700 INPS 46229 2232 B5
Grassy Creek Dr
10 WTLD 46184 2774 C6
2700 INPS 46229 2232 B5
Grassy Creek Ln
- GNWD 46143 2666 A4
Grassy Knoll Dr
17800 WTFD 46062 1684 D7
Grassy Meadow Cir
8100 INPS 46259 2558 B6
Grassy Meadow Ct
8100 INPS 46259 2558 B6
Grassy Meadow Ln
8100 INPS 46259 2558 B6
Grassyway Ct
10 WTLD 46184 2775 A3
Grattan Ln
6500 INPS 46220 2121 A2
Gravel Dr
- BCkT 46140 2234 C2
Gravelie Dr
3200 INPS 46227 2556 C4
3200 SPRT 46227 2556 C4
Graves Light Dr
- INPS 46217 2554 C3
N Gray Rd
- CRML 46240 2012 A1
- INPS 46240 2012 A1
9600 CRML 46280 2012 A1
9800 CRML 46033 2012 A1
11900 CRML 46033 1903 A4
14100 CRML 46033 1794 A6
14600 CRML 46062 1794 A6
14600 NbvT 46062 1794 A6
14600 WshT 46033 1794 A6
14600 WshT 46062 1794 A6
15100 NBVL 46062 1794 A4
15100 WTFD 46033 1794 A4
15100 WTFD 46062 1794 A4
17300 NbvT 46062 1685 A7
17300 WshT 46062 1685 A7
S Gray Rd
5000 INPS 46237 2447 D7
5600 INPS 46237 2556 D2
N Gray St
10 INPS 46201 2338 C2
10 NPLN 46163 2452 B3
S Gray St
10 INPS 46201 2338 C3
4400 INPS 46227 2447 C6
Gray Arbor Dr
3900 INPS 46237 2556 D2
Gray Arbor Wy
3900 INPS 46237 2556 D2
Gray Birch Ct E
2200 WshT 46123 2441 A1
Graybrook Cir
6300 INPS 46237 2557 E2
Graybrook Ct
6300 INPS 46237 2557 E2
Graybrook Dr
6700 INPS 46237 2557 E2
Graydon St
2400 INPS 46201 2338 B4
Gray Eagle Ct
5300 CRML 46033 1903 C1
Gray Eagle Dr
- FSHR 46038 1906 B5
Grayling Cir
6400 INPS 46241 2444 A5
Grayling Dr
4100 INPS 46241 2444 A5
Graylon Pl
14600 CRML 46062 1795 A6
14600 NBVL 46062 1795 A6
Graymont Dr
- INPS 46221 2553 B4
Gray Pond Ct
3800 INPS 46237 2556 D4
Graysford Dr
2300 INPS 46234 2225 B6
Grayson Dr
1100 GNFD 46140 2237 A6
4300 INPS 46228 2227 B1
Graystone Ct
10 ZNVL 46077 1898 E5
Graystone Ln
1600 ZNVL 46077 1898 E5
Grazing Ln
11700 INPS 46239 2341 D4
Great Blue Trc
- FSHR 46038 1905 E6
Great Lakes Cir E
300 AVON 46123 2333 B3
Great Lakes Cir W
200 AVON 46123 2333 A3
300 WshT 46123 2333 A3
Great Lakes Dr
300 NBVL 46060 1686 C6
Great Woods Dr
5300 INPS 46224 2335 C2
Grebe Cir
12000 CBLD 46229 2232 E7
Grebe Wy
5700 CRML 46033 1903 B2
Green Ct
10 CRML 46033 1902 E6
Green Pl
10 CRML 46033 1902 E5
Green St
300 PNFD 46168 2441 B4
11200 CRML 46033 1902 E6
E Green St
100 LEBN 46052 1677 A7
N Green St
10 BNBG 46112 2114 C5
1400 BrnT 46112 2114 C5
N Green St SR-267
10 BNBG 46112 2114 C5
1400 BrnT 46112 2114 C5
S Green St
10 BNBG 46112 2114 B7
500 BNBG 46112 2223 B2
1400 LcnT 46112 2223 B2
S Green St SR-267
10 BNBG 46112 2114 B7
500 BNBG 46112 2223 B2
1400 LcnT 46112 2223 B2
W Green St
200 LEBN 46052 1676 E7
Green Acre Ct
10 BNBG 46112 2114 C7
Green Acre Dr
10 BNBG 46112 2114 C7
Green Ash Ct
3500 INPS 46222 2227 A6
Greenbelt Ct
14300 CRML 46033 1794 C7
Green Braes Dr
8700 INPS 46234 2116 A6
Green Braes East Dr
5300 INPS 46234 2116 B6
Green Braes North Dr
8400 INPS 46234 2116 A6
Green Braes South Dr
8400 INPS 46234 2116 A6
Green Branch Ln
8600 INPS 46256 2014 A4
Greenbriar Ct
10 NWTD 46184 2774 D3
400 WshT 46123 2331 D3
Greenbriar Dr
10800 FCkT 46038 1905 B7
10800 FSHR 46038 1905 B7
N Greenbriar Dr
200 GNWD 46142 2664 D3
W Greenbriar Dr
1100 GNWD 46142 2664 E2
Greenbriar Ln
2200 INPS 46218 2229 B6
Greenbriar Mobile Home Pk
- LWNC 46235 2123 A6
- LWNC 46236 2122 E6
- LWNC 46236 2123 A6
Greenbrier Dr
10800 ClyT 46032 1900 D7
Greenbrook Ct
10 GNFD 46140 2237 A6
10200 INPS 46229 2341 A1
Greenbrook Dr
1000 GNFD 46140 2237 A6
1200 INPS 46229 2341 A1
Greenbrook Tr
10000 INPS 46229 2341 A1
W Greencastle Rd
600 BrnT 46158 2659 C3
600 MRVL 46158 2659 C3
900 BrnT 46158 2658 E3
1600 MnrT 46158 2658 E3
2200 MnrT 46158 2657 E3
Greencroft St
- CRML 46032 1900 D2
Greencycle Dr
- INPS 46221 2445 D1
Greene Ct
- WshT 46123 2333 C2
Greenfield Av
- NBVL 46060 1906 C1
1000 NBVL 46060 1795 D2
1600 NbvT 46060 1795 D2
2500 NBVL 46060 1796 B4
2500 NbvT 46060 1796 B4
5400 INPS 46219 2339 B4
10800 WynT 46060 1796 B4
12000 NBVL 46060 1797 A6
12000 WynT 46060 1797 A6
Greenfield Av SR-238
- NBVL 46060 1906 C1
1000 NBVL 46060 1795 D2
1800 NbvT 46060 1795 D2
2500 NBVL 46060 1796 B4
2500 NbvT 46060 1796 B4
10800 WynT 46060 1796 B4
12000 NBVL 46060 1797 A6
12000 WynT 46060 1797 A6
Greenfield Dr
1200 GNFD 46140 2236 D6
Greenfield Rd
11700 EglT 46077 1899 D4
Greenfield Village Ln
- GNFD 46140 2236 C5
Greengage Ct
6900 INPS 46237 2448 D6
Green Haven Pl
6500 INPS 46214 2334 E2
Green Haven Wy
6500 INPS 46214 2334 C1
Greenheart Dr
5000 INPS 46237 2447 D7
Greenheart Pl
- INPS 46237 2447 D7
Green Hills Ct
300 WRvT 46142 2664 B3
Greenhills Ct
10 GNFD 46140 2236 E6
Green Hills Dr
5000 LcnT 46112 2114 A7
Green Hills Ln
3000 INPS 46222 2227 B3
Green Hills Ovlk
3400 INPS 46222 2227 C3
Green Hills Rd
1300 GNFD 46140 2236 E5
1300 GNFD 46140 2237 A5
Green Hills Ln Middle Dr
3000 INPS 46222 2227 C3
Green Hills Ln North Dr
3000 INPS 46222 2227 C3
Green Hills Ln South Dr
2800 INPS 46222 2227 C3
Greenlawn Cir
1900 WshT 46123 2441 B1
Greenlawn St
1000 SDWY 46224 2335 D1
Green Leave Ct
9700 NbvT 46060 1686 D4
9700 NbvT 46060 1687 A4
Green Leaves Cir
6100 INPS 46220 2121 B4
Green Leaves Rd
6200 INPS 46220 2121 B3
Greenlee Cir
9000 INPS 46234 2333 E3
9000 INPS 46234 2334 A3
Greenlee Ct
800 INPS 46234 2334 A2
Greenlee Dr
400 INPS 46234 2334 A2
Green Meadow Cir
4400 INPS 46235 2232 B1
Green Meadow Ct
4400 INPS 46235 2232 A1
Green Meadow Dr
200 INPS 46229 2341 B3
500 GNWD 46143 2665 D5
Green Meadows Ct
19100 NbvT 46060 1686 E4
Green Meadows Dr
500 WshT 46123 2331 E5
E Green Meadows Dr
- GNFD 46140 2236 E6
W Green Meadows Dr
10 GNFD 46140 2236 C6
N Green Meadows Ests
7400 MrlT 46126 2670 A1
Green Mountain Ct
6200 INPS 46221 2553 A2
Green Pasture Ct
900 GNWD 46143 2666 A3
Green Ridge Dr
600 WshT 46123 2331 E5
Greenridge Dr
6400 INPS 46278 2008 A4
6600 INPS 46278 2007 E4
Green River Ct
1200 INPS 46229 2341 D1
Green Rock Ln
2000 INPS 46203 2339 A7
Greensboro Dr
16500 WTFD 46074 1792 D2
Greenshire Dr
6600 INPS 46220 2121 B2
Greenslope Ct
9200 FSHR 46038 1904 E1
Greenspire Dr
- CRML 46033 1903 A6
Greenspire Pl
6400 INPS 46221 2553 A1
6500 GNWD 46221 2552 E1
Green Spring Wy
1400 GNWD 46143 2665 E6
Greensprings Ct
200 WTLD 46184 2775 A6
Greensprings Dr
400 WTLD 46184 2775 A6
N Green Springs Rd
10 INPS 46214 2334 E3
W Green Springs Rd
7000 INPS 46214 2334 D3
Greensview Wy
5100 WshT 46123 2331 C6
Greensward Ln
5300 INPS 46224 2335 C3
Greenthread Ct
9500 ZNVL 46077 1898 D2
Greenthread Dr
- ZNVL 46077 1898 D1
Greenthread Ln
9200 ZNVL 46077 1898 D2
Greentree Ct
7500 GfdT 46168 2551 B5
Greentree Dr
9600 INPS 46032 2009 C2
10300 ClyT 46032 2009 B1
10400 ClyT 46032 1900 B7
Greentree St
2200 INPS 46227 2556 B5
Green Valley Ct
8500 INPS 46217 2554 D7
Green Valley Dr
- NBVL 46060 1686 E4
600 DNVL 46122 2329 E4
8500 INPS 46217 2554 D7
19200 NbvT 46060 1686 E4
19200 NbvT 46060 1687 A4
Green Valley Ln
2200 INPS 46217 2554 C7
Green Valley Rd
500 GNWD 46142 2664 D4
Greenview Cir
13400 WynT 46060 1797 C2
Greenview Dr
5500 INPS 46220 2120 E6
Greenview Rd
16600 WynT 46060 1797 C2
Greenview Wy
2800 INPS 46229 2232 B5
Greenville St
- WshT 46074 1792 A4
Greenway Dr
- FSHR 46038 2014 B2
4200 INPS 46220 2120 E6
Greenwich Dr
16300 WshT 46062 1793 E3
Greenwillow Ct
5200 INPS 46226 2121 B6
Greenwillow Rd
5200 INPS 46226 2121 B6
Greenwood Ct
19200 NbvT 46060 1686 E4
Greenwood Dr
10 MRVL 46158 2659 E2
Greenwood Pl
- INPS 46227 2555 E5
N Greenwood St
100 GNWD 46142 2665 C3
S Greenwood St
10 GNWD 46142 2665 C4
Green Woods Dr
700 INPS 46224 2335 C2
Greenwood Station Blvd
- GNWD 46143 2666 B5
Greenwood Trail East Dr
10 GNWD 46142 2665 D2
Greenwood Trail North Dr
10 GNWD 46142 2665 C1
Greenwood Trail South Dr
10 GNWD 46142 2665 C1
Greenwood Trail West Dr
900 GNWD 46142 2665 D2
Greer St
800 INPS 46203 2337 D5
Greer Dell Rd
1400 INPS 46260 2118 E3
Gregg Rd
10 INPS 46260 2010 C6
Gregory Cir
19900 NBVL 46062 1686 A2
Gregory Dr
6100 INPS 46241 2335 A5
Greighton Ct
7600 INPS 46227 2556 A5
Greighton Dr
1700 INPS 46227 2556 A5
Grenada Dr
8100 INPS 46227 2556 B6
Grenadier Ln
11700 INPS 46229 2232 E7
Grenville St
2100 CRML 46032 1900 D3
Gresham Pl
- NBVL 46060 1687 C4
- WynT 46060 1687 C4
E Greta Dr
8400 INPS 46239 2558 C1
Gretna Green Ln
18700 NBVL 46062 1685 E5
Greybudd Ct
3100 INPS 46268 2118 B1
Greybudd Dr
6800 INPS 46268 2118 B2
Greyfox Ct
400 GNWD 46142 2664 D4
Greyfrier Ct
2600 INPS 46220 2120 B2
Greyhound Cir
10 WshT 46032 1792 E5
Greyhound Ct
14800 WTFD 46032 1793 B6
E Greyhound Pass
- CRML 46033 1793 B6
10 WshT 46032 1792 D5
1100 WshT 46032 1793 A5
1400 WTFD 46032 1793 A5
1800 WTFD 46033 1793 B6
W Greyhound Pass
10 WshT 46032 1792 C5
Grey Oak Ln
400 GNWD 46142 2665 B4
Greyridge Blvd
- INPS 46237 2557 B3
Grey Spring Ct
2500 INPS 46239 2449 A1
Greystoke Ct
9700 FSHR 46038 1905 A3
Greystone Ct
2300 ClyT 46032 1900 D6
9000 INPS 46234 2225 B3
Greythorne Ct
7600 INPS 46239 2449 A1
Greythorne Dr
2400 INPS 46239 2449 A1
Greywell Cir
8400 INPS 46256 2013 D5
Gridley Av
1900 INPS 46241 2335 A7
S Gridley St
- INPS 46241 2335 A7
Griffin Rd
10 INPS 46227 2555 C5
Griffin Run
13200 CRML 46033 1903 E2
Griffin St
3300 INPS 46237 2447 C4
Griffith Rd
- ClkT 46143 2666 E7
7100 INPS 46227 2556 A4
Griggs Dr
6900 NBVL 46062 1794 E1
Grindstone Ct
1700 GNFD 46140 2237 B7
Grindstone Dr
10600 FSHR 46038 1905 C6
Grindstone Wy
1600 GNFD 46140 2237 B7
Gringo Dr
5000 INPS 46237 2448 B7
Grinnell Ln
2800 INPS 46268 2009 B2
Grinnell St
8900 INPS 46268 2009 C3
Grisson Estates Apartments
- CCRO 46034 1577 D4
Griswold Rd N
400 AVON 46123 2333 A2
1000 WshT 46123 2333 A1
2400 AVON 46112 2224 A5
2400 AVON 46123 2224 A5
2500 LcnT 46112 2224 A5
Groff Av
1000 INPS 46222 2336 B1
2200 INPS 46222 2227 B6
Grosbeak Ct
13300 CRML 46033 1903 D2
Grosbeak Ln
5600 LWNC 46235 2123 B5
Grosvenor Pl
6500 INPS 46220 2121 D2
Groton Ln
8100 INPS 46260 2010 A5
Grouse Ct
5400 INPS 46254 2226 C1
Grouse Point Tr
13100 CRML 46033 1903 D2
Grove Av
700 INPS 46203 2337 E5
Grove Cir
9400 FSHR 46038 1904 E7
Grove Ct
300 GNWD 46142 2664 C3
Grove Dr
- SGLK 46140 2343 E3
W Grove Dr
2800 SGLK 46140 2343 E3
Grove St
- GNWD 46184 2774 B2
500 GNFD 46140 2345 D2
Grove Berry Dr
8000 INPS 46239 2449 B3
Grove Berry Ln
3300 INPS 46239 2449 B3
Groveton Ct
3200 INPS 46227 2556 C6
Grove Tree Ct
5600 BHGV 46203 2448 B4
Grove Tree Ln
3800 BHGV 46203 2448 B4
Grove Walk Ct
6100 NBVL 46062 1685 C4
Grovewood Dr
100 BHGV 46107 2448 A5
300 BHGV 46107 2447 E5
Grovewood Pl
200 BHGV 46107 2448 A5
Grube St
900 INPS 46227 2555 E4
8300 INPS 46113 2552 B4
Guard Hill Ln
5600 INPS 46226 2121 B5
Guardhill Ln
10400 FSHR 46060 1905 B2
Guildhall Ct
1600 INPS 46260 2009 E4
Guilford Av
3300 INPS 46205 2228 E3
4900 INPS 46205 2119 E7
5200 INPS 46220 2119 E6
8600 INPS 46240 2010 E4
9600 CRML 46280 2010 E2
10000 ClyT 46280 2010 E2
N Guilford Av
8700 INPS 46240 2010 E4
Guilford Dr
9500 INPS 46240 2010 E3
N Guilford Rd
10 CRML 46032 1901 E2
S Guilford Rd
10 CRML 46032 1901 E3
Guinevere Dr
- INPS 46229 2231 E5
Guion Ln
3900 INPS 46268 2117 E3
3900 INPS 46268 2118 A3
Guion Rd
3700 INPS 46222 2227 A3
3800 INPS 46228 2227 A2
3800 INPS 46254 2227 A2
4500 INPS 46254 2117 E6
6200 INPS 46268 2117 E3
8600 INPS 46268 2009 A4
N Guion Rd
- INPS 46268 2118 A1
5600 INPS 46254 2117 E4
6600 INPS 46268 2117 E2
7900 INPS 46268 2008 E6
Guion Lakes Blvd
4200 INPS 46254 2117 E5
Guion Lakes Ct
5800 INPS 46254 2117 E4
Guion Lakes Dr
5700 INPS 46254 2117 E4
Guion Lakes Ter
4200 INPS 46254 2117 E4
Gulf Dr
1100 INPS 46217 2554 E7
1100 INPS 46217 2555 A7
Gulfstream Ct
9800 FCkT 46038 2014 D1
Gulfstream Dr
9700 FCkT 46038 2014 D1
11600 FSHR 46038 2014 D1
Gull Ct
1300 CCRO 46034 1577 B5
7800 INPS 46256 2013 C7
Gullane Ct
300 WshT 46123 2331 C4
Gullit Wy
7700 INPS 46214 2225 C7
Gull Lake Dr
9500 INPS 46239 2340 E5
Gumwood Ct
8800 INPS 46234 2334 A1
Gumwood Dr
1300 INPS 46234 2334 A1
Gunnery Cir
- INPS 46278 2007 E6
Gunnery Rd
6700 INPS 46278 2007 E6
Gunnison Ct
10800 FSHR 46038 1905 C3
Gunnison Dr
12500 LWNC 46236 2015 A6
Gunpowder Ct
8700 INPS 46256 2013 C4
Gunpowder Dr
8600 INPS 46256 2013 C4
Gunsmith Ct
7700 PNFD 46168 2441 D2
Gunwale Dr
11000 INPS 46236 2014 C6
Gunyon Ct
7500 INPS 46237 2557 D5
Gunyon Dr
7500 INPS 46237 2557 D5
Gunyon Wy
6000 INPS 46237 2557 C5
S Gurley St
10 WTFD 46074 1684 B7
10 WTFD 46074 1793 B1
Gusset Ct
18800 NBVL 46062 1685 C5
Guthrie Dr
4700 INPS 46221 2444 B6
Guthrie Rd
2000 GfdT 46168 2550 E6
Guy Rd
2000 Gfdl 46168 2550 E6
Guy St
11200 FSHR 46060 1905 D2
Guy Wy
12300 LWNC 46236 2015 A6
Gwin Dr
9900 ClyT 46280 2011 B1
Gwin Wy
8300 INPS 46256 2013 C4
Gwinnett Pl
7100 NBVL 46062 1685 E5
8100 INPS 46250 2011 E6
Gwynmere Run
1400 CRML 46032 1900 E4
Gwynn Ct
10 INPS 46222 2226 E5
Gypsy Hill Rd
7500 INPS 46240 2010 D7
Gyrfalcon Pl
5700 CRML 46033 1903 B1

H

H Ct
- WRvT 46142 2663 E1
H St
- BHGV 46107 2447 E3
Habig Rd
10 INPS 46217 2446 B4
Hacienda Ct
5700 INPS 46237 2448 B7
Hacienda Dr
1200 WshT 46123 2332 B1
Hacienda Pl
400 GNWD 46143 2665 E4
Hackberry Ct
7700 INPS 46227 2556 B5
10500 ClyT 46032 2011 B1

STREET
Block City ZIP Map# Grid

W Hackberry Tr
5500 SCkT 46163 2451 E3
Haddam Ln
16100 WshT 46062 1793 E3
Hadden Ln
- FSHR 46060 1905 D1
Haddington North Dr
8800 INPS 46256 2013 D3
Haddington West Dr
9300 INPS 46256 2013 C3
Hadleigh Dr
4000 INPS 46241 2444 A5
Hadley Dr
600 INPS 46202 2337 A2
Hadley Rd
900 MRVL 46158 2660 B4
4000 BrnT 46158 2660 B4
4300 MdnT 46158 2660 B4
5600 MdnT 46113 2660 D4
5600 MdnT 46113 2661 C4
5600 MdnT 46158 2661 C4
8300 MdnT 46113 2662 A4
E Hadley Rd
- GfdT 46168 2550 D2
1000 PNFD 46168 2550 D2
2300 PNFD 46168 2551 A2
Hadley St
200 MRVL 46158 2659 E3
Hadley Woodland St
10 BrnT 46158 2659 D2
Hadway Dr
9100 INPS 46256 2013 C3
Hague Rd
8500 INPS 46256 2013 B5
9600 FSHR 46256 2013 B2
9700 FSHR 46038 2013 B2
9900 DelT 46256 2013 B2
10400 DelT 46038 2013 B2
10600 DelT 46038 1904 B7
10600 FSHR 46038 1904 B7
18600 NBVL 46062 1686 B4
18600 NbvT 46062 1686 B1
20900 NBVL 46062 1577 B7
20900 NbvT 46062 1577 B7
N Hague Rd
6700 INPS 46256 2122 B1
7500 INPS 46256 2013 B7
9500 FSHR 46256 2013 B4
Haig Point Dr
10900 FSHR 46038 1905 C6
Haines Av
2100 INPS 46221 2336 D7
S Halcomb Cir
6500 INPS 46241 2444 A5
Halcomb Cir North Dr
6500 INPS 46241 2444 B4
Halcomb Cir South Dr
6500 INPS 46241 2444 B4
Haldale Dr
200 CRML 46032 1792 D7
200 CRML 46032 1901 D1
Halden Pl
7100 INPS 46214 2334 D2
Haley Ct
1000 CCRO 46034 1577 B6
Halfax St
- CRML 46032 1900 E2
Half Moon Ln
- CCRO 46034 1577 C4
Halfmoon Ln
6000 INPS 46220 2121 C2
Halifax Ct
- PNFD 46231 2333 D6
- WshT 46074 1792 B5
Halifax Dr
2800 INPS 46222 2227 C5
Halifax Ln
- PNFD 46231 2333 D6
Halite Ln
- FSHR 46060 1906 A1
Hall Ct
100 GNWD 46143 2665 C2
300 WynT 46060 1687 D1
Hall Dr
400 WRvT 46142 2663 C3
N Hall Pl
1600 INPS 46202 2228 C7
Hall Rd
2000 PNFD 46168 2550 B2
6300 GfdT 46168 2550 B3
Hall St
200 SPRT 46227 2556 B4
Halla Pl
7200 FSHR 46038 1904 A5
Hall Baker Rd
1400 CtrT 46052 1786 B2
1400 LEBN 46052 1786 B2
Halle Dr
11800 INPS 46229 2232 E7
Halleck Wy
10200 WshT 46123 2333 D2
Halliburton Dr
2400 PNFD 46231 2442 D1
2400 WshT 46231 2442 D1
Hallmark Dr
4400 GfdT 46231 2442 E6
4400 PNFD 46231 2442 E6
Hallwood Ct
5300 INPS 46254 2116 D6
Halsey Dr
9600 FCkT 46256 2014 D2
Hal Sharpe
- ZNVL 46077 1899 A5
Halsted Ct
400 INPS 46214 2334 D2
Halsted Dr
7300 INPS 46214 2334 D3
Halyard Wy
8000 INPS 46236 2014 C6
Hamble Dr
11600 LWNC 46235 2123 D6
Hamblen East Dr
1700 INPS 46231 2334 C7
Hamblen West Dr
1700 INPS 46231 2334 C7
S Hamblen West Dr
1800 INPS 46231 2334 C7
Hamblin Ct
9900 ClyT 46280 2011 B1
Hamburg Ct
9600 INPS 46256 2013 E5
Hamden St
600 BNBG 46112 2223 A1
N Hamilton Av
1400 INPS 46201 2338 A1
S Hamilton Av
200 INPS 46201 2338 A4
400 SRDN 46069 1573 A2
700 AdmT 46069 1573 A2
Hamilton Dr
- GNWD 46143 2666 B6
E Hamilton Dr
1200 NBVL 46060 1686 D5
Hamilton Ests
- CRML 46062 1795 A6
- NBVL 46062 1795 A6
- NbvT 46062 1795 A6
Hamilton Ln
1800 ClyT 46032 1902 B7
1800 ClyT 46280 1902 B7
Hamilton St
- PTBR 46167 2112 E3
200 BNBG 46112 2223 C1
700 LEBN 46052 1677 A7
W Hamilton St
9000 INPS 46234 2225 A3
9100 INPS 46234 2224 E3
Hamilton Commons Blvd
13100 FSHR 46060 1906 C1
Hamilton Crossing Blvd
- CRML 46032 1901 C2
Hamilton Hills Dr
9600 DelT 46038 2012 D2
Hamilton Hills Ln
9700 DelT 46038 2012 D2
Hamilton Pass
11100 FCkT 46038 1905 C6
11400 FSHR 46038 1905 D6
Hamlet Dr
600 AVON 46123 2332 B2
Hamlyn St
11000 INPS 46259 2559 C5
Hammer Rd
1800 MnrT 46158 2658 B2
Hammerstone Ct
4500 INPS 46239 2449 B5
Hammock Glen Dr
5200 LWNC 46235 2123 E6
Hammond Ct
3200 INPS 46268 2118 B3
Hammons Dr
10 LcnT 46112 2113 D5
Hamp Ct
10 CRML 46032 1792 E7
Hampshire Ct
10 NBVL 46062 1685 D1
500 CRML 46032 1901 B3
4000 INPS 46235 2231 D2
Hampshire Dr
7000 EglT 46077 1897 E7
Hampstead Ct
300 NBVL 46060 1795 D5
6600 INPS 46256 2122 A2
Hampstead Ln
7000 INPS 46256 2121 E2
7100 INPS 46256 2122 A2
Hampton Cir E
8200 INPS 46256 2013 E5
Hampton Cir N
9600 INPS 46256 2013 E5
Hampton Cir S
9600 INPS 46256 2013 E5
Hampton Cir W
8200 INPS 46256 2013 E5
Hampton Ct
- PNFD 46168 2442 B1
1000 INPS 46260 2010 A5
12000 CRML 46033 1902 D4
N Hampton Ct
1500 CBLD 46140 2232 E6
Hampton Dr
1500 ZNVL 46077 1898 E6
E Hampton Dr
10 INPS 46205 2228 D1
W Hampton Dr
10 INPS 46208 2228 B1
Hampton Dr E
6100 INPS 46226 2230 D1
6600 INPS 46226 2121 D7
Hampton Pl
10 WynT 46060 1687 D1
7800 FSHR 46038 1904 B5
Hampton Rd
600 WshT 46074 1792 B6
Hampton Wy
- INPS 46256 2013 E5
- INPS 46256 2014 A5
Hancock Av
200 INPS 46222 2336 C4
Hancock St
800 INPS 46221 2336 C5
12200 CRML 46032 1901 D4
Hancock Rd
200 PNFD 46168 2441 E5
Handball Ln
1400 INPS 46260 2009 E3
Handel Dr
14600 WshT 46032 1792 C6
Hanks Dr
6300 INPS 46224 2226 A7
Hanley Dr
- FSHR 46038 1906 B5
Hanley St
100 PNFD 46168 2441 C4
E Hanna Av
10 INPS 46227 2446 E4
1400 INPS 46227 2447 B4
3200 INPS 46237 2447 B4
6000 BHGV 46203 2448 C4
6400 INPS 46203 2448 D4
E Hanna Av
6600 INPS 46237 2448 D4
7000 INPS 46239 2448 E4
7000 INPS 46239 2449 A4
S Hanna Av
6200 INPS 46203 2448 D4
W Hanna Av
10 INPS 46217 2446 B5
1000 INPS 46217 2445 E5
4900 INPS 46221 2444 C5
5500 INPS 46241 2444 A5
6400 INPS 46241 2443 E5
Hanna Cir
3700 INPS 46241 2444 B4
Hanna St
700 PNFD 46168 2441 A5
7500 MCVL 46055 2015 C7
N Hanna St
7500 MCVL 46055 2015 C7
Hannah Ct
2100 LEBN 46052 1676 D4
3700 CRML 46033 2011 E2
Hanna Village Dr
4000 INPS 46227 2446 D5
Hannibal St
1900 NBVL 46060 1686 E7
E Hannibal St
1000 NBVL 46060 1686 D7
W Hannibal St
500 NBVL 46060 1686 C7
Hanover Ct
6200 FSHR 46038 1903 D6
Hanover Dr
600 NWTD 46184 2774 D4
2100 INPS 46227 2447 A6
Hansbrough Wy
6300 INPS 46268 2117 C3
Hansen Pl
- NBVL 46060 1687 C4
Hanson Av
- INPS 46202 2337 A2
N Hanson Av
- INPS 46202 2337 A2
Happy Hllw
5400 INPS 46268 2117 C3
Happy Hollow Ct
700 WRvT 46142 2664 B2
Happy House Dr
4700 LWNC 46235 2123 A7
Hapsburg Wy
3300 INPS 46239 2449 A3
Harbinger Ct
- NBVL 46060 1687 B4
17000 WTFD 46062 1793 D2
Harbison Av
- INPS 46219 2340 C3
N Harbison Av
1100 INPS 46219 2340 C1
1700 INPS 46219 2231 C7
5800 INPS 46239 2558 C1
Harbison Ct
1100 INPS 46219 2340 C1
S Harbison Rd
5800 INPS 46239 2558 C1
E Harbor Ct
9700 INPS 46229 2231 E6
W Harbor Ct
9700 INPS 46229 2231 E6
Harbor Dr
- WshT 46123 2332 E2
2200 INPS 46229 2231 E6
Harbor Ln
- WshT 46123 2332 E2
Harbor Wy
- WshT 46123 2332 E2
Harbor Bay Ct
10700 FCkT 46040 1906 E7
Harbor Bay Dr
10700 FCkT 46040 1906 D7
Harborton Wy
7800 INPS 46236 2014 B6
7800 LWNC 46236 2014 B6
Harbor Walk Ln
8000 INPS 46237 2557 C6
Harbor Walk Pl
8000 INPS 46237 2557 C6
Harbour Cir
200 FCkT 46038 1906 A7
N Harbour Dr
1900 NBVL 46062 1685 E1
2400 NBVL 46062 1576 D7
S Harbour Dr
100 NBVL 46062 1685 E4
Harbour Isl
7100 INPS 46240 2011 D7
7100 INPS 46240 2120 C1
Harbour Pt
7300 INPS 46240 2120 B1
Harbour Pines Ct
9800 INPS 46256 2014 A4
Harbour Point Dr E
300 NBVL 46062 1576 C7
300 NBVL 46062 1685 C1
Harbour Point Dr W
300 NBVL 46062 1576 D7
Harbourtown Ct
600 NBVL 46062 1576 D7
Harbour Town Dr
- NBVL 46062 1576 D7
Harbourtown Dr
200 NBVL 46062 1576 D7
Harbour Trees Ln
100 NBVL 46062 1685 E1
Harbourview Dr
300 NBVL 46062 1576 D7
Harbour Woods Ovlk
6800 NBVL 46062 1685 E5
Harbridge Rd
6200 INPS 46220 2121 C3
Harcourt Rd
7200 INPS 46260 2118 E1
7400 INPS 46260 2009 D7
Harcourt Springs Blvd
1900 INPS 46260 2009 C7
Harcourt Springs Ct
7800 INPS 46260 2009 D7
Harcourt Springs Dr
7800 INPS 46260 2009 D6
Harcourt Springs Pl
7700 INPS 46260 2009 D7
Harcourt Springs Ter
1900 INPS 46260 2009 C7
Hardegan St
4800 INPS 46227 2447 A7
8700 INPS 46227 2556 A7
8800 GNWD 46227 2665 A1
8800 INPS 46227 2665 A1
Hardin Blvd
300 INPS 46241 2335 B4
Hardin Ct
1500 PNFD 46168 2441 D6
Harding Av
200 GNFD 46140 2345 B1
Harding Ct
1000 INPS 46217 2445 E6
1000 INPS 46217 2446 A6
Harding Ln
5000 INPS 46217 2445 E7
7100 NBVL 46062 1576 E7
Harding St
400 PNFD 46168 2441 C6
N Harding St
10 INPS 46222 2336 E3
1400 INPS 46202 2227 E7
1400 INPS 46202 2336 E1
2200 INPS 46208 2227 E5
S Harding St
10 INPS 46222 2336 E7
200 INPS 46221 2336 E7
2100 INPS 46221 2445 E3
2700 INPS 46225 2445 E3
3000 INPS 46217 2445 D7
5500 INPS 46217 2554 E2
S Harding St SR-37
- INPS 46217 2445 D7
Hardin Oak Dr
7200 NBVL 46062 1686 A6
Hard Key Cir
9900 LWNC 46236 2123 A4
Hardwick Dr
11800 FSHR 46038 1904 B5
Hardwick Pl
7700 FSHR 46038 1904 B5
Hardwood Ct
9100 INPS 46250 2012 E4
Hardwood Dr
6900 INPS 46250 2012 E3
Hare Dr
5500 NBVL 46062 1576 B7
Harfield Dr
1700 INPS 46260 2009 E6
Hargeo Dr
10 INPS 46217 2555 B6
Harlan Av
2700 INPS 46203 2447 B3
3000 INPS 46237 2447 B3
Harlan Ct
2200 INPS 46227 2556 B1
Harlan Dr
300 MRVL 46158 2660 A3
Harlan St
100 INPS 46201 2338 A4
300 PNFD 46168 2441 C4
1000 INPS 46203 2338 A5
2500 INPS 46203 2447 B1
5000 INPS 46227 2447 B7
5800 INPS 46227 2556 B1
Harlem Dr
300 MRVL 46158 2660 A3
Harlequin Ln
11400 FSHR 46038 1903 E6
Harlescott Rd
6000 INPS 46220 2121 C2
Harlow Dr
10400 FSHR 46038 1905 B3
Harmon Av
7900 BrnT 46112 2006 D2
7900 EglT 46077 2006 D2
7900 EglT 46112 2006 D2
Harmon Ct
7000 INPS 46227 2556 C4
Harmon Dr
3200 INPS 46227 2556 C4
3200 SPRT 46227 2556 C4
Harmon St
400 INPS 46225 2337 C4
Harmon Wy
- LWNC 46216 2122 C6
- LWNC 46226 2122 C6
Harmon Ridge Ct
6300 INPS 46278 2008 A3
Harmony Dr
400 GNWD 46143 2665 B5
3900 INPS 46221 2444 E5
10600 GfdT 46231 2442 D5
10600 PNFD 46231 2442 D5
Harmony Ln
4000 INPS 46221 2444 E5
Harmony Rd
10 CRML 46032 1792 D7
S Harmony Tr
1300 SCkT 46140 2343 E4
W Harmony Tr
3000 SCkT 46140 2343 E3
Harmony Wy
- GNWD 46143 2666 D5
Harness Ct
10800 INPS 46239 2341 C6
Harness Wy
10700 INPS 46239 2341 C6
Harness Lakes Dr
- INPS 46217 2554 B4
Harnessmaker Ct
7600 PNFD 46168 2441 D2
Harney Ct
1600 LEBN 46052 1676 E5
Harney Dr
1000 LEBN 46052 1676 D5
Harper Rd
3200 INPS 46240 2011 C3
Harpers Ln
5000 INPS 46268 2117 D2
Harrier Cir
7000 INPS 46254 2116 E7
Harriet Dr
6800 INPS 46237 2557 E6
Harrington Ct
8400 INPS 46256 2013 D5
Harrington Ln
11100 FSHR 46038 1904 C6
Harrington Rd
8400 INPS 46256 2013 D5
S Harris Av
10 INPS 46222 2336 C4
E Harris St
1000 BNBG 46112 2223 D1
Harrison Av
- MRVL 46158 2659 D3
10 WTWN 46075 1788 D6
Harrison Cir
4900 CRML 46033 1903 A2
Harrison Ct
200 DNVL 46122 2330 A3
Harrison Dr
- PltT 46143 2665 B6
1300 GNWD 46143 2665 B6
8000 LWNC 46226 2122 B7
12800 CRML 46033 1903 A3
Harrison Pkwy
8300 FSHR 46038 1904 C1
14000 FSHR 46038 1795 D7
14100 FSHR 46060 1795 D7
Harrison Pt
- DelT 46060 1795 C7
Harrison St
200 DNVL 46122 2329 D3
700 INPS 46202 2337 D4
900 NBVL 46060 1686 D7
E Harrison St
10 MRVL 46158 2659 E3
1000 NBVL 46060 1686 D7
8700 INPS 46239 2449 C5
N Harrison St
10 CCRO 46034 1577 D2
10 GNFD 46140 2345 C1
600 CtrT 46140 2345 C1
S Harrison St
10 CCRO 46034 1577 D3
10 GNFD 46140 2345 C2
W Harrison St
10 MRVL 46158 2659 D3
Harrison Park Ct
- LWNC 46216 2122 D6
Harrison Park Dr
- LWNC 46216 2122 D6
Harrison Park Ln
- LWNC 46216 2122 D6
Harrison Ridge Blvd
6300 LWNC 46236 2122 E3
Harrison Ridge Dr
9700 LWNC 46236 2122 E3
Harrison Run Ct
8900 INPS 46256 2122 D2
Harrison Run Dr
9000 INPS 46256 2122 D2
Harrison Run Pl
9100 INPS 46256 2122 D2
Harriston Dr
11100 FSHR 46038 1905 C7
Harrow Pl
10300 ClyT 46280 2010 E1
Harrowgate Dr
- CRML 46033 1902 C2
Harshaw Dr
7800 INPS 46239 2449 B1
Harsin Ln
5900 LWNC 46235 2123 D4
Hart Dr
3100 INPS 46224 2226 D4
Hart Ln
7100 NBVL 46062 1576 E7
7100 NBVL 46062 1577 A7
Hartford Av
1800 INPS 46231 2334 B7
2100 PNFD 46168 2550 E1
2100 PNFD 46168 2551 A1
Hartford Dr
- AVON 46123 2332 D4
Hartford Ln
11300 FSHR 46038 1904 B6
Hartford St
1200 INPS 46203 2337 E6
Harting Ovlk
6400 INPS 46237 2557 C2
S Harting Farms Dr
3800 NPLN 46163 2452 A2
Hartington Pl
7000 INPS 46259 2558 B4
Hartland Dr
11700 INPS 46229 2341 E1
Hartle Dr
5700 LWNC 46216 2122 E5
N Hartman Dr
1000 INPS 46219 2340 A1
3400 INPS 46226 2231 A3
4500 LWNC 46226 2231 A1
4600 LWNC 46226 2122 A7
S Hartman Dr
3000 INPS 46239 2449 A3
Hartman Pl
7200 INPS 46226 2231 A3
Harts Ford Wy
200 BNBG 46112 2224 A2
Hartsford Wy
- LcnT 46112 2223 E1
Harvard Pl
300 INPS 46208 2228 B2
Harvest Av
3400 INPS 46226 2231 C3
Harvest Ct
10 DNVL 46122 2330 B2
900 GNWD 46143 2666 A3
1100 WTFD 46032 1792 E6
Harvest Ct
1100 WTFD 46032 1793 A6
3600 INPS 46226 2231 C3
Harvest Dr
14600 WTFD 46032 1792 E6
Harvest Ln
8000 INPS 46256 2013 B5
Harvest Wy
400 PNFD 46168 2442 A4
N Harvest Glen Ct
1100 CBLD 46229 2341 E1
E Harvest Glen Dr
11900 CBLD 46229 2341 E1
Harvest Lake Dr
- BNBG 46112 2114 E5
- BNBG 46112 2115 A5
Harvest Meadow Dr
- GNWD 46143 2665 B7
Harvest Meadows Dr E
18400 WTFD 46074 1684 B5
Harvest Meadows Dr S
1900 WTFD 46074 1684 B6
Harvest Meadows Dr W
18400 WTFD 46074 1684 B5
Harvest Moon Dr
- GNWD 46143 2774 D1
2100 INPS 46229 2232 C6
11500 NBVL 46060 1796 D1
Harvest Ridge Cir
800 AVON 46123 2332 C2
Harvest Ridge Ct
6600 INPS 46237 2557 D6
Harvest Ridge Dr
600 AVON 46123 2332 C2
Harway Ct
5000 INPS 46227 2447 B7
Harwich Dr
2600 INPS 46229 2232 A5
Haskell Pl
13100 CRML 46074 1900 A2
Hastings Blvd
2200 GNFD 46140 2236 C4
Hastings Ct
10400 FSHR 46038 2014 C1
Hastings Dr
10100 INPS 46235 2232 A2
Hastings Trc
9100 INPS 46234 2115 E6
Hathaway Dr
1000 INPS 46229 2340 E1
Hatherley Wy
10000 FCkT 46038 2014 E1
10000 FSHR 46038 2014 E1
Hatteras Ln
7100 INPS 46214 2225 D3
Haueisen Rd
- INPS 46231 2442 E6
- INPS 46241 2443 A6
Haugh St
700 INPS 46222 2336 C2
N Haugh St
400 INPS 46222 2336 C2
Haughey Av
4200 INPS 46208 2228 A1
Havana Av
1700 INPS 46241 2334 E7
W Haven Cir
9900 CRML 46033 2011 E2
Haven Ct
4400 ClyT 46077 1899 E6
9800 INPS 46235 2232 A3
S Haven Ct
7500 INPS 46217 2555 B5
S Haven Dr
- GNWD 46143 2665 E5
- SCkT 46163 2343 B3
900 GNWD 46143 2666 A5
E Haven Ln
9900 CRML 46033 2012 A1
Haven Point Blvd
- CRML 46033 2012 A2
4600 CRML 46033 2011 E2
Havens Dr
700 SCkT 46163 2343 B3
Haver Wy
9300 ClyT 46240 2011 C3
9300 INPS 46240 2011 C3
Haverford Av
4600 INPS 46205 2119 E7
5400 INPS 46220 2119 E7
Haverhill Ct
7200 INPS 46250 2120 E1
Haverhill Dr
2900 INPS 46240 2120 C1
Haverstick Rd
9300 ClyT 46240 2011 C3
9300 INPS 46240 2011 C3
9600 ClyT 46280 2011 C3
9800 CRML 46032 2011 C3
9800 CRML 46280 2011 C3
10600 CRML 46033 1902 E7
Haverton Wy
- CRML 46033 1903 D2
Hawes Ct
8300 INPS 46256 2013 A4
Hawk Ct
600 GNWD 46143 2665 E3
Hawkesbury Ln
2100 INPS 46260 2118 D1
Hawkeye Ct
4600 INPS 46254 2117 A7
Hawkins Av
- LWNC 46216 2122 D5
E Hawkins Ct
10000 INPS 46229 2232 A6
Hawks Ln
1100 INPS 46220 2119 E5
Hawks Wy
- WTFD 46033 1793 E4
Hawks Crescent Ct
5100 INPS 46254 2116 D6
Hawks Hill Dr
6900 LWNC 46236 2123 E1
Hawks Lake Dr
10100 FSHR 46038 2014 B1
Hawks Landing Dr
12500 FSHR 46038 1906 C4
Hawks Landing Pl
- INPS 46254 2225 D1
Hawks Point Rd
5100 INPS 46226 2121 A6
Hawks Ridge Ct
10500 FSHR 46038 2014 B1
Hawkstone Dr
13800 FCkT 46040 2015 D1
Hawley Dr
500 DNVL 46122 2329 D3
Hawthorn Dr
100 MdlT 46167 2113 B5
100 PTBR 46167 2113 B5
Hawthorn Ln
200 WRvT 46142 2663 D3
Hawthorn Rdg
- FSHR 46038 1905 D6
- FSHR 46038 2014 E1
- FSHR 46038 2015 A1
11100 FSHR 46038 1906 A6
Hawthorn Ter
4900 INPS 46220 2121 A3
Hawthorne Cir
5200 INPS 46250 2121 A1
Hawthorne Ct
10 CRML 46033 1902 D2
10 MdlT 46122 2222 A6
2200 WshT 46122 2222 A6
7900 INPS 46256 2122 B2
Hawthorne Dr
10 CRML 46033 1902 D1
400 WshT 46168 2441 C1
1000 CRML 46033 1793 D7
1600 PNFD 46168 2441 D4
5200 INPS 46226 2121 C6
N Hawthorne Dr
- INPS 46226 2121 C6
Hawthorne Dr W
3200 CRML 46033 1793 C7
Hawthorne Ln
300 GNFD 46140 2236 D7
700 BNBG 46112 2114 D4
N Hawthorne Ln
700 INPS 46219 2339 A1
3400 INPS 46218 2230 B3
3800 INPS 46226 2230 B2
7200 INPS 46250 2121 B1
S Hawthorne Ln
10 INPS 46219 2339 A3
1000 INPS 46203 2339 A6
Hawthorne Pl
2300 NBVL 46062 1685 C1
Hawthorne Rd
1000 WshT 46168 2441 B2
7900 INPS 46256 2122 B2
E Hawthorne St
10 ZNVL 46077 1899 B6
W Hawthorne St
100 ZNVL 46077 1899 B6
Hawthorne Wy
4800 WshT 46123 2331 C5
Hawthorn Park Dr
6700 INPS 46220 2121 B2
Haxton Pl
14500 FCkT 46040 1906 E5
Hayden St
12500 LWNC 46236 2015 A6
W Haydn Dr
200 WshT 46032 1792 C6
Haydon Ct
12400 FSHR 46038 1904 B4
Hayford Ct
6000 INPS 46254 2117 B7
Hayford Wy
6000 INPS 46254 2117 A7
Hayland Dr
- WshT 46123 2332 E2
Hay Meadow Ct
8600 INPS 46227 2555 E7
Haymount Dr
600 INPS 46241 2334 E5
Haynes Av
1500 INPS 46240 2120 A1
4800 INPS 46250 2121 A1
E Haynes Av
5400 INPS 46250 2121 B1
Haynes Ct
5000 INPS 46250 2121 A1
Hayworth Rd
7600 INPS 46221 2552 E5
Hazelchase Ct
2800 INPS 46268 2118 C3
Hazel Dell Pkwy
10300 CRML 46280 2012 B2
10600 CRML 46280 1903 B7
13700 CRML 46033 1903 C2
14000 CRML 46033 1794 C7
Hazel Dell Rd
14600 NBVL 46062 1794 C2
15600 NbvT 46062 1794 C2
17100 NbvT 46062 1685 C7
Hazel Foster Ct E
3200 CRML 46033 1793 D7
Hazel Foster Ct W
3100 CRML 46033 1793 C7
Hazel Foster Dr
2800 CRML 46033 1793 C7
Hazelhatch Ct
2800 INPS 46268 2118 C3
Hazelhatch Dr
6100 INPS 46228 2118 C4
6200 INPS 46268 2118 C3
Hazelnut Ct
6300 INPS 46268 2118 C3
Hazelrigg Rd
1900 CtrT 46052 1676 A2
Hazeltine Dr
2800 INPS 46234 2225 A5
Hazelview Ln
2800 INPS 46268 2118 B3
Hazelwood Av
6100 INPS 46228 2119 A4
7300 INPS 46260 2010 A7

STREET
Block City ZIP Map# Grid

Hazelwood Av
7300 INPS 46260 2119 A1
N Hazelwood Av
7300 INPS 46260 2119 B1
Hazelwood Cir
4600 CRML 46033 1902 E2
Hazelwood Ct
1100 INPS 46260 2119 A2
13100 CRML 46033 1902 E2
Hazelwood Ct E
1500 WRvT 46143 2664 C7
Hazelwood Ct W
1500 WRvT 46143 2664 C7
Hazelwood Dr
- GNWD 46143 2666 A6
13100 CRML 46033 1902 E2
Hazen Wy
8000 LWNC 46216 2122 B5
Hazy Cir
9100 INPS 46260 2009 E3
Hazy Ct
10 WRvT 46142 2663 E3
Hazy Ln
- WRvT 46142 2663 D3
N Hazy Ln
- WRvT 46142 2663 D3
Headwind Dr
7800 INPS 46241 2443 C1
Heady Ct
100 FSHR 46038 1904 B4
Heady Ln
100 FSHR 46038 1904 B4
Heaney Ct
4400 INPS 46228 2227 D1
Hearthside Ct
900 BNBG 46112 2223 E1
Hearthside Dr
- GNWD 46143 2666 D5
900 BNBG 46112 2223 E1
Hearthstone Ct
3500 INPS 46227 2556 C5
S Hearthstone Ct
3600 SCkT 46163 2451 E2
Hearthstone Dr
11100 FSHR 46038 1906 B6
Hearthstone Wy
7000 INPS 46227 2556 C5
Heartland Blvd
- GfdT 46113 2551 D7
- GfdT 46168 2551 D7
- INPS 46113 2551 E7
- INPS 46113 2552 A7
- INPS 46113 2661 A1
6700 MdnT 46113 2661 B1
Heartland Ct
6400 INPS 46278 2008 A7
Heartland Dr
- GNWD 46143 2666 E5
Heartland Rd
7500 INPS 46278 2008 A7
Heartland Bay
7400 INPS 46278 2008 A7
7400 INPS 46278 2117 A1
Heartwood Ct
14300 CRML 46033 1794 C7
Heath Cir
15400 WshT 46074 1792 C5
Heather Cir
1700 INPS 46229 2232 A7
Heather Ct
- BrnT 46112 2114 D1
1800 INPS 46229 2232 A7
Heather Dr
10 INPS 46214 2334 E3
300 CRML 46032 1902 B3
Heather Ln
- NBVL 46060 1687 A3
- NbvT 46060 1687 A3
7700 FSHR 46038 1904 B7
Heather Beach Ln
3000 INPS 46234 2225 B4
Heather Brook Ln
1200 CtrT 46122 2329 A1
Heatherdown Ct
7600 INPS 46259 2558 A5
Heatherglen Cir
9900 FSHR 46038 2014 A1
Heather Hills Rd
9900 INPS 46229 2232 A7
Heatherlea Ct
2700 INPS 46229 2232 B5
Heatherlea Dr
2700 INPS 46229 2232 B5
Heathermoor Crst
2400 CRML 46074 1900 C1
Heathermoor Park Dr N
2400 CRML 46074 1900 D1
Heathermoor Park Dr S
2500 CRML 46074 1900 C1
Heather Ridge Ct
7100 INPS 46214 2225 D4
Heather Ridge Dr
3200 INPS 46214 2225 D4
Heatherstone Pl
12100 CRML 46033 1903 A4
Heatherton Cir
8200 INPS 46256 2013 A5
Heatherton Ct
8200 INPS 46256 2013 A5
Heatherton Dr
8300 INPS 46256 2013 A4
Heatherwood Ct
600 NBVL 46062 1685 E4
Heatherwood Dr
1100 INPS 46241 2335 A5
Heatherwood Ln
10 MdnT 46113 2661 B2
Heathery Pl
8100 INPS 46214 2225 B6
Heathfield Ct
3800 CRML 46077 1900 A4
Heathmoore Dr
5800 INPS 46237 2448 C6
Heathmore Dr W
4800 INPS 46237 2448 C6
Heathrow Ct
1400 CRML 46033 1793 E6
W Heathrow Wy
- INPS 46221 2552 D1
- INPS 46241 2552 D1
E Heathwood Dr
5100 INPS 46237 2557 A6
Heaton Pass
5900 CRML 46033 1903 E3
Heckman Dr
500 WRvT 46142 2663 C2
Heckman Wy
5100 WRvT 46142 2663 C2
Hedback Dr
6500 INPS 46220 2120 C2
Hedback Wy
3200 INPS 46220 2120 C2
Hedge Ct
1400 GNFD 46140 2237 B5
Hedgerow Dr
5200 INPS 46226 2121 C6
S Heflin St
10 CBLD 46229 2341 E2
Heights Av
5200 INPS 46237 2447 E7
Heiney Rd
4000 INPS 46241 2444 B5
Heiny Rd
100 INPS 46217 2446 B3
Heirloom Ln
- GNWD 46143 2666 D4
E Helen Dr
1000 INPS 46240 2010 E7
Helena Av
5200 INPS 46237 2447 E7
Helena Ct
10 INPS 46222 2227 A5
100 LEBN 46052 1676 D4
Helena Dr
1100 LEBN 46052 1676 D4
Helen Keen Ct
600 CRML 46032 1901 E3
Helford Ln
1100 CRML 46032 1901 A4
1200 CRML 46032 1900 E4
Helm Dr
- WshT 46123 2333 C2
Helmsdale Dr
9300 INPS 46256 2013 D3
Helmsman Cir
7600 INPS 46256 2014 A5
Hemlock Av
3600 INPS 46205 2229 A2
Hemlock Ct
- BNBG 46112 2114 C3
400 NBVL 46062 1685 C3
Hemlock Ln
1700 PNFD 46168 2441 D3
Hemlock St
1100 CRML 46033 1902 D1
Hemlock Wy
3000 INPS 46203 2448 D3
Henderson Ct
14600 WshT 46074 1792 B6
Henderson Dr
5600 LcnT 46112 2114 A6
E Hendricks Dr
800 CtrT 46052 1786 B1
800 LEBN 46052 1786 B1
S Hendricks Dr
400 GNWD 46142 2664 D4
Hendricks Pl
10 INPS 46201 2338 A3
N Hendricks St
10 GNFD 46140 2345 C1
S Hendricks St
10 GNFD 46140 2345 C2
Hendricks County Rd
- GfdT 46113 2660 D1
- INPS 46113 2660 D1
9700 BrnT 46113 2660 C1
9700 BrnT 46168 2660 C1
9700 GfdT 46168 2660 C1
9700 MdnT 46113 2660 C1
9700 MdnT 46168 2660 C1
E Hendricks County Rd
500 LtyT 46118 2657 B5
500 LtyT 46157 2657 B5
500 MnrT 46157 2657 B5
700 BrnT 46158 2660 A1
700 BrnT 46168 2660 A1
700 GfdT 46158 2660 A1
700 GfdT 46168 2660 A1
700 MRVL 46158 2660 A1
800 MnrT 46118 2657 B5
6300 BrnT 46158 2658 E1
6300 BrnT 46158 2659 D1
6300 GfdT 46158 2658 E1
7700 GfdT 46158 2659 D1
7700 GfdT 46168 2659 D1
8300 MRVL 46158 2659 D1
Henley Cir
1000 CRML 46032 1901 A1
Henley St
700 PNFD 46168 2441 A5
Henly Dr
300 PNFD 46168 2441 A5
Henry St
400 LEBN 46052 1676 E6
1300 WshT 46123 2333 A1
E Henry St
10 INPS 46225 2337 C4
W Henry St
600 INPS 46225 2337 B4
1200 INPS 46221 2336 E4
3400 INPS 46241 2336 A4
4500 INPS 46241 2335 D4
7300 INPS 46231 2334 D4
Hensel Ct
10 CRML 46033 1902 C6
Hensel Dr
3000 CRML 46033 1902 C7
Herald Sq
9800 FSHR 46038 1905 A3
W Herbert St
1200 INPS 46202 2227 E7
Herbert Lord Rd
- LWNC 46216 2122 C6
Herford Dr
1900 INPS 46229 2232 E7
Heritage Ct
300 FSHR 46038 1904 B6
6400 MdnT 46158 2661 A4
7300 INPS 46256 2122 D1
S Heritage Ct
4100 SCkT 46163 2451 A2
Heritage Dr
- GNWD 46143 2666 E4
200 DNVL 46122 2330 B3
W Heritage Dr
7300 SCkT 46163 2451 A2
Heritage Ln
200 CRML 46032 1902 A1
1600 INPS 46227 2447 A3
5200 WRvT 46142 2663 C2
5400 EglT 46077 1898 D4
Heritage Pl
10 BNBG 46112 2114 C7
Heritage Commons Dr
8100 INPS 46219 2231 B7
Heritage Commons Ln
2000 INPS 46219 2231 B7
Heritage Hill Dr
6500 INPS 46237 2557 D6
Herman St
100 INPS 46202 2337 E3
Hermitage Ct
2200 SDWY 46224 2226 C6
Hermitage Ln
- CRML 46032 1900 D4
Hermitage Rd
3500 INPS 46217 2446 C4
Hermitage Wy
2300 SDWY 46224 2226 B6
Hermosa Ct
3400 INPS 46235 2231 D3
Hermosa Dr
10000 LWNC 46236 2014 A7
Herod Ct
2200 INPS 46229 2232 B6
Heroic Wy
13200 FSHR 46060 1906 A2
E Heron Ct
8300 INPS 46256 2013 C6
S Heron Ct
1000 SCkT 46163 2343 B3
S Heron Dr E
1200 SCkT 46163 2343 B4
S Heron Dr W
1200 SCkT 46163 2343 A4
Heron Neck Dr
6600 INPS 46217 2554 D3
Heron Pass
11300 FSHR 46038 1905 D6
Heron Ridge Blvd
1300 WRvT 46143 2664 B6
Heron Ridge Ct
- WRvT 46143 2664 B6
Herons Cove
9700 CRML 46280 2011 A2
Herriman Blvd
16300 NBVL 46060 1795 E3
16500 NbvT 46060 1795 E3
Herriman Ct
500 NBVL 46060 1795 D5
Herring Gull Dr
9700 CRML 46280 2011 A2
Herschell Av
1400 INPS 46202 2227 E6
Hervey Av
900 INPS 46203 2446 D1
Hervey St
- INPS 46203 2448 D1
2800 INPS 46203 2447 C1
Hesian Lp
300 ClyT 46032 1899 E6
300 ClyT 46032 1900 A6
Hess Av
- LWNC 46216 2122 C5
Hess Ct
10 LWNC 46216 2122 C4
E Hess St
1000 PNFD 46168 2441 C4
W Hess St
900 PNFD 46168 2441 C5
Hewes Ct
18800 NBVL 46062 1685 E5
18800 NBVL 46062 1686 A5
Hewes Pl
8100 INPS 46250 2011 E6
Hewlet Dr
8200 INPS 46268 2009 A5
Heyward Dr
8000 INPS 46250 2011 E6
Heyward Ln
4000 INPS 46250 2011 E6
Heyward Pl
4000 INPS 46250 2011 E5
Hialea Ct
1100 ClyT 46280 1901 E7
1100 ClyT 46280 1902 A7
Hiatt Av
- WRvT 46143 2663 D5
Hiatt St
800 INPS 46221 2336 D5
Hiawatha Dr
100 WRvT 46062 1578 D6
100 WynT 46062 1578 D6
Hibben Av
5200 INPS 46219 2339 A3
8500 INPS 46219 2340 C3
9000 INPS 46229 2340 D3
Hibiscus Ct
1000 CCRO 46034 1577 B2
Hibiscus Dr
1800 INPS 46219 2231 C7
Hickory Blvd
2000 CtrT 46140 2237 A4
2400 CtrT 46140 2236 E4
Hickory Cir
4100 INPS 46203 2448 D5
Hickory Ct
100 WRvT 46142 2664 A1
600 CBLD 46140 2233 A7
4600 ZNVL 46077 1899 A3
10700 CRML 46033 1902 E7
Hickory Ct E
4300 INPS 46203 2448 D5
Hickory Ct W
6500 INPS 46203 2448 D5
Hickory Dr
10 DNVL 46122 2330 B3
300 CBLD 46140 2342 A1
500 CBLD 46140 2233 A7
700 CRML 46032 1902 C3
W Hickory Dr
10 CtrT 46140 2345 A4
Hickory Ln
- CBLD 46140 2233 B7
- GNWD 46143 2666 A5
- SgCT 46126 2670 D7
10 LcnT 46112 2113 D5
100 GNFD 46140 2345 E4
100 WTLD 46184 2775 A6
400 PNFD 46168 2441 D3
1300 ZNVL 46077 1899 A7
6400 BrnT 46112 2113 D5
8300 INPS 46113 2552 B5
E Hickory Ln
10 INPS 46227 2555 C5
N Hickory Ln
200 SgCT 46126 2670 D7
W Hickory Ln
10 INPS 46217 2555 C5
Hickory Ln E
3400 INPS 46214 2225 C3
Hickory Ln W
3400 INPS 46214 2225 D3
Hickory Rd
100 BrnT 46112 2114 D2
S Hickory Rd
5000 INPS 46239 2449 E7
5000 INPS 46239 2558 E1
6000 INPS 46259 2558 E4
Hickory St
- NPLN 46163 2452 A3
Hickory Tr E
4000 INPS 46203 2448 D4
Hickory Tr S
6500 INPS 46203 2448 D5
Hickory Tr W
4100 INPS 46203 2448 D5
Hickory Wy
800 NBVL 46062 1685 D3
Hickory Forge Ct
6000 INPS 46254 2117 E4
Hickory Grove Ct
4100 LtyT 46118 2440 A7
Hickory Hill Dr
- LcnT 46112 2115 D5
Hickory Hill Tr
- GfdT 46158 2550 D7
Hickory Knoll Dr
4000 INPS 46203 2448 D5
Hickory Lake Dr
5100 LWNC 46235 2123 C6
Hickory Lake Ln
11000 LWNC 46235 2123 C6
Hickory Leaf Rd
10100 LWNC 46235 2123 A6
Hickorynut Cir
9300 FSHR 46038 1904 E1
Hickory Ridge Cir
10 JknT 46034 1577 A4
Hickory Ridge Ct
10400 ZNVL 46077 1899 A2
13700 CRML 46032 1792 A6
13700 CRML 46032 1901 C1
Hickory Ridge Dr
9900 ZNVL 46077 1898 E2
9900 ZNVL 46077 1899 A2
Hickory Wds
3000 BCkT 46140 2234 E6
Hickorywood Ct
100 BNBG 46112 2223 B2
2700 SDWY 46224 2226 C5
Hickorywood Dr
6000 SDWY 46224 2226 A5
Hickory Woods Dr
7400 FSHR 46038 1904 A6
Hickory Woods Dr S
7400 FSHR 46038 1904 C7
Hidden Ln
- CRML 46033 1902 D3
Hidden Rdg
7700 FSHR 46038 1904 B7
Hidden Bay
11400 LWNC 46236 2014 D6
Hidden Bay Dr
- GNWD 46142 2664 C3
Hidden Falls Cir
10000 FSHR 46038 1905 A6
Hidden Hills Ln
- LcnT 46112 2115 C5
Hidden Hollow Ct
- FSHR 46038 1905 C5
W Hidden Lake Ct
3200 BCkT 46140 2343 D1
Hidden Lake Dr
8400 INPS 46250 2012 E5
Hidden Meadow Ln
10100 INPS 46229 2341 B3
Hidden Oak Cir
10700 LWNC 46236 2123 B2
Hidden Oak Ln
6500 LWNC 46236 2123 B2
Hidden Oak Wy
10700 LWNC 46236 2123 B2
Hidden Orchard Ct
2200 INPS 46228 2227 D1
Hidden Orchard Ln
4300 INPS 46228 2227 D1
4400 INPS 46228 2118 C7
Hidden Pine Dr
3100 INPS 46235 2232 D4
Hidden Point Dr
8200 INPS 46256 2013 E5
Hidden Ridge Ct
5200 INPS 46221 2553 C2
Hidden Valley Dr
400 WshT 46168 2441 B1
Hidden Valley Ln
7500 INPS 46239 2340 A7
Hideaway Ct
900 GNWD 46142 2664 E1
N Hideaway Ln
10 BrnT 46158 2658 D5
Hideaway North Dr
2400 INPS 46268 2009 C6
Hideaway South Dr
2400 INPS 46268 2009 C6
Higdon Ct
7400 INPS 46214 2225 D7
High Ct
1000 CRML 46033 1902 C3
High Dr
400 CRML 46033 1902 C3
4300 LcnT 46112 2222 D2
7800 INPS 46240 2010 D6
High Dr E
4400 LcnT 46112 2222 D2
High Dr W
4200 LcnT 46112 2222 D2
High Grv
10300 ClyT 46032 2009 D1
High St
10 DNVL 46122 2329 C3
900 INPS 46225 2337 D5
E High St
10 MRVL 46158 2659 E4
300 MRVL 46158 2660 A4
400 BrnT 46158 2660 A4
E High St SR-42
10 MRVL 46158 2659 E4
300 MRVL 46158 2660 A4
400 BrnT 46158 2660 A4
W High St
10 MRVL 46158 2659 D4
W High St SR-42
10 MRVL 46158 2659 D4
S High Acres East St
2700 SCkT 46163 2342 E7
W High Acres North Ct
5600 SCkT 46163 2342 E7
W High Acres South Ct
5600 SCkT 46163 2342 E7
W High Acres West Ct
5600 SCkT 46163 2342 E7
S High Acres West St
2700 SCkT 46163 2342 E7
Highburry Ct
6700 INPS 46256 2122 A2
Highburry Dr
7200 INPS 46256 2122 A2
Highbury Pl
- FSHR 46060 1906 E3
High Cloister Ct
11800 FSHR 46038 1906 E5
High Eagle Tr
2000 SDWY 46224 2226 B7
Highfall Rd
5800 INPS 46226 2121 C4
Highfield Ct
3400 INPS 46222 2227 A3
E Highgate Cir
5900 FSHR 46250 2012 C2
N Highgate Cir
9600 FSHR 46250 2012 D2
Highland Av
- SCkT 46163 2452 B3
N Highland Av
200 INPS 46202 2337 E2
S Highland Av
10 INPS 46202 2337 E4
Highland Cir
3900 INPS 46221 2444 E5
Highland Dr
10 MRVL 46158 2659 E2
300 GNWD 46142 2665 C4
800 NWTD 46184 2774 D4
10600 ClyT 46280 1902 A7
Highland Ln
6500 MCVL 46055 2015 C3
Highland Pl
2100 INPS 46202 2228 B6
2300 INPS 46208 2228 B6
Highland Rd
7100 INPS 46268 2118 B1
Highland Cove
1800 ClyT 46280 1902 A7
Highlander Dr
800 PNFD 46168 2441 B6
Highland Manor Ct N
10 INPS 46228 2119 A5
Highland Manor Ct S
10 INPS 46228 2119 A5
Highland Meadows Bnd
- BrnT 46112 2114 D2
Highland Meadows Dr
- BrnT 46112 2114 D1
Highland Park Dr
- BrnT 46112 2114 D1
3600 WRvT 46143 2664 A7
Highlands Pl
12500 FSHR 46038 1904 A3
Highland Springs Cir
- BrnT 46112 2114 E1
Highland Springs Ct
13100 FCkT 46055 2015 C2
Highland Springs Dr
- BrnT 46112 2114 D1
13100 FCkT 46055 2015 C2
Highland Springs North Dr
9600 FCkT 46055 2015 C2
High Meadow Ct N
900 WRvT 46142 2663 E1
High Meadow Ct S
900 WRvT 46142 2663 E2
Highmount Ct
7000 INPS 46268 2118 C2
High Point Cir
13600 FSHR 46060 1905 B1
Highridge Cir
7700 INPS 46259 2558 A5
Highridge Dr
7600 INPS 46259 2558 A5
N High School Rd
10 INPS 46214 2335 A3
1000 INPS 46224 2335 A1
2500 SDWY 46224 2226 A1
3000 INPS 46224 2226 A1
3800 INPS 46254 2226 A1
4500 INPS 46254 2117 A7
S High School Rd
10 INPS 46241 2335 A7
2000 INPS 46241 2444 A1
4800 INPS 46221 2444 A1
5400 INPS 46221 2553 A1
High Timber Ln
5600 LWNC 46235 2123 C5
High View Cir
7700 LWNC 46236 2015 A7
High View Ct
12400 LWNC 46236 2015 A7
High View Dr
7600 LWNC 46236 2015 A7
High Vista Cir
- LcnT 46112 2115 C6
Highwood Dr
200 WTFD 46074 1684 A7
Highwood Ln
7600 BrnT 46112 2006 E7
Highwoods Ct
3200 INPS 46222 2227 B3
Highwoods Dr E
2900 INPS 46222 2227 C4
Highwoods Dr N
3300 INPS 46222 2227 B4
Highwoods Dr W
3100 INPS 46222 2227 B4
W Hiland Dr
3000 INPS 46268 2118 C1
Hilda Ct
10 CRML 46032 1902 A3
Hill Av
- PNFD 46168 2441 B4
Hill Ct
10 WRvT 46142 2663 E3
10 WRvT 46142 2664 A3
5400 INPS 46219 2339 B2
E Hill Dr
2400 CtrT 46140 2237 A4
5300 LWNC 46226 2122 A6
W Hill Dr
5300 LWNC 46226 2122 A6
N Hill Ln
- WRvT 46060 1579 B5
Hill St
10 WTLD 46184 2774 E5
5300 INPS 46219 2339 B2
13900 WynT 46060 1797 E2
Hillcot Ln
1300 INPS 46231 2334 A6
Hillcot Wy
1300 INPS 46231 2334 A6
Hill Crest Ct
13700 CRML 46032 1901 C1
Hillcrest Ct
10 DNVL 46122 2329 E3
4900 WshT 46123 2331 C5
6800 INPS 46227 2556 D3
Hillcrest Dr
10 WTFD 46074 1684 B7
700 GNWD 46142 2664 E2
1100 CRML 46033 1902 D3
1400 NBVL 46060 1795 E2
1400 NbvT 46060 1795 E2
3300 INPS 46227 2556 D3
6800 WshT 46168 2441 B2
7700 GfdT 46158 2550 C6
Hillcrest Ln
600 GNFD 46140 2236 D7
600 GNFD 46140 2345 D1
1500 INPS 46203 2447 A1
6100 INPS 46220 2121 C3
Hillcrest Rd
7900 INPS 46240 2010 D6
Hillcrest Country Club Rd
- INPS 46220 2121 C4
Hillendale Dr
400 WRvT 46142 2663 E3
400 WRvT 46142 2664 A3
Hill Gail Dr
8200 INPS 46217 2554 D6
Hill Pine Ct
8400 INPS 46227 2555 D6
Hill Rise Dr
5500 INPS 46237 2448 B6
Hillsboro Dr
5100 INPS 46224 2226 C4
Hillsborough Dr
10300 FSHR 46038 2014 B1
10400 FCkT 46038 2014 B1
Hillsdale Ct
6800 INPS 46250 2012 E7
Hillsdale Dr
10000 ClyT 46032 2011 B1
Hillside Av
3400 INPS 46218 2229 B3
4500 INPS 46205 2120 B7
4500 INPS 46205 2229 B1
6500 INPS 46220 2120 B2
N Hillside Av
3600 INPS 46218 2229 B3
3800 INPS 46205 2229 B2
Hillside Ct
- WTLD 46184 2774 C7
700 PNFD 46168 2441 C6
Hillside Dr
100 CRML 46032 1902 B1
W Hillside Dr
2500 SCkT 46140 2344 A2
2500 SGLK 46140 2344 A2
Hillside Ln
100 WTLD 46184 2774 C7
Hillside Av East Dr
5900 INPS 46220 2120 B4
Hillside Av West Dr
5900 INPS 46220 2120 B4
Hilltop Dr
10 DNVL 46122 2329 E3
10 DNVL 46122 2330 A4
W Hilltop Dr
600 GNWD 46142 2665 B3
8400 INPS 46234 2225 B4
Hilltop Ln
7700 INPS 46256 2122 B1
Hill Valley Ct
1900 ClyT 46280 1902 A7
Hill Valley Dr
5000 MdlT 46112 2113 C2
Hillvalley Dr
500 INPS 46217 2555 A6
E Hillvalley Dr
10 INPS 46227 2555 C6
Hillview Cir
6300 FSHR 46038 1903 D7
E Hilton Dr
3800 INPS 46237 2447 D6
Himalayan Dr
5300 INPS 46239 2449 B7
Himebaugh Ct
500 INPS 46231 2334 A5
Himebaugh Ln
8800 INPS 46231 2334 B4
Hinault Wy
1300 CRML 46032 1792 A7
Hine St
- WTWN 46075 1788 C6
1300 INPS 46202 2336 E2
Hiner Ln
7000 INPS 46219 2339 E1
7000 INPS 46219 2340 A1
Hines Dr
9800 LcnT 46112 2224 C3
Hinesley Av
5200 INPS 46208 2119 B6
Hinkle Rd
19900 NbvT 46062 1685 A2
19900 WshT 46062 1685 A2
20100 WshT 46062 1576 A7
21000 NbvT 46062 1576 A7
21600 JknT 46034 1576 A6
21600 JknT 46062 1576 A6
21600 WshT 46034 1576 A6
Hinshaw Wy
- WshT 46074 1793 C1
Hinsley Rd
24100 AdmT 46069 1573 B1
24100 SRDN 46069 1573 B1
Hintock Cir
- ClyT 46032 1900 B6
Hintocks Cir
- ClyT 46032 1900 A6
Historic Oaks Blvd
2100 INPS 46214 2225 C6
History Ct
7100 INPS 46239 2448 E6
S Hittle Dr
4700 INPS 46239 2449 D6
Hi-Vu Dr
6500 INPS 46227 2555 D3
Hobart Av
1900 INPS 46203 2338 C7
2200 INPS 46203 2447 C1
Hobbs Ct
5500 INPS 46271 2553 B1
Hobbs Rd
23800 WRvT 46060 1579 E2
Hobbs St
200 PNFD 46168 2441 C5
Hodges Dr
2000 ClyT 46280 2011 B1
Hoefgen St
200 INPS 46225 2446 C1
1100 INPS 46203 2446 E1
1500 INPS 46203 2447 A1
Hoff Ct
8500 INPS 46256 2013 C4
Hoffman Rd
2000 INPS 46231 2334 C7
W Hoffman Rd
2200 INPS 46241 2443 C1
Hogan Dr
2100 INPS 46229 2232 B6
Hohlier Ln
- AVON 46123 2332 C2
- WshT 46123 2332 C2
Hohum Ct
500 WRvT 46142 2664 B2
Holbrook Close
11700 FSHR 46038 1906 E5
Holden Ct
1300 CRML 46032 1792 A7
Holiday Ct
300 ZNVL 46077 1898 E4
Holiday Dr
200 PNFD 46168 2441 D4
9900 ClyT 46032 2011 B1
10400 ClyT 46032 1902 B7
Holiday Ln
10 MRVL 46158 2659 E2
Holiday Ln E
1300 BNBG 46112 2223 C2
Holiday Ln W
1400 BNBG 46112 2223 B2
Holiday Wy
- GNWD 46143 2666 D5
Holiday Pines Dr
- BNBG 46112 2224 A4
- LcnT 46112 2224 A4
Holland Dr
- MdnT 46158 2660 D7
6300 INPS 46224 2226 A7
11600 FSHR 46038 1904 C5

Street / Block	City	ZIP	Map#	Grid
N Holland Dr S				
10900	MdnT	46158	2660	D7
E Holland St				
1300	NBVL	46060	1795	D2
Hollaway Blvd				
10	BNBG	46112	2113	D3
Hollice Ln				
-	FSHR	46060	1906	E3
Holliday Cir				
9400	INPS	46260	2010	C2
Holliday Dr				
-	INPS	46260	2010	C3
Holliday Dr E				
6400	INPS	46260	2119	C2
Holliday Dr W				
6400	INPS	46260	2119	C2
Holliday Ln				
400	INPS	46260	2010	B7
Holliday East Dr				
7300	INPS	46260	2010	C7
7300	INPS	46260	2119	C1
Holliday West Dr				
7300	INPS	46260	2119	C1
7400	INPS	46260	2010	C7
Hollingsworth Dr				
7100	INPS	46268	2009	B7
7100	INPS	46268	2118	B1
Hollingsworth Rd				
5900	INPS	46254	2117	D4
Hollister Dr				
4400	INPS	46222	2226	D5
6300	SDWY	46224	2226	A5
Holl Oak Dr				
7400	NBVL	46062	1686	A6
Holloway Av				
1800	INPS	46218	2229	A7
Holloway Blvd				
-	BNBG	46112	2113	D3
Holloway Dr				
-	FSHR	46060	1906	D3
Hollow Brook Ct				
17800	NBVL	46062	1685	A7
Hollow Creek Ct				
8000	INPS	46250	2009	A6
Hollow Creek Dr				
4000	INPS	46268	2009	A6
Hollow Oak Ct				
5400	INPS	46250	2012	B3
Hollow Oak Tr				
5800	CRML	46033	1903	E1
Hollowood Ct				
1000	INPS	46234	2334	A1
10400	INPS	46060	1905	B2
Hollowood Dr				
8800	INPS	46234	2334	A1
Hollow Reed Ct				
7500	NBVL	46062	1686	A3
Hollow Ridge Cir				
7700	INPS	46256	2013	B6
Hollow Run Cir				
3500	INPS	46214	2225	E3
Hollow Run Dr				
6600	INPS	46214	2225	E3
6600	INPS	46214	2226	A2
Hollow Tree Ln				
10100	LWNC	46235	2123	A6
Hollowview Ct				
200	NBVL	46060	1686	B6
Hollowview Dr				
100	NBVL	46060	1686	B6
Holly Av				
600	INPS	46237	2337	A4
Holly Cir				
3500	INPS	46227	2556	D5
Holly Ct				
-	PNFD	46168	2444	C7
-	PNFD	46168	2550	C1
600	NBVL	46060	1686	C5
Holly Ct S				
500	NBVL	46060	1686	C6
Holly Dr				
1500	PNFD	46168	2550	C1
Holly Berry Ct				
10100	FSHR	46060	1796	B7
Hollybrook Ct				
8000	INPS	46250	2012	A6
Hollybrook Dr				
10	NWTD	46184	2774	D4
Hollybrook Ln				
7600	SPRT	46227	2556	B5
Holly Creek Ln				
7800	INPS	46240	2011	A7
Holly Hill Dr				
4100	INPS	46221	2444	D5
W Hollyhock Ct				
6300	SCkT	46163	2342	C7
Hollyhock Dr				
11800	FSHR	46038	1906	B5
Holly Oak Dr				
-	WTFD	46074	1793	C2
Holly Park Dr				
10	GNWD	46143	2665	C6
Hollypark Dr				
2800	INPS	46241	2444	C3
Holly Springs Cir				
6800	INPS	46254	2116	D6
Holly Springs Ct				
5300	INPS	46254	2116	E6
Holly Springs Dr E				
5200	INPS	46254	2116	E6
Holly Springs Dr W				
5200	INPS	46254	2116	E6
Holly Springs Pl				
6900	INPS	46254	2116	E6
Hollythorn Pl				
5800	CRML	46033	1903	C4
Hollywood Dr				
-	WshT	46123	2333	C2
Hollywood Tr				
6600	INPS	46214	2225	E7
Holman St				
800	GNWD	46142	2665	C2
Holmard Pl				
8200	INPS	46259	2558	B5

Street / Block	City	ZIP	Map#	Grid
Holmdale Rd				
700	INPS	46239	2341	A5
N Holmes Av				
10	INPS	46222	2336	C3
1600	INPS	46222	2227	C7
S Holmes Av				
10	INPS	46222	2336	C4
800	INPS	46221	2336	C5
Holmes Ct				
10	CtrT	46140	2236	D1
Holmes Rd				
1000	CtrT	46052	1787	C3
1000	WrhT	46052	1787	C3
Holm Mountain Cir				
-	WshT	46123	2332	E1
Holt Av				
200	GNWD	46142	2665	C4
N Holt Rd				
-	INPS	46222	2336	A1
-	INPS	46241	2336	A2
-	SDWY	46222	2336	A2
S Holt Rd				
-	INPS	46241	2336	A4
1700	INPS	46241	2445	A1
3000	INPS	46241	2445	A1
Holt St				
-	GNWD	46184	2774	B2
Holyoke Ct				
9200	INPS	46268	2009	C3
Holz Dr				
11800	INPS	46229	2341	E1
Holzkwecht Ct				
-	PNFD	46168	2441	B4
Home Av				
200	GNWD	46142	2665	C4
Home Dr				
7600	DelT	46038	1904	B5
7600	FSHR	46038	1904	B5
Homer Bray Rd				
-	MnrT	46157	2657	A4
Homeridge Dr				
1900	INPS	46203	2339	A7
Homeside Dr				
9200	INPS	46250	2012	E3
Homestead Cir E				
3600	PNFD	46168	2440	D4
Homestead Cir W				
3600	PNFD	46168	2440	D4
Homestead Ct				
5500	PNFD	46168	2440	D4
W Homestead Ct				
6300	SCkT	46163	2342	C6
Homestead Dr				
6100	INPS	46227	2556	A2
6500	HMCT	46227	2556	A2
S Homestead Dr				
3300	SCkT	46163	2451	E1
W Homestead Dr				
5700	SCkT	46163	2451	D2
Homestead Ln				
400	WRvT	46142	2663	C5
Homestead Pl				
3600	PNFD	46168	2440	D4
Homestead Wy				
-	BNBG	46112	2223	D1
Homewood Dr				
700	ClyT	46280	1901	C6
Honey Ln				
-	WRvT	46143	2664	C6
Honey Bee Ln				
-	WRvT	46143	2663	B6
Honeybee Ln				
-	WRvT	46143	2663	B6
Honey Comb Ln				
5200	INPS	46221	2444	C7
Honey Creek Cir				
-	MdnT	46113	2661	B1
Honey Creek Ct				
-	MdnT	46113	2661	B1
12000	FSHR	46038	1905	C5
S Honey Creek Rd				
700	GNWD	46143	2664	E7
1800	WRvT	46143	2664	E7
W Honey Creek Rd				
-	WRvT	46143	2664	E5
Honeylocust Dr				
12100	LWNC	46236	2014	E6
Honey Manor Ct				
5100	INPS	46221	2444	C7
Honey Manor Dr				
5200	INPS	46221	2444	C7
Honeysuckle Ct				
1000	MRVL	46158	2660	C3
S Honeysuckle Ct				
1300	CtrT	46140	2344	C3
Honeysuckle Dr				
1000	MRVL	46158	2660	C3
Honeysuckle Ln				
-	ZNVL	46077	1898	C2
6500	INPS	46237	2557	D2
Honeysuckle Wy				
8500	INPS	46256	2013	C5
Honey Tree Dr				
13800	CRML	46032	1901	A2
13900	CRML	46032	1791	E7
13900	CRML	46032	1900	E1
Honeywell Dr				
5900	LWNC	46236	2123	A4
Honeywell Ln				
10100	LWNC	46236	2123	A4
E Honnen North Dr				
7500	INPS	46256	2122	A2
Honnen South Dr				
7500	INPS	46256	2122	A2
Honnen West Dr				
6900	INPS	46256	2122	A2
Honors Dr				
12600	CRML	46033	1903	C3
Hooker St				
3200	LtyT	46168	2439	E6
Hoop Rd				
7700	INPS	46217	2554	E6
Hooper Pl				
4000	INPS	46250	2011	E5

Street / Block	City	ZIP	Map#	Grid
Hooper Strait Dr				
7700	LWNC	46236	2014	B7
Hoosier Ct				
10600	WshT	46234	2333	D1
Hoosier Rd				
10600	FCkT	46038	1905	D6
10600	FSHR	46038	1905	D6
Hoover Cir				
1000	INPS	46260	2010	A5
Hoover Ct				
7900	INPS	46260	2010	A6
Hoover Ln				
7900	INPS	46260	2010	A5
Hoover Rd				
5800	INPS	46228	2119	B3
2100	INPS	46260	2119	A3
7500	INPS	46260	2010	A7
11600	CRML	46032	1900	E4
E Hoover St				
300	WTFD	46074	1684	B6
W Hoover St				
10	WTFD	46074	1684	A6
Hope Ct				
300	GNWD	46142	2664	C4
Hope Dr				
300	WshT	46123	2332	B6
Hope Ln				
-	WshT	46234	2333	D3
Hopi Rd				
1700	WshT	46123	2222	E7
5900	WshT	46123	2331	E1
Hopi Tr				
7200	INPS	46219	2340	A3
Hopkins Ln				
8000	INPS	46250	2011	E6
Hopkins Rd				
100	CBLD	46229	2341	E1
800	LEBN	46052	1676	E4
Hopkins Tr E				
100	MRVL	46158	2660	B3
Hopkins Tr W				
300	MRVL	46158	2660	B3
Hopkinson Dr				
7300	NBVL	46062	1686	A5
Hopwood Dr				
2400	CRML	46032	1900	C4
Horatio Dr				
500	AVON	46123	2332	A2
Horbeck St				
-	CRML	46032	1900	D3
Horesham St				
12400	CRML	46032	1900	D4
Horizon Blvd				
2100	WRvT	46143	2663	C7
Horizon Ct				
6400	INPS	46260	2118	E3
11600	FCkT	46038	2014	E2
Horizon Ln				
1600	INPS	46260	2118	D3
Hornbean Ct				
5800	CRML	46033	1903	D1
Hornbill Pl				
5700	CRML	46033	1903	B1
Horner Dr				
3500	INPS	46239	2449	A3
S Horner Dr				
3800	INPS	46239	2449	A4
Hornet Av				
5100	BHGV	46107	2448	A4
Hornickel Cir				
11600	INPS	46235	2232	D2
Hornickel Dr				
-	INPS	46235	2232	D2
S Horniday Rd				
300	BNBG	46112	2114	D7
300	BNBG	46112	2223	D2
Hornton St				
10200	LWNC	46236	2123	B4
Horse Dr				
3500	INPS	46222	2336	B3
Horseferry Rd				
12800	CRML	46032	1900	D3
Horseguard Close				
1800	CRML	46032	1900	E3
Horse Hill East Dr				
2900	INPS	46214	2225	C5
Horse Hill West Dr				
2900	INPS	46214	2225	C4
Horseshoe Dr				
8900	EglT	46077	1789	C7
10900	WshT	46234	2224	C6
14900	WTFD	46033	1793	C6
Horseshoe Ln				
10	CRML	46033	1902	C4
Horseshoe Bend Dr				
2800	INPS	46214	2225	D5
Horth Ct				
3600	INPS	46235	2231	E3
Horton Rd				
19100	WshT	46069	1683	C4
19100	WTFD	46074	1683	C4
20800	WshT	46069	1574	C7
21600	AdmT	46069	1574	C7
Horton St				
600	GNWD	46142	2665	C2
Hosbrook St				
5600	INPS	46203	2337	E5
Hospital Ln				
10	DNVL	46122	2330	A4
Hoss Rd				
10	INPS	46217	2446	B6
Hoster Rd				
11700	CRML	46032	1903	C5
Hotze St				
7600	INPS	46259	2559	C5
E Hotze St				
7800	INPS	46259	2559	C5
S Hotze St				
7800	INPS	46259	2559	C5
Hough St				
10	GNFD	46140	2345	C1
Hounds Cross				
3500	ClyT	46032	1900	B7
Hourglass Dr				
1800	CRML	46032	1900	E3

Street / Block	City	ZIP	Map#	Grid
House St				
11000	INPS	46259	2559	C5
Houston St				
1900	INPS	46218	2229	C7
Hovey St				
3000	INPS	46218	2229	A4
3500	INPS	46205	2229	A4
Howard Av				
2700	INPS	46218	2229	B5
N Howard Rd				
100	GNWD	46142	2665	A2
S Howard Rd				
100	GNWD	46142	2665	A3
Howard St				
-	GNFD	46140	2345	E1
E Howard St				
300	LEBN	46052	1677	A6
N Howard St				
5900	CtnT	46052	1569	E3
W Howard St				
6000	INPS	46241	2335	A6
7000	INPS	46241	2334	D6
Howe Dr				
700	CRML	46032	1792	E7
5000	INPS	46201	2339	A3
Howe Rd				
10600	FSHR	46038	1905	B3
13100	FSHR	46060	1905	B1
13200	FCkT	46060	1905	B1
13500	FCkT	46060	1796	B7
13500	FSHR	46060	1796	B7
14100	NBVL	46060	1796	B5
15400	NbvT	46060	1796	B5
Howe St				
1100	SDWY	46224	2335	D1
Howell Ln				
500	INPS	46224	2335	B2
Hoy Av				
800	LEBN	46052	1676	D5
Hoyt Av				
1100	INPS	46203	2337	E5
3600	INPS	46203	2338	D5
7600	INPS	46239	2340	A5
Huber Av				
-	INPS	46226	2231	B4
Huber Ct				
7800	INPS	46226	2231	B4
N Huber Pl				
1300	INPS	46219	2340	B1
Huber St				
-	INPS	46219	2340	B2
-	NPLN	46163	2452	A3
N Huber St				
1000	INPS	46219	2340	B1
3600	INPS	46226	2231	B4
S Huber St				
1600	INPS	46239	2340	B3
1800	INPS	46239	2340	B5
900	INPS	46239	2340	B5
Huckleberry Ct				
10600	INPS	46236	2014	B6
Huddleston Dr E				
7500	INPS	46217	2555	C5
Huddleston Dr N				
10	INPS	46217	2555	B5
Huddleston Dr S				
100	INPS	46217	2555	B5
Huddleston Dr W				
7500	INPS	46217	2555	B5
Hudnut Blvd				
-	INPS	46221	2445	D1
N Hudnut Blvd				
-	INPS	46221	2445	D2
S Hudnut Blvd				
-	INPS	46221	2445	D3
Hudnut Pl				
-	INPS	46221	2445	D2
Hudson St				
500	INPS	46204	2337	D2
1200	INPS	46202	2337	D1
N Hudson St				
100	SRDN	46069	1573	C1
S Hudson St				
100	SRDN	46069	1573	C1
Hudson Bay Dr				
1000	GNWD	46142	2664	D3
Hudson Bay Ln				
10	GNWD	46142	2664	E3
Huff Blvd				
13100	FSHR	46060	1905	C2
S Huff St				
7000	INPS	46259	2559	D5
N Hugo St				
10	CBLD	46229	2341	D2
Hull Rd				
7000	EglT	46077	1898	E7
7000	EglT	46077	2007	E1
Hull St				
4200	LWNC	46226	2231	A1
4200	CBLD	46229	2233	A7
Hulman Blvd				
-	INPS	46222	2226	E5
-	SDWY	46222	2226	E5
Humber Ct				
-	ClyT	46032	1901	C7
Humble Blvd				
10	FSHR	46038	1906	A5
Humbolt Ln				
1900	INPS	46203	1900	E2
Hummel Dr				
7600	INPS	46239	2449	A2
Hummingbird Cir				
5100	CRML	46033	1794	B7
5100	CRML	46033	1903	B1
Hummingbird Ct				
8200	INPS	46256	2013	C5
Hummingbird Ln				
100	WTLD	46184	2775	A6

Street / Block	City	ZIP	Map#	Grid
Hunt Club Dr				
-	BrnT	46278	2006	D2
-	EglT	46077	1898	D7
Hunt Club Ln				
-	EglT	46077	2007	D1
Hunt Club Rd				
6700	EglT	46077	1897	D7
6700	EglT	46077	2006	D1
9300	EglT	46077	1898	D7
9600	ZNVL	46077	1898	D7
Hunt Country Ln				
-	EglT	46077	2006	E2
7300	EglT	46077	2007	A2
Hunt Country Pl				
-	EglT	46077	2006	E2
Hunter Ct				
15000	WshT	46074	1792	C5
Hunter Dr				
10	PNFD	46168	2441	B6
S Hunter Rd				
1000	INPS	46203	2339	E6
1000	INPS	46219	2339	E6
1000	INPS	46203	2448	E1
2200	INPS	46203	2448	E1
Hunterglen Rd				
5700	INPS	46226	2121	C5
Hunter Ridge Ln				
1700	WRvT	46143	2663	D7
Hunters Blvd				
11000	INPS	46235	2232	C3
N Hunters Ct				
3600	CtrT	46140	2236	D1
Hunters Dr				
500	CRML	46032	1902	B4
Hunters Dr E				
500	CRML	46032	1902	B4
500	AVON	46123	2332	E3
Hunters Dr W				
3400	INPS	46214	2225	D3
Hunters Gln				
500	CRML	46032	1902	B4
2600	INPS	46218	2229	C5
Hunters Ln				
1400	GNWD	46142	2664	C4
Hunters Pl				
8100	INPS	46236	2014	B6
Hunters Pth				
7800	INPS	46214	2225	C4
Hunters Rdg				
6300	EglT	46077	1897	D7
Hunters Tr				
-	BNBG	46112	2223	C3
200	ZNVL	46077	1898	E6
500	GNWD	46142	2664	C4
Hunters Cove Ct				
10300	INPS	46236	2014	B6
Hunters Cove Dr				
4800	INPS	46203	2339	A7
Hunters Creek Pl				
6400	INPS	46278	2116	D2
Huntersfield Dr				
10500	ClyT	46032	1900	B7
Hunters Green Cir				
6400	INPS	46278	2116	E2
Hunters Green Ct				
6400	INPS	46278	2116	E3
Hunters Green Ln				
6400	INPS	46278	2116	E2
Hunters Green Pl				
6400	INPS	46278	2116	D2
Hunters Green Wy				
-	BrnT		2006	E3
6700	INPS	46278	2116	E3
Hunters Meadow Ct				
8200	INPS	46259	2558	B5
Hunters Meadow Wy				
8300	INPS	46259	2558	C5
Hunters Point Dr				
-	INPS		1897	A5
-	INPS		2006	E3
Hunters Ridge Dr				
6000	PNFD	46168	2550	D2
S Hunters Ridge Ln				
1800	WRvT	46143	2663	E7
W Hunters Ridge Ln				
4200	WRvT	46143	2663	E7
Hunting Dr				
1600	INPS	46217	2554	D7
Hunting Tr				
8500	INPS	46217	2554	D7
Hunting Creek Ct				
13100	FSHR	46060	1905	C2
Hunting Creek Dr				
500	GNWD	46142	2664	D4
Huntington Cir				
12200	CBLD	46229	2232	E7
Huntington Ct				
1900	CBLD	46229	2233	A7
11100	CRML	46033	1903	B7
Huntington Dr				
-	INPS	46260	2009	E2
4900	INPS	46033	1903	A7
Huntington Ln				
9400	INPS	46260	2009	E3
Huntington Rd				
7100	INPS	46240	2120	D1
Huntington Woods Dr				
-	ZNVL	46077	2008	A1
Huntington Woods Rd				
-	ZNVL	46077	2008	A1
Huntleigh Cir				
-	PNFD	46168	2442	B1
Hunt Master Ct				
4500	INPS	46268	2117	E1
Huntsman Dr				
4200	EglT	46077	1899	C2
Huntsmen Ct				
6700	INPS	46250	2012	E3
E Huntstead Ln				
700	INPS	46227	2446	D7
W Huntstead Ln				
10	INPS	46217	2446	B7
Hunt St				
800	ZNVL	46077	1899	A6
3400	PNFD	46168	2442	A3
Huntwick Dr				
-	PNFD	46231	2333	D6

Street / Block	City	ZIP	Map#	Grid
Huntwick Dr				
-	PNFD	46231	2333	D6
11100	FSHR	46038	2014	C1
Huntwick Ln				
-	PNFD	46231	2333	E6
Hupa Wy				
400	INPS	46219	2340	A4
Hurbt St				
-	GNWD	46184	2774	A2
Hurley St				
-	GNWD	46143	2665	C7
Hurlock Dr				
-	FSHR	46038	1906	A4
Huron Dr				
-	AVON	46123	2332	C4
Huron Ln				
300	NBVL	46060	1686	C6
Huron Ter				
400	AVON	46123	2333	A3
400	WshT	46123	2333	A3
Hurst Dr				
10	AVON	46123	2332	C4
Hurstland Dr				
-	INPS	46237	2557	B6
Hussey Ln				
10400	ClyT	46032	1901	B7
10400	ClyT	46032	2010	B1
Huxley Ct				
-	FSHR	46038	2013	D1
Hyacinth Ct				
10500	NBVL	46060	1687	B4
12300	CRML	46032	1900	E4
Hyacinth Dr				
7200	WshT	46123	2223	C7
12300	FSHR	46038	1906	A6
Hyacinth Wy				
5600	INPS	46254	2117	D5
Hyannis Dr				
-	WshT	46123	2332	E3
600	AVON	46123	2332	E3
Hyannis Port Dr				
3400	INPS	46214	2224	E1
Hyche Av				
2600	INPS	46218	2229	C5
Hyde Pk				
10400	ClyT	46032	1900	D7
10400	ClyT	46032	2009	D1
Hyde Park Ct				
4100	INPS	46240	2011	E3
Hyde Park Dr				
500	EglT	46077	1897	D6
Hyde Park Row				
10	BNBG	46112	2223	B1
Hyde Park Wy				
4400	INPS	46240	2011	E3
Hylas Dr				
-	NBVL	46060	1687	C4
Hymera Grn				
16100	WTFD	46074	1792	D3
Hyperion Grn				
4800	INPS	46203	2339	A7
Hyperion Wy				
2100	INPS	46203	2339	B7
Hythe Rd				
6000	INPS	46220	2121	D2
I				
I Ct				
-	WRvT	46142	2663	E1
I St				
-	BHGV	46107	2447	E3
I-65				
-	BrnT		2006	A4
-	ClkT		2775	E6
-	CtrT		1567	A4
-	CtrT		1676	B2
-	CtrT		1786	A2
-	CtrT		1787	A7
-	EglT		1897	A5
-	EglT		2006	E3
-	GNWD		2557	B7
-	GNWD		2666	C7
-	INPS		2006	E3
-	INPS		2007	B7
-	INPS		2116	C1
-	INPS		2117	A4
-	INPS		2226	E1
-	INPS		2227	D3
-	INPS		2228	B7
-	INPS		2337	D1
-	INPS		2446	E1
-	INPS		2447	A3
-	INPS		2448	E1
-	LWNC		2121	E1
-	SDWY		2226	A4
I-865				
-	EglT		1897	C7
-	EglT		2006	D1
-	EglT		2007	C2
-	ZNVL		2008	A2
Ida Ct				
10	GNWD	46143	2665	D1
Ida St				
2600	INPS	46222	2336	C4
6300	INPS	46241	2334	A4
6300	INPS	46241	2335	A4
Idleway Ct				
10	WRvT	46142	2664	B4
Idlewild Ct				
3400	CRML	46033	2011	E1
Idlewood Ct N				
6900	INPS	46214	2225	E3
Idlewood Ct S				
6900	INPS	46214	2225	C2
Idlewood Dr				
-	FSHR	46038	1906	B6
11200	FCkT	46038	1906	B6
Idlewood Pkwy				
3700	INPS	46214	2225	E2
Idlewood Ter				
3500	INPS	46214	2225	E2
Idlewood Tr				
6800	INPS	46214	2225	E3
Igneous St				
-	FSHR	46060	1905	E2
Illinois St				
-	CRML	46290	1901	C7
-	CRML	46290	2010	C1
-	GNFD	46140	2236	D7
N Illinois St				
10	INPS	46204	2337	C3
1100	INPS	46202	2337	C1
1600	INPS	46208	2228	C6
2200	INPS	46208	2228	C6

Also listed in the I-70 / I-74 / I-465 / I-69 sections:

Street / Block	City	ZIP	Map#	Grid
I-69				
-	DelT		1904	D7
-	DelT		2013	C1
-	FCkT		1905	D3
-	FCkT		1906	A2
-	FCkT		1907	E1
-	FSHR		1904	D7
-	FSHR		1905	B4
-	FSHR		1906	A2
-	FSHR		2013	C1
-	GrnT		1907	A1
-	INPS		2012	D7
-	INPS		2013	C1
-	INPS		2014	E6
-	NBVL		1906	A2
-	NBVL		1907	A1
I-70				
-	BCkT		2232	D5
-	BCkT		2233	A5
-	BCkT		2234	C3
-	BCkT		2235	C3
-	CBLD		2232	D5
-	CtrT		2235	C3
-	CtrT		2236	C3
-	GfdT		2442	E7
-	GfdT		2549	D6
-	GfdT		2550	B5
-	GfdT		2551	D1
-	GNFD		2236	D3
-	INPS		2229	A7
-	INPS		2230	B6
-	INPS		2231	C6
-	INPS		2232	D5
-	INPS		2335	D7
-	INPS		2336	D5
-	INPS		2337	E1
-	INPS		2338	A1
-	INPS		2442	E7
-	INPS		2443	A7
-	INPS		2444	C2
-	INPS		2549	D6
-	LtyT		2657	C3
-	LtyT		2658	A1
-	MnrT		2657	C3
-	MnrT		2658	A1
-	PNFD		2442	E7
-	PNFD		2550	E3
-	PNFD		2551	D1
I-70 Anton T Hulman Jr Mem Wy				
-	CtrT		2236	C3
-	CtrT		2237	E3
-	GNFD		2236	E3
I-74				
-	BHGV		2448	C5
-	BNBG		2114	B4
-	BNBG		2115	B7
-	BrnT		2113	C2
-	BrnT		2114	D5
-	BwnT		2670	C3
-	INPS		2224	E1
-	INPS		2225	B2
-	INPS		2226	A5
-	INPS		2335	A3
-	INPS		2444	B5
-	INPS		2446	E6
-	INPS		2447	A6
-	INPS		2448	C5
-	INPS		2449	C2
-	INPS		2450	A6
-	INPS		2559	B1
-	LcnT		2114	D5
-	LcnT		2115	B7
-	LcnT		2224	D1
-	MdlT		2112	E1
-	MdlT		2113	C2
-	MrlT		2559	D3
-	MrlT		2560	A4
-	MrlT		2669	E1
-	MrlT		2670	E1
-	SDWY		2226	A5
-	SgCT		2670	C3
-	UnnT		2112	E1
I-465				
-	BHGV		2448	C5
-	ClyT		2010	D2
-	CRML		2010	D2
-	EglT		2008	C2
-	INPS		2008	C2
-	INPS		2009	E3
-	INPS		2010	A3
-	INPS		2116	E4
-	INPS		2117	E4
-	INPS		2226	A4
-	INPS		2231	A7
-	INPS		2448	C5
-	LWNC		2121	E1
-	SDWY		2226	A4

INDEX 28

N Illinois St — Indianapolis Street Index — Johnston Ct

STREET
Block City ZIP Map# Grid

N Illinois St
4500 INPS 46208 2119 C7
7200 INPS 46260 2119 C1
9400 INPS 46260 2010 C3
9500 CRML 46290 2010 C3
S Illinois St
- INPS 46260 2010 C3
10 INPS 46204 2337 C4
100 INPS 46225 2337 C4
2200 INPS 46225 2446 C1
5200 INPS 46217 2446 C7
8800 GNWD 46217 2664 E1
8800 INPS 46217 2555 C7
8800 INPS 46217 2664 E1
E Imperial Dr
9000 INPS 46239 2449 D5
Imperial Woods Cir
5600 INPS 46224 2335 B2
S In 267
- WshT 46123 2332 B7
- WshT 46123 2441 B1
- WshT 46168 2441 B1
W IN-36
1100 CtrT 46122 2329 A4
1100 DNVL 46122 2329 A4
Independence Av
- LcnT 46112 2115 E6
Independence Dr
4000 INPS 46227 2446 C4
Independence Rd
100 GNFD 46140 2345 A1
Independence Sq
4500 INPS 46203 2448 A6
Independence Wy
10700 ClyT 46032 1900 A7
N Indiana Av
300 INPS 46202 2337 B3
300 INPS 46204 2337 B3
Indiana Rd
3500 GfdT 46168 2550 E7
4000 GfdT 46168 2659 E1
Indiana St
- DNVL 46122 2329 D4
- MCVL 46055 2015 C7
200 PNFD 46168 2441 B5
400 GNFD 46140 2345 C1
N Indiana St
10 MRVL 46158 2659 E2
700 BrnT 46158 2659 E2
S Indiana St
10 DNVL 46122 2329 D4
10 MRVL 46158 2659 E4
S Indiana St SR-267
10 MRVL 46158 2659 E3
Indianapolis Av
100 LEBN 46052 1677 A7
1100 LEBN 46052 1786 B1
1200 CtrT 46052 1786 B1
3100 INPS 46208 2228 B4
Indianapolis Av SR-32
100 LEBN 46052 1677 A7
Indianapolis Rd
- BrnT 46278 2006 E3
- EglT 46278 2006 E3
- INPS 46278 2006 E3
300 MRVL 46158 2660 A2
500 BrnT 46158 2660 A3
1000 CtrT 46052 1786 C3
1100 GfdT 46158 2660 A2
2700 CtrT 46052 1787 A7
2700 PryT 46052 1787 A7
3400 PryT 46052 1896 B1
4300 WrhT 46052 1896 C2
5800 PryT 46052 1897 A5
6300 PryT 46112 1897 A5
7000 EglT 46112 1897 A5
7000 EglT 46112 2006 E3
7600 EglT 46077 2006 E3
S Indianapolis Rd
6500 EglT 46112 1897 B7
6500 PryT 46112 1897 B7
7500 EglT 46077 2006 D2
7500 EglT 46112 2006 D2
Indian Cove Rd
5400 INPS 46268 2117 B3
Indian Creek Rd
11300 LWNC 46236 2123 D3
E Indian Creek Rd
8400 INPS 46259 2558 E2
11600 INPS 46259 2559 D2
11600 MrlT 46259 2559 D2
Indian Lake Blvd
11000 LWNC 46236 2123 C2
Indian Lake Blvd N
9900 LWNC 46236 2123 A1
Indian Lake Blvd S
10600 LWNC 46236 2123 B2
Indian Lake Blvd W
6900 LWNC 46236 2123 A1
Indian Lake Rd
6800 LWNC 46236 2123 B1
7500 LWNC 46236 2014 B7
7800 INPS 46236 2014 B7
Indian Lake Blvd Dr S
10100 LWNC 46236 2123 A2
Indianola Av
4400 INPS 46205 2228 E1
4500 INPS 46205 2119 E7
4600 INPS 46205 2120 A7
5400 INPS 46220 2120 A5
7400 INPS 46240 2011 A7
Indian Pipe Cir
1000 CRML 46033 1902 C3
Indian Pipe Ln
1100 UnnT 46077 1790 B6
Indian Pipe Trc
4200 INPS 46237 2447 D5
Indian Pointe Dr
7800 INPS 46236 2014 B7
7800 LWNC 46236 2014 B7
Indian Spring Rd
400 LEBN 46052 1677 A5
Indian Trail Dr
700 CRML 46032 1902 C4

Indigo Ct
10700 FSHR 46038 1904 B7
Indigo Ln
800 INPS 46260 2119 A2
9500 FSHR 46038 1904 E1
9600 FSHR 46038 1905 A1
N Industrial Blvd
- INPS 46254 2226 E2
3800 INPS 46254 2227 A2
Industrial Dr
400 CRML 46032 1902 A3
1600 GNWD 46143 2665 D6
Industrial Ln
1100 INPS 46201 2338 D1
Industrial Pkwy
4700 LWNC 46226 2122 C7
Indy Ct
8200 INPS 46214 2225 B7
Indy Dr
- INPS 46214 2334 B1
W Indy Ln
8100 INPS 46214 2225 B7
Indy Pl
1200 INPS 46214 2334 B1
Indy Wy
1200 INPS 46214 2334 B1
Inez Setters Ln
14700 WTFD 46033 1793 E6
Inglenook Ln
1900 CRML 46032 1900 D1
13900 CRML 46032 1791 D7
Ingleside Ln
4400 INPS 46227 2447 B6
Inglewood Ct
4200 WRvT 46143 2663 E5
Ingomar Av
400 INPS 46241 2335 B4
Ingram St
1600 INPS 46218 2229 A7
Inisheer Ct
1800 INPS 46217 2554 D5
Inishmore Ct
2400 INPS 46214 2225 C6
Inishmore Dr
7800 INPS 46214 2225 C6
Inishmore Wy
7800 INPS 46214 2225 C6
Inland Cir
300 AVON 46123 2332 E3
Inland Dr
- WshT 46123 2333 A2
6800 INPS 46254 2225 E1
8300 AVON 46123 2332 E3
Inland Dr E
4200 INPS 46254 2225 E1
4500 INPS 46254 2116 E7
Inlet Dr
2600 CCRO 46034 1577 B6
Inn Wy
10 WRvT 46142 2663 C4
Innisbrook Blvd
9700 ClyT 46032 2009 B1
Innisbrooke Av
10 WRvT 46142 2663 C3
Innisbrooke Ct
5400 WRvT 46142 2663 C3
Innisbrooke Dr
200 WRvT 46142 2663 C3
Innisbrooke Ln
5300 WRvT 46142 2663 C3
10900 FSHR 46038 2014 C1
Innisbrooke Pl
5400 WRvT 46142 2663 C3
Innisbrooke Tr
10 WRvT 46142 2663 C3
Inside Tr
12100 NBVL 46060 1797 A5
Insignia Ct
3500 INPS 46214 2225 D3
Intech Blvd
6400 INPS 46278 2117 A2
Intech Commons Dr
6200 INPS 46278 2117 A2
International Dr
- INPS 46241 2334 E7
- INPS 46241 2443 E1
9400 INPS 46268 2009 B3
International Ln
9400 INPS 46268 2009 B3
International Wy
3000 INPS 46268 2009 B2
Inverness Blvd
- INPS 46032 2009 C2
3400 ClyT 46032 2009 C2
Inverness Ct
7800 INPS 46237 2557 D5
10400 FSHR 46038 2014 C1
Inverness Dr
- ClyT 46032 2009 C1
7500 INPS 46237 2557 D4
Inverness Pl
2000 WRvT 46143 2663 E7
Inverness Wy
6800 INPS 46237 2557 E5
Inverrary Ct
2900 INPS 46234 2225 A5
Inverrary Dr
2900 INPS 46234 2225 B4
Inwood Ln
4700 INPS 46250 2011 E6
4700 INPS 46250 2012 A7
E Iona Rd
6000 INPS 46203 2339 D7
Iowa St
10 INPS 46225 2337 C7
500 INPS 46203 2337 D7
4100 INPS 46203 2338 E7
E Iowa St
4800 INPS 46203 2339 A7
Ipswich Ct
6000 INPS 46254 2226 A1
Ira Ct
7000 INPS 46217 2554 E4
Ira Wy
400 CRML 46032 1901 B2

Ireland Ct
3600 INPS 46235 2231 E3
Ireland Dr
3800 INPS 46235 2231 E2
Iris Av
10 INPS 46241 2335 D4
Iris Ct
19300 NBVL 46060 1687 B4
Iris Dr
- BrnT 46112 2114 D1
Iris Ln
9000 ZNVL 46077 1898 D2
Irish Hill Dr
6100 EglT 46077 1898 D5
Irishman's Run
- EglT 46077 2007 E1
Irishmans Run Ln
9300 EglT 46077 2007 D1
Irishtown Pike
7000 ClkT 46162 2668 D7
Iron Tr E
1300 INPS 46234 2333 E1
Iron Tr W
1300 INPS 46234 2333 E1
Iron Bridge Rd
200 CCRO 46034 1577 D1
Ironbrook Ct
500 INPS 46239 2341 A4
Irongate Cir
1600 ZNVL 46077 1898 E6
Irongate Ct
8000 INPS 46268 2008 E6
Irongate Dr
10 ZNVL 46077 1898 E6
Iron Horse Ln
- ClyT 46032 2009 C1
7500 INPS 46256 2122 A1
Iron Liege Rd
1400 INPS 46217 2554 D6
Iron Oaks Ct
5800 INPS 46237 2557 C1
Ironridge Ct
500 INPS 46239 2341 A4
Iron Rock Rd
7300 LWNC 46236 2124 A1
Iron Springs Ct
1100 INPS 46240 2010 E5
Ironstone Ct
500 INPS 46239 2341 A4
W Ironton St
3800 INPS 46241 2445 A1
3900 INPS 46241 2444 E1
Ironway Dr
10000 INPS 46239 2341 A5
Ironwood Cir
200 NBVL 46062 1685 C2
Ironwood Ct
10 BNBG 46112 2223 D1
10 CRML 46033 1902 E2
800 GNWD 46143 2665 A5
9000 INPS 46260 2009 D3
Ironwood Dr
- BNBG 46112 2223 D1
200 CRML 46033 1902 D2
600 WshT 46123 2331 C5
900 CRML 46033 1793 D7
1200 MRVL 46158 2660 C2
Ironwood Dr W
1200 CRML 46033 1793 D7
Ironwood Ln
5200 PNFD 46168 2440 C4
Ironwood Tr
800 GNWD 46143 2665 A5
Ironwood East Dr
800 LcnT 46112 2224 C1
900 BNBG 46112 2223 E1
Ironwood West Dr
800 BNBG 46112 2223 D1
Iroquois Ct
9700 FCkT 46256 2014 C2
Iroquois Dr
2300 WshT 46234 2224 D6
Irredentism Ridge Rd
300 INPS 46202 2337 E3
Irving Ct
- INPS 46219 2339 B3
Irving Dr
- MCVL 46055 2124 B1
Irving St
400 NBVL 46060 1795 C2
N Irvington Av
900 INPS 46219 2339 B1
3600 INPS 46218 2230 B3
4200 INPS 46226 2230 B1
7200 INPS 46250 2121 B1
S Irvington Av
10 INPS 46219 2339 B3
1500 INPS 46203 2339 B6
N Irwin Av
- INPS 46219 2230 D5
4300 INPS 46226 2230 D1
Irwin Ct
6000 INPS 46237 2557 D2
Irwin Dr
6600 INPS 46219 2339 D2
W Irwin Dr
7800 BCkT 46140 2232 E3
Irwin Rd
3700 INPS 46218 2229 D4
N Irwin St
10 INPS 46219 2339 D3
1900 INPS 46219 2230 D6
S Irwin St
700 INPS 46219 2339 D5
2800 INPS 46203 2448 D2
6000 INPS 46237 2557 D2
Irwin Wy
13100 CRML 46032 1901 B2
Isenhour Hills Dr
400 ZNVL 46077 1899 B5
Ishnala St
2100 WshT 46234 2224 D6
Island Ct
7700 INPS 46214 2225 C4

Island Dr
3400 INPS 46214 2225 C4
12100 FCkT 46256 2015 A2
Island Wy
3400 INPS 46214 2225 C4
Island Club Cir
3100 INPS 46214 2225 C4
Island Club Ct
3100 INPS 46214 2225 C4
Island Club Dr
3100 INPS 46214 2225 C4
Island Club Ln
3000 INPS 46214 2225 C4
Islander Dr
7000 INPS 46214 2225 D4
E Island Woods Dr
1000 INPS 46220 2119 E2
Islay Ct
7900 INPS 46217 2554 D6
Islay Rd
7800 INPS 46217 2554 D5
Israel Ln
- FKLN 46131 2775 A7
- FKLN 46184 2775 A7
1400 FKLN 46131 2774 E7
Ithaca Wy
7800 INPS 46239 2449 B7
E Ivanhoe St
6000 INPS 46219 2339 C4
8500 INPS 46219 2340 C3
Ives Wy
- CRML 46032 1900 D3
Ivory Ct
4000 CRML 46074 1900 A2
4000 INPS 46237 2556 D5
Ivory Wy
3200 INPS 46227 2556 C5
3200 SPRT 46227 2556 C5
3900 INPS 46237 2556 D5
W Ivy Ct
7400 SCkT 46163 2342 A6
Ivy Ln
700 GNWD 46143 2665 B5
1100 INPS 46220 2119 E5
W Ivy Ln
7200 SCkT 46163 2342 A6
Ivybridge Dr
14100 CRML 46032 1792 B7
Ivydale Dr
7700 INPS 46250 2012 D7
Ivy Hill Dr
5200 CRML 46033 1903 C2
Ivy Knoll Ct
5600 INPS 46250 2012 C6
Ivy Knoll Dr
5600 INPS 46250 2012 C5
Ivy Knoll Ln
8100 INPS 46250 2012 B6
Ivy Tech Dr
5200 INPS 46268 2008 C4
Ivywood Cir
7500 INPS 46250 2012 C7
Ivywood Ct
4500 ZNVL 46077 1899 A3
Ivywood Dr
7500 INPS 46250 2012 C7

J

J Ct
- WRvT 46142 2663 E1
J St
- BHGV 46107 2447 E3
Jack Rd
- WshT 46069 1683 D1
Jack St
20500 WshT 46069 1683 D1
Jackie Ct
7300 INPS 46221 2553 A4
Jackie Ln
6000 INPS 46221 2553 A5
Jack Pine Ct
500 INPS 46224 2335 C2
7400 AVON 46123 2332 C5
Jacks Ln
1500 INPS 46227 2556 A2
Jackson Cir
- CRML 46032 1900 C3
Jackson Ct
10 BNBG 46112 2223 C1
S Jackson Ct
10 WRvT 46142 2663 D3
Jackson Ct S
200 WRvT 46142 2663 D2
Jackson Rd
- CRML 46032 1902 B5
600 WRvT 46142 2663 D2
Jackson St
10 MdnT 46113 2661 D4
600 BNBG 46112 2223 C1
800 LEBN 46052 1786 B1
900 LEBN 46052 1677 B7
2900 INPS 46222 2336 B4
5300 INPS 46241 2335 C4
6400 INPS 46241 2334 D4
E Jackson St
10 CCRO 46034 1577 D2
300 JknT 46034 1577 D2
W Jackson St
- INPS 46222 2336 D4
10 CCRO 46034 1577 C2
400 JknT 46034 1577 C2
8800 INPS 46231 2333 E4
8800 INPS 46231 2334 A4
W Jackson Place North Dr
10 INPS 46225 2337 B7
Jaclyn Dr
7800 INPS 46237 2557 C5
Jacob Ln
9500 LWNC 46235 2122 E6
S Jacobi Rd
1000 SCkT 46140 2343 E4
1000 SGLK 46140 2343 E4

Jacobs Ct
10700 FCkT 46040 1906 E7
Jacobsen Dr
12900 CRML 46033 1903 D3
Jacques Dr
1500 LEBN 46052 1676 D5
Jade Cir
8100 INPS 46268 2009 A6
Jade Ct
8100 INPS 46268 2009 A6
Jaden Ln
- GNWD 46143 2665 C7
Jade Stream Ct
6500 INPS 46237 2557 A3
Jaffa Ct East Dr
8600 INPS 46260 2010 C4
Jaffa Ct West Dr
8600 INPS 46260 2010 C4
Jagged Rock Ct
8500 INPS 46256 2013 C4
11500 FSHR 46038 1906 A5
Jaguar Pl
6400 INPS 46224 2226 A6
Jaguars Dr
12300 FCkT 46038 1906 A3
Jakes Pl
6200 INPS 46237 2557 D5
Jamaica Ct
8600 INPS 46219 2231 C7
James Blvd
1600 GNFD 46140 2236 E5
N James Blvd
- GNFD 46140 2236 E5
James Ct
- DNVL 46122 2330 A4
10 BNBG 46112 2223 B1
1300 ZNVL 46077 1899 A5
5200 CRML 46033 1794 B7
James Dr
400 NBVL 46060 1686 E7
1300 WshT 46123 2332 D6
1300 ZNVL 46077 1899 A5
James Rd
19600 NBVL 46062 1686 C2
19600 NbvT 46062 1686 C2
20600 NbvT 46062 1577 C7
James Blair Dr
- LcnT 46112 2115 D6
Jameson Ln
13900 CRML 46032 1792 B7
N Jameson St
200 LEBN 46052 1676 E6
S Jameson St
- LEBN 46052 1676 E7
Jamestown Ct
4400 INPS 46226 2230 C1
4500 INPS 46226 2121 C7
Jamestown Dr
- BCkT 46055 2124 B4
Jamestown North Dr
7600 FSHR 46038 1904 B5
Jamestown South Dr
7700 FSHR 46038 1904 B6
Jamestown Square Ln
- LcnT 46112 2115 E6
Jamestown West Dr
11400 FSHR 46038 1904 B6
Jamie Ct
4200 INPS 46226 2231 C1
Jamie Dr
14100 CRML 46033 1793 C7
Jamieson Ln
2800 INPS 46268 2009 C3
Janean Dr
10 BNBG 46112 2114 D3
100 BrnT 46112 2114 D2
Janel Cir
6000 INPS 46237 2557 C5
Janel Ct
7700 INPS 46237 2557 C5
Janel Dr
7700 INPS 46237 2557 C5
Janet Dr
1000 GNWD 46142 2665 C1
1100 INPS 46142 2665 C1
3500 INPS 46218 2229 E3
W Janet Dr
300 BNBG 46112 2223 A1
Janetta Ct
1400 DNVL 46122 2330 B2
Janson Dr
- INPS 46217 2554 A3
Jaques Dr
- LEBN 46052 1676 C5
Jarama Ln
- FSHR 46038 1906 C4
Jared Dr
800 GNWD 46143 2665 B5
Jaret Dr
100 SRDN 46069 1573 C1
Jarvis Dr
6500 INPS 46237 2557 D7
Jasmine Ct
8000 INPS 46219 2231 B7
14100 FSHR 46060 1795 D7
Jasmine Dr
- MRVL 46158 2660 C3
1100 GNFD 46140 2237 A7
1900 INPS 46219 2231 C7
10800 ClyT 46032 1900 C6
Jasmine Wy
4300 WRvT 46142 2663 E3
Jason Av
1400 FKLN 46131 2774 E7
Jason Dr
1400 GNFD 46140 2236 D6
2000 LEBN 46052 1676 D3
Jason Ln
700 NBVL 46062 1795 B1
Jason St
2800 CRML 46033 1793 C7
14400 WTFD 46033 1793 C7
Jasper Ct
9900 NBVL 46060 1796 A2
9900 NbvT 46060 1796 A2

Jasper St
- INPS 46221 2444 E7
1400 INPS 46227 2447 A7
N Jay Ct
2500 INPS 46229 2231 E5
E Jay Dr
9400 INPS 46229 2231 E5
Jaycee St
11600 FSHR 46038 1904 D5
Jaycees Av
100 SRDN 46069 1573 B2
Jaynes Cir
400 WRvT 46142 2663 D2
Jayson Cir
500 WTFD 46074 1792 D2
Jaytee Ln
14500 CRML 46033 1793 C6
Jaywick Dr
8900 FSHR 46038 2013 D1
10500 FSHR 46038 1904 D7
J Connector Expwy
- INPS 46225 2337 B7
- INPS 46225 2446 B1
Jean Ct
800 LEBN 46052 1676 D5
Jean Dr
- INPS 46235 2231 E3
Jean Ann Ct
7300 BrnT 46112 2114 D3
Jeanne Ct
- SCkT 46239 2342 A4
Jeans Ct
10 WTLD 46131 2774 E7
Jeff Rd
8000 INPS 46217 2555 A6
Jefferson Av
10 INPS 46201 2338 B3
1500 INPS 46201 2229 B7
2100 INPS 46218 2229 B6
Jefferson Blvd
10 GNFD 46140 2345 B1
600 CtrT 46140 2236 B7
600 GNFD 46140 2236 B7
W Jefferson Ct
- BCkT 46055 2124 B4
Jefferson Dr
1300 CRML 46032 1902 A6
2900 PNFD 46168 2441 C2
N Jefferson Dr
- BCkT 46055 2124 C4
Jefferson Dr E
1300 CRML 46032 1902 A6
Jefferson Dr W
1300 CRML 46032 1902 A5
Jefferson St
- DNVL 46122 2329 D3
N Jefferson St
10 BNBG 46112 2114 C6
10 DNVL 46122 2329 D4
10 MRVL 46158 2659 D3
S Jefferson St
10 BNBG 46112 2114 C7
10 DNVL 46122 2329 D4
10 MRVL 46158 2659 D4
500 BNBG 46112 2223 C1
W Jefferson St
4000 WshT 46069 1682 A7
4000 WshT 46074 1682 A7
Jefferson Roundabout
5200 CRML 46033 1794 B7
Jeffrey Ct
14300 CRML 46032 1792 E7
Jeffries Pl
12500 CRML 46033 1903 B4
Jekyll Ct
3900 INPS 46237 2556 D1
Jellico Blvd
- INPS 46229 2341 D1
Jena Dr
19300 NBVL 46062 1686 A4
Jene Ct
9100 INPS 46234 2224 E3
Jenkins Ct
2000 ClyT 46280 2011 B1
Jenkins Dr
1600 INPS 46218 2229 D7
Jennifer Ct
- AVON 46123 2332 D3
W Jennifer Ct
6800 BCkT 46140 2233 C7
Jennifer Dr
- BCkT 46140 2233 C7
800 GNWD 46143 2665 A5
7700 INPS 46214 2334 C1
N Jennifer Dr
800 BCkT 46140 2233 C6
W Jennifer Dr
6800 BCkT 46140 2233 B7
Jennifer Ln
10 BrnT 46112 2114 D2
W Jennifer Ln
6900 BCkT 46140 2233 C7
Jennings Dr
4900 CRML 46033 1903 A3
Jennings St
3300 INPS 46218 2229 C4
Jennings Farm Ln
- FSHR 46060 1796 B7
13800 FSHR 46060 1905 B1
Jenny Ln
10 INPS 46201 2338 E3
400 CRML 46032 1902 C3
Jennys Rd
4600 INPS 46228 2118 C7
Jeremy Ct
2800 CRML 46033 1793 C7
Jeremy Dr
14300 CRML 46033 1793 C7
Jerkwater Rd
24200 AdmT 46069 1573 B1
24200 SRDN 46069 1573 B1
Jerome Ct
3500 INPS 46235 2231 E3
Jerry Ct
5200 INPS 46254 2117 C6

W Jersey St
10 WTFD 46074 1793 A1
Jesse Cir
10800 LWNC 46236 2123 C3
Jessi Ln
14200 CRML 46033 1793 C7
Jessica Ct
- AVON 46123 2332 D2
Jessie Ct
10800 LWNC 46236 2123 C3
Jessman Rd East Dr
7100 INPS 46256 2122 A1
Jessman Rd North Dr
- INPS 46256 2122 A1
Jessman Rd South Dr
7300 INPS 46256 2122 A1
Jessman Rd West Dr
7100 INPS 46256 2122 B3
Jessup Blvd
10400 ClyT 46280 2010 E1
10500 ClyT 46280 1901 E7
Jessup Ct
1300 BrnT 46158 2659 B5
E Jessup Ct
- BrnT 46158 2659 A5
Jessup Wy
100 BrnT 46158 2659 B5
Jester Ct
6000 INPS 46254 2117 B4
Jesterwood Dr
11900 FSHR 46038 1906 D5
Jeto Lake Dr
1700 WshT 46123 2222 E7
Je to Lake Dr
1800 WshT 46123 2222 E7
Jeto Lake East Dr
1900 WshT 46123 2222 E7
Jet Stream Blvd
500 WshT 46074 1792 B4
Jewel Ln
7400 INPS 46250 2011 E7
7400 INPS 46250 2120 E1
10600 ClyT 46032 1900 C7
Jib Ct
8500 INPS 46236 2014 C5
Jill Ct
9400 INPS 46229 2231 E5
Jill Dr
2500 INPS 46229 2231 E5
N Jill Dr
2600 INPS 46229 2231 E5
Jill St
5100 INPS 46221 2444 C7
Jillison Ct
5500 INPS 46221 2553 B3
JJ Wy
200 NBVL 46060 1686 C6
Joan Av
200 BNBG 46112 2223 B1
Joan Pl
3400 INPS 46226 2231 B3
Joann Ct
400 WRvT 46142 2663 C3
800 CRML 46032 1792 E7
Joanna Ct
1300 WshT 46123 2332 D6
Jody Ct
1000 GNWD 46143 2665 D1
Joggins Ln
11800 FSHR 46038 1905 E5
John Ct
10 DNVL 46122 2330 A4
John St
- FCkT 46038 1906 D5
- FSHR 46038 1906 D5
100 CRML 46032 1793 A7
100 NBVL 46060 1686 C7
3300 CtrT 46052 1568 D7
3300 CtrT 46052 1677 E1
John Ambers Ln
- INPS 46260 2009 D5
Johnathan Dr
900 PNFD 46168 2441 D6
John-Bart Rd
500 CtrT 46052 1677 B5
800 LEBN 46052 1677 B5
John Charles Ct N
12800 MdnT 46113 2660 E3
John Glenn Ct
2200 INPS 46229 2232 A6
E John Jay Dr
10000 INPS 46235 2232 A3
E John Marshall Dr
10000 INPS 46235 2232 A3
John Muir Dr
- INPS 46240 2011 B6
John Paul Wy
14500 CRML 46032 1792 D7
Johns Dr
8700 INPS 46234 2225 A3
John Shaw Rd
1500 CtrT 46052 1785 E4
1500 LEBN 46052 1785 E4
Johnson Av
- SgCT 46126 2670 D7
10 INPS 46219 2339 B3
Johnson Ct
600 NBVL 46060 1795 D1
7100 BrnT 46112 2114 D3
Johnson Dr
600 CRML 46033 1902 E1
Johnson Ln
- BNBG 46112 2114 A6
Johnson Rd
400 MRVL 46158 2660 B5
500 BrnT 46158 2660 B5
6500 INPS 46220 2121 E1
7100 INPS 46250 2121 E1
7700 INPS 46250 2012 E7
S Johnson Rd
900 BrnT 46158 2660 B6
Johnson St
5000 WRvT 46143 2663 C5
Johnston Ct
- PTBR 46167 2113 B4

STREET
Block City ZIP Map# Grid

Johnston Ct
8100 INPS 46217 2554 E6
Johnwes Rd
6300 INPS 46241 2444 A5
Jo Honan Rd
10 WshT 46052 1568 A6
Joliet Rd
15600 WshT 46074 1791 A4
17600 WshT 46069 1682 A7
17600 WshT 46074 1682 A7
Jonathan Ct
6600 WshT 46123 2332 A6
Jonathan Dr
14800 WshT 46074 1792 B6
Jonathan Trc
5200 LWNC 46226 2122 A6
5300 LWNC 46226 2121 E6
Jones Rd
1800 UnnT 46077 1789 D4
Jones St
- INPS 46221 2336 E5
Jonquil Dr
10 INPS 46227 2555 C6
Jordan Ct
10 ClyT 46032 1902 C7
Jordan Dr
- GNWD 46143 2665 B5
Jordan Ln
8100 INPS 46240 2010 D5
Jordan Rd
10 INPS 46217 2555 B3
10600 ClyT 46032 1902 C7
Joseph Cir
1600 INPS 46227 2447 B7
Joseph Dr
4600 INPS 46227 2447 A6
Joseph Ln
10 WTLD 46184 2774 D7
Joseph Wy
400 CRML 46032 1901 C1
Joshua Cir
3100 WTFD 46033 1793 D4
Joshua Dr
2700 CRML 46033 1793 C7
Joshua Tree Pl
6200 INPS 46237 2448 D7
Josiah Ct
7200 INPS 46259 2558 A4
Joust Dr
- GNWD 46184 2774 A1
Joy Ct
1200 GNWD 46142 2664 D2
Joy Dr
600 GNWD 46142 2664 D2
Joyce Av
23400 WRvT 46034 1578 D2
E Joyce St
11000 INPS 46259 2559 C5
Jubilee Ln
700 AVON 46123 2332 C2
Judaco Dr
5800 INPS 46227 2556 C1
Judan Ct
4000 INPS 46221 2444 C5
Judan Dr
4100 INPS 46221 2444 C5
Judith Ln
1600 INPS 46227 2447 A6
Judith Anne Dr
5200 LWNC 46236 2122 E6
Jules Ln
8800 BrnT 46112 2006 E7
Julian Av
4900 INPS 46201 2339 A3
6000 INPS 46219 2339 C3
Julie Ln
3400 INPS 46228 2118 A5
Juliet Dr
6200 AVON 46123 2332 A2
6200 WshT 46123 2332 A2
Julietta St
11700 INPS 46239 2450 D1
Jumper Ln
10500 ClyT 46032 1901 B7
10500 ClyT 46032 2010 B1
Junco Cr
3900 INPS 46228 2118 A4
Junction Ln
6600 INPS 46220 2119 E2
Junction Pl
900 INPS 46220 2119 E2
Juniper Cir
- BrnT 46112 2114 D1
Juniper Ct
4100 INPS 46250 2011 E7
Juniper Ln
- GNWD 46143 2666 A7
Juniper Breeze Dr
10300 FSHR 46060 1796 B7
Jupiter Dr
7000 INPS 46241 2334 D4
Jupiter Pass
9700 ClyT 46032 2009 B2
Justice Cross
12600 FSHR 46060 1906 B2
Justice Dr
1900 GNFD 46140 2236 A7
Justin Av
1600 INPS 46219 2231 B7
Justin Ct
1600 INPS 46219 2231 A7
N Justin Dr
10500 MdnT 46158 2661 C7
Justin Ln
- MdnT 46158 2661 B7
7600 INPS 46219 2231 A7
Justin Morgan Dr
19400 WTFD 46074 1684 B4
Jutland Ct
9300 INPS 46250 2012 C3

K

K Ct
- WRvT 46142 2663 E1
K St
- BHGV 46107 2447 E3
Kain St
200 PNFD 46168 2441 B4
Kalmar Dr
3900 INPS 46222 2227 A5
4000 INPS 46222 2226 E4
Kane Ct
7700 FSHR 46038 1904 C4
Kankakee Ct
8400 INPS 46217 2555 B7
Kankakee St
- INPS 46204 2337 C2
- WynT 46062 1578 D7
Kansas Ct
8400 INPS 46217 2555 C6
Kansas St
10 INPS 46225 2337 B6
W Kansas St
3400 INPS 46241 2336 A6
Kanterbury Ln
400 MRVL 46158 2660 C3
Kaplan Ct
10800 FSHR 46038 1905 C2
Kappes St
800 INPS 46221 2336 D5
Kara Ct
600 GNFD 46140 2345 D2
Kara Ln
1000 GNWD 46142 2664 D1
Karcher St
10 INPS 46225 2337 C6
E Karcher St
10 INPS 46225 2337 C6
Karen Ct
- PTBR 46167 2113 A3
W Karen Ct
7800 MrlT 46126 2560 B4
Karen Dr
300 PTBR 46167 2113 A3
600 EglT 46077 1898 C6
4600 INPS 46226 2121 D7
4600 LWNC 46226 2121 D7
9300 WshT 46234 2224 D7
S Karen Dr
5800 INPS 46239 2559 C1
5800 INPS 46259 2559 C1
Karnes Dr
- MCVL 46055 2124 B2
Karri Ct
- INPS 46229 2232 A7
Karrington Blvd
100 MRVL 46158 2660 C4
Karst Ct
7100 INPS 46221 2553 A4
Karst Dr
6100 INPS 46221 2553 A4
Karstadt Dr
5300 INPS 46208 2119 B6
Karyl Anne Ct
1400 DNVL 46122 2330 B2
Karyn Dr
600 WshT 46123 2223 A7
600 WshT 46123 2332 B1
Kasan Ct
3100 INPS 46268 2118 B3
Kaskaskia Wy
2900 INPS 46217 2554 B5
Kasteel Wy
8900 INPS 46250 2012 C4
Katelyn Ct
3600 INPS 46228 2118 A6
Katelyn Dr
4800 INPS 46228 2118 A7
Katelyn Ln
3600 INPS 46228 2118 A7
Katelyn Wy
3600 INPS 46228 2118 A7
Kathcart Wy
5200 INPS 46254 2116 C6
N Katherine Dr
4800 LWNC 46226 2121 D7
S Katherine Dr
7400 INPS 46217 2555 B4
Kathi Dr
- BHGV 46237 2447 E6
Kathleen Av
- WshT 46123 2331 E2
8800 INPS 46234 2225 A4
9000 INPS 46234 2224 E4
Kathleen Dr
9200 INPS 46234 2224 E4
W Kathlene Ct
6000 BCkT 46055 2124 D6
Kathryn Dr
4500 GfdT 46231 2442 E6
5800 INPS 46228 2118 E5
Kathy Dr
7500 BrnT 46112 2114 C2
Kathy Ln
- WshT 46231 2333 D6
Kathy St
1900 GNWD 46143 2665 D7
Katie Ct
6900 GfdT 46168 2550 B1
Katie Ln
1000 CCRO 46034 1577 B6
Katie Knox Dr
1900 INPS 46260 2009 D5
Katydid Ct
- WRvT 46143 2663 B6
Katydid Ln
5200 INPS 46237 2448 C7
Kauai Ct
1200 INPS 46217 2554 E5
Kautsky Dr
900 INPS 46227 2555 E2
Kay Ct
- LEBN 46052 1676 D6
Kay Dr
- GNWD 46142 2664 E4
Kayak Ct
11400 INPS 46236 2014 D5
Kay Ellen Dr
2600 INPS 46229 2231 E5
Kayenta Ct
3300 INPS 46226 2231 D4
Kayla Dr
1600 INPS 46234 2225 B7
Kaymar Dr
100 CtrT 46122 2330 E3
Kayser Ct
5800 INPS 46226 2121 E6
N Kealing Av
1000 INPS 46201 2338 D1
1400 INPS 46201 2229 D7
S Kealing Av
900 INPS 46203 2338 D5
3700 INPS 46237 2447 D4
5700 INPS 46227 2556 D1
Kealing Ct
3600 INPS 46227 2556 D1
S Kealing St
1200 INPS 46203 2338 D6
Keating Dr
7500 INPS 46260 2009 E7
Keats Ct
200 CRML 46032 1901 C3
Kebil Ct
5000 INPS 46224 2226 D3
Kebil Dr
3400 INPS 46224 2226 D3
N Keefe Ct
3700 INPS 46235 2231 E3
Keego St
2100 WshT 46234 2224 D7
Keel Rd
15000 FCkT 46040 1907 A6
Keeler Dr
600 AVON 46123 2332 B2
Keeley Ct
12300 FSHR 46038 1904 D4
Keeneland Ct
1100 ClyT 46280 1901 E7
1100 ClyT 46280 1902 A7
6300 INPS 46278 2008 A7
Keeneland Ln
200 WRvT 46142 2663 D4
Keensburg Ct
1300 INPS 46228 2118 E4
1300 INPS 46228 2119 A4
Keensburg Dr
5900 INPS 46228 2118 E4
Keepsake Run
- GNWD 46143 2666 D5
Keevers Dr
8800 INPS 46234 2116 A6
Kegler Wy
3700 CRML 46074 1900 A2
Keith Dr
100 ZNVL 46077 1899 A6
Keller Ct
5100 INPS 46254 2117 C6
Keller Dr
10 BrnT 46158 2659 B4
100 GNFD 46140 2345 E4
1200 PNFD 46168 2441 D6
Keller Ter
14700 WTFD 46033 1793 E6
N Keller Heights Dr
11700 MnrT 46158 2658 B5
E Keller Hill Rd
10 BrnT 46158 2658 D5
200 BrnT 46158 2659 A5
W Keller Hill Rd
10 BrnT 46158 2658 C5
400 MnrT 46158 2658 C5
1900 MnrT 46158 2657 D5
2300 LtyT 46118 2657 D5
2300 LtyT 46158 2657 D5
2300 MnrT 46118 2657 D5
2300 MnrT 46157 2657 D5
N Kelley Dr
3600 CtrT 46140 2236 D1
Kelli Ct
100 LEBN 46052 1676 C5
Kellum Ct
6300 INPS 46221 2553 B2
Kellum Dr
6300 INPS 46221 2553 B3
10500 GfdT 46113 2551 D5
Kelly Ct
9500 WshT 46231 2333 D5
S Kelly Dr
4100 NPLN 46163 2452 A2
Kelly Ln
8200 INPS 46250 2012 B5
11000 WynT 46060 1687 D2
Kelly Pl
12500 FSHR 46038 1904 A4
E Kelly St
10 INPS 46225 2446 C1
1300 INPS 46203 2446 E1
1500 INPS 46203 2447 A1
W Kelly St
10 INPS 46225 2446 C1
3400 INPS 46241 2445 A1
4900 INPS 46241 2444 C1
Kelly Anne Wy
5400 NBVL 46062 1685 B1
Kelsay Ct
10 WTLD 46184 2775 A5
Kelsey Cir
3100 INPS 46268 2118 B3
Kelsey Ct
9100 FSHR 46038 2013 D2
Kelsey Dr
6200 INPS 46268 2118 B3
Kelsey Ln
8300 FSHR 46038 1904 C1
Kelso Dr
1100 INPS 46217 2554 C6
1100 INPS 46217 2555 A5
Kelvington Dr
4600 INPS 46254 2117 D6
Kelvington Ln
5400 INPS 46254 2117 E6
Kemble Ct
7700 FSHR 46038 1904 B4
Kemp Cir
12000 CBLD 46229 2232 E7
Kemp Ct
700 WshT 46123 2331 D5
10700 FCkT 46040 1906 E7
Kempton Pl
11100 FSHR 46038 1904 A6
W Ken Ln
4100 SCkT 46163 2343 C7
Kenasaw Ct
8500 INPS 46217 2555 B7
Kendale Ct
800 INPS 46234 2334 A2
Kendall Ct
1000 WTFD 46074 1792 E1
Kenderly Ct
5600 CRML 46033 1903 B4
Kenetta Ct
7700 FSHR 46038 1904 B4
Kenilworth Dr
3100 INPS 46228 2118 B7
Kenley Av
8400 INPS 46113 2552 A3
S Kenmore Av
2800 INPS 46203 2448 D2
N Kenmore Rd
1400 INPS 46219 2339 D1
1500 INPS 46219 2230 D7
4300 INPS 46226 2230 D1
5200 INPS 46226 2121 D6
S Kenmore Rd
200 INPS 46219 2339 D4
2600 INPS 46203 2448 D2
Kennard Ct
- MdnT 46113 2661 C1
Kennard Ln
500 WTFD 46074 1792 D2
Kennedy Ln
800 INPS 46260 2119 B3
Kennesaw Ln
8400 INPS 46227 2556 D7
Kenneth Av
4000 INPS 46226 2230 E2
Kenneth Ct
7700 BrnT 46112 2114 D2
Kennington St
- INPS 46225 2337 C7
Kenova Dr
10 INPS 46227 2555 C6
Kenruth Dr
1600 INPS 46260 2118 E3
Kensil St
10300 LWNC 46236 2123 B4
Kensington Blvd
5700 PNFD 46168 2440 D5
Kensington Cir
5700 PNFD 46168 2440 E5
Kensington Ct
10 PTBR 46167 2113 B4
400 WshT 46123 2223 C7
Kensington Dr
8600 NbvT 46060 1795 C6
E Kensington Dr
7000 INPS 46226 2230 E3
7100 INPS 46226 2231 A4
Kensington Pl
13500 CRML 46032 1902 A2
Kensington Rd
4500 CRML 46033 1903 A4
Kensington Wy
- MCVL 46055 2015 C7
- MCVL 46055 2124 C1
Kensington Wy N
4600 PNFD 46168 2440 E5
Kensington Wy S
4600 PNFD 46168 2440 E5
Kensington Park Ct
- GNWD 46142 2665 A3
Kensington Park Rd
200 GNWD 46142 2665 A3
Kensworth Dr
10400 LWNC 46236 2123 B3
Kent Av
400 LWNC 46216 2122 D4
Kent Ct
1400 GNWD 46143 2665 C6
12300 CRML 46032 1901 B3
Kent Ln
500 CRML 46032 1793 A7
Kentallen Ct
8200 LWNC 46236 2014 E5
Kentland Cir
6700 INPS 46237 2557 D3
Kentland Dr
6500 INPS 46237 2557 E3
Kentland Wy
6700 INPS 46237 2557 E3
Kentstone Dr
6200 INPS 46268 2118 B3
Kentucky Av
100 PNFD 46168 2441 D4
S Kentucky Av
300 INPS 46225 2337 A5
900 INPS 46221 2337 A5
1600 INPS 46221 2336 D7
2100 INPS 46221 2445 B2
2100 INPS 46241 2445 B2
3100 INPS 46221 2444 C4
3100 INPS 46241 2444 C4
5000 INPS 46221 2443 E7
5000 INPS 46241 2443 E7
5300 INPS 46221 2552 D1
5300 INPS 46241 2552 D1
6400 INPS 46113 2552 A4
7500 GfdT 46113 2551 D7
7500 INPS 46113 2551 D7
8600 GfdT 46168 2551 D7
8800 GfdT 46168 2660 C1
8800 GfdT 46168 2660 C1
8900 BrnT 46113 2660 C1
8900 BrnT 46158 2660 C1
8900 BrnT 46168 2660 C1
S Kentucky Av SR-67
4700 INPS 46221 2444 A6
4700 INPS 46241 2444 A6
5000 INPS 46221 2443 E7
5000 INPS 46241 2443 E7
5300 INPS 46221 2552 D1
5300 INPS 46241 2552 D1
6400 INPS 46113 2552 A4
7500 GfdT 46113 2551 D7
7500 INPS 46113 2551 D7
8600 GfdT 46168 2551 D7
8800 GfdT 46168 2660 C1
8900 BrnT 46113 2660 C1
8900 BrnT 46158 2660 C1
8900 BrnT 46168 2660 C1
N Kentucky St
10 DNVL 46122 2329 D4
S Kentucky St
100 DNVL 46122 2329 D4
800 CtrT 46122 2329 D5
S Kentucky St SR-39
800 CtrT 46122 2329 D5
800 DNVL 46122 2329 D5
N Kenwood Av
2100 INPS 46202 2228 C6
4400 INPS 46208 2228 C1
4600 INPS 46208 2119 C6
9300 INPS 46260 2010 C3
9500 CRML 46260 2010 C3
9500 CRML 46290 2010 C3
S Kenwood Av
800 INPS 46225 2337 C5
Kenwood Cir
100 INPS 46260 2010 C4
Kenwood Ct
100 INPS 46260 2010 C3
Kenwood Dr
1300 GNWD 46143 2665 C6
N Kenwood Dr
9100 INPS 46260 2010 C3
Kenwood Pl
5400 CRML 46033 1903 D4
N Kenyon Av
4300 INPS 46226 2230 D1
N Kenyon Dr
4700 LWNC 46226 2121 D7
5200 INPS 46226 2121 D6
S Kenyon Dr
2800 INPS 46203 2448 D2
N Kenyon St
10 INPS 46219 2339 D3
2100 INPS 46219 2230 D6
S Kenyon St
10 INPS 46219 2339 D3
Kenyon Tr
5700 NBVL 46062 1794 C5
Kenzie Ct
6100 LWNC 46236 2123 B4
Keough Ct
7700 LWNC 46236 2014 C7
Keough Dr
11000 LWNC 46236 2014 C7
Keran Manor Ct
- GNWD 46142 2665 C2
N Kercheval Dr
3800 INPS 46226 2231 A2
4000 LWNC 46226 2231 A2
5100 LWNC 46226 2122 A6
S Kercheval Dr
3000 INPS 46239 2449 A3
Kerf Ln
6200 NBVL 46062 1685 C5
Kern Rd
4000 WrhT 46052 1787 D4
Kerns Ct
2000 ClyT 46280 2011 B1
Kerns Ln
5400 INPS 46268 2117 C3
Kerria Ct
4800 CRML 46033 1903 A6
Kerry Ct
200 WshT 46032 1792 D6
S Kerry Dr
4100 INPS 46239 2449 B5
Kersey Dr
7900 LWNC 46236 2015 A6
Kersey St
500 LEBN 46052 1676 E6
Kerwood Dr
9100 INPS 46240 2011 B3
Kerwood Ln
5800 LcnT 46112 2114 A6
Kessler Ln
5900 INPS 46220 2120 E4
Kessler Blvd Dr N
3500 INPS 46222 2227 B4
3800 INPS 46228 2227 B4
4600 INPS 46228 2118 B7
Kessler Blvd East Dr
- INPS 46226 2121 A5
10 INPS 46208 2119 D4
10 INPS 46220 2119 D4
1400 INPS 46220 2120 A4
4900 INPS 46220 2121 A5
Kessler Blvd W Dr
10 INPS 46220 2119 C4
300 INPS 46208 2119 A5
300 INPS 46228 2119 A5
1100 INPS 46228 2118 D5
Kessler Blvd West Dr
- INPS 46208 2119 C4
Kessler Common Blvd
5700 INPS 46220 2121 A6
Kessler Ln Dr E
4200 INPS 46220 2120 E4
Kessler Ridge Rd
5900 INPS 46220 2120 D4
E Kessler View Dr
4700 INPS 46220 2120 E5
4900 INPS 46220 2121 A5
Kesslerwood Ct
1700 INPS 46228 2118 E5
Keston Cir
7000 INPS 46256 2121 E2
Kestral Ct
10600 NBVL 46060 1687 B4
Kestrel Ct
4200 INPS 46254 2225 D1
Keswick Ct
5400 WshT 46123 2331 D5
Keswick Dr
600 BNBG 46112 2114 B5
Keswick Rd
3100 INPS 46222 2226 E4
Ketcham St
700 INPS 46222 2336 C2
N Ketcham St
400 INPS 46222 2336 C3
Kettering Wy
2400 INPS 46214 2225 C6
Keuka Dr
2100 WshT 46234 2224 D6
Kevin Ct
- ZNVL 46077 1899 A5
Kevin Dr
100 ZNVL 46077 1899 A6
9300 LWNC 46236 2122 E6
Kevin Wy
3800 INPS 46254 2226 C2
Kewanna Ct
- MdnT 46113 2661 D1
Kewanna Dr
10100 WshT 46234 2224 C6
Key Ct
14400 FCkT 46040 1906 E7
W Key Ln
9000 INPS 46234 2224 E3
9000 INPS 46234 2225 A3
Key Club Dr
19000 NBVL 46062 1685 D5
Key Harbour Dr
8600 INPS 46236 2014 D4
Keyhole Cove
900 GNWD 46142 2664 D1
N Keystone Av
1000 INPS 46201 2338 B1
2400 INPS 46218 2229 B5
3800 INPS 46205 2229 B2
4600 INPS 46205 2120 B7
5200 INPS 46220 2120 B6
7100 INPS 46240 2120 B1
7400 INPS 46240 2011 C4
9200 ClyT 46240 2011 C4
9200 CRML 46240 2011 C4
9600 ClyT 46280 2011 C1
9800 CRML 46032 2011 C1
9800 CRML 46033 2011 C1
9800 CRML 46280 2011 C1
9900 ClyT 46032 1902 C6
9900 CRML 46032 1902 C4
9900 CRML 46033 1902 C6
N Keystone Av SR-431
8600 INPS 46240 2011 C1
9200 ClyT 46240 2011 C1
9200 CRML 46240 2011 C1
9600 ClyT 46280 2011 C1
9800 CRML 46032 2011 C1
9800 CRML 46033 2011 C1
9800 CRML 46280 2011 C1
9900 ClyT 46032 1902 C6
9900 CRML 46032 1902 C4
9900 CRML 46033 1902 C6
S Keystone Av
10 INPS 46201 2338 B3
500 INPS 46203 2338 B7
2200 INPS 46203 2447 B2
3000 INPS 46237 2447 B2
3500 INPS 46227 2447 B4
5500 INPS 46227 2556 B1
8700 GNWD 46227 2665 B1
8700 INPS 46227 2665 B1
Keystone Cross
8800 INPS 46240 2011 C4
Keystone Ct
5200 INPS 46220 2120 B6
Keystone Wy
- CRML 46032 1902 C5
2300 INPS 46218 2229 B6
Keystone Lakes Dr
1800 INPS 46237 2447 A3
Keystone Lakes Wy
3200 INPS 46237 2447 B3
Khaki Ct
4700 ZNVL 46077 1898 E3
Kiah Ct
- PNFD 46168 2550 A1
Kiawah Ct
5800 CRML 46033 1903 C2
Kiawah Dr
12700 CRML 46033 1903 C3
Kickapoo Tr
7200 INPS 46219 2340 A4
13300 CRML 46033 1903 C2
Kidwell Cir
5300 INPS 46239 2448 E7
Kidwell Ct
5400 INPS 46239 2449 A7
Kidwell Dr
7100 INPS 46239 2448 E7
7200 INPS 46239 2449 A7
Kiefer Ct
10 BHGV 46107 2447 E5
N Kiel Av
3600 INPS 46224 2226 B3
S Kiel Av
800 INPS 46241 2335 B5
Kilbarron Cir
7500 INPS 46217 2554 E5
Kilbarron Ct
7500 INPS 46217 2554 E5
Kilbourne Dr
700 GNWD 46142 2665 A2
Kilburn Ct
15400 WshT 46074 1792 B5
Kilda Dr
4800 WRvT 46142 2663 D4
Kildare Av
1600 INPS 46218 2230 A7
Kilder Ct
900 EglT 46077 1898 C4
Kileen Rd
7200 LWNC 46236 2124 A1
Kilkenney Cir
3300 CRML 46032 1900 B3
Kilkenny Ct
4800 INPS 46254 2116 C7
Killarey Hill Dr
7500 INPS 46217 2554 D5
Killarney Dr
7400 INPS 46217 2554 D5
Killarney Wy
1600 INPS 46217 2554 D4
Killarny Cir
10 BNBG 46112 2113 D3
Killdeer Dr
4100 INPS 46237 2556 D3
Killdeer Pl
5700 CRML 46033 1903 A2
Killian Dr
600 BHGV 46107 2447 E4
1000 MRVL 46158 2660 A5
Killimer Ct W
1400 INPS 46217 2554 E4
Killington Cir
10800 FSHR 46038 1905 C7
Killington Dr
5200 INPS 46237 2448 C7
Killington Ln
5200 INPS 46237 2448 C7
Killingworth Ct
9600 INPS 46256 2013 E5
Kilmer Ln
5200 INPS 46250 2012 A6
N Kilmer Ln
7500 INPS 46256 2013 A6
Kilroy Av
2200 INPS 46218 2229 B6
Kilworth Ct
10800 INPS 46235 2232 C2
Kim Wy
5400 INPS 46237 2448 B6
Kimberlite Dr
- FSHR 46060 1905 E2
E Kimberly Dr
7500 INPS 46256 2013 A6
Kimberly Ln
300 WshT 46168 2441 B1
Kimble Dr
7100 INPS 46217 2554 C4
Kimbrough Ct
10 BNBG 46112 2223 C3
Kimbrough Dr
200 GNWD 46143 2665 C6
Kimbrough Ln
300 CRML 46032 1902 A3
Kimcoe Ln
7600 INPS 46254 2116 C6
Kimkris Ct
6900 INPS 46278 2007 E7
Kimlough Cir
900 INPS 46240 2010 E5
Kimlough Dr
8200 INPS 46240 2010 E5
Kimmeridge Ln
4600 INPS 46254 2117 E7
Kincaid Dr
9600 FSHR 46038 2013 C2
9600 INPS 46038 2013 C2
10100 FSHR 46038 1904 C7
Kincannon Ln
1400 INPS 46217 2554 E4
Kinder Oak Dr
17800 NBVL 46062 1685 E7
17800 NBVL 46062 1686 A7
Kindig Rd
300 INPS 46217 2555 B4
Kindiwa Ct
3000 CRML 46033 2011 C1
King Av
500 INPS 46222 2336 C1
1400 INPS 46222 2227 C7
N King Av
6100 INPS 46228 2118 C4
King Ct
- AVON 46123 2332 B3
King Dr
500 INPS 46260 2010 B6
King St
700 LEBN 46052 1676 E5
King Arthur Ct
4400 CRML 46033 1902 E5
10100 INPS 46229 2232 A5
King Arthur Dr
10100 INPS 46229 2232 A5
Kingbridge St
1900 INPS 46203 2338 E7
S Kingbridge St
500 INPS 46203 2338 E5
Kingbury Dr
4700 LcnT 46167 2113 C5
4700 MdlT 46167 2113 C5
Kingdom Ct
14200 FCkT 46040 1906 E7
Kingfisher Cir
12000 INPS 46236 2014 E4
Kingfisher Ct
12000 INPS 46236 2014 E4
Kingfisher Pl
5700 CRML 46033 1903 B2
King George Dr
7300 INPS 46260 2010 B7
7300 INPS 46260 2119 B1
King James Ct
6400 INPS 46227 2555 C2
King John Ct
6500 INPS 46227 2555 C3
King John Dr
10 INPS 46227 2555 C3
King Lear Ct
6000 INPS 46254 2117 B4
King Lear Dr
5900 INPS 46254 2117 A4
King Lear Ln
6100 INPS 46254 2117 B4
Kinglet Ct
7300 INPS 46254 2225 D1

STREET Block City ZIP Map# Grid

N Kingman Cir
7200 INPS 46256 2122 A2
Kingman Dr
4100 INPS 46226 2230 E2
4100 LWNC 46226 2230 E2
4200 LWNC 46226 2231 A2
5100 LWNC 46226 2122 A7
6500 INPS 46256 2122 A2
N Kingman Dr
7000 INPS 46256 2122 A2
Kingmeadow Ct
8700 INPS 46217 2555 B7
Kingrail Wy
13400 CRML 46033 1903 B1
Kings Ct
1000 INPS 46260 2010 A5
2900 ClyT 46032 1900 C6
3300 AVON 46123 2332 A4
Kings Ln
300 NBVL 46060 1686 E7
500 NBVL 46060 1687 A7
4200 LtyT 46168 2440 B5
Kingsbee Ct
6100 INPS 46224 2226 A3
Kingsboro Cir
9300 LWNC 46235 2231 D1
Kingsboro Ct
9300 LWNC 46235 2122 D7
9300 LWNC 46235 2231 E1
Kingsboro Dr
4500 INPS 46235 2231 E1
4500 LWNC 46235 2122 D7
4500 LWNC 46235 2231 E1
Kingsbury Dr
13300 CRML 46032 1901 C1
Kingsbury Wy
6500 EglT 46077 1897 D6
Kings Canyon Dr
6200 INPS 46237 2448 D7
Kings Cove Ct
1200 INPS 46260 2010 A4
Kings Cross Ct
100 NBVL 46060 1795 E3
Kingscross Ct
9700 INPS 46235 2231 E4
Kings Cross St
400 WshT 46123 2223 C7
Kingsford Dr
7100 INPS 46260 2118 D1
Kings Gap Wy
- LcnT 46112 2115 D5
Kingsgate Dr
1300 CRML 46032 1792 A7
Kingsley Dr
4200 INPS 46205 2229 A1
4500 INPS 46205 2120 A7
6600 INPS 46220 2120 A2
7100 INPS 46240 2120 A1
9000 FSHR 46038 2013 D1
Kingsmead Dr
7900 LWNC 46226 2122 B7
Kingsmead Wy
- LWNC 46226 2122 B7
Kings Mill Dr
10600 ClyT 46032 1900 C7
Kings Mill Rd
800 GNWD 46142 2665 A1
Kings Point Ct
300 WshT 46032 1792 C5
Kingsport Rd
7500 INPS 46256 2012 E7
7500 INPS 46256 2013 A7
Kings Table Ct
10100 INPS 46229 2232 A4
Kings Table Dr
10100 INPS 46229 2232 A5
Kingston
- AVON 46123 2332 E4
Kingston Cir
700 BNBG 46112 2114 D4
Kingston Ct
10000 FSHR 46038 1905 A6
Kingston Dr
13500 FCkT 46055 2015 C1
Kingston St
- AVON 46123 2332 E4
Kingsview Dr
100 MRVL 46158 2660 B4
Kingsway Ct
400 MRVL 46158 2660 C3
Kingsway Dr
- AVON 46123 2332 B1
- WshT 46123 2332 B1
4700 INPS 46205 2120 B7
Kingswood Cir
7000 INPS 46256 2121 E3
7100 INPS 46256 2122 A3
Kingswood Ct
7000 INPS 46256 2121 E3
7000 INPS 46256 2122 A3
Kingswood Dr
4900 CRML 46033 1903 A7
6500 INPS 46256 2121 E2
Kingussie Ct
4400 INPS 46254 2225 E1
Kingwood Ct
11700 FSHR 46038 1906 D5
Kinlock Dr
8900 INPS 46256 2122 D1
Kinnard St
500 LEBN 46052 1677 A7
Kinnear Av
3400 INPS 46218 2229 A3
3800 INPS 46205 2229 A3
Kinnerton Dr
6600 INPS 46254 2116 E7
6600 INPS 46254 2117 A6
Kinnett Ln
3700 INPS 46228 2118 A6
Kinross Dr
- WshT 46123 2332 E1
Kinser Ct
200 FSHR 46038 1904 B5
Kinsey Av
18100 WshT 46074 1683 D6
Kinzer Av
600 CRML 46032 1902 C3
Kiowa Ct
3000 INPS 46235 2232 B4
Kiowa Dr
10000 FCkT 46256 2014 C1
10200 INPS 46235 2232 B4
Kira Ct
10400 LWNC 46236 2123 B4
Kirch Ct
6400 INPS 46268 2118 B3
Kirk Ct
2600 LEBN 46052 1677 A2
Kirk Dr E
10 INPS 46234 2334 B3
Kirk Dr W
10 INPS 46234 2334 A3
Kirk Allen Dr
9500 LWNC 46235 2122 E7
Kirkendall Ct
5900 CRML 46033 1903 E2
Kirkgate Ct
1300 CRML 46033 1793 D7
Kirkham Ct
9000 INPS 46260 2010 A3
Kirkham Ln
1200 INPS 46260 2010 A4
Kirkham Rd
8800 INPS 46260 2010 A4
Kirklees Dr
1300 CRML 46032 1792 A7
Kirklin Ct
8400 INPS 46237 2557 D6
Kirklin Dr
17000 WTFD 46074 1792 D2
Kirkpatrick Wy
- FSHR 46038 1904 E4
5700 INPS 46220 2121 B2
Kirkwood Ct
3100 GNWD 46142 2664 B1
Kirkwood Dr
1000 PNFD 46168 2441 C6
11500 CBLD 46229 2341 D2
Kirkwood Club Dr
6800 INPS 46241 2443 E7
Kirsch Dr
- LcnT 46234 2224 C3
3900 LcnT 46112 2224 C3
Kiser Pt
8900 INPS 46256 2013 C4
Kiskadee Ct
3700 INPS 46228 2118 A4
Kissel Rd
3000 EglT 46077 1789 B7
3000 WrhT 46075 1789 B7
3000 WrhT 46077 1789 B7
3700 EglT 46077 1898 A1
3700 WrhT 46075 1898 A1
3700 WrhT 46077 1898 A1
4900 EglT 46075 1898 A4
N Kissel Rd
9300 INPS 46278 2007 A3
Kit Dr
5300 INPS 46237 2557 B2
Kita Dr
7300 INPS 46259 2558 A6
Kitchen Rd
200 MdnT 46158 2661 A7
N Kitley Av
10 INPS 46219 2339 D3
2100 INPS 46219 2230 D6
3800 INPS 46226 2230 D1
4500 INPS 46226 2121 D7
4600 LWNC 46226 2121 D7
7300 INPS 46250 2012 D7
7300 INPS 46250 2121 D1
S Kitley Av
10 INPS 46219 2339 D3
1000 INPS 46203 2339 D6
2600 INPS 46203 2448 D2
S Kitley Rd
2400 INPS 46239 2450 D2
Kittery Dr
11600 FCkT 46038 1905 D5
Kittrell Dr
9600 ClyT 46280 2011 B2
Kitty Hawk Ct
3900 CRML 46033 1902 E7
Kivet Ct
3900 INPS 46235 2232 A2
Klay Ct
- GfdT 46158 2550 D7
Kline Dr
3600 INPS 46226 2231 A3
Klingesmith Blvd
- CRML 46033 1794 D7
Klintilloch Ct
4000 INPS 46237 2447 D5
Klotz St
500 LEBN 46052 1676 E6
Klotz Farm Blvd
11500 FSHR 46038 1905 A6
Knapbury Ln
3900 INPS 46235 2232 C2
Knaphill Ct
1800 CRML 46033 1793 E7
S Knapp Rd
7500 INPS 46259 2558 D5
Knapps Ct
1200 GNWD 46142 2664 E3
Knickerbocker Pl
3700 INPS 46240 2011 D4
Knickerbocker Wy
- INPS 46240 2011 D4
Knight Dr
10600 ClyT 46032 1900 C7
Knightbridge Ct
7200 WshT 46123 2223 C7
Knighton Ct
- WTFD 46074 1792 D4
Knights Ct
8900 INPS 46250 2012 C4
Knights Wy
4900 INPS 46217 2445 E7
Knights Bridge Blvd
9400 CRML 46240 2011 E3
9400 INPS 46240 2011 E3
Knightsbridge Ln
10700 FSHR 46038 1905 A7
Knob Creek Ovlk
3800 INPS 46234 2225 A2
Knob Hill Ct
7000 GfdT 46168 2551 B4
Knoblin Ln
- GNWD 46142 2665 C3
Knobstone Ln
- INPS 46203 2448 D3
Knobstone Wy
6500 INPS 46203 2448 D3
Knobwood Dr
7000 INPS 46260 2118 D1
Knoll Cross
8500 FSHR 46038 1904 C2
Knoll Ct
10 CRML 46032 1902 A2
100 NBVL 46062 1685 B1
Knoll Ln
10 BNBG 46112 2223 B4
Knoll Rdg
13100 FSHR 46038 1904 C2
Knoll St
- DNVL 46122 2329 C5
Knollcreek Cir
8100 INPS 46256 2122 B2
Knollcreek Dr
6700 INPS 46256 2122 C2
Knoll Crest Ct
5000 INPS 46228 2118 C6
Knollgate Ct
8000 INPS 46268 2008 E6
Knollridge Ct
11300 CBLD 46229 2341 D2
Knollton Ct
13100 FSHR 46038 1904 C2
Knollton Rd
3800 INPS 46228 2227 D2
6000 INPS 46228 2118 D4
6600 INPS 46260 2118 D2
Knoll Top Dr
4100 INPS 46237 2556 E2
Knollvalley Ln
7200 INPS 46256 2122 C1
Knollview Ct
8100 INPS 46256 2122 B2
Knollway Ct
8600 FSHR 46038 1904 C2
Knollwood Av
4000 FKLN 46131 2774 E7
Knollwood Ct
4100 FKLN 46131 2774 E7
Knollwood Dr
800 GNWD 46142 2665 A4
2400 INPS 46228 2118 C6
Knollwood Pl
13100 FSHR 46038 1904 C2
Knotty Pine Ct
8700 INPS 46227 2556 C7
Knox Cir
200 GNWD 46143 2665 D5
Knox Dr
1800 LtyT 46118 2548 C1
Knox St
500 INPS 46227 2446 D3
1500 INPS 46227 2447 A3
1600 INPS 46237 2447 A3
Knoxville Dr
5600 INPS 46221 2553 B2
Knue Rd
7900 INPS 46250 2012 D6
Knyghton Rd
6000 INPS 46220 2121 B3
Koefoot Dr
1900 INPS 46214 2225 E7
Koehne St
10 INPS 46222 2336 E3
2100 INPS 46202 2227 E6
2200 INPS 46208 2227 E6
N Koehne St
100 INPS 46222 2336 E3
Kokomo Ln
600 INPS 46241 2334 E5
Kolby Ct
5400 NBVL 46062 1685 B1
Koldyke Dr
7000 FSHR 46038 1903 E4
7000 FSHR 46038 1904 A5
Kollman Ct
6600 INPS 46241 2443 E6
Kollman Rd
3800 INPS 46241 2443 E5
Kopetsky Dr
5600 INPS 46217 2554 D1
Koster Dr
5800 INPS 46254 2117 A4
Kourtney Pl
- WTFD 46033 1793 D6
Kousa Dr
8300 INPS 46234 2225 B7
Kovey Ct
9900 ClyT 46280 2011 A1
S Koweba Ln
10 INPS 46201 2338 B4
Kozy Dr
2800 INPS 46241 2444 D2
Kramer Ct
9900 INPS 46235 2232 A2
Kreutzinger Ln
800 WshT 46123 2333 D2
Krewson St
100 PNFD 46168 2441 B5
W Krewson St
100 PNFD 46168 2441 B5
Kristen Cir
11400 INPS 46235 2232 D3
Kristen Ct
3300 INPS 46235 2232 D4
Kristen Dr
2500 INPS 46218 2230 B5
Kristen Dr E
2700 INPS 46218 2230 B5
Kristen Dr W
2700 INPS 46218 2230 B5
Kristen Ln
11300 INPS 46235 2232 D3
Kristen Erin Ct
1800 INPS 46234 2225 A7
S Kroft Dr
- GNWD 46143 2664 C5
Kruggle Ct
8600 INPS 46256 2013 C4
Krupp Rd
600 INPS 46217 2446 A4
Kungsholm Dr
9100 INPS 46250 2012 B3
Kunkel Ln
8600 INPS 46237 2557 D7
Kunkel Wy
6700 INPS 46237 2557 D7
Kurtis Blvd
6300 INPS 46224 2226 A7
Kylan Ct
7700 FSHR 46038 1904 B3
Kyle Ct
3000 INPS 46235 2232 D4
10600 FSHR 46038 1904 D7

L

L Ct
- WRvT 46142 2663 E1
L St
- BHGV 46107 2447 E2
Lablanca Bnd
13400 CRML 46074 1900 C2
La Canada Blvd
13100 DelT 46038 1904 C2
Lace Bark Ct
7400 AVON 46123 2332 C5
Lacebark Dr
3500 INPS 46235 2232 B3
Lacebark Ln
10600 INPS 46235 2232 B3
Lacey Ct
100 LEBN 46052 1676 C5
Lackwanna Ct
900 INPS 46217 2555 A6
Laclede Ct
4500 INPS 46221 2444 C6
Laclede St
300 INPS 46241 2335 D5
4500 INPS 46221 2444 D6
La Corrida Ct
8500 INPS 46227 2556 B7
La Corrida Dr
2600 INPS 46227 2556 B7
Lacosta Ln
5400 NBVL 46062 1685 B7
Lacosta Wy
18000 WTFD 46062 1684 E6
La Crosse Ct
3700 INPS 46235 2232 B3
Lacy Cir
500 WRvT 46142 2663 C2
Lacy Ct
10 BNBG 46112 2223 C2
5400 WRvT 46142 2663 C2
E Lacy Ct
3200 INPS 46227 2556 C5
Lacy Dr
400 WRvT 46142 2663 C2
S Lacy Dr
7800 INPS 46227 2556 C5
Lacy Ln
5100 WRvT 46142 2663 C2
Lacy Pl
5200 WRvT 46142 2663 C2
Lacy Rd
24100 WRvT 46034 1578 E1
Lacy Wy
5400 WRvT 46142 2663 C2
Ladson St
9600 FSHR 46038 1904 E3
Ladybug Ct
- WRvT 46143 2663 B6
Ladywood Dr
5200 INPS 46226 2121 A6
Lafayette Av
100 LEBN 46052 1676 D5
1700 CtrT 46052 1676 D5
Lafayette Blvd
4200 INPS 46254 2226 C1
Lafayette Ct
1000 LEBN 46052 1676 D5
Lafayette Dr
300 NBVL 46060 1686 B6
300 NBVL 46062 1686 B6
Lafayette Rd
1600 INPS 46222 2227 B6
3700 INPS 46222 2226 D2
3800 INPS 46254 2226 D2
4500 INPS 46254 2117 B5
6000 INPS 46278 2117 B5
6200 INPS 46278 2116 E3
N Lafayette Rd
6900 INPS 46278 2116 D1
9000 INPS 46278 2007 A3
W Lafayette Rd
3600 AdmT 46069 1573 B1
Lafayette St
1200 INPS 46202 2337 B1
5700 LtyT 46118 2548 C1
La Fleur Ct
5800 INPS 46237 2448 C7
La Fleur Wy
5100 INPS 46237 2448 C7
La Fontaine Ct
3700 INPS 46235 2232 B2
Lage Ct
- WshT 46123 2333 C3
Lagora Ln
4900 INPS 46224 2226 D3
La Grange Ct
3700 INPS 46235 2232 A3
E Lagrotte Dr
8500 INPS 46239 2449 C3
Laguna Dr
8100 INPS 46260 2009 E6
Laguna Ln
1000 GNWD 46143 2665 E5
La Habra Cir
8100 INPS 46236 2014 D5
La Habra Ln
8100 INPS 46236 2014 D5
Lahr Ct
8800 INPS 46256 2013 C4
Lake Cir
11600 FSHR 46038 1904 C5
Lake Ct
3100 WRvT 46142 2664 A3
E Lake Ct
5500 INPS 46220 2120 C6
Lake Dr
10 WRvT 46142 2664 A3
700 GNFD 46140 2236 E6
W Lake Dr
2500 SCkT 46140 2344 A2
2500 SGLK 46140 2344 A2
2700 SGLK 46140 2343 E2
5900 INPS 46224 2335 B3
Lake Dr E
1000 BNBG 46112 2223 C2
Lake Dr N
10 BNBG 46112 2223 B2
Lake Dr S
10 BNBG 46112 2223 B2
Lake Dr W
1000 BNBG 46112 2223 B2
Lake Rd
- INPS 46208 2119 B7
7000 INPS 46217 2554 A6
W Lake Rd
6800 INPS 46214 2334 E3
Lake Bodona Dr
10 BrnT 46158 2658 C4
10 MnrT 46158 2658 C4
Lake Boggs Ct
6000 INPS 46254 2117 B6
Lake Boggs St
5300 INPS 46254 2117 B6
Lake Breeze Wy
6000 SDWY 46224 2226 B7
Lake Cir Dr
2400 INPS 46268 2009 C4
Lake Clearwater Ln
8500 INPS 46240 2011 D5
Lake Clearwater Pl
3800 INPS 46240 2011 D5
Lake Crest Ct
9800 INPS 46229 2232 B5
Lake Crest Dr
2200 INPS 46229 2232 A6
Lakefield Ct
4200 INPS 46254 2117 E5
Lakefield Dr
4300 INPS 46254 2117 E5
Lakefield Trc
4300 INPS 46254 2117 E5
Lake Forest Dr
700 AVON 46123 2332 A5
700 WshT 46123 2332 A5
2800 INPS 46268 2009 C4
Lake Forest Pkwy
11600 CRML 46033 1903 B5
Lake Freeman Dr
6000 INPS 46254 2117 A6
Lake Front Dr
10900 INPS 46236 2014 C4
Lake Kessler Ct
5800 INPS 46220 2121 B4
Lakeknoll Dr
6500 INPS 46220 2121 C2
Lake Knoll Wy
5500 NBVL 46062 1685 B2
Lake Lakota Dr
7300 INPS 46217 2554 C4
Lake Lakota Pl
7300 INPS 46217 2554 C4
Lakeland Blvd
6300 LcnT 46112 2115 D5
Lakeland Ct
700 CRML 46032 1901 D1
6300 LcnT 46112 2115 E5
Lakeland Dr
- BrnT 46112 2115 D5
5500 INPS 46220 2121 B2
5700 LcnT 46112 2115 D5
10200 FSHR 46038 2014 A2
Lakeland Ln
5700 LcnT 46112 2115 D5
Lakeland Trails Blvd
7000 INPS 46259 2557 E5
7200 INPS 46259 2558 A5
Lakemanor Ct
6000 INPS 46254 2117 A6
Lakemanor Dr
5200 INPS 46254 2117 B6
Lake Mead Dr
6200 INPS 46237 2448 D7
Lakemore St
200 BNBG 46112 2114 D7
Lake Nora East Dr
8800 INPS 46240 2010 E4
Lake Nora North Dr
700 INPS 46240 2010 D3
Lake Nora South Dr
700 INPS 46240 2010 E4
Lake Nora West Dr
8900 INPS 46240 2010 E4
W Lake North Dr
5900 INPS 46224 2335 B2
Lake of Lanterns Rd
2100 WshT 46234 2224 C6
Lake of Lanterns North Dr
10000 WshT 46234 2224 D5
Lake of Lanterns West Dr
2100 WshT 46234 2224 C6
Lake of the Lanterns Dr
2100 WshT 46234 2224 C6
Lake of the Pines Dr
1800 INPS 46234 2225 A7
Lake Park Blvd
4000 INPS 46227 2447 C5
Lake Plaza Dr
6800 INPS 46220 2121 C2
Lake Point Blvd
5100 CRML 46033 1903 B5
Lake Point Cir
200 GNWD 46142 2664 D3
Lake Point Ct
8200 INPS 46256 2013 C5
Lake Point Ln N
1500 GNWD 46142 2664 C3
Lake Point Ln S
200 GNWD 46142 2664 C3
Lake Point Wy
300 NBVL 46062 1685 C2
8100 INPS 46256 2013 B5
Lakeridge Dr
4400 INPS 46234 2116 A7
4400 INPS 46234 2225 A1
Lake Ridge Ln
300 GNWD 46142 2664 D3
Lake Run Ct
1900 WRvT 46143 2664 C6
Lake Run Dr
- WRvT 46143 2664 A7
11000 FSHR 46038 1903 E7
Lakesedge Blvd
- INPS 46237 2448 D6
Lakesedge Dr
6500 INPS 46237 2448 D6
Lakeshire Ln
2600 INPS 46268 2009 C3
Lakeshore Cir
10 BNBG 46112 2223 E1
8300 INPS 46250 2012 A5
Lakeshore Ct
10 CRML 46033 1902 C6
2400 LEBN 46052 1676 E3
5100 INPS 46250 2012 A5
Lake Shore Dr
2900 INPS 46205 2120 B7
Lakeshore Dr
100 LEBN 46052 1676 E3
300 WshT 46123 2332 B4
E Lakeshore Dr
- LEBN 46052 1677 A3
9600 CRML 46280 2011 D1
9800 CRML 46033 2011 D1
10500 CRML 46033 1902 D7
W Lakeshore Dr
10600 CRML 46033 1902 D6
Lakeshore Pl
10 BNBG 46112 2223 E1
4800 INPS 46250 2012 A5
10400 CRML 46033 2011 D1
Lakeshore Trail East Dr
8200 INPS 46250 2012 A5
Lakeshore Trail West Dr
8200 INPS 46250 2012 A6
Lakeside Blvd
5900 INPS 46278 2117 B2
Lakeside Cir
900 GNWD 46143 2665 A5
Lakeside Ct
10 CtrT 46140 2236 D1
Lakeside Dr
600 PNFD 46168 2441 E5
7200 FSHR 46038 1904 A5
N Lakeside Dr
7100 INPS 46278 2116 E1
W Lakeside Dr
7100 INPS 46278 2116 E1
Lakeside Ln
1800 CBLD 46229 2232 E7
1800 CBLD 46229 2233 A7
Lakeside Pl
12000 FSHR 46038 1904 A4
Lakeside Green Dr
- FSHR 46038 2014 B2
Lakeside Manor Av
5800 INPS 46254 2117 A6
Lakeside Manor Blvd
5200 INPS 46254 2117 B6
Lakeside Manor Dr
5200 INPS 46254 2117 B6
Lakeside Manor Ln
5200 INPS 46254 2117 B6
Lakeside Woods Cir
6400 INPS 46278 2117 A1
Lakeside Woods Dr
7100 INPS 46278 2116 E2
7100 INPS 46278 2117 A1
Lake Springs Ct
8200 INPS 46236 2014 B5
Lake Station Ln
- NBVL 46062 1685 B5
Lakestone Ct
6600 INPS 46237 2448 D6
Lakestone Dr
4700 INPS 46237 2448 D6
Lake Stonebridge Ln
11400 FSHR 46038 1905 C6
Lake Terrace Ct
100 NBVL 46062 1685 C2
9700 INPS 46229 2232 A6
Lake Terrace Dr
2100 INPS 46229 2232 A6
Lake Terrace Pl
9800 INPS 46229 2232 A6
Lake Terrace North Dr
9700 INPS 46229 2231 E6
9800 INPS 46229 2232 A6
Lake Terrace South Dr
9800 INPS 46229 2232 A6
Lake Terrace West Dr
2100 INPS 46229 2231 E7
Laketon Dr
5800 INPS 46220 2121 C2
Lake Tree Cir
8000 INPS 46217 2555 B5
Lake Tree Ln
8000 INPS 46217 2555 A6
Lake Tree Pl
1100 INPS 46217 2554 E6
1100 INPS 46217 2555 A6
Lake Valley Ct
- NBVL 46062 1685 B1
Lake View Ct
100 AVON 46123 2332 D3
Lakeview Ct
- PTBR 46167 2113 B5
10 CRML 46033 1902 D7
Lakeview Ct N
100 GNFD 46140 2236 E6
Lakeview Ct S
100 GNFD 46140 2237 A7
Lakeview Dr
100 GNFD 46140 2236 E7
100 GNFD 46140 2237 A7
100 MdnT 46158 2660 E4
100 NBVL 46060 1686 C6
500 CCRO 46034 1577 C3
600 EglT 46077 1898 C6
600 NBVL 46062 1686 B5
1900 DNVL 46122 2330 B4
5900 INPS 46224 2335 A2
10600 CRML 46033 1902 D6
E Lakeview Dr
- LEBN 46052 1677 A3
Lakeview Ln
500 INPS 46224 2335 A2
Lakeview Pkwy
- FSHR 46038 1904 E7
Lakeview Pkwy South Dr
5200 INPS 46268 2117 C1
Lakeview Pkwy West Dr
7100 INPS 46268 2117 C1
Lakeville Cross
16400 WTFD 46074 1792 C2
Lake Vista Dr
100 FSHR 46038 1904 A4
Lake Vista Ln
7600 INPS 46217 2555 B5
Lakeway Dr
4200 INPS 46205 2229 C1
Lakewind Ct
9200 INPS 46256 2014 A3
Lakewind Dr
9100 INPS 46256 2014 A3
Lakewood Cir
9900 ZNVL 46077 1898 E2
9900 ZNVL 46077 1899 A2
Lakewood Ct
10 CtrT 46140 2236 C1
300 AVON 46123 2332 C3
4200 LtyT 46118 2549 A1
Lakewood Dr
3100 LcnT 46112 2224 B4
3600 CtrT 46140 2236 C1
8500 INPS 46256 2014 A5
9600 GfdT 46168 2551 B4
9700 ZNVL 46077 1898 E2
9700 ZNVL 46077 1899 A2
Lakewood Dr E
9800 CRML 46280 2011 D2
Lakewood Dr N
2700 CRML 46033 2011 C1
2700 CRML 46280 2011 C1
Lakewood Dr W
9800 CRML 46280 2011 C2
Lakewood Tr
4000 LtyT 46118 2549 A1
Lakewood North Dr
1000 BNBG 46112 2223 D1
Lakewood South Dr
1000 BNBG 46112 2223 D1
Lakewood Trails Ct
5400 LtyT 46118 2549 A1
Lakeworth Dr
6700 INPS 46220 2121 C2
Lalista Ct
5400 INPS 46254 2117 C5
Lamana Pl
13100 CRML 46074 1900 A2
Lamarque Pl
12900 FSHR 46038 1905 B3
Lambdin Ct
2800 INPS 46268 2118 C2
Lambert Ct
10 BrnT 46158 2659 A6
8800 FSHR 46060 1795 D7
Lambert Ln
- MdnT 46113 2661 A1
10 INPS 46113 2660 E1
10 MdnT 46113 2660 E1
Lambert St
1500 INPS 46221 2336 C6
3400 INPS 46241 2336 B6
6700 INPS 46241 2334 E6
W Lambert St
5600 INPS 46241 2335 B6
Lambeth Ct
9100 INPS 46278 2007 B3
Lambeth Wk
4600 CRML 46033 1902 E4
4700 CRML 46033 1903 A4
Lamboll St
12800 FSHR 46038 1904 E3
Lamira Ln
8300 INPS 46234 2225 B6
Lammermoor Cir
2300 INPS 46214 2225 B6
Lammermoor Ln
2200 INPS 46214 2225 B6
Lamong Rd
- SRDN 46069 1573 D4
19300 WshT 46069 1682 D2
20600 WshT 46069 1573 D7
21100 AdmT 46069 1573 D7
Lamplite Ct
- GNFD 46140 2236 D6
Lamsgate Dr
- WTFD 46074 1792 D4
S Lana Ct
5600 INPS 46239 2450 B7

INDEX 31

Lana Ct E — Indianapolis Street Index — E Lincoln Dr

STREET Block City ZIP Map# Grid

Lana Ct E
6500 SCkT 46163 2342 C3
Lana Ct W
6600 SCkT 46163 2342 C4
Lanarkshire Dr
1700 WRvT 46143 2664 A7
Lancashire Ct
1400 INPS 46260 2009 E5
Lancaster Cir
11800 CRML 46033 1902 E5
Lancaster Ct
1600 INPS 46260 2009 E4
Lancaster Ln
1400 ZNVL 46077 1898 E5
Lancaster Pl
- EglT 46077 1897 C6
Lancaster Rd
8600 INPS 46260 2009 E4
Lance Dr
- CRML 46074 1900 B2
Lancelot Dr
5100 INPS 46228 2118 C7
Lancelot Ln
12300 CRML 46033 1902 E3
Lancer Ln
7600 LWNC 46226 2122 A5
Lancet Ln
6900 INPS 46220 2119 D2
Landau Ln
7600 INPS 46227 2555 D5
Landborough North Dr
6200 INPS 46220 2121 D2
Landborough South Dr
6200 INPS 46220 2121 D2
Lander Dr
- WshT 46234 2224 C6
N Landersdale Ln
- MdnT 46158 2660 D3
Landersdale Rd
200 MdnT 46113 2660 D3
200 MdnT 46158 2660 D3
900 MdnT 46113 2661 A3
2100 MdnT 46113 2662 A3
Landings Cir
- INPS 46240 2011 B7
Landings Dr
7800 INPS 46240 2011 B6
11700 FCkT 46256 2014 E2
Landmark Dr
1900 INPS 46260 2009 D7
Landmark Tr
12300 FSHR 46038 1905 B4
Landola Ln
2800 INPS 46241 2444 C3
Landover Ln
12000 FSHR 46038 2014 E1
Landrum Cir
19500 NBVL 46062 1685 D3
Landsborough Ln
- CRML 46032 1900 C4
Lands End Cir
7100 NBVL 46062 1577 A7
Lands End Ln
6200 INPS 46220 2121 D2
Landser Ct
13500 CRML 46033 1902 E1
Landser Pl
13500 CRML 46033 1902 E1
Landwood Dr
11900 FSHR 46038 1906 C5
W Lane Rd
7200 BCkT 46055 2123 E6
7200 BCkT 46055 2124 A6
Lanett Ct
1300 BHGV 46107 2447 E6
Langham Cres
11600 FSHR 46038 1906 E5
Langham Wy
7900 INPS 46259 2558 B4
Langley Av
2000 INPS 46218 2229 A7
Langley Ct
13700 CRML 46032 1901 D2
Langley Dr
13700 CRML 46032 1901 E1
13700 CRML 46032 1902 A1
Langsdale Av
500 INPS 46202 2228 B6
Langston Dr
3700 INPS 46268 2009 A7
Langwood Ct
4100 INPS 46268 2009 B6
Langwood Dr
7700 INPS 46268 2009 A7
Lansdowne Ct
8600 INPS 46234 2334 A2
Lansdowne Dr
100 NBVL 46060 1795 E3
8500 FSHR 46038 1904 C3
Lansdowne Ln
10 CRML 46033 1902 C2
Lansdowne Rd
10 INPS 46234 2334 A3
Lansing Pl
14300 FSHR 46060 1795 D7
14400 FCkT 46060 1795 D7
Lansing St
300 INPS 46202 2336 E3
Lantern Ct
10 GNFD 46140 2236 D6
Lantern Ct S
10000 WshT 46234 2224 D6
Lantern Dr
4600 WRvT 46142 2663 D2
Lantern Ln
10 CRML 46032 1901 E3
8800 INPS 46256 2122 D1
Lantern Rd
- FSHR 46038 1904 C7
7700 INPS 46256 2013 D7
9600 FSHR 46038 2013 D2
9600 INPS 46038 2013 D2
11900 FCkT 46038 1904 D4
13100 DelT 46038 1904 D3

N Lantern Rd
6900 INPS 46256 2122 D1
7500 INPS 46256 2013 C7
Lantern Farms Dr
8500 FSHR 46038 1904 C3
Lantern Forest Ct
8700 INPS 46256 2122 C1
Lanterns Ct
10000 WshT 46234 2224 E6
Lantern View Dr
10800 FSHR 46038 1904 C7
Lantern Woods Blvd
- FSHR 46038 1904 C7
Lantry Ct
3600 INPS 46227 2556 D4
Lanyard Ct
900 CCRO 46034 1577 B3
N Lanyard Dr
800 CCRO 46034 1577 B3
S Lanyard Dr
800 CCRO 46034 1577 B3
La Paloma Ct
16300 NBVL 46060 1796 C3
La Pas Tr
6200 INPS 46268 2117 E3
Lapinta Dr
5400 LWNC 46236 2122 E6
La Placita St
600 GNWD 46143 2665 E4
Lappin Ct
2100 INPS 46229 2232 B6
Laramie Dr
6200 INPS 46237 2557 C6
Larch St
1100 INPS 46201 2338 A1
Laredo Ct
14700 WshT 46032 1792 C6
Laredo Dr
- MCVL 46055 2124 B1
5000 INPS 46237 2448 B7
13700 CRML 46032 1792 E7
13700 CRML 46032 1793 A7
13700 CRML 46032 1901 E1
Laredo Wy
100 WshT 46032 1792 C6
Laredo Wy N
10 WshT 46032 1792 C6
Laredo Wy S
100 WshT 46032 1792 D6
La Reforma Ct
400 GNWD 46143 2665 D4
La Reforma Dr
400 GNWD 46143 2665 D4
Largo Dr
12500 FSHR 46038 1906 B4
Larissa Pl
5400 CRML 46033 1903 C4
Lark Ct
400 CRML 46032 1902 A2
Lark Dr
100 CRML 46032 1902 A2
Larkfield Ct
1800 INPS 46260 2009 E6
Larkshall Rd
7100 INPS 46250 2121 D1
Larkspur Cir
1000 CRML 46033 1902 C3
Larkspur Ct
200 UnnT 46077 1790 B6
Larkspur Dr
7600 WshT 46123 2223 D7
Larkspur Ln
3500 ClyT 46032 1900 B6
Larkspur Trc
- INPS 46237 2447 D5
Larkwood Ct
6600 INPS 46241 2334 E4
Larman Ct
8100 INPS 46227 2556 B6
Larman Dr
2500 INPS 46227 2556 B6
Larnie Ln
2300 INPS 46219 2231 C6
E Larrabee St
10 NPLN 46163 2452 B4
W Larrabee St
10 NPLN 46163 2452 A3
Larwin Ct
- WshT 46234 2224 E6
La Salle Ct
3900 INPS 46205 2229 C2
Lasalle Ct
10 WTLD 46184 2775 A7
Lasalle Ln
- PTBR 46167 2113 B4
Lasalle Rd
10400 CRML 46033 2011 D1
10500 CRML 46033 1902 D7
La Salle St
2500 INPS 46218 2229 C5
4200 INPS 46205 2229 C1
4500 INPS 46205 2120 C7
N La Salle St
- INPS 46205 2229 C2
N Lasalle St
10 INPS 46201 2338 C3
1400 INPS 46201 2229 D7
5800 INPS 46220 2120 C4
7500 INPS 46240 2011 D7
S La Salle St
1900 INPS 46203 2338 C7
5000 INPS 46227 2447 C7
S Lasalle St
10 INPS 46201 2338 C3
3700 INPS 46237 2447 C4
Lasso Dr
9800 LcnT 46112 2224 C3
9800 LcnT 46234 2224 C3
Latitude Wy
14700 FCkT 46040 1907 A6
Latitudes Dr
8800 INPS 46237 2557 D7
Latitudes Pl
6600 INPS 46237 2557 D7

Latitudes Wy
8800 INPS 46237 2557 D7
Latona Ct
6300 INPS 46278 2117 B3
Latona Dr
6600 INPS 46278 2117 B2
Latonia Ln
1000 ClyT 46280 1901 E7
10800 ClyT 46280 1902 A7
11000 CRML 46280 1902 A7
La Tour Cir
6700 INPS 46278 2007 E7
Latrobe Ct
11800 FSHR 46038 1905 E3
Latta Dr
10 MNVA 46157 2657 C7
Lattice Ct
3700 ClyT 46032 2009 A2
Lattice Dr
7300 INPS 46217 2554 E4
Lauck Ln
10 INPS 46227 2446 C4
Laughlin Dr
8000 INPS 46219 2231 B6
Laughner St
10 WTWN 46075 1788 C7
Laura Ct
1100 GNWD 46143 2665 C1
Laura Dr
1000 GNWD 46143 2665 C1
2700 CRML 46033 1793 C7
Laura Lynne Ln
8100 INPS 46217 2555 B6
Laura Vista Dr
14200 CRML 46033 1793 C7
Laureate Ct N
3500 INPS 46214 2225 B2
Laureate Ct S
3500 INPS 46214 2225 B2
Laurel Av
600 ZNVL 46077 1899 A6
Laurel Cir
4600 INPS 46226 2120 E7
Laurel Cir N
4700 INPS 46226 2120 E7
Laurel Cir S
4600 INPS 46226 2120 E7
Laurel Ct
8500 FSHR 46038 1904 C3
Laurel Dr
7000 INPS 46227 2555 E4
Laurel Ln
900 NBVL 46062 1685 D3
Laurel St
2000 INPS 46203 2337 E7
3200 INPS 46227 2446 E3
5500 INPS 46227 2555 E1
Laurel Cherry Ln
3600 INPS 46239 2449 B4
Laurel Falls Cir
8600 WshT 46123 2333 A1
Laurel Falls Ln
11100 FSHR 46038 1905 A6
Laurel Hall Dr
4800 INPS 46226 2121 A6
Laurel Lakes Blvd
2400 CRML 46032 1900 C4
Laurel Leaf Ln
2000 WshT 46123 2440 E1
Laurel Oak Dr
1000 AVON 46123 2332 A1
Laurel Oak Pl
- INPS 46254 2117 D5
Laurel Oaks Dr
11800 LWNC 46236 2123 E1
Laurel Valley Dr
10 BNBG 46112 2113 D4
8400 INPS 46250 2012 E5
Laurelwood
1000 ClyT 46032 2010 A1
1200 ClyT 46032 1901 A7
Laurelwood Ct
12200 LWNC 46236 2014 E7
12200 LWNC 46236 2015 A7
Laurel Wood Dr
700 WRvT 46143 2663 E5
Laurelwood Dr
12000 LWNC 46236 2014 E7
Lauren Dr
3300 INPS 46235 2232 D4
Lauren Kelsey Dr
- LWNC 46235 2122 E7
Lauren Pass
10100 FSHR 46038 2014 A2
Laurens Ct
700 INPS 46217 2555 A5
Laurey Ct
3500 INPS 46214 2225 C3
Lava Ct
6400 INPS 46237 2557 A2
Lava Ln
5200 INPS 46237 2557 A2
Lava Rock Ct
11800 FSHR 46038 1905 E4
Lavender Ct
7000 INPS 46237 2557 B3
Lavender Dr
8800 NBVL 46060 1795 D6
Laverne Rd
7800 INPS 46217 2555 B5
E Laverock Rd
700 INPS 46220 2119 D3
W Laverock Rd
10 INPS 46208 2119 C5
10 INPS 46220 2119 C5
Lavonnie Av
19600 NbvT 46062 1686 C3
Lawndale Av
- INPS 46241 2335 B5
N Lawndale Av
- INPS 46224 2226 B2
10 INPS 46224 2335 B3
2900 SDWY 46224 2226 B4
3800 INPS 46254 2226 B2

S Lawndale Av
1100 INPS 46241 2335 B5
6500 INPS 46221 2553 A3
Lawndale Ct
1000 GNWD 46142 2665 A2
Lawndale Dr
400 PNFD 46168 2441 D5
500 GNWD 46142 2665 A2
Lawnhaven Cir
10400 INPS 46229 2232 B7
Lawnhaven Ct
10100 INPS 46229 2232 A7
Lawnhaven Dr
10100 INPS 46229 2232 A7
Lawnview Ln
3400 INPS 46222 2227 B6
Lawnwood Ct
1900 INPS 46219 2231 C6
Lawnwood Dr
600 GNWD 46142 2665 A2
Lawrence Av
500 INPS 46227 2446 D5
1400 INPS 46227 2447 A5
8200 INPS 46239 2449 B5
E Lawrence Av
8200 INPS 46239 2449 B5
Lawrence Ct
2600 INPS 46227 2447 B5
Lawrence Dr
- DNVL 46122 2330 A3
5800 INPS 46226 2121 C5
Lawrence Rd
1200 CRML 46033 1902 D3
Lawrence St
1900 INPS 46218 2229 A7
Lawrence Cir East Dr
4100 INPS 46241 2444 B4
Lawrence Cir West Dr
4100 INPS 46241 2444 A5
Lawrence Woods Blvd
7900 LWNC 46236 2015 A6
Lawrence Woods Cir
- LWNC 46236 2015 A6
Lawrence Woods Ct
7900 LWNC 46236 2015 A6
Lawson Ct
- DNVL 46122 2329 C5
Lawson Ln
- WRvT 46142 2663 C2
Lawton Av
10 DNVL 46122 2329 D3
Lawton Dr
- LWNC 46216 2122 C5
Lawton St
1200 INPS 46203 2337 E7
1400 INPS 46203 2338 A7
N Layman Av
800 INPS 46219 2339 B2
3400 INPS 46218 2230 B3
3800 INPS 46226 2230 B2
7100 INPS 46250 2121 B1
S Layman Av
2000 INPS 46203 2339 B7
N Layton Mills Ct
- MdnT 46113 2661 B1
Layton Park Dr
2200 INPS 46239 2340 B7
2200 INPS 46239 2449 B1
Lazy Ln
500 WRvT 46142 2664 B2
6000 INPS 46239 2558 A2
Lazy Hollow Dr
200 BNBG 46112 2114 D7
Lazy Hollow Ln
400 CRML 46032 1792 C7
Lea Ln
300 GNWD 46142 2664 D4
Leaf Dr
2200 INPS 46229 2232 C6
Leaf Ln
- WshT 46123 2440 E1
Leafy Branch Tr
400 CRML 46032 1902 A1
Leah Ln
- FSHR 46060 1906 E3
Leah Wy
500 GNWD 46142 2664 E4
Leander Ln
11300 INPS 46236 2014 D6
Leaning Tree Rd
10 WRvT 46142 2663 D3
Leanna Ct
7600 MdlT 46112 2113 C2
Leases Corner Dr
- GfdT 46168 2660 C1
Leatherbury Ln
3300 INPS 46222 2227 B3
Leatherwood Dr
400 DNVL 46122 2330 B2
700 GNWD 46143 2665 A5
13800 CRML 46033 1903 D1
N Lebanon St
100 LEBN 46052 1676 E3
2400 CtrT 46052 1676 E3
N Lebanon St SR-39
100 LEBN 46052 1676 E3
2400 CtrT 46052 1676 E3
S Lebanon St
- CtrT 46052 1785 E2
100 LEBN 46052 1676 E7
1200 LEBN 46052 1785 E2
S Lebanon St SR-32
100 LEBN 46052 1676 E7
S Lebanon St SR-39
- CtrT 46052 1785 E2
100 LEBN 46052 1676 E7
1200 LEBN 46052 1785 E2
Ledgerock Ct
11700 FSHR 46038 1906 A5
Ledgestone Cir
11700 FSHR 46038 1906 A5
Ledgestone Ct
6100 LWNC 46236 2123 B3
Ledgestone Dr
10300 LWNC 46236 2123 B3

Ledgewood Ct
1100 WshT 46123 2331 C2
Ledgewood Rd
1200 WshT 46123 2331 C1
Ledgewood Wy
14100 CRML 46032 1792 A7
Ledyard Ct
8300 INPS 46256 2013 E5
Lee Ct
2400 CCRO 46034 1577 B5
8300 LWNC 46226 2122 C6
Lee Dr
2100 INPS 46227 2556 B5
Lee Rd
200 LWNC 46216 2122 E4
6200 LWNC 46236 2122 E3
Lee St
1100 INPS 46221 2336 D6
Leeds Av
200 INPS 46201 2338 B4
500 INPS 46203 2338 B5
Leeds Cir
400 CRML 46032 1901 B3
Leeds Ct
100 ZNVL 46077 1899 A4
Leedy St
400 DNVL 46122 2329 E3
Leesburg Pl
700 WshT 46074 1792 B5
Lee Stewart Ln
14400 FSHR 46060 1796 B7
Leeward Blvd
9800 INPS 46256 2014 A3
Leeward Cir
9100 INPS 46256 2014 A3
Leeward Ct
9400 INPS 46256 2014 B3
Leewood Ct
12200 NBVL 46060 1797 A1
Leffler Dr
300 INPS 46231 2334 A4
Leffler Ln
8900 INPS 46231 2334 A4
Leftus Ct
3300 INPS 46268 2118 B3
Legacy Blvd
- GNWD 46143 2666 D4
Legacy Ct
1300 WshT 46234 2333 D1
8500 FSHR 46038 1904 C6
Legacy Ln
200 CRML 46032 1902 A2
1200 WshT 46234 2333 D1
Legare St
9600 FSHR 46038 1904 E4
Legend Ct
10 CCRO 46034 1577 B2
Legend Ln
6300 INPS 46254 2226 A1
Legends Creek Dr
9800 INPS 46229 2341 A3
Legends Creek Pl
200 INPS 46229 2341 A3
Legion Ln
8600 INPS 46231 2334 A5
Le Grande Av
10 INPS 46225 2337 C7
500 INPS 46203 2337 D7
1500 INPS 46203 2338 A7
4700 INPS 46241 2335 C7
Le Havre Dr
6100 INPS 46220 2120 E4
Lehigh Ct
3000 INPS 46268 2009 B3
Lehr St
16600 WynT 46060 1797 D2
Leichester Ct
100 NbvT 46060 1795 D6
Leighton Ct
- CRML 46032 1900 D4
Leisure Ct
500 WRvT 46142 2664 B2
Leisure Ln
300 WRvT 46142 2664 B3
1100 WRvT 46217 2664 A1
5900 MdlT 46167 2112 E6
Leisure Mnr
4700 INPS 46241 2444 D2
Leiters Ct
- MdnT 46113 2661 C1
Leith Ct
2200 INPS 46214 2225 C6
N Leland Av
700 INPS 46219 2339 A1
1300 INPS 46219 2230 A7
3400 INPS 46218 2230 A3
S Leland Av
1200 INPS 46203 2339 A6
Leland Museum
14300 FSHR 46038 1906 E5
Lema Cir
2200 INPS 46229 2232 B6
Lema Ct
2100 INPS 46229 2232 B6
Lemans Ct
1200 INPS 46205 2119 E7
1200 INPS 46205 2120 A7
Lemans Dr
4900 INPS 46205 2119 E7
Lemar Ln
9200 INPS 46234 2333 E2
Lemode Ct
8700 INPS 46268 2009 B4
Lemond Dr
- CRML 46032 1792 A7
Lemongrass Dr
- ClyT 46032 1899 E7
Lemongrass Ln
7700 INPS 46227 2556 A5
Lemont St
11200 INPS 46259 2559 C5
Lena Ln
200 CRML 46032 1901 D3
Lendsmith Cir
6300 INPS 46268 2118 C3

Lenna Ct
8500 INPS 46226 2231 C1
Lennington Dr
6200 INPS 46226 2230 D2
Lenora St
10 INPS 46231 2334 D4
Lenox Ln
900 CRML 46032 1901 E5
8200 INPS 46268 2009 C5
Lenwood St
9600 FSHR 46038 1904 E4
Leo Dr
11000 INPS 46235 2232 C2
Leon St
500 INPS 46204 2337 D2
Leonainie Ct
100 GNFD 46140 2345 D3
S Leonard Rd
3100 SCkT 46163 2343 A7
3200 SCkT 46163 2452 A1
Leonard St
1000 INPS 46203 2337 E5
Leone Ct
5500 INPS 46226 2121 D6
Leone Dr
4700 LWNC 46226 2121 E7
5200 INPS 46226 2121 D6
Leone Pl
5200 INPS 46226 2121 D6
Leota St
300 INPS 46202 2337 E4
400 INPS 46201 2337 E4
400 INPS 46203 2337 E4
Lepart Ct
8600 INPS 46278 2008 A4
Leroy Rd
9200 LcnT 46112 2224 B4
Le Sabre Dr
3800 INPS 46254 2226 D2
Lesley Av
7200 INPS 46250 2121 B1
N Lesley Av
800 INPS 46219 2339 B1
3400 INPS 46218 2230 B3
4200 INPS 46226 2230 B1
4400 INPS 46226 2121 B7
Lesley Ln
8800 BrnT 46112 2006 D7
Leslie Ct
3900 FKLN 46131 2774 E7
Lesta Ct
7000 INPS 46217 2554 D4
Lester St
5100 INPS 46208 2119 B6
Letterman Av
1400 LWNC 46216 2123 A5
E Levi Ln
400 BrnT 46158 2658 E4
Lewis Dr
100 GNWD 46142 2665 C1
Lewis Rd
7700 INPS 46256 2122 B2
Lewis St
300 PNFD 46168 2441 A6
1100 INPS 46202 2337 E1
1500 INPS 46202 2228 E7
Lewiston Dr
- WshT 46074 1792 A5
4900 INPS 46254 2117 D7
Lexi Ln
11000 FCkT 46040 1907 A6
Lexington Av
- INPS 46203 2339 A5
500 INPS 46203 2337 D4
4300 INPS 46203 2338 E5
5100 INPS 46219 2339 A5
9000 INPS 46239 2340 D5
Lexington Blvd
10 CRML 46032 1902 B3
Lexington Cir
6700 EglT 46077 1897 D7
Lexington Ct
100 ZNVL 46077 1898 E6
Lexington Dr
10 ZNVL 46077 1898 E6
10600 ClyT 46280 1901 E6
10800 CRML 46280 1901 E6
Lexington Ln
3700 CRML 46033 1902 E7
Lexington Tr
- CtrT 46140 2237 A6
1200 GNFD 46140 2237 A6
Liberty
- GNWD 46143 2666 A7
Liberty Blvd
400 WshT 46074 1792 C5
Liberty Dr
600 WshT 46074 1792 A5
1000 WshT 46234 2333 D1
4700 INPS 46241 2444 D3
Liberty Ln
8100 GfdT 46158 2550 D6
N Liberty Ln
200 GNFD 46140 2345 A1
400 GNFD 46140 2236 A7
W Liberty Ln
2100 GNFD 46140 2345 A1
Liberty Tr
2600 PNFD 46168 2441 D2
Liberty Blvd Pl
- INPS 46220 2120 A6
E Liberty Creek Dr
5600 INPS 46254 2117 C5
W Liberty Creek Dr
5600 INPS 46254 2117 B5
Liberty Creek Dr N
5800 INPS 46254 2117 B5
Liberty Creek Pkwy
5600 INPS 46254 2117 B5
Liberty Meadows Rd
100 LtyT 46168 2440 C4
100 WshT 46122 2440 C4
100 WshT 46168 2440 C4
Liberty Mills Dr
8600 INPS 46113 2552 A7

Liberty View Ct
10 GNFD 46140 2345 A1
Libra Ln
3800 INPS 46235 2232 C2
Library Blvd
1600 GNWD 46142 2664 C4
Library Plz
10 NBVL 46060 1687 A7
Library Park Dr
600 GNWD 46142 2664 C5
S Lichtenburg Rd
1100 INPS 46239 2340 E6
Lick Creek Blvd
400 INPS 46227 2446 D6
8300 INPS 46219 2340 C1
Lick Creek Cir
4700 INPS 46227 2447 B7
Lick Creek Ct
4700 INPS 46227 2447 A6
Lick Creek Dr
2000 INPS 46203 2339 B7
Lick Creek Pkwy South Dr
1400 INPS 46227 2446 E6
1400 INPS 46227 2447 B7
Lickridge Ct
4400 INPS 46237 2447 D5
Lickridge Ln
- CtrT 46122 2330 D6
3000 CtrT 46122 2439 C3
3000 LtyT 46122 2439 C3
Lickridge Ln North Dr
3700 INPS 46237 2447 D5
Lickridge Ln South Dr
3700 INPS 46237 2447 D5
S Lida Ln
5900 INPS 46239 2558 C1
Lieber Rd
5600 INPS 46228 2119 A5
7600 INPS 46260 2010 A7
Lighthorse Dr
8400 INPS 46231 2334 A4
Lighthouse Pt
1300 CCRO 46034 1577 B4
Lighthouse Wy
9400 INPS 46256 2014 B3
9500 FSHR 46256 2014 B3
Lightning Bug Wy
- WRvT 46143 2663 B6
Lightship Ct
- FSHR 46038 1904 A7
Lilac Cir
100 WRvT 46142 2663 E3
Lilac Ct
100 NBVL 46062 1685 C1
E Lilac Dr
1700 INPS 46227 2556 A7
W Lilac Ln
5000 SCkT 46163 2343 A4
5200 SCkT 46163 2342 E4
S Lillian Ct
4300 SCkT 46163 2451 A3
Lillians Ct
6500 INPS 46237 2557 B3
Lilly Lake Dr
6300 INPS 46278 2116 D3
Lilly Lake Tr
- INPS 46278 2116 D3
Lily Ct
- ZNVL 46077 1898 C1
S Lily Ct
1400 CtrT 46140 2344 C3
Lily Ln
4900 INPS 46254 2117 D6
N Lily Dale Ct
13900 MdnT 46113 2661 A1
Lily Pad Ln
5200 INPS 46237 2448 E7
Lima Ct
3600 INPS 46227 2556 D6
Lima East Dr
8100 INPS 46227 2556 D6
Lima North Dr
3700 INPS 46227 2556 D6
Limbach Cir
11000 LWNC 46236 2014 C7
Limbach Ct
10900 LWNC 46236 2014 C7
Limberlost Ct
8700 INPS 46113 2552 A7
Limberlost Dr
12600 CRML 46033 1903 A3
Limberlost Trc
4900 CRML 46033 1903 A2
Limberpine Dr
3600 INPS 46235 2232 B3
Limehouse St
1800 CRML 46032 1900 E3
Limerick Ct
6700 INPS 46250 2012 E3
Limestone Ct
5200 INPS 46237 2557 A2
Limestone Dr
6100 INPS 46237 2557 A2
12000 FSHR 46038 1906 A4
N Limestone St
300 INPS 46202 2336 E4
Lin Rd
15600 FCkT 46040 1907 B7
Lincoln Av
10 BNBG 46112 2114 C7
Lincoln Blvd
7900 INPS 46240 2011 B6
9600 ClyT 46280 2011 B2
N Lincoln Blvd
7900 INPS 46240 2011 B6
Lincoln Ct
10 CRML 46032 1902 B3
3200 INPS 46228 2118 B7
8500 FSHR 46038 1904 C6
Lincoln Dr
10 BNBG 46112 2114 C7
2300 CCRO 46034 1577 B5
E Lincoln Dr
1200 NBVL 46060 1686 D6

INDEX 32
Lincoln Ln
Lyric Dr

Indianapolis Street Index

STREET Block City ZIP Map# Grid

Lincoln Ln
10 MRVL 46158 2659 E3
W Lincoln Ln
2500 INPS 46228 2118 C4
Lincoln Rd
1600 SDWY 46224 2226 B7
3000 INPS 46222 2227 B4
4300 INPS 46228 2227 B1
4500 INPS 46228 2118 B7
Lincoln St
- GNWD 46142 2665 C4
100 PNFD 46168 2441 A4
200 INPS 46225 2337 D6
500 INPS 46203 2337 D6
E Lincoln St
10 DNVL 46122 2329 D5
10 GNFD 46140 2345 E1
100 PNFD 46168 2441 B4
800 GNFD 46140 2346 A1
N Lincoln St
10 GNFD 46140 2345 E2
10 GNFD 46140 2346 A1
W Lincoln St
10 DNVL 46122 2329 D5
W Lincoln St SR-39
200 DNVL 46122 2329 D5
Lincoln Tr
7600 PNFD 46168 2550 C2
11000 LWNC 46236 2123 C3
W Lincolncreek Cir
8800 INPS 46234 2225 A2
Lincoln Park Blvd
1200 GNWD 46142 2664 E1
Lincoln Park East Dr
900 GNWD 46142 2664 E1
Lincoln Park West Dr
800 GNWD 46142 2664 E1
Lincolnshire Blvd
3100 CRML 46074 1900 B2
Lincoln Trails Cir
11100 LWNC 46236 2123 C3
Lincolnwood Ln
800 INPS 46260 2119 A2
Linda Cir
9100 INPS 46239 2340 D6
Linda Ct
10500 WshT 46234 2224 D7
Linda Dr
- MdnT 46158 2660 D4
Linda Ln
6100 INPS 46241 2335 A4
Linda Wy
5200 WRvT 46142 2663 C2
17000 NBVL 46062 1794 B1
Linda Leigh Ln
8100 INPS 46217 2555 B6
Lindbergh Ct
- INPS 46237 2447 D6
Lindbergh Dr
2400 INPS 46227 2447 B6
3300 INPS 46237 2447 D6
E Lindbergh Dr
8400 INPS 46239 2449 C6
Lindel Ct
6800 INPS 46268 2118 B2
Lindel Ln
3200 INPS 46268 2118 B2
Linden Cir
1000 NBVL 46062 1685 D3
Linden Ct
7500 FSHR 46038 1904 B7
Linden Dr
6300 INPS 46227 2555 E2
Linden Ln
200 PNFD 46168 2441 D4
200 SRDN 46069 1573 C1
800 CRML 46033 1902 D1
Linden St
300 ZNVL 46077 1899 B5
1100 INPS 46203 2337 E6
3300 INPS 46227 2446 E4
Linden Wy
1000 WshT 46234 2333 D1
Linden Hill Cir
500 INPS 46224 2335 D2
Linden Ridge Tr
300 WRvT 46142 2663 D3
Lindenwald Dr
100 INPS 46217 2446 C3
Lindenwood Dr
7100 INPS 46227 2555 D4
Lindenwood St
600 GNWD 46142 2665 A2
Lindley Av
300 INPS 46241 2335 B4
S Lindley Av
1600 INPS 46241 2335 B6
Lindley Dr
12100 NBVL 46060 1796 E7
12100 NBVL 46060 1797 A7
Lindsay Ct
400 INPS 46214 2334 D2
Lindsay Dr
7400 INPS 46214 2334 C2
Lindsey Ct
- NBVL 46060 1686 E5
8700 FSHR 46060 1795 D7
Lindsey Ln
1300 LEBN 46052 1676 D4
Links Ln
- NBVL 46062 1686 B4
Link Side Ct
3500 ClyT 46032 2009 B2
Linkwood Cir
6200 LWNC 46236 2123 A3
Linn Ct
14600 WshT 46074 1792 B6
Linsburgh Cir
9200 INPS 46234 2224 E3
Linsburgh Ct
9100 INPS 46234 2224 E3
Linton Ln
4300 INPS 46226 2229 E1
4600 INPS 46226 2120 E7
5700 INPS 46220 2121 A4
Linville Av
500 WTWN 46075 1788 D6
Linville St
200 WTWN 46075 1788 D6
N Linwood Av
10 INPS 46201 2338 E2
3500 INPS 46218 2229 E3
S Linwood Av
10 INPS 46201 2338 E3
5200 INPS 46237 2447 E7
5800 INPS 46237 2556 E1
Linwood Ct
4400 INPS 46201 2338 E2
Linwood Dr
5600 INPS 46220 2120 E5
Lions Creek Blvd
10 NBVL 46062 1576 C7
Lions Creek Cir
200 NBVL 46062 1576 C7
Lions Creek Ct N
10 NBVL 46062 1576 C7
Lions Creek Ct S
10 NBVL 46062 1576 C7
Lions Creek Dr
500 NBVL 46062 1576 D6
N Lions Head Dr
7300 INPS 46260 2119 B1
7400 INPS 46260 2010 B7
Lions Head Ln
600 INPS 46260 2119 B1
800 WRvT 46143 2664 A5
Lions Wood Dr
1000 CCRO 46034 1577 B3
Lippan Wy
5400 INPS 46221 2553 B3
N Lippard Ln
3200 INPS 46234 2225 A4
Lippincott Wy
7400 INPS 46268 2009 A7
Liquori Ct
7400 INPS 46214 2225 D7
Lisa Cir
3500 INPS 46235 2232 D3
Lisa Ct
11100 INPS 46235 2232 D4
Lisa Ln
300 GfdT 46168 2440 E4
Liscannor Ln
7300 INPS 46217 2554 D4
Lisering Cir
8900 INPS 46256 2013 B4
Lismore Ln
1000 INPS 46227 2555 E6
Lismore East Dr
8300 INPS 46227 2555 E6
Lismore North Dr
900 INPS 46227 2555 E6
Lismore South Dr
900 INPS 46227 2555 E7
Lismore West Dr
8300 INPS 46227 2555 E6
Litchfield Pl
- FSHR 46060 1905 D1
Little Chicago Rd
17600 NBVL 46062 1685 C7
17600 NbvT 46062 1685 C7
21100 NBVL 46062 1576 C7
Little Cir Rd
8000 NBVL 46060 1686 B5
Little Creek Ct
5300 INPS 46254 2117 C5
Little Creek Dr
5700 INPS 46254 2117 C5
20200 NBVL 46062 1685 B2
20300 NbvT 46062 1685 B2
Little Eagle Ct
8300 INPS 46234 2334 B1
Little Eagle Dr
600 NbvT 46060 1796 A3
Little Eagle Creek Av
3000 EglT 46077 1790 C7
14300 CRML 46074 1790 E6
14300 CRML 46077 1790 E6
14600 WshT 46074 1790 E6
14600 WshT 46074 1791 A5
14600 WshT 46077 1790 E6
14600 WshT 46077 1791 A5
17200 WshT 46074 1682 D7
Little John Dr
7600 INPS 46219 2231 A7
Little Leaf Cir
4300 INPS 46203 2448 D5
Little Leaf Ct
4300 INPS 46203 2448 D5
Little Leaf Pl
6600 INPS 46203 2448 D5
E Little League Dr
9700 INPS 46235 2232 A1
S Little Oak Ln
7300 INPS 46259 2559 B4
Little Piney Dr
1300 INPS 46227 2446 E6
1300 INPS 46227 2447 A6
Little Piney Wy
1300 INPS 46227 2446 E6
1300 INPS 46227 2447 A6
Little River Ln
8000 INPS 46239 2558 B1
Little Rock Ct
11400 FSHR 46038 1906 B6
Littleton Dr
6700 INPS 46221 2553 B3
Littleton Pl
11500 FCkT 46040 1906 E5
Live Oak Ct
1800 WshT 46123 2331 E7
6700 INPS 46214 2225 E4
Live Oak Rd
6600 INPS 46214 2225 E3
Liverpool Dr
- ClyT 46032 1901 C7
Liverpool Ln
6000 LWNC 46236 2123 B4
Liverpool Wy
5900 LWNC 46236 2123 A4
N Livingston Av
1100 INPS 46222 2336 A1
1600 INPS 46222 2227 A7
S Livingston Av
400 INPS 46241 2336 A4
Lizton Ct
300 INPS 46231 2334 A4
E Lloyd St
4100 INPS 46239 2449 D5
Llyod Peterson Ln
- INPS 46202 2336 E1
Loam Ct
8300 INPS 46237 2557 E6
Lobo Dr
5300 INPS 46237 2448 B7
Loch Cir
- NBVL 46060 1796 E2
16900 NBVL 46060 1797 A2
Lochmere Dr
5300 CRML 46033 1903 D3
Loch Raven Blvd
11100 FSHR 46038 1906 B6
Loch Raven Ct
11500 FSHR 46038 1906 B5
Lockburn Pl
13000 FSHR 46038 1904 C2
S Lockburn St
300 INPS 46241 2336 A4
2400 INPS 46241 2445 A2
3000 INPS 46221 2445 A3
Lockefield Ct
700 INPS 46202 2337 A2
Lockefield Ln
700 INPS 46202 2337 A2
Lockefield St
700 INPS 46202 2337 A2
Lockerbie Cir
12600 CRML 46033 1902 E3
Lockerbie Cir N
500 INPS 46202 2337 B6
Lockerbie Cir S
500 INPS 46202 2337 B6
Lockerbie Ct
4400 CRML 46033 1902 E3
W Lockerbie Dr
6800 INPS 46214 2334 D3
8500 INPS 46234 2334 B3
Lockerbie Ln
200 PTBR 46167 2113 A4
12600 FSHR 46038 1905 A4
Lockerbie Pl
- CRML 46032 1901 E1
- CRML 46032 1902 A1
Lockerbie St
300 MRVL 46158 2659 D4
500 INPS 46202 2337 B6
Lockley Pl
12700 FSHR 46038 1905 B3
Lockport Dr
- WshT 46074 1792 A5
Lockwood Ct
100 INPS 46217 2555 B4
Lockwood Dr
3600 WTFD 46033 1793 D6
Lockwood Ln
6000 INPS 46217 2555 B2
Lockwood Pl N
8500 INPS 46217 2555 B7
Locus Ln
11800 NBVL 46060 1796 E4
Locust Cir
2800 INPS 46227 2556 C2
Locust Ct
10 NWTD 46184 2774 D3
Locust Dr
1500 PNFD 46168 2441 E4
2800 INPS 46227 2556 C2
Locust Ln
- SgCT 46126 2670 D7
200 MRVL 46158 2659 E2
S Locust Ln
500 BNBG 46112 2223 B2
1100 LcnT 46112 2223 B2
Locust St
- NPLN 46163 2452 A3
- ZNVL 46077 1899 B6
Locust Grove Dr
6500 INPS 46237 2557 D6
Locust Grove Ln
- GNWD 46143 2665 B7
Lodge Ct
10800 WshT 46231 2333 E5
Lodge Dr
400 WshT 46231 2333 E5
900 INPS 46231 2333 E5
Lodge St
- PTBR 46167 2112 E3
Lodgepole Dr
- GNWD 46184 2774 B2
Lodge Tree Cove
1600 CRML 46280 2011 A2
Loews Blvd
- GNWD 46142 2665 A1
Loew's Blvd
700 GNWD 46142 2665 A1
Lofton Ct
7800 INPS 46239 2340 B7
Logan Ln
9700 FSHR 46038 2013 D2
E Logan St
1000 BNBG 46112 2223 D1
1000 NBVL 46060 1686 D7
W Logan St
- NBVL 46062 1686 B7
10 NBVL 46060 1686 C7
S Loganberry Ct
3900 NPLN 46163 2452 A2
Loganberry Ln
9600 INPS 46256 2013 E6
9700 INPS 46256 2014 A6
Logan's Ct
23900 WRvT 46034 1578 E1
Loggia Dr
6100 INPS 46237 2448 C7
Loggia Pl
5400 INPS 46237 2448 C7
Loggia Wy
5400 INPS 46237 2448 C7
Logo Athletic Ct
8600 INPS 46219 2231 C5
Log Run Dr N
8600 INPS 46234 2225 A2
Log Run Dr S
8600 INPS 46234 2225 A2
W Log Run South Dr
9100 INPS 46234 2224 E2
9100 INPS 46234 2225 A2
Logwood Ct
9900 ClyT 46280 2011 B1
Logwood Dr
600 INPS 46227 2555 D7
Lohr Dr
2000 INPS 46214 2225 E7
Lohr Wy
6900 INPS 46214 2225 E7
Lois Ln
4500 INPS 46237 2447 E7
Lois Wy
400 CRML 46032 1901 C1
Lois Marie Dr
100 INPS 46214 2335 A3
E Lola Ct
7700 INPS 46219 2340 B1
Loma Ct
7700 DelT 46038 2013 B1
7700 DelT 46256 2013 B1
7700 FSHR 46038 2013 B1
7700 FSHR 46256 2013 B1
Lomax Dr
- WshT 46123 2333 B2
Lombard Ct
13000 FSHR 46038 1904 C3
Lombardi Dr
400 WshT 46168 2441 C2
Lombardy Pl
3400 INPS 46226 2231 C3
Lomond Ct
3700 WRvT 46143 2664 A7
Londa Ln
9600 PNFD 46231 2442 D5
London Ct
4400 INPS 46254 2117 E7
London Dr
4600 INPS 46254 2117 E7
London Ln
- GNWD 46142 2665 A1
300 AVON 46123 2332 B3
N London Rd
4000 SgCT 46110 2669 B6
5000 SgCT 46126 2669 B6
6000 MrlT 46110 2669 B6
6000 MrlT 46126 2669 B6
Londonberry Blvd
- ClyT 46032 1900 C7
Londonbury Dr
4900 LcnT 46167 2113 C5
4900 MdlT 46167 2113 C5
Londonderry Ct
10 WshT 46123 2331 B4
4600 INPS 46221 2444 D5
Londonderry Dr
4100 INPS 46221 2444 D5
Londonerry Ln
1100 GNWD 46142 2665 A1
Lonestar Dr
6300 INPS 46237 2557 D6
Lone Wolf Dr
10000 INPS 46235 2123 A7
10000 INPS 46235 2232 A1
Long St
- WshT 46123 2333 A1
Long Acre Dr
1400 INPS 46227 2447 A6
Long Acre Ter
1600 INPS 46227 2447 B7
Long Acre Wy
- NbvT 46062 1685 A5
- WshT 46062 1685 A5
Long Boat Dr
7100 INPS 46250 2013 A3
Longboat Key Cir
6500 NBVL 46062 1685 D4
Long Branch Dr
7700 INPS 46259 2558 B5
Long Branch Ln
- ClyT 46077 1900 A5
- CRML 46077 1900 A5
Long Cove Blvd
15100 WTFD 46033 1793 E5
Long Cove Vw
- WTFD 46033 1793 E5
Long Creek Dr
17100 NBVL 46060 1796 E2
17100 NBVL 46060 1797 A1
Longden St
10 GNWD 46142 2665 C3
Longest Dr
7000 CRML 46033 1903 E2
7000 CRML 46033 1904 A3
Longfellow Ct
300 GNFD 46140 2345 D3
Longfellow Dr
800 PNFD 46168 2441 C6
Longfellow Ln
10 GNFD 46140 2345 D3
Longford Dr
10100 WshT 46231 2333 C6
Longford Wy
500 NBVL 46062 1685 E1
700 NBVL 46062 1576 E7
Long Gravel Ln
- BCkT 46140 2125 D5
Long Grove Ln
8100 DelT 46038 1795 C7
8100 DelT 46038 1904 C1
8100 DelT 46060 1795 C7
8100 DelT 46060 1904 C1
8100 FSHR 46038 1904 C1
8100 FSHR 46060 1904 C1
Longhorn Ct
6400 INPS 46237 2557 D6
Longhorn Wy
- INPS 46259 2558 A4
Longiron Dr
- LWNC 46235 2123 D6
Long Lake Dr
- GNWD 46143 2665 B7
Long Lake Ln
- FSHR 46038 1905 C4
Longleaf Dr
- GNWD 46143 2665 B7
- GNWD 46143 2774 B1
- GNWD 46184 2774 B1
Longleaf Ln
12600 FSHR 46038 1905 A3
Longleat Rd
7400 INPS 46240 2011 D7
7400 INPS 46240 2120 D1
Longley Dr
10 LEBN 46052 1786 A1
Long Meadow Ct
6600 INPS 46268 2117 E2
Longmeadow Ct
5100 INPS 46221 2553 C3
Long Meadow Dr
9900 FSHR 46060 1796 A7
9900 FSHR 46060 1905 A1
Longmeadow Dr
6100 INPS 46221 2553 C2
Long Ridge Pl
5600 INPS 46221 2552 E1
Long Rifle Rd
- WRvT 46142 2664 A1
Long River Ln
6000 INPS 46221 2553 C2
W Long Run
9100 INPS 46234 2224 E2
9100 INPS 46234 2225 A2
Long Run Dr
6500 INPS 46268 2117 E2
Long Shore Cir
7100 INPS 46217 2554 E4
Long Shore Dr
1200 INPS 46217 2554 E4
Longspur Ct
8600 INPS 46234 2225 A6
Longstone Roundabout
5200 CRML 46033 1794 A7
Longstraw Dr
12000 LWNC 46236 2014 E5
12200 LWNC 46236 2015 A6
Long Sutton Cir
- FCkT 46038 1905 D4
Longview Bnd
200 BNBG 46112 2114 D6
Longview Ct
10 BNBG 46112 2114 D7
Longview Dr
- MCVL 46055 2124 B2
5400 NBVL 46062 1685 B7
Long Walk Ct
8200 NBVL 46060 1686 C5
Long Walk Ln
18600 NBVL 46060 1686 B5
Longwell Dr
1100 CRML 46240 2010 E3
1100 INPS 46240 2010 E3
Longwell Pl
1000 INPS 46240 2010 E2
Long Wharf Dr
3600 INPS 46235 2232 B3
Long Wharf Sq
10500 INPS 46235 2232 B3
Longwood St
300 CRML 46032 1902 A3
Longwoods Cir
6600 INPS 46254 2116 D6
Longwoods Ct
5300 INPS 46254 2116 E6
Longwoods Dr
- INPS 46254 2116 E5
Longworth Av
- INPS 46226 2231 A4
N Longworth Av
4400 LWNC 46226 2231 A1
4600 LWNC 46226 2122 A7
Longworth Pl
5200 LWNC 46226 2122 A6
Lookout Ct
8300 INPS 46217 2554 D6
Lookout Ln
- WshT 46234 2224 D6
Lookout Pass
1200 DNVL 46122 2331 A4
Lord St
700 INPS 46202 2337 D4
Lorene Cir
6400 INPS 46237 2557 D4
Lorene Ct
7400 INPS 46237 2557 D4
Lorenzo Blvd
13100 CRML 46074 1900 C2
Loretta Ct
6600 HMCT 46227 2555 E3
6700 AVON 46123 2332 B3
E Loretta Dr
1100 HMCT 46227 2555 E3
1100 INPS 46227 2555 E3
1400 HMCT 46227 2556 A3
1900 INPS 46227 2556 B3
W Loretta Dr
10 INPS 46217 2555 C3
6000 INPS 46221 2553 A3
Lori Ln
3600 INPS 46226 2231 A3
Lori Ann Dr
200 WTLD 46184 2774 E4
200 WTLD 46184 2775 A4
Loring Ct
5100 INPS 46268 2117 C1
Lorrain Rd
3400 INPS 46220 2120 C6
Lorraine St
1800 INPS 46203 2339 A7
Lorton Cir
9500 INPS 46239 2340 E5
Los Robles Rd
8200 DelT 46038 1904 B2
Lost Oaks Dr
5800 CRML 46033 1903 E1
Lostpine Ln
10600 INPS 46235 2232 B2
Lost Tree Ct
6600 INPS 46268 2117 E2
Lost Tree Dr
4500 INPS 46268 2117 D2
Lost Tree Pl
- NBVL 46060 1796 D3
Lothbury Cir
10100 FSHR 46038 2014 E1
Lott Dr
6200 INPS 46268 2118 C3
Lotus Dr
100 CRML 46032 1793 B7
100 CRML 46032 1902 B1
Lotus Ln
2900 SPRT 46227 2556 C5
N Louann Dr
9600 MrlT 46126 2560 B4
Loudon Dr
5600 LWNC 46235 2123 C5
Loudon Ln
11200 LWNC 46235 2123 C5
Loudoun Pl
- FSHR 46038 1905 E3
Loughery Ln
900 INPS 46228 2119 A4
Louise Av
3300 INPS 46234 2225 A3
Louise Dr
300 INPS 46217 2555 B5
500 NBVL 46060 1686 B5
E Louisiana St
300 INPS 46204 2337 C4
500 INPS 46202 2337 D4
W Louisiana St
100 INPS 46225 2337 C4
Louisville Dr
8000 LWNC 46226 2231 B1
8100 INPS 46226 2231 B1
Louisville Wy
8000 LWNC 46226 2231 B1
Lourdes Dr
6100 INPS 46220 2120 E4
Lovage Ct
7800 INPS 46237 2556 E5
7800 INPS 46237 2557 A5
Love Av
100 GNWD 46142 2664 C3
Love Ct
300 CRML 46032 1901 D1
Love Ln
5400 INPS 46268 2117 C3
Lovely Dove Ln
14800 NBVL 46060 1797 A6
Lovers Ln
1200 GNWD 46142 2664 E1
Lowanna Ct
6700 INPS 46220 2121 D2
Lowanna Wy
6500 INPS 46220 2121 D2
Lowe Dr
7300 LWNC 46226 2122 A6
Lowell Av
5300 INPS 46219 2339 C3
7600 INPS 46219 2340 A2
Lowell Ct
10 BNBG 46112 2223 C4
Lowell Dr
- NBVL 46060 1795 E2
- NbvT 46060 1795 E2
Lower Dr
- BNBG 46112 2114 B6
Lower Bay Ln
8000 INPS 46236 2014 C6
Lowry Rd
3600 INPS 46222 2226 D3
Loy St
1100 SDWY 46224 2335 D1
Loyola Ct
10900 FSHR 46038 1903 D7
Luann Dr
8600 NbvT 46062 1686 D3
Lucann St
2900 CRML 46033 1902 C6
Lucas Cir
17900 WTFD 46074 1684 C7
Lucas Dr
2700 WTFD 46074 1684 C7
Lucas Ln
10 WshT 46123 2331 B1
5000 INPS 46221 2444 C7
Lucas St
- WTWN 46075 1788 D6
Luce Creek Cir
1200 GNWD 46142 2664 E3
Lucerne Av
1700 INPS 46241 2334 E7
Lucia Ct
11000 FSHR 46038 1905 C7
Lucille Ct
1200 PNFD 46168 2550 C1
9600 FSHR 46038 1905 A1
Lucky Cir
4400 INPS 46203 2448 C5
Lucky Ct
4300 INPS 46203 2448 C5
Lucky Ln
4000 WRvT 46142 2664 B2
Lucky Dan Dr
- NBVL 46060 1796 D5
Ludlow Av
1600 INPS 46201 2229 A7
1600 INPS 46201 2338 A1
1800 INPS 46218 2229 A7
Ludwig Dr
2800 INPS 46239 2449 B2
N Luett Av
1200 INPS 46222 2336 A1
N Luett Av
1600 INPS 46222 2227 A7
S Luett Av
400 INPS 46241 2336 A4
Luewan Ct
3500 INPS 46235 2231 E3
Luewan Dr
3400 INPS 46235 2231 E3
Lufkin Ct
- MCVL 46055 2124 B2
Luke Ct
4600 INPS 46227 2447 A6
Luke Ln
1300 INPS 46227 2446 E6
1600 INPS 46227 2447 A6
Lullaby Blvd
300 GNFD 46140 2345 D3
Lullaby Ct
100 GNFD 46140 2345 D3
Lullwater Ln
2500 INPS 46229 2232 D5
Lumber Pine Dr
- GNWD 46184 2774 B2
Luna Ln
7800 INPS 46214 2334 C1
Lunsford Cir
5300 INPS 46237 2448 B7
Lunsford Dr
5500 INPS 46237 2448 B7
Lupine Ct
3000 INPS 46224 2226 A4
3000 SDWY 46224 2226 A4
19200 NBVL 46060 1687 A4
Lupine Dr
3000 INPS 46224 2226 A4
3000 SDWY 46224 2226 A4
Lupine Ter
6400 INPS 46224 2226 A4
Luther St
1700 INPS 46203 2338 B7
Lutherwood Dr
1600 INPS 46219 2231 D7
Lux Rd
- FCkT 46040 1907 B6
W Luxembourg Cir
4000 INPS 46228 2227 A2
Luxembourg Cir E
4000 INPS 46228 2227 A2
Luxor Chase
- FSHR 46060 1905 E1
Luzzane Ln
5200 INPS 46220 2120 A6
Lyle St
4400 LWNC 46226 2231 B1
Lynbrook Ct
8800 INPS 46219 2231 D7
N Lynbrook Dr
8700 INPS 46219 2231 D7
Lynch Ln
8000 INPS 46250 2011 E6
Lynchburg Wy
11200 INPS 46229 2341 D1
Lyndhurst Cross
- MCVL 46055 2124 C1
Lyngardens Cir
200 INPS 46224 2335 C3
Lynhaven Pl
8400 INPS 46256 2013 A5
N Lynhurst Dr
10 INPS 46224 2335 C1
800 SDWY 46224 2335 C1
1600 SDWY 46224 2226 C7
3400 INPS 46224 2226 C3
S Lynhurst Dr
10 INPS 46241 2335 C7
2200 INPS 46241 2444 C3
3900 INPS 46221 2444 C3
Lynn Av
14400 DelT 46060 1795 C7
14500 NbvT 46060 1795 C7
Lynn Ct
- PTBR 46167 2113 B4
100 ZNVL 46077 1898 E3
Lynn Dr
- FCkT 46038 1904 E6
10 MdnT 46158 2661 A7
8100 INPS 46237 2557 A6
E Lynn Dr
1400 INPS 46202 2337 B1
W Lynn Dr
1400 INPS 46202 2337 B1
Lynn St
200 INPS 46222 2336 D2
Lynne Dr
1200 CRML 46032 1901 D2
N Lynnfield Ct
6400 INPS 46254 2117 A7
S Lynnfield Ct
6400 INPS 46254 2117 A7
Lynnfield Rd
4600 INPS 46254 2117 A7
Lynnwood Blvd
12400 CRML 46033 1903 D4
Lynnwood Dr
2800 CtrT 46122 2330 E3
Lynton Ct
4700 INPS 46254 2117 E7
Lynwood Dr
10 NWTD 46184 2774 D5
N Lyon Av
500 INPS 46222 2335 E2
Lyon St
- INPS 46221 2444 E7
N Lyons Av
7100 INPS 46268 2117 E1
S Lyons Av
300 INPS 46241 2335 E4
2400 INPS 46241 2444 E2
3200 INPS 46221 2444 E4
Lyric Dr
10300 INPS 46235 2123 B7

Indianapolis Street Index

STREET
Block City ZIP Map# Grid

M

M Ct
- WRvT 46142 2663 E1
M St
- BHGV 46107 2447 E2
Mabel St
3000 INPS 46234 2224 E4
E Mac Cir
2600 WTFD 46033 1793 C5
Mac Ct
2000 INPS 46203 2447 B2
MacAlister Trc
12900 CRML 46033 1903 E3
MacAlpin St
700 WRvT 46143 2663 D5
MacArthur Ct
3200 INPS 46224 2226 B4
MacArthur Ln
2700 SDWY 46224 2226 B5
3200 INPS 46224 2226 B3
Macatuck Dr
6200 INPS 46220 2121 D3
Macaw Pl
13400 CRML 46033 1903 A1
Macbeth Ct
6100 INPS 46254 2117 B4
Macbeth Dr
600 AVON 46123 2332 B2
Macbeth Wy
6000 INPS 46254 2117 B4
Macduff Ct
- NBVL 46062 1794 D6
Macduff Dr
- NBVL 46062 1794 D6
Mace Dr
1600 CBLD 46229 2232 E7
Machledt Dr
- GNWD 46142 2665 C4
MacIntosh Ct
1400 WshT 46123 2332 A7
MacIntosh Dr
1400 WshT 46123 2332 A6
MacIntosh Ln
- DNVL 46122 2329 D3
Mackell Ct
7600 INPS 46268 2009 B7
MacKenzie Wy
4000 INPS 46221 2444 E5
Mackey Rd
10 DNVL 46122 2329 C4
Mack Farm Ln
6300 INPS 46237 2557 B2
Mackinac Ct
100 INPS 46227 2555 C5
Macklin Dr
3400 INPS 46237 2447 C4
MacPherson Av
2800 INPS 46205 2228 E5
Macy Dr
4600 WRvT 46142 2663 D2
Macy Ln
11500 CRML 46033 1902 B6
Macy Wy
400 WRvT 46142 2663 D2
Madan Park Dr
3000 INPS 46241 2444 B3
Madden Dr
7400 FSHR 46038 1904 B5
Madden Ln
7600 FSHR 46038 1904 B5
Madden Pl
7600 FSHR 46038 1904 B5
Madeira Ct
3400 INPS 46203 2338 C7
Madeira St
1100 INPS 46203 2338 C6
Madeline Ct
10800 FSHR 46038 1904 D7
Madeline Ln
3800 WTFD 46033 1793 D6
Madelynne Dr
2800 INPS 46229 2231 D5
Madison Av
- GNWD 46143 2665 C5
400 INPS 46225 2337 C4
N Madison Av
10 GNWD 46142 2665 C2
S Madison Av
10 GNWD 46142 2665 C4
700 GNWD 46143 2665 C4
1400 INPS 46225 2446 C1
1900 INPS 46225 2337 C7
3000 INPS 46227 2446 E5
5500 INPS 46227 2555 E1
5700 INPS 46227 2556 A2
6500 HMCT 46227 2556 A2
6900 SPRT 46227 2556 A4
Madison Ct
100 LEBN 46052 1677 A3
1900 CRML 46032 1902 A6
Madison Dr
300 GNFD 46140 2345 B1
1900 CRML 46032 1902 B5
S Madison Dr
- MRVL 46158 2659 E4
Madison St
- JknT 46011 1580 E1
22800 WRvT 46060 1579 A4
S Madison St
10 MRVL 46158 2659 E4
W Madison St
4000 WshT 46069 1682 A7
Madison Brooks Dr
10400 FCkT 46040 2015 E1
10500 FCkT 46040 1906 E7
Madison Village Ct
7200 INPS 46227 2556 A4
Madison Village Dr
- SPRT 46227 2556 A4
1800 INPS 46227 2556 A4
Madison Village East Dr
7200 INPS 46227 2556 A4

Madras Ct
4700 ZNVL 46077 1898 E3
Madrid Rd
1000 GNWD 46143 2666 A5
Madrone Ct
8100 LWNC 46236 2014 E6
Madrone Dr
12100 LWNC 46236 2014 E6
Madsion Ct
- WRvT 46142 2663 C4
Mae Dr
5300 CRML 46033 1794 B7
Magdalene Dr
5800 INPS 46224 2335 B2
Magdalene Ln
500 INPS 46224 2335 B2
Magenta Dr
10300 NBVL 46060 1687 B4
Magenta Ln
3700 INPS 46214 2225 D3
Maggie Ct
14900 WshT 46074 1792 C6
Magic Stallion Dr
13600 CRML 46032 1901 A1
13700 CRML 46032 1900 E1
13900 CRML 46032 1791 E7
14000 CRML 46032 1792 A7
Magnetic Acres St
10 BrnT 46158 2658 C5
Magnificent Ln
- LcnT 46112 2115 C6
Magnolia Av
4000 FKLN 46131 2774 E7
Magnolia Ct
10 LcnT 46112 2222 E1
600 DNVL 46122 2330 A3
Magnolia Dr
200 PNFD 46168 2441 E3
1200 GNFD 46140 2237 A6
4100 FKLN 46131 2774 E7
Magnolia Ln
100 NBVL 46062 1576 B7
200 GNWD 46143 2665 C6
9000 LWNC 46235 2231 D1
Magnolia Pl
2200 INPS 46219 2230 C6
Mahan Ln
10 BNBG 46112 2114 B6
Mahogany Ct
6900 WshT 46168 2441 B1
Mahogany Dr
- WRvT 46143 2663 E5
Mahony Ct
1400 INPS 46217 2554 E5
Maidstone Rd
6300 INPS 46254 2117 A7
W Maiellen Ct
6900 BCkT 46140 2233 B7
Maiellen Dr N
900 BCkT 46140 2233 B7
Maiellen Dr W
6900 BCkT 46140 2233 B7
Main Cross
10 SCkT 46140 2344 B2
Main Dr
10 SCkT 46163 2452 B2
Main Rd
- AVON 46123 2332 E5
- AVON 46123 2333 C5
- AVON 46231 2333 D4
Main St
- MdlT 46167 2112 A7
- UnnT 46149 2112 A7
- UnnT 46167 2112 A7
100 BHGV 46107 2448 A3
500 BHGV 46107 2447 C3
800 INPS 46220 2119 E3
1000 SDWY 46224 2335 D1
2100 SDWY 46224 2226 D6
2200 INPS 46107 2447 C3
3000 LtyT 46118 2439 E5
3000 LtyT 46168 2439 E5
3400 LtyT 46168 2440 A5
9400 MrlT 46126 2560 A4
E Main St
- CtrT 46140 2346 A1
10 BNBG 46112 2114 C7
10 CRML 46032 1902 D2
10 DNVL 46122 2329 E4
10 GNFD 46140 2345 E1
10 GNWD 46143 2665 D4
10 MRVL 46158 2659 E3
10 NPLN 46163 2452 C3
10 PTBR 46167 2112 E4
10 PTBR 46167 2113 A4
10 WTFD 46074 1684 B7
100 LEBN 46052 1677 A6
100 PNFD 46168 2441 C5
200 MNVA 46157 2657 D7
300 MRVL 46158 2660 A3
300 SgCT 46126 2670 E7
500 MnrT 46157 2657 D7
900 CRML 46033 1902 D2
900 GNFD 46140 2346 A1
900 GNWD 46143 2666 A4
1000 BNBG 46112 2223 E1
1200 BNBG 46112 2224 A1
1200 DNVL 46122 2330 A4
1400 LcnT 46112 2224 A1
1800 CtrT 46122 2330 C4
2300 PNFD 46168 2442 C2
3100 PNFD 46231 2442 C2
3200 WshT 46231 2442 C2
3300 CtrT 46122 2331 A4
3700 WshT 46122 2331 A4
3700 WshT 46123 2331 A4
4000 SCkT 46163 2452 C3
4600 CRML 46033 1903 A2
E Main St SR-32
10 WTFD 46074 1684 B7
100 LEBN 46052 1677 A6
E Main St SR-42
200 MNVA 46157 2657 D7
500 MnrT 46157 2657 D7

E Main St SR-267
300 PNFD 46168 2441 D4
E Main St US-36
10 DNVL 46122 2329 E4
1000 DNVL 46122 2330 A4
E Main St US-40
10 GNFD 46140 2345 E1
100 PNFD 46168 2441 C5
900 GNFD 46140 2346 A1
1000 CtrT 46140 2346 A1
2300 PNFD 46168 2442 C2
3100 PNFD 46231 2442 C2
3200 WshT 46231 2442 C2
E Main St US-52
10 NPLN 46163 2452 C3
4000 SCkT 46163 2452 C3
E Main St US-136
10 BNBG 46112 2114 C7
10 PTBR 46167 2112 E4
10 PTBR 46167 2113 A4
1000 BNBG 46112 2223 E1
1200 BNBG 46112 2224 A1
1400 LcnT 46112 2224 A1
N Main St
10 CCRO 46034 1577 C2
10 SPRT 46227 2556 B3
10 ZNVL 46077 1899 B6
N Main St E
200 WrhT 46075 1788 C6
200 WTWN 46075 1788 C6
S Main St
10 CCRO 46034 1577 C3
10 WTWN 46075 1788 D7
10 ZNVL 46077 1899 B6
100 SRDN 46069 1573 B1
S Main St SR-38
200 SRDN 46069 1573 B2
W Main St
- LEBN 46052 1676 D6
- WynT 46051 1689 E4
10 BNBG 46112 2114 B6
10 CRML 46032 1902 A2
10 DNVL 46122 2329 B4
10 GNFD 46140 2345 B1
10 LEBN 46052 1677 A6
10 MRVL 46158 2659 D3
10 NPLN 46163 2452 A3
10 PTBR 46167 2112 E3
10 WTFD 46074 1684 A7
100 PNFD 46168 2441 A5
200 LcnT 46112 2114 B6
400 BrnT 46158 2659 D3
500 MdlT 46167 2112 E3
700 CRML 46032 1901 D2
900 WshT 46074 1683 E7
900 WTFD 46074 1683 E7
1200 CtrT 46122 2329 B4
1600 PNFD 46168 2440 E6
2200 GNFD 46140 2344 E1
2500 CtrT 46140 2344 E1
7300 MrlT 46126 2669 C2
9000 SCkT 46051 1689 E4
W Main St SR-13
- WynT 46051 1689 E4
9000 SCkT 46051 1689 E4
W Main St SR-32
10 LEBN 46052 1677 A6
10 WTFD 46074 1684 A7
900 WshT 46074 1683 E7
900 WTFD 46074 1683 E7
W Main St SR-39
200 DNVL 46122 2329 B4
W Main St SR-267
10 MRVL 46158 2659 D3
W Main St US-36
10 DNVL 46122 2329 B4
1200 CtrT 46122 2329 B4
W Main St US-40
10 GNFD 46140 2345 B1
100 PNFD 46168 2441 A5
1600 PNFD 46168 2440 E6
2200 GNFD 46140 2344 E1
2500 CtrT 46140 2344 E1
W Main St US-52
10 NPLN 46163 2452 A3
W Main St US-136
10 BNBG 46112 2114 B6
10 PTBR 46167 2112 E3
200 LcnT 46112 2114 B6
500 MdlT 46167 2112 E3
Main St E
100 WTLD 46184 2774 E5
200 WTLD 46184 2775 A5
700 PltT 46184 2775 A5
Main St W
10 GNWD 46142 2665 A4
900 GNWD 46142 2664 D4
Main Cross St
10 SCkT 46140 2344 B2
Mainsail Ct
11300 FSHR 46038 1905 B6
Main St Sq
10 SPRT 46227 2556 B4
Maisons Ct
7500 INPS 46278 2007 D7
Maize Dr
12100 NBVL 46060 1796 E7
12200 NBVL 46060 1797 A7
Majestic Ln
4200 INPS 46254 2226 A1
Majestic Wy
12600 FSHR 46060 1906 A2
Majestic Perch Ct
- LcnT 46112 2115 D6
Major Run
8800 INPS 46256 2013 D4
Makena Ridge Ct
4500 WRvT 46142 2663 D3
Makenzie Ct
200 NBVL 46060 1686 C7
Malaga Dr
8600 INPS 46250 2012 A4
Malat Dr
10 GNWD 46143 2665 C7

Malden Ct
4300 BHGV 46107 2447 E6
Malden Ln
4000 BHGV 46107 2447 D6
Malibu Ct
3900 INPS 46226 2231 D2
Malibu Dr
3900 INPS 46226 2231 D2
Mall
- INPS 46226 2121 C5
Mallard Ct
300 CRML 46032 1901 C4
6700 MCVL 46055 2015 B3
7400 INPS 46260 2009 E7
10900 BrnT 46112 2115 E2
11300 FSHR 46038 1903 E6
11300 FSHR 46038 1904 A6
W Mallard Ct
7500 MrlT 46126 2560 C1
N Mallard Dr
8900 MCVL 46055 2015 C3
W Mallard Dr
7900 MCVL 46055 2015 C3
Mallard Lndg
6500 FSHR 46038 1903 D6
8000 BrnT 46112 2115 E2
Mallard Mnr
- BrnT 46112 2115 E2
Mallard Pt
9100 UnnT 46077 1789 D4
Mallard Wy
5900 PNFD 46168 2550 B2
7700 INPS 46256 2013 C7
10900 BrnT 46112 2115 E1
Mallard Green Dr
8800 INPS 46234 2225 A5
Mallard View Dr
5000 INPS 46226 2120 D7
Mallard View Ln
4700 INPS 46226 2120 D7
Mallery Dr
9700 NbvT 46060 1687 A4
9800 NBVL 46060 1687 A4
Mallery Rd
18100 WynT 46060 1687 D6
Mallway Dr
4000 INPS 46235 2231 D2
Malone Ct
1300 INPS 46217 2554 E5
Maloney Rd
7500 BrnT 46112 2005 D7
8000 BrnT 46112 2006 A7
9300 BrnT 46112 2115 D1
Malott St
1000 SRDN 46069 1573 B3
Malvina Av
1100 INPS 46229 2340 E1
Malvina Ct
9800 INPS 46229 2341 A1
Manasota Ct
4100 WTFD 46062 1684 E7
Manassas Dr
1000 WshT 46074 1792 A5
6600 INPS 46241 2334 E6
Manchester Ct
10 ClyT 46032 1901 C7
200 NBVL 46060 1795 D5
5900 MdlT 46167 2113 B6
Manchester Dr
- BNBG 46112 2223 E3
- BNBG 46112 2224 A4
- FSHR 46038 1903 D7
7300 INPS 46260 2118 D1
7500 INPS 46260 2009 D7
N Manchester Dr
1000 CBLD 46140 2232 E6
W Manchester Dr
1000 CBLD 46140 2232 E6
Manchester Ln
2000 INPS 46260 2118 D1
Mandan Ct
8400 INPS 46217 2555 B6
Manderley Dr
8600 INPS 46240 2011 B4
Mandren Dr
2400 WshT 46231 2442 C2
Manhattan Av
10 INPS 46241 2335 C4
2200 INPS 46241 2444 C1
S Manhattan Av
1500 INPS 46241 2335 C6
Manita Dr
2400 INPS 46234 2225 A5
Manitou Ct
11300 INPS 46236 2014 D4
Manker St
4800 INPS 46227 2446 E7
5100 INPS 46227 2555 E1
S Manker St
2600 INPS 46203 2446 E2
Manlove Av
2500 INPS 46218 2229 A5
Mann Dr
1800 BHGV 46107 2447 C3
Mann Rd
3400 INPS 46221 2444 D6
3400 INPS 46241 2444 D6
5000 INPS 46221 2553 C3
8500 INPS 46221 2662 B2
12000 MdnT 46113 2662 B2
N Mann Rd
11000 MdnT 46113 2662 A5
11000 MdnT 46158 2662 A5
11300 MdnT 46158 2661 E6
Mannan Ct
5200 INPS 46221 2444 B7
Manning Rd
3300 INPS 46228 2227 B1
5800 INPS 46228 2118 B4
N Manning Rd
5900 INPS 46228 2118 B4
Mannington Wy
- CRML 46032 1900 C4
Mann Village Dr
- INPS 46221 2444 D5

Mann Village Jct
4500 INPS 46221 2444 D5
Mann Village Ln
3900 INPS 46221 2444 E5
Mann Village Rd
3800 INPS 46221 2444 D5
Mann Village St
3900 INPS 46221 2444 D5
Mann Village Ter
4400 INPS 46221 2444 D5
Manor Blvd
11300 NBVL 46060 1796 D3
Manor Ct
800 PNFD 46168 2441 B6
3700 INPS 46218 2229 E3
Manor Dr
- CRML 46033 1902 C6
10 DNVL 46122 2330 B4
10 SCkT 46140 2342 C2
1600 LEBN 46052 1676 C5
Manor Dr N
7000 BNBG 46112 2223 B3
Manor Dr S
7000 BNBG 46112 2223 B3
Manor Hill Dr
3000 CRML 46033 1902 C5
Manor House Cir
5300 INPS 46226 2121 A6
Mansfield Ct
1500 WRvT 46143 2663 E6
Mansfield Pl
11500 ClyT 46032 1900 D5
Mansfield St
1800 INPS 46202 2227 E7
Manship Cir
7100 WshT 46123 2332 B2
Manship Ct
7100 WshT 46123 2332 B2
Manship Dr
8400 FSHR 46038 1904 C6
Manship Ln
8400 FSHR 46038 1904 C6
Manti Ct
10 INPS 46222 2226 E5
Maple Av
1700 NBVL 46060 1686 E7
E Maple Av
1000 NBVL 46060 1686 D7
W Maple Av
400 NBVL 46060 1686 D7
Maple Ct
300 CBLD 46140 2342 A1
600 BNBG 46112 2114 D7
Maple Dr
- GNFD 46140 2236 D7
10 AVON 46123 2332 B3
6200 INPS 46220 2120 B3
9600 ClyT 46280 2011 B2
11500 DelT 46038 1904 B5
E Maple Dr
10 WTLD 46131 2774 D7
10 WTLD 46184 2774 D7
N Maple Dr
100 WRvT 46142 2663 B3
4100 WTLD 46131 2774 D7
S Maple Dr
600 SGLK 46140 2343 E3
W Maple Dr
100 LEBN 46052 1677 A4
200 LEBN 46052 1676 E4
5600 WshT 46123 2331 D3
5700 WRvT 46142 2663 B3
Maple Ln
- GNWD 46143 2666 A5
10 BNBG 46112 2114 B7
10 MRVL 46158 2659 E3
600 BNBG 46112 2223 D1
700 WTFD 46074 1684 B6
4400 LWNC 46226 2122 C7
4400 LWNC 46226 2231 C1
5100 INPS 46219 2339 A2
11400 PNFD 46168 2442 A3
Maple Ln S
10 BNBG 46112 2114 B7
10 BNBG 46112 2223 C1
Maple Mnr
10 BrnT 46112 2113 D5
10 LcnT 46112 2113 D5
Maple Pt
100 NBVL 46062 1685 E1
Maple St
- NPLN 46163 2452 B3
10 DNVL 46122 2329 C4
10 WTFD 46074 1684 A6
10 WTLD 46184 2774 E5
200 GNWD 46142 2665 C2
200 WTFD 46074 1793 A1
300 MNVA 46157 2657 C7
6400 LWNC 46236 2123 D3
11600 FSHR 46038 1904 D5
13600 CRML 46033 1902 D1
N Maple St
100 PTBR 46167 2112 E3
100 ZNVL 46077 1899 B5
400 PTBR 46167 2113 A3
S Maple St
- NPLN 46163 2452 B4
- PTBR 46167 2112 E4
6600 MdlT 46167 2112 E4
Maple Wy
9400 INPS 46268 2009 C3
Maple Branch Pl
6000 INPS 46221 2553 A2
Maplebrook Dr
100 BNBG 46112 2223 C1
200 FSHR 46038 2012 C1
Maple Crest Dr
600 WTLD 46184 2774 E5
Maplecrest Dr
3000 CRML 46033 1902 C2
Maple Forge Cir
6000 INPS 46254 2117 E4
Maple Forge Ct
5900 INPS 46254 2117 E4

Maple Glen Dr
6600 INPS 46250 2012 D5
Maple Grove Dr
- INPS 46217 2554 E6
900 GNWD 46143 2665 E2
900 GNWD 46143 2666 A2
6600 INPS 46250 2012 D5
18600 NBVL 46062 1685 C5
Maple Grove Ln
8400 INPS 46250 2012 C5
Maple Grove Wy
- NBVL 46062 1685 C4
- NbvT 46062 1685 C4
Maple Hill Dr
8700 INPS 46239 2449 C6
Maple Hill St
200 PNFD 46168 2441 B5
Maplehurst Dr
10 BNBG 46112 2114 C4
Maple Lake Wy
- BNBG 46112 2114 E5
Maple Lawn Rd
6200 INPS 46241 2552 B3
Mapleleaf Cir
9400 FSHR 46038 1904 E1
Maple Leaf Ct
8200 INPS 46268 2009 A5
Maple Leaf Dr
6600 INPS 46250 2012 D5
Maple Leaf Ln
8400 INPS 46250 2012 E5
Maple Manor Dr
3800 INPS 46237 2556 D1
E Maple Park Dr
1900 WTFD 46074 1684 B6
Maple Ridge Ct
3300 INPS 46227 2556 C4
Maple Ridge Dr
7300 INPS 46227 2556 C4
Maples Ct
300 GNWD 46142 2665 B4
Maple Stream Blvd
8000 INPS 46217 2554 C6
8000 INPS 46217 2555 A6
Maple Stream Dr
1000 INPS 46217 2555 B5
1100 INPS 46217 2554 E6
Maple Stream Ln
8000 INPS 46217 2554 E6
Mapleton Ct
6900 INPS 46214 2225 E4
9900 FSHR 46038 2014 B2
Mapleton Pl
16900 WTFD 46074 1792 D2
Maple Tree Dr
8400 INPS 46250 2012 E5
Maple View Ct
800 INPS 46217 2555 A7
Maple View Dr
8600 INPS 46217 2555 A7
Maplewood Ct
1200 BNBG 46112 2223 D2
Maplewood Dr
100 NBVL 46062 1685 C3
5700 SDWY 46224 2226 B5
7100 INPS 46227 2555 E4
Maqua Ct
3000 CRML 46033 2011 C1
Marabou Mills Dr
3400 INPS 46214 2225 D3
Marabou Mills Ln
3400 INPS 46214 2225 C3
Marabou Mills Pl
3400 INPS 46214 2225 C3
Marabou Mills Wy
7600 INPS 46214 2225 C3
Maradona Dr
1700 INPS 46214 2225 C7
Maradona Dr S
7600 INPS 46214 2225 C7
Maralice Dr
2700 CRML 46033 1793 C7
Marana Dr
600 CRML 46032 1901 E1
600 CRML 46032 1902 A1
Maraschino Dr
16600 NBVL 46062 1794 E2
Marathon Run
- NBVL 46060 1796 E5
Marble Ct
5100 INPS 46237 2557 A2
Marble Dr
3600 INPS 46227 2556 D5
Marble Ln
700 GNFD 46140 2237 B7
6400 INPS 46237 2557 A2
Marble Arch Wy
13800 FSHR 46060 1906 D3
Marblehead Ct
11900 INPS 46236 2014 E3
Marborough Ln
1500 INPS 46260 2009 E6
Marbro Ln
1600 ClyT 46280 1902 A7
Marburn Dr
6200 INPS 46227 2556 C2
Marcella Ln
3600 INPS 46222 2227 A4
Marcia Dr
1600 MdnT 46158 2660 C4
Marcia Ln
5800 INPS 46217 2555 A1
Marcialee Dr
- SCkT 46163 2452 A1
Marco Pt
5700 CRML 46033 1903 D4
Marco St
- PNFD 46168 2550 A2
Marcy Ct
6900 PNFD 46168 2550 C2
Marcy Ln
- INPS 46205 2120 A7
- INPS 46205 2229 A1
100 GNWD 46143 2665 D2

Mardale Dr
10 BNBG 46112 2114 A6
Mardenis Ct
- MdnT 46113 2661 D1
Mardenis Dr
- MdnT 46113 2661 C1
Mardenna Av
3300 INPS 46218 2230 A4
Mardyke Ln
7000 LWNC 46226 2121 E6
7000 LWNC 46226 2122 A6
Mare Av
1800 INPS 46203 2339 B7
Maren Dr
4500 INPS 46222 2226 E5
6000 SDWY 46224 2226 A5
Marengo Tr
- WTFD 46074 1792 D3
Margaret Av
3500 INPS 46203 2447 D1
3700 BHGV 46203 2447 D1
Margaret Ct
6500 INPS 46237 2557 D4
Margate Ct
13000 FSHR 46038 1905 A2
Margate Dr W
100 WTLD 46184 2775 A6
Margate Rd
5300 INPS 46221 2444 C5
Margaux Ln
6000 INPS 46220 2121 D4
Margene Dr
10 BrnT 46112 2006 D6
Margie Dr
8100 BNBG 46112 2114 D4
8100 BrnT 46112 2114 D4
Margueritta Ct
500 GNWD 46143 2665 D5
Margueritta Wy
900 GNWD 46143 2665 E5
Mari Wy
400 CRML 46032 1901 B2
Maria Av
1400 FKLN 46131 2774 E7
1400 FKLN 46131 2775 A7
Maria Dr
400 GNWD 46143 2665 D4
Maria Ln
1400 WshT 46123 2332 C6
Marian Dr
1700 INPS 46240 2011 A3
Mariana Ct
10 BNBG 46112 2223 A1
Mari Ann Ct
6100 INPS 46237 2557 C5
Marianne Av
7200 INPS 46219 2231 A7
Marie Ct
20100 NBVL 46062 1686 B2
Marie Dr
9600 CRML 46280 2011 D2
Mariesi Dr
8600 INPS 46278 2008 A4
Marietta Cir
15500 WshT 46074 1792 B5
Marietta Ct
3900 INPS 46235 2232 A2
Marietta Dr
3800 INPS 46235 2232 A2
Marigold Cir
11700 FSHR 46038 1904 C5
Marigold Ln
4900 INPS 46254 2117 D5
Marilyn Ct
13900 CRML 46032 1792 D7
W Marilyn Dr
6500 INPS 46278 2116 D2
6500 INPS 46278 2117 A3
Marilyn Rd
5400 INPS 46226 2230 B1
13100 FSHR 46060 1905 E2
13600 FCkT 46060 1796 E7
13600 FCkT 46060 1905 E2
13600 FSHR 46060 1796 E7
14100 NBVL 46060 1796 E7
Marin Dr
- JknT 46034 1576 E3
Marina Dr
2500 INPS 46240 2011 B6
Marina View Dr
5900 INPS 46237 2557 C6
Marina View Ln
5900 INPS 46237 2557 C6
Mariner Ct
12900 FCkT 46055 2015 B2
Mariner Wy
7000 INPS 46214 2225 D4
Mariners Ln
7000 INPS 46214 2225 E4
Mario Creek Cir
2600 INPS 46234 2225 A5
Mario Creek Dr
8800 INPS 46234 2225 A5
Marion Av
- BCkT 46140 2233 A6
500 INPS 46221 2337 A4
Marion Ct
3800 ClyT 46032 1900 A7
E Marion St
10 DNVL 46122 2329 D4
W Marion St
10 DNVL 46122 2329 D4
Mariposa Dr
8800 INPS 46234 2334 A3
Marisa Ct
100 BrnT 46158 2658 D5
W Marisa Ct
100 BrnT 46158 2658 D5
Marisa Dr
8700 FSHR 46060 1795 D6
Maritime Dr
3400 INPS 46214 2225 C4
Mariway Cir
500 INPS 46234 2333 D2

Mariway Ct
- 9100 INPS 46234 2333 E2

Mariway Rd
- 400 INPS 46234 2333 E2

Mariwood
- 8000 BrnT 46112 2114 D4

Mariwood Dr
- 400 INPS 46234 2333 E2

Mariwood Pkwy
- 9200 INPS 46234 2333 E2

Marjac Wy
- 13400 FCkT 46055 2015 B1

Marjorie Ct
- 5500 MdnT 46113 2660 E3

Marjorie Ct E
- 5600 MdnT 46113 2660 E3
- 5600 MdnT 46113 2661 A3

Mark Ct
- 5400 WRvT 46142 2663 C2

Mark Ln
- 500 PNFD 46168 2441 D5
- 5000 INPS 46226 2121 D6

Mark Mnr
- 10 DNVL 46122 2329 C3

Markay Dr
- 12600 FCkT 46038 1904 D3
- 12600 FSHR 46038 1904 D3

Market Ct
- 18100 WTFD 46074 1684 A6

Market Plz
- 200 GNWD 46142 2665 C4

Market St
- — INPS 46222 2336 A4
- 10 SPRT 46227 2556 B4
- 1800 LtyT 46118 2548 C1

Market St SR-39
- — LtyT 46118 2548 B1

E Market St
- 10 INPS 46204 2337 C3
- 600 INPS 46202 2337 D3
- 3700 INPS 46201 2338 D3
- 5200 INPS 46219 2339 A3

W Market St
- — INPS 46222 2337 B3
- 10 INPS 46204 2337 C3
- 1600 INPS 46222 2336 D3
- 4400 INPS 46222 2335 D3
- 5400 INPS 46224 2335 B3
- 6300 INPS 46214 2335 A3

N Markland Dr
- 12100 BrnT 46158 2658 D5

Marksman Ct
- 6800 INPS 46226 2118 D2

Markville Ln
- — WTFD 46074 1792 C3

E Markwood Av
- 500 INPS 46227 2446 D5
- 1500 INPS 46227 2447 A5

W Markwood Av
- 4800 INPS 46221 2444 C5
- 6300 INPS 46241 2444 A5

Marla Dr
- 7100 INPS 46256 2122 B1
- 7400 INPS 46256 2013 C6

Marlee Ln
- 1400 LEBN 46052 1676 D4

Marlette Dr
- 300 INPS 46228 2228 B6

Marley Ct
- 10 WTLD 46184 2774 D7
- 2800 INPS 46268 2118 C2

Marlin Ct
- — NBVL 46060 1687 C4
- 10500 INPS 46256 2014 B3

Marlin Dr
- — GNWD 46142 2664 C3

E Marlin Rd
- 10700 INPS 46239 2450 D5
- 10700 SCkT 46239 2450 D5

Marlow Ct
- 13500 FSHR 46060 1905 A1

Marlowe Av
- 1100 INPS 46227 2337 E3
- 1400 INPS 46201 2337 E3
- 1400 INPS 46201 2338 A3

Marmon Cir
- 5300 INPS 46226 2121 B6

Marmont Cir
- 6600 INPS 46220 2121 D2

Marmont Ct
- 6800 INPS 46220 2121 E2

Marnan St
- — SgCT 46126 2670 D7

Marnette St
- 5500 INPS 46241 2335 B4

Marott Ct
- 5200 INPS 46226 2121 B6

Marquette Ct
- 3000 INPS 46268 2009 B3

Marquette Rd
- 10800 ZNVL 46077 1899 B3
- 10800 INPS 46268 2009 B3

Marquette Cir North Dr

Marquette Cir South Dr

Marquette Manor West Dr
- 2700 INPS 46268 2009 C5

Marquis Ln
- 7800 INPS 46260 2009 D7

Marrison Pl
- 3600 INPS 46205 2229 D1
- 3800 INPS 46226 2229 D1
- 4400 INPS 46226 2230 A1

Mars Dr
- 7000 INPS 46241 2334 D4

Marseille Ct
- 3900 INPS 46226 2231 C2

Marseille Rd
- 3800 INPS 46226 2231 C2

Marsh Rd
- — FSHR 46038 1904 A5

N Marsh Rd
- 7100 INPS 46278 2117 A1
- 7500 INPS 46278 2008 A7

Marsha Dr
- 1700 INPS 46214 2225 D7

Marshall Dr
- — SCkT 46163 2452 C2
- 4500 INPS 46237 2448 C6

Marsh Glen Ct
- 5700 CRML 46033 1903 B4

Mars Hill St
- 2600 INPS 46241 2444 E3
- 3000 INPS 46221 2444 E4

S Mars Hill St
- 2400 INPS 46241 2444 E1

Marstella Dr
- 7000 BrnT 46112 2114 B1

Marstella Ln
- 7000 BrnT 46112 2114 B1

Marten Ct E
- 4200 LWNC 46226 2231 B1

Marten Ct S
- — LWNC 46226 2231 B1
- — INPS 46226 2231 B1

Marten Ct W
- — LWNC 46226 2231 B1

Martha St
- 2100 INPS 46221 2336 D6
- 4800 INPS 46241 2335 D6
- 15400 FCkT 46040 1907 B7

W Martha St
- 5200 INPS 46241 2335 C6

Martin Dr
- 10 DNVL 46122 2329 C4

N Martin Ln
- 100 MdnT 46113 2660 D2

Martin Rd
- 3800 LtyT 46168 2439 E5
- 3800 LtyT 46168 2440 A5

Martin St
- 500 INPS 46227 2446 D3
- 1500 INPS 46227 2447 A3
- 1500 INPS 46227 2447 A3

E Martindale Dr
- — GNFD 46140 2236 D4

N Martindale Dr
- — GNFD 46140 2236 E4

Martinique Ln
- 6700 INPS 46227 2555 D3

Martin Luther Ln
- 5600 INPS 46218 2229 B6

Martin Pike
- 10100 FSHR 46038 1905 A4

Martin Road West Dr
- 700 LtyT 46168 2440 A5

Marwood Dr
- 900 ClyT 46280 2010 E1

Marwood Trail East Dr
- 10100 INPS 46280 2010 E2

Marwood Trail North Dr
- 900 ClyT 46280 2010 E1

Marwood Trail West Dr
- 900 ClyT 46280 2010 E2

Mary Ct
- 10 WTLD 46184 2774 D7
- 400 WRvT 46142 2663 C2
- 8400 BrnT 46112 2115 E1
- 13900 FSHR 46038 1796 A7
- 13900 FSHR 46038 1905 A1

Mary Dr
- 1400 LEBN 46052 1676 D4

S Mary Dr
- 1400 INPS 46241 2334 D6

Mary Ln
- 7100 MdnT 46158 2661 C7
- 7500 INPS 46217 2555 B5

Mary Wy
- 10 MdnT 46158 2661 B7

Maryann Ct
- 5500 INPS 46227 2556 C4

Mary Belle Ln
- 4500 INPS 46237 2556 E2

Mary Ellen Ct
- 300 CRML 46032 1901 B3

Mary Kay Dr
- 4000 INPS 46221 2444 E6

Maryland Ct
- 9300 FSHR 46038 1904 E7

E Maryland St
- 10 INPS 46204 2337 C4
- 700 INPS 46202 2337 D4
- 1700 INPS 46201 2338 A4

W Maryland St
- 10 INPS 46225 2337 B4
- 700 INPS 46204 2337 A3
- 1700 INPS 46222 2336 D4

Maryvale Ct
- 10 MRVL 46158 2659 E2
- 6900 INPS 46214 2334 E2

Marywood Ct
- 2900 SPRT 46227 2556 B5

Marywood Dr
- 10 GNFD 46140 2237 A6
- 2600 SPRT 46227 2556 B5

Mason Cir
- 5200 INPS 46254 2117 D6

Mason Dr
- 5000 INPS 46254 2117 D7

Mason St
- 200 INPS 46225 2446 C1
- 16600 WynT 46060 1797 D2

E Massachusetts Av
- 10 INPS 46204 2337 D2
- 500 INPS 46202 2337 D2
- 1300 INPS 46201 2337 D2
- 1400 INPS 46201 2229 D5
- 1800 INPS 46218 2229 D5
- 3300 INPS 46218 2230 B4
- 4500 INPS 46218 2230 B4
- 6000 INPS 46226 2230 B4

Mast Ct
- 11000 FCkT 46040 1907 A6

Masten Ct
- 100 PNFD 46168 2441 C5

Masters Cir
- 10 BNBG 46112 2113 C4

Masters Rd
- 8600 INPS 46250 2012 E4

Masters Rd
- 9200 FSHR 46250 2012 E4
- 9600 FSHR 46038 2012 E4

Maswa Ct
- 9900 CRML 46033 2011 D1

Matacumbe Dr
- 12000 FSHR 46038 1906 B4

Matchlock Ct
- 8700 INPS 46256 2013 C4

Match Point Ct
- 8600 INPS 46256 2014 A4

Matepaw Ln
- 3300 LcnT 46123 2222 E4

Mathews Av
- 4000 INPS 46227 2447 A5
- 5900 INPS 46227 2556 A1

Mathews Rd
- 8000 INPS 46259 2558 B6

S Mathews Rd
- 8000 INPS 46259 2558 A6
- 8800 ClkT 46143 2558 A6
- 8800 INPS 46143 2558 A6

Mathews Wy
- 4600 INPS 46227 2447 A6

Matrea More Ct
- 4300 INPS 46254 2225 E1

Matt Ct
- 2700 CRML 46033 1793 C7

Matt Dr
- 10100 LWNC 46235 2123 A6

Matt St
- 14200 CRML 46033 1793 C7

Matterhorn Ct
- 1000 LEBN 46052 1676 D4

Matterhorn Ln
- 1500 INPS 46234 2333 E1

Matterhorn Rd
- 9000 INPS 46234 2334 A1
- 9100 INPS 46234 2333 D1

N Matthews Rd
- 200 ClkT 46143 2667 B3
- 1500 ClkT 46143 2558 B7

Mattock Chase
- 13200 CRML 46033 1903 E1

Maumee Cir
- 10000 WshT 46234 2224 C6

Maumee Ct
- 3200 INPS 46235 2232 B4

Maumee Dr
- 10300 INPS 46235 2232 B4

Maupin St
- — NPLN 46163 2452 B3

Maura Ct
- 3400 INPS 46235 2231 D3

Maura Ln
- 3400 INPS 46235 2231 D3

Maureen Ter
- 7700 INPS 46214 2334 C1

Maurice Dr
- 8300 INPS 46234 2225 B6

Maurine Ct
- 3900 INPS 46235 2232 A2

Maurine Dr
- 9800 INPS 46235 2231 E4
- 9900 INPS 46235 2232 A2

Max Av
- 5000 WRvT 46143 2663 C6

Max Ct
- 8900 FSHR 46038 1904 D7

Maxine Dr
- 200 BNBG 46112 2223 B1

S Maxine Mnr
- 500 BNBG 46112 2223 B1

Maxine Rd
- 1400 INPS 46240 2120 A1

N Maxwell Ct
- 5000 ZNVL 46077 1899 A3

S Maxwell Ct
- 100 ZNVL 46077 1899 A4

Maxwell Ln
- 1000 ZNVL 46077 1899 A4

Maxwell Rd
- — INPS 46227 2446 C6
- 10 INPS 46217 2446 C6
- 400 GfdT 46168 2550 B4

Maxwellton St
- 200 GfdT 46158 2550 D7

W May Apple Cir
- 300 WshT 46074 1792 C5

Mayapple Ct
- 4400 INPS 46203 2448 C6
- 7600 WshT 46123 2223 C7
- 10400 NBVL 46060 1687 B4

Mayapple Dr
- — BNBG 46112 2223 E3
- — BNBG 46112 2224 A3
- 1900 WshT 46123 2223 D7

Mayfair Dr
- 1900 INPS 46260 2118 D3
- 2100 INPS 46268 2118 D3

Mayfair Ln
- 600 CRML 46032 1901 A3

Mayfield Dr
- — CBLD 46229 2341 E2
- 3600 INPS 46235 2231 E4
- 3600 INPS 46235 2232 A3

Mayfield Ln
- 6300 ZNVL 46077 1899 C6

Mayflower Dr
- 3500 INPS 46221 2444 E4

Mayflower Park Dr
- — ClyT 46032 2008 D1
- 7000 INPS 46077 2008 D1
- 7000 EglT 46032 2008 D1
- 7000 EglT 46077 1899 D7
- 7000 EglT 46032 2008 D1
- 9600 INPS 46032 2008 D2

Mayhew Dr
- 2300 INPS 46227 2556 B6

Maynard Dr
- 800 INPS 46227 2555 D3
- 1100 HMCT 46227 2555 E3
- 1400 INPS 46227 2556 A3
- 2400 INPS 46227 2556 B3

Mayor Blvd
- — INPS 46217 2554 A3

May Ridge Run
- 5400 INPS 46254 2117 B7

Maywood Rd
- 9900 INPS 46241 2445 B2
- — INPS 46241 2445 B2

S Maywood Rd
- 2500 INPS 46241 2445 B2

E Maze Rd
- 8500 INPS 46259 2558 C6
- 9000 INPS 46259 2559 B6

Maze Creek Dr
- 11800 INPS 46259 2559 C7

McClarney Ct
- — INPS 46217 2554 D4

E McClarnon Dr
- 200 GNFD 46140 2237 B5
- 1200 CtrT 46140 2237 B5
- 1200 GNFD 46140 2237 B5

W McClarnon Dr
- 200 GNFD 46140 2236 D5

McClellan Ct
- 6000 INPS 46254 2117 C4

McClellan Rd
- 100 GNFD 46140 2236 D7

McCloud Ct N
- 5700 INPS 46254 2117 B5

McCloud Ct S
- 5700 INPS 46254 2117 B5

McClure St
- 300 INPS 46241 2336 A4

N McClure St
- 900 INPS 46222 2336 A1

S McClure St
- 1100 INPS 46241 2336 A6
- 2400 INPS 46241 2445 A3
- 3000 INPS 46221 2445 A3

McCollough Ct
- 1500 INPS 46260 2009 E7

McCollough Dr
- 1500 INPS 46260 2009 E7

McCollum Ct
- 1600 PNFD 46168 2550 D1

McCollum Ln
- 1600 PNFD 46168 2550 D1

McConnell Wy
- 5000 INPS 46227 2446 E5

McCord Ln
- 7000 INPS 46217 2555 B4

N McCord Rd
- 9000 MCVL 46055 2015 D4
- 9000 VrnT 46055 2015 D4

W McCord Rd
- 5000 VrnT 46055 2015 E4
- 5000 VrnT 46055 2016 A3
- 5900 MCVL 46055 2015 E4

McCord St
- 1100 INPS 46203 2446 E2

N McCord St
- 7500 MCVL 46055 2015 C7

S McCord St
- — PTBR 46167 2112 E4

N McCorkle Ln
- 100 MdnT 46113 2661 E4

McCormick St
- — INPS 46203 2336 D3

McCormicks Dr
- 10 DNVL 46122 2329 B4

McCoy St
- 4400 LWNC 46226 2231 B1
- 4500 LWNC 46226 2122 B7

McCray St
- 4400 SDWY 46224 2226 D6

S McCrea St
- 200 INPS 46225 2337 C4

McCready Ct
- 1300 INPS 46217 2554 E5

McCullam Ct
- — MdlT 46167 2113 B5

McCullam Dr
- — MdlT 46167 2113 B5

McCully St
- 300 GNFD 46140 2345 D2

McCurdy Rd
- 4400 INPS 46234 2330 B3
- 4500 INPS 46234 2116 B7

McDougal St
- 1100 INPS 46203 2446 E2
- 6300 INPS 46203 2448 D2

McDowell Ct
- 1700 INPS 46229 2232 C7

McDowell Dr
- 11000 INPS 46229 2232 C7

McDuffee Run
- 13000 CRML 46033 1903 E2

McFarland Blvd
- 7000 INPS 46237 2556 E4
- 7300 INPS 46237 2557 A4

McFarland Ct
- — INPS 46227 2556 C6

McFarland Ln
- 7800 INPS 46237 2557 A6

McFarland Pl
- 3200 INPS 46227 2556 C6

S McFarland Rd
- 4900 INPS 46227 2447 C6
- 5500 INPS 46227 2556 C2
- 6900 SPRT 46227 2556 C5

McFarland Wy
- 3200 INPS 46227 2556 C6

E McGaughey Rd
- 8600 INPS 46239 2449 D5

McGreagor Rd
- — MrlT 46259 2559 E5
- — MrlT 46259 2560 A5

E McGregor Rd
- 8400 INPS 46259 2558 C4
- 9800 INPS 46259 2559 B5
- 11700 MrlT 46259 2559 B5
- 12100 MrlT 46126 2559 E5

W McGregor Rd
- 300 INPS 46217 2555 B5

McGuire Ct
- 4600 LWNC 46226 2122 A7

McHenry Ln
- 5100 INPS 46228 2118 D6

McIlvain Dr
- 8800 INPS 46256 2122 C1

N McIlvain Dr
- 9000 INPS 46256 2122 D2

McIntosh Ct
- 5300 LWNC 46226 2121 E6

McIntosh Ln
- 300 WshT 46074 1792 C4
- 7000 INPS 46226 2121 E6
- 7100 LWNC 46226 2122 A5

McKean Ln
- 4100 INPS 46250 2011 E6

McKenna Wy
- 17100 NBVL 46062 1794 E1

McKenzie Pkwy
- 11500 CRML 46032 1901 E6

E McKenzie Rd
- 6300 LWNC 46235 2124 A3

McKeon Ct
- 18700 NBVL 46062 1686 A5

McKim Av
- 100 INPS 46201 2338 A4

McKinges Cir
- 5900 CRML 46033 1903 E2

McKinley Ct
- 6200 INPS 46220 2120 B3

McKinley Dr
- 100 MRVL 46158 2659 E1

N McKinley St
- 10 GNWD 46143 2665 C3

S McKinley St
- — GNWD 46143 2665 C4

McKinstray Ct
- 11400 FSHR 46038 1903 E6

McLain Ct
- 7000 INPS 46217 2555 B4

McLaren Ln
- 400 ClyT 46032 1901 B6

McLaughlin Av
- 300 SPRT 46227 2556 C3

McLaughlin St
- — INPS 46227 2556 C3
- — SPRT 46227 2556 C3

McLean Pl
- 10 INPS 46202 2228 C6

McLeay Dr
- 2400 INPS 46220 2120 B5

McNutt Cir
- 8500 INPS 46256 2013 C4

McPherson St
- 10400 ClyT 46280 2010 E1
- 10800 ClyT 46280 1901 E7

Mead Ct
- 5600 INPS 46220 2120 C5
- 12600 FSHR 46038 1905 A3

Mead Dr
- 5600 INPS 46220 2120 C5

Meadow Cir
- 400 GNWD 46142 2664 C2

N Meadow Cir
- 6300 INPS 46268 2117 C3

Meadow Cres
- 800 CRML 46032 1792 E7

Meadow Ct
- — CRML 46033 1902 D5
- 800 MRVL 46158 2660 A5

Meadow Ct E
- 10 WTLD 46184 2774 E4

Meadow Ct W
- 10 WTLD 46184 2774 E4

Meadow Dr
- 10 NPLN 46163 2452 A3
- 10 MdnT 46113 2661 A2
- 200 DNVL 46122 2330 B3
- 200 GNWD 46142 2665 B2
- 2700 BrnT 46112 2114 C1

N Meadow Dr
- 5400 INPS 46268 2117 C3

S Meadow Dr
- 3300 INPS 46239 2449 A3

Meadow Ln
- 10 BrnT 46158 2660 A5
- 10 CRML 46032 1902 A2
- 10 MRVL 46158 2660 A5

N Meadow Ln
- 7000 ZNVL 46077 1899 C3

S Meadow Ln
- 500 ZNVL 46077 1899 C4

Meadow Bank Ct
- 100 DNVL 46122 2330 B3

Meadowbank Ct
- 100 DNVL 46122 2330 B3

Meadowbank Rd
- 200 DNVL 46122 2330 B3

Meadow Bend Cir
- 7900 INPS 46259 2558 B5

Meadow Bend Dr
- 7800 INPS 46259 2558 B5

Meadow Bend Ln
- 7800 INPS 46259 2558 B6

Meadowbrook Av
- 4900 INPS 46221 2444 C4
- 6800 LWNC 46226 2121 E7

Meadowbrook Ct
- 800 INPS 46240 2010 E7

Meadowbrook Dr
- 8100 INPS 46240 2010 E5
- 8400 FSHR 46038 1904 C6

E Meadowbrook Dr
- 1200 INPS 46240 2010 E5

W Meadowbrook Dr
- 1200 INPS 46240 2011 A5

Meadow Creek Blvd
- 10 WTLD 46184 2774 E7

Meadow Creek Blvd E
- 10 WTLD 46184 2775 A4

N Meadowcreek Dr
- 300 WshT 46074 1792 C4
- 14600 WTFD 46033 1793 C6

Meadow Creek South Dr
- 100 WTLD 46184 2774 E4

Meadowfield Blvd
- — LWNC 46236 2123 D4
- 6400 LWNC 46236 2123 D4

Meadowfield Cir
- 11500 CRML 46032 1901 E6

Meadowfield Dr
- 6300 LWNC 46235 2124 A3

Meadowgate Ct
- 8000 INPS 46268 2008 E5

Meadow Glen Dr
- 100 AVON 46123 2332 C3

Meadow Grass Wy
- 13900 FSHR 46038 1904 E1
- 14000 FSHR 46038 1795 E7

Meadowgreen Dr
- 6600 LWNC 46236 2123 C2

Meadow Lake Dr
- — LWNC 46062 1686 A5

W Meadow Lake Dr
- 4600 SCkT 46163 2343 A3

Meadowlands Ct
- — WshT 46074 1792 E3

Meadowlands Ln
- — WTFD 46074 1792 E3

Meadowlark Cir
- 11400 FSHR 46038 1903 E6

Meadowlark Ct
- 500 WTLD 46184 2775 A6
- 4200 INPS 46226 2231 C1

Meadowlark Dr
- 200 BNBG 46112 2224 A4
- 200 LcnT 46112 2224 A4
- 200 PNFD 46168 2442 A4
- 300 WTLD 46184 2775 A6
- 5800 INPS 46226 2230 C1
- 8200 INPS 46226 2231 C1
- 8400 LWNC 46226 2231 C1
- 9000 INPS 46235 2231 D1
- 9000 LWNC 46235 2231 D1
- 10000 INPS 46235 2232 B1

Meadow Lark Ln
- 3500 LcnT 46112 2224 B3

Meadowlark Ln
- 200 BNBG 46112 2223 C4
- 4200 INPS 46221 2444 B5

Meadowlark Mnr
- 9000 INPS 46235 2232 A1

Meadowlark Pl
- 12600 FSHR 46038 1905 A3

Meadowmor Ln
- 8100 INPS 46278 2007 B4

Meadowpond Wy
- 6300 LWNC 46236 2123 C3

Meadow Ridge Dr
- 7500 DelT 46038 1904 B7
- 7500 INPS 46038 1904 B7

Meadowridge Ln
- 8700 INPS 46217 2555 A7

Meadowridge Tr
- 500 INPS 46217 2555 B7

Meadow Rue Rd
- 7700 NBVL 46062 1686 B5

Meadows
- — PTBR 46167 2113 A3

Meadows Blvd
- 5400 INPS 46268 2117 C3

N Meadows Cir
- 900 BCkT 46140 2233 B7

Meadows Ct
- — WshT 46074 1684 A2
- — WTLD 46184 2774 C7
- 100 WshT 46074 1684 A2
- 100 PTBR 46167 2113 A4
- 3300 INPS 46205 2229 C2

Meadows Dr
- 100 PTBR 46167 2113 A3
- 400 PTBR 46167 2113 A3
- 3800 INPS 46205 2229 C2
- 11100 FSHR 46038 1904 C6

W Meadows Ln
- 7000 BCkT 46140 2233 B7

Meadows Pkwy
- 3000 INPS 46205 2229 C2

Meadows Edge Ln
- 500 INPS 46217 2555 B5

Meadow Side Ct
- 3800 CRML 46074 1900 A5

S Meadow Song Ct
- 400 SCkT 46163 2343 A3

Meadowsweet Ct
- 4300 INPS 46203 2448 B5

Meadow View Ct
- 6600 WshT 46123 2332 B7

Meadowview Ct
- 400 CRML 46032 1792 D7

Meadowview Dr
- 100 MRVL 46158 2660 C4
- 6800 LWNC 46226 2121 E7

W Meadowview Dr
- 3200 BCkT 46140 2334 B7

Meadowview Ln
- 8400 FSHR 46038 1904 C6
- 10 GNWD 46142 2664 E3

E Meadow Violet
- 1200 INPS 46123 2223 D7
- 1200 AVON 46123 2223 D7
- — AVON 46123 2332 D1
- — WshT 46123 2223 D7
- — WshT 46123 2332 D1

Meadow Violet Ct
- 7400 WshT 46123 2332 C1

Meadow Violet Dr
- 7600 WshT 46123 2223 C7
- 7600 WshT 46123 2332 C1

Meadow Vista Dr
- 8600 INPS 46217 2555 B7

Meadow Vue Ct
- 10 INPS 46227 2555 C4

Meadow Vue Ct North Dr
- 10 INPS 46227 2555 C4

Meadow Vue Ct South Dr
- 10 INPS 46227 2555 C4

Meadow Wing Ct
- — NBVL 46060 1687 B5

Meadwood Dr
- 1200 DNVL 46122 2329 B4

Meagan Dr N
- 12800 MdnT 46113 2661 A3

Meander Bnd
- 4000 INPS 46268 2009 A5
- 5600 BNBG 46112 2113 D3

Meander Wy
- 100 WRvT 46142 2664 B3

W Mecca Ct
- 4700 INPS 46241 2335 D7

Mechanic St
- — INPS 46225 2337 C4
- — SCkT 46163 2452 C2

Mechanicsburg Dr
- 3300 INPS 46227 2556 C7

Meckes Dr
- 5400 INPS 46237 2448 C7

Meckes Ln
- 5400 INPS 46237 2448 B7
- 5400 INPS 46237 2557 B1

Medalist Pkwy
- 12200 CRML 46033 1903 D4

Medallion Dr
- 6600 INPS 46260 2118 D2
- 10100 WshT 46231 2442 C2
- 10300 PNFD 46231 2442 C2

Medford Av
- 1000 INPS 46222 2336 C1
- 3000 INPS 46222 2227 C4

Media Dr
- 4900 INPS 46228 2118 D7

Medical Ct
- 1100 CRML 46032 1902 B4

Medical Dr
- 10 CRML 46032 1902 B4
- 900 INPS 46202 2337 A2
- 1200 INPS 46202 2336 E2

Medina Ct
- 10 INPS 46227 2446 C5

Medina Dr
- 10 INPS 46227 2446 C5

Medina Ln
- 10 INPS 46227 2446 C5

Medina Wy
- 4100 INPS 46227 2446 C5

Medinah Ct
- 700 INPS 46239 2341 E6

S Meek St
- 100 GNFD 46140 2345 E2
- 100 NBVL 46060 1686 E7
- 300 NBVL 46060 1795 E4

Meese Rd
- — LEBN 46052 1676 E2

Meeting St
- 9500 FSHR 46038 1904 B3

Meeting House Ct
- 3000 INPS 46222 2227 C3

Meeting House Ln
- 2800 INPS 46222 2227 C3

Meeting House Rd
- 12400 CRML 46033 1900 D3

Megan Ct
- 8500 INPS 46256 2013 A4

Megan Dr
- — CRML 46074 1791 D7
- 7400 INPS 46256 2013 A4

Megan Ln
- 7400 INPS 46256 2013 A4

Meganwood Ct
- 300 INPS 46234 2334 A3

Meganwood Dr
- 8300 INPS 46234 2334 A3

Meggs St
- 17200 WTFD 46062 1793 D4
- 17300 WTFD 46074 1794 A1

Meghan Lee Dr
- 9500 INPS 46235 2122 E7

Mehaffey St
- 4600 LWNC 46226 2122 A7

STREET Block City ZIP Map# Grid

Meikel St
800 INPS 46225 2337 B5
Meith St
15400 FCkT 46040 1907 B7
Melanie Ln
7000 INPS 46217 2555 C4
Melark Dr
500 CRML 46032 1902 C3
Melbourne Cir
3300 INPS 46228 2227 A2
Melbourne Ct
14700 WshT 46074 1792 C6
Melbourne Rd
4000 INPS 46228 2227 A1
5900 INPS 46228 2118 B4
7700 INPS 46268 2009 B7
Melbourne Rd East Dr
4200 INPS 46228 2227 B1
Melbourne Rd South Dr
3100 INPS 46228 2227 B2
Melissa Ann Ct
200 WshT 46234 2333 E3
Melissa Ann Dr
9400 WshT 46234 2333 D3
Mellen St
2200 INPS 46231 2443 A1
Mellis Ct
4100 INPS 46235 2231 E2
Mellis Dr
4100 INPS 46235 2231 E1
Mellon Ct
10 INPS 46222 2227 A5
Mellot Wy
8700 INPS 46113 2552 A7
Mellowood Dr
500 INPS 46217 2555 A7
Melody Av
200 GNWD 46142 2664 C4
Melody Ct
10 BHGV 46107 2447 E5
Melody Dr
- GNFD 46140 2236 E5
Melody Ln
2100 GNFD 46140 2236 E5
2200 BCkT 46140 2344 B1
10700 GfdT 46231 2442 D5
Melrose Av
4700 INPS 46241 2335 C7
Melrose Cir
12300 FSHR 46038 1904 D4
Melrose Ct
9100 INPS 46239 2449 D5
Melrose Dr
400 NWTD 46184 2774 D5
E Melrose Dr
9100 INPS 46239 2449 D5
Melrose Ln
300 WRvT 46142 2663 D3
Melton Dr
3900 INPS 46221 2444 E5
Melt Water Dr
8200 INPS 46268 2008 E5
Melvenia St
400 INPS 46219 2339 B4
Memorial Dr
10 MRVL 46158 2659 D3
500 BHGV 46107 2447 E4
Memorial Sq
10 GNFD 46140 2236 D7
Memorial Knoll Dr
- LcnT 46112 2115 D5
Memory Ln
500 CRML 46032 1901 D1
W Memory Ln
5900 SCkT 46163 2342 D2
Mendenhall Rd
5000 INPS 46241 2443 D7
5000 INPS 46241 2552 D3
5800 INPS 46221 2552 D3
7000 INPS 46113 2552 D4
Mendenhall St
7500 INPS 46113 2552 E5
7500 INPS 46221 2552 E5
Mendora Dr
5900 INPS 46228 2118 E4
5900 INPS 46228 2119 A4
Menlo Ln
2100 INPS 46240 2011 B5
Menlo Court West Dr
8100 INPS 46240 2011 B6
Menlo Ct East Dr
8100 INPS 46240 2011 B5
Mensa Dr
100 NBVL 46062 1686 B7
Mercantile Blvd
- NBVL 46060 1796 A2
Mercator Dr
10 GNWD 46143 2665 D5
Mercedes Dr
7900 INPS 46268 2009 C6
Mercer Rd
8600 INPS 46268 2009 B4
Merchant Dr
- AVON 46123 2332 D4
Merchants Dr
2700 INPS 46222 2227 A5
Merchants Square Dr
200 CRML 46032 1902 B5
Mercury Ct
2700 INPS 46229 2231 D5
14900 WshT 46032 1792 D6
Mercury Dr
9000 INPS 46229 2231 D5
10300 INPS 46229 2232 B5
Mercyside Ct
6200 LWNC 46236 2123 A3
Meredith Av
2800 INPS 46201 2338 C4
Merganser Dr
7000 FSHR 46038 1903 E5
7000 FSHR 46038 1904 A6
7300 INPS 46260 2118 E1
7400 INPS 46260 2009 E7
Merganser Pkwy
- GNWD 46143 2666 A6
Meridee Dr
3700 INPS 46237 2447 D5
Meridian Ct
200 PTBR 46167 2112 E3
E Meridian Ln
10 INPS 46220 2119 C5
Meridian Pkwy
6400 INPS 46220 2119 C3
Meridian Pl
10 INPS 46205 2119 C7
N Meridian Rd
200 GNFD 46140 2345 A2
300 CtrT 46140 2345 A1
400 GNFD 46140 2236 A7
3700 CtrT 46140 2236 A1
S Meridian Rd
10 CtrT 46140 2345 A3
10 GNFD 46140 2345 A3
2000 BwnT 46140 2345 A5
N Meridian St
- CRML 46032 1793 B6
- CRML 46033 1793 B6
10 GNWD 46142 2665 C3
10 GNWD 46143 2665 C3
10 PTBR 46167 2112 E3
100 INPS 46204 2337 C3
100 LEBN 46052 1677 A5
1100 INPS 46202 2337 C1
1200 INPS 46142 2665 C1
1200 INPS 46143 2665 C1
1200 PltT 46142 2665 C1
1200 PltT 46143 2665 C1
1600 INPS 46202 2228 C4
2200 INPS 46205 2228 C4
2200 INPS 46208 2228 C4
4500 INPS 46205 2119 C7
5200 INPS 46220 2119 C7
6100 INPS 46208 2119 D4
6200 INPS 46260 2119 D4
7100 INPS 46240 2119 C2
7300 INPS 46240 2010 C5
8800 INPS 46260 2010 C4
9200 CRML 46240 2010 C3
9600 CRML 46280 2010 C5
9600 CRML 46290 2010 C1
10400 CRML 46280 1901 C7
10400 CRML 46290 1901 C7
10600 ClyT 46032 1901 C7
10600 CRML 46032 1901 C7
13900 CRML 46032 1902 A1
14800 WTFD 46032 1793 B6
14800 WTFD 46033 1793 B6
15100 WshT 46032 1793 A4
15100 WshT 46033 1793 B6
N Meridian St US-31
- CRML 46032 1793 B6
- CRML 46033 1793 B6
9800 CRML 46280 2010 C1
9800 CRML 46290 2010 C1
10400 CRML 46280 1901 C7
10400 CRML 46290 1901 C7
10600 ClyT 46032 1901 C7
10600 CRML 46032 1901 C7
13900 CRML 46032 1902 A1
14800 WTFD 46032 1793 B6
14800 WTFD 46033 1793 B6
15100 WshT 46032 1793 A4
15100 WshT 46033 1793 B6
S Meridian St
- PTBR 46167 2112 E4
10 GNWD 46142 2665 C4
10 GNWD 46143 2665 C4
10 INPS 46204 2337 C4
100 INPS 46225 2337 C5
100 LEBN 46052 1677 A7
1200 LEBN 46052 1786 A1
2200 INPS 46225 2446 C4
3000 INPS 46217 2446 C4
3000 INPS 46227 2446 C4
5500 INPS 46217 2555 C1
6000 INPS 46227 2555 C3
S Meridian St SR-135
5600 INPS 46217 2555 C3
5600 INPS 46227 2555 C3
Meridian St S
1800 GNWD 46143 2665 C7
Meridian Ter
7200 INPS 46217 2555 C4
Meridian Corners Blvd
13100 CRML 46032 1901 C2
N Meridian Hills Blvd
10 INPS 46240 2119 C1
10 INPS 46260 2119 C1
Meridian Hills Ct
7300 INPS 46260 2119 B1
7400 INPS 46260 2010 B7
Meridian Hills Ln
7900 INPS 46240 2010 C6
Meridian Meadows Ct
1000 GNWD 46142 2664 C1
Meridian Meadows Rd
3000 GNWD 46142 2664 B1
Meridian Oaks Dr
1600 GNWD 46142 2664 C3
Meridian Parke Dr
3100 GNWD 46142 2664 B3
Meridian Parke Ln
300 GNWD 46142 2664 B3
E Meridian School Rd
10 INPS 46227 2555 C6
W Meridian School Rd
10 INPS 46217 2555 B6
Meridian Square Dr
8600 INPS 46240 2010 C4
N Meridian Sreet West Dr
6000 INPS 46208 2119 C3
6000 INPS 46220 2119 C3
6200 INPS 46260 2119 C3
Meridian Woods Blvd
6300 INPS 46217 2555 B2
Meriman Dr
- GNWD 46143 2666 A5
Merlin Ct
11300 FSHR 46038 1906 A6
Merlin Lake Ct
2700 INPS 46229 2232 A5
Merlin Lake Dr
10000 INPS 46229 2232 A5
Merom Ct
6400 INPS 46268 2117 C3
Merriam Rd
7200 INPS 46240 2120 D1
Merrick Ln
3100 INPS 46222 2227 B3
Merrick Wy
3600 INPS 46222 2227 B3
Merrill Ct
9000 FSHR 46060 1795 D7
E Merrill St
10 INPS 46225 2337 C5
500 INPS 46203 2337 D5
W Merrill St
10 INPS 46225 2337 C4
Merrimac Dr
- WshT 46032 1792 B6
400 WshT 46074 1792 B6
Merrimac Pl
10 INPS 46214 2335 A3
Merrit Rd
400 LWNC 46216 2122 D5
Merry Ln
200 GNWD 46142 2665 A3
Merry Hill Dr
6900 INPS 46237 2448 E6
Mersey Ct
10 ClyT 46032 1901 C6
Merts Dr
2800 INPS 46237 2447 C3
Mesa Ct
4200 INPS 46241 2444 D3
Mesa Dr
4400 INPS 46241 2444 D3
Mesa Valley Ct
11600 FSHR 46038 1906 A5
Mesa Verde Dr
5100 INPS 46237 2448 D7
Mesic Ct
8400 INPS 46278 2007 B6
Mesilla Ct
3300 INPS 46226 2231 C4
Mesquite Ct
- MCVL 46055 2124 B1
3400 INPS 46214 2225 D3
Messersmith Dr
4100 WRvT 46142 2663 E4
Messiah Pl
8300 INPS 46256 2013 A5
Messina Cir
12900 FSHR 46038 1905 A3
Metairie Dr
600 GNWD 46143 2665 E5
600 GNWD 46143 2666 A4
Metsker Ln
10 NbvT 46062 1686 A7
Metz Ct
3000 INPS 46268 2118 C2
Metzger Ct
8300 INPS 46256 2013 C4
Metzler Dr
1500 PNFD 46168 2550 D1
Meyer St
1800 GNWD 46143 2665 C6
Meyers Av
2300 SDWY 46224 2226 D6
Mia Ct
9500 PNFD 46168 2550 D2
Mia Dr
14900 WTFD 46033 1793 C6
Miami Ct N
1400 PNFD 46168 2441 D5
Miami Ct S
1400 PNFD 46168 2441 D5
Miami Dr
4500 INPS 46205 2120 C7
4500 INPS 46205 2229 D2
Miami St
10 WRvT 46062 1578 D7
10 WynT 46062 1578 D7
E Miami St
500 INPS 46202 2337 D3
500 INPS 46204 2337 D3
W Miami St
1700 INPS 46222 2336 D3
Mi Casa Av
3700 INPS 46237 2556 D3
Micawber Cir
7500 INPS 46256 2013 B7
Micawber Ct
7600 INPS 46256 2013 B7
Michael Ct
10 LcnT 46112 2114 A7
5300 WRvT 46142 2663 C2
Michael Dr
10 PNFD 46168 2441 E5
Michael Ln
2100 MdnT 46113 2661 C5
Michele Ln
1500 GNWD 46142 2664 C2
Michelle Mnr
1400 CtrT 46122 2329 A1
Michigan Pkwy
200 AVON 46123 2333 A3
200 WshT 46123 2333 A3
Michigan Pl
1100 INPS 46202 2337 E2
N Michigan Rd
- INPS 46208 2227 E1
- INPS 46208 2228 A2
- ZNVL 46077 1899 E7
10 UnnT 46077 1680 E7
1000 MrnT 46075 1680 C3
1000 UnnT 46075 1680 C3
3000 MrnT 46075 1571 B6
4000 MrnT 46052 1571 B6
4200 INPS 46228 2118 E7
4200 INPS 46228 2227 E1
5200 BwnT 46126 2670 E5
5800 MrlT 46126 2670 E5
5800 SgCT 46126 2670 E5
N Michigan Rd
6100 MrnT 46052 1570 E1
6100 MrnT 46069 1570 E1
6200 INPS 46260 2118 D4
6200 INPS 46268 2118 D4
7700 MrlT 46126 2560 D7
7700 MrlT 46126 2669 E1
8900 INPS 46268 2009 A3
9600 ClyT 46032 2009 A2
9600 INPS 46032 2009 A2
9800 ClyT 46032 2008 E1
10000 ClyT 46077 2008 E1
10500 ClyT 46032 1899 E7
10500 ClyT 46077 1899 E7
N Michigan Rd US-421
- ZNVL 46077 1899 E7
10 UnnT 46077 1680 E7
1000 MrnT 46075 1680 C3
1000 UnnT 46075 1680 C3
3000 MrnT 46075 1571 B6
4000 MrnT 46052 1571 B6
6100 MrnT 46052 1570 E1
6100 MrnT 46069 1570 E1
9500 INPS 46268 2009 A2
9600 ClyT 46032 2009 A2
9600 INPS 46032 2009 A2
9800 ClyT 46032 2008 E1
10000 ClyT 46077 2008 E1
10500 ClyT 46032 1899 E7
10500 ClyT 46077 1899 E7
S Michigan Rd
10 UnnT 46077 1789 E1
700 UnnT 46077 1790 A4
3000 EglT 46077 1790 B7
3400 EglT 46077 1899 C2
4500 ZNVL 46077 1899 C2
6000 ClyT 46077 1899 C2
S Michigan Rd US-421
10 UnnT 46077 1789 E1
700 UnnT 46077 1790 A4
3000 EglT 46077 1790 B7
3400 EglT 46077 1899 C2
4500 ZNVL 46077 1899 C2
6000 ClyT 46077 1899 C2
E Michigan St
10 INPS 46204 2337 D2
500 INPS 46202 2337 D2
1400 INPS 46201 2337 D2
1400 INPS 46201 2338 B2
4900 INPS 46201 2339 A2
6600 INPS 46219 2339 D2
8000 INPS 46219 2340 C2
9500 INPS 46229 2340 E2
9600 INPS 46229 2341 A2
11800 CBLD 46229 2341 E2
N Michigan St
600 GNFD 46140 2236 C7
W Michigan St
10 GNFD 46140 2236 D6
10 INPS 46204 2337 B2
300 INPS 46202 2337 B2
1200 INPS 46202 2336 E2
3300 INPS 46222 2336 A2
4000 INPS 46222 2335 E2
N Mickley Av
1100 INPS 46224 2335 B1
1400 SDWY 46224 2335 B1
1500 SDWY 46224 2226 B7
S Mickley Av
300 INPS 46241 2335 B4
Middle Dr
- NbvT 46062 1686 D1
- SCkT 46163 2452 B2
- WTFD 46062 1684 E7
800 NWTD 46184 2774 D4
1000 INPS 46202 2337 A2
10600 ClyT 46280 1902 B7
N Middle Dr
6000 LWNC 46235 2123 D4
N Middle St
10 GNWD 46143 2665 D3
S Middle St
10 GNWD 46143 2665 D4
Middle Bay Ln
8000 INPS 46236 2014 C6
Middleberry Pl
- WshT 46074 1792 B4
Middlebrook Ct
10300 FCkT 46055 2015 C1
Middlebury Dr
- WshT 46074 1792 A4
Middlebury Wy
9100 INPS 46113 2551 E6
Middlefield Ct
3300 INPS 46222 2227 B3
Middlefield Dr
3600 INPS 46222 2227 B3
Middleham Cir
600 INPS 46107 2447 D4
Middleham Ln
1200 INPS 46107 2447 D4
Middle Jamestown Rd
500 CtrT 46052 1785 D3
2500 HsnT 46052 1785 A5
Middleton Ct
6700 INPS 46268 2117 C2
Middletown Av
14300 WynT 46060 1688 D7
14300 WynT 46060 1689 A6
17200 WynT 46060 1797 B1
Middlewood Ln
13200 FSHR 46060 1905 C2
Midfield Service Rd
2900 INPS 46241 2443 D3
Midland Ct
10 DNVL 46122 2329 C5
Midland Dr
400 DNVL 46122 2329 C4
Midland Ln
- NBVL 46062 1794 C5
E Midland Rd
2400 INPS 46227 2447 B7
W Midland Rd
200 INPS 46217 2446 B7
Midlothian Ln
2200 INPS 46214 2225 C6
Midlothian Wy
7900 INPS 46214 2225 C6
Midnight Ct
600 INPS 46239 2341 B4
Midnight Dr
10500 INPS 46239 2341 B5
Midnight Pass
10700 FSHR 46038 1905 C7
E Midsummer Dr
8500 INPS 46239 2449 C4
Midvale Dr
3000 INPS 46222 2226 D4
Midway Ct
1300 CRML 46032 1792 A7
6100 INPS 46224 2226 A4
Midwest Blvd
1700 INPS 46214 2225 C7
Mignon Dr
5700 INPS 46254 2117 B5
Mignon Ln
- INPS 46254 2117 A5
Mikal Ln
600 BNBG 46112 2114 A5
Mikayla Ct
7700 INPS 46217 2554 C5
Mikco Ln
6000 INPS 46250 2012 C3
Mikes Wy
1000 GNWD 46143 2665 D1
1000 PltT 46143 2665 D1
Mikesell Dr
7000 INPS 46260 2118 E1
7300 INPS 46260 2009 E7
Milan St
3200 INPS 46222 2227 A4
Milburn Dr
- BNBG 46112 2223 D4
Milburn St
1200 INPS 46202 2337 A1
2200 INPS 46202 2228 A6
2200 INPS 46208 2228 A6
Mildred Dr
2900 INPS 46222 2226 E5
W Miles Dr
7300 INPS 46231 2334 D6
Miles Rd
5700 LtyT 46168 2440 B7
5700 LtyT 46168 2549 C1
5700 PNFD 46168 2440 B7
5700 PNFD 46168 2549 C1
Miley Av
400 INPS 46222 2336 D2
Milford Ct
10300 INPS 46235 2232 B4
Milford Rd
3200 INPS 46235 2232 B4
Milford St
- CRML 46032 1900 E3
Milhon
- BrnT 46158 2658 C7
Milhon Dr
10 BrnT 46158 2658 C7
Milhouse Ct
5900 INPS 46221 2553 B2
Milhouse Dr
5400 INPS 46221 2553 B2
Milhouse Rd
5100 INPS 46221 2553 C2
6300 INPS 46221 2552 D2
7500 INPS 46241 2552 D2
Milhousen Tr
- WTFD 46074 1792 C3
Mill Run
9900 ClyT 46032 2010 A1
Mill St
- BNBG 46112 2114 C6
10 WTFD 46074 1684 A7
200 WTFD 46074 1793 B1
1600 INPS 46202 2228 B7
E Mill St
10 NPLN 46163 2452 B3
100 DNVL 46122 2329 E4
N Mill St
100 PNFD 46168 2441 B5
S Mill St
100 PNFD 46168 2441 B5
W Mill St
- GNFD 46140 2345 D2
10 NPLN 46163 2452 A3
300 DNVL 46122 2329 C4
Millbrae Dr
- CRML 46074 1900 B1
Millbrook Cir
6800 INPS 46237 2557 D3
Millbrook Dr
600 AVON 46123 2332 C6
Millbrook Pkwy
- CRML 46032 2011 C1
Mill Creek Cir
6700 INPS 46214 2225 C2
6700 INPS 46214 2226 A2
Mill Creek Dr
3500 INPS 46214 2225 C2
3500 INPS 46214 2226 A2
Mill Creek Pl
9700 ClyT 46032 2010 A2
N Mill Creek Rd
10 NBVL 46062 1685 D5
20900 NBVL 46062 1576 D7
20900 NbvT 46062 1576 D7
20900 NbvT 46062 1685 D1
21600 JknT 46034 1576 D6
21600 NBVL 46034 1576 D6
21600 NbvT 46034 1576 D6
23600 JknT 46030 1576 D2
S Mill Creek Rd
16700 NbvT 46062 1794 D2
17100 NbvT 46062 1685 D7
W Milledgeville Av
1400 HsnT 46052 1894 C2
Millen Dr
12000 FSHR 46038 1906 C4
Miller Dr
300 GNWD 46142 2665 B2
400 MdnT 46113 2661 C2
S Miller Dr
3700 INPS 46239 2449 B4
Miller Ln
800 WshT 46123 2331 B2
W Miller St
1400 INPS 46221 2336 E6
3100 INPS 46241 2336 B6
5000 INPS 46241 2335 C6
7000 INPS 46241 2334 D6
Millers Ct
1100 NBVL 46060 1687 A6
Millersville
5400 INPS 46220 2121 A6
Millersville Dr
1800 INPS 46205 2229 A2
Millersville Rd
- INPS 46226 2121 A6
3900 INPS 46205 2229 A2
4500 INPS 46205 2120 D7
4600 INPS 46226 2120 E7
Millerwood Ct
1300 LEBN 46052 1677 B5
Millerwood Dr
800 LEBN 46052 1677 B4
Miller Woods Ln
6000 INPS 46237 2448 C5
Millet Ct
10 DNVL 46122 2330 B2
Mill Farm Ct
8500 INPS 46227 2555 E7
Mill Farm Rd
10 NbvT 46062 1685 D5
Mill Grove Dr
18900 NBVL 46062 1685 C4
Milliner Ct
7700 PNFD 46168 2441 D2
Millis Dr
7000 INPS 46113 2552 A4
Mill Oak Dr
6100 NBVL 46062 1685 C4
Mill Pond Ln
7900 INPS 46278 2007 C6
Mill Ridge Dr
300 ClyT 46290 2010 C1
Millridge Dr
1400 GNWD 46143 2665 C6
Mill Run Blvd
1000 GNFD 46140 2237 A7
E Mill Run Blvd
1100 GNFD 46140 2237 A7
N Mill Run Blvd
900 GNFD 46140 2237 A7
Mill Run Cir
3600 INPS 46214 2225 E3
Mill Run Ct
10 DelT 46038 1904 B1
Mill Run Dr
200 PNFD 46168 2441 B4
1100 NbvT 46062 1685 D6
6600 INPS 46214 2225 E3
Mill Run Ovlk
1100 NbvT 46062 1685 D6
E Mills Av
500 INPS 46227 2446 D5
1400 INPS 46227 2447 A5
W Mills Av
6300 INPS 46241 2444 A5
Mills Rd
8300 INPS 46241 2552 B3
W Mills Rd
5100 INPS 46221 2553 C3
6400 INPS 46221 2552 E3
E Mills St
200 GNFD 46140 2345 E2
Millside Dr
6600 INPS 46221 2553 A3
Millstone Ct
4800 INPS 46254 2116 D7
13800 CRML 46032 1792 D7
Mill Stream Cir
7900 INPS 46278 2007 B6
Mill Stream Ct
13700 CRML 46032 1792 C7
13700 CRML 46032 1901 C1
Millstream Rd
4000 WRvT 46143 2663 E7
Mill View Ct
4300 INPS 46226 2230 E1
Millview Ct
200 MRVL 46158 2660 B4
Mill View Dr
6800 INPS 46226 2230 E1
Mill Water Ln
1400 INPS 46227 2555 E7
Millwood Cir
2600 WTFD 46074 1684 C7
Millwood Ct
1000 INPS 46260 2010 A4
Millwright Ct
5000 INPS 46254 2116 D7
Milroy Rd
5400 LWNC 46216 2122 B6
Milton Ct
10500 FCkT 46040 2015 E1
Milton St
6600 INPS 46221 2552 E5
Milwaukee Ct
1100 INPS 46217 2554 E7
1100 INPS 46217 2555 A7
Mimi Dr
- BHGV 46237 2447 E6
Mimosa Ct
1400 GNFD 46140 2237 B6
13900 FSHR 46060 1796 A7
13900 FSHR 46060 1905 B1
19400 NBVL 46060 1687 B3
Mimosa Dr
- LcnT 46112 2115 E6
Mimosa Ln
6300 INPS 46259 2559 D3
Minden Dr
- FSHR 46060 1906 C2
Minden Dr
5700 INPS 46221 2553 B4
Mindy Ct
800 WTFD 46074 1793 B2
Mindy Dr
4700 LWNC 46235 2123 A7
Mindy Ln
100 BNBG 46112 2223 C4
Mineral Lake Ct
- BNBG 46112 2114 E5
Minerva St
600 LEBN 46052 1676 D6
N Minger Rd
3400 INPS 46222 2226 E3
Mingo Ct
2700 INPS 46217 2554 C4
Mingo Ln
2600 INPS 46217 2554 C4
Minlo Dr
6300 INPS 46227 2556 C2
E Minnesota St
10 INPS 46225 2337 C6
500 INPS 46203 2337 D6
3800 INPS 46203 2338 E6
4800 INPS 46203 2339 A6
W Minnesota St
10 INPS 46225 2337 C6
1500 INPS 46221 2336 D7
2300 INPS 46241 2336 A7
3800 INPS 46241 2335 E7
6300 INPS 46241 2334 E7
Minnow Dr
6800 INPS 46237 2448 E7
Minnow Ln
100 FCkT 46060 1798 B7
Minocqua Av
1400 INPS 46203 2338 C7
Minocqua St
2200 INPS 46203 2447 C1
Minor Ct
2800 INPS 46268 2118 C2
Mint Dr
4700 INPS 46237 2556 E5
Minton Ct
4700 CRML 46033 1903 A3
Minturn Ln
1600 INPS 46260 2009 E7
W Minturn Ln
1400 INPS 46260 2009 E7
Minuteman Cir
3800 ClyT 46032 1899 E7
Miracle Ct
3900 INPS 46237 2556 D5
Miracle Dr
7300 INPS 46237 2556 D4
Miracle Rd
7500 INPS 46237 2556 D5
Mirador Ln
- FSHR 46038 1905 D7
Mirafield Ln
9800 MCVL 46055 2015 C3
Miramar Ct
6400 INPS 46250 2012 D2
Miranda Cir
10000 FSHR 46038 1905 A3
Mission Dr
10 INPS 46241 2335 A4
3500 INPS 46224 2226 A3
4100 INPS 46254 2226 A1
4500 INPS 46254 2117 A7
N Mission Dr
- INPS 46214 2335 A3
Mission Ter
6300 INPS 46254 2226 A1
Mission Hills Dr
1000 GNWD 46143 2666 B3
Mission Hills Ln
2800 INPS 46234 2225 B5
N Missouri St
1400 INPS 46202 2337 B1
1500 INPS 46202 2228 A7
S Missouri St
- INPS 46204 2337 B3
900 INPS 46225 2337 B5
5400 INPS 46217 2446 B7
Mistflower Ct
3900 INPS 46235 2232 B2
Mistflower Ln
7600 NBVL 46062 1686 A4
Mistflower Wy
10600 INPS 46235 2232 B2
Mistletoe Dr
3600 INPS 46227 2556 D4
3800 INPS 46237 2556 D4
Misty Cir
9100 INPS 46260 2009 E3
Misty Ct
9100 INPS 46260 2009 E3
Misty Dr
8200 LWNC 46236 2014 E5
Misty Ln
1400 INPS 46260 2009 E3
Misty Wy
12100 LWNC 46236 2014 E5
12200 LWNC 46236 2015 A5
Misty Cove
8200 LWNC 46236 2014 E5
Misty Hollow Ln
10600 FSHR 46038 1904 B7
Misty Knoll Ct
10100 FSHR 46038 2014 A1
Misty Lake Cir
9100 INPS 46260 2009 E3
Misty Lake Ct
9100 INPS 46260 2009 E3
Misty Lake Dr
1500 INPS 46260 2009 E3
Misty Meadow Dr
7600 INPS 46217 2555 A5
Misty Pine Ct
14400 CRML 46032 1792 B7
Misty Ridge Cir
5600 INPS 46237 2557 B1
Misty Ridge Dr
5600 INPS 46237 2557 B1

STREET Block City ZIP Map# Grid

Misty Woods Ln
7000 INPS 46237 2557 B4
Mitchell Rd
11600 CRML 46032 1902 A5
Mitchell St
1000 INPS 46222 2336 B1
Mitchner Av
- INPS 46226 2231 A4
N Mitchner Av
1000 INPS 46219 2340 A1
4400 LWNC 46226 2231 A1
4600 LWNC 46226 2122 A7
Mitchner St
300 INPS 46219 2340 A4
500 INPS 46239 2340 A4
3400 INPS 46226 2231 A3
S Mitthoefer Rd
- ClkT 46259 2559 A7
- ClkT 46259 2668 A1
8000 INPS 46259 2559 A5
N Mitthoeffer Pl
2800 INPS 46229 2232 A4
N Mitthoeffer Rd
1300 INPS 46229 2341 A1
1600 INPS 46229 2232 A7
3000 INPS 46235 2232 A4
4400 INPS 46235 2123 A7
4400 LWNC 46235 2123 A7
4400 LWNC 46235 2232 A1
5300 LWNC 46236 2123 A6
S Mitthoeffer Rd
10 INPS 46229 2341 A4
500 INPS 46239 2341 A4
Moate Cir
- GNWD 46184 2774 A1
Moate Dr
11700 FSHR 46038 1906 D5
Mobile Dr
3400 INPS 46234 2224 E3
3400 LcnT 46234 2224 E3
Mobile Home Dr
4200 INPS 46241 2444 A5
Moccasin Ct
3200 INPS 46235 2232 B4
Moccosin Ct
200 WRvT 46142 2663 D2
Moccosin Pl
4500 WRvT 46142 2663 D2
Moccosin Rd
500 WRvT 46142 2663 D2
Mockernut Ct
12100 LWNC 46236 2014 E6
W Mockingbird Ct
7600 MrlT 46126 2560 C1
Mockingbird Ln
8300 INPS 46256 2013 C6
Model Sq
8400 INPS 46234 2334 B2
Modesto Ct
8600 INPS 46278 2008 A4
Modson Pl
5100 INPS 46241 2444 C3
Moffitt Ct
- CRML 46033 2011 E2
Moffitt St
1100 INPS 46227 2446 E6
Mohave Ct
10500 INPS 46235 2232 B4
Mohave Ln
3200 INPS 46235 2232 B4
Mohawk Ct
400 CRML 46033 1902 D3
Mohawk Dr
7100 LWNC 46236 2123 A1
Mohawk Ln
7100 INPS 46260 2119 A1
7800 INPS 46260 2010 A6
Mohawk Tr
- LcnT 46112 2115 D5
Mohawk Hills Dr
700 CRML 46032 1902 C3
Mohican Ct
13200 CRML 46033 1903 C2
Mohican Rd
5300 INPS 46220 2120 E6
N Mohr Dr
3500 CtrT 46140 2236 D1
E Mohr Rd
1600 CtrT 46140 2236 D1
Mohr Estate Middle Dr
4400 SCkT 46163 2452 B5
Mohr Estate South Dr
4500 SCkT 46163 2452 B6
Mojave Dr
12500 FSHR 46038 1906 A6
Moline Dr
4200 INPS 46221 2444 D4
Molique Blvd
- FSHR 46060 1906 C2
Moll Dr
8800 FSHR 46038 1904 D6
Mollenkopf Rd
9200 INPS 46256 2014 B3
9600 FCkT 46038 2014 B2
9600 FSHR 46038 2014 B2
Moller Ct
3600 INPS 46224 2226 C3
Moller Rd
2500 SDWY 46224 2226 C3
2900 INPS 46224 2226 C3
4400 INPS 46254 2226 B1
5200 INPS 46254 2117 C6
N Moller Rd
4300 INPS 46254 2226 C1
4400 INPS 46254 2117 C7
8400 INPS 46268 2008 C5
Moller Wy
4000 INPS 46254 2226 C1
Mollie Ct
9600 INPS 46259 2558 E4
Molly Ct
8400 FSHR 46038 1904 C6
Monaco Dr
4000 INPS 46220 2120 D4

STREET Block City ZIP Map# Grid

Monaghen Ln
7300 INPS 46217 2554 D5
Monahan Rd
10 ZNVL 46077 1898 E7
Monarch Cir
6100 INPS 46224 2226 A3
Monarch Ct
10300 NBVL 46060 1687 B4
Monarch Dr
6300 INPS 46224 2226 A3
Monarch Springs Dr
- NBVL 46060 1687 C5
Monarchy Ln
- GNWD 46184 2774 A1
11700 FSHR 46038 1906 E5
Monica Ct
3800 INPS 46226 2231 C2
N Monica Dr
5400 INPS 46254 2117 B6
Monitor Ct
5000 GNWD 46143 2666 B5
Monitor Dr
4300 INPS 46220 2120 E3
Monitor Ln
- ClyT 46032 1899 E7
6300 INPS 46220 2120 E3
Monmouth Dr
- WshT 46074 1792 A5
Monninger Dr
3400 INPS 46224 2226 D3
Monon Cir
400 WshT 46123 2331 E5
7300 INPS 46256 2122 A1
Monon Ct
7200 INPS 46256 2122 A1
Monroe Cres
100 LEBN 46052 1677 B3
Monroe Ct
11000 INPS 46229 2232 C7
Monroe Dr
1300 CRML 46032 1902 B5
Monroe St
100 GNFD 46140 2345 C1
300 MNVA 46157 2657 C7
600 CtrT 46140 2345 C1
1800 INPS 46229 2232 C7
N Monroe St
10 CBLD 46229 2341 C2
10 MRVL 46158 2659 D3
N Monroe St SR-267
10 MRVL 46158 2659 D3
S Monroe St
10 MRVL 46158 2659 D4
Montana Av
19600 WynT 46060 1689 D3
Montana St
1500 INPS 46218 2229 A7
Montauk Ct
3700 INPS 46214 2225 D3
Montavia Cir
5400 INPS 46239 2449 A7
Montavia Ln
5400 INPS 46239 2449 B7
Montcalm St
- CRML 46032 1900 D4
1600 INPS 46202 2228 A7
2300 INPS 46208 2228 A6
N Montcalm St
1300 INPS 46202 2337 A1
1500 INPS 46202 2228 A7
Montclair Dr
2800 INPS 46241 2444 C2
14900 WshT 46074 1792 A6
Monte Ln
9300 INPS 46256 2013 D3
Monteo Ct
11100 FCkT 46040 1907 A6
Monteray Cir
7300 AVON 46123 2332 C5
Monteray Rd
900 GNWD 46143 2665 D5
Monterey Ct
100 NBVL 46060 1686 B6
Monterey Dr
10 NBVL 46060 1686 B6
Montery Ct
8700 INPS 46226 2231 C2
Montery Rd
- INPS 46235 2232 A2
8400 INPS 46226 2231 C2
9700 INPS 46235 2231 E2
Monte Vista Ct
500 GNWD 46143 2665 D5
Monte Vista Dr
500 GNWD 46143 2665 D5
Montgomery Av
8300 INPS 46227 2556 C6
Montgomery Dr
400 WshT 46074 1792 B5
3200 INPS 46227 2556 C6
Montgomery Dr S
- BCkT 46140 2233 E2
Monticello Ct
10 GNWD 46142 2665 A3
100 NBVL 46060 1795 D2
400 GNWD 46142 2664 E4
Monticello Dr
10 GNWD 46142 2664 E3
10 GNWD 46142 2665 A3
10 INPS 46217 2446 B3
1900 GNFD 46140 2345 B1
Monticello Square Ln
- LcnT 46112 2115 E6
Montroff Cir
7000 INPS 46256 2121 E2
Montrose Ct
400 INPS 46234 2334 A2
Montrose Ln
16100 WshT 46074 1792 E3
Monty Cir
3700 ClyT 46032 2009 A1
Monument Cir
10 INPS 46204 2337 B7
6300 WshT 46123 2332 A4

STREET Block City ZIP Map# Grid

Monument Dr
900 CtrT 46052 1786 B2
900 LEBN 46052 1786 B2
Monument St
900 NBVL 46060 1686 D6
2100 NBVL 46060 1687 A6
E Monument St
1000 NBVL 46060 1686 D6
Moon Ct
7000 INPS 46241 2334 D4
Moon Dr
- INPS 46241 2334 D4
Moon Rd
5200 GfdT 46168 2549 E1
5200 PNFD 46168 2440 E7
5200 PNFD 46168 2549 E1
S Moon Rd
800 PNFD 46168 2440 E6
Moon Bay Cir
8600 INPS 46236 2014 D4
Moon Lake Ct
- NBVL 46060 1796 D1
Moonlight Ct
900 MRVL 46158 2660 A5
N Moonlight Dr
5000 INPS 46226 2121 D6
Moonlight Pth
14100 FSHR 46060 1796 B7
Moonlight Bay Cir
600 CCRO 46034 1577 B3
Moon Rd West Dr E
5700 GfdT 46168 2549 E1
5700 PNFD 46168 2549 E1
Moon River Ct
12300 INPS 46236 2015 A4
Moonseed Cir
6000 INPS 46203 2448 C2
Moonstone Pl
9800 MCVL 46055 2015 C3
Moonstone St
- INPS 46268 2009 B7
Moonstruck Pkwy
- INPS 46239 2558 A2
Moontown Rd
17600 NBVL 46062 1685 A5
17600 NbvT 46062 1685 A5
17600 WshT 46062 1685 A5
17600 WTFD 46062 1685 A5
Moore Av
2800 INPS 46201 2338 C4
Moore Dr
500 BNBG 46112 2223 D1
Moore Ln
- FSHR 46038 1904 C5
N Moore Rd
7800 INPS 46278 2007 D6
Moore St
10 NPLN 46163 2452 B4
11500 FSHR 46038 1904 D5
E Moore St
10 MRVL 46158 2659 E4
Moorefield Av
- INPS 46222 2336 D3
Mooreland Dr
600 NWTD 46184 2774 D4
Moores Cir
11200 INPS 46229 2341 C1
Moores Ct
1600 INPS 46229 2232 D7
N Moores Ct
10 MdnT 46113 2661 B4
Moores Mnr
1300 INPS 46229 2341 D1
1500 INPS 46229 2232 D7
Mooresville Byp
5500 INPS 46221 2444 B6
Mooresville Rd
7600 INPS 46113 2552 D5
7600 INPS 46221 2552 D5
S Mooresville Rd
6300 INPS 46221 2553 A3
7000 INPS 46221 2552 E4
7700 INPS 46113 2552 E5
W Mooresville Rd
- INPS 46241 2445 A3
2800 INPS 46221 2445 A3
3900 INPS 46221 2444 E4
7400 INPS 46113 2552 A6
9300 GfdT 46113 2551 E6
9300 INPS 46113 2551 E6
Moorgate Ct
400 NBVL 46060 1795 E3
Moorgate Rd
7100 INPS 46250 2121 D1
Moorhead Dr
9000 INPS 46268 2009 C3
Moorings Blvd
9200 INPS 46256 2014 B3
9500 FSHR 46256 2014 B3
Mopac Ct
1100 INPS 46217 2554 E7
1100 INPS 46217 2555 A7
Moqui Ct
10500 INPS 46235 2232 B4
Moraine Ct
5800 CRML 46033 1903 D2
Moran Ct
7600 INPS 46268 2009 B7
E Moray Ct
1900 INPS 46260 2009 D6
W Moray Ct
2000 INPS 46260 2009 D6
Morel Ct
9600 INPS 46256 2013 E6
Morel Dr
10 DNVL 46122 2330 B3
8200 INPS 46256 2013 E6
N Moreland Av
500 INPS 46222 2336 B2
1800 INPS 46222 2227 B7
S Moreland Av
1300 INPS 46241 2336 B6
2700 INPS 46241 2445 B2
Moreland Ct
2200 INPS 46222 2227 B6

STREET Block City ZIP Map# Grid

Morello Ln
- NBVL 46062 1794 E2
- NBVL 46062 1795 A2
- NbvT 46062 1794 E2
- NbvT 46062 1795 A2
Morenci Tr
6200 INPS 46268 2117 E3
S Morgan Av
6700 INPS 46113 2552 B3
Morgan Dr
700 INPS 46227 2446 E6
8500 FSHR 46038 1904 C6
Morgan St
- DNVL 46122 2329 D4
10 MRVL 46158 2659 D3
2100 INPS 46221 2336 D6
5600 LtyT 46118 2548 C1
Morgan St SR-39
5700 LtyT 46118 2548 C1
Morgantown Rd
8100 INPS 46217 2554 D7
8500 INPS 46217 2663 D1
N Morgantown Rd
200 WRvT 46142 2663 D3
S Morgantown Rd
10 WRvT 46142 2663 D6
700 WRvT 46143 2663 D6
Moriarty Dr
7000 INPS 46217 2554 E4
Morney Dr
5900 INPS 46254 2117 B5
Morney Pl
5700 INPS 46254 2117 B5
Morney Wy
5700 INPS 46254 2117 B5
Morningbird Ct
400 CRML 46032 1792 B6
Morning Dove Dr
- INPS 46228 2118 A4
S Morning Glory Cir
1400 CtrT 46140 2344 C4
Morning Glory Ct
12400 LWNC 46236 2124 A2
Morning Mist Ct
- NbvT 46062 1685 A2
Morningside Ct
10 NWTD 46184 2774 C4
600 ZNVL 46077 1899 A7
16100 NBVL 46060 1796 D3
Morningside Dr
100 BNBG 46112 2114 A5
600 NWTD 46184 2774 C4
600 ZNVL 46077 1899 A7
900 LEBN 46052 1677 B5
1000 GNFD 46140 2237 A6
7900 INPS 46240 2010 D5
Morningside Ln
7800 INPS 46240 2010 E7
Morning Song Dr
10300 FSHR 46060 1796 B7
Morningsong Dr
3000 INPS 46241 2444 C3
Morning Star Ct
9100 INPS 46229 2231 D5
Morning Star Dr
2500 INPS 46229 2231 D5
Morningstar Dr
500 MRVL 46158 2659 E2
N Morningstar Dr
100 MRVL 46158 2659 E3
Morning Sun Ln
1000 BHGV 46107 2447 E5
Mornington Dr
1200 INPS 46239 2341 B6
W Morning Walk Dr
1000 CtrT 46140 2344 C3
Moro Ln
800 CtrT 46122 2330 A2
Moroso Ct
6300 INPS 46224 2226 A6
Morphis Ln
800 WRvT 46142 2663 B1
Morris Rd
2100 INPS 46217 2554 C7
2100 INPS 46217 2663 B1
2100 WRvT 46217 2663 B1
E Morris St
10 INPS 46225 2337 C6
400 INPS 46203 2337 D6
3500 INPS 46203 2338 D6
W Morris St
10 INPS 46225 2337 A5
300 WshT 46122 2331 B6
300 WshT 46123 2331 B6
900 INPS 46221 2337 A5
1200 INPS 46221 2336 E6
2800 INPS 46241 2336 A6
3900 INPS 46241 2335 D6
6500 INPS 46241 2334 D6
7300 INPS 46231 2334 C6
8800 INPS 46231 2333 E6
Morrison Wy
19100 NBVL 46060 1686 E4
Morristown Ct
10600 ClyT 46032 1899 E7
S Morristown Pk
1700 BwnT 46140 2346 B5
1700 CtrT 46140 2346 B5
Morristown Pike
- GNFD 46140 2346 A1
S Morristown Pike
10 CtrT 46140 2346 A2
2800 BwnT 46140 2346 C6
Morse Cir
10 PTBR 46167 2113 B4
Morse Ct
10 CCRO 46034 1577 B2
W Morse Dr
1000 CCRO 46034 1577 B3
Morse Landing Dr
10 CCRO 46034 1577 A3
Morton Av
2100 INPS 46221 2336 D7
Morton Pl
5000 CRML 46033 1903 A3

STREET Block City ZIP Map# Grid

Morton St
1200 NBVL 46060 1686 D6
N Morton St
3800 FKLN 46131 2775 A7
3800 FKLN 46184 2775 A7
3800 FknT 46184 2775 A7
3800 WTLD 46131 2775 A7
3800 WTLD 46184 2775 A7
N Morton St US-31
3800 FKLN 46131 2775 A7
3800 FKLN 46184 2775 A7
3800 FknT 46184 2775 A7
3800 WTLD 46131 2775 A7
3800 WTLD 46184 2775 A7
Mortwood Av
7000 INPS 46241 2334 D4
Mosaic Dr
- INPS 46221 2553 B4
Mosey Mnr
8600 INPS 46231 2334 A5
Mosport Ct
6300 INPS 46224 2226 A6
Moss Cir
6600 INPS 46237 2556 E3
Moss Ct
6700 INPS 46237 2556 E3
Moss Dr
4100 CRML 46033 1902 E6
Moss Ln
- ZNVL 46077 1899 B3
4600 INPS 46237 2556 E3
Moss Creek Blvd
4300 INPS 46237 2556 D2
Moss Creek Cir
6500 INPS 46237 2556 E3
Moss Creek Ct
4700 INPS 46237 2556 E3
Moss Creek Pl
6500 INPS 46237 2556 E3
Moss Creek Ter
4400 INPS 46237 2556 E2
Moss Oak Ct
800 INPS 46217 2555 A5
Moss Ridge Cir
4300 INPS 46237 2556 E3
Moss Ridge Ct
4200 INPS 46237 2556 E3
Moss Ridge Ln
4100 INPS 46237 2556 D3
Moss Rock Ct
11500 FSHR 46038 1906 A5
Mosswood Ct
5200 INPS 46254 2116 D6
Moss Wood Dr
6100 FSHR 46038 2012 C1
Mosswood Dr
5200 INPS 46254 2116 D6
Mossy Bank Rd
- LcnT 46112 2224 E2
- LcnT 46234 2224 E2
Mossy Oak Ter
5400 INPS 46220 2120 E6
Mossy Rock Ln
6400 INPS 46237 2556 E3
Moultrie Ct
7600 INPS 46217 2555 A5
Moultrie Dr
7500 INPS 46217 2555 A5
Mounds Ct
300 CRML 46032 1901 C2
N Mount St
1000 INPS 46222 2336 C1
1400 INPS 46222 2227 C7
S Mount St
10 INPS 46222 2336 C4
300 GNFD 46140 2345 D2
800 INPS 46221 2336 C5
Mountain Air Dr
100 GNWD 46143 2666 A3
Mountain Ash Ct
700 CRML 46033 1793 E7
700 CRML 46033 1902 E1
Mountain Pine Dr
- GNWD 46143 2774 B1
N Mt Auburn Dr
1000 INPS 46224 2335 B1
W Mt Auburn Dr
5900 INPS 46224 2335 B1
Mountbatten Ct
4400 INPS 46254 2117 E7
Mountbatten Dr
4000 WRvT 46143 2663 E6
Mt Brook Ct
1200 WRvT 46143 2664 B6
Mt Dora Ln
500 INPS 46229 2340 E2
Mt Herman Av
7300 INPS 46231 2334 D5
Mt Pleasant Center St
5100 WRvT 46142 2663 C1
Mt Pleasant East St
1100 WRvT 46142 2663 D1
Mt Pleasant North St
5200 WRvT 46142 2663 C1
Mt Pleasant South St
5100 WRvT 46142 2663 C1
Mt Pleasant West Dr
1100 WRvT 46142 2663 C1
Mt Rainier Dr
600 INPS 46217 2555 A3
Mt Shasta North Dr
9000 INPS 46234 2334 C1
9100 INPS 46234 2333 E1
Mt Shasta South Dr
9000 INPS 46234 2333 D1
9000 INPS 46234 2334 C1
Mt Vernon Ct
1000 GNWD 46142 2664 E3
4100 INPS 46235 2231 D1
Mt Vernon Dr
1100 GNWD 46142 2664 E3
S Mt Vernon Dr
4800 INPS 46227 2446 D6
Mt Vernon Pl
3400 INPS 46217 2446 B3

STREET Block City ZIP Map# Grid

Mt Vernon Tr N
10900 INPS 46229 2341 C3
Mt Vernon Tr S
11000 INPS 46229 2341 B3
Mt Zion Rd
- LEBN 46052 1676 C6
N Mt Zion Rd
10 LEBN 46052 1785 C1
300 CtrT 46052 1785 C1
S Mt Zion Rd
800 CtrT 46052 1785 A3
W Mt Zion Rd
400 CtrT 46052 1785 B1
1400 LEBN 46052 1785 B1
Mowbray St
1900 CRML 46032 1900 D4
Mowrey St
4500 LWNC 46226 2122 C7
4500 LWNC 46226 2231 B1
W Mozart Dr
300 WshT 46032 1792 C6
Mozart Wy
2800 INPS 46239 2449 B2
Much Marcle Dr
- ClyT 46032 1899 E6
Mud Creek Ct
11200 FSHR 46038 1905 C6
S Mudcreek Ct
4700 SCkT 46163 2451 D4
Mud Creek Rd
8800 INPS 46256 2013 E4
9000 INPS 46256 2014 A3
9500 FCkT 46256 2014 A3
Muessing Rd
500 INPS 46239 2341 D4
S Muessing Rd
1500 INPS 46239 2341 D7
1700 INPS 46239 2450 D1
N Muessing St
10 CBLD 46229 2341 D2
S Muessing St
10 CBLD 46229 2341 D2
Mugo Dr
12400 LWNC 46236 2124 A2
Mugo Pine Ct
- GNWD 46143 2665 B7
Muir Ln
9100 FSHR 46038 2013 D1
10500 FSHR 46038 1904 D7
Muirfield Cir
7600 INPS 46237 2557 D5
S Muirfield Cir
300 LEBN 46052 1677 A3
Muirfield Ct
10 BNBG 46112 2114 D4
7600 INPS 46237 2557 D5
Muirfield Dr
600 BNBG 46112 2114 D4
Muirfield Pl
7200 INPS 46237 2557 C4
Muirfield Trc
10000 FSHR 46038 2014 C1
Muirfield Wy
3400 ClyT 46032 2009 C2
5600 WshT 46123 2331 D5
6300 INPS 46237 2557 D5
Mulberry
1300 GNFD 46140 2237 B6
Mulberry Cir
1700 NBVL 46062 1685 C2
Mulberry Ct
- BNBG 46112 2114 D3
1300 GNFD 46140 2237 B6
4000 FKLN 46131 2774 E7
Mulberry Ln
2300 INPS 46227 2556 B5
Mulberry Rd
- MrlT 46126 2560 A4
- MrlT 46259 2560 A4
Mulberry St
- JknT 46011 1580 E1
100 DNVL 46122 2329 D4
400 ZNVL 46077 1899 A4
1300 ZNVL 46077 1898 E4
1500 EglT 46077 1898 E4
1800 NBVL 46060 1795 E1
E Mulberry St
1300 NBVL 46060 1795 D1
N Mulberry St
200 SgCT 46126 2670 C7
6900 MrlT 46126 2669 C2
W Mulberry St
800 NBVL 46060 1795 D1
Mule Barn Rd
17600 WshT 46074 1682 B7
19300 WshT 46069 1682 B3
20600 WshT 46069 1573 B5
21600 AdmT 46069 1573 B5
22600 SRDN 46069 1573 B3
Mulford Ct
600 INPS 46234 2334 B2
Mullet Ct
9500 INPS 46256 2014 B3
Mulligan Wy
4200 INPS 46268 2117 E1
Mullinix Rd
700 WRvT 46143 2663 B6
Mullis Ln
7800 INPS 46237 2557 C5
Mulsanne Dr
1900 ZNVL 46077 1898 D7
Mundell St
11400 INPS 46259 2559 C5
Mundy Dr
- FSHR 46060 1795 E7
- NBVL 46060 1795 E7
Municipal Dr
10 FSHR 46038 1904 C5
Munsee Cir
1200 INPS 46228 2119 A3
Munsee Ct
1200 INPS 46260 2010 A7
Munsee Ln
6000 INPS 46228 2119 A4
6900 INPS 46260 2119 A2

STREET Block City ZIP Map# Grid

N Munsee Ln
7100 INPS 46260 2119 A1
Munsee Pth
13400 CRML 46033 1903 C1
Munsie Rd
200 INPS 46229 2341 D4
200 INPS 46239 2341 D4
N Munsie St
10 CBLD 46229 2341 D2
S Munsie St
10 CBLD 46229 2341 D3
Munter Ln
4700 INPS 46218 2229 E4
Murphy Cir
- BNBG 46112 2114 D7
Murphy Ct
10 BNBG 46112 2114 D7
8000 INPS 46256 2122 B1
Murphy Dr
7200 INPS 46256 2122 B1
Murphy Ln
100 BNBG 46112 2114 D7
Murphy's Landing Dr
1300 INPS 46217 2554 E3
Murphy's Landing Ln
- INPS 46217 2554 E4
Murray Pl
- NBVL 46060 1687 A7
Murray St
1400 GNWD 46143 2665 C6
4500 INPS 46241 2444 D3
E Murray St
8300 INPS 46239 2449 C3
W Murray St
1300 INPS 46217 2445 E3
3400 INPS 46221 2445 A3
3900 INPS 46221 2444 E3
E Murry St
400 INPS 46227 2446 D3
2100 INPS 46237 2447 B3
W Murry St
3800 INPS 46221 2445 A3
3800 INPS 46241 2445 A3
3900 INPS 46221 2444 E3
4100 INPS 46241 2444 E3
E Muskegon Dr
- GNFD 46140 2236 E5
W Muskegon Dr
400 GNFD 46140 2236 D5
Musket St
7800 INPS 46256 2012 E7
7800 INPS 46256 2013 A6
Muskingum St
- INPS 46202 2337 C1
600 INPS 46204 2337 C2
Mussman Dr
2800 INPS 46222 2226 E5
Mustang Ct
5800 INPS 46228 2118 A5
Mustang Chase Dr
1600 CRML 46074 1791 D7
Mustard Dr
- INPS 46203 2448 C2
Mutz Cir
11300 INPS 46229 2341 D1
Mutz Ct
11400 INPS 46229 2232 D7
Mutz Dr
1300 INPS 46229 2341 D1
1500 INPS 46229 2232 D7
Myers Dr
- SDWY 46222 2226 E7
Myers St
10 WTLD 46184 2774 E6
Myers Lake Dr
100 NBVL 46062 1685 B2
Myerwood Dr
100 CtrT 46122 2330 E3
Myron Av
10 INPS 46241 2335 C4
Myrtis St
500 INPS 46208 2228 B6
Myrtle Ln
- MrlT 46126 2560 D7
4700 WRvT 46142 2663 D3
6300 INPS 46220 2121 D3
13400 FSHR 46060 1905 D2
Myrtle Ter
100 WRvT 46142 2663 D3
Myrtle Grove Ct
9100 LWNC 46235 2231 D1
Myrtle Grove Dr
4400 LWNC 46235 2231 D1
Mystic Rd
16900 WynT 46060 1797 C1
19600 WynT 46060 1688 C3
Mystic Bay Ct
2000 INPS 46240 2011 A7
Mystic Bay Dr
7700 INPS 46240 2011 A6
Mystic Springs Dr
- GNWD 46143 2665 C7

N

N Ct
- WRvT 46142 2663 E2
N St
- BHGV 46107 2447 E2
Naab Rd
8200 INPS 46260 2009 D5
Nakomis St
10 WRvT 46062 1578 D7
10 WynT 46062 1578 D7
Nalon Ct
6100 SDWY 46224 2226 A6
Nalon Dr
2100 SDWY 46224 2226 A6
Nalon Ln
6000 SDWY 46224 2226 B6
W Nance Ln
4800 WRvT 46142 2663 D4
Nancy Ln
- INPS 46113 2552 D4
- INPS 46221 2552 D4

INDEX 37
Nancy Ln — Indianapolis Street Index — Oak Ct

STREET
Block City ZIP Map# Grid

Nancy Ln
10 GNWD 46142 2665 C1
Nansemond Ct
800 CRML 46032 1901 D1
Nansemond Dr
13800 CRML 46032 1901 E1
14000 CRML 46032 1792 E7
Nantucket Ct
7300 INPS 46214 2225 D3
Nantucket Dr
800 CCRO 46034 1577 B4
Nanwich Ct
1100 INPS 46217 2555 A4
E Naomi St
1100 INPS 46203 2337 E7
4100 INPS 46203 2338 E7
4800 INPS 46203 2339 A7
W Naomi St
4700 INPS 46241 2335 D7
Napa Cir
2100 INPS 46214 2225 E6
Napa Ct
23100 JknT 46034 1576 E3
Napa Valley Ln
11000 FSHR 46038 1906 A6
Naples Dr
13800 FSHR 46060 1905 A1
Napoleon Ct
16900 WTFD 46074 1792 D2
Napoleon St
2100 INPS 46203 2337 E7
2600 INPS 46203 2446 E2
Napoli Ct
4200 INPS 46235 2231 D1
Nappanee Dr
10 CRML 46032 1902 B4
Napponee Dr
- WynT 46062 1578 C7
Narcissus Dr
200 INPS 46227 2555 C7
Narita Rd
- INPS 46241 2552 C1
Narragansett Ct
8200 INPS 46256 2013 E5
Narrowleaf Ct
3900 INPS 46235 2232 D2
Narrowleaf Dr
11200 INPS 46235 2232 D2
Nash Cir
10 BNBG 46112 2223 C2
Nash Ct
10 BNBG 46112 2223 C2
Nash Ln
5800 SDWY 46224 2226 B7
Nashua Cir
15200 WshT 46074 1792 A5
Nashua Ct
1500 INPS 46260 2009 E5
Nashua Dr
8200 INPS 46260 2009 E5
Nashville Cir
1100 INPS 46229 2341 D1
Nassau Ln
10000 INPS 46229 2232 A6
Nassau St
- LcnT 46112 2115 D7
Natalie Ct
1400 FKLN 46131 2774 E7
Natalie Ln
400 INPS 46260 2010 B7
Natasha Ct
10 NBVL 46062 1795 B1
Natasha Dr
10 NBVL 46062 1795 B1
Natchez Ct
7500 INPS 46217 2555 A5
Nathan Ln
6500 INPS 46237 2557 B3
Nathan Pl
5400 INPS 46237 2557 B3
Nathaniel Cir
7300 LWNC 46236 2123 E1
National Av
1100 INPS 46227 2446 E4
1400 INPS 46227 2447 A4
3200 INPS 46237 2447 C4
E National Rd
1500 CtrT 46140 2346 D1
1500 GNFD 46140 2346 D1
E National Rd US-40
1500 CtrT 46140 2346 D1
1500 GNFD 46140 2346 D1
W National Rd
10 CtrT 46140 2344 A2
10 GNFD 46140 2344 A2
2100 SCkT 46140 2344 A2
2600 SGLK 46140 2344 A2
2700 SCkT 46140 2343 D2
2700 SGLK 46140 2343 D2
4200 SCkT 46163 2343 A2
5000 SCkT 46140 2342 C2
5000 SCkT 46163 2342 C2
6700 CBLD 46163 2342 C2
7000 CBLD 46229 2342 C2
7000 SCkT 46229 2342 C2
7600 CBLD 46229 2341 E2
7600 SCkT 46229 2341 E2
W National Rd US-40
10 CtrT 46140 2344 A2
10 GNFD 46140 2344 A2
2100 SCkT 46140 2344 A2
2600 SGLK 46140 2344 A2
2700 SCkT 46140 2343 D2
2700 SGLK 46140 2343 D2
4200 SCkT 46163 2343 A2
5000 SCkT 46140 2342 C2
5000 SCkT 46163 2342 C2
6700 CBLD 46163 2342 C2
7000 CBLD 46229 2342 C2
7000 SCkT 46229 2342 C2
7600 CBLD 46229 2341 E2
7600 SCkT 46229 2341 E2
Natural Lake Ct
- BNBG 46112 2114 E5
N Nature Dr
8900 INPS 46278 2007 A4
W Nature Dr
8500 INPS 46278 2007 A4
Nature Trail Dr
10800 FSHR 46038 1904 C7
Nautica Blvd
- MCVL 46055 2015 D4
Nautical Watch Dr
9000 INPS 46236 2014 C4
Nautilus Cir
9600 FCkT 46256 2014 D2
Navajo Ct
10 MdnT 46113 2661 E4
10 MdnT 46113 2662 A4
400 NbvT 46060 1796 A3
Navajo Dr
2200 WshT 46234 2224 D6
Navajo Wy
5200 CRML 46033 1903 C2
Navajo Trail South Dr
1000 INPS 46260 2010 A7
Navajo Trail West Dr
1200 INPS 46260 2010 A7
Navigate Wy
6700 INPS 46250 2012 E3
Navigator Dr
8700 INPS 46237 2557 D7
Navin St
- INPS 46201 2339 A4
Navy Cir
6100 INPS 46221 2553 B2
Neal Av
10 INPS 46222 2336 D4
Neal Ct
1200 WshT 46123 2332 C6
E Neal St
10 CCRO 46034 1577 D3
W Neal St
10 CCRO 46034 1577 D3
Needle Rdg
- BNBG 46112 2114 E5
Needles Dr
1100 INPS 46217 2555 A5
1200 INPS 46217 2554 E5
Neese St
100 WTWN 46075 1788 C7
Neitzel Rd
700 MdnT 46158 2660 D6
1000 MdnT 46158 2661 A6
Nekton Dr
8100 INPS 46236 2014 D5
Nellis Ct
13600 CRML 46032 1901 E1
Nelson
500 BNBG 46112 2114 D6
Nelson Av
200 INPS 46225 2446 C2
700 INPS 46203 2446 D2
1500 INPS 46203 2447 A2
E Nelson Av
2200 INPS 46203 2447 B2
Nelson Cir
10 BNBG 46112 2114 D6
100 NBVL 46060 1687 A6
Nelson Ct
6100 INPS 46219 2339 C1
Nelson Dr
600 MRVL 46158 2659 E2
600 MRVL 46158 2660 A2
Nelson Pl
6100 INPS 46219 2339 C1
Neptune Ct
2600 INPS 46229 2231 D5
Neptune Dr
- INPS 46219 2231 D5
9000 INPS 46229 2231 D5
E Neptune Dr
9500 INPS 46229 2231 E5
Nero Ct
800 CRML 46032 1792 E7
Nesbitt Rd
3800 INPS 46220 2120 D2
Nest Wy
8800 INPS 46231 2334 A6
Nester St
1200 SDWY 46224 2335 D1
Network Wy
6500 INPS 46278 2116 E2
6500 INPS 46278 2117 A2
Neva Ln
3700 CRML 46033 2011 E1
Nevelle Ln
700 CRML 46032 1792 E7
1000 CRML 46032 1793 A7
Never Mind Ct
10 WRvT 46142 2664 B3
Never Mind Wy
3900 WRvT 46142 2664 B3
E New Rd
500 GNFD 46140 2236 E4
W New Rd
- CtrT 46140 2235 C4
- GNFD 46140 2236 C4
New St
700 LEBN 46052 1677 A7
1700 INPS 46203 2337 D7
Newago Dr
2500 INPS 46217 2554 C5
New Amsterdam Dr
1000 GNWD 46142 2664 E3
Newark Ct
- GNWD 46143 2664 E6
Newark Dr
- NBVL 46062 1794 C5
New Augusta Rd
7100 INPS 46268 2117 E1
7400 INPS 46268 2008 E7
Newberry Ct
6200 INPS 46256 2122 A3
Newberry Ln
17000 WTFD 46074 1792 D1
Newberry Rd
6200 INPS 46256 2121 E3
6200 INPS 46256 2122 A3
Newbridge Ct
11500 ClyT 46032 1900 D5
New Britton Dr
13000 FSHR 46038 1904 C3
Newburg Pl
700 WshT 46074 1792 B4
Newburgh Dr
4100 INPS 46235 2232 B2
Newbury Ct
7300 FSHR 46038 1904 A7
Newbury St
600 CRML 46032 1902 A4
Newburyport Dr
14800 FCkT 46040 1907 A6
Newby Ct
200 WTFD 46074 1684 A7
Newby Ln
4900 GfdT 46168 2442 C6
Newcastle Dr
1300 CRML 46032 1792 A7
Newchurch Blvd
8800 INPS 46231 2334 A7
Newcomer Ln
1800 BHGV 46107 2447 C3
New Field Cir
8500 INPS 46231 2334 B6
New Field Ct
8500 INPS 46231 2334 B6
New Field Ln
1200 INPS 46231 2334 B6
Newgate Cir
- PNFD 46231 2333 E6
Newgate Ct N
3600 INPS 46235 2231 E3
Newgate Ct S
3600 INPS 46235 2231 E3
Newgate Ln
- PNFD 46231 2333 D6
3600 INPS 46235 2231 E4
Newhall Dr
5700 INPS 46239 2558 B1
Newhall Wy
7800 INPS 46239 2558 B1
New Harmony Cir
9000 INPS 46231 2333 E5
New Harmony Dr
900 INPS 46231 2333 E6
Newhart St
200 INPS 46217 2446 B7
2800 INPS 46217 2445 B7
New Haven Dr
2400 INPS 46241 2443 B1
15100 WshT 46074 1792 B5
Newhaven Dr
- INPS 46231 2443 B1
1800 INPS 46231 2334 B7
S New Haven Dr
2100 INPS 46231 2443 B1
2300 INPS 46241 2443 B1
New Heritage Dr
- INPS 46239 2449 C6
N New Jersey St
10 INPS 46204 2337 D3
1200 INPS 46202 2337 D1
1600 INPS 46202 2228 D7
3800 INPS 46205 2228 D2
5100 INPS 46205 2119 D6
5700 INPS 46220 2119 D5
10100 ClyT 46280 2010 D1
S New Jersey St
300 INPS 46204 2337 D4
400 INPS 46225 2337 D4
2500 INPS 46225 2446 D1
3200 INPS 46227 2446 D3
6600 INPS 46227 2555 D3
New London Ct
8400 INPS 46256 2013 E5
New London Dr
400 WRvT 46142 2663 D4
Newman St
1400 INPS 46201 2338 A1
E New Market St
12800 CRML 46032 1900 C3
N New Market St
- CRML 46032 1900 C3
S New Market St
- CRML 46032 1900 C3
W New Market St
- CRML 46032 1900 C3
New Oak Ln
7100 INPS 46237 2556 D4
Newport Av
- LcnT 46112 2115 D6
600 INPS 46203 2337 D5
Newport Cir
11500 LWNC 46236 2123 D3
Newport Ct
400 GNWD 46143 2666 B3
Newport Dr
11500 LWNC 46236 2123 D3
14700 WshT 46074 1792 B6
20700 NBVL 46062 1686 A1
Newport Ln
1400 ZNVL 46077 1898 E6
Newport Wy
7700 INPS 46256 2012 E7
Newport Bay Dr
7500 INPS 46240 2011 B7
New Salem Ovlk
3900 INPS 46234 2225 A2
Newstead Dr
6500 INPS 46217 2554 E3
Newton Av
2800 INPS 46201 2338 C4
23000 WRvT 46060 1579 D3
Newton St
7600 INPS 46221 2552 E5
New Tradition Tr
- FCkT 46038 1905 C4
- FSHR 46038 1905 C4
E New York St
10 INPS 46204 2337 D3
400 INPS 46202 2337 E3
1400 INPS 46201 2337 E3
1400 INPS 46201 2338 A3
4900 INPS 46201 2339 A3
E New York St
5100 INPS 46219 2339 A3
8100 INPS 46219 2340 C2
9000 INPS 46229 2340 D2
11300 CBLD 46229 2341 C2
W New York St
- INPS 46234 2334 B3
10 INPS 46204 2337 B3
200 INPS 46202 2337 B3
1200 INPS 46202 2336 E3
2400 INPS 46222 2336 C3
5500 INPS 46224 2335 B3
7700 INPS 46214 2334 C3
Niagara Dr
9900 FSHR 46038 1905 A6
Nice Pak Rd
10 BrnT 46158 2660 A2
S Nicholai Av
2300 INPS 46239 2450 D1
Nicholas Dr
14100 CRML 46074 1791 E7
14100 CRML 46074 1792 A7
Nicholas Rd
1200 INPS 46220 2119 E6
Nicholas St
3200 INPS 46218 2229 A4
Nicklaus Dr
600 GNWD 46143 2665 E4
Nicole Blvd
100 AVON 46123 2332 E3
500 WshT 46123 2332 E3
Nicole Ct
8300 AVON 46123 2332 E3
11400 ClyT 46032 1900 B6
11500 INPS 46236 2014 D5
Nicole Dr
500 GNWD 46143 2665 E5
500 GNWD 46143 2666 A5
1400 FKLN 46131 2775 A7
10000 BrnT 46112 2005 E4
Nicole Ln
9900 BrnT 46112 2005 E5
Nightengale Dr
300 WTLD 46184 2775 A6
Nighthawk Ct
4400 INPS 46254 2117 E5
Night Hawk Dr
10100 FSHR 46038 2014 B1
Nighthawk Dr
5400 INPS 46254 2117 E6
Nighthawk Wy
5400 INPS 46254 2117 E6
Nightingale Ct
7800 INPS 46256 2013 B7
Nightshade Dr
6300 INPS 46237 2557 E2
Nightshade Ln
- NbvT 46062 1685 A2
- WshT 46062 1685 A2
Nightsong Dr
3000 INPS 46241 2444 C3
Nikki Dr
4500 BHGV 46237 2447 E6
Nile Ridge Ct
7100 LWNC 46236 2123 B1
Niles St
11300 CBLD 46229 2341 D2
Niman Ct
10200 ClyT 46280 2011 A1
Nimitz Dr
6100 INPS 46219 2230 D6
Ninebark Ct
13800 CRML 46033 1903 D1
Nixon St
100 NBVL 46060 1686 C7
Noah Dr
4600 INPS 46227 2447 A6
Nob Ln
5200 INPS 46226 2121 A6
Nobbe Ln
400 INPS 46239 2341 B4
Noble Cir
8900 INPS 46250 2012 C4
Noble Ct
- LcnT 46112 2115 D6
Noble Dr
- LcnT 46112 2115 C6
Noble Run
900 NBVL 46060 1687 A7
Noble St
- GNFD 46140 2345 D1
100 GNWD 46142 2665 C3
600 INPS 46203 2337 D5
E Noble St
100 LEBN 46052 1677 A7
E Noble St SR-32
1000 LEBN 46052 1677 B7
N Noble St
100 GNFD 46140 2345 D1
100 GNFD 46140 2236 D7
S Noble St
10 GNFD 46140 2345 D1
W Noble St
100 LEBN 46052 1676 E7
Noble Creek Dr
200 NBVL 46060 1687 A7
200 NBVL 46060 1796 A1
Noblesville Commons Dr
- NBVL 46060 1687 A7
Noblet Ct
5400 INPS 46234 2116 A6
Nobris St
2300 WshT 46234 2224 D6
Nobscot Ct
3600 INPS 46222 2227 B3
Nobscot Dr
3100 INPS 46222 2227 B3
Nodlehs Ct
5600 INPS 46221 2553 B3
Nodlehs Dr
6600 INPS 46221 2553 B3
Noel Cir
- AVON 46123 2332 C2
Noel Ln
200 VrnT 46040 2016 E1
N Noel Rd
7100 INPS 46278 2116 D1
7400 INPS 46278 2007 D7
Noel Forest Ct
7400 INPS 46278 2007 C7
7400 INPS 46278 2116 D1
Noel Forest Ln
7400 INPS 46278 2116 D1
Nogales St
11800 LWNC 46236 2123 E3
Nolan Av
2000 INPS 46203 2338 C7
Nolan Dr
8500 FSHR 46060 1795 C7
Nolen Dr
3400 INPS 46234 2225 A3
Nolte St
- INPS 46241 2552 B2
6000 INPS 46221 2553 A2
Nonchelant Ct
700 WRvT 46142 2664 A1
Nonsense Av
- GNWD 46142 2664 E1
Nora Ln
9100 INPS 46240 2011 A3
9500 CRML 46240 2011 A2
Nora Woods Ct
1300 INPS 46240 2011 A4
Nora Woods Dr
8700 INPS 46240 2011 A4
Norbeck Ter
100 INPS 46217 2555 B4
Norcroft Ct
4500 INPS 46221 2444 C6
Norcroft Dr
5700 INPS 46221 2444 B6
Norcross Cir
1900 INPS 46260 2009 D2
Norcross Ct
9300 INPS 46260 2009 D1
Norcross Dr
1900 INPS 46260 2009 D3
Norden Ct
2200 INPS 46219 2230 D6
Nordyke Av
1200 INPS 46221 2337 A6
1400 INPS 46221 2336 E6
Norena Ct
6900 LcnT 46112 2223 B4
Norfolk
- INPS 46224 2335 C3
Norfolk Cir
1200 SDWY 46224 2335 C1
12800 CRML 46032 1901 A3
Norfolk Ct
1000 SDWY 46224 2335 C1
1600 SDWY 46224 2226 C7
Norfolk Dr
1500 ZNVL 46077 1898 E6
Norfolk Ln
12700 CRML 46032 1901 A4
Norfolk Pl
1000 INPS 46224 2335 C1
1000 SDWY 46224 2335 C1
N Norfolk St
1000 INPS 46224 2335 C1
1000 SDWY 46224 2335 C1
1600 SDWY 46224 2226 C7
1600 INPS 46224 2226 C7
3500 INPS 46224 2226 C3
8000 INPS 46268 2008 C5
S Norfolk St
300 INPS 46241 2335 C4
Norfolk Wy
5400 SDWY 46224 2335 C1
Norma Dr
5200 LWNC 46236 2122 E6
Norma Jean Dr
7400 INPS 46259 2558 A6
Normal Av
4600 LWNC 46226 2122 B7
Norman Ct
6300 LcnT 46112 2224 D2
Norman Rd
1000 LcnT 46112 2224 D2
Normandie Dr
10 WshT 46123 2332 C1
Normandy Blvd
7400 INPS 46278 2007 E7
Normandy Rd
3100 INPS 46222 2226 E4
Normandy Wy
7000 INPS 46278 2116 D1
Norriston Dr
1500 ClyT 46280 2011 A1
Norrose Dr
4100 INPS 46226 2229 E2
North Dr
- INPS 46220 2120 E4
- NbvT 46062 1686 D1
10 MRVL 46158 2659 E2
200 MdnT 46113 2661 D5
900 NBVL 46060 1686 D6
7300 LWNC 46226 2231 A1
North Lp
- WTFD 46074 1684 A6
N North Rd
300 AVON 46123 2332 C4
North St
- FSHR 46038 1904 D5
- INPS 46239 2450 D1
10 WTFD 46074 1684 B7
100 DNVL 46122 2329 D3
E North St
10 GNFD 46140 2345 E1
10 INPS 46204 2337 C2
10 LEBN 46052 1677 A6
10 NPLN 46163 2452 B3
100 PNFD 46168 2441 B4
300 INPS 46202 2337 D2
1100 NBVL 46060 1686 D6
2600 INPS 46201 2338 B2
5100 INPS 46219 2339 A2
W North St
- GNFD 46140 2345 B1
10 INPS 46204 2337 C2
W North St
10 NPLN 46163 2452 A3
100 LEBN 46052 1677 B4
100 PNFD 46168 2441 B4
200 LEBN 46052 1676 E6
500 INPS 46202 2337 B2
3400 INPS 46222 2336 A2
4200 INPS 46222 2335 E2
North Tr
- LcnT 46112 2115 C5
Northants Cir
12800 CRML 46032 1901 A3
Northbend Ct
6300 WshT 46123 2332 A7
Northbrook Cir
18900 WshT 46074 1684 C5
Northbrook Ct
8200 INPS 46260 2009 E5
Northbrook Dr
1400 INPS 46260 2009 E5
10300 FSHR 46038 2012 D1
North By Northeast Blvd
7800 FSHR 46038 2013 C2
9600 FSHR 46256 2013 C2
Northcrest Cir
7600 INPS 46256 2013 A4
Northcrest Ct
7500 INPS 46256 2013 A4
Northcrest Dr
7500 INPS 46256 2013 A5
Northcrest Pl
8400 INPS 46256 2013 A5
Northdale Lake Ct
5700 INPS 46220 2120 B5
Northdale Lake Dr
2000 INPS 46220 2120 A5
Northeast St
300 MRVL 46158 2659 E3
300 MRVL 46158 2660 A3
E Northeastern Av
4300 INPS 46239 2449 D5
S Northeastern Av
4300 INPS 46239 2449 C5
Northern Av
300 INPS 46208 2228 B2
Northern Dr
1400 WshT 46123 2332 E7
Northern Ln
6200 INPS 46220 2120 C3
Northern Dancer Dr
10500 WshT 46234 2224 D6
Northern Oaks Ct
9500 NBVL 46060 1686 D4
Northern Valley Tr
1300 WshT 46123 2333 A1
Northfield Blvd
7300 FSHR 46038 1904 A7
7400 DelT 46038 1904 A7
Northfield Cir
10700 FSHR 46038 1904 A7
Northfield Ct
600 INPS 46227 2446 D6
Northfield Dr
300 MRVL 46158 2659 E1
400 MRVL 46158 2660 A1
500 LEBN 46052 1676 E4
E Northfield Dr
10 BNBG 46112 2114 D5
N Northfield Dr
- BNBG 46112 2114 E6
- BNBG 46112 2115 A7
- BNBG 46112 2224 A1
- LcnT 46112 2224 A2
W Northfield Dr
400 BNBG 46112 2114 A5
1500 BNBG 46112 2113 E5
Northfield Pl
10600 FSHR 46038 1904 A7
Northfield Rd
500 PNFD 46168 2441 B4
Northgate Ct
9100 NBVL 46060 1686 D5
Northgate Dr
500 GNWD 46143 2665 C1
W Northgate Dr
3100 INPS 46228 2118 B4
E Northgate St
1200 INPS 46220 2119 E5
1300 INPS 46220 2120 A4
W Northgate St
1800 INPS 46228 2118 D4
Northgreen Pkwy
10 BNBG 46112 2114 C6
Northhampton Dr
10600 FSHR 46038 1904 A7
Northhampton Row
700 DNVL 46122 2329 D2
Northlake Dr
1100 NBVL 46060 1687 A6
Northland Ct
100 FSHR 46038 1904 B3
Northland Rd
5900 INPS 46228 2118 A4
Northland St
1000 FSHR 46038 1904 B3
Northlane Dr
100 NWTD 46184 2774 D3
North Point Cir
3600 DNVL 46122 2329 C3
North Point Dr
- BrnT 46112 2114 E1
Northpointe Dr
1200 GfdT 46158 2659 E1
1200 MRVL 46158 2659 E1
Northport Cir
8700 INPS 46236 2015 A4
Northport Dr
5500 INPS 46221 2553 B2
Northridge Ct
10 BNBG 46112 2114 C5
Northridge Dr
10 MRVL 46158 2659 D2
200 BrnT 46158 2659 D2
18600 NBVL 46060 1686 E5
Northridge St
1400 CtrT 46122 2329 D1
North Shore Dr
- FCkT 46038 1906 C5
Northside Dr
6700 BNBG 46112 2223 A2
6700 LcnT 46112 2223 A2
Northview Av
700 INPS 46220 2119 E5
2400 INPS 46220 2120 B5
Northview Ct
6200 MCVL 46055 2015 C3
Northview Dr
10 DNVL 46122 2329 D3
10 INPS 46208 2119 C5
6300 MCVL 46055 2015 C3
Northview Pl
18600 NBVL 46060 1686 E5
North Vista Run
1600 ClyT 46280 2011 A2
1600 CRML 46280 2011 A2
Northway Ln
9500 INPS 46268 2009 C3
Northwest Blvd
8500 INPS 46278 2008 B5
Northwestern Av
1400 INPS 46202 2228 A7
1400 INPS 46202 2337 B1
Northwestern Dr
4400 ClyT 46077 2008 E1
Northwest Plaza East Dr
4500 ClyT 46077 2008 E1
Northwest Plaza West Dr
4500 ClyT 46077 2008 E1
Northwind
- BNBG 46112 2114 A2
Northwind Cir
9900 INPS 46256 2014 A3
Northwind Ct
9500 INPS 46256 2014 A3
Northwind Dr
9800 INPS 46256 2014 A3
Northwood Dr
10 GNWD 46143 2665 C7
100 FSHR 46038 1904 A4
200 MdnT 46113 2661 C3
1400 INPS 46240 2011 A6
5800 CRML 46033 1903 C4
Norton Av
500 INPS 46227 2446 D4
1400 INPS 46227 2447 A4
Norwaldo Av
4200 INPS 46205 2229 A1
4500 INPS 46205 2120 A7
5600 INPS 46220 2120 A5
Norwalk Ct
- INPS 46226 2231 B2
Norwalk Dr
14400 CRML 46033 1794 B7
Nor-Way Dr
5100 INPS 46219 2339 A3
Norway Spruce Ln
17200 WTFD 46074 1792 D1
Norwich Ct
3100 INPS 46224 2226 B4
Norwich Ln
3100 INPS 46224 2226 B4
Norwick Cir
900 GNWD 46143 2665 E4
E Norwood St
100 INPS 46225 2337 B5
600 INPS 46203 2337 D5
W Norwood St
400 INPS 46225 2337 B5
Nostalgia Ln
7100 INPS 46214 2334 D3
Notre Dame Dr
9300 INPS 46240 2010 E3
Nottingham Ct
600 CRML 46032 1901 A3
E Nottingham Ct
700 INPS 46240 2119 E1
Nottingham Dr
1600 INPS 46240 2011 A3
Nottingham Ln
200 LEBN 46052 1677 A2
Nottingham Rd
13100 FCkT 46038 1904 D2
Nottinghill Ct
300 INPS 46234 2334 B3
Nottinghill Dr
8300 INPS 46234 2334 B3
Nowland Av
3000 INPS 46201 2338 C1
4900 INPS 46201 2339 A1
Nowling Ct
2300 WshT 46234 2224 C6
Nowling Ln
2100 WshT 46234 2224 C7
Noyes St
10 PTBR 46167 2113 A4
Nuckols Ct
5600 INPS 46237 2557 B6
Nuckols Ln
8000 INPS 46237 2557 B6
Nuthatch Dr
500 EglT 46077 1898 D4
Nuthatcher Dr
3600 INPS 46228 2118 A4
Nutmeg Ct
7400 INPS 46237 2556 D4
Nyla Ct
4700 WTFD 46062 1685 A6

O

O St
- BHGV 46107 2448 A2
Oak Av
5700 INPS 46219 2339 C4
7400 INPS 46219 2340 A3
Oak Blvd
700 GNFD 46140 2236 D7
Oak Ct
900 GNFD 46140 2236 D7

INDEX 38

Oak Dr — Indianapolis Street Index — Orkney Ct

Block	City	ZIP	Map#	Grid
Oak Dr				
-	MdnT	46113	2661	C3
-	SgCT	46126	2670	D7
-	SGLK	46140	2343	E3
400	CRML	46032	1901	E3
600	GNWD	46142	2665	A2
11400	FCkT	46038	1904	E6
11400	FSHR	46038	1904	E6
S Oak Dr				
700	SGLK	46140	2344	A3
7500	INPS	46227	2555	E5
W Oak Dr				
4700	SCkT	46163	2343	A4
Oak Ln				
-	BCkT	46140	2233	B7
-	GNWD	46143	2666	A5
N Oak Ln				
6900	INPS	46220	2119	D2
Oak Rd				
-	WTFD	46033	1793	B6
15100	WshT	46033	1793	C4
16100	WshT	46074	1793	C4
16100	WTFD	46074	1793	C2
Oak St				
-	AVON	46234	2333	D1
-	MrlT	46126	2560	A4
-	WshT	46234	2333	D1
E Oak St				
10	ZNVL	46077	1899	B6
N Oak St				
10	NPLN	46163	2452	B3
S Oak St				
-	NPLN	46163	2452	B3
800	LEBN	46052	1677	A7
W Oak St				
100	ZNVL	46077	1899	A6
1500	ZNVL	46077	1898	E6
9400	EglT	46077	1898	E6
W Oak St SR-334				
100	ZNVL	46077	1899	A6
1500	ZNVL	46077	1898	E6
9400	EglT	46077	1898	E6
Oakbay Cir				
7000	NBVL	46062	1576	E7
Oakbay Ct				
6100	INPS	46237	2557	C1
Oakbay Dr				
7000	NBVL	46062	1576	E7
7000	NbvT	46062	1576	E7
7100	NBVL	46062	1577	A7
7300	JknT	46062	1577	A7
Oakbend Ct				
-	LEBN	46052	1677	A2
Oak Blvd Dr N				
-	BCkT	46140	2342	A1
800	CBLD	46140	2342	A1
Oak Blvd Dr S				
100	BCkT	46140	2342	A1
100	CBLD	46140	2342	A1
Oak Blvd Dr W				
500	CBLD	46140	2233	A7
500	CBLD	46140	2342	A1
Oakbrook Ct				
4900	INPS	46254	2117	D4
14200	CRML	46033	1793	E7
14200	CRML	46033	1794	A7
Oakbrook Dr				
4800	INPS	46254	2117	D4
5300	PNFD	46168	2440	D4
Oakbrook Ln				
4900	INPS	46254	2117	D4
Oakbrook Rd				
4900	INPS	46254	2117	D4
Oak Brooke Ln				
300	GNWD	46142	2665	B4
Oak Cove Ln				
7100	NBVL	46062	1577	A7
Oakcrest Ct				
9800	FSHR	46038	2014	A2
Oakcrest Dr				
5500	INPS	46237	2448	E7
5700	INPS	46237	2557	C1
Oakdale Ln				
7900	INPS	46214	2225	C6
Oakden Ct				
-	NWTD	46184	2774	D2
-	PltT	46184	2774	D2
Oakden Rd				
300	NWTD	46184	2774	D3
Oak Edge Cir				
-	NBVL	46062	1685	E7
Oakenshaw Dr				
7100	FSHR	46038	1903	E5
7100	FSHR	46038	1904	A5
Oak Farm Dr				
5000	INPS	46237	2447	D7
Oakfield Dr				
4000	INPS	46237	2447	D7
Oakforge Dr				
4600	INPS	46254	2117	D4
Oakforge Ln				
5900	INPS	46254	2117	E4
Oak Grove Ct				
10	MRVL	46158	2659	D2
7800	INPS	46259	2558	B5
13800	FSHR	46038	1905	A1
Oak Grove Dr				
7600	INPS	46259	2558	B5
Oakham Pl				
400	FCkT	46038	1904	D1
Oak Harbor Ct				
5300	INPS	46237	2447	D7
Oak Harbor Ln				
-	INPS	46237	2447	D7
Oak Harbour Cir				
7100	NBVL	46062	1577	A7
Oakhaven Ct				
9600	INPS	46256	2013	E6
Oak Haven Dr				
10	MdnT	46113	2661	B3
Oakhaven Pl				
7900	INPS	46256	2013	E6
Oak Hill Dr				
10	BNBG	46112	2113	C4
10	BrnT	46112	2113	C4
7900	INPS	46250	2012	A6
7900	PNFD	46168	2550	C1
Oak Hill Ln				
-	CCRO	46034	1577	C4
Oak Hill Apartments				
-	LWNC	46226	2122	A6
Oak Hill East Dr				
5900	PNFD	46168	2550	D2
Oak Hill West Dr				
5900	PNFD	46168	2550	C2
Oak Hollow Cir				
6500	LWNC	46236	2123	B2
Oakhurst Ct				
4600	INPS	46254	2117	D7
Oakhurst Dr				
4900	INPS	46254	2117	D7
Oakhurst Ln				
3800	LcnT	46112	2224	C3
4700	INPS	46254	2117	D7
Oakhurst Pl				
4600	INPS	46254	2117	D7
Oakhurst Wy				
4600	INPS	46254	2117	D7
Oak Knoll Ct				
1200	INPS	46217	2554	E4
Oak Knoll Dr				
7300	INPS	46217	2554	E4
Oak Knoll Ln				
9100	FSHR	46038	1904	E7
Oak Lake Cir				
-	INPS	46268	2009	A5
Oak Lake Cir N				
3700	INPS	46268	2009	A4
Oak Lake Cir S				
3700	INPS	46268	2009	A5
Oak Lake Dr				
6700	INPS	46214	2225	E4
N Oakland Av				
1000	INPS	46201	2338	C1
6600	INPS	46220	2120	C2
7100	INPS	46240	2120	C1
S Oakland Av				
200	INPS	46201	2338	C4
2800	INPS	46203	2447	C2
3200	INPS	46237	2447	C3
W Oakland Dr				
9000	INPS	46241	2443	A1
N Oakland Rd				
7900	INPS	46240	2011	A6
Oakland Ter				
5700	INPS	46220	2120	C5
Oakland Wy				
600	NWTD	46184	2774	C4
Oakland Hills Cir				
7400	LWNC	46236	2014	C7
7400	LWNC	46236	2123	C1
Oakland Hills Ct				
7300	LWNC	46236	2123	C1
7400	LWNC	46236	2014	E6
Oakland Hills Dr				
7300	LWNC	46236	2123	C1
Oaklandon Rd				
6200	LWNC	46235	2123	E3
6200	LWNC	46236	2123	E3
7500	LWNC	46236	2014	E7
7900	INPS	46236	2014	E6
Oak Leaf Dr				
5200	INPS	46220	2120	A6
Oakleaf Dr				
3900	CRML	46077	1899	D1
3900	EglT	46077	1899	D1
Oakleaf Wy				
9700	FCkT	46055	2015	C2
Oak Limb Ct				
6200	INPS	46221	2553	B2
Oak Manor Dr				
-	WTFD	46074	1793	C2
Oak Meadows Ct				
300	GNWD	46142	2665	B4
Oak Meadows Ln				
700	GNWD	46142	2665	B4
Oakmere Ter				
-	GNWD	46142	2664	C2
Oakmere Wy				
1600	GNWD	46142	2664	C2
Oakmont Ct				
10	BHGV	46107	2447	E7
Oakmont Ct E				
8900	GfdT	46168	2551	A5
Oakmont Dr				
-	NBVL	46062	1686	A6
10	BNBG	46112	2113	D4
18300	NBVL	46062	1685	E6
Oakmont Ln				
8500	INPS	46260	2010	B4
Oakmont West Dr				
2400	GfdT	46168	2551	A5
Oaknoll Dr				
4500	INPS	46221	2444	B6
Oak Park Cir				
2700	WTFD	46033	1793	C3
Oak Park Ct				
15900	WTFD	46033	1793	C4
Oak Park Dr				
8300	INPS	46227	2556	A6
Oak Point Cir				
7100	NBVL	46062	1577	A7
Oak Ridge Ct				
600	WshT	46123	2331	E5
14300	CRML	46032	1792	E7
Oak Ridge Dr				
1200	INPS	46220	2119	E4
9800	ZNVL	46077	1898	E2
10000	ZNVL	46077	1899	A3
Oakridge Dr				
600	AVON	46123	2332	A1
600	WshT	46123	2332	A1
5100	GfdT	46168	2549	C6
10900	FSHR	46038	1903	E7
Oak Ridge Rd				
13600	CRML	46032	1901	E1
13800	CRML	46032	1792	E7
14600	WshT	46032	1792	E7
14600	WTFD	46032	1792	E7
15200	WshT	46074	1792	E4
16100	WTFD	46074	1792	E4
17500	WshT	46074	1683	E7
17500	WTFD	46074	1683	E7
20600	WshT	46069	1574	E5
20600	WshT	46069	1683	E1
21400	AdmT	46069	1574	E5
Oakridge Wy				
500	GNWD	46142	2664	E2
Oak Ridge Spring Lake Dr				
-	BNBG	46112	2114	E6
Oak Run Cir				
9200	INPS	46260	2009	D3
Oak Run Ct				
2000	INPS	46260	2009	D3
Oak Run Pl				
2100	INPS	46260	2009	D3
Oak Run East Dr				
9200	INPS	46260	2009	D3
Oak Run North Dr				
2000	INPS	46260	2009	D3
Oak Run South Dr				
2000	INPS	46260	2009	D3
Oakshot Ln				
7700	INPS	46268	2009	A7
Oak Spring Ct				
11100	INPS	46239	2341	C4
Oak Spring Dr				
11000	INPS	46239	2341	C4
Oak Trail Dr				
3800	INPS	46237	2447	D7
Oak Tree Cir				
3500	INPS	46227	2556	C7
Oak Tree Ct				
3400	INPS	46227	2556	C7
Oak Tree Dr				
10	BNBG	46112	2113	D4
10	BrnT	46112	2113	D4
Oak Tree Dr N				
3200	INPS	46227	2556	C7
Oak Tree Dr S				
3200	INPS	46227	2556	C7
Oak Tree Ln				
7400	FSHR	46038	1904	A6
9700	LWNC	46235	2122	E6
9800	LWNC	46235	2123	A6
Oak Tree Wy				
11600	ClyT	46032	1900	B5
11600	CRML	46032	1900	B5
Oakview Cir				
7100	NBVL	46062	1576	E7
7100	NBVL	46062	1577	A7
Oakview Dr				
100	MRVL	46158	2660	B4
21200	NBVL	46062	1576	E7
21400	JknT	46062	1576	E7
21400	JknT	46062	1577	A6
21400	NBVL	46062	1577	A6
Oakview Dr N				
6400	INPS	46278	2116	D2
6400	INPS	46278	2117	A3
Oakview Dr S				
6400	INPS	46278	2116	E3
6400	INPS	46278	2117	A3
Oakville Blvd				
-	FKLN	46131	2775	A7
-	WTLD	46184	2775	A7
Oakwood Cir				
7000	JknT	46062	1576	E6
7000	NBVL	46062	1576	E6
Oakwood Ct				
10	BNBG	46112	2223	D2
200	GNWD	46142	2665	B4
500	INPS	46260	2010	B5
900	PNFD	46168	2441	D6
10600	CRML	46033	1902	C7
13700	CRML	46032	1792	A6
W Oakwood Ct				
7500	SCkT	46239	2342	A5
Oakwood Dr				
400	INPS	46260	2010	B5
4500	EglT	46077	1899	C2
4500	ZNVL	46077	1899	C2
S Oakwood Dr				
300	GNWD	46142	2665	A4
2400	SCkT	46239	2342	A6
W Oakwood Dr				
600	GNWD	46142	2665	A4
Oakwood Tr				
900	INPS	46260	2119	A2
1300	INPS	46260	2118	E2
4800	INPS	46268	2117	D2
Oakwoods Ln				
2100	WshT	46074	1793	C3
Oakwood Trail Dr				
6800	INPS	46260	2119	A2
Obara Ct				
1600	CRML	46033	1902	E1
Oberlies Wy				
5900	PNFD	46168	2550	B1
Oberlin Ct				
3000	INPS	46268	2009	B3
Oceanline Dr				
3300	INPS	46214	2225	C4
Oceanline East Dr				
3100	INPS	46214	2225	D4
Ochs Av				
5200	INPS	46254	2117	D6
S Octavi Ct				
10	BNBG	46112	2114	B5
Odam Ct				
9900	LWNC	46236	2123	A3
O'Dell Ln				
-	GNWD	46143	2665	C6
O'Dell St				
-	BNBG	46112	2114	D6
1500	BNBG	46112	2223	D3
N O'Dell St				
400	BNBG	46112	2114	D6
S O'Dell St				
10	BNBG	46112	2114	D7
500	BNBG	46112	2223	D1
S Oden Dr				
1300	CtrT	46140	2346	B3
Odessa Cir				
11200	FCkT	46040	1907	A6
Odessa Wy				
-	MCVL	46055	2124	B2
Odom				
-	INPS	46113	2552	A7
Office Park Dr				
8400	INPS	46260	2009	E5
Office Plaza Blvd				
3900	INPS	46254	2226	D2
Offutt Dr				
13700	CRML	46032	1902	A1
E Ogden St				
1000	INPS	46202	2337	D1
N Ogden St				
300	INPS	46204	2337	D3
1200	INPS	46202	2337	D1
1600	INPS	46202	2228	D7
S Ogden St				
700	INPS	46204	2337	D4
Ogden Dunes Ct				
9100	INPS	46113	2551	E7
Ogden Dunes Dr				
8700	GfdT	46113	2551	E7
8700	INPS	46113	2551	E7
8800	GfdT	46113	2660	D1
8800	INPS	46113	2660	D1
Oglethorpe Ct				
2700	INPS	46268	2009	C3
Ohara Ct				
-	NBVL	46062	1685	E5
O'Hara Ct				
3300	INPS	46224	2226	C4
O'Hara Ln				
5300	INPS	46224	2226	C4
Ohio St				
-	GNFD	46140	2236	D7
-	INPS	46202	2337	A3
E Ohio St				
10	INPS	46204	2337	C3
600	INPS	46202	2337	D3
3500	INPS	46201	2338	D3
N Ohio St				
-	MCVL	46055	2015	C7
S Ohio St				
100	SRDN	46069	1573	B1
W Ohio St				
10	INPS	46204	2337	C3
200	INPS	46202	2337	C3
400	FTVL	46040	2016	E1
400	VrnT	46040	2016	E1
1400	INPS	46222	2336	E3
4500	INPS	46222	2335	E3
5500	INPS	46224	2335	B3
6300	INPS	46214	2335	A3
6500	INPS	46214	2334	E3
8400	INPS	46234	2334	A3
Ohmer Av				
200	INPS	46219	2339	B4
Oil Creek Ct				
8200	INPS	46268	2008	E5
Oil Creek Dr				
3600	INPS	46268	2009	A6
4100	INPS	46268	2008	E5
Oklahoma Ct				
900	INPS	46231	2333	E5
Old Barn Cir				
5300	INPS	46268	2117	C3
Old Barn Ct				
6200	INPS	46268	2117	C3
Old Barn Dr				
5300	INPS	46268	2117	C3
Old Briar Ln				
-	WTFD	46032	1793	A5
Old Bridge Rd				
6000	LcnT	46112	2222	E1
W Old Colony Dr				
7500	SCkT	46163	2451	A2
7700	SCkT	46163	2450	E2
Old Colony Rd				
5300	LWNC	46226	2121	E6
5600	INPS	46226	2121	D5
Old Course Pl				
6100	INPS	46237	2448	C7
Old Dominion Ct				
8600	INPS	46231	2334	A5
Old Eagle Wy				
1100	WRvT	46143	2664	A5
S Old Emerson Av				
2400	INPS	46203	2448	A1
Olde Mill Run				
8500	INPS	46260	2010	C4
Olde Mill Trc				
8500	INPS	46260	2010	C4
Olde Mill Bay				
100	INPS	46260	2010	C5
Olde Mill Circle East Dr				
8400	INPS	46260	2010	C4
Olde Mill Circle North Dr				
100	INPS	46260	2010	D4
Olde Mill Circle South Dr				
100	INPS	46260	2010	C5
Olde Mill Circle West Dr				
8400	INPS	46260	2010	C4
Olde Mill Cove				
200	INPS	46260	2010	D4
Oldenburg Cir				
-	WTFD	46074	1792	D3
Olde Village Ln				
-	NBVL	46062	1685	C7
Old Farm Ln				
8100	INPS	46214	2225	B7
Old Farm Rd				
400	DNVL	46122	2330	B3
8200	INPS	46256	2013	B5
Oldfield Ct				
5100	CRML	46033	1903	A6
Oldfield Dr				
11100	CRML	46033	1903	A6
Oldfield Ln				
10	BrnT	46158	2659	C6
Oldfield Commons Dr				
600	GNWD	46142	2664	E5
Oldfields Circle North Dr				
1900	INPS	46228	2227	D2
Oldfields Circle South Dr				
1900	INPS	46228	2227	D2
Old Glory Cir				
300	GNFD	46140	2345	A1
Old Glory Dr				
400	GNFD	46140	2345	B1
12700	FSHR	46060	1906	B2
Old Grayce Ln				
100	CRML	46032	1902	A1
Oldham Dr				
7000	INPS	46221	2553	B4
Old Heritage Pl				
-	GNWD	46143	2666	B5
Old Hickory Cir				
1300	GNWD	46142	2664	D3
Old Hickory Ct				
7600	INPS	46259	2558	A5
Old Hickory Dr				
1200	GNWD	46142	2664	D3
Old Hickory Ln				
400	GNWD	46142	2664	D3
Old Honey Creek Ln				
1000	WRvT	46143	2663	C5
Old House Rd				
7000	INPS	46256	2012	E7
7100	INPS	46256	2013	A7
Old IN-37				
1600	WRvT	46143	2662	E7
N Old IN-67				
-	BrnT	46113	2660	A2
400	BrnT	46158	2660	A2
400	MRVL	46158	2660	A2
S Old IN-67				
1200	MRVL	46158	2659	D7
Old Market Sq				
-	GNWD	46143	2666	B6
Old Meridian St				
11900	CRML	46032	1901	D4
13800	CRML	46032	1902	A1
Old Mill Cir				
1500	CRML	46032	1792	C6
Old Mill Ct				
5500	INPS	46221	2553	B2
14000	CRML	46032	1792	C7
Old Mill Dr				
5700	INPS	46221	2553	B2
Old Mission Cove				
1600	CRML	46280	2011	A2
Old National Rd				
10000	PNFD	46168	2442	C2
10000	PNFD	46231	2442	C2
10500	WshT	46231	2442	D2
Old North Salem Rd				
10	DNVL	46122	2329	C3
Old Oak Dr				
-	FSHR	46038	1795	E7
9900	FSHR	46038	1904	E1
Old Oak Tr				
7200	LWNC	46236	2123	E1
Old Oakland Cir				
11400	LWNC	46236	2014	D7
Old Oakland Boulevard East Dr				
7500	LWNC	46236	2014	D7
Old Oakland Boulevard North Dr				
11400	LWNC	46236	2014	D7
Old Oakland Boulevard West Dr				
7500	LWNC	46236	2014	D7
Old Orchard Dr				
11800	LWNC	46236	2123	E2
12300	LWNC	46236	2124	A1
Old Orchard Rd				
6000	INPS	46226	2121	C5
Old Otto Ct				
-	MdnT	46113	2661	A1
Old Prairie Ct				
8100	INPS	46256	2013	B5
Old Raymond St				
1500	INPS	46221	2445	D1
2200	INPS	46241	2445	D1
Old Smith Valley Rd				
4500	WRvT	46143	2663	C5
Old Springfield Wy				
-	INPS	46239	2449	C6
Old Stone Dr				
11100	INPS	46236	2014	D4
12200	INPS	46236	2015	A4
Old Stone Pl				
7100	FSHR	46038	1903	E5
Old Town Ln				
-	WRvT	46142	2663	B4
8600	INPS	46260	2010	A4
Old Town East Dr				
8700	INPS	46260	2010	A4
Old Town North Dr				
1200	INPS	46260	2010	A4
Old Town South Dr				
1200	INPS	46260	2010	A4
Old Town West Dr				
8700	INPS	46260	2010	A4
S Old Trail Rd				
7500	INPS	46219	2340	A3
Old US-36				
-	WshT	46123	2331	D4
Old US-421 N				
-	INPS	-	2448	D1
-	INPS	-	2449	A1
-	INPS	46203	2448	D1
Old US-421 S				
-	INPS	-	2448	E1
-	INPS	-	2449	A1
-	INPS	46203	2448	E1
Old Vines Dr				
-	WTFD	46074	1793	C2
Olea Ct				
-	WRvT	46143	2664	A7
Olender Dr				
3500	INPS	46221	2444	D4
Oles Dr				
1600	INPS	46228	2118	D6
4000	LcnT	46112	2222	E2
N Oles Dr				
5500	INPS	46228	2118	E6
Oleta Dr				
10	INPS	46217	2555	B4
Oligocene St				
-	INPS	46218	2229	D7
Olin Av				
1000	INPS	46222	2336	A1
1000	SDWY	46222	2336	A1
1500	SDWY	46222	2227	A7
Olin Rd				
8400	INPS	46278	2007	B5
Olio Rd				
9800	FCkT	46055	2015	D2
10900	FCkT	46038	1906	D7
10900	FCkT	46040	1906	D7
10900	FCkT	46040	2015	D2
10900	FCkT	46055	1906	D7
11600	FSHR	46038	1906	D4
12600	FCkT	46060	1906	D3
12600	FSHR	46060	1906	D3
13900	NBVL	46060	1797	D7
13900	NBVL	46060	1906	D3
14600	WynT	46060	1797	D7
19600	WynT	46060	1688	D2
20600	WRvT	46060	1579	D7
20600	WynT	46060	1579	D7
Olive St				
6900	INPS	46227	2555	E3
S Olive St				
100	INPS	46202	2337	E4
2000	INPS	46203	2337	E7
3300	INPS	46227	2446	E3
Olive Branch Ct				
6600	INPS	46237	2557	D1
Olive Branch Ln				
1500	WRvT	46143	2663	D6
6500	INPS	46237	2557	D1
Olive Branch Rd				
-	WRvT	46143	2662	E7
-	WRvT	46143	2663	E7
-	WRvT	46143	2664	A7
Olive Branch Wy				
5600	INPS	46237	2557	D1
Oliver Av				
-	INPS	46225	2337	A4
900	INPS	46221	2337	A4
1300	INPS	46221	2336	E5
3400	INPS	46241	2336	A5
5300	INPS	46241	2335	B5
E Oliver Av				
900	PNFD	46168	2441	C5
W Oliver Av				
1100	PNFD	46168	2441	C5
Oliver Ln				
13800	CRML	46074	1900	C1
Olivewood Dr				
1900	INPS	46219	2231	B7
Olivia Dr				
6400	INPS	46226	2230	D4
N Olney St				
1000	INPS	46201	2338	C1
1400	INPS	46201	2229	C7
1900	INPS	46218	2229	C6
4300	INPS	46205	2229	C1
6500	INPS	46220	2120	D2
7100	INPS	46240	2120	D1
S Olney St				
3700	INPS	46237	2447	D4
Olsen				
-	PTBR	46167	2112	E4
Olvey St				
6600	LWNC	46236	2123	E2
Olympia Cir				
4900	INPS	46228	2118	D7
Olympia Ct				
5000	INPS	46228	2118	C7
Olympia Dr				
5200	INPS	46228	2118	D6
9700	FSHR	46038	2014	B2
Olympic Cir				
-	LcnT	46112	2115	C5
Olympic Ct				
6200	INPS	46237	2448	C7
Omega Ln				
10	PNFD	46168	2441	E4
O'Neal Av				
3700	EglT	46077	1899	A1
One West Dr				
8500	INPS	46260	2010	C4
Onslow Ct				
4900	WRvT	46142	2663	D4
Ontario Cir				
3600	INPS	46268	2009	A5
Ontario Ct				
200	NBVL	46060	1686	C6
300	AVON	46123	2333	B3
Ontario Ln				
8200	INPS	46268	2009	A5
Onward Dr				
-	WTFD	46074	1792	C2
Onyx Cir				
6300	INPS	46237	2557	A2
Onyx Dr				
10700	ClyT	46032	1900	C7
Opal Rd				
8200	INPS	46217	2555	B6
Opal St				
-	INPS	46268	2009	B7
Opal Ridge Ln				
4900	INPS	46237	2557	A3
S Opel St				
1000	SRDN	46069	1573	C2
Opelika Ct				
7700	INPS	46217	2555	A5
Opera Pl				
3500	INPS	46226	2231	D3
Ophelia Ct				
700	AVON	46123	2332	A2
Ophelia Dr				
500	AVON	46123	2332	A2
Opus Dr				
-	GfdT	46168	2442	C7
-	GfdT	46168	2551	C1
-	PNFD	46168	2442	C7
1500	PNFD	46168	2551	C1
5700	CRML	46033	1903	B3
Orange St				
10	INPS	46225	2337	C6
500	INPS	46203	2337	D6
4700	INPS	46203	2338	E6
6100	INPS	46203	2339	C6
7400	INPS	46239	2340	A5
Orange Blossom Ct				
2100	INPS	46229	2232	C6
Orange Blossom Tr				
9800	FSHR	46060	1796	A6
Orchard Av				
3000	INPS	46218	2229	A4
3800	INPS	46205	2229	A3
Orchard Blvd				
10	FSHR	46038	1904	B4
400	DNVL	46122	2329	C3
Orchard Ct				
10	DNVL	46122	2329	D3
1900	ClyT	46280	1902	A6
Orchard Dr				
-	SGLK	46140	2343	E2
N Orchard Dr				
7100	LWNC	46236	2124	A1
Orchard Ln				
-	WRvT	46142	2663	C4
10	CtrT	46122	2329	D3
10	DNVL	46122	2329	D3
800	GNWD	46142	2665	A4
W Orchard Ln				
400	GNWD	46142	2665	B4
Orchard Ln W				
100	GNWD	46142	2665	C4
Orchard Pt				
200	ZNVL	46077	1899	A3
Orchard Ter				
3000	INPS	46218	2229	A4
Orchard Wy				
10600	ClyT	46280	1902	A6
Orchard Crossing Dr				
10600	ClyT	46280	1902	A6
Orchardgrass Ln				
5600	INPS	46254	2117	C6
Orchard Grove Dr				
8600	INPS	46113	2552	A7
Orchard Hill Ln				
1600	GNWD	46142	2664	C1
N Orchard Hill Ln				
6000	INPS	46220	2121	B4
Orchard Park Dr				
-	ClyT	46280	2011	A1
Orchard Park Dr N				
1200	ClyT	46280	1902	A7
1400	ClyT	46280	2011	A1
Orchard Park Dr S				
10400	ClyT	46280	2011	A1
Orchard Park Dr W				
10000	ClyT	46280	2011	A1
Orchard Park South Dr				
10100	ClyT	46280	2011	A1
Orchard Valley Blvd				
4000	INPS	46235	2232	C2
Orchard Valley Ln				
4000	INPS	46235	2232	B2
Orchard Valley Wy				
10800	INPS	46235	2232	B1
Orchardview Ln				
400	GNWD	46142	2664	C2
Orchard Village Dr				
7600	INPS	46217	2555	B5
Orchestra Wy				
1500	INPS	46231	2333	E6
1500	INPS	46231	2334	A7
Orchid Ct				
1700	INPS	46219	2231	B7
15000	NBVL	46060	1795	D5
15000	NbvT	46060	1795	D5
Orchid Ln				
8000	INPS	46219	2231	B7
Orchid Bloom Dr				
1900	INPS	46231	2334	A7
Orchid Bloom Ln				
1900	INPS	46231	2334	A7
Orchid Bloom Pl				
8900	INPS	46231	2334	A7
Oregon St				
-	INPS	46202	2337	B1
Oriental Ct				
8600	INPS	46219	2231	C7
N Oriental St				
10	INPS	46201	2337	E2
10	INPS	46202	2337	E2
S Oriental St				
100	INPS	46201	2337	E4
100	INPS	46202	2337	E4
Oriental Oak Ct				
18400	NBVL	46062	1685	E6
18400	NBVL	46062	1686	A6
Orinoco Av				
6000	INPS	46227	2555	E3
6500	HMCT	46227	2555	E3
7500	INPS	46227	2556	A5
Oriole Ct				
-	PNFD	46231	2333	E6
Oriole Dr				
5100	CRML	46033	1794	B7
5100	CRML	46033	1903	B1
Orion St				
4900	INPS	46201	2339	A4
Oris Ct				
8200	INPS	46259	2558	B2
E Oris Rd				
8200	INPS	46259	2558	C2
Orkney Ct				
400	WRvT	46142	2663	D4

STREET
Block City ZIP Map# Grid

Orland Ovlk
300 WTFD 46074 1792 C3
Orlando Ct
4600 INPS 46228 2118 C7
Orlando St
2400 INPS 46228 2118 C7
Orleans Ct
18800 NBVL 46060 1686 E5
Orleans St
1700 INPS 46203 2337 D7
Orphant Annie Dr
1100 GNFD 46140 2345 D3
Orth Cir
5800 INPS 46221 2444 B7
Orth Ct
5500 INPS 46221 2444 B7
Orth Dr
5100 INPS 46221 2444 B7
Orville Ln
6500 INPS 46237 2557 A3
Osage Dr
5800 CRML 46033 1903 C1
E Osage St
100 GNFD 46140 2345 E2
200 CtrT 46140 2345 E2
W Osage St
10 GNFD 46140 2345 D2
Osborn Dr
6300 INPS 46226 2230 D1
Osborne Av
- PTBR 46167 2112 E3
Osborne St
- NBVL 46060 1686 B7
Osceola Ct
10300 INPS 46235 2232 B4
Osceola Dr
10000 WshT 46234 2224 C6
Osceola Ln
3000 INPS 46235 2232 A4
Oshawa St
11600 LWNC 46236 2123 D3
Oslo Pl
3700 INPS 46228 2227 A2
Osman Ln
2300 BCkT 46140 2235 A7
Osprey Cir
8200 INPS 46256 2013 C7
Osprey Ln
- GNWD 46143 2665 E6
Osprey Wy
5700 CRML 46033 1903 B1
Ossington Ct
4700 INPS 46254 2116 E7
Ossington Dr
6700 INPS 46254 2116 E7
Ostara Ct
12300 FSHR 46038 1906 A6
Oswasco Cir
10200 WshT 46234 2224 C6
Oswasco Dr
10000 WshT 46234 2224 C5
Oswego Dr
700 CRML 46032 1902 B4
10000 LWNC 46236 2123 A1
Othello Wy
600 AVON 46123 2332 B2
Otis Av
600 LWNC 46216 2122 D5
Ottawa Dr
300 INPS 46217 2555 B7
Ottawa Pass
5500 CRML 46033 1903 B2
Otter Pl
10200 CRML 46033 2011 D1
Otterbein Av
4000 INPS 46227 2446 E5
4200 INPS 46227 2447 A5
Otter Cove Cir
8700 INPS 46236 2014 C4
Ottercreek Dr
10000 WshT 46234 2224 C6
Outback Ct
5100 NBVL 46062 1685 A1
N Outer Dr
700 LEBN 46052 1677 A5
Outer Dr S
900 LEBN 46052 1677 A5
Outer Bank Rd
- NBVL 46062 1685 D4
5700 INPS 46239 2558 B1
Outrigger Ct
11100 INPS 46236 2014 C5
Outrigger Ln
10100 FSHR 46038 1905 B5
Outside Tr
15400 NBVL 46060 1796 E4
15400 NBVL 46060 1797 A4
Outside Trail Ct
12200 NBVL 46060 1797 A4
Over Dr
- NBVL 46060 1687 A7
Overbrook Cir
5500 INPS 46226 2121 B5
Overbrooke Ln
- AVON 46123 2332 D5
Overcrest Dr
5700 INPS 46237 2557 A1
9600 FSHR 46038 2013 E1
Overdorf Rd
20200 NbvT 46060 1687 B2
20600 NbvT 46062 1687 B1
20900 NbvT 46062 1578 B6
21100 WRvT 46062 1578 B6
22600 WRvT 46034 1578 B2
Overland Ct
100 NBVL 46060 1795 D2
600 BNBG 46112 2223 D3
5100 INPS 46268 2117 C2
Overland Dr
400 GNWD 46143 2665 B6
Overlook Cir
- CCRO 46034 1577 B5
Overlook Ct
200 WshT 46123 2332 A3
2000 INPS 46229 2232 A7
Overlook Ct
10700 FSHR 46038 1904 B7
Overlook Dr
11400 FSHR 46038 1905 A6
Overlook Pkwy
8500 INPS 46260 2010 A5
Overlook Pl
11500 EglT 46077 1899 D3
Overlook Pt
9800 EglT 46077 2007 E1
Overlook Tr
300 PNFD 46168 2441 A3
Overlook Pass
- WshT 46123 2332 A3
Overman Blvd
- WTFD 46074 1792 D4
Overture Dr
12600 CRML 46033 1903 B3
Overview Dr
12900 FSHR 46060 1906 D2
Owl Ct
4300 INPS 46268 2008 E5
Owls Head Dr
6500 INPS 46217 2554 C3
Owls Nest Ct
6800 INPS 46254 2116 D6
Owls Nest Dr
- INPS 46254 2116 E7
Owls Nest Pl
4600 INPS 46254 2116 E7
Owster Ct
4100 INPS 46237 2447 D5
Owster Ln
3600 INPS 46237 2447 D5
Owster Wy
3900 INPS 46237 2447 D4
Oxbow Wy
6300 INPS 46220 2119 E3
6300 INPS 46220 2120 A3
Oxbridge Pl
12800 FSHR 46060 1906 D3
Oxford Dr
400 NBVL 46062 1685 D2
Oxford Ln
- MCVL 46055 2124 C1
2800 INPS 46218 2229 B5
Oxford Pl
4500 CRML 46033 1902 E4
4500 CRML 46033 1903 A4
Oxford Run
1300 GNWD 46143 2665 B6
N Oxford St
- INPS 46205 2120 C7
1000 INPS 46201 2338 C1
3400 INPS 46218 2229 C3
4100 INPS 46205 2229 C1
6400 INPS 46220 2120 C2
S Oxford St
10 INPS 46201 2338 C3
1400 INPS 46203 2338 C6
2800 INPS 46203 2447 B2
3200 INPS 46237 2447 C3
6600 INPS 46227 2556 C3
Oxmoor Wy
- WshT 46123 2333 C3
200 AVON 46123 2333 D3
Oyster Bay Ct
10700 LWNC 46236 2014 B6

P

P Ct
- WRvT 46142 2663 E2
P St
- BHGV 46107 2448 A3
N Paca St
800 INPS 46202 2337 B2
Pacer Ct
14900 WshT 46032 1792 C6
Pacific St
300 INPS 46227 2446 D4
1700 INPS 46227 2447 A4
Pacifica Pl
- NBVL 46060 1687 D4
Packard Dr
10200 FSHR 46038 2014 B1
Packard Ln
6500 INPS 46237 2557 D1
Paddington Cir
3600 INPS 46268 2009 A6
Paddington Ln N
3700 INPS 46268 2009 A6
Paddington Ln W
7700 INPS 46268 2009 A7
Paddington Pkwy
- FSHR 46060 1906 D3
Paddlebrook Dr
400 DNVL 46122 2329 B4
N Paddock Dr
300 WRvT 46142 2663 C3
Paddock Rd
200 WRvT 46142 2663 C4
700 MdnT 46158 2661 D6
3200 PryT 46052 1896 B1
3600 PNFD 46168 2440 D4
9200 MdnT 46113 2661 D2
S Paddock Rd
700 WRvT 46143 2663 C6
8000 INPS 46113 2552 D7
8000 INPS 46221 2552 D7
8500 INPS 46113 2661 D1
8500 MdnT 46113 2661 D1
Padre Ln
700 GNWD 46143 2665 E5
800 GNWD 46143 2666 A5
5200 INPS 46237 2448 B7
Pagoda Dr
- INPS 46203 2446 D1
- INPS 46225 2446 D1
Pagosa Ct
3300 INPS 46226 2231 C4
Painted Maple Ct
5500 INPS 46254 2116 D6
Painter Ct
13800 CRML 46032 1901 D1
Palace Ct
2900 ClyT 46032 1900 C7
Palace Dr
2800 INPS 46241 2444 D2
Palais Cir
7300 INPS 46278 2116 E1
Palais Ct
7500 INPS 46278 2007 D7
7500 INPS 46278 2116 D1
Palais Dr
7400 INPS 46278 2116 E1
Palamaro Cir
7900 INPS 46239 2340 B7
Palatka Ct
11000 LWNC 46236 2123 C2
Palawan Dr
7800 INPS 46239 2340 B5
Palawan Wy
7800 INPS 46239 2340 B5
Palimino Ct
10 ZNVL 46077 1899 A6
Palisade Ct
5200 INPS 46237 2448 A7
Palisade Wy
5200 INPS 46237 2448 A7
Palisades Ct
- GNWD 46143 2774 A1
11600 FCkT 46038 1906 D5
11600 FSHR 46038 1906 D5
Palm Ct
1300 GNFD 46140 2237 B6
8500 INPS 46219 2231 C7
Palmaire Pl
9900 FSHR 46060 1796 A7
Palmbrook Blvd
- NBVL 46062 1685 A6
- NbvT 46062 1685 A6
- WshT 46062 1685 A6
Palmer Dr
700 NBVL 46062 1576 D7
Palmer Ln
300 GNWD 46143 2665 E4
Palmer St
- INPS 46225 2337 C6
E Palmer St
10 INPS 46225 2337 C6
900 INPS 46203 2337 E6
1500 INPS 46203 2338 A6
Palmetto Ct
800 INPS 46217 2555 A6
Palmetto Ln
8100 INPS 46217 2555 A6
Palmetto Wy
16700 NBVL 46062 1794 E2
Palm Grove Ct
7800 INPS 46219 2231 B7
Palmyra Cir
10700 INPS 46239 2341 B4
Palmyra Ct
10700 INPS 46239 2341 B4
Palmyra Dr
200 INPS 46239 2341 B4
300 WTFD 46074 1792 D3
Palmyra Grn
16100 WTFD 46074 1792 E3
Palo Alto Ct
- CRML 46074 1900 B1
Palomar Vista Cir
- LcnT 46112 2115 C5
Palomino Run
7200 INPS 46278 2117 A1
Palomino Tr
4600 INPS 46239 2449 B6
Palo Verde Ct
2700 INPS 46227 2556 B6
Palo Verde Dr
8400 INPS 46227 2556 B6
Palo Verde Ter
8400 INPS 46227 2556 B7
Palo Vista Rd
1100 GNWD 46143 2665 E4
Pam Rd
100 ClyT 46280 1901 D7
Pamela Dr
1000 PNFD 46168 2550 C1
2100 INPS 46220 2120 B3
E Pamela Pkwy
100 BNBG 46112 2223 C1
Pamona Cir
6600 INPS 46214 2226 A7
Pamona Ct
1900 INPS 46214 2225 E7
10100 FSHR 46060 1905 B2
Pamona Dr
1800 INPS 46214 2225 E7
1800 INPS 46214 2226 A7
Panama Av
1200 INPS 46241 2334 E6
Pann Ct
8100 INPS 46217 2555 C6
Panola Ct
400 INPS 46239 2341 B4
Panorama Ct
9000 INPS 46234 2333 E3
9000 INPS 46234 2334 A3
Panther Wy
6600 INPS 46237 2557 D4
Panthers Wy
- FCkT 46038 1905 E3
Pantina Ln
6800 INPS 46237 2448 E6
Pantina Wy
4600 INPS 46237 2448 E6
Papan Ct
2200 WshT 46168 2441 C1
Pappas Dr
5000 INPS 46237 2448 B7
5500 INPS 46237 2557 B1
Par Dr
3900 INPS 46268 2118 A1
4200 INPS 46268 2117 E1
Paradise Ct
600 GNWD 46143 2666 A4
6500 LWNC 46236 2123 E2
Paradise Dr
12000 LWNC 46236 2123 E2
Paradise Ln
- NbvT 46062 1578 B7
6500 LWNC 46236 2123 E2
10200 NbvT 46062 1687 B1
Paradise Wy E
500 GNWD 46143 2666 A4
Paradise Wy N
1000 GNWD 46143 2666 B3
Paradise Wy W
500 GNWD 46143 2666 A4
Paragon Ct
400 GNFD 46140 2236 D5
Paragon Ln
- WTFD 46074 1792 D3
Paragon Wy
400 GNFD 46140 2236 C6
Parallel St
7400 INPS 46268 2009 C7
Parcrest Ct
8000 INPS 46259 2558 B3
Paree Ct E
600 INPS 46224 2335 A2
Paree Ct W
600 INPS 46224 2335 A2
Paris Av
2200 INPS 46208 2228 B6
Parish Ct
10 LEBN 46052 1676 D5
Parish Ln
8300 INPS 46217 2555 B6
Park Av
500 GNWD 46143 2665 D4
E Park Av
- GNFD 46140 2237 A7
100 GNFD 46140 2236 E7
N Park Av
10 INPS 46204 2337 D2
1200 INPS 46202 2337 D1
1600 INPS 46202 2228 D7
3600 INPS 46205 2228 D2
4400 INPS 46205 2119 D7
6900 INPS 46220 2119 D2
7400 INPS 46240 2119 D1
9100 INPS 46240 2010 D3
10000 ClyT 46280 2010 D1
10600 ClyT 46280 1901 D7
S Park Av
100 INPS 46202 2337 D4
400 INPS 46203 2337 D4
700 SRDN 46069 1573 B2
W Park Av
100 GNFD 46140 2236 D7
S Park Blvd
10 GNWD 46143 2666 A3
Park Ct
1400 GNWD 46143 2666 A3
Park Dr
- NBVL 46060 1686 C5
- WTWN 46075 1788 D6
100 PNFD 46168 2441 A5
200 MRVL 46158 2659 E4
400 GNWD 46143 2665 D3
700 FCkT 46040 2016 D2
800 LEBN 46052 1677 A5
N Park Dr
5300 INPS 46220 2120 D6
S Park Dr
200 MRVL 46158 2659 E4
500 SGLK 46140 2343 E2
1100 GNWD 46143 2666 A3
Park Ln
10 CRML 46032 1902 A3
300 LcnT 46112 2223 B5
6900 WshT 46123 2223 B6
Park Pl
1000 ZNVL 46077 1899 A4
Park Rd
- BNBG 46112 2114 B6
Park St
10 CCRO 46034 1577 D1
300 NBVL 46060 1686 C6
E Park St
200 PNFD 46168 2441 B5
300 WTFD 46074 1793 B1
N Park St
200 LEBN 46052 1677 A6
W Park St
10 WTFD 46074 1793 A1
Park 32 West Dr
100 NbvT 46062 1685 D7
100 NbvT 46062 1794 E1
Park 65 Dr
4000 INPS 46254 2226 E1
4000 INPS 46254 2227 A2
Park 800 Dr
400 GNWD 46143 2665 D7
Park Castle Wy
1600 INPS 46229 2232 A7
Park Central Ct
800 INPS 46260 2119 A3
Park Central Dr
- INPS 46260 2119 A3
Park Central Dr N
800 INPS 46260 2119 A3
Park Central Dr S
800 INPS 46260 2119 A3
Park Central Dr W
6400 INPS 46260 2119 A3
Park Central Wy
6400 INPS 46260 2119 A2
Park Chase Pl
1600 INPS 46229 2232 A7
Parkdale Pl
6600 INPS 46254 2225 E2
Park Davis Cir
3400 INPS 46235 2232 A3
Park Davis Dr
9600 INPS 46235 2231 E3
9900 INPS 46235 2232 A3
Park Davis Ln
3500 INPS 46235 2232 A3
Parke Dr
300 WshT 46123 2332 B6
Parke Dr
6200 LtyT 46118 2548 B2
Park East Ct
- FSHR 46038 1904 E1
Park Emerson Dr
5200 BHGV 46203 2448 A5
Parker Av
- INPS 46218 2229 C5
N Parker Av
1000 INPS 46201 2338 C1
3400 INPS 46218 2229 C3
3900 INPS 46205 2229 C2
4500 INPS 46205 2120 D7
5600 INPS 46220 2120 C4
7100 INPS 46240 2120 C1
S Parker Av
10 INPS 46201 2338 C3
2800 INPS 46203 2447 C2
2900 BHGV 46203 2447 C2
3200 INPS 46237 2447 C3
Parker Ct
3900 INPS 46205 2229 C2
Parker Ln
6500 INPS 46220 2120 C2
Parker Rd
- MdlT 46167 2221 C1
3700 MdlT 46122 2221 C1
Parker St
- WTLD 46184 2774 E5
2200 INPS 46218 2229 C6
Parker Oaks Wy
600 BNBG 46112 2114 D6
Park Forest Ct
4400 INPS 46226 2121 C7
4400 INPS 46226 2230 C1
Park Forest Dr E
200 WTLD 46131 2774 D7
200 WTLD 46184 2774 D7
Park Forest Dr N
10 WTLD 46184 2774 D7
Park Forest South Dr
10 WTLD 46131 2774 D7
10 WTLD 46184 2774 D7
Parkgate Av
500 INPS 46239 2341 B4
Park Glen Ct
10000 INPS 46229 2232 A7
Park Hill Dr
1600 INPS 46229 2232 A7
Park Hoover Village Dr
900 INPS 46260 2119 A2
Parkhurst Ct
- GNWD 46142 2664 E4
Park Hurst Dr
1600 INPS 46229 2232 A7
Parkia Ct
6200 INPS 46203 2448 C3
Parklake Cir
7100 INPS 46217 2554 C4
Parklake Ln
2600 INPS 46217 2554 C4
Parkland Ct
10900 FSHR 46038 1905 C5
Parkland Pl
8400 INPS 46256 2013 A5
Park Lodge Ct
3500 INPS 46205 2120 D7
Park Madison Ct
600 GNWD 46142 2665 C2
Park Madison Dr
600 GNWD 46142 2665 C2
Park Meadow Ct
400 INPS 46107 2447 E4
Park Meadow Dr
1200 BHGV 46107 2447 D4
1200 INPS 46107 2447 D4
Park Meadow Wy
1300 INPS 46107 2447 D4
Park Meadows Ct
- BrnT 46112 2114 D2
11300 NBVL 46060 1796 D2
Park Meadows Dr
- BrnT 46112 2114 D1
Park North Bnd
1700 INPS 46260 2009 E6
Park North Cir
7800 INPS 46260 2009 E6
Park North Ct
7700 INPS 46260 2009 E7
Park North Ln
1700 INPS 46260 2009 E7
Park North Wy
1600 INPS 46260 2009 E7
Park North Lake Dr
7700 INPS 46260 2009 E7
Park Place Blvd
100 AVON 46123 2332 C3
Park Place Ct
200 AVON 46123 2332 C3
Park Plaza Ct
5700 INPS 46220 2121 B2
Park Ridge Dr
10100 INPS 46229 2232 A7
10100 INPS 46229 2341 A1
Parkridge Dr
100 DNVL 46122 2329 E4
Park Ridge Wy
1600 INPS 46229 2232 B7
Park Royal Wy
13800 FSHR 46060 1906 D3
Park Royale Dr
10100 INPS 46229 2232 A7
Parkshore Dr
9800 FSHR 46060 1905 A1
Parkside Av
- SCkT 46163 2343 B2
Parkside Cres
11100 ClyT 46032 1901 B6
Parkside Ct
- SCkT 46163 2343 B2
10 BNBG 46112 2114 D6
Parkside Ct E
1100 PNFD 46168 2550 C1
Parkside Ct N
1000 PNFD 46168 2550 C1
Parkside Ct S
1000 PNFD 46168 2550 C1
Parkside Dr
7300 LWNC 46226 2122 A6
12600 FSHR 46038 1904 E3
S Parkside Dr
- SCkT 46163 2452 A1
3300 SCkT 46163 2451 E1
Park Square Dr
- AVON 46123 2332 B1
Park Stream Dr
10100 INPS 46229 2341 A1
Park Terrace Ct
1600 INPS 46229 2232 B7
Parkthorne Dr
1500 INPS 46229 2341 A1
1600 INPS 46229 2232 A7
Park Valley Dr
10000 INPS 46229 2232 A7
Parkview Av
10 INPS 46201 2338 A3
Parkview Ct
100 CRML 46032 1792 D7
12000 FSHR 46038 1904 C4
Parkview Dr
- BrnT 46112 2114 D1
10 MRVL 46158 2659 D2
10 NWTD 46184 2774 D4
Parkview Ln
11900 FSHR 46038 1904 C4
Parkview Pl
200 CRML 46032 1902 A2
300 NBVL 46060 1686 D7
Parkview Rd
10 CRML 46032 1792 D7
Park Vista Ct
1500 INPS 46229 2341 A1
10700 FSHR 46038 1904 E7
Park Ward Pl
7800 INPS 46259 2558 B6
Parkway Av
200 INPS 46225 2337 D6
800 INPS 46203 2337 D6
Parkway Cir
300 WTFD 46074 1793 A1
Parkway Dr
1200 ZNVL 46077 1899 A6
9900 FSHR 46038 2014 A1
Parkway St
300 NWTD 46184 2774 D5
400 WTLD 46184 2774 D5
Parkway East Dr
- INPS 46254 2116 D5
Parkwood Cross
- CRML 46280 2010 D2
Parkwood Ct
5900 INPS 46254 2226 B2
Parkwood Dr
10 BNBG 46112 2223 E2
1500 LEBN 46052 1676 E5
2400 SDWY 46224 2226 B6
Parkwood Pl
- PNFD 46168 2550 E1
Parliament Ct
100 NBVL 46060 1795 E3
Parliament Dr
6200 INPS 46220 2120 E3
6200 INPS 46220 2121 A3
Parliament Ln
3800 INPS 46235 2231 E2
Parliament Pl
800 GNWD 46142 2665 A1
Parmer Cir
10300 FSHR 46060 1796 B7
Parr Dr
2500 INPS 46220 2120 B2
Parrington Dr
6000 LWNC 46236 2123 B4
Parrish Ct
3500 INPS 46227 2556 C1
Parrot Cir
10800 FSHR 46038 1905 C7
Parsley Ln
8100 INPS 46237 2557 A6
Parsons Dr
1700 INPS 46224 2226 A7
Parson's Gate
- CRML 46032 1900 E3
Parterra Ct
5000 INPS 46237 2448 C7
Parterra Dr
5800 INPS 46237 2448 C7
Parthenia Av
100 BNBG 46112 2114 C6
Partridge Ct
7900 SPRT 46227 2556 C5
Partridge Dr
- PNFD 46231 2333 D6
Partridge Pl
900 EglT 46077 1898 C4
10000 CRML 46033 2011 D1
Partridge Rd
7500 SPRT 46227 2556 C5
Pasadena Av
1600 INPS 46219 2230 D7
4300 INPS 46226 2230 D1
N Pasadena Av
3800 INPS 46226 2230 D2
Pasadena Rd
100 NbvT 46062 1685 E5
N Pasadena St
10 INPS 46219 2339 D3
2000 INPS 46219 2230 D6
S Pasadena St
700 INPS 46219 2339 D5
1900 INPS 46203 2339 D7
2700 INPS 46203 2448 D2
Pascal Ct
8100 INPS 46268 2008 E5
Pasco Ln
- PNFD 46168 2550 A2
Paso del Norte Ct
8300 INPS 46227 2556 B7
Paso del Norte Dr
2700 INPS 46227 2556 B6
Passage Cir
6700 INPS 46250 2012 E3
Pasture View Ct
12300 CRML 46033 1903 B4
Pathfinder Ct
6300 INPS 46203 2448 D3
Pathway Dr N
1600 WRvT 46143 2664 C7
Pathway Dr S
1700 WRvT 46143 2664 C7
Pathway Pointe
19100 NBVL 46062 1685 D4
Pathwood Cir
11800 FSHR 46038 1906 E5
Patoka Cir
10200 WshT 46234 2224 C6
Patoka Dr
10200 WshT 46234 2224 D6
Patoka Pl
300 CRML 46032 1901 C1
Patoka Lake Dr
6000 INPS 46254 2117 A6
Patricia Ct
300 CRML 46033 1902 C5
Patricia Dr
3000 CRML 46033 1902 C5
E Patricia Dr
7300 MdnT 46113 2661 D4
Patricia St
3900 INPS 46222 2227 A4
4700 INPS 46222 2226 D4
5300 INPS 46224 2226 C4
Patrick Ct
12800 FSHR 46038 1905 A3
Patrick Pl
800 BNBG 46112 2114 D5
7000 INPS 46256 2012 E6
Patrick's Pl
- BNBG 46112 2114 D5
Patriot Ct
10 GNFD 46140 2345 A1
3600 ClyT 46032 1900 A6
Patriot Ln
1100 WshT 46234 2333 D1
Patriot Wy
5600 INPS 46254 2117 B5
Patriotic Wy
13200 FSHR 46060 1906 B2
Patriots Ct
5500 WRvT 46142 2663 B4
Patterson Dr
7800 WshT 46123 2223 D7
Patterson St
10 GNWD 46143 2665 E3
300 INPS 46202 2337 A3
5100 INPS 46208 2119 A6
N Patterson St
100 LEBN 46052 1676 E6
S Patterson St
200 LEBN 46052 1676 E7
Patton Dr
10 GNWD 46143 2665 C6
1900 SDWY 46224 2226 B7
3400 INPS 46224 2226 B3
8100 LWNC 46226 2122 B6
Paul Dr
1000 INPS 46229 2341 E1
Paula Lane East Dr
4300 INPS 46228 2227 D1
Paula Lane South Dr
2100 INPS 46228 2227 D1
Pauls Ct
10 GNFD 46140 2237 A5
Pauls Dr
1000 GNFD 46140 2237 A5
1300 GNFD 46140 2236 E5
Pavestone Ct
12700 FSHR 46038 1906 B6
Pavetto Ln
3200 INPS 46203 2448 D3
Pawleys Ct
11700 LWNC 46235 2123 D6
Pawnee Ct
3000 INPS 46235 2232 B4
Pawnee Dr
700 CRML 46032 1902 B4
2600 INPS 46229 2232 B5
3000 INPS 46235 2232 B4
10200 WshT 46234 2224 E6
Paw Paw Ct
6400 INPS 46203 2448 D2
Pawtucket Ct
7400 INPS 46250 2012 C7
7400 INPS 46250 2121 C1
8200 INPS 46256 2013 E5
Pawtucket Dr
- WshT 46074 1792 A5
Paxson Pl
19400 NBVL 46060 1687 C4
Paxton Pl
700 INPS 46220 2119 E4
1400 INPS 46220 2120 A4
Payne Rd
3200 INPS 46227 2556 C2
E Payne Rd
6500 INPS 46203 2448 D3
7000 INPS 46239 2448 E3
N Payne Rd
7900 INPS 46268 2009 A5
Payne Branch Rd
3900 INPS 46268 2009 A4
Payne South Dr
3000 INPS 46227 2556 C2
Payton Av
- INPS 46226 2231 A4
4500 LWNC 46226 2122 A7
4500 LWNC 46226 2231 A1
Payton Rd
1000 INPS 46219 2340 A1
Payton St
300 INPS 46219 2340 A2
N Paz Dr
1000 GNWD 46142 2665 C1
W Paz Dr
10 GNWD 46142 2665 C1

STREET
Block City ZIP Map# Grid

Peace Pl
6400 INPS 46268 2117 C3
S Peace St
1200 SCkT 46140 2343 E4
Peaceful Pl
4000 WRvT 46142 2664 B3
Peaceful View Dr
600 MRVL 46158 2660 A5
Peacemaker Ln
6100 NbvT 46062 1794 C2
Peach Ct
10 BNBG 46112 2223 D3
Peach Ln
16800 NBVL 46062 1794 E2
Peach Blossom Pl
7500 INPS 46254 2116 C6
Peachtree Ct
300 GNWD 46143 2665 C6
Peach Tree Ln
10 NWTD 46184 2774 D3
500 DNVL 46122 2329 C3
Peachtree Ln
200 GNWD 46143 2665 C6
300 INPS 46219 2340 A4
Peachwood Ct
4500 LWNC 46235 2122 E7
4500 LWNC 46235 2231 E1
Peacock Ct
7000 GfdT 46168 2550 B1
7000 PNFD 46168 2550 B1
11600 LWNC 46236 2123 D3
Peacock Dr
11300 LWNC 46236 2123 D3
Peak Ln
6400 INPS 46214 2335 A3
Peak Pl
6400 INPS 46214 2335 A3
Pearl
10 SCkT 46140 2344 A2
Pearl St
100 CRML 46032 1793 A7
300 GNWD 46142 2665 C3
7200 INPS 46221 2552 E5
E Pearl St
10 GNWD 46143 2665 C4
10 INPS 46204 2337 C3
100 LEBN 46052 1677 A7
200 WTLD 46184 2774 E6
400 WTLD 46184 2775 A5
2400 INPS 46201 2338 B3
N Pearl St
10 CCRO 46034 1577 D2
S Pearl St
10 CCRO 46034 1577 C3
W Pearl St
400 LEBN 46052 1676 E6
Pearl Bay Rdg
12100 INPS 46236 2014 E4
Pearlbush Av
3600 BHGV 46203 2448 B4
Pearlbush Ln
5400 BHGV 46203 2448 B4
Pearson Dr
- WshT 46062 1684 E6
Pearson Pkwy
- LEBN 46052 1676 D7
Pearson Pl
8000 INPS 46237 2556 E6
Peartree Rd
10100 LWNC 46235 2123 A6
Pebble Ct
4900 WRvT 46142 2663 D2
Pebble Ln
4900 WRvT 46142 2663 D3
Pebble Wy
400 WRvT 46142 2663 D2
Pebble Wy E
2800 INPS 46268 2117 D3
Pebble Wy W
2800 INPS 46268 2117 E3
Pebble Beach Ct
8300 INPS 46234 2225 A5
Pebble Beach Dr
2100 ClyT 46032 1900 D7
Pebble Brook Blvd
- NBVL 46062 1685 B6
Pebble Brook Cir
300 NBVL 46062 1685 B6
Pebblebrook Ct
10 BrnT 46112 2114 B1
Pebble Brook Dr
- NBVL 46062 1685 B6
Pebblebrook Dr
8000 BrnT 46112 2114 B2
Pebblebrook Ln
11700 CRML 46033 1903 C5
Pebble Brook Pl
700 NBVL 46062 1685 B6
Pebblebrooke Ct
12000 LWNC 46236 2123 E1
Pebblebrooke East Dr
7300 LWNC 46236 2123 D1
7400 LWNC 46236 2014 E7
Pebblebrooke West Dr
7300 LWNC 46236 2123 E1
7400 LWNC 46236 2014 E7
Pebble Center Dr
- NBVL 46062 1685 C7
- NbvT 46062 1685 C7
Pebble Creek Ct
8000 INPS 46268 2009 A6
Pebble Creek Dr
- GNWD 46143 2665 C7
3600 INPS 46268 2009 A6
Pebble Knoll Wy
12300 CRML 46033 1903 C4
Pebble Point Dr
3000 INPS 46214 2225 D4
Pebblepointe Pass
11600 CRML 46033 1903 A5
Pebblestone Ct
5700 CRML 46033 1903 B4
Pebblestream Dr
5800 CRML 46033 1903 C3

Pebble Village Ln
- NBVL 46062 1685 B7
Pecan Ct
900 INPS 46217 2555 A5
N Peck Av
1000 INPS 46202 2337 D1
Peck Dr
10 GNWD 46143 2665 C7
Peck St
1200 INPS 46202 2337 D1
1500 GNWD 46143 2665 C6
1500 INPS 46202 2228 A7
Pecos Ct
- CRML 46033 1794 D7
- CRML 46033 1903 D1
5400 INPS 46237 2448 B7
W Peg Ct
6800 MrlT 46130 2560 D6
Pegasus Dr
- NBVL 46060 1796 D6
Peggy Ln
10 LcnT 46112 2113 D5
Pele Pl
1600 INPS 46214 2225 D7
Pelham Pl
8100 LWNC 46216 2122 B6
Pelham Wy
5300 LWNC 46216 2122 B6
Pelican Pl
5000 CRML 46033 1903 B1
Pemberly Ct
700 NBVL 46060 1795 E3
Pemberly Dr
5700 INPS 46221 2553 B3
Pemberton Cir
8600 INPS 46260 2009 E4
Pemberton Ln
1700 INPS 46260 2009 D4
Pemboke Ct
- MdnT 46113 2661 A2
Pembridge Dr
4800 INPS 46254 2116 E7
Pembridge Wy
6600 INPS 46254 2116 D6
Pembroke Ln
- INPS 46226 2121 D5
Pembroke Pl
6000 INPS 46220 2120 E4
Pembrooke Cir
12400 CRML 46032 1900 E3
Pendleton Wy
3800 INPS 46226 2231 A2
E Pendleton Pike
6800 INPS 46226 2230 E2
7000 LWNC 46226 2230 E2
7200 INPS 46226 2231 A2
7200 LWNC 46226 2231 A2
8400 LWNC 46226 2122 E6
9000 LWNC 46235 2122 E6
9000 LWNC 46236 2122 E6
9800 LWNC 46236 2123 A5
10000 LWNC 46235 2123 A5
12300 LWNC 46236 2124 A1
12600 MCVL 46055 2124 A1
12600 MCVL 46236 2124 A1
E Pendleton Pike SR-67
7500 INPS 46226 2231 B1
7500 LWNC 46226 2231 B1
8400 LWNC 46226 2122 E6
9000 LWNC 46235 2122 E6
9000 LWNC 46236 2122 E6
9800 LWNC 46236 2123 A5
10000 LWNC 46235 2123 A5
12300 LWNC 46236 2124 A1
12600 MCVL 46055 2124 A1
12600 MCVL 46236 2124 A1
E Pendleton Pike US-36
7500 INPS 46226 2231 B1
7500 LWNC 46226 2231 B1
8400 LWNC 46226 2122 E6
9000 LWNC 46235 2122 E6
9000 LWNC 46236 2122 E6
9800 LWNC 46236 2123 A5
10000 LWNC 46235 2123 A5
12300 LWNC 46236 2124 A1
12600 MCVL 46055 2124 A1
12600 MCVL 46236 2124 A1
W Pendleton Pike
3000 VrnT 46040 2016 B4
3000 VrnT 46055 2016 B4
5000 VrnT 46055 2015 E6
5600 MCVL 46055 2015 E6
6500 LWNC 46236 2124 B1
6500 MCVL 46055 2124 B1
6500 MCVL 46236 2124 B1
W Pendleton Pike SR-67
3000 VrnT 46040 2016 B4
3000 VrnT 46055 2016 B4
5000 VrnT 46055 2015 E6
5600 MCVL 46055 2015 E6
6500 LWNC 46236 2124 B1
6500 MCVL 46055 2124 B1
6500 MCVL 46236 2124 B1
W Pendleton Pike US-36
3000 VrnT 46040 2016 B4
3000 VrnT 46055 2016 B4
5000 VrnT 46055 2015 E6
5600 MCVL 46055 2015 E6
6500 LWNC 46236 2124 B1
6500 MCVL 46055 2124 B1
6500 MCVL 46236 2124 B1
Pendragon Blvd
4800 INPS 46268 2117 D2
Pendula Dr
4800 CRML 46033 1903 A6
10100 LWNC 46236 2123 A4
Penguin Cir
7600 INPS 46239 2449 A7
Penjerrack Ct
3700 ClyT 46032 2009 A1
Penn Dr
10 WshT 46123 2332 A4
10600 ClyT 46280 1901 D7
Penn Pl
10 ZNVL 46077 1899 A4

Penn Pl
8100 INPS 46250 2011 E6
Penn St
10 WTFD 46074 1684 B7
Pennan Ct
6400 NBVL 46062 1794 D6
Penneagle Dr
13100 CRML 46033 1903 C2
Penneramp Dr
- PNFD 46168 2550 B2
Pennie Ln
- PTBR 46167 2113 A2
Penninger Dr
13300 CRML 46074 1900 A1
Pennington Ct
4600 INPS 46254 2116 C7
Pennington Rd
10 MdnT 46158 2660 C7
12600 FCkT 46038 1906 C2
12600 FCkT 46060 1906 C2
12600 FSHR 46038 1906 C2
12600 FSHR 46060 1906 C2
17300 WynT 46060 1688 C7
17300 WynT 46060 1797 C1
23800 WynT 46060 1579 C2
Pennover Ct
7700 INPS 46217 2554 C5
Pennridge Dr
100 INPS 46240 2119 D1
Pennswood Ct
- PNFD 46168 2440 D4
Pennswood Dr
200 WRvT 46142 2663 B4
Pennsylvania Ct
100 INPS 46225 2446 C2
Pennsylvania Pkwy
10 ClyT 46280 2010 D1
10 CRML 46280 2010 D1
Pennsylvania St
10 GNFD 46140 2345 D1
N Pennsylvania St
10 INPS 46204 2337 C3
800 INPS 46202 2337 C3
1600 INPS 46202 2228 C6
2600 INPS 46205 2228 C5
4500 INPS 46205 2119 C7
6700 INPS 46220 2119 C1
7100 INPS 46240 2119 C1
9200 INPS 46240 2010 D3
9500 CRML 46240 2010 D3
10300 CRML 46280 2010 D1
10900 ClyT 46280 1901 D7
10900 CRML 46280 1901 D7
11000 CRML 46032 1901 D6
S Pennsylvania St
10 GNFD 46140 2345 D2
10 INPS 46204 2337 C5
2000 INPS 46225 2337 C7
2200 INPS 46225 2446 C1
3000 INPS 46227 2446 C3
7600 INPS 46227 2555 C5
Pennwood Ct
8900 INPS 46240 2010 D4
Pennwood Dr
4600 INPS 46205 2120 B7
Pennwood Ln
200 BNBG 46112 2114 D7
Penny Ct
2400 INPS 46229 2232 B6
Penny Ln
- GfdT 46168 2440 E4
10200 INPS 46229 2232 A6
Pennycroft Dr
7500 LWNC 46236 2014 C7
8000 INPS 46236 2014 C7
Pennyroyal Ln
7700 INPS 46237 2556 E5
Penobscot Dr
7800 INPS 46239 2340 B5
Penridge Ct
- GNWD 46143 2666 A7
Penright Ct
500 INPS 46217 2555 B7
Penrith Dr
10000 INPS 46229 2232 A5
E Pentecost Rd
9300 INPS 46239 2449 E5
9300 INPS 46239 2450 A5
Pentwater Ct
12200 INPS 46236 2015 A4
Penway Cir
6000 INPS 46224 2226 B3
Penway Ct
5400 INPS 46224 2226 C2
Penway St
100 INPS 46205 2228 D3
5900 INPS 46224 2226 B3
E Penway St
7500 INPS 46226 2231 A3
W Penway St
4600 INPS 46222 2226 E3
Penzance Pl
3800 ClyT 46032 2009 A1
Peony Pl
4900 INPS 46254 2117 D5
Pepin Pl
14100 CRML 46032 1792 A7
Pepper Cir
4600 INPS 46237 2556 E4
Pepper Ct
4500 INPS 46237 2556 E4
Peppergrass Ct
5000 INPS 46254 2117 C6
Pepperidge Cir
4400 INPS 46235 2232 B1
Pepperidge Ct
4400 INPS 46235 2232 A1
Pepperidge Dr
9400 INPS 46235 2231 E1
10000 INPS 46235 2232 A1
Peppermill Ct
12900 CRML 46033 1902 E3
Peppermill Ln
11000 FSHR 46038 1905 C5

Peppermill Run
700 GNWD 46143 2665 B5
Peppermint Ct
- GNWD 46143 2665 B5
Pepperwood Dr
12000 LWNC 46236 2014 E6
Perched Owl Run
- FCkT 46055 2015 C2
Percheron Ln
2900 INPS 46227 2447 C4
Percheron Pl
- INPS 46227 2447 C4
Peregrine Blvd
- INPS 46228 2118 A4
Pergola Ln
6300 INPS 46241 2335 A5
Perilla Ct
7500 INPS 46237 2556 E5
7500 INPS 46237 2557 A4
Perimeter Pkwy
- PNFD 46168 2551 A2
N Perimeter Rd
- INPS 46231 2442 E2
- INPS 46241 2442 E2
6600 INPS 46241 2334 E7
7300 INPS 46231 2334 D7
7800 INPS 46231 2443 B1
7800 INPS 46241 2443 B1
S Perimeter Rd
- INPS 46241 2444 A4
6700 INPS 46241 2443 E4
Periwinkle Ct
4500 WTFD 46062 1684 E7
4700 INPS 46221 2444 C6
Periwinkle Ln
5600 INPS 46220 2120 C5
Periwinkle Wy
3400 INPS 46220 2120 C5
Perkins Av
10 BHGV 46107 2447 C3
10 INPS 46107 2447 C3
10 INPS 46237 2447 C3
1400 INPS 46203 2338 C7
2200 INPS 46203 2447 C1
Perkins St
11500 CRML 46032 1901 E6
E Perlinda Ln
9500 INPS 46259 2558 E4
Perlita Pl
10000 FSHR 46038 1905 A3
Perrault Dr
6200 INPS 46227 2556 B2
Perrier Ct
6700 INPS 46278 2116 E1
Perrier Dr
7400 INPS 46278 2007 E7
7400 INPS 46278 2116 E1
Perrin Dr
13700 CRML 46032 1792 E7
13700 CRML 46032 1901 E1
Perry Av
3600 INPS 46221 2445 A3
W Perry Av
3400 INPS 46221 2445 B3
Perry Ct
6800 INPS 46219 2339 E3
Perry Dr
6700 INPS 46219 2339 D2
Perry Rd
- GfdT 46168 2442 B7
- GfdT 46168 2551 B1
900 PNFD 46168 2442 B7
S Perry Rd
- PNFD 46168 2442 B3
Perry St
10 GNWD 46142 2665 B3
E Perry St
500 INPS 46227 2446 D3
1500 INPS 46227 2447 A3
1600 INPS 46237 2447 A3
W Perry St
3700 INPS 46221 2445 A3
4000 INPS 46221 2444 E3
4200 INPS 46241 2444 D3
Perry Commons Av
7000 INPS 46217 2554 D4
Perry Commons Blvd
1500 INPS 46217 2554 E4
Perry Pear Dr
- ClyT 46032 1899 E6
Perry Pines Ct
6300 INPS 46237 2556 D2
Perry Woods Ct
5700 INPS 46227 2556 B1
Perry Woods Wy
5800 INPS 46227 2556 C1
S Perry Worth Rd
1000 CtrT 46052 1786 D3
2000 CtrT 46052 1787 B7
2000 PryT 46052 1787 B7
3000 PryT 46052 1896 C1
4000 WrhT 46075 1896 D3
4600 PryT 46075 1896 D3
5000 PryT 46075 1897 A4
6100 EglT 46075 1897 B6
6100 EglT 46077 1897 B6
Pershing Av
6900 INPS 46268 2118 C1
N Pershing Av
- INPS 46222 2227 D7
1000 INPS 46222 2336 D1
6000 INPS 46228 2118 C4
S Pershing Av
700 INPS 46221 2336 D5
Pershing Rd
7500 INPS 46268 2009 B7
Persimmon Cir
1400 GNFD 46140 2237 B6
Persimmon Dr
12400 LWNC 46236 2124 A2
Persimmon Ln
- WRvT 46143 2663 E5
Persimmon Pl
1500 NBVL 46062 1685 C2

Persimmon Pass
6300 PNFD 46168 2550 D2
Personality Ct
5500 INPS 46237 2448 B6
N Peru St
- JknT 46030 1577 D1
10 CCRO 46034 1577 D1
700 JknT 46034 1577 D1
N Peru St SR-19
- JknT 46030 1577 D1
10 CCRO 46034 1577 D1
700 JknT 46034 1577 D1
S Peru St
10 CCRO 46034 1577 D3
S Peru St SR-19
10 CCRO 46034 1577 D3
Petalon Trc
12300 FSHR 46038 1906 A6
Pete Dye Blvd
- WTFD 46033 1793 D5
Pete Moore Dr
- BNBG 46112 2223 D1
Peter Dr
2200 INPS 46229 2232 C6
Peterman Rd
10 WRvT 46142 2664 A3
N Peterman Rd
400 WRvT 46142 2664 A2
S Peterman Rd
100 WRvT 46142 2664 A4
Peters St
100 WTWN 46075 1788 D7
Petersburg Dr
5900 INPS 46254 2117 B4
Petersburg Pkwy
5700 INPS 46254 2117 A4
Peterson Ct
- GNWD 46143 2666 A6
5800 INPS 46254 2117 B5
Petree Ct
3400 CtrT 46122 2331 A4
Pewter Pl
12400 FSHR 46038 1904 C3
PGA Dr
7000 INPS 46250 2012 E4
Phaeton Pl
500 INPS 46227 2555 D5
Phantom Ct
500 ZNVL 46077 1898 E7
Pheasant Ct
5400 INPS 46254 2226 C1
5800 CRML 46033 1903 D2
6400 INPS 46237 2556 E2
Pheasant Dr
6400 INPS 46237 2556 E2
Pheasant Run
500 EglT 46077 1898 D3
N Pheasant Run
11000 MrlT 46126 2560 C1
11300 MrlT 46126 2451 C7
Pheasant Wy
1800 WRvT 46143 2663 E7
Pheasant Ridge Ct
6300 INPS 46237 2557 D4
Pheasant Ridge Dr
7100 INPS 46237 2557 D4
Phi Delta Kappa Dr
100 DNVL 46122 2330 A4
Philadelphia Ct
5600 INPS 46254 2117 B5
Philadelphia Dr
- BCkT 46055 2124 C4
8000 FSHR 46038 1904 C6
Philip Ct
10 INPS 46222 2226 E5
Philips Dr
1300 INPS 46241 2335 D6
Phillip Dr
- NBVL 46060 1687 A6
Phillips Ct
10 WTLD 46184 2775 A4
Phillips Pl
10 ZNVL 46077 1898 E6
Philwood Dr
2500 SDWY 46224 2226 B5
Phoenix Cir
3200 INPS 46241 2444 E3
Phoenix Dr
4200 INPS 46241 2444 D3
Phylis Dr
5100 INPS 46254 2117 D6
Physics Wy
4500 INPS 46239 2448 E6
Picadilly Ct
10 BNBG 46112 2223 C1
2000 INPS 46260 2009 D3
8300 INPS 46256 2013 C5
Picadilly Ln
8200 INPS 46256 2013 C5
Picadilly Pl
1900 INPS 46260 2009 D2
Picadilly Rd
10 BNBG 46112 2223 B1
Piccadily Cir
12700 FSHR 46060 1906 D3
Pickens Ct
10800 ClyT 46032 1900 A6
Picket Fence Pl
10800 FSHR 46038 1905 C5
Pickett St
400 PNFD 46168 2441 B4
Pickford Ct
3000 INPS 46227 2556 C6
Pickford Dr
8000 INPS 46227 2556 C6
Pickwick Ct
300 NBVL 46062 1685 E2
6300 EglT 46077 1897 C7
Pickwick Dr
8800 INPS 46260 2010 A4
Pickwick Pl
1200 INPS 46208 2227 E3
Picnic Rd
4900 INPS 46268 2008 D4

Picton Dr
7000 LWNC 46226 2230 E2
7200 LWNC 46226 2231 A2
Piedmont Dr
500 WshT 46074 1792 B5
Pierce Dr
1000 PNFD 46168 2441 D7
E Pierce St
10 WTWN 46075 1788 D6
500 WrhT 46075 1788 D6
W Pierce St
10 WTWN 46075 1788 C6
800 WrhT 46075 1788 C6
Piermont Dr
3500 INPS 46227 2556 D6
Piers End Dr
18400 NBVL 46062 1685 E5
Pierson Ct
19100 NBVL 46060 1687 C4
Pierson Dr
6400 INPS 46241 2335 A7
6500 INPS 46241 2334 E7
Pierson St
- NPLN 46163 2452 A4
900 INPS 46204 2337 C2
1600 INPS 46202 2228 C7
2400 INPS 46208 2228 C6
E Pierson St
10 GNFD 46140 2345 E2
N Pierson St
- INPS 46204 2337 C3
W Pierson St
300 GNFD 46140 2345 D2
Pigeon Creek Ln
3900 INPS 46234 2225 A2
Pike Ln
5200 GfdT 46168 2441 A4
Pike Pkwy
5700 INPS 46254 2117 B5
Pike Pl
10 PNFD 46168 2441 C5
Pike Creek Blvd
5000 INPS 46254 2117 C6
Pike Creek Ln
5100 INPS 46254 2117 C7
W Pike Plaza Rd
5000 INPS 46254 2226 C2
Pike Side Dr
- LWNC 46235 2123 D4
Pike View Ct
6500 INPS 46268 2117 D2
Pike View Dr
4900 INPS 46268 2117 D2
Pilgram Rd
100 GNWD 46142 2664 E4
Pilgrim Ct
100 GNWD 46142 2664 E4
Pilgrim Dr
5500 INPS 46254 2117 B5
Pilgrim Rd
15900 WynT 46060 1688 D4
Pillory Cir
6100 INPS 46254 2117 B4
Pillory Dr
6000 INPS 46254 2117 C4
Pillory Pl
6000 INPS 46254 2117 B4
Pillory Wy
5400 INPS 46254 2117 B3
Pilot Mills Ct
- NBVL 46062 1685 C5
Pilot Mills Dr
18600 NBVL 46062 1685 C5
Pimbury Ct
1100 INPS 46260 2010 A3
Pimlico Cir
1000 ClyT 46280 1901 E7
Pine Dr
10 INPS 46260 2010 C3
W Pine Dr
100 INPS 46260 2010 C3
Pine St
- NPLN 46163 2452 A3
10 SPRT 46227 2556 B4
1000 BNBG 46112 2223 B2
E Pine St
10 ZNVL 46077 1899 B6
N Pine St
100 INPS 46202 2337 E3
800 BCkT 46140 2233 B7
S Pine St
- NPLN 46163 2452 A4
10 INPS 46202 2337 E4
400 INPS 46203 2337 D5
W Pine St
10 ZNVL 46077 1899 B6
Pinebark Dr
2300 INPS 46217 2554 C2
Pine Bluff Dr
10600 FSHR 46038 1904 E7
10700 FSHR 46038 1905 B6
W Pine Bluff Dr
5000 SCkT 46163 2452 A1
Pinebrook Dr
4800 NBVL 46062 1685 A6
5200 INPS 46254 2117 D6
Pine Cone Wy
8900 INPS 46268 2009 C3
Pinecreek Cir
9300 INPS 46256 2013 D3
Pinecreek Ct
9000 INPS 46256 2013 D3
Pinecreek Dr
9400 INPS 46256 2013 D3
Pinecreek Wy
9000 INPS 46256 2013 D3
Pine Crest Cir
5500 NBVL 46062 1685 B2
Pinecrest Dr
10 GNWD 46143 2665 C7
Pinecrest Rd
3100 INPS 46234 2225 B3
Pinecroft Dr
- INPS 46254 2117 D6

Pinedale Dr
10 WshT 46123 2331 D3
100 WTLD 46184 2775 A6
Pine Forge Cir
6000 INPS 46254 2117 E4
Pine Forge Ct
6000 INPS 46254 2117 E4
Pine Grove Ct
- LcnT 46112 2115 C5
12600 LWNC 46236 2015 A7
Pine Grove Ln
2000 GfdT 46168 2550 E5
Pine Grove Wy
- LcnT 46112 2115 C5
Pine Hill Dr
5000 NBVL 46062 1685 B1
5000 NbvT 46062 1685 B1
5900 LWNC 46235 2123 D4
Pine Hill Wy
1000 CRML 46032 1792 A7
Pinehollow Ct
4500 INPS 46254 2117 A7
4500 INPS 46254 2226 A1
Pinehurst Av
100 FCkT 46038 1905 B7
Pinehurst Dr
2100 ClyT 46032 1900 D6
Pinehurst Dr E
4000 INPS 46235 2231 D2
Pinehurst Dr N
9000 INPS 46235 2231 D2
Pinehurst Dr S
9000 INPS 46235 2231 D2
Pine Knoll Blvd
5400 NBVL 46062 1685 B1
Pine Lake Dr
- GNWD 46184 2774 A1
- PltT 46184 2774 A1
Pine Lake Rd
7900 INPS 46268 2008 E6
Pine Lake Wy
4500 INPS 46268 2008 E6
Pinellas Park Dr
10900 INPS 46229 2232 C6
Pine Meadow Cir
11800 FSHR 46038 1905 E5
Pine Meadow Dr
10 BNBG 46112 2113 D4
600 ZNVL 46077 1899 B5
Pine Mountain Pl
11200 INPS 46229 2341 D1
Pine Mountain Wy
1000 INPS 46229 2341 C1
Pine Needle Ct
10700 FSHR 46038 1905 B7
Pineneedle Ct
10100 INPS 46235 2232 A1
Pineneedle Dr
12400 LWNC 46236 2124 A2
Pine Oak Dr
- ZNVL 46077 1898 C1
Pine Park Ln
4600 INPS 46268 2008 E6
Pine Ridge Dr
8600 INPS 46260 2010 B4
E Pine Ridge Dr
10 WTFD 46074 1792 D1
W Pine Ridge Dr
10 WTFD 46074 1792 C1
Pine Ridge Dr E
9600 FSHR 46038 2012 D2
Pine Ridge Wy
- BNBG 46112 2114 E4
Pine Ridge North Dr
9600 UnnT 46077 1680 E7
9700 FSHR 46038 2012 D2
Pine Ridge South Dr
- UnnT 46077 1680 E7
Pine Royal Dr
7500 INPS 46256 2122 A2
Pines Pointe Cir
7200 INPS 46268 2118 A1
Pine Springs Ct
7500 INPS 46256 2013 B7
Pine Springs Dr
7500 INPS 46256 2013 C6
Pine Springs East Dr
7500 INPS 46256 2013 B7
Pine Springs West Dr
7500 INPS 46256 2013 B7
Pinetop Ct
3200 INPS 46227 2556 C4
Pinetop Dr
3300 INPS 46227 2556 C4
3900 INPS 46237 2556 D4
Pine Tree
- AVON 46123 2332 D5
Pine Tree Blvd
8300 INPS 46256 2013 C4
Pinetree Ct
9300 INPS 46235 2231 D2
Pine Tree Ln
100 WynT 46060 1796 C1
Pine Valley Ct
10700 FSHR 46038 1905 B7
Pine Valley Dr
10 CRML 46032 1902 B6
Pine Valley Ln
7500 INPS 46250 2011 E7
Pineview Cir
4000 INPS 46237 2556 D4
10500 FSHR 46038 2012 D1
Pineview Ct
7800 INPS 46250 2011 E7
Pine View Dr
100 CRML 46032 1793 B7
100 CRML 46032 1902 B1
Pineview Dr
200 MRVL 46158 2660 B5
700 EglT 46077 2008 A2
700 INPS 46077 2008 A2
7800 EglT 46077 2007 C2
7800 INPS 46077 2007 C2
7800 INPS 46278 2007 C2

Indianapolis Street Index

STREET
Block City ZIP Map# Grid

Pineview Ln
3900 WRvT 46142 2664 A1
Pineview East Ct
- EglT 46077 2008 A2
Pineview West Ct
- EglT 46077 2008 A2
Pineway Dr
7100 BrnT 46112 2006 D7
Pinewood Ct
1000 INPS 46240 2010 E3
Pinewood Ct N
900 PNFD 46168 2441 E6
Pinewood Ct S
1000 PNFD 46168 2441 E6
Pinewood Dr
- PNFD 46168 2441 E6
4300 LcnT 46112 2223 A2
Pine Wood Ln
17300 WTFD 46074 1792 D1
Piney Wood Ct
7900 INPS 46214 2225 C4
Pinnacle Blvd
6100 INPS 46237 2448 C5
Pinnacle Ln
200 PNFD 46168 2441 A4
Pin Oak Cir
6400 AVON 46123 2332 A1
Pin Oak Ct
- WTLD 46184 2775 A7
10 WRvT 46142 2664 A1
100 NBVL 46062 1685 E4
1900 INPS 46260 2009 D4
Pin Oak Dr
- ZNVL 46077 1898 C2
1000 MRVL 46158 2660 B6
5000 INPS 46254 2117 C5
6300 MCVL 46055 2015 C3
7100 BNBG 46112 2223 B3
Pin Oak Tr
12000 LWNC 46236 2123 E1
Pin Oak Wy
5200 INPS 46254 2117 C5
Pinon Dr
- INPS 46227 2447 C7
Pintail Ct
300 CRML 46032 1901 C4
Pintail Dr
6900 FSHR 46038 1903 E5
Pinto Cir
5600 INPS 46228 2118 A5
Pinto Ct
5600 INPS 46228 2118 A5
Pinto Wy
3600 INPS 46228 2118 A5
Pinyon Ct
8900 INPS 46260 2009 D4
Pioneer Cir
100 BrnT 46158 2660 A4
E Pioneer Cir
3500 BrnT 46158 2660 A4
Pioneer Ct
100 MRVL 46158 2659 D1
Pioneer Dr
500 INPS 46217 2555 A1
Pioneer Pl
100 MRVL 46158 2659 D1
Pioneer Tr
8400 FSHR 46038 1904 C6
Pioneer Woods Dr
700 INPS 46224 2335 C2
Piper Lake Dr
9600 INPS 46239 2340 E5
Piping Rock Ln
6400 INPS 46254 2226 A1
Pippin Ct
1400 WshT 46123 2332 A7
1500 GNFD 46140 2345 E4
Pippin Dr
1500 GNFD 46140 2345 E4
Pisa Ct
4200 INPS 46235 2231 D1
Pitch Pine Dr
- GNWD 46184 2774 B2
Pitney Dr
500 NBVL 46062 1685 B5
Pittman Pl
4000 INPS 46254 2118 A7
Pittsboro Rd
- DNVL 46122 2329 E3
7500 HsnT 46052 2003 E3
7700 MdlT 46052 2003 E3
10200 MdlT 46167 2003 E3
Pittsburo Rd
2500 CtrT 46052 1785 E7
3300 HsnT 46052 1785 E7
3300 HsnT 46052 1894 E1
7000 HsnT 46052 2003 E1
Pittwood Dr
1400 INPS 46240 2011 A3
Piute Dr
10000 WshT 46234 2224 C6
Pixley Ct
3500 INPS 46235 2231 D3
Pixley Ln
500 NBVL 46062 1685 D1
Pixy Ct
100 GNFD 46140 2345 D4
Placing Rd
7500 INPS 46226 2231 A3
W Plainfield Av
4800 INPS 46241 2335 D6
Plainfield Commons Dr
- PNFD 46168 2442 B3
N Plainview Av
1100 INPS 46214 2334 E1
Plainview Dr
200 WshT 46123 2331 C4
S Plainview St
10 INPS 46241 2334 E4
Plainville Dr
- WTFD 46074 1792 D3
Planer Dr
18800 NBVL 46062 1685 C5
Planes Dr
2500 INPS 46219 2231 C5
Planewood Dr
3800 INPS 46235 2232 D2
Plantana Blvd
9800 FSHR 46060 1796 A7
9800 FSHR 46060 1905 A1
Plantation Dr
4800 INPS 46250 2012 A6
Plantation Ln
7300 AVON 46123 2332 C2
W Plantation Row
1800 BCkT 46140 2235 B5
1800 CtrT 46140 2235 B5
Plantation Wood Ln
14000 CRML 46033 1794 D7
14000 CRML 46033 1903 E1
Planters Rd
800 INPS 46239 2341 D5
Plantree Dr
13800 CRML 46033 1903 E1
Platini Pl
7700 INPS 46214 2225 C7
Platinum Dr
10400 NBVL 46060 1796 B5
Platinum Pl
- INPS 46203 2448 C2
Platte Dr
13900 CRML 46033 1794 C7
13900 CRML 46033 1903 C1
Player Cir
13100 CRML 46033 1903 C2
Players Dr
10800 INPS 46229 2232 C7
Playview Wy
- DelT 46038 1903 D7
- FSHR 46038 1903 D7
Plaza Dr
100 GNFD 46140 2236 E6
2700 INPS 46268 2009 C5
Plaza Ln
8200 INPS 46268 2009 C5
Plaza Central St
100 WRvT 46143 2664 B7
Plaza Chica St
100 WRvT 46143 2664 B7
Plaza Granda St
100 WRvT 46143 2664 B7
Pleasant Dr
300 NWTD 46184 2774 D4
N Pleasant Dr
9500 MrlT 46126 2560 B4
W Pleasant Dr
3100 SCkT 46140 2343 E4
Pleasant Ln
200 GNWD 46142 2665 C4
Pleasant Run
- GNWD 46142 2665 A4
2000 WTFD 46074 1793 B1
Pleasant St
10 GNWD 46143 2665 D3
800 LEBN 46052 1677 A7
1100 INPS 46203 2337 E5
1300 NBVL 46060 1795 E1
1500 INPS 46203 2338 A5
2100 NBVL 46060 1796 A1
9000 INPS 46239 2340 D5
E Pleasant St
1000 NBVL 46060 1795 D1
W Pleasant St
100 NBVL 46060 1795 C1
Pleasant Wy
9700 ClyT 46280 2011 C2
Pleasant Wy W
2500 ClyT 46280 2011 C2
Pleasant Creek Ct
8600 INPS 46227 2556 C7
Pleasant Creek Dr
3400 INPS 46227 2556 C7
Pleasant Garden Ct
9000 INPS 46113 2551 E7
9000 INPS 46113 2660 D1
Pleasant Garden Ln
8800 INPS 46113 2660 D2
8800 INPS 46113 2661 A1
Pleasant Hill Cir
5400 INPS 46224 2335 C2
Pleasant Hill Ct
10 JknT 46034 1577 A4
Pleasant Lake Cir
8700 INPS 46227 2556 D7
Pleasant Lake Ct
8700 INPS 46227 2556 C7
Pleasant Lake Dr
3300 INPS 46227 2556 D7
Pleasant Point Cir
700 CCRO 46034 1577 B3
Pleasant Run Dr
400 GNWD 46142 2665 C1
E Pleasant Run Pkwy North Dr
- INPS 46203 2338 A5
- INPS 46203 2446 C1
10 INPS 46225 2446 C1
600 INPS 46203 2337 D7
3700 INPS 46201 2338 D4
4800 INPS 46201 2339 A3
6700 INPS 46219 2339 D1
W Pleasant Run Pkwy North Dr
10 INPS 46225 2446 B1
E Pleasant Run Pkwy South Dr
10 INPS 46225 2446 C1
700 INPS 46203 2337 E7
1500 INPS 46203 2338 A6
3700 INPS 46201 2338 D4
6000 INPS 46219 2339 D2
6800 INPS 46219 2230 E7
7100 INPS 46219 2231 A7
W Pleasant Run Pkwy South Dr
10 INPS 46225 2446 B1
Pleasant Tree Ct
8200 INPS 46237 2557 B6
Pleasantview Blvd
300 GNWD 46142 2664 B2
Pleasantview Dr
300 GNWD 46142 2664 B3
10800 CRML 46033 1902 D7
Pleasant View Ln
10500 FSHR 46038 1905 B3
Pleasant View Rd
- MrlT 46126 2560 A4
1000 UnnT 46077 1789 E4
2700 EglT 46077 1789 E6
3000 EglT 46077 1898 E2
4300 ZNVL 46077 1898 E2
W Pleasant View Elm St
8500 MrlT 46126 2560 A4
W Pleasant View Mulberry St
9700 MrlT 46126 2560 A4
Pleasant Woods Ln
6300 LWNC 46236 2123 A3
Plum St
- SgCT 46126 2670 D7
1000 LcnT 46112 2223 D3
1200 NBVL 46060 1795 D1
E Plum St
1000 NBVL 46060 1795 D1
W Plum St
300 NBVL 46060 1795 C1
Plum Creek Blvd
5800 CRML 46033 1903 C3
Plum Hollow Cir
11000 FSHR 46038 1905 C6
Plummer St
- LWNC 46226 2231 A1
Plumtree Dr
9900 LWNC 46235 2123 A6
Plumwood Ln
8200 INPS 46256 2013 E6
Pluto Dr
7000 INPS 46241 2334 D5
N Plymouth Ct
- BCkT 46055 2124 B4
Plymouth Rock Ct
100 GNWD 46142 2664 E4
Plymouth Rock Dr
14400 CRML 46033 1794 B7
Plymouth Rock Wy
100 GNWD 46142 2664 E4
Pock Rd
5000 EglT 46077 1899 C7
5000 ZNVL 46077 1899 C7
Pocket Hollow Ct
8100 INPS 46256 2013 B4
Pocono Mesa N
5800 SDWY 46224 2226 B7
Pocono Mesa S
5800 SDWY 46224 2226 B7
Poindexter Dr
5400 LWNC 46235 2123 B6
Poinsettia Dr
3600 INPS 46227 2556 D4
W Point Dr
8700 INPS 46231 2334 A4
9100 INPS 46268 2009 B3
Point Ln
10 JknT 46030 1577 C1
Point Bar Rd
3900 INPS 46268 2009 A3
N Pointe Blvd
14600 NBVL 46060 1795 E6
Pointe Ct
9100 FSHR 46038 1904 E7
Pointe East Ct
6500 INPS 46250 2012 D3
Pointer Pl
12500 FSHR 46038 1904 C3
Pointers Ct
8200 INPS 46256 2013 C5
Point to Point Line
- LtyT 46118 2548 D2
Pokagon Dr
200 CRML 46032 1901 C2
Polaris Dr
300 INPS 46241 2334 E4
N Polco St
- INPS 46222 2335 E1
1000 SDWY 46222 2335 E1
Polk Dr
- NBVL 46062 1794 B6
Polk Pl
- GNWD 46143 2665 D4
Polk St
100 GNFD 46140 2345 B1
200 GNWD 46143 2665 D4
1100 INPS 46202 2337 E2
Polk Manor Dr
200 GNWD 46143 2665 D4
Polk Village Rd
200 GNWD 46143 2665 D4
Pollard Pk
- LcnT 46112 2115 D6
Pollard St
7200 INPS 46268 2117 E1
N Pollard St
7100 INPS 46268 2117 E1
Polley Dr
- DNVL 46122 2330 B2
Polo Ct
11100 INPS 46239 2341 C6
Polo Chase Ct
1400 CRML 46032 1900 E1
Polonius Ct
6000 INPS 46254 2117 B4
Polonius Dr
5900 INPS 46254 2117 B4
Polonius Ln
5900 INPS 46254 2117 A4
Pomander Pl
1000 INPS 46208 2228 A3
1100 INPS 46208 2227 E3
Pommel Ct
5400 INPS 46203 2339 B7
Pomona Ct
300 GNFD 46140 2345 D3
2700 INPS 46268 2009 C3
Pompano Dr
11600 INPS 46236 2014 D5
Pomroy Dr
4000 INPS 46237 2556 D6
Ponderosa Blvd
4100 INPS 46250 2011 E7
Ponderosa Ct
7700 AVON 46123 2332 D5
Ponderosa Pine Dr
- GNWD 46184 2774 B1
Ponderosa Pines Ln
7300 INPS 46239 2449 A7
Ponderosa Pines Pl
7200 INPS 46239 2448 E7
7200 INPS 46239 2449 A7
Ponds Pointe Dr
400 CRML 46032 1792 B7
Pond View Ct
10 BNBG 46112 2223 B3
Pondview Ct
3300 INPS 46268 2118 B2
Pondview Dr
1400 CRML 46032 1792 C7
Ponsonby Ct
10 INPS 46214 2334 D3
Pontell Pl
12800 CRML 46077 1900 A3
Pontiac Dr
5800 INPS 46224 2335 B2
Ponza Ct
4200 INPS 46235 2231 D1
Poole Pl
5700 NBVL 46062 1576 C6
Poplar Av
7600 BrnT 46112 2114 D2
Poplar Ct
10 NWTD 46184 2774 D3
200 NBVL 46062 1576 B7
Poplar Dr
200 NBVL 46062 1576 B7
500 GNWD 46142 2664 D5
500 PTBR 46167 2112 E3
500 PTBR 46167 2113 A3
Poplar Rd
300 INPS 46219 2339 A3
Poplar St
10 WTFD 46074 1684 A6
200 WTFD 46074 1793 A1
600 PNFD 46168 2441 C4
600 WTLD 46184 2775 A5
E Poplar St
10 ZNVL 46077 1899 B6
200 DNVL 46122 2329 D4
W Poplar St
10 DNVL 46122 2329 D4
700 ZNVL 46077 1899 A6
Poplar Byrd Ct
700 CRML 46032 1901 E1
Poplar Grove Dr
200 WshT 46123 2331 D3
Poppy Dr
- INPS 46231 2334 A7
Poppy Ln
8900 INPS 46231 2334 A7
Poppyseed Dr
7300 INPS 46237 2556 E4
Porchester Dr
13000 NBVL 46062 1794 B5
Porchester Ln
- GNWD 46143 2665 B5
Porchester Pl
- PNFD 46168 2440 E5
Porsche Dr
7900 INPS 46268 2009 C6
Port Ct
- WshT 46123 2333 A2
E Port Ct
1500 CCRO 46034 1577 B6
Port Dr
- MCVL 46055 2015 D3
- VrnT 46055 2015 D3
- WshT 46123 2332 E2
- WshT 46123 2333 A2
500 AVON 46123 2332 E3
N Port Dr
1500 CCRO 46034 1577 B6
Portage Av
7500 INPS 46227 2556 A5
Portage Cir
100 FCkT 46038 1906 A7
Portage Ct
1700 INPS 46227 2556 A5
Portage Ter
1700 INPS 46227 2556 A5
Portage Wy
12500 FCkT 46038 1906 A7
12500 FSHR 46038 1906 A7
Portalan Dr
1000 BCkT 46140 2233 D6
Port au Prince
5700 INPS 46224 2335 B3
Porter Av
- WTWN 46075 1788 D7
Porter Dr
9700 WshT 46123 2333 B4
Porter Ln
6000 NBVL 46062 1794 C5
Porter St
- INPS 46220 2120 C5
10 WTWN 46075 1788 C7
S Porter St
2300 INPS 46231 2443 A1
Portia Dr
6100 BCkT 46140 2233 D6
Portillo Pl
5900 INPS 46254 2117 B4
Port Irving Dr
5700 INPS 46224 2335 B3
Portland Dr
- WshT 46074 1792 A5
Portland Sq
7100 INPS 46260 2118 D1
Port Lillian Dr
5700 INPS 46224 2335 B3
Portman Dr
5300 NBVL 46062 1794 B5
Portman Pl
5900 PNFD 46168 2440 E5
N Porto Alegre St
300 INPS 46202 2336 E2
Port Ocall Dr
10 INPS 46224 2335 B3
Port Ohope Dr
5700 INPS 46224 2335 B3
Port Omonaco St
5800 INPS 46224 2335 A3
Portrait Dr
- INPS 46217 2554 C4
Port Robert Dr
10 INPS 46224 2335 B3
Portside Ct
10700 INPS 46236 2014 B5
Portside Dr
8100 AVON 46123 2332 E3
Portside Wy
- FCkT 46256 2015 A2
Portsmouth Av
5500 INPS 46224 2335 B1
Portsmouth Ct
400 CRML 46032 1901 B3
Portsmouth Dr
12900 CRML 46032 1901 C2
Port Sylvia Dr
10 INPS 46224 2335 B3
Port View Ln
10200 FCkT 46055 2015 B1
Portwood Ct
6000 INPS 46254 2117 B4
Portwood Pl
5600 INPS 46254 2117 B4
Post Dr
2300 INPS 46219 2231 D6
N Post Rd
10 INPS 46219 2340 D2
10 INPS 46229 2340 D2
1600 INPS 46219 2231 D5
1600 INPS 46229 2231 D5
3000 INPS 46226 2231 D5
3000 INPS 46235 2231 D5
4200 LWNC 46226 2231 D3
4300 LWNC 46235 2231 D3
4500 LWNC 46226 2122 D7
4500 LWNC 46235 2122 D7
5200 LWNC 46216 2122 D5
S Post Rd
10 INPS 46219 2340 D3
10 INPS 46229 2340 D3
500 INPS 46239 2340 D7
2200 INPS 46239 2449 D1
Post Acres Mobile Home Pk
- LWNC 46226 2122 D6
- LWNC 46236 2122 D6
Post Cliff Rd
8700 WshT 46123 2333 A1
Post Master Ln
2300 BCkT 46140 2235 A7
Potomac Av
7400 INPS 46226 2231 A4
Potomac Ct
500 WshT 46074 1792 B5
Potomac Dr
- LWNC 46236 2014 B6
W Potomac Dr
4200 SCkT 46140 2343 B2
Potomac Ln
5200 WRvT 46142 2663 C4
Potomac Square Dr
- INPS 46268 2117 C2
Potomac Square Ln
6400 INPS 46268 2117 C2
Potomac Square Pl
4900 INPS 46268 2117 D2
Potomac Square Wy
4900 INPS 46268 2117 D3
Potters Bridge Rd
19100 NBVL 46060 1686 E4
19400 NbvT 46060 1686 E4
Potters Cove Ct
8700 INPS 46234 2116 A6
Potters Pike
5000 INPS 46234 2116 A7
Powder Dr
14000 CRML 46033 1794 C7
14000 CRML 46033 1903 C1
Powderhorn Ct
4300 CRML 46033 2011 E1
8700 INPS 46256 2013 D3
Powderhorn Ln
8700 INPS 46256 2013 C3
Powderhorn Wy
8700 INPS 46256 2013 D3
Powder River Ct
5400 INPS 46221 2553 C1
Powell Dr
5900 INPS 46221 2444 A7
Powell Pl
500 INPS 46205 2228 D3
Powell St
300 INPS 46227 2446 D7
500 LEBN 46052 1676 E6
W Powell St
5600 INPS 46221 2444 B7
Power Dr
3600 CRML 46033 2011 E1
Power Pl
3600 CRML 46033 2011 D1
Powhatan Dr
700 INPS 46231 2334 A5
Prague Av
800 INPS 46227 2446 D7
Prague Rd
3100 INPS 46227 2447 C7
W Prairie Ct
6300 SCkT 46163 2342 C7
Prairie Dr
700 BNBG 46112 2223 C1
1000 LEBN 46052 1676 C5
8300 INPS 46256 2013 B5
Prairie Pkwy
10 BNBG 46112 2223 B1
Prairie Pl
11700 CRML 46033 1903 C5
Prairie Tr
8900 WshT 46123 2333 A3
Prairie Baptist Rd
13000 FCkT 46060 1907 A2
13000 FSHR 46060 1907 A2
14100 FCkT 46060 1798 A7
14100 NBVL 46060 1798 A7
14600 WynT 46060 1798 A5
16700 WynT 46060 1689 A7
20600 WynT 46060 1580 A7
21000 WRvT 46060 1580 A7
Prairie Bluff Ct
5100 INPS 46221 2553 C2
Prairie Clover Ln
- INPS 46254 2117 C5
Prairieclover Ln
- INPS 46254 2117 D5
Prairie Clover Wy
5100 INPS 46254 2117 C5
Prairie Creek Ct
1300 CRML 46032 1901 D1
Prairie Creek Dr
5800 INPS 46254 2117 B6
Prairie Crossing Dr
18700 NBVL 46062 1686 B5
Prairie Depot
600 INPS 46241 2334 E5
Prairie Dog Dr
5500 INPS 46237 2448 A7
5500 INPS 46237 2557 A1
Prairie Fire Dr
11300 INPS 46229 2232 C5
Prairie Fire Ln
2200 INPS 46229 2232 D6
Prairie Fox Dr
10400 FSHR 46038 2014 B1
Prairie Lake Dr
7300 INPS 46256 2013 A7
Prairie Meadow Dr
5700 INPS 46221 2553 C2
Prairie Ridge Cir
9100 INPS 46256 2013 D7
Prairie Ridge Ct
9100 INPS 46256 2013 D7
Prairie Ridge Pl
9100 INPS 46256 2013 D7
Prairie Rose Ln
5200 INPS 46254 2117 C7
Prairie View Dr
7500 INPS 46256 2013 D7
Prairieview Dr
7600 FSHR 46038 1904 B4
Prairie View Ln
7500 INPS 46256 2013 D7
Prairie View Tr
- CtrT 46122 2330 E3
3200 DNVL 46122 2331 A4
3600 DNVL 46122 2330 E4
Prairiewood Wy
9600 ClyT 46032 2009 D2
Prarie Dr
3100 GNWD 46142 2664 B1
Prarie Fire Ct
- BrnT 46112 2114 D1
Pratt St
- GNFD 46140 2236 E7
10 GNFD 46140 2345 E1
Preakness Dr
800 WRvT 46143 2663 D5
Preamble Ct
7300 INPS 46259 2558 A4
Precision Dr
9000 INPS 46235 2231 D4
E Preddy Dr
2500 INPS 46227 2556 B7
Preidt Ct
4800 INPS 46237 2556 E6
Preidt Pl
8000 INPS 46237 2556 E6
8000 INPS 46237 2557 A6
Prelude Ln
5700 CRML 46033 1903 B3
Prentis Cir
6000 INPS 46254 2117 C4
Prentiss Wy
- WshT 46123 2333 C2
Presbyterian Dr
11000 LWNC 46236 2123 C3
Prescott Ct
800 INPS 46214 2334 E2
Preservation Dr
7700 INPS 46278 2007 A7
Preservation Pt
11000 FSHR 46038 1905 D6
Preservation Wy
8500 INPS 46278 2007 B7
President Cir
100 GNFD 46140 2345 A1
10900 INPS 46229 2341 C3
President Ct
100 INPS 46229 2341 C3
President St
- CRML 46032 1900 D2
President Tr E
100 INPS 46229 2341 C3
President Tr W
100 INPS 46229 2341 C3
Presidential Ct
100 GNFD 46140 2345 B1
Presidential Wy
100 BNBG 46112 2223 D3
Presley Dr
- NBVL 46060 1687 B7
Prestbury Dr
10500 LWNC 46236 2123 B3
Presto Av
1600 SDWY 46224 2226 D7
Preston Ct
1400 WRvT 46143 2664 B6
1500 ClyT 46032 1900 E7
10100 FSHR 46038 2014 A1
Preston Dr
500 GNFD 46140 2236 C5
700 ClyT 46280 2010 E1
10700 LWNC 46236 2123 B3
Preston Tr
1400 ClyT 46032 1900 E6
1400 ClyT 46032 1901 A6
Prestonwood Ct
5600 INPS 46254 2117 C5
Prestonwood Dr
5700 INPS 46254 2117 C5
Prestwick Cir
1200 GNWD 46143 2664 D5
1500 ClyT 46032 1900 E6
Prestwick Ct
6500 INPS 46214 2334 C1
Prestwick Dr
900 INPS 46214 2334 C1
900 INPS 46214 2335 A2
Prestwick Ln
900 INPS 46214 2335 A3
1400 ClyT 46032 1900 E6
1400 ClyT 46032 1901 A6
Prestwick Pl
900 INPS 46214 2334 C1
Prestwick Wy
800 GNWD 46143 2664 D5
Price Ct
1000 WshT 46123 2332 B6
5800 INPS 46254 2226 B2
Price Ln
5800 INPS 46254 2226 B2
Price Rd
400 WshT 46123 2332 B6
Primo Wy
13800 CRML 46074 1900 B1
13900 CRML 46074 1791 B7
Primrose Av
4400 INPS 46205 2229 A1
4500 INPS 46205 2120 A7
5200 INPS 46220 2120 A7
Prim Rose Ct
700 WRvT 46142 2664 B2
Primrose Ct
- BrnT 46112 2114 D1
Primrose Ln
300 AVON 46123 2332 A5
Prim Rose Pth
4000 WRvT 46142 2664 A2
Primrose Pth
100 NbvT 46062 1795 A6
Prince Dr
100 WRvT 46142 2663 D4
Prince George Ct
10 INPS 46217 2555 B3
Prince George Dr
- CRML 46032 1900 E1
Prince Regent Ct
6700 INPS 46250 2012 E3
Princess Ln
300 AVON 46123 2332 B3
Princeton Av
2900 INPS 46205 2228 D5
Princeton Cir
- PNFD 46168 2442 B1
Princeton Ct
- PNFD 46168 2442 B1
Princeton Dr
600 NWTD 46184 2774 D3
Princeton Ln
600 WshT 46074 1792 B6
Princeton Pl
1100 ZNVL 46077 1899 A3
Princeton Gate
1000 CRML 46032 1901 A1
Princewood Ct
12100 FSHR 46038 1906 E4
Princewood Dr
11900 FSHR 46038 1906 D5
Prince Woods Cir
5600 INPS 46224 2335 B2
Priority Pl
1200 INPS 46227 2555 E5
Priority Way South Dr
3500 INPS 46240 2011 D3
Priority Way West Dr
9100 INPS 46240 2011 D3
9500 CRML 46240 2011 D3
Priscilla Av
1400 INPS 46219 2339 C1
1600 INPS 46218 2230 C7
4200 INPS 46226 2230 C1
4400 INPS 46226 2121 C7
N Priscilla Av
3000 INPS 46218 2230 C4
3800 INPS 46226 2230 C2
Priscilla Cir
5700 INPS 46226 2121 C7
Priscilla Ct
3500 INPS 46218 2230 C3
Priscilla Pl
13800 FSHR 46038 1904 C1
Prissy Ln
10700 INPS 46259 2559 B2
Pritchett Ln
400 DNVL 46122 2329 C3
N Private Road 100 W
10700 MnrT 46158 2658 B6
Pro Am Pl
1900 INPS 46229 2232 C7
Producers Dr
- INPS 46218 2229 E6
Production Dr
200 AVON 46123 2332 D4
1700 INPS 46241 2335 B7
1900 INPS 46241 2444 B1
Professional Cir
5600 INPS 46241 2444 B1
Professional Dr
3000 CRML 46280 2011 C2
Profit Dr
2200 INPS 46241 2444 B1
Profit St
1700 GNWD 46143 2665 D6
Progress Av
900 LEBN 46052 1676 D6

STREET
Block City ZIP Map# Grid

Progress St
5400 INPS 46241 2335 B7
Pro-Med Ln
600 CRML 46032 1901 E1
600 CRML 46032 1902 A2
Promenade Cir
900 CCRO 46034 1577 B4
Promenade Ct
6100 INPS 46224 2226 A3
Promise Rd
12600 FCkT 46038 1905 C3
12600 FSHR 46038 1905 C3
12600 FSHR 46060 1905 C1
13100 FCkT 46060 1905 C1
13700 FCkT 46060 1796 C6
14100 NBVL 46060 1796 C6
14400 WynT 46060 1796 C4
17600 WynT 46060 1687 C7
18600 NBVL 46060 1687 C4
Promontory Cir
9200 INPS 46236 2014 E3
Promontory Ct
11900 INPS 46236 2014 E3
Promontory Rd
8400 LWNC 46236 2014 E5
8400 LWNC 46236 2015 A5
8600 INPS 46236 2014 E4
Promontory Tr
11600 EglT 46077 1899 D2
Pronghorn Cir
- NBVL 46060 1796 E6
Proper Pt
- FSHR 46038 1905 E6
Proper Pass
- FSHR 46038 1905 E6
Proposal Pointe Wy
10500 FCkT 46040 1906 D7
10500 FCkT 46040 2015 D1
Prospect St
100 WTWN 46075 1788 C7
6000 INPS 46203 2339 C5
7500 INPS 46239 2340 A5
E Prospect St
200 INPS 46225 2337 D5
500 INPS 46203 2337 D5
3900 INPS 46203 2338 E5
4800 INPS 46203 2339 A5
9000 INPS 46239 2340 E5
9700 INPS 46239 2341 C5
Prosperity Cir
- GfdT 46113 2551 D7
- GfdT 46168 2551 D7
Prosperity Dr
- NBVL 46060 1795 E3
Providence Blvd
200 CRML 46032 1901 D3
Providence Cir
7800 INPS 46250 2011 E7
Providence Ct
- GNWD 46143 2774 D1
Providence Dr
- GNWD 46143 2665 D7
- GNWD 46143 2774 D1
8300 FSHR 46060 1795 C7
Provincetown Cir
5900 INPS 46250 2121 C1
Provincial Ln
200 AVON 46123 2333 B3
200 WshT 46123 2333 B3
W Pruitt St
1400 INPS 46208 2227 E6
Ptarmigan Ct
11000 WynT 46060 1796 C3
Publishers Dr
13000 FSHR 46038 1904 E2
Pueblo Ct
5300 CRML 46033 1903 C1
Puffin Pl
5100 CRML 46033 1903 B1
Pullman Ct
7300 INPS 46256 2122 A1
Pump Rd
- PNFD 46168 2442 B5
Pumpkinvine Rd
5000 CtnT 46052 1570 A1
N Pumpkinvine Rd
7000 MrlT 46130 2560 C3
8800 MrlT 46126 2560 C5
Punkin Ct
100 GNFD 46140 2345 D3
Puntledge Dr
16900 WTFD 46062 1793 E2
Punto Alto Cir
2800 INPS 46227 2556 B7
Punto Alto Ct
400 GNWD 46143 2665 D4
2800 INPS 46227 2556 B7
Punto Alto Dr
8300 INPS 46227 2556 B6
Punto Baho Dr
400 GNWD 46143 2665 D4
Purcell Cir
1500 INPS 46231 2334 B7
Purdue Rd
8600 INPS 46268 2009 B3
N Purdy St
7100 INPS 46268 2117 E1
Purity Dr
300 LEBN 46052 1676 B7
300 LEBN 46052 1785 B1
Purple Cress Dr
7500 WshT 46123 2223 D7
Purple Lilac Cir
5400 INPS 46254 2116 C6
Purpura Dr
1500 CtrT 46122 2439 B1
1500 DNVL 46122 2439 B1
5400 LWNC 46236 2123 A6
Pursel Dr
- CRML 46033 1903 B5
Pursel Ln
5100 CRML 46033 1903 B5
Puryear St
100 INPS 46202 2337 C1
Putnam Pl
10700 ClyT 46032 1900 A7
Putnam Wy
- LWNC 46216 2122 C5
Putter Ct
3100 WRvT 46143 2664 B7
Putters Ln
2500 INPS 46222 2227 C6
Pymbroke Cir
7100 FSHR 46038 1904 A4
Pymbroke Dr
7300 FSHR 46038 1904 A4
Pymbroke Pl
11900 FSHR 46038 1904 A4
Pymbroke Wy
7200 FSHR 46038 1904 A4
Pyrite Ct
10000 NBVL 46060 1796 A3

Q

Q Ct
- WRvT 46142 2663 E1
Q St
- BHGV 46107 2448 A2
Quail Cir
6400 INPS 46278 2117 B3
Quail Ct
8300 INPS 46256 2013 C6
S Quail Ct
1000 SCkT 46163 2343 B3
Quail Rd
5600 INPS 46278 2117 B3
Quail Rd E
6200 PNFD 46168 2550 D3
Quail Rd N
7600 PNFD 46168 2550 C2
Quail Rd S
6400 PNFD 46168 2550 D3
Quail Rd W
6200 PNFD 46168 2550 D3
Quail Run
500 GNWD 46142 2664 D2
6500 FSHR 46038 1903 D6
Quail Trc S
4300 MdlT 46167 2113 B2
Quail Wy
5800 INPS 46237 2557 C1
Quail Chase Dr
5800 INPS 46237 2557 B1
Quail Cove Ct
5700 INPS 46237 2557 B1
Quail Creek Blvd
6000 INPS 46237 2556 E1
Quail Creek Dr
4700 INPS 46237 2556 E2
Quail Creek Trc
- MdlT 46167 2113 A2
- PTBR 46167 2113 A2
Quail Crescent Ct
4800 INPS 46254 2116 E7
Quail Crossing Ct
- INPS 46237 2557 B1
Quail Crossing Dr
5700 INPS 46237 2557 B1
Quail Feather Ct
- INPS 46237 2557 A1
Quail Glen Ct
1500 CRML 46032 1902 A5
Quail Hollow Rd
8400 INPS 46260 2010 A4
Quail Pointe Dr
14300 CRML 46032 1792 B7
Quail Pointe Ln
5700 INPS 46237 2557 B1
E Quail Ridge Dr
400 WTFD 46074 1792 D1
Quail Ridge Ln
4800 INPS 46254 2116 E7
Quail Roost Ct
5800 INPS 46237 2557 C1
Quail Run Ct
5900 INPS 46237 2557 C1
Quail Run Dr
5800 INPS 46237 2557 C1
W Quail Run Dr
4500 SCkT 46163 2343 A3
Quails Nest Dr
4700 INPS 46237 2556 E2
Quail Valley Dr
500 EglT 46077 1898 D4
E Quail Wood Ln
10 WTFD 46074 1792 D1
W Quail Wood Ln
10 WTFD 46074 1792 C1
Quaker Av
7600 INPS 46221 2552 E5
Quaker Blvd
1600 PNFD 46168 2550 E2
4600 PNFD 46168 2441 E6
Quaker Blvd SR-267
1600 PNFD 46168 2550 E2
4600 PNFD 46168 2441 E6
Quaker Ridge Ct
10100 FSHR 46038 1905 A7
Qualmish Av
200 INPS 46202 2337 A3
Quarry Ct
11900 FSHR 46038 1905 E4
Quarry Face Ct
- FSHR 46038 1906 A4
Quarterback Ln
- FCkT 46038 1906 A3
Quarterhorse Dr
8600 INPS 46256 2013 B4
Quarter Path Rd
- CCRO 46034 1577 C4
Quartz Dr
16200 NBVL 46060 1796 B3
16200 NbvT 46060 1796 B3
Quartz Rock Rd
7300 LWNC 46236 2124 A1
7400 LWNC 46236 2015 A7
Queen St
500 INPS 46231 2334 D4
Queen Anne Ct
7200 INPS 46227 2556 B4
Queen Elizabeth Ct
2200 INPS 46227 2556 B4
Queen Gates Dr
800 WRvT 46143 2664 A5
Queen Mary Ct
7200 INPS 46227 2556 A4
Queens Ct
8300 INPS 46260 2010 A5
Queens Ln
100 NBVL 46060 1687 A7
Queens Wy
1300 ClyT 46032 1901 A6
Queensborough Ct
900 CRML 46033 1793 E7
Queensborough Dr
1400 CRML 46033 1793 D7
Queensbridge Cir
1800 INPS 46219 2231 B7
Queensbridge Com
7800 INPS 46219 2231 B7
Queensbridge Dr
1600 INPS 46219 2231 B7
Queensbridge Sq
1600 INPS 46219 2231 B7
Queensbury Ct
100 NBVL 46062 1685 D1
7100 INPS 46214 2334 D2
10800 CRML 46033 1902 D7
Queensbury Dr
900 NBVL 46062 1685 D1
Queens Troop Close
12900 CRML 46032 1900 D3
Queensway Ct
400 MRVL 46158 2660 C3
Queensway Dr
100 AVON 46123 2332 B4
Queenswood Ct
800 INPS 46217 2555 A7
Queenswood Dr
500 INPS 46217 2555 A7
Queens Wy Cir
11000 ClyT 46032 1901 A6
Queen Victoria Ct
7200 INPS 46227 2556 B4
Queen Victoria Pl
2200 INPS 46227 2556 B4
Queenwood Ct
11800 FSHR 46038 1906 D5
Quemetco Dr
900 INPS 46231 2334 C5
Questend Dr
2900 INPS 46222 2227 B5
N Questend Dr
2800 INPS 46222 2227 C5
S Questend Dr
2800 INPS 46222 2227 C5
Questover Cir
700 INPS 46228 2119 A5
Quetico Dr
8100 INPS 46268 2009 A5
Quicksilver Rd
20600 NBVL 46062 1685 B1
Quiet Ct
2300 INPS 46239 2450 B1
Quiet Dr
10300 INPS 46239 2450 B1
Quiet Wy
2300 INPS 46239 2450 B1
N Quiet Bay Cir
900 CCRO 46034 1577 B3
S Quiet Bay Cir
1000 CCRO 46034 1577 B4
Quiet Haven Cir
1700 INPS 46229 2232 E7
Quill St
1600 INPS 46203 2338 A6
Quincy Ct
7400 INPS 46254 2116 D7
Quincy Pl
400 WshT 46074 1792 C5
Quinlan Ct
1400 INPS 46217 2554 E4
Quinn Dr
- SDWY 46222 2226 D6
Quinn Creek Dr
- BNBG 46112 2224 A2

R

R Ct
- WRvT 46142 2663 E1
R St
- BHGV 46107 2448 A3
Raccoon Ct
10 BNBG 46112 2223 C3
21400 NBVL 46062 1576 B6
Raccoon Run
700 GNWD 46142 2664 D2
Racebrook Ct
17900 NBVL 46062 1685 A7
Raceway Rd
- GfdT 46113 2551 D7
- GfdT 46113 2660 D1
- GfdT 46168 2551 D7
- GfdT 46168 2660 D1
- INPS 46113 2551 D7
N Raceway Rd
10 AVON 46234 2333 E2
1000 INPS 46234 2333 E2
1000 WshT 46234 2333 E2
1500 INPS 46234 2224 E7
1500 WshT 46234 2224 E7
2400 LcnT 46234 2224 E7
3700 LcnT 46112 2224 E3
4200 INPS 46112 2224 E3
4600 INPS 46234 2115 E7
4600 LcnT 46112 2115 E7
4900 LcnT 46234 2115 E7
5500 INPS 46112 2115 E7
5800 BrnT 46234 2115 E3
6200 INPS 46278 2115 E3
6300 BrnT 46112 2115 E3
S Raceway Rd
10 AVON 46123 2333 E7
10 INPS 46231 2333 E7
300 AVON 46231 2333 E7
300 INPS 46123 2333 E7
400 WshT 46231 2333 E7
800 PNFD 46231 2333 E7
1800 INPS 46231 2442 E1
1800 PNFD 46231 2442 E1
1800 WshT 46231 2442 E1
6400 GfdT 46113 2551 E3
8000 INPS 46113 2551 E7
Rachel Dr
1700 PNFD 46168 2550 D1
Rachel Ln
3900 WTFD 46033 1793 D6
Racine Ln
5900 INPS 46254 2117 A5
Racoon Lake Dr
- INPS 46254 2117 A6
Racoon Run Rd
9000 MdnT 46113 2660 C1
N Racoon Run Rd
- MdnT 46113 2660 E1
Racquet Ct
10 WRvT 46142 2663 C4
Racquet Ball Dr
9200 INPS 46260 2009 E3
Racquet Ball Ln
9300 INPS 46260 2009 E3
Racquet Ball Wy
9200 INPS 46260 2009 E3
Racquet Club Dr
9300 INPS 46260 2010 A3
Racquet Club North Dr
1100 INPS 46260 2010 A3
Racquet Club South Dr
1100 INPS 46260 2010 A3
Radburn Cir
7400 INPS 46214 2334 D2
Radburn Ct
7300 INPS 46214 2334 D2
Radburn Dr
400 INPS 46214 2334 D2
Radcliffe Av
2000 INPS 46227 2447 B5
Radcliffe Ct
2100 INPS 46227 2447 B5
Radcliff North Ln
- PNFD 46168 2440 E4
Rader St
3100 INPS 46208 2228 A4
Radford Ct
- WTFD 46074 1792 D4
N Radford Dr
3000 INPS 46226 2230 E4
3000 INPS 46226 2231 A4
Radiance Dr
- NBVL 46060 1796 B5
Radnor Rd
4300 INPS 46226 2120 E7
6200 INPS 46226 2121 D7
Radnor Wy
13100 FSHR 46060 1905 B2
Raesner Dr
5000 SCkT 46163 2343 A7
W Raesner North Dr
5000 SCkT 46163 2343 A7
W Raesner South Dr
5000 SCkT 46163 2343 A7
Raesta Dr
10 MRVL 46158 2659 D2
Ragcoon Run Rd
9000 MdnT 46113 2660 E1
Ragland St
1400 INPS 46241 2335 D6
Ragsdale Pl
11100 FSHR 46038 1905 A6
Rahke Rd
3500 INPS 46217 2446 B4
5500 INPS 46217 2555 B1
Rahkewood Dr
500 INPS 46217 2555 A1
Raiders Blvd
12600 FCkT 46038 1905 E3
Railhead Ct
7300 INPS 46256 2122 A1
N Railroad Av
10 WTLD 46184 2775 A5
S Railroad Av
100 WTLD 46184 2775 A6
Railroad Rd
- INPS 46217 2664 A2
- WRvT 46217 2664 A2
8000 INPS 46217 2555 A7
Railroad St
- LWNC 46236 2123 E2
10 BNBG 46112 2114 C6
7700 MCVL 46055 2015 C7
N Railroad St
6100 MCVL 46055 2015 C7
S Railroad St
- MCVL 46055 2015 D7
Railway Ct
7300 INPS 46256 2122 A1
Railwood Dr
8800 INPS 46234 2225 A3
Rainbow Blvd
10 WshT 46234 2333 D3
Rainbow Ct
4500 INPS 46221 2444 C6
Rainbow Ln
10 BrnT 46158 2659 E7
400 INPS 46260 2119 B2
10000 LWNC 46236 2123 B1
Rainbow Falls Ln
9900 FSHR 46038 1905 A6
Rainbow North Ln
7200 LWNC 46236 2123 B1
7300 LWNC 46236 2014 B7
Rainbow View Dr
4000 INPS 46221 2444 D5
Raindance Tr
8000 INPS 46239 2449 B6
Rainer Dr
6500 INPS 46214 2334 E2
6500 INPS 46214 2335 A3
Rainer Ln
800 INPS 46214 2335 A2
Rainer Wy
6500 INPS 46214 2334 E2
6500 INPS 46214 2335 A2
Raines St
100 PNFD 46168 2441 C4
Rains Ln
5600 INPS 46254 2117 B4
Raintree Dr
- GNFD 46140 2237 A6
10 ZNVL 46077 1899 C5
200 DNVL 46122 2330 B3
500 AVON 46123 2332 C3
Raintree Ln
6200 LWNC 46236 2123 D3
Raintree Rd
- LcnT 46112 2224 E2
- LcnT 46234 2224 E2
Raleigh Dr
6100 INPS 46219 2230 C6
Raleigh Ln
7600 FSHR 46038 1904 B6
Rally Ct
- WynT 46060 1797 A5
Ralph Ct
6900 INPS 46220 2119 E2
Ralston Av
2200 INPS 46218 2229 A5
4200 INPS 46205 2229 A1
4500 INPS 46205 2120 A7
6900 INPS 46220 2120 A2
7100 INPS 46240 2120 A1
11400 CRML 46032 1902 A6
N Ralston Av
7300 INPS 46240 2120 A1
7400 INPS 46240 2011 A7
Ralston Ct
8500 INPS 46217 2555 B7
E Ralston Rd
300 INPS 46227 2555 D7
W Ralston Rd
500 INPS 46217 2555 A7
5300 INPS 46221 2553 B7
6400 INPS 46221 2552 E7
6500 INPS 46113 2552 C7
Ramblewood Dr
3000 INPS 46268 2009 B5
Ramblin Ct
1100 WRvT 46142 2664 B1
Ramblin Rd
500 WRvT 46142 2664 B2
Rambling Rd
8100 INPS 46239 2558 B1
12100 FSHR 46038 1905 C4
Ramona Dr
9700 PNFD 46231 2442 D6
Rams Ct
12600 FCkT 46038 1905 E3
Ramsey Dr
5800 NBVL 46062 1794 C4
Ramsey Ln
1700 PNFD 46168 2550 D1
Ramsgate Ct
1100 ClyT 46280 2011 A1
12800 FSHR 46038 1905 A3
Rams Gates Rd
800 WRvT 46143 2664 A5
Rand Rd
2600 INPS 46241 2444 C2
Randall Ct
1800 INPS 46240 2011 A7
1800 INPS 46240 2120 A1
Randall Dr
- CRML 46280 2011 E2
8600 FSHR 46038 1904 C3
10300 CRML 46033 2011 E2
Randall Rd
1300 INPS 46240 2010 E7
1400 INPS 46240 2011 A7
1800 INPS 46240 2120 A1
Randall Wy
1000 BNBG 46112 2223 C2
N Randolph St
10 INPS 46201 2338 A3
S Randolph St
100 INPS 46201 2338 A4
600 INPS 46203 2338 A5
2200 INPS 46203 2447 A1
3700 INPS 46227 2447 A4
5500 INPS 46227 2556 A1
Randue Ct
7600 INPS 46278 2007 D7
N Range Line Rd
10 CRML 46032 1902 B2
1000 CRML 46032 1793 B7
S Range Line Rd
10 CRML 46032 1902 B5
Rangeview Ct
- FSHR 46038 1905 E6
Ransburg Dr N
500 CRML 46032 1901 E3
Ransburg Dr S
600 CRML 46032 1901 E3
Ransdall Ct
300 INPS 46227 2555 D6
Ransdall St
5800 INPS 46227 2555 D2
Ransdell Ct
1200 LEBN 46052 1676 D7
Ransdell Rd
400 LEBN 46052 1676 D7
Ransdell St
2100 INPS 46225 2337 D7
2500 INPS 46225 2446 D1
3300 INPS 46227 2446 D3
W Ransom St
500 INPS 46202 2337 B1
Rapidan Ln
5400 INPS 46254 2117 C4
Rapid Hill Ln
- BNBG 46112 2224 A2
Rapp Dr
8500 INPS 46237 2557 E7
Raritan Ct
6700 INPS 46221 2553 B3
Raritan Dr
6700 INPS 46221 2553 B3
Ratcliff Ct
- INPS 46113 2552 A3
9200 INPS 46234 2224 E3
Rathmann Dr
6300 INPS 46224 2226 A7
Ratliff Rd
6300 INPS 46241 2552 A3
6500 INPS 46113 2552 A3
Ratliff Run
12900 FSHR 46060 1906 D2
Raton Ct
3300 INPS 46226 2231 C4
Raven Ct
9800 INPS 46235 2232 A3
10600 FSHR 46038 1905 B3
S Raven Ct
4100 NPLN 46163 2452 A2
W Ravenfield Blvd
3300 BCkT 46140 2234 D7
N Ravenfield Ct
700 BCkT 46140 2234 D7
Ravenna Wy
11000 LWNC 46236 2123 C1
Raven Ridge Rd
900 EglT 46077 1898 D4
Raven Rock Ct
8000 INPS 46256 2013 C6
N Raven Rock Dr
8000 INPS 46256 2013 C6
Ravenswood Blvd
7300 INPS 46240 2120 A1
Ravine Ct
10 CCRO 46034 1577 B2
Ravine Rd
5700 INPS 46220 2120 E4
14200 DelT 46060 1795 C7
Rawles Av
5500 INPS 46219 2339 B4
8000 INPS 46219 2340 C4
8000 INPS 46239 2340 C4
E Rawles Av
9000 INPS 46229 2340 E4
9000 INPS 46239 2340 E4
9600 INPS 46229 2341 A4
9600 INPS 46239 2341 A4
E Rawles Ter
5500 INPS 46219 2339 B4
Rawlings Ct
12900 FSHR 46038 1905 B3
Rawlings Pl
10200 FSHR 46038 1905 B3
Rawlins Sq
7200 INPS 46260 2118 D1
Ray Cir
8600 INPS 46256 2013 C4
E Ray St
10 INPS 46225 2337 C5
W Ray St
500 INPS 46225 2337 B5
900 INPS 46221 2337 A5
1400 INPS 46221 2336 E5
3900 INPS 46241 2335 E5
Rayham Ct
600 INPS 46234 2334 B2
Raylin Dr
3200 INPS 46227 2556 C1
Raymond Ln
14700 WshT 46032 1792 D6
Raymond St
900 PNFD 46168 2441 C5
E Raymond St
10 INPS 46225 2337 D7
500 INPS 46203 2337 D7
600 PNFD 46168 2441 C5
1300 INPS 46203 2338 A7
4900 INPS 46203 2339 A7
6800 INPS 46239 2339 E7
6800 INPS 46239 2340 A7
9300 INPS 46239 2341 A7
W Raymond St
- INPS 46225 2337 B7
200 INPS 46225 2446 B1
800 INPS 46221 2337 B7
900 INPS 46221 2446 A1
1100 INPS 46221 2445 C1
1100 PNFD 46168 2441 D5
2000 INPS 46241 2445 D1
4700 INPS 46241 2444 D1
Raymond Park Dr
2200 INPS 46239 2340 B7
Rayners Ln
14000 FSHR 46060 1906 D3
Rea Rd
7800 INPS 46227 2556 A5
Reading Sta
300 WshT 46123 2331 E4
Real St
- CRML 46240 2011 A2
- CRML 46280 2011 A2
- INPS 46240 2011 A2
Real Quiet Dr
- WshT 46234 2224 D6
Reavest Dr N
2400 INPS 46203 2338 B6
Reavest Dr S
2400 INPS 46203 2338 B6
Rebecca Dr
10 INPS 46241 2335 C4
Rebecca Ln
1400 FKLN 46131 2774 E7
Rebel Run
700 INPS 46237 2447 D5
Records St
7700 LWNC 46226 2231 B1
Rector Ct
1100 INPS 46229 2341 A1
Reda Rd
600 INPS 46227 2555 D5
Red Alder Dr
6200 WshT 46123 2440 E1
6200 WshT 46123 2441 A1
Redan Dr
6700 INPS 46254 2116 E7
Red Barn Cir
8000 INPS 46239 2449 B7
Red Barn Ct
8000 INPS 46239 2449 B7
Redbay Ct
10 NBVL 46062 1685 C3
Redbay Dr
300 NBVL 46062 1685 C3
Red Berry Ct
10600 FSHR 46038 1905 D7
Redberry Ct
5400 INPS 46254 2116 D6
Redbird Dr
3900 INPS 46222 2226 E5
3900 INPS 46222 2227 A5
Red Bird Ln
- GfdT 46168 2550 D4
S Redbird Tr
3700 NPLN 46163 2452 A2
Red Bluff Dr
7400 INPS 46214 2225 D3
Redbrook Ct
1200 INPS 46229 2341 A1
Redbud Cir
700 NBVL 46062 1685 D3
W Redbud Cir
2900 BCkT 46140 2234 E6
Red Bud Ct
1700 PNFD 46168 2441 A4
Redbud Ct
3300 WTFD 46062 1684 D7
Red Bud Ln
9800 ClyT 46032 2009 B2
Redbud Ln
10 LcnT 46112 2222 E1
400 GNWD 46142 2665 A3
400 ZNVL 46077 1899 B3
600 GNFD 46140 2236 D7
8200 INPS 46256 2013 D6
Redbud Pl
300 GNWD 46142 2665 B3
Red Bud East Ln
8200 INPS 46256 2013 D6
Red Bud West Ln
8200 INPS 46256 2013 D6
Red Bush Ct
11200 INPS 46229 2232 C6
Red Bush Dr
11300 INPS 46229 2232 D6
Red Cedar Ct
8800 INPS 46256 2013 C4
Red Cedar Wy
5800 CRML 46033 1903 D1
Red Chalice Rd
6200 INPS 46268 2117 C3
Redcliff Dr
14700 NBVL 46062 1794 B6
Redcliff Rd
7400 INPS 46256 2122 A1
Redcliff North Ln
4400 PNFD 46168 2440 E5
Redcliff South Ln
- PNFD 46168 2440 E5
Red Clover Dr
7700 INPS 46227 2556 A5
Redcoach Cir
7800 INPS 46250 2012 C7
Redcoach Ct
6000 INPS 46250 2012 C7
Redcoach Dr
7600 INPS 46250 2012 C7
Redcoach Ln
6000 INPS 46250 2012 D7
Red Delicious Ln
1400 WshT 46123 2332 A6
Redding Ct
200 ZNVL 46077 1898 E4
7900 INPS 46226 2231 B2
Redfern Dr
500 BHGV 46107 2447 E6
2000 INPS 46227 2447 A6
3800 INPS 46237 2447 D6
4100 BHGV 46237 2447 D6
4900 BHGV 46107 2448 A6
E Redfern North Dr
8400 INPS 46239 2449 C5
E Redfern South Dr
8400 INPS 46239 2449 C5
Redford Ct
9100 INPS 46260 2010 A3
Redfox Ct N
500 GNWD 46142 2664 D4
Redfox Ct S
600 GNWD 46142 2664 D4
Red Fox Run
- DelT 46038 1903 E6
11200 FSHR 46038 1903 E6
Red Fox Tr
- SCkT 46239 2342 A5
Redgold Run
12100 CRML 46032 1900 E4
Red Haw Ln
6200 LWNC 46236 2123 D3
Red Hawk Dr
12000 FSHR 46038 1906 C5
Red Hawk Ln
5200 WRvT 46142 2663 C1
Red Hawk Sta
6100 MCVL 46055 2015 C3
Red Horizon Blvd
4700 INPS 46221 2444 C6
Red Lake Ct
7000 INPS 46217 2554 B4
Redland Dr
6500 INPS 46217 2554 C3
Redland Ln
2400 INPS 46217 2554 C3
Redland Wy
6500 INPS 46217 2554 B3

Indianapolis Street Index

STREET
Block City ZIP Map# Grid

Red Leaf Ct
1900 INPS 46229 2232 D7
Redman Dr
4000 WRvT 46142 2663 E2
Red Maple Ct
900 GNWD 46143 2666 A2
Red Maple Dr
5700 INPS 46237 2556 E1
Red Maple Ln
9300 FSHR 46038 1904 E1
Redmill Ct
3800 INPS 46226 2231 B2
Redmill Dr
7700 INPS 46226 2231 B2
Redmill Pl
3800 INPS 46226 2231 B2
Redmill Wy
3800 INPS 46226 2231 B2
Redmond Ct
9900 LWNC 46236 2123 A4
Red Oak Ct
- INPS 46227 2555 E7
- INPS 46227 2556 A7
100 CRML 46033 1902 D2
Red Oak Dr
1000 AVON 46123 2332 A1
Red Oak Ln
10 CRML 46033 1902 D2
Red Oak Rdg
200 CRML 46033 1902 D2
Red Oak Wy
600 MRVL 46158 2660 A6
Redondo Ct
1000 GNWD 46143 2666 A4
Redondo Dr
8200 INPS 46236 2014 E5
Red Phister Dr
1700 WshT 46123 2223 C7
Red Pine Dr
10700 FSHR 46038 1904 E7
Red River Ct
5300 INPS 46221 2553 C2
Red Robin Dr
- INPS 46107 2448 A6
4800 BHGV 46107 2448 A6
Red Rock Rd
7300 LWNC 46236 2124 A1
Red Rose Ln
300 AVON 46123 2332 A4
Redsail Ct
8200 INPS 46236 2014 C5
Redskin Dr
3000 INPS 46235 2232 D4
Redskin Ln
11200 INPS 46235 2232 C4
Redskin Pl
11200 INPS 46235 2232 C4
Redskins Av
12600 FCkT 46038 1906 A3
Red Sky Rd
10800 FSHR 46038 1905 C5
Red Stone Ln
5200 WRvT 46142 2663 C1
Red Sunset Dr
- BNBG 46112 2113 E6
Red Sunset Wy
7900 AVON 46123 2332 D3
Red Tail Ct
6900 INPS 46241 2334 E4
Red Tail Dr
10100 FSHR 46038 2014 B1
Red Tail Ln
300 INPS 46241 2334 E4
Red Wing Ct
- FSHR 46038 1905 D6
Redwood Cir
200 NBVL 46062 1685 E4
Redwood Ct
- ZNVL 46077 1898 C2
10 BNBG 46112 2223 D2
400 GNWD 46143 2666 A4
Redwood Dr
400 MRVL 46158 2660 C2
1000 BNBG 46112 2223 D2
1000 LEBN 46052 1676 D3
1400 CRML 46032 1792 C7
3200 INPS 46227 2447 C7
3200 INPS 46227 2556 C1
Red Yarrow Wy
5100 INPS 46254 2117 C5
Red Yorrow Wy
5100 INPS 46254 2117 D5
Reed Ct
500 GNWD 46143 2665 B6
Reed Rd
5000 INPS 46254 2116 D7
6700 MdlT 46167 2112 D4
Reeder St
5000 INPS 46203 2339 A6
Reedy Ct
12800 CRML 46032 1900 B3
Reef Ct
8300 INPS 46236 2014 C5
Reel Creek Dr
- BrnT 46112 2115 E1
Reel Creek Ln
- BrnT 46112 2115 D1
Reese Ct
5300 CRML 46033 1794 B7
Reeves Rd
- GfdT 46168 2442 C7
- GfdT 46168 2551 C1
- PNFD 46168 2442 C7
- PNFD 46168 2551 C1
1200 PNFD 46168 2550 C1
Reflection Ct
- GNWD 46143 2666 E4
15200 NBVL 46060 1796 B5
Reflection Point Dr
11200 FSHR 46038 1905 B6
Reflections Dr
7500 INPS 46214 2225 C3
Reflections Ln
3600 INPS 46214 2225 D3
Reformers Av
2000 INPS 46203 2338 A7
Refreshing Garden Ln
14400 FSHR 46060 1796 B7
Regal Ct
- LcnT 46112 2115 D6
100 INPS 46227 2555 C1
Regal Dr
1300 ClyT 46032 1901 A7
Regatta Ct
9500 INPS 46229 2231 E6
Regency Ct
5600 INPS 46224 2226 B3
Regency Dr
5600 INPS 46224 2226 B3
11600 FSHR 46038 1904 C4
Regency Ln
11200 CRML 46033 1903 A6
Regency Pl
4900 CRML 46033 1903 A6
Regent Cir
12900 CRML 46032 1901 B3
Regent Ct
200 NBVL 46060 1795 D5
E Regent St
10 INPS 46225 2337 C7
W Regent St
200 INPS 46225 2337 B7
4700 INPS 46241 2444 D1
4800 INPS 46241 2335 C7
Regents Park Ln
100 NBVL 46062 1685 E1
Regina Cir
6100 INPS 46224 2226 A3
Regina Dr
200 LcnT 46112 2114 A7
Regis Ct
10600 INPS 46239 2341 B3
Registry Dr
7200 INPS 46217 2554 E4
Reichwein Av
10 INPS 46222 2336 D4
Reid Pl
1100 INPS 46203 2338 A6
N Reisner St
100 INPS 46222 2336 E3
S Reisner St
1000 INPS 46221 2336 E5
W Rembrandt Cir
7400 SCkT 46163 2451 A3
Rembrandt St
2000 INPS 46202 2228 A7
N Rembrandt St
1400 INPS 46202 2337 A1
1500 INPS 46202 2228 A7
Remington Ct
1600 INPS 46227 2556 A6
Remington Dr
3200 INPS 46227 2556 C6
16200 FCkT 46060 1907 C2
Remington Pl
1800 INPS 46227 2556 A6
Remington Pt
400 GNWD 46143 2666 A4
Rene Dr
6300 INPS 46221 2553 B2
Renee Dr
1200 PNFD 46168 2550 D1
Renegade Ct
2000 CRML 46032 1900 D1
Renfrew Dr
- INPS 46226 2231 A4
W Renn Ln
5500 INPS 46254 2226 B1
Reno St
500 INPS 46225 2337 B5
Rentham Ln
1000 INPS 46217 2555 A4
Renton Av
1400 INPS 46203 2338 B6
S Renton Av
1700 INPS 46203 2338 B7
Republic Dr
- FSHR 46060 1906 B2
Republic Ln
7000 INPS 46259 2558 A4
Research Wy
1500 INPS 46231 2334 C7
Reserve Dr
6600 INPS 46220 2119 E2
Reserve Wy
1100 INPS 46220 2119 D1
Residence Dr
6500 INPS 46278 2007 E4
6500 INPS 46278 2008 A4
Restin Rd
10 WRvT 46142 2664 B4
S Restin Rd
400 WRvT 46142 2664 B4
Reston Dr
- PNFD 46168 2440 D4
Reston Ln
9600 FCkT 46055 2015 C2
Retail Pkwy
- ClyT 46032 2008 E1
- ClyT 46032 2009 A1
Retford Ct
- GNWD 46143 2664 E6
Retreat Rd
8700 GfdT 46113 2551 E7
S Retriever Ln
7800 BrnT 46278 2006 E2
7800 EglT 46077 2006 E2
7800 EglT 46278 2006 E2
Reunion Ln
- GNWD 46143 2666 D5
6800 INPS 46250 2012 E5
Revere Ct
800 GNWD 46142 2665 A4
Revere Ln
1100 WshT 46234 2333 D1
6700 INPS 46237 2557 D3
Revere Pl
- CRML 46032 1902 B5
Revere Run
10 ZNVL 46077 1899 A5
Revere Wy
9700 FSHR 46250 2012 C2
Revolutionary Dr
5500 INPS 46254 2117 B5
Rex Ct
2800 INPS 46222 2227 C4
N Rex Dr
3300 INPS 46222 2227 C4
W Rex Dr
2800 INPS 46222 2227 C4
Rexford Rd
8800 INPS 46260 2009 E4
Rexham Ln
200 FCkT 46038 1904 D2
Rexmill Dr
8000 INPS 46227 2556 C6
S Rex Ridge Rd
7400 SCkT 46239 2342 A4
Reynolds Dr
100 LEBN 46052 1676 E4
100 LEBN 46052 1677 A4
12300 FSHR 46038 1904 E4
W Reynolds Rd
7300 INPS 46113 2552 C4
7300 INPS 46221 2552 C4
Rhettsbury St
- CRML 46032 1900 D3
Rhodes Ln
- WshT 46123 2333 C2
Rhonda Ct
3400 INPS 46203 2447 C1
Rhone Ter
8600 INPS 46250 2012 B4
Rialto Tr
9600 CRML 46280 2011 A2
Ribble Rd
4700 INPS 46218 2229 E5
5000 INPS 46218 2230 A4
Ribbon Dr
3500 INPS 46227 2556 D5
Richard St
5000 INPS 46221 2444 D7
N Richardson St
200 LEBN 46052 1677 A6
S Richardson St
100 LEBN 46052 1677 A6
N Richardt Av
2700 INPS 46219 2231 A5
3000 INPS 46226 2231 A3
4300 LWNC 46226 2231 A1
4600 LWNC 46226 2122 A7
S Richardt Av
3000 INPS 46239 2449 A3
Richardt St
7900 INPS 46256 2013 A6
N Richardt St
3800 INPS 46226 2231 A2
Richart Ln
800 GNWD 46142 2665 A4
Richelieu Ct
3900 INPS 46226 2231 C2
Richelieu Rd
3800 INPS 46226 2231 C2
Richfield Ln
10 WshT 46123 2332 B1
Richie Av
10 INPS 46234 2334 A3
Richie Cir
7300 LWNC 46236 2123 E1
N Richland St
10 INPS 46222 2336 E3
S Richland St
- INPS 46221 2336 D5
Richland Wy
500 WshT 46074 1792 B5
Richland Center Dr
- GfdT 46113 2551 D7
Richlane Dr
12500 INPS 46236 2015 A3
Richmond Ct
3800 ClyT 46032 1900 A7
Richmond Dr
1400 ZNVL 46077 1898 E6
Richmond Ln
5900 INPS 46254 2117 B4
Richters Blvd
- WTFD 46074 1792 D3
Richwood Dr
1000 AVON 46123 2332 A1
1000 WshT 46123 2332 A1
Rick Ln
400 INPS 46217 2555 B2
Ricks Av
100 GNFD 46140 2236 E6
N Ricks Dr E
8500 VrnT 46055 2016 B5
N Ricks Dr W
8500 VrnT 46055 2016 A5
W Ricks Dr S
4700 VrnT 46055 2016 B5
Riddell Ln
3700 WTFD 46062 1793 D3
Ridge Ct
10 WRvT 46142 2663 D2
1000 CRML 46033 1902 C3
10900 FCkT 46256 2014 C2
10900 FSHR 46038 1903 E7
W Ridge Ct
12300 LWNC 46236 2015 A7
Ridge Dr
9700 FCkT 46256 2014 C2
E Ridge Dr
800 CtrT 46140 2237 A5
Ridge Rd
400 WRvT 46142 2663 D2
1100 CRML 46033 1902 D3
5700 INPS 46226 2121 C5
7700 INPS 46240 2010 D6
Ridgebrook Dr
600 AVON 46123 2332 C5
Ridgecreek Ct
9400 INPS 46256 2013 D3
Ridgecreek Dr
9000 INPS 46256 2013 D3
Ridge Field Dr
10000 INPS 46235 2232 A3
Ridge Gate Dr
600 BNBG 46112 2114 A5
Ridgegate East Dr
8000 INPS 46268 2008 E5
Ridgegate West Dr
7900 INPS 46268 2008 E6
Ridge Harvest Ln
7700 INPS 46259 2557 E5
Ridge Hill Av
1600 INPS 46217 2554 D7
Ridge Hill Dr
8500 INPS 46217 2554 D7
8900 INPS 46217 2663 D1
8900 WRvT 46217 2663 D1
Ridge Hill Ln
1600 INPS 46217 2554 E7
Ridge Hill Wy
4400 WshT 46123 2331 D5
Ridgehill Wy
800 WshT 46123 2331 E5
Ridgeland Dr
5700 LcnT 46112 2222 E3
7800 INPS 46250 2011 E7
Ridge Line Ct
10300 LWNC 46236 2123 B3
Ridgeline Rd
10 BNBG 46112 2114 B6
Ridgemere Cir
4600 WRvT 46143 2663 D7
Ridgemere Pl
2000 WRvT 46143 2663 D7
Ridgemere Wy
2000 WRvT 46143 2663 D7
Ridgepoint Dr
300 CRML 46032 1902 A4
Ridgepointe Ct
8900 INPS 46234 2334 A1
Ridgepointe Dr
1000 INPS 46234 2334 A1
Ridgeside Rd
12200 FCkT 46256 2015 A2
Ridge Top Dr
1000 GNWD 46142 2664 E1
1200 GNWD 46142 2665 A1
Ridgeview Cir
10400 FSHR 46038 2012 D1
Ridgeview Ct
800 WshT 46123 2331 D6
6500 MRVL 46158 2660 B4
N Ridgeview Dr
1000 INPS 46219 2339 D1
1400 INPS 46219 2230 D7
3800 INPS 46226 2230 D2
S Ridgeview Dr
10 INPS 46219 2339 D3
Ridgeview Wy
5100 WshT 46123 2331 C5
Ridgewater Cir
11100 FSHR 46038 1904 E6
Ridgeway Ct
- PTBR 46167 2113 B4
N Ridgeway Ct
9800 MCVL 46055 2015 C3
Ridgeway Dr
10 BNBG 46112 2114 B5
Ridgewind Cir
8000 BrnT 46112 2005 D3
Ridgewood Av
700 WshT 46074 1792 E3
Ridgewood Ct
1200 PNFD 46168 2441 C7
Ridgewood Dr
800 PNFD 46168 2441 C6
4600 EglT 46077 1899 D2
7400 INPS 46226 2231 A4
Ridge Wy Dr
4000 INPS 46221 2444 E6
Ridley Ct
8100 INPS 46260 2010 B5
Rigging Ct
9000 INPS 46256 2014 B3
Riley Av
10 GNFD 46140 2345 D2
N Riley Av
500 INPS 46201 2339 A2
3100 INPS 46218 2230 A3
4100 INPS 46226 2230 A1
6600 INPS 46220 2121 A2
7300 INPS 46250 2121 A1
S Riley Av
200 INPS 46201 2339 A3
1300 INPS 46203 2339 A6
2200 INPS 46203 2448 A1
Riley Ct
- GNFD 46140 2345 D2
7200 INPS 46250 2121 A1
Riley Mw
4900 CRML 46033 1903 A2
Riley Pl
- INPS 46203 2339 A6
Riley Rd
1800 CtrT 46052 1676 C5
1800 LEBN 46052 1676 C5
12200 LWNC 46236 2123 E1
12200 LWNC 46236 2124 A1
E Rimwood Dr
8400 INPS 46256 2013 A5
W Rimwood Dr
8400 INPS 46256 2013 A5
Rimwood Ln
7500 INPS 46256 2013 A5
Rinaldi St
- INPS 46241 2335 E6
Rinehart Av
5400 INPS 46241 2335 B4
Ring Rd
- INPS 46250 2012 C5
Ringer Rd
- FCkT 46038 1906 E6
Ringgold St
1500 INPS 46203 2337 E6
Ringgold St
2200 INPS 46203 2446 E1
Ring Necked Dr
2200 INPS 46234 2225 A6
Ringstead Wy
- INPS 46235 2123 B7
4400 INPS 46235 2232 B1
Ringtail Ct
7000 INPS 46254 2116 E7
Ringtail Pl
10300 FSHR 46060 1905 B2
Rio Grande Dr
6900 INPS 46217 2555 A3
Rioux Grove Ct
19100 NBVL 46062 1685 C4
Rio Vista Rd
900 GNWD 46143 2665 E5
Ripon Ct
9000 INPS 46268 2009 B3
Ripple Rd
300 INPS 46208 2119 B6
Ripplewood Dr
100 WRvT 46142 2663 E3
1400 DNVL 46122 2329 B4
Rippling Wy N
2200 INPS 46260 2009 D4
Rippling Wy S
2200 INPS 46260 2009 D4
Rippling Brook Wy
5300 CRML 46033 1794 C7
Rippling Wy Ct
2200 INPS 46260 2009 D4
Rising Rd
400 LWNC 46216 2122 D5
Rising Sun Ct
- MdnT 46113 2661 D1
Rising Sun Wy
12100 FCkT 46038 1905 C4
12100 FSHR 46038 1905 C4
Rita Dr
900 WRvT 46143 2664 B5
N Ritter Av
10 INPS 46219 2339 B3
1600 INPS 46218 2230 B7
4000 INPS 46226 2230 B1
4600 INPS 46226 2121 B7
7200 INPS 46250 2121 B1
7400 INPS 46250 2012 B7
S Ritter Av
10 INPS 46219 2339 B4
1500 INPS 46203 2339 B6
2200 INPS 46203 2448 B2
2700 BHGV 46203 2448 B2
Ritter St
5500 BHGV 46203 2448 B4
Ritterskamp Ct
4000 INPS 46250 2011 E7
Riva Ridge Ct
- WshT 46234 2224 E6
4500 INPS 46237 2448 B6
Riva Ridge Dr
6000 INPS 46237 2448 C5
E Riva Ridge Dr
5500 INPS 46237 2448 B5
River Av
600 INPS 46221 2337 A5
1000 INPS 46221 2336 E5
14600 CRML 46062 1795 B5
14600 NBVL 46062 1795 B5
14600 NbvT 46062 1795 B5
17500 NBVL 46062 1686 B7
River Dr E
11400 CRML 46280 1903 C6
River Dr W
11400 CRML 46280 1903 C5
River Rd
10000 CRML 46280 1903 B7
10000 CRML 46280 2012 B1
11600 CRML 46033 1903 C5
13600 CRML 46033 1795 A7
13600 CRML 46033 1904 A1
N River Rd
8500 INPS 46240 2011 D4
S River Rd
7500 INPS 46240 2011 B7
Riverbank Wy
200 AVON 46123 2333 B3
200 WshT 46123 2333 B3
River Bay Ct
2900 INPS 46240 2011 C6
River Bay Dr E
7900 INPS 46240 2011 C6
River Bay Dr N
2900 INPS 46240 2011 C6
River Bay Dr W
8000 INPS 46240 2011 C6
River Bend Ct
8900 INPS 46250 2012 B4
River Bend Pkwy
5200 INPS 46250 2012 A4
River Birch Ct
2300 WshT 46123 2440 E1
River Birch Dr
2300 WshT 46123 2440 E1
3000 INPS 46235 2232 C4
River Birch Ln
7200 LWNC 46236 2123 B1
River Birch Rd
15600 WshT 46074 1792 C4
Riverbirch Run
4200 EglT 46077 1899 D2
River Birch Wy
13800 CRML 46033 1903 E1
Riverbrook Ln
4400 INPS 46254 2117 D5
Riverby Ln
1000 INPS 46240 2010 E7
River Chase Dr
2700 INPS 46214 2225 D5
River Chase Ln
- MCVL 46055 2015 D4
River Crossing Blvd
- INPS 46240 2011 D5
N River Crossing Blvd
8600 INPS 46240 2011 D4
River Crossing Pkwy
3600 INPS 46240 2011 D4
River Edge Ln
7600 INPS 46240 2011 C6
Riverfront Av
6900 INPS 46220 2120 A2
Riverfront Dr
6600 INPS 46220 2120 A2
River Glen Dr
7200 FSHR 46038 1904 A5
11800 FSHR 46038 1903 E5
E River Heights Dr
1200 INPS 46240 2119 E1
1200 INPS 46240 2120 A1
River Highlands Dr
7400 FSHR 46038 1904 A4
River Mist Ln
8100 INPS 46237 2557 C6
River Mist Pl
8100 INPS 46237 2557 C6
River Oak Ln E
9600 FSHR 46038 2012 D2
River Oak Ln N
9700 FSHR 46038 2012 D2
River Oak Ln W
9800 FSHR 46038 2012 D2
River Park Wy
- LcnT 46112 2115 D5
River Promenade
- INPS 46222 2336 E3
- INPS 46222 2337 A3
River Ridge Dr
4600 INPS 46240 2011 E3
4900 INPS 46240 2012 A3
11600 FSHR 46038 1903 E5
River Run Dr
6300 INPS 46221 2553 C3
River Run Pl
8100 NBVL 46062 1795 B1
River Shore Pkwy
1600 INPS 46208 2227 E4
River Shore Pl
1700 INPS 46208 2227 E4
Riverside Dr
700 GNWD 46142 2665 B2
E Riverside Dr
1400 INPS 46202 2336 E1
1500 INPS 46202 2227 E7
2200 INPS 46208 2227 E5
River Side Wy
6600 FSHR 46038 1903 E5
Riversport Ct
6000 INPS 46221 2553 C2
Riverstone Ct
1800 WTFD 46074 1684 B5
2000 WshT 46123 2441 B1
River Valley Dr
12300 FSHR 46038 1906 A4
River Valley Wy
6300 INPS 46221 2553 C2
Riverview Ct
10 GNFD 46140 2237 A6
Riverview Dr
1100 GNFD 46140 2237 A6
6000 INPS 46208 2119 C4
6200 INPS 46220 2119 D3
6200 INPS 46260 2119 C4
N Riverview Dr
6600 INPS 46220 2119 D2
River Walk Dr
7200 INPS 46214 2225 D5
Riverwalk Wy
7200 NBVL 46062 1686 A7
7200 NbvT 46062 1686 A7
Riverwood Av
9800 NbvT 46060 1687 A2
10200 WynT 46060 1687 B2
10200 WynT 46062 1687 C1
20600 WynT 46060 1578 C6
20600 WynT 46062 1578 C6
21500 WRvT 46062 1578 C6
Riverwood Blvd
- LcnT 46112 2224 D2
- LcnT 46234 2224 D2
Riverwood Ct
5700 INPS 46250 2012 B3
Riverwood Dr
200 WRvT 46062 1578 D6
200 WynT 46062 1578 D6
3600 INPS 46214 2225 C3
5700 INPS 46250 2012 C3
Riverwood Wy
13800 CRML 46032 1792 C7
Riviera Ct
4500 WRvT 46142 2663 D3
Riviera Dr
300 WshT 46123 2332 B6
1000 INPS 46220 2119 E3
Riviera St
1900 INPS 46260 2118 D3
Rivington Dr
6200 LWNC 46236 2123 A3
Rix Ct
2500 CRML 46033 1793 B7
Rixon Av
4800 INPS 46221 2444 C5
Roach St
3200 INPS 46218 2229 C5
W Roache St
700 INPS 46208 2228 A5
1200 INPS 46208 2227 E5
Roamin Ct
10 WRvT 46142 2664 B4
Roamin Dr
4000 WRvT 46142 2664 B4
Roan Ln
12600 LWNC 46236 2124 A2
12700 MCVL 46236 2124 A2
Roanoke Dr
1000 WshT 46074 1792 A5
1500 ZNVL 46077 1898 E6
N Roanoke St
500 INPS 46204 2337 C2
600 INPS 46202 2337 C2
Rob Ln
8100 INPS 46237 2557 A6
Robbins Dr
200 GNWD 46142 2665 A4
Robbins Rd
8600 INPS 46268 2008 C4
Roberson Blvd
400 MRVL 46158 2660 C2
Robert Ct
1300 ZNVL 46077 1899 A6
Robert Dr
1300 ZNVL 46077 1899 A6
Robert Rd
5100 WRvT 46142 2663 C3
Roberta Ct
600 BNBG 46112 2114 D6
Roberta Dr
3100 INPS 46222 2227 B5
Roberts Dr
8600 FSHR 46038 2013 C2
20600 WshT 46069 1683 C1
Roberts Pl
6100 INPS 46220 2121 A4
E Roberts Rd
10 INPS 46227 2446 C6
W Roberts Rd
10 INPS 46217 2446 B6
Roberts Creek Ln
6200 INPS 46221 2553 A3
Robertson Av
2700 INPS 46218 2229 B5
Robertson Blvd
4100 INPS 46228 2227 A1
Robertson Ct
4100 INPS 46228 2227 A2
Robertson St
10 MdnT 46113 2661 D3
Robey Rd
8700 INPS 46234 2225 A4
Robey Glen Dr
- INPS 46234 2224 E5
Robin Dr
4000 INPS 46221 2444 C5
Robin Ln
600 GNFD 46140 2236 E6
N Robin Ln
9200 INPS 46240 2011 A3
Robin Run
6100 INPS 46254 2117 D4
Robin Run E
- INPS 46268 2117 C3
Robin Run W
6300 INPS 46268 2117 C3
Robinbrook Dr
12500 CRML 46033 1903 C4
Robin Hood Ct
6700 INPS 46227 2555 C3
Robin Hood Dr
100 INPS 46227 2555 C3
Robin Run Wy
- WshT 46123 2332 E2
- WshT 46123 2333 A2
Robinson Run
13800 FSHR 46038 1904 C1
Robinsrock Dr
6300 INPS 46268 2117 D3
Robinsrock Ln
6400 INPS 46268 2117 C3
Robinsrock Wy
5000 INPS 46268 2117 C2
Robinwood Dr
6100 INPS 46237 2448 C7
Robinwood Ln
6200 INPS 46237 2448 D7
Robinwood Rd
10 BNBG 46112 2223 D2
W Robison Rd
4900 INPS 46268 2008 D3
Robson Ln
10 GfdT 46168 2551 B7
10 GfdT 46168 2660 B1
Robson St
2800 INPS 46201 2338 C2
Robton St
300 INPS 46241 2335 E4
Robwes Rd
6300 INPS 46241 2444 A5
Rochelle Ct
9200 INPS 46235 2231 D3
Rochelle Dr
9100 INPS 46235 2231 E3
N Rochester Av
1000 INPS 46222 2336 A1
1600 INPS 46222 2227 A7
S Rochester St
400 INPS 46241 2336 A4
Rockberry Dr
200 CRML 46032 1793 A7
Rockcress Ct
4600 ZNVL 46077 1898 D2
Rockford Ct
10300 INPS 46229 2232 B7
12100 NBVL 46060 1796 E2
Rockford Dr
1800 INPS 46229 2232 B7
Rock Hampton Ct
5300 INPS 46268 2008 C4
Rockhill Ct
- MdnT 46113 2661 A1
Rock Hollow Cir
8500 INPS 46256 2013 C4
Rocking Chair Rd
4000 WRvT 46142 2664 B2
Rockingham Cir
- FCkT 46038 1905 C6
Rockingham Pl
1400 INPS 46260 2009 E5
Rock Island Ct
8900 INPS 46217 2555 A7
8900 INPS 46217 2664 A2
8900 WRvT 46217 2664 A2
Rocklane Rd
1500 GNWD 46143 2666 C3
2600 ClkT 46143 2666 C3
3200 ClkT 46143 2667 B4

STREET Block City ZIP Map# Grid
Rocklane Rd
5500 ClkT 46143 2668 A5
E Rocklane Rd
7000 ClkT 46143 2668 D6
7000 ClkT 46162 2668 D6
Rockleigh Av
7300 INPS 46214 2334 D3
Rock Maple Dr
3500 INPS 46235 2232 C3
Rockne Cir
4900 CRML 46033 1903 A3
Rock Oak Ct
500 INPS 46227 2555 D6
Rock Oak Dr
8300 INPS 46227 2555 D6
Rockport Pl
600 WshT 46074 1792 B5
Rock Ridge Ct
7900 INPS 46268 2008 E6
Rock River Ct
14300 CRML 46033 1794 C7
Rock Rose Ct
7800 INPS 46237 2556 E5
Rockrose Ct
10 WshT 46074 1792 C4
Rockshire Rd
100 INPS 46241 2335 A4
Rockspray Cir
5400 INPS 46254 2116 D6
Rockspray Ct
5800 CRML 46033 1903 D1
Rockstone Ct
6300 INPS 46268 2117 D3
Rockview Cir
2400 AVON 46123 2332 D5
Rockville Av
3800 INPS 46241 2336 A4
3900 INPS 46241 2335 E4
4000 INPS 46222 2335 E4
Rockville Rd
3500 INPS 46222 2336 A4
3500 INPS 46241 2336 A4
3900 INPS 46222 2335 B3
3900 INPS 46241 2335 B3
4600 INPS 46224 2335 B3
6200 INPS 46214 2335 B3
6400 INPS 46214 2334 D4
6400 INPS 46241 2334 D4
7300 INPS 46231 2334 D4
8300 INPS 46234 2334 B4
8800 INPS 46231 2333 E4
8800 INPS 46234 2333 E4
Rockville Rd US-36
- INPS 46224 2335 A4
6200 INPS 46214 2335 A4
6200 INPS 46241 2335 A4
6400 INPS 46214 2334 D4
6400 INPS 46241 2334 D4
7300 INPS 46231 2334 D4
8300 INPS 46234 2334 B4
8800 INPS 46231 2333 E4
8800 INPS 46234 2333 E4
W Rockway Dr
5500 SCkT 46163 2451 E1
Rockwell Ct
300 ZNVL 46077 1898 E3
Rockwell Dr
- GNWD 46143 2664 E6
5300 INPS 46237 2448 D7
Rockwell Ln
6200 INPS 46237 2448 D7
Rockwell Pl
6100 INPS 46237 2448 D7
Rockwood Ct
9300 NBVL 46060 1686 E4
W Rockwood Ln
6700 SCkT 46163 2451 B3
Rocky Beach Dr
19300 NBVL 46062 1685 D4
Rocky Cay Ct
5100 CRML 46033 1903 B5
Rocky Forge Dr
5000 INPS 46221 2553 C1
Rocky Hill Rd
8800 INPS 46217 2554 D7
Rocky Knob Ln
4600 INPS 46254 2118 A7
Rocky Meadow Dr
- GNWD 46143 2665 B6
Rocky Meadows Ct
8000 INPS 46259 2558 B5
Rocky Mountain Ct
12500 FSHR 46038 1906 A6
Rocky Mountain Dr
5000 INPS 46237 2448 D7
Rocky Pointe Rd
12900 FCkT 46055 2015 B1
Rocky Ridge Rd
8800 INPS 46217 2554 D7
8900 INPS 46217 2663 D1
8900 WRvT 46217 2663 D1
Rocky River Dr
6000 INPS 46221 2553 C2
Rod Ct
6300 INPS 46237 2557 D2
Rodebaugh Rd
6200 INPS 46268 2118 A3
Rodeo Ct
8800 INPS 46217 2555 B7
Rodeo Dr
300 INPS 46217 2555 B7
Roderick Ct
10 BHGV 46107 2447 E6
Rodney Ct
10 BHGV 46107 2447 E6
Rodney Dr
8300 INPS 46234 2225 B6
Rodney Pl
7100 NBVL 46062 1686 A5
E Rodney St
400 BNBG 46112 2114 C6
S Roena St
300 INPS 46241 2335 E5
2400 INPS 46241 2444 E2

STREET Block City ZIP Map# Grid
Roeriver Ct
14600 NBVL 46060 1796 E6
Rogers Cir
1600 INPS 46214 2225 D7
Rogers Ct
- CRML 46032 1901 E2
1600 INPS 46214 2225 D7
Rogers Dr
1100 PNFD 46168 2441 C6
7300 INPS 46214 2225 D7
Rogers Rd
10 CRML 46032 1902 A2
1500 INPS 46227 2556 A4
Rohan Ct
8700 INPS 46278 2007 A4
Rohrer Rd
- CRML 46032 1901 E1
800 CRML 46032 1902 A1
1000 CRML 46032 1793 A7
Roland Dr
5200 INPS 46228 2118 D6
Roland Rd
4200 INPS 46228 2227 D1
Rolling Ct
1300 WshT 46032 1793 A3
11400 CRML 46033 1902 D5
Rolling Ct W
1300 WshT 46032 1793 A4
Rolling Bluff Ln
5700 INPS 46221 2553 C2
Rolling Dunes Dr
2900 INPS 46214 2225 E4
Rolling Hill Dr
100 CRML 46032 1793 A6
Rolling Hill Rd
1000 GNWD 46142 2664 E1
E Rolling Hill Rd
1000 GNWD 46142 2664 E1
1500 GNWD 46142 2665 A1
Rolling Hills Ct
1300 INPS 46214 2334 D1
Rolling Hills Dr
7100 INPS 46214 2334 D1
Rolling Hills Ln
1000 WshT 46168 2441 B1
Rolling Meadow Blvd
5200 INPS 46237 2448 C7
Rolling Meadow Dr
6100 INPS 46237 2448 D7
Rolling Meadow Ln
6100 INPS 46237 2448 D7
Rolling Meadows Ct
10600 MdnT 46158 2661 B7
Rolling Oak Dr
2200 INPS 46214 2225 C6
Rolling Pines Ct
5700 INPS 46220 2120 D5
Rolling Ridge Dr
1200 NBVL 46060 1795 E2
1400 NbvT 46060 1795 E2
Rolling Ridge Rd
5600 INPS 46220 2120 D5
Rolling River Ct
5300 INPS 46221 2553 C2
Rolling Springs Ct
10 CRML 46033 1902 D6
Rolling Springs Dr
2900 CRML 46033 1902 C6
9600 WshT 46234 2333 D2
Rolling Trails Rd
300 WRvT 46142 2663 E3
Rollingview Ct
200 MRVL 46158 2660 B5
Rollingwood Cir
2600 WTFD 46074 1684 C7
Rollins Ct
2600 INPS 46268 2009 C3
Rolls Dr
2400 INPS 46268 2009 C6
Rollshore Ct
3000 CRML 46033 1902 C6
Roma Wy
- WshT 46123 2332 A7
Romalong Ct
14800 WshT 46032 1792 C5
W Romalong Ct
100 WshT 46032 1792 C5
Romalong Ln
15100 WshT 46032 1792 C5
Roman Ct
15200 WshT 46032 1792 D5
Romar Dr
3600 LcnT 46112 2223 B4
Rome Dr
2100 INPS 46228 2227 D2
Rome Ter
3700 INPS 46228 2227 A1
Romeo Ct
- AVON 46123 2332 B3
Romeo Dr
500 AVON 46123 2332 A3
6200 WshT 46123 2332 A3
Romeo Pl
11300 FCkT 46040 1907 A6
Rommel Dr
3900 INPS 46228 2227 D2
Romney Dr
19300 NBVL 46060 1687 C4
Romo Bnd
13200 CRML 46074 1900 C2
Ronald Ct
400 WRvT 46142 2663 C3
10200 INPS 46229 2232 B7
Ronald Reagan Pkwy
- AVON 46123 2224 C7
- AVON 46123 2333 C1
- AVON 46234 2333 C1
- WshT 46123 2333 C2
Rook Rd
8500 INPS 46234 2225 A1
Rooker Rd
1000 BrnT 46158 2660 A5
1000 MRVL 46158 2660 A5
Rooker Trc
- BrnT 46158 2660 B6

STREET Block City ZIP Map# Grid
Rooker Trc
- MRVL 46158 2660 B6
Rookwood Av
3800 INPS 46208 2228 B2
4600 INPS 46208 2119 B7
Rooses Dr
7100 INPS 46217 2554 E5
Rooses Ln
1600 INPS 46217 2554 D5
Rooses Wy
7300 INPS 46217 2554 D4
E Roosevelt Av
- INPS 46201 2229 A7
1300 INPS 46201 2337 E1
1300 INPS 46202 2337 E1
1400 INPS 46201 2338 A1
2800 INPS 46218 2229 C6
Roosevelt Dr
100 GNFD 46140 2345 B1
E Roosevelt Dr
1000 NBVL 46060 1686 D6
Roosevelt St
10 WTFD 46074 1793 B1
400 PNFD 46168 2441 B6
Rosalind Ct
2900 INPS 46268 2118 C2
Roscommon Ct
4800 INPS 46254 2116 C7
Rose Ct
1400 PNFD 46168 2441 D7
11600 CRML 46033 1903 B5
Rose Dr
7100 INPS 46227 2556 A4
Rose Ln
100 GNWD 46143 2665 D5
100 INPS 46227 2555 C5
600 MRVL 46158 2659 E2
700 BNBG 46112 2114 D4
Rose St
- WRvT 46143 2664 B5
Roseapple Dr
9500 INPS 46256 2013 E6
Rosebay Ct
800 INPS 46240 2010 E5
Rosebay Dr
900 INPS 46240 2010 E5
Rosebay Ln
1900 CRML 46033 1902 E1
Roseberry Ct
1300 MRVL 46158 2660 C3
Rosebery Ct
200 INPS 46214 2334 D3
Rosebery Ln
200 INPS 46214 2334 D3
Rosebrock Ct
- INPS 46217 2446 B7
Rosebrock Ln
- INPS 46217 2446 B7
Rosebud Dr
- FSHR 46060 1795 D6
14700 NBVL 46060 1795 D6
14700 NbvT 46060 1795 D6
Rosebud Ln
1500 WRvT 46143 2664 C7
6600 INPS 46237 2557 D5
Rosebush Dr
7800 INPS 46237 2557 D5
Rosebush Ln
6500 INPS 46237 2557 D5
Rosecrans Ct
10 BNBG 46112 2223 C3
Rosedale Ct
100 NBVL 46060 1795 E4
Rosedale Dr
1800 INPS 46227 2447 A6
Rosedowne Ct
200 NBVL 46060 1795 E3
Rosefinch Dr
3800 INPS 46228 2118 A3
Rosegate Av
- INPS 46237 2557 A5
Rosegate Dr
7500 INPS 46237 2557 A5
Rosegate Ln
5100 INPS 46237 2557 A5
Rosegate Pl
5100 INPS 46237 2557 A5
Rose Haven Dr
12300 LWNC 46235 2124 A3
Rosehill Dr
7000 INPS 46260 2118 D1
Roselawn Av
- INPS 46226 2230 A2
10 BNBG 46112 2223 D2
Roselawn Dr
2200 LEBN 46052 1676 E3
4100 INPS 46226 2229 E2
6000 INPS 46226 2230 C2
Roselawn Ln
5600 INPS 46221 2444 B5
Roselyn Dr
10 MdnT 46158 2661 A7
Rosemary Dr
5200 INPS 46250 2121 A1
Rosemead Ln
8100 INPS 46240 2011 A6
Rosemeade Dr
11600 CRML 46032 1902 A5
Rosemere Av
10 INPS 46229 2340 D3
E Rosemill Dr
1300 WTFD 46032 1793 A6
Rosemont
1000 CRML 46032 1901 A1
Rosemont Ct
5700 INPS 46254 2117 C5
Rosemont Dr
5700 INPS 46254 2117 C4
Rosemoss Cross
15400 WshT 46074 1792 D5
Rosengarten Dr
1000 GNWD 46142 2664 D1
Roses Rd
8300 DelT 46038 1904 C2

STREET Block City ZIP Map# Grid
Rose Tree Ct
6900 INPS 46237 2448 E6
Roseway Ct
7800 INPS 46226 2231 B4
Roseway Dr
3400 INPS 46226 2231 B3
N Roseway Dr
1000 INPS 46219 2340 B1
Roseway Ln
3700 INPS 46226 2231 B3
S Rosewind Dr
3200 SCkT 46163 2451 C1
Rosewood Ct
10400 CRML 46033 2011 C1
Rosewood Dr
10 BrnT 46158 2659 E7
10 CCRO 46034 1577 B2
Rosewood Ln
1200 MRVL 46158 2660 C2
8600 INPS 46240 2011 B4
Rosewood Commons Ct
4400 INPS 46254 2117 E7
Rosewood Commons Dr
5300 INPS 46254 2117 E6
Rosewood Commons Pl
4400 INPS 46254 2117 E7
Rosewood Commons Wy
4500 INPS 46254 2117 E6
Rosner Dr
1000 SDWY 46224 2335 C1
Ross Cross
10400 FSHR 46038 1905 B3
Ross Ln
9500 INPS 46268 2008 E2
Rossburn Dr
11500 FCkT 46038 1905 E5
11500 FSHR 46038 1905 E5
Rossi Dr
12000 LWNC 46236 2123 E1
Rosslyn Av
4600 INPS 46205 2120 A6
5200 INPS 46220 2120 A6
7500 INPS 46240 2011 A7
Rosston Av
9300 UnnT 46077 1680 D6
Rost Ln
7600 GfdT 46168 2551 B5
Roswell Ct
400 INPS 46234 2334 A2
Roswell Dr
13600 CRML 46032 1901 E1
13700 CRML 46032 1792 E7
Roswill Dr
- INPS 46241 2444 B5
Rotary Cir
700 INPS 46202 2337 A2
Rothbury Dr
8400 INPS 46260 2009 E4
Rothe Ln
2800 INPS 46229 2232 D5
Rothe Wy
11600 INPS 46229 2232 D5
Rotherham Cir
900 BHGV 46107 2447 E5
Rotherham Ln
900 BHGV 46107 2447 E4
1100 INPS 46107 2447 E4
Rotterdam Dr
4400 INPS 46228 2227 A1
Rouark Cir
2800 INPS 46229 2232 A4
Rouark Ln
10300 INPS 46229 2232 B5
Roudebush Blvd
19100 NBVL 46060 1687 C4
Rough Cedar Ln
7800 INPS 46250 2012 C7
Round Ct
700 ZNVL 46077 1899 C5
Roundabout Cir
- PTBR 46167 2113 A2
Round Hill Ct
10 DNVL 46122 2329 C3
8100 INPS 46260 2010 B5
Round Hill Rd
10 DNVL 46122 2329 C3
400 INPS 46260 2010 B6
Round Lake Ct
- LEBN 46052 1676 C4
Round Lake Rd
4600 INPS 46205 2120 B7
18600 NBVL 46060 1686 B5
Roundrock Ct
6700 WshT 46123 2441 B1
Roundtable Ct
900 INPS 46260 2010 A5
Roundtree Ct
6600 INPS 46214 2225 E4
6600 INPS 46214 2226 D5
Roundtree Rd
10700 FSHR 46038 1905 C4
Round Up Tr
100 DelT 46038 1903 D7
Roundwood Ct
11300 INPS 46235 2232 D2
Roundwood Dr
3800 INPS 46235 2232 D2
N Routiers Av
10 INPS 46219 2340 D2
2500 INPS 46219 2231 C5
S Routiers Av
200 INPS 46219 2340 C4
6000 INPS 46259 2558 C2
Routiers Ct
8700 INPS 46219 2231 C5
Routiers Dr
- INPS 46226 2231 C2
N Routiers Rd
1000 INPS 46219 2340 D1
Rovene Dr
1500 LEBN 46052 1676 D4
Rowan Ct
5200 INPS 46237 2557 A6
W Rowan Ct
200 WshT 46074 1792 C5

STREET Block City ZIP Map# Grid
E Rowan Run
10 WshT 46074 1792 C5
W Rowan Run
10 WshT 46074 1792 C5
Rowin Rd
1200 INPS 46220 2119 E6
Rowlett Pl
3900 CRML 46074 1900 A2
Rowney St
4500 INPS 46203 2338 E6
4800 INPS 46203 2339 A6
Roxanne Dr
- CRML 46033 1903 B4
Roxburgh Ct N
3600 INPS 46234 2225 B3
Roxburgh Ct S
3600 INPS 46234 2225 B3
Roxbury Cir
5700 INPS 46226 2121 B6
Roxbury Ct
4900 MdlT 46167 2113 C6
5700 INPS 46226 2121 B6
Roxbury Dr
4600 MdlT 46167 2113 B5
9600 FSHR 46038 2012 D2
Roxbury Ln
100 NBVL 46062 1685 D2
Roxbury Pl
6400 EglT 46077 1897 D6
12100 CRML 46033 1902 E4
Roxbury Rd
5200 INPS 46226 2121 B6
Roxbury Ter
5500 INPS 46226 2121 B6
Roxie Dr
4400 LWNC 46235 2231 D1
4500 LWNC 46235 2122 D7
Roy Rd
7800 INPS 46219 2231 B5
Royal Av
7900 BrnT 46077 2006 D2
7900 BrnT 46112 2006 D2
7900 EglT 46077 2006 D2
7900 EglT 46112 2006 D2
Royal Blvd
2400 ClyT 46032 1900 D6
Royal Cir
11300 ClyT 46032 1900 D6
Royal Ct
11300 ClyT 46032 1900 D6
Royal Dr
8600 FSHR 46038 1904 C6
10700 ClyT 46032 1901 A7
Royal Ln
6600 AVON 46123 2332 B3
Royal Pl
11300 ClyT 46032 1900 D6
Royal Rd
100 BHGV 46107 2447 C2
100 INPS 46107 2447 C2
W Royal St
200 LEBN 46052 1676 E5
Royal Fern Ln
7500 NBVL 46062 1686 A4
Royal Lake Cir
1400 INPS 46228 2118 E4
Royal Lake Dr
1400 INPS 46228 2118 E4
Royal Meadow Dr
8400 INPS 46217 2555 A6
8900 INPS 46217 2664 A2
8900 WRvT 46217 2664 A2
Royal Oak Ct
200 ZNVL 46077 1899 A3
5500 INPS 46227 2556 C1
Royal Oak Dr
3300 INPS 46227 2556 C1
Royal Oak Ln
4600 CRML 46033 1902 E4
Royal Oakland Ct
7100 LWNC 46236 2123 D1
Royal Oakland Dr
7100 LWNC 46236 2123 D1
7400 LWNC 46236 2014 E6
Royal Oakland Pl
6500 LWNC 46236 2123 D2
Royal Oaks Ct
700 GNWD 46143 2665 A5
Royal Orbit Ct
4900 INPS 46237 2448 B6
Royal Pine Blvd
4000 INPS 46250 2011 E7
Royal Pine Ln
10 JknT 46034 1576 E6
10 JknT 46034 1577 A6
Royal Run Blvd
- EglT 46077 1897 D6
Royal Saddle Dr
13600 CRML 46032 1900 E1
13600 CRML 46032 1901 A2
Royal St. George Dr
600 GNWD 46143 2665 E5
Royalton Dr
1600 ClyT 46032 2009 E1
Royal Troon Ct
700 WshT 46123 2331 D5
Royal Troon Wy
4700 WshT 46123 2331 D5
Royalwood Ct
12000 FSHR 46038 1906 E4
Royalwood Dr
11900 FSHR 46038 1906 D5
Royce Ct
12500 CRML 46033 1902 E3
Royce Dr
9800 INPS 46235 2232 A3
Ruby Blvd
- INPS 46268 2009 C7
Ruby Ct
10800 ClyT 46032 1900 C6
Ruby St
6400 LWNC 46236 2123 E3
Ruby Ter
100 GNWD 46143 2665 D5

STREET Block City ZIP Map# Grid
Ruby Bee Dr
4600 INPS 46221 2444 E6
Rucker Cir
5200 INPS 46250 2012 B7
Rucker Rd
5800 INPS 46220 2121 B4
7700 INPS 46250 2012 A7
Ruckle St
1700 INPS 46202 2228 D7
3700 INPS 46205 2228 D3
10100 ClyT 46280 2010 D1
11000 ClyT 46280 1901 D6
11100 CRML 46032 1901 D6
Ruddy Ln
11300 FSHR 46038 1903 E6
Rudgate Dr
200 WshT 46123 2223 B7
Rue Biscay St
4200 LWNC 46226 2231 C1
Rue Cezanne St
3900 INPS 46220 2120 D6
Rue Chanel
3200 INPS 46227 2447 C6
Rue Delacroix St
3800 INPS 46220 2120 D6
Rue de Margot Dr
7200 INPS 46260 2118 D1
Rue Deville St
5200 INPS 46220 2120 D6
Rue Flambeau St
3800 INPS 46220 2120 D6
Rue le Blanc St
4200 LWNC 46226 2231 D1
Rue Lemans St
4200 INPS 46226 2231 D1
4200 LWNC 46226 2231 D1
Ruelling Dr
5200 INPS 46254 2117 C6
Rue Madeleine St
8700 LWNC 46226 2231 C1
Rue Marceau St
5500 INPS 46220 2120 D6
Rue Monet St
5400 INPS 46220 2120 D6
Rue Rabelais
3900 INPS 46220 2120 D6
Rue Renoir St
3900 INPS 46220 2120 D6
Rue Riviera St
8200 LWNC 46226 2231 C1
Rue Royale
5500 INPS 46227 2555 C1
Rue Vallee
4900 INPS 46227 2447 C6
Rue Verlaine St
3800 INPS 46220 2120 D6
Rue Voltaire St
3800 INPS 46220 2120 D5
Rugby Ct
10 NbvT 46060 1795 C6
10300 ClyT 46280 2010 E1
Rulon Rd
23400 WRvT 46034 1578 C2
Rum Cherry Wy
5500 INPS 46237 2447 D7
5500 INPS 46237 2556 D1
Rumford Rd
8000 INPS 46219 2340 B1
Runaway Dr
1900 SDWY 46224 2226 B7
Runaway Ln
- NBVL 46060 1797 A4
Runaway Bay Ln
1800 SDWY 46224 2226 A7
Rundle Ct
5600 INPS 46220 2120 D5
Runningbrook Ct
1100 WshT 46123 2332 B6
7400 INPS 46254 2116 D6
Runningbrook Dr
- WshT 46123 2332 B6
Running Brook Rd
- LcnT 46112 2224 E2
Runningbrook Ter
4600 WRvT 46143 2663 D7
Runningbrook Wy
7300 INPS 46254 2116 D7
Running Creek Ct
8700 INPS 46268 2009 B4
Running Springs Rd
12100 FSHR 46038 1905 C4
Running Tide Ct
10900 INPS 46236 2014 C6
Runnymede Ct
- MdnT 46113 2661 A1
Runview Cir
10400 FSHR 46038 2012 D1
Runyon Ct
200 WRvT 46142 2663 D4
Runyon Rd
200 WRvT 46142 2663 D4
S Runyon Rd
1200 WRvT 46143 2663 D6
Runyon Deer Ln
4500 WRvT 46142 2663 D4
W Runyon Lake Dr
4500 WRvT 46143 2663 D5
Rural Dr
6000 INPS 46227 2556 D2
N Rural St
500 INPS 46201 2338 C2
2700 INPS 46218 2229 B5
3800 INPS 46205 2229 C2
7000 INPS 46220 2120 C1
7200 INPS 46240 2120 C1
S Rural St
10 INPS 46201 2338 B4
500 INPS 46203 2338 B4
2500 INPS 46203 2447 B1
3000 INPS 46237 2447 B3
3600 INPS 46227 2447 B4
Rush Ct
100 FSHR 46038 1904 B5
Rush Dr
11700 FSHR 46038 1904 B5

STREET Block City ZIP Map# Grid
Rush Pl
8100 INPS 46250 2011 E6
Rushing River
6400 NBVL 46062 1685 D4
Rushmore Blvd E
1200 INPS 46234 2334 A1
Rushmore Blvd N
- INPS 46234 2333 E1
Rushmore Blvd S
9000 INPS 46234 2334 A1
9200 INPS 46234 2333 E1
Rushmore Blvd W
1200 INPS 46234 2333 D1
Rushmore Dr
17100 WshT 46074 1793 B1
17100 WTFD 46074 1793 B1
Ruskin Ct
6100 INPS 46224 2226 A2
Ruskin Pl
400 INPS 46205 2228 D3
E Ruskin Pl
7500 INPS 46226 2231 A2
W Ruskin Pl
5200 INPS 46224 2226 C2
Ruskin Pl W
5800 INPS 46224 2226 B2
Russell Av
600 INPS 46225 2337 C4
Russell Dr
- FSHR 46060 1905 B2
8700 EglT 46077 1898 C6
Russell Ln
5000 WRvT 46143 2663 C5
E Russell Lake Dr
600 EglT 46077 1898 C6
W Russell Lake Dr
600 EglT 46077 1898 C6
Russet Ct
2100 WshT 46168 2441 B1
Russet Dr
6800 WshT 46168 2441 B1
Rustic Ct
6700 LWNC 46236 2124 A2
Rustic Ln
10 PltT 46184 2774 B4
Rustic Wood Ct
21000 WynT 46062 1578 C7
21000 WynT 46062 1687 C1
Rutgers Ln
10800 FSHR 46038 1903 D7
Rutgers Rd
2400 INPS 46227 2447 B6
19800 WynT 46060 1688 D3
Ruth Dr
1700 INPS 46240 2120 A1
9600 NbvT 46060 1687 A5
E Ruth Dr
1000 INPS 46240 2119 E1
1400 INPS 46240 2120 A1
Rutherford Dr
6900 INPS 46237 2557 E7
15000 WshT 46074 1792 A6
Rutherglen Wy
7600 INPS 46254 2116 C6
Rutherwood Ct
1100 ClyT 46280 2010 D2
Rutledge Ct
1100 NBVL 46062 1686 A4
Rutledge Dr
3200 INPS 46228 2227 B1
Rutledge Rd
4800 WshT 46123 2331 C1
Ryan Dr
2400 INPS 46220 2120 B5
8500 FSHR 46060 1795 C7
S Ryan St
100 LEBN 46052 1676 E6
Ryan Tr
300 BNBG 46112 2223 C2
N Rybolt Av
400 SDWY 46222 2335 E3
500 INPS 46222 2335 E2
3400 INPS 46222 2226 E3
S Rybolt Av
500 INPS 46241 2335 E5
2300 INPS 46241 2444 E2
3200 INPS 46221 2444 E4
Rydal Ct
4700 INPS 46254 2117 D7
Rylan Cir
600 WRvT 46142 2663 D4
Rymark Ct
5700 INPS 46250 2012 C3
Rymark Dr
9100 INPS 46250 2012 C3
Rympa Pl
- NWTD 46184 2774 C4
Rypma Pl
- NWTD 46184 2774 C4
Rypma Row
10 NWTD 46184 2774 C4

S

S Ct
- WRvT 46142 2663 E1
Saben Ct
13800 CRML 46032 1792 C7
Sable Dr
- INPS 46221 2553 B5
Sable Run
900 CRML 46032 1901 A1
Sable Chase
400 BNBG 46112 2114 D6
Sable Chase Cir
10 BNBG 46112 2114 D6
Sable Creek Ct
3000 GNWD 46142 2664 B2
Sable Creek Ln
700 GNWD 46142 2664 B2
Sable Ridge Cir
- GNWD 46142 2664 C2
Sable Ridge Dr
700 GNWD 46142 2664 C1

STREET
Block City ZIP Map# Grid

Sable Ridge Ln
3100 GNWD 46142 2664 B2
Sable Ridge Pl
3000 GNWD 46142 2664 B1
Sabre Ct
- NBVL 46060 1687 C4
Sabrina Cir
1400 PNFD 46168 2441 D6
Sachs Dr
6200 SDWY 46224 2226 A7
Sackett Dr
9800 LcnT 46112 2224 C2
W Sacramento Dr
7300 BCkT 46140 2233 A6
Saddle Ct
8700 INPS 46256 2013 B4
Saddleback Dr
14400 CRML 46032 1792 E7
Saddle Barn East Dr
2800 INPS 46214 2225 D5
Saddle Barn West Dr
2800 INPS 46214 2225 D5
Saddlebrook Cir
1300 INPS 46228 2119 A4
Saddlebrook Ct
200 UnnT 46077 1789 D5
1300 INPS 46228 2119 A4
Saddlebrook Dr
200 UnnT 46077 1789 D5
6000 INPS 46228 2119 B4
Saddle Hill Ct
400 WshT 46234 2333 D3
Saddlehorn Ct
14800 WTFD 46033 1793 C6
Saddlehorn Dr
2800 WTFD 46033 1793 C6
Saddle Point Dr
8300 INPS 46256 2013 E6
Saddle Ridge St
3500 INPS 46222 2336 B3
Saddlestone Dr
10400 FCkT 46040 2015 D1
10600 FCkT 46040 1906 D7
Saddletree Dr
6200 EglT 46077 1897 D6
Sadie St
800 INPS 46221 2336 B5
N Sadlier Dr
10 INPS 46219 2340 A2
3800 INPS 46226 2231 A2
4100 LWNC 46226 2231 A2
5200 LWNC 46226 2122 A6
S Sadlier Dr
3400 INPS 46239 2449 A3
Sadlier Circle East Dr
1300 INPS 46239 2340 A6
Sadlier Circle North Dr
- INPS 46239 2340 A6
Sadlier Circle South Dr
1300 INPS 46239 2340 A6
Sadlier Circle West Dr
1300 INPS 46239 2340 A6
Safari Dr
5700 INPS 46237 2557 D1
Saffron Cir
14200 CRML 46032 1792 A7
Saffron Dr
4100 INPS 46237 2556 E4
Sagamore Tr
4200 INPS 46220 2120 E6
Sagamore Woods Dr
12100 FSHR 46038 1905 C4
Sage Ct
5700 INPS 46237 2448 B7
10300 NBVL 46060 1687 B4
Sagebrush Av
5400 BHGV 46203 2448 B4
Sagemeadow Dr
- BNBG 46112 2224 A3
Sagewood Ct
4000 WRvT 46143 2663 E6
6200 INPS 46268 2117 D3
Saguaro Ct
6400 INPS 46268 2117 E3
Saguaro Tr
4200 INPS 46268 2117 E3
E Sahm St
10 INPS 46204 2337 C2
100 INPS 46202 2337 D2
W Sahm St
10 INPS 46204 2337 C2
200 INPS 46202 2337 C2
Sailing Ct
1800 INPS 46260 2118 E2
Sailors Ln
7800 INPS 46254 2116 C7
Sail Place Dr
12000 FCkT 46256 2014 E2
12000 FCkT 46256 2015 A2
St. Andrews Cir
2000 ClyT 46032 1900 D6
St. Andrews Dr
900 WshT 46123 2331 D5
4000 INPS 46221 2444 E5
St. Andrews Ln
11100 ClyT 46032 1900 D6
St. Andrews Wy
12800 FSHR 46038 1905 A3
12900 FSHR 46038 1904 E2
St. Annes Ct
10 GNWD 46143 2665 E5
St. Armands Cir
12300 CRML 46033 1903 D4
St. Charles Ct
11000 CRML 46033 1903 A7
St. Charles Pl
700 GNWD 46143 2665 A5
3100 INPS 46227 2447 C7
4900 CRML 46033 1903 A7
St. Charles Wy
200 WTLD 46184 2774 E4
300 WTLD 46184 2775 A4
St. Clair Ct
800 INPS 46214 2334 D2

St. Clair St
10 MRVL 46158 2659 E3
400 MRVL 46158 2660 A3
E St. Clair St
10 INPS 46204 2337 D2
100 INPS 46202 2337 E2
4100 INPS 46201 2338 E2
5100 INPS 46219 2339 B2
W St. Clair St
10 INPS 46204 2337 B2
200 INPS 46202 2337 B2
1500 INPS 46222 2336 D2
7300 INPS 46214 2334 D2
St. Croix Ln
7300 INPS 46214 2225 D3
St. Francis Av
300 BHGV 46107 2447 C3
St. George Blvd
7500 FSHR 46038 1904 B6
St. George Ct
7400 FSHR 46038 1904 B6
St. Helen's Wk
11800 FSHR 46038 1906 E4
St. James Blvd
1700 GNFD 46140 2236 E5
St. James Dr
6300 INPS 46217 2555 B3
N St. James Dr
- GNFD 46140 2236 E4
St. James Pl
700 NBVL 46060 1795 D4
St. Jean Dr
6300 INPS 46217 2555 A2
St. Joe Dr
6300 INPS 46217 2555 B2
St. John Cir
4600 ZNVL 46077 1898 E3
St. John Ct N
400 BHGV 46107 2447 E6
St. John Ct S
1500 BHGV 46107 2447 E6
N St. John St
100 SRDN 46069 1573 B1
S St. John St
100 SRDN 46069 1573 B1
St. Joseph St
11300 CBLD 46229 2341 D2
E St. Joseph St
10 INPS 46204 2337 C2
100 INPS 46202 2337 C2
3100 INPS 46201 2338 C2
6000 INPS 46219 2339 C2
7800 INPS 46219 2340 B2
W St. Joseph St
10 INPS 46204 2337 C1
St. Jude Dr
3100 INPS 46227 2447 C7
St. Luke Dr
500 PNFD 46168 2441 C5
St. Marcel Ln
5700 INPS 46254 2117 A5
St. Patrick Dr
- BrnT 46112 2114 D1
St. Patrick St
1000 INPS 46203 2337 E5
St. Paul St
400 INPS 46201 2338 B4
1900 INPS 46203 2338 B7
2200 INPS 46203 2447 B1
3000 INPS 46237 2447 B3
St. Peter St
400 INPS 46201 2338 B4
1100 INPS 46203 2338 B5
2200 INPS 46203 2447 B1
8700 GNWD 46227 2665 B1
8700 INPS 46227 2556 B7
8700 INPS 46227 2665 B1
St. Petersburg Wy
10800 INPS 46229 2232 B6
St. Simons Ct
3800 INPS 46237 2556 D1
St. Simons Dr
5700 INPS 46237 2556 D1
St. Thomas
- INPS 46214 2225 D2
- INPS 46254 2225 D2
St. Thomas Blvd
3500 INPS 46214 2225 D3
St. Thomas Ln
3500 INPS 46214 2225 D3
St. Vail Ct
5200 NBVL 46062 1685 B1
Saksons Blvd
12400 FSHR 46038 1904 C4
Salamone Wy
13300 CRML 46074 1900 A2
Salamonie Dr
- INPS 46203 2448 D3
Salanie Pl
6000 INPS 46254 2117 A6
Salatheal Ct
8400 FSHR 46038 1904 C6
Salazar Dr
7300 INPS 46214 2225 D7
Salem Cir
5400 CRML 46033 1794 B7
Salem Ct
18900 NBVL 46060 1686 E5
N Salem Ct
- CBLD 46140 2232 E5
Salem Dr
6400 FSHR 46038 1903 D6
N Salem Dr
1300 CBLD 46140 2232 E6
1300 CBLD 46229 2232 E6
Salem Dr E
14300 CRML 46033 1794 C7
Salem Dr N
5500 CRML 46033 1794 B7
Salem Dr S
5500 CRML 46033 1794 B7
Salem Dr W
14300 CRML 46033 1794 B7
Salem Rd
6000 EglT 46077 1898 A5

Salem Rd
7000 EglT 46077 2007 A2
7900 INPS 46077 2007 A2
Salem Sq
1800 INPS 46227 2447 A5
Salem St
3400 INPS 46208 2228 C3
Salem Creek Blvd
1200 INPS 46231 2333 E6
Salem Park Ct
2300 INPS 46239 2449 B1
Salem Park Dr
2200 INPS 46239 2340 B7
2200 INPS 46239 2449 B1
Salimonia Ln
16500 WTFD 46074 1792 D2
Salisbury Ln
1400 INPS 46227 2446 E3
6000 NBVL 46062 1794 C5
Sally Ann Cir
6000 INPS 46237 2557 C5
Sally Ann Ct
7800 INPS 46237 2557 C5
Salmon Dr
- CRML 46033 1794 D7
- CRML 46033 1903 D1
Salsbury Creek Dr
13800 CRML 46032 1901 C1
13900 CRML 46032 1792 A6
Salter Ct
5100 INPS 46250 2012 A7
Saltford Cir
12400 FCkT 46038 1905 D3
Saltford Ln
11500 FCkT 46038 1905 D3
Salt Fork Wy
8100 INPS 46256 2013 B6
N Salt Fork Wy
8100 INPS 46256 2013 B5
Salt Lake Rd
3000 INPS 46214 2225 C4
N Salt Lake Rd
3200 INPS 46214 2225 B4
Samantha Dr
- LWNC 46235 2122 E7
N Samoa Av
1400 INPS 46201 2338 A1
1600 INPS 46201 2229 A6
Samoa St
14300 FSHR 46060 1795 D7
Sampson Dr
5300 INPS 46237 2557 B2
Sam Ralston Rd
500 LEBN 46052 1676 D6
Samuel Dr
300 WTLD 46131 2774 D7
300 WTLD 46184 2774 D7
7000 INPS 46259 2557 E6
7300 INPS 46259 2558 A6
Sanatorium Av
- INPS 46222 2336 B4
San Carlos Ct
8200 INPS 46256 2013 B5
San Carlos Dr
400 WRvT 46142 2663 E2
San Clemente Dr
5700 INPS 46226 2121 D4
San Clemente Ln
5800 INPS 46226 2121 D4
Sanctuary Ct
1100 CRML 46032 1901 A3
Sand Pt
7500 INPS 46240 2011 C7
Sand St
500 INPS 46225 2337 B5
Sandalwood Dr
300 WshT 46123 2332 B1
5800 CRML 46033 1903 C3
7500 INPS 46217 2555 A5
Sandbar Dr
19200 NBVL 46062 1685 D4
Sandbria Dr
11000 LWNC 46235 2123 C6
Sand Brook Cir
200 NBVL 46062 1685 B7
Sand Brook Ct
300 NBVL 46062 1685 B6
Sand Brook Dr
200 NBVL 46062 1685 B6
Sandbury Rd
9100 INPS 46256 2013 D7
9100 INPS 46256 2122 D1
Sand Cherry Ct
13900 CRML 46033 1903 D1
Sandcherry Dr
5900 LWNC 46236 2123 A4
Sandcherry Ln
10100 LWNC 46236 2123 A4
Sand Creek Blvd
10300 FSHR 46038 1905 B5
Sand Dollar Cir
11900 FCkT 46256 2014 E2
Sand Dollar Ct
11800 FCkT 46256 2014 E2
Sanderling Trc
12300 FSHR 46038 1906 A6
Sanders Ct
100 PryT 46052 1896 D5
Sanders Dr
- FSHR 46060 1905 D1
Sanders Gln
- WTFD 46074 1793 B1
Sanders St
- INPS 46203 2338 A6
200 INPS 46225 2337 C6
500 INPS 46203 2337 D6
Sandhill Ct
2000 INPS 46217 2554 D7
Sandhill Rd
1700 INPS 46217 2554 D7
Sand Hill Crane Run
- GNWD 46143 2665 E6
- GNWD 46143 2666 A6
Sandhill Crane Run
800 GNWD 46143 2665 E6

Sandhurst Dr
5000 INPS 46217 2445 A7
Sandi Ct
8000 INPS 46260 2009 E6
Sandi Dr
1400 INPS 46260 2009 E6
San Diego Dr
4500 INPS 46241 2444 A6
San Diego Ln
6400 INPS 46241 2444 A6
Sand Key Cir
10700 INPS 46256 2014 B3
Sand Key Ln
9100 INPS 46256 2014 B4
Sandoval Ct
1700 INPS 46214 2225 D7
Sandover Ln
10000 LWNC 46236 2123 A4
Sandpebble Ct
4700 INPS 46221 2444 C6
Sand Piper Ct
8400 INPS 46256 2013 C6
Sandpiper Ct
10600 NBVL 46060 1687 B3
Sandpiper East Dr
9400 INPS 46268 2009 B2
Sandpiper North Dr
3000 INPS 46268 2009 B2
N Sandpiper North Dr
3100 INPS 46268 2009 B1
Sandpiper South Dr
3000 INPS 46268 2009 B3
Sandpiper West Dr
9400 INPS 46268 2009 B2
Sand Point Wy
8300 INPS 46240 2011 C5
Sandra Ln
300 INPS 46227 2446 C3
Sand Ridge Cir
8100 INPS 46237 2557 D6
Sandringham Cir
2200 INPS 46214 2225 C6
Sand Run Ct
7600 INPS 46259 2557 E5
Sand Shoal Ct
7800 LWNC 46236 2014 B7
Sandstone Ct
1000 CBLD 46140 2233 A6
5200 INPS 46237 2557 A3
Sandstone Dr
- GNWD 46143 2666 B5
Sandstone Run
12500 CRML 46033 1903 B4
Sandwell Ct
6300 LWNC 46236 2123 A3
Sandwood Ct
11600 LWNC 46235 2123 D6
Sandwood Dr
5200 LWNC 46235 2123 D6
Sandy Ct
5100 MdlT 46112 2113 C2
Sandy Dr
11800 EglT 46077 1899 D5
Sandy Ann Ln
1300 INPS 46220 2119 E6
Sandy Bay Dr
- GNWD 46142 2664 C3
Sandy Creek Ct
13800 CRML 46032 1792 D7
Sandy Forge Dr
5100 INPS 46221 2553 C1
Sandy Run Ct
17800 NBVL 46062 1685 A7
Sandy Spring Ln
3400 INPS 46222 2227 C3
San Fernando Dr
4500 INPS 46268 2008 D7
San Gabriel Dr
4500 INPS 46268 2008 E7
San Gabriel Wy
4500 INPS 46268 2008 E7
Sanger Dr
10000 FSHR 46038 1905 A3
Sangster Av
2500 INPS 46218 2229 A5
Sanibel Cir
17600 WTFD 46062 1684 E7
17700 WshT 46062 1684 E7
Sanitary Dr
- INPS 46221 2445 D2
San Jacinto Dr
9300 INPS 46250 2012 C3
9400 FSHR 46250 2012 C3
San Jose Dr
3000 WRvT 46143 2664 B7
San Jose St
- INPS 46241 2336 C7
San Marco Pass
9700 CRML 46280 2011 A2
San Marcos Cir
8300 INPS 46256 2013 B5
San Marcos Dr
400 WRvT 46142 2663 E3
San Miguel Cir
5900 INPS 46250 2012 C3
San Miguel Ct
5800 INPS 46250 2012 C3
San Miguel Dr
9400 INPS 46250 2012 C3
Sanner Ct
300 ClyT 46290 2010 C1
Sanner Dr
1400 GNWD 46143 2665 C6
San Paulo Cir
5700 INPS 46226 2121 E5
San Ricardo Ct
600 WRvT 46142 2663 E2
7900 INPS 46256 2013 B5
San Ricardo Dr
400 WRvT 46142 2663 E2
Santa Ana Dr
900 WRvT 46143 2664 B7
Santa Ana Ln
6500 INPS 46214 2226 A7

Santa Anita Ct
10800 ClyT 46280 1901 E7
Santa Barbara Dr
7600 INPS 46268 2008 E7
Santa Clara Dr
3900 WRvT 46142 2664 A2
Santa Cruz Dr
4600 INPS 46268 2008 E7
Santa Fe Ct
4200 INPS 46241 2444 D4
Santa Fe Dr
4500 INPS 46241 2444 D4
Santa Maria Dr
900 WRvT 46143 2664 B7
Santa Monica Dr
7500 INPS 46268 2008 E7
Santana Cir
7800 INPS 46278 2007 C4
Santana Ln
8700 INPS 46278 2007 C4
Santaro Ct
2500 INPS 46217 2554 C4
Sante Fe Cir
500 WshT 46123 2331 E5
Santiago Dr
900 WRvT 46143 2664 B7
Santolina Dr
7500 INPS 46237 2556 E5
7800 INPS 46237 2557 A5
San Vincente Blvd
13100 DelT 46038 1904 C2
13100 FSHR 46038 1904 C2
Sanwela Dr
1600 INPS 46260 2118 E3
Sapelo Dr
5800 INPS 46237 2556 D1
Sapling Cir
11900 NBVL 46060 1796 E5
W Sapphire Blvd
3000 INPS 46268 2009 B7
Sapphire Dr
400 WshT 46032 1792 D6
5600 CRML 46033 1903 B2
Sapphire Berry Ln
9900 FSHR 46060 1796 A6
Sara Ct
10 WTLD 46131 2774 E7
6700 PNFD 46168 2550 B1
8000 INPS 46217 2555 B6
10800 FSHR 46038 1904 D7
Sarah Ct
- GNWD 46142 2664 E4
Sarah Ln
100 MdnT 46158 2661 B7
Saraina Ln
600 NWTD 46184 2774 C5
Sarasota Ct
8500 INPS 46219 2231 C7
Saratoga Cir
1000 ClyT 46280 1901 E7
Saratoga Dr
9000 INPS 46235 2231 D1
S Saratoga Dr
500 BNBG 46112 2223 B1
Saratoga Pkwy
- PNFD 46168 2440 D4
Saratoga Pl
5700 PNFD 46168 2440 E4
Sarazen Cir
1400 INPS 46239 2341 C6
Sarazen Ln
11000 INPS 46239 2341 C6
Sardonyx St
- INPS 46268 2009 B7
Sargent Ln
8500 INPS 46256 2013 C6
N Sargent Rd
6600 INPS 46256 2122 B2
7500 INPS 46256 2013 D5
8800 FSHR 46256 2013 D5
Sargent Rdg
8000 INPS 46256 2013 C6
Sargent Creek Ct
8800 INPS 46256 2013 D4
Sargent Creek Dr
8900 INPS 46256 2013 D4
Sargent Creek Ln
8600 INPS 46256 2013 D4
Sargent Manor Ct
9100 INPS 46256 2013 D4
Sarto Dr
7100 INPS 46240 2120 C1
Sarton Ln
5600 INPS 46221 2553 B3
Sassafern Dr
13900 CRML 46033 1903 E1
Sassafras Cir
300 NBVL 46062 1685 D3
Sassafras Ct
8900 INPS 46260 2009 E4
Sassafras Dr
200 DNVL 46122 2330 B3
Sassafras Tr
- GNWD 46143 2666 A6
Saturn Dr
2400 INPS 46229 2231 D6
E Saturn St
11600 CBLD 46229 2341 D2
Saulcy St
1400 INPS 46222 2336 E3
Sault Sainte Marie Dr
7800 INPS 46227 2555 C5
Saunders Field Dr
2000 WshT 46123 2441 B1
2000 WshT 46168 2441 B1
Sauterne Ct
7400 INPS 46278 2007 E7
Sauterne Dr
6700 INPS 46278 2007 E7
Savannah Dr
300 GNWD 46142 2664 E4
7500 INPS 46217 2555 A5
Savannah Ln
400 WTFD 46074 1684 B7

Saville Rd
8700 NBVL 46060 1795 D6
8700 NbvT 46060 1795 D6
Saville Row Rd
600 GNWD 46142 2665 A3
Savin Dr
6100 INPS 46254 2117 B4
Sawgrass Ct
100 LEBN 46052 1677 A2
9700 ClyT 46032 2009 B2
Sawgrass Dr
8300 INPS 46234 2225 B4
10700 FSHR 46038 1905 C7
Sawgrass Ln
- GNWD 46143 2666 A6
Sawleaf Rd
8700 INPS 46260 2009 E4
Saw Mill Ct
- SCkT 46163 2452 B2
Sawmill Ct
8900 INPS 46236 2014 D4
Saw Mill Dr
6000 NBVL 46062 1685 C5
Sawmill Rd
- MdnT 46158 2660 C6
- PltT 46184 2774 D6
- WTLD 46184 2774 D6
Sawyer Av
4300 INPS 46226 2230 C1
Sawyer St
4000 INPS 46226 2230 C2
E Saxon St
11800 CBLD 46229 2341 E2
Saxony Blvd
12900 FSHR 46060 1906 C2
Saybrook Ct
11100 FCkT 46038 1905 C6
11100 FSHR 46038 1905 C6
Saybrooke Ct
5900 INPS 46237 2557 D1
Saylor Ct
1300 ZNVL 46077 1899 A6
Saylor Dr
1300 ZNVL 46077 1899 A5
1500 ZNVL 46077 1898 E6
Sayre Ct
500 GNWD 46143 2665 E2
Sayre Dr
10 GNWD 46143 2665 D1
900 GNWD 46143 2666 A2
Scarborough Cir
100 NBVL 46062 1685 D2
Scarborough Ct
8000 INPS 46256 2122 B1
Scarborough Ln
- CRML 46033 1794 C6
- NBVL 46033 1794 C6
1100 GNWD 46142 2665 A1
2400 CRML 46032 1900 C5
14600 NBVL 46062 1794 C6
Scarborough Ln N
14700 NBVL 46062 1794 D6
Scarborough Wy
300 NBVL 46060 1795 D4
Scarborough Boulevard East Dr
7300 INPS 46256 2013 C7
7300 INPS 46256 2122 B1
Scarborough Boulevard South Dr
7700 INPS 46256 2122 B1
Scarlet Ct
3400 INPS 46224 2226 B3
Scarlet Dr
5500 INPS 46224 2226 B3
Scarlet Ter
5500 INPS 46224 2226 B3
Scarlet Oak Ct
3400 INPS 46222 2227 B6
7100 NBVL 46062 1685 E5
Scarlet Oak Dr
2100 WshT 46123 2441 A1
Scarlet Oak Ln
1000 MRVL 46158 2660 A5
Scarsdale Ct
8300 INPS 46256 2013 C5
Scarsdale Dr E
8400 INPS 46256 2013 C5
Scarsdale Dr W
8300 INPS 46256 2013 C5
Scatterwood Ct
5300 INPS 46221 2553 D2
Scatterwoods Ln
7500 INPS 46239 2340 A7
Scearce Av
100 DNVL 46122 2329 C4
Scenic Ct
6400 INPS 46260 2118 E2
Scenic Dr
7900 INPS 46260 2010 B6
Scenic View Dr
8400 FSHR 46038 1904 C7
Schaefer Dr
- CRML 46032 1901 B1
Schaefer Ln
3700 INPS 46235 2231 E3
Schaff St
100 BHGV 46107 2448 A3
Scheel Ln
11500 CRML 46032 1901 E6
Schieling Ct
6000 CRML 46033 1903 C5
Schiller St
10 INPS 46225 2337 C7
Schilling Pl
3900 INPS 46221 2444 E5
Schleicher Av
1000 INPS 46229 2340 E1
Schmitt Cir
1700 INPS 46239 2341 D5
Schmitt Ct
11700 INPS 46239 2341 D4
Schmitt Ln
- INPS 46239 2341 E5

Schmitt Rd
500 INPS 46239 2341 E5
Schmus Ct
6400 INPS 46268 2117 C3
Schoen Ct
800 CRML 46032 1901 E3
Schoen Dr
8100 LWNC 46226 2122 B7
Schofield Av
3200 INPS 46218 2229 A3
School Dr
- GNWD 46143 2665 B5
5700 SDWY 46224 2226 B5
School Ln
- INPS 46241 2335 A5
School Pkwy
10400 ClyT 46280 1902 A7
10400 ClyT 46280 2011 A1
School Rd
- LWNC 46216 2122 E4
300 AVON 46123 2332 B4
N School St
- NPLN 46163 2452 B3
10 GNFD 46140 2345 D1
700 GNFD 46140 2236 D7
11400 FSHR 46038 1904 D6
S School St
- NPLN 46163 2452 A3
- SCkT 46163 2452 A3
10 BNBG 46112 2114 C7
500 BNBG 46112 2223 C1
Schooley Dr
400 GNWD 46142 2664 D4
Schoolhouse Rd
- FCkT 46038 1905 C4
- FSHR 46038 1905 C4
Schoolmaster Dr
2700 PNFD 46168 2441 C2
Schoolwood Dr
5800 SDWY 46224 2226 A5
Schooner Cir
- MCVL 46055 2015 C4
Schooner Ct
10500 INPS 46256 2014 B4
Schooner Wy
3000 CCRO 46034 1577 B6
Schrier Dr
9700 WshT 46123 2333 B4
Schubert Pl
18900 NBVL 46060 1686 E5
Schulley Rd
21000 NBVL 46062 1576 E7
21000 NBVL 46062 1685 E1
21000 NbvT 46062 1576 E7
21000 NbvT 46062 1685 E1
21100 JknT 46034 1576 E7
21100 JknT 46062 1576 E7
Schultz Ct
10 MdnT 46113 2661 B4
W Schultz St
- NPLN 46163 2452 A3
Schwier Ct
1800 INPS 46229 2232 A7
Schwier Dr
1800 INPS 46229 2232 A7
Scicor Dr
8200 INPS 46214 2334 B3
N Scioto St
- INPS 46202 2228 C7
- INPS 46202 2337 C1
900 INPS 46204 2337 C1
S Scioto St
- INPS 46204 2337 C4
- INPS 46225 2337 C4
Scmahorn Dr
10 PTBR 46167 2112 E3
Scotch Pine Ct
9700 FSHR 46038 1905 A7
Scotch Pine Dr
- GNWD 46184 2774 B1
Scotch Pine Ln
9700 INPS 46256 2014 A4
Scoter Ct
8900 INPS 46234 2225 A5
Scotia Ct
6800 INPS 46254 2225 E1
Scotland Blvd
- INPS 46231 2334 A6
Scotland Dr
- INPS 46231 2334 A6
Scotland St
- LcnT 46112 2115 D6
Scots Tr
- CtrT 46140 2237 A5
- GNFD 46140 2237 A5
Scott Ct
9800 INPS 46235 2232 A2
Scott Dr
13700 CRML 46032 1792 E7
13700 CRML 46032 1901 E1
N Scott Dr
600 WRvT 46142 2663 C2
W Scott Dr
600 WRvT 46142 2663 C2
Scott Rd
7300 INPS 46241 2443 D6
Scott St
- PTBR 46167 2112 E3
Scott Ian Ct
5800 INPS 46254 2117 B4
Scottish Bnd
12400 CRML 46033 1903 C4
Scottsdale Dr
2400 CRML 46033 1793 B7
2900 INPS 46234 2225 B4
Scout Rd
700 LWNC 46216 2122 C5
Scranton Ct
100 ZNVL 46077 1898 E4
Screech Owl Cir
3700 INPS 46228 2118 A4
Seabiscuit Dr
11300 NBVL 46060 1796 D5
Seabreeze Cir
300 AVON 46123 2332 E3

STREET
Block City ZIP Map# Grid

Seabreeze Cir
9000 INPS 46256 2014 A3
Seabreeze Ct
9000 INPS 46256 2014 A4
Seabreeze Dr
- WshT 46123 2332 E2
Seabreeze Wy
10100 INPS 46256 2014 A4
Seabridge Wy
8300 INPS 46240 2011 C5
Seabrook Dr
8000 INPS 46237 2557 B5
Seabrook Ln
5900 INPS 46237 2557 C6
Seabury Ct
11100 FSHR 46038 1904 A6
Seacrest Wy
- NBVL 46062 1686 B3
- NbvT 46062 1686 B3
Seacrest Wy N
7500 NBVL 46062 1686 A3
Seacrest Wy S
7500 NBVL 46062 1686 A3
Sea Eagle Ct
7000 INPS 46254 2116 D7
Seafan Ct
11500 INPS 46236 2014 D5
Seagrave Dr
10100 FSHR 46038 1905 B5
Seagull Wy
1000 CCRO 46034 1577 B6
Seahawks Ln
12000 FCkT 46038 1905 E3
Sea Kerd Ct
- WshT 46234 2224 E6
Sealord Ct
10600 LWNC 46236 2014 B7
Sealy Rd
3200 INPS 46241 2444 D3
Sea Oats Dr
9100 INPS 46250 2012 E3
Sea Oats Ln
7000 INPS 46250 2012 E3
Sea Pine Dr
7000 INPS 46250 2012 E3
7100 INPS 46250 2013 A3
Sea Pine Ln
9200 INPS 46250 2013 A3
Seaport Dr
1000 CCRO 46034 1577 B6
1900 INPS 46240 2011 B6
Searay Dr
- NBVL 46060 1687 D4
12000 LWNC 46236 2014 E5
Sears Rd
10 DNVL 46122 2330 C4
1500 CtrT 46122 2221 C7
1500 CtrT 46122 2330 C1
1500 MdlT 46122 2221 C7
Sears St
1100 INPS 46239 2340 A5
Seascape Ct
10700 INPS 46256 2014 B3
Seascape Dr
9200 INPS 46256 2014 C3
Seaside Dr
- CRML 46280 2011 A2
Seasons Bnd
13600 CRML 46032 1902 A1
Seasons Dr
- GNWD 46143 2666 D5
Sea Star Cir
11700 FCkT 46038 2014 D1
Sea Star Ct
9900 FCkT 46038 2014 E1
Sea Star Dr
11700 FCkT 46256 2014 E2
Sea Star Wy
10000 FCkT 46038 2014 D1
11600 FSHR 46038 2014 D1
Seattle Av
6400 INPS 46241 2443 E6
6400 INPS 46241 2444 A6
Seattle Slew Ct
8400 INPS 46217 2554 E6
11400 NBVL 46060 1796 D5
Seattle Slew Dr
- WshT 46234 2224 E6
11300 NBVL 46060 1796 D5
Seattle Slew Ln
8400 INPS 46217 2554 E7
Seaview Ln
10700 LWNC 46236 2014 B7
Seaward Ct
8600 INPS 46256 2014 B5
Seaward Ln
8600 INPS 46256 2014 B5
Seaway Cir
12300 INPS 46236 2015 A4
Seaway Dr
- FCkT 46038 1906 C5
3400 INPS 46214 2225 C3
Seawood Ct
8000 INPS 46268 2008 E6
Sebring Ct
5800 INPS 46254 2117 D4
Sebring Dr
5700 INPS 46254 2117 D5
Secretarial Dr
- WshT 46234 2224 E6
Secretariat Ct
14100 CRML 46074 1791 D7
Secretariat Dr
- WshT 46234 2224 E6
1300 LEBN 46052 1676 D4
Secretariat Ln
1300 INPS 46217 2554 E6
Section St
1100 PNFD 46168 2441 D5
Sedge Ct
4200 ZNVL 46077 1898 D2
Sedgegrass Cross
5800 CRML 46033 1903 D1
Sedgegrass Dr
10500 LWNC 46235 2123 B5
Sedgehill Dr
10200 INPS 46239 2341 A5
Sedgehill Ln
1100 INPS 46239 2341 B5
Sedgemoor Cir
- ClyT 46032 1900 A7
Sedgewick Wy
7300 INPS 46256 2122 A1
Sedgwick Ln
15200 CRML 46074 1900 B2
Sedlak Ct
1500 INPS 46229 2232 C7
1500 INPS 46229 2341 C1
E Sedlak Ln
11000 INPS 46229 2341 C1
Sedona Ct
14000 CRML 46032 1792 C7
Sedona Dr
1300 CRML 46032 1792 C7
Sedona Pass
1000 CRML 46280 2011 A2
Sedona Ridge Ln
8500 INPS 46239 2449 C4
Sedwick Ct
200 NBVL 46062 1685 C1
Seekonk Ct
8400 INPS 46256 2013 E5
Seerley Rd
5300 INPS 46241 2444 C3
Seerley Creek Rd
5000 INPS 46241 2444 C3
Segundo Pl
11400 FCkT 46040 1907 A5
S Seifert Ct
4100 NPLN 46163 2452 B2
Seine Ct
3400 INPS 46226 2231 D3
Selago Dr
6200 INPS 46203 2448 D3
Selby Ct
6000 NBVL 46062 1576 C7
Selkirk Ct
9200 INPS 46260 2010 A3
Selkirk Ln
1000 INPS 46260 2010 A3
Sellers St
4300 INPS 46226 2231 A1
4300 LWNC 46226 2231 A1
Sellerton Dr
11900 FSHR 46038 1905 E4
Seminole Dr
3500 ClyT 46032 2009 B2
10300 WshT 46234 2224 D6
E Seminole Dr
6200 INPS 46259 2559 C2
Seminole Rd
16100 NbvT 46062 1794 D3
Senate Av
- INPS 46217 2555 B1
N Senate Av
10 INPS 46204 2337 C3
100 INPS 46202 2337 C3
1600 INPS 46202 2228 C7
S Senate Av
10 INPS 46204 2337 B3
1200 INPS 46225 2337 B6
4600 INPS 46217 2446 B6
Senate Blvd
1600 INPS 46202 2228 B7
E Senator Wy
10 WshT 46032 1792 D5
W Senator Wy
10 WshT 46032 1792 C5
Senators Dr
6800 INPS 46217 2554 C3
Senators Wy
2500 INPS 46217 2554 C3
Seneca Cir
1500 WshT 46074 1792 A5
Seneca Dr
5200 INPS 46220 2120 E6
10200 WshT 46234 2224 C6
Seneff Ct
800 PNFD 46168 2441 C5
Senie Ln
11500 CRML 46032 1901 E5
11500 CRML 46032 1902 A6
S Senour Rd
2300 INPS 46239 2341 B7
2300 INPS 46239 2450 B1
5600 INPS 46239 2559 B1
Sentiment Ln
- GNWD 46143 2666 D5
Sentinel Tr
7600 INPS 46250 2012 A7
Sequoia Ct
4300 WRvT 46143 2663 E5
8000 INPS 46240 2011 B6
Sequoia Ln
2100 INPS 46240 2011 B5
Sequoia Tr
1000 AVON 46123 2332 D6
Sequoia Stone Ct
12600 FSHR 46038 1906 A6
Serenity Ct
4000 WRvT 46142 2664 B3
Serenity Ln
11700 INPS 46229 2232 D7
N Serenity Wy
200 WRvT 46142 2664 B3
S Serenity Wy
10 WRvT 46142 2664 B4
Sergi Canyon Ct
7900 INPS 46217 2554 C5
Sergi Canyon Dr
7500 INPS 46217 2554 C5
Serpent Cir
8900 INPS 46236 2014 D4
Serpentine Rd
- INPS 46226 2121 C5
Sester St
1200 NBVL 46060 1795 D2
Setters Rd
14600 WTFD 46033 1793 E5
14800 WshT 46033 1793 E5
Settlement Dr N
6500 INPS 46250 2012 D2
Settlement Dr S
6500 INPS 46250 2012 E3
Settlement Dr W
9400 INPS 46250 2012 D3
Settlers Ct
11100 FSHR 46038 1904 C7
Settlers Ridge Tr
13900 CRML 46033 1903 D1
Seumin St
10 BNBG 46112 2114 B6
Seven Oaks Dr
- FSHR 46060 1905 D1
Seven Oaks Dr E
7100 LWNC 46236 2123 E1
Seven Oaks Dr N
11800 LWNC 46236 2123 E1
Severn Ct
1200 GNWD 46142 2664 D3
Severn Dr
10 GNWD 46142 2664 E3
Severn Wy
13100 FCkT 46060 1905 A2
Seville Ct
4900 INPS 46228 2118 C7
Seville Dr
4800 INPS 46228 2118 C7
Seville Rd
11600 FSHR 46038 1905 E5
Sextant Ct
10300 FSHR 46038 1905 B6
Sextant Dr
6700 INPS 46260 2118 D2
Sextant Wy
1900 INPS 46260 2118 D2
Sexton St
6000 INPS 46219 2230 C5
N Shadeland Av
- INPS - 2339 E2
- INPS 46226 2121 E1
- INPS 46226 2230 E1
500 INPS 46219 2339 E2
1600 INPS 46219 2230 E5
3900 LWNC 46226 2230 E2
4500 LWNC 46226 2121 E7
6200 INPS 46220 2121 E1
6200 INPS 46256 2121 E1
7100 INPS 46250 2121 E1
7500 INPS 46250 2012 E6
7500 INPS 46256 2012 E6
Shadeland Av N
- INPS - 2339 E5
- INPS - 2340 A6
6200 INPS - 2448 E1
Shadeland Av S
- INPS - 2339 E5
- INPS - 2340 A7
Shadeland Dr
10 BwnT 46140 2345 D5
10 GNFD 46140 2345 D5
Shadeland Sta
7100 INPS 46256 2122 A1
7300 INPS 46256 2121 E1
Shadeland Wy
- LWNC 46226 2122 A6
5000 LWNC 46226 2121 E6
Shadeland Station Wy
7100 INPS 46256 2013 A7
7100 INPS 46256 2122 A1
Shades Ct
300 CRML 46032 1901 C2
Shade Tree Ct
100 GNFD 46140 2345 E2
Shadoan Wy
17100 WshT 46074 1793 D1
Shadow Cir
8200 INPS 46260 2009 E5
Shadow Ct
1400 ZNVL 46077 1898 E7
Shadow Dr
8100 INPS 46260 2009 E5
9800 LcnT 46112 2224 C3
Shadow Rd
300 WRvT 46142 2664 A3
Shadow Brook Ct
6800 INPS 46214 2225 E4
Shadow Brook Dr
3100 INPS 46214 2225 E4
3100 INPS 46214 2226 D5
Shadowbrook Dr
- PNFD 46168 2442 A2
- WshT 46168 2442 A2
Shadow Cove Wy
12400 CRML 46033 1903 C4
W Shadow Creek Wy
7700 BCkT 46140 2232 E3
Shadowcrest Ct
500 NBVL 46060 1795 E4
Shadow Hill Ct
3900 WRvT 46142 2664 A3
Shadow Hill Dr
300 WRvT 46142 2664 A3
Shadow Hill Ln
3900 WRvT 46142 2664 A3
Shadow Lake Dr
2800 INPS 46217 2554 B4
W Shadow Lakes Dr
14600 WTFD 46032 1793 A6
Shadow Lakes Dr E
14600 WTFD 46032 1793 A6
Shadow Lakes Dr N
1300 WTFD 46032 1793 A6
Shadowlawn Dr
100 FSHR 46038 1903 E6
100 FSHR 46038 1904 C7
Shadow Lawn St
1000 INPS 46260 2010 A5
Shadow Pointe Dr
4700 INPS 46254 2118 A7
Shadow Pointe Ln
3900 INPS 46254 2118 A7
Shadow Ridge Ln
8600 INPS 46239 2449 C4
Shadow Ridge Rd
1000 CRML 46280 2011 A2
Shadowridge Run
1900 WshT 46123 2332 B7
1900 WshT 46123 2441 A2
Shadow Rock Cir
4900 CRML 46033 1903 A5
Shadowview Cir
200 MRVL 46158 2660 B4
Shadowview Wy
1000 INPS 46241 2335 B5
Shadow Wood Ct
5300 INPS 46254 2116 D6
Shadowwood Ct
11600 CRML 46077 1900 A5
Shadow Wood Dr
7300 INPS 46254 2116 D6
Shadwell Ct
8200 INPS 46237 2557 B6
Shady Ct
8200 INPS 46217 2555 B6
Shady Ln
10 CRML 46032 1902 A3
400 WRvT 46142 2664 B2
3500 PNFD 46168 2442 A3
4200 INPS 46226 2230 B1
4400 INPS 46226 2121 B7
Shady Pl
- GNWD 46142 2664 D2
Shady Ter
1100 INPS 46241 2335 B5
Shady Acres Pk
100 MrlT 46126 2669 C3
Shadybend Ct
9300 INPS 46256 2122 D1
Shady Brook Hts
10 WRvT 46142 2663 E1
Shady Creek Ct
600 GNWD 46142 2664 E2
Shady Creek Dr
500 GNWD 46142 2664 E2
S Shady Creek Dr
1000 SCkT 46140 2343 D3
W Shady Creek Dr
1200 GNWD 46142 2664 E2
Shady Grove Ct
3100 INPS 46222 2227 B3
Shady Hills Dr
7600 INPS 46278 2007 C7
Shady Hills Dr E
7600 INPS 46278 2007 C7
Shady Hills Dr W
7600 INPS 46278 2007 C7
Shady Hollow Ln
11300 INPS 46229 2232 D7
Shady Maple Wy
3200 INPS 46227 2556 C5
3200 SPRT 46227 2556 C5
Shady Meadow Pl
11600 FSHR 46038 1905 D5
Shady Nook Rd
17500 WTFD 46062 1684 E6
17800 WshT 46062 1684 E6
Shady Oak Dr
2800 INPS 46229 2232 A5
4100 INPS 46235 2232 A2
Shady Tree Ln
8900 INPS 46256 2013 C3
Shady View Ct
4300 INPS 46226 2230 E1
Shady View Dr
4300 INPS 46226 2230 E1
Shady Woods Dr
7700 INPS 46259 2558 B4
Shaelynn Ct
17600 WTFD 46074 1684 C7
Shafer Cir
3700 CRML 46033 1902 D7
3700 CRML 46033 2011 E1
Shafer Ct
3700 CRML 46033 2011 E1
Shafter Rd
- LWNC 46256 2122 A3
600 LWNC 46216 2122 C4
800 LWNC 46226 2122 A3
Shaftesbury Rd
2100 CRML 46032 1900 D4
Shagbark Ct
7700 BrnT 46112 2114 B2
Shagbark Rd
8700 INPS 46260 2009 D4
Shag Bark Tr
11100 CRML 46032 1901 D6
Shag Oak Dr
7200 NBVL 46062 1686 A6
Shahan Ct
9800 INPS 46256 2014 A4
Shakamac Dr
13400 CRML 46032 1901 C2
Shaker Ln
2300 LEBN 46052 1676 E3
Shakerwood Dr
6300 INPS 46241 2552 A3
Shakespeare Dr
500 AVON 46123 2332 A3
500 WshT 46123 2332 A3
2500 SPRT 46227 2556 B5
Shale Ln
12700 LWNC 46236 2124 A1
Shalimar Ct
6700 INPS 46214 2334 E2
Shallow Brook Ct
- CRML 46074 1900 C1
Shallowbrook Ct
10200 INPS 46229 2341 A1
Shamel Dr
6300 INPS 46278 2008 A4
Shamrock Blvd
10 WTFD 46074 1684 A7
Shamrock Dr
7200 INPS 46217 2555 A4
Shamus Dr
5200 LWNC 46235 2123 D6
S Shan Crest Hl
2100 INPS 46239 2340 D7
Shandon Ln
12900 FSHR 46038 1905 A3
Shane Dr
- INPS 46259 2558 E4
Shanghai Rd
6200 INPS 46278 2116 E3
N Shanghai Rd
- INPS 46278 2116 E2
Shank Ln
- INPS 46214 2225 D6
Shanna Cir
7300 LWNC 46236 2124 A1
Shannon Av
1000 INPS 46201 2338 E1
1500 INPS 46201 2229 D7
1500 INPS 46218 2229 D7
Shannon Ct
600 NBVL 46062 1685 D1
Shannon Rd
10 ZNVL 46077 1898 E7
Shannon Lakes Dr
1500 INPS 46217 2554 D5
Shannon Lakes Ln
1300 INPS 46217 2554 E5
Shannon Lakes Wy
7500 INPS 46217 2554 E5
Shannon Pointe Rd
11700 INPS 46229 2341 E1
Shannonway Wy
6800 INPS 46241 2334 D7
Sharer Dr
1500 PNFD 46168 2550 D1
Sharon Av
1000 INPS 46222 2336 C1
3000 INPS 46222 2227 C4
Sharon Ct
10 MRVL 46158 2659 E1
700 PNFD 46168 2441 A5
Sharon Dr
900 WshT 46123 2223 D7
W Sharon Dr
3000 BCkT 46140 2343 E1
Sharon Ln
4300 INPS 46226 2229 E1
N Sharon Rd
5700 INPS 46228 2119 A5
Sharrob Rd
6300 INPS 46241 2444 A6
Sharsted Ct
9900 LWNC 46236 2123 A3
Sharzad Pl
7400 INPS 46227 2556 A4
Shasta Dr
7500 INPS 46217 2554 B5
9500 FSHR 46038 1904 E1
9500 FSHR 46038 1905 A1
Shattuck Dr
8200 AVON 46123 2332 E3
8400 WshT 46123 2332 E3
Shaw Av
2400 SDWY 46224 2226 D6
Shaw Dr
- SDWY 46222 2226 E6
Shaw St
100 PNFD 46168 2441 C5
Shawnee Rd
1300 INPS 46260 2118 E2
1300 INPS 46260 2119 A2
Shawnee Trail North Dr
6100 INPS 46220 2121 A4
Shawnee Trail South Dr
5500 INPS 46220 2121 B4
Shea Ct
900 CRML 46032 1901 E3
Shearer Rd
7900 INPS 46219 2231 B6
Sheehan Pl
4600 INPS 46254 2117 A7
Sheek Rd
10 GNWD 46143 2666 A4
1300 PltT 46143 2666 A7
Sheets Rd
6000 EglT 46077 1898 D6
6300 ZNVL 46077 1898 D6
N Sheffield Av
10 INPS 46222 2336 D3
S Sheffield Av
700 INPS 46221 2336 D5
Sheffield Blvd
12800 CRML 46032 1901 C3
Sheffield Ct
400 CRML 46032 1901 B3
1100 GNWD 46143 2664 E5
4800 WshT 46123 2332 C2
10300 INPS 46229 2232 B5
10700 FSHR 46038 1904 A7
Sheffield Dr
- WshT 46123 2332 B1
700 GNWD 46143 2664 E5
N Sheffield Dr
2500 INPS 46229 2232 B5
Sheffield Rd
1500 WshT 46123 2223 C7
1500 WshT 46123 2332 B1
Shefford Ct
5200 INPS 46254 2117 E6
Sheila Dr
7500 BrnT 46112 2114 D2
9300 LWNC 46235 2122 D6
9300 LWNC 46236 2122 D6
Shelborne Ct
3600 ClyT 46032 1900 A7
Shelborne Rd
9600 ClyT 46032 2009 A2
9600 INPS 46032 2009 A2
11400 ClyT 46077 1900 A7
11600 ClyT 46032 1900 B5
11600 CRML 46032 1900 B5
11600 CRML 46077 1900 B5
13100 CRML 46074 1900 B1
13900 CRML 46074 1791 B7
14600 WshT 46074 1791 B5
Shelburne Dr
2100 INPS 46260 2118 D2
Shelburne Wy
- ZNVL 46077 1898 D2
Shelby Ct
6600 HMCT 46227 2555 E3
Shelby St
10 INPS 46202 2337 E3
S Shelby St
100 INPS 46202 2337 E4
300 INPS 46203 2337 E5
2200 INPS 46203 2446 E1
3000 INPS 46227 2446 E5
5500 INPS 46227 2555 E1
6500 HMCT 46227 2555 E3
E Shelbyville Rd
4100 INPS 46237 2447 E7
4500 INPS 46237 2448 A7
5200 INPS 46237 2557 B1
6800 INPS 46259 2557 D3
8500 ClkT 46259 2558 C7
8500 INPS 46259 2558 C7
Sheldon St
- INPS 46201 2229 A7
1400 INPS 46201 2338 A2
1600 INPS 46218 2229 A7
Shellbark Dr
3000 INPS 46235 2232 C4
15400 NBVL 46062 1794 C4
Shelley Ct
6800 INPS 46219 2339 E2
Shelley St
6600 INPS 46219 2339 D2
Shelly Wy
6100 INPS 46237 2557 C2
Shelton
- GNFD 46140 2345 E4
Shelton Dr
- WshT 46123 2333 B4
10 AVON 46123 2333 C4
Shelton Pl
200 NWTD 46184 2774 D4
Shenandoah Ct
9200 INPS 46229 2231 E7
E Shenandoah Dr
9000 INPS 46229 2231 D7
Shenandoah Pl
1900 INPS 46229 2231 E7
Shepard St
800 INPS 46221 2336 D5
Shepherd Ct
200 GNFD 46140 2345 E4
Shepherds Wy
12700 FSHR 46060 1906 D3
W Sherbern Dr
13100 CRML 46032 1900 E2
13100 CRML 46032 1901 A2
Sherborne Rd
10600 FSHR 46038 1904 A7
Sherbrook St
2000 INPS 46218 2229 A7
Sherburne Cir
3300 INPS 46222 2227 B3
Sherburne Ct
3300 INPS 46222 2227 B3
Sherburne Ln
3300 INPS 46222 2227 A3
Sheri Cir
1500 PNFD 46168 2441 D6
N Sheridan Av
1000 INPS 46219 2339 C1
2400 INPS 46219 2230 D5
4300 INPS 46226 2230 D1
S Sheridan Av
10 INPS 46219 2339 C3
600 SRDN 46069 1573 B2
900 AdmT 46069 1573 B2
2200 INPS 46203 2339 C7
2200 INPS 46203 2448 C1
Sheridan Ct
2500 CCRO 46034 1577 B5
Sheridan Rd
100 NBVL 46060 1686 B6
100 NBVL 46062 1686 B6
1400 NBVL 46062 1686 B6
1400 NbvT 46062 1686 B6
1900 NbvT 46062 1685 C4
3200 WshT 46062 1685 A3
4400 WshT 46062 1684 E2
4400 WshT 46074 1684 E2
4400 WTFD 46074 1684 E2
Sheridan Rd SR-38
100 NBVL 46060 1686 B6
100 NBVL 46062 1686 B6
1400 NBVL 46062 1685 C4
1400 NbvT 46062 1686 B6
1900 NbvT 46062 1685 C4
3200 WshT 46062 1685 A3
4400 WshT 46062 1684 E2
4400 WshT 46074 1684 E2
4400 WTFD 46074 1684 E2
Sherlock Dr
3900 INPS 46254 2226 B2
Sherman Av
5700 INPS 46220 2120 D5
N Sherman Av
100 SRDN 46069 1573 A1
200 AdmT 46069 1573 A1
N Sherman Av SR-38
100 SRDN 46069 1573 A1
200 AdmT 46069 1573 A1
S Sherman Av
10 SRDN 46069 1573 A1
S Sherman Av SR-38
10 SRDN 46069 1573 A1
Sherman Ct
1300 CCRO 46034 1577 B5
3800 INPS 46220 2120 D2
Sherman Dr
- INPS 46143 2665 D1
- PltT 46143 2665 D1
10 BHGV 46107 2447 D4
10 CRML 46032 1902 A3
200 INPS 46107 2447 D4
1100 GNWD 46143 2665 D1
3400 INPS 46237 2447 D4
N Sherman Dr
1500 INPS 46201 2229 D7
1500 INPS 46201 2338 D1
2100 INPS 46218 2229 D7
3800 INPS 46205 2229 D1
3800 INPS 46226 2229 D1
4500 INPS 46205 2120 D7
4500 INPS 46226 2120 D7
5800 INPS 46220 2120 D4
7600 INPS 46240 2011 D7
S Sherman Dr
- BHGV 46107 2447 D1
10 INPS 46201 2338 D6
500 INPS 46203 2338 D6
2200 INPS 46203 2447 D1
2400 BHGV 46203 2447 D1
4000 INPS 46237 2447 D5
6300 INPS 46227 2556 D2
7000 INPS 46237 2556 D4
Sherman Towne Dr
3800 INPS 46237 2447 D6
Sheroak Ct
8100 INPS 46227 2556 C6
Sherri Ln
1000 LEBN 46052 1677 B3
Sherry Ct
10 WshT 46032 1792 E5
Sherry Ln
10 BrnT 46112 2114 C2
100 INPS 46227 2555 C5
6100 INPS 46241 2335 A5
Sherwood Ct
10 GNFD 46140 2237 A6
200 ZNVL 46077 1898 E3
1000 GNWD 46142 2665 A1
5000 LcnT 46167 2113 C5
5000 MdlT 46167 2113 C5
5200 CRML 46033 1903 A6
Sherwood Dr
300 MRVL 46158 2659 D2
1100 DNVL 46122 2330 A3
1200 GNFD 46140 2236 E6
1200 GNFD 46140 2237 A6
E Sherwood Dr
700 INPS 46240 2119 E1
Sherwood Ln
9100 INPS 46240 2011 A3
Sheryl Av
10 MdnT 46113 2661 C4
Shetland Ct
700 WshT 46074 1792 B6
8900 INPS 46278 2007 A4
Shetland Ln
8600 INPS 46278 2007 A4
Shibler Dr
8000 INPS 46219 2231 B5
Shick Dr
3100 INPS 46218 2229 E4
Shiloh Cir
- WshT 46123 2333 C2
Shiloh Ct
8200 INPS 46227 2555 E6
Shiloh Creek Wy
- WshT 46234 2333 D2
Shiloh Crossing Dr
100 AVON 46123 2333 D3
Shiloh Falls
5200 CRML 46033 1903 C2
Shiloh Park Dr
- AVON 46123 2333 C4
Shiloh Professional Dr
- AVON 46123 2333 C3
Shiloh Wood Ct
9400 WshT 46234 2333 D3
Shimer Av
5500 INPS 46219 2339 B4
Shine Ct
4200 WTFD 46033 1793 E6
Shingle Oak Ct
500 INPS 46224 2335 C2
Shipwatch Ln
5800 INPS 46237 2557 B5
Shipwatch Pl
5800 INPS 46237 2557 B5
Shire Close
14500 FSHR 46038 1906 E5
Shireton Ct
4600 INPS 46254 2116 C7
Shirk Wy
- GNWD 46143 2666 D4
Shirley Dr
2600 INPS 46222 2226 E5
Shirley Ln
1500 INPS 46227 2447 A6
Shoal Pl
11400 NBVL 46060 1796 D3
Shoal Creek Ln
2200 BrnT 46112 2115 B4
8500 INPS 46234 2225 B1
Shoals Wy
6700 INPS 46237 2557 D6
Shoemaker Dr
400 CRML 46032 1901 B2
Shoe Overlook Dr
8300 FSHR 46038 1904 C3
Shore Cir
10 CRML 46033 1902 D6
Shore Dr
- INPS 46214 2225 E2
3300 WRvT 46143 2664 B6
3800 INPS 46254 2225 E2
Shore Ter
6800 INPS 46254 2225 E2
Shore Cove Ct
13600 CRML 46074 1900 C1
N Shore Island Dr
6600 INPS 46220 2119 E2
Shoreland Ct
9500 INPS 46229 2231 E6
Shoreland Dr
2100 INPS 46229 2231 E6
Shoreland Ln
9500 INPS 46229 2231 E6
Shorelane Dr
500 CCRO 46034 1577 C3

Indianapolis Street Index

STREET
Block City ZIP Map# Grid

Shoreline Blvd
12900 FCkT 46055 2015 B2
Shoreline Cir
900 CCRO 46034 1577 C3
Shoreline Ct
100 NBVL 46062 1685 C1
Shoreline Dr
700 CCRO 46034 1577 C3
Shoreridge Ter
8000 INPS 46236 2014 D6
Shores Edge Pl
8100 INPS 46237 2557 B5
Shores Edge Wy
8100 INPS 46237 2557 B5
Shoreview Cir
11200 INPS 46236 2014 C6
Shoreview Ln
11300 INPS 46236 2014 E6
Shorevista Dr
12600 INPS 46236 2015 A3
Shore Vista Ln
21500 NBVL 46062 1577 B7
Shorewalk Dr
8100 INPS 46236 2014 D6
Shoreway E
15000 WshT 46032 1792 E5
Shoreway Ct
3200 INPS 46240 2011 C5
Shoreway Dr
8400 INPS 46240 2011 C5
Shorewood Dr
2400 LEBN 46052 1677 A3
5200 INPS 46220 2120 B6
E Shorewood Dr
2400 LEBN 46052 1676 E3
2400 LEBN 46052 1677 B2
Short St
- LtyT 46118 2548 B1
10 NPLN 46163 2452 B4
300 GNWD 46142 2665 C3
300 PNFD 46168 2441 B5
3300 LtyT 46168 2439 E6
Short Ter
4200 WTFD 46033 1793 E6
Shorter Ct
1700 INPS 46214 2225 D7
Shorter Dr
1700 INPS 46214 2225 D7
Short Iron Ln
11500 LWNC 46235 2123 D7
Shortleaf Ct
8100 LWNC 46236 2014 E6
8100 LWNC 46236 2015 A6
Shortleaf Dr
700 AVON 46123 2332 C5
Short Ridge Dr
1300 WRvT 46143 2664 B6
Shortridge Dr
1200 WRvT 46143 2664 B6
N Shortridge Rd
10 INPS 46219 2340 A2
1600 INPS 46219 2231 A7
3000 INPS 46226 2231 A4
S Shortridge Rd
10 INPS 46219 2340 A4
500 INPS 46239 2340 A6
3000 INPS 46239 2449 A2
Shoshone Dr
10 CRML 46032 1902 B4
7100 LWNC 46236 2123 B1
Shot St
- LtyT 46118 2548 C1
Shottery Ter
8000 INPS 46268 2009 B6
Shower Ct
14600 WshT 46032 1792 C6
Shrewsbury Ln
7000 INPS 46260 2118 D1
Shrike Ct
7800 INPS 46256 2013 B7
Shriver Av
3100 INPS 46208 2228 B4
Shut Out Ct
1500 INPS 46217 2554 E6
Sickle Rd
2400 INPS 46219 2231 B5
Sidewinder Ct
900 WRvT 46142 2664 B1
Siear Ct
2500 INPS 46227 2556 B6
Siear Dr
8100 INPS 46227 2556 B6
Slear Ter
8000 INPS 46227 2556 B6
Sienna Cir
5700 INPS 46239 2558 C1
Sienna Ct
10600 NBVL 46060 1687 B3
Sienna Dr
10400 NBVL 46060 1687 B3
Sierra
200 LEBN 46052 1676 E3
200 LEBN 46052 1677 A3
Sierra Cir
400 NWTD 46184 2774 D5
Sierra Ct
200 INPS 46234 2333 E3
Sierra Dr
- INPS 46231 2333 E5
100 CCRO 46034 1577 B2
Sierra Madre Dr
1000 GNWD 46143 2666 A4
Sierra Pass
1400 DNVL 46122 2330 E4
Sierra Ridge Dr
8500 INPS 46239 2449 C4
Sierra Ridge Ln
8500 INPS 46239 2449 C4
Sierra Springs Dr
1300 CRML 46280 2011 A2
Sigmond Cir
11100 FSHR 46038 1903 D6
Signature Dr
8800 INPS 46268 2009 A3
Signet Ln
11500 LWNC 46235 2123 D5
N Sigsbee St
10 INPS 46214 2334 E3
S Sigsbee St
1200 INPS 46241 2334 E6
Silas Ct
5800 CRML 46033 1903 D2
Silas Moffitt Wy
5900 CRML 46033 1903 E2
Silk Cir
8100 INPS 46256 2013 B4
Silver Av
1300 INPS 46221 2337 A6
E Silver Ct
2400 WTFD 46033 1793 B5
Silver Spur
13500 CRML 46032 1901 D2
Silverado Dr
8300 INPS 46237 2557 D6
11700 FSHR 46038 1906 A5
Silver Bay Cir
12400 INPS 46236 2015 A4
Silverbell Ln
- FSHR 46060 1905 D1
Silverberry Ct
100 MRVL 46158 2660 C3
Silver Creek Ct
1000 WRvT 46142 2663 E1
Silver Creek Dr
4800 INPS 46237 2557 A3
Silver Creek Wy
900 WRvT 46142 2663 E2
Silver Dawn Ct
600 ZNVL 46077 1898 E7
Silver Drift Ct
2000 INPS 46229 2232 D6
Silver Drift Wy
11300 INPS 46229 2232 D7
Silver Fox Ct
500 INPS 46217 2555 A5
Silver Fox Dr
7700 INPS 46217 2555 A5
Silver Grove Ct
6800 INPS 46237 2448 E6
Silver Hill Dr
4500 WRvT 46142 2663 D1
Silver Hill Ln
900 WRvT 46142 2663 D1
Silver Lake Cir
1000 WRvT 46142 2663 D1
7800 INPS 46259 2557 E5
Silver Lake Ct
1000 WRvT 46142 2663 E1
Silver Lake Dr
400 WTFD 46074 1684 B7
7100 INPS 46259 2557 E5
7200 INPS 46259 2558 A5
Silver Lake Pl
7700 INPS 46259 2557 E5
N Silverleaf Ct
8500 INPS 46278 2007 D5
Silverleaf Dr
7900 INPS 46260 2009 E6
Silver Ln Dr
2300 INPS 46203 2339 C7
2300 INPS 46203 2448 B1
Silver Maple Ct
900 GNWD 46143 2666 A2
2200 INPS 46222 2227 B6
3000 CRML 46033 1902 B6
Silver Meadow Ct
11600 FSHR 46038 1905 D5
Silvermere Dr
1200 INPS 46239 2341 B5
Silver Moon Ct
11400 NBVL 46060 1796 D1
Silver Oaks Dr
2400 ClyT 46032 2009 C1
5700 INPS 46237 2557 C1
Silverpine Ct
7500 INPS 46250 2011 E7
Silver Ridge Cir
- BNBG 46112 2114 E6
10400 FSHR 46038 2012 C1
N Silver Ridge Ct
8500 INPS 46278 2007 D5
Silver Ridge Ln
- BNBG 46112 2114 E5
Silver Shore Ct
12000 INPS 46236 2014 E3
Silver Spring Dr
19300 NBVL 46062 1685 D4
Silver Springs Blvd
4900 WRvT 46142 2663 D1
Silver Springs Ct
4900 WRvT 46142 2663 D1
Silver Springs Dr
4300 WRvT 46142 2663 D1
Silverstone Dr
13200 FSHR 46038 1906 C4
Silver Stream Dr
13800 CRML 46032 1792 C7
Silver Thorne Wy
14900 WTFD 46033 1793 C6
Silverton Ct
6400 INPS 46237 2557 B2
Silverton Wy
6300 INPS 46237 2557 B2
Silvertree Ct
11000 FSHR 46038 1905 A6
Silver Tree Dr
6600 LWNC 46236 2123 D2
Silver Valley Cir
900 WRvT 46142 2663 D2
Silver Valley Ct
900 WRvT 46142 2663 D2
Silver Valley Dr
900 WRvT 46142 2663 D1
Silver Wraith Dr
600 ZNVL 46077 1898 D7
Simcoe St
11800 LWNC 46236 2123 E3
Simien Rd
6000 INPS 46237 2557 B2
Simmerman Ct
3700 CRML 46033 2011 E1
Simmons Ln
- INPS 46229 2232 D5
Simmons St
100 PNFD 46168 2441 D5
Simmul Cir
5800 INPS 46221 2553 B3
Simmul Ln
5600 INPS 46221 2553 B3
Simone Dr
7300 SPRT 46227 2556 C4
Simsbury Ct
10500 LWNC 46236 2123 B4
Sinclair Dr
11600 LWNC 46235 2123 D6
Sinclair Pl
12700 FSHR 46038 1905 A3
Sinclair Wood Dr
2900 INPS 46240 2011 C4
Singleton St
2000 INPS 46203 2337 D7
5000 INPS 46227 2555 D1
Singletree Ct
13600 CRML 46032 1901 B1
Singletree Dr
2700 INPS 46234 2225 A5
Sinking Cr
- MdnT 46158 2661 D6
Sioux Cir
200 NBVL 46062 1686 A2
Sioux Dr
- WshT 46234 2224 C5
Sioux Run
7200 INPS 46219 2340 A4
Sioux Tr
7700 INPS 46250 2012 A7
13300 CRML 46033 1903 C1
Six Points Rd
- GfdT 46168 2442 D6
- GfdT 46231 2442 D6
- INPS 46241 2551 E1
- INPS 46241 2552 A2
- PNFD 46168 2442 D6
- PNFD 46231 2442 D6
- PNFD 46231 2551 E1
- PNFD 46241 2551 E1
13100 CRML 46032 1901 B2
19300 WshT 46069 1683 B1
20600 WshT 46069 1574 B7
21600 AdmT 46069 1574 B7
Skeeter Ct
3100 INPS 46214 2225 E4
Skelton St
4800 WRvT 46143 2663 D5
Skerries Ct
7700 INPS 46217 2554 E5
Skiles Pl
8600 INPS 46234 2225 A7
Skiles St N
- INPS 46234 2225 A7
Skiles St North Dr
1800 INPS 46234 2225 A7
Skipjack Dr
8200 INPS 46236 2014 C5
Skipper Ct
14200 CRML 46033 1793 C7
Skippers Ct
8400 AVON 46123 2332 E3
10100 INPS 46256 2014 A4
Skippers Wy
8700 INPS 46256 2014 A4
Skipping Rock Ct
4800 CRML 46033 1903 A3
Skipping Stone Dr
5200 INPS 46237 2448 E7
5600 INPS 46237 2557 E1
Skipton Ct
5700 NBVL 46062 1576 C7
Skybridge Dr
- INPS 46241 2444 A1
Skycrest Tr
7800 INPS 46214 2334 C3
Skyhawk Ct
11600 FSHR 46038 1906 B5
Skylark Ct
14100 CRML 46033 1903 B1
Skylark Dr
4300 INPS 46239 2449 D5
Skyline Ct
- WRvT 46143 2663 C7
Skyline Dr
1700 WRvT 46143 2663 C7
2800 INPS 46241 2444 D3
Skyline Ln
5200 WRvT 46143 2663 C7
Skyridge Dr
5200 INPS 46250 2012 B6
Skyward Dr
- LcnT 46112 2115 C6
Skyway Dr
8300 INPS 46219 2231 C7
Slabtown Rd
2500 CtrT 46052 1679 C2
2500 MrnT 46052 1679 C2
7000 MrnT 46075 1679 D2
7800 MrnT 46075 1680 A2
Slate Dr
- FSHR 46038 1906 A4
Sleeping Ridge Dr
7500 INPS 46217 2554 C5
Sleeping Ridge Wy
- INPS 46217 2554 B5
Sleepy Hollow Ct
- GNWD 46142 2665 A3
10 WTFD 46074 1684 B7
Sleepy Hollow Dr
10 WTFD 46074 1684 B7
400 PNFD 46168 2441 B4
Sleepy Hollow Ln
10 CRML 46032 1902 A3
Sleepy Hollow Pl
800 GNWD 46142 2665 A3
Sleet Dr
5400 INPS 46237 2448 B7
5400 INPS 46237 2557 B1
Sleet Ln
5400 INPS 46237 2448 B7
Sleuth Cir
6100 INPS 46221 2553 A2
Slideoff Rd
8700 INPS 46113 2661 A2
8700 MdnT 46113 2661 A2
Slippery Elm Ct
8400 INPS 46227 2555 D6
Slippery Rock Ct
- WTFD 46062 1793 D3
Slippery Rock Rd
12500 LWNC 46236 2124 A1
Sloan Av
1600 INPS 46203 2338 E6
1600 INPS 46203 2339 A6
S Sloan Av
2200 INPS 46203 2338 E7
2200 INPS 46203 2447 E1
Sloan Ter
4800 WRvT 46143 2663 D7
Sloane Muse
11800 FSHR 46038 1906 E4
Sloop Cir
7500 FSHR 46038 1904 A6
Sloop Ct
11100 INPS 46236 2014 C5
Sludge Av
- INPS 46221 2445 D2
Sly Run
100 NbvT 46062 1685 D5
Slyrun Ovlk
600 NbvT 46062 1685 E6
Sly Run Rd
- NBVL 46060 1795 E2
- NbvT 46060 1795 E2
Small Rd
3000 CtrT 46052 1568 A7
3000 CtrT 46052 1677 A1
Smallwood Ln E
3600 INPS 46214 2225 C3
Smallwood Ln W
3600 INPS 46214 2225 B2
N Smart St
10 GNWD 46142 2665 C3
S Smart St
10 GNWD 46142 2665 C3
Smethwick Cir
8400 INPS 46256 2013 D5
Smiley St
700 LEBN 46052 1676 D5
E Smith Ct
4700 INPS 46201 2338 E1
Smith Ln
7000 EglT 46077 2007 E1
Smith Rd
- AVON 46123 2333 A5
- WshT 46123 2333 A5
6400 LWNC 46236 2123 D3
Smith St
10 PTBR 46167 2113 A4
10 WTWN 46075 1788 C7
100 LEBN 46052 1676 D6
Smithfield Blvd
6700 INPS 46237 2557 D7
Smithfield Dr
6500 INPS 46237 2557 D6
15100 WshT 46074 1792 A5
Smithfield Ln
8400 INPS 46237 2557 D6
Smith Valley Rd
- GNWD 46142 2665 C5
- GNWD 46143 2665 C5
- WRvT 46142 2663 B5
- WRvT 46143 2663 B5
E Smith Valley Rd
- GNWD 46142 2665 D5
- GNWD 46143 2666 A4
10 GNWD 46143 2665 D5
W Smith Valley Rd
100 GNWD 46142 2665 B5
100 GNWD 46143 2665 B5
900 GNWD 46142 2664 C5
900 GNWD 46143 2664 C5
900 PltT 46143 2664 C5
1300 WRvT 46142 2664 C5
1300 WRvT 46143 2664 C5
4000 WRvT 46142 2663 D5
4000 WRvT 46143 2663 D5
Smock Dr
100 GNWD 46143 2665 D5
Smock St
5200 INPS 46227 2555 D1
Smoketree Dr
1200 BHGV 46107 2447 D5
1200 INPS 46107 2447 D5
Smokey Ln
600 CRML 46033 1902 E1
600 CRML 46033 1903 A1
Smokey Hollow Ct
13700 CRML 46032 1901 C1
Smokey Hollow Pl
13600 CRML 46033 1902 C1
Smokey Quartz Ln
- FSHR 46060 1905 E2
Smokey Ridge Cir
3200 CRML 46033 1902 C1
Smokey Ridge Ct
3200 CRML 46033 1902 C1
Smokey Ridge Dr
13600 CRML 46033 1902 C1
13800 CRML 46033 1793 C7
Smokey Ridge Ln
3100 CRML 46033 1793 C7
3100 CRML 46033 1902 B1
Smokey Ridge Ovlk
13700 CRML 46033 1902 C1
Smokey Ridge Pl
13600 CRML 46033 1902 C1
Smokey Ridge Tr
3100 CRML 46033 1902 C1
Smokey Ridge Trc
13600 CRML 46033 1902 C1
Smokey Ridge Wy
3200 CRML 46033 1902 B1
Smokey Row Ct
500 CRML 46033 1902 D1
Smokey Row Ln
1200 CRML 46033 1902 D1
Smokey Row Rd
- CRML 46032 1901 E1
100 MdnT 46143 2662 A6
100 MdnT 46158 2662 A6
2700 CRML 46033 1902 C1
4500 CRML 46033 1903 A1
E Smokey Row Rd
- CRML 46033 1902 B1
1800 CRML 46033 1902 B1
N Smokey Row Rd
10 MdnT 46158 2662 A6
W Smokey Row Rd
200 CRML 46032 1902 A1
500 CRML 46032 1901 E2
500 MdnT 46143 2662 A7
500 MdnT 46158 2662 A7
Smoothbark Dr
11300 INPS 46235 2232 D2
Snaffle Bit Rd
4000 PryT 46052 1896 B2
Snap Dragon Ct
19300 NBVL 46060 1687 C3
Snapdragon Ln
5400 BHGV 46203 2448 B4
Snapper Ct
10400 INPS 46256 2014 B3
Snead Cir
2100 INPS 46229 2232 B6
Snider Ct
7200 INPS 46221 2553 A4
Snowberry Ct
500 NBVL 46062 1685 E4
5500 INPS 46221 2553 A1
Snowberry Bay Ct
4800 CRML 46033 1903 A4
N Snowden Sq
9000 INPS 46234 2334 C1
S Snowden Sq
9000 INPS 46234 2334 C1
Snowdrop Wy
10800 INPS 46235 2232 B2
Snowflake Cir
10 GNWD 46143 2665 D7
Snowflake Dr
7200 INPS 46227 2556 D4
Snow Owl Dr
13200 CRML 46033 1903 B2
Snug Harbor Ct
1600 INPS 46227 2556 A6
Snug Harbor Dr
8000 INPS 46227 2556 A6
Snug Harbor Ln
8000 INPS 46227 2556 A6
Soaring Eagle Ct
3500 INPS 46214 2225 C3
Soaring Eagle Dr
1200 WRvT 46143 2664 A6
Soaring Eagle Ln
9800 FCkT 46055 2015 D2
Soaring Hawk Rd
7800 EglT 46077 2007 D2
7800 INPS 46077 2007 D2
Soaring Heights Cir
- LcnT 46112 2115 D6
Sobax Dr
8200 INPS 46268 2009 A5
Sofia Pl
3500 INPS 46228 2227 A2
Softwood Ct
7800 INPS 46239 2340 B7
Solitude Ct
- MdnT 46113 2661 A1
Solomon St
200 MRVL 46158 2659 E2
200 MRVL 46158 2660 A2
Solomons Ct
11600 FCkT 46038 2014 D2
Solun Ct
4200 INPS 46221 2444 B5
Solun Rd
4100 INPS 46221 2444 B5
Somerby Ct
- PNFD 46168 2441 B4
Somers Dr
5500 INPS 46237 2557 B1
N Somerset Av
1000 INPS 46222 2336 A1
1600 INPS 46222 2227 A7
S Somerset Av
400 INPS 46241 2336 A4
Somerset Cir
10 BNBG 46112 2114 D6
Somerset Ct
100 NBVL 46060 1795 D5
Somerset Dr
- FCkT 46038 1905 D4
100 GNWD 46143 2666 A3
700 LEBN 46052 1677 A5
Somerset Dr W
400 INPS 46260 2010 B6
Somerset Ln
5000 ZNVL 46077 1899 B3
Somerset Wy E
11800 CRML 46033 1902 E4
Somerset Wy S
4400 CRML 46033 1902 E5
Somerset Bay
2700 INPS 46240 2011 C7
2700 INPS 46240 2120 B1
Somerville Dr
8300 LWNC 46216 2122 C5
Sommer Awning Blvd
6300 INPS 46220 2121 A3
Sommersworth Ln
3600 INPS 46228 2118 A4
Sommerwood Dr
8600 NBVL 46060 1795 D6
8600 NbvT 46060 1795 D6
Sondridge Cir
7200 INPS 46256 2122 A2
Sonesta Dr
6500 INPS 46217 2554 D3
Sonesta Ln
1600 INPS 46217 2554 D3
Sonesta Wy
1700 INPS 46217 2554 D3
Song Ct
14000 CRML 46032 1792 D7
Songbird Ct
10 CRML 46033 1902 C6
10 GNFD 46140 2236 E6
400 MRVL 46158 2660 A6
4100 WRvT 46142 2663 E5
Songbird Ln
10800 CRML 46033 1902 C7
11300 FSHR 46038 1903 E6
Sonhatsett Dr
400 WTFD 46074 1684 B7
Sonna Dr
100 CRML 46032 1901 D2
Sonnefield Ct
5400 INPS 46224 2335 C3
Sonoma Dr
- JknT 46034 1576 E3
Sonoma Ln
- JknT 46034 1576 D3
Sonora Cir
400 NWTD 46184 2774 D4
Soper Cir
7600 INPS 46214 2225 C7
Sorbonne Pl
8800 INPS 46268 2009 B4
Sorbus Ct
5700 INPS 46254 2117 B5
Sorbus Dr
6000 INPS 46254 2117 B5
S Sorel St
2300 INPS 46239 2450 E1
Sorrel Ct
10 ZNVL 46077 1899 A7
Sorrel Dr
8600 INPS 46260 2009 D4
Sorrell Ct
800 LEBN 46052 1677 B5
Sourwood Ct
8900 INPS 46260 2009 E4
Sourwood Ln
14000 CRML 46033 1794 D7
14000 CRML 46033 1903 E1
Souter Dr
7700 INPS 46219 2231 B5
South Ct
300 MRVL 46158 2659 D7
South Dr
- NbvT 46062 1686 D1
- WTFD 46074 1684 A6
6500 LcnT 46112 2223 A2
South Lp
- WTFD 46074 1684 A6
South St
10 INPS 46227 2556 A4
10 SPRT 46227 2556 A4
10 WTFD 46074 1793 B1
500 NBVL 46060 1795 C2
8500 FSHR 46038 1904 C6
E South St
10 INPS 46225 2337 C4
10 MRVL 46158 2659 E4
100 GNFD 46140 2345 E1
100 INPS 46204 2337 C4
100 LEBN 46052 1677 A6
200 PNFD 46168 2441 B5
300 MRVL 46158 2660 A4
1000 CtrT 46140 2346 A1
1000 NBVL 46060 1795 D2
E South St SR-32
100 LEBN 46052 1677 A6
W South St
10 INPS 46225 2337 B4
10 MRVL 46158 2659 D4
100 PNFD 46168 2441 B5
200 LEBN 46052 1676 C6
600 GNFD 46140 2345 C2
600 NBVL 46060 1795 D2
7400 MrlT 46126 2669 C2
W South St SR-32
200 LEBN 46052 1676 C6
Southampton Ct
13000 CRML 46032 1901 B3
South Bay Dr
6000 FSHR 46250 2012 C2
Southbridge
1100 GNWD 46142 2665 B1
1200 GNWD 46227 2665 B1
1200 INPS 46227 2665 B1
Southbridge Ct
300 GNWD 46142 2665 C1
Southbridge St
200 MRVL 46158 2659 E5
Southbrook Dr
1200 INPS 46240 2010 E6
Southcreek Ct
8700 INPS 46217 2555 B7
12100 LWNC 46236 2014 E5
Southcreek Dr N
300 INPS 46217 2555 B7
Southcreek Dr S
300 INPS 46217 2555 B7
Southcrest Ct
7400 INPS 46217 2555 C4
South Crossing Dr
100 AVON 46123 2333 D3
South Ct Dr
1400 INPS 46227 2555 E3
1400 INPS 46227 2556 A3
Southdale Dr
5200 INPS 46217 2446 B7
Southeast Pkwy
1100 BHGV 46107 2447 D3
Southeastern Av
- MrlT 46259 2559 E3
- MrlT 46259 2560 A4
12500 MrlT 46126 2560 A4
E Southeastern Av
1000 INPS 46202 2337 E3
1400 INPS 46201 2337 E3
1400 INPS 46201 2338 D5
2800 INPS 46203 2338 D5
4800 INPS 46203 2339 A7
5600 INPS 46203 2448 C1
6800 INPS 46239 2448 D2
7200 INPS 46239 2449 C5
9700 INPS 46239 2450 A7
9700 INPS 46239 2559 B1
10700 INPS 46259 2559 B1
11800 MrlT 46259 2559 E3
Southern Av
1000 BHGV 46107 2447 D1
1500 BHGV 46203 2447 D1
8300 INPS 46241 2443 B1
E Southern Av
10 INPS 46225 2446 D2
500 INPS 46203 2446 D2
3000 INPS 46203 2447 C1
3100 BHGV 46107 2447 C1
3500 BHGV 46203 2447 C1
5000 INPS 46203 2448 A1
W Southern Av
400 INPS 46225 2446 B1
3800 INPS 46241 2445 A2
5100 INPS 46241 2444 C2
Southern Cross Dr
6500 INPS 46237 2557 D6
Southern Lakes Dr
7300 INPS 46237 2557 D5
Southern Lakes Dr N
6400 INPS 46237 2557 D4
Southern Mist Dr
5500 INPS 46237 2557 B6
Southern Oaks Dr
7900 INPS 46217 2555 A6
Southern Pines Dr
- GNWD 46184 2774 A2
- PltT 46184 2774 A2
Southern Plaza Dr
10 INPS 46227 2446 C5
Southern Ridge Dr
6500 INPS 46237 2557 D6
Southern Springs Av
5800 INPS 46237 2557 C6
Southern Springs Blvd
8000 INPS 46237 2557 C6
Southern Springs Cir
8100 INPS 46237 2557 C6
Southern Springs Ct
8100 INPS 46237 2557 B6
Southern Springs Dr
8300 INPS 46237 2557 B6
Southern Springs Ln
5800 INPS 46237 2557 B6
Southern Springs Wy
8200 INPS 46237 2557 C6
Southern Trails Dr
- INPS 46237 2557 B5
Southern Trails Pl
8000 INPS 46237 2557 D6
Southernwood Dr
- INPS 46231 2333 E7
Southernwood Ln
1800 INPS 46231 2333 E7
Southernwood Wy
9000 INPS 46231 2333 E7
9000 INPS 46231 2334 A7
Southfield Ct
700 INPS 46227 2446 C6
Southfield Dr
900 PNFD 46168 2441 E6
7500 SPRT 46227 2556 B5
Southgate Dr
400 GNWD 46143 2665 D3
4200 INPS 46268 2008 E6
Southgreen Dr
5000 INPS 46227 2446 D7
Southhampton Ct
500 NBVL 46060 1795 D4
Southlane Dr
10 NWTD 46184 2774 D4
Southmore St
400 PNFD 46168 2441 D5
Southpark Dr
- WTFD 46074 1792 E3
16600 WTFD 46074 1793 A2
Southpoint Dr
- FSHR 46256 2013 B2
Southpointe Dr
8800 INPS 46227 2555 E7
Southport Pl
- INPS 46217 2553 E3
- INPS 46217 2554 A3
E Southport Rd
10 INPS 46227 2555 D4
1400 INPS 46227 2556 A4
1600 SPRT 46227 2556 A4
3700 INPS 46237 2556 D3
4800 INPS 46237 2557 A3
7000 INPS 46259 2557 E3
7000 INPS 46259 2558 A3
9600 INPS 46259 2559 B4
W Southport Rd
10 INPS 46217 2555 A4
1200 INPS 46217 2554 B3
3800 INPS 46217 2553 D4
3800 INPS 46221 2553 D4
6800 INPS 46221 2552 E5
Southport Ter
4600 INPS 46237 2556 E3
4600 INPS 46237 2557 A3
Southport Crossings Dr
4300 INPS 46237 2556 D4
Southport Crossings Wy
4300 INPS 46237 2556 E4
Southport Trace Dr
4100 INPS 46237 2556 D2
Southridge Cir
7600 LWNC 46236 2015 A7
Southridge Ct
600 WTFD 46074 1793 A1
2600 SPRT 46227 2556 B5

INDEX 48

Southridge Dr — Indianapolis Street Index — SR-267

STREET
Block City ZIP Map# Grid

Southridge Dr
5700 LcnT 46112 2222 E2
Southridge Ln
100 WTFD 46074 1793 A1
Southshore Dr
400 WshT 46123 2332 B5
E Southshore Dr
- FCkT 46038 1906 C5
W Southshore Dr
- FCkT 46038 1906 C6
Southview Dr
800 INPS 46227 2555 E3
1000 HMCT 46227 2555 E3
1400 HMCT 46227 2556 A3
1400 INPS 46227 2556 A3
Southway Ct
10 WRvT 46142 2663 E2
S Southway Dr
3300 SCkT 46163 2451 B1
Southway Pl
10 WRvT 46142 2663 D2
Southway Rd
4300 WRvT 46142 2663 E2
Southwest Dr
3000 INPS 46241 2444 D3
Southwick Ct
2400 INPS 46268 2118 C1
Southwind
- BNBG 46112 2114 A3
- BrnT 46112 2114 A3
Southwind Cir
9900 INPS 46256 2014 A3
Southwind Ct
100 WRvT 46142 2664 A3
9200 INPS 46256 2014 A3
Southwind Dr
9800 INPS 46256 2014 A3
Southwind Ln
10 WRvT 46142 2664 A3
N Southwind Ln
10 WRvT 46142 2664 A3
South Wind Pt
- WRvT 46142 2664 A3
Southwind Ter
3800 WRvT 46142 2664 A3
Southwind Wy
10 WRvT 46142 2664 A3
Southwood Cir
14000 FSHR 46038 1906 D4
Southwood Ct
300 INPS 46217 2555 B2
Southwood Dr
800 INPS 46227 2555 E2
Southwood St
2000 GNWD 46143 2665 C7
Sovereign Ln
12600 FSHR 46038 1905 A3
Sowers Dr
14400 DelT 46060 1795 C7
Spanish Fir Ln
8300 INPS 46227 2555 D6
Spanish Lake Dr
1000 WshT 46123 2333 A1
Spann Av
1100 INPS 46203 2337 E5
3500 INPS 46203 2338 D5
Spannwood Rd
900 INPS 46228 2119 A4
N Sparks Rd
2600 BCkT 46140 2233 E3
Sparks St
10 PTBR 46167 2112 E4
Sparrow Av
700 INPS 46227 2446 D3
1700 INPS 46227 2447 A3
Sparrow Ct
- NBVL 46060 1687 B3
Sparrowood Blvd
6500 LWNC 46236 2124 A2
Sparrowood Ct
6500 LWNC 46236 2124 A2
Sparrowood Dr
6500 LWNC 46236 2123 E2
6500 LWNC 46236 2124 A2
Sparrows Point Ct
7700 LWNC 46236 2014 B7
Speedway Av
4900 SDWY 46224 2226 C7
Speedway Dr
5300 SDWY 46224 2226 B6
Speedway Woods Dr
700 INPS 46224 2335 B2
Speights Dr
6400 INPS 46278 2116 E3
6400 INPS 46278 2117 A3
Spellman Ct
7000 INPS 46259 2558 B4
Spencer Av
900 LEBN 46052 1677 B7
Spencer Av SR-32
900 LEBN 46052 1677 B7
N Spencer Av
2100 INPS 46218 2230 A6
S Spencer Av
10 INPS 46219 2339 A3
1200 INPS 46203 2339 A6
Spencer Dr
- BNBG 46112 2223 E4
- GNWD 46143 2666 A6
- LcnT 46112 2223 E4
W Spencer St
300 AdmT 46069 1573 B1
300 SRDN 46069 1573 B1
Spend A Buck Ct
8700 INPS 46217 2554 E7
Spend A Buck Dr
8500 INPS 46217 2554 E7
Spice Ln
11000 FSHR 46038 1905 C5
Spicebush Ct
13400 CRML 46033 1903 D2
Spicebush Dr
5500 INPS 46254 2116 D6
Spicewood Ct
8900 INPS 46260 2009 D4

Spicewood Dr
200 INPS 46227 2446 C4
Spider Bay Ct
8900 INPS 46236 2014 C4
Spillwater Wy
- WTFD 46062 1793 E3
Spindriff Ln
5600 INPS 46220 2120 D5
Spiney Ln
- GNWD 46184 2774 A2
Spinnaker Ct
8800 INPS 46256 2014 B4
Spinnaker Bay
- GNWD 46143 2666 A4
Spinner Ct
1000 CCRO 46034 1577 B3
Spire Dr
4200 INPS 46237 2448 C5
Spire Pl
6100 INPS 46237 2448 C5
Spireview Dr
- FSHR 46038 1905 E4
Spirit Lake Dr
6600 INPS 46220 2119 D1
6600 INPS 46220 2120 A2
Splendor Wy
- LcnT 46112 2115 D6
Split Granite Dr
12100 FSHR 46038 1906 A4
Split Rock Wy
- LcnT 46112 2115 C5
Split Tree Ct
9000 INPS 46256 2013 C3
Spoon Dr
8800 INPS 46219 2340 D1
N Sportest Rd
- WRvT 46060 1579 C3
Sportsman Ct
9600 INPS 46239 2340 E7
Sportsman Dr
9500 INPS 46239 2340 E7
Spotswood St
- CRML 46032 1900 E2
Spotted Owl Dr
10 BNBG 46112 2223 C3
Sprague St
600 INPS 46217 2446 A5
Spring Ct
- ZNVL 46077 1898 E2
200 INPS 46214 2334 E3
1100 WshT 46123 2332 A6
Spring Ct E
4600 INPS 46239 2449 D6
Spring Dr
10 ZNVL 46077 1899 C5
100 PNFD 46168 2441 C4
400 GNWD 46143 2665 D1
Spring Ln
7400 INPS 46268 2009 B7
Spring St
10 DNVL 46122 2329 C4
200 INPS 46202 2337 D3
E Spring St
10 CCRO 46034 1577 D2
N Spring St
10 GNFD 46140 2345 E1
600 GNFD 46140 2236 E7
S Spring St
- GNFD 46140 2345 E1
W Spring St
10 CCRO 46034 1577 D2
Spring Blossom Ln
11200 FSHR 46038 1904 D6
N Springbrook Dr
6600 INPS 46219 2339 D2
S Springbrook Dr
6600 INPS 46219 2339 D2
Springbrooke Run
12400 CRML 46033 1903 B4
Spring Creek Cir
5300 INPS 46254 2117 C6
Spring Creek Ct
100 NBVL 46062 1685 B2
5200 INPS 46254 2117 C6
9900 WshT 46123 2333 C3
Spring Creek Pl
5400 INPS 46254 2117 C6
Springcrest St
1000 PNFD 46168 2441 C7
Springdale Dr
400 WTLD 46184 2775 A6
9700 FCkT 46038 1904 E5
Springer Av
6600 INPS 46219 2339 D2
Spring Farms Dr
13300 CRML 46032 1901 C2
Springfield Cir
300 GNWD 46143 2665 B7
Springfield Ct
1200 WshT 46123 2332 B6
11800 FSHR 46038 1904 C5
Springfield Dr
1100 WshT 46123 2332 A6
2500 INPS 46228 2118 C3
Springfield Ln
11800 FSHR 46038 1904 C5
Springfield Overlook St
3800 INPS 46234 2225 A2
Spring Flower Ct
4700 INPS 46237 2448 D6
Spring Flower Dr
6500 INPS 46237 2448 D6
Spring Forest Dr
9200 INPS 46260 2010 A3
Spring Highland Dr
10300 ClyT 46290 2010 C1
Spring Hill Ct
100 MRVL 46158 2660 A4
2400 INPS 46268 2009 C6
Spring Hill Dr
10500 ClyT 46032 1902 B7
10500 ClyT 46032 2011 B1
Springhill Wy
6400 INPS 46254 2226 A1

Spring Hills Dr
600 EglT 46077 1898 D6
Springhollow Ct
5600 WshT 46123 2331 D6
Spring Hollow Dr
9100 INPS 46260 2010 B3
Spring Hollow Rd
1300 INPS 46208 2227 E3
Spring Lake Dr
- BNBG 46112 2114 E5
Springlake Dr
10 WTFD 46074 1792 D2
Spring Lake Rd
10 SCkT 46140 2344 A3
10 SGLK 46140 2344 A3
2200 MdnT 46158 2661 A7
Spring Lakes Dr
9200 INPS 46260 2010 A3
Spring Meadow Ct
2800 INPS 46268 2009 C4
Spring Meadow Dr
900 GNWD 46143 2666 A3
Spring Meadow Ln
100 GNWD 46143 2665 E3
100 GNWD 46143 2666 A3
E Springmeadow Ln
3100 WTFD 46033 1793 D6
Springmill Blvd
1400 CRML 46032 1792 C7
13600 CRML 46032 1901 C1
Spring Mill Cir
1400 CRML 46032 1901 C1
Spring Mill Ct
10 MRVL 46158 2660 A4
300 ClyT 46032 1901 C7
8400 INPS 46260 2010 C5
Spring Mill Dr
100 MRVL 46158 2660 A4
1100 WshT 46123 2332 A6
Spring Mill Ln
400 INPS 46260 2010 B7
400 MRVL 46158 2660 A5
10900 ClyT 46032 1901 C7
Spring Mill Rd
- INPS 46208 2119 B3
5900 INPS 46228 2119 B3
5900 INPS 46260 2119 B3
7400 INPS 46260 2010 B7
9500 ClyT 46260 2010 C3
9500 CRML 46260 2010 C3
10600 ClyT 46032 1901 C5
13600 CRML 46032 1901 C2
13900 CRML 46032 1792 C7
14700 WshT 46032 1792 C7
14700 WshT 46074 1792 C3
16100 WTFD 46074 1792 C3
17600 WshT 46074 1683 C5
22100 AdmT 46069 1574 C5
Springmill Rd
- WshT 46074 1683 B7
9600 ClyT 46032 2010 C1
9600 CRML 46032 2010 C1
9600 CRML 46290 2010 C1
9900 ClyT 46290 2010 C1
10500 ClyT 46032 1901 C7
10500 ClyT 46290 1901 C7
Springmill Ponds Blvd
- CRML 46032 1792 C7
Springmill Ponds Cir
1500 CRML 46032 1792 C7
Springmill Ponds Cir W
13800 CRML 46032 1792 C7
Spring Mist Cir
5600 INPS 46237 2557 A1
Spring Oaks Dr
6000 INPS 46237 2557 C1
Spring Oaks Wy
5700 INPS 46237 2557 C1
Springridge Cir
10300 FSHR 46038 2013 E1
10300 FSHR 46038 2014 B1
Spring Ridge Ct
300 ClyT 46032 1901 C7
Spring Ridge Dr
- ClyT 46032 1901 C7
Springs Ct
100 CRML 46033 1902 C6
Springside Ln E
8700 INPS 46260 2009 D4
Springside Ln N
2300 INPS 46260 2009 C5
Springside Ln W
8800 INPS 46260 2009 D4
Springside Ln Ct
2300 INPS 46260 2009 C5
Spring Song Blvd
5300 INPS 46241 2444 C3
Springston Ct
10600 FSHR 46038 2014 B1
Springstone Rd
9600 FCkT 46055 2015 C2
Springtime Rd
2100 GNWD 46143 2774 C1
Springtree Pl
11000 INPS 46239 2341 C4
Spring Valley Ct
700 INPS 46231 2334 A5
Spring Valley Dr
600 INPS 46231 2334 A5
8000 GfdT 46168 2550 D5
Spring Valley Ln
8600 INPS 46231 2334 A5
Springview Ct
- BNBG 46112 2114 D3
Springview Dr
- MCVL 46055 2015 D5
6600 WshT 46123 2332 A6
8400 INPS 46260 2010 B5
Spring Violet Pl
12500 CRML 46033 1903 B4
Springwater Cir
7900 INPS 46256 2013 B6
Spring Water Ct
100 WTLD 46184 2775 A6

Springwater Ct
- GNWD 46143 2666 A6
6200 WshT 46123 2332 A7
7900 INPS 46256 2013 B6
Springwater Dr
- GNWD 46143 2666 A5
N Springwater Dr W
8100 INPS 46256 2013 B3
Springwater Dr W
7900 INPS 46256 2013 B6
Springway Dr
8500 INPS 46239 2449 C5
Spring Wind Dr
8200 INPS 46239 2449 C3
Spring Wind Ln
3300 INPS 46239 2449 C3
Springwood Ct
4200 INPS 46228 2227 C1
9900 FCkT 46055 2015 C2
Springwood Dr
100 AVON 46123 2332 D3
Springwood Tr
4200 INPS 46228 2227 C1
Springwood Wy
400 ClyT 46032 1901 B7
Spring Wy Dr
11500 CRML 46033 1902 C6
Sprong Rd
- EglT 46077 1897 E7
7500 EglT 46077 1898 A7
Spruance Ct
9600 FCkT 46256 2014 D2
Spruce Ct
1500 CRML 46033 1793 E7
7300 WshT 46168 2441 C1
Spruce Dr
- GNWD 46184 2774 B1
700 CRML 46033 1902 E1
800 CRML 46033 1793 D7
1900 CRML 46033 1903 A1
Spruce Ln
17500 WshT 46074 1683 E7
17500 WshT 46074 1792 E1
Spruce Ln W
9600 FSHR 46038 2012 D2
Spruce St
- NPLN 46163 2452 B3
200 PNFD 46168 2441 C4
400 INPS 46201 2338 A6
1500 INPS 46203 2338 A6
1800 LcnT 46112 2223 E4
2800 INPS 46203 2447 A2
S Spruce St
- NPLN 46163 2452 B3
Spruce Knoll Cir
5700 INPS 46220 2120 D3
Spruce Knoll Ct
5700 INPS 46220 2120 E5
Spruce Knoll Ln
4500 INPS 46220 2120 D3
Spur Ct
- GNWD 46143 2665 B7
Spur Ln
900 INPS 46220 2119 E2
Spur Wy
6600 INPS 46220 2119 E2
Spurlock Ln
- GNWD 46143 2666 D4
Spur Point Dr
2300 INPS 46217 2554 C3
Spurrington Cir
7100 LWNC 46236 2124 A1
Spurrington Wy
12600 LWNC 46236 2124 A1
Spyglass Ct
- LEBN 46052 1677 A2
Spyglass Dr
8200 INPS 46260 2009 D5
Spyglass Pl
- INPS 46260 2009 C5
Spyglass Ridge Dr
11300 FSHR 46038 1905 B6
Spy Run Dr N
900 CBLD 46229 2341 E2
Spy Run Dr S
800 CBLD 46229 2341 E2
Squire Ct
8900 INPS 46250 2012 C4
Squire Dr
4700 INPS 46241 2444 D2
Squire Boone Ct
8800 INPS 46113 2552 A7
Squirrel Hllw
11200 FSHR 46038 1903 E6
Squirrels Run
5800 INPS 46254 2117 D5
SR-9
3000 CtrT 46140 2236 D1
SR-9 S 200 E
2000 BwnT 46140 2345 E6
2000 CtrT 46140 2345 E5
2000 GNFD 46140 2345 E5
SR-9 N State St
10 GNFD 46140 2345 D1
2300 GNFD 46140 2236 D4
2700 CtrT 46140 2236 D4
SR-9 S State St
10 GNFD 46140 2345 D1
1900 CtrT 46140 2345 E5
SR-13 N Atlantic Rd
100 JknT 46011 1580 E6
100 SCkT 46011 1580 E6
100 WRvT 46011 1580 E6
100 WRvT 46060 1580 E6
100 WynT 46011 1580 E6
100 WynT 46060 1580 E6
SR-13 N Atlantic Rd E
- JknT 46011 1580 E2
- WRvT 46011 1580 E2
1000 WRvT 46060 1580 E4
1500 JknT 46060 1580 E3
SR-13 Atlantic Rd E
100 SCkT 46051 1580 E7
100 SCkT 46051 1689 E1
100 WynT 46051 1580 E7

SR-13 Atlantic Rd E
100 WynT 46051 1689 E1
100 WynT 46060 1580 E7
100 WynT 46060 1689 E1
SR-13 W Main St
100 WynT 46051 1689 E4
9000 SCkT 46051 1689 E4
SR-19
- CCRO 46034 1577 D4
- JknT 46034 1577 D4
SR-19 Cicero Rd
100 NBVL 46060 1686 D5
700 NbvT 46060 1686 D5
1300 NbvT 46062 1686 D5
3200 JknT 46062 1577 D6
3200 NbvT 46062 1577 D7
SR-19 N Peru St
- JknT 46030 1577 D1
10 CCRO 46034 1577 D2
700 JknT 46034 1577 D1
SR-19 S Peru St
10 CCRO 46034 1577 D1
SR-32
- WynT 46060 1687 D7
- WynT 46060 1688 E6
700 CtrT 46052 1677 B7
1200 CtrT 46052 1676 B6
1200 LEBN 46052 1676 B6
1500 CtrT 46052 1678 A7
9400 SCkT 46051 1689 E4
9800 WynT 46051 1689 E4
9800 WynT 46060 1689 E4
SR-32 E 176th St
10 WTFD 46074 1683 D7
600 WshT 46074 1683 E7
SR-32 W 176th St
10 WshT 46074 1683 C7
10 WTFD 46074 1683 C7
1600 WshT 46074 1682 E7
4000 WshT 46069 1682 A7
4100 WshT 46069 1681 A7
4100 WshT 46074 1681 A7
4200 UnnT 46069 1681 A7
4200 UnnT 46074 1681 A7
SR-32 W Base Line Rd
4000 CtrT 46052 1678 D7
4000 WrhT 46052 1678 D7
5000 CtrT 46052 1679 D7
5000 WrhT 46052 1679 D7
6000 UnnT 46052 1679 D7
6500 UnnT 46075 1679 D7
6500 WrhT 46075 1679 D7
6900 UnnT 46077 1679 D7
6900 WrhT 46077 1679 D7
7100 UnnT 46075 1680 A7
7100 UnnT 46077 1680 A7
10000 UnnT 46077 1681 A7
SR-32 Conner St
100 NBVL 46060 1686 C7
SR-32 E Conner St
1000 NBVL 46060 1686 D7
1900 NBVL 46060 1687 A7
3100 NbvT 46060 1687 B7
3100 WynT 46060 1687 B7
SR-32 W Conner St
500 NBVL 46060 1686 C7
SR-32 Indianapolis Av
100 LEBN 46052 1677 D7
SR-32 S Lebanon St
100 LEBN 46052 1676 E6
SR-32 E Main St
10 WTFD 46074 1684 B7
100 LEBN 46052 1677 A6
SR-32 W Main St
10 LEBN 46052 1677 A6
10 WTFD 46074 1684 B7
900 WshT 46074 1683 E7
900 WTFD 46074 1683 E7
SR-32 E Noble St
1000 LEBN 46052 1677 B7
SR-32 E South St
100 LEBN 46052 1677 A6
SR-32 W South St
100 LEBN 46052 1677 B7
200 LEBN 46052 1676 E6
SR-32 Spencer Av
900 LEBN 46052 1677 B7
SR-32 Westfield Rd
- WshT 46074 1684 E7
- WTFD 46074 1684 E7
200 NBVL 46060 1686 C7
500 NBVL 46062 1686 A7
900 NbvT 46062 1686 A7
1400 NBVL 46062 1685 D7
1400 NbvT 46062 1685 D7
3100 WshT 46062 1685 B7
3500 WshT 46062 1684 E7
3500 WTFD 46062 1684 E7
SR-37
- BHGV - 2448 D4
- DelT - 1904 D6
- DelT - 2013 C1
- FCkT 46060 1795 E7
- FSHR - 1904 D6
- FSHR - 2013 A4
- FSHR 46038 1795 E7
- FSHR 46038 1904 E2
- FSHR 46060 1795 E7
- INPS - 2012 E6
- INPS - 2013 C1
- INPS - 2231 B5
- INPS - 2339 E7
- INPS - 2340 A1
- INPS - 2445 E6
- INPS - 2446 B6
- INPS - 2447 E5
- INPS - 2448 D4
- INPS 46142 2663 B1
- INPS 46217 2554 C7
- INPS 46217 2663 B1
- LWNC - 2121 E6
- NBVL 46060 1687 D1
- NBVL 46060 1795 E7
- NBVL 46060 1796 A2
- NbvT 46060 1687 B4

SR-37
- NbvT 46060 1796 A2
- WRvT 46060 1578 E6
- WRvT 46060 1579 D2
- WRvT 46060 1580 B1
- WRvT 46142 2663 B1
- WRvT 46143 2662 E7
- WRvT 46143 2663 A5
- WynT 46060 1578 E6
- WynT 46060 1687 D1
SR-37 S Harding St
- INPS 46217 2445 D7
SR-38
- AdmT 46069 1573 A1
- AdmT 46069 1574 A4
- GrnT 46051 1798 C3
- GrnT 46060 1798 C3
- GrnT 46064 1798 C3
- NBVL 46060 1796 E1
- NBVL 46060 1797 A1
- SRDN 46069 1573 C2
- WshT 46062 1575 A7
- WshT 46069 1574 D6
- WshT 46069 1575 A7
- WshT 46074 1575 A7
- WynT 46060 1687 D7
- WynT 46060 1796 E7
- WynT 46060 1797 A1
- WynT 46060 1798 C3
SR-38 W 2nd St
100 SRDN 46069 1573 B1
SR-38 E 6th St
100 SRDN 46069 1573 B2
SR-38 Conner St
100 NBVL 46060 1686 C7
SR-38 E Conner St
1000 NBVL 46060 1686 D7
1900 NBVL 46060 1687 A7
3100 NbvT 46060 1687 B7
3100 WynT 46060 1687 B7
SR-38 W Conner St
500 NBVL 46060 1686 C7
SR-38 S Main St
200 SRDN 46069 1573 B1
SR-38 Sheridan Rd
100 NBVL 46060 1686 B6
100 NBVL 46062 1686 B6
1400 NBVL 46062 1685 E5
1400 NbvT 46062 1686 A6
1900 NbvT 46062 1685 E5
3200 WshT 46062 1685 A3
4400 WshT 46062 1684 E2
4400 WshT 46074 1684 D2
4400 WTFD 46074 1684 D1
SR-38 N Sherman Av
100 SRDN 46069 1573 B1
200 AdmT 46069 1573 B1
SR-38 S Sherman Av
10 SRDN 46069 1573 B1
SR-38 Westfield Rd
200 NBVL 46060 1686 C7
SR-38 S White Av
600 SRDN 46069 1573 B1
700 AdmT 46069 1573 B1
SR-39
- DNVL 46122 2329 D5
500 CtrT 46122 2329 C3
1000 CtrT 46052 1785 E2
2500 HsnT 46052 1785 D6
2800 CtrT 46052 1676 E2
2800 LEBN 46052 1676 E2
3000 CtrT 46052 1567 E7
3000 HsnT 46052 1894 C1
3700 WshT 46052 1567 E7
5200 LtyT 46118 2439 A7
5200 LtyT 46118 2548 A1
8800 LtyT 46118 2657 C1
11000 MnrT 46157 2657 C6
SR-39 N Chestnut St
300 MNVA 46157 2657 C7
SR-39 S Cross St
10 DNVL 46122 2329 D4
SR-39 S Kentucky St
800 CtrT 46122 2329 D5
800 DNVL 46122 2329 D5
SR-39 N Lebanon St
100 LEBN 46052 1676 E1
2400 CtrT 46052 1676 E1
SR-39 S Lebanon St
- CtrT 46052 1785 E2
100 LEBN 46052 1676 E5
1200 LEBN 46052 1785 E2
SR-39 W Lincoln St
200 DNVL 46122 2329 D5
SR-39 W Main St
200 DNVL 46122 2329 B4
SR-39 Market St
- LtyT 46118 2548 C1
SR-39 Morgan St
5700 LtyT 46118 2548 C1
SR-39 Urban St
10 DNVL 46122 2329 C2
SR-42
800 BrnT 46158 2659 B6
900 BrnT 46158 2658 E6
900 MnrT 46158 2658 A6
1600 MnrT 46158 2657 E7
2000 MnrT 46157 2657 E7
2000 MNVA 46158 2657 E7
SR-42 E High St
10 MRVL 46158 2659 E4
300 MRVL 46158 2660 A4
400 BrnT 46158 2660 A4
SR-42 W High St
10 MRVL 46158 2659 E4
SR-42 E Main St
200 MNVA 46157 2657 D7
500 MnrT 46157 2657 E7
SR-47
10 WshT 46052 1567 E2
10 WshT 46052 1568 A2
700 CtnT 46052 1568 D2
2000 CtnT 46052 1569 A2
2200 WshT 46071 1567 A2

SR-47 E 10th St
100 SRDN 46069 1573 A2
SR-47 W 10th St
10 SRDN 46069 1573 B2
300 AdmT 46069 1573 B2
SR-47 W 236th St
3700 AdmT 46069 1572 C2
3700 AdmT 46069 1573 A2
3900 MrnT 46069 1572 C2
SR-47 Strawtown Rd
5000 CtnT 46052 1570 B2
6000 MrnT 46052 1570 E2
7400 MrnT 46052 1571 B2
8000 MrnT 46069 1571 B2
9000 MrnT 46069 1572 A2
SR-67
- BrnT 46113 2660 A4
- BrnT 46158 2660 A4
- BrnT 46168 2660 A4
- MRVL 46113 2660 B1
- MRVL 46158 2660 B1
- VrnT 46040 2016 D3
11000 BrnT 46158 2659 D7
11000 MRVL 46158 2659 E4
SR-67 S Kentucky Av
4700 INPS 46221 2444 A6
4700 INPS 46241 2444 A6
5000 INPS 46221 2443 E7
5100 INPS 46241 2443 E7
5300 INPS 46221 2552 A4
5300 INPS 46241 2552 A4
6400 INPS 46113 2552 A4
7500 GfdT 46113 2551 D6
7500 INPS 46113 2551 D6
8600 GfdT 46168 2551 D6
8900 BrnT 46113 2660 C1
8900 BrnT 46158 2660 C1
8900 BrnT 46168 2660 C1
8900 GfdT 46168 2660 C1
SR-67 E Pendleton Pike
7500 INPS 46226 2231 B1
7500 LWNC 46226 2231 B1
8400 LWNC 46226 2122 C7
9000 LWNC 46235 2122 C7
9000 LWNC 46236 2122 E6
10000 LWNC 46235 2123 A6
10000 LWNC 46236 2123 A6
12300 LWNC 46236 2124 A2
12600 MCVL 46055 2124 B1
12600 MCVL 46236 2124 B1
SR-67 W Pendleton Pike
3000 VrnT 46040 2016 E3
3000 VrnT 46055 2016 C4
5000 VrnT 46055 2015 E6
5600 MCVL 46055 2015 E6
6500 LWNC 46236 2124 B1
6500 MCVL 46055 2124 B1
6500 MCVL 46236 2124 B1
SR-134 N Girls School Rd
2600 INPS 46214 2225 D5
SR-135
- INPS 46217 2446 C7
- INPS 46217 2555 C1
- INPS 46227 2446 C7
- INPS 46227 2555 C1
200 GNWD 46142 2664 C3
SR-135 S 300 Rd W
- GNWD 46142 2664 C3
SR-135 300 W Rd
200 GNWD 46142 2664 C4
700 GNWD 46143 2664 C5
700 WRvT 46143 2664 C5
SR-135 S Meridian St
5600 INPS 46217 2555 C1
5600 INPS 46227 2555 C1
8900 INPS 46217 2664 C1
8900 INPS 46227 2664 C1
SR-135 E Thompson Rd
10 INPS 46217 2446 C7
10 INPS 46227 2446 C7
SR-144
- MdnT 46158 2660 C6
500 MRVL 46158 2660 C6
800 BrnT 46158 2660 C6
SR-213
- WRvT 46060 1579 B2
SR-234
2100 VrnT 46040 2016 C6
2100 VrnT 46055 2016 C6
SR-234 W 800 N
3000 VrnT 46055 2016 D6
5000 MCVL 46055 2015 E6
5000 VrnT 46055 2015 E6
SR-236
1000 CtrT 46122 2329 B1
SR-238
- FCkT 46064 1907 E7
- GrnT 46040 1907 E7
- GrnT 46064 1907 E7
- VrnT 46040 1907 E7
2600 VrnT 46040 2016 E1
SR-238 Greenfield Av
- NBVL 46060 1906 D1
1000 NBVL 46060 1795 D2
1800 NbvT 46060 1795 E3
2500 NBVL 46060 1796 C4
2500 NbvT 46060 1796 C4
10800 WynT 46060 1796 C4
12000 NBVL 46060 1797 A6
12000 WynT 46060 1797 A6
SR-267
- PNFD 46168 2550 E2
10 AVON 46123 2332 B4
300 WshT 46123 2332 B4
500 MRVL 46158 2659 D2
1500 WshT 46123 2223 B7
1800 WshT 46123 2441 B3
1900 WshT 46168 2441 B3
2100 LcnT 46123 2223 B6
2500 LcnT 46112 2223 B5
2500 PNFD 46168 2441 B3
2800 GfdT 46168 2441 B3
3500 BNBG 46112 2223 B3
4100 PryT 46052 1896 C3

INDEX 49
SR-267 Indianapolis Street Index N Strathmore Dr

STREET Block City ZIP Map# Grid

SR-267
7000 PryT 46052 2005 C2
7300 BNBG 46112 2114 C3
7500 BrnT 46112 2114 C2
7600 BrnT 46112 2005 C2
7600 GfdT 46158 2550 C6
7600 GfdT 46158 2550 D5
7600 PryT 46112 2005 C2
8700 BrnT 46158 2659 D2
8700 GfdT 46158 2659 D2
SR-267 S 400 E
- PryT 46052 1896 C2
- PryT 46075 1896 C2
SR-267 E 750 S
- GfdT 46168 2550 E5
SR-267 Avon Av
100 PNFD 46168 2441 B5
SR-267 County Rd 400 E
- PryT 46052 1896 C1
- PryT 46075 1896 C1
- WrhT 46075 1896 C1
SR-267 N Green St
10 BNBG 46112 2114 B7
1400 BrnT 46112 2114 C2
SR-267 S Green St
10 BNBG 46112 2114 C7
500 BNBG 46112 2223 B1
1400 LcnT 46112 2223 B1
SR-267 S Indiana St
10 MRVL 46158 2659 E3
SR-267 E Main St
300 PNFD 46168 2441 E6
SR-267 W Main St
10 MRVL 46158 2659 E3
SR-267 N Monroe St
10 MRVL 46158 2659 D3
SR-267 Quaker Blvd
1600 PNFD 46168 2550 E1
4600 PNFD 46168 2441 E6
SR-334
- EglT 46112 1897 C6
6000 EglT 46077 1897 C6
7000 EglT 46077 1898 A6
11200 ZNVL 46077 1899 C6
11700 EglT 46077 1899 C6
SR-334 S 1st St
100 ZNVL 46077 1899 B6
SR-334 E 650 S
5800 EglT 46112 1897 B6
5800 PryT 46052 1897 B6
5800 PryT 46112 1897 B6
SR-334 W Oak St
100 ZNVL 46077 1899 B6
1500 ZNVL 46077 1898 D6
9400 EglT 46077 1898 D6
SR-334 E Sycamore St
10 ZNVL 46077 1899 B6
SR-431
- CRML 46032 1793 B7
- CRML 46032 1902 B1
- CRML 46033 1793 B7
- CRML 46033 1902 B1
SR-431 N Keystone Av
8600 INPS 46240 2011 C1
9200 ClyT 46240 2011 C1
9200 CRML 46240 2011 C1
9600 ClyT 46280 2011 C1
9800 CRML 46032 2011 C1
9800 CRML 46033 2011 C1
9800 CRML 46280 2011 C1
9900 ClyT 46032 1902 C7
9900 CRML 46032 1902 C7
9900 CRML 46033 1902 C4
W Staat St
400 VrnT 46040 2016 E2
Stable Cir
1600 INPS 46239 2341 B6
Stable Dr
10700 INPS 46239 2341 B6
Stable Chase
- NBVL 46060 1796 E5
Stacey St
14100 CRML 46033 1793 C7
Stacie Cir
12100 LWNC 46236 2123 E1
Stack Ct
10600 INPS 46229 2232 B5
Stacy Lynn Ct
8300 INPS 46231 2334 B7
Stacy Lynn Dr
1500 INPS 46231 2334 B7
Stadium Dr
- INPS 46202 2337 A1
N Stadium Dr
1100 INPS 46202 2337 A1
1500 INPS 46202 2227 E7
1500 INPS 46202 2336 E1
S Stadium Dr
300 BNBG 46112 2114 D7
400 BNBG 46112 2223 D1
Stafford Ct
8000 INPS 46260 2010 A6
Stafford Ln
8200 INPS 46260 2010 A5
Stafford Pl
6400 EglT 46077 1897 D6
Stafford Rd
- GfdT 46168 2442 C6
- GfdT 46231 2442 C6
- PNFD 46168 2442 C6
- PNFD 46231 2442 C6
100 PNFD 46168 2441 D6
5800 INPS 46228 2119 B4
Stafford Wy
5800 INPS 46228 2119 A4
Stafford Castle Ln
5700 INPS 46250 2012 C4
Staffordshire Cir
5900 INPS 46254 2117 B4
Stage Coach Tr
- FCkT 46038 1905 B4
- FSHR 46038 1905 B4
Stagg Hill Dr
13200 CRML 46033 1903 C2

Staghorn Ct
13900 CRML 46033 1903 E1
Staghorn Dr
14000 CRML 46032 1792 A7
14000 CRML 46032 1901 A1
Staghorn Rd
8700 INPS 46260 2009 E4
Stallion Ct
14100 CRML 46074 1791 D7
Stamford Ct
7400 FSHR 46038 1904 A7
Stamford Dr
- MdlT 46167 2112 E5
- MdlT 46167 2113 A5
Stamm Av
2900 INPS 46240 2120 C1
Stamm St
1500 INPS 46240 2120 A1
Standard Av
1200 INPS 46221 2336 E5
1200 INPS 46221 2337 A5
Standing Tree Wy
10100 FSHR 46038 1905 A4
Standish Av
700 INPS 46227 2446 D4
1400 INPS 46227 2447 A4
Standish Ct
3700 INPS 46221 2444 D4
Standish Dr
1100 GNWD 46142 2664 E3
4400 INPS 46221 2444 D4
Standish Pl
10500 NBVL 46060 1687 B4
Standish St
- CRML 46032 1902 A4
Stanford Ct
2600 INPS 46268 2009 C3
Stanford Dr
- CRML 46074 1900 B1
Stanhope Dr
6600 INPS 46254 2116 E7
Stanhope Ln
5100 INPS 46254 2116 E7
Stanhope St
1900 CRML 46032 1900 D3
Stanhope Wy
6600 INPS 46254 2116 E6
6600 INPS 46254 2117 A6
Stanley Av
- INPS 46203 2446 D2
3000 INPS 46227 2446 D3
Stanley Dr
1000 ZNVL 46077 1899 B3
Stanley Dr E
- WshT 46123 2331 E2
Stanley Rd
- PNFD 46168 2442 A7
900 PNFD 46168 2441 D7
5200 INPS 46241 2443 A7
5500 INPS 46241 2552 A1
S Stanley Rd
6500 INPS 46113 2552 A3
Stanley Ter
11800 FSHR 46038 1906 E5
N Stansbury Blvd
- BCkT 46055 2124 B4
Stansbury Ct
1300 WRvT 46143 2664 B6
4600 INPS 46254 2116 C7
Stansbury Ln
4600 INPS 46254 2116 D7
Stansfield Dr
900 CRML 46032 1901 E6
E Stanton Av
3600 INPS 46201 2338 D4
Stanton Ct
800 CRML 46033 1902 D1
Stanwich Pl
12600 CRML 46033 1903 C3
Star Cir
13100 FSHR 46060 1906 B2
Star Dr
12800 FSHR 46060 1906 B2
Star Ln
10 MRVL 46158 2659 E1
Starboard Rd
14800 FCkT 46040 1907 A6
Starboard Wy
10400 INPS 46256 2014 B4
Starcross Dr
1200 INPS 46239 2341 A6
Stardust Blvd
800 NbvT 46060 1686 D5
Stardust Dr
9000 INPS 46229 2231 D6
9800 INPS 46229 2232 A6
Star Fire Dr
1900 INPS 46229 2232 D7
E Stargrass Dr
10 WshT 46074 1792 C4
Stargrass Ln
15700 WshT 46074 1792 C4
Starhaven Cir
10300 INPS 46229 2232 B5
Starhaven Ct
10300 INPS 46229 2232 A5
Stark Dr
- GNWD 46142 2664 B3
8300 LWNC 46216 2122 C5
Stark Rd
200 AVON 46123 2333 B3
Starkey Av
1100 ZNVL 46077 1899 A7
Starkey Rd
500 ZNVL 46077 1899 A7
Starkey Ridge Ln
6800 INPS 46268 2118 A1
Starlight Ct
20100 NbvT 46062 1685 A2
Starlight Dr
4300 INPS 46239 2449 D5
Starsong Dr
5300 INPS 46241 2444 C3
Stars Pride Ct
15100 WshT 46032 1792 D5

N Starter St
10 CBLD 46229 2341 E2
S Starter St
10 CBLD 46229 2341 E3
Starview Ct
10400 INPS 46229 2232 B5
Starview Dr
10300 INPS 46229 2232 A5
N State Av
1200 INPS 46201 2338 A1
S State Av
10 INPS 46201 2338 A4
500 INPS 46203 2338 A7
2200 INPS 46203 2447 A1
3000 INPS 46237 2447 A3
3300 INPS 46227 2447 A4
5500 INPS 46227 2556 A1
N State St
10 GNFD 46140 2345 D1
100 WTLD 46184 2775 B5
2300 GNFD 46140 2236 D3
2700 CtrT 46140 2236 D3
N State St SR-9
10 GNFD 46140 2345 D1
2300 GNFD 46140 2236 D3
2700 CtrT 46140 2236 D3
S State St
10 GNFD 46140 2345 E3
10 WTLD 46184 2775 B6
1900 CtrT 46140 2345 E5
S State St SR-9
10 GNFD 46140 2345 E3
1900 CtrT 46140 2345 E5
E Staten Ln
10 MdnT 46113 2661 E3
10 MdnT 46113 2662 A3
Staten Pl
10 ZNVL 46077 1899 A4
S State Road 267
- GfdT 46168 2441 B3
- PNFD 46168 2441 B3
- WshT 46168 2441 B3
States Bend Dr
7800 INPS 46239 2449 B3
States Bend Ln
7800 INPS 46239 2449 B3
Statesman Ct
10 BNBG 46112 2223 E3
Statesman Dr
1000 BNBG 46112 2223 D3
Statesmen Dr
- INPS 46250 2012 A6
4000 INPS 46250 2011 E6
Statesmen Pl
4600 INPS 46250 2011 E6
Statesmen Wy
4400 INPS 46250 2011 E6
Station Dr
600 CRML 46032 1902 C5
Station St
2300 INPS 46218 2229 D5
7600 INPS 46240 2011 D7
8700 FSHR 46038 1904 D5
N Station St
3300 INPS 46218 2229 D3
W Station Wy
6000 BCkT 46140 2233 D2
Station Hill Dr
5500 WshT 46123 2331 D4
Staton Place East Dr
700 INPS 46234 2334 C1
Staton Place West Dr
700 INPS 46234 2334 C1
Statuette Ct
3500 INPS 46214 2225 B2
Stauffer Row
2900 INPS 46268 2009 B3
Staughton Dr
4300 INPS 46226 2120 E7
5900 INPS 46226 2121 C7
Stave Oak Ct
1200 BHGV 46107 2447 E5
Stave Oak Dr
900 BHGV 46107 2447 E5
1100 INPS 46107 2447 E5
Steambrook Dr
10300 FSHR 46038 2012 C1
Stearns Hill Ct
6600 INPS 46237 2557 D2
Stearns Hill Dr
6500 INPS 46237 2557 D3
Steele St
1500 INPS 46201 2338 A1
Steelers Blvd
- FCkT 46038 1906 A3
Steel Ford Rd
100 CtrT 46140 2345 E5
100 GNFD 46140 2345 E5
200 CtrT 46140 2346 A4
E Steel Ford Rd
2600 CtrT 46140 2346 A5
Steelwater Ct
11100 INPS 46235 2232 C2
Steelwater Ln
3900 INPS 46235 2232 C2
Steelwater Wy
3900 INPS 46235 2232 C2
Steeplebush Ct
10300 NBVL 46060 1687 B3
Steeplechase Dr
- WshT 46123 2333 D2
10 ClyT 46032 1900 B7
10 ClyT 46032 2009 B1
9100 INPS 46250 2012 D3
10200 AVON 46123 2333 C3
Steer St
3500 INPS 46222 2336 B3
Stein Rd
- ClkT 46143 2668 A3
Steinmeier Ct
5400 INPS 46250 2121 B1
Steinmeier Dr
6800 INPS 46220 2121 B2
7100 INPS 46250 2121 B1
7400 INPS 46250 2012 A7

Steinmeier Dr N
5300 INPS 46220 2121 B1
Steinmeier Dr W
6800 INPS 46220 2121 B2
Steinmeier Ln
6800 INPS 46220 2121 B2
Steinmetz Dr
3900 INPS 46254 2226 B2
Stella Ct
14300 FCkT 46040 1906 E7
Stella Dr
3100 WRvT 46143 2664 B5
Stella St
6300 LWNC 46236 2123 E3
Stelor Ct
10500 FCkT 46038 1905 B7
Sten Ct
8400 INPS 46227 2556 A6
Stephan Cir
5000 INPS 46203 2337 D5
Stephanie Ln
200 INPS 46227 2446 C3
Stephanie St
- WTFD 46033 1793 C7
14400 CRML 46033 1793 C7
Stephanie Ann Dr
9500 LWNC 46235 2122 E7
Stephen Ct
200 ClyT 46280 1901 D7
Stephen Dr
500 BNBG 46112 2223 B1
Stepping Stone Dr
11700 FSHR 46038 1905 E4
Sterling Coms
13000 FSHR 46038 1905 A2
Sterling Ct
100 PTBR 46167 2112 E3
Sterling Dr
100 PTBR 46167 2112 E3
Sterling St
1000 INPS 46201 2338 A1
Sterling Apple Dr
10600 INPS 46235 2232 B2
Sterling Bluff Ct
4100 WTFD 46033 1793 E4
Sterling Ridge Run
8900 INPS 46236 2014 E4
Stern Dr
12000 FCkT 46256 2014 E2
12000 FCkT 46256 2015 A2
Sterrett Blvd
11500 LWNC 46236 2014 D7
Stetson Ln
- GNWD 46143 2665 B7
Stevedon Ct
1000 PNFD 46168 2550 C1
Steven Ln
- WRvT 46142 2663 B2
Steven St
1400 BrnT 46158 2660 B7
6900 INPS 46260 2119 B1
N Steven St
- BrnT 46158 2660 A6
Stevens Ct
10 GNFD 46140 2236 D7
Stevens Dr
10 PNFD 46168 2441 E4
Stevens Rd
1100 ZNVL 46077 1899 C3
Stevens St
500 INPS 46203 2337 D5
1400 INPS 46227 2555 E2
1400 INPS 46227 2556 A2
Stevenson St
1600 INPS 46228 2118 E5
Steward Ct
10600 FCkT 46040 1906 E7
Stewart Cir
14500 FSHR 46060 1796 B6
Stewart Ct
7000 INPS 46256 2122 D1
Stewart Rd
2500 PryT 46052 1895 E1
2500 PryT 46052 1896 A1
Stiles Dr
- FCkT 46060 1907 D1
Stiles Rd
500 BrnT 46158 2658 D2
1800 MnrT 46158 2658 D2
Stillcreek Dr
10600 INPS 46239 2341 B4
Stillcrest Ln
2800 INPS 46217 2554 D4
Still Haven Ct
11700 INPS 46229 2232 E7
Stillman Av
2800 INPS 46268 2009 C3
Stillmeadow Dr
3100 INPS 46214 2225 B4
Stillwater Ct
1200 GNWD 46142 2664 E2
10900 FSHR 46038 2014 C1
Stillwater Ln
500 GNWD 46142 2664 E2
6900 INPS 46268 2118 C2
W Stillwater Ln
1200 GNWD 46142 2664 D2
Stillwater Rd
- LcnT 46112 2224 E2
Stillwell Ct
10300 WshT 46123 2333 D2
Stillwell Dr
10200 WshT 46123 2333 D2
Stillwell Ln
- AVON 46123 2333 D3
- WshT 46123 2333 D3
Stillwell St
900 INPS 46202 2337 E2
Stillwood Ct
300 INPS 46239 2341 B4
Stillwood Ln
10500 INPS 46239 2341 B4
Stilton Ct
6000 LWNC 46236 2123 B4

Stilton Dr
3000 CCRO 46034 1577 B6
W Stinemeyer Ct
5800 SCkT 46163 2451 D3
Stinemyer Rd
- SCkT 46163 2451 E4
W Stinemyer Rd
5500 SCkT 46163 2451 D4
7800 INPS 46163 2450 E4
7800 INPS 46239 2450 E4
7800 SCkT 46163 2450 E4
Stingray Dr
10300 INPS 46256 2014 B3
Stirling Point Dr
- INPS 46221 2443 E7
5100 INPS 46241 2443 E7
Stirrup Ct
8700 INPS 46256 2013 C4
Stockard St
7500 INPS 46239 2340 A7
Stockberger Pl
5800 INPS 46241 2444 B3
Stockbridge Dr
400 WshT 46074 1792 B5
2400 INPS 46268 2118 C1
Stockport Rd
6400 INPS 46254 2117 A7
Stockton Ct
1300 INPS 46260 2010 A6
Stockton Dr
18700 NBVL 46062 1685 E5
18900 NBVL 46062 1686 A5
Stockton St
900 INPS 46260 2010 A6
Stockwell Ct
5500 INPS 46237 2557 B2
Stockwell Dr
6300 INPS 46237 2557 B3
10100 FSHR 46060 1905 A1
Stoeppelwerth Dr
11300 INPS 46229 2232 D7
Stokley Blvd
400 GNWD 46143 2665 D4
Stolz St
500 LEBN 46052 1676 E6
Stone Dr
12400 INPS 46236 2015 A4
13600 CRML 46032 1901 B1
Stone Ln
600 AVON 46123 2332 D5
Stone Rd
900 WRvT 46143 2663 B5
S Stone Wy
3700 SCkT 46163 2451 E2
W Stone Wy
5200 SCkT 46163 2451 E1
5200 SCkT 46163 2452 A1
Stonebluff Ln
- NBVL 46062 1685 B5
Stonebranch East Dr
7900 INPS 46256 2013 B4
Stonebranch North Dr
7800 INPS 46256 2013 B3
Stonebranch South Dr
7700 INPS 46256 2013 B6
Stonebridge Ct
10300 FSHR 46038 1905 B5
Stonebridge Dr
700 WshT 46123 2332 C2
9100 INPS 46240 2011 E3
Stonebrook Pl
11600 FSHR 46038 1903 E5
Stonechat Ln
5700 INPS 46237 2557 B3
Stonecreek Ct
6400 INPS 46268 2117 D3
Stonecreek Dr
6000 PNFD 46168 2550 D2
6300 INPS 46268 2117 C3
Stonecrest Ct
4100 INPS 46226 2230 A1
Stone Crossing Ln
- NBVL 46062 1685 B5
Stonegate Ct
7300 INPS 46256 2013 B7
7300 INPS 46256 2122 B1
14500 CRML 46032 1792 A6
Stonegate Dr
10400 FCkT 46040 2015 D1
Stonegate Ln
700 INPS 46227 2555 C7
6200 EglT 46077 1898 A6
Stonegate Rd
- GNWD 46227 2664 C1
- INPS 46142 2664 C1
- INPS 46227 2664 C1
1100 GNWD 46142 2664 C1
8900 INPS 46227 2555 C7
Stonegate Run
6100 EglT 46077 1898 A6
Stoneham Dr
2000 INPS 46260 2009 D7
2000 INPS 46260 2118 D1
Stone Harbour Dr
- NBVL 46062 1685 E5
Stone Haven Dr
13500 CRML 46033 1903 D2
Stonehaven Ln
4900 SCkT 46163 2451 D1
S Stonehaven Ln
3600 SCkT 46163 2451 E2
W Stonehaven Ln
- SCkT 46163 2451 E2
4800 NPLN 46163 2452 A2
Stonehedge Ct
10 CRML 46032 1793 A7
1500 GNWD 46142 2664 C1
Stonehedge Dr
300 CRML 46032 1793 A7
Stonehedge East Dr
1100 GNWD 46142 2664 D1
1200 INPS 46142 2664 D1
1200 INPS 46227 2664 D1
Stonehedge West Dr
1500 GNWD 46142 2664 C1

Stone Hill Dr
5700 INPS 46208 2119 C5
Stonehinge Cir
8000 INPS 46260 2009 E6
Stonehinge Ct N
8000 INPS 46260 2009 E6
Stonehinge Ct S
7900 INPS 46260 2009 E6
Stonehinge Dr
1600 INPS 46260 2009 C7
Stonehurst Ct
7400 INPS 46256 2122 B1
Stonehurst Dr
7800 INPS 46256 2122 B1
Stone Key Wy
13900 FCkT 46038 1906 D6
Stoneleigh Ct
500 INPS 46231 2334 A5
Stonemill Cir
1300 CRML 46032 1792 D7
Stonemill Cir N
1300 CRML 46032 1792 C7
Stonemill Cir S
1400 CRML 46032 1792 C7
Stone Mill Ct
10700 FSHR 46038 1904 B7
Stone Mill Dr
4100 INPS 46237 2556 E1
Stonemill Dr
600 GNWD 46143 2665 B5
Stone Pine Tr
5800 CRML 46033 1903 D1
Stonereath Cts
8000 INPS 46237 2557 B6
Stoneridge Ct
2800 CRML 46032 2011 C1
Stoneridge Dr
4100 LcnT 46112 2222 E2
5800 INPS 46226 2121 E5
Stone Ring Cir
8200 INPS 46268 2009 A6
Stones Bluff Ln
9000 INPS 46113 2551 E7
Stones Bluff Pl
9000 INPS 46113 2551 E7
Stones Ferry Pl
9200 INPS 46278 2007 B3
Stones Ferry Rd
8300 INPS 46278 2007 B3
Stones Ferry Wy
9200 INPS 46278 2007 B3
Stones River Cir
8000 INPS 46259 2558 B5
Stones River Ct
7600 INPS 46259 2558 B5
Stones River Dr
7500 INPS 46259 2558 B4
Stoneview Ln
200 MRVL 46158 2660 B4
Stonewall Dr
1500 GNFD 46140 2237 B7
8400 INPS 46231 2334 A5
Stone Wall Ln
- ZNVL 46077 1898 E7
Stonewall Ln
- WshT 46123 2333 D2
Stoneway Ln
2800 CRML 46032 2011 C1
Stonewick Dr
- CRML 46033 1903 A5
Stonewood Ct
14000 FSHR 46038 1906 D4
Stonewood Dr
1600 INPS 46239 2341 B6
Stonewood Pl
14100 FSHR 46038 1906 D4
Stoney Bay Cir
11800 CRML 46033 1903 A4
Stoney Bend Cir
8100 INPS 46259 2558 B5
Stoney Bend Ct
7900 INPS 46259 2558 B5
Stoneybrook Ct
100 GNWD 46142 2664 D3
Stoneybrook Dr
10 BNBG 46112 2114 B5
10 GNWD 46142 2664 D3
Stoneybrook Grove Dr
300 GNWD 46142 2664 E2
Stoneybrook Grove Ln
1500 GNWD 46142 2664 C3
Stoney Creek Cir
500 NBVL 46060 1795 D3
1300 CRML 46032 1792 C7
1300 CRML 46032 1901 C1
Stoney Creek Ct
10900 INPS 46239 2341 C5
Stoney Creek Ovlk
100 NBVL 46060 1795 D3
Stoney Croft Ln
- SPRT 46227 2556 C5
Stoney Moon Dr
- NBVL 46060 1796 D1
Stoney Side Ct
7600 INPS 46259 2558 A5
Stoney Side Ln
7500 INPS 46259 2558 A5
Stony Ln
100 WynT 46060 1796 D1
Stonybrook Cir
10000 INPS 46229 2341 A1
Stony Brook Dr
11200 INPS 46229 2232 C5
Stony Creek Dr
500 WshT 46234 2333 D2
Stony Creek Rd
1600 NBVL 46060 1795 E2
1600 NbvT 46060 1795 E2
1800 NBVL 46060 1796 A1
Stony Creek Wy
15200 NBVL 46060 1795 D5
S Stony Ridge Ct
3700 SCkT 46163 2452 A1
Stony Ridge Dr
16200 NBVL 46060 1796 A3

Stony Ridge Dr
16200 NbvT 46060 1796 A3
Stony Ridge Wy
6500 INPS 46260 2119 A3
E Stop 10 Rd
1100 INPS 46227 2555 E4
1400 INPS 46227 2556 A4
2400 SPRT 46227 2556 B4
Stop 10 St
10 SPRT 46227 2556 B4
E Stop 11 Rd
500 INPS 46227 2555 D6
1300 INPS 46227 2556 A5
2700 SPRT 46227 2556 B6
3800 INPS 46237 2556 D6
4800 INPS 46237 2557 A5
7000 INPS 46259 2557 E5
7200 INPS 46259 2558 A5
W Stop 11 Rd
1000 INPS 46217 2555 A6
1300 INPS 46217 2554 E6
E Stop 12 Rd
1100 INPS 46227 2555 E7
1500 INPS 46227 2556 A7
E Stop 13 Rd
1900 INPS 46227 2556 A7
Stop 18 Rd
- GNWD 46143 2665 E6
- GNWD 46143 2666 A6
- PltT 46143 2666 A6
E Stop 18 Rd
10 GNWD 46143 2665 D6
W Stop 18 Rd
10 GNWD 46143 2665 B6
500 PltT 46143 2665 B6
E Stop Eleven Rd
10 INPS 46227 2555 C5
W Stop Eleven Rd
10 INPS 46217 2555 B5
1200 INPS 46217 2554 E6
E Stop Ten Rd
1500 INPS 46227 2556 A4
3800 INPS 46237 2556 D4
E Stop Thirteen Rd
10 INPS 46227 2555 C7
2200 INPS 46227 2556 B7
Storm Bay Cir
- MCVL 46055 2015 D4
Stormhaven Ct
8900 INPS 46256 2014 B4
Stormhaven Wy
10300 INPS 46256 2014 B4
Storms Av
1500 INPS 46203 2447 A2
Stormy Ln
10 MRVL 46158 2659 D3
Stormy Port
- MCVL 46055 2015 C4
Stormy Ridge Ct
1400 CRML 46032 1901 C1
Story Ct
5500 INPS 46221 2552 E1
15000 WshT 46074 1792 B5
Story Dr
8700 GfdT 46113 2551 E7
Stouffer Ct
9400 INPS 46235 2231 E1
Stouffer Ln
4200 INPS 46235 2231 E1
Stoughton Ct
4700 INPS 46254 2116 D7
Stout Dr
14900 NBVL 46062 1794 C6
Stout Field Ter
1700 INPS 46241 2335 E7
Stout Field East Dr
1700 INPS 46241 2335 E7
1800 INPS 46241 2444 E1
Stout Field North Dr
4300 INPS 46241 2444 E1
Stout Field South Dr
4300 INPS 46241 2444 D1
Stout Field West Dr
1700 INPS 46241 2335 E7
4300 INPS 46241 2444 E1
Stover Av
500 INPS 46227 2446 D5
Stradford Ct
1200 GNWD 46142 2664 E3
N Strahl Dr
3600 CtrT 46140 2236 D1
Straley Ct
14700 WTFD 46033 1793 D6
Strand Ct
19100 NBVL 46060 1686 D4
Strand Ln
200 AVON 46123 2333 B4
Stratfield Dr
7700 LWNC 46236 2014 E7
Stratford Av
4500 INPS 46201 2338 E4
4800 INPS 46201 2339 A4
Stratford Ct
10 CRML 46033 1902 D7
4000 INPS 46235 2231 D2
Stratford Dr N
6300 FSHR 46038 1903 D6
Stratford Dr S
6300 FSHR 46038 1903 D6
Stratford Pl
3600 CRML 46033 1902 D7
Stratford Wy
- DNVL 46122 2329 E3
100 DNVL 46122 2330 A3
10800 FSHR 46038 1903 D6
Stratford Hall St
1000 INPS 46260 2010 A4
Strathdon Pl
- INPS 46236 2014 D6
E Strathmore Ct
9800 INPS 46235 2231 E4
9800 INPS 46235 2232 A3
N Strathmore Dr
3800 INPS 46235 2231 E2

STREET Block City ZIP Map# Grid

Stratton Cir
10700 ClyT 46032 1900 B7
Stratton Ct
9100 FSHR 46038 2013 D2
Stratton Sq
6900 INPS 46260 2118 D2
Strauss Dr
14600 WshT 46032 1792 C6
Strawberry Ln
300 INPS 46219 2340 A3
Strawbridge Ln
- BNBG 46112 2223 D1
Strawbridge St
4500 INPS 46237 2447 D6
Strawflower Dr
4300 INPS 46203 2448 C5
Straw Hat Ct
5300 INPS 46237 2448 B7
Straw Hat Dr
5200 INPS 46237 2448 B7
Strawtown Av
12000 WRvT 46034 1578 D3
12000 WRvT 46060 1578 D3
12000 WRvT 46060 1579 B4
13000 WRvT 46060 1580 B2
Strawtown Rd
5000 CtnT 46052 1570 B2
6000 MrnT 46052 1570 B2
7400 MrnT 46052 1571 A2
8000 MrnT 46069 1571 A2
9000 MrnT 46069 1572 A2
Strawtown Rd SR-47
5000 CtnT 46052 1570 B2
6000 MrnT 46052 1570 B2
7400 MrnT 46052 1571 A2
8000 MrnT 46069 1571 A2
9000 MrnT 46069 1572 A2
Streamside Ct
6400 INPS 46278 2117 B2
Streamside Dr
- CRML 46033 1794 C7
5600 INPS 46278 2117 B2
Stream View Ct
8100 INPS 46217 2554 E6
Streamwood Ln
5900 INPS 46237 2557 B5
Street 1
- WshT 46069 1683 D1
Stringtown Pike
1000 CCRO 46034 1577 C4
2000 JknT 46034 1577 C4
Strobus Dr
- GNWD 46184 2774 B1
Strongbow Rd
- FCkT 46040 2015 E1
Stuart Ct
1200 CCRO 46034 1577 B5
Stuart Dr
400 LcnT 46112 2224 E2
Stuart St
2500 INPS 46218 2229 C5
Stubbington Ln
- MCVL 46055 2124 C1
Studebaker Ct
6700 INPS 46214 2225 E4
Studebaker Ln
6700 INPS 46214 2225 E4
Sturbridge Rd
1600 INPS 46260 2009 E4
Sturgeon Wy
4800 INPS 46237 2448 B6
Sturgeon Bay Ln
8600 INPS 46236 2014 D4
Sturm Av
1200 INPS 46202 2337 E3
1400 INPS 46201 2337 E3
1500 INPS 46201 2338 A3
Stutsman Dr
100 GNFD 46140 2345 B2
Styleline Dr
300 MRVL 46158 2659 D3
Stymie Ct
1100 INPS 46217 2555 B5
1200 INPS 46217 2554 E5
Suburban Dr
5600 INPS 46224 2226 B3
Subway St
- BHGV 46203 2448 A2
4800 BHGV 46107 2448 A2
4800 INPS 46107 2448 A2
4800 INPS 46203 2448 A2
Suda Dr
2000 ClyT 46280 2011 B1
Sudbury Ct
400 INPS 46234 2334 A2
Sue Dr
5100 CRML 46033 1794 A7
Sue Springs Ct
10 CRML 46033 1902 C5
Suffolk Ct
3300 WRvT 46143 2664 B6
Suffolk Ln
600 CRML 46032 1901 A4
1900 INPS 46260 2009 D7
Sugar Bay Ln
4500 INPS 46237 2448 E6
N Sugar Bend Run
1100 BCkT 46140 2235 A6
Sugarberry Ct
1300 MRVL 46158 2660 C2
7800 LWNC 46236 2014 E6
7800 LWNC 46236 2015 A6
Sugarbush Dr
600 ZNVL 46077 1899 A7
Sugar Bush Ln N
300 BNBG 46112 2223 C2
Sugar Bush Ln S
200 BNBG 46112 2223 C2
Sugarbush Rd
800 ZNVL 46077 1899 A7
800 ZNVL 46077 2008 A1
Sugar Cay Ct
5000 CRML 46033 1903 A3
Sugar Creek Av
- SCkT 46163 2452 C3
Sugar Creek Dr
- SCkT 46140 2343 E3
- SGLK 46140 2343 E3
Sugarcreek Dr
- NPLN 46163 2452 B4
N Sugar Creek Dr
10 NPLN 46163 2452 B3
S Sugar Creek Dr
10 NPLN 46163 2452 B3
W Sugar Creek Dr
2500 SCkT 46140 2344 A3
2500 SGLK 46140 2344 A3
2700 SGLK 46140 2343 E3
Sugar Creek Rd
11900 NBVL 46060 1796 E2
N Sugar Creek Tr
1800 CtrT 46140 2235 C5
Sugar Creek Addition
- MrlT 46126 2560 C7
N Sugar Creek Lee Dr
8000 MrlT 46126 2560 D7
N Sugar Creek Myrtle Ln
8000 MrlT 46126 2560 D7
Sugar Grove Av
1800 INPS 46202 2227 E7
2300 INPS 46208 2227 E6
N Sugar Grove Av
1600 INPS 46202 2227 E7
Sugarleaf Pl
9800 FSHR 46060 1905 A1
Sugar Loaf Ct
3400 CRML 46033 2011 D2
Sugar Loaf Dr
3500 CRML 46033 2011 D2
Sugar Maple Ct
3000 CRML 46033 1902 C5
3200 INPS 46227 2556 C4
Sugar Maple Dr
- GNWD 46143 2666 A6
Sugar Maple Ln
600 MRVL 46158 2660 A6
Sugar Pine Ct
7400 AVON 46123 2332 C5
Sugar Pine Pt
8700 INPS 46256 2013 C4
Sugar Tree Ln
400 INPS 46260 2010 B4
Sugarwood Dr
600 MRVL 46158 2659 D2
Sugarwood Ln
100 WshT 46123 2331 C5
Suggins Dr
- NbvT 46062 1685 D7
- NbvT 46062 1794 C1
Sulky Ct
500 INPS 46227 2555 D5
Sulky Wy
14800 WshT 46032 1792 C6
Sullivan Ct
6300 INPS 46224 2226 A6
Sullivan Dr
1500 LtyT 46118 2548 B1
Sullivan Pl
9400 EglT 46077 2007 D1
Sullivans Rd
- ZNVL 46077 2008 A1
Sumac Ct
1300 CRML 46033 1902 D2
Sumac Ln
9900 LWNC 46236 2014 A7
Summer Ct
400 GNWD 46143 2665 D1
Summer Hl
900 CRML 46032 1901 A1
Summer Rd
800 GNWD 46143 2665 D1
15100 NBVL 46060 1796 E5
15100 WynT 46060 1796 E5
19100 WynT 46060 1687 E4
Summer Wy
- ZNVL 46077 1898 E2
300 PNFD 46168 2442 A4
Summer Breeze Cir
3300 INPS 46239 2449 C3
Summer Breeze Dr
- INPS 46239 2449 C3
Summer Breeze Ln
3300 INPS 46239 2449 C3
Summer Breeze Wy
- GNWD 46143 2665 C7
- GNWD 46143 2774 C1
Summerbrook Ct
5900 CRML 46033 1903 C4
Summer Estate Dr
8800 INPS 46256 2013 D5
Summerfield Cir
3200 INPS 46214 2225 E4
Summerfield Dr
- PNFD 46168 2442 B1
3100 INPS 46214 2225 E3
N Summerfield Dr
300 BCkT 46140 2343 D1
Summerfield Dr N
6900 INPS 46214 2225 E3
S Summerhaven Ct
- SCkT 46163 2343 B3
Summerhaven Dr
4200 SCkT 46163 2343 B3
Summerhill Blvd
5400 INPS 46254 2117 C5
Summerhouse Dr
1200 INPS 46217 2554 E4
Summerlakes Ct
1600 ClyT 46032 2009 D2
Summerlakes Dr
9600 ClyT 46032 2009 D2
Summer Lea Ct
7300 INPS 46217 2554 E4
Summerlin Wy
10100 FCkT 46038 2015 A1
Summer Meadow Ct
1300 INPS 46217 2554 D3
Summer Oak Dr
7000 NBVL 46062 1685 E6
7200 NBVL 46062 1686 A6
Summer Ridge Pl
9500 ClyT 46260 2009 E3
9500 INPS 46260 2009 E3
Summersby Ln
700 BNBG 46112 2114 D4
Summersong Dr
3000 INPS 46241 2444 C3
Summersong Rd
- ZNVL 46077 1899 B3
Summer Sweet Ln
1900 CRML 46033 1902 C2
1900 CRML 46033 1903 A1
Summer Time Dr
6800 INPS 46226 2230 D1
Summertree Ct
8100 INPS 46256 2013 B5
Summertree Ln
8400 INPS 46256 2013 B5
Summer Walk Dr E
8700 INPS 46227 2556 C7
8900 INPS 46227 2665 C1
Summer Walk Dr S
8900 INPS 46227 2556 D7
Summer Walk Dr W
8800 INPS 46227 2556 C7
Summerwood
600 CBLD 46229 2341 C1
Summerwood Blvd
900 CtrT 46140 2237 B7
Summerwood Ln
- GNWD 46143 2774 D1
10600 FSHR 46060 1905 B2
Summet St
4100 LtyT 46168 2439 E5
Summit Cir
11500 EglT 46077 1899 D3
Summit Ct
400 PNFD 46168 2441 A4
N Summit Ct
100 INPS 46201 2338 A3
Summit Dr
500 PNFD 46168 2441 A3
1000 CRML 46032 1902 A4
Summit Rd
20600 NBVL 46062 1685 A1
N Summit St
300 INPS 46201 2338 A3
S Summit St
100 INPS 46201 2338 A4
Summitcrest Dr
600 INPS 46241 2334 E5
N Summit Hill Dr
8100 INPS 46250 2012 E6
Summit Ridge Ct
10 WRvT 46142 2664 A4
Summit Ridge Dr
10 WRvT 46142 2663 E3
10 WRvT 46142 2664 A4
Summit Ridge Rd
4000 WRvT 46142 2663 E3
4000 WRvT 46142 2664 A3
E Sumner Av
1100 INPS 46227 2446 E3
1300 INPS 46227 2447 A4
2800 INPS 46237 2447 C4
3200 BHGV 46107 2447 C4
3200 INPS 46107 2447 C4
W Sumner Av
10 INPS 46217 2446 B4
900 INPS 46217 2445 E4
5300 INPS 46241 2444 C4
Sumter Rd
6100 INPS 46250 2121 C1
Sumter St
2100 SDWY 46224 2226 C6
Sumter Wy
3700 ClyT 46032 1900 A6
Sun Ct
7000 INPS 46241 2334 D4
Sun Dr
- INPS 46241 2334 D4
Sunbeam Cir
600 INPS 46231 2334 A5
Sunbeam Ln
200 GNWD 46143 2774 B1
Sunbird Cir
600 INPS 46231 2334 A5
Sunblest Blvd
600 FSHR 46038 1904 B4
Sunblest Blvd S
100 FSHR 46038 1904 B5
Sunblest Ct
10 FSHR 46038 1904 B5
4700 INPS 46221 2444 C6
Sunbow Cir
800 INPS 46231 2334 A5
Sunbow Dr
8800 INPS 46231 2334 A5
Sunbow Ln
700 INPS 46231 2334 A5
Sunbriar Ct
5000 CRML 46033 1903 A1
Sunburst Cir
8900 INPS 46227 2556 D7
Sunburst Ct
8800 INPS 46227 2556 C7
10700 NBVL 46060 1687 C3
Sunburst Ln
300 GNWD 46143 2774 B1
Sunburst Wy
- NBVL 46060 1687 C3
Sunbury Dr
10 MRVL 46158 2659 E2
6600 INPS 46241 2334 E6
Suncatcher Dr
11500 FCkT 46038 1905 E5
Sunchase Dr
4000 INPS 46239 2449 C4
W Suncloud Dr
6700 SCkT 46163 2451 C1
Suncoral Cir
9800 FSHR 46060 1796 A7
Suncrest Cir
1100 INPS 46241 2335 B6
Suncrest Dr
10 GNWD 46143 2665 D1
E Suncrest Dr
1100 INPS 46241 2335 C5
N Suncrest Dr
1000 INPS 46241 2335 C5
W Suncrest Dr
1000 INPS 46241 2335 C5
Sundad Dr
2400 INPS 46239 2449 B1
Sundance Ct
3900 CRML 46077 1900 A5
Sundance Dr
7400 INPS 46237 2556 E4
7400 INPS 46237 2557 A4
S Sundance Tr
4600 INPS 46239 2449 B6
Sunday Dr
1300 INPS 46217 2554 E1
Sundew Cir
15700 WshT 46074 1792 C4
Sundial Cir
600 INPS 46231 2334 A5
S Sundial Ct
17700 WTFD 46062 1684 E7
N Sundial Dr
17800 WTFD 46062 1684 E7
Sundisk Ct
700 INPS 46231 2334 A5
Sundown Cir
500 PNFD 46168 2440 E5
600 PNFD 46168 2441 A6
Sundown Ct
600 PNFD 46168 2441 A4
Sundown Dr
- INPS 46239 2450 A2
Sundown Dr N
6600 INPS 46254 2225 E1
Sundown Dr S
6600 INPS 46254 2225 E1
Sundrop Rd
8800 INPS 46231 2334 A5
Sunfield Ct
7900 INPS 46214 2225 C4
Sunfish Ct
1200 CCRO 46034 1577 A4
1200 JknT 46034 1577 A4
8000 INPS 46236 2014 C6
Sunflower Ct
4500 ZNVL 46077 1898 D3
6600 INPS 46214 2225 E4
6600 INPS 46214 2226 D5
Sunflower Dr
7600 NBVL 46062 1686 A4
Sun Gate Ct
4000 INPS 46239 2449 C5
Sunglow Cir
700 INPS 46231 2334 A5
Sunglow Ct
8800 INPS 46231 2334 A5
Sun Gold Ct
10200 FSHR 46038 1905 B4
Sunland Ct
- WshT 46074 1792 E3
- WTFD 46074 1792 E3
Sunloch Ct
6600 INPS 46250 2012 E4
Sunmeadow Cir
3900 INPS 46228 2227 C2
Sunmeadow Ct
2900 INPS 46228 2227 C2
Sunmeadow Dr
3000 INPS 46228 2227 B2
Sunmeadow Ln
4000 INPS 46228 2227 C1
Sunmeadow Wy
2800 INPS 46228 2227 C2
Sunningdale Blvd
8400 INPS 46234 2225 A5
Sunningdale Ct
2600 INPS 46234 2225 A5
Sunny Dr
2200 LcnT 46112 2223 B4
Sunny Ln
500 NWTD 46184 2774 C4
6500 INPS 46220 2120 D2
Sunnybay Ln
11000 LWNC 46236 2014 C7
Sunnybrook Ct
1200 INPS 46229 2341 A1
S Sunnybrook Dr
500 BNBG 46112 2223 B1
Sunnybrook Ln
- GNWD 46143 2666 B6
10 LEBN 46052 1676 E6
10 LEBN 46052 1677 A4
Sunnybrook Pl
11600 FSHR 46038 1903 E5
Sunny Creek Ln
11100 LWNC 46235 2123 C4
11100 LWNC 46236 2123 C4
Sunnyfield Ct
2800 INPS 46228 2227 C2
Sunny Meade Ln
9800 ClyT 46280 2011 C2
9800 CRML 46032 2011 C2
9800 CRML 46280 2011 C2
Sunnymeade St
5100 INPS 46208 2119 A7
Sunny Ridge Dr
9000 INPS 46250 2012 B4
Sunnyside Dr
6300 INPS 46268 2117 D3
Sunnyside Ln
1100 LEBN 46052 1677 B5
Sunnyside Rd
5700 LWNC 46235 2123 C2
5700 LWNC 46236 2123 C2
7500 LWNC 46236 2014 C7
7900 INPS 46236 2014 C7
Sun Park Dr
17500 WTFD 46074 1683 E7
17500 WTFD 46074 1684 A7
Sun Pass Dr
5500 INPS 46254 2116 E5
Sunpoint Cir
4800 INPS 46237 2556 E4
Sunray Ct
8200 INPS 46278 2007 E5
Sunridge Cir
18000 NBVL 46062 1685 A6
Sun Ridge Ct
800 INPS 46239 2341 C5
Sunrise Cir
200 WRvT 46142 2664 A3
1700 CBLD 46229 2233 A7
11900 FSHR 46038 1904 C4
Sunrise Ct
12100 CBLD 46229 2232 E7
S Sunrise Ct
2700 SCkT 46163 2342 A7
Sunrise Dr
6900 WshT 46168 2441 B3
12200 CBLD 46229 2232 E7
12200 CBLD 46229 2233 A7
S Sunrise Dr
2700 SCkT 46163 2342 A7
Sunrise Rd
4200 INPS 46228 2227 C1
Sunrise Tr
1100 INPS 46241 2335 B5
Sun River Dr
6700 FSHR 46038 1903 E5
Sunscape Cir
4900 INPS 46237 2557 A4
Sunset Av
4200 INPS 46208 2228 B1
5200 INPS 46208 2119 B6
Sunset Blvd
200 GNWD 46142 2665 B2
Sunset Cir
6300 INPS 46241 2444 A4
Sunset Ct
100 CCRO 46034 1577 B1
7200 EglT 46077 2007 E1
N Sunset Ct
500 BCkT 46140 2234 D7
500 BCkT 46140 2343 D1
Sunset Dr
400 NBVL 46060 1686 B6
700 DNVL 46122 2329 C5
900 LEBN 46052 1676 E7
S Sunset Dr
5800 INPS 46239 2559 B1
W Sunset Dr N
3200 BCkT 46140 2343 D1
W Sunset Dr S
3200 BCkT 46140 2234 D7
3200 BCkT 46140 2343 D1
Sunset Ln
5500 INPS 46208 2119 B5
5900 INPS 46228 2119 B4
7300 INPS 46260 2119 B1
8400 INPS 46260 2010 B5
8900 LcnT 46112 2115 A6
19700 NbvT 46060 1687 B3
N Sunset Ln
6500 INPS 46260 2119 B2
Sunset Mnr
10 MRVL 46158 2659 E2
Sunset Pl
6800 WshT 46168 2441 B2
Sunset Bay
7900 LWNC 46236 2014 E6
Sunset Cove Ct
11500 LWNC 46236 2014 E6
Sunset Cove Dr
- INPS 46236 2014 D6
8000 LWNC 46236 2014 D6
Sunset Cove Ln
11500 LWNC 46236 2014 D6
Sunset Point Dr
7000 INPS 46259 2557 E2
7100 INPS 46259 2558 A2
Sunset Point Ln
10600 FSHR 46038 1905 B6
Sunset Ridge Pkwy
7000 INPS 46259 2557 E2
7100 INPS 46259 2558 A2
Sunshine Av
3900 INPS 46228 2227 A1
Sunshine Ct
700 WRvT 46142 2664 B2
Sunshine Dr
2000 SCkT 46140 2344 B1
Sunshine Wy
700 WRvT 46142 2664 A1
Sun Valley Ct
600 INPS 46217 2555 A3
Sunview Cir
4800 INPS 46237 2556 E4
4800 INPS 46237 2557 A4
Sunwood Dr
5800 INPS 46224 2226 B3
Sunwood Wy
9600 ClyT 46032 2009 D2
Superior Ln
400 AVON 46123 2333 A3
400 WshT 46123 2333 A3
Superior Rd
4000 INPS 46221 2444 D5
Superior St
- CRML 46290 2010 C1
E Superior St
100 LEBN 46052 1677 A7
W Superior St
1000 LEBN 46052 1676 D6
Super Star Ct
500 WshT 46032 1792 D5
Super Star Dr
15000 WshT 46032 1792 E5
Surina Wy
100 GNWD 46143 2665 C4
Surrey Ct
7500 INPS 46227 2555 D5
W Surrey Ct
- SCkT 46163 2451 A3
Surrey Dr
7500 INPS 46227 2555 D5
Surrey Ln
5000 CRML 46033 1903 A2
S Surrey Ln
4100 SCkT 46163 2451 A2
W Surrey Ln
7700 INPS 46163 2450 E3
7700 SCkT 46163 2450 E3
Surrey Rd
3500 INPS 46228 2118 A3
Surrey Hill Cir
5400 INPS 46226 2121 B5
Surrey Hill Ct
200 CRML 46032 1902 A3
200 NBVL 46062 1685 C1
800 GNWD 46142 2665 A4
5400 INPS 46226 2121 B6
Surrey Hill Ln
800 GNWD 46142 2665 A4
Surrey Hill Rd
5400 INPS 46226 2121 B6
Susan Ct
10 WshT 46032 1792 E5
10 WshT 46032 1793 A5
100 NbvT 46062 1794 D3
Susan Dr E
5400 INPS 46250 2012 B6
Susan Dr S
7700 INPS 46250 2012 B7
Susan Ln
5300 INPS 46226 2230 B1
Sussex Cir
300 NBVL 46062 1685 D2
Sussex Dr
6500 EglT 46077 1897 C7
Sussex Ln
2100 INPS 46229 2231 D6
Sussex Ter
9200 INPS 46229 2231 D6
Susy Ct
4000 INPS 46221 2444 E6
Susy Ln
4500 INPS 46221 2444 E6
Suter Dr
- FSHR 46060 1906 D3
Sutherland Av
500 INPS 46205 2228 D5
3300 INPS 46205 2229 A3
3300 INPS 46218 2229 A3
Sutters Ct
10100 INPS 46229 2341 A1
Sutton Av
2500 ClyT 46032 1900 D6
Sutton Dr
700 WRvT 46143 2663 C5
Sutton St
5300 INPS 46218 2230 A7
W Sutton Park Dr
3100 GNWD 46142 2664 C4
Sutton Place Dr E
11400 ClyT 46032 1900 D6
Sutton Place Dr S
2400 ClyT 46032 1900 D6
Sutton Place Dr W
11400 ClyT 46032 1900 D6
Suwanee Ct
800 INPS 46217 2555 A5
Suzanne Ct
8700 INPS 46234 2225 A7
Suzy Ln
10700 INPS 46259 2559 B1
Swails St
7500 INPS 46259 2559 C5
Swallow Ln
400 WshT 46168 2441 B1
Swallowtail Dr
7700 INPS 46214 2334 C1
Swan Ct
- PNFD 46231 2333 D6
Swan Dr
- FSHR 46038 1905 E3
Swans Wy
8400 INPS 46260 2010 A5
Swan Sea Dr
2500 INPS 46239 2449 B1
Swanson Dr
4200 INPS 46228 2227 B1
Sweeping Ridge Dr
11700 CRML 46077 1900 A5
Sweet Bay Ct
9000 INPS 46260 2009 D3
Sweet Birch Dr
8400 INPS 46239 2449 C3
Sweet Blossom Ln
1800 INPS 46229 2232 C7
Sweetbriar Av
- NWTD 46184 2774 E4
- WTLD 46184 2774 E4
Sweetbriar Dr
- GNWD 46143 2666 A5
Sweet Briar Pkwy
12800 FSHR 46038 1905 B3
13300 FSHR 46060 1905 B1
Sweet Cherry Mdws
- LEBN 46052 1676 C4
Sweet Cherry Pk
- LEBN 46052 1676 C3
Sweetclover Ct
8200 INPS 46256 2013 E6
Sweet Clover Dr
7400 WshT 46123 2223 C7
Sweetclover Dr
8200 INPS 46256 2013 E6
Sweet Clover Wy
9500 FSHR 46038 1904 E1
Sweet Creek Dr
600 INPS 46239 2340 E4
W Sweet Creek Dr
6500 SCkT 46163 2451 B3
Sweet Creek Tr
- FSHR 46038 1905 C4
Sweetgrass Ln
6800 JknT 46034 1576 E5
Sweet Gum Ct
200 NBVL 46062 1685 D3
Sweet Gum Dr
1600 INPS 46260 2009 E4
2000 WshT 46123 2331 E7
2000 WshT 46123 2440 E1
Sweet Gum Dr S
1400 BNBG 46112 2223 C3
Sweetheart Ct
100 GNFD 46140 2345 D4
Sweetleaf Ct
3500 INPS 46235 2232 C3
Sweetleaf Dr
11300 INPS 46235 2232 C3
Sweetmeadow Blvd
- BNBG 46112 2223 E2
Sweet River Dr
5500 INPS 46221 2553 B1
Sweet River Wy
5000 INPS 46221 2553 C1
Sweet Saddle Ct
1400 CRML 46032 1791 E7
Sweetsen Rd
10700 GfdT 46113 2551 D7
10700 GfdT 46113 2660 E1
Sweet Spring Ct
13000 FSHR 46038 1904 C3
Sweetwater Dr
5200 LWNC 46235 2123 A6
Sweetwood Dr
10 MRVL 46158 2659 E2
10 MRVL 46158 2660 A2
Swift Ct
8400 INPS 46237 2556 D6
Swiftsail Cir
8800 INPS 46256 2014 B4
Swiftsail Ct
8600 INPS 46256 2014 A4
Swiftsail Ln
10200 INPS 46256 2014 A4
N Swope St
200 GNFD 46140 2345 E1
600 GNFD 46140 2236 E7
S Swope St
10 GNFD 46140 2345 E1
Sycamore Ct
- GNWD 46143 2666 A5
10 BNBG 46112 2223 D1
10 NWTD 46184 2774 D3
600 EglT 46077 1898 B6
700 PNFD 46168 2441 C6
4100 FKLN 46131 2774 E7
Sycamore Dr
10 NBVL 46062 1686 A4
800 SCkT 46140 2344 A3
800 SGLK 46140 2344 A3
1600 PNFD 46168 2441 E5
2800 SGLK 46140 2343 E3
7200 AVON 46123 2332 C3
9600 ClyT 46032 2009 B2
9600 INPS 46032 2009 B2
12100 LWNC 46236 2123 E1
12200 LWNC 46236 2124 A1
W Sycamore Dr
2600 SGLK 46140 2343 E2
Sycamore Hl
6200 INPS 46220 2121 D3
Sycamore Ln
100 GNWD 46142 2665 C1
200 GNFD 46140 2345 D1
900 DNVL 46122 2330 A3
E Sycamore Ln
3400 INPS 46239 2450 A3
Sycamore Rd
- MrlT 46126 2560 A4
10 CRML 46033 1902 D2
7900 INPS 46240 2010 D6
N Sycamore Rd
8100 INPS 46240 2010 D5
W Sycamore Rd
8000 MrlT 46126 2560 A4
Sycamore St
10 BNBG 46112 2223 C2
200 LEBN 46052 1677 A7
400 WTFD 46074 1684 B7
E Sycamore St
10 INPS 46225 2337 C5
10 ZNVL 46077 1899 C6
E Sycamore St SR-334
10 ZNVL 46077 1899 C6
W Sycamore St
400 ZNVL 46077 1899 B6
Sycamore Forge Ct
5900 INPS 46254 2117 E4
Sycamore Forge Dr
5900 INPS 46254 2117 D4
Sycamore Forge Ln
5900 INPS 46254 2117 D4
Sycamore Grove Ct
7500 INPS 46260 2009 E7
S Sycamore Hills Dr
3000 SCkT 46163 2343 C7
Sycamore Ridge Ct
300 WshT 46123 2332 A3
Sycamore Run Dr
- INPS 46237 2557 B4
Sycamore Springs Tr
8000 INPS 46239 2340 B5
Sydney Bay Ct
12200 INPS 46236 2015 A4
Sylvan Ct
6600 WshT 46123 2332 B7
Sylvan Dr
200 WynT 46060 1687 D1
5800 INPS 46228 2118 B5
Sylvan Ln
100 CRML 46032 1902 B2
Sylvan Rd
4300 INPS 46228 2227 B1
4500 INPS 46228 2118 B7
Sylvan Tr
100 WynT 46060 1687 D1
Sylvan Ridge Ct
3500 INPS 46240 2120 D1
Sylvan Ridge Rd
6500 INPS 46220 2120 D2
7100 INPS 46240 2120 D1

STREET
Block City ZIP Map# Grid

Sylvan Ridge Rd
7400 INPS 46240 2011 C7
Symphony Blvd
15700 NbvT 46060 1796 B4
Symphony Pl
1500 INPS 46231 2333 E7
Symphony Wy
9200 INPS 46231 2333 E6
Syracuse Ct
1900 LEBN 46052 1676 E4
Syracuse Dr
- WshT 46074 1792 B5
700 LEBN 46052 1676 E4

T

T Ct
- WRvT 46142 2663 E1
Tabor St
- INPS 46203 2448 D1
- INPS 46239 2448 E1
E Tabor St
10 INPS 46225 2446 C1
900 INPS 46203 2446 E1
1500 INPS 46203 2447 A1
W Tabor St
10 INPS 46225 2446 C1
N Tacoma Av
1000 INPS 46201 2338 B1
3400 INPS 46218 2229 B3
3800 INPS 46205 2229 B2
6900 INPS 46220 2120 B2
7100 INPS 46240 2120 B1
9100 INPS 46240 2011 B3
S Tacoma Av
10 INPS 46201 2338 B3
3000 INPS 46237 2447 B3
6300 INPS 46227 2556 B2
Tacoma Cir
2500 INPS 46220 2120 B3
Tacoma Pl
13100 FSHR 46060 1905 B2
N Tade Ct
3700 INPS 46234 2225 B2
W Tade Ln
3700 INPS 46234 2225 A3
Tadpole Ct
6800 INPS 46237 2557 E1
Taegart Dr
10 MRVL 46158 2659 D3
N Taft Av
3400 INPS 46222 2226 E3
S Taft Av
10 INPS 46241 2335 E4
2700 INPS 46241 2444 E3
Taftwood Dr
11500 CBLD 46229 2341 D2
Taggart Dr
10 MRVL 46158 2659 D3
8700 GfdT 46113 2551 D7
Tague St
10 GNFD 46140 2345 E2
Tahoe Cir
20000 NBVL 46062 1686 B3
Tahoe Ct
3600 CRML 46033 2011 D2
Tahoe Dr
200 LEBN 46052 1676 E3
Tahoe Rd
3400 CRML 46033 2011 D1
Tailwind Dr
7700 INPS 46241 2443 C1
S Talbott Av
8100 INPS 46227 2555 C6
Talbott St
- INPS 46202 2337 C2
- INPS 46204 2337 C3
N Talbott St
- INPS 46202 2337 C1
- INPS 46204 2337 C2
1600 INPS 46202 2228 C7
2200 INPS 46205 2228 C6
S Talbott St
1200 INPS 46225 2337 C6
Talisman Dr
10500 NBVL 46060 1687 C4
Talladega Ct
10100 FSHR 46060 1905 B2
Tallgrass Ct
17800 NBVL 46062 1685 A7
Talliho Dr
8000 INPS 46256 2014 A6
Tallman Av
1800 INPS 46218 2229 A7
Tallowtree Ct
12200 LWNC 46236 2014 E7
12200 LWNC 46236 2015 A7
Tallow Wood Ln
10800 LWNC 46236 2123 B2
Tall Pines Ln
3100 INPS 46235 2232 D4
Tall Timber Dr
- GNWD 46184 2774 B1
Tall Timber Run
5800 CRML 46033 1903 D1
Tall Timber Wy
6800 INPS 46241 2334 E4
Tall Trees Dr
11200 FSHR 46038 1903 D6
Talnuck Cir
- FSHR 46038 1905 D6
Talon Ln
4000 INPS 46234 2225 A2
Talon Trc
11200 FSHR 46038 1905 E6
11200 FSHR 46038 1906 A6
Talping Row
2900 INPS 46268 2009 C3
Tamara Tr
100 INPS 46217 2555 B2
Tamara Trc
13900 FSHR 46038 1904 C1
Tamara Wy
3900 FKLN 46131 2774 E7

Tamarack Ct
1800 WshT 46123 2223 C7
Tamarack Dr
- ClyT 46260 2010 A2
400 DNVL 46122 2330 B2
400 NBVL 46062 1685 D3
2200 INPS 46227 2556 B5
9100 INPS 46260 2010 A3
Tamarack Ln
- DNVL 46122 2330 B2
500 NBVL 46062 1685 D3
Tamarack Circle North Dr
900 INPS 46260 2010 A3
Tamarack Circle South Dr
900 INPS 46260 2010 A3
Tamarisk Blvd
11600 FSHR 46038 1905 E5
Tamarisk Ct
5200 INPS 46237 2557 A6
Tamenend Ct
600 FCkT 46038 2015 A1
Tamenend Trc
700 FCkT 46038 2015 A1
Tammany Tr
5200 CRML 46033 1903 C1
Tammer Dr
10200 ClyT 46032 2009 A1
Tammin Dr
6000 INPS 46254 2117 A7
Tammin Ln
- INPS 46254 2117 A7
Tammy Dr
7300 SPRT 46227 2556 C4
Tammy Renee Dr
- LWNC 46235 2122 E7
Tamoha Tr
7800 INPS 46214 2334 C2
Tam O'Shanter Ct
2200 ClyT 46032 1900 D7
Tam O'Shanter Dr
10800 ClyT 46032 1900 D6
Tam O'Shanter Ln
- ClyT 46032 1900 D6
Tampa Ct
4500 INPS 46241 2444 A6
Tampa Ln
6400 INPS 46241 2443 E6
6400 INPS 46241 2444 A6
Tampico Rd
1100 GNWD 46143 2665 E4
Tanager Ct
8000 INPS 46256 2013 B7
Tanager Ln
5800 CRML 46033 1903 D2
7700 INPS 46256 2013 B7
Tanana Dr
5900 CRML 46033 1903 C1
Tanbark Dr
10600 LWNC 46235 2123 B5
Tanbark Ln
5800 CRML 46033 1794 D7
Tanfield Ct
6400 INPS 46268 2118 A2
Tanglewood Ct
9900 GfdT 46168 2660 C1
9900 MdnT 46168 2660 C1
Tanglewood Dr
600 WynT 46060 1687 D1
1000 GNWD 46142 2664 E1
1200 GNWD 46227 2664 E1
Tanglewood Sq
1700 INPS 46260 2009 E6
Tanner Dr
8800 FCkT 46038 1904 D4
8800 FSHR 46038 1904 D4
Tanninger Dr
500 INPS 46239 2341 B4
Tanoan Ln
10500 INPS 46235 2232 B4
Tansel Cir
9100 INPS 46234 2333 E2
Tansel Ct
9100 INPS 46234 2224 E2
9100 INPS 46234 2225 A2
Tansel Rd
9100 INPS 46234 2333 E2
N Tansel Rd
2100 INPS 46234 2225 A6
4000 INPS 46234 2224 E2
Tansel Crossing Cir
2200 INPS 46234 2224 E7
Tansel Crossing Dr
9100 INPS 46234 2224 E7
Tansel Forge Dr
2200 INPS 46234 2224 E6
Tansel Grove Ln
2200 INPS 46234 2225 A6
W Tansey Cross
100 WshT 46074 1792 C4
Tansy Ct
5700 INPS 46203 2448 B5
Tantara Bnd
13200 CRML 46032 1900 B2
Tanya Dr
2200 WshT 46123 2441 A1
Tanzanite Cir
13100 CRML 46033 1903 B2
Taos Tr
7200 INPS 46219 2340 A3
Tapp Dr
11800 INPS 46229 2341 E1
11900 CBLD 46229 2341 E1
Tappan Dr
7100 INPS 46268 2118 A1
Tappan St
600 CRML 46032 1902 A5
Tapwood Ln
2900 INPS 46217 2554 B4
Tara Cir
400 WRvT 46142 2663 E3
Tara Ct
3600 CRML 46074 1900 A1

Tara Ct E
3200 INPS 46224 2226 C5
Tara Ct N
5400 INPS 46224 2226 C4
Tara Ct S
5300 INPS 46224 2226 C4
Tara Ct W
3200 INPS 46224 2226 C4
Tara Ln
3200 INPS 46224 2226 C3
Tara Wy
5700 BrnT 46112 2004 D6
Tardelli Ln
7700 INPS 46214 2225 C7
Tarkington Cmn
12900 CRML 46033 1903 A3
Tarpon Av
1600 PNFD 46168 2441 D4
Tarpon Dr
10300 INPS 46256 2014 B3
Tarpon Bay Dr
4000 WTFD 46062 1684 E7
Tarragon Ct
7100 INPS 46237 2556 E4
10600 FSHR 46038 1904 B7
Tarragon Dr
4200 INPS 46237 2556 E4
Tarragon Ln
7200 INPS 46237 2556 D4
Tarragon Pl
7400 INPS 46237 2556 E4
7600 INPS 46237 2557 A5
Tarragon Ter
4200 INPS 46237 2556 E4
Tarry Ct
10 WRvT 46142 2664 B4
Tarry Ln
4000 WRvT 46142 2664 B4
Tarrynot Ln
11600 CRML 46033 1903 A5
Tartan Ct
6800 INPS 46254 2225 E1
Tarver Ct
11800 FSHR 46038 1906 B5
Tasman Cir
11600 FSHR 46038 1906 C5
Tassel Ct
7300 AVON 46123 2332 C3
Tassel Meadow Dr
7000 INPS 46217 2554 E4
Tates Wy
3200 INPS 46268 2118 B1
Tattersall Dr
4200 LtyT 46168 2440 B4
Taunton Rd
7800 INPS 46260 2010 A6
Tavarez Ct
10400 FCkT 46040 2015 E1
Tavernier Dr
11000 FSHR 46038 1906 A4
Tavistock Dr
400 MRVL 46158 2660 B3
Taylor Ct
10 DNVL 46122 2329 C4
E Taylor Dr
1200 INPS 46219 2339 D1
W Taylor Dr
1200 INPS 46219 2339 C1
Taylor Rd
10 UnnT 46077 1681 B7
10 UnnT 46077 1790 A1
Taylor St
10 MRVL 46158 2659 E3
Taylor Trace Dr
14500 CRML 46033 1793 D6
14500 WTFD 46033 1793 D6
Tayside Ct
8300 LWNC 46236 2014 E5
TC Steele Ln
5000 CRML 46033 1903 A3
Teague Pl
4000 CRML 46074 1900 A2
Teak Ct
6300 INPS 46217 2555 B2
Teakwood Dr
700 PNFD 46168 2441 C6
3200 INPS 46227 2446 E3
3200 INPS 46227 2447 A3
Teakwood Ln
4200 WRvT 46143 2663 E5
Teal Ln
12100 CRML 46032 1901 C4
Teal St
11300 FSHR 46038 1903 E6
Tealpoint Cir
1200 INPS 46229 2341 B1
Tealpoint Ct
1200 INPS 46229 2341 C1
Tealpoint Dr
10800 INPS 46229 2341 C1
Tealpoint Ln
1200 INPS 46229 2341 C1
Tealwood Dr
12500 LWNC 46236 2015 A5
Tealwood Ln
8400 LWNC 46236 2015 A5
Teasel Ct
7600 INPS 46237 2556 E5
Technology Dr
9000 FSHR 46038 1904 D4
11600 CRML 46032 1901 D5
Technology Ln
11700 FSHR 46038 1904 D5
Technology Wy
5200 INPS 46268 2117 C1
Tecumseh Dr
100 SRDN 46069 1573 C1
Tecumseh St
1000 INPS 46201 2338 A1
Teddy Ln
300 INPS 46227 2446 D3
N Teel Wy
8100 INPS 46256 2013 C6
Teesdale Ct
9900 FSHR 46038 1905 A2

Teeter Cir
10900 LWNC 46236 2123 C3
Teeter Ct
10800 LWNC 46236 2123 B3
Teeter Ln
6400 LWNC 46236 2123 C3
Tegler Dr
- NBVL 46060 1797 C7
Tekesbury Ct
4200 LtyT 46168 2440 B5
Telecom Dr
6600 INPS 46278 2117 A2
Telfair St
1900 CRML 46032 1900 D3
Telford Ct
5200 INPS 46254 2117 E6
Telford Dr
9000 FSHR 46038 2013 D1
Telluride Dr
12700 LWNC 46236 2015 A6
Tembroke Ln
8100 INPS 46260 2010 B6
Tempe Ct
4600 INPS 46241 2444 D3
Tempe Dr
3200 INPS 46241 2444 D3
Tempelhof Dr
7400 INPS 46241 2443 D7
Temperance Av
1100 INPS 46203 2338 E6
S Temperance Av
500 INPS 46203 2338 E5
Tempest Dr
5800 INPS 46237 2557 D1
Temple Av
1800 ZNVL 46077 1899 B4
N Temple Av
1000 INPS 46201 2338 B1
3400 INPS 46218 2229 B3
3800 INPS 46205 2229 B2
7000 INPS 46220 2120 B2
7100 INPS 46240 2120 B1
9100 INPS 46240 2011 B3
S Temple Av
10 INPS 46201 2338 B3
500 INPS 46203 2338 B5
2300 INPS 46203 2447 B1
3000 INPS 46237 2447 B3
Temple Ct
1300 DNVL 46122 2330 B2
2400 INPS 46240 2011 B3
Temple Dr
1400 DNVL 46122 2330 B2
Templin Av
13400 FSHR 46060 1906 C2
Templin Rd
10800 ZNVL 46077 1899 C4
11100 EglT 46077 1899 C4
Tenacious Dr
10800 INPS 46236 2014 C6
N Tennessee St
10 DNVL 46122 2329 D4
S Tennessee St
10 DNVL 46122 2329 D5
Tennessee Wk
6200 INPS 46278 2117 A1
Tennis Ct Cir
1000 INPS 46260 2010 A3
Tennison Ct
6200 LWNC 46236 2123 B3
Tennison Dr
10600 LWNC 46236 2123 B3
Tennison Wy
6200 LWNC 46236 2123 B3
Tennyson Ln
12500 CRML 46032 1901 C3
Tenor Dr
9100 INPS 46231 2333 E6
Tenor Pl
- INPS 46231 2333 E6
Tenor Wy
9100 INPS 46231 2333 E6
15900 NbvT 46060 1796 B3
Ten Point Dr
15200 NBVL 46060 1796 E5
Tenton Ct
9000 INPS 46278 2007 B3
Tequista Cir
8300 INPS 46236 2014 D5
Tequista Ct
8300 INPS 46236 2014 D5
Teresa Ln
- LWNC 46236 2123 B5
600 NBVL 46062 1795 B1
Terhune Ct
- MdnT 46113 2661 A1
Terminal Rd
1200 INPS 46217 2445 E5
Tern Ct
8200 INPS 46256 2013 C7
Terra Dr
4000 INPS 46237 2447 D5
W Terra Ln
6000 MCVL 46055 2015 C3
Terrace Av
- INPS 46225 2337 B6
500 INPS 46203 2337 D6
2800 INPS 46203 2338 C6
4800 INPS 46203 2339 A6
W Terrace Av
8800 INPS 46234 2225 A4
Terrace Bch
7500 INPS 46240 2011 A7
Terrace Ct
10 CRML 46032 1901 E2
100 LEBN 46052 1677 A3
700 WshT 46123 2331 E5
Terrace Dr
10 MNVA 46157 2657 C7
100 NBVL 46060 1686 B6
600 ZNVL 46077 1899 B5
12600 CRML 46033 1903 A3
Terrace Ln
300 LEBN 46052 1676 E3
2000 LEBN 46052 1677 A4

Terrace Mnr
- GNWD 46143 2666 B5
Terrace Pl
8600 DelT 46060 1795 C6
Terrace Tr
10 MRVL 46158 2659 D2
Terra Cotta Ct
12100 FSHR 46038 1905 B4
Terra Vista Ln
3300 INPS 46220 2120 C2
Terrell Dr
10 PTBR 46167 2113 A3
Terrents Ct
300 CRML 46032 1901 C2
Terri Ln
10000 BrnT 46112 2006 D7
Terry Dr
1200 PNFD 46168 2441 D7
Terry Ln
11100 INPS 46239 2559 C1
Terrytown Pkwy
5600 INPS 46254 2117 B4
Tesh Dr
2400 INPS 46203 2447 D1
Tesh Pl
3600 INPS 46203 2447 D1
Teton Tr
500 INPS 46217 2555 A3
Tewksbury Ct
1100 MRVL 46158 2660 B2
Texarkana Ct
9200 INPS 46231 2333 E5
Texarkana Dr
900 INPS 46231 2333 E5
Thackery Ct
8300 INPS 46256 2013 C5
Thaddeus St
1700 INPS 46203 2337 E7
Thames E
10300 INPS 46229 2232 B5
Thames W
10200 INPS 46229 2232 A5
Thames Ct
9000 NBVL 46060 1795 D6
9000 NbvT 46060 1795 D6
Thames Dr
1400 WRvT 46143 2663 E6
Thatcher Dr
7100 INPS 46256 2122 A1
Thayer St
3100 INPS 46222 2227 A4
The Arbors
- CRML 46032 1901 D4
The Legends Blvd
- FSHR 46038 1905 C6
Thelma Dr
5300 LWNC 46236 2122 E6
Theo Ct
9100 INPS 46234 2333 E2
Theodore Cir
7100 INPS 46214 2225 D7
Theodore Ct
7100 INPS 46214 2225 E7
Theodore Dr
1900 INPS 46214 2225 D7
S Theodore Ln
3100 SCkT 46163 2342 E7
The Springs Dr
2300 INPS 46260 2009 D4
The Village Grn
- CRML 46032 1793 A7
Thicket Trc
4400 EglT 46077 1899 D2
Thicket Grove Ln
4800 INPS 46237 2448 E6
Thicket Hill Cir
12100 CRML 46033 1903 B4
Thicket Hill Ln
5300 INPS 46226 2121 A6
Thickett Dr
7000 INPS 46254 2225 D2
Thimbleberry Dr
- WshT 46123 2332 C1
Thistle Bnd
6300 AVON 46123 2332 A4
Thistle Ct
1700 WshT 46123 2223 C7
Thistle Dr
6300 INPS 46224 2226 A4
Thistle Rdg
10600 FSHR 46038 1904 B7
Thistle Finch
- BrnT 46112 2114 D1
Thistleridge Ct
6700 INPS 46221 2552 E1
Thistleridge Pl
- INPS 46221 2552 E1
Thistlewood Ct
1200 CRML 46032 1901 D1
Thistlewood Dr
13600 CRML 46032 1901 D1
Thistlewood Dr E
13600 CRML 46032 1901 D1
Thistlewood Dr W
13600 CRML 46032 1901 D1
E Thomas Ct
2700 CtrT 46140 2346 B4
Thomas Dr
- CRML 46032 1792 B6
1200 LEBN 46052 1676 D4
Thomas Rd
- INPS 46234 2225 A5
6000 INPS 46259 2559 C2
Thomas St
10 GNWD 46143 2665 D3
Thomas Marion Ct
8700 INPS 46234 2225 A7
Thomas Morris Trc
13100 CRML 46033 1903 E2
Thomas Woods Tr
1500 INPS 46260 2118 E3
Thompson Rd
100 GNFD 46140 2345 B2
E Thompson Rd
- INPS 46126 2450 D6

E Thompson Rd
- INPS 46239 2450 D6
- MrlT 46126 2450 D6
- MrlT 46239 2450 D6
10 INPS 46217 2446 E7
10 INPS 46227 2446 E7
1400 INPS 46227 2447 B6
3500 INPS 46237 2447 D6
4100 BHGV 46107 2447 D6
4100 INPS 46107 2447 D6
4900 BHGV 46107 2448 A6
4900 INPS 46107 2448 A6
4900 INPS 46237 2448 A6
5100 BHGV 46237 2448 A6
7000 INPS 46239 2448 A6
7200 INPS 46239 2449 A6
E Thompson Rd SR-135
10 INPS 46217 2446 C7
10 INPS 46227 2446 C7
W Thompson Rd
- INPS 46221 2443 C7
1000 INPS 46217 2445 E7
1000 INPS 46217 2446 A7
6300 INPS 46221 2444 A7
6500 INPS 46241 2443 C7
E Thompson St
200 LEBN 46052 1786 A1
W Thompson St
100 LEBN 46052 1785 E1
100 LEBN 46052 1786 A1
Thompson Park Blvd
5100 INPS 46237 2448 D7
5600 INPS 46237 2557 D1
Thompson Village Dr
5100 INPS 46227 2446 C7
Thompson Village Pl
5100 INPS 46227 2446 C7
Thompson Village Tr
100 INPS 46227 2446 C7
Thompson Village Wy
100 INPS 46227 2446 C7
Thoreau Ct
- FSHR 46038 2013 D1
Thornapple Ln
9400 INPS 46250 2012 C3
Thorn Bend Dr
8200 INPS 46278 2007 B3
Thornberry Ct
10 CRML 46032 1793 A7
7900 AVON 46123 2332 D3
Thornberry Dr
300 CRML 46032 1793 A7
Thornberry St
- INPS 46221 2336 D7
Thornbird Ln
1200 CRML 46032 1901 D1
Thornburg Rd
10 BNBG 46112 2223 B3
Thorncrest Ct
3600 INPS 46234 2225 A3
Thorncrest Dr
200 GfdT 46158 2550 C7
3500 INPS 46234 2225 A3
Thorndale Ln
- FSHR 46060 1905 A2
Thorndale St
1200 INPS 46214 2334 E1
1600 INPS 46214 2225 E7
Thorne Dr
400 BNBG 46112 2223 E1
Thornebush Ln
9500 FSHR 46038 1904 E6
Thorneycroft Dr
2900 INPS 46268 2009 B6
Thorney Wood Dr
7600 INPS 46239 2449 A1
Thornhill Dr
8400 INPS 46256 2013 D5
Thornhill Ln
- GNWD 46143 2666 B6
Thornhill Run
9900 FCkT 46060 1905 A2
Thornhurst Dr
10 CRML 46032 1901 E2
10 CRML 46032 1902 A2
Thornleigh Ct
- BNBG 46112 2223 B1
Thornleigh Dr
100 BNBG 46112 2223 B1
Thornleigh Rd
4300 INPS 46226 2120 E7
4600 INPS 46226 2121 A7
Thornmeadow Cir
1200 GNWD 46143 2664 D5
Thornmill Ct
7300 AVON 46123 2332 C6
Thornridge Dr
6200 AVON 46123 2332 A4
Thornridge Ln
5300 INPS 46237 2448 D7
Thornridge Pl
5300 INPS 46237 2448 D7
Thornton Ln
2800 INPS 46268 2009 C3
Thornwood Ct
6000 INPS 46250 2012 C3
Thornwood Dr
- CRML 46033 1903 D1
800 WRvT 46143 2663 E5
9300 INPS 46250 2012 C3
9400 FSHR 46250 2012 C3
Thorny Ridge Trc
10600 FSHR 46038 1905 D7
Thorny Ridge Pass
- FSHR 46038 1905 D7
Thoroughbred Blvd
- BrnT 46278 2006 E3
Thoroughbred Ct
8200 INPS 46278 2007 E5
Thoroughbred Dr
6700 INPS 46278 2007 E5
Thoroughbred Run
8100 INPS 46256 2013 B4
Thor Run Dr
14600 FCkT 46040 1906 E7

Thor Run Dr
14600 FCkT 46040 1907 A7
14600 FCkT 46040 2016 A1
Thousand Oaks Blvd
2000 INPS 46214 2225 E7
Thousand Oaks Dr
6700 INPS 46214 2225 E7
Thousand Oaks Ln
6800 INPS 46214 2225 E7
Thradd St
9500 FSHR 46038 1904 E3
Thrasher Dr
5200 INPS 46254 2117 D6
Three Hundred Yard Dr
10900 FSHR 46038 1905 E7
Threel Rd
9400 CRML 46240 2011 C3
9400 INPS 46240 2011 C3
N Threshing Ct
1000 CBLD 46229 2341 E1
Thrine Rd
1500 WshT 46052 1567 B4
W Thrush Dr
3900 INPS 46222 2227 A4
4000 INPS 46222 2226 E4
4800 INPS 46224 2226 D4
Thrush Ln
14000 CRML 46033 1903 B1
Thrushwood Cir
6100 INPS 46250 2012 C3
Thrushwood Ct
9100 INPS 46250 2012 C3
Thrushwood Dr
6000 INPS 46250 2012 C3
Thrushwood Ln
9200 INPS 46250 2012 D3
Thunder Bay Ct
12300 INPS 46236 2015 A3
Thunderbird Dr
10800 ClyT 46032 1900 D7
Thunderbird Rd
5700 LWNC 46235 2123 B5
5700 LWNC 46236 2123 B5
Thurman Dr
10 WTLD 46184 2774 E6
5700 INPS 46217 2555 B1
Thurmond Wy
12900 CRML 46077 1900 A2
Thurston Ct
10 WynT 46060 1687 D5
7900 FSHR 46038 1904 C4
Thurston Dr
100 WynT 46060 1687 C6
3200 INPS 46224 2226 B4
Thyme Ln
6800 INPS 46241 2334 E6
Tiara Ct
3600 INPS 46224 2226 A3
N Tibbs Av
10 INPS 46222 2336 B1
1600 INPS 46222 2227 B6
S Tibbs Av
10 INPS 46241 2336 B5
2200 INPS 46241 2445 B1
2900 INPS 46221 2445 B2
5000 INPS 46217 2445 D7
6500 INPS 46217 2554 B3
Ticen Av
10 BHGV 46107 2447 C3
Ticen Ct
1800 BHGV 46107 2447 C3
Ticonderoga Ln
5700 INPS 46254 2117 A5
Tidewater Ct
8500 INPS 46236 2014 D5
Tidewater Dr
11700 FSHR 46038 1905 B5
E Tidewater Dr S
11700 INPS 46236 2014 C4
11700 LWNC 46236 2014 C4
Tidewater Dr S
11500 INPS 46236 2014 D5
Tidewater Dr W
8500 INPS 46236 2014 D5
Tidsa Ct
- MdnT 46113 2661 C1
Tiffany Ct
3000 CRML 46033 1902 C5
Tiffany Dr
3400 INPS 46226 2231 B3
Tiger Tr
- MrlT 46126 2560 A3
Tilbury Ct
3600 INPS 46234 2224 E3
E Tilden Rd
10 BNBG 46112 2114 B7
10 BNBG 46112 2223 C1
W Tilden Rd
10 BNBG 46112 2114 B7
100 BNBG 46112 2223 B1
200 LcnT 46112 2223 B1
Tilden Ter
- LcnT 46112 2222 D1
Tilden Sunset Dr
5500 LcnT 46112 2222 D1
Tillage Rd
1700 INPS 46239 2341 D5
Tiller Ct
17400 WTFD 46074 1792 D1
Tillson Dr
900 ZNVL 46077 1899 D6
Tilly Mill Ln
8200 INPS 46278 2007 B4
Tilly Mill Rd
9000 INPS 46278 2007 B4
Tilmor Dr
10 NWTD 46184 2774 D3
Timber Ct
4100 INPS 46250 2011 E7
W Timber Dr
7100 SCkT 46163 2451 B3
Timber Ln
10 BNBG 46112 2114 B5
300 GNWD 46142 2664 C2
10600 ClyT 46032 1902 C7

STREET	Block	City	ZIP	Map#	Grid
Timber Tr	1300	GNWD	46142	2664	C2
N Timber Tr	400	GNWD	46142	2664	C2
Timber Trc	900	BrnT	46112	2115	B5
	6400	LcnT	46112	2115	B5
Timberbend Ct	6000	WshT	46123	2440	E1
Timberbend Dr	6000	WshT	46123	2440	E1
Timberbluff Cir	6300	WshT	46123	2441	A1
Timberbluff Ct	8700	INPS	46234	2225	A6
Timberbrook Ct	3300	LcnT	46123	2222	D4
S Timberbrook Run	100	WTFD	46074	1684	C7
	200	WTFD	46074	1793	B1
Timber Climb Dr	1100	AVON	46123	2332	A1
Timber Creek Dr	800	INPS	46239	2341	B5
	1000	CRML	46032	1901	E3
	1000	CRML	46032	1902	A4
Timber Creek Ln	900	GNWD	46142	2664	C1
	1200	INPS	46142	2664	C1
Timber Crest Bnd	12600	CRML	46033	1903	B3
Timber Crest Ct	7600	INPS	46256	2013	E7
Timber Crest Ln	-	INPS	46256	2013	E7
Timberfield Ct	7700	INPS	46259	2558	A5
Timberfield Ln	7500	INPS	46259	2558	A5
Timber Glen Wy	300	INPS	46241	2334	E4
Timber Grove Dr	300	WshT	46123	2332	B2
Timber Grove Pl	900	BHGV	46107	2447	E4
Timber Grove Wy	300	BHGV	46107	2447	E4
Timber Heights Dr	1700	ClyT	46280	2011	B1
Timber Hill Ct	7900	INPS	46217	2554	D6
S Timber Hill Dr	1900	INPS	46217	2554	D5
Timber Hill Tr	7800	INPS	46217	2554	D5
Timber Hill North Dr	7600	INPS	46217	2554	D5
Timber Lake Blvd	5800	INPS	46237	2448	C7
Timberlake Ct	100	FSHR	46038	1904	A6
Timber Lake Ln	6100	INPS	46237	2448	D7
Timberlake Ln	11300	FSHR	46038	1904	B6
Timber Lake Pl	6100	INPS	46237	2448	D7
Timber Lake Wy	5800	INPS	46237	2448	C7
Timberland Ct	6200	INPS	46221	2553	B2
Timberland Wy	6000	INPS	46221	2553	B2
Timberlane Dr	-	INPS	46260	2010	A7
	7400	FSHR	46038	1904	A6
	11400	DelT	46038	1904	A6
N Timberlane Dr	8700	MrlT	46126	2560	D6
	8700	MrlT	46130	2560	D6
Timberlane Pl	7400	FSHR	46038	1904	A6
Timber Leaf Ct	10300	LWNC	46236	2123	A3
Timber Leaf Ln	6400	LWNC	46236	2123	A3
Timberline Ct	9500	INPS	46256	2013	E7
Timberline Dr	-	CCRO	46034	1577	B2
	10	GNWD	46143	2665	C7
	9200	INPS	46256	2013	E7
Timberline Wy	9300	INPS	46256	2013	E7
Timber Ln Cir	300	GNWD	46142	2664	C3
Timberly Dr	2400	INPS	46220	2120	B2
Timbermill Ct	6400	WshT	46123	2332	A7
Timber Mill Ln	600	INPS	46260	2010	B7
Timber Ridge Ct	10	JknT	46034	1576	E5
	10	JknT	46034	1577	A5
Timber Ridge Dr	7900	INPS	46219	2231	B7
Timber Ridge Trc	10	LcnT	46112	2114	A7
Timber Run Ct	7800	INPS	46256	2013	E7
Timber Run Ln	7800	INPS	46256	2013	E7
Timbersedge Ct	3500	INPS	46222	2227	A3
Timbersedge Dr	3400	INPS	46222	2227	A3
Timber Springs Ct	3500	CRML	46033	1902	D6
Timber Springs Dr	7500	FSHR	46038	1904	B6
Timber Springs Dr E	10700	FSHR	46038	1904	B7
Timber Springs Dr S	7500	FSHR	46038	1904	B7
Timber Valley Rd	9400	INPS	46250	2012	B3
Timber View Dr	9300	INPS	46250	2012	C3
Timberview Dr	11000	FSHR	46038	1904	E6
Timber Village Dr	1500	GNWD	46142	2664	C1
Timber Walk Dr	6400	LWNC	46236	2123	B3
Timberwolf Ln	9100	UnnT	46077	1789	D2
Timberwood Ct	1600	GfdT	46168	2550	D5
Timberwood Dr	1800	GfdT	46168	2550	D5
	8700	INPS	46234	2334	A1
Timbrook Cir	500	INPS	46107	2447	D4
Timbrook Ln	1200	INPS	46107	2447	D4
Timeless Run	-	GNWD	46143	2666	E5
Timken Cir	11600	FSHR	46038	1906	C5
Timothy Ln	-	NBVL	46060	1687	B4
N Timothy Ln	8700	MrlT	46130	2560	D6
Timpani Wy	1600	INPS	46231	2333	E7
	15900	NbvT	46060	1796	B4
Tim Tam Cir	4600	INPS	46237	2448	B6
Tim Tam Ct	5700	INPS	46237	2448	C6
W Tina Dr	7000	INPS	46214	2225	D7
Tina Marie Ct	1500	INPS	46229	2232	C7
	1500	INPS	46229	2341	C1
Tincher Rd	4500	INPS	46221	2444	B6
	5200	INPS	46221	2553	B1
E Tincher Rd	200	BrnT	46158	2658	E7
	700	BrnT	46158	2659	A7
Tindall St	2700	INPS	46203	2447	A2
W Tinker St	300	AdmT	46069	1573	B1
	300	SRDN	46069	1573	B1
Tinkersfield Ln	3100	INPS	46214	2225	D4
Tinsel Av	7500	INPS	46237	2556	D5
Tinton Ct	10100	INPS	46235	2232	A1
Tip St	800	INPS	46221	2336	B5
Tippecanoe Dr	10	WynT	46062	1578	D6
	100	WRvT	46062	1578	D6
Tippecanoe St	-	INPS	46202	2337	D3
	-	INPS	46204	2337	B6
W Tippecanoe St	-	INPS	46204	2337	B6
Tipton St	2000	INPS	46218	2229	A7
Tiptop Dr	2400	INPS	46239	2449	B1
Tisbury Ct	11100	FSHR	46038	1904	A6
Tishman Ln	1300	INPS	46260	2010	A7
Titan Dr	2800	INPS	46241	2444	D2
Titan Run	10400	ClyT	46032	1900	C7
	10400	ClyT	46032	2009	C1
Titania Cir	11900	LWNC	46236	2123	E3
Titania Dr	6300	LWNC	46236	2123	E3
Titans Dr	-	FCkT	46038	1906	A3
Titleist Ln	2000	INPS	46229	2232	C7
Titleist Wy	1900	INPS	46229	2232	C7
Tito Ct	8900	FSHR	46038	1904	D4
Tiverton Dr	1100	MRVL	46158	2660	B3
Toad Hollow Ln	5600	INPS	46220	2120	D5
Tobello Blvd	-	WshT	46234	2224	D6
Tobermory Rd	8300	LWNC	46236	2014	E5
Tobey Dr	2500	INPS	46219	2231	C5
N Tocovi Ct	10	BNBG	46112	2114	B5
S Tocovi Ct	10	BNBG	46112	2114	B5
Todd Rd	900	WshT	46123	2332	B7
E Todd Rd	3800	INPS	46237	2556	E7
	4100	INPS	46237	2557	A6
Todd Ter	10	DNVL	46122	2329	C3
Todda Dr	2700	INPS	46229	2231	E5
Tolbert Pl	3900	CRML	46077	1900	A3
Toledo St	-	INPS	46202	2337	B3
Tollgate Rd	22600	CCRO	46034	1577	A3
	22600	JknT	46034	1577	A3
	23600	CCRO	46030	1577	B2
	23600	JknT	46030	1577	B2
Tollhouse Wy	10200	FSHR	46038	1905	B4
Tolliston Dr	600	LWNC	46236	2123	B4
Tolliston Ln	-	LWNC	46236	2123	C3
Tomahawk St	-	AdmT	46069	1573	A3
Tomahawk Tr	400	INPS	46214	2334	C2
Tomke Dr	-	SCkT	46163	2452	A1
Tomlinson Dr	-	INPS	46222	2226	E3
	500	INPS	46222	2336	A2
	3300	INPS	46222	2227	A4
Tomlinson Rd	18600	WshT	46074	1684	A5
	19600	WTFD	46074	1684	A4
	19900	WshT	46069	1684	A4
Tommy Lee Ct	1200	INPS	46217	2554	E5
Tooley Ct	21300	NBVL	46062	1576	C7
Topaz Dr	8100	INPS	46227	2556	B6
Topaz Ln	2900	ClyT	46032	1900	C6
Topeka Ct	6700	INPS	46241	2443	E6
Topeka Ln	6400	INPS	46241	2444	A6
Topeka Tr	4600	INPS	46241	2443	E6
	4700	INPS	46241	2444	A6
Toponas Pl	14500	FCkT	46040	1906	E5
Topp Dr	5100	INPS	46218	2230	A5
Topp Creek Ct	7100	INPS	46214	2334	D1
Topp Creek Dr	1300	INPS	46214	2334	E1
Top Rock Ct	12200	FSHR	46038	1905	E4
Torbay Cir	7500	INPS	46254	2116	D7
Torberg Pl	12300	FSHR	46038	1904	D4
Torchwood Ct	600	INPS	46227	2555	D7
Torino Ct	4200	INPS	46235	2231	D1
Toronto Ct	3600	INPS	46268	2009	A5
Toronto St	100	INPS	46202	2337	C2
Torrance Pl	8800	FSHR	46038	1904	D4
Torrey Ct	500	AVON	46123	2332	D5
	17000	WTFD	46074	1793	C1
Torrey Pine Dr	10	BNBG	46112	2113	D4
Torrey Pines Cir	10700	ClyT	46032	1900	D7
Totem Ln	3600	INPS	46208	2227	E3
Totten Dr	100	GNWD	46143	2665	D1
Tottenham Dr	7200	INPS	46250	2121	D1
	10800	ClyT	46032	1901	C7
Touchdown Dr	12600	FCkT	46038	1906	A3
Touch Stone Dr	10000	FSHR	46038	1905	A3
Touchstone Dr	1200	INPS	46239	2341	C5
Touchstone Wy	1600	INPS	46239	2341	C6
Tourmaline Dr	1800	WTFD	46074	1793	B2
Tournament Ln	10800	INPS	46229	2232	C7
Tournon Dr	10100	FSHR	46038	2015	A1
Tours Ct	6100	INPS	46220	2120	E4
Tousley Ct	10	INPS	46224	2226	D4
Tousley Dr	7100	INPS	46256	2122	B1
Tower Ct	400	NBVL	46060	1795	D5
	7000	INPS	46214	2334	D2
Tower Ln	9400	INPS	46235	2231	E2
Tower Rd	600	PNFD	46168	2441	C3
Tower Bridge Rd	9100	INPS	46240	2011	E3
Towe String Rd	1600	INPS	46217	2554	D7
Towhees Dr	3900	INPS	46237	2556	D6
Town & Country Blvd	-	NBVL	46060	1795	E2
	-	NBVL	46060	1796	A2
Town Center S	-	MRVL	46158	2660	B3
Town Center Dr	300	MRVL	46158	2660	A3
Town Center Rd S	300	MRVL	46158	2660	B3
Towne Ct	4300	INPS	46254	2226	A1
Towne Dr	2500	ClyT	46032	2009	C1
Towne Ln	-	ClyT	46032	2009	C1
Towne Rd	9500	ClyT	46032	2009	C2
	9500	INPS	46032	2009	C2
	11500	ClyT	46032	1900	D5
Towne Rd	11600	CRML	46032	1900	D6
	13100	CRML	46074	1900	D2
	13700	CRML	46032	1791	D5
	13700	CRML	46074	1791	D5
	14600	WshT	46074	1791	D5
Towne Center Dr N	400	MRVL	46158	2660	B3
Towne Lake Dr	3500	ClyT	46032	2009	B1
Townsend Ct	600	PNFD	46168	2441	C5
Townsend Dr	-	GNWD	46143	2666	B5
Townsend Wy	6400	INPS	46268	2118	C2
Township Dr	7700	INPS	46260	2009	D7
	7700	INPS	46268	2009	D7
Township Ln	8200	INPS	46268	2009	C5
Township Line Rd	-	GfdT	46168	2441	C3
	-	PNFD	46168	2441	C3
	-	WshT	46168	2441	C3
	6800	INPS	46260	2118	C2
	6800	INPS	46268	2118	C2
	7900	INPS	46260	2009	D4
	7900	INPS	46268	2009	D4
Towpath Ln	7400	INPS	46214	2225	D4
Trace Blvd N	-	WTFD	46074	1792	E2
Trace Blvd W	-	WTFD	46074	1792	E3
Trace Cir	8300	INPS	46260	2009	E5
Trace Ln	1500	INPS	46260	2009	E5
Trace Run	100	BrnT	46158	2659	A5
Trace Edge Ln	4200	INPS	46254	2226	E1
Trace Wood Ct	4300	INPS	46254	2226	E1
Trace Wood Dr	4200	INPS	46254	2226	E1
Traction St	-	INPS	46268	2009	B6
Tracy Ct	1700	INPS	46234	2225	A7
Tracy Dr	-	WTLD	46184	2774	E5
	8600	LtyT	46118	2548	B7
	8800	LtyT	46118	2657	B1
Tracy Ln	300	GNWD	46143	2665	E4
	500	BNBG	46112	2223	C4
Tracy Rd	-	ClkT	46184	2775	D3
	-	NWTD	46184	2775	A3
	-	PltT	46184	2775	D3
	-	WTLD	46184	2774	E3
	-	WTLD	46184	2775	A3
	10	NWTD	46184	2774	D3
	10	PltT	46184	2774	D3
Tracy Jo Ct	5400	WRvT	46142	2663	C2
Tracy Jo Rd	5100	WRvT	46142	2663	C3
Tracy Ridge Blvd	100	NWTD	46184	2774	D3
Tradd St	-	CRML	46032	1900	D2
Trade Center Dr	13800	FSHR	46038	1795	E7
	13800	FSHR	46038	1904	E1
Traders Ct	8400	FSHR	46038	1904	C6
Traders Ln	7400	INPS	46278	2007	C7
	7400	INPS	46278	2116	C1
W Traders Ln	7900	INPS	46278	2007	C7
Traders Lndg	8700	BrnT	46112	2006	E7
Traders Cove Ln	7700	INPS	46254	2116	C6
Traders Hollow Ct	8200	INPS	46278	2007	C5
Traders Hollow Ln	7700	INPS	46278	2007	B5
Traders Pass	10	BrnT	46112	2006	D7
Tradewind	-	BNBG	46112	2114	A3
Trade Winds Ct	-	CtrT	46052	1676	E2
	-	LEBN	46052	1676	E2
Tradewinds Ct	-	LEBN	46052	1676	E2
Trade Winds Dr	2200	INPS	46229	2232	A6
Tradewinds Dr	19100	NBVL	46062	1686	A4
Trading Post Pl	5900	CRML	46033	1903	E2
Tradition Ln	200	DNVL	46122	2330	B3
Tradition Pass	-	GNWD	46143	2666	D4
Traditions Dr	5200	LWNC	46235	2123	A6
Traditions Ln	9800	NBVL	46060	1687	A5
Traditions Rd	5200	LWNC	46235	2123	B6
Traditions Wy	5200	LWNC	46235	2123	A6
Trafalger Ln	5800	INPS	46224	2335	B3
Trager Ct	8800	INPS	46256	2013	B4
Trail Creek Ct	1400	CRML	46032	1792	C7
Trail End	-	GNWD	46142	2665	C1
	100	BNBG	46112	2114	C3
N Trailer Ct Rd	700	LWNC	46216	2122	C5
Trailgate Dr	4300	INPS	46268	2008	E6
Trail Ridge Ct	800	MRVL	46158	2660	A5
Trails End Dr	11300	DelT	46038	1903	C6
Trailside Dr	-	GNWD	46143	2666	B6
	6600	WshT	46123	2441	B1
Trails Pointe Dr	7800	LWNC	46236	2014	B7
Trails Run Ct	1800	INPS	46217	2554	D7
Trails Run Rd	8500	INPS	46217	2554	D7
Trailview Cir	17400	NBVL	46062	1795	B1
Trail View Dr	100	CRML	46032	1793	B7
	100	CRML	46032	1902	B1
Trailwind Ct	14200	CRML	46032	1792	A7
Trailwind Dr	7400	BrnT	46112	2114	B3
Trailwood Dr	10600	FSHR	46060	1905	B2
Trainers Cir	1500	INPS	46239	2341	C6
Trainers Ct	11000	INPS	46239	2341	C6
Tralee Ct	13200	CRML	46074	1900	C2
Tram Ln	12600	CRML	46032	1900	B3
Trammel Ct	5500	CRML	46033	1903	B4
Tranquil Tr	700	WRvT	46142	2664	A2
Tranquility Ct	8400	FSHR	46038	1904	C1
Transfer Dr	10	INPS	46214	2334	C3
Transportation Dr	10300	LWNC	46236	2123	B5
Trappers Ct	8400	FSHR	46038	1904	C6
N Traub Av	1000	INPS	46222	2336	D1
S Traub Av	10	INPS	46222	2336	D4
Travers Pl	7300	INPS	46226	2231	A3
Traverse Pl	12300	FSHR	46038	1904	D4
	12400	FCkT	46038	1904	D4
Travertine Wy	-	FSHR	46060	1905	E2
Travis Dr	2200	LEBN	46052	1677	B3
	4700	LWNC	46235	2123	A7
Travis Ln	4100	FKLN	46131	2774	E7
Traymoore Dr	-	FSHR	46060	1905	E1
Treasure Tr	10700	FSHR	46038	1905	C4
Treasure Pt	-	INPS	46236	2015	B3
Treasury Row	2300	INPS	46229	2231	E6
Treaty Line St	12600	CRML	46032	1900	D3
Trebah Cir	10400	ClyT	46032	2009	A1
Treefork Dr	-	LWNC	46235	2122	E7
Tree Fox Pl	6000	INPS	46237	2557	B2
Treehouse Pass	-	GNWD	46143	2666	D5
Treeline Ct	10300	FCkT	46038	2015	A1
Treeline Dr	8400	INPS	46256	2013	A4
Treeline Pl	7400	INPS	46256	2013	A5
E Trees Ct	10	NPLN	46163	2452	B3
Treesdale Cir	-	ClyT	46032	2009	D1
Tree Top Ct	-	NBVL	46062	1794	E2
Tree Top Dr	8500	INPS	46260	2010	B4
Tree Top Ln	1000	GNWD	46142	2665	A1
	6900	NBVL	46062	1794	E2
Treewood Dr	10100	LWNC	46235	2123	A6
Trem Kamp Ct	10200	LWNC	46236	2123	A4
Tremont Cir	10500	FSHR	46038	2014	B1
Tremont Ct	300	NBVL	46062	1685	D1
Tremont Dr	10100	FSHR	46038	2014	A1
N Tremont Dr	10500	FSHR	46038	2014	B1
Tremont Ln	10400	FSHR	46038	2014	A1
N Tremont St	1000	INPS	46222	2336	C1
	1400	INPS	46222	2227	C7
	5700	INPS	46228	2118	C5
	6400	INPS	46260	2118	C2
	6400	INPS	46268	2118	C2
S Tremont St	10	INPS	46222	2336	C4
	700	INPS	46221	2336	C5
Trent Ct	10300	INPS	46229	2232	A6
Trenton Av	300	INPS	46205	2228	D5
Trenton Ct	400	ZNVL	46077	1898	E4
	11400	FSHR	46038	1904	B6
Trerice Pl	10400	ClyT	46032	2009	A1
Tresa Cir	7100	INPS	46239	2448	E7
Tresa Dr	7100	INPS	46239	2448	E7
	7100	INPS	46239	2449	A7
Trester Ln	12500	FSHR	46038	1904	D4
Trestle Wy Cir	7300	INPS	46256	2122	B2
Trestle Wy Ct	7200	INPS	46256	2122	A1
Trevellian Wy	8100	INPS	46217	2555	A6
Trevia Ct	6500	LWNC	46236	2123	A2
Trevia Dr	9700	LWNC	46236	2122	E3
	9700	LWNC	46236	2123	A3
Treving Dr	2000	CCRO	46034	1577	B6
E Trevor St	400	BNBG	46112	2114	D6
Trewithen Ln	3700	ClyT	46032	2009	A1
Treybourne Dr	-	GNWD	46142	2664	C2
Treyburn Cir	6800	INPS	46237	2557	E3
Treyburn Dr	10900	FSHR	46038	2014	C1
Treyburn Green Blvd	-	INPS	46239	2340	E5
Treyburn Green Dr	700	INPS	46239	2340	E5
Treyburn Green Wy	9600	INPS	46239	2340	E5
Treyburn Lakes Blvd	-	INPS	46239	2340	E4
Treyburn Lakes Dr	9500	INPS	46239	2340	E4
Treyburn Lakes Wy	500	INPS	46239	2340	E5
Tributary Ct	3700	WTFD	46062	1793	D3
Trigger Ln	9800	LcnT	46112	2224	C3
Trilbey Ct	400	NBVL	46062	1685	E2
	3900	INPS	46235	2232	A2
Trilbey Dr	3800	INPS	46235	2232	A2
Trillium Ct	10400	NBVL	46060	1687	B4
N Trillium Ct	1000	INPS	46219	2340	C1
S Trillium Ct	1200	INPS	46219	2340	C1
Trillium Woods Ct	6100	INPS	46221	2553	B2
Trillum Ct	3400	WTFD	46062	1684	D6
Trilobi Dr	9600	LWNC	46236	2122	E2
Trinity Pl	9100	INPS	46229	2231	D7
Trinity Wy	-	MRVL	46158	2660	A2
	100	MRVL	46158	2659	E1
Triple Crown Dr	13800	CRML	46032	1792	A6
	13800	CRML	46032	1901	A1
E Triple Crown Ln	10	MdnT	46113	2661	D1
Tripler Rd	100	LWNC	46216	2122	E5
	100	LWNC	46216	2123	A5
Tripps Av	-	LEBN	46052	1676	D6
	-	LEBN	46052	1677	A5
E Tripps Av	100	LEBN	46052	1677	A5
Tri-Sab Ln	10	INPS	46217	2446	C3
Trolley Rd	11900	LWNC	46236	2123	E2
Troon Ct	7500	INPS	46237	2557	D4
	9600	ClyT	46032	2009	C2
Troon Dr	7400	INPS	46237	2557	D4
Troon Wy	6500	INPS	46237	2557	D4
Trophy Dr	12400	FCkT	46038	1904	D4
	12400	FSHR	46038	1904	D4
Trophy Ln	6800	NBVL	46062	1794	E1
Trophy Club Dr	7500	INPS	46214	2225	C3
Trophy Club Dr N	7500	INPS	46214	2225	C3
Trophy Oaks Ct	5800	INPS	46237	2557	C1
Tropic Ct	6500	INPS	46237	2557	D7
Trotter Av	200	INPS	46222	2336	C3
Trotter Ct	800	WRvT	46143	2663	E5
	14900	WshT	46032	1792	C6
Trotter Rd	6100	INPS	46241	2552	B2
	7000	INPS	46113	2552	B5
	8500	INPS	46113	2661	B1
Trotters Run	10	BNBG	46112	2223	C3
Trotwood Cir	7800	INPS	46256	2013	B7
Trotwood Ln	-	ZNVL	46077	1899	A6
Trout St	-	WrhT	46075	1788	D6
	-	WTWN	46075	1788	D6
Trowbridge St	200	INPS	46201	2338	B4
	500	INPS	46203	2338	B5
	2200	INPS	46203	2447	B1
Trowbridge High St	1800	CRML	46032	1900	D2
Trowbridge Pass	-	CRML	46032	1900	C2
Troy Av	2900	BHGV	46203	2447	C3
	2900	BHGV	46237	2447	C3
	2900	INPS	46203	2447	C3
	2900	INPS	46237	2447	C3
E Troy Av	-	BHGV	46203	2448	C2
	10	INPS	46225	2446	D3
	10	INPS	46227	2446	D3
	500	INPS	46203	2446	D3
	1500	INPS	46203	2447	B2
	1500	INPS	46227	2447	B2
	1500	INPS	46237	2447	B2
	7000	INPS	46203	2448	E2
	7000	INPS	46239	2448	E2
	7300	INPS	46239	2449	A2
	9000	INPS	46239	2450	B2
W Troy Av	10	INPS	46217	2446	B2
	10	INPS	46225	2446	B2
	1000	INPS	46217	2445	E3
	1000	INPS	46225	2445	E3
	3600	INPS	46221	2445	A3
	3800	INPS	46241	2445	A3
	3900	INPS	46241	2444	D3
Troy Dr	-	WshT	46074	1792	A5
Troy Ln	17000	WTFD	46074	1792	D2
Truax Comer Ln	1000	MRVL	46158	2660	A5
Trull Brook Dr	5000	NBVL	46062	1685	A7
Trumbull Cir	10800	ClyT	46032	1900	A6
Trumbull Ct	12400	FSHR	46038	1904	D4
Trumbull St	1700	INPS	46218	2229	A2
Trump Dr	4700	LWNC	46235	2123	A7
Trumpeter Ct	8800	INPS	46234	2225	A6
Trumpeter Dr	8600	INPS	46234	2225	A6
Trumpeter Pl	-	FSHR	46038	1906	E5
Truro Ct	3900	INPS	46228	2227	A2
Tryon Dr	-	CRML	46033	1903	B5
Tuck Ct	11300	CBLD	46229	2341	D2
Tuckahoe St	1000	INPS	46260	2010	A5
Tuckaway Ct	-	FSHR	46038	1905	C4
Tucker Av	500	PNFD	46168	2441	C4
Tucker Ln	8000	MrlT	46126	2560	E6
Tucson Dr	4400	INPS	46241	2444	D3
Tudor Av	-	INPS	46241	2335	D6
Tudor Cir	5000	CRML	46033	1903	A2
Tudor Ct	9900	FSHR	46038	2013	D2
Tudor Dr	13100	CRML	46033	1903	A2
Tudor Pl	4900	CRML	46033	1903	A2
Tudor Park Dr	3600	INPS	46235	2231	E3
	3700	INPS	46235	2232	A3
Tufton Ct	7800	FSHR	46038	1904	B6
Tufton Dr	5200	INPS	46254	2116	E6
	5200	INPS	46254	2117	A6
Tufton Pl	7800	FSHR	46038	1904	C6
Tufton St	7700	FSHR	46038	1904	B6
Tufts Ct	5500	INPS	46221	2553	B3
Tulane Rd	2400	INPS	46268	2009	C3
Tulip Ct	10	NWTD	46184	2774	D3
	400	PNFD	46168	2441	E3
	600	NBVL	46062	1685	D4
	1500	FKLN	46131	2774	E7
	3300	INPS	46227	2556	D3
Tulip Dr	10	INPS	46227	2555	C3
	400	MRVL	46158	2660	B2
	1400	INPS	46227	2556	A3
	1600	HMCT	46227	2556	A3
	5500	LcnT	46112	2222	E1
W Tulip Dr	11400	PNFD	46168	2442	A3
Tulip Dr S	2300	INPS	46227	2556	B3
Tulip Poplar Ct	600	MRVL	46158	2660	A5
Tulip Poplar Crst	400	CRML	46033	1902	D2

STREET
Block City ZIP Map# Grid

W Tulip Tree Dr
3200 BCkT 46140 2234 E6
Tuliptree Tr
7000 INPS 46256 2122 C1
Tullamore Ct
5100 INPS 46254 2116 C6
Tulloride Sta
9600 MCVL 46055 2015 C3
Tumbleweed Ct
12500 FSHR 46038 1906 A6
Tumbleweed Dr
5000 SCkT 46163 2451 E1
5000 SCkT 46163 2452 A1
Tundra Dr
9200 UnnT 46077 1789 D2
Tupelo Ct
8500 INPS 46239 2449 C3
Tupelo Dr
3200 INPS 46239 2449 C3
Turfgrass Wy
11000 LWNC 46236 2123 C2
Turfway Cir
5400 INPS 46228 2118 A6
Turfway Ct
3700 INPS 46228 2118 A5
4600 WRvT 46143 2663 D5
Turin Ct
8800 FSHR 46038 1904 D4
Turk St
1000 INPS 46227 2446 E7
Turkel Ct
8000 FSHR 46038 1904 C4
Turkel Dr
7800 FSHR 46038 1904 C4
Turkel Pl
12400 FSHR 46038 1904 C4
Turkey Foot Rd
4100 EglT 46077 1899 B2
4800 ZNVL 46077 1899 B3
Turkey Pen Cir
3000 WRvT 46143 2664 C6
Turkey Pen Dr
3000 WRvT 46143 2664 C6
Turnberry Ct
- LEBN 46052 1677 A2
400 WshT 46123 2331 C4
7500 INPS 46237 2557 E5
9600 ClyT 46032 2009 C2
Turnberry Dr
- LEBN 46052 1677 A3
Turnberry Wy
6700 INPS 46237 2557 E4
Turnbridge Ct
9100 INPS 46260 2010 A3
Turnbridge Dr
6300 WshT 46123 2332 A7
Turnbull Ct
5700 CRML 46033 1903 D2
Turnbury Ln
1100 BNBG 46112 2114 D4
Turne Grv
10800 FSHR 46038 1906 A7
Turner Av
2100 INPS 46222 2336 C3
Turner Ct
10 MdnT 46158 2661 A4
Turner Dr
6200 LtyT 46118 2548 B2
W Turner Dr
6300 INPS 46241 2444 A2
Turner Rd
10 MdnT 46158 2661 A5
Turner St
10 WTWN 46075 1788 C7
Turnham Ct
12900 FSHR 46038 1905 B3
Turnham Dr
12700 FSHR 46038 1905 B3
Turning Leaf Ln
2400 ClyT 46032 2009 C1
6400 LWNC 46236 2123 B2
Turnleaf Cir
11300 FSHR 46038 1905 E6
Turnstone Ct
8600 INPS 46234 2225 A6
9300 NBVL 46060 1686 E4
Turquoise Cir
13100 CRML 46033 1903 B2
Turtle Creek Ct
5000 INPS 46227 2446 D7
Turtle Creek East Dr
5200 INPS 46227 2446 D7
Turtle Creek North Dr
500 INPS 46227 2446 D7
Turtle Creek South Dr
500 INPS 46227 2446 D7
Tuscany Blvd
12600 CRML 46032 1900 B3
Tuscany Ln
4900 INPS 46254 2117 D7
Tuscarora Ln
2900 INPS 46217 2554 B5
E Tuxedo Ln
6500 INPS 46220 2120 C2
N Tuxedo St
500 INPS 46201 2338 C2
1400 INPS 46201 2229 D7
4800 INPS 46205 2120 C7
6900 INPS 46220 2120 C2
7100 INPS 46240 2120 C1
S Tuxedo St
10 INPS 46201 2338 C3
Twelve Oaks
900 CRML 46032 1901 A1
Twelve Oaks Blvd
- INPS 46278 2116 E2
Twilight Dr
1200 NbvT 46060 1686 D5
4200 INPS 46254 2226 A2
W Twilight Dr
7900 MrlT 46126 2560 B4
Twilight Hills Dr
23900 JknT 46034 1575 B1
Twin St
10 BNBG 46112 2114 C6

Twin Acre Ln
4900 LWNC 46235 2122 E7
Twin Beech Dr
7300 LWNC 46226 2122 A6
Twin Beech Ln
7700 LWNC 46226 2122 B6
Twin Bridge Blvd
5300 INPS 46239 2449 A7
Twin Bridge Cir
5400 INPS 46239 2449 A7
Twin Bridge Ct
5400 INPS 46239 2449 A7
E Twin Bridges Rd
100 CtrT 46122 2330 A5
100 DNVL 46122 2330 A5
Twin Brooks Dr
6600 INPS 46227 2556 B3
Twin Creeks Dr
6200 INPS 46268 2117 C3
Twin Lakes Ct
5600 INPS 46237 2557 B1
Twin Leaf Ct
1900 INPS 46229 2232 D7
Twin Oaks Dr
400 CRML 46032 1792 B7
7000 INPS 46226 2230 E3
7100 INPS 46226 2231 A3
Twin Pines Ct
11700 INPS 46235 2232 D4
Twin Pointe Cir
8200 INPS 46236 2014 D5
Twin Rivers Dr
8000 INPS 46239 2558 B1
Twin Rivers Ln
5700 INPS 46239 2558 B1
Twinshore Ct
10 CRML 46033 1902 C6
Twin Springs Ct
10 CRML 46033 1902 D5
Twin Springs Dr
3500 CRML 46033 1902 D6
Twyckenham Ct
10000 LWNC 46236 2123 A4
Twyckenham Dr
6000 LWNC 46236 2123 A4
Tybalt Cir
5900 INPS 46254 2117 A4
Tybalt Ct
6100 INPS 46254 2117 B3
Tybalt Dr
6000 INPS 46254 2117 A4
10100 FSHR 46038 1905 B3
Tybalt Ln
5900 INPS 46254 2117 B4
Tybalt Pl
6200 INPS 46254 2117 A4
Tyler Av
10 GNFD 46140 2345 B1
Tyler Ct
- WRvT 46142 2664 A3
10 BNBG 46112 2223 C2
Tyler Ln
7000 INPS 46217 2554 C4
Tylers Close
11600 FSHR 46038 1906 E5
Tynan Wy
8800 FSHR 46038 1904 D3
Tyne Cir
800 DNVL 46122 2330 C2
Tyre Dr
700 LEBN 46052 1677 A4
Tyre Rd
200 CtrT 46052 1785 E3
E Tyre Rd
200 CtrT 46052 1785 E1
200 CtrT 46052 1786 A1
200 LEBN 46052 1785 E1
200 LEBN 46052 1786 A1
Tyrone Dr
3000 INPS 46222 2227 C4

U

U Ct
- WRvT 46142 2663 E1
Udell St
500 INPS 46208 2228 B5
1400 INPS 46208 2227 E5
Uitts St
600 WTWN 46075 1788 C6
Ulen Blvd
100 LEBN 46052 1677 A4
100 ULEN 46052 1677 A4
E Ulen Dr
100 LEBN 46052 1677 A5
300 ULEN 46052 1677 A5
W Ulen Dr
100 LEBN 46052 1676 E5
Ulen Ovlk
300 BneC 46052 1677 A3
300 LEBN 46052 1676 E3
300 LEBN 46052 1677 A3
300 ULEN 46052 1677 A3
Underwood Ct
- GNWD 46184 2774 A2
5300 CRML 46033 1903 B6
Underwood Dr
- GNWD 46184 2774 A2
N Union Dr
500 INPS 46202 2336 E2
Union St
800 INPS 46225 2337 B5
2500 INPS 46225 2446 C1
4000 INPS 46227 2446 C5
8200 INPS 46227 2555 C6
N Union St
18700 WTFD 46074 1684 B5
S Union St
10 WTFD 46074 1684 C6
900 WTFD 46074 1793 A2
Union Chapel Rd
8100 INPS 46240 2011 C5
10700 NBVL 46060 1796 C2
10700 WynT 46060 1796 C2
15500 NbvT 46060 1796 C4

W Union Church Rd
100 MnrT 46157 2657 D6
100 MNVA 46157 2657 D6
900 MnrT 46158 2657 E7
900 MNVA 46158 2657 E7
Union Mills Dr
- GfdT 46168 2551 D7
- GfdT 46168 2660 D1
- MdnT 46168 2660 D1
United Dr
13200 FSHR 46060 1906 B2
United Church Dr
4000 INPS 46237 2447 C5
United Church Ln
4000 INPS 46237 2447 C5
Unity Tr
5400 INPS 46268 2117 C3
University Av
4800 INPS 46201 2339 A4
5100 INPS 46219 2339 A4
N University Blvd
900 INPS 46202 2337 A2
University Cres
12800 CRML 46032 1900 D3
Unser Blvd
6200 SDWY 46224 2226 A7
Updike Cir
4400 WTFD 46033 1793 E6
Upland Ct
8000 INPS 46278 2007 B6
W Upland Ct
1000 MnrT 46158 2658 B5
Upland Wy
10700 NBVL 46060 1687 C4
Upper Dr
- BNBG 46112 2114 B6
Upper Bay Ln
8000 INPS 46236 2014 E6
Upper Simmons Rd
- WshT 46052 1568 A5
1500 WshT 46052 1567 A5
Upton Ct
9900 ClyT 46280 2011 B1
Uptown Dr
9300 FSHR 46256 2013 A3
9300 INPS 46256 2013 A3
Urban St
10 DNVL 46122 2329 C3
Urban St SR-39
10 DNVL 46122 2329 C3
Ursal Ln
100 GNWD 46143 2665 C5
US-31
- AdmT 46034 1575 B1
- AdmT 46069 1575 B1
- FKLN 46184 2775 A7
- GNWD 46142 2665 A1
- GNWD 46143 2665 D6
- GNWD 46143 2774 D1
- INPS 46227 2555 D4
- INPS 46227 2556 A7
- INPS 46227 2665 D6
- JknT 46034 1575 B1
- JknT 46062 1575 B7
- JknT 46069 1575 B7
- LWNC - 2121 E7
- WshT 46032 1793 A2
- WshT 46062 1575 B7
- WshT 46069 1575 B7
- WshT 46069 1684 B2
- WshT 46074 1575 B7
- WshT 46074 1684 B2
- WshT 46074 1793 A2
- WTFD 46032 1793 A2
- WTFD 46033 1793 A2
- WTFD 46074 1684 B2
- WTFD 46074 1793 A2
- WTLD 46184 2775 A7
100 WTLD 46184 2774 E6
1000 NWTD 46184 2774 E3
6000 GNWD 46184 2774 D2
6000 PltT 46184 2774 D2
US-31 N
15700 WshT 46032 1793 A4
17600 WTFD 46074 1684 A7
US-31 S East St
4900 INPS 46227 2446 D7
5500 INPS 46227 2555 E5
US-31 N Meridian St
- CRML 46032 1793 B6
- CRML 46033 1793 B6
9800 CRML 46280 2010 C1
9800 CRML 46290 2010 C1
10400 CRML 46280 1901 C7
10400 CRML 46290 1901 C7
10600 ClyT 46032 1901 C7
10600 CRML 46032 1901 C7
13900 CRML 46032 1902 A1
14800 WTFD 46032 1793 B6
14800 WTFD 46033 1793 B6
15100 WTFD 46033 1793 B5
15100 WshT 46033 1793 B5
US-31 N Morton St
3800 FKLN 46131 2775 A7
3800 FKLN 46184 2775 A7
3800 FknT 46184 2775 A7
3800 WTLD 46131 2775 A7
3800 WTLD 46184 2775 A7
US-31 US Highway 31 N
300 GNWD 46142 2665 B3
1200 GNWD 46227 2665 A1
US-31 US Highway 31 S
200 GNWD 46142 2665 B4
600 GNWD 46143 2665 C5
1400 GNWD 46143 2774 E5
US-36
- CtrT 46122 2330 E4
- CtrT 46122 2331 A4
- CtrT 46123 2331 A4
- DNVL 46122 2329 B4
- DNVL 46122 2330 E4
- DNVL 46122 2331 A4
- VrnT 46040 2016 D3
1300 CtrT 46122 2329 B4
5200 WshT 46123 2331 E4

US-36
5800 AVON 46123 2331 E7
5800 WshT 46123 2332 D4
6400 AVON 46123 2332 B4
8400 AVON 46123 2333 B4
9400 WshT 46123 2333 B4
10500 AVON 46234 2333 E4
US-36 E Main St
10 DNVL 46122 2329 D4
900 DNVL 46122 2330 A4
US-36 W Main St
10 DNVL 46122 2329 E4
1200 CtrT 46122 2329 B4
US-36 E Pendleton Pike
7500 INPS 46226 2231 B1
7500 LWNC 46226 2231 B1
8400 LWNC 46226 2122 E6
9000 LWNC 46235 2122 E6
9000 LWNC 46236 2122 E6
10000 LWNC 46235 2123 A6
10000 LWNC 46236 2123 A6
12300 LWNC 46236 2124 A2
12600 MCVL 46055 2124 B1
12600 MCVL 46236 2124 B1
US-36 W Pendleton Pike
3000 VrnT 46040 2016 E3
3000 VrnT 46055 2016 C4
5000 VrnT 46055 2015 D6
5600 MCVL 46055 2015 D6
6500 LWNC 46236 2124 B1
6500 MCVL 46055 2124 B1
6500 MCVL 46236 2124 B1
US-36 Rockville Rd
- INPS 46224 2335 A4
6200 INPS 46214 2335 A4
6200 INPS 46241 2335 A4
6400 INPS 46214 2334 E4
6400 INPS 46241 2334 E4
7300 INPS 46231 2334 E4
8300 INPS 46234 2334 A4
8800 INPS 46231 2333 E4
8800 INPS 46234 2333 E4
US-40
2200 LtyT 46118 2548 D1
3300 LtyT 46118 2439 E7
3600 LtyT 46118 2440 A7
4100 LtyT 46168 2440 A7
4600 PNFD 46168 2440 C7
4800 GfdT 46168 2440 C6
US-40 Cumberland St
- LtyT 46118 2548 C1
US-40 E Main St
10 GNFD 46140 2345 E1
100 PNFD 46168 2441 A5
900 GNFD 46140 2346 C1
1000 CtrT 46140 2346 C1
2300 PNFD 46168 2442 A3
3100 PNFD 46231 2442 E1
3200 WshT 46231 2442 E1
US-40 W Main St
10 GNFD 46140 2345 D1
100 PNFD 46168 2441 D4
1600 PNFD 46168 2440 A7
2200 GNFD 46140 2344 D2
2500 CtrT 46140 2344 D2
US-40 E National Rd
1500 CtrT 46140 2346 B1
1500 GNFD 46140 2346 B1
US-40 W National Rd
10 CtrT 46140 2344 D2
10 GNFD 46140 2344 D2
2100 SCkT 46140 2344 B2
2600 SGLK 46140 2344 A2
2700 SCkT 46140 2343 D2
2700 SGLK 46140 2343 D2
4200 SCkT 46163 2342 E2
5000 SCkT 46140 2342 E2
5000 SCkT 46163 2342 E2
6700 CBLD 46163 2342 B2
7000 CBLD 46229 2342 B2
7000 SCkT 46229 2342 B2
7300 SCkT 46229 2341 E2
7600 CBLD 46229 2341 E2
US-40 E Washington
7700 CBLD 46229 2341 E2
7700 SCkT 46229 2341 E2
US-40 E Washington St
7800 CBLD 46229 2341 E2
7800 INPS 46219 2340 C3
7800 SCkT 46229 2341 E2
9000 INPS 46229 2340 C3
9500 INPS 46229 2341 A2
US-40 W Washington St
6000 INPS 46241 2335 A6
6600 INPS 46241 2334 D7
7300 INPS 46231 2334 D7
8000 INPS 46231 2443 A1
9200 INPS 46231 2442 E1
9200 PNFD 46231 2442 E1
9200 WshT 46231 2442 E1
US-47 E 236th St
10 AdmT 46069 1574 D2
10 AdmT 46069 1575 A2
US-47 W 236th St
10 AdmT 46069 1574 D2
900 AdmT 46069 1573 E2
2400 SRDN 46069 1573 E2
US-52
- ClyT - 2010 B2
- CRML - 2010 B2
- CtrT - 1786 E5
- CtrT - 1787 A7
- CtrT 46052 1676 A2
- EglT - 1897 C7
- EglT - 2006 D1
- EglT - 2007 C2
- EglT - 2008 C2
- INPS - 2008 A2
- INPS - 2009 E3
- INPS - 2010 B2
- INPS - 2231 B5
- INPS - 2340 A1
- LEBN - 1676 D7
- LEBN - 1785 E1
- LEBN - 1786 B2

US-52
- LWNC - 2121 E7
- PryT - 1787 A7
- PryT - 1896 E4
- PryT - 1897 C7
- WrhT - 1896 C1
- ZNVL - 2008 A2
2000 SCkT 46163 2452 E4
5300 SCkT 46163 2451 D2
7300 INPS 46163 2450 E1
7300 SCkT 46163 2450 E1
US-52 E Brookville Rd
7700 INPS 46239 2340 D6
9600 INPS 46239 2341 A7
10700 INPS 46239 2450 E1
US-52 E Main St
10 NPLN 46163 2452 B3
4000 SCkT 46163 2452 C3
US-52 W Main St
10 NPLN 46163 2452 B3
US-136
300 UnnT 46149 2112 A3
800 MdlT 46149 2112 A3
1000 MdlT 46167 2112 A3
4000 PTBR 46167 2113 C5
4200 MdlT 46167 2113 C5
4800 LcnT 46167 2113 C5
5500 LcnT 46112 2113 E5
5700 BNBG 46112 2113 E5
6000 BNBG 46112 2114 B6
6000 LcnT 46112 2114 B6
9000 LcnT 46112 2224 C2
10000 LcnT 46234 2224 C2
10800 INPS 46234 2224 C2
US-136 Crawfordsville Rd
6200 SDWY 46224 2226 A6
6300 INPS 46224 2226 A6
6600 INPS 46214 2225 E5
6600 INPS 46214 2226 A6
US-136 W Crawfordsville Rd
8300 INPS 46234 2225 B4
9100 INPS 46234 2224 E3
9200 LcnT 46234 2224 E3
US-136 E Main St
10 BNBG 46112 2114 C7
10 PTBR 46167 2112 E4
10 PTBR 46167 2113 A4
1000 BNBG 46112 2223 E1
1300 BNBG 46112 2224 A1
1400 LcnT 46112 2224 A1
US-136 W Main St
10 BNBG 46112 2114 C6
10 PTBR 46167 2112 E4
200 LcnT 46112 2114 B6
500 MdlT 46167 2112 E3
US-421
- BwnT - 2670 D3
- ClyT - 2010 B2
- CRML - 2010 B2
- INPS - 2009 B3
- INPS - 2010 B2
- INPS - 2231 B5
- INPS - 2339 E7
- INPS - 2340 A7
- INPS - 2448 E1
- INPS - 2449 E6
- INPS - 2450 A7
- INPS - 2559 B1
- LWNC - 2121 E6
- MrlT - 2559 D3
- MrlT - 2560 A5
- MrlT - 2669 E1
- MrlT - 2670 D3
- SgCT - 2670 D3
US-421 N Michigan Rd
- ZNVL 46077 1899 C2
10 UnnT 46077 1680 D6
1000 MrnT 46075 1680 C2
1000 UnnT 46075 1680 D6
3000 MrnT 46075 1571 B7
4000 MrnT 46052 1571 B7
6100 MrnT 46052 1570 E2
6100 MrnT 46069 1570 E2
9500 INPS 46268 2009 A2
9600 ClyT 46032 2009 A2
9600 INPS 46032 2009 A2
9800 ClyT 46032 2008 E1
10000 ClyT 46077 2008 E1
10500 ClyT 46032 1899 E7
10500 ClyT 46077 1899 E7
US-421 S Michigan Rd
10 UnnT 46077 1789 E1
700 UnnT 46077 1790 A3
3000 EglT 46077 1790 B6
3400 EglT 46077 1899 C2
4500 ZNVL 46077 1899 C2
6000 ClyT 46077 1899 E7
USA Dr
10900 FSHR 46038 1904 D7
USA Pkwy
- DelT 46038 1904 D6
- FSHR 46038 1904 D6
11500 FCkT 46038 1904 E6
Useppa Ct
4200 WTFD 46062 1684 E7
US Highway 31 N
300 GNWD 46142 2665 B1
1200 GNWD 46227 2665 B1
US Highway 31 N US-31
300 GNWD 46142 2665 B1
1200 GNWD 46227 2665 B1
US Highway 31 S
200 GNWD 46142 2665 B4
600 GNWD 46143 2665 B4
1400 GNWD 46143 2774 D1
US Highway 31 S US-31
200 GNWD 46142 2665 B4
600 GNWD 46143 2665 B4
1400 GNWD 46143 2774 D1
Ute Dr
100 CRML 46032 1902 B4
Uxbridge Ln
300 CRML 46032 1901 D3

V

Vail Dr
3800 CRML 46033 2011 D2
Valburn Ct
900 BHGV 46107 2447 E5
Val-Del Ct
200 INPS 46227 2555 C6
Valdosta Pl
1300 WshT 46074 1792 A5
Valeside Cres
11100 ClyT 46032 1901 B6
Valhalla Dr
16400 NBVL 46060 1796 C3
16400 WynT 46060 1796 C3
Valhalla Ln
12500 FSHR 46038 1906 A4
Valhalla Wy
- LWNC 46235 2123 D5
Vali Ct
200 ClyT 46280 1901 D7
Vali Dr
10600 ClyT 46280 1901 D7
Valiant Dr
2700 INPS 46241 2444 D2
Valley Av
1900 INPS 46218 2229 A7
2000 INPS 46201 2229 B7
Valley Cir
100 BNBG 46112 2114 C3
Valley Ct
10 WshT 46032 1793 A5
W Valley Ct
1200 CtrT 46140 2235 C5
Valley Dr
- WRvT 46143 2663 C5
10 CtrT 46140 2346 A1
10 GNFD 46140 2346 A1
1800 ClyT 46280 1902 A7
Valley Ln
10 MdnT 46113 2661 B4
6000 INPS 46221 2444 A7
E Valley Ln
- INPS 46218 2229 B7
N Valley Ln
400 GNWD 46142 2665 C3
1900 CtrT 46140 2235 D5
S Valley Ln
300 GNWD 46142 2665 B3
Valley Rd
10300 ClyT 46280 2011 A1
N Valley Tr
- AVON 46123 2224 A7
- WshT 46123 2224 A7
- WshT 46123 2333 A1
Valley Vw
10 BNBG 46112 2114 C2
Valley Brook Ct
12000 CBLD 46229 2232 E7
Valley Brook Dr
1600 CBLD 46229 2232 E7
1600 CBLD 46229 2233 C7
Valleybrook Pl
11600 CRML 46033 1902 E5
Valley Creek Dr N
11700 INPS 46229 2232 D6
Valley Creek Ln E
2200 INPS 46229 2232 E6
Valley Creek Ln S
2200 INPS 46229 2232 D6
Valley Creek Ln W
2200 INPS 46229 2232 E6
Valley Creek Wy
2200 INPS 46229 2232 D6
Valley Creek East Ln
2200 INPS 46229 2232 E6
Valley Estates Dr
8300 INPS 46227 2555 C6
Valley Farms Cir
8000 INPS 46214 2225 B3
Valley Farms Ct
100 FCkT 46038 1905 A7
7900 INPS 46214 2225 C4
Valley Farms Ln
8000 INPS 46214 2225 C4
Valley Farms Pl
3200 INPS 46214 2225 B3
Valley Farms Rd
3000 INPS 46214 2225 C4
Valley Farms Tr
8000 INPS 46214 2225 B3
Valley Farms Wy
3200 INPS 46214 2225 B3
Valley Forge Cir
10900 ClyT 46280 1900 A6
Valley Forge Ct
6500 INPS 46237 2557 D3
Valley Forge Dr
- WshT 46234 2333 E1
3700 INPS 46240 2011 D4
E Valley Forge Ln
6700 INPS 46237 2557 D3
Valleygrass Dr
- BNBG 46112 2223 E3
Valley Lake Ct
8600 INPS 46227 2556 C7
Valley Lake Dr
3400 INPS 46227 2556 C7
Valley Ln Ct
600 GNWD 46142 2665 B3
Valley Meadow Dr
11300 ZNVL 46077 1899 C4
Valley Mills Av
6500 INPS 46241 2443 E7
6500 INPS 46241 2444 A7
Valley Oaks Rd
400 GNWD 46143 2665 D5
Valley Ridge Cir
10200 FSHR 46038 1905 A5
Valley Springs Blvd
- FCkT 46038 1905 A7
9500 FSHR 46038 1904 E7
9600 FSHR 46038 1905 A7

Valley Stream Dr
7800 INPS 46237 2556 E5
Valley Trace Ct
4400 INPS 46237 2556 E5
Valley Trace Dr
4300 INPS 46237 2556 E5
Valley Trace Ln
7800 INPS 46237 2556 E5
Valley View Cir
12200 CBLD 46229 2232 E7
Valley View Ct
9700 NbvT 46060 1686 D4
9700 NbvT 46060 1687 A4
Valley View Dr
15200 WshT 46032 1793 A5
Valleyview Dr
600 ZNVL 46077 1899 B6
900 PNFD 46168 2441 C6
6200 FSHR 46038 1903 D7
6200 FSHR 46038 2012 D1
E Valley View Dr
10 INPS 46227 2555 C6
W Valley View Dr
600 INPS 46217 2555 A6
Valley View Ln
11500 LWNC 46236 2014 D6
Valley Vista Ct
- WshT 46123 2331 C2
Valley Vista Dr
- WshT 46123 2331 C2
Valleywood Ct
6400 WshT 46123 2441 A1
Valleywood Dr
1700 WshT 46123 2332 A7
1900 WshT 46123 2441 A1
Valley Wy Ct
10 WRvT 46142 2663 E2
Valley Wy Pl
10 WRvT 46142 2663 E2
Valley Wy Rd
400 WRvT 46142 2663 E2
Valor Wy
2500 INPS 46239 2449 C1
N Valparaiso Ct
9500 INPS 46268 2009 A3
Van Buren Ct
1900 INPS 46203 2338 C7
Van Buren St
10 GNFD 46140 2345 B1
1300 INPS 46203 2337 E7
3100 INPS 46203 2338 C7
Van Camp Dr
5200 INPS 46268 2008 C5
Van Camp Sq
400 GNWD 46143 2665 D4
Vance Ct
3500 INPS 46268 2118 A3
Vanceburg Dr
600 INPS 46241 2334 E5
Van Cleave St
4600 LWNC 46226 2122 C7
Vancouver Ct
6200 LWNC 46236 2123 B3
Vandalia St
- INPS 46222 2336 C5
4100 INPS 46241 2335 D6
Vandeman St
900 INPS 46203 2338 C5
E Vandergriff Rd
9200 INPS 46239 2449 E4
10700 INPS 46239 2450 D3
Van Dyke St
- INPS 46227 2556 A4
10 SPRT 46227 2556 A4
Vanguard Cir
3800 ClyT 46032 1900 A7
Vanguard Ln
8400 INPS 46239 2449 C1
Vanherp Ct
11900 LWNC 46236 2014 E7
Vanhoy Dr
500 WRvT 46142 2663 E4
Van Ness Pl
2200 INPS 46240 2011 B6
Van Ness Wy
8000 INPS 46240 2011 B6
Vannice Blvd
10 DNVL 46122 2329 D2
Van Spronsen Ct
12200 LWNC 46236 2123 E1
12200 LWNC 46236 2124 A1
Van Spronsen Wy
12300 LWNC 46236 2124 A1
Vantage Point Rd
4900 WshT 46123 2331 C5
Van Tassel Dr
3200 INPS 46240 2120 C1
Varna Dr
5400 INPS 46221 2444 B5
Varner Rd
4100 LcnT 46112 2224 C2
Vassar Ln
9200 INPS 46240 2010 E3
Vassar St
600 CRML 46032 1902 A4
Vauxhall Rd
7000 INPS 46220 2121 D2
7100 INPS 46250 2121 D1
Veatch St
- WTLD 46184 2775 A5
Venable Dr
10 AVON 46123 2332 B4
Venetian Ct
11400 NBVL 46060 1796 D5
Venetian Wy
7500 INPS 46217 2555 A5
Venice Ct
4200 INPS 46235 2231 D1
Venice Dr
- CRML 46280 2011 A2
E Venoy Dr
300 INPS 46227 2555 C3
W Venoy Dr
7300 INPS 46221 2552 D4

INDEX 54

Ventana Ct — Indianapolis Street Index — N Washington Blvd

Indianapolis Street Index

STREET
Block City ZIP Map# Grid

Ventana Ct
300 ClyT 46290 2010 B1
Ventanna Ln
5500 NBVL 46062 1685 B7
Ventnor Ct
300 INPS 46217 2555 B3
Ventnor Ln
- INPS 46217 2555 B3
Ventura Ct
1000 GNWD 46143 2666 A4
Ventura Dr
2800 INPS 46241 2444 C3
Venus Dr
300 INPS 46241 2334 D4
Veon Dr
10800 FSHR 46038 1905 C2
Vera Dr
4100 INPS 46220 2120 E4
S Vera Dr
1100 SCkT 46163 2342 C4
Veranda Ct
- GNWD 46143 2664 E6
Verbena Ct
6300 INPS 46224 2226 A4
10300 NBVL 46060 1687 B3
Verdin St
11600 LWNC 46236 2123 D3
Verdun Ct
6100 INPS 46220 2120 E4
Verdure Ln
3700 CRML 46077 1900 A5
Vermillion Ct
4800 WshT 46123 2331 B4
Vermillion Ln
9200 LWNC 46235 2122 D7
Vermont Ct
16300 NBVL 46060 1796 B3
Vermont Pl
500 INPS 46202 2337 D3
Vermont St
10 BNBG 46112 2114 C6
10800 WshT 46234 2333 E3
E Vermont St
10 BNBG 46112 2114 C6
10 INPS 46204 2337 C3
500 INPS 46202 2337 D3
2800 INPS 46201 2338 C3
7800 INPS 46219 2340 B2
W Vermont St
- SDWY 46222 2335 E3
10 BNBG 46112 2114 C6
10 INPS 46204 2337 C3
900 INPS 46202 2337 A3
1300 INPS 46202 2336 E3
1500 INPS 46222 2336 D3
4300 INPS 46222 2335 E3
4500 INPS 46224 2335 D3
8700 INPS 46234 2334 A3
Vernon Av
4500 LWNC 46226 2122 B7
4500 LWNC 46226 2231 B1
Vernon Dr
10 BrnT 46158 2660 A6
800 WRvT 46143 2663 C5
Vernon Ln
200 BNBG 46112 2114 B7
Vernon Pl
400 WTFD 46074 1792 D1
W Vernon St
300 GNFD 46140 2345 D2
Verona Ct
4200 INPS 46235 2231 D1
Versaille Dr
5500 INPS 46227 2555 C1
Versailles Dr
13400 CRML 46032 1901 C1
Verwood Ct
400 INPS 46234 2334 A2
Vesta Ct
8500 INPS 46226 2231 C1
Vestal Ct
- CRML 46033 1794 D7
Vestal Ln
600 PNFD 46168 2441 A5
Vestal Rd
100 PNFD 46168 2441 A5
2000 WshT 46173 2440 E2
2000 WshT 46168 2440 E2
3000 GfdT 46168 2440 E2
5700 GfdT 46168 2441 A5
Vestman Ct
- GNWD 46143 2664 E6
Vestry Ct
4200 INPS 46237 2448 D5
Vestry Pl
4300 INPS 46237 2448 D5
Vets Cir
5800 INPS 46221 2553 B2
Viburnum Ct
8400 INPS 46260 2010 A5
Viburnum Dr
1100 INPS 46260 2010 A5
Viburnum Run
300 WshT 46074 1792 D5
Vickery Ln
- CRML 46033 1902 E2
S Vickie Dr
1700 INPS 46239 2340 D6
Vickie Ln
6200 EglT 46077 1898 D5
Vicksburg Dr
5400 INPS 46254 2117 B4
Vicksburg Ln
5800 INPS 46254 2117 B4
Vicksburg North Dr
900 GNWD 46143 2666 B5
Vicksburg South Dr
1000 GNWD 46143 2666 A6
Vicky Ln
- BrnT 46112 2006 D7
Vics Ct
7800 NBVL 46062 1686 B5
Victor Dr
10 MRVL 46158 2659 E2
N Victor Rd
6000 WshT 46052 1568 A1
Victor St
1500 INPS 46241 2334 E7
Victoria Ct
100 LEBN 46052 1676 D4
1500 WRvT 46143 2663 E6
11600 CRML 46033 1903 B5
Victoria Dr
1200 LEBN 46052 1676 D4
N Victoria Dr
6000 INPS 46228 2118 B4
S Victoria Dr
5200 INPS 46217 2446 A7
Victoria Ln
400 MRVL 46158 2660 C3
4000 DNVL 46122 2331 A4
4000 WshT 46123 2331 A4
Victoria Rd
4800 INPS 46228 2118 B7
Victoria St
- INPS 46241 2336 B4
2600 INPS 46222 2336 C4
Victoria Park Dr
10300 INPS 46229 2232 B6
Victory Av
200 GNWD 46142 2664 C4
5800 INPS 46203 2448 C5
Victory Blvd
4300 INPS 46203 2448 C5
Victory Cir
4400 INPS 46203 2448 C5
Victory Ct
4200 INPS 46203 2448 C5
14700 WshT 46032 1792 D6
Victory Dr
5200 INPS 46203 2448 B5
E Victory Dr
- BHGV 46107 2448 A5
5100 BHGV 46203 2448 A5
5100 INPS 46203 2448 A5
Victory Wy
6100 INPS 46278 2117 B3
Victory Chapel Rd
19600 WynT 46060 1688 C2
20600 WRvT 46060 1579 C7
20600 WynT 46060 1579 C7
Vienna Pl
3700 INPS 46228 2227 A2
Viewpoint Dr
700 PNFD 46168 2441 A3
Viewside Dr
3900 INPS 46221 2444 E6
Vigo Dr
6100 LtyT 46118 2548 B2
Viking Hills Ct
9200 INPS 46250 2012 B3
Vikings Ln
12600 FCkT 46038 1906 A3
Villa Av
100 INPS 46201 2338 A4
800 INPS 46203 2338 A5
2200 INPS 46203 2447 A1
3000 INPS 46237 2447 B3
4900 INPS 46227 2447 B6
Villa Ct
5200 WshT 46123 2331 D4
Villa Ln
5600 INPS 46227 2556 B1
Village Blvd
400 MRVL 46158 2660 B3
Village Cir
10 ZNVL 46077 1898 E6
Village Cir E
2500 INPS 46229 2232 A5
Village Cir W
2500 INPS 46229 2232 A5
Village Cross
700 GNWD 46143 2665 E6
Village Ct
10 ZNVL 46077 1898 E6
4500 INPS 46254 2225 C1
10000 AVON 46123 2333 C3
10000 WshT 46123 2333 C3
Village Dr
10 CRML 46032 1792 D7
600 CRML 46032 1901 D1
S Village Dr
3700 SCkT 46163 2451 A2
5700 INPS 46239 2559 B1
W Village Dr
5200 SCkT 46163 2342 E7
5200 SCkT 46163 2343 A7
Village Dr E
100 CRML 46032 1792 D7
1800 GNFD 46140 2236 C5
Village Dr W
1700 GNFD 46140 2236 C5
Village Ln
200 GNWD 46143 2665 C5
4400 INPS 46254 2225 D1
Village Pl
10 ZNVL 46077 1898 E6
S Village Row
3800 SCkT 46163 2451 A2
Village Wy
8600 INPS 46256 2013 C4
17900 NBVL 46062 1685 B7
N Village Wy
7500 INPS 46239 2340 A4
S Village Wy
7500 INPS 46239 2340 A5
W Village Wy
7500 SCkT 46163 2451 A2
Village Bend Ct
4200 INPS 46254 2226 E1
Village Bend Dr
4200 INPS 46254 2226 E1
Village Bend Ln
4200 INPS 46254 2226 E1
Village Brooke Dr E
- NBVL 46062 1685 C7
Village Brooke Dr S
- NBVL 46062 1685 C7
Village Brooke Dr W
- NBVL 46062 1685 C7
Village Center Dr
- NbvT 46062 1685 B7
17800 NBVL 46062 1685 B7
Village Cir Dr
900 GNWD 46143 2665 A5
Village Crossing Dr
- NBVL 46062 1685 C6
Village Glen Dr
- NBVL 46062 1685 B7
Village Green Dr
10 INPS 46227 2446 C6
N Village Green Dr
1000 CBLD 46140 2232 E6
Village Green Ln
100 CRML 46032 1902 A3
Village Oak Ct
6300 LWNC 46236 2123 D3
Village Oak Dr
11700 LWNC 46236 2123 D3
E Village Park Cir
3000 WTFD 46033 1793 D5
Village Park East Dr
14600 WTFD 46033 1793 C6
E Village Park North Dr
2900 WTFD 46033 1793 C6
E Village Park South Dr
2900 WTFD 46033 1793 D5
Village Parkway Cir E
4200 INPS 46254 2225 D1
Village Parkway Cir N
- INPS 46254 2225 D1
Village Parkway Cir W
4200 INPS 46254 2225 D1
Village Parkway Dr
7200 INPS 46254 2225 D1
Village Park West Dr
14700 WTFD 46033 1793 C6
Village Place North Dr
600 ClyT 46280 2010 E1
Village Place South Dr
600 ClyT 46280 2010 D1
Village Plaza North Dr
5800 INPS 46219 2339 C2
Village Plaza South Dr
5800 INPS 46219 2339 C1
Village Square Ln
11000 FSHR 46038 1904 A6
Village Trace Blvd
3900 INPS 46254 2227 A1
4100 INPS 46254 2226 E1
Village Trace Ct
4300 INPS 46254 2226 E1
Village Trace Dr
4200 INPS 46254 2226 E1
Village View Cir
5400 NBVL 46062 1685 B7
Village Walk Ct
10 ZNVL 46077 1898 E5
Village Walk Dr
1500 ZNVL 46077 1898 E5
Village Winds Dr
- NBVL 46062 1685 B7
Villanova
10 GNFD 46140 2345 B1
Villanova Dr
- GNFD 46140 2345 B2
Villa Paree
6100 INPS 46220 2120 E4
Villa Paree Dr
- INPS 46220 2120 E4
Villard Av
4000 INPS 46226 2230 E2
Villas Dr
3900 WRvT 46142 2664 A2
Vincennes Cir
4000 INPS 46268 2008 E3
8800 INPS 46268 2009 A4
Vincennes Rd
3500 INPS 46268 2009 A4
Vincennes St
1100 INPS 46221 2337 A5
Vincent Ct
7700 INPS 46217 2555 B5
W Vincz Dr
3100 INPS 46228 2118 B5
Vindale Dr
1700 GNWD 46143 2665 C7
Vindohurst Wy
- GNWD 46143 2666 A3
Vine St
10 GNFD 46140 2345 E1
E Vine St
100 NBVL 46060 1795 D1
N Vine St
10 INPS 46222 2335 E3
100 PNFD 46168 2441 B4
S Vine St
100 PNFD 46168 2441 B5
300 INPS 46241 2335 D4
W Vine St
100 NBVL 46060 1795 C1
8500 MrlT 46126 2560 A4
Vine St S
10 SCkT 46140 2344 A2
Vinewood N
300 BNBG 46112 2223 C1
Vinewood S
300 BNBG 46112 2223 C1
N Vinewood Av
1000 INPS 46224 2335 B1
4200 INPS 46254 2226 B1
4500 INPS 46254 2117 B7
S Vinewood Av
1300 INPS 46241 2335 A6
Vinewood Dr
- GNWD 46143 2666 A6
2500 SDWY 46224 2226 B5
Vinewood St
1000 INPS 46224 2335 B1
Vineyard Cir
1600 INPS 46260 2009 E6
Vineyard Ct
1600 INPS 46260 2009 E6
Vineyard Dr
7400 FSHR 46038 1904 A6
7900 INPS 46260 2009 E6
Vinings Dr
2800 CRML 46032 2011 C1
Vin Rose Ln
5400 LWNC 46226 2122 B6
Vintage Cir
7400 AVON 46123 2332 C2
7600 LWNC 46226 2122 A6
Vintage Ct
7600 LWNC 46226 2122 A6
Vintage Dr
5400 LWNC 46226 2122 A6
Vintner Ct
8600 INPS 46256 2014 A4
Vintner Wy
- INPS 46256 2014 A4
N Vinton Hills Dr
5700 MrlT 46126 2670 D5
5700 SgCT 46126 2670 D5
Viola Ct
6800 INPS 46237 2448 E6
Violet Wy
13400 CRML 46032 1901 B2
Virgil Ct
- GNWD 46142 2665 C1
E Virgil St
11000 INPS 46259 2559 C5
Virginia Av
- LcnT 46112 2115 D6
10 INPS 46204 2337 D5
300 INPS 46202 2337 D5
300 INPS 46225 2337 D5
400 INPS 46203 2337 D5
Virginia Dr
- DNVL 46122 2330 B2
Visionary Wy
12100 FSHR 46038 1904 D4
Vista Ct
- WshT 46123 2331 D5
600 PNFD 46168 2441 A3
Vista Dr
400 ClyT 46280 1901 D6
Vista Cove Ct
- LEBN 46052 1676 C4
Vista Park Wy
10 AVON 46123 2332 D4
N Vista Ridge Ln
10500 MdnT 46158 2661 C7
Vista Village Dr
- NBVL 46062 1685 C7
Vivian Dr
1200 CRML 46032 1901 D2
Voigt Ct
3200 INPS 46224 2226 B4
Voigt Dr
3100 INPS 46224 2226 B4
Volcanic Rock Dr
- FSHR 46038 1906 A5
11900 FSHR 46038 1905 E5
Volney St
1500 INPS 46201 2230 B6
1500 INPS 46201 2339 A1
Volta Dr
5700 INPS 46254 2117 B5
Volunteer Dr
5900 INPS 46254 2117 B4
Vos Hiatt Av
22400 CCRO 46034 1577 C4
22400 JknT 46034 1577 C4
Voyager Dr
- FCkT 46038 1906 D6
Voyageur Ct
12200 INPS 46236 2015 A4

W

Wabash Dr
13800 FSHR 46038 1904 D1
Wabash St
100 PNFD 46168 2441 B5
E Wabash St
300 INPS 46204 2337 D3
600 INPS 46202 2337 D3
W Wabash St
- INPS 46204 2337 C3
Wabesa Wy
6800 LWNC 46236 2123 C2
Waddy St
4600 LWNC 46226 2122 B7
Wade Ct
3100 INPS 46203 2447 C1
Wade St
1100 INPS 46203 2446 E1
1500 INPS 46203 2447 A1
Wade Hill Ct
8100 INPS 46256 2013 B6
Wading Crane Av
9900 FCkT 46055 2015 C2
Wadsworth Cir
6500 INPS 46250 2012 D3
Wadsworth Ct
9100 FSHR 46038 2013 D1
Wadsworth St
- INPS 46250 2012 E6
Wadsworth Wy
7000 INPS 46219 2230 E7
Wagner Ln
1800 INPS 46203 2338 D7
Wagner Rd
- INPS 46234 2225 A3
Wagon Tr
100 MRVL 46158 2659 D1
Wagon Trail Cir
100 MRVL 46158 2659 D1
Wagon Trail Ct
100 MRVL 46158 2659 D1
Wagon Trail Dr
19200 NBVL 46060 1687 A4
19200 NbvT 46060 1687 A4
Wagon Wheel Ct
5300 INPS 46237 2448 A7
Wagon Wheel Tr
5200 INPS 46237 2448 A7
Wagon Wheel Tr
5500 INPS 46237 2557 A1
Wahpihani Dr
6100 DelT 46038 1903 C5
Wainwright Blvd
11600 FSHR 46038 1904 A5
Wakefield Cir E
- WRvT 46142 2663 C4
Wakefield Cir N
300 WRvT 46142 2663 C4
Wakefield Cir S
- WRvT 46142 2663 C4
Wakefield Ct
8400 INPS 46256 2013 B5
Wakefield Dr
100 WRvT 46142 2663 C4
Wakefield Pl
100 WRvT 46142 2663 C4
13900 FSHR 46038 1904 D1
Wakefield Rd
5400 WRvT 46142 2663 B4
6300 INPS 46254 2117 A7
Wakefield Trc
- WRvT 46142 2663 B4
Wakulla Ct
800 INPS 46217 2555 A5
Walbridge St
500 CRML 46032 1902 A4
N Walcott St
10 INPS 46201 2338 A3
S Walcott St
200 INPS 46201 2338 A4
2600 INPS 46203 2447 A2
3400 INPS 46227 2447 A3
5500 INPS 46227 2556 A1
Waldemar Dr
7100 INPS 46268 2117 C1
Waldemar Rd
9100 INPS 46268 2009 A3
Waldemere Av
600 INPS 46241 2335 B5
S Waldemere Av
1200 INPS 46241 2335 B6
Waldemere Rd
4000 INPS 46241 2444 B5
Walden Ln
- ClyT 46280 2011 B1
5600 INPS 46228 2119 A5
Walden Pl
3600 CRML 46033 1902 D4
Walden Glen Ct
8100 INPS 46278 2007 B5
Walden Trace Ct
8500 INPS 46278 2007 C5
Walden Trace Dr
8500 INPS 46278 2007 B5
Waldmer Ln
100 WynT 46060 1689 A4
Waldon Ct
1600 ZNVL 46077 1898 E6
Waldorf Ln
8200 INPS 46268 2009 C5
Wales Ct
10 INPS 46222 2227 A5
300 WRvT 46142 2663 D4
1400 FKLN 46131 2774 E6
Wales Dr
1600 INPS 46218 2229 D7
Walker Av
1400 INPS 46203 2446 E1
1500 INPS 46203 2447 A1
Walker Dr
- LWNC 46216 2122 C5
Walker Ln
11800 FSHR 46038 1906 C5
Walker Pl
2500 INPS 46203 2447 A1
Walker St
10 GNFD 46140 2236 E7
4600 WRvT 46143 2663 D5
Walking Wood Ln
11200 FSHR 46038 1905 B6
Wall St
400 GNWD 46143 2774 D1
E Wall St
10 MdlT 46167 2113 A2
10 PTBR 46167 2113 A2
W Wall St
10 MdlT 46167 2112 E2
10 MdlT 46167 2113 A2
10 PTBR 46167 2112 E2
10 PTBR 46167 2113 A2
Wallace Av
10 INPS 46201 2338 E2
3000 INPS 46218 2229 E4
3800 INPS 46226 2229 E2
5300 INPS 46220 2120 E6
Wallace Ln
10 INPS 46201 2338 E3
Wallard Dr
6300 INPS 46224 2226 A7
Wallbridge Dr
600 INPS 46241 2334 E5
Walleye Ct
100 INPS 46227 2555 C5
Wallien Ct
8000 INPS 46237 2556 E6
8000 INPS 46237 2557 A5
Wallington Cir
1000 GNWD 46143 2665 C5
Wallingwood Dr
5600 LWNC 46226 2122 A5
8000 INPS 46256 2013 A6
E Wall St Pike
300 WshT 46123 2222 E6
300 WshT 46123 2223 A6
Wallstreet Cir
1700 INPS 46234 2225 A7
Wallstreet Dr
8600 INPS 46234 2225 A7
W Wallstreet Pike
- MdlT 46167 2112 E2
- PTBR 46167 2112 E2
Wally Ct
10 BHGV 46107 2448 A5
Walma Ct
8700 INPS 46219 2231 D7
Walma Dr
8700 INPS 46219 2231 C7
Walney Ct
12600 FSHR 46038 1905 A3
Walnut Ct
- BCkT 46140 2234 E7
- BCkT 46140 2343 E1
100 NBVL 46062 1685 C1
3000 LcnT 46112 2222 E4
Walnut Dr
- DNVL 46122 2330 A3
900 WshT 46123 2223 D7
3000 LcnT 46112 2222 E4
7600 INPS 46268 2009 C7
N Walnut Dr
10 BCkT 46140 2344 A1
10 SCkT 46140 2344 A1
S Walnut Dr
800 SGLK 46140 2344 A3
W Walnut Dr
2800 SGLK 46140 2343 E3
Walnut Grv
10700 GfdT 46113 2551 E7
10700 GfdT 46168 2551 E7
10800 INPS 46113 2551 E7
Walnut Ln
200 BNBG 46112 2114 C6
Walnut St
- JknT 46011 1580 E1
- WTWN 46075 1788 C6
10 DNVL 46122 2329 D4
10 PTBR 46167 2113 A4
400 PNFD 46168 2441 B5
600 WTLD 46184 2775 A5
2200 SCkT 46140 2344 A2
E Walnut St
- NPLN 46163 2452 B3
- ZNVL 46077 1899 B5
100 INPS 46204 2337 C2
200 LEBN 46052 1677 A7
300 INPS 46202 2337 D2
1000 NBVL 46060 1795 D1
3800 INPS 46201 2338 D2
4900 INPS 46201 2339 A2
5100 INPS 46219 2339 A2
N Walnut St
- SgCT 46126 2670 C7
10 WTFD 46074 1684 B7
6900 MrlT 46126 2669 C2
S Walnut St
10 WTFD 46074 1684 C7
500 WTFD 46074 1793 B1
W Walnut St
- INPS 46234 2224 E3
10 INPS 46204 2337 C2
10 NPLN 46163 2452 A3
100 LEBN 46052 1677 A7
100 NBVL 46060 1795 C1
100 ZNVL 46077 1899 B6
200 LEBN 46052 1676 E7
800 GNFD 46140 2345 C1
900 INPS 46202 2337 A2
3700 INPS 46222 2336 A2
5400 WRvT 46142 2663 B3
9700 SCkT 46051 1689 E3
9900 WynT 46051 1689 E3
Walnut Trc
1600 GNFD 46140 2236 E5
N Walnut Trc
1700 GNFD 46140 2236 E5
Walnut Wy
10 BrnT 46112 2113 D4
10 LcnT 46112 2113 D4
1800 NBVL 46062 1685 C1
8200 INPS 46256 2122 B1
Walnut Bend Rd
6800 INPS 46254 2116 E6
Walnut Creek Cross
7200 WshT 46123 2223 C6
Walnut Creek Ct
3300 ClyT 46032 1900 B7
Walnut Creek Dr N
2900 ClyT 46032 1900 B7
Walnut Creek Dr W
10600 ClyT 46032 1900 B7
Walnut Grove
- GfdT 46168 2551 D7
Walnut Grove Dr
9100 INPS 46236 2015 A3
Walnut Meadow Dr
2100 INPS 46234 2225 A6
Walnut Point Rd
7600 INPS 46254 2116 C4
Walnut Ridge Ln
2200 INPS 46234 2225 A6
Walnut Ridge Pl
12500 FSHR 46038 1904 A3
Walnut Wy Ct
6500 BrnT 46112 2113 D4
Walpole Ln
1600 INPS 46231 2334 A7
Walpole Wy
1600 INPS 46231 2334 A6
Walrond Rd
12600 FCkT 46038 1906 A3
Walsham Wy
5800 INPS 46254 2226 B1
Walston Ct
1300 INPS 46260 2010 A7
Walter Ct
200 CRML 46032 1793 A7
Walter St
10 CRML 46032 1793 A7
Walter Barrick Wy
- BHGV 46107 2448 A3
Walter Grove Dr
19100 NBVL 46062 1685 C4
Walter Reed Rd
- LWNC 46216 2122 E5
Walthan Wy
10000 FSHR 46038 2013 D2
Walton Av
8900 INPS 46231 2333 E4
Walton Av
8900 INPS 46231 2334 A4
Walton Dr
- MdnT 46113 2661 B2
800 PNFD 46168 2441 D6
7600 INPS 46214 2334 C2
Walton St
5300 INPS 46241 2335 C4
7200 INPS 46241 2334 D4
Wanamaker Dr
4100 INPS 46239 2449 C5
Wanatah Cir
300 WTFD 46074 1792 D2
Wanatah Tr
16500 WTFD 46074 1792 D3
Wander Ct
3200 INPS 46268 2118 B2
Wander Wy
4000 WRvT 46142 2664 B4
Wandering Wy
6600 INPS 46241 2334 E4
15100 NBVL 46060 1796 E4
Wandflower Dr
9000 INPS 46231 2334 A7
9100 INPS 46231 2333 E7
Wanessa Dr
2100 WshT 46234 2224 C6
Wapiti Wy
11800 NBVL 46060 1796 E5
War Admiral Ct
11500 NBVL 46060 1796 D5
War Admiral Dr
11300 NBVL 46060 1796 D5
Warbler Ct
7800 INPS 46256 2013 B6
Warbler Wy
900 EglT 46077 1898 C4
7700 INPS 46256 2013 B7
Warbler Wy N
14100 CRML 46033 1903 B1
Warbler Wy S
5100 CRML 46033 1903 B1
Ward Dr
6200 SDWY 46224 2226 A7
Ware St
6300 LWNC 46236 2123 D3
Warehouse St
11900 CBLD 46229 2341 D3
War Emblem Dr
15000 NBVL 46060 1796 D6
Waring Dr E
900 CBLD 46229 2341 D2
Waring Dr W
900 CBLD 46229 2341 D2
N Warman Av
700 INPS 46222 2336 C1
2800 INPS 46222 2227 C5
S Warman Av
10 INPS 46222 2336 C4
700 INPS 46221 2336 C4
5000 INPS 46217 2445 C7
5300 INPS 46217 2554 C1
Warner Tr
14600 WshT 46074 1792 B6
Warren Av
- INPS 46241 2336 C7
- INPS 46241 2445 C1
500 INPS 46221 2337 A4
Warren Cir
9900 INPS 46229 2232 A7
Warren Ct
400 GNFD 46140 2236 D5
Warren Ln
6200 BNBG 46112 2113 D5
6200 LcnT 46112 2113 D5
Warren Wy
400 GNFD 46140 2236 D5
3000 CRML 46033 1902 C5
Warrenburg Wy
12200 CRML 46032 1900 D3
Warren Lake Ct
1400 INPS 46229 2232 E7
1400 INPS 46229 2341 D1
Warrington Ct
- MdlT 46167 2113 A5
800 INPS 46234 2333 E2
Warrington Dr
- MdlT 46167 2112 E5
- MdlT 46167 2113 A5
8300 INPS 46234 2334 B2
9200 INPS 46234 2333 E2
Warrior Tr
7200 INPS 46260 2118 D1
E Warsaw St
500 INPS 46203 2337 D4
Warwick Ct
1400 CRML 46033 1793 E7
Warwick Dr
1000 NWTD 46184 2774 D3
Warwick Ln
7700 INPS 46256 2013 B5
Warwick Rd
6900 INPS 46220 2119 D2
N Warwick Rd
9100 INPS 46240 2010 D3
Warwick Castle Ln
8900 INPS 46250 2012 B4
E Washington
7700 CBLD 46229 2341 E2
7700 SCkT 46229 2341 E2
E Washington US-40
7700 CBLD 46229 2341 E2
7700 SCkT 46229 2341 E2
Washington Av
10 CCRO 46034 1577 D3
600 INPS 46202 2337 B3
600 INPS 46204 2337 B3
Washington Blvd
8600 INPS 46240 2010 D4
11400 CRML 46032 1901 D6
N Washington Blvd
2700 INPS 46205 2228 D4
4500 INPS 46205 2119 D7
6900 INPS 46220 2119 D2
7100 INPS 46240 2119 D1

STREET Block City ZIP Map# Grid

N Washington Blvd
9100 INPS 46240 2010 D3
10100 ClyT 46280 2010 D1
10500 ClyT 46280 1901 B7
Washington Blvd W
6700 INPS 46220 2119 D2
Washington Ct
200 INPS 46205 2228 D4
Washington St
- LtyT 46118 2548 B1
10 BNBG 46112 2114 B7
10 SPRT 46227 2556 A4
1900 WshT 46074 1682 D7
E Washington St
10 INPS 46204 2337 E3
10 MRVL 46158 2659 E3
100 LEBN 46052 1677 B6
300 MRVL 46158 2660 A3
500 INPS 46202 2337 E3
900 CtrT 46052 1677 B6
1100 NBVL 46060 1795 D1
1400 INPS 46201 2338 A3
4900 INPS 46201 2339 B3
5100 INPS 46219 2339 B3
7200 INPS 46219 2340 A3
7800 CBLD 46229 2341 E2
7800 SCkT 46229 2341 E2
9000 INPS 46229 2340 D3
9500 INPS 46229 2341 B2
E Washington St US-40
7800 CBLD 46229 2341 E2
7800 INPS 46219 2340 D3
7800 SCkT 46229 2341 E2
9000 INPS 46229 2340 D3
9500 INPS 46229 2341 B2
N Washington St
10 DNVL 46122 2329 D3
10 GNWD 46143 2665 C3
500 CtrT 46122 2329 D3
2700 JknT 46011 1580 E1
S Washington St
10 DNVL 46122 2329 D4
100 GNWD 46143 2665 D4
W Washington St
10 INPS 46204 2337 A4
10 MRVL 46158 2659 D3
100 LEBN 46052 1676 E6
100 NBVL 46060 1795 C1
500 INPS 46202 2337 A4
700 INPS 46225 2337 A4
900 INPS 46222 2337 A4
1200 INPS 46222 2336 B4
3500 INPS 46241 2336 B4
3900 INPS 46241 2335 C5
6600 INPS 46241 2334 D7
7300 INPS 46231 2334 D7
8000 INPS 46231 2443 A1
9200 INPS 46231 2442 E1
9200 PNFD 46231 2442 E1
9200 WshT 46231 2442 E1
W Washington St US-40
6000 INPS 46241 2335 A6
6600 INPS 46241 2334 D7
7300 INPS 46231 2334 D7
8000 INPS 46231 2443 A1
9200 INPS 46231 2442 E1
9200 PNFD 46231 2442 E1
9200 WshT 46231 2442 E1
Washington St N
17600 WshT 46069 1682 A7
17600 WshT 46074 1682 A7
Washington St S
17400 WshT 46074 1682 D7
17400 WshT 46074 1791 D1
Washington Bay Dr
10800 FSHR 46038 1904 E7
Washington Boulevard West Dr
8600 INPS 46240 2010 D4
Washington Cove Ln
800 CBLD 46229 2341 E2
Washington Cove Wy
600 CBLD 46229 2341 E2
Washington Pointe Dr
10 INPS 46229 2341 B2
Washita Ct
13900 CRML 46033 1903 C1
Water St
- GNWD 46143 2665 D3
9000 JknT 46011 1580 E1
S Water St
10 GNWD 46143 2665 D3
W Water St
9700 SCkT 46051 1689 E4
9900 WynT 46051 1689 E4
Water Trc
8000 INPS 46256 2013 B6
Waterbar Dr
2300 WshT 46234 2224 D7
Water Bay Cir
- MCVL 46055 2015 D4
Water Birch Dr
11300 INPS 46235 2232 D2
Waterburn Ct
1300 CCRO 46034 1577 B5
Waterbury Ct
- GNWD 46142 2665 C3
E Waterbury Rd
10 INPS 46227 2555 C4
W Waterbury Rd
10 INPS 46217 2555 C4
Waterbury St
300 GNWD 46142 2665 C3
Watercress Wy
- BNBG 46112 2224 A2
Watercrest Ct
5800 INPS 46278 2117 B3
Water Crest Dr
9800 FSHR 46060 1905 A1
10400 FCkT 46060 1905 B1
Watercrest Ln
100 MRVL 46158 2660 C4
Watercrest Wy
200 AVON 46123 2332 E3
6300 INPS 46278 2117 B3
Waterfield Dr
3900 INPS 46235 2232 C2
Waterfield Ln
11000 INPS 46235 2232 C2
Waterfield Pl
11000 INPS 46235 2232 C2
Waterford Ct
10 ZNVL 46077 1898 E5
100 AVON 46123 2332 D3
Waterford Dr
400 ZNVL 46077 1898 E5
1000 GNWD 46142 2664 B1
1000 WshT 46231 2333 C6
Waterford Ln
300 AVON 46123 2332 D3
11900 CRML 46033 1902 C5
Waterford Pl
2000 INPS 46260 2118 D1
Waterford Wy
400 DNVL 46122 2329 B4
Waterfront Ct
200 NBVL 46062 1685 C1
Waterfront Dr
6900 INPS 46214 2225 D5
Water Front Ln
10600 FCkT 46040 1907 A7
Waterfront Wy
- MCVL 46055 2015 C4
Waterfront Parkway East Dr
2600 INPS 46214 2225 E5
Waterfront Parkway West Dr
2700 INPS 46214 2225 E5
Watergate Ct
3300 INPS 46224 2226 C4
Watergate Pl
3100 INPS 46224 2226 C4
Watergate Rd
3000 INPS 46224 2226 C4
Watergate Wy
3000 INPS 46224 2226 C5
Watergate Mall N
3300 INPS 46224 2226 C5
Watergate Mall S
3200 INPS 46224 2226 C4
Watergate Turn St
3000 INPS 46224 2226 C5
Waterlilly Ct
4000 INPS 46254 2225 D2
Waterloo Cir
3100 INPS 46268 2118 B2
Waterloo Dr
3000 INPS 46268 2118 B2
Waterloo Ln
6400 INPS 46268 2118 B2
Waterman Av
2200 INPS 46203 2339 C7
2200 INPS 46203 2448 C1
Waterman Dr E
100 NBVL 46060 1796 A4
Waterman Dr W
100 NBVL 46060 1796 A4
Watermark Ct
12000 INPS 46236 2014 E4
Watermead Dr
700 NBVL 46062 1686 B7
Water Oak Ct
1800 WshT 46123 2331 E7
Water Oak Wy
1900 WshT 46123 2440 E1
2000 WshT 46123 2331 E7
Water Ridge Dr
12900 FCkT 46055 2015 B2
Waterscape Wy
20700 NBVL 46062 1686 A1
Waters Edge Ct
- MdnT 46113 2661 B3
20900 NBVL 46062 1686 B1
Waters Edge Dr
- MdnT 46113 2661 B3
7300 INPS 46256 2013 A4
Watershed Ct
200 NBVL 46062 1686 A1
Waterside Cir
4900 CRML 46033 1903 A5
Waterside Ct
6700 INPS 46278 2007 E4
Waterside Dr
8700 INPS 46278 2007 E4
9900 NBVL 46060 1687 A5
Watersite Cir
5000 INPS 46254 2116 C6
Watersonway Cir
500 INPS 46217 2555 A1
Waterstone Cir
3500 INPS 46268 2118 A2
Waterstone Ct
3500 INPS 46268 2118 A2
Waterstone Dr
3500 INPS 46268 2118 B3
Waterstone Wy
4800 CRML 46033 1903 A5
Waterthrush Dr
4000 INPS 46254 2225 D2
Waterton Pl
8900 FCkT 46038 1904 D1
8900 FSHR 46038 1904 D1
Waterton Lakes Dr
5200 INPS 46237 2448 D7
Watertown Dr
1000 WshT 46074 1792 A5
8300 LWNC 46216 2122 C5
Waterview Blvd
400 GNFD 46140 2236 E7
400 GNFD 46140 2237 A7
Water View Cir
12200 CBLD 46229 2232 E7
Waterview Ct
6300 MCVL 46055 2015 C3
Waterview Dr
200 MRVL 46158 2660 B5
600 INPS 46224 2335 B2
Waterview Pt
7000 NBVL 46062 1576 E7
Waterview Pt
7000 NBVL 46062 1577 A7
Waterway Blvd
1400 INPS 46202 2336 E1
1600 INPS 46202 2227 D7
13800 FCkT 46040 1906 D7
W Waterway Blvd
1000 INPS 46202 2336 E1
1000 INPS 46202 2337 A1
W Waterway Dr
- SCkT 46163 2343 A2
Waterwood Dr
7600 INPS 46214 2225 C3
Waterwood Pkwy
3700 INPS 46214 2225 B2
Waterwood Wy
600 CRML 46032 1901 E6
Watford Wy
- FSHR 46060 1906 D3
Watham Ct
6400 INPS 46250 2012 B2
Watkins Dr
10100 WshT 46123 2333 D2
Watson Blvd
15200 NBVL 46060 1796 D5
Watson Ct
5800 LWNC 46226 2122 A5
Watson Ln
300 GNWD 46143 2665 E4
Watson Rd
3500 INPS 46205 2228 D3
S Watt Lndg
9700 GrnT 46064 1907 E5
Watterson Ct
500 INPS 46217 2555 A7
Wattles Dr
5700 INPS 46224 2335 B2
Watts Bar Ct
11300 INPS 46229 2341 D1
Waveland Cir
900 GNWD 46143 2664 E5
10300 FSHR 46060 1796 B7
Waveland Ln
800 GNWD 46143 2664 E5
Waverhill Dr
6700 INPS 46217 2554 C3
Waverly Ct
6700 INPS 46220 2120 C2
Waverly Rd
14400 CRML 46033 1794 C6
Wawasee Ct
7800 INPS 46250 2012 B7
Wawasee Dr
7700 INPS 46250 2012 B7
Waybridge Ct
6500 INPS 46237 2557 A3
Waybridge Ln
5100 INPS 46237 2557 A2
N Wayburn St
10 CBLD 46229 2341 E2
S Wayburn St
10 CBLD 46229 2341 E3
Waycross Dr
13800 FSHR 46038 1904 D1
Wayfield Dr
1800 WshT 46123 2332 B7
1800 WshT 46123 2441 A1
Wayforest Ct
7800 INPS 46239 2340 B7
E Wayland Dr
7000 INPS 46239 2448 E3
Waymen Dr
9100 INPS 46268 2009 B3
Wayne Av
5100 INPS 46241 2335 C4
Wayne Dr
2200 BCkT 46140 2344 A1
5400 INPS 46219 2339 B1
Wayne St
- NBVL 46060 1686 E7
E Wayne St
1000 NBVL 46060 1686 D7
N Wayne St
10 DNVL 46122 2329 E3
S Wayne St
10 DNVL 46122 2329 D4
W Wayne St
800 NBVL 46060 1686 D7
Waynecroft Av
10 INPS 46241 2334 D4
Waypoint Ct
- INPS 46240 2011 C5
Wayside Ct
500 PNFD 46168 2441 D5
Wayside Dr
200 PNFD 46168 2441 D5
400 INPS 46260 2010 B2
Wayside Rd
12200 FCkT 46256 2015 A2
Wayward Wind Dr
2400 INPS 46239 2450 A1
Waywing Ct
13800 CRML 46033 1903 D2
Weald St
- GNWD 46184 2774 A2
Weathered Edge Dr
11700 FSHR 46038 1905 E4
11900 FSHR 46038 1906 A4
Weatherly Ct
10000 INPS 46236 2014 B5
Weatherstone Dr
2900 CRML 46032 2011 C1
Weathervane Cir
8200 INPS 46239 2449 C4
Weathervane Ct
8300 INPS 46239 2449 C3
Weathervane Dr
12100 NBVL 46060 1796 E7
12100 NBVL 46060 1797 A6
Weaver Av
3100 INPS 46227 2446 D3
Weaver Ct
4800 INPS 46227 2447 A6
Weaver Woods Pl
8300 FSHR 46038 1795 C7
Webb Dr
200 INPS 46227 2555 C4
Webb St
2100 INPS 46225 2337 D7
2500 INPS 46225 2446 D1
Webber Wy
300 GNWD 46142 2664 D3
Weber Blvd
- INPS 46241 2442 E3
- INPS 46241 2443 A3
Weber Dr
1300 INPS 46227 2555 E4
1500 INPS 46227 2556 A4
W Weber Rd
10 BwnT 46140 2345 D5
10 GNFD 46140 2345 D5
800 CtrT 46140 2345 D5
N Webster Av
10 INPS 46219 2339 C3
2800 INPS 46219 2230 C5
3900 INPS 46226 2230 C2
S Webster Av
10 INPS 46219 2339 C3
1100 INPS 46203 2339 C6
Webster St
- GNWD 46142 2665 A2
Wedding Ln
10 PNFD 46168 2441 A5
Wedgefield Ct
11200 FSHR 46038 2014 D1
Wedgefield Dr
7500 INPS 46217 2555 A5
Wedgeport Ln
11600 FSHR 46038 1905 E5
Wedgewood Ct
4200 INPS 46254 2226 B1
Wedgewood Dr
1700 WRvT 46143 2664 A7
3100 SPRT 46227 2556 C5
3200 INPS 46227 2556 C5
Wedgewood Ln
700 CRML 46033 1793 E7
700 CRML 46033 1794 A7
700 CRML 46033 1902 E1
Wedgewood Wy
6000 INPS 46254 2226 A1
Weeping Cherry Dr
9900 FSHR 46060 1796 A7
Weeping Willow Ct
14300 CRML 46033 1794 C7
Weeping Willow Dr
- LWNC 46235 2123 B6
Weeping Wy Ln
700 AVON 46123 2332 C5
Weesner Dr
500 PNFD 46168 2441 A5
Weghorst St
500 INPS 46203 2337 D6
Weil Dr
6500 BrnT 46112 2114 D4
Welch Cir
7400 AVON 46123 2332 C3
Welch Dr
3400 INPS 46224 2226 D3
Welch Lake Dr
800 GfdT 46158 2550 C7
Welchwood Cir
1800 INPS 46260 2009 D6
Welchwood Dr
7900 INPS 46260 2009 E6
Welcome Wy
- GNWD 46143 2666 D5
Welcome Wy Blvd E
100 INPS 46214 2334 D3
Welcome Wy Blvd W
100 INPS 46214 2334 D3
Welford Wy
14100 CRML 46032 1792 A7
Welham Ct
300 NBVL 46060 1795 E3
Welham Rd
6200 INPS 46220 2121 D2
Welker Dr
6100 LWNC 46236 2123 A3
N Welker Dr
10 BCkT 46140 2343 E2
10 SCkT 46140 2343 E2
Welkin Ct
19100 NBVL 46060 1686 E4
E Welland St
11600 CBLD 46229 2341 D2
Wellborne Dr
10100 LWNC 46236 2123 A3
Wellcroft Ln
9900 LWNC 46236 2123 A3
Weller Cir
6200 INPS 46268 2118 B3
Weller Dr
3200 INPS 46268 2118 B3
Wellesley Blvd
1600 INPS 46219 2231 A7
Wellesley Coms
1800 INPS 46219 2231 B7
Wellesley Ct
1600 INPS 46219 2231 B7
Wellesley Dr N
7700 INPS 46219 2231 C6
Wellesley Dr S
7700 INPS 46219 2231 C6
Wellesley Ln
1600 INPS 46219 2231 C6
13700 CRML 46032 1901 B1
Wellingshire Blvd
- INPS 46217 2554 C5
Wellingston Ct
14600 NbvT 46060 1795 C6
Wellington Av
1700 INPS 46219 2231 B7
3200 INPS 46226 2231 B4
4600 LWNC 46226 2122 B7
N Wellington Av
1300 INPS 46219 2340 B1
Wellington Cir
4400 CRML 46033 1902 E4
Wellington Ct
1600 WshT 46123 2223 C7
Wellington Ln
800 GNWD 46142 2665 A1
Wellington Ovlk
300 NBVL 46060 1795 C5
Wellington Pkwy
100 NBVL 46060 1795 D3
Wellington Rd
400 INPS 46260 2119 B3
W Wellington Rd
10 INPS 46260 2119 C3
Wellington Bluff Ct
100 NbvT 46060 1795 C6
Wellington West Dr
6400 INPS 46260 2119 B3
Wells Dr
1500 PNFD 46168 2550 C1
Wells St
6700 INPS 46250 2012 E6
Wellsbrook Dr
8000 INPS 46278 2007 E6
Wellsford Cir
9900 LWNC 46236 2123 A3
Wellston Ct
400 INPS 46234 2333 E3
Wellston Dr
9100 INPS 46234 2333 E3
Wellwood Dr
- INPS 46217 2554 C4
Wellworth Dr
- CCRO 46034 1577 B1
Welton Cir
4600 WRvT 46143 2663 D5
Welton St
4600 WRvT 46143 2663 D5
Wembley Ct
1000 INPS 46260 2010 A6
Wembly Cir
13000 CRML 46033 1903 A2
Wembly Ct
12900 CRML 46033 1903 A3
Wembly Ln
4600 CRML 46033 1902 E3
Wembly Rd
3300 WRvT 46143 2664 B6
12700 CRML 46033 1902 E3
12700 CRML 46033 1903 A3
Wemouth Ct
8300 INPS 46256 2013 C5
Wendell Av
2100 INPS 46202 2228 B7
Wendessa Dr
- FSHR 46060 1905 E1
Wendy Ln
- INPS 46218 2229 A6
200 LEBN 46052 1676 E3
200 LEBN 46052 1677 A3
Wentworth Blvd
4500 INPS 46201 2338 E4
4800 INPS 46201 2339 A4
Wentworth Ct
1300 WRvT 46143 2664 B6
9700 ClyT 46032 2009 B1
Wentz Dr
4200 WTFD 46033 1793 E6
E Werges Av
300 INPS 46227 2446 D3
1800 INPS 46237 2447 A3
Werges St
3800 INPS 46221 2445 A3
3900 INPS 46221 2444 E3
Wesley Cir
- INPS 46227 2447 A4
100 NBVL 46062 1685 E1
Wesley Ct
6700 PNFD 46168 2550 B1
6900 INPS 46220 2119 E2
12000 FSHR 46038 1904 D4
Wesley Pl
12200 FSHR 46038 1904 D4
Wesleyan Rd
8700 INPS 46268 2009 A3
Weslynn Dr
2400 INPS 46228 2118 C7
N Wesminster Ct
1300 CBLD 46140 2232 D6
Wespler St
- INPS 46239 2450 E1
Wessex Cir
300 NBVL 46062 1685 D2
West Brch
10 BNBG 46112 2114 C3
West Dr
- INPS 46239 2340 B6
- SCkT 46163 2452 B2
- SGLK 46140 2343 E2
- WshT 46074 1684 A6
- WshT 46234 2333 D1
- WTFD 46074 1684 A6
200 FCkT 46040 2016 D2
500 INPS 46202 2337 A2
1000 AVON 46234 2333 D1
West Ln
2400 WshT 46231 2442 C2
West Rd
12600 CRML 46077 1899 E3
13100 CRML 46074 1899 E1
13800 CRML 46074 1790 E7
23600 AdmT 46069 1572 E2
West St
- NPLN 46163 2452 A3
10 MRVL 46158 2659 D3
10 SPRT 46227 2556 B4
10 WTLD 46184 2775 A6
100 PNFD 46168 2441 B5
N West St
10 INPS 46202 2337 B3
10 INPS 46204 2337 B3
100 LEBN 46052 1676 E6
S West St
10 INPS 46204 2337 B3
100 LEBN 46052 1676 E7
200 GNFD 46140 2345 C2
800 INPS 46225 2337 B6
S West St
2200 INPS 46225 2446 B1
Westbay Cir
21100 NBVL 46062 1577 A7
Westbay Ct
1600 INPS 46260 2009 E6
N West Bay Dr
2000 GNFD 46140 2236 E4
Westbourne Dr
100 BNBG 46112 2114 B5
4200 INPS 46205 2229 D1
4500 INPS 46205 2120 D7
Westbridge Dr
300 PNFD 46168 2441 A5
Westbrook Av
800 INPS 46241 2335 D6
2600 INPS 46241 2444 D2
Westbrook Blvd
200 NBVL 46062 1795 B1
Westbrook Cir
400 NBVL 46062 1795 B1
Westbrook Dr
200 NWTD 46184 2774 D5
300 WTLD 46184 2774 D5
800 MRVL 46158 2659 E2
Westbury East Dr
500 INPS 46224 2335 B2
Westbury North Dr
5800 INPS 46224 2335 B2
Westbury Place Dr
11500 ClyT 46032 1900 D6
Westbury West Dr
700 INPS 46224 2335 B2
Westchester Blvd
100 NBVL 46062 1685 E3
Westchester Dr
- CRML 46033 1903 A7
7300 LWNC 46226 2122 A6
Westcliff Dr
- WshT 46123 2332 E1
Westcreek Ct
12100 LWNC 46236 2014 E5
Westdrum Ct
9100 INPS 46231 2333 E5
Westdrum Rd
6300 INPS 46241 2335 A5
6700 INPS 46241 2334 E5
Westerbeck Ct
8000 INPS 46237 2556 E6
W Western Ct
6800 SCkT 46163 2451 B1
Western Dr
400 DNVL 46122 2329 C4
800 INPS 46241 2334 D5
Western Rd
10 MdnT 46113 2660 E2
10 MdnT 46113 2661 A1
Western Wy
- WTFD 46032 1793 A6
Western Select Dr
- INPS 46219 2230 E6
7000 INPS 46219 2231 A6
Westerville Dr
7800 LtyT 46118 2548 D6
Westfall Pkwy
2000 CRML 46033 1902 D6
Westfield Blvd
- WshT 46032 1793 B4
- WTFD 46032 1793 B4
7100 INPS 46240 2119 E1
7400 INPS 46240 2010 E7
10200 ClyT 46280 2011 B1
10500 ClyT 46032 1902 B7
10500 ClyT 46280 1902 B7
11000 CRML 46280 1902 B7
11100 CRML 46032 1902 B7
15000 WTFD 46033 1793 B4
E Westfield Blvd
- INPS 46208 2119 C4
800 INPS 46220 2119 C4
9600 ClyT 46280 2011 B2
9600 CRML 46280 2011 B2
N Westfield Blvd
7800 INPS 46240 2011 A6
9400 ClyT 46240 2011 A4
9400 CRML 46240 2011 A4
S Westfield Blvd
15400 WTFD 46033 1793 B4
16100 WshT 46074 1793 B4
16100 WTFD 46074 1793 B4
W Westfield Blvd
10 INPS 46208 2119 B6
10 INPS 46220 2119 B6
Westfield Ct
1200 INPS 46220 2119 D1
1500 CtrT 46140 2237 B7
Westfield Ct W
1100 INPS 46220 2119 E1
Westfield Dr
1100 CtrT 46140 2237 B6
Westfield Rd
- WshT 46074 1684 D7
- WTFD 46074 1684 D7
200 NBVL 46060 1686 A7
500 NBVL 46062 1686 A7
900 NbvT 46062 1686 A7
1400 NBVL 46062 1685 D7
1400 NbvT 46062 1685 D7
3100 WshT 46062 1685 A7
3500 WshT 46062 1684 D7
3500 WTFD 46062 1684 D7
Westfield Rd SR-32
- WshT 46074 1684 D7
- WTFD 46074 1684 D7
200 NBVL 46060 1686 A7
500 NBVL 46062 1686 A7
900 NbvT 46062 1686 A7
1400 NBVL 46062 1685 D7
1400 NbvT 46062 1685 D7
3100 WshT 46062 1685 A7
3500 WshT 46062 1684 D7
3500 WTFD 46062 1684 D7
Westfield Rd SR-38
200 NBVL 46060 1686 C7
Westfield Wy
8800 INPS 46240 2011 A3
Westfield Park Rd
16900 WTFD 46074 1792 E2
16900 WTFD 46074 1793 A1
17300 WTFD 46074 1684 A6
Westgate Blvd
- LEBN 46052 1676 B6
Westhaven Dr
6300 INPS 46254 2226 A2
West Lake South Dr
5900 INPS 46224 2335 A3
Westlane Rd
1400 INPS 46260 2118 D1
2400 INPS 46268 2118 D1
Westlea Dr
10 WTFD 46074 1684 A7
Westleigh Dr
2900 INPS 46268 2009 B5
Westmere Dr
9000 PNFD 46168 2442 B2
9000 WshT 46168 2442 B2
Westminster Ct
1100 GNWD 46142 2665 A1
4900 CRML 46033 1903 A7
8800 INPS 46256 2122 D1
Westminster Dr
100 NBVL 46060 1795 D5
600 NbvT 46060 1795 D4
7100 INPS 46256 2122 D1
Westminster Row
- GNWD 46142 2665 A1
Westminster Wy
11100 CRML 46033 1903 A7
West Mont Ln
200 NbvT 46062 1686 A7
Westmoor Dr
200 LEBN 46052 1676 E3
Westmore Cir
7500 INPS 46214 2334 C2
Westmore Dr
500 INPS 46214 2334 C2
Westmorland Dr
- FCkT 46038 1905 E4
Westmount Ct
400 INPS 46234 2334 B3
Weston Av
8100 AVON 46123 2332 D4
Weston Ct
7000 INPS 46214 2334 D2
Weston Dr
- ClyT 46032 1899 E7
10700 ClyT 46032 1900 A6
Weston St
400 BNBG 46112 2223 A1
Weston Pointe Dr
- ClyT 46032 1899 E7
- ClyT 46077 1899 E7
Westover Cir
8000 INPS 46268 2009 A6
Westover Dr
4000 INPS 46268 2008 E6
4000 INPS 46268 2009 A6
Westover Rd
- AVON 46123 2332 D5
Westpark Wy
1000 INPS 46214 2334 C1
Westpoint Dr
9800 FSHR 46256 2013 B2
West Point Pl
9300 INPS 46268 2009 B3
Westport Ct
1600 CCRO 46034 1577 A6
Westport Ln
8400 INPS 46234 2334 B2
Westridge Blvd
10 GNWD 46142 2664 D3
Westridge Cir
800 NBVL 46062 1795 B1
Westridge Ct
1300 GNWD 46142 2664 D3
Westridge Dr
8400 INPS 46234 2225 B6
Westridge Dr N
800 NBVL 46062 1795 B1
Westridge Pl
10 GNWD 46142 2664 D4
Westridge South St
700 NBVL 46062 1795 B1
Westside Dr
4300 LcnT 46112 2223 A2
S Westside Dr
10 NPLN 46163 2452 A3
Westview Dr
200 GNWD 46142 2665 B4
800 NWTD 46184 2774 D4
1800 INPS 46221 2336 D5
Westview St
200 DNVL 46122 2329 B4
Westwind Dr
1500 WshT 46123 2332 D6
Westwood Ct
4900 CRML 46033 1903 A6
Westwood Dr
1000 MRVL 46158 2659 E1
1200 GfdT 46158 2659 E1
11600 CRML 46033 1903 C5
Westwood Ln
13200 FSHR 46060 1905 C2
Westwood Rd
400 INPS 46240 2010 D5
Westwood St
10 GNWD 46143 2665 C7
Wetherby Ct
5200 INPS 46254 2117 D6
Wetherby Lake Dr
400 CRML 46032 1792 B7
Wetland Pt
- FSHR 46038 1905 E6
Wetmore Ct
7100 INPS 46259 2557 E5
Wet Rock Ct
7200 LWNC 46236 2124 A1
Wexford Ct
500 NBVL 46062 1685 D2

STREET
Block City ZIP Map# Grid

Wexford Dr
- WshT 46231 2333 C6
7100 INPS 46250 2121 B1
Wexford Rd
4200 INPS 46226 2230 A1
4500 INPS 46226 2121 A7
5900 INPS 46220 2121 A4
Wexley Ct
3400 CRML 46032 1900 B3
Weymouth Dr
5600 LWNC 46216 2122 C5
Weyworth Pl
- GNWD 46142 2664 E4
Whalen Av
2000 INPS 46227 2556 A1
Wharfside Ln
7100 INPS 46214 2225 E3
Wharton Ln
10800 FSHR 46038 1903 E7
Wheatcroft Ct
5200 INPS 46226 2121 B6
Wheatfield Ct
1100 WTFD 46032 1793 A6
Wheatfield Ln
14700 WTFD 46032 1792 E6
14700 WTFD 46032 1793 A6
14900 WshT 46032 1793 A6
Wheatgrass Ln
7500 NBVL 46062 1686 A4
Wheat Ridge Ct
7900 INPS 46268 2008 E6
Wheatstone Ct
5500 INPS 46221 2552 E1
Wheeler Av
200 MRVL 46158 2659 E3
Wheeler Rd
- LWNC 46216 2122 D5
17600 WshT 46074 1683 E7
17600 WTFD 46074 1683 E7
Wheeler St
2200 INPS 46218 2229 C6
Wheel Estates Ct
9400 LWNC 46236 2122 E6
Wheel Estates East Dr
5200 LWNC 46236 2122 E6
Wheel Estates North Dr
9500 LWNC 46236 2122 E5
Wheel Estates West Dr
5200 LWNC 46236 2122 E6
Wheelhorse Dr
5700 INPS 46221 2553 B1
Wheeling Ct
14000 FSHR 46038 1795 D7
Wheelwright Ct
7700 PNFD 46168 2441 D2
Whenner Dr
3700 INPS 46226 2230 E3
Whichman Wy
4800 INPS 46237 2556 E6
Whidbey Ct
900 CBLD 46229 2341 D2
Whidbey Dr
11600 CBLD 46229 2341 D2
Whipplewood Ct
5200 INPS 46226 2121 A6
Whippoorwill Ln
- PNFD 46231 2333 D7
Whippoorwill Wy
5700 CRML 46033 1903 B2
Whipporwill Cir
1300 GNWD 46142 2664 D2
Whipporwill Ct
500 GNWD 46142 2664 D2
Whipporwill Dr
8400 INPS 46256 2013 A5
Whipporwill Pl
7400 INPS 46256 2013 A5
Whirlaway Cir
5500 INPS 46237 2448 B6
Whirlaway Ct
2300 WshT 46234 2224 E6
5600 INPS 46237 2448 B6
Whirlaway Dr
4500 INPS 46237 2448 B6
Whirlaway Ln
5500 INPS 46237 2448 B6
Whirlway Dr
- NBVL 46060 1797 A6
Whisenand Dr
4900 INPS 46254 2117 B7
Whisper Ln
400 GNWD 46142 2664 D2
Whisper Wy
12600 FCkT 46038 1905 E3
Whisper Bay Ct
11600 CRML 46033 1903 A5
Whisper Cove Dr
11700 FCkT 46038 1905 D3
S Whispering Dr
2300 INPS 46239 2341 B7
2300 INPS 46239 2450 B1
Whispering Ln
9200 INPS 46234 2333 D2
Whispering Tr
600 GNWD 46142 2664 C2
800 GNFD 46140 2236 E6
900 GNFD 46140 2237 A6
3000 CRML 46033 1902 C6
Whispering Wy
2300 INPS 46239 2450 A1
4400 EglT 46077 1899 D2
10200 INPS 46239 2341 A7
Whispering Mist Ln
8200 MdnT 46158 2661 E7
8200 MdnT 46158 2662 A7
Whispering Willow Ct
200 NBVL 46060 1686 B6
Whispering Willow Dr
500 NBVL 46060 1686 B6
Whispering Winds St
10300 WshT 46234 2224 D7
Whispering Wood Cir
10 GNFD 46140 2237 A6
Whispering Woods Ct
19400 NBVL 46060 1686 E4
Whisper Knoll Dr
12700 FCkT 46038 1905 D3
Whisper Oaks Ct
6800 INPS 46214 2225 E4
Whisper Wind Dr
14300 CRML 46032 1792 B7
Whisperwood Ct
10 BNBG 46112 2223 D1
Whisperwood Ln
5200 INPS 46226 2121 A6
Whisperwood Tr
- CtrT 46122 2330 B2
1700 DNVL 46122 2330 B2
Whisperwood Wy
- FCkT 46038 1905 D3
Whistler Cir
1600 INPS 46229 2232 D7
Whistler Dr
11000 INPS 46229 2232 C7
11300 INPS 46229 2341 D1
W Whistler Dr
7600 MrlT 46126 2560 C1
Whistler Ter
1600 INPS 46229 2232 C7
Whistlewood Ct
8100 INPS 46239 2449 B4
Whistlewood Dr
8000 INPS 46239 2449 B4
Whistlewood Ln
3500 INPS 46239 2449 B4
Whistling Ln
15300 WTFD 46033 1793 D5
Whitaker Dr
4000 INPS 46254 2226 B2
Whitaker Rd
- PNFD 46168 2551 C1
1100 PNFD 46168 2442 C6
Whitaker Farms Dr
6200 INPS 46237 2557 C5
Whitaker Farms Ln
7800 INPS 46237 2557 D5
Whitaker Valley Blvd
7700 INPS 46237 2556 E5
N Whitcomb Av
1000 INPS 46224 2335 C1
1000 SDWY 46224 2335 C1
2700 SDWY 46224 2226 C5
3500 INPS 46224 2226 C3
S Whitcomb Av
300 INPS 46241 2335 B4
Whitcomb Ct
5500 INPS 46224 2335 B1
Whitcomb Pl
18700 NBVL 46062 1685 E5
18700 NBVL 46062 1686 A5
Whitcomb Ter
5600 INPS 46224 2335 B1
White Av
1000 BNBG 46112 2223 D1
2100 INPS 46202 2227 E6
2500 INPS 46208 2227 E5
S White Av
200 SRDN 46069 1573 B1
700 AdmT 46069 1573 C2
S White Av SR-38
600 SRDN 46069 1573 C2
700 AdmT 46069 1573 C2
E White Ln
7900 LWNC 46226 2122 B6
N White Ln
5200 LWNC 46226 2122 B6
White Rd
- INPS 46259 2558 D3
White Alder Ct
6200 WshT 46123 2441 A1
White Ash Ct
1000 MRVL 46158 2660 B6
6000 WshT 46123 2440 E1
White Ash Dr
1500 CRML 46033 1902 E1
White Ash Rd
1200 WRvT 46143 2664 B6
White Ash Tr
600 MRVL 46158 2660 B6
White Bark Ct
7700 AVON 46123 2332 D5
Whitebark Ct
17000 WTFD 46074 1793 B1
Whitebark Dr
12100 LWNC 46236 2014 E6
Whitebirch Dr
5900 FSHR 46038 2012 C1
Whitebridge Dr
12800 FSHR 46038 1906 B5
Whitecap Cir
8600 INPS 46256 2014 A4
Whitecap Wy
10100 INPS 46256 2014 A4
White Cedar Ct
3400 INPS 46222 2227 A6
Whitecliff Ct
2300 INPS 46234 2224 E7
Whitecliff Dr
2200 INPS 46234 2224 E6
Whitecliff Wy
9200 INPS 46234 2224 E6
White Cloud Ct
- MdnT 46113 2661 B2
White Dove Ct
7800 INPS 46256 2013 B7
White Dove Dr
7700 INPS 46256 2013 B7
White Fir Dr
8800 INPS 46256 2013 C4
White Hall Cir
14500 CRML 46033 1794 B6
Whitehall Ct
9200 INPS 46256 2122 D1
Whitehall Dr
7100 INPS 46256 2122 D1
Whitehall Pl
700 CRML 46033 1902 D3
White Hall Wy
5500 CRML 46033 1794 B6
White Haven Ct
200 NBVL 46060 1795 D5
Whitehaven Ln
12900 FSHR 46038 1905 A3
Whitehaven Rd
6300 INPS 46254 2117 A7
White Horse Ln
100 DelT 46038 1903 C7
White Horse Rd
5300 SDWY 46224 2226 C6
White House North Dr
400 GNWD 46143 2665 D4
White House South Dr
400 GNWD 46143 2665 D4
White Knight Blvd
2700 INPS 46229 2231 E5
Whiteland Rd
10 NWTD 46184 2774 D5
10 PltT 46184 2774 D5
10 WTLD 46184 2774 D5
1600 PltT 46184 2775 B5
2300 ClkT 46184 2775 B5
Whitelick Cr
10 PryT 46052 1896 D4
White Lick Ct
4600 INPS 46227 2446 C6
5800 PNFD 46168 2550 C1
White Lick Dr
10 INPS 46227 2446 C6
4100 PryT 46052 1896 C2
Whitelick Dr
2600 BrnT 46112 2114 C1
White Lick Ln
600 PNFD 46168 2441 A4
White Lick Rd
- MRVL 46158 2659 C2
200 BrnT 46158 2659 C2
White Marsh Ln
5300 INPS 46226 2121 B6
White Oak Ct
600 EglT 46077 1898 B6
5800 INPS 46220 2120 E5
White Oak Dr
100 GNFD 46140 2345 D4
6700 AVON 46123 2332 B1
10400 CRML 46033 2011 C1
10500 CRML 46033 1902 C7
S White Oak Dr
3700 SCkT 46163 2451 A2
W White Oak Dr
7300 SCkT 46163 2451 A2
White Oak Tr
7100 LWNC 46236 2123 E1
White Oaks Dr
- FSHR 46060 1795 C7
100 DelT 46060 1795 C7
White Oaks Rd
2200 SDWY 46224 2226 C6
White Pine Dr
600 NBVL 46062 1685 C2
7800 AVON 46123 2332 D6
White Pines Ct
6900 INPS 46217 2555 A3
White River Dr
7800 INPS 46240 2011 C6
White River Pl
6600 FSHR 46038 1903 E5
White River St
5100 WRvT 46143 2663 C5
N White River Parkway East Dr
- INPS 46208 2227 D4
300 INPS 46202 2227 D6
S White River Parkway East Dr
1000 INPS 46225 2337 A5
N White River Parkway West Dr
- INPS 46228 2227 D4
500 INPS 46222 2336 D2
3000 INPS 46222 2227 D4
S White River Parkway West Dr
- INPS 46222 2337 A5
10 INPS 46221 2337 A6
N White River Pkwy West Dr
300 INPS 46222 2336 E3
White Rock Ct
12700 LWNC 46236 2124 A1
White Sail Ct
10900 INPS 46236 2014 C5
Whitestone Rd
7100 INPS 46256 2012 D7
7100 INPS 46256 2013 A7
Whitestown Rd
4200 WrhT 46075 1897 E2
7500 WrhT 46075 1898 A2
8000 EglT 46077 1898 C3
8000 WrhT 46077 1898 A2
Whitetail Cir
10200 FSHR 46038 2014 A1
Whitetail Ct
2000 WshT 46123 2441 B1
2100 WRvT 46143 2663 A7
White Tail Dr
6200 EglT 46077 1898 D6
Whitetail Ln
7100 INPS 46254 2225 D2
Whitetail Run
6100 WRvT 46143 2663 A7
14600 NBVL 46060 1796 E6
White Tail Tr
- MCVL 46055 2015 C5
Whitethorn Ct
6000 INPS 46220 2120 B2
White Water Ct
1300 CCRO 46034 1577 A4
Whitewater Dr
6200 LWNC 46236 2123 C3
Whitewater Ln
10200 FSHR 46038 1905 B4
Whitewater Wy
11200 FSHR 46038 1905 A6
White Willow Ct
5400 INPS 46254 2116 D6
White Willow Dr
2600 WTFD 46074 1684 C7
Whitewood Ct
10 BHGV 46107 2447 E6
2000 INPS 46260 2009 D4
Whitham Dr
8100 INPS 46237 2556 E6
Whitham Ln
4600 INPS 46237 2556 E6
Whitley Ct
700 NBVL 46062 1685 D1
Whitley Dr
9300 INPS 46240 2011 C3
9400 ClyT 46240 2011 C3
Whitley Ln
6400 INPS 46260 2118 E3
Whitlock Ct
7500 INPS 46268 2009 B7
Whitman Ct
9000 FSHR 46038 2013 D1
Whitney St
- INPS 46222 2227 C7
Whitney Wy
10000 FSHR 46038 2013 D2
Whitridge Ln
4600 INPS 46237 2556 E6
Whitten Dr
- FSHR 46060 1906 C2
Whitten Dr S
- FSHR 46060 1906 C2
Whittier Ct
5400 INPS 46250 2012 B7
Whittier Dr
13900 FSHR 46038 1904 D1
14000 FSHR 46038 1795 D7
Whittier Ln
5400 INPS 46250 2012 B7
Whittier Pl
- INPS 46218 2230 B6
N Whittier Pl
1100 INPS 46219 2339 B1
3600 INPS 46218 2230 B2
4200 INPS 46226 2230 B1
7900 INPS 46250 2012 B6
S Whittier Pl
400 INPS 46219 2339 B4
1500 INPS 46203 2339 B6
Whittington Dr
10 BNBG 46112 2114 C4
Whitton Pl
4900 INPS 46220 2121 A3
Whitty Ln
1300 INPS 46229 2340 E1
1400 INPS 46229 2231 E7
Whitview Dr
8000 INPS 46237 2556 E6
Whitview Ln
4700 INPS 46237 2556 E6
Whitworth Dr
4300 INPS 46237 2556 E5
14300 CRML 46033 1793 D7
Wichita Hill Dr
- INPS 46217 2554 B6
Wichser Av
300 INPS 46241 2335 E4
Wichser Ct
4500 INPS 46228 2227 D1
Wicker Rd
2300 INPS 46217 2554 C7
3500 INPS 46217 2553 E7
Wickerwood Dr
400 CBLD 46229 2341 C1
Wickfield Ct
7800 INPS 46256 2013 B7
Wickfield Dr
7600 INPS 46256 2013 B7
Wickfield Wy
7600 INPS 46256 2013 C6
Wickham Ct
900 CRML 46032 1901 E5
Wickham Rd
8900 INPS 46260 2010 A4
Wickland Ct
9600 FSHR 46038 2013 D2
Wicklow Ln
- FCkT 46040 2015 D1
Wicksworth Wy
14100 CRML 46032 1792 A7
Widland Pass
- INPS 46226 2121 C5
Wiebeck Ct
- INPS 46226 2121 D5
Wigeon Ct
2400 INPS 46234 2225 A6
Wigeon Dr
- INPS 46234 2225 A5
Wigeon Rd
7000 FSHR 46038 1903 E6
7000 FSHR 46038 1904 A6
Wigmaker Ct
7700 PNFD 46168 2441 D3
Wilcore Dr
100 WynT 46060 1687 C6
Wilcox St
2800 INPS 46222 2336 C2
Wildcat Dr
6000 INPS 46203 2448 C3
13800 CRML 46033 1794 C7
13800 CRML 46033 1903 C1
Wildcat Ln
3000 INPS 46203 2448 C3
Wildcat Run Ct
7300 INPS 46239 2449 A7
Wildcat Run Dr
5200 INPS 46239 2449 A7
5600 INPS 46239 2558 A1
Wildcat Run Ln
7300 INPS 46239 2449 A7
Wild Cherry Dr
6700 FSHR 46038 1903 E6
Wild Cherry Ln
9600 ClyT 46280 2011 B2
Wilder Wy
5300 LWNC 46216 2122 C6
Wilderness Ln
800 GNWD 46142 2665 A4
Wilderness Rd
- WshT 46074 1792 C4
- WTFD 46074 1792 C4
Wilderness Tr
3700 INPS 46237 2447 D5
6500 FSHR 46038 1903 D6
Wildflower Cir
5800 INPS 46254 2117 D5
Wildflower Ct
5000 INPS 46254 2117 C5
11500 FSHR 46038 1903 E6
15400 WshT 46074 1792 C5
W Wildflower Ct
1000 MnrT 46158 2658 B6
Wildflower Dr
5800 INPS 46254 2117 D5
Wildflower Ln
- GNWD 46143 2774 A1
15400 WshT 46074 1792 D5
Wild Horse Dr
5500 INPS 46239 2449 B7
Wild Horse Ln
6900 INPS 46241 2334 E5
Wild Ivy Cir
3300 INPS 46227 2556 C7
Wild Ivy Ct
3600 INPS 46227 2556 D7
Wild Ivy Dr
3400 INPS 46227 2556 C7
Wild Lake Cir
- BNBG 46112 2114 E5
Wildman Ln
3000 CRML 46032 1900 B3
Wild Opera Ct
900 NBVL 46060 1687 A6
Wild Ridge Blvd
- BNBG 46112 2114 E4
Wild Ridge Ct
600 WynT 46060 1687 E1
Wild Ridge Dr
400 WynT 46060 1687 E1
Wildridge Rd
6800 INPS 46256 2122 C2
Wild Rose Ln
400 AVON 46123 2332 A5
700 WRvT 46142 2663 C2
Wildrye Dr
15700 WshT 46074 1792 D4
Wild Turkey Row
9800 FCkT 46055 2015 C2
Wildwood Av
5700 INPS 46220 2119 E5
Wildwood Ct
10 BNBG 46112 2223 D2
1500 PNFD 46168 2441 D6
6800 INPS 46268 2117 D2
Wildwood Dr
10 CRML 46032 1901 E2
700 BCkT 46140 2235 A7
700 BCkT 46140 2344 A1
1500 PNFD 46168 2441 D6
9900 ZNVL 46077 1899 A2
10600 FCkT 46038 1905 B7
S Wildwood Dr
3700 INPS 46239 2449 B4
Wildwood Ln
- GNWD 46143 2666 A5
900 MdnT 46113 2661 D5
2100 INPS 46239 2341 C7
7400 FSHR 46038 1904 A6
E Wildwood Ln
11100 INPS 46239 2341 C7
Wildwood Farms Blvd
- INPS 46239 2449 B3
Wildwood Farms Dr
8000 INPS 46239 2449 B3
Wildwood Farms Ln
7900 INPS 46239 2449 B3
Wiley Av
5300 INPS 46226 2121 D6
Wiley St
10 CCRO 46034 1577 D3
E Wiley St
10 GNWD 46143 2665 C3
W Wiley St
100 CCRO 46034 1577 C3
Wiley St W
300 GNWD 46142 2665 B3
Wilford Ln
1300 INPS 46229 2341 E1
1500 INPS 46229 2232 E7
Wilkens St
- NPLN 46163 2452 A4
W Wilkins Av
5300 INPS 46241 2335 C5
Wilkins St
- NPLN 46163 2452 A3
W Wilkins St
500 INPS 46225 2337 B5
2800 INPS 46221 2336 C5
5700 INPS 46241 2335 B5
Willa Bonn Ct
9800 NbvT 46060 1687 A2
Willard St
400 INPS 46225 2337 C4
Willark Dr
800 NWTD 46184 2774 D4
Willcreek Ln
400 INPS 46260 2010 B6
Willcrest Dr
2500 INPS 46228 2118 C7
Willesden Cir
13800 FSHR 46060 1906 E2
William Av
4000 FKLN 46131 2774 E7
4000 FKLN 46131 2775 A7
William Dr
9600 NbvT 46060 1687 A5
W William Dr
10 BNBG 46112 2223 B1
W William St
200 DNVL 46122 2329 D4
William Conner Wy
- CRML 46033 1903 D2
William Penn Cir
8800 INPS 46256 2013 D7
William Penn Dr
7600 INPS 46256 2013 D7
William Penn Pl
7500 INPS 46256 2013 D7
Williams Cir
5000 CRML 46033 1903 A6
Williams Ct
200 INPS 46260 2010 C6
300 AVON 46123 2332 B4
600 WRvT 46142 2663 D2
11200 CRML 46033 1903 A6
Williams Dr
10 MRVL 46158 2659 E2
200 INPS 46260 2010 C6
4900 CRML 46033 1903 A6
5900 PNFD 46168 2550 D2
Williams Ln
200 INPS 46260 2010 C6
Williams St
1400 INPS 46201 2337 E3
1400 INPS 46201 2338 A4
E Williams St
500 LEBN 46052 1677 A6
W Williams St
100 LEBN 46052 1677 B4
200 LEBN 46052 1676 E6
Williams Trc
100 PNFD 46168 2442 C2
Williamsburg Ct
10 ZNVL 46077 1899 A4
6000 INPS 46226 2230 C1
Williamsburg Dr
7500 PNFD 46168 2441 C2
14100 CRML 46033 1794 A7
Williamsburg Ln
600 GNWD 46142 2664 E2
900 ZNVL 46077 1899 A4
Williamsburg Wy
1000 WshT 46234 2333 E1
Williams Cove Ct
8400 INPS 46260 2010 B5
Williams Cove Dr
700 INPS 46260 2010 B5
Williams Creek Blvd
10 INPS 46240 2010 C6
10 INPS 46260 2010 C6
Williams Creek Dr
7100 INPS 46220 2119 E1
7100 INPS 46240 2119 E1
11600 CRML 46032 1901 B5
Williamshire East Dr
8600 INPS 46260 2010 A4
Williamshire West Dr
8600 INPS 46260 2010 A4
N Williamshire West Dr
- INPS 46260 2010 B4
Williamson Pkwy
- CRML 46033 1902 E7
10400 CRML 46033 2011 D1
Williamson St
500 WTLD 46184 2775 A5
W Williamswood Dr
7500 SCkT 46163 2450 E2
7500 SCkT 46163 2451 A2
Willis Dr
17100 NBVL 46062 1794 E1
Williston Ct
9100 INPS 46260 2010 A3
Willman Dr
3300 GfdT 46168 2551 B5
Willoughby Ct
500 PNFD 46168 2441 B4
6800 INPS 46214 2334 E2
Willow Ct
700 DNVL 46122 2330 A2
1300 NBVL 46062 1685 D3
4000 FKLN 46131 2774 E7
6600 INPS 46214 2334 E3
Willow Dr
- GNWD 46142 2664 E1
500 DNVL 46122 2330 A3
500 MRVL 46158 2659 D2
600 WTLD 46184 2775 A5
1000 INPS 46203 2446 E2
8600 DelT 46060 1795 C7
Willow Ln
- INPS 46254 2117 A7
Willow Rd
100 GNFD 46140 2236 D7
4400 EglT 46077 1899 C2
4400 ZNVL 46077 1899 C2
N Willow Rd
3500 EglT 46077 1790 D7
3500 EglT 46077 1899 D1
6800 INPS 46220 2119 D2
Willow Rdg
7500 FSHR 46038 1904 B7
E Willow St
100 ZNVL 46077 1899 B5
Willow Wy
1200 NBVL 46062 1685 D2
N Willow Wy
2400 INPS 46268 2009 C4
Willow Bend Ct
- WshT 46123 2331 E7
- WshT 46123 2440 E1
10200 FSHR 46038 2014 B1
Willow Bend Dr
1800 WshT 46123 2331 E7
4000 BHGV 46107 2447 D6
Willowbrook Dr
500 FSHR 46038 2012 D2
700 AVON 46123 2332 C5
Willowbrook Pkwy
2400 INPS 46205 2120 B7
Willow Creek Wy
17600 WTFD 46074 1684 C7
Willow Forge Ct
4500 INPS 46254 2117 E4
Willowgate Dr
100 INPS 46260 2010 C3
Willowgate Ln
100 INPS 46260 2010 C3
Willow Glen Cir
2600 INPS 46229 2232 A5
Willow Glen Ct
2600 INPS 46229 2232 A5
Willow Glen Dr
4000 BHGV 46107 2447 D6
4900 INPS 46107 2447 D6
Willow Glen Ln
4200 BHGV 46107 2447 D6
S Willow Grove Dr
3300 SCkT 46163 2451 C1
W Willow Grove Dr
6700 SCkT 46163 2451 B1
Willowick Dr
600 CRML 46032 1902 C2
Willow Lake Dr
2100 WRvT 46143 2664 A7
2800 INPS 46268 2009 C4
Willowleaf Ct
- NBVL 46062 1794 E1
- NbvT 46062 1794 E1
Willowmere Dr
10800 ClyT 46280 1902 A7
10800 CRML 46032 1902 A7
10800 CRML 46280 1902 A7
Willowmette Ln
11200 INPS 46235 2232 C3
Willow Oak Ct
1300 AVON 46123 2332 A1
Willowood Dr
3600 INPS 46235 2232 C3
Willowood Ln
100 FSHR 46038 1904 A4
Willowood St
7600 INPS 46214 2225 B2
Willow Pointe Dr
- GfdT 46168 2441 A6
Willow Pointe North Dr
- GfdT 46168 2440 E4
- GfdT 46168 2441 A6
Willow Pointe South Dr
- GfdT 46168 2440 E4
- GfdT 46168 2441 A6
Willow Pond Dr
- NBVL 46062 1794 E1
- NbvT 46062 1794 E1
- NbvT 46062 1795 A1
Willow Ridge Ct
4900 ZNVL 46077 1899 A3
Willowridge Ct
- GfdT 46168 2440 E4
5600 INPS 46221 2553 A1
W Willow Run Ct
- MnrT 46158 2658 B6
Willowrun Dr
9100 INPS 46260 2010 C3
Willowrun Wy
100 INPS 46260 2010 C3
Willow Spring Rd
- INPS 46240 2010 D6
Willow Springs Blvd
1100 BNBG 46112 2223 B2
Willowtree Ln
9700 INPS 46229 2231 E5
9900 INPS 46229 2232 A5
Willowview Cir
2300 INPS 46239 2449 B1
Willowview Dr
- INPS 46239 2340 A7
2300 INPS 46239 2449 A1
Willow View Rd
9600 DelT 46038 2012 E2
9600 FSHR 46038 2012 E2
17100 NBVL 46062 1794 E1
17100 NbvT 46062 1794 E1
17300 NBVL 46062 1685 D7
17300 NbvT 46062 1685 D7
Willow Wind Cir
7900 INPS 46239 2340 B7
Willow Wind Ct
2100 INPS 46239 2340 B7
4400 WRvT 46142 2663 E4
Willow Wind Dr
- WRvT 46142 2663 E4
Will Scarlet Ln
5200 INPS 46228 2118 C6
Willsey Ct
3500 GfdT 46168 2550 E5
Willshire Dr
1300 WRvT 46143 2664 B6
Wilmet St
- INPS 46219 2340 D1
- INPS 46229 2340 D1
Wilmett Ct
5600 CRML 46033 1903 D3
Wilmington Cir
11400 FSHR 46038 1904 B6
Wilmington Dr
10800 CRML 46033 1902 E7
Wilshire Ct
100 NBVL 46062 1685 D2
Wilshire Dr
4300 LcnT 46112 2224 D2
6000 INPS 46259 2559 C2
Wilshire Pl
6500 EglT 46077 1897 E6
Wilshire Rd
2000 INPS 46228 2227 D1
Wilshire Glen Dr
9000 INPS 46234 2224 E3
9000 INPS 46234 2225 A3
Wilson Dr
10 BrnT 46158 2660 A6
10 CRML 46032 1901 E3
10 CRML 46032 1902 A3
100 NPLN 46163 2452 B3
Wilson Rd
5200 PryT 46112 2006 A1
6500 EglT 46077 2006 A1
6500 EglT 46112 2006 A1
7300 INPS 46278 2116 C1

STREET
Block City ZIP Map# Grid

Wilson Rd
9000 INPS 46278 2006 E7
9000 INPS 46278 2007 A7
9200 BrnT 46112 2006 E7
10400 BrnT 46278 2006 E7
Wilson St
10 CCRO 46034 1577 D3
10 GNFD 46140 2345 D1
100 NPLN 46163 2452 B4
600 DNVL 46122 2329 C4
700 GNFD 46140 2236 C7
N Wilson St
800 INPS 46202 2337 A2
W Wilson St
- CCRO 46034 1577 C3
Wilson Terrace Ct
700 CRML 46032 1901 E2
Wilton Ct
6700 INPS 46214 2334 E2
Wiltonwood Ct
5200 INPS 46254 2116 D6
Wimbledon Ct
9400 INPS 46250 2012 B2
Wimbledon Dr
- EglT 46077 2006 D1
6600 EglT 46077 1897 C7
Wimbly Wy
18800 NBVL 46060 1686 E5
18900 NbvT 46060 1686 E5
Wimmenauer Dr
1500 INPS 46203 2339 B6
Winamac Ct
13400 CRML 46032 1901 C1
Winchester Dr
1700 INPS 46227 2556 A6
3400 WRvT 46143 2664 B6
9800 LcnT 46112 2224 C3
N Winchester Dr
1200 CBLD 46140 2232 E6
Winchester Pl
8000 INPS 46227 2556 D6
10300 ClyT 46280 2010 E1
10300 ClyT 46280 2011 A1
W Wind Cir
1300 CRML 46032 1901 D1
W Wind Ln
5400 INPS 46250 2012 B3
Windage Dr
- FCkT 46038 1906 C6
Windbreak Ct
9500 FSHR 46038 1904 E7
Windbush Wy
12400 CRML 46033 1903 B4
Windcastle Tr
1300 CRML 46280 2011 A2
Wind Chime Cir
- GNWD 46143 2666 D4
Windcombe Blvd
8100 INPS 46240 2010 E5
Winddoor Rd
6400 INPS 46226 2121 D4
Wind Drift Cir
8000 BrnT 46112 2005 D4
Wind Drift Ct
10 MdlT 46167 2113 B5
10 PTBR 46167 2113 B5
Wind Drift Dr
3800 INPS 46254 2225 D2
Wind Drift Dr E
3900 INPS 46254 2225 D2
Wind Drift Dr W
3800 INPS 46254 2225 D2
Windemere
10300 ClyT 46032 2009 D1
10500 ClyT 46032 1900 D7
Windemere Rd
100 NWTD 46184 2774 D3
Windermere Blvd
- FSHR 46038 2014 B2
Windermire St
1000 INPS 46227 2446 E5
1300 INPS 46227 2447 A5
Windfall Ln
- GfdT 46113 2551 E6
- INPS 46113 2551 E6
Windflower Ct
- BrnT 46112 2114 B2
Windham Ct
10 BNBG 46112 2223 B3
Windham Dr
3300 WRvT 46143 2664 B6
Windham Lake Cir
3400 INPS 46214 2225 B4
Windham Lake Ct
3400 INPS 46214 2225 B3
Windham Lake Dr
8000 INPS 46214 2225 B3
Windham Lake Pl
3400 INPS 46214 2225 C3
Windham Lake Rd
3400 INPS 46214 2225 B3
Windham Lake Ter
- INPS 46214 2225 B3
Windham Lake Trc
- INPS 46214 2225 B3
Windham Lake Wy
7900 INPS 46214 2225 B3
Windham Pass
12600 CRML 46032 1901 E3
E Windhaven Blvd
11500 INPS 46236 2014 D5
11600 LWNC 46236 2014 D5
Windhaven Cir
- BNBG 46112 2114 E5
8200 INPS 46236 2014 D5
Windhaven Ct
900 SCkT 46163 2343 B3
11400 INPS 46236 2014 D5
Windhaven Ln
2300 LEBN 46052 1676 C3
Windhill Dr
4000 INPS 46235 2231 D2
7900 INPS 46256 2013 E6
N Windhill Dr
7900 INPS 46256 2013 E6
Windhorst Wy
1100 GNWD 46143 2666 A3
Winding Tr
600 GNWD 46142 2664 D2
Winding Wy
100 CRML 46062 1795 A6
100 NbvT 46062 1795 A6
200 CtrT 46052 1677 B3
300 CRML 46032 1901 E3
300 CRML 46032 1902 A3
3900 INPS 46220 2120 D5
7500 FSHR 46038 1904 B7
Winding Brook Dr
600 WynT 46060 1687 E1
Windingbrook Dr
11000 ClyT 46280 1902 A7
11000 CRML 46280 1902 A7
Winding Brook Ln
800 GNWD 46142 2665 A2
Winding Brook Pkwy
800 INPS 46234 2333 E2
Winding Brook East Dr
800 INPS 46234 2333 E2
Winding Creek Cir
12300 LWNC 46236 2015 A7
Winding Creek Ct
100 FSHR 46038 1904 C3
12700 LWNC 46236 2015 A7
Winding Creek Dr
7600 LWNC 46236 2015 A7
Winding Creek Ln
12400 LWNC 46236 2015 A7
12500 FSHR 46038 1904 B3
Winding Creek Pl
7700 LWNC 46236 2015 A7
Winding Creek Tr
1500 BNBG 46112 2114 C4
1500 BrnT 46112 2114 C4
Winding Hart Dr
1000 INPS 46229 2341 E1
Winding Hill Dr
1900 INPS 46239 2340 B7
Winding Lake Dr E
20800 NBVL 46062 1686 B1
Winding Lake Dr N
7600 NBVL 46062 1686 A1
Winding Lake Dr S
7600 NBVL 46062 1686 A1
Winding Lake Dr W
20800 NBVL 46062 1686 B1
Winding Pine Rd
5400 NBVL 46062 1685 B7
Winding Ridge Av
1800 INPS 46217 2554 D7
Winding Ridge Ct
1800 INPS 46217 2554 D7
Winding Ridge Rd
8500 INPS 46217 2554 D7
Winding Trail Cir
- GNWD 46142 2664 D2
Winding Wood Ct
11200 LWNC 46235 2123 D5
Winding Wood Dr
11400 LWNC 46235 2123 D5
Winding Wy Ln
5800 INPS 46220 2120 E5
Windjammer
6500 BrnT 46112 2114 B2
Windjammer Cir
10400 INPS 46236 2014 B6
Windjammer Ct
6700 BrnT 46112 2114 B2
10400 INPS 46236 2014 B6
10900 FCkT 46256 2014 E1
Windjammer Trc
10900 FCkT 46038 2014 D2
Windjammer North Dr
10900 FCkT 46256 2014 C2
Windjammer South Dr
10900 FCkT 46256 2014 C2
Windledge Cir
4500 ClyT 46077 1899 E6
Windmill Cir
15000 WTFD 46033 1793 C6
Windmill Dr
1600 BrnT 46112 2005 A6
1600 WshT 46123 2332 D7
5600 INPS 46254 2226 B2
14900 WTFD 46033 1793 D6
Windmill Tr N
100 WRvT 46142 2663 E3
Windmill Tr S
200 WRvT 46142 2663 E4
Windmill Wy
- NPLN 46163 2452 A2
W Windmill Wy
5000 SCkT 46163 2452 A1
Windovers Dr
8300 INPS 46259 2558 B6
Windpointe Pass
11700 CRML 46033 1903 A4
Windrider Ct
6800 BrnT 46112 2114 B2
Windridge Dr
4900 INPS 46226 2121 A6
Windridge Dr N
800 NBVL 46062 1795 A1
Windridge Lndg
- BNBG 46112 2114 A3
Windridge Wy
7000 BrnT 46112 2114 B4
7400 BNBG 46112 2114 B3
Windrift Wy
4800 CRML 46033 1903 A5
Wind River Ct
9200 INPS 46234 2333 E1
N Wind River Run
9900 MCVL 46055 2015 C3
Wind Run Cir
7700 INPS 46256 2013 B6
Wind Skip Cir
400 WTFD 46074 1684 B7
Windsong Ct
2200 INPS 46229 2232 A6
6800 BrnT 46112 2114 B3
W Windsong Ct
4400 SCkT 46163 2343 B2
Windsong Dr
2200 INPS 46229 2232 A6
N Windsong Ln
200 WRvT 46142 2663 E3
Wind Song Tr
700 MRVL 46158 2660 A5
Windsor Ct
2500 LEBN 46052 1677 A2
4100 WRvT 46142 2663 E4
Windsor Dr
- FSHR 46038 1904 D3
- MCVL 46055 2124 C1
6000 INPS 46219 2230 C6
12100 CRML 46033 1902 E4
Windsor Ln
100 NBVL 46060 1795 D5
100 NbvT 46060 1795 D5
800 DNVL 46122 2330 C2
Windsor Pkwy
2100 INPS 46227 2556 A4
Windsor Pl
- PNFD 46168 2442 A2
Windsor Rd
1000 LcnT 46112 2224 D2
Windsor St
1000 INPS 46201 2338 A1
Windsor East Dr
12100 FSHR 46038 1904 E4
Windsor Lakes Dr
- INPS 46237 2557 B4
Windsor Lakes Pl
7200 INPS 46237 2557 B4
Windsor South Dr
12000 FSHR 46038 1904 D4
Windsor West Dr
12100 FSHR 46038 1904 D4
Windstone Cir
18400 NBVL 46062 1685 E6
Windswept Dr
- FSHR 46038 1906 B6
N Windswept Rd
10 CtrT 46140 2344 D1
10 GNFD 46140 2344 D1
800 CtrT 46140 2235 D7
Windtree Rd
- BrnT 46112 2005 E3
Wind View Cir
4300 WRvT 46142 2663 E3
Windview Dr
- BNBG 46112 2114 B3
Windward Cir
200 AVON 46123 2332 E3
Windward Ct
5700 INPS 46278 2117 B2
6600 BrnT 46112 2114 B2
Windward Dr
- BrnT 46112 2005 E4
- LcnT 46112 2115 D6
1700 WRvT 46143 2663 E7
Windward Ln
400 PNFD 46168 2441 A4
Windward Wy
3500 ClyT 46032 2009 B1
5600 INPS 46278 2117 B2
Windward Pass
10000 FSHR 46038 2014 C2
Windwood Cir
8900 INPS 46256 2013 C4
17700 WTFD 46074 1684 D7
Windwood Pkwy
19300 NBVL 46062 1686 B4
Windy Ln
10800 INPS 46239 2341 C5
E Windy Acres Ln
10 MdnT 46158 2662 A5
Windy Hill Ct
2100 INPS 46239 2340 A7
Windy Hill Ln
1800 INPS 46239 2340 A7
Windy Hill Wy
7600 INPS 46239 2340 A7
Windy Knoll Ln
- CRML 46074 1900 B2
Winesap Wy
1800 CRML 46032 1900 E4
Winfield Av
1000 INPS 46222 2336 C1
3000 INPS 46222 2227 C4
Winfield Dr
2400 CRML 46032 1900 C4
Winfield St
400 GNFD 46140 2345 B1
500 CtrT 46140 2345 B1
Winfield Park Ct
100 GNFD 46140 2345 A1
Winfield Park Dr
1500 GNFD 46140 2345 A1
Winford Dr
6100 LWNC 46236 2123 B3
Wingate Blvd
3600 INPS 46235 2232 B3
Wingate Ct
3600 INPS 46235 2232 B3
Wingate Dr
3700 INPS 46235 2232 B3
Wingate Ter
3600 INPS 46235 2232 A3
Winged Foot Ct
6000 INPS 46254 2117 D4
Winghaven Dr
- NBVL 46060 1796 B3
Wings Ct
500 LcnT 46112 2223 A1
Wings Dr
4800 BNBG 46112 2223 A1
4800 LcnT 46112 2223 A1
Wingstem Ct
12900 FSHR 46038 1905 A3
Wining Ln
- AVON 46123 2332 B5
Winings Av
3400 INPS 46221 2445 A3
Winlee Ct
10200 LWNC 46236 2123 A3
Winnebago Dr
5000 INPS 46241 2444 C2
Winners Cir
- BrnT 46278 2006 E3
4400 INPS 46203 2448 C6
Winners Ct
4400 INPS 46203 2448 C5
Winning Ln
7000 WshT 46123 2332 B6
Winning Colors Dr
15100 NBVL 46060 1796 D5
Winnings Ln
7000 WshT 46123 2332 B7
Winnock Dr
6600 INPS 46220 2121 C2
Winnpeny Ln
6000 INPS 46220 2120 E4
6000 INPS 46220 2121 A4
Winoma St
- WRvT 46062 1578 D6
Winona Dr
10 CRML 46032 1902 B3
6300 LWNC 46236 2123 A3
Winship Ct
5500 INPS 46221 2553 B1
Winship Dr
5500 INPS 46221 2553 B1
Winslow Dr
1000 WTFD 46074 1792 D1
6200 INPS 46237 2557 D6
Winslow Wy
- FSHR 46038 2013 D1
Winsome Ct
9600 INPS 46256 2013 E6
Winsted Dr
8600 INPS 46231 2443 A1
Winston Ct
18900 NBVL 46060 1686 E5
Winston Dr
4800 INPS 46226 2120 E6
4800 INPS 46226 2121 A6
Winston Ln
10400 FCkT 46038 1905 B7
Winston Pl
5200 INPS 46218 2230 A3
Winter Av
- INPS 46218 2229 B6
Winter Ct
700 CRML 46032 1792 E7
Winter Wy
- ZNVL 46077 1898 E2
700 CRML 46032 1792 E7
Winterberry Cir
5100 INPS 46254 2117 C5
Winter Berry Ct
7600 NBVL 46062 1686 B3
Winterberry Ct
8900 ZNVL 46077 1898 D2
Winterberry Dr
5100 INPS 46254 2117 C5
Winterberry Ln
100 MRVL 46158 2660 C3
Wintercove Wy
10800 FSHR 46038 1904 A7
Wintergreen Dr
- NBVL 46062 1685 C2
Wintergreen Ln
4800 CRML 46033 1903 A1
Wintergreen Wy
- WshT 46234 2224 D6
8700 INPS 46256 2013 C4
Winter Haven Ln
4700 CRML 46033 2012 A1
Winterhawk Dr
400 INPS 46241 2334 E5
Winterhazel Dr
5400 INPS 46254 2116 D6
Winterking Pass
10600 FSHR 46038 1905 D7
Winters Rd
700 WshT 46123 2223 B7
Winterset Cir
8000 INPS 46214 2225 B6
Winterset Dr
2900 ClyT 46032 1900 C7
Winterset Wy
200 GNWD 46143 2774 B1
Wintersong Dr
3000 INPS 46241 2444 C3
Winterspring Cres
4500 EglT 46077 1899 D2
Winterstill
- EglT 46077 1899 B2
- ZNVL 46077 1899 B2
Winterthur
1000 INPS 46260 2010 A5
Winterwind Ct
5600 INPS 46237 2557 B4
Winterwind Ln
5600 INPS 46237 2557 B4
Winterwood
10600 ClyT 46032 1901 B7
Winter Wood Ct
- ZNVL 46077 2008 A1
Winterwood Dr
- GNWD 46143 2665 C7
300 AVON 46123 2332 D3
Winterwood Ln
11200 LWNC 46235 2123 C6
Winthorp Pl
8800 FCkT 46038 1904 D1
8800 FSHR 46038 1904 D1
Winthrop Av
3700 INPS 46205 2228 E2
4900 INPS 46205 2119 E7
5200 INPS 46220 2119 E6
N Winthrop Av
8300 INPS 46240 2010 E5
Winthrop Rd
100 NWTD 46184 2774 D3
Winton Av
1000 SDWY 46224 2335 D1
1600 SDWY 46224 2226 D7
Winton Av
3000 INPS 46224 2226 D4
N Winton Av
3100 INPS 46224 2226 D4
Winton Ct
2300 SDWY 46224 2226 C6
Winton Dr
7100 INPS 46268 2117 D1
7500 INPS 46268 2008 D7
Wipperwill Ct
1500 GNWD 46142 2665 A1
S Wisby Dr
10 INPS 46241 2335 D4
Wisconsin St
10 INPS 46225 2337 B6
W Wisconsin St
3400 INPS 46241 2336 A6
Wise St
7400 INPS 46113 2552 D5
7400 INPS 46221 2552 D5
Wiser Av
100 MdnT 46113 2661 C4
Wish Av
3600 INPS 46268 2009 A6
Wish Ct
8000 INPS 46268 2009 A6
Wishard Blvd
1000 INPS 46202 2337 A2
1200 INPS 46202 2336 E2
Wishbone Blvd
3600 INPS 46268 2009 A6
S Wishmeyer Ln
1500 INPS 46239 2340 E6
Wismar Dr
11000 INPS 46235 2232 C3
Wisteria Dr
4900 INPS 46254 2117 D5
E Wisteria Wy
10 WshT 46074 1792 C4
Witch Hazel Dr
11300 INPS 46235 2232 C3
Witherbee Ct
12400 FSHR 46038 1906 B4
Witherbee Ln
12900 FSHR 46038 1906 B4
Witherington Rd
7900 INPS 46268 2009 C6
Witherspoon Dr
11100 LWNC 46236 2123 C3
Witt Ct
1600 WRvT 46143 2663 A5
Witt Dr
6000 WRvT 46143 2663 A5
Witt Rd
1600 LEBN 46052 1676 D4
2700 CtrT 46052 1676 C1
3000 CtrT 46052 1567 C6
3700 WshT 46052 1567 C6
W Witt Rd
- LEBN 46052 1676 C4
Wittfield Ct
9300 INPS 46235 2231 D1
Wittfield St
1000 INPS 46229 2340 D1
N Wittfield St
4200 INPS 46235 2231 D1
4400 LWNC 46235 2231 D1
S Wittfield St
100 INPS 46229 2340 D3
Wixshire Ct
4400 INPS 46254 2226 A1
Wixshire Dr
6000 INPS 46254 2226 A1
Wixson Ct
5900 INPS 46254 2226 B1
Woburn Dr
6200 INPS 46250 2121 D1
Wolf Cir
1300 INPS 46229 2341 D1
Wolf Ct
1300 INPS 46229 2341 D1
Wolf Ln
11200 INPS 46229 2341 D1
Wolf Creek Cir
3800 CRML 46033 2011 D1
Wolfe Rd
7500 PryT 46112 2005 E2
7500 PryT 46112 2006 A2
7900 BrnT 46112 2006 A2
Wolff Ct
1400 FKLN 46131 2774 E7
Wolffe Dr
7200 FSHR 46038 1904 A5
Wolfgang Dr
2900 INPS 46239 2449 A2
Wolford Ct
7900 FSHR 46038 1904 C4
Wolford Dr
12500 FSHR 46038 1904 D4
Wolford Pl
12500 FSHR 46038 1904 D4
Wolf Run Ct
15200 NBVL 46060 1797 A5
Wolf Run Rd
12000 NBVL 46060 1796 E5
12100 NBVL 46060 1797 A5
S Wollenweber Rd
2600 SCkT 46163 2342 C7
Wolverine Wy
2500 UnnT 46077 1790 A6
6600 INPS 46237 2557 D4
Wonderland Ct
5600 INPS 46239 2450 C7
E Wonderland Dr
10800 INPS 46239 2450 B7
Wood Ct
700 ZNVL 46077 1899 C5
1100 INPS 46227 2555 E2
7400 FSHR 46038 1903 E7
11100 CRML 46033 1902 E6
Wood Rd
- LWNC 46216 2122 D4
Wood St
10 GNFD 46140 2345 E1
600 GNFD 46140 2236 E7
Woodacre Blvd
9200 INPS 46234 2115 E6
Woodacre Ct
5500 INPS 46234 2115 E6
Woodacre Dr
10 CRML 46032 1902 A2
Woodacre Ln
8800 INPS 46234 2116 A6
Woodacre Boulevard North Dr
9100 INPS 46234 2115 E6
Woodacre Boulevard South Dr
9000 INPS 46234 2115 E6
9000 INPS 46234 2116 A6
Woodale Ct
3500 INPS 46234 2225 A3
Woodale Rd
3600 INPS 46234 2225 A3
Woodall Dr
8200 INPS 46268 2009 A5
Woodberry Dr
700 DNVL 46122 2330 C4
Woodbine Ct
900 INPS 46217 2555 A6
1900 CRML 46033 1903 A1
Woodbine Dr
8100 INPS 46217 2555 A6
Woodbine Dr E
600 CRML 46033 1902 C2
600 CRML 46033 1903 A1
Woodbine Dr W
600 CRML 46033 1902 E1
Wood Blaize Dr
- BrnT 46112 2114 D2
Woodbluff Ct
8600 INPS 46234 2225 A6
Woodbridge Ct
9100 INPS 46260 2010 A3
Woodbridge Ln
1000 INPS 46260 2010 A3
S Woodbridge Ln
4200 NPLN 46163 2452 B3
W Woodbridge Ln
4300 NPLN 46163 2452 B2
Woodbridge Pl
9400 EglT 46077 2007 D1
Woodbrier Ln
9700 ClyT 46280 2011 B2
Woodbrook Dr
5200 INPS 46254 2117 D6
Woodbrook Ln
11600 CRML 46033 1902 E5
Woodbrush Ct
8300 INPS 46256 2013 C3
W Woodburn Dr
8300 INPS 46234 2225 B6
Woodbury Ct
7400 INPS 46237 2557 B4
Woodbury Dr
11100 CRML 46033 1903 A6
Woodchuck Ln
10 INPS 46239 2449 A1
Woodcliff Cir
600 EglT 46077 1897 D7
Woodcliff Dr
3500 INPS 46203 2447 D1
Woodcock Dr
1900 WshT 46123 2441 A1
Woodcote Dr
5700 INPS 46221 2553 A4
Woodcote Ln
700 BNBG 46112 2114 D4
Woodcreek Cross
7300 WshT 46123 2223 C6
Wood Creek Ct
5200 CRML 46033 1903 B6
Woodcreek Ct
700 WRvT 46142 2664 A1
Woodcreek Dr
1200 WRvT 46142 2664 A1
1200 WRvT 46217 2664 A1
2200 WshT 46123 2223 C6
4900 CRML 46033 1903 A6
8100 INPS 46256 2122 B2
Wood Creek Pl
700 WRvT 46142 2664 A2
Woodcrest
6800 BCkT 46140 2342 B1
Woodcrest Ct
2100 INPS 46227 2447 B6
Woodcrest Dr
6200 WshT 46123 2441 A1
W Woodcrest Dr
5800 SCkT 46163 2451 D3
Woodcrest Rd
1900 INPS 46227 2447 A6
Woodcroft Av
4600 LWNC 46226 2121 E7
Woodcroft Ct
1700 WRvT 46143 2664 A7
Woodcross Ct
800 WshT 46123 2331 E5
Wooddale Ter
600 GNWD 46142 2665 B2
Wood Duck Ct
5000 CRML 46033 1903 A4
7300 INPS 46254 2225 D1
Wooded Glen Ct
2700 INPS 46268 2009 C4
Wooden Ln
7900 INPS 46260 2010 B6
Wooden Branch Dr
5600 INPS 46221 2552 E1
Wooden Shoe Cir
7800 WshT 46123 2332 D7
Woodfield Blvd
- CRML 46033 1794 B7
Woodfield Cir
500 AVON 46123 2332 C5
14100 CRML 46033 1794 A7
Woodfield Ct
- GNWD 46143 2666 A5
Woodfield Dr
4800 CRML 46033 1794 A7
S Woodfield Dr
3800 SCkT 46163 2451 A2
Woodfield Dr N
5200 CRML 46033 1794 A7
Woodfield Dr S
5200 CRML 46033 1794 B7
Woodfield Grn
10 DNVL 46122 2329 C2
E Woodfield Ln
200 BrnT 46158 2658 D7
Woodfield Pl
10 DNVL 46122 2329 C2
Woodfield Wy
5400 CRML 46033 1794 A7
Woodfield Crossing Blvd
8300 INPS 46240 2011 B5
Woodfield Crossing Ln
8200 INPS 46240 2011 B5
Woodford Ln
6500 INPS 46237 2557 D3
Woodfox Ct
6100 INPS 46226 2230 C1
Woodfront Ct
3500 INPS 46222 2227 B3
Woodfront Dr
3400 INPS 46222 2227 A3
Woodfront Pl
3400 INPS 46222 2227 B3
Woodgate Blvd
- GNWD 46143 2666 A6
Woodgate Cir
1400 CRML 46033 1793 D7
7000 FSHR 46038 1903 E7
Woodgate Ct
8000 INPS 46268 2008 E6
Woodgate Dr
1100 CRML 46033 1793 E7
1300 WTFD 46033 1793 E7
7100 FSHR 46038 1903 E6
Woodgate Ln
- GNWD 46143 2665 E6
- GNWD 46143 2666 A6
Woodglen Ct
8000 INPS 46260 2009 D6
Woodglen Dr
2100 INPS 46260 2009 C6
Woodglen Pl
8000 INPS 46260 2009 D6
Woodhaven Cir
10300 INPS 46229 2232 A5
Woodhaven Ct
1800 WRvT 46143 2663 E7
6300 WshT 46123 2332 A7
Woodhaven Dr
4400 ClyT 46077 1899 E6
Woodhill Dr
10 INPS 46227 2555 C2
Wood Hollow Dr
400 WTFD 46074 1684 B7
400 WTFD 46074 1793 A1
5300 INPS 46239 2449 B7
5500 INPS 46239 2558 B1
Wood Hollow Ln
8100 INPS 46239 2449 B7
Woodhouse Dr
- LWNC 46235 2122 E7
Woodington Ct
8100 INPS 46259 2558 B4
Woodington Pl
7200 INPS 46259 2558 B4
Wood Knoll Ln
6300 INPS 46260 2118 E3
Woodlake Ct
1500 ClyT 46032 1900 E6
Woodland Av
3700 INPS 46205 2229 A2
Woodland Cir
10 ClyT 46032 1902 C6
Woodland Ct
600 PNFD 46168 2441 C5
4500 INPS 46254 2117 B7
4500 INPS 46254 2226 B1
9500 LcnT 46112 2224 B4
Wood Land Dr
- BCkT 46140 2233 A6
Woodland Dr
10 INPS 46201 2338 D3
100 ClyT 46032 1902 B6
100 CRML 46032 1902 B6
100 NWTD 46184 2774 D5
200 GNWD 46142 2665 B3
200 LEBN 46052 1677 A5
2400 BrnT 46112 2114 C1
1600 NBVL 46060 1795 E2
4200 INPS 46254 2226 B1
4500 INPS 46254 2117 B7
7100 INPS 46278 2117 B1
8000 INPS 46278 2008 B6
N Woodland Dr
4600 INPS 46254 2117 B7
Woodland Pl
- PTBR 46167 2113 A2
10 DNVL 46122 2329 C3
500 GNWD 46142 2665 B3
Woodland Trc
1000 WshT 46168 2441 C1
Woodland Wy
5600 INPS 46254 2226 B1
Woodland East Dr
300 CBLD 46140 2342 B1
Woodland Hills Dr
- MdlT 46167 2113 B5
- PTBR 46167 2113 B5
Woodlands Dr
9600 FSHR 46038 2014 A2
Woodland Trace Blvd
5600 INPS 46237 2557 D1
Woodland Trail Dr
300 INPS 46229 2341 C4
300 INPS 46239 2341 C4
Woodland West Dr
300 CBLD 46140 2342 B1
Woodlane Ct
3100 INPS 46268 2118 B1

Indianapolis Street Index

STREET Block City ZIP Map# Grid

Woodlark Dr
10 CBLD 46229 2341 D2
8800 FSHR 46038 1795 D7
Woodlawn Av
900 INPS 46203 2337 E5
1700 INPS 46203 2338 A5
7500 INPS 46239 2340 A5
Woodlawn Dr
- SCkT 46163 2451 D3
600 GNWD 46142 2665 B3
10400 ClyT 46280 1902 A7
10400 ClyT 46280 2011 A1
N Woodlawn Dr
10 BrnT 46158 2658 C4
Woodlea Ct
7400 INPS 46256 2013 A5
Wood Lily Ct
- NBVL 46060 1687 C3
Woodlook Ln
10800 INPS 46239 2341 C4
Woodmere Cir
6500 INPS 46260 2119 A2
Woodmere Ct
6600 INPS 46260 2119 A2
Woodmere Dr
400 INPS 46260 2119 B2
Woodmill Ct
7200 AVON 46123 2332 C5
13600 CRML 46032 1901 C1
Woodmill Dr
5900 FSHR 46038 2012 C1
Woodmizer Wy
- INPS 46214 2334 B1
Woodmont Ct
- PNFD 46168 2442 B2
10 BHGV 46107 2447 E6
Woodmont Ln
10600 FSHR 46038 2014 B2
Woodmore Ct
500 WRvT 46142 2664 A2
Woodmore Dr
500 WRvT 46142 2664 A2
Woodmore Trc
7600 INPS 46260 2009 D7
Woodmoss Ln
8900 INPS 46250 2012 B4
N Woodnotes Addition
7100 MrlT 46126 2669 B2
Woodpointe Cir
8700 INPS 46234 2225 A7
Woodpointe Dr
1000 INPS 46234 2334 A1
1600 INPS 46234 2225 A7
Woodpond North Roundabout
1200 CRML 46033 1793 D6
Woodpond South Roundabout
1400 CRML 46033 1793 D6
Woodreed Ct
8600 INPS 46278 2007 B6
Woodridge Blvd
4200 INPS 46205 2229 C1
Woodridge Ct
10 NWTD 46184 2774 D3
700 WshT 46123 2332 B2
1000 CRML 46032 1793 B7
1000 CRML 46032 1902 B1
3800 AVON 46123 2332 B2
Woodridge Dr
- BNBG 46112 2223 E3
- MdlT 46167 2112 E4
300 WshT 46123 2332 B2
1000 LcnT 46112 2223 E3
Wood Ridge Ln
10800 FSHR 46038 1903 E7
Woodridge Pl
1700 WRvT 46143 2663 E7
Woodridge North Dr
- MdlT 46167 2112 E4
- MdlT 46167 2113 A4
Woodridge South Dr
- MdlT 46167 2112 E4
- MdlT 46167 2113 A4
Woodrow Av
800 INPS 46241 2335 D5
2600 INPS 46241 2444 D2
Woodruff St
600 WTLD 46184 2774 E5
Woodruff Cross Dr
1600 INPS 46201 2338 A2
N Woodruff Pl East Dr
500 INPS 46201 2338 A2
N Woodruff Pl Middle Dr
500 INPS 46201 2338 A2
N Woodruff Pl West Dr
500 INPS 46201 2338 A2
Woods Dr
- NBVL 46060 1797 A7
W Woodsage Ct
10 WshT 46074 1792 C4
Wood Sage Dr
1300 WshT 46123 2332 D1
Woodsage Trc
- INPS 46237 2447 D5
Woods Bay Ct
11900 CRML 46033 1903 A4
Woods Bay Ln
10900 INPS 46236 2014 C4
Woods Bay Pl
12100 CRML 46033 1903 A4
Woods Crossing Av
7700 INPS 46239 2340 B4
Woods Crossing Dr
500 INPS 46239 2340 A5
Woods Crossing Ln
600 INPS 46239 2340 A5
Woods Edge Ct
- PTBR 46167 2113 B5
13800 CRML 46032 1792 C7
Woods Edge Dr
4500 EglT 46077 1899 D3
9900 FSHR 46038 2014 A1
Woods Edge East Dr
8400 INPS 46250 2012 D4
Woods Edge North Dr
6300 INPS 46250 2012 D5
Woods Edge South Dr
6400 INPS 46250 2012 D5
Woods Edge West Dr
8400 INPS 46250 2012 D5
Woodshire Pl
4000 LtyT 46118 2549 A1
7400 INPS 46217 2555 B3
Woodshore Ct
3000 CRML 46033 1902 C6
Woodside Av
10 INPS 46219 2340 A3
Woodside Ct
- BNBG 46112 2114 C3
- ZNVL 46077 1899 A7
5100 CRML 46033 1903 A6
Woodside Dr
- MRVL 46158 2659 D7
- ZNVL 46077 1899 B3
10 BrnT 46158 2659 D7
700 WshT 46168 2441 B3
1400 WTFD 46074 1793 A2
1500 DNVL 46122 2330 B3
2900 GfdT 46168 2441 B3
5900 INPS 46228 2118 E4
7000 INPS 46260 2118 D1
7300 AVON 46123 2332 C3
7300 INPS 46260 2009 E7
Woodsmall Dr
9800 INPS 46229 2232 B5
Woodsmall Ln
2200 INPS 46229 2232 A6
Woodsong Ln
9600 INPS 46229 2340 E3
9600 INPS 46229 2341 A3
Woodsong Wy
9600 INPS 46229 2340 E3
9600 INPS 46229 2341 A3
Wood Spring Dr
3000 CRML 46033 1902 C6
Woodstock Ct
200 ZNVL 46077 1899 A3
Woodstock Dr
- INPS 46208 2227 E2
100 BNBG 46112 2223 E3
Woodstock Wy
8900 FSHR 46038 2013 D2
Woodstone Ct
8500 INPS 46256 2013 C4
9600 FSHR 46038 2014 A2
Woodstone Dr
8700 INPS 46256 2013 C4
Woodstone Wy S
8300 INPS 46256 2013 C4
Woodstone Way West Dr
8500 INPS 46256 2013 C4
Woodstream Ct
1800 WTFD 46074 1684 B6
Wood Stream Dr
7300 INPS 46254 2116 D6
7700 INPS 46239 2340 A6
Woodstream Dr
2100 WshT 46123 2441 A1
Woodsway Dr
2000 WRvT 46143 2664 B7
Woodthrush Dr
5700 INPS 46278 2117 B3
Woodtrace Ct
900 CtrT 46140 2237 C6
Wood Valley Ct
- ZNVL 46077 2008 A1
Wood Valley Dr
1700 CRML 46032 1902 B6
Woodview Ct
- BrnT 46112 2114 D2
100 MRVL 46158 2660 B4
11300 FSHR 46038 1904 A6
Woodview Dr
- LtyT 46118 2549 B1
- PTBR 46167 2113 B5
300 NBVL 46060 1686 C6
600 WTLD 46184 2774 D7
Woodview Ln
- INPS 46222 2227 A7
Woodview Tr
- MCVL 46055 2015 D5
Woodview Trc
3500 INPS 46268 2009 A3
Woodview East Dr
11400 CRML 46032 1901 E6
Woodview North Dr
700 CRML 46032 1901 E5
Woodview South Dr
700 CRML 46032 1901 E6
Woodview West Dr
11400 CRML 46032 1901 E6
Woodville St
12500 WRvT 46060 1579 A4
Woodward Dr
10800 FSHR 46038 1905 C7
Woodwind Ct
7600 BrnT 46112 2114 B2
Woodwind Dr
6300 INPS 46217 2555 B3
Woodwind Wy
2700 INPS 46268 2009 C4
Woodworth Ct
6500 INPS 46237 2557 B2
Woodworth Wy
5600 INPS 46237 2557 B3
N Woody Creek Cross
- MCVL 46055 2015 C3
Woolco Ln
5500 SDWY 46224 2226 B6
Woonsocket Ct
8200 INPS 46256 2013 E5
Wooster Ct
8900 FSHR 46038 1904 D1
Worcester Av
200 INPS 46201 2339 A4
500 INPS 46203 2339 A4
Worcester Wy
1200 GNFD 46140 2237 A6
Worchester Ct
4300 CRML 46033 1793 D7
Worchester Dr
1300 CRML 46033 1793 D7
Wordsworth Ct
600 NBVL 46060 1795 E3
Worman St
10 SPRT 46227 2556 A4
E Worman St
10 WshT 46069 1683 C2
W Worman St
10 WshT 46069 1683 C1
N Worth Av
10 INPS 46224 2335 C3
1400 SDWY 46224 2335 C1
1500 SDWY 46224 2226 C7
S Worth Av
300 INPS 46241 2335 C4
Worth Ct
100 MRVL 46158 2659 D7
400 WshT 46032 1792 D6
Wortham Wy
2700 INPS 46268 2009 C7
2700 INPS 46268 2118 C1
Worthington Blvd
9800 FSHR 46060 1796 A7
Worthington Cir
8800 INPS 46278 2008 A4
Worthington Ct
8700 INPS 46278 2008 A4
W Worthsville Rd
- GNWD 46143 2665 A7
- PltT 46143 2665 A7
Wrangler Ct
8600 INPS 46217 2555 B7
Wren Ct
5100 CRML 46033 1903 B1
Wren St
3000 INPS 46222 2336 C1
Wren Wy
500 EglT 46077 1898 D4
Wright St
800 INPS 46203 2337 D5
WTLC Cir
- INPS 46203 2447 C1
Wyandott Tr
4600 INPS 46250 2011 E7
4800 INPS 46250 2012 A7
Wyandotte Ct
200 NbvT 46060 1796 A3
Wyandotte Dr
4200 INPS 46220 2120 E6
Wyandotte Pl
13700 FCkT 46038 1904 D1
13700 FSHR 46038 1904 D1
Wyandotte Tr
3700 INPS 46240 2011 D7
Wychwood Pl
18500 NBVL 46062 1685 E5
Wyckfield Wy
5700 INPS 46220 2121 B2
Wyckford Ct
7600 INPS 46214 2334 C2
Wyckford Dr
800 INPS 46214 2334 C2
Wycliff East Dr
4800 INPS 46221 2444 B7
Wycombe Ln
4400 INPS 46226 2121 A7
4400 INPS 46226 2230 A1
5800 INPS 46220 2121 B4
Wyman Ct
6500 INPS 46220 2121 D2
Wynbrook Blvd
2300 WshT 46234 2224 D6
Wynbrooke Blvd
- WshT 46234 2224 D7
Wyndham Dr
10 BNBG 46112 2223 C3
Wyndham Ln
10 BNBG 46112 2223 C3
Wyndham Wy
- GNWD 46142 2664 E4
Wyndotte Dr
200 CRML 46032 1901 C2
Wyngate Cir
1100 GNWD 46143 2664 E5
Wyngate Wy
1100 GNWD 46143 2664 E5
Wynham Ct
10000 FSHR 46038 2014 B2
Wynne St
6600 LWNC 46236 2123 E2
Wynnedale Rd
2000 INPS 46228 2227 D2
Wynridge Ct
5600 LWNC 46235 2123 B5
Wynstone Wy
5100 CRML 46033 1903 A4
Wynter Wy
7100 INPS 46250 2121 C1
W Wyoming St
10 INPS 46225 2337 B5
2800 INPS 46221 2336 C5
Wysom Ct
- FSHR 46060 1905 E1
Wysong Dr
7700 INPS 46219 2231 B6
Wysteria Ct
10 LcnT 46112 2222 E2
Wythe Dr
7100 NBVL 46062 1685 E5
7200 NBVL 46062 1686 A5
Wythe Ln
- LcnT 46112 2115 D6
4100 INPS 46250 2011 E6

X

Xenia Cir
3400 INPS 46227 2556 C6
Xenia Dr
8000 INPS 46227 2556 C6

Y

Yacht Harbor Cir
1900 INPS 46260 2118 D2
Yale Dr
9300 INPS 46240 2010 E3
Yancey Pl
- CRML 46077 1900 A3
Yandes St
1200 INPS 46202 2337 E1
1600 INPS 46202 2228 E7
2200 INPS 46205 2228 E6
Yardley Ct
8700 INPS 46268 2009 C4
Yarmouth Pl
11200 FSHR 46038 1904 A6
Yates Ln
1200 AVON 46123 2333 C1
1200 WshT 46123 2333 C1
Yates St
1400 LEBN 46052 1676 D5
Yazoo Dr
1400 BHGV 46107 2447 E6
1700 INPS 46107 2447 E6
Yeager Ct
5500 INPS 46237 2557 B1
Yeager Dr
5800 INPS 46237 2448 C7
Yeager Ln
5400 INPS 46237 2448 C7
Yeagy Ct N
600 WRvT 46142 2663 D2
Yeagy Ct S
500 WRvT 46142 2663 D2
Yeagy Dr
4600 WRvT 46142 2663 D2
Yeagy Rd
400 WRvT 46142 2663 D2
Yearling Run
6200 INPS 46278 2117 A1
Yellow Birch Ct E
6000 WshT 46123 2440 E1
6100 WshT 46123 2441 A1
Yellow Birch Wy
5400 INPS 46254 2116 D6
Yellowood Ct
9000 INPS 46260 2009 E4
Yellow Pine Ct
900 INPS 46217 2555 A5
Yellow Poplar Ct
3500 INPS 46222 2227 A6
Yellowstone Pkwy
6500 INPS 46217 2555 A3
Yellowwood Cir
1100 NBVL 46062 1685 D3
Yellowwood Dr
- WRvT 46143 2663 E5
Yeoman Wy
16600 WTFD 46074 1792 E2
Yoke St
10 INPS 46225 2446 C2
E Yoke St
700 INPS 46203 2446 E2
Yolanda Ct
7200 LWNC 46236 2124 A1
Yolander Ln
4500 WshT 46123 2331 B7
York Cir
600 NBVL 46062 1685 D2
York Dr
- ZNVL 46077 1898 E4
- ZNVL 46077 1899 A4
10 CRML 46032 1902 A2
York Pl
600 FSHR 46038 1904 A5
York Rd
800 BNBG 46112 2223 C2
York St
- GNWD 46143 2665 C3
900 INPS 46221 2337 A6
Yorkbend Ct
5100 INPS 46254 2117 C7
Yorkshire Blvd
10 CBLD 46229 2342 A2
W Yorkshire Blvd
10 CBLD 46229 2342 A2
Yorkshire Cir
200 NBVL 46060 1795 D4
6400 EglT 46077 1897 E7
W Yorkshire Ct
2100 INPS 46229 2231 E6
Yorkshire Dr
3300 WRvT 46143 2664 B6
Yorkshire Ln
11800 CRML 46033 1902 E5
Yorkshire Pl
6700 WshT 46123 2332 B2
Yorktown Cross
10900 ClyT 46032 1900 A6
Yorktown Dr
4100 INPS 46235 2231 D1
Yorktown Ln
- AVON 46123 2333 D3
- WshT 46123 2333 C2
200 WRvT 46142 2663 C4
Yorktown Rd
- GNWD 46143 2664 E4
200 GNWD 46142 2664 E4
Yorkville Ct
5600 INPS 46254 2117 B5
Yosemite Ct
6900 INPS 46217 2555 A4
11000 FSHR 46038 1906 A6
Yosemite Dr
600 INPS 46217 2555 A3
1000 LEBN 46052 1676 D3
Yosemite Ln
- BrnT 46112 2115 C5
- LcnT 46112 2115 C5
Young Av
4400 INPS 46201 2338 E4
4800 INPS 46201 2339 A4
Youngberry Ct
2900 INPS 46217 2554 B3
Youngberry Dr
6800 INPS 46217 2554 C3
Young Lakes Dr
10600 INPS 46239 2341 B3
10700 INPS 46229 2341 B3
Youngs Creek Ln
8800 INPS 46113 2552 A7
Youngwood Ln
9800 FSHR 46060 1905 A1
Younkin Dr
5400 INPS 46268 2117 C3
Yount Blvd
- INPS 46224 2335 C2
Yucatan Dr
5200 INPS 46237 2448 B7
Yuma Ct
3300 INPS 46241 2444 D3
Yuma Dr
4500 INPS 46241 2444 D4
Yvette Dr
9100 WshT 46123 2333 A1

Z

Zeenat Ct
3900 INPS 46254 2227 A1
Zeenat Dr
3900 INPS 46254 2227 A1
Zeenat Ln
4400 INPS 46254 2227 A1
4500 INPS 46254 2118 A7
Zelda St
1300 NBVL 46060 1795 D2
Zellwood Ct
13200 CRML 46033 1903 C2
Zenas Ct
- MdnT 46113 2661 C1
Zephtr Wy
- WshT 46074 1792 B4
Zephyr Dr
- CtrT 46122 2330 A2
- DNVL 46122 2330 A2
8500 INPS 46217 2555 A7
Zephyr Wy
400 WshT 46074 1792 B4
Zinfandel Pl
10300 FSHR 46060 1905 B2
Zinfandel Wy
4000 INPS 46254 2225 E2
Zinnia Dr
1700 INPS 46219 2231 B7
Zion Ct
10 INPS 46222 2227 A5
Zion Ln
500 EglT 46077 1899 D4
Zionsville Rd
4000 WrhT 46075 1897 E2
6200 INPS 46268 2117 B3
7100 INPS 46278 2117 B1
7500 INPS 46278 2008 B7
8600 INPS 46268 2008 B3
9600 EglT 46077 2008 B3
9600 EglT 46278 2008 B3
9900 EglT 46077 1899 B7
9900 ZNVL 46077 1899 B7
N Zionsville Rd
- INPS 46268 2008 B4
- INPS 46278 2008 B4
6500 INPS 46268 2117 B2
6500 INPS 46278 2117 B2
Zoeller Cir
5300 CRML 46033 1903 D3
Zoeller St
4400 LWNC 46226 2122 C7
4400 LWNC 46226 2231 C1
Zona Dr
8100 INPS 46227 2556 B6
Zonda Blvd
- ClyT 46032 2009 A2
Zuker Ct
3700 ClyT 46032 2009 A1
Zurich Ter
3700 INPS 46228 2227 A1
Zwieback St
2100 INPS 46202 2228 A6

#

N 1st Av
3300 INPS 46234 2225 A4
1st Av NE
100 CRML 46032 1902 B2
1st Av NW
100 CRML 46032 1902 B2
1st Av SE
10 CRML 46032 1902 B3
1st Av SW
10 CRML 46032 1902 B3
1st Ct
100 CRML 46033 1902 D2
1st St
- AVON 46234 2333 D1
- MCVL 46055 2015 D7
- UnnT 46077 1680 D6
2300 PNFD 46168 2441 E3
2300 PNFD 46168 2442 A3
E 1st St
100 AdmT 46069 1573 B1
100 SRDN 46069 1573 B1
1000 GNFD 46140 2346 A1
N 1st St
10 ZNVL 46077 1899 B6
S 1st St
10 ZNVL 46077 1899 B6
S 1st St SR-334
100 ZNVL 46077 1899 B6
W 1st St
100 AdmT 46069 1573 B1
100 SRDN 46069 1573 B1
1st St NE
10 CRML 46032 1902 B2
1st St NW
10 CRML 46032 1902 A2
1st St SE
10 CRML 46032 1902 B2
1st St SW
10 CRML 46032 1902 A2
1st Bomar
800 GNWD 46142 2664 D1
1st Flight Cir
4100 EglT 46077 1899 C2
N 2nd Av
10 BHGV 46107 2448 A2
3300 INPS 46234 2225 A4
S 2nd Av
10 BHGV 46107 2448 A3
2nd Av NE
100 CRML 46032 1902 B2
2nd Av NW
10 CRML 46032 1902 A2
2nd Av SW
10 CRML 46032 1902 A2
2nd St
- AVON 46234 2333 D1
- MCVL 46055 2015 D7
10 SPRT 46227 2556 A3
2300 PNFD 46168 2441 E3
E 2nd St
100 SRDN 46069 1573 C1
700 AdmT 46069 1573 C1
1000 GNFD 46140 2346 A1
N 2nd St
10 ZNVL 46077 1899 B6
S 2nd St
10 ZNVL 46077 1899 B6
600 NBVL 46060 1795 C1
W 2nd St
100 SRDN 46069 1573 A1
W 2nd St SR-38
100 SRDN 46069 1573 B1
2nd St NE
10 CRML 46032 1902 B2
2nd St NW
10 CRML 46032 1902 A2
2nd St SE
10 CRML 46032 1902 B2
2nd St SW
200 CRML 46032 1902 A3
E 2nd Wy
1400 CRML 46033 1902 D2
2nd Bomar St
1400 GNWD 46142 2664 D1
N 3rd Av
10 BHGV 46107 2448 A3
S 3rd Av
10 BHGV 46107 2448 A3
3rd Av NE
100 CRML 46032 1902 B2
3rd Av NW
10 CRML 46032 1902 A2
3rd Av SW
10 CRML 46032 1902 A2
3rd St
- AVON 46234 2333 D1
- MCVL 46055 2015 C7
E 3rd St
100 SRDN 46069 1573 B1
1000 GNFD 46140 2346 A1
N 3rd St
10 ZNVL 46077 1899 B5
S 3rd St
10 ZNVL 46077 1899 B6
600 NBVL 46060 1795 C1
W 3rd St
100 SRDN 46069 1573 B1
3rd St NE
10 CRML 46032 1902 B2
3rd St NW
10 CRML 46032 1902 A2
3rd St SE
10 CRML 46032 1902 B3
3rd St SW
10 CRML 46032 1902 A3
N 4th Av
10 BHGV 46107 2448 A3
S 4th Av
10 BHGV 46107 2448 A3
600 BHGV 46107 2447 E4
4th Av E
3000 INPS 46221 2445 A3
4th Av NE
10 CRML 46032 1902 B2
4th Av SE
10 CRML 46032 1902 B2
4th Av SW
10 CRML 46032 1902 A3
4th Ct E
300 CRML 46033 1902 D2
4th Ct W
300 CRML 46033 1902 D2
4th St
- AVON 46234 2333 D1
- SDWY 46222 2226 E7
- ZNVL 46077 1898 E3
E 4th St
100 SRDN 46069 1573 B1
1000 GNFD 46140 2346 A1
N 4th St
10 ZNVL 46077 1899 B6
S 4th St
300 ZNVL 46077 1899 B6
600 NBVL 46060 1795 C1
W 4th St
10 GNFD 46140 2345 D1
400 SRDN 46069 1573 A1
4th St NE
10 CRML 46032 1902 B2
4th St NW
10 CRML 46032 1902 A2
4th St SE
10 CRML 46032 1902 B3
N 5th Av
10 BHGV 46107 2447 E2
S 5th Av
10 BHGV 46107 2447 E3
5th Av E
3000 INPS 46221 2445 A3
5th St
- AVON 46234 2333 D1
- SDWY 46222 2226 E7
E 5th St
100 SRDN 46069 1573 B2
1000 GNFD 46140 2346 A1
N 5th St
10 ZNVL 46077 1899 B6
S 5th St
10 NBVL 46060 1686 C7
300 ZNVL 46077 1899 B6
400 NBVL 46060 1795 C1
W 5th St
400 GNFD 46140 2345 C1
400 SRDN 46069 1573 A2
5th St NE
10 CRML 46032 1902 B2
5th St NW
10 CRML 46032 1902 A2
5th St SE
10 CRML 46032 1902 B3
N 6th Av
10 BHGV 46107 2447 E2
S 6th Av
10 BHGV 46107 2447 E3
6th Av E
3000 INPS 46221 2445 A3
6th St
- SDWY 46222 2226 E7
E 6th St
100 SRDN 46069 1573 B2
1000 GNFD 46140 2237 A7
E 6th St SR-38
100 SRDN 46069 1573 B2
N 6th St
10 ZNVL 46077 1899 B6
S 6th St
10 NBVL 46060 1686 D7
10 ZNVL 46077 1899 B6
400 NBVL 46060 1795 D1
W 6th St
200 SRDN 46069 1573 A2
500 AdmT 46069 1573 A2
500 GNFD 46140 2345 C1
6th St NW
10 CRML 46032 1902 A2
6th St SE
10 CRML 46032 1902 B3
N 7th Av
10 BHGV 46107 2447 E3
S 7th Av
10 BHGV 46107 2447 E3
7th St
- SDWY 46222 2226 E6
E 7th St
200 SRDN 46069 1573 B2
300 INPS 46202 2337 D2
1000 GNFD 46140 2237 A7
S 7th St
300 NBVL 46060 1686 D7
800 NBVL 46060 1795 D1
W 7th St
100 SRDN 46069 1573 B2
500 GNFD 46140 2345 C1
1000 CtrT 46140 2345 C1
7th St NE
100 CRML 46032 1902 B1
N 8th Av
10 BHGV 46107 2447 E3
S 8th Av
10 BHGV 46107 2447 E3
8th St
- SRDN 46069 1573 B2
1000 GNFD 46140 2237 A7
E 8th St
300 SRDN 46069 1573 C2
N 8th St
10 NBVL 46060 1686 D7
200 ZNVL 46077 1899 A6
S 8th St
10 NBVL 46060 1686 D7
100 ZNVL 46077 1899 A6
400 NBVL 46060 1795 D2
1700 NbvT 46060 1795 D2
W 8th St
100 SRDN 46069 1573 B2
400 AdmT 46069 1573 B2
8th St NE
10 CRML 46032 1902 B1
8th St NW
10 CRML 46032 1902 B1
N 9th Av
10 BHGV 46107 2447 E2
S 9th Av
10 BHGV 46107 2447 E3
1100 BHGV 46237 2447 E6
1700 INPS 46107 2447 E6
E 9th St
- SRDN 46069 1573 B2
10 INPS 46204 2337 C2
100 INPS 46202 2337 C2
1000 GNFD 46140 2237 A7
3300 INPS 46201 2338 D2
4900 INPS 46201 2339 A2
5100 INPS 46219 2339 A2
9600 INPS 46229 2340 E2
11700 CBLD 46229 2341 E2
N 9th St
10 NBVL 46060 1686 D6
100 ZNVL 46077 1899 A6
S 9th St
10 NBVL 46060 1686 D7
100 ZNVL 46077 1899 A6
400 NBVL 46060 1795 D1
W 9th St
100 INPS 46204 2337 C2
100 SRDN 46069 1573 B2
400 AdmT 46069 1573 B2
600 GNFD 46140 2236 C7
600 INPS 46202 2337 B2
3100 INPS 46222 2336 B2
W 10 N
9000 JknT 46011 1580 E6
9000 SCkT 46011 1580 E6
9000 SCkT 46051 1580 E6
9000 WRvT 46011 1580 E6
9000 WynT 46011 1580 E6
9000 WynT 46051 1580 E6

STREET
Block City ZIP Map# Grid

N 10th Av
400 BHGV 46107 2447 E2
S 10th Av
10 BHGV 46107 2447 E3
10th St
800 CtrT 46122 2330 A3
800 DNVL 46122 2330 A3
E 10th St
10 INPS 46204 2337 D1
100 SRDN 46069 1573 B2
500 INPS 46202 2337 D1
1400 INPS 46201 2338 A1
4900 INPS 46201 2339 A2
5100 INPS 46219 2339 B2
7200 INPS 46219 2340 A1
9000 INPS 46229 2340 E1
9600 INPS 46229 2341 A1
10500 CBLD 46229 2341 B1
E 10th St SR-47
100 SRDN 46069 1573 B2
N 10th St
10 NBVL 46060 1686 D5
1200 NbvT 46060 1686 D5
S 10th St
10 NBVL 46060 1686 D7
400 NBVL 46060 1795 D2
W 10th St
- WshT 46234 2333 E2
10 INPS 46204 2337 A2
10 SRDN 46069 1573 B2
200 INPS 46202 2337 A2
300 AdmT 46069 1573 B2
1300 INPS 46202 2336 D1
1500 INPS 46222 2336 D1
3900 INPS 46222 2335 D1
3900 SDWY 46222 2335 D1
3900 SDWY 46222 2336 A1
4500 SDWY 46224 2335 D1
5900 INPS 46224 2335 A2
6300 INPS 46214 2335 A2
8100 INPS 46214 2334 A1
8300 INPS 46234 2334 A1
9000 INPS 46234 2333 E2
W 10th St SR-47
10 SRDN 46069 1573 B2
300 AdmT 46069 1573 B2
N 11th Av
400 BHGV 46107 2447 E1
S 11th Av
10 BHGV 46107 2447 E3
11th St
11100 WshT 46123 2333 A1
E 11th St
- INPS 46202 2337 C1
- SRDN 46069 1573 B2
10 INPS 46204 2337 C1
1400 INPS 46201 2337 E1
1400 INPS 46201 2338 A1
4900 INPS 46201 2339 A1
5100 INPS 46219 2339 A1
7200 INPS 46219 2340 A1
9700 INPS 46229 2340 E1
9800 INPS 46229 2341 A1
N 11th St
600 NBVL 46060 1686 D6
S 11th St
200 NBVL 46060 1686 D7
400 NBVL 46060 1795 D1
W 11th St
100 INPS 46202 2337 C1
100 INPS 46204 2337 C1
2900 INPS 46222 2336 C1
5300 SDWY 46224 2335 C1
6500 INPS 46214 2335 A1
6800 INPS 46214 2334 E1
N 12th Av
400 BHGV 46107 2447 E1
S 12th Av
10 BHGV 46107 2447 E3
E 12th St
10 INPS 46204 2337 C1
200 INPS 46202 2337 C1
3900 INPS 46201 2338 E1
4900 INPS 46201 2339 A1
6000 INPS 46219 2339 C1
8000 INPS 46219 2340 B1
9000 INPS 46229 2340 D1
9700 INPS 46229 2341 A1
N 12th St
600 NBVL 46060 1686 D6
S 12th St
10 NBVL 46060 1686 D7
800 NBVL 46060 1795 D1
W 12th St
10 INPS 46204 2337 C1
400 INPS 46202 2337 B1
2100 INPS 46222 2336 D1
5100 SDWY 46224 2335 D1
6400 INPS 46214 2335 A1
6800 INPS 46214 2334 E1
12th Man Al
- INPS 46225 2337 B4
N 13th Av
10 BHGV 46107 2447 E3
S 13th Av
10 BHGV 46107 2447 D3
E 13th St
100 INPS 46202 2337 D1
2400 INPS 46201 2338 B1
4900 INPS 46201 2339 A1
6100 INPS 46219 2339 C1
7200 INPS 46219 2340 A1
9000 INPS 46229 2340 D1
N 13th St
300 NBVL 46060 1686 D7
S 13th St
200 NBVL 46060 1686 D7
400 NBVL 46060 1795 D1
W 13th St
10 INPS 46204 2337 C1
500 INPS 46202 2337 B1
4900 SDWY 46224 2335 D1
6400 INPS 46214 2335 A1
6500 INPS 46214 2334 E1
E 14th Av
- INPS 46219 2339 C1
N 14th Av
200 BHGV 46107 2447 D2
E 14th St
100 INPS 46202 2337 C1
3800 INPS 46201 2338 D1
4800 INPS 46201 2339 A1
6400 INPS 46219 2339 D1
7200 INPS 46219 2340 A1
9600 INPS 46229 2340 E1
9800 INPS 46229 2341 A1
N 14th St
10 NBVL 46060 1686 E7
S 14th St
10 NBVL 46060 1686 D7
300 NBVL 46060 1795 E1
W 14th St
1000 INPS 46202 2337 A1
3000 INPS 46222 2336 C1
4700 SDWY 46222 2335 E1
4900 SDWY 46224 2335 D1
6300 INPS 46214 2335 A1
6500 INPS 46214 2334 E1
N 15th Av
200 BHGV 46107 2447 D2
S 15th Av
10 BHGV 46107 2447 D3
15th St
- WRvT 46060 1579 A3
E 15th St
- INPS 46202 2337 C1
3900 INPS 46201 2338 D1
6000 INPS 46219 2339 C1
8700 INPS 46219 2340 D1
N 15th St
600 NBVL 46060 1686 E6
S 15th St
400 NBVL 46060 1795 E1
W 15th St
100 INPS 46202 2337 B1
1000 INPS 46202 2228 A7
1700 INPS 46202 2227 D7
3500 INPS 46222 2336 A1
4900 SDWY 46224 2335 C1
6300 INPS 46214 2335 A1
6500 INPS 46214 2334 E1
N 16th Av
200 BHGV 46107 2447 D2
S 16th Av
10 BHGV 46107 2447 D3
E 16th Ct
2600 INPS 46201 2338 B1
2600 INPS 46218 2338 B1
E 16th Pl
8700 INPS 46219 2231 D7
W 16th Pl
- INPS 46222 2227 A7
400 INPS 46202 2228 B7
E 16th St
10 INPS 46202 2228 D7
1300 INPS 46201 2228 D7
1400 INPS 46218 2228 D7
2200 INPS 46201 2338 B1
2200 INPS 46218 2338 B1
2800 INPS 46201 2229 A7
3800 INPS 46218 2229 E7
4800 INPS 46201 2230 A7
4800 INPS 46218 2230 A7
5100 INPS 46219 2230 A7
8800 INPS 46219 2231 D7
9000 INPS 46229 2231 D7
9700 INPS 46229 2232 A7
N 16th St
10 NBVL 46060 1686 E6
S 16th St
10 NBVL 46060 1686 E7
300 NBVL 46060 1795 E1
1400 NbvT 46060 1795 E2
W 16th St
10 INPS 46202 2228 A7
1200 INPS 46202 2227 D7
2100 INPS 46222 2227 D7
3800 SDWY 46222 2226 E7
3800 SDWY 46222 2227 B7
4700 SDWY 46224 2226 C7
6300 INPS 46214 2226 A7
6600 INPS 46214 2225 E7
6700 INPS 46214 2334 E1
8900 INPS 46234 2224 E7
8900 INPS 46234 2225 A7
10000 WshT 46234 2224 D7
N 17th Av
10 BHGV 46107 2447 D2
17th St
11300 WshT 46123 2224 A7
E 17th St
10 INPS 46202 2228 C7
1400 INPS 46218 2229 A7
5500 INPS 46218 2230 C7
6700 INPS 46219 2230 D7
7200 INPS 46219 2231 A7
9000 INPS 46229 2231 D7
9700 INPS 46229 2232 A7
N 17th St
400 NBVL 46060 1686 E6
S 17th St
10 NBVL 46060 1686 E7
300 NBVL 46060 1795 E1
W 17th St
- INPS 46202 2228 C7
1100 INPS 46202 2227 E7
3400 INPS 46222 2227 A7
N 18th Av
10 BHGV 46107 2447 D3
S 18th Av
200 BHGV 46107 2447 D3
200 INPS 46107 2447 D3
E 18th St
- INPS 46201 2229 A7
10 INPS 46202 2228 C7
4200 INPS 46218 2229 E7
5500 INPS 46218 2230 C7
6600 INPS 46219 2230 D7
8700 INPS 46219 2231 D7
9000 INPS 46229 2231 E7
9100 INPS 46229 2232 A7
N 18th St
400 NBVL 46060 1686 E7
S 18th St
10 NBVL 46060 1686 E7
300 NBVL 46060 1795 E1
W 18th St
1000 INPS 46202 2228 A7
1100 INPS 46202 2227 D7
2500 INPS 46222 2227 C7
5700 SDWY 46224 2226 B7
N 19th Av
10 BHGV 46107 2447 D2
E 19th Pl
5300 INPS 46218 2230 B7
E 19th St
100 INPS 46202 2228 C7
4400 INPS 46218 2229 E7
4800 INPS 46218 2230 A7
6600 INPS 46219 2230 D7
7200 INPS 46219 2231 A7
N 19th St
400 NBVL 46060 1686 E7
S 19th St
10 NBVL 46060 1686 E7
400 NBVL 46060 1795 E1
W 19th St
10 INPS 46202 2228 C7
1200 INPS 46202 2227 E7
2400 INPS 46222 2227 C7
N 20th Av
200 BHGV 46107 2447 D2
E 20th Pl
5100 INPS 46218 2230 B7
E 20th St
600 INPS 46202 2228 D7
1600 INPS 46218 2229 A7
4900 INPS 46218 2230 A7
6600 INPS 46219 2230 D7
8000 INPS 46219 2231 B7
S 20th St
200 NBVL 46060 1795 E1
W 20th St
10 INPS 46202 2228 C7
1200 INPS 46202 2227 E7
2700 INPS 46222 2227 C7
5300 SDWY 46224 2226 C7
20th St Ct
5500 SDWY 46224 2226 C7
N 21st Av
200 BHGV 46107 2447 D2
E 21st Pl
10200 INPS 46229 2232 B6
E 21st St
100 INPS 46202 2228 E6
3200 INPS 46218 2229 C6
4900 INPS 46218 2230 A6
6000 INPS 46219 2230 C6
8300 INPS 46219 2231 D6
9000 INPS 46229 2231 D6
9800 INPS 46229 2232 A6
W 21st St
900 INPS 46202 2228 C7
1100 INPS 46202 2227 E6
2700 INPS 46222 2227 C6
5800 SDWY 46224 2226 B6
6300 INPS 46224 2226 B6
6500 INPS 46214 2225 E6
6500 INPS 46214 2226 B6
8300 INPS 46234 2225 A6
9200 INPS 46234 2224 E7
E 22nd St
10 INPS 46202 2228 D6
10 INPS 46205 2228 D6
3500 INPS 46218 2229 D6
5500 INPS 46218 2230 A6
6500 INPS 46219 2230 D6
W 22nd St
10 INPS 46202 2228 C6
10 INPS 46208 2228 C6
1400 INPS 46202 2227 E6
1400 INPS 46208 2227 E6
3100 INPS 46222 2227 B6
4800 SDWY 46224 2226 D6
N 23rd Av
300 BHGV 46107 2447 C2
E 23rd St
- INPS 46229 2232 C6
10 INPS 46205 2228 D6
1500 INPS 46218 2229 A6
5100 INPS 46218 2230 A6
6400 INPS 46219 2230 D6
W 23rd St
- SDWY 46224 2226 D6
1000 INPS 46208 2228 A6
1100 INPS 46208 2227 E6
3300 INPS 46222 2227 B6
N 24th Av
400 BHGV 46107 2447 C2
E 24th St
10 INPS 46205 2228 D6
1500 INPS 46218 2229 A6
5200 INPS 46218 2230 A6
6000 INPS 46219 2230 C6
9500 INPS 46229 2231 E6
9800 INPS 46229 2232 A6
W 24th St
500 INPS 46208 2228 B6
4800 SDWY 46224 2226 D6
E 25 S
7100 AVON 46123 2332 C4
N 25th Av
- BHGV 46237 2447 C2
10 BHGV 46107 2447 C2
10 INPS 46107 2447 C2
10 INPS 46237 2447 C2
100 BHGV 46203 2447 C2
100 INPS 46203 2447 C2
E 25th St
- INPS 46218 2229 A5
10 INPS 46205 2228 D5
5200 INPS 46218 2230 A5
6000 INPS 46219 2230 C5
8500 INPS 46219 2231 C6
9000 INPS 46229 2231 E5
9800 INPS 46229 2232 A5
W 25th St
400 INPS 46208 2228 A5
1400 INPS 46208 2227 E5
4800 SDWY 46224 2226 B6
E 26th St
600 INPS 46205 2228 D5
3200 INPS 46218 2229 C5
5200 INPS 46218 2230 A5
6000 INPS 46219 2230 C5
W 26th St
700 INPS 46208 2228 A5
1400 INPS 46208 2227 E5
5300 SDWY 46224 2226 C5
E 27th St
10 INPS 46205 2228 C5
2900 INPS 46218 2229 C5
5200 INPS 46218 2230 B5
W 27th St
700 INPS 46208 2228 A5
1300 INPS 46208 2227 E5
E 28th St
1200 INPS 46205 2228 E5
1700 INPS 46218 2229 A5
5200 INPS 46218 2230 A5
W 28th St
400 INPS 46208 2228 A5
1300 INPS 46208 2227 E5
4400 INPS 46222 2226 E5
4700 SDWY 46222 2226 E5
W 29th Pl
5800 SDWY 46224 2226 B5
E 29th St
10 INPS 46205 2228 D5
3100 INPS 46218 2229 C5
W 29th St
- INPS 46222 2227 E5
10 INPS 46208 2228 A5
1200 INPS 46208 2227 E5
E 30th St
10 INPS 46205 2228 E4
1400 INPS 46218 2229 C4
4900 INPS 46218 2230 A4
6000 INPS 46219 2230 E4
6000 INPS 46226 2230 E4
8900 INPS 46219 2231 E4
8900 INPS 46226 2231 E4
9000 INPS 46229 2231 E4
9000 INPS 46235 2231 E4
9700 INPS 46229 2232 A4
9700 INPS 46235 2232 A4
11700 BCkT 46229 2232 D4
11700 BCkT 46235 2232 D4
W 30th St
10 INPS 46208 2228 A4
1200 INPS 46208 2227 C4
2100 INPS 46222 2227 C4
3900 INPS 46222 2226 E4
4800 INPS 46224 2226 E4
5600 SDWY 46224 2226 B4
8700 INPS 46234 2225 A5
9000 INPS 46234 2224 E5
E 31st St
200 INPS 46205 2220 D4
4100 INPS 46218 2229 E4
4900 INPS 46218 2230 A4
6000 INPS 46226 2230 C4
W 31st St
900 INPS 46208 2228 A4
1100 INPS 46208 2227 E4
3100 INPS 46222 2227 B4
E 32nd Ct
6300 INPS 46226 2230 D4
W 32nd Pl
6000 INPS 46224 2226 A4
E 32nd St
10 INPS 46205 2228 D4
1400 INPS 46218 2229 A4
4900 INPS 46218 2230 A4
6000 INPS 46226 2230 C4
7200 INPS 46226 2231 A4
W 32nd St
10 INPS 46208 2228 C4
1200 INPS 46208 2227 E4
3600 INPS 46222 2227 A4
5300 INPS 46224 2226 C4
W 33rd Pl
3300 INPS 46222 2227 B4
5700 INPS 46224 2226 B3
E 33rd St
10 INPS 46205 2228 D4
10 INPS 46208 2228 D4
4600 INPS 46218 2229 E4
5700 INPS 46218 2230 C4
7000 INPS 46226 2230 E4
7200 INPS 46226 2231 A4
9000 INPS 46235 2231 D4
10000 INPS 46235 2232 A4
W 33rd St
10 INPS 46208 2228 C4
1200 INPS 46208 2227 E4
2800 INPS 46222 2227 C4
4000 INPS 46222 2226 E4
5100 INPS 46224 2226 D4
E 34th Pl
8300 INPS 46226 2231 C3
W 34th Pl
5200 INPS 46224 2226 C3
E 34th St
10 INPS 46205 2228 E3
1500 INPS 46205 2229 A3
1500 INPS 46218 2229 A3
4900 INPS 46218 2230 A3
6000 INPS 46226 2230 D3
7200 INPS 46226 2231 A3
9000 INPS 46235 2231 D3
W 34th St
10 INPS 46208 2228 C3
1200 INPS 46208 2227 E4
3800 INPS 46222 2226 E3
3800 INPS 46222 2227 A3
4800 INPS 46224 2226 D3
6600 INPS 46214 2225 E3
6600 INPS 46214 2226 B3
E 35th Pl
8000 INPS 46226 2231 B3
W 35th Pl
6300 INPS 46224 2226 A3
E 35th St
1100 INPS 46205 2228 E3
1500 INPS 46205 2229 A3
4600 INPS 46218 2229 E3
5100 INPS 46218 2230 A3
7200 INPS 46226 2231 A3
W 35th St
900 INPS 46208 2228 A4
1300 INPS 46208 2227 E4
5300 INPS 46224 2226 C3
W 35th Ter
5000 INPS 46224 2226 D3
W 36th Ct
5200 INPS 46224 2226 C3
E 36th Pl
8000 INPS 46226 2231 B3
9200 INPS 46235 2231 E3
E 36th St
10 INPS 46205 2228 C3
1600 INPS 46205 2229 A3
1600 INPS 46218 2229 A3
4800 INPS 46218 2230 A3
7500 INPS 46226 2231 A3
9000 INPS 46235 2231 D3
W 36th St
10 INPS 46208 2228 C3
1100 INPS 46208 2227 E3
4500 INPS 46222 2226 E3
5100 INPS 46224 2226 C3
W 36th Ter
5000 INPS 46224 2226 D3
E 37th Pl
7600 INPS 46226 2231 A3
9400 INPS 46235 2231 E3
E 37th St
10 INPS 46205 2228 C3
3800 INPS 46218 2229 E3
4900 INPS 46218 2230 A3
7300 INPS 46226 2231 A3
10400 INPS 46235 2232 B2
W 37th St
1000 INPS 46208 2228 A3
1100 INPS 46208 2227 E3
4600 INPS 46222 2226 D3
4700 INPS 46224 2226 D3
E 38th Pl
9000 INPS 46235 2231 D2
E 38th St
- INPS 46218 2229 A2
10 INPS 46205 2228 D2
1200 INPS 46205 2229 A2
3800 INPS 46226 2229 D2
4900 INPS 46218 2230 A2
4900 INPS 46226 2230 A2
7200 INPS 46226 2231 A2
9000 INPS 46235 2231 E2
9800 INPS 46235 2232 A2
W 38th St
- INPS 46214 2226 B2
- INPS 46254 2227 C2
10 INPS 46208 2228 A2
1200 INPS 46208 2227 C2
1400 INPS 46222 2227 E2
1400 INPS 46228 2227 E2
3900 INPS 46222 2226 B2
3900 INPS 46254 2226 B2
4800 INPS 46224 2226 B2
6600 INPS 46214 2225 D2
6600 INPS 46254 2225 D2
38th N Dr
2800 INPS 46205 2229 C2
2800 INPS 46218 2229 C2
4100 INPS 46226 2229 E2
5200 INPS 46226 2230 A2
E 39th Pl
9000 INPS 46235 2231 D2
W 39th Pl
3200 INPS 46228 2227 B2
E 39th St
10 INPS 46205 2228 C2
1600 INPS 46205 2229 A2
3800 INPS 46226 2229 D2
5700 INPS 46226 2230 C2
7500 INPS 46226 2231 A2
9500 INPS 46235 2231 E2
W 39th St
400 INPS 46208 2228 B2
2700 INPS 46228 2227 C2
S 40 E
4700 HsnT 46052 1895 A3
40 & 8 Av
- INPS 46204 2337 C2
E 40th Pl
8200 INPS 46226 2231 B2
E 40th St
10 INPS 46205 2228 E2
2200 INPS 46205 2229 B2
4000 INPS 46226 2229 D2
4900 INPS 46226 2230 A2
9200 INPS 46235 2231 D2
W 40th St
10 INPS 46208 2228 C2
E 40th Street North Dr
4100 INPS 46226 2229 E2
E 40th Street South Dr
4100 INPS 46226 2229 E2
E 41st Pl
8200 INPS 46226 2231 C1
W 41st Pl
5800 INPS 46254 2226 B1
E 41st St
400 INPS 46205 2228 D2
4700 INPS 46226 2229 E2
4900 INPS 46226 2230 A2
8200 INPS 46226 2231 C2
9200 INPS 46235 2231 D2
W 41st St
200 INPS 46208 2228 B2
2100 INPS 46228 2227 D2
W 41st Ter
3600 INPS 46228 2227 A2
E 42nd Pl
8200 INPS 46226 2231 C1
E 42nd St
- INPS 46235 2231 D1
500 INPS 46205 2228 E1
2800 INPS 46205 2229 C1
3800 INPS 46226 2229 E1
6800 INPS 46226 2230 E1
7100 LWNC 46226 2230 E1
7500 INPS 46226 2231 B1
7500 LWNC 46226 2231 C1
9800 INPS 46235 2232 B1
W 42nd St
200 INPS 46208 2228 B1
2000 INPS 46228 2227 D2
5500 INPS 46254 2226 B1
8500 INPS 46234 2225 A1
8700 INPS 46234 2224 E1
W 42nd Ter
3700 INPS 46228 2227 A1
43rd Ct
4200 INPS 46226 2230 C1
E 43rd Pl
6100 INPS 46226 2230 C1
E 43rd St
10 INPS 46205 2228 D1
1700 INPS 46205 2229 A1
7000 INPS 46226 2230 E1
7000 LWNC 46226 2230 E1
7200 LWNC 46226 2231 A1
9300 INPS 46235 2231 E1
W 43rd St
100 INPS 46208 2228 B1
5400 INPS 46254 2226 C1
W 43rd Ter
3700 INPS 46228 2227 A1
E 44th Pl
6200 INPS 46226 2230 D1
E 44th St
100 INPS 46205 2228 D1
1700 INPS 46205 2229 A1
5400 INPS 46226 2230 B1
9300 INPS 46235 2231 D1
W 44th St
100 INPS 46208 2228 B1
2000 INPS 46228 2227 C1
5500 INPS 46254 2226 B1
W 44th Ter
3600 INPS 46228 2227 A1
E 45th St
10 INPS 46205 2228 C1
1300 INPS 46205 2119 E7
1600 INPS 46205 2229 A1
5800 INPS 46226 2121 C7
6700 INPS 46226 2230 D1
7000 LWNC 46226 2230 E1
8000 LWNC 46226 2122 B7
8600 LWNC 46226 2231 D1
W 45th Ter
3700 INPS 46228 2227 A1
46th Pl
- LWNC 46226 2122 B7
E 46th St
10 INPS 46205 2119 D7
1400 INPS 46205 2120 A7
3800 INPS 46226 2120 E7
4700 INPS 46226 2121 B7
6500 LWNC 46226 2121 D7
8600 LWNC 46226 2122 B7
9000 LWNC 46235 2122 E7
9600 INPS 46235 2123 B7
9600 LWNC 46235 2123 B7
W 46th St
10 INPS 46208 2119 C7
3100 INPS 46228 2118 B7
5200 INPS 46254 2117 B7
6500 INPS 46254 2116 E7
7500 INPS 46254 2225 D1
8500 INPS 46234 2116 A7
8700 INPS 46234 2115 E7
E 47th St
600 INPS 46205 2119 D7
2900 INPS 46205 2120 C7
6600 LWNC 46226 2121 D7
7300 LWNC 46226 2122 A7
W 47th St
400 INPS 46208 2119 B7
4100 INPS 46254 2118 A7
4200 INPS 46254 2117 E7
E 48th St
100 INPS 46205 2119 D7
3100 INPS 46205 2120 C7
6800 LWNC 46226 2121 E7
7300 LWNC 46226 2122 A7
W 48th St
3100 INPS 46228 2118 B7
E 49th St
10 INPS 46205 2119 D7
1500 INPS 46205 2120 A7
6500 LWNC 46226 2121 D7
7300 LWNC 46226 2122 A7
W 49th St
- INPS 46254 2117 E7
- INPS 46254 2118 A7
10 INPS 46208 2119 B7
3100 INPS 46228 2118 B7
E 50 N
400 CtrT 46122 2329 E3
400 DNVL 46122 2329 E3
700 CtrT 46122 2330 A3
700 DNVL 46122 2330 A3
E 50 S
300 WshT 46123 2331 D5
8000 UnnT 46077 1789 C1
N 50 E
500 CtrT 46122 2329 E3
500 DNVL 46122 2329 E3
1800 CtrT 46122 2221 A7
1800 CtrT 46122 2330 A1
3000 CtrT 46140 2236 B1
S 50 E
2500 CtrT 46052 1786 A6
3500 HsnT 46052 1786 A7
3500 HsnT 46052 1895 A1
7000 HsnT 46052 2004 A1
7000 MdlT 46052 2004 A1
S 50 W
3000 BwnT 46140 2344 E7
W 50 S
1300 CtrT 46122 2329 A5
1300 DNVL 46122 2329 A5
2200 CtrT 46052 1785 A1
E 50th Pl
6300 INPS 46226 2121 D7
E 50th St
100 INPS 46205 2119 D7
3300 INPS 46205 2120 C7
7200 LWNC 46226 2121 C7
7200 LWNC 46226 2122 A7
W 50th St
3100 INPS 46228 2118 B7
E 51 S
6500 AVON 46123 2332 B5
W 51st Dr N
5600 INPS 46254 2117 B7
W 51st Dr S
5600 INPS 46254 2117 C7
E 51st St
100 INPS 46205 2119 D7
3300 INPS 46205 2120 C6
7200 LWNC 46226 2122 A7
W 51st St
800 INPS 46208 2119 A7
3100 INPS 46228 2118 B7
5500 INPS 46254 2117 C7
E 52nd Pl
6000 INPS 46226 2121 C6
6800 LWNC 46226 2121 E6
52nd St
- LWNC 46235 2123 C6
E 52nd St
10 INPS 46205 2119 D6
10 INPS 46220 2119 D6
1400 INPS 46205 2120 A6
1400 INPS 46220 2120 A6
6300 INPS 46226 2121 D6
6400 LWNC 46226 2121 D6
7200 LWNC 46226 2122 A6
9400 LWNC 46235 2122 E6
9400 LWNC 46236 2122 E6
9600 LWNC 46235 2123 A6
9600 LWNC 46236 2123 A6
W 52nd St
10 INPS 46208 2119 B6
1000 INPS 46228 2118 E6
1000 INPS 46228 2119 A6
3900 INPS 46254 2117 E6
3900 INPS 46254 2118 A6
8800 INPS 46234 2115 E6
8800 INPS 46234 2116 A6
E 53rd Pl
7500 LWNC 46226 2122 A6
E 53rd St
100 INPS 46220 2119 D6
1500 INPS 46220 2120 A6
7300 LWNC 46226 2122 A6
W 53rd St
600 INPS 46208 2119 A6
1700 INPS 46228 2118 E6
5300 INPS 46254 2117 C6
E 54th Pl
6000 INPS 46226 2121 C6
6700 LWNC 46226 2121 D6
7600 LWNC 46226 2122 A6
E 54th St
10 INPS 46220 2119 D6
1400 INPS 46220 2120 A6
5700 INPS 46226 2121 C6
7300 LWNC 46226 2122 A6
W 54th St
500 INPS 46208 2119 B6
1600 INPS 46228 2118 E6
4000 INPS 46254 2117 E6
E 55th Pl
2400 INPS 46220 2120 B5
6200 INPS 46226 2121 D6
E 55th St
10 INPS 46220 2119 D6
3700 INPS 46220 2120 D6
7300 LWNC 46226 2122 A5
W 55th St
3400 INPS 46228 2118 B6
E 56th St
- INPS 46226 2121 E5
10 BNBG 46112 2114 D5
10 INPS 46220 2119 D5
1300 INPS 46220 2120 A5
4900 INPS 46220 2121 A5
7000 LWNC 46226 2121 E5
7100 LWNC 46226 2122 A5
7900 LWNC 46216 2122 B5
9600 LWNC 46236 2122 D5
9800 LWNC 46236 2123 A5
10000 LWNC 46235 2123 B5
W 56th St
10 INPS 46208 2119 C5
700 INPS 46228 2119 A5
2000 INPS 46228 2118 D5
3900 INPS 46254 2117 E5
3900 INPS 46254 2118 A5
6800 INPS 46254 2116 E5
7900 INPS 46234 2116 B5
9000 INPS 46234 2115 E5
E 57th St
10 INPS 46220 2119 D5
1300 INPS 46220 2120 A5
W 57th St
10 INPS 46208 2119 C5
1600 INPS 46228 2118 E5
4800 INPS 46254 2117 D5
E 58th St
10 INPS 46220 2119 D5
1300 INPS 46220 2120 B5
W 58th St
10 INPS 46208 2119 C4

INDEX 60

W 58th St — Indianapolis Street Index — E 146th St

STREET Block City ZIP Map# Grid

W 58th St
900 INPS 46228 2119 A5
3400 INPS 46228 2118 B5
59th Pl
- INPS 46220 2120 B4
E 59th St
9300 LWNC 46216 2122 E4
9600 LWNC 46216 2123 A4
9600 LWNC 46236 2123 A4
11400 LWNC 46235 2123 D4
W 59th St
10 INPS 46208 2119 C4
800 INPS 46228 2119 A4
2100 INPS 46228 2118 D4
4200 INPS 46254 2117 E4
W 59th St A
4900 INPS 46254 2117 D4
W 59th St B
4900 INPS 46254 2117 D4
E 60 S
7700 UnnT 46077 1789 A1
E 60th St
500 INPS 46220 2119 D4
1300 INPS 46220 2120 A4
W 60th St
1700 INPS 46228 2118 C4
E 61st Pl
2000 INPS 46220 2120 B4
E 61st St
- INPS 46208 2119 D4
100 INPS 46220 2119 D4
3200 INPS 46220 2120 D4
W 61st St
10 INPS 46208 2119 C4
10 INPS 46220 2119 C4
3200 INPS 46228 2118 B4
E 62nd Pl
- INPS 46220 2121 C4
500 INPS 46220 2119 D3
W 62nd Pl
3200 INPS 46228 2118 B4
E 62nd St
500 INPS 46220 2119 D3
2400 INPS 46220 2120 B3
4700 INPS 46220 2121 A3
7500 BCkT 46055 2124 A3
7500 BCkT 46235 2124 A3
7500 LWNC 46235 2124 A3
7800 BCkT 46235 2123 E3
7800 LWNC 46235 2123 E3
W 62nd St
- INPS 46254 2116 D3
- INPS 46278 2116 D3
10 INPS 46208 2119 C4
300 INPS 46228 2119 B3
300 INPS 46260 2119 B3
1600 INPS 46228 2118 E3
1600 INPS 46260 2118 E3
2200 INPS 46268 2118 A3
3900 INPS 46254 2118 A3
4100 INPS 46254 2117 E3
4100 INPS 46268 2117 E3
5600 INPS 46278 2117 A3
E 63rd Pl
700 INPS 46220 2119 E3
E 63rd St
- LWNC 46216 2122 E3
100 INPS 46220 2119 D3
2300 INPS 46220 2120 B3
9700 LWNC 46236 2122 E3
9900 LWNC 46236 2123 A3
W 63rd St
800 INPS 46260 2119 A3
1900 INPS 46260 2118 D3
E 64th St
- INPS 46220 2120 E3
300 INPS 46220 2119 D3
4800 INPS 46220 2121 A3
W 64th St
- INPS 46260 2119 B3
1000 INPS 46260 2118 E3
2100 INPS 46268 2118 D3
64th Street S
1900 INPS 46220 2120 A3
E 64th Street South Dr
1800 INPS 46220 2120 A3
E 65th Pl
5900 INPS 46220 2121 C2
W 65th Pl
1700 INPS 46260 2118 E2
65th St
- INPS 46278 2116 D2
E 65th St
700 INPS 46220 2119 E3
1800 INPS 46220 2120 A2
6600 INPS 46220 2121 D2
7000 INPS 46256 2121 E2
7200 INPS 46256 2122 A2
7400 LWNC 46256 2122 A2
11900 LWNC 46236 2123 E2
12000 LWNC 46235 2123 E2
12400 LWNC 46235 2124 A2
12400 LWNC 46236 2124 A2
12500 VrnT 46235 2124 A2
12500 VrnT 46236 2124 A2
W 65th St
400 INPS 46260 2119 B2
1900 INPS 46260 2118 D2
2300 INPS 46268 2118 D2
8900 INPS 46278 2115 E3
8900 INPS 46278 2116 A2
E 66th St
500 INPS 46220 2119 D2
2700 INPS 46220 2120 C2
5000 INPS 46220 2121 A2
W 66th St
1700 INPS 46260 2118 D2
2400 INPS 46268 2118 D2
E 67th Ct
3400 INPS 46220 2120 C2
E 67th St
700 INPS 46220 2119 E2
2700 INPS 46220 2120 C2
5000 INPS 46220 2121 A2

W 67th St
2200 INPS 46260 2118 D2
2400 INPS 46268 2118 D2
E 68th Ct
3200 INPS 46220 2120 C2
E 68th St
900 INPS 46220 2119 E2
1600 INPS 46220 2120 A2
5000 INPS 46220 2121 A2
E 69th St
1500 INPS 46220 2120 A2
4900 INPS 46220 2121 A2
W 69th St
3000 INPS 46268 2118 C2
E 70th Pl
700 INPS 46220 2119 E1
E 70th St
10 INPS 46220 2119 D2
4800 INPS 46220 2120 E2
4800 INPS 46220 2121 A2
W 70th St
400 INPS 46260 2119 B1
E 71st St
- INPS 46256 2122 E2
- LWNC 46216 2122 E2
- LWNC 46236 2122 E2
- LWNC 46256 2122 E2
10 INPS 46220 2119 D1
10 INPS 46240 2119 D1
1200 INPS 46220 2120 A1
1200 INPS 46240 2120 A1
4100 INPS 46250 2120 E1
4800 INPS 46220 2121 B1
4800 INPS 46250 2121 B1
7000 INPS 46256 2121 D1
11800 LWNC 46236 2123 E2
W 71st St
3300 INPS 46268 2118 A1
4200 INPS 46268 2117 D1
5600 INPS 46278 2117 B1
6600 INPS 46278 2116 E1
E 72nd Ct
5100 INPS 46250 2121 A1
E 72nd Pl
4900 INPS 46250 2121 A1
W 72nd Pl
1700 INPS 46260 2118 E1
E 72nd St
300 INPS 46240 2119 D1
2900 INPS 46240 2120 C1
4800 INPS 46250 2121 A1
W 72nd St
900 INPS 46260 2119 A1
1500 INPS 46260 2118 E1
4500 INPS 46268 2117 D1
E 73rd Ct
5200 INPS 46250 2121 A1
W 73rd Pl
1600 INPS 46260 2118 E1
E 73rd St
700 INPS 46240 2119 E1
1400 INPS 46240 2120 A1
4100 INPS 46250 2120 E1
W 73rd St
10 INPS 46260 2119 B1
5500 INPS 46268 2117 C1
5600 INPS 46278 2117 B1
E 74th Ct
5100 INPS 46250 2121 A1
E 74th Pl
5100 INPS 46250 2121 A1
5300 INPS 46250 2012 B7
W 74th Pl
1500 INPS 46260 2009 E7
E 74th St
1000 INPS 46240 2119 E1
1400 INPS 46240 2011 A7
2200 INPS 46240 2120 B1
W 74th St
- INPS 46260 2119 C1
1900 INPS 46260 2118 D1
5000 INPS 46268 2117 C1
5600 INPS 46278 2117 B1
E 75 N
900 CtrT 46052 1677 C6
2500 CtrT 46052 1678 A6
5700 AVON 46123 2331 D2
5700 WshT 46123 2331 D2
E 75 S
1500 CtrT 46122 2330 C5
N 75 E
7900 UnnT 46149 2112 A2
8000 UnnT 46149 2003 A7
N 75 W
4300 FknT 46131 2774 B6
4300 PltT 46131 2774 B6
4900 PltT 46184 2774 B4
S 75 W
- DNVL 46122 2329 C5
700 CtrT 46122 2329 C5
5000 HsnT 46052 1894 D4
7500 HsnT 46052 2003 D2
7700 MdlT 46052 2003 D2
E 75th Pl
1800 INPS 46240 2011 A7
W 75th Pl
1900 INPS 46260 2009 D7
75th St
- MCVL 46055 2015 C7
- VrnT 46055 2015 C7
E 75th St
10 INPS 46240 2010 D7
1700 INPS 46240 2011 A7
4000 INPS 46250 2011 E7
4300 INPS 46250 2012 A7
7000 INPS 46256 2012 D7
7200 INPS 46256 2013 A7
8200 INPS 46256 2122 C1
10300 LWNC 46236 2014 B7
12200 LWNC 46236 2015 A7
W 75th St
10 INPS 46260 2010 C7
2700 INPS 46268 2009 C7
3100 INPS 46268 2118 B1

W 75th Ct Ter
1200 INPS 46260 2010 A7
76th Ct
5000 INPS 46250 2012 A7
W 76th Pl
1500 INPS 46260 2009 E7
E 76th St
1000 INPS 46240 2010 E7
3200 INPS 46240 2011 C7
5000 INPS 46250 2012 A7
W 76th St
2000 INPS 46260 2009 D7
2700 INPS 46268 2009 C7
5100 INPS 46268 2008 C7
77th St
10900 LWNC 46236 2014 C7
E 77th St
100 INPS 46240 2010 D7
3600 INPS 46240 2011 D7
4600 INPS 46250 2011 E7
6800 INPS 46250 2012 E7
W 77th St
- INPS 46260 2010 B7
3000 INPS 46268 2009 B7
W 77th Street North Dr
800 INPS 46260 2010 A7
W 77th Street South Dr
800 INPS 46260 2010 A7
E 78th Pl
5200 INPS 46250 2012 B7
E 78th St
700 INPS 46240 2010 E6
2500 INPS 46240 2011 B6
4600 INPS 46250 2011 E7
4600 INPS 46250 2012 A7
W 78th St
1000 INPS 46260 2010 A6
2700 INPS 46268 2009 C6
4900 INPS 46268 2008 D7
E 79th St
600 INPS 46240 2010 D6
1500 INPS 46240 2011 A6
4000 INPS 46250 2011 E6
4600 INPS 46250 2012 A6
9800 INPS 46256 2014 A6
10000 INPS 46236 2014 A6
10000 LWNC 46236 2014 A6
12300 LWNC 46236 2015 A6
W 79th St
10 INPS 46260 2010 C6
1400 INPS 46260 2009 D6
2400 INPS 46268 2009 A6
4100 INPS 46268 2008 D6
5600 INPS 46278 2008 A6
6500 INPS 46278 2007 D6
E 80th St
1100 INPS 46240 2010 E6
1200 INPS 46240 2011 A6
4400 INPS 46250 2011 E6
7500 INPS 46256 2013 A6
W 80th St
10 INPS 46260 2010 C6
1800 INPS 46260 2009 E6
3900 INPS 46268 2009 A6
4000 INPS 46268 2008 D6
5600 INPS 46278 2008 B6
W 81st Pl
4500 INPS 46268 2008 E5
E 81st St
500 INPS 46240 2010 D5
1400 INPS 46240 2011 A6
5200 INPS 46250 2012 B6
W 81st St
100 INPS 46260 2010 C6
4900 INPS 46268 2008 C6
8900 INPS 46278 2007 A6
E 82nd Pl
8300 INPS 46256 2013 C5
E 82nd St
- INPS 46256 2012 E5
10 INPS 46240 2010 D5
1500 INPS 46240 2011 A5
4000 INPS 46250 2011 E5
6500 INPS 46250 2012 D6
7200 INPS 46256 2013 A6
9700 INPS 46256 2014 A6
W 82nd St
10 INPS 46260 2010 C5
2900 INPS 46268 2009 B5
5600 INPS 46278 2008 B6
8100 INPS 46278 2007 B5
9000 INPS 46278 2006 E6
9100 BrnT 46278 2006 E5
W 83rd Pl
400 INPS 46260 2010 B5
E 83rd St
800 INPS 46240 2010 E5
1400 INPS 46240 2011 A5
W 83rd St
500 INPS 46260 2010 B5
E 84th St
100 INPS 46240 2010 D5
W 84th St
1100 INPS 46260 2010 A5
4600 INPS 46268 2008 E5
5800 INPS 46278 2008 B5
8400 INPS 46278 2007 B5
E 85th Pl
8400 INPS 46256 2013 C5
E 85th St
900 INPS 46240 2010 E5
W 85th St
5600 INPS 46278 2008 B5
8400 INPS 46278 2007 B5
E 86th St
10 INPS 46240 2010 D4
1400 INPS 46240 2011 B4
5100 INPS 46250 2012 A4
7000 INPS 46250 2013 A4
7000 INPS 46256 2012 E4
7300 INPS 46256 2013 C4
9800 INPS 46256 2014 A4
11800 INPS 46236 2014 E4
11800 LWNC 46236 2014 E4
12200 INPS 46236 2015 A5

E 86th St
12200 LWNC 46236 2015 A5
W 86th St
10 INPS 46260 2010 A4
1400 INPS 46260 2009 D4
2400 INPS 46268 2009 D4
4000 INPS 46268 2008 E4
5600 INPS 46278 2008 A4
8800 INPS 46278 2007 A4
9100 INPS 46278 2006 E5
E 87th St
700 INPS 46240 2010 E4
1700 INPS 46240 2011 A4
7100 INPS 46256 2013 A4
W 87th St
8200 INPS 46278 2007 B4
E 88th Pl
7500 INPS 46256 2013 A4
E 88th St
1200 INPS 46240 2011 A4
7700 INPS 46256 2013 B4
W 88th St
100 INPS 46260 2010 C4
7200 INPS 46278 2007 C4
E 89th St
7700 INPS 46256 2013 B4
E 90th Pl
1700 INPS 46240 2011 A3
E 90th St
1000 INPS 46240 2010 E4
1200 INPS 46240 2011 A4
7300 INPS 46256 2013 A4
E 91 North Rd
5900 AVON 46123 2331 E2
5900 WshT 46123 2331 E2
5900 WshT 46123 2332 A2
6200 AVON 46123 2332 A2
E 91st St
10 INPS 46240 2010 D3
1200 INPS 46240 2011 A3
5800 INPS 46250 2012 C3
W 91st St
10 INPS 46260 2010 C3
W 92nd St
400 INPS 46260 2010 B3
3800 INPS 46268 2009 A3
7400 INPS 46278 2007 D3
E 93rd Dr
700 INPS 46240 2010 E3
93rd St
- INPS 46256 2013 A3
E 93rd St
400 INPS 46240 2010 D3
W 93rd St
400 INPS 46260 2010 B3
4000 INPS 46268 2008 E3
4000 INPS 46268 2009 A3
7200 INPS 46278 2007 D3
E 94th St
- INPS 46240 2011 C3
W 94th St
4000 INPS 46268 2008 E3
4000 INPS 46268 2009 A3
E 95th St
200 INPS 46240 2010 D3
E 96th Pl
6100 INPS 46250 2012 D3
E 96th St
- CRML 46038 2012 D2
- CRML 46250 2012 D2
- FCkT 46256 2014 A2
- INPS 46240 2012 D2
10 CRML 46240 2010 D2
10 CRML 46280 2010 D2
10 INPS 46240 2010 D2
200 INPS 46280 2010 D2
1300 CRML 46280 2011 C2
2000 ClyT 46240 2011 C2
2000 ClyT 46280 2011 C2
2200 INPS 46240 2011 C2
4100 CRML 46240 2011 E2
4300 CRML 46240 2012 D2
4300 CRML 46280 2012 D2
5400 FSHR 46038 2012 D2
5400 INPS 46250 2012 D2
6000 FSHR 46250 2012 D2
6400 DelT 46038 2012 D2
6400 DelT 46250 2012 D2
7000 FSHR 46038 2013 B2
7000 FSHR 46250 2013 B2
7000 INPS 46250 2013 B2
7500 FSHR 46256 2013 B2
7500 INPS 46256 2013 B2
7800 INPS 46038 2013 B2
9200 FCkT 46038 2013 E2
9200 FCkT 46256 2013 E2
9800 FCkT 46038 2014 A2
9800 FSHR 46038 2014 A2
9800 INPS 46256 2014 A2
10300 FSHR 46256 2014 A2
10600 INPS 46038 2014 A2
12900 FCkT 46055 2015 D2
12900 MCVL 46055 2015 D2
14000 FCkT 46055 2016 A2
14000 VrnT 46055 2015 D2
14000 VrnT 46055 2016 A2
14700 FCkT 46040 2016 A2
14700 VrnT 46040 2016 A2
W 96th St
- ClyT 46260 2010 A2
- CRML 46240 2010 C2
- EglT 46278 2008 B2
- INPS 46240 2010 C2
- INPS 46260 2010 A2
- INPS 46278 2008 B2
10 CRML 46290 2010 C2
100 CRML 46260 2010 C2
400 ClyT 46032 2010 C2
400 CRML 46032 2010 C2
1400 ClyT 46032 2009 A2
1400 ClyT 46260 2009 E2
1400 INPS 46260 2009 E2
1500 INPS 46032 2009 A2
3800 INPS 46268 2009 A2
4100 ClyT 46032 2008 E2

W 96th St
4800 EglT 46032 2008 E2
4800 EglT 46077 2008 E2
4800 INPS 46032 2008 E2
4800 INPS 46268 2008 E2
6200 INPS 46077 2008 B2
6700 EglT 46077 2007 E2
6700 INPS 46077 2007 E2
6700 INPS 46278 2007 E2
6800 EglT 46278 2007 E2
E 97th St
10600 FCkT 46038 2014 B2
W 97th St
3700 ClyT 46032 2009 A2
E 98th St
- ClyT 46280 2011 B2
3000 CRML 46280 2011 C2
3400 CRML 46033 2011 D2
6300 FSHR 46038 2012 D2
10600 FCkT 46038 2014 B2
W 98th St
3700 ClyT 46032 2009 A2
E 99th St
- CRML 46033 2011 B1
2100 ClyT 46280 2011 B1
2200 ClyT 46032 2011 B1
2400 CRML 46032 2011 B1
2400 CRML 46280 2011 B1
W 99th St
4500 ClyT 46032 2008 E2
E 100 N
- CtrT 46122 2330 A2
400 CtrT 46122 2329 E2
400 DNVL 46122 2329 E2
1000 DNVL 46122 2330 A2
3000 CtrT 46052 1678 B5
3400 CtrT 46140 2237 C6
3600 CtrT 46122 2331 A2
3800 CtrT 46123 2331 A2
3800 WshT 46122 2331 A2
3800 WshT 46123 2331 A2
4900 AVON 46123 2331 D2
5000 CtrT 46052 1679 B5
6000 UnnT 46052 1679 B5
6300 AVON 46123 2332 B2
6300 WshT 46123 2332 B2
6500 UnnT 46075 1679 E5
7500 UnnT 46075 1680 A5
8100 WshT 46123 2333 A2
8500 UnnT 46077 1680 B5
9000 AVON 46123 2333 A2
9300 UnnT 46075 1681 A5
9300 UnnT 46077 1681 A5
10000 AVON 46234 2333 E2
10000 UnnT 46069 1681 A5
10600 WshT 46234 2333 E2
E 100 S
- CtrT 46122 2330 C6
400 CtrT 46122 2329 E7
1200 CtrT 46052 1786 D2
1900 CtrT 46140 2346 C3
2000 CtrT 46052 1787 A2
2700 BRvT 46140 2346 E3
3800 WrhT 46052 1787 C2
5200 WshT 46123 2331 D6
5800 AVON 46123 2331 D6
5800 AVON 46123 2332 E6
5800 WshT 46123 2332 A6
8200 AVON 46123 2333 A6
8200 WshT 46123 2333 A6
9000 AVON 46231 2333 D6
9000 WshT 46231 2333 B6
9600 UnnT 46077 1789 E2
9600 UnnT 46077 1790 A2
10500 PNFD 46231 2333 D6
N 100 E
1100 CtrT 46122 2330 A3
1400 DNVL 46122 2330 A2
1700 CtrT 46122 2221 A6
1900 MdlT 46122 2221 A6
3800 UnnT 46122 2221 A2
5400 MdlT 46167 2112 A7
5400 UnnT 46149 2112 A7
5400 UnnT 46167 2112 A7
7100 MdlT 46149 2112 A2
N 100 W
2500 CtrT 46140 2235 D1
S 100 E
2500 CtrT 46052 1786 B6
4000 HsnT 46052 1895 B2
4000 PryT 46052 1895 B2
9200 LtyT 46118 2657 A2
S 100 W
6500 HsnT 46052 1894 C7
7000 HsnT 46052 2003 C1
W 100 N
600 CtrT 46140 2235 D6
600 CtrT 46140 2236 A6
1500 BCkT 46140 2235 A6
2400 CtrT 46052 1676 A5
2700 BCkT 46140 2234 E6
4000 BCkT 46140 2233 E6
9300 JknT 46011 1580 E4
W 100 S
100 CtrT 46140 2344 E3
100 CtrT 46140 2345 A3
1100 CtrT 46122 2329 B6
1700 SCkT 46140 2344 A3
2500 SGLK 46140 2344 A3
2600 SCkT 46140 2343 E3
2600 SGLK 46140 2343 E3
3800 SCkT 46163 2343 B3
6000 SCkT 46163 2342 C3
9300 SCkT 46051 1689 E1
9300 WynT 46051 1689 E1
S 100 Rd E
10200 LtyT 46118 2657 A3
S 101 E
3100 LtyT 46118 2439 A4
E 101st St
700 ClyT 46280 2010 E2
700 FCkT 46040 2016 D1
700 VrnT 46040 2016 D1
1000 CRML 46280 2010 E2
1500 ClyT 46280 2011 A1

E 102nd St
- DelT 46038 2012 D1
- FSHR 46038 2012 D1
400 ClyT 46280 2010 D1
E 103rd St
100 ClyT 46280 2010 D1
100 CRML 46280 2010 D1
W 103rd St
200 CRML 46290 2010 C1
E 104th St
700 ClyT 46280 2010 E1
1200 ClyT 46280 2011 A1
3200 CRML 46033 2011 C1
14000 FCkT 46040 2015 E1
14000 FCkT 46055 2015 E1
14500 FCkT 46040 2016 B1
E 105th St
700 ClyT 46280 2010 E1
106th Pl
10600 CRML 46033 1902 D7
E 106th St
- CRML 46032 1902 D7
10 CRML 46280 1901 D7
100 ClyT 46280 1901 D7
1300 ClyT 46280 1902 B7
1700 ClyT 46032 1902 B7
3000 CRML 46033 1902 D7
4300 CRML 46033 1903 A7
5000 CRML 46280 1903 A7
6100 DelT 46038 1903 D7
6100 FSHR 46038 1903 D7
7000 DelT 46038 1904 A7
7000 FSHR 46038 1904 A7
8000 FSHR 46256 1904 A7
9100 FCkT 46038 1904 E7
9700 FCkT 46038 1905 A7
9700 FSHR 46038 1905 A7
W 106th St
10 CRML 46032 1901 A7
10 CRML 46290 1901 A7
100 ClyT 46032 1901 A7
100 ClyT 46290 1901 A7
1400 ClyT 46032 1900 E7
4300 ClyT 46032 1899 E7
E 107th St
500 ClyT 46280 1901 D7
W 107th St
300 ClyT 46032 1901 C7
E 108th St
500 ClyT 46280 1901 D7
7100 DelT 46038 1903 E7
7100 DelT 46038 1904 A7
7100 FSHR 46038 1903 E7
E 109th St
1600 ClyT 46280 1902 A7
1900 ClyT 46032 1902 B7
E 110th St
700 ClyT 46280 1901 E7
1600 ClyT 46280 1902 A7
2100 ClyT 46032 1902 C7
E 111th St
10 CRML 46032 1901 E6
10 CRML 46280 1901 E6
100 ClyT 46032 1901 E6
100 ClyT 46280 1901 E6
1400 CRML 46032 1902 A6
1400 CRML 46280 1902 A6
2100 ClyT 46032 1902 C6
11100 DelT 46038 1903 E6
11100 DelT 46038 1904 C7
11100 FSHR 46038 1903 E6
11300 FCkT 46038 1905 D7
11300 FSHR 46038 1905 D7
W 111th St
10 ClyT 46032 1901 C6
10 CRML 46032 1901 C6
E 113th St
13800 FCkT 46038 1906 E6
14300 FCkT 46040 1906 E6
14600 FCkT 46040 1907 A6
E 114th St
400 CRML 46032 1901 D6
13500 FCkT 46038 1906 C6
E 115th St
8000 DelT 46038 1904 B6
115th St E
300 CRML 46032 1901 D5
E 116th St
10 CRML 46032 1901 D5
1100 CRML 46032 1902 A5
2800 CRML 46033 1902 D5
4200 CRML 46033 1903 B5
5500 CRML 46280 1903 B5
6000 CRML 46033 1903 B5
6000 DelT 46038 1903 B5
6200 FSHR 46038 1903 E5
7100 FSHR 46038 1904 A5
7400 DelT 46038 1904 A5
9600 FCkT 46038 1904 C5
9700 FCkT 46038 1905 A5
9700 FSHR 46038 1905 A5
11900 FCkT 46038 1906 B5
11900 FSHR 46038 1906 B5
W 116th St
10 CRML 46032 1901 A5
400 ClyT 46032 1901 A5
1400 ClyT 46032 1900 E5
1400 CRML 46032 1900 E5
3700 ClyT 46077 1900 A5
3700 CRML 46077 1900 A5
4000 ClyT 46077 1899 E5
4000 CRML 46077 1899 E5
11800 EglT 46077 1899 E5
117th St
- CRML 46032 1901 D5
E 117th St
13800 FSHR 46038 1906 D5
E 118th St
13600 FCkT 46038 1906 D5
E 121 N
6000 WshT 46123 2331 E1
S 121 E
5900 LtyT 46118 2548 A2
E 121st St
8800 FCkT 46038 1904 D4

E 121st St
8800 FSHR 46038 1904 D4
9800 FCkT 46038 1905 A4
9800 FSHR 46038 1905 A4
W 121st St
3900 CRML 46077 1900 A4
4100 CRML 46077 1899 E4
4400 EglT 46077 1899 E4
E 122nd St
5900 CRML 46033 1903 D4
W 122nd St
200 CRML 46032 1901 D4
N 125 E
2600 MdlT 46122 2221 B5
N 125 W
2600 CtrT 46140 2235 C3
6100 PltT 46184 2774 A3
6500 GNWD 46184 2774 A3
6600 GNWD 46143 2665 A7
6600 GNWD 46143 2774 A3
6600 GNWD 46184 2665 A7
6600 PltT 46143 2665 A7
6600 PltT 46143 2774 A3
6600 PltT 46184 2665 A7
S 125 E
2800 PryT 46052 1786 C6
3500 PryT 46052 1895 C1
S 125 W
3000 BwnT 46140 2344 C7
3000 HsnT 46052 1785 C7
W 125 N
9500 JknT 46011 1580 E4
126th St
- CRML 46032 1901 E3
E 126th St
- CRML 46033 1903 C3
10 CRML 46032 1902 B3
1000 CRML 46033 1902 D3
7600 DelT 46038 1904 B3
7600 FSHR 46038 1904 B3
8800 FCkT 46038 1904 C3
9700 FSHR 46038 1905 A3
9900 FCkT 46038 1905 A3
11900 FCkT 46038 1906 A3
11900 FSHR 46038 1906 A3
13200 FCkT 46060 1906 A3
13200 FSHR 46060 1906 A3
13900 FCkT 46038 1907 A3
13900 FSHR 46060 1907 A3
15000 FCkT 46060 1907 D3
W 126th St
2400 CRML 46032 1900 C3
4000 CRML 46077 1899 E3
E 131st St
- FSHR 46060 1906 D2
5200 CRML 46033 1903 B2
8200 DelT 46038 1904 C2
8200 FSHR 46038 1904 C2
8800 FCkT 46038 1904 C2
9700 FSHR 46038 1905 A2
9800 FCkT 46038 1905 A2
9800 FSHR 46060 1905 C2
11900 FCkT 46060 1905 E2
11900 FCkT 46060 1906 A2
W 131st St
10 CRML 46032 1901 A2
1400 CRML 46032 1900 D2
2400 CRML 46074 1900 A2
3600 CRML 46077 1900 A2
3800 CRML 46074 1899 D2
11500 EglT 46077 1899 D2
11900 CRML 46077 1899 D2
E 132nd St
- DelT 46038 1904 B2
133rd Pl
9000 FSHR 46038 1904 D2
134th St
- FSHR 46060 1906 D2
S 135 W
2700 CtrT 46052 1785 C6
E 136th St
1000 CRML 46032 1901 D1
11000 FCkT 46060 1905 E1
11000 FSHR 46060 1905 D1
12000 FSHR 46060 1906 A1
12000 NBVL 46060 1906 A1
12800 FCkT 46060 1906 E1
14000 FCkT 46060 1907 A1
W 136th St
- CRML 46074 1900 A1
700 CRML 46032 1901 A1
1400 CRML 46032 1900 E1
W 138th St
4300 CRML 46074 1899 E1
E 141st St
- FSHR 46038 1904 C1
- FSHR 46060 1904 C1
8700 FSHR 46038 1795 E7
8700 FSHR 46060 1795 E7
8900 FCkT 46060 1795 E7
9300 NBVL 46060 1795 E7
9700 FSHR 46038 1796 A7
9700 FSHR 46060 1796 A7
9700 NBVL 46060 1796 A7
9800 FCkT 46060 1796 A7
13800 NBVL 46060 1797 E7
13800 NBVL 46060 1798 A7
W 141st St
400 CRML 46032 1792 B7
1400 CRML 46032 1791 E7
1400 CRML 46074 1791 E7
1400 CRML 46074 1792 B7
3600 CRML 46074 1790 E7
4400 CRML 46077 1790 E7
4400 EglT 46077 1790 E7
146th St
- NBVL 46060 1796 E6
- NBVL 46060 1797 A6
E 146th St
- DelT 46033 1795 D6
- DelT 46062 1795 D6
- NBVL 46060 1797 B6
1800 CRML 46033 1793 B6
1800 WTFD 46033 1793 B6
4200 CRML 46033 1794 A6

INDEX 61

E 146th St — Indianapolis Street Index — E 400 N

STREET Block City ZIP Map# Grid

E 146th St
4200 WshT 46033 1793 C6
4200 WshT 46033 1794 A6
4800 CRML 46062 1794 A6
4800 NbvT 46033 1794 A6
4800 NbvT 46062 1794 A6
5100 NBVL 46033 1794 A6
5100 NBVL 46062 1794 A6
6600 CRML 46033 1795 A6
6600 CRML 46062 1795 A6
6600 NBVL 46062 1795 A6
7200 NbvT 46062 1795 A6
8200 DelT 46060 1795 D6
8200 NbvT 46060 1795 D6
8700 FSHR 46060 1795 D6
8700 HlnC 46060 1795 D6
9000 NBVL 46060 1795 D6
9100 FCkT 46060 1795 D6
9500 NBVL 46060 1796 A6
13800 WynT 46060 1797 C6
13800 WynT 46060 1798 A6
14800 FCkT 46060 1798 B6
14800 NBVL 46060 1798 A6
W 146th St
- CRML 46032 1792 A6
- WshT 46032 1792 A6
- WshT 46074 1792 A6
10 CRML 46032 1793 A6
10 WTFD 46032 1793 A6
800 WTFD 46032 1792 D6
1600 CRML 46074 1791 E6
1600 CRML 46074 1792 A6
1600 WshT 46074 1791 E6
3600 CRML 46074 1790 E6
3600 WshT 46074 1790 E6
4500 CRML 46077 1790 E6
4500 EglT 46077 1790 E6
4500 UnnT 46077 1790 E6
4500 WshT 46077 1790 E6
147th Pl
8800 NbvT 46060 1795 D6
E 147th Pl
8800 NbvT 46060 1795 D6
E 148th St
9600 NBVL 46060 1795 E6
9600 NBVL 46060 1796 A6
E 150 N
1000 CtrT 46052 1677 C4
1000 LEBN 46052 1677 C4
4200 WshT 46123 2331 B1
5800 AVON 46123 2331 E1
6500 UnnT 46052 1679 D4
6500 UnnT 46075 1679 D4
E 150 S
10 CtrT 46052 1785 E3
10 CtrT 46052 1786 A3
10 LEBN 46052 1785 E3
10 LEBN 46052 1786 A3
200 CtrT 46122 2330 D7
2400 WshT 46123 2332 A7
5000 WrhT 46052 1787 E3
5000 WrhT 46052 1788 A3
N 150 E
- MdlT 46122 2221 B4
8400 MdlT 46167 2003 B7
8400 MdlT 46167 2112 B1
10200 MdlT 46052 2003 B3
N 150 W
10 CtrT 46140 2235 C7
10 CtrT 46140 2344 C1
S 150 E
100 CtrT 46122 2330 B7
100 CtrT 46122 2439 B1
100 DNVL 46122 2330 B7
100 DNVL 46122 2439 B1
1700 LtyT 46118 2548 B1
4000 LtyT 46118 2439 B5
S 150 W
10 CtrT 46140 2344 C3
2000 BwnT 46140 2344 C6
7500 HsnT 46052 2003 B2
7500 MdlT 46052 2003 B2
W 150 N
4000 BCkT 46140 2233 E5
4000 BCkT 46140 2234 A5
W 150 S
2500 CtrT 46052 1785 A3
150 W
- MnrT 46118 2658 A1
- MnrT 46158 2658 A2
E 150 Rd S
800 AVON 46123 2332 C7
800 WshT 46123 2332 C7
E 150th St
- NBVL 46060 1795 E5
- NBVL 46060 1796 A5
E 151 N
- WshT 46123 2223 A7
E 151st St
1300 WshT 46032 1793 A5
1300 WTFD 46032 1793 A5
1800 WTFD 46033 1793 B5
2500 WshT 46033 1793 E5
4300 WshT 46033 1794 A5
4300 WTFD 46033 1794 A5
W 151st St
1800 WshT 46074 1791 E5
1800 WshT 46074 1792 A5
E 156th St
- WTFD 46032 1793 B4
10 WshT 46032 1792 E4
10 WshT 46032 1793 A4
1700 WTFD 46033 1793 B4
4800 NBVL 46062 1794 B4
4800 NbvT 46062 1794 B4
4800 WTFD 46062 1794 B4
11000 WynT 46060 1796 D4
11800 NBVL 46060 1796 D4
11900 NBVL 46060 1797 A4
12200 WynT 46060 1797 A4
13800 WynT 46060 1798 A4
15800 GrnT 46060 1798 D4
W 156th St
10 WshT 46074 1792 D4
10 WTFD 46074 1792 D4
1400 WshT 46074 1791 E4
3800 UnnT 46074 1790 E4
3800 UnnT 46077 1790 E4
3800 WshT 46074 1790 E4
3800 WshT 46077 1790 E4
3800 WshT 46077 1791 A4
W 159th St
2400 WshT 46074 1791 C4
E 160th St
7500 NBVL 46062 1795 A4
7500 NbvT 46062 1795 A4
E 161st St
- WTFD 46032 1793 B3
10 WshT 46074 1792 D3
10 WTFD 46074 1792 D3
700 WshT 46032 1792 D3
700 WshT 46032 1793 B3
700 WshT 46074 1793 B3
1500 WTFD 46033 1793 B3
1500 WTFD 46074 1793 B3
1600 WshT 46033 1793 B3
3300 WshT 46062 1793 E3
3300 WTFD 46062 1793 E3
3900 WshT 46033 1794 A3
3900 WshT 46062 1794 A3
4800 NbvT 46062 1794 A3
6400 NBVL 46062 1794 C3
6400 NbvT 46062 1795 A3
W 161st St
10 WshT 46074 1792 A3
10 WTFD 46074 1792 A3
1400 WshT 46074 1791 E3
E 166th St
9800 NBVL 46060 1796 C2
9800 NbvT 46060 1796 C2
10800 WynT 46060 1796 C2
12100 NBVL 46060 1797 A2
12100 WynT 46060 1797 A2
W 166th St
1800 WshT 46074 1791 E2
1800 WshT 46074 1792 A2
4200 UnnT 46074 1790 E2
4200 WshT 46074 1790 E2
E 169th St
300 WTFD 46074 1792 D2
700 WshT 46074 1792 E2
1200 WTFD 46074 1793 A2
3300 WshT 46062 1793 E2
3300 WTFD 46062 1793 E2
4000 WshT 46062 1794 A2
4800 NBVL 46062 1794 B2
4800 NbvT 46062 1794 B2
15800 SCkT 46060 1798 D2
15800 WynT 46060 1798 D2
W 169th St
10 WshT 46074 1792 B2
10 WTFD 46074 1792 C2
E 171 N
- CtrT 46122 2221 A7
E 171st St
300 WTFD 46074 1793 B1
700 WshT 46074 1793 B1
6300 NbvT 46062 1794 D1
6800 NBVL 46062 1794 D1
6900 NBVL 46062 1795 A1
6900 NbvT 46062 1795 A1
N 175 E
3700 CtnT 46052 1568 D6
3700 CtrT 46052 1568 D6
S 175 W
5000 HsnT 46052 1894 C7
7000 HsnT 46052 2003 C1
175th St
- WTFD 46074 1792 D1
E 176th St
- SCkT 46051 1689 D7
- WynT 46051 1689 D7
10 WTFD 46074 1683 D7
600 WshT 46074 1683 D7
14800 WynT 46060 1689 A7
15800 SCkT 46060 1689 D7
E 176th St SR-32
10 WTFD 46074 1683 D7
600 WshT 46074 1683 D7
W 176th St
10 WshT 46074 1683 A7
10 WTFD 46074 1683 A7
1600 WshT 46074 1682 C7
4000 WshT 46069 1682 C7
4100 WshT 46069 1681 E7
4100 WshT 46074 1681 E7
4200 UnnT 46069 1681 E7
4200 UnnT 46074 1681 E7
W 176th St SR-32
10 WshT 46074 1683 A7
10 WTFD 46074 1683 A7
1600 WshT 46074 1682 C7
4000 WshT 46069 1682 C7
4100 WshT 46069 1681 E7
4100 WshT 46074 1681 E7
4200 UnnT 46069 1681 E7
4200 UnnT 46074 1681 E7
E 179th St
13300 WynT 46060 1688 D7
S 180 W
3200 HsnT 46052 1785 B7
3200 HsnT 46052 1894 B1
E 181st St
500 WshT 46074 1683 E6
500 WTFD 46074 1683 E6
900 WshT 46074 1684 A6
900 WTFD 46074 1684 A6
11000 WynT 46060 1687 D6
11500 WynT 46060 1688 A6
S 185 W
3200 HsnT 46052 1785 B7
3200 HsnT 46052 1894 B1
7000 HsnT 46052 2003 B1
E 186th St
- WshT 46074 1683 D5
2100 WshT 46074 1684 A5
4000 WshT 46062 1684 E5
4000 WshT 46062 1685 A5
9800 NBVL 46060 1687 A5
9800 NbvT 46060 1687 A5
10000 WynT 46060 1687 B5
12800 WynT 46060 1688 C5
15800 WynT 46060 1689 D5
W 186th St
10 WshT 46074 1683 A5
1200 WshT 46074 1682 C5
4100 UnnT 46069 1681 E5
4100 WshT 46069 1681 E5
4100 WshT 46069 1682 C5
E 191st St
10 WshT 46074 1683 D4
10 WshT 46074 1684 A4
1700 WTFD 46074 1684 A4
3300 WshT 46062 1684 E4
4000 WshT 46062 1685 B4
4800 NbvT 46062 1685 B4
5000 NBVL 46062 1685 B4
9300 NBVL 46060 1686 E4
9300 NbvT 46060 1686 E4
9600 NbvT 46060 1687 B4
9800 NBVL 46060 1687 B4
11000 WynT 46060 1687 E4
11800 WynT 46060 1688 A4
14200 WynT 46060 1689 B4
W 191st St
10 WshT 46074 1683 C4
E 192nd St
9500 NbvT 46060 1686 E4
W 193rd St
10 WshT 46069 1683 B4
10 WshT 46074 1683 B4
1200 WshT 46069 1682 B4
1200 WshT 46074 1682 B4
E 196th St
1100 WshT 46074 1684 A3
1100 WTFD 46074 1684 A3
3300 WshT 46062 1684 E3
4000 WshT 46062 1685 A3
7400 NBVL 46062 1686 A3
7500 NbvT 46062 1686 C3
11000 NBVL 46060 1687 D3
11000 WynT 46060 1687 D3
12000 WynT 46060 1688 A3
14200 WynT 46060 1689 A3
W 196th St
4400 MrnT 46069 1681 E3
4400 UnnT 46069 1681 E3
4400 WshT 46069 1681 E3
4400 WshT 46069 1682 A3
E 199th St
10 WshT 46069 1683 D3
10 WshT 46069 1684 A3
10 WshT 46074 1683 D3
10 WshT 46074 1684 A3
W 199th St
10 WshT 46069 1683 C3
10 WshT 46074 1683 C3
E 200 N
- CtrT 46140 2236 E4
- GNFD 46140 2236 E4
100 CtrT 46122 2221 B7
100 MdlT 46122 2221 B7
2000 CtrT 46052 1677 E3
2500 CtrT 46052 1678 A3
2500 CtrT 46140 2237 A4
5400 WshT 46123 2222 C7
6700 MrnT 46075 1679 E3
6700 UnnT 46075 1679 E3
7000 WshT 46123 2223 C7
7500 MrnT 46075 1680 A3
7500 UnnT 46075 1680 A3
7900 WshT 46112 2223 E7
8000 AVON 46112 2223 E7
8000 AVON 46112 2224 A7
8000 AVON 46123 2223 E7
8000 AVON 46123 2224 A7
8000 WshT 46112 2224 A7
8000 WshT 46123 2224 A7
9800 MrnT 46075 1681 A3
9800 UnnT 46075 1681 A3
10000 AVON 46234 2224 C7
10000 WshT 46234 2224 C7
10100 MrnT 46069 1681 A3
10100 UnnT 46069 1681 A3
E 200 S
10 CtrT 46122 2439 A1
100 DNVL 46122 2439 A1
1600 AVON 46168 2441 E1
1600 WshT 46123 2441 E1
1600 WshT 46168 2441 E1
2000 BwnT 46140 2345 E5
2000 BwnT 46140 2346 A5
2000 CtrT 46140 2345 E5
2000 CtrT 46140 2346 A5
2500 AVON 46168 2442 A1
2500 WshT 46123 2442 A1
2500 WshT 46168 2442 A1
3500 CtrT 46122 2440 A1
3500 WshT 46122 2440 A1
3600 BRvT 46140 2346 C5
4000 WrhT 46052 1787 D4
4700 WshT 46123 2440 B1
4700 WshT 46168 2440 B1
5500 WrhT 46075 1788 A4
6000 WrhT 46052 1788 C4
7000 WrhT 46075 1789 B4
8100 UnnT 46075 1789 B4
8100 UnnT 46077 1789 B4
9000 WshT 46231 2442 A1
9200 PNFD 46168 2442 B1
9500 UnnT 46077 1790 A4
10600 PNFD 46231 2442 D1
N 200 E
700 CtrT 46052 1677 D6
6000 CtnT 46052 1568 E1
10100 MdlT 46167 2003 C5
10400 MdlT 46052 2003 C3
N 200 W
10 CtrT 46052 1676 B7
S 200 E
- DNVL 46122 2330 C5
100 CtrT 46122 2330 C5
1500 CtrT 46052 1786 D4
2000 BwnT 46140 2345 E6
2000 CtrT 46140 2345 E6
2000 GNFD 46140 2345 E6
3500 LtyT 46118 2439 C4
5000 LtyT 46118 2548 C1
S 200 E SR-9
2000 BwnT 46140 2345 E6
2000 CtrT 46140 2345 E6
2000 GNFD 46140 2345 E6
S 200 W
10 CtrT 46052 1676 B7
10 CtrT 46052 1785 A1
100 CtrT 46140 2344 B3
100 SCkT 46140 2344 B3
2000 BwnT 46140 2344 B7
W 200 N
10 CtrT 46140 2236 A4
10 GNFD 46140 2236 A4
900 CtrT 46140 2235 E4
1800 BCkT 46140 2235 C4
2000 BCkT 46140 2234 E4
5000 BCkT 46140 2233 E4
7800 BCkT 46140 2232 E4
7800 BCkT 46229 2232 E4
W 200 S
10 BwnT 46140 2344 E5
10 BwnT 46140 2345 A5
10 CtrT 46140 2344 E5
10 CtrT 46140 2345 A5
1500 SCkT 46140 2344 B5
2500 SCkT 46140 2343 E5
3700 SCkT 46163 2343 C5
5300 SCkT 46163 2342 E5
7000 SCkT 46239 2342 A5
7600 INPS 46239 2341 E5
7600 SCkT 46239 2341 E5
N 201 E
7000 MdlT 46167 2112 C3
E 201st St
13500 WynT 46060 1688 C2
E 202nd St
1700 WshT 46074 1684 B2
1700 WTFD 46074 1684 B2
E 203rd St
1000 WshT 46069 1684 A2
1000 WTFD 46069 1684 A2
1000 WTFD 46074 1684 A2
2500 WshT 46074 1684 C2
E 206th St
10 WshT 46069 1683 E1
7500 NBVL 46062 1686 C1
7500 NbvT 46062 1686 C1
8800 NbvT 46060 1686 C1
9300 NbvT 46060 1687 B1
9300 NbvT 46062 1687 B1
10200 WynT 46060 1687 C1
10200 WynT 46062 1687 C1
12000 WynT 46060 1688 B1
14800 WynT 46060 1689 D1
W 206th St
10 WshT 46069 1683 C1
900 WshT 46069 1682 C1
4100 MrnT 46069 1681 E1
4100 WshT 46069 1681 E1
E 210 N
4000 CtrT 46052 1678 D3
E 211th St
4800 WshT 46062 1576 A7
6200 NBVL 46062 1576 D7
6300 NbvT 46062 1576 D7
7500 NbvT 46062 1577 B7
10200 NbvT 46062 1578 C7
10200 WynT 46062 1578 C7
11000 WynT 46060 1578 D7
14800 WynT 46060 1580 B7
W 211th St
1800 WshT 46069 1573 D7
E 214th St
500 WshT 46069 1574 D7
E 216th St
- AdmT 46069 1575 A6
- JknT 46069 1575 A6
- WshT 46069 1575 A6
2500 JknT 46034 1575 E6
2500 JknT 46062 1575 E6
2500 WshT 46062 1575 E6
3300 JknT 46034 1576 B6
3300 WshT 46034 1575 E6
3300 WshT 46062 1576 B6
4800 JknT 46062 1576 B6
4800 NbvT 46062 1576 B6
5500 NBVL 46034 1576 B6
5500 NBVL 46062 1576 B6
5500 NbvT 46034 1576 B6
7700 CCRO 46034 1577 C6
7700 CCRO 46062 1577 C6
7700 JknT 46034 1577 C6
7700 JknT 46062 1577 C6
7700 NBVL 46062 1577 C6
7700 NbvT 46034 1577 C6
7700 NbvT 46062 1577 C6
11000 WRvT 46060 1578 E6
12000 WRvT 46060 1579 B6
12000 WynT 46060 1579 B6
15800 WRvT 46060 1580 D6
15800 WynT 46060 1580 D6
W 216th St
300 AdmT 46069 1574 B6
300 WshT 46069 1574 B6
800 AdmT 46069 1573 E6
800 WshT 46069 1573 E6
3600 AdmT 46069 1572 E6
3600 MrnT 46069 1572 E6
3600 WshT 46069 1572 E6
E 221st St
6300 JknT 46034 1576 D6
7800 JknT 46034 1577 E5
8900 JknT 46034 1578 A5
8900 WRvT 46034 1578 A5
9800 WRvT 46062 1578 C5
W 221st St
400 AdmT 46069 1574 B5
900 AdmT 46069 1573 E5
E 225 N
3000 MdlT 46122 2221 E6
3600 MdlT 46122 2222 A6
3800 WshT 46122 2222 A6
E 225 S
6600 WrhT 46075 1788 D5
N 225 E
- MdlT 46167 2003 D6
200 MdlT 46122 2221 D6
3300 CtrT 46052 1677 E1
3400 CtnT 46052 1568 E7
3400 CtrT 46052 1568 E7
4200 PltT 46184 2775 C6
7200 MdlT 46167 2112 D3
8100 PTBR 46167 2112 D3
N 225 W
6000 WshT 46052 1567 A1
6000 WshT 46071 1567 A1
S 225 E
100 CtrT 46122 2330 D7
200 CtrT 46122 2439 D3
200 LtyT 46122 2439 D3
S 225 W
500 CtrT 46052 1785 A2
W 225 N
5700 BCkT 46140 2233 D4
E 225th St
4000 JknT 46034 1575 E5
4000 JknT 46034 1576 A5
4800 JknT 46062 1576 A5
E 226th St
- AdmT 46034 1575 A4
300 AdmT 46069 1574 D4
700 AdmT 46069 1575 A4
1800 JknT 46034 1575 D4
4100 JknT 46034 1576 C4
7100 JknT 46034 1577 A4
8800 JknT 46034 1578 A4
8800 WRvT 46034 1578 A4
9800 WRvT 46062 1578 A4
12400 WRvT 46060 1580 D4
W 226th St
10 AdmT 46069 1574 C4
900 AdmT 46069 1573 E4
3600 AdmT 46069 1572 E4
4300 MrnT 46069 1572 E4
E 230 S
6700 WrhT 46075 1788 D5
8700 UnnT 46077 1789 C5
E 231st St
10 AdmT 46069 1574 D3
4000 JknT 46034 1575 E3
6300 JknT 46034 1576 E3
6700 JknT 46034 1577 A3
W 231st St
10 AdmT 46069 1574 C3
E 234th St
1100 AdmT 46069 1575 A3
9600 JknT 46034 1577 E2
9600 JknT 46034 1578 C3
9900 WRvT 46034 1578 C3
E 235th St
9500 JknT 46034 1577 E2
9500 JknT 46034 1578 A2
E 236th St
- AdmT 46034 1575 A2
10 AdmT 46069 1574 E2
10 AdmT 46069 1575 A2
1700 JknT 46034 1575 E2
4000 JknT 46034 1576 B2
6300 JknT 46034 1577 B2
7500 CCRO 46034 1577 B2
E 236th St US-47
10 AdmT 46069 1574 E2
10 AdmT 46069 1575 A2
W 236th St
10 AdmT 46069 1574 D2
2400 SRDN 46069 1573 D2
3700 AdmT 46069 1572 E2
3700 AdmT 46069 1573 A2
3900 MrnT 46069 1572 E2
W 236th St SR-47
3700 AdmT 46069 1572 E2
3700 AdmT 46069 1573 A2
3900 MrnT 46069 1572 E2
W 236th St US-47
10 AdmT 46069 1574 D2
900 AdmT 46069 1573 D2
2400 SRDN 46069 1573 D2
E 239th St
12800 WRvT 46060 1579 C2
E 241st St
- AdmT 46069 1575 C1
- JknT 46069 1575 C1
1700 JknT 46034 1575 C1
6400 CCRO 46030 1577 A1
6400 JknT 46030 1576 E1
6400 JknT 46030 1577 A1
8700 CCRO 46034 1577 E1
8700 JknT 46034 1577 E1
9400 JknT 46034 1578 A1
9700 WRvT 46034 1578 D1
W 241st St
3900 AdmT 46069 1572 E1
3900 AdmT 46069 1573 A1
4300 MrnT 46069 1572 E1
E 244th St
6100 JknT 46034 1576 C1
E 250 N
2600 MdlT 46122 2221 A6
5000 CtrT 46052 1679 A2
E 250 S
10 CtrT 46052 1785 E5
10 CtrT 46052 1786 B5
10 LEBN 46052 1785 E5
10 LEBN 46052 1786 B5
7700 WrhT 46075 1789 B5
7800 UnnT 46077 1789 B5
7800 WrhT 46077 1789 B5
N 250 E
- CtrT 46122 2330 D3
- GNWD 46143 2666 D3
- MdlT 46122 2221 D1
2000 CtrT 46052 1678 A1
4900 MdlT 46167 2221 D1
5000 CtnT 46052 1569 A5
5200 MdlT 46167 2112 E6
6600 PltT 46184 2775 D3
7200 PltT 46184 2666 D7
N 250 W
1600 CtrT 46052 1676 A3
S 250 W
1000 SCkT 46140 2344 A5
W 250 N
400 CtrT 46052 1676 D2
W 250 S
10 CtrT 46052 1785 E5
E 251 S
10600 WshT 46168 2440 E2
10600 WshT 46168 2441 A2
E 275 N
6000 CtrT 46052 1679 C2
6000 MrnT 46052 1679 C2
N 275 E
7500 MdlT 46167 2112 E2
7500 PTBR 46167 2112 E2
8000 MdlT 46167 2003 E7
S 275 E
2300 BwnT 46140 2346 A6
6500 LtyT 46118 2548 D3
W 275 N
1100 CtrT 46052 1676 C2
W 275 S
1300 CtrT 46052 1785 B6
E 300 N
10 CtrT 46052 1677 A1
10 CtrT 46140 2236 A2
10 LEBN 46052 1677 A1
300 CtrT 46122 2221 A5
300 MdlT 46122 2221 A5
2000 GNFD 46140 2236 E2
2300 CtrT 46140 2237 A2
6700 MrnT 46052 1679 D1
7000 BNBG 46112 2223 C5
7000 LcnT 46112 2223 C5
8000 LcnT 46112 2224 A4
8500 MrnT 46075 1680 B1
9600 MrnT 46075 1681 B1
10000 LcnT 46234 2224 C4
10000 MrnT 46069 1681 B1
E 300 S
- AVON 46168 2441 E3
- GfdT 46168 2440 E3
- GfdT 46168 2441 C3
- GfdT 46168 2442 A3
- PNFD 46168 2442 A3
- WshT 46168 2440 E3
- WshT 46168 2441 E3
- WshT 46168 2442 A3
10 BwnT 46140 2345 B7
200 CtrT 46122 2439 D3
200 LtyT 46122 2439 D3
400 CtrT 46052 1786 A6
400 HsnT 46052 1786 A6
2000 BwnT 46140 2346 A7
3000 CtrT 46052 1787 B6
3000 PryT 46052 1787 B6
3700 BRvT 46140 2346 D7
4000 CtrT 46075 1787 D6
4000 PryT 46075 1787 D6
4000 WrhT 46075 1787 D6
6900 WrhT 46075 1788 E6
7100 WrhT 46075 1789 A6
8000 EglT 46077 1789 A6
8000 UnnT 46077 1789 A6
8000 WrhT 46077 1789 A6
9700 EglT 46077 1790 A6
9700 UnnT 46077 1790 A6
N 300 E
10 CtrT 46052 1678 A7
10 DNVL 46122 2330 E3
1000 CtrT 46122 2330 E1
1700 CtrT 46122 2221 E7
1700 MdlT 46122 2221 E7
3000 CtrT 46140 2237 B1
5500 ClkT 46143 2775 E1
5500 ClkT 46184 2775 E1
5500 PltT 46184 2775 E1
6400 CtnT 46052 1569 B1
10000 ClkT 46143 2557 E7
10000 ClkT 46143 2666 E3
10000 GNWD 46143 2666 E3
10000 INPS 46143 2557 E7
10000 PltT 46143 2557 E7
10000 PltT 46143 2666 E1
N 300 W
10 BCkT 46140 2343 E1
10 SCkT 46140 2343 E1
2300 BCkT 46140 2234 E1
3000 BCkT 46140 2125 E6
6000 VrnT 46055 2125 E3
6000 VrnT 46140 2125 E3
7100 VrnT 46055 2016 E7
8400 VrnT 46040 2016 E5
S 300 E
10 CtrT 46052 1678 B7
10 CtrT 46052 1787 A1
10 CtrT 46122 2330 E4
10 DNVL 46122 2330 E4
1600 CtrT 46122 2439 E1
2700 LtyT 46122 2439 E2
7500 PryT 46052 2005 A2
7500 PryT 46112 2005 A2
7700 BrnT 46112 2005 A2
S 300 W
10 SCkT 46140 2343 E2
200 SGLK 46140 2343 E2
3000 SCkT 46140 2452 E1
3000 SCkT 46163 2343 E7
3000 SCkT 46163 2452 E1
W 300 N
10 CtrT 46052 1677 A1
10 CtrT 46140 2236 A2
10 LEBN 46052 1677 A1
100 CtrT 46140 2235 E2
300 CtrT 46052 1676 E1
300 LEBN 46052 1676 E1
1700 BCkT 46140 2235 A2
2000 BCkT 46140 2234 D2
5000 BCkT 46140 2233 E2
7500 BCkT 46140 2232 E2
7700 INPS 46140 2232 E2
W 300 S
10 BwnT 46140 2344 B7
10 BwnT 46140 2345 A7
700 CtrT 46052 1785 C6
700 HsnT 46052 1785 C6
2000 SCkT 46140 2344 B7
2500 SCkT 46140 2343 C7
3000 SCkT 46163 2343 C7
6000 SCkT 46163 2342 A7
7700 SCkT 46163 2341 E7
7700 SCkT 46239 2341 E7
9500 SCkT 46051 1689 E5
9500 WynT 46051 1689 E5
300 E
- ClkT 46184 2775 E5
- PltT 46184 2775 E5
S 300 Rd W
- GNWD 46142 2664 C3
S 300 Rd W SR-135
- GNWD 46142 2664 C3
300 W Rd
200 GNWD 46142 2664 C5
700 GNWD 46143 2664 C5
700 WRvT 46143 2664 C7
300 W Rd SR-135
200 GNWD 46142 2664 C5
700 GNWD 46143 2664 C5
700 WRvT 46143 2664 C7
E 325 S
1000 CtrT 46052 1786 B6
1000 HsnT 46052 1786 B6
1000 PryT 46052 1786 C7
W 325 S
1200 HsnT 46052 1785 B7
325 E
100 ClkT 46143 2666 E4
100 GNWD 46143 2666 E4
330 S
6000 SCkT 46163 2451 D1
E 350 N
1000 MdlT 46122 2221 B4
4100 MdlT 46122 2222 B4
4200 MdlT 46123 2222 B4
4900 LcnT 46122 2222 B4
4900 LcnT 46123 2222 B4
5000 LcnT 46112 2222 B4
6100 LcnT 46112 2223 A4
11000 MrnT 46069 1572 C7
E 350 S
200 LtyT 46122 2439 E4
200 LtyT 46168 2439 E4
300 HsnT 46052 1786 B7
300 LtyT 46122 2440 A4
300 LtyT 46168 2440 A4
600 PryT 46052 1786 B7
1500 GfdT 46168 2440 E4
1500 PNFD 46168 2440 C4
8700 EglT 46077 1789 D7
8700 ZNVL 46077 1789 D7
N 350 E
4700 CtnT 46052 1569 C4
N 350 W
10 BCkT 46140 2343 D2
10 SCkT 46140 2343 D2
600 BCkT 46140 2234 D7
6000 VrnT 46055 2125 D2
W 350 N
6000 BCkT 46140 2233 C1
7000 BCkT 46140 2232 E1
7000 INPS 46140 2232 E1
E 375 N
1100 CtrT 46052 1568 C7
1900 MdlT 46122 2221 D3
E 375 S
9500 EglT 46077 1898 E1
9700 EglT 46077 1899 A1
N 375 E
3000 CtrT 46140 2237 C1
6000 CtnT 46052 1569 C1
6400 MdlT 46167 2112 E5
6400 MdlT 46167 2113 A6
S 375 E
- LtyT 46118 2657 E1
- MnrT 46118 2657 E1
7300 LtyT 46118 2548 E4
W 375 N
- CtrT 46140 2236 A1
200 CtrT 46052 1567 D7
200 CtrT 46052 1568 A7
200 CtrT 46140 2235 E1
W 375 S
300 HsnT 46052 1894 D1
375 E
10 ClkT 46143 2667 A6
W 380 N
2000 BCkT 46140 2235 B1
E 400 N
900 BNBG 46112 2223 C2
1700 FKLN 46131 2775 A7
1700 FknT 46131 2775 A7
1700 FknT 46184 2775 A7
1700 WTLD 46131 2775 A7
1700 WTLD 46184 2775 A7
2200 PltT 46131 2775 C7
2200 PltT 46184 2775 C7
3100 ClkT 46184 2775 E7
3100 NdmT 46131 2775 E7
3100 NdmT 46184 2775 E7
3400 MdlT 46122 2221 E3
4200 MdlT 46122 2222 C3
5000 CtnT 46052 1570 B6
6000 CtnT 46052 1570 B6
6000 MrnT 46052 1570 C6
7000 MrnT 46052 1571 A6
8000 MrnT 46075 1571 B6
8500 BNBG 46112 2224 A2
8500 LcnT 46112 2223 C2
8500 LcnT 46112 2224 A2
9400 MrnT 46075 1572 A6
10000 MrnT 46069 1572 A6

INDEX 62

E 400 S

Indianapolis Street Index

E 925 North Rd

STREET Block	City	ZIP	Map#	Grid
E 400 S				
10	HsnT	46052	1895	A1
400	LtyT	46118	2439	A5
1000	PryT	46052	1895	D1
3300	PryT	46052	1896	B1
4400	WrhT	46075	1896	D1
4800	GfdT	46168	2440	C6
4800	LtyT	46168	2440	C6
6000	WrhT	46075	1897	B1
6000	WTWN	46075	1897	B1
7500	WrhT	46075	1898	A1
8000	EglT	46077	1898	A1
8000	WrhT	46077	1898	A1
8700	ZNVL	46077	1898	D1
N 400 E				
10	CtrT	46052	1678	C7
100	CtrT	46140	2237	D7
100	CtrT	46140	2346	D1
3500	CtnT	46052	1569	D7
3500	CtrT	46052	1569	D7
3800	MdlT	46122	2222	A3
4200	MdlT	46167	2222	A3
8200	MdlT	46167	2113	A1
10000	MdlT	46167	2004	A3
N 400 W				
-	SgCT	46126	2670	E5
100	BCkT	46140	2234	C7
100	BCkT	46140	2343	C1
100	SCkT	46140	2343	C1
3000	BCkT	46140	2125	C6
4300	BwnT	46126	2670	E7
5300	BCkT	46055	2125	C6
6000	VrnT	46055	2125	C3
6100	MrlT	46126	2670	E3
7000	MrlT	46126	2561	E6
7500	VrnT	46055	2016	C7
8900	VrnT	46040	2016	C5
9200	MrlT	46130	2561	E6
11000	MrlT	46130	2452	E7
11700	SCkT	46130	2452	E7
S 400 E				
-	PryT	46052	1896	C2
-	PryT	46075	1896	C2
10	BRvT	46140	2346	D2
10	CtrT	46052	1678	C7
10	CtrT	46052	1787	C1
10	CtrT	46122	2331	A5
10	CtrT	46140	2346	D2
10	WrhT	46052	1678	C7
10	WrhT	46052	1787	C1
10	WshT	46122	2331	A5
10	WshT	46123	2331	A5
100	DNVL	46122	2331	A5
300	CtrT	46123	2331	A5
1400	BwnT	46140	2346	D4
5200	LtyT	46118	2440	A7
5300	LtyT	46118	2549	A1
S 400 E SR-267				
-	PryT	46052	1896	C2
-	PryT	46075	1896	C2
S 400 W				
10	SCkT	46140	2343	C2
300	SCkT	46163	2343	C4
3100	SCkT	46163	2452	C1
5100	MrlT	46163	2452	C6
W 400 N				
2600	BCkT	46140	2125	D7
6000	BCkT	46055	2124	C7
6000	BCkT	46140	2124	C7
W 400 S				
2000	SCkT	46140	2452	E2
2000	SCkT	46163	2452	E2
2200	HsnT	46052	1894	A1
4000	NPLN	46163	2452	B2
9700	SCkT	46051	1689	E7
9700	WynT	46051	1689	E7
400 E				
-	CtrT	46140	2346	D1
400 W				
1300	MnrT	46157	2657	A6
N 401 E				
7500	MdlT	46167	2113	A2
7500	PTBR	46167	2113	A2
E 425 N				
-	MdlT	46122	2222	B2
-	MdlT	46167	2222	B2
3000	CtnT	46052	1569	C6
4000	CtnT	46052	1570	A6
6700	BNBG	46112	2223	B2
E 425 S				
7000	WrhT	46075	1897	E2
N 425 E				
1400	WshT	46122	2331	B1
1400	WshT	46123	2331	B1
2100	WshT	46122	2222	B7
2100	WshT	46123	2222	B7
2300	MdlT	46122	2222	B5
2300	MdlT	46123	2222	B5
9300	MdlT	46167	2004	B6
N 425 W				
11700	MrlT	46130	2452	D7
S 425 E				
3100	LtyT	46118	2549	B7
3100	LtyT	46118	2658	A1
3100	MnrT	46118	2658	A1
6900	PryT	46052	1896	D7
6900	PryT	46052	2005	D1
S 425 W				
2000	SCkT	46163	2343	B6
E 450 N				
700	CtnT	46052	1568	C5
700	MdlT	46122	2221	A2
700	UnnT	46122	2221	A2
700	WshT	46052	1568	C5
2200	CtnT	46052	1569	A5
2800	MdlT	46167	2221	E1
4900	LcnT	46167	2222	C1
4900	MdlT	46167	2222	C1
5300	LcnT	46112	2222	D2
10200	LcnT	46112	2224	D1
E 450 S				
-	GfdT	46168	2442	A6
1000	PryT	46052	1895	C2
4100	WrhT	46052	1896	D2
4300	WrhT	46075	1896	E2
5500	WrhT	46075	1897	A2
8500	PNFD	46168	2441	E6
8500	PNFD	46168	2442	A6
N 450 E				
-	MdlT	46167	2222	B2
200	WshT	46123	2331	B3
3000	CtrT	46140	2237	E1
6000	CtnT	46052	1569	E1
N 450 W				
4500	SgCT	46126	2670	D6
S 450				
4000	NPLN	46163	2452	B2
4000	SCkT	46163	2452	B2
S 450 E				
100	WshT	46122	2331	B6
100	WshT	46122	2440	B1
100	WshT	46123	2331	B6
100	WshT	46123	2440	B1
3100	WrhT	46075	1787	D7
3600	WrhT	46075	1896	D1
7500	PryT	46052	2005	D2
7500	PryT	46112	2005	D2
7900	BrnT	46112	2005	D2
S 450 W				
10	NPLN	46163	2452	B4
100	SCkT	46163	2452	B4
W 450 N				
10	WshT	46052	1567	D5
10	WshT	46052	1568	A5
3300	BwnT	46126	2670	E7
3300	SgCT	46126	2670	E7
W 450 S				
1000	HsnT	46052	1894	D2
450 W				
700	WRvT	46143	2663	E5
E 451 S				
1300	LtyT	46118	2439	B6
N 460 W				
11000	MrlT	46130	2561	D1
N 471 E				
10000	MdlT	46167	2004	C4
E 475 N				
3500	CtnT	46052	1569	D5
4000	CtnT	46052	1570	A5
N 475 E				
-	WshT	46123	2222	C7
1000	WshT	46123	2331	C1
6400	MdlT	46167	2113	C4
N 475 W				
7000	VrnT	46055	2016	B7
7000	VrnT	46055	2125	B1
S 475 E				
5200	PryT	46052	1896	E5
6500	PryT	46052	2005	E1
N 480 W				
11000	MrlT	46130	2561	C1
N 490 W				
11000	MrlT	46130	2561	C1
E 500 N				
-	LcnT	46112	2223	A1
10	UnnT	46122	2221	A1
10	UnnT	46149	2221	A1
10	UnnT	46167	2221	A1
10	WshT	46052	1568	B4
700	CtnT	46052	1568	B4
1000	MdlT	46122	2221	A1
1000	MdlT	46167	2221	A1
5700	CtnT	46052	1570	B4
5900	LcnT	46112	2222	E1
6000	LcnT	46112	2114	A7
6000	MrnT	46052	1570	D4
7000	MrnT	46052	1571	A4
8300	MrnT	46069	1571	C4
8300	MrnT	46075	1571	C4
9600	MrnT	46069	1572	A4
E 500 S				
10	HsnT	46052	1895	A3
1000	PryT	46052	1895	B3
4500	PryT	46052	1896	E3
4500	WrhT	46052	1896	E3
5200	PryT	46075	1896	E3
5200	PryT	46075	1897	A3
5200	WrhT	46075	1896	E3
5200	WrhT	46075	1897	A3
5700	EglT	46075	1897	C3
5800	EglT	46077	1897	C3
11500	EglT	46077	1899	D3
N 500 E				
10	AVON	46123	2331	C3
10	CtrT	46052	1678	E7
10	WrhT	46052	1678	E7
10	WshT	46123	2331	C3
500	CtrT	46052	1679	A6
2000	LcnT	46123	2222	C4
2000	MdlT	46123	2222	C4
2000	WshT	46123	2222	C6
3500	CtrT	46052	1570	A7
3700	LcnT	46112	2222	C3
3700	LcnT	46122	2222	C3
3700	MdlT	46122	2222	C3
4000	CtnT	46052	1570	A6
4300	LcnT	46167	2222	C3
4300	MdlT	46167	2222	C3
4900	LcnT	46112	2113	C7
4900	LcnT	46167	2113	C7
4900	MdlT	46112	2222	C1
4900	MdlT	46167	2113	C7
7600	BNBG	46112	2113	C1
7600	MdlT	46112	2113	C1
8900	MdlT	46112	2004	C6
8900	MdlT	46167	2004	C6
N 500 W				
2600	BCkT	46140	2234	A3
5000	SgCT	46126	2670	C5
5200	BCkT	46055	2125	A4
6000	VrnT	46055	2125	A3
7100	MrlT	46126	2670	C1
7100	VrnT	46055	2016	A7
7200	MrlT	46126	2561	C5
9300	MrlT	46130	2561	C5
11300	MrlT	46130	2452	C7
11300	SCkT	46130	2452	C7
S 500 E				
-	PNFD	46168	2440	C6
600	GfdT	46168	2440	C6
600	LtyT	46168	2440	C6
1000	WrhT	46052	1787	E4
2000	WrhT	46075	1787	E4
3900	WrhT	46075	1896	E1
S 500 W				
10	SCkT	46140	2343	A3
10	SCkT	46163	2343	A7
3200	SCkT	46163	2452	A1
3400	NPLN	46163	2452	A1
W 500 N				
10	PltT	46184	2774	A5
10	WshT	46052	1567	D4
10	WshT	46052	1568	A4
2000	BCkT	46140	2125	E5
3600	BCkT	46055	2125	B5
3700	BwnT	46126	2670	E6
4000	SgCT	46126	2670	D6
6000	BCkT	46055	2124	C5
6000	SgCT	46110	2669	E6
6000	SgCT	46126	2669	E6
7700	BCkT	46055	2123	E5
7700	BCkT	46235	2123	E5
W 500 S				
700	HsnT	46052	1894	C3
9000	GrnT	46051	1798	E2
9000	SCkT	46051	1798	E2
S 521 E				
6000	GfdT	46168	2549	D2
E 525 S				
6900	EglT	46077	1897	D4
N 525 W				
10	BCkT	46140	2233	E7
10	BCkT	46140	2342	E1
10	SCkT	46140	2342	E1
S 525 E				
-	BrnT	46158	2658	D1
-	GfdT	46158	2658	D1
-	PryT	46112	2006	A1
10	WshT	46123	2331	D6
1800	WshT	46123	2440	D1
6500	PryT	46052	1897	A7
7300	GfdT	46168	2549	D4
8300	GfdT	46168	2658	D1
S 525 W				
10	SCkT	46140	2342	E2
W 525 N				
1500	WshT	46052	1567	A3
7800	SgCT	46110	2669	A6
8300	SgCT	46110	2668	E6
W 525 S				
200	HsnT	46052	1894	D4
E 550 N				
3800	MdlT	46167	2113	A7
4100	LcnT	46167	2113	D7
5100	BNBG	46112	2113	D7
5100	LcnT	46112	2113	D7
5500	CtnT	46052	1570	B3
E 550 S				
500	HsnT	46052	1895	B4
1000	PryT	46052	1895	D4
4000	PryT	46052	1896	C4
5000	PryT	46052	1897	A5
5500	EglT	46075	1897	B4
5500	PryT	46075	1897	B4
5700	PNFD	46168	2550	E1
7000	EglT	46077	1897	E4
7300	EglT	46077	1898	A4
8600	GfdT	46168	2550	E1
8600	GfdT	46168	2551	A1
8600	PNFD	46168	2551	A1
N 550 E				
2500	CtrT	46052	1679	B1
3500	CtrT	46052	1570	B7
5500	BNBG	46112	2113	D6
5500	LcnT	46112	2113	D6
6000	CtnT	46052	1570	B1
6600	BrnT	46112	2113	D5
9000	BrnT	46112	2004	D5
9000	MdlT	46112	2004	D5
9900	MdlT	46167	2004	D5
10900	BrnT	46167	2004	D3
N 550 W				
4000	SgCT	46126	2670	B7
S 550 E				
200	WshT	46123	2331	D4
S 550 W				
4200	SCkT	46163	2451	E3
550 E				
10	ClkT	46143	2667	E6
E 551 N				
5100	LcnT	46112	2113	D6
S 565 W				
-	SCkT	46163	2451	E2
N 571 E				
100	AVON	46123	2331	E3
100	WshT	46123	2331	E3
E 575 S				
9000	EglT	46077	1898	D5
N 575 E				
2000	LcnT	46112	2222	E5
2000	LcnT	46123	2222	E5
5000	CtnT	46052	1570	B4
S 575 E				
-	AVON	46123	2331	E4
-	WshT	46123	2331	E4
1700	WrhT	46052	1788	B4
1700	WrhT	46075	1788	B4
3500	WrhT	46075	1897	B1
4900	PryT	46075	1897	B3
8800	GfdT	46158	2549	E6
8800	GfdT	46158	2658	E1
8800	GfdT	46168	2549	E6
8800	GfdT	46168	2658	E1
E 600 N				
500	UnnT	46149	2112	A6
1400	MdlT	46167	2112	C6
1400	UnnT	46167	2112	A6
8500	BNBG	46112	2114	E6
8500	BNBG	46112	2115	B5
8500	LcnT	46112	2114	E6
8500	LcnT	46112	2115	B5
E 600 S				
2300	LtyT	46118	2548	D2
2700	LtyT	46118	2549	A2
4900	GfdT	46168	2549	D2
4900	LtyT	46168	2549	D2
6400	GfdT	46168	2550	A2
6400	PNFD	46168	2550	A2
7000	EglT	46077	1897	E5
8600	GfdT	46168	2551	A2
8600	PNFD	46168	2551	A2
9600	GfdT	46231	2551	B2
9600	PNFD	46231	2551	B2
N 600 E				
10	UnnT	46052	1679	C6
800	AVON	46123	2331	E1
800	WshT	46123	2331	E1
1000	MrnT	46052	1679	C4
1500	WshT	46123	2222	E7
2200	LcnT	46123	2222	E6
2500	LcnT	46112	2222	E5
2900	CtrT	46052	1679	C2
3200	LcnT	46112	2223	A5
3300	CtrT	46052	1570	C7
3300	MrnT	46052	1570	C7
3500	CtnT	46052	1570	C7
5000	LcnT	46112	2113	E7
5400	BNBG	46112	2113	E7
N 600 W				
10	BCkT	46140	2233	D6
10	BCkT	46140	2342	D1
10	SCkT	46140	2342	D1
3600	BCkT	46140	2124	D7
4000	BCkT	46055	2124	D7
6000	VrnT	46055	2124	D2
6500	MCVL	46055	2124	D2
7500	MCVL	46055	2015	D7
S 600 E				
1000	WrhT	46052	1788	B3
1000	WrhT	46075	1788	B3
5600	GfdT	46168	2549	E1
5600	PNFD	46168	2549	E1
7500	BrnT	46112	2006	B2
7500	EglT	46112	2006	B2
7500	PryT	46112	2006	B2
S 600 W				
10	SCkT	46163	2342	D4
3000	SCkT	46163	2451	D1
W 600 N				
-	SgCT	46126	2670	D4
2000	BCkT	46140	2125	D3
2000	VrnT	46140	2125	D3
2900	VrnT	46055	2125	D3
3000	BCkT	46055	2125	D3
5000	BCkT	46055	2124	E3
5000	VrnT	46055	2124	E3
6000	MrlT	46126	2669	E4
6000	MrlT	46126	2670	A4
6000	SgCT	46126	2669	E4
8400	MrlT	46110	2668	E4
8400	MrlT	46110	2669	A4
8400	SgCT	46110	2668	E4
8400	SgCT	46110	2669	A4
8900	ClkT	46110	2668	E4
8900	ClkT	46143	2668	E4
8900	MrlT	46143	2668	E4
600 E				
7000	ClkT	46143	2668	A7
10000	ClkT	46259	2668	A2
600 N				
3000	ClkT	46184	2775	E3
E 601 S				
4200	LtyT	46118	2549	B2
E 625 S				
8000	EglT	46077	1898	B6
N 625 E				
-	LcnT	46112	2114	A5
200	WshT	46123	2332	A3
500	AVON	46123	2332	A3
6300	BNBG	46112	2114	A5
6700	BrnT	46112	2114	A4
S 625 E				
10	WshT	46123	2332	A4
100	AVON	46123	2332	A4
1700	WshT	46123	2441	A1
2200	WshT	46168	2441	A2
2600	GfdT	46168	2441	A2
3100	PNFD	46168	2441	A3
N 630 W				
5600	SgCT	46126	2669	E5
S 630 W				
3000	SCkT	46163	2342	C7
3000	SCkT	46163	2451	C1
E 650 N				
9600	BrnT	46112	2115	E4
E 650 S				
3800	PryT	46052	1896	D6
4700	PryT	46052	1897	A6
5700	PryT	46112	1897	B6
5800	EglT	46112	1897	B6
6100	EglT	46077	1897	C6
9500	GfdT	46113	2551	D3
9500	GfdT	46231	2551	D3
9500	GfdT	46241	2551	E3
E 650 S SR-334				
5800	EglT	46112	1897	B6
5800	PryT	46052	1897	B6
5800	PryT	46112	1897	B6
N 650 E				
10	UnnT	46052	1679	D5
10	UnnT	46075	1679	D5
7500	BNBG	46112	2114	A3
7500	BrnT	46112	2114	A3
8000	BrnT	46112	2005	A7
N 650 W				
6500	MrlT	46126	2669	E2
7200	MrlT	46126	2560	E7
11100	MrlT	46130	2451	E7
11100	MrlT	46130	2560	E1
11800	SCkT	46130	2451	E7
S 650 E				
3000	GfdT	46168	2550	A4
3200	WrhT	46075	1788	C7
3200	WrhT	46075	1897	C1
3200	WTWN	46075	1788	C7
3200	WTWN	46075	1897	C1
4000	EglT	46075	1897	C4
5000	EglT	46077	1897	C4
7200	EglT	46077	2006	C1
7200	EglT	46112	2006	C1
8300	BrnT	46158	2659	A1
8300	GfdT	46158	2549	E6
8300	GfdT	46158	2550	A7
8300	GfdT	46158	2659	A1
8300	GfdT	46168	2549	E6
S 650 W				
4100	SCkT	46163	2451	C3
W 650 N				
6200	MCVL	46055	2124	B2
6200	VrnT	46055	2124	B2
W 650 S				
700	HsnT	46052	1894	D6
9000	GrnT	46064	1798	E5
650 E				
8400	ClkT	46143	2668	B4
650 N				
7400	MrnT	46052	1570	E1
7400	MrnT	46069	1570	E1
7400	MrnT	46069	1571	A1
11000	MrnT	46069	1572	D1
S 650 Blvd E				
6900	EglT	46077	1897	D7
E 651 N				
2300	MdlT	46167	2112	E5
N 670 E				
7000	ClkT	46143	2668	B7
7000	ClkT	46162	2668	B7
N 671 E				
100	AVON	46123	2332	B3
N 675 E				
1500	UnnT	46052	1679	D3
1500	UnnT	46075	1679	D3
2100	MrnT	46052	1679	D2
2100	MrnT	46075	1679	D2
N 675 W				
9100	MrlT	46126	2560	D5
9100	MrlT	46130	2560	D5
S 675 E				
500	GfdT	46168	2550	B6
S 675 W				
5000	SCkT	46163	2451	B4
5600	MrlT	46163	2451	B6
E 700 N				
500	UnnT	46149	2112	A3
5500	BNBG	46112	2113	E3
5500	BrnT	46112	2113	E3
5700	BrnT	46112	2114	A3
6400	BNBG	46112	2114	B3
8200	BrnT	46112	2115	A3
E 700 S				
10	HsnT	46052	1894	E7
10	HsnT	46052	1895	A7
600	GfdT	46168	2550	A4
600	PryT	46052	1895	C7
3000	LtyT	46118	2548	E4
3800	LtyT	46118	2549	B4
5100	GfdT	46118	2549	B4
6100	GfdT	46168	2549	E4
9200	GfdT	46168	2551	B4
9200	PNFD	46168	2551	B4
10500	GfdT	46113	2551	D4
N 700 E				
100	UnnT	46075	1679	E7
3000	MrnT	46052	1570	E7
3000	MrnT	46052	1679	E1
N 700 W				
10	BCkT	46140	2342	B1
10	CBLD	46140	2342	B1
10	SCkT	46140	2342	B1
700	BCkT	46140	2233	B7
3500	BCkT	46140	2124	B7
4000	BCkT	46055	2124	B7
6000	SgCT	46126	2669	D4
6700	MrlT	46126	2669	D2
10600	MrlT	46126	2560	D2
11400	MrlT	46130	2451	D7
11400	MrlT	46130	2560	D1
11700	SCkT	46130	2451	D7
S 700 E				
10	UnnT	46077	1788	E1
10	WrhT	46075	1788	E1
10	WrhT	46077	1788	E1
4000	WrhT	46075	1897	D2
4800	GfdT	46168	2550	B1
4800	PNFD	46168	2441	B7
4800	PNFD	46168	2550	B1
5100	EglT	46075	1897	D3
5100	EglT	46077	1897	D3
S 700 W				
10	SCkT	46140	2342	B2
10	SCkT	46229	2342	B2
200	CBLD	46163	2342	B3
200	CBLD	46229	2342	B2
200	SCkT	46163	2342	B3
1200	SCkT	46239	2342	B4
3000	SCkT	46163	2451	B1
W 700 N				
2200	VrnT	46055	2125	E1
3600	MrlT	46126	2670	E2
5100	VrnT	46055	2124	E1
5800	MCVL	46055	2124	E1
6000	MrlT	46126	2669	D2
7700	MrlT	46110	2669	B2
8200	MrlT	46110	2668	E2
8200	MrlT	46126	2668	E2
8700	MrlT	46259	2668	E3
W 700 S				
10	HsnT	46052	1894	E7
9300	GrnT	46064	1798	E6
700 S				
4700	ClyT	46077	1899	E7
N 700 Rd E				
7700	ClkT	46143	2668	C6
7700	ClkT	46162	2668	C6
10000	ClkT	46259	2668	C3
10700	ClkT	46259	2559	C7
700 North Ct				
700	INPS	46240	2010	E3
700 South Ct				
700	INPS	46240	2010	E4
S 701 E				
8300	GfdT	46168	2550	B7
N 710 W				
8600	MrlT	46126	2560	D6
E 725 N				
8300	BrnT	46112	2114	E3
S 725 E				
7000	GfdT	46168	2550	C5
E 750 N				
10	GNWD	46143	2665	D7
900	GNWD	46143	2666	A7
1200	PltT	46143	2666	B7
1700	PltT	46184	2666	B7
2700	ClkT	46143	2666	E7
2700	ClkT	46184	2666	E7
4000	MdlT	46167	2113	B2
5000	BNBG	46112	2113	C2
5000	MdlT	46112	2113	C2
8500	BrnT	46112	2114	E2
8500	BrnT	46112	2115	A2
E 750 S				
-	GfdT	46168	2550	D5
-	GfdT	46168	2551	A5
2100	LtyT	46118	2548	D5
5400	GfdT	46168	2549	E5
E 750 S SR-267				
-	GfdT	46168	2550	D5
N 750 E				
1000	UnnT	46075	1680	A4
2700	MrnT	46052	1680	A1
2700	MrnT	46075	1680	A1
3000	MrnT	46052	1571	A7
9800	BrnT	46112	2005	C5
N 750 W				
7300	MrlT	46126	2560	C7
7300	MrlT	46126	2669	C1
S 750 E				
6500	GfdT	46168	2550	D4
W 750 N				
5300	MCVL	46055	2015	E7
5300	VrnT	46055	2015	E7
5300	VrnT	46055	2016	A7
W 750 S				
200	HsnT	46052	2003	C1
E 775 N				
-	PTBR	46167	2112	D2
E 775 S				
500	GfdT	46168	2550	B6
6500	EglT	46077	2006	D2
6500	EglT	46112	2006	D2
N 775 E				
10700	ClkT	46259	2559	D7
10700	ClkT	46259	2668	D1
S 775 E				
10	UnnT	46077	1680	A7
10	UnnT	46077	1789	A1
1400	WrhT	46075	1789	A3
W 775 S				
200	HsnT	46052	2003	D2
S 780 E				
2300	WrhT	46075	1789	A5
E 800 N				
-	PTBR	46167	2112	D1
800	MdlT	46149	2112	A1
800	UnnT	46149	2112	A1
1200	MdlT	46167	2112	A1
5300	MdlT	46112	2113	D1
5400	BrnT	46112	2113	D1
5900	BrnT	46112	2114	A1
E 800 S				
-	GfdT	46158	2550	C6
-	GfdT	46168	2550	C6
200	LtyT	46118	2548	A6
1800	GfdT	46168	2549	D6
6500	BrnT	46112	2006	D2
7600	EglT	46077	2006	E2
7600	EglT	46077	2007	A2
7600	EglT	46278	2006	E2
7600	EglT	46278	2007	A2
7600	INPS	46077	2007	A2
7600	INPS	46278	2007	A2
9400	GfdT	46168	2551	C6
10700	GfdT	46113	2551	D6
N 800 E				
200	UnnT	46075	1680	B7
200	UnnT	46077	1680	B7
700	AVON	46123	2332	D2
700	WshT	46123	2332	D2
1600	WshT	46123	2223	D7
2000	MrnT	46075	1680	B1
2400	BNBG	46112	2223	D5
2400	LcnT	46112	2223	D5
2400	WshT	46112	2223	D5
2700	MrnT	46052	1571	B7
2700	MrnT	46052	1680	B1
2700	MrnT	46075	1571	B7
7000	BNBG	46112	2114	D3
7000	BrnT	46112	2114	D3
7300	MrnT	46069	1571	B1
8800	BrnT	46112	2005	D6
N 800 W				
7000	MrlT	46126	2669	B1
10000	MrlT	46126	2560	B3
11000	MrlT	46126	2451	B7
S 800 E				
10	AVON	46123	2332	D4
100	UnnT	46077	1680	B7
100	UnnT	46077	1789	B1
1200	WshT	46123	2332	D7
1600	AVON	46123	2441	D2
1600	WshT	46123	2441	D2
2100	AVON	46168	2441	D2
2100	WshT	46168	2441	D2
2500	PNFD	46168	2441	D2
W 800 N				
3000	VrnT	46055	2016	D6
3300	MrlT	46126	2561	E7
5000	MCVL	46055	2015	E6
5000	VrnT	46055	2015	E6
6400	MrlT	46126	2560	D7
8200	MrlT	46259	2560	A7
8600	MrlT	46259	2559	E7
W 800 N SR-234				
3000	VrnT	46055	2016	D6
5000	MCVL	46055	2015	E6
5000	VrnT	46055	2015	E6
W 800 S				
9200	FCkT	46064	1907	E1
9200	GrnT	46064	1907	E1
800 E				
6200	MrnT	46052	1571	B2
6200	MrnT	46069	1571	B2
800 North Rd				
4400	WRvT	46143	2663	E6
E 825 S				
6800	GfdT	46168	2550	B6
N 825 W				
4000	SgCT	46110	2669	A7
6000	MrlT	46110	2669	A7
S 825 E				
1000	UnnT	46077	1789	B3
S 840 E				
500	UnnT	46077	1789	B1
E 850 N				
4200	MdlT	46167	2004	B7
E 850 S				
-	LtyT	46118	2548	E6
4300	GfdT	46118	2549	C7
4300	GfdT	46168	2549	C7
4300	LtyT	46118	2549	C7
N 850 E				
7400	BrnT	46112	2114	E3
N 850 W				
9900	MrlT	46126	2560	A3
S 850 E				
6900	EglT	46077	1898	B7
7000	EglT	46077	2007	B1
N 875 W				
-	INPS	46259	2559	E7
-	MrlT	46259	2559	E7
5200	SgCT	46110	2668	E5
6000	MrlT	46110	2668	E4
7000	MrlT	46126	2668	E1
7000	MrlT	46259	2668	E1
S 875 E				
2300	UnnT	46077	1789	C6
2900	EglT	46077	1789	C7
3500	EglT	46077	1898	C1
3500	ZNVL	46077	1789	C7
3500	ZNVL	46077	1898	C1
875 N				
-	BrnT	46112	2005	C7
S 875 East Rd				
3100	GfdT	46168	2550	E4
6000	GfdT	46168	2551	A2
6000	PNFD	46168	2551	A2
E 875 South Rd				
800	BrnT	46158	2658	D1
800	GfdT	46158	2658	D1
3000	LtyT	46118	2548	D7
5600	GfdT	46168	2658	D1
E 900 N				
100	MdlT	46167	2003	C6
100	UnnT	46149	2003	C6
100	UnnT	46167	2003	C6
5100	BrnT	46112	2004	D6
5100	MdlT	46112	2004	D6
5100	MdlT	46167	2004	D6
6100	BrnT	46112	2005	B6
7600	WRvT	46142	2662	E5
7600	WRvT	46142	2663	A5
7600	WRvT	46143	2662	E5
7600	WRvT	46143	2663	A5
E 900 S				
800	LtyT	46118	2657	A1
N 900 E				
-	BrnT	46112	2006	A7
1400	AVON	46123	2224	A7
1400	AVON	46123	2333	A1
1400	WshT	46123	2224	A7
1400	WshT	46123	2333	A1
2900	LcnT	46112	2224	A4
3400	MrnT	46075	1571	D7
3400	MrnT	46075	1680	D1
4000	MrnT	46052	1571	D5
4400	BNBG	46112	2224	A3
4600	LcnT	46112	2115	A7
6500	BNBG	46112	2115	A5
6500	BrnT	46112	2115	A4
10900	PryT	46112	2006	A3
S 900 E				
10	UnnT	46077	1680	D7
10	UnnT	46077	1789	D2
100	AVON	46123	2333	A4
1000	WshT	46123	2333	A7
1000	WshT	46231	2333	A7
1900	WshT	46123	2442	A1
1900	WshT	46231	2442	A1
2000	WshT	46168	2442	A1
2100	PNFD	46168	2442	A1
W 900 N				
2100	VrnT	46040	2016	D4
3000	VrnT	46055	2016	D4
3200	MrlT	46126	2561	E5
3200	MrlT	46130	2561	E5
5000	MCVL	46055	2015	E4
5000	VrnT	46055	2015	E4
6000	MrlT	46126	2560	D5
6000	MrlT	46130	2560	D5
W 900 S				
9400	FCkT	46064	1907	E3
9400	GrnT	46064	1907	E3
900 East Rd				
5300	MrnT	46052	1571	D4
6400	MrnT	46069	1571	D2
900 North Ct				
900	INPS	46240	2010	E3
900 South Ct				
900	INPS	46240	2010	E4
N 901 East Rd				
5700	LcnT	46112	2115	A6
W 925 N				
2600	VrnT	46040	2016	E4
N 925 East Rd				
8900	BrnT	46112	2006	B7
8900	BrnT	46112	2115	B1
E 925 North Rd				
300	UnnT	46149	2003	A6

STREET Block	City	ZIP	Map#	Grid
S 950 E				
3500	EglT	46077	1789	E7
3500	EglT	46077	1898	E1
W 950 N				
4200	MrlT	46130	2561	D4
7400	MrlT	46126	2560	B4
N 950 East Rd				
3000	LcnT	46112	2224	B4
9700	BrnT	46112	2006	B5
E 950 North Rd				
-	MdlT	46167	2003	D5
9000	BrnT	46112	2006	B5
10700	BrnT	46278	2006	D5
E 951 North Rd				
3800	MdlT	46167	2004	A5
S 975 East Rd				
3700	GfdT	46168	2551	C5
E 975 North Rd				
500	UnnT	46149	2003	A5
700	MdlT	46167	2003	A5
700	UnnT	46167	2003	A5
E 1000 N				
3000	MdlT	46167	2003	E4
3000	MdlT	46167	2004	C4
5300	MdlT	46112	2004	C4
6300	BrnT	46112	2004	C4
6300	BrnT	46112	2005	B4
7100	ClkT	46143	2668	D2
7100	ClkT	46259	2668	D2
7800	ClkT	46110	2668	D2
8300	BrnT	46112	2006	A4
10700	BrnT	46278	2006	E4
E 1000 S				
800	LtyT	46118	2657	B3
2600	MnrT	46118	2657	D3
N 1000 E				
2400	AVON	46123	2224	C6
2400	AVON	46234	2224	C6
2400	WshT	46234	2224	C6
2500	AVON	46112	2224	C6
2500	LcnT	46112	2224	C6
2500	LcnT	46234	2224	C6
5000	LcnT	46112	2115	C7
6300	BrnT	46112	2115	C5
10700	BrnT	46112	2006	C3
W 1000 N				
3000	MrlT	46130	2561	E3
6000	MrlT	46130	2560	E3
6700	MrlT	46126	2560	E3
E 1025 N				
-	UnnT	46167	2003	C4
600	UnnT	46149	2003	C4
1500	MdlT	46167	2003	C4
N 1025 E				
4100	LcnT	46112	2224	D2
4100	LcnT	46234	2224	D2
9700	BrnT	46112	2006	D5
S 1025 E				
6000	GfdT	46168	2551	C3
6000	GfdT	46231	2551	C3
6800	PNFD	46168	2551	C3
8700	GfdT	46168	2660	C1
8700	MdnT	46168	2660	C1
N 1050 E				
10	AVON	46123	2333	D2
500	WshT	46123	2333	D2
1300	AVON	46234	2333	D1
1300	WshT	46234	2333	D1
1500	WshT	46234	2224	D7
1600	AVON	46234	2224	D7
8100	BrnT	46112	2115	D1
8400	BrnT	46112	2006	D7
S 1050 E				
700	AVON	46123	2333	D5
700	AVON	46231	2333	D5
700	WshT	46123	2333	D5
700	WshT	46231	2333	D5
1700	PNFD	46231	2333	D7
1900	PNFD	46231	2442	D1
1900	WshT	46231	2442	D1
3000	GfdT	46231	2442	D2
4500	GfdT	46168	2442	D7
5800	GfdT	46231	2551	D1
5800	PNFD	46231	2551	D1
6600	GfdT	46113	2551	D4
6600	GfdT	46168	2551	D4
W 1050 N				
3000	MrlT	46130	2561	E2
6500	MrlT	46130	2560	E2
E 1075 N				
7100	ClkT	46259	2668	C1
N 1075 E				
9500	BrnT	46278	2006	E5
10400	BrnT	46112	2006	E3
S 1075 E				
5800	PNFD	46231	2551	E2
5800	PNFD	46241	2551	E2
6700	GfdT	46231	2551	E2
N 1100 E				
10	UnnT	46077	1681	C7
1900	UnnT	46069	1681	C4
S 1100 E				
300	UnnT	46077	1681	C7
300	UnnT	46077	1790	C2
W 1100 N				
3100	MrlT	46130	2561	E1
6000	MrlT	46130	2560	E1
7200	MrlT	46126	2560	C1
8500	MrlT	46126	2559	E1
8500	MrlT	46259	2559	E1
W 1110 N				
4800	MrlT	46130	2561	C1
W 1120 N				
4600	MrlT	46130	2561	C1
N 1150 E				
3600	MrnT	46069	1572	D7
1150 N				
-	MdnT	46143	2662	A6
-	MdnT	46158	2661	E6
-	MdnT	46158	2662	A6
W 1175 N				
4000	MrlT	46130	2452	D7
W 1200 N				
2000	MrlT	46130	2452	E6
2000	SCkT	46163	2452	E6

STREET Block	City	ZIP	Map#	Grid
W 1200 N				
3000	MrlT	46163	2452	D6
4700	SCkT	46130	2452	A6
5000	MrlT	46130	2451	E6
5000	SCkT	46130	2451	E6
5000	SCkT	46163	2451	E6
6000	MrlT	46126	2451	C6
6000	MrlT	46163	2451	D6
7000	MrlT	46126	2450	E6
7000	MrlT	46163	2450	E6
7000	MrlT	46239	2450	E6
7000	SCkT	46163	2450	E6
1200 E				
600	UnnT	46074	1681	E5
600	UnnT	46074	1790	E1
600	UnnT	46077	1681	E5
600	UnnT	46077	1790	E1
600	WshT	46074	1790	E1
2000	WshT	46077	1790	E5
6000	AdmT	46069	1572	E1
6000	MrnT	46069	1572	E1
17600	WshT	46069	1681	E5
18600	UnnT	46069	1681	E5
19600	MrnT	46069	1681	E1
20600	WshT	46069	1572	E7
1300 N				
2500	MnrT	46118	2657	E3
2500	MnrT	46158	2657	E3

INDEX 64

Airports — Colleges & Universities

Indianapolis Points of Interest Index

Airports

FEATURE NAME Address City ZIP Code	MAP#	GRID
Boone County, CtrT	1786	D5
Eagle Creek Airpark, INPS	2225	C2
Greenwood Municipal, INPS	2665	E1
Hendricks County, CtrT	2330	D6
Indianapolis International, INPS	2444	A1
Indianapolis Metropolitan, FSHR	2012	E2
Indianapolis Terry, UnnT	1790	C1
Mount Comfort, BCkT	2125	A7
Mount Comfort Airfield, BCkT	2124	E6
Noblesville, NBVL	1796	D5
Post-Air, INPS	2340	C6
Speedway, AVON	2224	B6
Westfield, WshT	1683	C6

Beaches, Harbors & Water Rec

FEATURE NAME Address City ZIP Code	MAP#	GRID
Geist Lake Marina, FCkT	2014	E2
Morse Lake Marina, NBVL	1686	B1

Buildings

FEATURE NAME Address City ZIP Code	MAP#	GRID
Airport Technology Center INPS, 46214	2334	C3
Allison Transmission Div-GMC INPS, 46222	2335	D2
Andrade Industrial Park EglT, 46077	1899	D7
Beech Grove Industrial Park BHGV, 46203	2448	C5
Carmel Industrial Park CRML, 46032	1902	A5
Carmel Science & Technology Center CRML, 46032	1901	D4
Chevrolet Motor Division INPS, 46222	2337	A4
Citizens Coke & Gas S Keystone Av, INPS, 46203	2338	B5
Citizens Gas Company INPS, 46225	2337	B4
Country Club Industrial Park INPS, 46214	2334	B1
Daimler Chrysler Foundry INPS, 46241	2336	A5
Dow Chemical EglT, 46278	2008	B3
Eastwood Industrial Park INPS, 46219	2230	C5
Federal Express S High School Rd, INPS, 46241	2443	E3
FFA National Headquarters INPS, 46278	2008	B3
FMC Bearing Division INPS, 46214	2334	C4
FMC Chain Division INPS, 46221	2336	C4
Ford Plant INPS, 46219	2339	E4
Greenwood Industrial Air-Park GNWD, 46143	2665	E2
Greenwood Industrial Park GNWD, 46143	2665	D7
Indianapolis Disposal Plant INPS, 46221	2445	D3
Indianapolis Power & Light 1 Monument Cir, INPS, 46204	2337	C3
Indianapolis Power & Light INPS, 46217	2445	D4
Indianapolis Sewage Disposal Plant INPS, 46217	2554	A3
Jackson Industrial Park INPS, 46226	2231	C4
Keystone Enterprise Park INPS, 46218	2229	B6
Kroger Bakery INPS, 46219	2339	E4
Kroger Dairy INPS, 46219	2339	E4
Lilly Corporate Center INPS, 46225	2337	C5
Lilly Industrial Center INPS, 46221	2336	E7
Meridian Technology Center CRML, 46032	1901	D4
Navistar International Facility INPS, 46219	2339	B5
Near North Industrial Park INPS, 46202	2337	B1
Olin Brass INPS, 46241	2336	A7
Park 65 North Industrial Park INPS, 46254	2227	A2
Park Fletcher Industrial Park INPS, 46241	2444	B2
Raytheon Technical Services Company INPS, 46219	2230	C7
RCA INPS, 46219	2231	A6
Reilly Tar & Chemical INPS, 46241	2336	A7
Rock Island Refinery INPS, 46268	2008	C4
Rolls Royce Allison INPS, 46241	2336	B7
South Park Business Center GNWD, 46143	2666	A3
Speedway Industrial Park INPS, 46222	2335	E1
Stafford Business Park Quaker Blvd, PNFD, 46168	2441	E6
Stokely Van Camp INPS, 46203	2337	D7
Stony Creek Industrial Park Herriman Blvd, NBVL, 46060	1795	E4
Tobey Drive Industrial Park INPS, 46219	2231	C5
Western Select Industrial Park INPS, 46219	2231	A5

Buildings - Governmental

FEATURE NAME Address City ZIP Code	MAP#	GRID
Avon Town Hall AVON, 46123	2332	A4
Beech Grove City Hall 806 Main St, BHGV, 46107	2447	E3
Boone County Government Building 212 Courthouse Sq, LEBN, 46052	1677	A6
Boone County Health Department 116 W Washington St, LEBN, 46052	1676	E6
Brownsburg Town Hall 80 E Vermont St, BNBG, 46112	2114	C6
Carmel City Hall 1 Civic Sq, CRML, 46032	1902	B4
Cicero City Hall 150 W Jackson St, CCRO, 46034	1577	D2
Crows Nest Town Hall 700 W 56th St, INPS, 46228	2119	A5
Cumberland Town Hall 11501 E Washington St, CBLD, 46229	2341	D2
Danville Town Hall 147 W Main St, DNVL, 46122	2329	D4
Fishers City Hall 1 Municipal Dr, FSHR, 46038	1904	C5
Governor's Mansion 4750 N Meridian St, INPS, 46208	2119	C7
Greenfield City Hall 110 S State St, GNFD, 46140	2345	D2
Greenwood City Hall 2 N Madison Av, GNWD, 46142	2665	C3
Hamilton County Circut Court 1 N 8th St, NBVL, 46060	1686	D7
Hamilton County Court W Conner St, NBVL, 46060	1686	D7
Hamilton County Government Building W Conner St, NBVL, 46060	1686	D7
Hamilton County Health Department W Conner St, NBVL, 46060	1686	D7
Hancock County Government Building 9 E Main St, GNFD, 46140	2345	E1
Hancock County Health Department 111 American Legion Pl, GNFD, 46140	2345	C2
Hancock Superior Court 9 E Main St, GNFD, 46140	2345	D1
Hendricks County Government Building 355 S Washington St, DNVL, 46122	2329	D4
Hendricks County Health Department 355 S Washington St, DNVL, 46122	2329	D4
Indianapolis Juvenile Correctional Facility 2569 N Girls School Rd, INPS, 46214	2225	D6
Indianapolis-Marion Co Municipal Building 200 E Washington St, INPS, 46204	2337	C3
Indianapolis Men's Work Release Center 448 W Norwood St, INPS, 46225	2337	B5
Indianapolis Supreme Court 115 W Washington St, INPS, 46204	2337	C3
Indianapolis Women's Work Release 512 E Minnesota St, INPS, 46203	2337	D6
Indiana State Capitol 200 W Washington St, INPS, 46204	2337	B3
Indiana Womens Prison E New York St, INPS, 46201	2338	A2
Judicial Center W Conner St, NBVL, 46060	1686	D7
Lawrence City Hall 4455 McCoy St, LWNC, 46226	2231	B1
Lebanon City Hall 201 E Main St, LEBN, 46052	1677	A6
Marion County Health Department 3838 N Rural St, INPS, 46205	2229	B2
Marion County Jail 40 S Alabama St, INPS, 46204	2337	C3
Marion County Municipal Court 1410 N Lynhurst Dr, SDWY, 46224	2335	C1
Marion County Superior Court 200 E Washington St, INPS, 46204	2337	C3
McCordsville Town Hall 5759 W Pendleton Pike, VrnT, 46055	2015	D6
Meridian Hills Town Hall 7530 N Washington Blvd, INPS, 46240	2010	D7
Mooresville Town Hall 26 S Indiana St, MRVL, 46158	2659	E3
Municipal Building E South St, LEBN, 46052	1677	A6
New Palestine Town Hall 15 E Larrabee St, NPLN, 46163	2452	B3
New Whiteland Town Hall 401 Mooreland Dr, NWTD, 46184	2774	D5
Noblesville City Court 135 S 9th St, NBVL, 46060	1686	D7
Noblesville City Hall 16 S 10th St, NBVL, 46060	1686	D7
North Crows Nest Town Hall 6225 Sunset Ln, INPS, 46260	2119	C4
Pittsboro Town Hall 80 N Meridian St, PTBR, 46167	2112	E3
Plainfield Correctional Facility 727 S Moon Rd, PNFD, 46168	2440	E6
Plainfield Juvenile Correctional Facility 501 W Main St, PNFD, 46168	2441	A5
Plainfield Municipal Building 206 W Main St, PNFD, 46168	2441	B5
Plainfield Town Hall 206 W Main St, PNFD, 46168	2441	B5
Rocky Ripple Town Hall 508 W 54th St, INPS, 46208	2119	B6
Sheridan Town Hall 506 S Main St, SRDN, 46069	1573	B2
Southport City Hall 6901 Derbyshire Rd, SPRT, 46227	2556	B3
Speedway Town Hall 1450 N Lynhurst Dr, SDWY, 46224	2335	C1
Spring Lake Town Hall 2668 W Sugar Creek Dr, SGLK, 46140	2344	A3
Supreme Court of Indiana 200 W Washington St, INPS, 46204	2337	C3
Warren Twp Government Center E 10th St, INPS, 46229	2340	D2
Westfield Town Hall 130 Penn St, WTFD, 46074	1684	B7
Whitestown Town Hall 3 S Main St, WTWN, 46075	1788	C6
Zionsville Town Hall 110 S 4th St, ZNVL, 46077	1899	B6

Cemeteries

FEATURE NAME Address City ZIP Code	MAP#	GRID
Acton Cem, INPS	2559	C5
Anderson Cem, INPS	2339	D2
Bell Cem, INPS	2445	D7
Bethel Cem, INPS	2117	C6
Bethel Cem, MrnT	1680	D1
Calvary Cem, INPS	2446	B3
Carmel Cem, CRML	1902	A1
Center Cem, CtrT	1678	A7
Chester Cem, WshT	1684	A3
Cicero Cem, CCRO	1577	B2
Concordia Cem, INPS	2446	C2
Cotton Cem, INPS	2008	A3
Crown Hill Cem, INPS	2228	A2
Crownland Cem, NBVL	1686	E6
Crown Point Cem, INPS	2007	B7
Dowden Cem, CtrT	1787	C2
Eagle Creek Cem, WshT	1791	A4
Ervin Cem, NBVL	1797	C6
Floral Park Cem, INPS	2336	A3
Floral Park West Cem, INPS	2224	E7
Flower-Mundy Cem, INPS	2554	C4
Forest Lawn Cem, WRvT	2664	C7
Friends Cem, INPS	2552	E5
Green Lawn Cem, BNBG	2114	C5
Greenwood Cem, GNWD	2665	B3
Hair Cem, WynT	1689	B4
Hamilton Memorial Park, WTFD	1684	D7
Hebrew Cem, INPS	2446	B1
Highland Cem, FCkT	1905	C6
Hurlock Cem, NBVL	1796	A2
Jones Chapel Cem, INPS	2116	A5
Lincoln Memory Gardens Cem, EglT	1897	C7
Lowery Cem, FCkT	1905	C1
Maple Hill Cem, PNFD	2441	C5
Memorial Park Cem, INPS	2340	D2
Mount Jackson Cem, INPS	2336	B3
Mount Pleasant Cem, INPS	2553	C3
Mount Pleasant Cem, WRvT	2663	D1
Mt. Olive Cem, MdnT	2662	A4
New Crown Cem, INPS	2338	B7
New Palestine Cem, SCkT	2452	A4
Oak Hill Cem, CtrT	1677	B6
Oaklandon Cem, LWNC	2123	E1
Oaklawn Memorial Gardens Cem, FSHR	2012	C2
Our Lady of Peace Cem, INPS	2011	C4
Park Cem, CtrT	2345	E2
Parr-Jones Cem, MrnT	1681	B3
Pleasant Hill Cem, INPS	2007	D5
Prairie Cem, WynT	1688	E1
Riverview Cem, NBVL	1686	C7
Robinson Cem, LEBN	1785	E5
Round Hill Cem, INPS	2446	C7
St. Joseph & Holy Cross Cem, INPS	2446	B1
St. Malachy West Cem, MdlT	2113	B4
Sparks Cem, BrnT	2113	D2
Stony Creek Cem, WynT	1797	A1
Sugar Grove Cem, WshT	1791	A4
Summit Lawn Cem, WshT	1793	B2
Sutherland Park Cem, INPS	2229	B1
Union Chapel Cem, INPS	2011	C4
Union Grove Cem, AdmT	1573	D6
Washington Park Cem, CBLD	2341	B2
Washington Park North Cem, INPS	2118	C5
Weaver Cem, MdlT	2113	D1
West Newton Cem, INPS	2552	E5
White Lick Cem, MdlT	2113	B5
Zionsville Cem, EglT	1899	C7

Colleges & Universities

FEATURE NAME Address City ZIP Code	MAP#	GRID
American College of Sports Medicine 401 W Michigan St, INPS, 46202	2337	B2
Butler University 4600 Sunset Av, INPS, 46208	2119	A7
Christian Theological Seminary 1000 W 42nd St, INPS, 46208	2228	A1
Concordia Univ of WI Indp Adult Lrn Ctr 11350 N Meridian St, CRML, 46032	1901	C6
George Roger's Clark College 1840 N Meridian St, INPS, 46202	2228	C7
Heritage Baptist University 1301 E County Line Rd, GNWD, 46142	2664	D1
Indiana Business College 802 N Meridian St, INPS, 46204	2337	C2
Indiana Business Coll-Indp Bus Div Campus 550 E Washington St, INPS, 46204	2337	D3
Indiana Business Coll-Indp Med Div Campus 8150 E Brookville Rd, INPS, 46239	2340	B6
Indiana Tech 3500 De Pauw Blvd, INPS, 46268	2009	A3
Indiana University-Purdue University 355 Lansing St, INPS, 46202	2336	E2
Indiana University School of Nursing 1111 Middle Dr, INPS, 46202	2337	A2
Indiana Unversity School of Dentistry 1121 W Michigan St, INPS, 46202	2337	A2
Indiana Wesleyan University INPS, 46240	2011	C3
International Business College 7205 Shadeland Station Wy, INPS, 46256	2122	A1
ITT Technical Institute 9511 Angola Ct, INPS, 46268	2009	A3
Ivy Tech State College 510 Essex Dr, LEBN, 46052	1677	A5
Ivy Tech State College-Central Indiana 1 W 26th St, INPS, 46208	2228	C5
Lincoln Technical Institute 1201 N Stadium Dr, INPS, 46202	2337	A1
Marian College 3200 Cold Spring Rd, INPS, 46222	2227	C4

Indianapolis Points of Interest Index

FEATURE NAME Address City ZIP Code	MAP#	GRID
Sheridan Police Dept 506 S Main St, SRDN, 46069	1573	B2
South District Police Dept E Morris St, INPS, 46203	2337	E6
Southport Police Dept 6901 Derbyshire Rd, SPRT, 46227	2556	B3
Speedway Police Dept 1410 N Lynhurst Dr, SDWY, 46224	2335	C1
Westfield Police Deptartment 17535 Dartown Rd, WTFD, 46074	1683	D7
Whitestown Police Deptartment 7 S Main St, WTWN, 46075	1788	C6
Zionsville Police Dept Parkway Dr, ZNVL, 46077	1899	A6

Libraries

FEATURE NAME Address City ZIP Code	MAP#	GRID
Avon-Washington Twp Public AVON, 46123	2332	B3
Beech Grove 1102 Main St, BHGV, 46107	2447	E3
Break-O-Day Branch 700 Centerline Rd, NWTD, 46184	2774	D4
Brownsburg Public 450 S Jefferson St, BNBG, 46112	2223	C1
Carmel Clay Public 515 E Main St, CRML, 46032	1902	B2
College Avenue Branch 4180 N College Av, INPS, 46205	2228	D1
Danville-Center Twp Public 101 S Indiana St, DNVL, 46122	2329	D4
East 38th Street Branch 5420 E 38th St, INPS, 46226	2230	B2
Fishers Branch 5 Municipal Dr, FSHR, 46038	1904	C5
Fountain Square Branch 1066 Virginia Av, INPS, 46203	2337	E5
Franklin Road Branch 5500 S Franklin Rd, INPS, 46239	2449	C7
Garceau W 86th St, INPS, 46260	2009	D4
Glendale Branch 6101 N Keystone Av, INPS, 46220	2120	B4
Greenwood Public 310 S Meridian St, GNWD, 46142	2665	C4
Hamilton North Public 209 Brinton Rd, CCRO, 46034	1577	D3
Hancock County Public 700 N Broadway St, GNFD, 46140	2345	C1
Hussey-Mayfield Memorial Public 250 N 5th St, ZNVL, 46077	1899	B6
Indianapolis-Brightwood 2435 N Sherman Dr, INPS, 46218	2229	D5
Indianapolis-Broad Ripple 1550 Broad Ripple Av, INPS, 46220	2120	A3
Indianapolis-Brown 5427 E Washington St, INPS, 46219	2339	B3
Indianapolis-Decatur 5301 S Kentucky Av, INPS, 46221	2443	E7
Indianapolis-Eagle 3325 Lowry Rd, INPS, 46222	2226	E4
Indianapolis-East Washington 2822 E Washington St, INPS, 46201	2338	C3
Indianapolis-Flanner House 2424 Dr Martin Luther King Jr S, INPS, 46208	2228	B6
Indianapolis-Haughville 3815 W Michigan St, INPS, 46222	2336	A2
Indianapolis-Lawrence 7898 N Hague Rd, INPS, 46256	2013	A6
Indianapolis Marion County Lib-Wayne 198 S Girls School Rd, INPS, 46231	2334	D4
Indianapolis Marion County Public 202 N Alabama St, INPS, 46204	2337	D3
Indianapolis-Marion County Public 2450 N Meridian St, INPS, 46208	2228	C6
Indianapolis Marion-Haughville 2121 W Michigan St, INPS, 46222	2336	D2
Indianapolis-Nora 8625 Guilford Av, INPS, 46240	2010	E4
Indianapolis-Pike 6525 N Zionsville Rd, INPS, 46268	2117	B2
Indianapolis-Prospect 1831 E Prospect St, INPS, 46203	2338	A5
Indianapolis-Shelby 2502 S Shelby St, INPS, 46203	2446	E1
Indianapolis-Southport 2630 E Stop 11 Rd, INPS, 46227	2556	B5
Indianapolis-Spades Park 1801 Nowland Av, INPS, 46201	2338	A1
Indianapolis-Speedway 5633 W 25th St, SDWY, 46224	2226	B6
Indianapolis-Wanamaker 8822 E Southeastern Av, INPS, 46239	2449	D5
Indianapolis-Warren 9701 E 21st St, INPS, 46229	2231	E7
Indianapolis-West Indianapolis 1216 Kappes St, INPS, 46221	2336	D6
Indiana State 140 N Senate Av, INPS, 46202	2337	B3
Indiana University W Michigan St, INPS, 46202	2337	A2
Infozone At The Children's Museum 3000 N Meridian St, INPS, 46208	2228	C4
Irvington Branch 5625 E Washington St, INPS, 46219	2339	B3
Lebanon Public 104 E Washington St, LEBN, 46052	1677	A6
Mooresville Public 220 W Harrison St, MRVL, 46158	2659	D3
Noblesville Southeastern Public 1 Library Plz, NBVL, 46060	1687	A7
Plainfield Public 1120 Stafford Rd, PNFD, 46168	2441	D6
Riley Family 702 Barnhill Dr, INPS, 46202	2337	A2
Sheridan Public 214 S Main St, SRDN, 46069	1573	B1
Sugar Creek Branch 11 E Main St, NPLN, 46163	2452	B3

FEATURE NAME Address City ZIP Code	MAP#	GRID
Westfield 333 W Hoover St, WTFD, 46074	1684	A6
White River 1664 Library Blvd, GNWD, 46142	2664	C4

Military Installations

FEATURE NAME Address City ZIP Code	MAP#	GRID
Armory E Fordice St, LEBN, 46052	1677	A5
Indiana Army National Guard 2002 S Holt Rd, INPS, 46241	2336	A7
National Guard Armory 2021 Field Dr, NBVL, 46060	1686	E5
Reserve Center Walter Reed Rd, LWNC, 46216	2122	E5
US Army Reserve INPS, 46222	2227	C5

Museums

FEATURE NAME Address City ZIP Code	MAP#	GRID
Academy Building Mus 250 N Monroe St, MRVL, 46158	2659	D3
Center for Agricultural Science & Heritage 1201 E 38th St, INPS, 46205	2228	E2
Conner Prairie 13400 Allisonville Rd, FSHR, 46038	1904	B1
Eiteljorg Mus 500 W Washington St, INPS, 46202	2337	B3
Emil A Blackmore Mus of Amer Lgn Nat'l HQs 700 N Pennsylvania St, INPS, 46204	2337	C2
Hooks Discovery & Learning Center 1305 W 29th St, INPS, 46208	2227	E4
Hoosier Salon Gallery 714 E 65th St, INPS, 46220	2119	D3
Indiana Historical Society 450 N West St, INPS, 46202	2337	B3
Indiana Medical History Mus 3045 W Vermont St, INPS, 46222	2336	B3
Indianapolis Mus of Art 4000 W 38th St, INPS, 46208	2228	A2
Indiana State Mus 650 W Washington St, INPS, 46202	2337	B3
Indiana Transportation Mus 325 Cicero Rd, NBVL, 46060	1686	C7
IUPUI Cultural Arts Gallery 815 W Michigan St, INPS, 46202	2337	B2
James Whitcomb Riley Birthplace & Mus 250 W Main St, GNFD, 46140	2345	C1
Lilly Pavilion of Decorative Arts 4000 N Michigan Rd, INPS, 46208	2227	E2
Morris-Butler House Mus 1204 N Park Av, INPS, 46202	2337	D1
Motor Speedway Hall of Fame W 16th St, SDWY, 46222	2226	E7
Museum of Miniature Houses 111 E Main St, CRML, 46032	1902	B2
National Art Mus of Sport 850 W Michigan St, INPS, 46202	2337	A2
NCAA Hall of Champions 700 W Washington St, INPS, 46204	2337	A4
Old Log Jail & Chapel Muss E Main St, CtrT, 46140	2346	A1
PH Sullivan Mus & Genealogy Library 225 W Hawthorne St, ZNVL, 46077	1899	B6
Ropkey Armor Mus 6424 W 79th St, INPS, 46278	2008	A6
The Children's Mus of Indianapolis 3000 N Meridian St, INPS, 46208	2228	C4

Open Space

FEATURE NAME	MAP#	GRID
Marott Pk Woods Nature Preserve, INPS	2119	E2
Ritchey Woods Nature Preserve, FSHR	2013	A1
Watson Road Bird Preserve Pk, INPS	2228	E3

Other

FEATURE NAME Address City ZIP Code	MAP#	GRID
Bastine Pottery 16509 Cyntheanne Rd, WynT, 46060	1798	C2
Camp Beltzer-Boy Scouts Boy Scout Rd, LWNC, 46226	2121	E4
Camp Dellwood Girl Scouts N Girls School Rd, INPS, 46214	2225	D6
Canterbury Arabians 12131 E 191st St, WynT, 46060	1687	E4
Canterbury Hotel 123 S Illinois St, INPS, 46225	2337	C4
Garfield Park Conservatory 2450 S Shelby St, INPS, 46203	2446	D1
Guardians Home University Av, INPS, 46219	2339	B4
Holcomb Observatory & Planetarium 4600 Sunset Av, INPS, 46208	2119	B7
Holy Trinity Catholic Church 2618 W St. Clair St, INPS, 46222	2336	C1
IMAX 3-D Theater W Washington St, INPS, 46204	2337	A3
Indiana Law Enforcement Academy Forest Ridge Dr, PNFD, 46168	2441	A7
Indianapolis Art Center 820 E 67th St, INPS, 46220	2119	E2
Indianapolis Boys Club Camp E 216th St, NbvT, 46062	1576	A7
Indianapolis City Market 222 E Market St, INPS, 46204	2337	C3
Indianapolis Sailing Club Portside Wy, FCkT, 46256	2015	A2
Indianapolis Yacht Club Fall Creek Rd, FCkT, 46055	2015	B2
Internexus English Language Study Center E Hanna Av, INPS, 46227	2447	A5
McKenzie Career Center 7250 E 75th St, INPS, 46256	2013	A7
Nat'l Association of Miniature Enthusiasts 130 N Range Line Rd, CRML, 46032	1902	B2
National Institute for Fitness & Sport 250 N University Blvd, INPS, 46202	2337	A3
Noblesville Soccer Club 8600 E 196th St, NBVL, 46062	1686	C3

FEATURE NAME Address City ZIP Code	MAP#	GRID
Omni Severin Hotel 40 W Jackson Place North Dr, INPS, 46225	2337	C4
St. Maur Theological Center N Michigan Rd, INPS, 46228	2118	E7
Shagbark Ridge Llama Farm 10912 E 166th St, NBVL, 46060	1796	C2
Stonycreek Farm WynT, 46060	1796	D1
Stuckey Farm Market 19995 1200 E, WshT, 46069	1681	E1
The Church Federation of Great Indianapolis 1100 W 42nd St, INPS, 46208	2228	A2
Union Station 39 W Jackson Place North Dr, INPS, 46225	2337	C4
Univ of Indianapolis Theater E Hanna Av, INPS, 46227	2446	E4
Veteran's Memorial Plaza N Pennsylvania St, INPS, 46204	2337	C2
Zionsville Munce Art Center 205 W Hawthorne St, ZNVL, 46077	1899	B6

Parks & Recreation

FEATURE NAME	MAP#	GRID
61 Street Broadway Pk, INPS	2119	D4
Abner Longley Pk, LEBN	1786	A1
Anderson Pk, PNFD	2441	B6
Arbuckle Acres Pk, BNBG	2114	B6
Arsenal Pk, INPS	2119	E7
Asa Bales Pk, WTFD	1684	B7
Audubon Pk, INPS	2339	B4
Avon Town Hall Pk, AVON	2332	A3
Azionaqua Swim Club, ZNVL	1899	C3
Badger Pk, CRML	1903	B3
Barton Pk, INPS	2228	C6
Bellamy Pk, INPS	2231	E3
Belmont Pk, INPS	2336	D1
Bertha Ross Pk, INPS	2228	A3
Bethel Pk, INPS	2338	C7
Biddle Memorial Pk, SRDN	1573	C2
Billericay Pk, FSHR	1905	C3
Bluff Pk, INPS	2446	B5
Bowman Pk, INPS	2226	D3
Broad Ripple Pk, INPS	2120	A3
Brookside Pk, INPS	2229	C7
Brooks School Pk, FSHR	1906	A5
Carey Grove Pk, CRML	1793	D7
Carmel Clay Community Soccer Complex, CRML	1900	B3
Carmel Ice Stadium, CRML	1902	A4
Carmelot Pk, CRML	1903	A7
Carson Pk, INPS	2444	A7
Centennial & Groff Pk, INPS	2227	B6
Chapel Hill Pk, INPS	2334	D2
Cherry Tree Softball Complex, CRML	1794	B7
Christian Pk, INPS	2338	D4
Cicero Community Pk, CCRO	1577	C3
City Pk, INPS	2446	D2
Clayton & Lasalle Pk, INPS	2338	C4
Cool Creek Pk, WTFD	1793	B5
Craig Pk, GNWD	2665	D4
Cumberland Pk, CBLD	2342	A1
Cumberland Pk, FCkT	2013	E1
Denver Pk, INPS	2336	C1
Douglas Pk, INPS	2229	A5
Dubarry Pk, INPS	2231	C3
Eagle Creek Pk, INPS	2116	A3
Ellenberger Ice Rink, INPS	2339	B2
Ellenberger Pk, INPS	2339	A2
Fall Creek & 16th Pk, INPS	2337	A1
Fall Creek Pk, INPS	2122	C2
Flowing Well Pk, CRML	1903	A5
Forest Manor Pk, INPS	2229	D7
Forest Pk, NBVL	1686	C5
Fort Harrison State Pk, INPS	2122	B3
Fortville Pk, VrnT	2016	E2
Forum Ice Stadium, FSHR	1904	D3
Fox Hill Manor Pk, INPS	2118	E4
Franklin Pk, PNFD	2441	A4
Franklin Twp Community Pk, INPS	2558	D2
Frank R Beckwith Pk, INPS	2229	B4
Friendship Gardens Pk, PNFD	2441	B6
Garden Pk, PNFD	2441	D5
Gardner Pk, INPS	2121	E7
Garfield Pk, INPS	2446	D1
Gateway Pk West, INPS	2226	A1
Geist Pk, FCkT	1907	B7
George Washington Pk, INPS	2229	C4
German Church & 30th Pk, INPS	2232	B4
German Pk, INPS	2555	B7
Gustafson Pk, INPS	2226	B4
Habig Field Sports Complex, WshT	1793	C4
Harrison Pk, CRML	1900	E3
Harrison Thompson Pk, FCkT	1904	C1
Haughville Pk, INPS	2336	C2
Hawthorne Pk, INPS	2336	C3
Highland Pk, INPS	2337	E3
Holiday Pk, BNBG	2223	C1
Holiday Pk, INPS	2119	C3
Hummel Pk, PNFD	2441	C7
Irvington & 41st Pk, INPS	2230	A2
Jake Greene Pk, INPS	2231	B7
Jennings Field, ZNVL	1899	A5
John Ed Pk, INPS	2229	A7
JTV Hill Pk, INPS	2228	E7
Juan Soloman Pk, INPS	2118	E3
Krannert Pk, INPS	2335	A5
Lake Sullivan Sports Complex, INPS	2227	D3
Lawrence Community Pk, LWNC	2122	C6
Lee Road Pk, LWNC	2122	E4
Lentz Pk, INPS	2336	D2
Leonard Pk, SDWY	2335	C1
Lions Pk, ZNVL	1899	C6
Longacre Pk, INPS	2447	A6
Louis J Jenn Memorial Pk, LWNC	2123	B3
Martin Luther King Jr Pk, INPS	2228	D7
Mary Moore Pk, GNFD	2236	C7
Max Bahr Pk, INPS	2336	C3
Meadowlark Pk, CRML	1902	A2
Meadowood Pk, SDWY	2226	B5
Military Pk, INPS	2337	B3
Moreland Pk, INPS	2227	B5

Indianapolis Points of Interest Index

FEATURE NAME Address City ZIP Code	MAP# GRID	FEATURE NAME Address City ZIP Code	MAP# GRID	FEATURE NAME Address City ZIP Code	MAP# GRID
DeWitt Morgan School 200 W 49th St, INPS, 46208	2119 C7	**Greenwood Montessori School** 824 N Madison Av, GNWD, 46142	2665 B2	**Lebanon Middle School** 1800 N Grant St, LEBN, 46052	1677 A4
Divine Savior Lutheran Elementary 7315 E 75th St, INPS, 46256	2122 A1	**Greenwood NE Elementary School** 99 Crestview Dr, GNWD, 46143	2665 D2	**Lebanon Schools Alternative School** 403 W Main St, LEBN, 46052	1676 E6
Doe Creek Middle School 2279 S 600 W, SCkT, 46163	2342 D6	**Greenwood SW Elementary School** 619 W Smith Valley Rd, GNWD, 46143	2665 B5	**Lebanon Senior High School** 510 Essex Dr, LEBN, 46052	1677 A5
Douglas A MacArthur Elementary School 454 E Stop Eleven Rd, INPS, 46227	2555 D5	**Guion Creek Elementary School** 4301 W 52nd St, INPS, 46254	2117 E6	**Lew Wallace Elementary School** 3307 Ashway Dr, INPS, 46224	2226 A4
Durbin Elementary School 18000 Durbin Rd, WynT, 46060	1688 E6	**Guion Creek Middle School** 4401 W 52nd St, INPS, 46254	2117 E6	**Lil Touch of Love Academy** 4439 Dabny Cir, INPS, 46254	2226 B1
Eagle Creek Elementary School 6905 W 46th St, INPS, 46254	2116 E7	**Hamilton Southeastern High School** 13910 E 126th St, FSHR, 46038	1906 D3	**Lincoln Elementary School** 310 S Stadium Dr, BNBG, 46112	2114 D7
Eagledale Christian School 4950 W 34th St, INPS, 46224	2226 D3	**Hamilton Southeastern Junior High School** 12001 Olio Rd, FSHR, 46038	1906 C5	**Lincoln Middle School** 5353 W 71st St, INPS, 46268	2117 C1
Eagle Elementary School 555 Sycamore St, BNBG, 46112	2223 C1	**Hamilton Southeastern Middle School** 13257 Cumberland Rd, FSHR, 46038	1905 A2	**Louis B Russell Junior Elementary School** 3445 Central Av, INPS, 46205	2228 D3
Eagle Elementary School 350 N 6th St, ZNVL, 46077	1899 B5	**Harcourt Elementary School** 7535 Harcourt Rd, INPS, 46260	2009 E7	**Love & Faith Christian Academy** 1414 Mary Dr, LEBN, 46052	1676 D4
Eastbrook Elementary School 7839 New Augusta Rd, INPS, 46268	2008 E7	**Harney Elementary School** 1500 Garfield St, LEBN, 46052	1676 E5	**Lutheran High School** 5555 S Arlington Av, INPS, 46237	2448 C7
Eastridge Elementary School 10930 E 10th St, INPS, 46229	2341 C1	**Harriett Becher Stowe School** 2710 Bethel Av, INPS, 46203	2338 B7	**Lynwood Elementary School** 4640 Santa Fe Dr, INPS, 46241	2444 D3
Eastwood Middle School 4401 E 62nd St, INPS, 46220	2120 E3	**Harris Elementary School** 725 S Green St, BNBG, 46112	2223 B1	**Maple Elementary School** 7237 Business Center Dr, AVON, 46123	2332 C4
Edgar Evans Academy 3202 E 42nd St, INPS, 46205	2229 C1	**Harris Elementary School** 200 W Park Av, GNFD, 46140	2236 D7	**Maplewood Elementary School** 1643 Dunlap Av, INPS, 46241	2335 D6
Elder W Diggs Elementary School 1002 W 25th St, INPS, 46208	2228 A5	**Harrison Hill Elementary School** 7510 E 53rd St, LWNC, 46226	2122 A6	**Margaret McFarland Middle School** 3200 E Raymond St, INPS, 46203	2338 C7
Eleanor Skillen Elementary School 1410 Wade St, INPS, 46203	2446 E1	**Harrison Parkway Elementary School** 14135 Harrison Pkwy, FSHR, 46060	1795 D7	**Mary Adams Elementary School** 7341 E Stop 11 Rd, INPS, 46259	2558 A5
Eliza A Blaker School 55 1349 E 54th St, INPS, 46220	2120 A6	**Hasten Hebrew Academy** 6602 Hoover Rd, INPS, 46260	2119 A2	**Mary Bryan Elementary School** 4355 E Stop 11 Rd, INPS, 46237	2556 E6
Emma Donnan Junior High School 1202 E Troy Av, INPS, 46203	2446 E2	**Hattie B Stokes Elementary School** E Hendricks Dr, LEBN, 46052	1786 B1	**Mary E Nicholson Elementary School** 510 E 46th St, INPS, 46205	2119 D7
Emmaus Lutheran School 1224 Laurel St, INPS, 46203	2337 E6	**Hawthorne Elementary School** 8301 Rawles Av, INPS, 46239	2340 C4	**Mary Evelyn Castle Elementary School** 8502 E 82nd St, INPS, 46256	2013 C5
Emmerich Manual High School 2405 S Madison Av, INPS, 46225	2446 D1	**Hazel Dell Elementary School** 3025 Westfield Rd, NBVL, 46062	1685 B7	**McClelland Elementary School** 6740 W Morris St, INPS, 46241	2334 E6
Ernie Pyle Elementary School 3351 W 18th St, INPS, 46222	2227 B7	**Hazel Hart Hendricks School** 2605 E 25th St, INPS, 46218	2229 B6	**Meredith Nicholson Elementary School** 3651 N Kiel Av, INPS, 46224	2226 B3
Excel Academy 3421 N Park Av, INPS, 46205	2228 D3	**Heather Hills Elementary School** 10502 E 21st St, INPS, 46229	2232 B6	**Meridian Academy of the Arts** 1640 Fry Rd, GNWD, 46142	2664 C2
Fall Creek Elementary School 12131 Olio Rd, FSHR, 46038	1906 D5	**Henry W Longfellow Middle School** 510 Laurel St, INPS, 46203	2337 E4	**Merle Sidener Middle School** 2424 Kessler Blvd East Dr, INPS, 46220	2120 B4
Fall Creek Intermediate School Olio Rd, FSHR, 46038	1906 D5	**Heritage Christian School** 6401 E 75th St, INPS, 46250	2121 D1	**Metro Middle School** 5108 S High School Rd, INPS, 46221	2444 A7
Fall Creek Valley Middle School 9701 E 63rd St, LWNC, 46236	2122 E3	**Hickory Elementary School** AVON, 46123	2332 B6	**Metropolitan School** 8425 E Raymond St, INPS, 46239	2340 C7
Fishback Creek Public Academy 8301 W 86th St, INPS, 46278	2007 B5	**Hinkle Creek Elementary School** 595 S Harbour Dr, NBVL, 46062	1685 E4	**Minnie Hartmann Elementary School** 3734 E Vermont St, INPS, 46201	2338 D3
Fishers Elementary School 11442 Lantern Rd, FSHR, 46038	1904 D6	**HL Harshman Middle School** 1501 E 10th St, INPS, 46201	2338 A1	**Mohawk Trails Elementary School** 4242 E 126th St, CRML, 46033	1902 E3
Fishers High School E 131st St, FSHR, 46060	1905 D2	**Holy Angels School** 2822 Dr Martin Luther King Jr S, INPS, 46208	2228 B5	**Montessori Children's House** 222 S 4th Av, BHGV, 46107	2448 A3
Florence Fay Elementary School 2815 E English Av, INPS, 46203	2338 C4	**Holy Cross Central School** 125 N Oriental St, INPS, 46201	2338 A3	**Montessori International School** 620 Kinzer Av, CRML, 46032	1902 C3
Floro Torrence Elementary School 5050 E 42nd St, INPS, 46226	2230 A1	**Holy Name School** 21 Sherman Dr, BHGV, 46107	2447 D3	**Montessouri Community School** 8383 Craig St, INPS, 46250	2012 D5
Forest Dale Elementary School 10721 W Lakeshore Dr, CRML, 46033	1902 C7	**Holy Spirit School** 7241 E 10th St, INPS, 46219	2340 A2	**Moorehead Elementary School** 2150 S Hunter Rd, INPS, 46203	2339 D7
Forest Glen Elementary School 6333 Lee Rd, LWNC, 46236	2122 E3	**Homecroft Elementary School** 1551 Southview Dr, INPS, 46227	2556 A3	**Mooresville Christian School** MRVL, 46158	2660 A4
Forest Hill Elementary School 470 Lakeview Dr, NBVL, 46060	1686 C6	**Hoosier Road Elementary School** Hoosier Rd, FSHR, 46038	1905 D4	**Mooresville High School** 550 N Indiana St, MRVL, 46158	2659 D2
Forest Manor Junior High School 4501 E 32nd St, INPS, 46218	2229 E4	**Horizon Christian School** 7702 Indian Lake Rd, LWNC, 46236	2014 B7	**Moorhead Elementary School** 8400 E 10th St, INPS, 46219	2340 C1
Fox Hill Elementary School 802 Fox Hill Dr, INPS, 46228	2119 B4	**Horizons Middle School** 1401 E 10th St, INPS, 46201	2338 A1	**Mount Comfort Elementary School** 5694 W 300 N, BCkT, 46140	2233 E2
Francis Bellamy Elementary School 9501 E 36th Pl, INPS, 46235	2231 E3	**Hornet Park Elementary School** 5249 Hornet Av, BHGV, 46107	2448 A4	**Nativity School** 3310 S Meadow Dr, INPS, 46239	2449 A3
Francis Scott Key Elementary School 3920 N Baker Dr, INPS, 46235	2231 E2	**Immaculate Heart of Mary School** 317 E 57th St, INPS, 46220	2119 D5	**Nazarene Christian School** 5152 Hornet Av, BHGV, 46107	2448 A4
Francis W Parker School 2353 Columbia Av, INPS, 46205	2228 E6	**Indiana Boys School** S 700 E, PNFD, 46168	2441 A6	**Neil Armstrong Elementary School** MRVL, 46158	2660 A4
Frank H Wheeler Elementary School 5700 School Dr, SDWY, 46224	2226 B5	**Indianapolis Christian School** 620 E 10th St, INPS, 46202	2337 D1	**New Augusta Public Academy North** 6450 Rodebaugh Rd, INPS, 46268	2118 A3
Franklin Central High School 6215 S Franklin Rd, INPS, 46259	2558 C2	**Indianapolis Junior Academy** 2910 E 62nd St, INPS, 46220	2120 C3	**New Augusta Public Academy South** 6250 Rodebaugh Rd, INPS, 46268	2118 A3
Franklin Twp Middle School 6019 S Franklin Rd, INPS, 46259	2558 C1	**Indiana School for the Blind** 7725 N College Av, INPS, 46240	2010 E7	**New Beginnings Alternative School** 1840 N Meridian St, INPS, 46202	2228 C7
Frederick Douglas Middle School 2020 Dawson St, INPS, 46203	2338 A7	**Indian Creek Elementary School** 10833 E 56th St, LWNC, 46235	2123 C5	**New Britton Elementary School** 8660 E 131st St, FSHR, 46038	1904 C2
Fulton Junior High School 7320 W 10th St, INPS, 46214	2334 D1	**Isom Central Elementary School** 50 E Broadway St, GNWD, 46143	2665 C3	**Newby Memorial Elementary School** 240 N Monroe St, MRVL, 46158	2659 D3
Garden City Elementary School 4901 Rockville Rd, INPS, 46241	2335 D4	**James A Allison Elementary School** 5240 W 22nd St, SDWY, 46224	2226 C6	**New Palestine Elementary School** 4801 County Road 500 W, SCkT, 46163	2452 A4
Geist Elementary School 14051 E 104th St, FCkT, 46040	2015 D1	**James A Garfield Elementary School** 307 Lincoln St, INPS, 46225	2337 D6	**New Palestine High School** S School St, NPLN, 46163	2452 A3
George B Loomis Elementary School 338 S Arlington Av, INPS, 46219	2339 C4	**James Whitcomb Riley School** 150 W 40th St, INPS, 46208	2228 C2	**Noblesville High School** 18111 Cumberland Rd, NBVL, 46060	1687 A6
George Buck Elementary School 2701 N Devon Av, INPS, 46219	2231 C5	**JB Stephens Elementary School** 1331 N Blue Rd, CtrT, 46140	2237 B6	**Noblesville Intermediate School** 1625 Field Dr, NBVL, 46060	1686 E5
George H Fisher Elementary School 7151 E Kensington Dr, INPS, 46226	2230 E3	**Jewel Christian Academy** 5750 E 30th St, INPS, 46218	2230 C4	**Noblesville Middle School** 300 N 17th St, NBVL, 46060	1686 E7
George Washington Community School 2215 W Washington St, INPS, 46222	2336 D3	**John Marshall Junior High School** 10101 E 38th St, INPS, 46235	2232 A3	**Nora Elementary School** 1000 E 91st St, INPS, 46240	2010 A4
George W Carver Elementary School 2411 Indianapolis Av, INPS, 46208	2228 B6	**John Strange Elementary School** 3660 E 62nd St, INPS, 46220	2120 D3	**North Central High School** 1801 E 86th St, INPS, 46240	2011 A4
George W Julian School 57 5435 E Washington St, INPS, 46219	2339 B3	**Jonathan Jennings Elementary School** 6150 Gateway Dr, INPS, 46254	2226 A2	**Northeast Christian Academy** 2825 N Ritter Av, INPS, 46218	2230 B5
Glenns Valley Elementary School 8239 Morgantown Rd, INPS, 46217	2554 D6	**Joseph J Bingham Elementary School** 440 E 57th St, INPS, 46220	2119 D5	**North Elementary School** 440 N 10th St, NBVL, 46060	1686 D7
Goddard School 11437 Fishers Pointe Blvd, FSHR, 46038	1904 C6	**Joyce Kilmer Academy School 69** 3421 N Keystone Av, INPS, 46218	2229 B3	**North Grove Elementary School** 3280 W Fairview Rd, GNWD, 46142	2664 B5
Goddard School 1640 W Oak St, ZNVL, 46077	1898 E6	**Julian D Coleman Elementary School** 1740 E 30th St, INPS, 46218	2229 A4	**North Madison Elementary School** 7456 Hadley Rd, MdnT, 46113	2661 D4
Grassy Creek Elementary School 10330 E Prospect St, INPS, 46239	2341 B5	**Kingsway Christian School** 7979 E 100 N, AVON, 46123	2332 D2	**North Park Academy** 5735 W 73rd St, INPS, 46278	2117 B1
Gray Road Christian School 5500 S Gray Rd, INPS, 46237	2447 D7	**Lakeside Elementary School** 9601 E 21st St, INPS, 46229	2231 E7	**Northside Montessori School** 1224 E 52nd St, INPS, 46220	2119 E6
Greenbriar Elementary School 8201 Ditch Rd, INPS, 46260	2010 A5	**Lakeview Christian Academy** 47 Beachway Dr, INPS, 46224	2335 B3	**North Star Christian Academy** 5350 E 38th St, INPS, 46226	2230 B2
Greenfield Central High School 810 N Broadway St, GNFD, 46140	2236 C7	**Lantern Road Elementary School** 10595 Lantern Rd, FSHR, 46038	2013 D1	**Northview Middle School** 8401 N Westfield Blvd, INPS, 46240	2011 A4
Greenfield Middle School 204 W Park Av, GNFD, 46140	2236 D7	**Lawrence Central High School** 7300 E 56th St, LWNC, 46226	2122 A5	**North Wayne Elementary School** 6950 W 34th St, INPS, 46214	2225 D7
Greenwood Community High School 615 W Smith Valley Rd, GNWD, 46143	2665 B5	**Lawrence North High School** 7802 N Hague Rd, INPS, 46256	2013 A7	**Northwest High School** 5525 W 34th St, INPS, 46224	2226 B3
Greenwood Middle School 523 S Madison Av, GNWD, 46142	2665 C4	**Lebanon Christian Academy** 504 E Elm St, LEBN, 46052	1677 A7	**Northwood Elementary School** 630 N Indiana St, MRVL, 46158	2659 E2

Shopping Centers

FEATURE NAME Address City ZIP Code	MAP#	GRID
Lafayette Square Shopping Center 3919 Lafayette Rd, INPS, 46254	2226	E2
Lebanon Plaza N Lebanon St, LEBN, 46052	1676	E4
Linwood Shopping Center 4215 E 10th St, INPS, 46201	2338	D2
Menard's Shopping Center 6800 E Pendleton Pike, INPS, 46226	2230	E2
Merchants Square Mall 2160 E 116th St, CRML, 46032	1902	C5
Noblesville Square River Av, NBVL, 46062	1686	B7
Nora Plaza Shopping Center E 86th St, INPS, 46240	2011	A4
Norgate Shopping Center N Keystone Av, INPS, 46240	2120	B1
North Eastwood Shopping Center 8901 E 38th St, INPS, 46226	2231	D3
North Willows Commons W 86th St, INPS, 46260	2009	E4
Parkwood Shopping Center 1600 N Lebanon St, LEBN, 46052	1676	E5
Plainfield Commons Shopping Center E Main St, PNFD, 46168	2442	A3
Plainfield Shoppes E Main St, PNFD, 46168	2442	A3
Plainfield Shopping Center E Main St, PNFD, 46168	2441	C4
Riverplace Shopping Center W Logan St, NBVL, 46060	1686	C6
Shadeland Plaza N Shadeland Av, INPS, 46219	2230	E7
Shadeland Station Shopping Center N Shadeland Av, INPS, 46256	2121	E1
Shiloh Crossing AVON, 46123	2332	C4
Southbridge Shopping Center Southbridge St, MRVL, 46158	2659	D5
Southern Plaza Shopping Center 4200 S East St, INPS, 46227	2446	D5
Southpointe Centre 901 Grube St, INPS, 46227	2555	D4
Speedway Shopping Center 5852 Crawfordsville Rd, SDWY, 46224	2226	B6
Stony Creek Marketplace Pleasant St, NBVL, 46060	1796	A1
Target Northwest Shopping Center N Michigan Rd, INPS, 46268	2118	C2
Target Plaza E Main St, PNFD, 46168	2442	B3
Target Washington West Shopping Center S High School Rd, INPS, 46241	2335	A6
Target West Shopping Center Lafayette Rd, INPS, 46222	2227	C6
The Village at Eagle Creek Eagle Creek Pkwy, INPS, 46214	2225	E3
The Village Shopping Center S Indiana St, MRVL, 46158	2659	D4
Town & Country Shopping Center Aulton Dr, NBVL, 46060	1795	E2
Towne Center Shopping Center Towne Center Dr N, MRVL, 46158	2660	B3
Twin Aire Shopping Center E Southeastern Av, INPS, 46203	2338	C5
Village North Shopping Center N Lebanon St, CtrT, 46052	1676	E2
Village Park Plaza E 151st St, WTFD, 46033	1793	B5
Wal-Mart Plaza E Main St, PNFD, 46168	2442	A3
Washington Shoppes E Washington St, INPS, 46229	2341	A3
Washington Square Mall 10202 E Washington St, INPS, 46229	2341	A2
Washington Village Shoppes E Washington St, INPS, 46229	2340	E3
West 40 Plaza W Washington St, INPS, 46222	2336	D3
Western Plaza Westfield Rd, NBVL, 46062	1686	B7
Westfield Market Place Westfield Rd, WTFD, 46062	1684	D7
Willow Lake Shopping Center 2550 Lake Cir Dr, INPS, 46268	2009	C4
Zionsville Shopping Center 1201 W Oak St, ZNVL, 46077	1899	A6

Subdivisions & Neighborhoods

FEATURE NAME	MAP#	GRID
Avalon Hills, INPS	2121	D2
Bacon, INPS	2120	B5
Ben Davis, INPS	2335	A6
Bowman Acres, GNFD	2345	E4
Brendan Wood, LEBN	1676	E4
Brendonwood, INPS	2121	C5
Bridgeport, INPS	2443	A1
Brightwood, INPS	2229	C5
Broad Ripple, INPS	2119	E4
Brookfield, MrlT	2560	A5
Castleton, INPS	2012	D5
Centre East, INPS	2341	B3
Chapel Hill, INPS	2334	E2
Charle Sumac Estates, INPS	2559	B2
Clermont, INPS	2225	A3
Clermont Heights, LcnT	2224	D3
Crestview Heights, MdnT	2660	D6
Crows Nest, INPS	2119	B5
Devonshire, INPS	2121	D2
Drexel Gardens, INPS	2335	C7
Eastgate, INPS	2339	E2
Edgewood, INPS	2555	E1
Fairwood Hills, INPS	2122	B1
Five Points, INPS	2448	E2
Fort Benjamin Harrison, LWNC	2122	E6
Glenns Valley, INPS	2554	C6
Green Meadows, MrlT	2670	A2
Highwoods, INPS	2118	E7
Imperial Hills, GNWD	2664	B1
Indian Creek Estates, INPS	2559	C2
Indian Lake, LWNC	2123	A1

Indianapolis Points of Interest Index

FEATURE NAME Address City ZIP Code	MAP#	GRID
Ivanhoe, INPS	2340	C4
Ivy Hills, INPS	2012	B6
Lindenwood, INPS	2555	C4
Linwood, INPS	2338	E2
London Heights, MrlT	2669	D2
Mapleton, INPS	2228	C6
Mars Hill, INPS	2445	A3
Maywood, INPS	2445	B2
McCarty, GNWD	2664	E4
Meridian Hills, INPS	2010	C7
Mickleyville, INPS	2335	B6
Millersville, INPS	2120	E6
Monterey Village, NBVL	1686	B6
New Augusta, INPS	2117	E1
Nora, INPS	2337	B6
North Crows Nest, INPS	2119	C4
Northern Meadows, ZNVL	1899	B4
Northfield Village, LEBN	1676	C4
Oaklandon, LWNC	2123	D3
Park Fletcher, INPS	2335	B7
Perry Manor, INPS	2556	C2
Rainbow, INPS	2227	B7
Ravenswood, INPS	2120	A1
Ridgewood, MRVL	2660	A5
Rocky Ripple, INPS	2119	A6
Rosedale Hills, INPS	2447	A7
Sherwood Forest, INPS	2011	A3
Southeast Manor, MrlT	2669	E2
Spring Hills, INPS	2227	D1
Sundown Manor, BrnT	2659	E7
Sunshine Gardens, INPS	2445	B7
Traders Point, INPS	2007	C7
Twin Brooks, INPS	2556	B3
University Heights, INPS	2446	E5
Valley Mills, INPS	2443	E7
Wanamaker, INPS	2449	C5
Warren Park, INPS	2339	D1
Washington Place, INPS	2340	C2
West Indianapolis, INPS	2336	C5
West Newton, INPS	2552	D5
West Noblesville, NBVL	1686	C7
Williams Creek, INPS	2010	D6
Windsor Village, INPS	2230	D6
Woodruff Place, INPS	2338	A2
Wynnedale, INPS	2227	D1
Young, BrnT	2660	A4

Transportation

FEATURE NAME	MAP#	GRID
Amtrak-Indianapolis, INPS	2337	C4
Greyhound-Indianapolis, INPS	2337	C3
IndyGo, INPS	2336	E3
Trailways-Indianapolis, INPS	2227	D7

Visitor Information

FEATURE NAME Address City ZIP Code	MAP#	GRID
Hamilton County Convention & Visitors Bureau 11601 Municipal Dr, FSHR, 46038	1904	C5
Hendricks County Conv & Visitors Bureau W Main St, DNVL, 46122	2329	D4
Pumphouse Visitor Center W Maryland St, INPS, 46204	2337	B3

RAND McNALLY

Thank you for purchasing this Rand McNally Street Guide!
We value your comments and suggestions.

Please help us serve you better by completing this postage-paid reply card.
This information is for internal use ONLY and will not be distributed or sold to any external third party.

Missing pages? Maybe not... Please refer to the "Using Your Street Guide" page for further explanation.

Street Guide Title: **Indianapolis & Vicinity**   ISBN# 0-528-85542-5   Edition: 7th   MKT: IND

Today's Date: _____ Gender: ☐M ☐F   Age Group: ☐18-24 ☐25-31 ☐32-40 ☐41-50 ☐51-64 ☐65+

1. What type of industry do you work in?
    ☐Real Estate   ☐Trucking   ☐Delivery   ☐Construction   ☐Utilities   ☐Government
    ☐Retail   ☐Sales   ☐Transportation   ☐Landscape   ☐Service & Repair
    ☐Courier   ☐Automotive   ☐Insurance   ☐Medical   ☐Police/Fire/First Response
    ☐Other, please specify: _____
2. What type of job do you have in this industry?_____
3. Where did you purchase this Street Guide? (store name & city) _____
4. Why did you purchase this Street Guide? _____
5. How often do you purchase an updated Street Guide?   ☐Annually   ☐2 yrs.   ☐3-5 yrs.   ☐Other:_____
6. Where do you use it?   ☐Primarily in the car   ☐Primarily in the office   ☐Primarily at home   ☐Other: _____
7. How do you use it?   ☐Exclusively for business   ☐Primarily for business but also for personal or leisure use
    ☐Both work and personal evenly   ☐Primarily for personal use   ☐Exclusively for personal use
8. What do you use your Street Guide for?
    ☐Find Addresses   ☐In-route navigation   ☐Planning routes   ☐Other: _____
    Find points of interest: ☐Schools   ☐Parks   ☐Buildings   ☐Shopping Centers   ☐Other:_____
9. How often do you use it?   ☐Daily   ☐Weekly   ☐Monthly   ☐Other: _____
10. Do you use the internet for maps and/or directions?   ☐Yes   ☐No
11. How often do you use the internet for directions?   ☐Daily   ☐Weekly   ☐Monthly   ☐Other:_____
12. Do you use any of the following mapping products in addition to your Street Guide?
    ☐Folded paper maps   ☐Folded laminated maps   ☐Wall maps   ☐GPS   ☐PDA   ☐In-car navigation   ☐Phone maps
13. What features, if any, would you like to see added to your Street Guide? _____
    _____
14. What features or information do you find most useful in your Rand McNally Street Guide? (please specify)
    _____
    _____
15. Please provide any additional comments or suggestions you have. _____
    _____

16. Did the free CD-ROM influence your purchase?   ☐Yes   ☐No
17. What do you use the CD-ROM for? _____
18. Do you have comments or suggestions for the CD-ROM? _____

We strive to provide you with the most current updated information available if you know of a map correction, please notify us here.

Where is the correction?   Map Page #:_____   Grid #:_____   Index Page #:_____

Nature of the correction: ☐Street name missing   ☐Street name misspelled   ☐Street information incorrect
    ☐Incorrect location for point of interest   ☐Index error   ☐Other: _____

Detail: _____

I would like to receive information about updated editions and special offers from Rand McNally
    ☐via e-mail   E-mail address: _____
    ☐via postal mail
    Your Name: _____   Company (if used for work): _____
    Address:_____   City/State/ZIP: _____

Thank you for your time and help. We are working to serve you better.
This information is for internal use ONLY and will not be distributed or sold to any external third party.

CUT ALONG DOTTED LINE

SG.06

get directions at
randmcnally.com

BUSINESS REPLY MAIL
FIRST-CLASS MAIL   PERMIT NO. 388   CHICAGO IL
POSTAGE WILL BE PAID BY ADDRESSEE

NO POSTAGE
NECESSARY
IF MAILED
IN THE
UNITED STATES

**RAND MCNALLY
CONSUMER AFFAIRS
PO BOX 7600
CHICAGO IL 60680-9915**

⊕ RAND MᶜNALLY
The most trusted name on the map.

You'll never need to ask for directions again with these Rand McNally products!

- EasyFinder® Laminated Maps
- Folded Maps
- Street Guides
- Wall Maps
- CustomView Wall Maps
- Road Atlases
- Motor Carriers' Road Atlases